Playing with Canons

Explosive New Works from Great Literature by America's Indie Playwrights

Edited by

Martin Denton

Published by The New York Theatre Experience, Inc.
P.O. Box 1606, Murray Hill Station, New York, NY 10156
www.nyte.org
email: info@nyte.org

ISBN-10: 0-9670234-8-3
ISBN-13: 978-0-9670234-8-9
Library of Congress Control Number: 2006933951

 Playing with Canons is made possible, in part, with public funds from the New York State Council on the Arts, a state agency.

 Playing with Canons is also made possible, in part, with public funds from the New York City Department of Cultural Affairs.

Playing with Canons is also made possible, in part, by support from the Peg Santvoord Foundation.

Book and cover designed by Nita Congress

PERMISSIONS

TABLE OF CONTENTS

PREFACE

Martin Denton

It has taken seven years for *Playing with Canons* to come to life, so to speak: from the time when I first got the idea to create this anthology until this moment, when it is poised to go to press and see the light of day as a finished book.

Not long after the publication of *Plays and Playwrights for the New Millennium*—the first volume in what has turned into an annual series showcasing new plays by never-before-published playwrights—it became clear that a whole kind of new dramatic literature was being overlooked, namely, plays drawn from classic literary and theatrical sources. The fact is that brilliant playwrights and directors and their collaborators find new ways to make the books and plays of yesteryear fresh and relevant and important for today, and the work they create when they take an old piece of writing and put their own spin and imprint on it is worth celebrating and remembering.

And so, here's *Playing with Canons*, a collection of eighteen theatre pieces that translate works we thought we knew into something we've never seen before, something meaningful and lucid that helps us redefine how we look at the world and/or reshape how we look at theatre.

As I gathered the scripts together, I decided that some kind of organizing principle was needed to help make sense of them, and as a result I've divided *Playing with Canons* into six sections, each consisting of three plays that tackle a particular literary/dramatic type. Part I offers a trio of plays that react to the work of William Shakespeare. Kirk Wood Bromley's *Want's Unwisht Work*, the earliest chronologically of the plays in this volume, comes from the early heyday of this contemporary downtown theatre bard, when his eclectic subjects and pyrotechnic poetics electrified a lot of people in the then-nascent indie theatre movement. A sort of cyberpunk response to *Love's Labour's Lost*, *Want's* debuted at Nada on the Lower East Side in 1996 and has had several subsequent productions; I'm delighted to have it touch down on these pages. Bromley actually was with me when I encountered *Titus X*, Shawn Northrip's deliciously audacious punk rock *Titus Andronicus*. What I love about this piece, which was part of the very first New York Musical Theatre Festival in 2004, is how right the fit is: if any classic play demands to be the text of a punk rock opera, it's *Titus*. Larry Loebell's *La Tempestad* takes characters and situations from *The Tempest* and transplants them to Puerto Rico in the early twenty-first century to tell an entirely new and timely story with elegance and intelligence. I saw it in its New York premiere at the Ohio Theatre, under the auspices of the excellent company Resonance Ensemble.

Part II consists of pieces drawn from a variety of "sacred" sources. Matt Freeman's *Genesis* updates five medieval Mystery plays to tell some of the most familiar stories from the Bible with an ingenious mix of old and new sensibilities. Freeman directed the play in a very particular, pointed way in its premiere, under the aegis of Handcart Ensemble, and I'm happy that he's notated some of his staging ideas to accompany the text in this volume. Greek myth and legend are represented here by David Johnston's *Eumenides*, a startling take on the final play in Aeschylus's *Oresteia*. It was originally conceived as the concluding third of an evening drawn from three playwrights in three different styles. Happily, Johnston has since written the rest of his own *Oresteia* adaptation, and at this writing it's about five months away from its world premiere.

The last of our "sacred" plays is from a much newer source: Michael Maeillo's *Principia* is based, in part, on the mid-twentieth century phenomenon known as the *Principia Discordia*. I came to this funny, loopy satire via its director, Joe Tantalo, whose work with Godlight Theatre Company has impressed me for some time. Tantalo, Maeillo, and composer Andrew Recinos created a special kind of magic with this piece. I wish you could hear Recinos's delightfully varied and catchy score; I hope what you read here will do the show justice.

In Parts III, IV, and V, we look at adaptations from the literature of a particular country or region. Part III is called "Chekhov and Other Russians" because Chekhov's work inspired two of the three pieces here. Jeff Cohen's *Uncle Jack*, staged in 1999, places the characters, stories, and themes of *Uncle Vanya* in contemporary West Virginia. Thanks in part to Cohen's sensitive direction of an extraordinary cast, that production remains the most realized *Vanya* I think I've ever seen; certainly Cohen finds, in his script, the deep humanity that characterizes Chekhov's work, and presents it in an accessible and resonant way for a modern American audience. Anthony P. Pennino's *Story of an Unknown Man* is taken mostly from a Chekhov story of that title which was unfamiliar to me until I saw this play; but there's more to it than that, because Pennino has added elements from other Chekhov pieces and even placed Chekhov himself in the thick of the thing. (A side note for those interested in trivia: Matt Freeman, author of *Genesis*, was one of the actors in *Story of an Unknown Man*; indeed, I first encountered him in this show, making me doubly lucky to have gotten to see it.) The "Other Russians" is, I now see, a misnomer, as there is only one other, Dostoevsky. Alec Harrington's audacious eight-hour adaptation of *The Brothers Karamazov* is a singular theatrical achievement, bringing the depth and complexity of a modern literary classic quite wholeheartedly and stunningly to the stage for audiences to experience in all its honest enormity. I hope someday Harrington will have an opportunity to mount both parts in repertory, as they should be done (the original productions happened nearly a year apart, at two different theatres).

Three American masters figure in Part IV. Reneé Flemings's *Bel Canto* takes one of Edgar Allan Poe's most famous stories, "The Tell-Tale Heart," and translates it to a jazzy, noir-ish setting among two-bit gangsters. *Bel Canto* originated at Metropolitan Playhouse as part of an evening of short plays based on famous American literature; among offerings derived from Wharton, Dickinson, and Whitman, this stark, poetic piece stood out as something both original and remarkably deeply felt; I've come to learn that that's almost always the case with Flemings's idiosyncratic work. Metropolitan is also the home of Alex Roe's *Salem*, which is inspired by Nathaniel Hawthorne's "Young Goodman Brown." It's fitting that this fine but perhaps undervalued off-off-Broadway company located in the heart of Alphabet City in New York's East Village is represented in this volume, because this troupe, under the leadership of David Zarko and, now, Roe himself, has made its reputation as an interpreter of classic, often "lost" American drama. This piece—part ghost story, part spiritual exercise—is a splendid addition to that canon. The other great mid-nineteenth century American author, Herman Melville, also gets his due here, in R. L. Lane's terrific *Bartleby the Scrivener*. This play, which debuted at the now (sadly) defunct Blue Heron Arts Center in late 2005, is terrifically well-realized theatre; what makes it more exciting is the way that it redefines a story that a lot of people think they know. Lane's Bartleby is not the existential hero that many of us recall from school. Indeed, he's not even the protagonist of the play—that honor goes to his employer, the attorney Standard, whose transformation is the moving subject of this finely wrought drama.

Part V takes us across the ocean to Europe, where three nineteenth century novels serve as fodder for three spectacular theatrical excursions. Rob Reese's *Frankenstein* tells the familiar story of Mary Shelley's novel quite faithfully. There have been lots of *Frankenstein* plays, but Reese's is extraordinary: with its multilayered framing device and its use of theatrical techniques such as multiple actors playing the Creature simultaneously, it becomes an exploration of storytelling and playmaking as a kind of creation. Jane Austen's *Northanger Abbey* is dramatized by Lynn Marie Macy, but this playful piece is not content just to put Austen's charming story onto the stage—it also puts large chunks of the gothic romance *The Mysteries of Udolpho* up there as well. That novel is the one that *Northanger*'s spunky heroine Catherine is so enamored of; it's a spark of grand inspiration to let us see that piece unfold side by side with Catherine's own adventures. Kiran Rikhye's *The Man Who Laughs*, the final offering in this section, recasts Victor Hugo's macabre tale of a young man whose mouth has been carved into a permanent smile as a live "silent film." As you'll see, the script is shaped like a movie scenario, complete with titles but not a word of spoken dialogue. As directed by Jon Stancato for Stolen Chair Theatre Company (the troupe for which he and Rikhye serve as co-artistic directors), this piece is a lively and exciting exemplar of the physical theatre movement that is gaining rapid currency on American stages.

The final section of this volume is dubbed "Fresh Looks," and here we have three diverse, challenging pieces that cast three of the most influential masterworks in the Western canon in riveting new light. *Bald Diva!: The Ionesco Parody Your Mother Warned You About*, by David Koteles, is just what its title implies—a dead-on parody of Ionesco's seminal absurdist work *The Bald Soprano*. But look beneath the glossily hilarious surface and you'll see that there's as much astute and incisive commentary about the state of the world today as there was in the original. John Clancy's *Fatboy* aims to be as unsettling and profane and sensational as Alfred Jarry's *Ubu the King* was a century ago, and I think it succeeds brilliantly; I started my review of the show by noting the number of times that "fuck" appears in the script (139). Clancy, more than anyone else in this book (or anywhere, for that matter), is a seminal figure in the indie theatre movement that this collection celebrates; I'm proud and happy that this volume marks the first publication of one of his plays. *The Persians…a comedy about war with five songs*, is the final selection. Created by the rising young theatre troupe Waterwell, it starts with Aeschylus and then riffs on it masterfully, translating it into a surreal, off-kilter vaudeville that nonetheless retains the majesty and potency of the original in chronicling the horrors of war.

≈ ≈

Playing with Canons, like the theatrical work it seeks to represent on paper, is the result of a collaboration among many dedicated people. First and foremost are the playwrights who have entrusted their scripts to me; my sincere gratitude to all of them for placing their work here. The six gentlemen who composed the introductory essays for each section I likewise thank for their generosity and clear-eyed vision.

Thanks to all the people who helped me find the plays and get to know the playwrights: Rachel Reiner, Karen Greco, Scott Reynolds, Joe Tantalo, Christopher Carter Sanderson, Carol Fineman, Jim Baldassare, David Scott, Judith Jarosz, and Jon Stancato.

Tim Cusack and Anthony Pennino assisted with copy editing; thanks to both of them for their excellent efforts. Thanks also to Sarah Congress for proofreading the entire manuscript. Michael Criscuolo, NYTE's staff associate, wrote the playwrights' bios and performed numerous other tasks to help bring the book to fruition. Rochelle Denton, our managing director, handles all the myriad details that make a book such as this possible, and I am indebted to her for all the hard work that she will deny having done.

Thanks beyond measure to my sister, Nita Congress, who single-handedly guided this volume through its long production process. She is our editor, designer, graphic artist, and the utterly invaluable shaper of the product you now hold in your hands. Without her, there would be no *Playing with Canons*. I appreciate her extraordinary efforts more than I can adequately say.

Finally, I must mention Leo Farley, dedicated actor, director, playwright, and friend, who was the inspiration for this book in the first place. *Playing with Canons* is dedicated to him.

Part I

REFLECTIONS ON SHAKESPEARE

For the past ten years, I've worked in theatre companies dedicated to verse plays and to Shakespeare (as the executive director for Inverse Theater and the director of development for the New Globe Theater), and in that time I've received scores of scripts "inspired" by "the Bard": verse plays packed with Elizabethan vernacular, rhyming couplets, and heartfelt soliloquies. The results are almost always unpleasant for both audience and writer, and have the primary effect of stifling the playwright's voice and hampering his or her career in the theatre.

However, aspiring to write in Shakespeare's *style*—and employing his language, cadences, and plots—and striving to match his *spirit*, are worlds apart. The former is futile, as such texts (and the authors behind them) are generally incinerated as they approach the Shakespearean star; but the latter is the key to unlocking the power and persistence of the world's most successful playwright and strongest poet.

To write in the spirit of Shakespeare is to smash words and syntax and then build new meaning from the shards. To limn the workings of the human mind and the maneuverings of modern society. To follow in Shakespeare's footsteps is to hide your self, withhold your judgments, and mask your worldview. To fill the world with a multitude of people as real and fascinating as any your audience is likely to meet. And above all, to tell stories that provide medicine against despair, an excuse for joy, and a guide to wisdom.

The following playwrights aim to merge Shakespeare's style with his spirit—and as such, are his truest progeny and greatest legacy.

—*Chad Gracia*

WANT'S UNWISHT WORK

aka A Birthday Play

Kirk Wood Bromley

KIRK WOOD BROMLEY was born in 1966 in Corvallis, Oregon, but raised primarily in both Madison, Wisconsin, and Phoenix, Arizona. He is an NYC-based playwright, actor, theatre writer, and musician, and artistic director of Inverse Theater Company. His other produced plays include *All Must Be Admitted* (1992), *The Sickness and the Cure* (1997), *Icarus and Aria* (1997), *Faust—The Musical* (1997), *Lost Labor's Loved* (1998), *The Death of Griffin Hunter* (1998), *The American Revolution* (1999), *Midnight Brainwash Revival* (1999; published in NYTE's *Plays and Playwrights for the New Millennium*), *The Death of Don Flagrante Delicto* (2000), *Syndrome* (2001), *The Burnt Woman of Harvard* (2001), *Lost—The Musical* (2003), *On the Origin of Darwin* (2004), *The Banger's Flopera* (2005), *Three Dollar Bill* (2005), and *That American Shakespeare Thing* (2005). His plays and musicals have been presented and positively reviewed in New York City, Los Angeles, San Francisco, Cleveland, and London, and at several U.S. colleges. Inverse Theater was awarded Best Downtown Theater by the New York Press in 2001; Bromley is the recipient of the 2001 Berrilla Kerr Foundation Playwrights Award, and his plays have won two FringeNYC Awards—for Excellence in Playwriting (2002) and Excellence in Music and Lyrics (2003). Inverse Theater won the first ever Caffe Cino Award for Excellence in Off-Off-Broadway by the New York Innovative Theater Awards. More information on Bromley, his plays, and his theater company can be found at www.inversetheater.org.

Want's Unwisht Work was first presented on March 21, 1996, at Nada, New York City, with the following cast and credits:

Richard (Vazoline).. Douglas Gregory
Elisa.. Billie James/Suzanne Goldklang
Bertha Lerner.. Lisa Colbert/Ginny Hack
Marla ....Jody Booth/Billie James
Lydia ....Melanie Martinez
Corme.. Kate Hampton/Tara Bahna-James
Leavus ....P. J. Sosko/Dan Flamhaft
Warren .... Rizwan Manji/Hank Wagner
Dr. Kling.. Ian W. Hill/Al Foote III
Erad...Spencer Aste
Nichedigger...Will Newman/Sven Holmberg
Dick...Hank Wagner/Yuri Lowenthal
Laptop ....Alexander Stephano/Tim Ellis
Rem .... Sven Holmberg/Ian W. Hill
Gene.. Pietro Gonzalez/Todd Woodard
Rock..Al Foote III/Adam Wald
Art .... Dan Flamhaft/Steven Eng
Nicelle...Christine Mascott/Laura Knight

Directed and dramaturged by: Aaron Beall
Sets and Props: Raphaele Shirley
Lighting: Laura Zambrano
Costumes: Cheree Colucelli
Stage Management: Jennifer Kroll

It was revived by Inverse Theater Company on May 3, 2001, at the Kraine Theatre, New York City, with the following cast: Spencer Aste, Alan Benditt, Elisa Blynn, Christopher Briggs, Bill Coelius, Matt Daniels, Eve Eaton, Lars Engstrom, Tom Epstein, Emily Greenhill, Brad Haines, Bob Laine, Elizabeth London, Matt Oberg, Christina Pastor, Shirley Roeca, Dave Shalansky, and Darius Stone. Alexander Stephano directed. Chad Gracia produced and dramaturged. Sets and lighting by Morgan von Prelle Pecelli. Costumes by Karen Flood. Music by Aaron Hondros. Props by Andrew Theodorou.

CAST OF CHARACTERS

RICHARD (VAZOLINE, a cross-dresser), a man with a house, Elisa's husband
ELISA, a woman with a house, and Richard's wife
BERTHA LERNER, a professor of women's studies
MARLA, her student
LYDIA, her student
CORME, her student
LEAVUS, Marla's boyfriend
WARREN, Lydia's boyfriend
DR. KLING, an analyst and author
ERAD, his student
NICHEDIGGER, DICK, LAPTOP, and REM, Rambling Fanatics
GENE, ROCK, ART, and NICELLE, the Wishful Waiters

ACTION

Richard and Elisa's house in Athens, Georgia, now.

Enter RICHARD.

RICHARD: O, welcome, all! And thanks for your attendance
To celebrate with me my other's birth.
But while she's out, I'll intimate this chance
To tell my play's untold motive and worth:
Soon, here, my wife, art's most-appreciant,
Will from bit work return, wholly unversed
That I this birthday show extravagant
Have for her eager, open mind rehearsed.
From fiction's menu, truth persuaded me
To click the icon of her sex. I scanned
Her muting drudge for psychic spontany,
And thus, from her own past, this present planned.
Now, though my bent is straight with subtle phrase,
Low gest, loose term, wild image and character,
Be sure, my wife's aware in fable's maze
What lives on stage, dies there healthier.
Yet, we must rush—she's home, each day, same time.
That none's offended, I'll the politic
And moral of this rowdy, startling rhyme
Relate. Let's see, it starts, I think, with Dick.

(Enter ELISA, at the door of her house.)

ELISA: Rich! The door is jammed! Come lemme in!

RICHARD: Too late! That last you'll have to get your-selves.
Coming, Elisa, my love! Look how I sweat!

(Enter RICHARD, from inside the house.)

RICHARD: O, sweet Elisa, happy birthday!

ELISA: Richard, when ya gonna fix this knob?

RICHARD: Tomorrow, dear! Today, I fix your spirit!

ELISA: You ever heard my daddy sayin no man's his own neighbor?

RICHARD: Yes.

ELISA: Can my daddy be heard and not heeded?

RICHARD: No.

ELISA: This house is fallin to pieces, Rich!

RICHARD: And you will fall to pieces when you see my piece, Elisa!

ELISA: Richard, it ain't fair. You make plays, I make payroll. You funambules all day, while I punch keys for crooks at Pilfer Pharmaceutic. Be a man, Richard. Quit dreamin diddlysquawk up in that attic, and contribute to our tangibles.

RICHARD: My plays, Elisa, are not diddlysquawk.

ELISA: Well, I don't get em, so they're diddlysquawk. I'm goin to bed.

RICHARD: But I made this work for you.

ELISA: And Richard, I am tired of workin for you. My mind is on screensaver, my fingers have devolved into staple removers, and I got a burnin case of sec-retary spread. You wanna give me a gift? Put down

the unprofiting pen, haul your hausfrau up them
stairs, and then, for her birthday, you can pour her
a Concha y Toro.

RICHARD: O, please, sit in the comfy chair and let the
show revive you.

ELISA: It's just a bunch a high-falutin fancy schmansy,
Rich!

RICHARD: But words are birth, Elisa, and new ones
nurture us.

ELISA: Ya, well, sleep's a word, so don't mind me if I
nurture a doze.

RICHARD: Of course, my love.

ELISA: Ah, Rich, you're nothin nuts, but still my honey
man.

RICHARD: O, happy birthday, love! My gift? A play!
But what? Eyes open, open! Feel the cheer
That pounced with you into our world this day,
For soon, your lust enacted visits here.
So, may my urgency have your patience,
My whim your work, my stress your distress ease,
Engendering a core of recompense,
That we, in sharing pleasures, pains appease.
For as they say, the tale must fall out
As naturally as it was first attached.
Just so, in asking you to join this bout,
I hope, once all's diverged, our wants be matched.
If darkly seated, you should snuggle sleep,
Then we our clash into your dreams will seep,
And recreating you in this show's run,
Be self reborn, if not more free for fun.

(ELISA falls asleep, and RICHARD exits with her. Enter
BERTHA, CORME, MARLA, and LYDIA on the porch
of the house.)

BERTHA: May woman, utera of knowings new,
Within this dreamt-of house her self reclaim.
May she, the caring, altruistic sex,
Replenish here her fruitful, fertile traits.
And may she, who lames life if she is lost,
Fresh menses from her moral organ feel.
Now, Corme, Marla, Lydia, to you,
In Georgia's Athens, Sophia of the South,
This house is here awarded, that, as one,
You concentrate against your degradation,
And build the femine shelter of our world.
For man, fear's nepotist to relevance,
With acts revolting, does its berth assault.

For man, fat war and form-forcing suppression
Quick-stagnant gifts to devolution are.
For man, his staged, stage-frighting, asocial self
Thrusts into woman, rupturing her peace,
As talkshows unacquit of fact or merit
Insert in public prescience petty clack.
Woman, man's beginning, has he betrayed.
Therefore, I formally request you now:
Of woman's truth alone can you research?
Will you sans man discourse on sex and urge?
Can you your body's variant questing fix
Free of men, upon a lustless fulcrum?
Can you, not thru men, not for men, not by men,
Be altered to your own discoveries?
Marla, can you promise this to woman?

MARLA: That won't be hard. To me, man's optional.
At tigress pride, he lingers t'importune.
No men, I say, and feel it natural
As restriction of the weapon from the womb.

BERTHA: Honest, ravaged Marla. You may enter.

(MARLA goes in.)

BERTHA: Lydia, can you promise this to woman?

LYDIA: It's women who genetic change emote.
Man's a necessary-nothing, a go-between,
A futile fringe device, creating bloat.
I won't be used like easy oxygen.

BERTHA: A victim, Lydia, you proudly are.
You may enter.

(LYDIA goes in.)

BERTHA: Well, as we celebrate this house's birth,
We happy birthday wish to our Corme,
Who will, of course, our present promise try,
And make her day a present to us all.

CORME: By this promise, all's tried by us but us.

BERTHA: Speak plain, Corme. We are all sisters here.

CORME: Suits woman wrath? Can she, in hiding,
flourish?
Her problem's route I've followed, her issues
Have pervaded me, yet new stimulus
I wish us to attract and not diffract.
Stasis is no thesis. Isolation
Is healthless life. Pointing fingers point back.
Let's balance rage and reticence, and accept
Into our congress of inclusive strife
An acting arbitration with all life.

BERTHA: But Corme, you have signed the grant with
    pen,
And see its strict deletioning of men.

CORME: I've done as much. It was inhuman.

MARLA: What are we, Corme, moon to moon con-
    venience?
One hour developing? Instant obedience?

CORME: What of those countless comedies, where men
Adopt the closure of depraving rules,
Which then they break, yet mend to squelch again,
In stupid, cycling symbolry of fools?
Must we relive this universal farce,
Copying man's limits but not his range?
Can we across the ancient scriptings parse,
To then all errors barely rearrange?
For woman, truer study is expressed
Rebonding molecules of every style,
And making motive of another's mess
Of strain and stress, she dissipates his guile.
If nothing else, as travertines are made,
Let frames collect the silt of trust betrayed.

LYDIA: When resistance wiggles, none can resist;
Will cancer cure by cooing "please, don't spread"?
The stress of man marks beauty to a cyst,
Dividing life to cells that grow when dead.

MARLA: Man's a homicidal basket case.

CORME: Yet open baskets calm what they embrace.

LYDIA: We're shutting him out, not shutting him
    down.

CORME: If out and not down, he'll come back around.

MARLA: We want to be a part by being apart.

CORME: Your parts will then for parts well-known
    depart.

LYDIA: Separation's often opportunity.

CORME: And yet exclusion has no intimacy!
If, to project past man, you act like him,
He'll harder jut, turgescing at the thrill.
So let your better self his better win
By war of woman's inclusant words and will.

MARLA: The rule is set.

LYDIA: Isn't it, Ms. Lerner?

BERTHA: As good persuasion as Corme has made,
And full of aperturing delegant,

It seems contingence would not too dissuade
The purpose of the spirit from this grant.
So, I have a thought: By vote we'll choose.
A man may enter if two women wish.

MARLA: A great idea!

LYDIA: And free of prejudice.

BERTHA: Corme?

CORME: Though setting up decisions such as these
Could cause this house to on itself implode
Thru problematic sneaks and jealousies,
I'll enter, trusting woman is no fraud.

BERTHA: It's set. May woman, now, man's history of
Hustled lust and crazing rules reprove.

*(CORME enters the house, and VAZOLINE, cross-dress-
ing, enters.)*

BERTHA: Who are you?

VAZOLINE: I'm the sun after the brainstorm. Who
    are you?

BERTHA: Bertha Lerner, director of the women's
    studies department, and the university's granted
    me this house.

VAZOLINE: Oh, ain't that sweet?
I thought this menudo nest was mine,
Living in its attic since the embryo,
But 'long comes senorita manicure,
Sent from swindle's guru,
Who's granted it to her and pearly swine.
Sorry, babe, but this norm grotto's mine.

MARLA: What are you?

VAZOLINE: I am a peloric lily, perfectly unnatural.
    What are you?

LYDIA: We are women.

VAZOLINE: What, do say, is a we-men?

LYDIA: Woman is life's only perpetual resource.

VAZOLINE: O, then she is death.

MARLA: Woman is the backbone of society.

VAZOLINE: Society needs less backbone, and more
    forebrain.

BERTHA: No men is now a bylaw of this house.

VAZOLINE: Oh, but how can a bi-law say no men?

LYDIA: Are you a man or are you not?

VAZOLINE: I am a man, though to manliness I am awol.

LYDIA: Why a wall?

VAZOLINE: I am absence without leaving.

MARLA: Then we, as women, are staying with presence.

VAZOLINE: Presence is the present that won't stay.

BERTHA: You cannot stay, being a man.

VAZOLINE: If I can't stay being a man, I become a woman.

LYDIA: If you must become a woman, then you are a man, and may not enter.

VAZOLINE: Being a man, I can only enter;
Being a woman, you may never.
So don't you see? Your law is inapplicable
When applied. Besides, it's very dull.

MARLA: Whatever you are, you're a man in a woman's house.

BERTHA: Women, let's claim our rights!

VAZOLINE: Oh goody, leave me what's left, and I'll be rich again!

(BERTHA, MARLA, and LYDIA enter the house.)

CORME: Hello.

VAZOLINE: O hell.

CORME: I didn't catch your name.

VAZOLINE: Because it's Vazoline, and it slippt away.

CORME: I'm Corme.

VAZOLINE: Did these subdermal birthmarks
Of black hole funny faces suck you in?

CORME: Your chatter is all clatter.

VAZOLINE: Then I will suck
My speech like a vacuum: Corme, do you swear
To dance in this booth, this holed booth, and to wear
Nothing in this booth, so helpless dog?

CORME: I've joined them, hesitantly, yes, I have.

VAZOLINE: Then listen, girl, and I will teach
The fact that no fact-finders reach:

Neurotic is that saming game
Of dying to rename a name.
Every object errors light,
And thus eradicates on sight.
What you are is what you're not;
Identity is mental clot.
So let no group or plot define
Hers and his, yours and mine.
Get it?

CORME: Yes.

VAZOLINE: Then give it!

CORME: Goodbye.

VAZOLINE: Bye, good.

(CORME exits.)

VAZOLINE: Ever pleading after power,
When will each be its own flower?
Once again, in my own brambles,
I must bray, and stir up shambles! (Exits.)

(Enter DR. KLING and ERAD, onto the porch of the house.)

ERAD: Do the women expect us, Doctor Kling?

DR. KLING: They expect us, Erad, or, ex-pectus, from the pectorals, they churn a curd.

ERAD: Churn a curd, doctor?

DR. KLING: I say churn a curd; I mean learn a word; episteme identicus, lapsus parturitibus; one hysterik mutter.

ERAD: Hysteric mother?

DR. KLING: Hysterik mutter, Erad, not hysteric mother. The nuance does not miscegenate.

ERAD: The nuance does not miscegenate as symbols, crossing cultures, being the symbol of that cross, represent the method and not the meaning, correct?

DR. KLING: Obviously. We must say ego-gruppe, not ego-group, maintaining the menacing marvel in the former. Bett, not bed, as in LibidoBettstruktur, keeping the dutch etymology of "to beg." And in the extensively firm and rotundative german Name, pronounced Na-ma, neben zie nasal and puny english "name," we see the cripplings castratives of bastardo-bardometry, poor translation, or bad copulating.

ERAD: From copula, meaning to conjoin.

DR. KLING: Ach, jugendwork ist profitlos!

(Enter BERTHA, CORME, MARLA, and LYDIA.)

BERTHA: Doctor Kling! Women, this is Doctor Kling, my therapist.

DR. KLING: And who is this myophore?

CORME: Excuse me?

ERAD: Isn't the myophore the section of the clam to which the ambulatory muscle affixes, doctor?

DR. KLING: I glomagglutinate my ploche. Myo is muscle; phore, to move; thus signifying, in sensu nonsensa, muscle mover, which, via coital prolepsis, infers the activity of "unconches coupling conches."

ERAD: You mean conscious, doctor?

DR. KLING: No, conches.

CORME: Shells?

DR. KLING: Bivalves.

CORME: What has therapy to do with the engendering of crustaceans?

ERAD: Doctor Kling?

DR. KLING: Crustacean, students, is crusty crawdad. Qua crust? Topping. Qua craw? The belly. And dad, via metonym antonymical, is das UberTuber! So, women, being pulp-filled logic pastries, or pie (that indefinitely mysterious series of unknown digit-places), more readily shuck thru therapy, as men are unconches; women, conches.

ERAD: Does this relate to your study on the synecdoche of toddler repetition, doctor?

DR. KLING: It does. "Mama, look at the baby. It's so cute" becomes "I'm a kook. I need therapy. My pain's acute."

CORME: Then female comes to mean speech disorder caused by stout, from phemia and ale.

DR. KLING: And woman signifies man-wooer or womb followed by indefinite article.

BERTHA: Doctor Kling, thru dissecting our discourse,
Inquisits of our mind's primordial source.
His recent book, "O, Woman," is pure brilliance!

DR. KLING: "On Woman" describes my entire position to date.

(Enter LEAVUS.)

LEAVUS: Yo, Merl, ya action babe. Where ya been?

MARLA: Not now, Leavus. Men aren't allowed here.

LEAVUS: So what are these? Chemotherapy chimps?

MARLA: They're doctors!

LYDIA: Hello, Leavus.

LEAVUS: Yah, same to ya.
Look, docs, all due respect to gettin high,
You infect my squeeze's head with that froydo gab,
I'll pop your puny skulls, then you'll need doctors.

MARLA: Leavus, go away!

BERTHA: Yes, Mr. Leavus,
Do as you are named. Marla seeks herself.

LEAVUS: Yo, me and my woman seek stuff together:
We're a team; I coach, she takes the ball.
She's a bumper crop, I am the weather.
When the twisters rip, we rip out Twister
And get snarled in the basement, til we blister.
Our love is ready made, and as I've said,
Woman's like tile; fragile til laid.

BERTHA: How rude.

MARLA: I'll salt you where I shell you, Mr. Peanut.
Now skat, and I will see you in five months.

LEAVUS: Five months? Now Merl, you know my latenight love
Don't pause for station identification.
My love's pounds per square inch; its pressure valve
Has two settings: sloucht or sockets blown.
Make my love wait one minute, it's decrepit,
Sagged to an ornery state, with ice caps melted.
Five months does to love what it does to grits.
From youngest calf, the softest leather's pelted.

MARLA: Are you insinuating that my body
Is your piece of produce pedigree?

LEAVUS: No, but mine'll be if yours'll be!

MARLA: Am I then some farm animal to you?

LEAVUS: That depends how loudly you can moo.

MARLA: You best back off; before I moo, I kick.

LEAVUS: I'll brand you then, and rope ya to my stick.

MARLA: So full of bull, I'd cut it and you'd crumble!

LEAVUS: Til my bull's cut, I'll bellow, and not
    mumble!

MARLA: Witness, women, here, all that's wrong
With man, that fancy pro of vulgar con.

LYDIA: No, O, no! Leavus is a specimen
Of manly riddle, riled for his woman,
Unlike my non-boycotting boyfriend Warren,
Who'd second my choice were I a manikin!
Leavus wrestles; Warren pins himself;
Warren strokes, but Leavus deeply rolfs.
A man should be of spunk just gobs and gobs,
Cuz I'd rather die by fire than choke on sobs.

(Enter WARREN.)

WARREN: I've come!

LYDIA: O, yahoo yippy, Warren's come.

WARREN: Woman, how beguiling are your knees!
Disks, as cute or sweet as baby peas!
Perfect beyond any need to bend,
Yet able, if must, to spread and contend!
Woman, your knees are everything, yet more!
Round and hard, yet soft! Not for the floor!
They hold your thigh and shin together, there,
In that spot, like a lock, sans hair!
O woman, stand erect, and do not kneel;
My gravel-cherishing knees for you ordeal.

LYDIA: Gracias, Warren, now go, and not so gladly;
In one semester, we'll each other see.

MARLA: How sweet a poem!

LYDIA: Such stalking rarely sprouts.

MARLA: And here I thought that men could only
    shout.

LEAVUS: The more I stalk, the more Marla surges.

MARLA: No, the more you talk, the less my urge is.

WARREN: When a lifetime of a year has passt,
Lonely, lonely, lonely, lonely ages,
I, with champagne and petunias vast,
Will return, with reams of praising pages
For Lydia, who is my love in sphere:
Circling me, my everywhere is here.

MARLA: Sphere? I've only been called a basketball.

LEAVUS: You work the perimeter, and drive to the
    rim.

LYDIA: Trust me, words can never do it all.

BERTHA: Well, enough. Doctor Kling, come in.

CORME: How, this house of sisterhood begun
For researches and studies feminine,
Do we to raise our subtle selves devise,
When in the crib our first conviction dies?

LYDIA: One man must have two votes to enter in.

BERTHA: But Doctor Kling is genius! These boys are
    skin.

LEAVUS: What?

MARLA: Quiet.

WARREN: Lydia?

LYDIA: O, shut up.

ERAD: Can I speak?

DR. KLING: You'd say nothing, so do not.

CORME: We ought to follow the grant, as amended.

BERTHA: Yes, we ought. Marla, whom do you choose?
But know, to grovel for is to abuse.

MARLA: As Lydia wants me to, I vote Warren.

LEAVUS: Yah? Then I will veto from Bar Mundi,
Where the women value my dexterity! *(Exits.)*

BERTHA: Lydia?

LYDIA: For Marla, I vote Leavus!

(LEAVUS enters.)

LEAVUS: But never run when you're in the running.

WARREN: That choice I honor and adore, though
    weeping.

BERTHA: Think of the grant, and how we swore to
    study!
As prisoners, by cureless poison tempted,
Express themselves most truly by not taking
Man's unembossed pill, so must we!
From Doctor Kling's important book "For Woman"…

DR. KLING: "On Woman."

BERTHA: "On Woman," to which I wrote
The foreword, I recite this potent passage:
"Woman is an alembic tactical,
Or a Nustern, mistranslated to nostril,
As her logic's sense is due to holes,

Which are gaps, where she picks her roles."
So, I say the doctor, and his young guest,
Must enter, as good intuition's best.

WARREN: Brava, donna!

LEAVUS: What a crock a lugnuts!

DR. KLING: Men are just inherently skeptical
About ideas skeptical of their inherency.
Mann ist Nachurlaublich, which has, ja schon,
No exact english equivalent yet.

ERAD: It means that man is always late to return.

(Enter VAZOLINE.)

VAZOLINE: Mommy, where am I? Son, you're at the
    Festival of Yawns.

LEAVUS: What is that?

WARREN: A transgender activist!

VAZOLINE: O, I knew I came to the zoo to talk!
Educate me then, you slackademics,
Why do all children love cinnamon toast?

LEAVUS: Every child loves cinnamon toast
Cuz it's crunchy and soft, like teeth on tits.

VAZOLINE: He passes such gases, I'll call him a star!
Outgab this gagging man, you gliberator.

WARREN: As sugar is the mother of memory,
So every child loves cinnamon toast.

VAZOLINE: Is he awake, or am I a nightlight?
Doctor Take-It-Back? You could take it all!

DR. KLING: Every child does not love cinnamon
    toast.

VAZOLINE: Buzz! Sorry! The answer is…

ERAD: Every child loves cinnamon toast because
Cinnamon toast rhymes with synonym ghost,
And that each child knows before itself.

VAZOLINE: Son, you shall be number one,
Thus closest be to none. *(Exits.)*

WARREN: What a clever other kind of person.

LEAVUS: That's one woman I won't study.

BERTHA: Corme?

CORME: To be for woman, not against man, I
Came to this house, and yet those I am for

Are now against each other, that my vote
In any way will seem a fit to fit
Into what's fitting, which still cannot fit
My basic tenet of being here for woman.
I am in a spot, and must mischoose
One of you to choose another's one,
Making myself a despot. So, seeing clear
Distinction between a doctor and a lover,
As doctors lead us to our many goals,
While lovers pull us to their one distraction,
I vote, and do it for the group's objective,
For Doctor Kling, and his student, Erad.

LEAVUS: Holy day-old cannoli! Blah blah blah
Blah blah blah blah blah blah blah blah blah blah!
I bet my neck: When Merl skips the pit
With her guzzling racer, I will do drag!

WARREN: I trust this is another fey endeavor
To extract more worship from me, Lydia.
Well, it worked. I love you more than ever,
And will return, with stanzas on your tibia!

MARLA: Leavus, goodbye.

LYDIA: So long, Warren. Sigh.

(LEAVUS and WARREN exit.)

MARLA: Lydia, as woman, has been betrayed.

LYDIA: Not as much as Marla is denied.

MARLA: So, she votes for one, and brings in two.

LYDIA: She has greater interests.

MARLA: She'll double her loss.

(They enter the house.)

BERTHA: I could gulp forever now, and still not swal-
    low pride!

DR. KLING: Each choice, Corme, is a mix of ache and
    ease, and empowers the organ to organize.

BERTHA: In you, Corme, I see my better sex.

DR. KLING: Note it, Erad: Macht ist rein Gerausch.

(They enter the house.)

ERAD: The doctor says that power is silent noise.

CORME: His impotence is blaring information.

ERAD: You study under her?

CORME: He talks over you?

ERAD: I am not out to get you, Corme.

CORME: Good,
Because I am not in to take you, Erad.

ERAD: Why so radical?

CORME: Why so obedient?

ERAD: Let's not read, but just look at, each other.

CORME: Men of your science cannot stare on woman,
But as an author fondling his first text.
And I am here to learn, not to gawk.

ERAD: My science, Corme, seeks to reconfigure
The graph of lust's relations, to deconstruct
Humanity's commuting, basic language,
And wage some compensation for inborn labors.
To saw down walls in habit's bleary maze,
I analyze forlorn and sexfull ways.

CORME: That does sound sexy: grafting woman's
    flesh
With graphics judged by man to up his graft.

ERAD: Perhaps, to you, sex is but exhibition.
To me, who am not timid in its dark,
Our sex is extract of our body's birth.
It's all the meanings, histories, and dreams
Of every tincture of uncome detail;
The plastic, vital, moving communiqué
Of form decreeing law, law begging space,
Space urging time, time talking love,
That binds creation to a coupling code,
Which I intend by cracking to reset:
To you, sex may be just some simple action;
It is, to me, the logic of attraction.

CORME: So says the poet, pornstar, and psychologist:
Sex is all, so let's just all have sex.

ERAD: I am professional.

CORME: Another term
For websites of invisible invasion.

ERAD: You are so stoned with dope conspiracy,
You probly say earth spins to make you dizzy.

CORME: And you are so abstracted with your lust,
Your thoughts are limp, and lack a certain thrust.

ERAD: That was low.

CORME: In earshot of a snake.

ERAD: What have I done to you?

CORME: You cling too much.

ERAD: I'll have you know, the doctor has been called
Messiah of our language's miscarriage.

CORME: And yet, his phrases are so clumped and
    broken,
I thought his thesaurus had aborted.

ERAD: He's famous!

CORME: All that fame can ever do
Is push the past, until our tolerance
To newness is so low, we sell tomorrow
For its fix of loitering arrogance.

ERAD: He is, Corme, the palette of his field!

CORME: My, how much life's spectrum has con-
    gealed.

ERAD: No man, in word's captivity, is freer.

CORME: Of great men's freedom I am prisoner.

ERAD: O, how the glass of genius is here stained
By jealousy, yet scintillates the more
It is besmirched! Must every man, from slugs
That feed upon the compost of old newspaper,
To he whose head deserves the title planet,
Be ever slopped into mundanity
By high frustration's dealer, jealousy?
I'm trained, Corme, to see the swarms of faces
Grimacing the truth around your face:
You're insecure, and so secure this place.

CORME: So dumb is genius, it calls insecure
What it cannot knock down with axioms.

ERAD: If you're so certain, drop Bertha the Bomb.

CORME: Bertha Lerner is a force of nature!

ERAD: O were she so and not a farce of nurture!

CORME: My future traces her.

ERAD: You trace a blur.

CORME: She is of woman's statement architect.

ERAD: Fashionable militants start progressive sect.

CORME: If you don't like it, don't go in it.

ERAD: If I don't enter, I'll miss my victor's exit.

CORME: There is no winning when you beat yourself.

ERAD: To penetrate is triumph in itself.

CORME: You will not go too deeply in, I'm sure.

ERAD: Deep enough to find your cure.

CORME: O! This house is due to men like you.

ERAD: What? Who wish they knew what women knew?

CORME: Don't men, should woman once think for herself,
Instantly turn thinking to love's stealth.
What do you want?

ERAD: I want to know of woman,
Without glamour, gimmicks, or absolute
Design, to touch her simple permutation.
In life's absurding path, she is acute
Of truths both tiny and magnanimous:
She rules both life and love: she calibrates
The mixtures of emotion's rich vicarious;
She sees all secrets; yet, in stranger states
She's curious: of wilderness unlicked,
The art of rounding corners, the extra toe,
The milk that slips from lettuce when it's picked:
In these minutia, she feels a crucial flow.
What is she, being so material,
That renders immaterial all else?
What tugs her, sluices thru her, makes her call
So tirelessly to our better self,
Desiring man, who is so death-adept?
Why is she? From what music has she leapt?
If your eyes see with mine, we will perceive
What man and woman can as one conceive.

CORME: Are you for real?

ERAD: If you say so, I am.

CORME: I say, so I am.

ERAD: I am, so I need.

CORME: You can't come in.

ERAD: But you are my sponsor!

CORME: Why would Doctor Kling have such a student?

ERAD: We each, in some commitment, hide our love.

CORME: We should, for love, not hide what we are of.

ERAD: Corme, do not go in.

CORME: And why not, Erad?

ERAD: We will be posed, in there, opposingly.

CORME: Then let aversion our allure be.

(They enter the house. Enter DICK, LAPTOP, and REM, on the street.)

DICK: Ah, Friday is my day, Laptop! Fishfry!

LAPTOP: What's on the pulldown menu, Dick?

DICK: Well, Paptip, I'll pull down a pint, pull down the curtains, and then I'll pull my own leg.

LAPTOP: No, like, what's the dos?

DICK: I'm the boss, that's who!

LAPTOP: No, man, the dos, like, ya know, the demented order of shakedown?

DICK: What are you, cliffnotes?

REM: Girls.

DICK: O, ya shoulda said so! Well, Squeezetop, seein's I ain't so regular round here, comin from up North there, yack to me of them southern ways, and I will reconnoiter the situation for acquiring us some postal service, cuz man, my bag is bloatin!

LAPTOP: Snail mail?

DICK: Snail trail, Lollipop!

LAPTOP: Escargot!

DICK: Ya, I gotta go too. So what ya get down here, Yapcrop, for shootin the president in public?

LAPTOP: Eighty-sixed.

DICK: Come sixty-nine.

LAPTOP: Sixty-nine from eighty-six is seventeen, Dick.

DICK: Mmmminors.

LAPTOP: Like spelunkin?

REM: Girls.

DICK: Girls, Creamtop, girls!

LAPTOP: Major miscommunication.

DICK: Man, in Brooklyn, babes ooze out the bricks! The gutter's carpeted with babes! Forty ounce babes, half pint babes, even plastic bottle vodka babes! My favorite brand of babe? Boarshead—but we got them others too. Santa Ria babes, O choke my chicken! Petrushka babes, with lots a little ones inside. Hindu babes, with very good hinder; Ganja babes, waftin wit da wailers, singin "One glove, one part, them stick togetha but ya tear them apart." Man, Brooklyn got babes as black as the pyramid's shadow, and as pale as a peel'd potato! I swear, Moptop, Brooklyn babes are as abundant as jockitch at a Red Hook junior high.

LAPTOP: Like, transfer my files to Booklyn.

(Enter NICHEDIGGER.)

NICHEDIGGER: Boys, we got wood.

DICK: Yo, where's the action, Nichedigger?

NICHEDIGGER: I have spotted, via these schnapps goggles, the bellijissimest Georgia peachfuzz ever found on infant behind!

DICK: Jerkin juicyfruits, I'm droolin here!

NICHEDIGGER: With curves like a Chickamauga footlong, and tight as the Tech pomsquad, the air ignit sternoid before her, singeing my eyebrows and palmhairs.

DICK: I'm guyserin! I'm Yomessity!

NICHEDIGGER: She was one big full-body smile, and did prance so pretty like, I bethunk me in a fresh tub a bobblin waters. Hoodoggey, woman's my favorite food!

DICK: Lemme at her!

NICHEDIGGER: I shall then: boys, peer o'er yonder. There on that curb, curbed by none, none but the best, and better than butter, you will find Dick's mama. Park in close, I pray you.

DICK: Ah, ya kudzu cracker!

LAPTOP: Hey, Nichedigger, can I merge your swill?

NICHEDIGGER: And swap your sissy spit? I'd rather rump ya! Move over!

DICK: Hey, talkin a mamas.

NICHEDIGGER: Don't. You are beneath her.

DICK: Ya, but up North we call it on top.

NICHEDIGGER: She wouldn't even glance at you.

DICK: It's hard to look back when you're crawlin in place.

NICHEDIGGER: Shut it, boy.

DICK: I seen a sign that pointed to your mama: Men Working, Next Ten Thousand Feet.

NICHEDIGGER: Mention my dear mother again, I'll make sure you never have one.

DICK: Over and out! Hey, d'ya hear? Nichedigger's mama just got a patent as an alarm clock!

REM: Cool!

LAPTOP: What features?

DICK: She wakes ya up to get turned off; gots a button called smooze makes her buzz all over, and she can do it in digilog or anital, though either methodonology ends up in what ya might call headway. Every man's mama should be an alarm clock, Hosechigger.

NICHEDIGGER: You slimy piece a northern man-dirt.

DICK: Don't hit me!

NICHEDIGGER: And porkwa?

DICK: This highgrade diesel sauce mixed down with my bodily salts and peppers makes one highly explosive mixturation. The whole neighborhood could go.

NICHEDIGGER: Then there goes the neighborhood! Biff!

(NICHEDIGGER hits him.)

DICK: Cronko!

(DICK hits him.)

NICHEDIGGER: Swapp!

(NICHEDIGGER hits him.)

DICK: Thwacky!

(DICK hits him.)

NICHEDIGGER: Womp!

(NICHEDIGGER hits him.)

DICK: Allright already!

NICHEDIGGER: You boys hear a boom?

DICK: I'd a done it, but you're so butt ugly.

LAPTOP: It's the nooks, not the looks.

REM: Wo.

NICHEDIGGER: Do you think our southern ladies would wanna ride the electric bull of corpal greed if a bigcity scumbag like yourself lets this nation's righteous gears get viscous, cuzza all them incapacities from spirits? Hu? Did the great Thamas Jeffson drink his self so dry?

DICK: He brewed his own.

LAPTOP: Monticello means "Pile of Winos."

NICHEDIGGER: Then what about Ulushious S. Grant?

DICK: "I shall meet Robert P. Wee at Atopamax… Appotimox…Amapickax."

LAPTOP: He drank so much whole armies leaked themselves.

NICHEDIGGER: Then Franky Jellono Ruskyvelt. He most definitely never bibed like you.

DICK: I drank with him.

NICHEDIGGER: No way!

DICK: Me and his foxy wife Theodore did port bongs with Franko on the porch, and he'd get so proppt he'd jump out his wheelchair and salsa on the billiards table with his pinkies extended! That man bumrushed the dike!

LAPTOP: The great society was firstly termed "I Hate Sobriety."

DICK: Face it, Pinchtrigger, history is sousery.

NICHEDIGGER: Why, you blasfemin tramps!

LAPTOP: Backspace!

(NICHEDIGGER chases them. Enter LEAVUS and WARREN.)

LEAVUS: Yo, I'm truckin my ass downtown right now,
And pick me up a pierced and wild waif.

WARREN: Yah, I'm headed uptown. I hear those girls
Keep every form of danger in their safe!

LEAVUS: Rock on!

WARREN: Until the sticky, blinking dawn!

LEAVUS: I'm free!

WARREN: De langue de non va langue d'oui!

NICHEDIGGER: Pardon me, men.

WARREN: I give at home.

LEAVUS: Here's a dollar. Psych!

NICHEDIGGER: My name's Nichedigger, the great-grandpuppy of the late and far greater father of all bad mothers, Andrew Long Knife Jackson, and I's wonderin if ya might clue me on, ya know, in a, whadda ya say, tit to tit, where I might pluck me up some apple pie, for the hotdog, via your baseballin?

LEAVUS: That house, right there.

WARREN: My love awaits you all!

(They exit.)

NICHEDIGGER: Well gall damn, it's world serious day!
Oh, you salacious founding padres,
How did I not perceive in your fine nation
There dwelt, derived by you, with starspangled mayonnaise,
Fine breasts a walleye in their cute wrappins?
What else, from the nation that invented foreplay?
Boys, write me up a slit for babeous porpoise!
Cuz as an American, I must pursue my lascivious purpose!
Froward!

REM: Yah.

DICK: Man, you are wordy.

(They exit. Enter MARLA, in the house.)

MARLA: O, what a gentle, pliant man have I
In supple-speaking Warren finally found!
His words, that gift for Lydia wrappt, ensky
With light the gloom that's been my loving-ground.
Leavus is all action-packt shebang,
While Warren works in image, not in gym.
Leavus is a skin flick boomerang,
But Warren is more mystic, more french film.
Were I to talk to Leavus about culture,
He'd flinch as if his blow up doll bit him!
Yet Warren's such a sweet biographer,
The self I want to be I hear in him.
It's time my love matured, became proctress
Of an arousal radical and pure,
That I to music grow, and groans repress,
Played to pitch thru Warren's embouchure.
O, but then, I must abbreviate
These longings, and on this place concentrate!
It's in the sisterhood I breathe, and must
Not choke my source with hoping's underdust.
But here is Lydia, whom I betray.
Go off, reenter, and more honest play. (Exits.)

(LYDIA enters.)

LYDIA: I'm done. My body, lowered into fields
Where spine and brain and pelvis dance apart,
To delirial exogenesis so yields,
Love's lattice swirls me another heart.
Leavus! O, when soon, they say, the sun
Shall eat the earth, why should you not consume me?
How strong you are, and I, so unbegun,
Hard arms demand to force my fantasy.
That pawing Warren's limericks make me sick!
He blinks, and it is fault to make me quake!
I was cloth-mother to that monkey geek,
Who's had nor ate life's ever-moistly cake.
It seems now I have loved a million Warrens,
And yet it seems I've never loved at all!
But O, Leavus, that firm mellifluence,
Throbs into me new vibrants palatal.
Warren's so weak, he weeps when a t-shirt dyes!
He's air, a ghost, a fleshless, junior blip!
Leavus, I think, for greater things is sized,
Will more concretely at the soil grip.
For in this stage of me, I should rehearse
Beside a man of talents substantive.
Yet chasing him I fumble and respin,
And am, to my convictions, fugitive!
How can I swoonly savor, crave, and sip
At all I have denounced as deathmanship?
Betraying my ideals, my own ideas
Become an anarchy I can't betray!
O, where's the pass in passion? Why now, rude lust?

(MARLA enters.)

MARLA: Lydia?

LYDIA: O love, no shame, but smiles.

MARLA: Lydia!

LYDIA: O, my sister, Marla!

MARLA: Isn't this house incredible?

LYDIA: Ineffably!

MARLA: Are you okay?

LYDIA: Are you?

MARLA: Are you?

LYDIA: Are you?

MARLA: We, like african-amazons, beat one drum.

LYDIA: But the mouths of mothers must not falseness bear.

MARLA: I knew you knew what I felt that you felt.

LYDIA: I do.

MARLA: Then let me gush my reservoir
Of withheld worry.

LYDIA: Gush on, you crazy thing!
Reserved, I listen; seat truth where you wish.

MARLA: Though travesty to woman, and thus repuls-
ing,
I'll vote for he it is so clear you love.

LYDIA: Clear I love?

MARLA: Clear as cappuccino!

LYDIA: How do you know?

MARLA: The swarming stares, the lowly, torrid ges-
tures,
The coy rejection whispering full acceptance,
Seeing these, I muttered, "They are perfect."

LYDIA: Really?

MARLA: I would know.

LYDIA: O, Relief, gorge me
To your repletion! What women are we,
So readily exchanging!

MARLA: And accepting.

LYDIA: Marla, he and you, like double dreams
That bookend days diverse, do prove one urge.

MARLA: No.

LYDIA: I'll torch my diary when it's false.

(Enter CORME.)

CORME: May we talk?

MARLA: O, Corme! We've lots to say
On you and me and us and our type stuff!

LYDIA: I'll start.

MARLA: I will.

LYDIA: No me.

MARLA: Warren is in.

LYDIA: Warren?

MARLA: Yes!

LYDIA: I meant Leavus!

MARLA: You love Leavus?

LYDIA: No.

MARLA: Then you meant Warren.

LYDIA: You love Warren?

MARLA: No.

CORME: Women, are we weak? Do we expect
In some man's dusk of self our dawn to see?
No! Thru our own night we must endeavor
To meet that sparkling picture of reform!
Nomads once within the world we bear,
Our roof is anger, saying no to men.
The ghetto of our gender has created
These lexicons of obliged dependency,
From which it is our inmost obligation
To escape, as hard as it may be.
But let your member-selves also remember:
This abstinence is only a semester.
Then, refreshed, and stronger for our struggle,
We'll back into the whirl of common need.
So let us now, as we intended, plan
The role of woman without the reel of man.

(Enter VAZOLINE.)

VAZOLINE: Well, looky who it is; Why, Ms. Belief,
Ms. Conduct, and O, Ms. Taken, too!
Have I missed anyone?

MARLA: Yourself, self missed.

VAZOLINE: I miss myself, you wish to lose yourself.

LYDIA: This ersatz chick calls foul what is not he!

VAZOLINE: Okay, you're chickens, and you taste
like me.

CORME: Such quick responses show you are not free.

VAZOLINE: Let's plod and plume and tweeze the
issues, then,
And longly pause, and ululate of men.

MARLA: Men are a pain.

VAZOLINE: Compared to what?

MARLA: To nothing.

VAZOLINE: Ah, but girl, pain must have its partner,
Cuz for every killer, there's a kiss.
Just like eye needs eye, so pain needs pleasure;
Not seeing the same, they show us synthesis.

LYDIA: Fine, relative to all, man is a pain.

VAZOLINE: If relative to all, then he is Pan,
That ancient, hairy goat-god of deception,
And now, the mix m.c. of all sensation,
Who at his board, lays tracks to each event
And keeps the party pure flirtation.
Pan's body is a satellite omnipotent,
With telefiber wig, a flashing hat
Of movie screens, where slogans reconcile.
Pan's dress is stitched of tiles heat-resistant,
To plummet thru the ozone of denial.
Two luxury ocean liners are his boots,
And he struts the ever-wriggling map of nations;
Pan's languages don't wallow, they transmute;
On his rings twinkle the die of ideations.
Pan is a massive ambling Las Vegas,
Born up from the desert of your addictions.
And at his service bop,
Like fleshy agitprop,
Three null-adoring, duty-free
Daughters of ambiguity:
Lazy, loose as a baptist's hose;
Loud, screaming like the iceman unfroze;
And Laughy, giggling her cortex out her nose!
These fly-on-the-handle,
Gang-of-flummox,
Enemies to energy,
From all-spice shakers,
Dribble their magic milk
Upon you famous fakers,
Breaking down all families
And their pertinent loyalties
Of ethic, of prude, and of ilk!
So life by death by dream by mom by dog can be
enticed,
And the cable box to the comet to the fussflux gets
spliced,
And cohesive xenophobic segregrating judgment's
brain
By Pan is jolted, mixing up our pleasure with our pain!
(Making good things bad, and bad things entertain.)
It's Pan first pierced the nipple with amulet.
Of another's drool, he brews love's sucklant soda.
How much bliss he crams into your debt!
What boring-glory to drive thru South Dakota!
You scratch a crabsore til its gold of puss
Drains out; it's Pan compels your frantic nails.
What horrid joy's the act adulterous!
Why do you shop at Bloomingdale's?
Pan hungers you for that hell. In tattooed skins
He needles the beautiful agony of style.
Look how much a losing boxer wins!

Pan perfumes the owner to its pile.
And in the groanings of a punctured teen,
He enters pain as life's first pleasure scene.
Why do tightpants feel so good?
Who's the hood within the hood?
Pan! The most-talked-about misunderstood!
And at his swimming meet,
Pain and pleasure race the waters,
Like daughters hurdling over daughters,
Putting chic into the slaughters,
As encroaching each other's lane they beat,
Lapping, stroking, choking to swipe
The ultimate trophy, "First in Hype."
But here is Pan, in velvet chair, smoking a fat Robusto,
Laughing so unfoundedly, "O, they drown with
    gusto!"
While in the booth his pale announcers jabber pitch-
    lessly,
It's pain this year, as we with pleasure see.
Cuz pleasure's finishline is death,
And pain's goal is limitless,
So the game is started done,
As to compete for all's to play for none!
You who fly
To call the sky
Tiny, when you go
On jets of pain
It's pleasure's plane
To Pan's imbroglio.

MARLA: Allright, then! Only some men are pains!

VAZOLINE: So, your meat's a waffle; your core, a
    fudge,
And your argument's point is your circular head.
In squirms the can of worms to squirming judge,
Followed by the part-pregnant and half-dead!

LYDIA: I know one thing: you're a pain.

VAZOLINE: Find my pain and say you feel,
Feel my pain and say you heal,
Heal my pain and call me better,
Steal my pain and say I never.
I quote when I say the wise shouldn't quote,
But…

CORME: Vazoline, go off somewhere and gloat.

VAZOLINE: (Sings.) O, can the strong still survive?
Are my emotions recorded live?
O what came first? I will confirm
The chicken egg is chicken sperm! (Exits.)

MARLA: I'm tired, and going upstairs.

LYDIA: So too am I.

(They exit.)

CORME: Though none condone, to be myself I try.
    (Exits.)

(Enter THE WISHFUL WAITERS at the door of the
house.)

GENE: Wishful Waiters, group grope. I call the roll, in
    order of appearance. Art!

ART: Arturo.

GENE: Rock!

ROCK: Present.

GENE: Nicelle.

NICELLE: That's my name.

GENE: Now, we've a birthday gram to give, birthdays
    are very special days, so we must be very, very spe-
    cial. Therefore, I, your author, have crafted a play in
    verse, rich with thoughtful emotion and passionate
    intellect, entitled "The Blueberry Play." This very,
    very, very special skit tells how Sky (played by Art),
    and Earth (Rock, please), fight for the love of Bush
    (Nicelle), consummating in the creation of the blue-
    berry, the perfect birthday fruit. So, breathe, stretch,
    and smile, cuz, people, this is pay. One gimp thru,
    we sprint. O happy happy…

ART: When's my sexy farm-hand scene with Bush?

GENE: There are no sexy farm-hand scenes in birthday
    grams. O happy happy…

ROCK: He, Sky, she, Bush, and I but lowly Earth? Will
    I not be upstaged?

GENE: All parts are equal in my play. O happy
    happy…

NICELLE: I am not Bush.

GENE: The line was cut. O happy happy…

NICELLE: I am not Bush.

GENE: The line is in. O happy happy…

NICELLE: I mean I will not take the part of Bush.

GENE: Nicelle, there are sound dramatic principles
    why you should play the bush.

NICELLE: Name me one.

GENE: You more readily imagine bushy-type super-objectives by utilizing your affective memory of past bushy experiences, just as I, who inhabit the sky of genius…

NICELLE: I've had no bushy experiences.

ART: Liar on the stage.

GENE: People, no real conflicts!

NICELLE: I will not play the bush.

ART: Yo, the bush is a juicy part.

ROCK: Your gifts are best revealed in your bush, as my airy gifts…

GENE: The audience loves your bush, Nicelle.

NICELLE: Look, you histrionic hunks. It is rude, sexist, demeaning, regressive, and totally un-American that I should play the bush.

GENE: My dear Nicelle, this is a birthday gram, not a day at the Grammys. We are the Wishful Waiters, not waited upon by well wishers. This is not grand marquis, but tiny margin. Not star-studded, but deep space nine. Not tourist driven, but tourette's driven. So leave the identity politics to the public and play what I say, or no pay.

ROCK: I shall inform Equity of this.

GENE: My Equity is bigger than Equity.

ART: Disempowering Gene! Equity is our union. Our bubblewrap against abuse. Our assurance against naked auditions. In a world where the faux are not free and the free cannot be faux, how dare you defy Equity?

GENE: I own the Wishful Waiters, I write the checks, so you are my actors.

NICELLE: My actors?

ART: No one owns me, man.

ROCK: Impudent pig operative, thou!

NICELLE: So I'm a bimbo in a spot to save your limbo plot?

ART: The play frickin stinks.

ROCK: It doth offendeth my strills.

NICELLE: And verse? What is this, Elizabethan Rome?

ART: Eat me, Gino, eat me!

ROCK: The union declareth a strike!

ART: Strike!

NICELLE: Strike!

GENE: Fine, you videots, write the script yourselves.

ROCK: We will improvise.

ART: Ya.

NICELLE: Ya.

ROCK: Improvisor, I. Come with me, people, come with me. I'm a jelly fish, bobbling in a clam, violent sea, when a friendly shark bites me in half, O! But I'm rescued by a manly fishergirl, who heals me, as we quiver and shriek, til O blammobajinsky, I am born again as Sky, or me, Rock Random, dancing, nude, juggling the sun, and now you enter singing…

ART: End of strike.

NICELLE: I think we found our bush.

GENE: People, scrunch up cozy. Art, you are Earth. Rock, you are Sky. And Nicelle, you are Bush. Nicelle, this is a theater of creations, not of operations. The stage is a wishful word-worn place. The plot is a ploy to garner cash. And character? What is a character? A dash of dark across a screen of white? Character is nada. Sliver moons, holey socks, and the philanthropies of genius longer last. Do not let pride wage you out of wonder. Do not deprive your image of her action. There are as many characters as inconsistencies, but there is only one consistent you. Though your character is bush, you are ever you, so find your bush, embrace your bush, spread wide with wild pride your bush, and do not be, just play the bleepin bush!

(They all exit. Enter NICHEDIGGER, DICK, LAPTOP, and REM.)

NICHEDIGGER: Troops, subside. The first amenmint says "no soldier shall be stripped and gizzard in a house lessen that owner's lower quadrants are will-fully stripped thereto." Orgo, my right to distend and enter is secured by the same irreputable laws accorded woman that she may wear her nighties all day long. Inward crusty soldiers to the house of hoseable hootaninnys!

DICK: And who says you're the best man for the job?

NICHEDIGGER: You sayin I'm the worst man for the job?

DICK: I'm sayin you're the best man for the job.

NICHEDIGGER: You sayin I'm the best man for the job?

DICK: I'm sayin you're the best man for the job!

NICHEDIGGER: And I'm sayin you're the best man for the job!

DICK: Then I'll do the job!

LAPTOP: See, we need like protocol: Expensively extensive modem surveys prove there are women in houses throughout much of the phoneable world. Each man should expound his attributes, experiences, and references and include an objective statement on how to like enter the house, for the best of us is the test of us. Rem, cue up.

NICHEDIGGER: My name's Nichedigger. Country? Mine. On a finite globe, America, the infinite. Acclitudes? I can clean up after myself, when forced. Experiences? I can chase panty, preferably with a Blatz. References? I can tap kegs (ting! ting! She's empty!), I can fry up a topbutt t-bone that'll grow your gut over your molars, and I can flush any GTO on a flat nevada mile if there's T-and-A at the ribbon, so I am the man for the job!

LAPTOP: How does this spreadsheet get them to spread under the sheets?

DICK: We could throw him in front of a bus, and ask to use their phone.

LAPTOP: If we're to like execute this object exchange without downtime, we must poll all channels for optimal database entries. So, like I have a plan.

NICHEDIGGER: Make it quick.

LAPTOP: Surfing the cyberwaves of virtual nature, we see a coherent bitmap showing that reality is based in realty. So, like dragging our image into a custom box, and inserting it into their graphic, it's clear that we should load up on women's garments, and like then bearing the appearance of these multimedia treats, we'll coolly chill into their webby software domain.

REM: What?

NICHEDIGGER: Does this mean you do not think I am the best man for the job?

LAPTOP: Government reports say no one listens to government reports.

DICK: Both a you deadbeats remind me of a piece a liverwurst I threw up once: Me—"How come you're comin up steada goin down?" It—"There ain't no worse liver than you, Dick Skills."

NICHEDIGGER: Boy, your only skill's poppin corks and zits.

DICK: You forget cherries and questions, in that order.

LAPTOP: Maybe Rich is the man for the job.

DICK: Dick. My name is Dick.

NICHEDIGGER: And whatsoever makes him the man for the job?

DICK: I can take a dive, but not give a damn; I can hit the ground, even if it's moving.

LAPTOP: And Confuseus say: brain like cookie; made bad by raisin. Drunk head like drunk soup: make you feel you're in. Man with no mind must be minded.

NICHEDIGGER: What language is that country from?

DICK: Man, you southern boys is a bunch of gumbo dumbies! We'll just head to Bunhugger's house, grab his camera equipment, then pop into this voluptuant pooter pavilion, posing as Big Fashion Deal photographers, and we're in as a bellybutton!

LAPTOP: Sources say going to the source is highly reensourcing.

NICHEDIGGER: Let's go to Lipcrap's house.

LAPTOP: Laptop, and I like forgot my password.

NICHEDIGGER: Then let's go to Richard's.

DICK: Dick! The name is Dick! And my house is what ya call spacially sensitive: its space is my senses.

NICHEDIGGER: Can't you do nothin, Rem?

REM: Eat pizza.

DICK: Shazam!

NICHEDIGGER: Then I say we cruise on up there, in a southern and sexual manner, and offering pie for pie, we're in the house.

LAPTOP: File save.

NICHEDIGGER: O, you lusty men! We have been called
To test our bunny-guns up at the dogtrack!
So let's howl! Dammit, you are good men,
And you're rowdy men, and bad also!
You are range-pigs of the American desert,
Starved for quailbroth, with thronking trunks
And a javalina's hankerin for Glad bags!
Let your Decorations of Dependence
Call out to these far-lips' louisiana.
For this is it, my men. Manfest density!
Rich, Lipcrap, Rem, march!

DICK: Dick!

LAPTOP: Laptop!

REM: Dood!

NICHEDIGGER: Whatever!

(They exit. Enter LYDIA, at MARLA's window.)

LYDIA: The lute of lust I follow without control,
Even to the room of my ally.
I should leave!

(Enter LEAVUS.)

LEAVUS: Hey, Marla, is that you?

LYDIA: O, temptation, you shyly, slyly serve.

LEAVUS: Yo, Marlin, can't we work this whole thing out,
And get back to the funky-futon biz?

LYDIA: Macho one, woman zilch.

LEAVUS: If twice a night
Ain't doin it for you, I'll up the dose.

LYDIA: Another ace for Urge Overkill.

LEAVUS: Come on, Merl. We can work it out.

LYDIA: Match point, and I'm in love.

LEAVUS: Remember how I oiled your body down?

LYDIA: Yes, Leavus, yes, yes, how I remember!

LEAVUS: Well, could I peruse the goods?

LYDIA: No. I'm in mud-mask.

LEAVUS: Marla?

LYDIA: Leavus, we have to talk.

LEAVUS: Hey, I can talk.

LYDIA: When on the porch Lydia first approached,
Your rapture at her beauty was so blatant,
You gazed and gulped like mutt upon a meal.
Don't say it isn't so; her gorgeous frame
Went up like scaffolding in which you weaved
And wobbled with the wind of lust's effusion.
Of course, you go as wolf to baby deer,
In carnal homage to delicious wonder,
Guiltless to ravish she so ravishing.
But do you love her, Leavus, more than me?

LEAVUS: Me, love Lydia? That victim to vogue?
That tasteless tofu patty with the multi-grain bun?
Babe, I'd rather get ganged by whoopin cranes
Than nibble that gamehen; she is way pretentious.

LYDIA: Might such repulsion hide a lover's taste,
That is afraid to eat, and thus to waste?

LEAVUS: I would spank my privates out in public
Before I'd much as let her flick my Zippo.

LYDIA: You go too far to prove your object worthless;
There must be some desire in your distress.

LEAVUS: I'd sooner love a bunsen-burner belt.

LYDIA: Such a loss would be too hugely felt.

LEAVUS: Girls like her, they breathe out anesthesia.

LYDIA: Then she, the cause, could cure the phobia.

LEAVUS: Marla, what's up?

LYDIA: O, if only I weren't me,
But her he loves, or that, unknown to him,
I could somehow construct another we,
Where he'd love me, not being among them
I am among, so, loving he his hate
For us, he'd savor me, and we could mate!

LEAVUS: Marla, I'll do anything to get inside!

LYDIA: The only way is you become a woman.

LEAVUS: Anything does not include that shit.

LYDIA: If you desire me, you will become me.

(She throws him women's clothing and wig.)

LEAVUS: Are you psycho? What is this, plasma week?

LYDIA: Do it, Leavus. The reward is ecstasy.

(She exits. She enters.)

LYDIA: When as a woman you meet me at the door,
Take the name Hormonia, my whore. (Exits.)

LEAVUS: Hormonia? O, man, that bitch is crooked!
I do not do this. This I do not do.
Man is stuck together by a stud
Of mottoes. Mine is like I said.
We'd all be sluts, if we just upped and changed
Every time the currency rearranged.
No way, Merl! This here dog ain't whippt!
Before I dress the way you want, I'll strip! (Exits, with
    the clothes.)

(Enter MARLA, at LYDIA's window.)

MARLA: O would he came, yet would he wouldn't,
    and yet!
Below highwires of love, is there no net?

(Enter WARREN.)

WARREN: If tied, O hateful love, unto the earth
In Yunnan's woods, where bamboo fields grow,
That sprouting shoots pierce thru my tender girth,
Still would I yet much deeper horror know!
Love's centrifugal, total-bonding hole
In this war of gentle-jabbing jaws and shanks,
Do your all-scrambling moods and cranky soul
Explode into cosmogonies of angst!
You rage, my thankful sorrow calls it peace;
You bite and pour your brandy where I bleed;
You ditch my love thus I thru loss increase;
You staple me to all and call me freed.
Yet well! Above, there's shadow, as if night
To one spot came. Lydia, is this a fight?

MARLA: No, Warren, it's a hug.

WARREN: Is that my precious?

MARLA: I am the one forgetful lovers call "you."

WARREN: Why am I from your softness now removed?

MARLA: Cuz by removal I a favor seek.

WARREN: Though I must lose my torso, I will do it!

MARLA: Your voice, that choir of complimenting tease,
To me alone has throated songs of late,
Yet when you rhymed my charm in peas and knees,
Another me felt not so desolate.

WARREN: Whatever other, I've no other ever;
To them I happen; to you, I persever.

MARLA: O, but Warren, might your jaw not cramp,

Chewing always round a single name?
Commitment is a maiming, laming clamp
To crush our sensual infatuations!
One lover is but one from everything;
Two lovers more than twice, as competition
Brings about delirious multiplying.
O, go, be fat!
Be Mr. Natural, the sex-offender,
Whose one offense is knowing where it's at.

WARREN: Whereto, love, these dizzy metaphors?

MARLA: My friend, Marla, needs your praises, Warren.
Though she's perfunct to tight commendment's needs,
She has not dated the verbalest of men.
Sprinkle on her, for me, your metric seeds.

WARREN: Marla?

MARLA: Do it, Warren.

WARREN: What's she to praise?

MARLA: Her mind.

WARREN: Were it as yours, then I would praise it.

MARLA: Her shape—what shades and colors show
    it best?

WARREN: The ones that augur darkness in the west.

MARLA: Then, her face—what does it bring to view?

WARREN: Big pores, small eyes, and a don't hairdo.
Lydia, must I praise her, and not you?

MARLA: Yes! What else has she of quality?

WARREN: None else that having seen her once I see.
She is noisy, sass, and nebulous;
You are tuneful, bunt, and rich.
Her talk is droll, her points ambiguous,
While you all thoughts-exact together stitch.
Of every talent you own rights to boast;
Marla has the flair of Wonder toast.

MARLA: Have you any poems yet written for her?

WARREN: I've one for you, Lydia.

MARLA: That will do.

WARREN: Wait, Lydia,

MARLA: No, say "Wait, Marla."

WARREN: Wait, Marla, wait
There for my word,

hat off from the sweetest of scentust end,
That you sway, Marla, sway,
And you play, Marla, play.

MARLA: O, how personal, go on, go on!

WARREN: Come, Marla, come
To where you belong,
Push, Marla, push
The weak to the strong,
For you stir me to wait,
And you kiss me to sting,
And you sparkle me glum
For the moments you rush,
Cuz it's wrong, Marla, it's wrong
To love as if living were long,
Rather sing, Marla, a song,
That I may sing along.
Lydia, can I come in now?

MARLA: If you so badly want her, put these on.

(She throws him women's clothing and wig.)

WARREN: Brilliant, love!

MARLA: I'll meet you at the door.

WARREN: One more ode to you, and I will go.

MARLA: No! Love must wait til only lovers know.

(They exit. Enter BERTHA, ERAD, and DR. KLING.)

BERTHA: How thrilling to try new therapies, radical yet structured, heuristic yet didactic, intuitive yet purposive, involving Corme in the stereotypes of her own emotions! Enter the patient!

ERAD: May I ask the objectives of these methodologies, Doctor Kling?

DR. KLING: Today, we will be utilizing my recent exigency of therapeusis, "Gegensatzunterbrechungsuberlisten," or the disruption of resistance thru prescient frolic. My third book on the psychogenesis of gynecosemantics, "VulvaMetaforik," may be referenced.

BERTHA: An exciting text!

DR. KLING: The human female is tertiad.

BERTHA: A three-part thing.

DR. KLING: First, the labio section, from "labo," indicating "I hesitate." This perimeter system, signifying the anxieties, ecstasies, and humidities of the patient, I term the prope, or almost, system.

BERTHA: We effect this system thru a roleplay on relation.

DR. KLING: Next, durch stimulatio, the patient's self-concept, or fold, expands and puffs, exposing the clito-complex, or summer stock. Stemmed in clitella, or saddle; clivosus, or hill; and clio, the muse of history, we ride audibliating to the top of the patient's past, where we reveal, or rub off, the tenant of mentations responsible for mood and habit, or the clito-complex, which forms the nunc, or now, system.

BERTHA: It's here that Corme questions her control.

DR. KLING: Lastly, in the semper, or always, system, we ramble to the cervix, or channel of creation, where we split the patient's personal traits from her impersonal drives, finding the ventricles of her somatic jargon, venting them, that they trickle, thereby incurring the insemination of equilibrium, the parturition of placidity, and bringing, finally, relaxation for our efforts.

BERTHA: O, how intense!

DR. KLING: By these methods, we cure Corme of her problem.

ERAD: What problem, Doctor Kling?

DR. KLING: She resists manipulation.

ERAD: Does not that prove she has no problem, doctor?

DR. KLING: He is so thoroughly confused.

BERTHA: Manipulation, Erad, is education. Corme's recalcitrance is more self-easing than self-izing, and we merely stroke her unreachable parts, being so, as it were, unstretched.

DR. KLING: Society, or Gesellschaft, is manipulation under dreamlight. A shaft enters a companion, genus feels union, there is cramming, durcheindringen, and the surling of nubs. All things cling to nubs, therefore are nubs all things. So, we concentrate on the nubs.

BERTHA: And concentrate, in german, is, I think, dich.

DR. KLING: It is, and it means thick.

BERTHA: Thru this treatment, we open Corme to herself.

DR. KLING: Not "treatment," Ms. Lerner, but "treat me nt."

ERAD: nt?

DR. KLING: To the nth, as you wish.

BERTHA: It's all about existence.

DR. KLING: Existenz, Ms. Lerner, pronounced "Ek! Cyst ends!," recircling to the nubs.

BERTHA: The nubs.

ERAD: Thank you, doctor, for clarifying.

DR. KLING: Behind the screen.

(They go behind the screen, and CORME enters.)

CORME: Where am I born, within me or without?
Have I the single sense of my own being,
Or in relation's teeming roundabout
Am I a breath from others' meandering?
How can I say "I wish myself to be,"
If wishing is a self that isn't yet?
Can wishes dredge the tiding from the sea,
Sideswipe the sun, and force the moon's regret?
She I trusted, now trusts in Dr. Pun;
My sisters, firm of plan, now romp unraveling;
And this boy, so brilliant yet outshone,
Desires my figure for his figuring!
Our high ideals are lowly deprivations;
A shallow plot refracts deep honesty;
To dream? To doubt? To fear? To hate? To love?
All's but the cast of thought, that rerun comedy,
Where sameness lives for difference, and ends the same.
If to the wild ventured, you are eaten.
If to the garden, you are clippt and tame.
What is it then to be a strong woman?
Must she, forsaking men, herself forsake,
As none's the gift of giving in to none,
Or, wanting of her image, can she partake

Of man, and doubled be, by taking one?
O, love's a fleurage from our simpleness,
Yet I must rescue him from an addling spell!
But then, if I'm the Prince, who is my Princess,
When him I want is by his want compelled?
O, and I do want him. So, from deceit
I'll save his over-wonder-blunted spirit,
For what is strength, but in some love complete
To strive to settle with one's opposite?
I am afraid, which I to him will show,
And bravely there, to love say yes or no.

(Enter BERTHA and ERAD.)

BERTHA: O, you salty peanut!

ERAD: I said no!

BERTHA: But I asked you should I stop!

ERAD: Corme!

BERTHA: O, Corme.

ERAD: Hello, Corme.

CORME: Hello.

BERTHA: We're doing research, for doctor Kling.

ERAD: Yes, research.

CORME: What have you lost that you must research it?

BERTHA: O, you know, this and that and the other.

ERAD: Nothing, really.

BERTHA: Isn't he cute?

CORME: What?

BERTHA: Back to the lab!

CORME: Erad, wait.

(They exit. Enter DR. KLING.)

DR. KLING: How wend your widsithians, Corme?

CORME: Weirdly.

DR. KLING: What's wrong?

CORME: I'm not sure.

DR. KLING: Why are you stammering?

CORME: I'm not.

DR. KLING: Why are you pausing?

CORME: I'm not.

DR. KLING: What does this evasion mean?

CORME: What are Bertha and Erad researching, Doctor Kling?

DR. KLING: Why do you ask?

CORME: They passed by here just now, and acting very intimate, told me they were doing research for you.

DR. KLING: Intimate?

CORME: Acting very strangely, close.

DR. KLING: Close is strange, Corme?

CORME: No, but for them it is not normal.

DR. KLING: You now predominate upon normalcy?

CORME: No.

DR. KLING: You fixate on the loss of relation.

CORME: I do not.

DR. KLING: But forgive me. I am informing you. *(Exits.)*

(Enter BERTHA, dragging ERAD by a leash around his neck.)

CORME: Erad?

ERAD: Yes, Corme?

CORME: Why are you wearing a leash?

ERAD: I am empowered by being on a leash, Corme.

CORME: This is a joke.

BERTHA: Erad and I are performing bondage therapies to reify our structural power assumptions, Corme. Does that concern you?

CORME: Does it concern me? No. Yes. Yes, I have a concern.

ERAD: What concern could you have?

CORME: It is stupid. That's my concern.

ERAD: You call stupid what I wish to do?

CORME: I call dumb what others convince you to do.

BERTHA: He asked I place him on a leash.

CORME: I thought we had sworn to celibacy!

BERTHA: Are you inferring this infers I have deferred from that?

CORME: No.

BERTHA: You obviously have a problem with having problems, Corme.

ERAD: An extremely problematic problem.

CORME: This is a joke.

BERTHA: Jokes are immature revolutions, Corme.

ERAD: I am a naughty, excessive, gifted boy,
And, by my beggings balsamiferous,
Madam Lerner makes my id her toy,
Enacting little pranks upon my tush.
Will you honestly deny me this education?

BERTHA: Crawl, puerile minor.

ERAD: I have shame
I have thanks
The two are one
When I get spanks.

BERTHA: By being humbled, Erad transcends himself.

ERAD: Let's go diaper Mr. Menial!

(They exit. Enter DR. KLING.)

CORME: What is happening?

DR. KLING: Events, mysteries, defecations.

CORME: You are the clown behind this chaos.

DR. KLING: Do you want me to be?

CORME: You're playing a stunt.

DR. KLING: Are you stunted?

CORME: I am soaring so above it.

DR. KLING: No. You are losing control. *(Exits.)*

CORME: The thoughts that capture them, don't rapture me;
Kling's zony cage holds them, but I am free.

(Enter BERTHA in dog mask, ERAD in pig mask.)

CORME: Ah, but this is captious! Wait, I'll guess: Men are pigs, women are bitches, so you mask yourselves in sexist taxonomies to finally tear them off. I'm catching on.

BERTHA: What are you catching?

CORME: The plague of plaques and games.

ERAD: How juvenile to call rebirth a game.

BERTHA: When I have barked to the phenomenal epicenter of my canine conscience, Corme calls it Scattergories.

ERAD: And when I can at last relax, knowing the emotional sustenance of wearing my pig mask about the house, Corme accuses me of monopoly.

CORME: This justified insanity is very old. Let me be.

BERTHA: Be what?

CORME: Alone.

ERAD: Be a gerbil, Corme.

CORME: Excuse me?

BERTHA: Be the gerbil in yourself.

ERAD: You are the archetype of gerbilesque.

CORME: Why am I a gerbil?

ERAD: You are fuzzy, delicate, and a great pet for the kids.

BERTHA: And you scamper on your dainty habit trail!

ERAD: Here, we brought you a gerbil mask.

CORME: No thank you.

BERTHA: Put it on, Corme!

ERAD: You'll feel free!

CORME: I don't want to be a gerbil!

ERAD: We must become what we don't want to be to be ourselves!

BERTHA: Lydia's a walking stick!

ERAD: Marla's a horny toad!

BERTHA: Doctor Kling is a silver-backed stud gorilla!

CORME: No!

(Enter VAZOLINE.)

VAZOLINE: What's the racket?

(BERTHA and ERAD run off.)

CORME: I don't know!

VAZOLINE: It's a tool for hitting balls, you hermit. (Exits.)

(Enter DR. KLING.)

DR. KLING: What do you want, Corme?

CORME: I want to know who decided I'm a gerbil.

DR. KLING: Are you a baby frozen in a Popsicle?

CORME: No.

DR. KLING: Is this an atmosphere of Johnsons and Johnsons?

CORME: No.

DR. KLING: Are you horse-piddle waterfalls on ham and cheese croissants?

CORME: I am myself.

DR. KLING: Self is addiction, Corme, or a rodent, dreamt to a flinch.

CORME: I'm going.

DR. KLING: Being drained, you cannot go, as we go by signs, like "loose rocks" or "soft shoulder," for signs are clusters of excitations, or aureoles, which nozzle the Brustsemiotik.

CORME: The what?

DR. KLING: The breast signifiers, reservoirs recuperant, or, in some tongues, jugs.

CORME: Jugs?

DR. KLING: Which I can replenish.

CORME: Speech has never lied so well.

DR. KLING: Speech never lies, and when it does, not on its front, due to its breasts.

CORME: I'm going.

DR. KLING: Come with me, Corme, into the thirteen steps.

CORME: I thought there were only twelve steps.

DR. KLING: The thirteenth, being the loss of identity, means you will be in therapy for the rest of your life, with me.

CORME: I'll lay upon your couch when he is she. (Runs off.)

DR. KLING: To deny me is to want me, Corme!

(Enter BERTHA and ERAD.)

BERTHA: Your prognosis, Doctor Kling?

DR. KLING: We must win
The ego of the patient thru a play.

(They exit. Enter LEAVUS, dressed as a woman, at door of the house.)

LEAVUS: Finally, love has let me down so low
I see the bottom of the mine of man:
Will he cut off his head to get some head? Yep.
Will he wear weird things to be in? Yep.
The soul of man is like a stripclub:
The nudity's free, the beers are pricy,
And ya get yourself ejected if ya touch.
Wow, that's some heady stuff. My Merl best be
Wearin her Victory's Secret lunge-array!
But wo! I got knockers, so I'll knock. *(Knocks.)*

(Enter VAZOLINE.)

VAZOLINE: What are you?

LEAVUS: None of your backwards business. Tell Marla, Hormonia's here.

VAZOLINE: Hormonia? Then this must be puberty!

LEAVUS: Looky, Captain Covert Corndog. Go get her.

VAZOLINE: I got her last night, and like birth, I don't repeat myself.

LEAVUS: Let me in!

VAZOLINE: I'd sooner drown you in the gene pool.

(Enter LYDIA.)

LYDIA: Hormonia!

LEAVUS: Lydia?

VAZOLINE: And I'm Testy Ester, from the Vast Albuminal Deference, and I was wondering if you wouldn't be too dead to sign my petition against extinction?

LEAVUS: Step it back.

LYDIA: Hurry, Hormonia!

LEAVUS: Where is Marla?

LYDIA: It's I that dressed you as I desired, Leavus!

VAZOLINE: And they call this shit straight?

LEAVUS: You want me? That's it! I'm out!

VAZOLINE: Then come back to my closet!

LEAVUS: This shack is a nuthouse!

VAZOLINE: And this earth is a blueball.

LEAVUS: You tell Marla that she can smooch my buttocks pasta la vista!

VAZOLINE: Can I, can I?

LYDIA: No, Hormonia, wait, and I'll explain!

(LYDIA chases LEAVUS off.)

VAZOLINE: Hurry! Hurry! Crepes on fire!
Emergency! Peach perspire!
Spray the hose at puppy's owy!
Helpy yelpy! Bowy wowy! *(Exits.)*

(Enter WARREN, dressed as a woman, at door of the house.)

WARREN: Ha! I do look fine! This lipstick color
Like flame to forest does match my haut couture.
The blouse? Vintage Salvation Armani.
The hair? Get-with-it wigs, by Connie.
And these pumps? Push em, and they squeal.
Boy, if realness is, then I am real. *(Knocks.)*

(Enter VAZOLINE.)

VAZOLINE: Why, you must be Fabia!

WARREN: Who?

VAZOLINE: Hormonia just left!

WARREN: O.

VAZOLINE: So you're first!

WARREN: Good.

VAZOLINE: But she knocked first.

WARREN: O.

VAZOLINE: And knocking is intentful.

WARREN: It is.

VAZOLINE: And being is incidental.

WARREN: Yes.

VAZOLINE: So?

WARREN: Is Lydia here?

VAZOLINE: She's dead.

WARREN: O, dead?

VAZOLINE: What are you, dial-a-flood?

WARREN: How dead?

VAZOLINE: Did I say dead? Sorry. I meant busy.

WARREN: Can Lydia come out and play?

(Enter MARLA.)

VAZOLINE: La Fabia nouveaux est arrivé!

MARLA: Be scarce.

VAZOLINE: But this girlscout's selling thin-mints.

MARLA: Ciao, bella.

VAZOLINE: Or is this a boyscout selling fat-gum?

MARLA: Arrivederci.

VAZOLINE: Or is this den-mother packing brownies?

WARREN: Is Lydia here?

MARLA: Lydia doesn't want you, Furbia. I do.

VAZOLINE: Rip the retina from reason, I'm versch-mutzed!

WARREN: It's you that dressed me?

MARLA: Yes.

VAZOLINE: I'll get my gun.

WARREN: You tell false-Lydia here that Freebia's gone.
There's only so much even I can stand.
Though I'm the one she calls the one,
I won't be a man in no-man's-land!

MARLA: No, Fobia, I need you!

(MARLA chases WARREN off.)

VAZOLINE: Quick! Let's all exit as Greed
And enter as What We Need! (Exits.)

(Enter DR. KLING, BERTHA, dressed as a man, and ERAD, dressed as a woman.)

BERTHA: Are we certain this role-play won't harm her, doctor?

DR. KLING: Learning begins when bowels move vowels, da-da becomes do-do, ma-ma turns to we-we, in a process termed Umgestalten, or rolling over. Venturing to Corme's parental anima, we schismatize her clanic-membrane, strobing where we'd probe.

BERTHA: Of course.

DR. KLING: And, as I have written, "Women are saucy, sauces are fungible, so the catharctic goulash grows fungus without friction."

ERAD: You wrote that?

DR. KLING: Do not smuggle dope across the borders of my hallucinogenic state.

ERAD: What?

DR. KLING: You are inferior to me in mind, age, stamina, reading, assets, outlets, and cathexis; You are a mess, I am a message. And nota bene: to flunk, in german, is to fail.

BERTHA: I trust you, Doctor Kling.

DR. KLING: To the phones.

(They go behind the screen. Enter CORME, composing a letter.)

CORME: "Dear Marla and Lydia." But why to them? They quit the minute they joined. "To Ms. Lerner." Yet why to her? What entrust to whom I do not trust? Then, "Dear Erad." Right. Why cram such wheeze and warrant into abandon? "Dear departed: This house has shown the meaning of coalition: disdain-contriving, false-defining, envy-shouting silence. I am giving up the study, and joining my parents in L.A. In them I know, in all I know, reality." Yet is it not the surest sign of despair to use this word "reality"? "I truly hope to never see you again, or, if I do, I hope you are all someone else. Not shaken by my perceptions, I am moved to shake them away. My thanks to your ingratitude, my regards to your irregard, and my awe at your apathy. Severely, Corme." This letter is harsh, but harsh am I within, tough to hurt I'll later feel.
So, like the cat I steal the spoon,
And let these cows slump over the moon,
The moon so sad behind exhaust,
That shines defaced on the place I've lost. (Goes to exit.)

ERAD: My yellow fingers will not walk the dial.

(BERTHA dials the phone near her and the one near CORME rings. The answering machine picks up.)

MACHINE: Sorry, no one's home right now but you,
So while you talk, why don't you listen, too.
Beep.

BERTHA: Hello? Corme? It's me, your mother.

CORME: (Picks up.) Mom? You're hard to hear.

BERTHA: I'm on the carphone. O, it's horrible!

CORME: What is?

BERTHA: Your father threw a fit and kicked me out!

CORME: What?

BERTHA: You're not mine, Corme, you're hers. They said she wouldn't come when I adopted. She scared me, cuz she's big like a man.

CORME: What are you talking about?

BERTHA: She's wearing a gingham dress and a sunflower scarf. Oh, you're not my baby! *(Hangs up.)*

CORME: Mom? *(Hangs up.)*

(The phone rings. CORME picks up.)

CORME: Hello?

ERAD: Corme, honey, it's your father.

CORME: Dad? This phone is really bad.

ERAD: She lied to me. You're not mine, you're his, that scrawny, bearded, pin-stripe suited wimp! I have no child! *(Hangs up.)*

CORME: Dad? *(Hangs up.)* My father has no child? What's going on?

(Enter DR. KLING, BERTHA, and ERAD.)

DR. KLING: Please, not now.

ERAD: Looka, that's my baby!

CORME: Gingham dress and a sunflower scarf?

BERTHA: She sure as shuckin beats you for looks.

CORME: Pin-striped suit and a beard?

DR. KLING: People, these things take time!

ERAD: My longlost baby, O, how I did you bad! We's livin in a Dodge down next the bayou, eatin pigeons and drinking rain, and splat, ya just felled out.

DR. KLING: That's enough!

ERAD: We had to give ya up, cuz we couldn't a raised ya none proper.

BERTHA: I fought it like a fart on fire!

ERAD: You never did!

BERTHA: Ah, blow it out your barndoor!

ERAD: You was durable, though, layin there all wet and red on the newspaper.

BERTHA: Don't think I can't read or nothin.

ERAD: And despite the chemical factory hissin, I could hear ya mewin sure enuf!

BERTHA: Wrong! That was the possum ya had after her!

ERAD: We want ya back. You're ours, not them others.

BERTHA: Damn right ya is. We did ya, so now we wanna keep ya.

DR. KLING: Okay, I will talk to her.

ERAD: Doctor Kling's been real darn nice.

BERTHA: You trust in Doctor Kling now, ya hear?

DR. KLING: Please, let me talk to her.

ERAD: We love you!

BERTHA: Ah, don't say that!

(They exit.)

CORME: Is this for real?

DR. KLING: Real is a loose fitting term, Corme. Let us say, it happened.

CORME: I am not well at all.

DR. KLING: Tell me how you feel, and watch my watch.

CORME: I am…

DR. KLING: A bowl of forgotten food?

CORME: Yes.

DR. KLING: You are a dish of unsucked shrimps.

CORME: I am…

DR. KLING: An empty wildlife reserve?

CORME: Yes.

DR. KLING: You are lowlying shrub, awaiting the squalls of aquarius that call the dingo to grub. Freely associate.

CORME: I am a sprout, with hung, husk-heavy head,
The ocean scent above an empty bed.
What am I?

DR. KLING: Und in der Nacht die nackte Nectarinen Unter des Verfalls Nachbauten essen.

CORME: Yes.

DR. KLING: Naked nectarines inside the night
Nibble empty structures of neglect.

CORME: O.

DR. KLING: Your prana moans of discontent. You spill.

CORME: I spill.

DR. KLING: Your semantics are my stealth;
No name annuls you are not yourself.
Come with me, Corme. I am your health.

(He leads her off, hypnotized. Enter ERAD and BERTHA from behind the screen.)

ERAD: This is obscene!

BERTHA: There must be purpose in it.

ERAD: That the puss may purr? Or the lame may nt?

BERTHA: He leads her to her feminine end.

ERAD: Ms. Lerner, listen to yourself, just once!
In nature's name, what toxins won't he spray,
To make her mind some man-made demutation?
Why yank the real and wild rose, to shunt
Its math inherent, to give, unreal, a rose?
Why tack the butterfly upon a board,
Its sunbeam-dusted pinions grayly pinned,
To tab the freckles that once so feckless flew?
Will you snipe the felt of woman to a fur
That she then wears in glamorous self-betrayal?
Creation, not corruption, is innate,
So only Corme should Corme create.

BERTHA: His therapy has helped me be myself!

ERAD: So, here's why humans betterment resist:
All say "I'm proof perfection does exist."

BERTHA: Doctor Kling is good, Erad.

ERAD: Good at what?
I will not be Kling's theory-sucking drone,
And must, without his help, make myself my own.
    (Exits.)

BERTHA: Oh how confused and pure pretend am I!
In meaning to a learnful place profound
Develop in this house, what sanctified
And sense-repulsing sleazery I've found!
In therapy, the doctor was my worship,
And seemed in raptures of discursiveness
To soothe, but viewing his contortionship
Of others, I am crouched in horridness.

I almost am the father-false I am,
Falling blind into his cryptogram.
I must confront him, or my post dispense:
No tenure should survive such negligence. *(Exits.)*

(Enter LEAVUS, in a peach orchard.)

LEAVUS: Man! This world's a farm for freaky babes!
I'm used, dumpt, degraded, reused, dumpt;
That's my cycle. You almost gotta be
Some puppy at the pound to get pickt up,
Like Warren, who could talk that there buddha dead.
Zap! I smell my dandruff stokin! Women
Want a man, like Warren, whose rickshaw rap
Rolls em round all day and spoons em syrup tea.
The next woman I meet, I'll Warren be.
So long, Barbie gear, and a fat bon vagy.

(Enter WARREN.)

WARREN: Marla has gone totally berzerk!
I'll hide within this orchard, for a bit.

LEAVUS: (Baborama! Wow's that wobbly thing!
I'll poke my pick in this free sampling.)
O you peach in your fresh-linen nest,
It's you we georgians love the best,
Sweet and fuzzy, juicy and good,
You grow on what you give us: wood!

WARREN: I'm sorry, but are you talking to me?

LEAVUS: I am not worthy, so I'll gesture;
But gesture's lewd, so I'll stare;
But staring scares, so I my eyes detour;
And looking, looping far, I see you there.

WARREN: Very pretty. Now, just go away.

LEAVUS: Where can I go, if you are here?
You're Everclear; the rest, near beer.
O girl, your peach in faded jeans
Would shame the earth its gold and beans.

WARREN: Look, I'm just not into sapphic fragments.

LEAVUS: Oops! Going for it, I forgot! Wig out! *(Rips off his wig.)*

WARREN: (O, insanity! It's that Leavus guy!
If he finds out I'm me, I'll get hard whoopt!)

LEAVUS: Come, sit on my lap, and tell your story.

WARREN: My tale is long, and doing laps bores me.

LEAVUS: Boring is the drill to muscular bliss.

WARREN: Your tip can't even crack my avarice.

LEAVUS: You'll get more than a tip for serving me.

WARREN: You pay my check, you'll get the shaft for free!

LEAVUS: My motor needs a fuel not so crude.

WARREN: I will not be refined. I am too prude.

LEAVUS: Can no man unsnarl your pleasures free?

WARREN: The only man is Warren, and he's inside me.

LEAVUS: Then nix the new, and opt the old; get beasty!

WARREN: O!

(LEAVUS goes for WARREN. WARREN hits LEAVUS.)

LEAVUS: Kick the boiler, and out my mad juice flows!

(WARREN hits him.)

WARREN: Unplug the furnace, and in the tenants shrivel!

(WARREN hits him.)

LEAVUS: Once you knock me down, I'll knock you up.

(WARREN hits him.)

WARREN: Once I beat you up, I'll put you down!

(WARREN hits him.)

LEAVUS: Seduction mode complete! It's Twister time!

(LEAVUS kisses him. Enter LYDIA.)

LYDIA: Hormonia!

LEAVUS: O, boy.

LYDIA: It's round-up time
At the heeby-jeeby livestock rodeo!
Boy: Me, boss; you, butt; your slipp'ry booty's mine;
This cowchick's gonna brand her up some bovine!

LEAVUS: It's best I scram this crosseyed wigwam powwow.
Fabia, stay. Woman, I ain't your cow!

(LYDIA chases LEAVUS off, who puts his wig back on.)

WARREN: Lydia? My delicate Lydia?
O, space, lift up your lid, for I must spew!
Was that my love, lassooing after Leavus
In a skirt, calling him hind quarters?
After we took back the night, will she

Make her back his salt-lick; her chew, his cud?
O, my insides press at the window of my skin!
If Lydia for this distortion onanates,
Why chased she never me? What's Leavus got?
Well, no man has so saliently seduced
A woman, though I'm not one, as he did me.
O, sick! Yet is there drug in this disease?
I will round Lydia up, and sir her loins!
No! Some flowers seed when smackt, not she!
I'll cry forgiveness! O, she hates my clouds!
I'll shout! She'll scream. I'll kiss her. She'll bite me.
I have mistook my fiction for my font,
And must rework my wishes to my want!

(Enter MARLA.)

MARLA: Warren! There you are! O, sing to me!

WARREN: I will sing at your funeral, "I am free!"

(MARLA chases WARREN off. Enter ERAD, on the porch of the house.)

ERAD: Was ever more insidious torture known
Than that I suffer being just myself?
I am a hollow-headed, whiny failure,
A theory-propping, word-regretting cheat,
A lazy, timid turd, a crook of cheap respect,
A goo of subsidized ungroundedness,
Who, with a baby's bliss, makes the teethed
And spit-on ring of success his pacifier.
Destroy the mirrors! I'll kill who films me now!
O hopeless, hopeless, hopeless! What can I do?
I'd beg for change at Corme's midnight teller,
But I'm to change so long unpracticed,
I'd need a life to read the manual!
I'd take a risk, but my soul is a public park,
That's lamped to prevent danger, and thus prevents
Also groping strangers on a bench.
So, I must be systematic then,
And walk the whole way thru this half-way house,
Counseling Kling's closure on himself.
For what is schoolish learning, if it blots
The independent passions of reflection?
What breathe, if we the uncut green deforest,
To golf our course and drive at numbered holes?
I am a bug born buried, that must dig
Its sensing-pod above the gestate soil
With those same mandibles that dug it in,
To chrysalis a winged and clingless man.
And once I dissertate this Dr. Dork,
I'll go declare to Corme all I know.
Listen, love, and I will call your cue,

And then, all gorgeous pleasures we'll outdo! *(Takes off his wig.)*

(Enter DR. KLING.)

DR. KLING: Erad?

ERAD: (O coward, you'd sell your choice for a chair!) *(Puts the wig back on.)*

DR. KLING: I am latensificating Corme's underphotos. If you insist on bursting out of the picture, her infantile leaflets will not develop as I desire.

ERAD: Yes, doctor.

DR. KLING: Impress on her your destructive gravid tendencies.

ERAD: Yes, doctor.

DR. KLING: I bring her in. *(Exits.)*

ERAD: I am a storm up from the soggy south,
A ton of slush, that precipitantly melts.

(Enter DR. KLING and CORME.)

DR. KLING: Look, Corme, it's your mother.

CORME: Hello, mother.

ERAD: (O, she was the mint among the muck,
And now she's trampled by this migrant quack!)

DR. KLING: Tell your mother who you are, Corme.

CORME: I am a child from cuddling stroller thrown;
I am the family cabin mossy grown.

DR. KLING: Mutter, kann sie sprechen zur seine Saugling?

ERAD: (All dark and heavy things steep on my tongue!)

DR. KLING: Corme, go expect me in your womb.
It's there we'll reenact what mothers mute.

(CORME exits.)

ERAD: I couldn't.

DR. KLING: Do you suffer inelasticity of the privates?

ERAD: My privacy is stretched beyond return.

DR. KLING: Look at you. Fear is your bib. Time, the moil, has raggled your rose end, and that liquor of frenzy, estrogen, dribbles down your chin, like nanny milch. You are a minor, heedless, warp-rapt male, your desire's default denied. I, the Illustrierte-

Mensch, juggle the tongs of philos, while you but fondle undescended goonads in the dying, backward biote of your brain.

ERAD: What could this nefarious harangue have to do with the project of healing, doctor?

DR. KLING: Humans are a dermal-upholstered memory-mattress. Corme has much work to do beneath herself, and I will be there, in the overposition.

ERAD: Are you inferring you will analyze Corme in accords with your personal motives?

DR. KLING: "To be at" is the end, "to beat" is the means, ab lapsus eradicatione.

ERAD: What?

DR. KLING: Her verbs "to want" and "to do" are merely a difference of letters! Let her want this! Let her do that!

ERAD: Let her do what?

DR. KLING: I must record the beeps and pounds, the quicks and creeps of her! Don't you see?

ERAD: Don't I see what, Doctor Kling?

DR. KLING: The sack, the castration, the discharge? I remove you from the Corme sessions. Go home, and never study the mind again. *(Exits.)*

ERAD: Droppt? I have been droppt upon my head!
And this doctor delivers himself to my love's bed!
I am that breed of man that should not breed.

(Enter NICHEDIGGER, DICK, LAPTOP, and REM.)

DICK: Yo! Pizza shmeeza! Honeys hangin out the house!

NICHEDIGGER: Fetch me my solderin nipple! I wanna get stuck!

DICK: I got dibs.

NICHEDIGGER: I got dibs!

DICK: You got dibs!

NICHEDIGGER: I got dibs!

DICK: Ooo, man, don't spread them dibs!

(They fight.)

LAPTOP: Pardon me, mam, but if you'd like click on drive "u," directory "ought," file #2, you'd call up the web between us, in a window called "you ought to"…

ERAD: What ought I do?

DICK: Yarbles, you should strip!

ERAD: Like this?

DICK: No, no, no! Ya gotta slinky strip, like a slug slippin down sandpaper.

ERAD: Piece by piece?

DICK: Bit by thread, thread by bead, bead by flick, and flick the bit!

ERAD: And you?

DICK: I get the bongos revin, the plush interior pricklin, and shout margaritas and bullion cubes all round!

ERAD: And then?

DICK: My steroids put their storm trooper suit upon them!

ERAD: Skywalker, skywalker.

DICK: Now ya pole dance, like in my favo-filmo *Showgirls*, and I, your bodyguard, will that pole provide.

ERAD: Provide, provide.

DICK: Dive, dive, dive!

NICHEDIGGER: Now my dear Debbie, or assumin you are so named,
Pay no attention to this beggar of attenuations.
I and this quasi-viril posse represent
Our species' national ambit. Why have we come?
Simple. We are spurned, and our body endemic
Wields far too little. The symptoms, I recite:
Our brain, Laptop, for expulging less datas,
Miscomputes, and spills upon his f-keys.
Dick, our gut, as you, I'm sorry, see here,
Has fallen, not being chewed, to bottle-biting.
Rem, he is the mass of our silent hopes.
But I, my Debbie, I am our polity's gamut,
That gigantomungous necessary hub,
Who, unjustly as bad cookin, has been locked
Out of congress, housing, and your interior.
So, let me implore, respectin this vetoed abode,
That you allow democracy to thrive,
Which is that each has access unto each,
Particuly between our private properties,

That we who are not commonists, can quit
Hangin out in the lawn, over there.
For we are men, and citizens, my Debbie,
That much prefer your mutter to that fodder.

ERAD: You want a girl?

NICHEDIGGER: I have spoken well.

LAPTOP: Gigo! Gigo!

REM: Score!

NICHEDIGGER: Bigmac, I like your secret sauce.

ERAD: Do you now?

NICHEDIGGER: Yes, mam, I do.

ERAD: Wanna know the secret?

DICK: Yes, I do!

ERAD: Come a little closer!

DICK: Swoony, I'm in love!

LAPTOP: Boot up!

NICHEDIGGER: Victory.

REM: Ya.

ERAD: If you can take it, I can fake it. Boo! *(Rips off his wig.)*

REM: Wo!

NICHEDIGGER: Retreat!

LAPTOP: Reboot!

DICK: Recoil!

(They exit. Enter CORME, unseen by ERAD.)

ERAD: There, you grunge! Worship at my bra!
Shatter, shrapnel, slough, and putrefy!
Jihad on Lethargy and Oolala!
O, my anger's sponge is squoze, and I
Am raging! Are these the claws of conceit
That everyday at women grab to eat?
These pummeling, intrusive pick-up lines?
She leads a life to the left of less-than signs!
O, nothing's known but thru immersion swum!
How gravity must sulk at apples tosst,
And gloom so loathe the celebrated sun,
As one, not crosst by other, self-exhausts,
And yet, x-like, is canceled crossbecoming.
But the tool that takes takes not the tool of taking.

He takes his watch and mock-hypnotizes himself.
Be as you have never been,
Do what you should have done then,
Get Ms. Lerner, and closet-brave
Bust this lecher, then Corme save! *(Exits.)*

CORME: Mother? Erad? All's swirling in charade!
Father, where? O, I'm too crudely made!
Is this my voice, or a static-stifled tune
Stippling sleep, waking me to confusion?
Some ploy's been laid. Who else but Kling? None else.
He is the misfit, me-despoiling elf
That did this house's wiring unwind.
So, I must some good craftsman-cohort find
To my own ploy deploy, and it is Pan
This pain of pleasure will overplan.
But now, my absence, stay, and emulate;
Your presence will, most missed, most perpetrate.
(Exits.)

(Enter THE WISHFUL WAITERS, at the front door.)

GENE: Fine! I will play the Bush. Set?

ART: Set.

ROCK: Set.

NICELLE: Set.

GENE: Good, then in we go. *(Knocks.)*

(Enter VAZOLINE.)

VAZOLINE: O, yippy, a roving troupe of merry pranksters!

ALL: Birthday gram for Corme
From her parents in L.A.!

VAZOLINE: I'm her parents, and I ordered a snuff-gram.

NICELLE: He is playing the Bush.

ROCK: Equity code clearly states no snuffing.

VAZOLINE: Fine, but I must sample you before I buy the bun. You, first.

ART: I can jump a flaming village in a jeep, I can smoke and drink heavily, I can say simple things in a simple way, and I'll cram your box office til it bursts, baby!

VAZOLINE: Holy wood, Bat Dork, that's a thriller. Next!

ROCK: Rock Random, thespian and Yale graduate. My roles include Esophagus in "Six Lazy Vivisectionists," The Loud Party Goer in "What's up with Birds?," Grey Poupon in "10 lbs. of Ground Chuck," and the Seal Pup Mother in the almost reviewed "O, Eskimo!" I can do cockney, southern, and New Yawk dialects, juggle, knucklewalk, play the tambourine, drive, and whistle. I have a nurse's uniform. I'm good with pets and power tools, and I am a state certified psychosexual interviewer. Hey! If there's a part, I'll make it whole! Rock Random!

VAZOLINE: You need your head shot.

GENE: I have a monologue.

VAZOLINE: Not too long and mono, please.

GENE: "Why i before e, except after c?
Is "cliché" an exception? O, rules, rules, rules!
Look, it's her. No! Look it's she?
Subject? Object? O, Fools, fools, fools!"

VAZOLINE: O, actors, actors, actors!
Woman, why do you wait?

NICELLE: Because I cannot act.

VAZOLINE: Well, follow me. Now, were I, out of naughtiness, to request your gram be played at a certain unique moment, when elements such as audience, timing, and location were neither ideal nor particularly responsive, could you tiny hams, for a big tip, overgive it?

GENE: Yes, sir. The Wishful Waiters love to serve!

VAZOLINE: O, help these days. Go into the basement, and get warm.

(ALL enter the house. Enter ERAD and BERTHA, in CORME's room.)

ERAD: Corme's not here!

BERTHA: What if he's taken her?

ERAD: No. I hear him. Go, upon the bed.
Within this closet, I will listen. Then,
Say "Peal my labels," and I will come out.

BERTHA: Peal my labels.

ERAD: Say it when he's nearest.

(ERAD hides in the closet. BERTHA sits on CORME's bed, in the dark. Enter DR. KLING.)

DR. KLING: Soon, onto my censure-shrinking couch
Will Corme give, symbatic to my sense,
The perk, tender, and copyright of her desire.
She, once pure-resistant, yields now
Beneath my qualming pang of phrase, and waits
To at my prompt her ripest extract utter.
O, how her words will word my life anew!
How I, in converse seminal, will untap
The alchemies of life's tableau cryptique
From her repressed, thus ever-youngful, diction.
O, she has such a great subconscious,
Thru which I'll rise regendering ingenious!
In her I scrawl the screed of my career;
How funny humans cannot close their ears.

BERTHA: Doctor Kling?

DR. KLING: Ah, Corme, you are in season.

BERTHA: Your voice the orbit is, doctor, that tugs
Thru me the seas that suck back sucking seas.

DR. KLING: Ignorance is such sweet aphrodisia!
I wish the light.

BERTHA: No!

DR. KLING: An unconscious "no"?

BERTHA: Let love butt at heads.

DR. KLING: She speaks of love?

BERTHA: My candy, my recovery, which is first?

DR. KLING: Such words do bring an April to my eyes.

BERTHA: Doctor?

DR. KLING: Just as two lips make one mouth to flower,
And two near humps become a stair to somewhere,
So we'll delimit the world's wordless width.

BERTHA: O, Doctor Kling, label my peals!

DR. KLING: What?

BERTHA: No! I mean, peal my doctors, label.

DR. KLING: This is verb soup.

BERTHA: Peal my labels, doctor!

DR. KLING: Yes, my dream!

(Enter ERAD.)

ERAD: Doctor, I have made a stunning find!

DR. KLING: Not now.

ERAD: Corme is a man!

DR. KLING: What?

ERAD: I smelled her he-sore thru her she-shell. Repeat after me.

DR. KLING: I will not.

ERAD: She-shells over he-sores are he-held for the she-sell. Repeat after me!

DR. KLING: I can't do such things.

ERAD: Do it, you recalled zygote.

DR. KLING: Corme, come.

ERAD: She will not, Doctor Kling. She is a Gleitschutz-reifen.

DR. KLING: A no skid tire?

ERAD: She will not rub herself on asphalts.

DR. KLING: Corme, I said come!

ERAD: She cannot. She has Einwegsflaschesyndrom.

DR. KLING: Non-returnable bottle sickness?

ERAD: Once used, she cannot be turned in.

DR. KLING: Corme, up!

BERTHA: Corme is not Corme.

DR. KLING: Ms. Lerner! I am had.

ERAD: That is Projektion: no one will have you, so you think you are had.

DR. KLING: I will have your grade!

ERAD: This is Ambivalenz: I am your double, so you halve my grade.

DR. KLING: Absurd!

ERAD: Transferenz: All is absurd, because you are an "or."

DR. KLING: "or"?

ERAD: You follow either with a phrase, you stand between devolving the involved, and what's more, your briefs are "overripe."

DR. KLING: Ms. Lerner, we must talk.

BERTHA: You do not talk, doctor. You stamp and sign.

DR. KLING: Bertha, I am your physician.

BERTHA: Marvin, you have lost my patience.

ERAD: The german for this, I think, is "can't."

DR. KLING: You are unreal!

BERTHA: No, Marvin, we are you.

DR. KLING: I'll exit now that mystery has entered!
Wunschenbild, sie sind auch Schweifelei!

*(ERAD grabs him and accompanies him out of the house.
Enter MARLA and WARREN, in the peach orchard.)*

MARLA: Why won't you have me, Warren? Am I gross?
Do I secrete some sour expectoration?
Am I not hot? Are my portions not choice?
Do I not have it? Yes! I am desirable!
Lydia calls your poems noxious pollen;
They are to me the spray of nature's sex.
She sneezes at them; I their gusts imbibe!
Has any man been hounded ever so?
Just tell me straight, if we're to kiss or not.
No more chasing. Take me now, or rot.

WARREN: Marla, you are nice, persistent, and direct,
And though I won't love you, I'll be your friend.

MARLA: Friend? So it is that way you'll escape!
Men have no friends, but words in place of love.
To call me friend's to cancel me, you pud!
Would you revert my tulips to a bud?

WARREN: Marla, we are simply not compatible!

MARLA: Compatible? O how I hate the word!
Will you make the baby feed the bottle?
Compatible has no management in love!
Speak me compatible! Invent our bind.

WARREN: No! I will not budge! I do not like you!

MARLA: Which means, invertedly, you do like me!
Or, as Kling would say, you're ego-reticent.
No more "love is"; say love may and love how!
All may alter all; come, change me now.

WARREN: Your syllogism's sound, but I am deaf,
And being strangled, I run to catch my breath!

(MARLA chases him off. Enter LYDIA and LEAVUS.)

LEAVUS: No, you virus, no and no and no!
When a man says no, Lydia, he means no!
Now just let me alone!

LYDIA: O, you are real!
You tell it like it is. You drive it home

Into that dirty dark. O, yes, Leavus,
Plant me to the soil of my sexiness!

LEAVUS: (The more I dis her, the less our distance is.
She's no bagel; I'll smear her other side.)

LYDIA: Are you contemplating how to seize me?

LEAVUS: Yes! How seize a thing so delicate
As are the ticklish earnerves of a cat?

LYDIA: You mean as tough as are the sluts of porn.

LEAVUS: No, as soft as breath on winter's morn.

LYDIA: Am not I rock and roll?

LEAVUS: No, you are sway and tumble.

LYDIA: That's my cocaine attitude!

LEAVUS: You're a powder-precious prude.

LYDIA: Call me priestess of the pitch abyss!

LEAVUS: You're as light as a grandma's kiss!

LYDIA: Call me fierce Electra!

LEAVUS: Sweet Melissa!

LYDIA: Brutal!

LEAVUS: Cute!

LYDIA: Blunt!

LEAVUS: Shy like stars!

LYDIA: That's it! War on Warren!

*(LYDIA chases LEAVUS off. Enter WARREN and
MARLA.)*

WARREN: (What should I do? I've always been sensitive!
I'll try unsensitive.) My, you are strong!

MARLA: I am?

WARREN: You've got to be, with all that fat!

MARLA: Fat?

WARREN: And you have such somber, seldom eyes!

MARLA: Why seldom?

WARREN: Cuz they seldom emerge from fat!

MARLA: I am not fat!

WARREN: Your voice—I've heard the surf sing so!

MARLA: You have?

WARREN: I'm wrong—It was at the seal cage.

MARLA: These sniglets seeped in blubber harm me not.
I am slender, and nothing's wrong with fat.

WARREN: Then I'll sing your sections.

MARLA: Fine, one more poem.

WARREN: How unguzzled guppies grip
In her mishandled mulch
And the gushing gerkins drip
Inside go-get-em gulch,
When Marla, the ramblant pudding,
Rolls cross her cookie sheet,
With those gut dimples crumpling,
Drippy gunks of meat!
Fat is she. All fat. My ass, she's fat.

MARLA: Patience has its limit, which I am at!
It's twister time!

(MARLA kisses WARREN. Enter LEAVUS and LYDIA.)

LYDIA: Marla?

LEAVUS: Fabia!

MARLA: Lydia?

WARREN: O, no.

LYDIA: Why are you with this woman in the woods?

MARLA: I am sick of men, and she's my type?

LEAVUS: Aren't you with Leavus?

WARREN: Aren't you with Warren?

LYDIA: What love I've had from Moron until now
Would not seduce a child to recess.

WARREN: What?

MARLA: Love? At least you got it! That inbreed Leavus
Was like a he-wolf humping on the pipeline!

LEAVUS: Not!

LYDIA: Really?

MARLA: I was suet for his seed.

WARREN: Many girls tell me the same.

LEAVUS: They lie!

LYDIA: Unleavened Warren's loaf just never rose.

WARREN: Now that I never heard!

LEAVUS: It's true, Fabia!

MARLA: Don't Warren's poems prove he loves to serve?

LYDIA: Warren served me like snakes play volleyball.

MARLA: He's so creative!

LYDIA: All's a teeny bang.

WARREN: I think Warren's gifted.

LEAVUS: Fabia, wrong!

LYDIA: Tiny no deep would do better with sheep,
And little boy blue's got no horn.

MARLA: Tiny no deep?

WARREN: O, death!

LEAVUS: But Fabia,
Leavus is a better man than Warren!

MARLA: Leavus's gums and teeth are Chia Pets.

WARREN: Botanical gardens!

LEAVUS: Leavus brushes!

MARLA: And how soever do you know, girl?

LEAVUS: Heard it.

MARLA: There are only two things in his room: sweat
and sweat.

LEAVUS: Viva la sweat! Death to the deodorized!

MARLA: Warren is a self-cleaning appliance.

WARREN: Then Lydia's a Frigidaire!

LYDIA: Wouldn't you be
If Mr. Ice-tongs were midwifing your kitties?

MARLA: Mr. Ice-Tongs?

WARREN: Warren has good qualities!

LEAVUS: Like what?

WARREN: Curly black hair!

LYDIA: On his back!

MARLA: Nasty.

WARREN: Manly!

LEAVUS: Sex is where you shave.

WARREN: He's lyric!

LYDIA: He's an epic of mistakes.

WARREN: He's thoughtful!

LYDIA: His medium? Tedium.

WARREN: Inspired!

LYDIA: Out of breath.

LEAVUS: Don't tell me, Fabia,
You love that loser Warren?

WARREN: O, shut up!

LYDIA: Leavus can't be that bad.

LEAVUS: Leavus rocks.

WARREN: I hate Leavus!

LEAVUS: Fabia?

MARLA: I'll top that:
Leavus totally shirked man's basic labor.

LYDIA: Working?

MARLA: Nope.

LYDIA: Sharing?

MARLA: Nope.

LYDIA: Craving?

MARLA: Nope.
Wiping.

LYDIA: He doesn't wipe?

MARLA: Not counter, face or…

LEAVUS: Tell Fabia I wipe!

MARLA: And who are you?

LYDIA: She's talking Leavus, that dump-its-duty gland!

MARLA: She's talking Warren, the vertically challenged!

WARREN: O, I'm fainting.

LEAVUS: Tell Fabia Leavus wipes!

WARREN: O, go die.

LEAVUS: No, Fabia, I need you!
Take Marla, Lydia, and go on back
To that house of tantrums! But see me now
As I truly am, and as I fully love
Fabia, real woman. Goodbye, cruel head-glove! (Rips off his wig.)

MARLA: Leavus?

WARREN: Play on, self. Open and close. (Rips off his wig.)

LEAVUS: Warren!

LYDIA: Warren?

MARLA: Warren.

WARREN: It's Twister time.

(ALL fall down. Enter BERTHA, ERAD, and DR. KLING.)

BERTHA: Marla, Lydia, lying on the ground?

ERAD: Leavus, Warren, dressed in women's clothes?

BERTHA: Is everyone okay?

ERAD: What are you doing?

MARLA: Acting dead.

LEAVUS: Molting to mulch.

LYDIA: Digging a grave.

WARREN: Rotting.

BERTHA: Where is Corme?

ERAD: Where is she, Doctor Kling?

DR. KLING: I'm speechless.

ERAD: Then I'll untwist your nettled tongue!

(ERAD goes for DR. KLING. Enter NICHEDIGGER, DICK, LAPTOP, and REM, dressed as pizza delivery men.)

ALL FOUR: Pizza delivery!

BERTHA: But we didn't order any pizza!

NICHEDIGGER: And why not?

BERTHA: We have personal issues to deal with!

NICHEDIGGER: Now you listen up! That I, in order to form a more direct union, establish juices, and secure domestic transactivity, yea, that I this pie can deliver, what quoth that mean? It is a dumpster, large, signifying my nation's hodgepodge pile of peoples. There's a tripod of them, indicating life, liberty, and the prostitute of happiness; and for this lambasto bravo of my coglimative efforts, I get tipped, which tip shall drill tap oils, which oils will lubricate, which lubrificatives will supple the sausage of my freedom and wealth. Feel my point? So, before you go pullin the world's unused muscle of self-review with your I-gotta-be-me pliers, go ahead and tell me flat-eyed that you didn't order this pizza.

BERTHA: We didn't order any pizza!

DICK: Just a slap-happy minute here! Haven't we so loudly flailed for this cheese's fast steaming?

MARLA: No, we haven't.

DICK: Didn't we see our peppers glare red when bombs flew by us with blonde hair?

LYDIA: No, we didn't.

DICK: And ain't we drunk proof with our pie cuz our flag was that hair?

BERTHA: Another aberrant we!

NICHEDIGGER: Then did Washington…

DICK: Yo, I'm talkin here!

NICHEDIGGER: Sorry.

DICK: Then did Washington, his prosciutto in his pants,
Not cross the cold caviling Mississip?
And pussy-slapping Patton, wasn't he
Of as many repasts, or slices, as all wars are?
If Ned and Warren Beatty's insatiabilities
Call not your rustling uzos to the uzi,
Then what, e plunderus ovum, could untap
Your buds of taste to caw beyond the frigid fold,
And order you a jumbo dumpster pie? Hu?

NICHEDIGGER: The Bull of Rights secures our ordering
Of pizzas and chilled brewskies, mushrooms free!

DICK: Are you not Americans?

NICHEDIGGER: Is this not the superbowl?

DICK: Then grasp and glower!

NICHEDIGGER: Chewing is genetic!

DICK: Humans just gotta devour the superpie!

ERAD: We didn't order a pizza!

NICHEDIGGER: Leapin Weebelows, it's that taste-tester for the queen! Men, prepare for flight.

(ALL are about to fight. Enter CORME, on the roof of the house.)

CORME: Who is weaker, asked he,
The wanter or the wanted?
Who is weaker, she asked,
The daunting or the daunted?
He is stronger, said he,
Who gets all that he's after.
She is stronger, she laught,
Who has it before it's asked her.
With parrot parents, maybe I can fly.

BERTHA: Corme, no!

CORME: O, to soar above the fair!
To be of ambience a zillionaire!

DR. KLING: Leave the ledge, Corme! Leave the ledge! Leave the ledge! Leave the ledge!

CORME: Some students throw their caps into the air. Me? I throw myself. Beware, beware!

NICHEDIGGER: We'll break her fall with our delivery bags!

LEAVUS: Does no somber moment shut you fuckers up?

ERAD: Corme, come down!

CORME: Father? Mother! Sisters! Enemies! O, it's a party!

MARLA: What's wrong, Corme? You always seemed so grounded!

CORME: I want to whack the ball I lob.
I want to chafe the man I coddle.
Quiche, Quiche, my name is Quiche,
The only thing real men won't eat!

DICK: Yo, I eat quiche!

LYDIA: These are good things, Corme, and we like you for them.

CORME: O, I am Joan of Archallaxis screaming,
"How wondrous to be first, but for the skinning!"

BERTHA: O, sad Corme, come down!

CORME: No, Father, no!
I am frozen like a fish
Into the gizmo stare of viscid death;
And you're not the woman I thought you were, Dad;
O belly laugh! O, belly sad!

ERAD: She's suffering an Identifizierungskrankheit!

DR. KLING: No, she is Schuldgefuhlsverschiebtend.

CORME: See the sparrows? They are words.
See the trees? They are we.
Sparrows for a seat are fighting,
To rouse and fight again! O, spare me!

ERAD: It's me, Corme! Erad!

CORME: Mother! It's the boy of love impaired,
Never found, forever bidden;
Love him, try; his name is Dare spellt backward,
And he's riding a chairlift to Eden.

ERAD: I am Erad, Corme! I cannot love myself!

CORME: And I'm an upling cotyledon,
In a June monsoon,
And so I must fly,
And so I must fly,
Into the shadows of Athen's leaves,
Under the porches, over the eaves,
I must fly that another may be
A floating, blooming illusion of me!

ERAD: Corme!

CORME: With your displacement, I myself replace:
Of lineage, life, and loss, I push erase! *(Jumps.)*

ALL: No!

(ALL exit but RAMBLING FANATICS.)

DICK: That's it! I need a Wild Turkey!

NICHEDIGGER: We must assemblem a bivouac bravo-bravo squadroon!

LAPTOP: I'll alert the space shuttle.

REM: My mind is so totally blown!

(They exit. Enter ALL, looking for CORME.)

BERTHA: She's gone!

ERAD: But how?

LYDIA: She crawled away!

MARLA: Corme!

(Enter VAZOLINE, carrying CORME's falsely dead body.)

VAZOLINE: Look, O world, upon your beaten child!
Killers! Betrayers! Environmental hazards!
O, dead density of good! O, tender tortured!
Doom, like smoth'ring, red autumnal fungus,
O'ercreeps the fallen stalks and stones of her!

Before death's sputum glued its muzzle on
Her mouth, your vying's gentle victim cried:
"Am I a gerbil? Do I scratch and snivel?
Are my pullulate and nimble wants
Merely nodes, polyps, buttons for the bored?
I hear the unk, unk, unk of one great shell!
So then, into the beak of buzzard death
Myself I feed, as one confused-complete,
To wade no more in being, but not to be."
All said, her alphabet passed into z's.
Why, O why, must she that stays herself
Be ever she we let not with us stay?
That's that. I nine one-one, and end the play.

(He lays her down, and exits.)

BERTHA: Corme's dead?

ERAD: This blurb-surgeon performed it,
But vengeance can't the final act acquit.

(Enter THE WISHFUL WAITERS.)

ALL: Birthday gram for Corme
From her parents in L.A.!

SKY: I think that's her!

GENE: She looks dead.

EARTH: I never lost an audience so fast.

SKY: Whether the seats be coffins or cribs, Equity says "act on!"

MARLA: Please, she does not need a birthday gram.

GENE: And why not?

LYDIA: She isn't feeling well.

GENE: Doctor? I prescribe a birthday gram!

ALL: Birthday gram for Corme!

GENE: Hurray!

ALL: Hurray!

LEAVUS: Look, just go away.

GENE: Now seal your chops in a Tupperware of tact, or I will barbecue them to a crisp! We are the Wishful Waiters! It is her birthday! This is the receipt! She gets a gram! You best wholeassedly squat yourself upon the forget-me-nots, or I will most amateurishly break my leg on you!

SKY: Happy birthday Corme!

GENE: Hurray!

ALL: Hurray!

GENE: If Corme, you'll fix your eyes,
Upon our little play,
You will have a big surprise
On this berry special day!

WARREN: Okay, thank you! Very nice! Goodbye!

GENE: How the blueberry came to be
Is our gram's brief progeny;
Part earth, part sky, the blueberry
Is born for you on your birthday!

SKY: Bush! Bush! Enter Bush!

BUSH: Here I am.

GENE: Bush I am.

BUSH: Bush I am,
Swoosh, swoosh,
A twisty replica in twig;
Upon a crag
My roots I push,
But still I bulge no bushels big.

SKY: O bush, sweet bush, dry bush!
How I love you truly!
But why, O why, must you clutch
Into that globe so globby!

EARTH: Yo, fat bush! Forget that airhead!
Curl them toes in my prairie bed!
What's the wind got you lately?
Quit reachin to the sky, and dig me, baby!

BERTHA: We are dealing with an emergency here!

GENE: You're telling me! Bush, O, bush!
The sky, so blue, is jealous for you!
The earth, so round, is zealous too!
So neither share their vitals lush!

SKY: I refuse to gleak or rain
Til you from hunky humus refrain!

EARTH: And I ain't swappin minerals
Til you dump Mr. Above-it-alls!

GENE: How you, Corme, so giftlessly
Must feel blue unberryably!

BUSH: What can I do? O all is wrong!
My two friends won't get along!
The sky is blue, the earth is round,
The one is air, the other is ground!
But I am barren, bleak, and brown!

GENE: You're killing Corme so softly with that song!

ERAD: Look, you freaks! We think that she is dead!
Gone! Finished! Blotted out! Caput!
Do you understand that word, you goons?
She doesn't need a birthday gram right now!
O, how I loved her, but I was a lie,
And as she lies here now, I murder I.

GENE: Fine, we will expedite the process.

BUSH: Blue sky? Round earth?
One at a time, I will seduce,
While one naps, the other's juice!

GENE: So, as night curls up in dark's duvet,
And constellations cross its lids plie,
Bush, in a naughty sorta mood,
Woos the sky with woosy word.

BUSH: Sky?

SKY: Bush.

BUSH: Show me where the jetstreams push.

SKY: Eons, ions, oons I release!

BUSH: Hail, snow, and geese.

GENE: Then bush tricks sky to outward go.

BUSH: Fetch me a dreambar from venus snow.

GENE: Exit, sky. Enter earth.

BUSH: Earth?

EARTH: Giggle, gurgle, gaggle, Bush!

GENE: Sky comes back!

BUSH: Sky, meet jack.

GENE: He's sorta perturbed.

SKY: I see no snow on venus!

EARTH: Word.

GENE: So, each tumbles tidy to its spot,
And our world crumbles to a plot.
But wait! As dawn in pinkening panoramas
Sparkles over Earth's plaid pajamas,
What's that on bush's once bare-limbs?
Berries round, with bluish skins!

BUSH: Sky's been trickt! Earth's bamboozled,
But look what they've together oozled!

GENE: Earth lurkt up,
Sky plopt down,

Their cheeks clean-jerkt
The sagging dumbbells of their frowns!

SKY: My children, they are blue, like me!

EARTH: My babies, how they roundful be!

GENE: Then both joined hips, hands, head, and feet
And jangled round their newborn treat!

BUSH: I, the bush, blueberries sprout
For Corme's birthday. Shout it out!

GENE: Corme's in the house!

ALL: Happy birthday!

GENE: We're berry glad for you, Corme,
As clearly, you've enjoyed our play!
So, from sky, earth, bush, and I,
This gift we give; a blueberry!

BUSH: Eat the fruit that on this day
Grew for you in a play.

(They feed her a blueberry.)

GENE: Thank you, we are done.

EARTH: She ain't gettin up.

REM: I got a birthday song.

DICK: Gig it, Rem.

REM: *(Sings.)* Maybe planets share no secret,
Maybe passion's lost in space,
Sensation has no set,
And the morning's out of place.
But girl, you are born,
Wild and laughingly,
From a picture torn,
A picture none can see.
So maybe time can talk,
And distance never lies,
And maybe when we walk,
The world round us flies.
Cuz girl, you are born,
Serious and suspectingly,
From a nothing torn,
A nothing all must see.

CORME: *(Rises.)* Thanks Rem, and all. It's thru your
    work, I waken
From my stiff-posing play against your play,
Which, though immoral, a moral gave to these,
So needy of a stern sashay thru self.

LEAVUS: I've seen it all!

MARLA: All but yourself, girlfriend.

CORME: Friends, no grudge! The strafings of conten-
    tion
Soothe into blush, outcoloring your gripes.
Humans are a sugar, so be not bitter,
But let your genes more snugly fit the time,
As I, in fashion now, must cut our finish.

MARLA: I see no clean conclusion to this conflict.

CORME: Look!
Don't fights, past effort's punch, gasp into ease?
Don't days to dreaming lost, refind us soon?
Our wants, like bricks mislaid, here topple down
Into a mull of scrambled sediment,
Sounder, being settled naturally;
And where there's litter, is there not then life?

LYDIA: Why blend with him? Our compounds barely
    fizzle.

CORME: Barely fizzle? The day itself exploded!
Laying goads beneath deception's bludgeon,
Bungling thru the props of stumbling's stage,
And leaving solid sense for furor's haze,
You blundered into animacy's maze
That you might find yourselves thru confusion!
Am I right?

WARREN: My tongue's yankt out at my waist.

CORME: What's disaster taught us?

WARREN: I am dumb.

CORME: Listen!
No structure can defend us from our sex,
As sex is harvest driving to itself.
Every want with other want's imbued,
And every plan another's past renews.
This doctor's choreography of concepts,
Though verbal thrash, our dance interpreted.
The risks these gender-rangers took, they took
For us, proving their love cannot be neutered.
Even this house, where self evicted self,
That the self-within and the self-without
To oneself turned, so losing all self-want,
By disillusioning all, left none deceived.
So weird and worrysome things grow to meaning,
Yelling at us: cross over to yourselves!

LEAVUS: I've looked both ways, and I want neither side.

CORME: Then it is side by side that you should go,
That then for neither side you need decide!
Our wishes, from their dragging wants dismantled,
Have floated to this play, as children do,
Who play at flight to learn to crawl to work.
Like in the old and over-coupling stage
Extravaganzas, revocably concluded,
We should, our spears outshaked, our wills rewrote,
As these here like it, liken here ourselves
To them, who, hopefully, will leave in pairs.
For we are a thriving, ever-stranger
Alloy'nce of both the do and don't of dreams,
The wish of was, the want in wasn't, the like
Unlikely, the angry-happy stash of now.
So touch; with each awakening pinch, be free;
If mixed up, only mixing you can be!
And help a lover fumble to love's home,
For love's a plaything, and is never grown.

LEAVUS: I can't.

MARLA: I won't.

LYDIA: Too much, too soon.

WARREN: Too late.

CORME: Fine, my soul will be our sole example
In making learn and love identical.
Erad, you have failed as a mother;
Would you consent to undertake a lover?

ERAD: For you, I will be anything you wish,
And out my love, for therein all is bliss.

CORME: Then be yourself, and I will be a kiss.

(They kiss.)

NICHEDIGGER: Men, the great Aluminum Lincoln
   hath said it best:
"She is alltogether fitting and proper to do this."

DICK: Yo! Let's all make up, and make out!

LYDIA: Warren, I've slighted you.

WARREN: And none too slightly!

LYDIA: I'm sorry.

WARREN: And still I hurt.

LYDIA: I was swept up
In my own sting for lust.

WARREN: Lust, Lydia?

LYDIA: Lust, Warren.

WARREN: And could you not see my lust?

LYDIA: Not then, but now, unstung, I see you better,
(And better like you in such sexy get-ups!)
What you have I want; what you might, we'll work on.

WARREN: I, Lydia, was also swept away.

LYDIA: You, Warren?

WARREN: Into an urge most guttural.

LYDIA: O, Warren!

WARREN: Into the lurches of my nature.

LYDIA: O, Warren! Is it real?

WARREN: It's really real.

LYDIA: O, I will strap you belly-up to me,
And out thru the tingling expanse
We'll gambol on our radiating mustangs,
Thumping the orb of wild things to a dream!
But, in our love, can my words speak my want?

WARREN: I have, in rend'ring you, made you unfree,
And so must liberate you bodily.
The you I need is lovely-all without me;
Speak your want, then be my wild thing.

LYDIA: I am a kiss!

MARLA: Leavus, you come here.

LEAVUS: What?

MARLA: You look so stupid in that dress.

LEAVUS: Then dresses make ya stupid, don't they,
   woman?

MARLA: Have you not changed at all?

LEAVUS: You know I have lived thru it, Merl. You know
I am shell-shockt, shook down, and out of bounds
When it comes to hearin door-lockin ideas.
I got no flow control, no gauge on me
When someone tells me no. I gotta have
What I don't have. But all my life, the loss
I've seen from love put out beneath a tarp
To mold away, cuz other things came first,
Has spookt me, like someday there won't be none.
I say, if you love something, go and get it,
And if you got something, do not waste it.
If this house is open to all, my mouth is shut,
Cuz I'll do anything to have you, Merl.

MARLA: To fill the final order of my being
Requires a more diverse provisioning

Than the muddy and quick-wilting greens of lust,
But the knocks I jabbed at you were lies unjust.
I want you, Leavus. And all I ask of you
Is an occasional flattering review.

LEAVUS: Yo, Fabia's taught me a tune; I'll do it, for you.

MARLA: Then we can kiss.

BERTHA: Marvin, we have by rote
This rout of youth effected for our affect.
Can you unspeak it, and make us again a kiss?

DR. KLING: I do not know. Words seem cruel to me.
I think I will go hum beneath a tree. (*Exits.*)

BERTHA: I am at fault.

CORME: But no, Ms. Lerner, no.
For here are all excuses viable
Emerging from the muddled and unmutual.
We who followed, lead ourselves to you.
To mean the best is not the best to do.
Stay with us.

BERTHA: Stay where? Nowhere will do.

NICELLE: Hey, isn't it Corme's day today?

NICHEDIGGER: Let's have a party, here, and another play!

LAPTOP: Restart!

(*RICHARD enters.*)

VAZOLINE: Your dream channel's been cut.

ELISA: (*Calls from side.*) Richard, you there?

CORME: Come, let's go.

LYDIA: O, Vazoline, come with!

RICHARD: What? And leave myself? Then I'd be you.
And what would she, who must stay here, then do?

MARLA: Fine, we'll leave, but first, I'd like to know
How'd you ever end up here, ya ho?

RICHARD: How'd you ever end up here, ya ho?

LYDIA: An end that parodies where it began.

CORME: Let's go. Man before woman, woman before man.

(*They all exit, except VAZOLINE. Enter ELISA.*)

ELISA: Richard?

RICHARD: Ah, my bluffin muffin, how were the sleepy-deepys?

ELISA: Not so hot. What was all that noise?

RICHARD: I heard nothing, love.

ELISA: Ya.

RICHARD: Now you just go upstairs. I'll bring up some Concha Y Toro, and then tigerbalm your temples.

ELISA: Will you, now?

RICHARD: For your birthday, yes.

ELISA: Godot is waiting, Dick. (*Exits.*)

RICHARD: Isn't there that story no one's told
How someone once set out to live a story
And found that stories start with their theme's death?
With my story's self, I felt concurrent,
But it was that paradox of the heart's design
Wherein the pulse is vital most at pause.
My play on birth is thru, unheard by she
It's acted for, my significant other me.
Forever ends, mundane shadows surprise,
So I, back to the attic, lonely rise.

(*Enter DICK, outside the house.*)

DICK: Hey there, pretty girl! Come out, come out whatever ya are!

RICHARD: O, you quaint, slurring boy. Chantes-tu pour moi?

DICK: Now, this may be a shanty, but seeins as it's stufft with you, I'll call it a manshun, so I am not above comin up it.

RICHARD: Will you climb thru the window then?

DICK: Now, pretty girl, I ain't zactly been sloggin microbiotic leapgerm all them years, and that window there seems to have a showvanism against ladder-type ladders.

RICHARD: Are you strong, fly-guy? Are you a man?

DICK: Last times I whifft myself I was.

ELISA: (*Calls from above.*) Dick, get up here quick!

DICK: I'm comin as fast as I can, baby! Don't it never be said that Dick Skills from up North there didn't dare his do-dads to wangle up and scramble in the hooters! I'm assendin, one callous at a time. I ain't so steady, but least I'm dizzy.

RICHARD: That's my boy. Whisper when you fall. (*Exits.*)

(*End of play.*)

LA TEMPESTAD

Larry Loebell

LARRY LOEBELL was born in 1951 in Philadelphia and has lived there most of his life. He is a playwright and dramaturg and holds both a BA in English and an MFA in film and television from Temple University. He also holds an MA in English, with a concentration in creative writing, from Colorado State University. He began his career in 1987 dramaturging a new musical for the American Music Theater Festival and wrote his first play in 1992. His plays include *Pride of the Lion* (2000), *Angie and Arnie Sanguine* (2002), *The Ballad of John Wesley Reed* (2005), and *Girl Science*. Loebell's work has been developed at Playwrights Theater of New Jersey, Seven Devils Playwrights Conference, Ensemble Studio Theatre, InterAct Theater Company, and New Jersey Repertory. He won the Pennsylvania Playwriting Prize in 1999, is a four-time recipient of the Playwriting Fellowship from the Pennsylvania Council on the Arts (1996, 1998, 2004, 2006), and was awarded a New Play Commission from the National Foundation for Jewish Culture (2006). From 1998 to 2005, Loebell was literary manager and dramaturg at InterAct Theater Company in Philadelphia. He currently teaches playwriting and dramaturgy at Arcadia University, and narrative film history at the University of the Arts. He lives in the Mount Airy section of Philadelphia with his wife Diane, an attorney.

La Tempestad was first presented by Resonance Ensemble (Eric Parness, Artistic Director) on October 9, 2005, at the Ohio Theatre, New York City, with the following cast and credits:

Prospero	Gordon Stanley
Ferdinand	Alberto Bonilla
Stephano	Brian Flegel
Miranda	Vivia Font
Ariel	Felipe Javier Gorostiza
Alonso	Ed Jewett
Iris	Lori McNally
Trinculo	Patrick Melville
Caliban	Ray A. Rodriguez
Sprite	Frank Tamez
Gonzolo	James T. Ware

Directed by: Eric Parness
Scenic Design: Martin T. Lopez
Lighting Design: Aaron Copp
Costume Design: Sidney Shannon
Sound Design: Nick Moore
Stage Management: Katie Kring
Produced by: Rachel Reiner

The writing of *La Tempestad* was supported in part by a grant from the Pennsylvania Council on the Arts. The play was given a staged reading in 2004 by the Resonance Ensemble and workshopped by them in the fall of 2004.

THANKS

Thanks to Eleanor, Diane, David, Pam, Clara, and Amy, living generations of my own family, and to Becky Wright, who has served as first reader, dramaturg, conscience, and voice of reason throughout the writing, workshopping, and production of this play. All my love. Also to Gordon Smith, Shakespeare professor extraordinaire, and all of the teachers whose love of the written word inspired me. To Eric Parness and Rachel Reiner of Resonance Ensemble, who believed in this play from its first draft onward, and to Kittson O'Neill, former literary manager of New Jersey Repertory Theater, who gave the play to Eric. To Bob Lohrmann and John Lilly, who first persuaded me to visit Vieques and who have a lovely oceanfront house for rent there. And finally to all the members of Working Writers Group, whose support and insight helped me to find the landscape of this play and many of my previous ones: Robin Black, Doug Gordon, Miriam Seidel, Ann De Forest, Debra Leigh Scott, Lou Greenstein, and David Sanders.

CHARACTERS

PROSPERO: Founder and curator of the local island history museum, housed in the Fortín Conde de Mellado; sixty-two. Highly educated, degreed, erudite, eccentric. Puerto Rican of Spanish descent.

MIRANDA: Prospero's daughter; early twenties. Island raised, American educated, a chic mix of cultures.

FERDINAND: Miranda's intended, mid- to late twenties. Island born, American raised, of Puerto Rican descent, but very assimilated.

TRINCULO: A museum curator from the States; gay, late thirties. Handsome, smart.

STEPHANO: His significant other, early thirties.

ALONSO: A U.S. Marine officer on special assignment; forties.

GONZOLO: A military attaché, thirties–forties; also on special assignment. African American.

CALIBAN: Bartender, concierge, tour guide, disgruntled employee of Prospero. Native islander, arguably of Taíno descent.

ARIEL: Another of Prospero's employees, taken by everyone for less than he is. Puerto Rican of mixed descent.

IRIS: Young twenty-something tourist from the States; NYC born and bred, but of Puerto Rican extraction.

SPRITE: Iris's intended, same age, same background.

SETTING

This play is set on the Caribbean island of Vieques, Puerto Rico, largely in the terrace bar and on the beach directly in front of the Fortín Conde de Mellado. This restored Spanish fort and now modest but very well-regarded museum of Spanish Caribbean history contains significant artifacts from pre-Columbian times to the present. The Fortín Conde de Mellado has a commanding view of the island coastline and the sea. On the same site there is a small hotel. The name of the terrace bar, which serves both the museum and hotel patrons, is La Casita del Amor.

TIME

Late 2002, hurricane season in the Caribbean, and just before the 2003 invasion of Iraq.

AUTHOR'S NOTE

There is a real museum on the island of Vieques, Puerto Rico, called the Fortín Conde de Mirasol wherein resides a fascinating historical and anthropological collection. I visited that museum first in 1999, while the U.S. military was still engaged in nearly daily bombing practice in Vieques. One week after I visited the island, a civilian security guard named David Sanes was killed and several others were injured when a U.S. Navy jet practicing maneuvers missed the target zone and dropped a five-hundred-pound bomb on a manned observation post. That incident and my visit to the museum at Fortín Conde de Mirasol were significant inspirations for this play. The real museum has a good collection of pre-Columbian pottery and implements, and other local artifacts, as well as information about the history of Vieques, including the history of the military occupation of the island and the protests against that occupation. However, unlike the one in the play, it has no swagger sticks, *santos*, or Taíno petroglyphs. The building itself sits on a hill, not on the seashore, and is, in fact, the last Spanish fort built in the Caribbean.

ACT ONE

In the darkness the noise of thunder is heard in the distance. A flash of lightning. Lights up on TWO MEN standing on a beach, looking out to sea. These are ALONSO, a naval officer, and GONZOLO, a civilian attaché.

ALONSO: *(Shouting to be heard above the wind and thunder.)* "Cheerly, cheerly, my hearts. Take in the topsail. Tend to th' master's whistle. Blow till thou burst thy wind, if room enough." You recognize that?

GONZOLO: I don't, no.

ALONSO: "Keep your cabins: you do assist the storm."

GONZOLO: Sorry.

ALONSO: You're my what, advisor? Counselor?

GONZOLO: Attaché.

ALONSO: Well, relax, attaché. When the sky's in turmoil, the land is calm.

GONZOLO: I'm just not getting the references.

ALONSO: The planes are grounded until the storm passes. Although grounded is a term of art when the "ground" is the deck of a supercarrier. You're not one of those weather geeks, are you? A fan of tropical storms?

GONZOLO: I don't have much experience with them.

ALONSO: You spend enough time here, you come to resent the wild weather. Down here, most days are perfect.

GONZOLO: For sunbathing, you mean?

ALONSO: For flying sorties. *(Gives GONZOLO a hard once over.)* It's determined the outcome often enough.

GONZOLO: What has?

ALONSO: The defeat of the Spanish Armada. Battle of Trenton. Stalingrad. Inchon Landing. The Battle of the Bulge, for God's sake.

(GONZOLO is blank.)

ALONSO: Weather. A day's delay for rain allows the defenders to fortify a redoubt. A gale swamps a gunship. Weather can change the outcome of war.

GONZOLO: This is practice.

ALONSO: This is war. I'd love to find the asshole who first called them war games. It's no game. We strafe or bomb here every day. Navy and Marine fliers, Army and Air Force, recon and rescue, military storm spotters, even CIA black ops.

GONZOLO: You mean because we're building up and there's an intention—

ALONSO: Why are you here exactly?

GONZOLO: Command thought—

ALONSO: Who? Who in command?

GONZOLO: I don't know.

ALONSO: So someone in command, and the word came down.

GONZOLO: Someone thought you needed…assistance.

ALONSO: Sir.

GONZOLO: *(A beat.)* Things could be brewing here. With increased activity there'll be responsive protests, more mainland press, possibly security issues. Sir.

ALONSO: I've got things pretty well under control.

GONZOLO: Someone thought an extra set of hands, an extra pair of eyes, when things heat up. *(Brings his binoculars to his eyes, scans the horizon.)*

ALONSO: If. *(A beat.)* Nothing to do now but wait. They're hunkered down.

GONZOLO: How does a supercarrier hunker?

ALONSO: Maybe a little early in our relationship for the junior officer to be making jokes.

GONZOLO: Yes sir.

ALONSO: They take in the topsails.

GONZOLO: The topsails?

ALONSO: Though it is never too early for a senior officer to make jokes.

GONZOLO: Ah. Good one, sir.

ALONSO: About now, I'd bet they'd give a thousand miles of sea for an acre of solid ground. "The wills above be done, but I would fain die a dry death."

(GONZOLO is blank.)

ALONSO: It's Shakespeare. I'm quoting Shakespeare. You've read him, right?

GONZOLO: In college. But I don't remember—

(*There is an extremely loud thunder crack.*)

ALONSO: Never mind. Come on.

(*ALONSO and GONZOLO exit. Lights up on PROSPERO and ARIEL on the terrace of Fortin Conde de Mellado Museum. PROSPERO watches the sea through binoculars, much as ALONSO had in the last scene. Wind whips the fort's flag, which is the Puerto Rican flag, at a high rate. The sky is dark. Rain has begun falling.*)

ARIEL: It's as you guessed, Prospero. Our fishermen have seen them. Still far out at sea, but closer every hour. And there's another thing. Alonso has returned. He walks the beaches, studies the water and the sky.

PROSPERO: Looking for signs of our strategy. Now they will all come, Ariel. All the enemies of my person and state.

ARIEL: What would you have me do?

PROSPERO: Remain invisible. Record his every move. He takes you for nothing but a bit of breeze. Be my eyes, Ariel. Be my ears.

ARIEL: Three days more, Prospero. Then you will need a new man.

(*MIRANDA enters. As ARIEL exits, MIRANDA and ARIEL acknowledge each other in the familiar way the master's man and the master's daughter would. PROSPERO shifts his focus to his daughter.*)

MIRANDA: They took off. I called the airport.

PROSPERO: (*Scanning the sky.*) Yes, I see them. Making a run for it.

MIRANDA: I wish they'd waited. This will blow over in an hour. (*Looking out.*) Turn back.

PROSPERO: You're sure Ferdinand's on the plane?

MIRANDA: He flies in this dangerous weather because *you* insisted he come here.

PROSPERO: Does he think this will impress me?

MIRANDA: Let's not argue.

PROSPERO: In perfect weather, the flight from San Juan is one of the sweetest crossings in the world. The plane floats like a gull on the breeze, first past El Yunque and then over the sparkling stretch of sea that separates our tiny island from its greater sister.

MIRANDA: Look again. Can you still see the plane?

PROSPERO: But in a squall, there is no telling how long it will take. In that soupy sky pilots can lose their orientation to the earth so completely they crash into it.

MIRANDA: You've told me this a hundred times. Just to scare me. To scare me into staying here.

(*MIRANDA takes his binoculars.*)

PROSPERO: When you are up in such a sky, it can feel as if the delicate fingers that hold the plane aloft have suddenly dropped you, like a child drops a toy in which he has lost interest. Many times I have been thrown against some stranger in a suddenly sodden sky, hoping that those invisible fingers will grab us back up.

MIRANDA: (*Upset by this but working to ignore him.*) I don't see them. Where were they?

PROSPERO: (*Gently shows her where he last spotted them.*) Then, one time, crossing in a violent gale, it occurred to me that it was not the pilot's skill nor the airframe's reliability that saved us from otherwise certain tragedy, but the simple fact that I have a destination, a determination, which is stronger than the will of nature to stop me.

MIRANDA: Do you think they could have turned back?

PROSPERO: Does your Ferdinand have such a determination?

MIRANDA: Do not ask me to compare. You will not be pleased with my conclusion.

PROSPERO: When this occurred to me, in the midst of raindrops the size of oranges hammering the windows, when my belly seemed miles above my body, I understood that if I could will myself to arrive, I could also will others.

MIRANDA: Father, if you have this power, now is the time to use it. I want Ferdinand here with me.

PROSPERO: You don't believe me I know, *mijita,* but I am the one who saves the shrieking tourist from his certain doom. Now each time I make this crossing, I say under my breath to the *gringa* fearfully eyeing the darkening sky, "Do not fear. I will get you across."

MIRANDA: (*Affectionately.*) You are really full of shit. Do you know that? How did Mother put up with you as long as she did?

PROSPERO: Do not disrespect me, daughter. I have done nothing but care for you dearly, and I have taught you everything about this little drift of dirt where we have chosen to live in our exquisite exile.

MIRANDA: *You* have chosen.

PROSPERO: Fine. Have it your way. It is only that I do not want to see you waste yourself on someone who doesn't appreciate—

MIRANDA: Have I ever, for one moment, been angry with you that I was here and my mother was in New York? Have I ever disputed you when you say you have given me a charmed childhood?

PROSPERO: You do not dispute it because it is true.

MIRANDA: I love it here. I had no idea there were other ways to grow up. But I have come to see other possibilities. I have developed different desires.

PROSPERO: You fell in love with that *Americano.*

MIRANDA: You, too, are *Americano*, Father.

PROSPERO: Just because they say so doesn't make it so. I am *Viequense.*

MIRANDA: His family comes from Dorado and his aunts still live there.

PROSPERO: He's a *Nuyorican.* My worst nightmare. Come to steal my daughter.

MIRANDA: Don't be so melodramatic. I can think of lots of worse nightmares than living in New York. You fight so many enemies, Father. The evil employers who lured your wife away with their good pay and health benefits. The sneaky academics who want to plunder your museum and cart away our treasures. I know them all; I have been hearing about them all my life. But I don't see them.

PROSPERO: You see the military surely. You see the barbed wire that cuts us off from two-thirds of our island. You see the jets diving toward our eastern bays.

MIRANDA: Father, I see them. I just choose not to focus on them as you do. My studies, working in the museum with you, these take my attention. Can we please stop arguing now? I'm worried. They should be nearly across. We should see them. Where are they?

(PROSPERO closes his eyes and concentrates. If we had not just heard that PROSPERO thinks he can have an

impact on nature, we might think he was praying. The sound of the plane comes up slowly under what follows.)

MIRANDA: Look. Coming out of the clouds. Is that their plane? Please, please, let them come out of that horrible sky.

PROSPERO: They have started their descent.

MIRANDA: *Menos mal. Gracias a Dios!* I'm going into town now to retrieve my fiancé. Stay out here in the rain if you like. Believe you have magical powers if it makes you happy. Thankfully, the Airlink has good pilots, and they know how to fly in the tempest.

PROSPERO: *(A beat.)* Alright, fine. Go to the airport. Ariel can drive you.

MIRANDA: I can drive myself.

PROSPERO: Do not let him stay in town. Bring him back here. If he wants to take you away from me, he must come and ask, man to man.

MIRANDA: He does not need to ask you. He has already asked me.

(MIRANDA and then PROSPERO exit. The sound of the descending plane fades. A light and sound change signals that time has passed and the weather has cleared. STEPHANO and TRINCULO enter and move with dispatch to one end of the terrace bar, taking up residence on woven cane stools to survey the patio. CALIBAN, the bartender, enters during the following, barely visible at first under a staggering load of glasses or other bar equipment he has retrieved from elsewhere. He does not immediately seem to recognize their presence and does not jump to serve them. He puts away glasses, restocks the bar shelves, folds the napkins, straightens up the tables in the room, and comes to pay attention to them only belatedly.)

STEPHANO: That was maybe the worst experience of my life.

TRINCULO: Shake it off. We're here. Terra firma. The enchanted isle. Let's have a drink to celebrate our arrival.

STEPHANO: Survival.

TRINCULO: Something frufie with an umbrella. To elevate your mood.

STEPHANO: I don't want to be elevated, thank you very much. I've had enough off-earth experience for one day. I feel battered. First that woman, then the storm—

TRINCULO: What woman?

STEPHANO: In the airport in San Juan.

TRINCULO: What did she do?

STEPHANO: She spoke Spanish.

TRINCULO: She called our flight.

STEPHANO: How did you know that?

TRINCULO: Four years of high school Spanish and, oh yeah, I'm standing in an airport waiting for someone to announce "flight to Vieques." Even without the Spanish, I think I'd guess what someone opening a door to the runway and saying *Vuelo para Vieques* was trying to get across.

STEPHANO: (*Completely affectionately.*) God, I worship you.

TRINCULO: So you can file it away for next time. They just come up from the tarmac and call when the plane's ready. That's what they do.

STEPHANO: There's going to be a next time?

(*IRIS and SPRITE enter. They stand in the doorway, totally absorbed in each other, kissing deeply. CALIBAN works, apparently without recognizing he has customers.*)

IRIS: I love you.

SPRITE: I love you.

(*IRIS and SPRITE kiss and cuddle through all of what follows.*)

STEPHANO: (*A beat. Looking around.*) I thought you said there weren't going to be any breeders here.

TRINCULO: I said very few. We're off season. There's the possibility of hurricanes.

STEPHANO: But look. This place is a regular haven for honeymooners, a luau of love.

TRINCULO: Luau would be Hawaii. Do the addition. There's as many of us as them. Two each.

STEPHANO: I just wish that once I could hold you or kiss you in public without feeling—

TRINCULO: Oh Christ, here we go.

STEPHANO: No. I mean it. Don't you wish? Outside of New York? Without feeling conspicuous?

TRINCULO: You can hold me. Anywhere you want. I don't give a damn. I put my hands all over you whenever I want. I was rubbing your back in the airport, remember?

STEPHANO: And I felt the averted stares of everyone in that waiting room.

TRINCULO: No one could see us where we were sitting.

STEPHANO: What about that woman at the ticket counter?

TRINCULO: And you can't feel averted stares.

STEPHANO: Okay. That's true.

TRINCULO: Just forget it, will you? You want to hold my hand, you want to kiss me, you even want to grab my ass for a little squeeze, just go for it. You have my permission.

(*STEPHANO reaches out, hesitates for the briefest moment for a look around, and then, satisfied it's alright, gives TRINCULO a squeeze through his pants.*)

TRINCULO: (*A beat, indulging him.*) Okay. Got that out of your system?

STEPHANO: Here's another thing.

TRINCULO: Why don't you relax?

STEPHANO: You said the best beaches here are on the military base?

TRINCULO: Not on the active base. I mean, they let tourists on. Us regular Americans with folding money in our pockets and our frighteningly pale legs sticking out of our Speedos. You go through a checkpoint, they write down your name.

STEPHANO: I should feel good about giving them my name?

TRINCULO: They make sure you come back out later. They want to keep protesters off. I told you. Been going on for thirty years. It's not going to have an impact on us.

STEPHANO: What's going to happen when we drive through those checkpoints? Do they practice don't ask, don't tell? Because I hate to point this out to you, Mister I Never Swish, but one look at us, and they won't have to ask and we won't have to tell.

TRINCULO: Anyone can get on the beach. Just like back home. If you want to worry about something, worry about how much sunscreen it's going to take to keep you from crisping up like a pork rind while you're snorkeling in that thong you brought with you. I promise you, if you get thrown in a military jail for going to the beach with me, I'll visit as often as I can.

STEPHANO: Very reassuring.

TRINCULO: Look, here's our man. Let's move out to a table in the sun—now that we have some sun. *Señor. Por favor, una mesa para dos en la terraza.*

(CALIBAN comes to seat TRINCULO and STEPHANO and takes their order.)

IRIS: Kiss me again.

(SPRITE does.)

IRIS: Again.

(SPRITE does.)

IRIS: Again.

SPRITE: Iris—

IRIS: Again.

(He kisses her a final time, deeply.)

IRIS: Okay. Officially here. Officially started. Off and running. Now take me upstairs and fuck me.

SPRITE: *(Playfully.)* Can't we get a drink first? I want a planter's punch.

IRIS: Screw the planter's punch. I want you to take me upstairs right now. You're going to have more sex than you've ever had. Than you ever dreamed of having. Starting right now. Let's go.

SPRITE: You have a quota?

IRIS: I want you. That's all. Come on now.

SPRITE: I want you, too. But I want to do this for a few more minutes. I like it that people see me with you. I want everyone to know that you are mine.

IRIS: You know what I want? I want it to be perfect. I want to have the perfect honeymoon. Not a good one, not a nice one. Not a here's-another-picture-of-us-on-the-beach-sunbathing one. I want a honeymoon so gloriously filled with great sex that in seven years when you get your first idea about leaving me, you will have to say to yourself, well, I might find love with Rosa or Maria or whoever she may be, but I will never have a honeymoon as perfect as the one I had with Iris. I will never have more sex, never have better sex, never have a woman more willing to fulfill all of my fantasies than Iris. Get it? I am your love slave, you foolish boy.

SPRITE: I'm not going to leave you. Not in seven years. Not ever.

IRIS: I want to make absolutely sure.

SPRITE: There's one problem with your plan.

IRIS: What's that?

SPRITE: We're not married.

IRIS: A technicality.

SPRITE: Not to your parents.

IRIS: Look, you get a deal like this once in a lifetime. I saw that fare pop up on Priceline, New York/San Juan, companion flies free, I jumped on it.

SPRITE: You're sure this is how you want this to go?

IRIS: Absolutely. Let the honeymoon begin.

SPRITE: You promise you're going to marry me eventually?

IRIS: You're killing me.

SPRITE: In a church so our parents will be happy.

IRIS: In a church.

SPRITE: You're not just using me now. Because I'm not that guy. I'm traditional. I want it on paper.

IRIS: I'm going to count to three, at which point you better be coming upstairs with me. Because I'm pretty much ready to explode, and I'm sure if I needed to I could find one of those guys here. One. Two.

(SPRITE leaps up, takes her hand and runs. IRIS happily follows. CALIBAN has returned with the drinks for TRINCULO and STEPHANO. During what follows, ALONSO and GONZOLO enter. They seat themselves. ALONSO pays a lot of attention to the activity in the bar. GONZOLO works on his Palm Pilot.)

CALIBAN: Caliban at your service, gentlemen. *Dos martinis, con Stoli.* As wicked a poison as ever my mother dredged from the unwholesome fen.

STEPHANO: Your mother was a bartender?

CALIBAN: She was a *bruja.* A witch. I learned a lot of useful secrets from her.

TRINCULO: You speak English very well.

CALIBAN: I learned so I could make a living. With the military here, English makes me invaluable. But as a consequence, I use my native tongue less and less.

STEPHANO: Are you the proprietor?

CALIBAN: In my dreams. My master is Prospero. He owns this bar, the hotel, and the museum with its rooms of Indian trinkets and its underwhelming gift shop. Vertical integration, that's the ticket. Package-deal tourism for the hunters of the arcane. Scholars. Librarians. A one-stop wet dream for *gringo* geeks.

STEPHANO: Uh-oh.

CALIBAN: Are you… Oh, man, Caliban puts his foot in it again. I thought you were military.

STEPHANO: Us? Us!?

CALIBAN: So which are you?

TRINCULO: Museum curator, not academic. Special exhibits planner, freelance. *Gringo* geek.

CALIBAN: My humble apologies. And you, sir?

STEPHANO: Me? Just a hanger-on. A *bon vivant.* A friend of the fabulous.

TRINCULO: You know your Mister Prospero is proprietor of a treasure.

CALIBAN: He may be proprietor of the museum, and giving him all due credit, it's a good one. But it is *my* culture he presents up there in his fort, not his own. He is descended from Spanish imperialists who tortured and enslaved my forebearers. I am Taíno. Look at my skin, eh? See how it shimmers like a penny in the sun? That is the mark of the Taíno they could not erase. The copper color. To them, we were savages. To be converted by the sword or taken for sex. No one is pure anymore. But I am as close as you get.

TRINCULO: Could I get another one of these?

CALIBAN: I am at your service. I hope you will consider, *señor*, when you speak to my master about this culture, whose culture it is you are perusing. If you see what I mean?

TRINCULO: I do.

CALIBAN: But I did not mean to damage your mood. What you do for profit is your business. This is a magical place. If you have time for its more intangible virtues, in addition to being an excellent host, I am also an excellent guide.

STEPHANO: For a small fee, no doubt.

CALIBAN: No, my friend. Not a small fee. A large fee. But then, Caliban is the best there is. Ask around.

Because I followed my mother into the bogs and ponds along the beaches and back bays, I know the secrets the guide books won't lead you to.

(CALIBAN exits with their empty glasses. MIRANDA and FERDINAND enter and go to the bar. MIRANDA makes him a drink.)

MIRANDA: You are the most composed man I have ever laid eyes upon. Handsome and composed.

FERDINAND: Give me a break, Miranda.

MIRANDA: *(A little breathless, smitten.)* No, seriously. Look at you. You fly four hours from New York, run across the terminal to the Airlink and ride out a gale, and you look like you have just stepped out of a Bloomingdale's ad. You have come to me despite adversity. You take challenges in your stride.

FERDINAND: Now you sound like a commercial. Are you trying to sell me?

MIRANDA: In a way.

FERDINAND: The Airlink flight was horrible, but the storm ended as quickly as it came.

MIRANDA: My father will take credit for that.

FERDINAND: Yes. Prospero's magic. Doesn't that alone make you want to get away from him as fast as you can? Superstitious explanations, occult ravings. *(Only half teasing.)* It worries me how much may have rubbed off.

MIRANDA: Tell me about your sister's wedding. Was she a beautiful bride?

FERDINAND: Not as beautiful as you will be.

MIRANDA: *(Kissing him.)* You see? So many good qualities. Handsome and diplomatic. You just need to say the right things and my father will melt, too. *(Kisses him again.)*

FERDINAND: My new brother-in-law is a very black African, so my father told everyone who would listen that he was a tribal prince. But I think that's just made up.

MIRANDA: He is worried, *limpieza de sangre.* What the family will say.

FERDINAND: She announced at the party that they are going to live in Tanzania. To my father, they might as well have been saying they were going to live on the moon. He has one idea about what his children should do. Live on Long Island and be successful like he is. He expected them to be living nearby.

MIRANDA: Our fathers have the same desire.

FERDINAND: What about your mother? You have a mother, too. She misses you terribly. She wants you in New York, near her.

MIRANDA: You talk to her about this?

FERDINAND: Only a couple of times a week. She thinks I'm her best hope of bringing you back permanently. She loved having you in New York when you were in school. She worries that the longer you're here under your father's influence, the more you will want to stay here forever.

MIRANDA: That's your worry.

FERDINAND: She worries, too. She thinks your father will convince you to marry a *jíbaro* and live in a *bohío*.

MIRANDA: My father's opinions mean a great deal to me.

FERDINAND: Miranda.

MIRANDA: You will have to talk to him, Ferdinand. He needs to understand that you are the right man for me. If you do not convince him, there will always be tension.

FERDINAND: I am going to talk to him, Miranda, but it is not likely to be a conversation. I've tried before, you know I have. Your father is totally intractable on the subject of your future. Our conversations always seem to go wrong. I know he shouldn't, but he intimidates me.

MIRANDA: You don't need to tell me. But there is something else.

FERDINAND: What's that?

MIRANDA: He is also right. You would have me live on Long Island in a split level. You would offer me the comforts of a suburban life insulated from whatever danger and magic you imagine—

FERDINAND: What's wrong with being insulated from danger? I want my children—

MIRANDA: Your children?

FERDINAND: Yes, my children. *(Then, realizing his gaff.)* Miranda, I just meant, thinking about…imagining the future we will…

MIRANDA: *(Teasing him, though with serious undertones.)* You see, my father worries with cause. He worries you have made all our plans without ever consulting me.

FERDINAND: This is the kind of trap I fall into with him.

MIRANDA: You will need to avoid his traps if you want to win him over.

FERDINAND: What's wrong with split levels? I grew up in a split level.

(MIRANDA and FERDINAND exit. CALIBAN reenters with his tray and serves STEPHANO and TRINCULO. ARIEL enters, distributing bar supplies, then moves from table to table, doing a busboy's job.)

ALONSO: *(Loudly, to CALIBAN.)* Can we get some service here?

CALIBAN: Right away, gentlemen.

ALONSO: *(To GONZOLO.)* He's my man.

GONZOLO: That guy?

ALONSO: He's in deep.

CALIBAN: What can I get you?

ALONSO: Bring us a couple of *mojitos.*

CALIBAN: Vodka not rum, as usual.

ALONSO: Right. I outrank my friend here, so he's drinking what I'm drinking.

(CALIBAN goes to the bar to fill their order. ARIEL goes to ALONSO and GONZOLO's table and wipes the surface, very slowly and deliberately.)

ALONSO: The way it works is, the carrier groups rotate in for training. They have to get the sorties they can fly off of their decks up to a certain number. The crews are green. If Desert Storm taught us anything, it was the value of air superiority. In Kuwait, we shut the Iraqis down like a storm cellar in a Kansas twister.

GONZOLO: *(Focusing on ARIEL, but speaking to ALONSO.)* What's with this guy? *(To ARIEL.)* Do you want something?

(ARIEL does not respond)

ALONSO: I don't think he speaks English. *(To ARIEL, very loudly.)* Do you speak English?

(ARIEL is silent. He merely continues doing his work.)

ALONSO: Right.

(ARIEL finishes, and moves slightly away, but busies himself nearby, in listening range).

GONZOLO: What are our orders? What's our status?

ALONSO: On-site observation. Make sure the operation goes as planned. Deal with the locals who want to get too close to the action. I represent the Marine brass on shore.

GONZOLO: The flack catcher.

ALONSO: We don't want a full-court press. They didn't used to have anyone with a rank on the ground. For years the island was pretty much deserted beyond the fence line. We booted ten thousand people off of here in the forties. Sliced this place up like pie.

GONZOLO: No wonder the natives are restless.

(CALIBAN brings their drinks.)

ALONSO: For a long time, we had the remaining locals under pretty good control. But for the last couple of decades, we're in this rear guard with protesters.

GONZOLO: They red-filed the guy who owns this place.

ALONSO: Prospero.

GONZOLO: I read his dossier. I assume that's why we're here.

ALONSO: We're here because this place makes the world's best *mojitos*.

GONZOLO: *(Inclining his chin toward STEPHANO and TRINCULO.)* I'm surprised to see *that*.

ALONSO: Sure. There's a lot of them here.

GONZOLO: Really? Why here? There's no nightlife.

ALONSO: Who knows. Maybe they figure they need the military to protect their life-style.

(CALIBAN works his way back over to ALONSO and GONZOLO.)

ALONSO: What do you hear?

CALIBAN: *(Whispering.)* Nothing. Very quiet. Maybe too quiet, if you get my meaning.

GONZOLO: What happens next?

CALIBAN: What they do depends on what you do. If you escalate, they will. As always.

ALONSO: You will keep us posted.

CALIBAN: At your service.

(CALIBAN returns to his work at the bar. ARIEL sweeps the floor near where the MEN are talking. They ignore him as if he were not there.)

GONZOLO: You trust this guy is really with us?

ALONSO: I don't trust anyone. But his information's been good. We can head them off as long as we know their plans. It's mostly flotillas of creaky fishing boats. We don't want anyone hurt, so we let them come ashore. They wave some banners. We arrest them. I let their local paper take pictures. They preach to the local converted, so there's no harm. Then I call Fox News in Miami and tsk tsk to mainland viewers who vote in the congressmen who keep our military funded.

GONZOLO: It's a pain in the ass to defend a place where you aren't wanted.

ALONSO: This Prospero guy thinks we should just get out of Dodge. In a perfect world, he's probably right. But we're the law in Dodge and we're supposed to stay here, my President says so. Alright, we've got the "all quiet," so let's go get in a couple of hours of surf-casting. You ever surf-cast? It's a spiritual experience. You can hook tarpon right off the beach here that will cook up as juicy as can be. Come on.

(ALONSO throws money on the table, and he and GONZOLO exit. CALIBAN picks it up, goes to the register, rings a sale, then takes his tip and pockets it. He exits. MIRANDA and PROSPERO enter and sit together. ARIEL serves them coffees.)

PROSPERO: He's here?

MIRANDA: Upstairs in his room. Collecting his thoughts.

PROSPERO: For a simple conversation?

MIRANDA: I love him father. Is it really necessary—

PROSPERO: Love is hardly a persuasive argument. There is nothing to falling in love. I have done it dozens of times.

MIRANDA: Father.

PROSPERO: It's true. You want to believe that your mother was the only one, and that aside from her desire to leave here, we would still be together. But I was not a faithful husband. Not in my heart. I fell in love with every woman I saw. To me, all women are beautiful. And interesting.

MIRANDA: What are you trying to say, Father?

PROSPERO: Just that this Ferdinand whom you love is not the only fish in the sea. And that love may be overrated as a way to choose a mate. Lack of love was not what made your mother leave me or made me decide not to follow her.

MIRANDA: This is all just talk to you, Father. Love as another of your intellectual pursuits, a philosophical game in which I am your current opponent. But I am a real girl and Ferdinand is a real boy, and you know that in the end it is not going to matter what you say to me. I am going to marry him, and we are going to live in New York.

PROSPERO: Despite my saying to you that you should look around some more. You fall in love with the first man who shows you any attention. You dote on him. You give him an advantage over you.

MIRANDA: I have no interest in other men, Father. This one is a good man.

PROSPERO: He knows nothing of our life here.

MIRANDA: This is his third visit. I will show him what he needs to see. And you could help in this.

PROSPERO: Help him to see my home as a tourist sees it? As a storybook place, charmed but unreal, visited on a whim and easily left behind. That is how you will come to think of it when you come for your yearly visit. Swaying palms. Turquoise sea. And that eccentric concierge living on his Fantasy Island.

MIRANDA: That is not how I will think of it at all. And I'll be living on an island, too.

PROSPERO: Manhattan doesn't count.

MIRANDA: It's his intention you must look at, Father. He is coming in here to talk to you now. Please say you will give us your blessing.

PROSPERO: I need more time to think about it.

MIRANDA: No, you don't. You just want to delay the inevitable. You think if you withhold your blessing you will stall my growing up?

PROSPERO: Everything I love, they want.

MIRANDA: Who is this "they," Father? No one has sent Ferdinand to take me. Damn the military and their stolen property. You confuse them with everything else in the world. America is not taking me. I am going of my own accord.

PROSPERO: This is your home. Persuade him to live here with you.

MIRANDA: Father, I love it here. I carry this place inside of me. I do not need to be here to have it. You have given this to me. But what I want now is elsewhere.

PROSPERO: Ferdinand. America.

MIRANDA: Yes.

PROSPERO: Every one of us who leaves this island admits defeat. It breaks my heart.

MIRANDA: That is such an old-fashioned attitude, Father.

PROSPERO: Perhaps that is the most radical kind.

(FERDINAND enters, very nervous.)

FERDINAND: *Buenas noches, Papa.*

PROSPERO: I am not your father-in-law yet. Do not rush things.

MIRANDA: Father—

PROSPERO: Alright, alright. Sit down. Drink?

MIRANDA: I will be on the terrace if you need me.

(MIRANDA kisses her FATHER on the cheek and exits, leaving FERDINAND a little before he is ready. PROSPERO pours FERDINAND a drink. There is an awkward moment.)

PROSPERO: Did you know that my great-great-grandfather once governed here? By popular acclamation?

FERDINAND: Miranda told me.

PROSPERO: And that I am genuine heir to his legacy, a legacy taken from him and all of us without compensation, without consideration, by invaders who had no interest here other than to exploit this place for whatever they could squeeze from it.

FERDINAND: I have read the history.

PROSPERO: His blood flows through Miranda's veins, too. His desires, passed down father to child.

FERDINAND: What desires do you think are pulsing in her, Prospero? The desire to farm sugarcane? Or to be an overseer of *jibaros*? To make sure our people do their quota to enrich others?

PROSPERO: Our people?

FERDINAND: I was born on Puerto Rico's north coast. I am no less native to these islands than you. And there are millions of us *en el vaivén.* You know this. We go and we come back.

PROSPERO: You think because there is a name for this transit that makes it reasonable? You think because you came to a museum like this once a year as a child or on a rainy day when there was no baseball on television that you know our history? You think having seen Taíno petroglyphs you've done the important things?

FERDINAND: I think wanting with all my heart to marry your daughter and take care of her wherever we live is the important thing.

PROSPERO: After 9/11 I heard people who were born here—my former neighbors returned to visit—say it is treason to want the Marines to stop practicing here.

FERDINAND: I have heard the same. Though there are an equal number of us who will stand shoulder to shoulder with you and march to the beach chanting "*Fuera la marina.*" Pride doesn't vanish when you change your address.

PROSPERO: You want to talk to me about giving your engagement my blessing.

FERDINAND: Frankly? No. I do not want a discussion with you, Prospero. Miranda has asked me to ask you, and out of respect I am doing so. But we are returning to New York in two days with or without your blessing. So I am asking for her sake. Don't let her leave defying you. She loves you.

(PROSPERO and FERDINAND face each other for a moment, and then FERDINAND turns on his heel and exits. ARIEL appears.)

ARIEL: I think he has located his *cajones.* He spoke better than I expected he would.

PROSPERO: She does not see what she is going to lose, Ariel.

ARIEL: She is not a child any longer, Prospero.

PROSPERO: She is as headstrong as her mother. *(A beat, changing gears.)* Come on now. What do you hear?

ARIEL: You know I am leaving here in three days. I am going to the mainland for good.

PROSPERO: So you keep threatening. I don't think it's going to suit you.

ARIEL: I am just reminding you because you will owe me three weeks' wages, plus what you have promised me for all these years as severance for good service.

PROSPERO: Have I ever not made good on a promise? I have saved for you for your old age.

ARIEL: You may be tempted to renege because I am leaving. Or you may be angry because she is leaving. I have served you faithfully. I hope this will not be difficult.

PROSPERO: You wound me, Ariel. I am deeply loyal to those who have been loyal to me.

ARIEL: You could see my leaving as an act of desertion.

PROSPERO: I do. But I am not angry. You have prepared me. You are going to live with your family. I understand. Now, what do you hear?

ARIEL: There is a second man with Alonso. He is unknown to me. In the bar I heard them talking about how they lie to the mainland press. They have gotten word from Caliban that there are no protests planned.

PROSPERO: Has the new carrier group arrived? It is always worse in the first few days of training.

ARIEL: I did not hear them say, but in the past when Alonso appears at the bar, the next wave begins within two days.

PROSPERO: Why do the Americans, with all of their secret skill and expertise, think we won't calculate the timing from when their advance men appear? Do they think they are so devious and we so stupid that we will not put this two and that two together and over time come up with four?

ARIEL: It is no different from how they treat me. If they believe I speak no English, they talk openly around me. I am invisible to them, as if I wore a cloak of night. Even Caliban does not think I understand what they say in English, and he knows I speak it.

PROSPERO: What else do you hear?

ARIEL: They have gone off fishing. They think we have nothing planned.

PROSPERO: Then we will surprise them with our rag-tag army on the beach when the bombardment starts. Go now. Let everyone know the time is soon. And keep yourself alert for changes in their plans.

ARIEL: You are going to pay me in cash, right?

PROSPERO: You will get your reward. Go.

(ARIEL exits. Lights shift. It is later in the day. TRINCULO enters, dressed for the beach, in a thong and open-fronted shirt. He sits in a beach chair which bears the logo of La Casita Del Amour. ALONSO and GONZOLO also enter, with fishing gear. ALONSO teaches GONZOLO how to surf-cast. TRINCULO sunbathes. After a moment, STEPHANO enters, wearing snorkeling gear and surprising TRINCULO.)

TRINCULO: Where have you been? I was getting worried.

STEPHANO: Snorkeling.

TRINCULO: Alone?

STEPHANO: With Caliban as my guide.

TRINCULO: Really? I thought he was just showing you around town.

STEPHANO: It was so amazing, Trinculo. Now I know why you like it so much.

TRINCULO: I wish you had come to get me.

STEPHANO: I wanted to try it without you first. I wanted to learn it without feeling like I was keeping you from enjoying it.

TRINCULO: Stephano.

STEPHANO: We'll go again, I promise. It'll be better now that I know I can do it. Really.

TRINCULO: So what did you see?

STEPHANO: Once I got the hang of the mask and breathing, it was like flying in the water. I know you told me it would be like that. Caliban gave me this card and this wax marker, and as we were swimming, he pointed out all of the fish and I checked them off. They have amazing names that must have been made up by flaming fishermen, or whoever makes up fish names.

TRINCULO: Biologists, I'd guess.

STEPHANO: You think academics have all the fun. But these are something else. The great hind. Bright-red hind. The smallmouth grunt. The Spanish grunt. The goatfish. The large trunkfish and the somewhat more diminutive small trunkfish. Half of them look like they're in drag. Oh, there's the honey damselfish, and my personal favorite, the queen angelfish.

TRINCULO: I assume you didn't share any of this with your guide.

STEPHANO: I'm not sure he'd have seen the humor. Decent hind for an older guy.

TRINCULO: Water distorts the body.

STEPHANO: He changed into his trunks right on the beach.

TRINCULO: My my. You have had quite the time.

STEPHANO: So I did.

TRINCULO: Come here, you honey damselfish. Make my small mouth grunt.

(They kiss. Then they settle into their chairs once again for sunbathing.)

STEPHANO: *(Noticing ALONSO and GONZOLO.)* What are they doing?

TRINCULO: I'd say fishing.

STEPHANO: Fishing? They're going to murder my colorful friends?

TRINCULO: Down, Aqua Boy. They're after tarpon. Tarpon are gray. Food fish, not entertainment fish.

STEPHANO: Talk about fish out of water. What's their deal?

TRINCULO: They're probably a couple of old fags like us, here for a jaunt.

STEPHANO: They're not fags. They have no fashion sense. Oh shit. Did he hear me say that?

(ALONSO notices STEPHANO and TRINCULO, plants his fishing rod in the sand and comes over to them.)

ALONSO: Excuse me. You boys from the mainland? I've been coming here so long speaking my Pidgin Spanish, English is a sound for sore ears. Mind if I sit? *(He does, before they answer.)*

ALONSO: So, are you here for business or pleasure?

TRINCULO: Mostly business.

ALONSO: I have you pegged for travel writers. On assignment from *Condé Nast*? *Travel and Leisure*? *Caribbean Preview*?

STEPHANO: You've got it wrong, Mister—I don't think I caught your name.

ALONSO: The name's Alonso.

STEPHANO: We're not writers.

ALONSO: Really? What're you doing here then? If you don't mind my asking. It's hurricane season. Kind of an odd time for a trip to the tropics.

STEPHANO: Visiting the museum. I'm Stephano. This is Trinculo.

ALONSO: Pleasure.

(They shake hands.)

ALONSO: So now I'm guessing you boys are a couple. Don't worry. It makes no never mind to me. Live and let live. That's my motto. I'll take a boatload of American boys no matter what their orientation over the people who live here. You been in town yet? Just let me warn you. Don't leave anything unattended. There's no good citizenship.

STEPHANO: What brings you here?

ALONSO: Training. There's a couple of beaches further up the coast where pilots learn the playbook.

TRINCULO: You're military.

ALONSO: You've caught me in my civvies, I'm afraid.

TRINCULO: I thought the President agreed we'd stop training here.

ALONSO: Assuming we can find someplace else as good. You've probably heard about the controversies. The locals have this theory that their elevated cancer rates are because of something the military is doing—as opposed to the fact that they get ten times the UV the rest of the planet gets or they eat a lot of imported junk food and salty meat with nitrates. But it's patent nonsense. Targeting beaches they've never been on and flying touch-and-goes is hardly making cancer rates go up. Hell, we do the same damn things at McGuire Air Force Base. You hear anyone screaming New Jersey is carcinogenic?

(STEPHANO is about to say something, but TRINCULO gives him a look that stops him.)

ALONSO: This used to be a military beach, you know.

TRINCULO: Really?

ALONSO: We're far downrange from the target area. Look at this place. Pristine sand, turquoise water. It's damn near perfect. Tourists have been swimming here for years. Soldiers, too. You think we'd let our boys recreate here… *(The thought goes unfinished. A beat, then.)* You boys are staying at the La Casita Del Amour right? I saw you in the bar. I've stayed there myself on occasion. Decent beds. Almost didn't recognize you without clothes. You haven't met the guy who owns the place, have you?

STEPHANO: *(Happy to have the subject changed.)* Not yet. He's taking us on a private tour of the museum this evening.

ALONSO: Really? Well, enjoy. You've got a perfect day today.

(ALONSO returns to GONZOLO and his fishing gear.)

STEPHANO: That was weird.

TRINCULO: You certainly were Mister Chatty Kathy. Is there some reason you wanted to tell him all of our plans?

STEPHANO: You think that was an accident?

TRINCULO: What?

STEPHANO: Him talking to us.

TRINCULO: We're the only ones out here.

(We hear the sounds of IRIS and SPRITE's lovemaking.)

STEPHANO: Not anymore.

STEPHANO: *(To TRINCULO.)* Oh brother.

TRINCULO: Maybe it's time for us to head back to the hotel.

(TRINCULO and STEPHANO gather their stuff and exit. After they are gone, IRIS enters, tying on her bikini top, and looks around to see if anyone is there. SPRITE follows, dragging slightly.)

SPRITE: Was that okay?

IRIS: Okay? It was great! Let's go do it in the water now.

SPRITE: Hold on. Hold on.

IRIS: You're good, right?

SPRITE: Yes. I mean, no. I don't know.

IRIS: Sprite? What? What is it?

SPRITE: I don't know.

(She waits.)

SPRITE: I don't know!

IRIS: Oh, no. You can't do this. You have to tell me. This is crucial, Sprite. We have to be able to talk about this. If we can't, it's going to go bad between us. I've been through this with other guys. Everything seems great at first and then there is this "thing," and it's just there but not discussed, and soon it starts to grow and then it's just too big to talk about, and then it's easier to pretend it isn't there and just back away from each other. I don't want you backing away from me, so just say it, okay? Whatever it is. I'm not afraid of anything you can say. But I'd be totally freaked out if I felt there was something you couldn't.

SPRITE: It scares me, Iris.

IRIS: What does?

SPRITE: What you want... I don't know.

IRIS: What I want? I want love, friendship, and comfort. I want us to be together forever. I want romance and sex and passion. I want crashing orgasms. I want to be so exciting to you that you throb with desire every time you think of me. I want you to be sitting at your desk at work counting the agonizing minutes until you get to come home to me. I want what every woman wants.

SPRITE: I want all those things, too. And it's not the sex. I love making love to you. I'm totally up for that.

IRIS: So? And? But? Come on, Sprite. You have to be able to do this.

SPRITE: It's your intensity.

IRIS: You're scared of my intensity?

SPRITE: Not scared of, exactly.

IRIS: What is it exactly?

SPRITE: Everything is right up to the edge with you. We've been making love every minute we've been here, and now you want to do it in the water and then you want to sneak onto the restricted beaches. I'm not sure I can keep up with you, Iris. And I'm afraid of what you'll think if I don't.

IRIS: Oh, Sprite.

SPRITE: What?

IRIS: You're doing just fine. You're not going to disappoint me. I'm sure of it.

SPRITE: You are?

IRIS: I am. You're the one... I love you. Just kiss me, now.

(PROSPERO appears in the café, goes to the edge of the wall with his binoculars. First, he scans the sea and sky through the binoculars, and then he watches IRIS and SPRITE making out. When MIRANDA enters, he quickly scans the beach. She watches him for a moment.)

MIRANDA: There's no need to hide behind your binoculars. We don't have to talk. I'm just out here for some air. (Seeing what PROSPERO was originally looking at.) They're cute. And sexy. Playful as puppies.

PROSPERO: Not much younger than you. Sowing some wild oats.

MIRANDA: Don't you have an appointment?

PROSPERO: In a few minutes.

MIRANDA: The day has turned out alright. After a rough start.

PROSPERO: Yes. And it is going to be a lovely night. We'll have stars.

MIRANDA: I am taking Ferdinand night swimming in *la luminosa*.

PROSPERO: *La bahia luminiscente*. Do you remember the first time we went swimming there?

MIRANDA: I remember. It was just after Mother left. You put me in your canoe. I didn't want to go. I was angry, the way only a seven-year-old can be. I had no idea where you were taking me. Everything seemed so strange to me then, like I had crossed into another world.

PROSPERO: You had. We had.

(IRIS and SPRITE get up quietly and exit.)

MIRANDA: I remember we paddled up the coast a long way and then turned into a break between the mangroves. Suddenly, there was flash of lightning in the water, then another, then another.

PROSPERO: Yes. The effect of motion on a tiny organism, a creature that makes light.

MIRANDA: I didn't believe you when you told me that. I thought it was one of your tricks.

PROSPERO: And I remember exactly how you looked, delighted despite yourself. And when we dropped into the water to swim...

MIRANDA: Imagine loving the world so much that you glow when it touches you.

PROSPERO: There are such wonders here.

MIRANDA: I have thought of that bay many times, at my most lonely or homesick moments.

PROSPERO: But from above, from a bird's-eye view or from the cockpit of an F-15 say, you might see it as a target, the green interior surrounded by a white ring of beach, on which to unleash forces that rival—

MIRANDA: *(Gently.)* Father…

PROSPERO: *(A beat, then.)* Alright.

MIRANDA: You cannot protect me from the world, Father. Please give me your blessing going out into it.

PROSPERO: Watch the stars with me for a moment before you run off to Ferdinand. Let me pretend you are still mine and mine alone. Let me grieve this way for what time has taken.

(MIRANDA hugs him. They walk together slowly and exit. ALONSO and GONZOLO enter, still with their fishing poles.)

ALONSO: I was wrong. They're museum guys, not reporters. But we'll go by La Casita and buttonhole them again tomorrow. They might have heard something.

GONZOLO: Twist my arm and make me drink another *mojito*.

ALONSO: Where'd you get the name Gonzolo?

GONZOLO: It's an old Italian name.

ALONSO: Italian? But you're—

GONZOLO: My mom. My friends call me Gonzo.

ALONSO: Really? Gonzo like from the *Fear and Loathing* guy or Gonzo from *The Muppets*?

GONZOLO: I got the nickname when I was twelve.

(ALONSO's cell phone rings. He answers it.)

ALONSO: Speak to me. Right. Copy that. Yes, sir. Copy that. Right.

(ALONSO snaps shut his cell and begins to reel in his line. GONZOLO reels in his as well.)

GONZOLO: What is it?

ALONSO: We've got work to do. The sea is churning. The timetable has shifted. We're close to liftoff. A thousand sorties, raining bombs, louder than weather.

GONZOLO: When?

ALONSO: Not for me to know exactly. For now, they coil like a cloud over the decks of the carriers. Soon they will swirl inland like a swarm of bees, to sting the body of this island. The sky will pop like Fourth of July fireworks, and we will be known by the traces of light we leave in the air.

GONZOLO: You're a poet.

ALONSO: No, my friend, I am a soldier. What I love arises from what I believe. This work we do, this is the work of civilization. Let's get ready.

(ARIEL rolls out of the place where he has been hiding. He sneaks away from GONZOLO and ALONSO, and then goes off to tell his master. Lights change. TRINCULO, STEPHANO, and PROSPERO enter from the museum and take a table.)

TRINCULO: Thank you so much for the tour. You have a wonderful museum. And as I always feel when I visit a new place, there are so many things I do not understand about the history and the nuances of the culture.

PROSPERO: Why would you? It is not your history.

TRINCULO: It's my job. When a museum hires me to plan a show, I read everything I can about the world of the artifacts. I go to see similar exhibitions to get a sense of the material. Museum-goers want to understand *why* they should look at something. With some things, it's clear. You look at tomb treasure, you understand that you are looking at a reflection of glory from antiquity. But if it's more complex, someone has to digest it to be able to make sense of it for the casual observer. That someone is often me.

PROSPERO: What did you like best? It is always interesting to get an expert's impression of my collection.

TRINCULO: The *santos*, of course. I heard before I left New York that your collection was superb. Felipe de la Espada's work from the eighteenth century. Extremely rare.

PROSPERO: There is a revival in this carving. Boredom and unemployment have encouraged our people to become artists.

STEPHANO: What do your people like best?

PROSPERO: Regular museum visitors?

STEPHANO: Yes.

PROSPERO: Children seem to like the military uniforms—the dress grays of the officers who have been sent here to oversee us. They do not yet understand what hundreds of years of occupation have meant here. Spanish, Dutch, British, and American forces have all held power here. We are among the most occupied people on earth, did you know that?

TRINCULO: The people I represent—

PROSPERO: Who are they, exactly?

TRINCULO: I am not at precise liberty to say. They do not want word of this to become public prematurely.

PROSPERO: They think I would announce—

TRINCULO: No. Hardly. Though one of your employees might accidentally leak it, or perhaps you are in negotiations with someone else and might use a public announcement as leverage. As they have no history of dealing with you—

PROSPERO: They do not trust me. I understand.

TRINCULO: *(Does not rise to the bait.)* I can tell you this. They are a major museum. If I told you the city, you could probably guess which it is.

PROSPERO: But you will not tell me that.

TRINCULO: The people I represent have the notion to do an exhibition about the arts and culture here from pre-Columbian times to the present. They would not want the military displays. Or the political material about the beach blockades and protests. There are many relevant artifacts in my client's collection, but you have dozens of high-quality items that they do not.

PROSPERO: The glyphs, for instance.

TRINCULO: Yes. That would be one example.

PROSPERO: The *jibaro* household goods. The wood- and metalwork. The antique handicrafts.

TRINCULO: Yes. You have a rather complete timeline.

PROSPERO: How about the swagger sticks?

STEPHANO: I liked the swagger sticks.

TRINCULO: Yes. That's quite an impressive collection. Because they are also craft, I'd make a case for them.

PROSPERO: You know that swagger sticks were never part of the American officer's official uniform? Hundreds were made here from our hardwoods. Parents ordered them as gifts for graduation from Annapolis. Sticks that represented a naval officer's power when he walks onshore, a baton a strutting sailor twirls to demonstrate his imperious nature. A gentleman's bully accessory.

TRINCULO: I hardly think that. It was a style, not necessarily meaningful in the same way to each man or in each situation.

PROSPERO: Well, each scholar to his own interpretation.

TRINCULO: Can we set a time for serious negotiation?

PROSPERO: You want to offer me a rental fee to empty my cases and strip my walls. For how long?

TRINCULO: The institution I represent would want a nine-month minimum. And a regional exclusive.

PROSPERO: Aside from the money, why should I do this?

TRINCULO: The money could be a strong inducement. I can see just from walking around you need repairs. Your security and humidity devices are antiquated. You could close for the period of time your contents were on exhibit at my client's museum, complete your upgrades, and have a grand reopening. Raise your prices when you reopen.

PROSPERO: Raise my prices?

TRINCULO: Or lower them. Perhaps a several-hundred-thousand-dollar windfall allows you to do that. Make a big splash.

PROSPERO: Do you have any idea why I do this?

TRINCULO: To preserve your heritage? Because history and archeology appeal to you?

PROSPERO: Yes. But not entirely. I do it because if I don't do it, my history will be gone.

TRINCULO: Gone? You mean, lost?

PROSPERO: No, I mean gone. All of these items would find their way somewhere else. To the museum on the big island or to New York. Gone. But now, the moment a schoolchild gets interested in why his skin is copper and the next kid's is black, he can come here and see why. Here, where he lives, where it happened. In a Spanish fort. On an old plantation. Near a slave graveyard. Here.

STEPHANO: That boy will still be here nine months from now.

PROSPERO: But his interest may not.

(ARIEL enters. He signals to PROSPERO. They speak privately.)

PROSPERO: Excuse me, gentlemen.

ARIEL: There are planes on the way. Spotted in the east. This is not the usual daily runs. This is something else. Bigger. You must come right away. We are gathering at the gates of the base.

STEPHANO: *(To TRINCULO.)* What is he saying?

TRINCULO: Something about planes.

PROSPERO: You are going to get quite a show, my friend. Only once in a while do we get this kind of buildup. You are going to see the awesome power of your military. They must be planning to make a move overseas. We are guessing that the exercises will begin tonight.

TRINCULO: Our military.

PROSPERO: What?

TRINCULO: Our military. Yours and mine. Not just mine.

PROSPERO: As you wish.

TRINCULO: No. I'm sorry. I had to listen to you tell me your views of having your culture usurped for two hours now, and I think you should listen to mine for a moment. You think I could sit on a beach with the man I love in Iraq, Saudi Arabia, or even in our dear friend, Pakistan?

STEPHANO: Trinculo, I don't think you want to—

TRINCULO: No. I do want to. You think my intellectual interests would be tolerated by the fundamentalist mullahs? Because those same bastards who'd stone me to death would smash your *santos* to bits without a second thought. You enjoy your right to hold us *gringos* in contempt *because* our military is here.

STEPHANO: I think we need to take a breather now. Let's talk again tomorrow after everyone has the opportunity to think about things. Trinculo?

TRINCULO: Yes. Fine.

PROSPERO: Thank you for enlightening me about your position. It is useful to be reminded that there are people who believe other than I do.

TRINCULO: Let us leave it, then, that your collection continues to be of great interest to me personally and to my employer.

PROSPERO: I understand.

TRINCULO: And everything may look different to you upon reflection.

PROSPERO: Yes. Or nothing will.

(PROSPERO exits and ARIEL follows, leaving TRINCULO and STEPHANO alone.)

STEPHANO: What's gotten into you? I've never seen you like that.

TRINCULO: I'm sorry. It was stupid. Very unprofessional of me.

STEPHANO: Don't be sorry.

TRINCULO: I am.

STEPHANO: You really love me, don't you.

TRINCULO: What? Yes, I do. Don't you know that?

STEPHANO: I didn't. I mean, I know you say it. But we all say it, right? It's easy to say it. But you said it there. In anger. At the risk of losing… well, I was dumbstruck. No one has ever—

TRINCULO: Stephano, there is going to be a moment when we are going to be able to say it, out loud, formally, in front of everyone. And I want to be able to do that. I want to be able to take your hand in front of my friends and family and declare that I love you, that I never want to be apart from you.

STEPHANO: Are you proposing to me?

TRINCULO: This is the most romantic place I know to do it. I was planning to do it better, I mean more articulately. But this will do. Will you marry me? I have been carrying this ring, waiting for the perfect moment—

STEPHANO: Yes! Yes. Yes, yes, yes, yes.

(STEPHANO throws himself into TRINCULO's arms. IRIS and SPRITE reenter.)

IRIS: I need to ask you something.

SPRITE: Okay.

IRIS: Do you *want* to marry me?

SPRITE: What?

IRIS: I know this has all been my idea and that I want it all to be a certain way, but I need to know.

SPRITE: If I will marry you.

IRIS: If you *want* to.

SPRITE: First you throw yourself at me with the force of a hurricane and now you ask if I want you?

IRIS: Yes.

SPRITE: I love you, Iris. I love you with all of my soul. I would have come here with you simply to sit under these stars and stare at you across the sand.

IRIS: But you're okay with all the sex, right?

SPRITE: You're all I'll ever want.

IRIS: You're sure?

SPRITE: Absolutely.

(They kiss deeply. MIRANDA and FERDINAND enter.)

MIRANDA: Wasn't that amazing?

FERDINAND: It was.

MIRANDA: I'm always struck by how little we matter to the creatures in *la luminosa*. How incidental we are.

FERDINAND: Uh-huh.

MIRANDA: But how at the same time, if we did not see them, their glow would not exist.

FERDINAND: Miranda, we might never get your father's blessing.

MIRANDA: It's possible.

FERDINAND: I need to know, Miranda. And I am asking. Even if he says no. Will you marry me?

MIRANDA: *(She deflects him, but only for a moment.)* I wonder how many people have proposed to each other here.

FERDINAND: In Vieques?

MIRANDA: On this stretch of beach. Since the dawn of time.

FERDINAND: Marry me, Miranda.

(No words are necessary to seal the answer. They simply kiss, as the other couples have done. But as they do, lights up slightly on ALONSO and GONZOLO.)

ALONSO: Do you copy? *(He pauses to await the reply.)* There's a stray bird headed our way. Do you see him? He's off course. What is it? Guidance problems? Dead stick? Jesus man, there are civilians on this beach. He's what? Disoriented?

GONZOLO: Ask what he's carrying.

ALONSO: What is he carrying? He's what? *(To GON-ZOLO.)* He's fully loaded.

GONZOLO: What?

ALONSO: Fully loaded. Tell him to dump his armaments. Now, goddamn it!

GONZOLO: *(Shouting.)* NO! He's too close. If he drops now, he'll light up the whole beach. They'll hop over the water like skipping stones right into us. Tell him to pull up. Tell him there are people out here. Tourists. Civilians. Tell him to—

(The sound of a plane screaming in. PROSPERO and ARIEL run out to the patio and look out to sea. CALIBAN joins them. The THREE COUPLES, now illuminated, turn as the explosion lights up the beach. There is a moment of sheer terror on all their faces, then blackout.)

ACT TWO

CALIBAN alone on the beach, his clothes in awful disarray. Broken palm branches cover him. It is morning; the sky is bright.

CALIBAN: Ohhh. Dreams, do not go. *(Covering his eyes.)* Shit. I am blinded awake. Where am I? What day is this? What is that light? Did I sleep here, in the open, under the stars? Oh, I hurt. What has turned my soothing sun to sadistic swordsman stabbing my eyes? I will stand. Survey. There. Nothing. But something. Itches. Nags. What? A flash of light, a cry. When was that? My head. Did I drink all of this? *(Examining the bottle.)* From Prospero's private reserve. I was working at the bar I remember. *(A beat.)* Then there was a sound. What was it? A sudden squall? Thunder? *Don't be afraid,* I remember telling myself. The island is full of sounds and sweet airs that usually give delight. Sometimes a sound like a thousand tingling instruments hums in your ears. I do not think it was a storm. I am dry as toast, my clothes sand streaked, not rain splattered. What then? I think there were shouts. Were they shouts? Run. Run! RUN! And I was afraid then. Did I run? From what? From where? My head. Then, I remember, there was a flash and I was flying, a marionette, jerked upward by unseen hands, somersaulting over the scenery, a soaring angel swimming up the sky on a wave of heat. I remember near the top noticing this claret clenched in my fist and thinking, *I didn't pay for this. (Teetering. Head pounding.)* And then, in an instant, angelic puppet flight curtailed, I was condemned, discarded, plunged down to sand. The beach breaking my fall. Stumbling on my knees and thinking, *This is not right, this is not a thing a man can do, propelled into sky on no force other than wind.* And then there were the voices again, softer, anguished. But I couldn't move. Couldn't. And then crawling out of range of the heat, in the sudden darkness, where there was no sound but lapping water, and the breeze was the breeze of scented night, I sank down to the succor of sleep. *(A beat.)* Was there more than this? I must have dreamed the rain. The clouds, I dreamt, had opened and dropped their riches down on me, so much so that when I woke, I would cry to dream again.

(CALIBAN exits. PROSPERO enters. He is on the veranda of his café, looking out at the sea. He studies the sky for a moment, and then raises a pair of binoculars to his face for a closer study of the horizon. In the distance we hear the sound of a small plane drawing nearer. ARIEL enters, waits nearby.)

PROSPERO: Today the sky is cloudless and calm, Ariel. Blue as a baby's blanket, serene as a song. No jets are scrambling today.

ARIEL: They flew yesterday, and for twenty thousand days before that. They will fly today. Why should this stop them?

PROSPERO: Perhaps this is their brief penitence, a moment of silence before they come with their checkbooks to see if there is anything we need to help us forget the sight of that beautiful girl eviscerated before her lover's eyes. I have to go and meet the parents.

ARIEL: The boy does not want to go with you. He is afraid her parents will blame him.

PROSPERO: Do you know what face her parents will see in their grief? The radiant one of her looking up from her first steps, first communion, first day in school. The

face of innocence. But unless they see his grief as well they will never be able to look past their anger. Thrown clear as if by magic, this one and not the other. What can possibly explain this? They must see his grief to understand.

ARIEL: Is there anything else you need from me?

PROSPERO: Can you turn back time, Ariel? Two days, that's all I ask. Can we work that magic together, you and I? Perhaps together we might accomplish it.

ARIEL: Not even God can exercise that power.

PROSPERO: Why should He be so inflexible? Just a few moments out of all the millennia. To set a thing right? Give those children a chance? *(A beat.)* Do you remember before they came?

ARIEL: It is only two days. Though it seems a lifetime.

PROSPERO: I mean before the military. Was there a moment from your childhood—

ARIEL: No. They were always here, or so it seems to me. In the sky or up on the eastern tip. We did not go there.

PROSPERO: Off limits to us, yes. Parents kept their children away to keep them safe. *(A beat.)* I did.

ARIEL: Yes.

PROSPERO: That is what her parents will feel. That they have failed to protect their child. To keep her from the precipice. From the place where danger waits. They will feel we have failed as well, we who were here, her implied guardians.

ARIEL: Do you know that I was proud of them?

PROSPERO: Who?

ARIEL: The Marines. The Navy. As a child. I felt pride. I did not understand the difference between us. I ran on the beach with my toy bomber, swooping my sand castle Vieques, protecting it from invaders, a hero to my people.

PROSPERO: Child's play.

ARIEL: Is there anything else I can do?

PROSPERO: Bring that bastard Alonso to me. This afternoon. That weasel who blithely sits in my café, who corrupts my employees to spy on me. Bring him here so I can spit curses at him face to face. That's his job, to stand at attention and take it like a good soldier. Let us make him do it.

ARIEL: He will spit back.

PROSPERO: Let him dare.

(SPRITE appears, bandaged and banged up. He is ashen. ARIEL ushers him forward and then exits. PROSPERO puts his arms around SPRITE's shoulders and helps him to a chair. PROSPERO kneels in front of him.)

PROSPERO: How old are you, young man?

SPRITE: Twenty-two.

PROSPERO: So young.

SPRITE: Are you going to tell me I am young enough that I will recover from this? That is what the priest tried—

PROSPERO: No. *(A long beat.)* You were born in the States?

SPRITE: Philadelphia.

PROSPERO: May I ask you why you decided to vacation here and not at Isla Verde or Dorado?

SPRITE: Iris heard it was magical here. *(A long beat. He is barely containing his grief.)* What do I say to her parents? How do I face them?

PROSPERO: I have been asking myself the same questions.

SPRITE: They say the plane was airworthy. That it was an accident.

PROSPERO: Listen to me, son. You are deep in grief now. There is nothing I can say to you that will provide any real comfort. But later, when you can reflect, you must remember that an airplane flew toward us, its own citizens, as if it was at war. There is no margin for error when you are moving at five hundred miles an hour. *(With growing anger.)* They have put us in harm's way every day for sixty years. Training for Normandy. Training for Korea. Training for Vietnam. Training for Grenada. Training for Panama. Training for Desert Storm. Training the pilots who patrolled the no-fly zone. And now, training for whatever is next. In the name of what? This was not an accident. You must carry that with you in your heart, next to your love for her, in equal measure. You must use her death in your life. It will give you what you need.

SPRITE: But how will I live without her?

(A wail of sadness escapes from SPRITE. PROSPERO comforts him a moment and then MIRANDA enters.)

PROSPERO: Are they here?

MIRANDA: Upstairs. In the first suite.

PROSPERO: *(To SPRITE.)* Go on. Go see them. You will know what to say.

(SPRITE exits.)

PROSPERO: How are they?

MIRANDA: Awful. Inconsolable. What is going to happen?

PROSPERO: The government will try to put the best face on it. A tragic consequence of keeping our shores protected. *Carbones.*

MIRANDA: Father.

PROSPERO: Do I become extreme in my anger? My reasonable responses do not seem to have produced results.

MIRANDA: This may not be the moment for that kind of anger.

PROSPERO: When are you leaving?

MIRANDA: What?

PROSPERO: I asked when you were leaving?

MIRANDA: I'm not leaving.

PROSPERO: Of course you are.

MIRANDA: No. I'm staying here. For the first time, the world is watching. We have the chance to be heard. Maybe even the chance to win. I know you, Father. You are already planning the response. I can assist you with—

PROSPERO: You cannot stay here.

MIRANDA: What are you talking about?

PROSPERO: It is dangerous, that's all. I will not have you—

MIRANDA: You will not have me? It is not for you to say.

PROSPERO: Their planes are falling out of the sky. You are my only child. It could have just as easily been you.

MIRANDA: Or you. Or anyone on that beach, including their spotters.

PROSPERO: Go to New York. I will speak to your mother. I will tell her that you have my blessing to marry Ferdinand if that is what you desire, and that I will help pay for the wedding. Give yourselves a year to test your love, to find your stride together. And then you can proceed—

MIRANDA: Father! Listen to yourself. Two days ago you were lecturing me for even thinking about going to the mainland. Now you are writing checks for champagne and flowers?

PROSPERO: Two days was another lifetime.

MIRANDA: Our quarrel is the same. You are still trying to tell me what to do.

PROSPERO: There is going to be trouble here, Miranda. I am going to make trouble, as you have guessed. I do not want you to be hurt as a consequence. I want to know you are safe. I want to take what action I feel is necessary. I don't want to have to worry—

MIRANDA: Are you going to put yourself in harm's way? You're a sixty-two-year-old man.

PROSPERO: What does that have to do with anything?

MIRANDA: I want to be here for whatever is coming. This is my home. That was my beach they showered with blood. Those were my guests. And this is my country. Mine as much as yours.

PROSPERO: I cannot tell you how proud I am to hear you say it, but I cannot let you stay here.

MIRANDA: You do not think I should stand with you in this? I have skills, Father. I have things to offer. And I am not going until I know you are safe.

PROSPERO: My safety is not your concern. Your safety is mine.

MIRANDA: You are not responsible for me any longer, Father, in any decisions I make.

PROSPERO: I could have protected them, Miranda. Warded off that terrible moment. But I was distracted, worrying about you, about the collection. But no more. This is the time to end it. This is within my power.

MIRANDA: Father, this was not your fault.

PROSPERO: Two days ago you dismissed my saying I could change the course of events as the ravings of an old man lost in his own beliefs—

MIRANDA: You rave, Father, at many things. But I have never thought you lost. You are the most found man I know. Rooted like a mangrove, Father, tentacled down into the deep soil tethered to the sea. When you rave, Father, it is like watching a great tree shake in the wind, making a great noise as it brushes the air. But you stand, Father, solid as steel, for where you are.

PROSPERO: Could a man ask for a daughter with more understanding? But I beg you, leave here now. Take this man who loves you and go.

MIRANDA: I am too close to the tree, Father. I am rooted here, too. I will not go.

(MIRANDA and PROSPERO exit. STEPHANO and TRINCULO enter on the beach. STEPHANO steps carefully as if he cannot bear to walk here. TRINCULO looks out over the water. They do not seem to be connected.)

STEPHANO: I don't want to walk near there.

TRINCULO: Where?

STEPHANO: There. Where the plane…where it happened.

TRINCULO: Okay.

STEPHANO: It's too weird.

TRINCULO: Okay.

STEPHANO: What are we doing out here anyway?

TRINCULO: Contemplating the weather. Standing in the sunshine. Having a breath of fresh air.

STEPHANO: Why?

TRINCULO: Because as nice as our little suite is, we have been holed up in our room too long.

STEPHANO: I don't want to be out here.

TRINCULO: I am trying to figure out which would be harder. Getting you on a plane and flying you home, or staying here and trying to persuade you to do something comforting until you relax. But I can't sit around anymore in the midst of your gloom.

STEPHANO: *(Blowing him off at first.)* So don't. *(A beat, then engaging him.)* I fly a thousand white-knuckled miles in a jet and I cross the channel in a storm in a tuna fish can, and then my own country, which you defend for its openness and honor, kills a kid almost in front of me. And you want to go swimming?

TRINCULO: I want to conclude my business here and go home. It was an accident, Stephano. The same as a car wreck.

STEPHANO: No. It was not. It may not have been premeditated, but it was not an accident. If you are raining bombs on a place every day, at some point someone is going to get rained on.

TRINCULO: You're right. Okay? Does that make you feel better?

STEPHANO: When you proposed to me two days ago, it was one of the happiest moments of my life. But frankly, now I feel—

TRINCULO: Stephano—

STEPHANO: Let me finish…that my desire to be with you, the pure, unadorned love I felt in that moment, has been replaced by something baser, a terror I guess I would call it, a terror of being alone, of dying alone, and that anything I do now, anything I choose, is not about—

TRINCULO: Nothing's going to happen—

STEPHANO: …being with you because I love you. It would be because I have been made rudely aware of my mortality—and how scary the world is.

TRINCULO: Look. Would you—and just indulge me here for a minute—at home would you, crawl under a rock if you saw a car wreck?

STEPHANO: I might. It depends what I saw.

TRINCULO: Go into our apartment and hide? Go into deep mourning for a stranger? Rend your clothes? Tear your hair?

STEPHANO: I'm not doing that.

TRINCULO: Remember that time we watched the bike messenger get clipped by that truck? Gone in an instant. It was awful, but we went on with our lives.

STEPHANO: Trinculo…

TRINCULO: Or here's a better example. Did we stop living our lives after the Trade Towers fell? Did we? I mean for all of our paranoia about New York under siege? Sure, the city felt subdued for a time. We stayed home a little more. We held each other a little tighter in bed. We ate out less. We watched more TV than usual. We went to Ground Zero. We stood and wept. We shook our fists in anger. A real enemy had attacked us, blocks from where we live. It was personal. We knew

people. People we partied with. Lovers of friends. We were dazed for a while. But then—

STEPHANO: Trinculo—

TRINCULO: No. Let me finish. Then we went back to work and to the restaurants we love and to the theatre and all of the pleasures of our lives. We went back to them because without those things we have no lives.

STEPHANO: I have been sitting here for two days waiting for something to occur to me. Something to unknot my stomach, something that might dissolve my anger.

TRINCULO: What do you have to be angry about?

STEPHANO: There's lots to be angry at. I'm angry at my country. I'm angry at the sad history of this place. I'm angry things in life are so random. I'm angry at you.

TRINCULO: At me? For what?

STEPHANO: I'm angry at love.

TRINCULO: At love?

STEPHANO: Yes.

TRINCULO: What's love got to do with it?

STEPHANO: Oooo. Catchy.

TRINCULO: I'm serious.

STEPHANO: Everything that happened on that beach in that moment was about love. Love of country, love between two people, love of place, love of self. I know that pilot didn't want to kill anybody. The men who sent that plane on its mission believe in their jobs, love their country, love the ideals they are defending, I have no doubt. You have convinced me of that. But here I am, turned to stone by all this for looking at it. I cannot move. I cannot think. And every time I start to, I just get angry. I want to smash the whole world.

TRINCULO: Stephano, we live our lives. That's all. We get on the plane or we don't. We kiss on the beach or we don't. We don't always get to choose.

STEPHANO: Well, there it is, anyway.

TRINCULO: I make my living looking at the past, at the evidence that gets left behind. I believe in the idea that if you add history up it gets better, not in all ways at all times, but overall. There is no time I want to go back to, no place I'd rather be than here and now. I recognize that despite intermittent oppression we endure—

STEPHANO: Intermittent?

TRINCULO: Yes, compared to other oppressions one might have had to endure historically. As a Jew in Europe, say, or a native in the New World. This is the culmination of history so far. I cannot hold these two beliefs simultaneously—that life has purpose and progress is imminent, and that things are random and nothing matters. So I choose the former. I choose it, that's all.

STEPHANO: *(After a moment, allowing himself to feel mildly comforted.)* Have you decided what you are going to do about Prospero?

TRINCULO: We have to talk again, to see where things stand.

STEPHANO: You know the girl's parents are here?

TRINCULO: I know. *(A beat.)* I am perfectly willing to go on playing houseboy to you until you feel better, but let me point out, and hear me out here before you jump down my throat, that activity of any kind might be good for you. Another snorkeling trip might remind you that there are other ways to see the world. Other worlds to see.

STEPHANO: Let me think about it.

TRINCULO: Okay.

STEPHANO: I do love you, you know.

TRINCULO: *Love in the Time of Cholera.*

STEPHANO: What?

TRINCULO: Nothing. It's a book by—

STEPHANO: I know what it is. And what you meant. Just because I'm blithering does not mean I am a complete idiot.

TRINCULO: I know.

STEPHANO: I'm okay. I will be.

TRINCULO: I know.

(TRINCULO hugs STEPHANO and then they exit. ALONSO is at his command post. ARIEL stands in front of him. GONZOLO watches the conversation but does not participate.)

ALONSO: I was told you spoke no English.

ARIEL: You were misinformed.

ALONSO: So it's what, some sort of island joke on us *gringos*?

ARIEL: Prospero wants to see you this afternoon.

ALONSO: He wants to see me? He thinks he can command and I will come running? Who the fuck does he think he is?

ARIEL: He thinks he is someone you should talk to just now.

ALONSO: I have plenty on my plate at this particular moment. Do you think I don't know he's pissed off? Do you think I don't know he's going to do everything he can to drive a truckload of bad press and blame up my ass?

ARIEL: He has asked me to tell you that he wants to see you. I am not here to debate your point of—

ALONSO: There is no debate. This isn't some little pissant operation we got here. I have a dead pilot who's got parents, too, and they aren't coming down here to parade their grief in front of the wire service photographers and point fingers of blame. They're waiting for the body at Dover where there will be no pictures of their bravery. They attend their grief in private like…

ARIEL: What? What were you going to say?

ALONSO: I have half of the Fourth Fleet sitting out there waiting to get back to work. You think we're going to stop because one of our planes went down?

ARIEL: It doesn't matter what I think.

ALONSO: You tell your boss that terrorism creeps in when you let your guard down.

ARIEL: Terrorism?

ALONSO: That's the lesson of our time. You respond with passivity, the next thing that happens is boatloads of radicalized fanatics are landing on your beaches with dirty bombs in their Zodiacs. You think Bin Laden gives a crap about the fine distinction between this island and that, or mainland versus Caribbean? You're safe because this base is here. America is safer because of what we are doing here. And the more of these guys we learn to dig out of their hidey holes, the safer we'll all be.

ARIEL: You may be right about this. I am just delivering a message.

ALONSO: Yeah, well, in those places they kill the messenger. So here's the deal. You tell your Mister Prospero, when we start our training runs again, he should watch from his veranda. Tell him to get that Caliban fellow to mix him up a double rum planter's punch. Then you tell him to turn his eyes to the sky. You watch with him, too. And you will see the glory of U.S. air power coming in, as it has done for the last sixty years and as it will for the next sixty, and then you thank your lucky stars that you live in this country and not in one of those places that would as soon cut your throat as look at you.

ARIEL: You may be right.

ALONSO: You tell him. Freedom costs. We will deal with the parents of that child. We will not negotiate policy with him.

ARIEL: When shall I tell him you will be coming to see him?

(MIRANDA and FERDINAND enter the café.)

FERDINAND: You've just decided to stay here. Just like that. Your father has put you up to this.

MIRANDA: My father is your best friend right now. He would probably pay you to hogtie me and hoist me onto the Airlink.

FERDINAND: You have decided you will never convince him and you are using this as an excuse.

MIRANDA: You don't understand.

FERDINAND: What then?

MIRANDA: My father spent this morning telling me all the reasons I had to go to the States with you.

FERDINAND: What?

MIRANDA: He doesn't want me here, you see, because he is going to go stand on the beach and let himself get arrested, or worse, so he can call the *New York Times* from jail or a hospital bed and tell them he is a political prisoner in his own country.

FERDINAND: They'll Homeland Security him. He'll be held as a traitor. They will do it.

MIRANDA: He is willing to take the risk that they won't do that to someone with a national profile.

FERDINAND: Has he heard of Camp X-Ray? Has he heard that they deny security prisoners lawyers?

MIRANDA: I cannot leave him here to do this with no one—

FERDINAND: He's got his troops, his warriors.

MIRANDA: He's got me, too.

FERDINAND: How long?

MIRANDA: What?

FERDINAND: How long do you plan to be on the barricades?

MIRANDA: As long as it takes.

FERDINAND: You need to do better than that.

MIRANDA: Are you going to give me an ultimatum?

FERDINAND: Two weeks? Three weeks? Give me a plan, Miranda.

MIRANDA: There is no plan.

FERDINAND: I have been at your father's mercy ever since you and I met. What he wants, what he doesn't want. Now you must decide.

MIRANDA: We must respond to this.

FERDINAND: Why? Who was this girl, Miranda? I mean who was she to you? To him?

MIRANDA: Our visitors. Our guests. Puerto Ricans returning to the place their parents came from to make their vows. You think that means nothing? She is the name of our struggle now.

FERDINAND: The name of our struggle? Give me a break! She is not OUR struggle. She is his struggle.

MIRANDA: Not only his.

FERDINAND: Kids making love on a beach. Pumping up the rhetoric doesn't make her a hero. (A beat.) What do you want to do?

MIRANDA: I want to be on that beach every day with my father until we make them stop. I want to defend my place by staying in it.

FERDINAND: Two days ago you were ready to run screaming back to New York. Your father was driving you—

MIRANDA: Love is not always a sensible emotion.

FERDINAND: Now we're talking about love?

MIRANDA: Love of country. Love of family. Many kinds of love. Love for you. Desire to protect you. Desire to fix this awful thing so you and your wife can come back here and be at home. So the world is a better place to live in.

FERDINAND: I am afraid of this. I do not want you to do this. Please don't ask me to stay here.

MIRANDA: I haven't asked.

FERDINAND: No. But if you stay, I will stay.

MIRANDA: What?

FERDINAND: I want to be with you. If it will make you understand how much you mean to me, I will make his fight my own. Many kinds of love. Here's mine.

MIRANDA: You would do that.

FERDINAND: Yes.

MIRANDA: Even knowing he wants you to take me away from here. You would defy him.

FERDINAND: He wants you to be safe. He wants to hold onto you. He wants many things at once. But what he really wants is for you to have a future.

MIRANDA: You can barely speak to him. How do you know what he wants?

FERDINAND: He wants what all fathers want. What I will want for our children. And before you jump down my throat about—

MIRANDA: *(Understanding exactly where he is headed, throwing herself into his arms.)* Shut up. Just shut up now and say nothing more.

(He does. As MIRANDA and FERDINAND hold each other, lights shift to ALONSO and GONZOLO at their command post.)

ALONSO: This is a nightmare. I have the governor up my ass, the Adjutant General's office screaming at me, and now this guy wants a personal audience. Who the hell does he think—

GONZOLO: He's the guy who the press at home is quoting.

ALONSO: What are they saying?

GONZOLO: All the usual stuff. The history. The cancer stats. The indifference to public safety.

ALONSO: Indifference? What the hell do they think you and I were doing on that beach? Twenty yards the other way, it could have just as easily been… Screw it. What do you think?

GONZOLO: Permission to speak freely?

ALONSO: Sure.

GONZOLO: I think you have to ratchet it down. I think you have to be a little less dismissive. You want it to go away?

ALONSO: Where does he come off making propaganda out of this? A horrible accident kills a kid, not to mention a pilot, and this guy wants to suggest, what, we planned to ditch a ten-million-dollar aircraft just to piss him off? He thinks I wanted this? He thinks we have that kind of disregard—

GONZOLO: He's got the parents at his hotel. You've let him parade them in front of the cameras without being there to tell your…our side of the story.

ALONSO: There is no side to the story. It was an accident. End of story.

GONZOLO: That's a side to the story. You have to say that.

ALONSO: They were two kids fucking on the beach. In public, for Christ's sake. Not even all that discreetly. We can tell from the pictures what they were doing. It's a hell of a camera we've got in the nose of those planes. Survived the crash completely intact. We've got pornographic close-ups. Let's show the press what they were up to.

GONZOLO: They are lovers, returning to their ancestral home for a marriage proposal. That is what the press has already got. Are you crazy enough to want to run your morality up the flagpole here? You think you got something that will trump lovers holding each other on the beach?

ALONSO: Fucking each other.

GONZOLO: Let me tell you this as clearly as I can. You cannot torch their reputations.

ALONSO: It's obscene.

GONZOLO: The way she died was obscene.

ALONSO: Whose side are you on?

GONZOLO: I'm trying to tell you what you need to do.

ALONSO: So I let them say what? Anything they want?

GONZOLO: Do you have kids?

ALONSO: What?

GONZOLO: Do you have kids?

ALONSO: Two. A boy and a girl. Eleven and fifteen.

GONZOLO: You can't protect them.

ALONSO: What?

GONZOLO: You can't protect them. Not really. Not the way you want to.

ALONSO: The hell I can't. It's my duty.

GONZOLO: I agree with that. We do the best we can. Maybe your daughter would never do something like this.

ALONSO: Trust me. She wouldn't.

GONZOLO: Maybe. But she's going to do something you don't like at some time.

ALONSO: And I'll deal with it when it happens. If it happens.

GONZOLO: She has parents who love her as much as you love your kids. You can't make them feel—

ALONSO: Okay. I get it.

GONZOLO: You need to suck it up. Say you're sorry. Make a few promises.

ALONSO: What do you think I can promise?

GONZOLO: To take it up with your superiors.

ALONSO: I can't take it up. I'm the backstop. That's my job.

GONZOLO: You can take it up and you have to. You can tell your superiors exactly what happened and what resulted from what happened. You do not have to take a position. But you can tell the press that you are sorry, which you are, and that you feel for the parents, which you do, and that you are saddened by all loss of life and that sometimes there are unintended consequences of vigilance. You can and you must.

ALONSO: Unintended consequences of vigilance. PR crap.

GONZOLO: Without the attitude.

ALONSO: How long do we tell the fleet to hold off the touch-and-goes? How long until they can start to train again?

GONZOLO: Until her parents fly the body out of here. Until the national press is looking elsewhere.

ALONSO: That could be days. This isn't some little candy-ass flyover we're delaying. This is something global. While we're waiting, this guy is sitting there in Baghdad—

GONZOLO: Do the right thing here and you will preserve your ability to continue to practice here. Push them to the edge, and you will be fighting a rear-guard action against the *New York Times* and the goddamned *Washington Post* for the next ten years. You want to be the guy who's remembered for finally getting us kicked out of here?

ALONSO: This is why they sent you.

GONZOLO: Yes.

ALONSO: An attaché.

GONZOLO: I'm really more of an advisor. For when things need…diplomacy.

ALONSO: A flack's flack.

GONZOLO: Call me what you want.

ALONSO: You know that real soldiers hate guys like you. I should have guessed when you told me you never surf-cast.

GONZOLO: Military men are not diplomats. But diplomats are sometimes required.

ALONSO: Well fuck that.

GONZOLO: Yeah, fuck it. Fuck doing the right thing. Fuck the moral high ground. Fuck trying to make us look like we have our shit together for once, and we are doing something because we believe it and not because it's politically compelling or to avenge someone's daddy. Fuck all the soldiers who are going to stick their necks out for it, and fuck having ideals. Do whatever the hell you want. Take your swagger stick and smack these assholes around. You're right. That's the right way to handle it. Fuck everyone. Sir.

ALONSO: *(After a long beat.)* Set it up.

(GONZOLO exits, then ALONSO. PROSPERO is in his museum office. ARIEL enters.)

ARIEL: Your man has arrived.

PROSPERO: Thank you.

ARIEL: I do not wish him on you. He's a piece of work.

PROSPERO: I know.

ARIEL: He was shocked to learn I understood his language. He thought we had conspired to trick him.

PROSPERO: I wish I had seen his face when he realized.

ARIEL: You would have enjoyed it.

PROSPERO: I will miss you, Ariel, your loyalty.

ARIEL: I was hoping to see this end before I left.

PROSPERO: I know. You have served me well. All these years.

(MIRANDA enters.)

MIRANDA: Father told me you were leaving.

ARIEL: Bad timing, eh?

MIRANDA: This is your home. You will always be welcome here.

ARIEL: I will send him in.

MIRANDA: Wait. Give me a moment with my father.

(ARIEL starts to exit. MIRANDA calls him. She goes to ARIEL and hugs him. Then he exits.)

MIRANDA: Father, there is something I need to say to you.

PROSPERO: Go on.

MIRANDA: Nothing is simple, is it, Father? You make one choice and immediately every other seems better. I said before that I would stay, but I am torn between wanting to be here with you and wanting to begin my life with the man who loves me.

PROSPERO: I know.

MIRANDA: Ferdinand says he's willing to stay here with me, but I don't think he should do that. He has opportunities to pursue, and I don't want to send him back without me. But we need someone in the States to speak for us, someone who knows our cause intimately. So I am asking, Father, give me your blessing to go to New York. I will raise my voice there in your name. Let me begin my life with Ferdinand by making this commitment to you.

PROSPERO: *(Takes a long beat before he answers.)* You have my blessing.

MIRANDA: Promise me you are not just saying this now because you think I will be safer elsewhere?

PROSPERO: I promise. But there is something you must promise me.

MIRANDA: What is it?

PROSPERO: If anything happens to me, you will come back here and find a way to keep the museum open. You will make it your duty.

MIRANDA: Nothing is going to happen to you. You will be here forever.

PROSPERO: Perhaps. I seem to be in exile in my own land.

MIRANDA: You are not in exile. You are home.

PROSPERO: Do you think there is anywhere in the world where people actually feel safe?

MIRANDA: What do you mean?

PROSPERO: Actually never worry about their lives ending suddenly before they have concluded their important work.

MIRANDA: Father—

PROSPERO: Somewhere in the States, perhaps, an idyllic small town, where no one believes there is danger to them personally.

MIRANDA: What are you trying to talk yourself into?

PROSPERO: Nothing. I simply want a safe place to get to know my grandchildren. And for them to get to know me.

MIRANDA: Why is everyone so preoccupied with my having children?

PROSPERO: A man at my age—seeing his daughter yearn to move beyond him, not quite finished with what he has set out to accomplish—thoughts turn to mortality.

MIRANDA: You will live a long life, Father. You will finish what you have set out to do.

PROSPERO: Promise me. Promise me you will come back if—

MIRANDA: I promise.

(She kisses her father and exits. ARIEL brings ALONSO.)

ARIEL: Don Prospero—

(ALONSO enters. ARIEL leaves.)

ALONSO: Quite a lot of hoopla out there.

PROSPERO: Hoopla? That's what this is to you? A little excitement?

ALONSO: I didn't mean—

PROSPERO: That angry crowd you walked through, all the press, all the hoopla as you call it, you understand you have brought this on yourselves. Not simply because of the death of that child but because of your lack of respect for us. If you had been wiser, you could have avoided—

ALONSO: Are you advising the American military now? Give me a break, Prospero. You think anyone cares what these political opportunists say? Robert fucking Kennedy? Al Sharpton? A couple of card-carrying liberals on a junket who say what everyone expects them to say? They could have saved the airfare. You think patriots are a parody. But I owe my country something. People died to give me what I have. People I loved. An uncle in Korea. A cousin in Vietnam. Once upon a time the idea of making compromises for your country didn't seem like a simpleton's choice. Plato proposed it in *The Republic*.

PROSPERO: We are not building an ideal society. And I think of myself as a patriot.

ALONSO: That's your opinion.

PROSPERO: *(Bargaining.)* One day.

ALONSO: So you could say to the *New York Times* you made us stop flying?

PROSPERO: Respecting the dead. One afternoon.

ALONSO: It is not in my hands.

PROSPERO: You are the ranking—

ALONSO: On the island, yes. On the seas, it is someone else. On a carrier. Or in Washington.

PROSPERO: Always at a safe distance.

ALONSO: That's how the military operates.

PROSPERO: No one on the hot seat. No one taking responsibility. No place the buck stops.

ALONSO: There is, but you wouldn't understand.

PROSPERO: Try me.

ALONSO: Chain of command is not simply about order, or orders. It is about mission, about weighing information, about need to know, about perspective. I do not have the perspective of whoever has said keep flying. From their vantage point, something trumps respect for the dead.

PROSPERO: What could that possibly be?

ALONSO: Respect for the living. Defending the nation. She is simply collateral damage.

PROSPERO: That famous phrase.

ALONSO: Used because it is accurate. Collateral to the mission. To what someone with a broader perspective deems most important.

PROSPERO: Military intelligence.

ALONSO: You say it with derision, but yes. There is such a thing. Even if it serves your cause not to believe it.

PROSPERO: Collateral damage is an evasion of the facts.

ALONSO: It is a description. Without judgment.

PROSPERO: Without respect.

ALONSO: And we have come full circle. We have nothing to say to one another, nothing one of us can persuade the other to accept. We are set in our beliefs. I can live with that.

PROSPERO: You live with it *because* there is no argument. You set the terms. You've won before we engage.

ALONSO: I have a duty to perform.

PROSPERO: A duty? You have murdered an innocent child.

ALONSO: You do not want to accept it, but part of that duty is to you. *(Begins to exit.)*

PROSPERO: *(As ALONSO exits.)* We will not forget this. This is not over.

(ALONSO exits. TRINCULO waits in the café. PROSPERO goes to him.)

TRINCULO: Thank you for seeing me. I know this is a hard time and that there may be bad feelings associated with, well, us mainlanders.

PROSPERO: You think?

TRINCULO: I understand. But Prospero, I think your collection, properly curated for my client's space, would do more to bring a positive awareness—

PROSPERO: Yes. Fine. I have made up my mind. You have a number?

TRINCULO: Sir?

PROSPERO: A number. An offer. A specific amount of time and money.

TRINCULO: Yes.

(TRINCULO hands PROSPERO a paper. PROSPERO reads it.)

PROSPERO: I accept.

TRINCULO: You do? *(With relief.)* That's great. Although I am somewhat surprised.

PROSPERO: Yes. Well. Provided.

TRINCULO: Provided?

PROSPERO: Provided that you take the political material as well. The news photos, as well as the *santos* and swagger sticks.

TRINCULO: I don't think that my client will consent—

PROSPERO: That is my bottom line. The whole collection, including the political material, or nothing. There is no negotiation on this point.

TRINCULO: You must understand the position I am in, Prospero. My client wants an artistic and cultural exhibition. They get money from the NEH, the NEA. They can't appear to have a political agenda.

PROSPERO: But I do. Curate it however you like, I don't care. Just as long as you display this as well.

TRINCULO: You realize this will probably be a deal breaker.

PROSPERO: No, it won't. You tell that son-of-a-bitch client of yours that this bombing makes what he sent you here to get twice as marketable. The death of that child has given you a huge bump in ticket sales. Vieques, the troubled isle. Vieques, first line in our last stand against terrorism. Get the marketing machine cranked up. They'll know how to spin it. I'll take what comes.

TRINCULO: It is none of my business, but what do you plan to do while the pieces are traveling?

PROSPERO: Is that your way of saying you'll accept my terms?

TRINCULO: I will need to make some calls.

PROSPERO: Don't come back to me with a counteroffer. These numbers are for the whole exhibit.

TRINCULO: I think I can probably convince them.

PROSPERO: I will do as you suggested. I will make upgrades to the building. I will try to write an end to the military story.

TRINCULO: You may not be able to.

PROSPERO: This is the best opportunity we have. That kid should not have died.

TRINCULO: That is the same thing they are saying about the pilot now.

PROSPERO: I know. Sides. Spin.

TRINCULO: May I give you a piece of advice?

PROSPERO: Advice?

TRINCULO: Yes. From someone who has a personal stake in a progressive view of things.

PROSPERO: You would hardly have convinced me you were a progressive the other day.

TRINCULO: We differ on how progress is made.

PROSPERO: Yes. But I may be feeling my oppression more than you are feeling yours at the moment. What is your advice?

TRINCULO: When you win, and you will win eventually, forgive history.

PROSPERO: What?

TRINCULO: You and I, we work in the same world. I've come to think there is only one lesson in the pileup of accumulata and ephemera and symbolized beliefs that we boil down to a few feet of evidence in a display case or on a wall. Forgive history or relive it. For me, it's that simple.

PROSPERO: You can forgive the years of exclusion, the absurd moralizing—

TRINCULO: I can forgive anything if I believe it will help us move beyond it. I came here to propose marriage to the man I love. I stood on your beach and asked for his hand. I am going back to a country where there are people serious about legalizing our union. Ten years ago, even that thought was unimaginable. Forgive history, Prospero.

PROSPERO: I will keep that in mind for the time when we have the opportunity to do that.

TRINCULO: Thank you for not being offended.

PROSPERO: How is your friend doing? I hear he is morose.

TRINCULO: He doubts he will make it home.

PROSPERO: Tell him I will ensure that he does.

TRINCULO: Caliban said you believe you have this power. If you did, it would be remarkable. Enviable.

PROSPERO: Even if it was my will that has also kept them flying all these years?

TRINCULO: The bombers?

PROSPERO: To protect my home, my little strip of sanity.

TRINCULO: What happened with the plane that crashed?

PROSPERO: On that beach, on that night, torn between sorrow at my own obsolescence and pride imagining my daughter's future, my guard was down.

TRINCULO: You'll forgive me if prefer to trust the laws of physics.

PROSPERO: But on the off chance it is my will that can keep your plane aloft, don't you want me to be exercising it?

TRINCULO: Sure. (After a moment.) Take care of yourself, Prospero. I'd hate to see you get hurt in this fight of yours. It would be a loss to…

PROSPERO: To whom?

TRINCULO: I was going to say "your people" but I think it is more than that. To us. To everyone.

PROSPERO: And you take care of my treasures, Trinculo. I may yet learn to forgive history, but if these objects are mishandled, I will not forgive you.

TRINCULO: You have my word. (Exits.)

(Light shift signals time shift. PROSPERO is on the beach—not in front of his museum but in the military reserve.)

PROSPERO: Now they all have gone. Ariel to his new home. Miranda and Ferdinand gone this morning to the States. The Navy flacks back to their base, secure that they have made their problem disappear. My collection, packed in crates, tomorrow sails. Pray for calm seas, auspicious gales. And here I am. Beyond the horizon the warriors wait to train on my spit of sand. They will fly in the formation of geese, a leader at the tip of the V searing forward. Soon enough they will find me, off limits, over the fence, defending this blasted place. I will use my will to draw them here, then whatever powers I formerly had, I will abjure. I face them with my native strength alone. Today or tomorrow, or whenever it comes, I will give them my life, and if necessary my death. This is the problem with parenthood. To make our children safe, we put the world under a spell. We tell ourselves it is in our power to prevent their pain. But it's a lie. We have no power but this: to stand in the face of wrong and yell at the wind. If death finds me, make it be for reasons anyone can understand—freedom or a cause that is just. So here I declare: I will not forgive history. But can I change it with my death? I offer it here, on this beach. Come do your worst. Pick me up in your hands and swat me down that my death be the cause for wails of sorrow, screams of murder, or else my project fails.

(During the above, CALIBAN has entered and stands listening.)

CALIBAN: What is this? Ranting like a madman at the sky? I have always suspected madness. Do I let him shout himself out? Dare I approach him? Prospero.

PROSPERO: What are you doing here?

CALIBAN: I was about to ask you the same.

PROSPERO: I am waiting for our airborne warriors. I have decided to give them a real target.

CALIBAN: No, Prospero. You can't.

PROSPERO: Let them practice on me.

CALIBAN: It will be a long wait.

PROSPERO: What do you mean?

CALIBAN: You haven't heard? They are finished.

PROSPERO: Finished?

CALIBAN: All finished. This is the first day for sixty years with no planes.

PROSPERO: They took the day off. Finally decided to respect our dead. The first day in sixty years. A tiny victory.

CALIBAN: No, Prospero. They are gone.

PROSPERO: Are you mocking me, Caliban? I fire you for spying on me and now you seek some advantage over me? Have your military masters sent you to get me to abandon this beach?

CALIBAN: No.

PROSPERO: What then? Why don't they fly?

CALIBAN: They decided. For reasons of their own. No relation to the killing of that kid.

PROSPERO: I don't believe you.

CALIBAN: Go look, Prospero. As we speak, work crews strip the barbed wire from the fence posts. I'm the crew boss. This is my reward for years of good service to my country.

PROSPERO: Good service? Informing on your friends? Being a traitor to your people?

CALIBAN: Look at my badge. Environmental Consultant, United States Department of the Interior. I have a GS grade. A pension.

PROSPERO: Unbelievable.

CALIBAN: Why so dejected? You've won, Prospero. No more target practice. No more bombs. Listen. There is nothing coming.

PROSPERO: What convinced them?

CALIBAN: They didn't tell me. The military operates in mysterious ways.

PROSPERO: No they don't. They are obvious. They are unsubtle.

CALIBAN: I have to go back to work now. Be careful walking the beach. There may be unexploded ordinances, and there is no military here to clear them for us. Whatever happens now, we are on our own. *(Exits.)*

PROSPERO: *(Watches the sky. Shouting.)* Where are you? I know you haven't gone. I know you're out there, revving up. Taking aim. Bearing down. Somewhere in the world, some acre of ground is under your siege. *(Unfurls his protest banner. It says "Fuera la marina." He scans the sky through his binoculars.)* I know you are out there. I am watching for you. Where are you? I am watching.

(The sounds of a storm rise, lightning and thunder, PROSPERO scans the sky. Blackout.)

(End of play.)

TITUS X

Shawn Northrip

SHAWN NORTHRIP is a playwright, composer-lyricist, and teacher. He was born in suburban Washington, D.C., on February 23, 1977, and grew up in Arlington, Virginia. He received a bachelor's degree in theatre education from Catholic University in Washington, D.C. (where he studied with Bill Foeller and Roland Reed), and an MFA in musical theatre writing from New York University (under the tutelage of Sybille Pearson, Martin Epstein, Sarah Schlesinger, and Robert Lee). Initially an aspiring sound mixer, Northrip got his start in show business volunteering (i.e., mopping the stage) for Arlington Dance Theatre, which, in turn, inspired him to start writing musicals. His theatre credits include the musicals *Lunch* (2006 New York Musical Theatre Festival) and *Cautionary Tales for Adults* (2006 MadCap Winter Carnival). He has also written two short film scripts, *Breakfast 101* and *Shopping List*, both for director Tak Inagaki. Additionally, Northrip writes songs for the self-tribute band, Baboon Ass. He teaches film studies at George Mason High School in Falls Church City, Virginia, and divides his time between his home in Arlington and Joe DeFeo's couch on Roosevelt Island, New York. He is currently forming a new theatre company with collaborators Shirley Serotsky and Caehlin Bell: Bouncing Ball Theatrical Productions.

Titus X was first presented as *Titus, the Musical* at Source Theatre (Joe Banno, Artistic Director), Washington, D.C., in September 2003, with the following cast and credits:

Tribune/Lavinia ....Patricia Hurley
Saturninus/Martius/Demetrius/Messengerius ....Joe Pindelski
Bassanius/Mutius/Quintus/Chiron/Lucius/Young Lucius................Evan Omerso
Titus..Jason Stiles
Tamora...Marybeth Fritzky
Aaron...Tyee Tighlman

Directed by: Shirley Serotsky
Music Direction: Amandia Daigneault
Lighting Design: Heather Pagella
Musicians: Boinkee (Guitar), Derrick Decker (Drums), Jacob Jackovich (Bass)

The New York production of *Titus X* premiered at the New York Musical Theatre Festival in September 2004, and was subsequently presented by Fugly Productions (Joe DeFeo, Producer) with Braden Chapman Productions and Chashama on November 5, 2004, at Chashama, New York City, with the following cast and credits:

Tribune/Lavinia ....Amanda Bond
Saturninus/Martius/Demetrius/Messengerius ....Joe Pindelski
Bassanius/Mutius/Quintus/Chiron/Lucius/Young Lucius......................Ben Pryor
Titus.. Peter Schuyler
Tamora...Bat Parnas
Aaron.. T-Boy

Directed by: Peter Sanfilippo
Assistant Director/Fight Choreographer: Ty Robinson
Lighting Design: Eric Cope
Hair and Makeup: Erin Kennedy Lundsford
Set Designer: Andrea Steiner
Assistant Set Designer: Jesse Belsky
Graphics and Website Design: Rowan Bordewieck
Musicians: Boinkee (Guitar), Derrick Decker (Drums), Jacob Jackovich (Bass)

Titus X was originally developed in readings at the Kennedy Center, and in workshop at the Catholic University of America. *Titus X* would not have been possible without the following who participated in these developmental productions: Kathryn Conte (director), Ellen Hause (dramaturg), Steve McWilliams (Titus), Michael John Casey (Titus), Anne Marie Dalton (Lavinia), John Bryson (Young Lucius), Dwayne Scott (Aaron), and Jim Ferry (drums).

A NOTE FROM THE DIRECTOR

It has been a while since I removed my tongue ring, I have long since taken out my eyebrow rings, and for some time now my hair has stayed one color. But even with all the physical assemblages of my punk adolescence gone and the angst of teenage life past, I still feel like that same punk kid.

When I read Shawn's script and heard the music for the first time, I was reminded of myself today—if you look beyond the loud music, look beyond the clothes and hair, beyond the revelry in its position outside of the mainstream; if you take all that away—you will find that the punk in *Titus X* (as I like to believe it does in myself) extends beyond the physical and topical. It's the story of those wronged by society, who have to turn their backs to the mainstream and take on a personal mission to tear down the system in order to exact change, and at the core of Shakespeare's *Titus Andronicus* are the same prevailing feelings that make up punk culture—rebellion and anarchy.

So we can tear apart Shakespeare, reconstruct it with loud music, find joy and humor in our own irreverence to a classic, and know that this will work, because this rebellion and this destructiveness are at the root of the story we are telling.

—*Peter Sanfilippo*

ON THE OTHER HAND: A NOTE FROM THE PLAYWRIGHT

Not so long ago, I was sitting in a cardboard box in an otherwise unfurnished Roosevelt Island apartment, trying to figure out what I was going to do to pass the two weeks until my roommates moved in with furniture. Unable to think of anything better, I decided to write a musical. After all, I was going to be attending NYU's graduate musical theatre writing program in the fall; perhaps, I thought to myself, I should have written at least one musical by then. Armed with a cheap guitar I traded for a cheap amp, and a Boss Metal Zone distortion pedal that cost more than the guitar, I set out to write. Having misspent most of my youth playing in suburban D.C. garage bands, I wanted to find a story that could be told through good, old-fashioned, ear-splittingly loud punk rock music. I found Elizabethan England's answer to a Gwar show: *Titus Andronicus*. The first draft was finished shortly thereafter, and sent to my friends at the Fun With Classics Theatre Company, a company that I had helped create and for whom I wrote all the material. They refused to perform it.

The project was shelved while I wrote about alien abduction for my MFA thesis. It is very likely *Titus* would never have seen the light of day again if it were not for a bad case of writer's block I developed the summer after graduating from NYU. Catholic University was presenting alumni work at the Kennedy Center's 2002 Page-to-Stage Festival, and just my luck, I was an alumnus. After failing all summer to write something new, I pulled out the old *Titus* recording and played it for a friend, who said to me, "Wow, most of this sucks." She was, however, gracious enough to tell me which songs were good, and suggested a composer to rewrite the others for me. After the composer never set the lyrics I sent him, I realized I was only going to finish on time if I wrote the thing myself. Before long I had written a solid twenty-minute version of the show. I got the cast from a movie I had just finished shooting, called my old bandmates to play the music, and we put on a good show. Catholic offered me a chance to workshop it, which in turn became a concert reading, which in turn got the show into the 23rd Annual Washington New Play Festival, which got us a production at the Source Theatre in Washington, D.C., which led to the New York Musical Festival and to here. This show. The seventh incarnation of a show that has had four titles, twenty-eight performances, and thirty-four different artists work on it (to all of whom I say thanks).

Titus X, like some dumb punk-ass kid, continues to grow up. Like that same punk-ass kid in his adolescence, the show will not give up as it struggles to find its own identity, and refuses to simply be what others expect it to be. The show has come a long way, and I am not just speaking geographically. It's bigger, bloodier, and louder than ever.

In the words of Crankcase's Phil Venable: come out, stay late, get drunk and throw shit.

—Shawn Northrip

PROLOGUE

THE BAND is upstage. THE BAND is called THE DEAD SONS OF TITUS. Downstage are four microphones. The beat starts on the bass drum. It is low and slow. The bass guitar is added, thumping like a heart. The guitar wails.

Song 1. Prologue

(LUCIUS enters and rocks out.)

LUCIUS: TITUS! TITUS!

(SATURNINUS, LAVINIA, and TAMORA enter.)

LUCIUS and SATURNINUS: TITUS! TITUS!

LUCIUS: Come on, I want to hear you all singing out loud!

ALL: TITUS! TITUS!

LAVINIA: HUMAN SACRIFICE

LUCIUS and SATURNINUS: GANG RAPE

TAMORA: DISMEMBERMENT

TAMORA and SATURNINUS: CANNIBALISM

ALL: TITUS IMPALES, DESTROYS!
TITUS PLUNDERS, THAT'S JOY!

TAMORA: HE MAKES WIDOWS CRY AND ORPHANS HOWL

LAVINIA: HE'S MAKING HIS WAY, THE ONLY WAY HE KNOWS HOW

TAMORA: AND THAT'S JUST A LITTLE BIT MORE THAN THE LAW WILL ALLOW

LUCIUS: DECAPITATE

LAVINIA: OBLITERATE

SATURNINUS: HIS BLOOD LUST CANNOT WAIT

TAMORA and SATURNINUS: HE'S MAKING HIS WAY, THE ONLY WAY HE KNOWS HOW

LUCIUS and LAVINIA: AND THAT'S JUST A LITTLE BIT MORE THAN THE LAW WILL ALLOW

ALL: TITUS!

(Exeunt.)

SCENE 1
The Cemetery

THE TRIBUNE, played by LAVINIA wearing a large white hooded robe which conceals her face, enters.

Song 2. Eulogy

THE TRIBUNE: ON THIS DAY WE MOURN FOR CAESAR
THERE NOW DEAD HE DIED OF SEIZURE
ROME NOW NEEDS TO FIND A NEW HEAD
TO GUIDE HER TO BETTER DAYS
SO SING YOUR PRAISE
OF THE LORD YOU WANT FOR ROME,
OUR HOME
OUR HOME
OUR HOME
OUR HOME

ROMANS: *(Voices of offstage cast.)* TITUS! TITUS!

(SATURNINUS enters.)

SATURNINUS: As eldest son of Caesar, I, Saturninus, have been ordained by God to be the new emperor.

ROMANS: TITUS! TITUS!

(BASSANIUS enters.)

BASSANIUS: Rome is a democracy, and will vote as Rome sees fit: for Bassanius, Caesar's heir by choice, though not by birth.

SATURNINUS: Pretender! Pretender!

ROMANS: TITUS! TITUS!

THE TRIBUNE: With love and loyalty, Rome does favor our victorious general: Titus Andronicus. Hear them chant his illustrious name.

ROMANS: TITUS! TITUS!

SATURNINUS: Come on now! Don't do that. Stop it! SATURNINUS! SATURNINUS!

BASSANIUS: Give it up.

Song 3. At the Tribune, Part I

SATURNINUS: NOBLE ROMANS! HOW DARE YOU
YOU KNOW I DON'T MEAN TO MOTHERFUCKIN' SCARE
   YOU
BUT TO FOLLOW MY FATHER IS MY RIGHT
AND IF I HAVE TO, I'LL PUT UP A FIGHT

LET MY FATHER'S HONOR LIVE IN ME
DON'T WRONG ME WITH THIS INDIGNITY
BUT IF I DON'T SWAY YOU WITH MY WORDS
I'LL PLEAD MY TITLE WITH MY SWORDS

VOTE FOR ME TO BE THE NEW EMPEROR

BASSANIUS: DON'T BE SWAYED BY MY BROTHER'S
   TEMPER
YOU ARE FREE TO VOTE AS YOU CHOOSE

SATURNINUS: BUT IF YOU'RE SMART YOU WON'T LET
   ME LOSE

ROMANS: TITUS! TITUS!

ROMANS and BASSANIUS: TITUS! TITUS!

(*SATURNINUS looks at BASSANIUS angrily, BASSANIUS flicks him off.*)

SATURNINUS: WHY OLD ANDRONICUS? WHAT THE
   FUCK IS WRONG WITH US?

BASSANIUS: WITH YOU.

SATURNINUS: YOU'VE MADE ME VERY MAD
I'M GOING TO BE VERY BAD
HOW YOU VOTED WAS A SIN
GOD HAS PROMISED THAT I SHOULD WIN
I'M SO CROSS, DON'T KNOW WHERE TO BEGIN-IA

BASSANIUS: I GOT THE HOTS FOR HIS DAUGHTER
   LAVINIA

SATURNINUS: IN MY LIFE I'VE NEVER LOST
IF I LOSE THERE WILL BE A COST
DON'T THINK I'LL FORGET THIS
YOU'VE ALL MADE ME VERY PISSED

THE TRIBUNE: Princes that strive by factions, lay aside your quarrel. General Titus Andronicus, here named in election by Rome, returns bleeding and victorious from the battlefield today. With him, twenty-two of his own flesh lost in the war,
Today shall here be entombed, their souls baptized
With the blood of the baby of the vanquished
Queen of the Goths.
Be humble for his holy rites, his loss, and him.

SATURNINUS: I will be humble… for now.

BASSANIUS: And me, a poor competitor.

(*TITUS enters with TAMORA in shackles. She carries a baby. He carries an urn, or more precisely a Folger's Crystals coffee tin. Written on the side of the tin are the words: Dead Sons' Ashes, Do Not Use In Coffee.*)

TITUS: Hey Rome! I'm back!

(*The CROWD cheers.*)

ROMANS: TITUS! TITUS!
TIT—

(*TITUS waves his hand, cutting off the chant.*)

Song 4. At the Tribune, Part II

TITUS: HAIL ROME, VICTORIOUS IN THY MOURNING
   WEEDS
IT WAS ALL FOR YOU, I DID THESE DEADLY DEEDS.

(*Holding up the urn.*)

BEHOLD THE POOR REMAINS OF ANDRONICUS'S SONS,
TWENTY-TWO FUNERALS FOR TWENTY-TWO DEAD ONES.
HOLY RITES OF SACRIFICE I WILL NOW DO
BUTCHER TAMORA'S BABY, FOR MY BOYS THAT SHE SLEW

TAMORA: OH! PLEASE DON'T SACRIFICE MY SON
THE WAR IS OVER AND YOU WON
THERE'S NO NEED TO DESECRATE
AND MUTILATE AND VIOLATE
AND AMPUTATE, AND DECIMATE, AND DEVASTATE,
   EVISCERATE, EMASCULATE, HUMILIATE,
REGURGITATE, DISCOMBOBULATE
LEAVING MY BOY AT HELL'S GATE

TITUS: YOUR PLEAS HAVE NOT FALLEN ON A HEART
   OF STONE
BUT IN THIS WAR I LOST SONS OF MY OWN
AND FOR THAT YOUR SON'S SOUL MUST SUFFER
LOOK AT THAT SHINY SWORD, IT LUSTERS!

(*TITUS rips baby from TAMORA's arms and prepares the sacrifice.*)

TITUS: SACRIFICE!

TAMORA: NO!

TITUS: SACRIFICE!

TAMORA: NO!

(TITUS cuts open the baby. TAMORA crumples.)

TITUS: SACRIFICE!

ROMANS: SACRIFICE!

TITUS: SACRIFICE!

ROMANS: SACRIFICE!

TITUS: NOW MY BOYS ARE SATISFIED
MUTILATED PEOPLE DIED
SUFFERING RELIEVES SUFFERINGS
LOOK WHAT A SMILE IT BRINGS

THERE GREET IN SILENCE
WORDS ARE NO MORE
SLEEP IN PEACE, SLAIN IN THE WAR
STAIN THE TOMB WITH BLOOD

(He baptizes the urn in the baby's blood.)

TITUS: DO IT FOR ROME'S GOOD

(TAMORA draws herself up.)

SONG 5. TAMORA'S CURSE

TAMORA: TITUS WILL PAY
FOR THIS INJUSTICE TODAY
I WILL REVENGE
'CAUSE I'M HARD LIKE STONEHENGE
THERE IS GOING TO BE A MASSACRE
MY VENGEANCE IS PURE
I WILL KILL EVERY LAST ONE
THE CRUEL FATHER AND TRAITOROUS SONS
AND MAKE THEM KNOW WHAT IT IS TO LET A QUEEN
KNEEL IN THE STREETS AND BEG FOR GRACE IN VAIN

SONG 6. THE CORONATION

THE TRIBUNE: TITUS ANDRONICUS, ROME'S CITIZENS,
WHOSE FRIEND IN JUSTICE THOU HAST BEEN,
SEND THEIR TRUST FROM ME, THE TRIBUNE, TO YOU,
WITH THIS ROYAL ROBE OF SPOTLESS HUE,
AND NAME YOU IN ELECTION FOR THE EMPIRE,
IT'S YOU THEY DESIRE.

TITUS: AND I THANK YOU FOR THIS HONOR
BUT LET THE SON OF CAESAR CONTINUE THE LINE
HE WAS RAISED TO LOVE THIS EMPIRE
I JUST WANT TO RETIRE
LONG LIVE EMPEROR SATURNINE

THE TRIBUNE: Come again?

TITUS: Now, trust me on this one, everything is gonna be okay. (Thumbs up.) Long live our emperor!

SATURNINUS: TITUS ANDRONICUS,
FOR THIS FAVOR DONE TO US
ON ELECTION DAY I GIVE YOU THANKS.
AND TO THE ADVANCE
OF YOUR NAME AND YOUR FAMILY,
YOUR DAUGHTER, LAVINIA, I'LL MAKE QUEEN OF ME.

BASSANIUS: (Tries to interject.) Buh…

SATURNINUS: What do you think? Dad?

TITUS: Welcome to the family.

BASSANIUS: But…

TITUS: (To THE TRIBUNE.) Could you go find my daughter? I'm sure she's around… somewhere.

(THE TRIBUNE goes out and returns as LAVINIA.)

SATURNINUS: Is there something you'd like to say to my father-in-law, baby brother?

BASSANIUS: No. Nothing, bro.

TITUS: As a dowry, my noble lord, I present to you, my prisoner: Tamora, Queen of the Goths.

(TITUS gives TAMORA to SATURNINUS.)

SATURNINUS: (To TAMORA.) Girl, I think you might be even hotter than I am. (To TITUS.) Cool. Very cool. I set my prisoner free.

TAMORA: Brave emperor: my sons Chiron and Demetrius, and my servant, the Moor, are still in Titus's custody.

SATURNINUS: Freedom for all!

TITUS: They're prisoners of war!

SATURNINUS: No one is free when others are oppressed. (Turning his attention to LAVINIA.) And now Lavinia!

(SATURNINUS grabs LAVINIA and tries to stick his tongue in her ear. She turns and looks desperately at BASSANIUS. She indicates for him to say something.)

BASSANIUS: Lavinia is not your property to just give away as you please.

(TITUS turns his attention to BASSANIUS. TAMORA grabs SATURNINUS and lures him into lovemaking.)

TITUS: She's my daughter.

BASSANIUS: She's a person, with a free will, and she is married to me. *(He indicates the chains and padlocks they both wear around their necks.)*

TITUS: Is this true, Lavinia?

LAVINIA: Yes, Daddy.

BASSANIUS: You abandoned this precious jewel here so you could go play soldier in the jungle.

TITUS: I got a chunk of shrapnel in my ass making the world safe for punks like you!

(TITUS steps up to BASSANIUS, who turns, grabs LAVINIA's hand, and runs out.)

TITUS: Don't worry, sir, I'll bring her back.

(TITUS notices SATURNINUS making out with TAMORA. SATURNINUS pulls himself off of her.)

SATURNINUS: She's not worth my time.

(TAMORA fixes herself.)

SATURNINUS: Instead, I choose lovely rockin' Tamora, sexy Queen of Goth punks.

TAMORA: Oh my God, I didn't see this coming.

SATURNINUS: Come, it's time to make you a Roman… by injection.

(They kiss and exit. Enter MUTIUS. He is dressed as a Boy Scout.)

MUTIUS: Welcome back, General Dad.

(MUTIUS tries to hug TITUS, who stops him. Instead he salutes.)

TITUS: Mutius, it's time for a talk, son. I know you're just a boy, but during the war you were the only man of the house. It was your job to look after the family.

MUTIUS: Totally. I did a great job.

TITUS: Lavinia is married.

MUTIUS: Yeah, it was so cool. I got to stand in for you at her wedding.

TITUS: You did what…?

MUTIUS: They were like, who's gonna give Lavinia away. And I was like, I can do it…

(TITUS stabs MUTIUS. He stumbles out, bleeding.)

TITUS: NOW I'M FACED WITH DISHONOR

(Offstage we hear crashes and screams, then finally MUTIUS's death scream and a loud thud.)

TITUS: THE YOUNGER SON OF CAESAR IS NO FRIEND OF MINE
WHO ELSE KNEW THIS CONSPIRED?
I JUST WANTED TO RETIRE
BASSANIUS HAS STOLEN MY SUNSHINE

Fuck!

(QUINTUS and MARTIUS enter.)

QUINTUS: Persecution.

MARTIUS: Oppression.

TITUS: Quintus and Martius…

MARTIUS: Injustice!

TITUS: Damn, right! I'm the father of this family, I deserve respect.

QUINTUS: Where's the respect for your children?

MARTIUS: Yeah! Children are people too. Just shorter.

TITUS: Don't talk to me like that. Where's your brother, Lucius, he knows how to respect his father.

QUINTUS: Mutius respected his father. Lavinia respected her father.

TITUS: She could have been the empress of Rome.

MARTIUS: Well, she would have been if you gave the throne to Bassanius.

TITUS: She disgraced the Andronici. Lucius would never disgrace me.

MARTIUS: How can you think about your reputation, you just killed one of your sons.

TITUS: No. He was no son of mine. He, apparently, was Lavinia's father. Where's Lucius?

QUINTUS: Where's Lucius? Where's Lucius? Do you care about any of your other children? Do you even know which one of us is Quintus and which is Martius?

(TITUS thinks about it.)

MARTIUS: Maybe you'd like to kill us too?

QUINTUS: Yeah!

MARTIUS: We're gonna put Mutius in the tomb.

TITUS: In this tomb? With my sons who gave their lives in the service of their county?

QUINTUS: With our brothers, our brother shall lie. *(Takes the urn.)*

TITUS: Well, bury him then, and bury me next.

(LAVINIA enters. Sensing impending drama, QUINTUS and MARTIUS duck out. TITUS notices LAVINIA and turns to go.)

Song 7. I'm Sorry Dad

LAVINIA: I'M SORRY DAD, YOUR LITTLE GIRL IS GONE

IT USED TO MEAN SO MUCH, TO HAVE YOU WATCHING
  OVER ME
IT USED TO SEEM SO SAFE, TO BE WHERE YOU COULD SEE
THEN YOU LEFT AND I HAD TO DO WHAT WAS BEST
  FOR ME
AND THAT DOESN'T MEAN YOU MEAN ANY LESS TO ME

I'M SORRY DAD, YOUR LITTLE GIRL IS GONE

WHY'S IT SO HARD TO ADMIT THAT I'VE GROWN UP
WHY'S IT SO HARD TO SEE
WHY'S IT SO HARD TO ADMIT, NOW THAT YOU'VE
  SHOWN UP
DO I STILL LOOK THE SAME AS WHEN I WAS THREE?

I'M SORRY DAD, YOUR LITTLE GIRL IS GONE
YOUR LITTLE GIRL IS

ALWAYS AWAY FROM YOU
ALWAYS FAR FROM YOUR MIND
ALWAYS CRYING AND WONDERING
WHY YOU LEFT ME BEHIND

YOUR DUTY CAME FIRST
YOUR DUTY CAME FIRST

NOW YOUR LITTLE GIRL IS GONE
YOUR LITTLE GIRL IS GONE
YOUR LITTLE GIRL IS GONE
YOUR LITTLE GIRL IS GONE

(She looks at TITUS for acceptance and forgiveness. He stares at her for a minute, and then turns his back and leaves. She leaves disappointed.)

SCENE 2
A ROMAN SQUARE

Enter BASSANIUS and SATURNINUS.

SATURNINUS: Baby brother, I'm sorry I set you up like that. I'm spiteful.

BASSANIUS: I thought Andronicus was going to kill me.

SATURNINUS: You don't need to worry about him. You're the emperor's baby brother, and I love you. Besides, I'm gonna nail that Tamora chick.

BASSANIUS: Nice.

(Noticing TITUS approaching.)

BASSANIUS: Shoot, here he comes.

(BASSANIUS runs out. Enter TITUS.)

SATURNINUS: Titus, my brother is worthy of being called "son."

TITUS: I will not acknowledge them.

SATURNINUS: Do you spit in my face? Where is your loyalty, Andronicus?

TITUS: My emperor, I gave your father a lifetime of service, and since his death, that loyalty I have bestowed upon you, with my crown, my daughter, and my prisoner.

SATURNINUS: Why don't you brag about it some more. You make it sound like I begged you to be emperor. *(Storms out.)*

Song 8. What the Hell

TITUS: WHAT THE HELL WAS THAT ABOUT?!

(Enter TAMORA.)

TAMORA: Titus, I want what is mine returned to me. And I want it now.

TITUS: And what do I have of yours?

TAMORA: Two sons, one slave.

TITUS: Hmmm, I don't have any recollection…

TAMORA: Saturninus told you to free them. I heard him say it. Rome heard him say it. *(To THE BAND.)* They heard him say it.

THE BAND: Yeah!

TAMORA: It's a direct order from your emperor. Will you disobey it? If everyone blatantly disregards the laws established by society, well then we'd have anarchy. So go ahead, ignore me, tear down the system from the inside.

TITUS: *(Defeated.)* Have it your way.

(He snaps his fingers. THE GUITAR PLAYER looks annoyed, then goes out momentarily.)

TAMORA: I'm almost disappointed, Titus. I was hoping you'd prove you weren't just an unthinking automaton, another cog in the machine.

TITUS: Good God, this day keeps getting worse and worse. What else could go wrong?

(CHIRON, DEMETRIUS, and AARON emerge. CHIRON and DEMETRIUS kiss their mother incestuously.)

TAMORA: Titus, my sons are returned to me, let's be friends. Today, let all our quarrels die.

TITUS: Tomorrow. *(Exits.)*

TAMORA: Boys, your momma needs a few minutes alone with Aaron. Go play.

(CHIRON and DEMETRIUS exit, pushing each other.)

TAMORA: My darling Aaron, I need you to plan my revenge against Titus Andronicus. Make him pay for the life of a son and the loss of a kingdom and I will reward you with kisses, anywhere on your body you like.

AARON: Even…

TAMORA: Anywhere. Just tell me how evil you can be.

AARON: There was this one time, I knew this guy who "died." And even as his wife's wounds were healing, I dug him up, propped him against her door, rang her doorbell, and ran. As if that wasn't funny enough, in his chest I carved the words, "Let not your sorrow die though I am dead."

TAMORA: Oh, that makes me so hot. Put your evil genius to work while I go placate the emperor.

AARON: Grrrrrr.

TAMORA: Baby, please, you will find there are perks to being the empress's stud. *(Exits.)*

Song 9. Beware

AARON: ONE TWO THREE FOUR
EVIL GENIUS
WORK IS PLAY
LIVE OR DIE
YOU'RE IN MY WAY
FRIEND OR FOE
YOU HAVE TO PAY
SO BEWARE
I DON'T FIGHT FAIR
FLESH WOUNDS HEAL TOO EASY

PSYCHO WARS HURT MUCH MORE
CRACKED RIBS MEND IN TIME
MENTAL BREAKS NEVER HEAL
MIND FUCKING

AARON and BAND: THAT'S FOR ME

AARON: MIND FUCKING

AARON and BAND: THAT'S FOR ME

(LAVINIA enters. CHIRON and DEMETRIUS come in behind her, both looking at her lasciviously.)

AARON: SO, BEWARE ROME
I WILL DO WHAT MY MISTRESS COMMANDS OF ME

(LAVINIA exits. CHIRON and DEMETRIUS get into a fight over her.)

AARON: WHEN I STRIKE THERE'LL BE NO MARKS LEFT
    TO SEE
I WILL DO WHAT MY MISTRESS COMMANDS OF ME.

I DON'T LIKE TO USE MY FISTS
THERE'S A CHANCE I MIGHT FEEL PAIN

(DEMETRIUS unplugs the bass and takes the cable as a weapon against CHIRON.)

AARON: SO INSTEAD I RACK MY BRAIN
ALL BEWARE, I DON'T FIGHT FAIR

(CHIRON takes the mic stand from AARON, leaving the mic in AARON's hand, and uses the stand as a weapon against DEMETRIUS.)

AARON: KNIFE WOUNDS ONLY KILL YOU
THERE ARE THINGS WORSE THAN DEATH…

(The song comes to a crash as the fight between CHIRON and DEMETRIUS peaks with the TWO of them falling into the drum kit.)

AARON: What the hell do you think you're doing?

(CHIRON and DEMETRIUS start rolling around the floor fighting. AARON parts them.)

CHIRON: I get her!

DEMETRIUS: I get her!

CHIRON: No, I do.

DEMETRIUS: I don't think so.

AARON: What's going on, Demetrius?

DEMETRIUS: Chiron and I just met a girl named Lavinia…

AARON: Lavinia Andronicus…?

DEMETRIUS: You know her?

AARON: By reputation.

DEMETRIUS: Well, Chiron says she's his, and I say she's mine, and now we're gonna fight for her.

CHIRON: Yeah!

AARON: You don't need to fight.

CHIRON: You're not our dad.

AARON: Boys, it's not that it's wrong to fight. It's only wrong because you want to love her.

CHIRON: Is that how you feel about Mom?

AARON: Ask yourself, why do you really want her? Do you want a lifelong lover and friend, or do you just want her chastity?

BOTH: Chastity.

CHIRON: But I want it more.

DEMETRIUS: I want it more.

CHIRON: I want it more.

DEMETRIUS: I want it more.

Song 10. She, Woman

CHIRON: FISHNETS, AND COMBAT BOOTS,
NEON HAIR WITH GROWING ROOTS
TIGHT LITTLE ABS AND PERFECT GLUTES
SHE STEALS MY HEART EVERY TIME SHE LOOTS

CHIRON and DEMETRIUS: SHE, WOMAN! SHE, WOMAN!

DEMETRIUS: PIERCED THIS AND PIERCED THAT
HER BODY COVERED OVER IN SEXY TATS
SHE CAN BEND LIKE AN ACROBAT
SHE'S A CUTEY POUTY BRAT

CHIRON and DEMETRIUS: SHE, WOMAN! SHE, WOMAN!

CHIRON: MINE MINE MINE MINE MINE MINE MINE
MINE MINE MINE MINE MINE MINE MINE

DEMETRIUS: MINE MINE MINE MINE MINE MINE MINE
MINE MINE MINE MINE MINE MINE MINE

CHIRON and DEMETRIUS: SHE, WOMAN! SHE,
WOMAN! SHE, WOMAN! SHE, WOMAN!

DEMETRIUS: MINE MINE MINE MINE MINE MINE MINE
MINE MINE MINE MINE MINE MINE MINE

CHIRON: MINE MINE MINE MINE MINE MINE MINE
MINE MINE MINE MINE MINE MINE MINE

BOTH: MINE MINE MINE MINE MINE MINE MINE
MINE MINE MINE MINE MINE MINE MINE

CHIRON and DEMETRIUS: SHE, WOMAN!

AARON: LISTEN UP, BOYS
LISTEN UP, BOYS
WHY LOVE A WOMAN FOR THE REST OF YOUR LIFE
WHY LET A WOMAN GET TO BE YOUR WIFE
WHEN ALL YOU WANT IS THAT JEWEL BELOW
AND ONE CHANCE TO GET TO BIBLICALLY KNOW

CHIRON and DEMETRIUS: SHE, WOMAN!

AARON: HEAR ME NOW, BOYS
HEAR ME NOW, BOYS
WOULD IT OFFEND IF I WOULD SUGGEST
THAT BOTH OF YOU BOYS PUT HER TO THE TEST
THAT BOTH OF YOU BOYS SHOULD GET TO SPEED
AND FORCE THAT LITTLE GIRL UP TO THE DEED

CHIRON and DEMETRIUS: SHE, WOMAN!

AARON: DO IT NOW, BOYS
DO IT NOW, BOYS
KILL BASSANIUS BEFORE HE CAN WED

DEMETRIUS: BEFORE HE CAN WED

AARON: AND TAKE HER TO HIS WEDDING BED

CHIRON: HIS WEDDING BED

AARON: IGNORE THE GIRL AS SHE BEGS AND PLEADS

DEMETRIUS: SHE BEGS AND PLEADS

AARON: AND IF SHE'S A VIRGIN, SHE WILL BLEED

CHIRON: SHE WILL BLEED

CHIRON and DEMETRIUS: SHE, WOMAN!

CHIRON: Stop! Wait! Hold up! Are you suggesting we…?

AARON: Yes.

CHIRON and DEMETRIUS: Okay. (*Exit with excitement.*)

AARON: VENGEANCE IN MY HEART
DEATH IN MY HAND
BLOOD AND REVENGE
HAMMER MY HEAD
HAMMER MY HEAD

(*DEMETRIUS and CHIRON, come back in, suddenly confused.*)

CHIRON: Hate to be a bother, Mr. Aaron, sir, but isn't she gonna tell on us?

AARON: Not if you cut out her tongue and cut off her hands.

DEMETRIUS: That makes sense.

(*Enter TAMORA.*)

TAMORA: Come here, boys, give your mother a kiss.

(*They kiss her in a very naughty incestuous way. THE BAND is grossed out.*)

TAMORA: (*With love.*) My boys. I brought you some dinner.

(*She gives them a case of beer and a carton of cigarettes.*)

DEMETRIUS: (*Almost disappointed.*) Beer and cigarettes again?

TAMORA: Now run along and get into mischief.

(*They exit, punching each other.*)

TAMORA: I love those boys. (*Turns her attention to AARON.*)

AARON: That was quick. Did you and Saturninus consummate?

TAMORA: Are you jealous?

AARON: Me, jealous, over a woman?

(*She seduces AARON.*)

Song 11. Serenade

TAMORA: THERE'S NOTHING THERE FOR YOU TO FEAR
NOTHING TO BE ENVIOUS OF
NOTHING CAN DESTROY OUR LOVE

THERE'S LITTLE THERE TO CHALLENGE YOU
NOTHING TO BE THREATENED BY
YOU'VE GOT TO KNOW THAT YOU'RE MY GUY

AND THOUGH YOU'RE SWEET
THIS IS JUST A PIECE OF MEAT
ONE DAY IT WILL ROT AWAY
IT'S ONLY FLESH AND WILL DECAY

SO LET GO OF YOUR SOMBER MOOD
DON'T JUST SIT THERE AND CONTINUE TO BROOD
IT'S JUST A BODY, IT'S NOT A SOUL
HE'S NOT THE ONE WHO FILLS MY HOLE

DON'T WORRY, LET ME CALM YOUR RAGE
I KNOW WHEN IT RAINS IT POURS
LET ME PROVE THAT I'M STILL YOURS

(*They go out together.*)

SCENE 3
The Forest

BASSANIUS and LAVINIA enter.

Song 12. The Love Song

LAVINIA: YOU HATE EVERYTHING MAINSTREAM
YOU HATE EVERYTHING EXTREME
BUT YOU DON'T HATE ME
THAT'S WHY I DON'T HATE YOU TOO

BASSANIUS: YOU HATE SOCIAL INJUSTICE
YOU HATE WITNESSING PREJUDICE
BUT YOU DON'T HATE ME
THAT'S WHY I DON'T HATE YOU TOO

BOTH: HATE YOU
YOU DON'T HATE ME
THAT'S WHY I DON'T HATE YOU TOO

BASSANIUS: I DON'T HATE YOU, I DON'T HATE YOU

LAVINIA: YOU SAY SUCH SWEET THINGS

BOTH: LOVE IS LIKE A BLUNT FORCE TRAUMA
LOVE IS LIKE A BLUNT FORCE TRAUMA

(*TAMORA and AARON enter.*)

ALL: LOVE IS LIKE A BLUNT FORCE TRAUMA
LOVE IS LIKE A BLUNT FORCE TRAUMA

(*BASSANIUS and LAVINIA realize they are not singing alone and find TAMORA singing with AARON.*)

BASSANIUS: What have we here?

LAVINIA: I do believe it's the empress and her boy toy.

AARON: I'll fetch your sons. (*Exits.*)

Song 13. For the Love of Mother

BASSANIUS: Aren't thou Rome's royal empress?
Or is it Diane, chaste nymphet of the hunt?
Have you abandoned your holy groves
To see the general hunting in the forest?

TAMORA: Had I the power that some say Diane had,
Your temples would be growing horns.

LAVINIA: Sure, the way you give your husbands horns.

BASSANIUS: Spotted, detested, and abhorred.

LAVINIA: God, shield the emperor from his dogs on this day,
Else, they should take him for a stag.

TAMORA: Why have I patience to endure all this?
Am I not the empress of Rome?

LAVINIA: 'Cause you are caught in sport with your raven-colored love.

BASSANIUS: The emperor my brother will know of this.

(LAVINIA and BASSANIUS exit. However, they are pushed back onstage by DEMETRIUS. BASSANIUS has been replaced by a dummy.)

TAMORA: Where's your brother?

DEMETRIUS: He's coming.

LAVINIA: I pray you, let us go.

(CHIRON runs in.)

CHIRON: I'm sorry I'm late.

DEMETRIUS: How now, dear gracious Mother,
Why do you look so pale?

CHIRON: Why do you charge our mother?

TAMORA: HAVE I NO REASON TO LOOK PALE
WHEN THEY TRAPPED ME IN THIS DARKENED DALE
WHERE THE TREES DROOP WITH SORROW AND THEY
    WAIL
HERE THE SUNLIGHT SEEMS TO FAIL
THESE TWO HIDE UNDER THE NIGHT'S VEIL
HERE WHERE THE WATER IS STILL AND THE AIR IS STALE
BUT NOW THAT YOU'VE COME TO ASSAIL
I CAN SEE THE TIP OF THE SCALE
SO LET THE VENGEANCE FALL LIKE HAIL
ELSE YOU LOVE YOUR MOTHER NOT
SO COME ON AND SHOW ME WHAT YOU'VE GOT
OR YOU ARE NOT MY SONS,
PROVE YOU ARE MY SONS!

DEMETRIUS: FOR THE LOVE OF MOTHER
BEAR WITNESS I'M THY SON

(Stabs the DUMMY BASSANIUS.)

CHIRON: FOR THE LOVE OF MOTHER
HERE COMES ANOTHER ONE

(Stabs the DUMMY BASSANIUS.)

BOTH: FOR THE LOVE OF MOTHER
THERE'S NOTHING WE WON'T DO

(They start closing in on LAVINIA.)

BOTH: FOR THE LOVE OF MOTHER
AND BROTHER FOR THE LOVE OF YOU

LAVINIA: NOW IT'S MY TURN TO LOOK PALE
I AM SO SMALL AND FRAIL
WHAT HARM CAN I DO TO YOU, I WON'T TELL MY TALE

TAMORA: I will not hear her speak. Take her away.

DEMETRIUS: CRY!

LAVINIA: PLEASE, LADY, YOU SEEM TO BE FEMALE
CAN'T YOU TELL WHAT THEIR LOOKS ENTAIL
BUT I'M BEGGING TO NO AVAIL

TAMORA: Take her away.

DEMETRIUS: CRY!

LAVINIA: HOW'D I FALL TO THIS BETRAYAL
MY HEART SINKS, FLESH WILL AIL
WHAT WILL I DO IF MY TEARS FAIL?

CHIRON: Let's use Bassanius's body as a pillow.

LAVINIA: SWEET LADY, KILL ME IF YOU MUST
BUT SAVE ME FROM THEIR LUST
AND SINCE I SEE YOU'LL LET THEM HAVE IT ALL,
CONFUSION FALL!

FOR THE LOVE OF FATHER
THE MAN WHO SPARED YOUR LIFE
FOR THE LOVE OF FATHER
WHO SPARED YOU FROM HIS KNIFE
FOR THE LOVE OF FATHER
WHO I'LL NEVER AGAIN BE ABLE TO SEE
FOR THE LOVE OF FATHER
PLEASE DON'T LET THEM DO THIS TO ME

TAMORA: THOUGH YOU NEVER OFFENDED ME
FOR YOUR FATHER'S SAKE I HAVE NO PITY
REMEMBER, I POURED FORTH TEARS IN VAIN
TO SAVE THE SOULS OF MY BABIES SLAIN
BUT YOUR CRUEL FATHER WOULD NOT RELENT
AND THIS CRUEL MOTHER WILL NOT REPENT
SO SHOULD I ROB MY SWEET BOYS OF THEIR FEE
NO, LET THEM SATISFY THEIR LUST ON THEE

DEMETRIUS: FOR THE LOVE OF MOTHER
BEAR WITNESS I'M THY SON

CHIRON: FOR THE LOVE OF MOTHER
HERE COMES ANOTHER ONE

BOTH: FOR THE LOVE OF MOTHER
THERE'S NOTHING WE WON'T DO
FOR THE LOVE OF MOTHER
AND BROTHER FOR THE LOVE OF YOU

(LAVINIA breaks away. THE BOYS give chase.)

TAMORA: FAREWELL, BOYS. SEE THAT YOU MAKE
   HER SURE
THAT SHE KNOWS WHY SHE KEPT HERSELF PURE.
AND NOW TO CONTINUE SPREADING SUCH JOYS,
FOR THIS I'LL FRAME THE OLD MAN'S YOUNGEST BOYS.
BECAUSE MY HEART WILL NEVER KNOW MERRY CHEER
'TIL ALL ARE DEAD THAT ANDRONICUS HOLDS DEAR
NOW I WILL FIND MY LOVELY MOOR
WHILE MY SPLEENFUL SONS DEFLOWER THE WHORE.

(She exits. AARON enters. He kicks BASSANIUS'S BODY out of view.)

AARON: *(Calls.)* Come on, young Andronici!

(QUINTUS and MARTIUS enter.)

QUINTUS: Who are you again?

AARON: I told you, Quintus, I'm a friend of your father's. He's so disappointed in you two. Ever since your little mutiny, he doesn't know if he can trust you anymore. *(Smiles wickedly.)*

MARTIUS: Why'd you bring us here?

AARON: Well, Martius, he said the only way he would ever be able to trust you again is if you proved yourselves by killing a black panther. Well, today while I was walking along, I saw a black panther trapped in a pit and thought to myself, this must be divine intervention. I can help Titus's wayward sons. Here, take these bloody hunting knives.

(AARON holds out a Zip Lock bag which contains CHIRON and DEMETRIUS's knives. QUINTUS and MARTIUS each take a knife.)

QUINTUS: How do we know we can trust you?

AARON: Didn't I bring you candy?

MARTIUS: Yes.

AARON: So trust me. *(Looks around.)* Here's the place.

MARTIUS: Where is it?

AARON: *(Opens a trap door in the drum riser.)* It's fallen into this pit.

MARTIUS: I don't see anything.

AARON: Look closer.

MARTIUS: Where?

AARON: Lean a bit more precariously over the edge and you'll just see it.

(AARON pushes MARTIUS in, unnoticed by QUINTUS.)

QUINTUS: Marty, did you fall? Reach your hand up to me. Marty? Marty?

(AARON pushes QUINTUS in, then closes the trap. Immediately, he moves BASSANIUS'S BODY back into view and poses it into a surprised position. TAMORA enters, calling back to SATURNINUS.)

TAMORA: Hurry, sweet Saturninus. Here is Bassanius's corpse as Aaron said. It's still warm. His love was his undoing.

(SATURNINUS enters. AARON points at the BODY OF BASSANIUS.)

AARON: I told you, my most gracious lord, I found the body of your brother.

SATURNINUS: Bassanius. Baby brother? Who did this?

AARON: I saw two of Titus's army brats: Quintus and Martius.

(AARON shoots TAMORA a look.)

TAMORA: *(Suddenly remembering.)* Me, too. And I heard Quintus say, "Now is the house of Andronicus clean wiped of the shame Bassanius levied upon it."

QUINTUS: *(Offstage.)* I did not.

SATURNINUS: Where are they?

AARON: In this hole. *(Opens the trap.)*

SATURNINUS: Hello? Who's down there?

QUINTUS: *(Offstage.)* The unhappy sons of old Andronicus: Quintus and Martius.

(SATURNINUS closes the trap, stomps and jumps on it.)

SONG 14. EXECUTE THEM

SATURNINUS: WHAT WERE THE PROCEEDINGS
THAT LEFT MY BLOOD A-BLEEDING
THEY'LL PAY A GREAT FINE

FOR THIS LOSS OF MINE
I'LL BE DEAF TO EXCUSES
NOR TEARS NOR PRAYERS OR ABUSES
THE EVIDENCE CAN'T BE DISPUTED
SO HAVE THEM EXECUTED

(TAMORA and SATURNINUS exit. AARON kicks BASSANIUS'S BODY. THE BASSIST gives it a few kicks as well. LAVINIA runs in. HER CAPTORS chase her and try to box her in.)

SONG 15. SWEET LAVINIA

CHIRON: SWEET LAVINIA
I WANT TO GET IN YA, LAVINIA
LAVINIA LAVINIA
OH, LAVINIA

(Guitar solo.)

DEMETRIUS: SWEET LAVINIA
I WANT TO GET IN YA, LAVINIA
LAVINIA LAVINIA
OH, LAVINIA

CHIRON and DEMETRIUS: SWEET LAVINIA
I WANT TO GET IN YA, LAVINIA
LAVINIA LAVINIA
OH, LAVINIA

(Blackout. In darkness:)

CHIRON and DEMETRIUS: SWEET LAVINIA
I WANT TO GET IN YA, LAVINIA
OH, OH, LAVINIA
OH, OH, LAVINIA
OH, OH, LAVINIA

SCENE 4
SEVERAL LOCATIONS

SONG 16. ROME IS BURNING DOWN

(TAMORA enters, isolated stage left, and TITUS enters, isolated stage right.)

TAMORA and TITUS: ROME IS BURNING DOWN

(AARON enters, escorting the prisoners: QUINTUS— once again, the stunt dummy—and MARTIUS. They are chained together. They exit.)

TAMORA and TITUS: ROME IS BURNING DOWN

(AARON pushes LUCIUS in. LUCIUS wears an olive drab green army jacket with his name stenciled on it in white spray paint. AARON pushes LUCIUS to the ground.)

AARON: Lucius Andronicus, it is my ill duty, as messenger of Rome, to inform you, that in light of recent actions taken by your family against Rome, you are to suffer either immediate banishment or execution by sunset. I want you to know, it's nothing personal. I'm just doing my job.

ALL: ROME IS BURNING DOWN

AARON: Let fools do good, and fair men call for grace:
Aaron will have his soul black like his face.

(AARON and TAMORA exit.)

SCENE 5
THE ANDRONICUS HOME

TITUS: Lucius.

(TITUS helps LUCIUS to his feet. They embrace.)

TITUS: You better go.

LUCIUS: If I leave, who's gonna take care of you?

TITUS: I still have Quintus and Martius.

LUCIUS: Quintus and Martius have been arrested.

TITUS: What'd they do this time?

LUCIUS: They killed Bassanius.

TITUS: Are you sure?

LUCIUS: That's why I'm being banished. Saturninus is afraid of my retribution. Check this out: Mutius let Lavinia marry Bassanius, so you kill him; Quintus and Martius bury Mutius, so you kick them out of the family; they kill Bassanius to win you back; Saturninus wants to kill them for killing his brother; so naturally, I'll have to do something to him for killing my brothers. And that's why I'm being sent into exile.

TITUS: And with that, Titus has no more sons.

LUCIUS: Say the word and I'll break them out.

TITUS: Justice will protect them. So, go, get out of here before it's too late.

(TITUS throws a few playful punches at LUCIUS.)

TITUS: Don't worry about me. I'll be fine. I'll find Lavinia, and if she'll forgive me…

(LAVINIA drags herself in. LUCIUS sees her first.)

LUCIUS: Holy sh…?

TITUS: Watch your mouth! (*Noticing LAVINIA.*) What the fuck?

LUCIUS: I think I'm gonna throw up.

TITUS: Faint-hearted boy, you look at her.

LUCIUS: If I do dream, would all the world wake me up,
If I do wake, God strike me down.

TITUS: (*To LAVINIA.*) Speak Lavinia, speak, whose accursed hand
Made you handless in your father's sight?

(*LAVINIA opens her mouth, spitting a mouthful of blood onto herself.*)

TITUS: No tongue to tell me who has martyred you?

LUCIUS: What happened to her tongue?

TITUS: It's been cut out. See for yourself!

(*They force her jaws open and look in her mouth.*)

LUCIUS: Oh God.

(*LUCIUS tries to touch it.*)

TITUS: Don't put your fingers in there.

LUCIUS: No tongue, no hands, someone didn't want her to tell us something really important.

(*TITUS, LAVINIA, and THE BAND give LUCIUS a look.*)

TITUS: Bassanius is dead, and your brothers are accused of his murder.

(*LAVINIA shakes her head, "No." Blood spatters.*)

LUCIUS: She's shaking.

TITUS: It's all my fault.

LUCIUS: No, come on.

TITUS: It is. I'm sorry, Lavinia. I was only hurt because I adore you so much. You're my only girl.

LUCIUS: Oh, what a sympathy of woe is this,
As far from help as limbo is from bliss.

(*Again TITUS and LAVINIA look at LUCIUS.*)

LUCIUS: This sucks. This completely sucks.

(*AARON enters.*)

AARON: Titus Andronicus, you have been ordered by Saturninus to appear before the Tribune to defend the lives of your sons: Quintus and Martius, on the charge: murder. (*Exits.*)

LUCIUS: Father, don't waste your time. The Tribune is infected, and won't listen. You'll tell your sorrow to the stones.

TITUS: Lucius, let me go to plead for your brothers. As for you, boy, get out of sight. Go back to the Goths, and raise an army there, and come back to make things right.

LUCIUS: Take care of Young Lucius for me.

TITUS: Rome has befriended you by banishing you. For Rome is a den of tigers. Tigers need prey, and in Rome there is no better meal than me and mine.

(*TITUS and LAVINIA exit.*)

Song 17. Exile

LUCIUS: EXILE, EXILE, EXILE, EXILE
IF I LIVE TO SEE THE DAY
I WILL RIGHT, I WILL RIGHT, I WILL RIGHT YOUR WRONGS
IF I LIVE I'LL MAKE THEM PAY
I WILL FIGHT, I WILL FIGHT, I WILL FIGHT
I WILL RAISE THE THRONGS
I WILL FELL THE STRONG
COME BACK WHERE I BELONG

JUST LIKE TARQUIN AND HIS QUEEN
YOU WILL FALL, YOU WILL FALL, YOU WILL FALL ON DOWN
I'LL CUT YOU OFF LIKE YOU'RE GANGRENE
YOU'RE SO SMALL, YOU'RE SO SMALL, YOU'RE SO SMALL:
YOU ARE JUST A CLOWN
WHEN YOU WEAR YOUR CROWN
WHY SEND ME OUT OF TOWN

CORRUPTION, DECADENCE, GREED
YOU'RE GONNA PAY
GLUTTONY, DEPRAVITY, HEDONISM
YOU'RE GONNA PAY
PUGNACIOUS, RAPACIOUS, LOOK IT UP
YOU'RE GONNA PAY
REPUBLICAN, DESPOT, YOU SUCK
YOU'RE GONNA PAY

I'LL GO TO SEE THE ENEMY
I WILL RAISE, I WILL RAISE, I WILL RAISE A FORCE
I'LL COME BACK TO SET ROME FREE
THEY WILL PRAISE, THEY WILL PRAISE, THEY WILL PRAISE ME
KNOW THAT YOU'RE THE SOURCE
OF THIS ROYAL DIVORCE
NOW THAT YOU'VE SET THE COURSE

(*LUCIUS exits.*)

SCENE 6
THE TRIBUNE

TAMORA enters wearing the Tribune's robe from the opening scene. She wears the hood which conceals her face. Enter AARON, escorting TITUS and LAVINIA.

AARON: Honorable Tribune of Rome, will you hear the case now before you?

(TAMORA motions with her hand for them to continue. AARON presents TITUS and then exits.)

TITUS: High Tribune, I know the evidence is overwhelming: they seem to have a motive; the emperor himself discovered them near the body, bloody daggers in hand; but my sons are not murderers. And look at Lavinia, would they have done this to their own sister?

TAMORA: Lavinia, who has killed your husband? Speak up, girl.

TITUS: She can't, she doesn't have a tongue.

TAMORA: Isn't that convenient?

TITUS: Tribune, please consider the service the Andronici have always given Rome.

TAMORA: We cannot be partial. We must be fair, and within the law. Or else Rome will become an anarchy.

TITUS: *(Aside.)* Where have I heard that before? *(To TAMORA.)* Then if they are found guilty, we will willingly face the consequences.

(AARON escorts in QUINTUS and MARTIUS on the opposite side.)

SONG 18. QUINTUS AND MARTIUS

QUINTUS: WAITING FOR THE VERDICT
TRYING TO BE STRONG
WAITING AND WATCHING AND PROTECTING MY BROTHER

MARTIUS: MY EYES ARE GROWING DIM JUST LIKE IN
    A DREAM
IT'S A BAD OMEN THAT THINGS ARE ALL GOING WRONG

TITUS: HEAR ME, GRAVE FATHERS
PITY MY SONS
LET ME TRADE MY OWN LIFE FOR THEIR YOUNG ONES

BEGGING ON MY KNEE
HELP ME, DEAR TRIBUNE: REMEMBER I FOUGHT WHILE
    YOU SLEPT IN BED
I NEVER BEFORE CRIED FOR THE DEATHS OF MY SONS

BECAUSE THEY DIED AT WAR AND NOT FOR ONE PICA-
    YUNE

MARTIUS and QUINTUS: HERE'S OUR GRAVE, FATHER
TODAY WE DIE
THOUGH WE'RE BRAVE WE CAN'T HELP BUT CRY

TITUS, MARTIUS, and QUINTUS: AND WE'RE LOS-
    ING A FAMILY
AND WE'RE LOSING OUR BLOOD
WHICH THE EARTH WILL DRINK AND TURN INTO MUD
AND WE'RE SHEDDING OUR TOUGH FAÇADE
AND WE'RE SHEDDING OUR TEARS
WHICH THE EARTH WILL DRINK FOR MANY MORE YEARS

QUINTUS: WAITING FOR THE VERDICT

TITUS: HELP ME DEAR TRIBUNE

MARTIUS: MY EYES ARE GROWING DIM, JUST LIKE IN
    A DREAM

TITUS, MARTIUS, and QUINTUS: IF WE DIE NOW IT
    WILL BE TOO SOON

TAMORA: Guilty.

(TITUS mourns.)

TAMORA: Andronicus, I hope you are satisfied with the service of justice.

(AARON escorts QUINTUS and MARTIUS out. TAMORA removes her hood and exits, noticed only by LAVINIA.)

SCENE 7
THE ANDRONICUS HOME

TITUS turns to LAVINIA and tries to find comfort.

TITUS: Lavinia, you can be happy, the murderers of your husband will face justice.

(He hugs her. She spits a mouthful of blood down his back.)

TITUS: Are you weeping because your brothers killed your husband, or because you know they are innocent?

(Enter AARON.)

AARON: Titus Andronicus, my lord, there has been a reprieve. The Emperor Saturninus will overturn the verdict on one condition: If you love your sons, chop off your hand, and send it to him, and for it you will have your sons returned.

TITUS: (*Whacks off his hand.*) Take it, for hands that serve Rome, serve in vain.

(*AARON takes it, gives TITUS a bandage, and exits. TITUS is forlorn. LAVINIA attempts to bandage his hand. Unsuccessful, LAVINIA starts indicating.*)

TITUS: Speechless communicator, I will learn your thoughts. You can sigh, or wink, or nod, or kneel, or flail your stumps, and that will be our language.

(*LAVINIA enacts a mime show.*)

TITUS: I'm sorry?

(*LAVINIA tries again.*)

TITUS: Come again? I'll get better with practice.

Song 19. Ballad

LAVINIA: ii ii oo ee mah amay [i'd like to tell
   my family]
aaaeeee oo ee [what really happened to me]
uu ib ib aaah oo aa [but it's so hard to chat]
ie oot a oo oo ee [without a tongue for that]
i ee oo i um ay [i need to find some way]
oo aa aeeeouay [to say what i have to say]
oo ill i abbi ii iiii [so while my father is killing]
ee ill et ib illi [he will get his filling]
ab oobi ebaa [and goodbye demetrius]
ba oobi iaa [and goodbye chiron]
oo ow oo oo eaved [for how you both behaved]
ii aa oo oo ave [i'll dance on your grave]
i ii [i will]
i ii [i will]
i ii [i will]

(*TITUS, sensing her woe at the lack of communication, whistles to join her in the song.*)

LAVINIA: i ii! [i will]
ah oo! [my book!]

(*She runs offstage. She returns with a book clasped to her chest.*)

TITUS: Will you read to pass the time?

(*Frustrated, she gives him the book.*)

TITUS: You want me to read? But my eyes are too old and tired, and cannot make out the letters.

(*LAVINIA is annoyed by having to accomplish yet another feat. She sighs, exhausted, then indicates for TITUS to wait, and runs off.*)

YOUNG LUCIUS: (*Offstage.*) What the hell is that?

(*YOUNG LUCIUS skates onstage. He tries to use his skateboard as a shield against LAVINIA.*)

TITUS: Lucius! You should be in exile!

YOUNG LUCIUS: But I'm Young Lucius. I'm like a small pizza, I'm smaller, but just as good.

TITUS: Did I ever tell you how much you look like your father?

YOUNG LUCIUS: (*Annoyed.*) Yes.

(*LAVINIA lunges at YOUNG LUCIUS. He swings at her with his skateboard.*)

YOUNG LUCIUS: Don't touch me! I'll jack you up.

TITUS: Stand by me, boy.

(*YOUNG LUCIUS stands by TITUS. He stares at TITUS's hand.*)

TITUS: Don't be afraid of your aunt. I'm sure she's just trying to tell you how much she loves you.

YOUNG LUCIUS: What happened to your hand?

TITUS: I cut it off.

YOUNG LUCIUS: Can I see the stump?

(*TITUS holds out his stump to show YOUNG LUCIUS, but when YOUNG LUCIUS goes closer, TITUS draws it back like he is going to smack him.*)

TITUS: I'll show you the stump.

(*LAVINIA stops TITUS from hitting YOUNG LUCIUS, and then indicates the book in his other hand.*)

TITUS: What book is this?

YOUNG LUCIUS: It's Ovid's *Metamorphosis*.

(*YOUNG LUCIUS takes the book. She indicates a page.*)

YOUNG LUCIUS: Oh, gross, she's bleeding on the book.

TITUS: On which story?

YOUNG LUCIUS: The story of Philomel. We read it in English class. It's about a girl and her loom… (*He snores.*)

TITUS: Your sight is young, and you will read when mine begin to dazzle.

YOUNG LUCIUS: Huh?

TITUS: Read it!

SONG 20. THE RAPE OF PHILOMEL

YOUNG LUCIUS: TEREUS DRAGGED HER TO THE FOREST
PHILOMEL CALLING FOR HER FATHER AND SISTER
TEREUS TURNED, HE COULD NO LONGER RESIST HER
SHE CRIED, "WHAT ARE YOU GONNA DO?"
"I'M GONNA RAPE YOU!"

TITUS: MAGNI DOMINATOR POLI
TAM LENTUS AUDIS SCELERA TAM LENTUS VIDES

Read it!

YOUNG LUCIUS: TEREUS SATISFIED HIMSELF
PHILOMEL CRYING AS HE'S TRYING TO KISS HER
SHE WONDERS IF SOMEONE WILL MISS HER
BUT HE DOESN'T KILL HER WHEN HE'S FINISHED WITH HER
HE CUTS OUT HER TONGUE AND LETS IT SLITHER

TITUS and YOUNG LUCIUS: MAGNI DOMINATOR POLI
TAM LENTUS AUDIS SCELERA TAM LENTUS VIDES

YOUNG LUCIUS: NO TONGUE TO HELP HER TELL HER TALE

TITUS: WAS IT RAPE? WRITE THE NAMES IN THE SAND WITH THIS STAFF.

YOUNG LUCIUS: SHE TOOK UP THE ART OF THE LOOM

(She takes it and writes.)

TITUS: DEMETRIUS AND CHIRON.

YOUNG LUCIUS: AND SHE WOVE THE STORY OF HER DOOM

TITUS: DEMETRIUS AND CHIRON!

YOUNG LUCIUS: WHILE THE POISON GREW INSIDE HER WOMB

TITUS: KNEEL DOWN, KNEEL DOWN, SWEET BOY
KNEEL DOWN, KNEEL DOWN, SWEET BOY
KNEEL DOWN, KNEEL DOWN, SWEET BOY
KNEEL DOWN, KNEEL DOWN, SWEET BOY
AND LIKE BRUTUS FOR LUCRECE'S RAPE
SWEAR TO SEE BLOOD AND LET NONE ESCAPE

TITUS and YOUNG LUCIUS: GREAT RULER OF HEAVEN
THE MORE CRIMES YOU SEE AND HEAR, THE LESS YOU CARE
GREAT RULER OF HEAVEN
THE MORE CRIMES YOU SEE AND HEAR, THE LESS YOU CARE

(MESSENGERIUS enters with a sack. He opens the sack, spilling out the heads and TITUS's hand. The music begins.)

SONG 21. FEARFUL SLUMBER

MESSENGERIUS: WORTHY ANDRONICUS, ILL ART THOU REPAID
FOR THAT GOOD HAND YOU SENT TO SATURNINE
HERE IS YOUR SEVERED HAND, AND HERE ARE YOUR SONS' HEADS
SENT IN SCORN BACK TO YOU AGAIN

YOUNG LUCIUS: THIS SIGHT MAKES A WOUND TOO DEEP TO GRIEVE
WHERE LIFE HAS NO MORE INTEREST BUT TO BREATHE

TITUS: WHEN WILL THIS FEARFUL SLUMBER HAVE AN END?

MESSENGERIUS: WORTHY ANDRONICUS, FIND SOME COMFORT HERE
TAKE A KISS FROM YOUR DAUGHTER AND BE RELIEVED

Oh, God what happened to her?

TITUS: WHEN WILL THIS FEARFUL SLUMBER HAVE AN END?

YOUNG LUCIUS: FAREWELL, FLATTERY; JUST DIE, ANDRONICUS!
YOU DO NOT SLEEP, AND THIS IS NOT A DREAM
SEE TWO SONS' HEADS, ONE WARLIKE HAND, AND YOUR MANGLED DAUGHTER HERE,
AND MY FATHER IS BANISHED TOO AND IT'S ALL BECAUSE OF YOU!

TITUS: WHEN WILL THIS FEARFUL SLUMBER HAVE AN END?
WHEN WILL THIS FEARFUL SLUMBER HAVE AN END?

Go! Go!

(MESSENGERIUS and YOUNG LUCIUS go out. TITUS cries. LAVINIA nudges the heads of her brothers over to TITUS. TITUS looks at them and his demeanor changes. His cries turn to laughs. He wipes his tears and then, with the blood of his stump, writes "Saturninus" on the wall. He then scratches through it.)

TITUS: I have in blood thus set it down: beware Saturninus. (Grabs up the heads by their hair.)

SONG 22. NO TEARS

TITUS: I HAVE NOT A TEAR TO SHED
FOR MY BOYS NOW ARE ALL DEAD

THIS SORROW IS MY ENEMY
IT WILL DESTROY WHAT IS LEFT OF ME
LAVINIA
LAVINIA

(He holds the heads up to his ear.)

AND NOW THESE TWO HEADS SEEM TO SPEAK
REVENGE THEY URGE ME TO SEEK
AND THEY TELL ME I WON'T COME TO BLISS
IF I CONTINUE TO BE FUCKED LIKE THIS
LAVINIA
LAVINIA

AS I HOLD THESE HEADS IN MY HAND
I PREPARE TO MAKE A FINAL STAND
AND KILL ALL WHO NEED KILLING
I AM READY NOW, AND WILLING
LAVINIA
LAVINIA

I'LL IMPALE A FEW
AND QUARTER A FEW
AND WHEN IT'S TIME FOR SOMETHING NEW
I'LL SLICE A FEW
AND DICE A FEW
FOR CROSSING ME THEY ALL WILL RUE
THE DAY THEY MET ANDRONICUS
WHILE SPEWING BLOOD AND DRIPPING PUS
IT WILL BE THE END OF US
BUT WHO CARES
IT WILL BE THE END OF US
BUT WHO CARES

I'LL BURN A FEW
AND STRETCH A FEW
HANGING CORPSES WILL BLOCK THE VIEW
WHEN I CUT A FEW
AND GUT A FEW
THE SPANISH INQUISITION WILL HAVE NOTHING ON ME
SOON THEY ALL WILL SEE
THERE IS NO END TO MY BLOOD LUST
IT WILL BE THE END OF US
IT WILL BE THE END OF US
OH, IT WILL BE THE END OF US
BUT WHO CARES

(Exeunt.)

SCENE 8
THE PALACE

AARON's chamber. Enter AARON, then DEMETRIUS and CHIRON with a baby.

CHIRON: We are screwed. And not the fun way.

DEMETRIUS: Mom had a son today.

AARON: Good for her and Scatterninny.

CHIRON: Oh, it's not his baby.

DEMETRIUS: Do you know whose it is?

CHIRON: It's not mine.

DEMETRIUS: Well, it's not mine.

CHIRON: Then it must be the drummer's.

AARON: Let me see the baby you keep.

CHIRON: In this family, he's the black sheep.

DEMETRIUS: He's black. Black as you.

AARON: Is black so base a hue?

CHIRON: Mother sends it to you for your stamp and your seal,
She wants you to christen it with your knife's steel.

DEMETRIUS: What have you done?

AARON: That which you cannot undo.

CHIRON: You have undone our mother.

AARON: Boy, I have done your mother.

CHIRON: Let's cut to the chase. If the emperor sees the color of this baby's face, you're one dead duck.

DEMETRIUS: Is that worth a fuck?

AARON: Then it shall be done. The baby will die. (To BABY.) Kiss your ass goodbye. (To CHIRON.) Go. Tell your mother, I'll do what you say.

CHIRON: Okay.

DEMETRIUS: No. Kill the baby first.

AARON: Leave me alone, for my heart will burst when this baby I strike. (AARON is about to kill it with a meat cleaver.)

DEMETRIUS: Alright, then.

(They exit.)

CHIRON: (While going out.) Hey, did you notice we were rhyming?

(AARON works himself up to do the deed. He pumps the knife a few times. Then he swings, stopping just shy of the baby.)

AARON: Psych! (Grabs up the baby and exits.)

SCENE 9
A ROMAN SQUARE

Enter TITUS. He marches back and forth.

TITUS: *(Calls.)* Write for me, boy.

(YOUNG LUCIUS enters, rolls his eyes, then produces a Sharpie and paper.)

SONG 24. TITUS'S GRIEVANCES

TITUS: "JUSTICE, JUSTICE
JUSTICE HAS ABANDONED THE EARTH.
WHICH ONE OF MY HANDS HAD NOT DEFENDED THE
    LAND I LOVED?
AND NOW THIS SINISTER HAND WILL MAKE ME ITS FOE.
I LIFT MY STUMP UP TO HEAVEN AND BEG FOR JUSTICE
FOR MY DUTIES, AND MY SONS WHO DIED
'MUTINY, MUTINY,' I CRY
I PUT YOU ON THE THRONE, WHEN IT COULD HAVE
    BEEN MINE
DEATH SHALL COME TO SATURNINE."

(SATURNINUS enters.)

SATURNINUS: Andronicus!

TITUS: Aye, aye, the name of a fly, come hither to entertain the emperor with my buzzing. But beware, to the emperor, for even a fly, when swatted at one too many times, may return to sting the emperor in his pride. Do you know the emperor?

SATURNINUS: I am the emperor.

TITUS: Then deliver this to him from me. *(Grabs the paper, balls it up, and throws the ball in SATURNINUS's face. To YOUNG LUCIUS.)* You see that, fascism isn't just for fascists anymore.

(SATURNINUS uncrumples the letter and reads it.)

SONG 25. WHY LORD?

SATURNINUS: WHY, LORD, WHAT WRONGS ARE
    THESE?
WAS EVER AN EMPEROR IN ROME THUS OVERBORNE?
WHY, OH WHY, LORD, I FALL TO MY KNEES?
SHALL I BEG MERCY AND FACE THE SCORN?
FACE THE SCORN!

(TAMORA enters; SATURNINUS hands her the letter.)

SATURNINUS: OLD MAN ANDRONICUS
IT SEEMS LIKE SORROW OVERWHELMS YOUR WITS
HAVE YOU LOST YOUR MIND OR SEEK REVENGE ON US?

'CAUSE I FEAR YOUR VENGEFUL FITS
I THINK YOU'RE FAKING IT

IF HE THINKS IN ROME
THAT THERE IS NO JUSTICE
HE WILL WAKE HER UP
WITH HIS OUTRAGES
AND IF HE AND HIS
GET AWAY WITH THIS
HE WILL FIND HER FURY
FOR THE WAR HE WAGES

TAMORA: MY GRACIOUS LORD, MY SATURNINE
YOU NEED NOT WORRY, SO REST YOUR MIND
IF YOU LOOK CLOSER YOU WILL FIND
THE OLD MAN'S A VICTIM OF HIS AGE
NO REASON TO FEAR HIS RAGE

SATURNINUS: SHALL I ENDURE THIS VILLAINY?

TAMORA: YOU DON'T HAVE TO
YOU DON'T HAVE TO
I WILL

SATURNINUS: I'M THE EMPEROR AND I'LL DO WHAT
    I CAN

TAMORA: YOU DON'T HAVE TO
YOU DON'T HAVE TO
I WILL

SATURNINUS: FIND HIM, AND BRING HIM HERE TO ME

TAMORA: YOU DON'T HAVE TO
YOU DON'T HAVE TO
I WILL

SATURNINUS: AND I MYSELF WILL BE THE SLAUGH-
    TERMAN

BOTH: TIME JUSTICE BEGAN
THAT SOUNDS LIKE FUN

TAMORA: Ooh, wait, we can't kill him yet.

SATURNINUS: Oh, baby, you made me go limp.

TAMORA: I have some bad news.

SATURNINUS: Can it wait? I want Titus dead. It's time for debauchery and he makes me flaccid.

TAMORA: Do you remember Lucius?

SATURNINUS: Andronicus?

TAMORA: Yes.

SATURNINUS: I haven't seen him in a while.

TAMORA: Well, you banished him.

SATURNINUS: Did I?

TAMORA: Okay, I banished him. But I did it for you. He was gonna kill you for killing his brothers for killing your brother for marrying Lavinia.

SATURNINUS: Well, what about him?

TAMORA: I just heard from one of the band members that Lucius has raised the Goth army.

(THE BAND MEMBERS are suddenly doing other things.)

TAMORA: And right now they are on their way to besiege Rome.

SATURNINUS: Which band member?

TAMORA: Boinkee.

(BOINKEE waves innocently.)

SATURNINUS: Well, shit in my bucket. Rome loves the Andronici, and if Lucius invades the city, all of Rome will rise in support of him, and overthrow me.

TAMORA: Don't worry about the baby. I have a plan.

SATURNINUS: What baby?

TAMORA: I mean, don't worry about that, baby. I have a plan to destroy Titus and the Goths at the same time. Chiron, Demetrius, and I will go see the old fart. I'll disguise myself as the Muse of Revenge, and Chiron and Demetrius can be Rape and Murder, respectively. We'll mess with Titus's mind by doing a spectacular dance number. We'll trick him into bringing Lucius home, decapitating the Goth army. And when we have the two of them together, we'll slaughter them both.

SATURNINUS: God, you're an evil bitch.

(Exeunt.)

SCENE 10
OUTSIDE OF ROME

LUCIUS enters, and addresses GOTHS.

LUCIUS: My faithful Goth friends, gather around. I have just received a letter from my father. (Reads.) "My beloved boy, Lucius, I hope you are having fun at camp. At home, Rome grows ill. It has a tummy ache from eating too much of my flesh and blood. I hope you will come soon with the cure." He then rambles at length about spiders. And signs it, "Your loving father, Stumps Andronicus."

(AARON stumbles in.)

AARON: I think I made a wrong turn. Shit, Lucius.

LUCIUS: Well, well, well… looks like a good day for a hanging.

(GOTHS grab AARON.)

AARON: Aren't you Lucius? Banished son of old Andronicus?

LUCIUS: Aye.

AARON: I have information about plots against your father, which I will gladly trade for my escape.

LUCIUS: I don't know any plots against my father, except ones made by you.

AARON: Not me. I am the empress's slave.

LUCIUS: You're the empress's whore, and by your side the evidence of your bastardy.

(LUCIUS grabs the baby.)

AARON: Unhand the boy, he has royal blood.

LUCIUS: I have a son in Rome. If anything has happened to him…

(LUCIUS puts a knife to the baby's neck.)

AARON: Lucius, save the child, and I'll tell you wondrous things.
If you will not, befall what may befall,
I'll say no more, but "Vengeance rot you all!"

LUCIUS: Say on, and if you please me, the child will live.

AARON: If I please you? It will vex your very soul to hear my story. But swear, by Jesus, like a good Roman Catholic, that my son will live or all shall be buried in my death.

LUCIUS: I swear.

SONG 26. CONFESSION

AARON: LET ME START WITH YOUR LOVELY SISTER
I WISH I WAS THE ONE TO DEFLOWER, DE-FIST HER
I WAS NOT, BUT I WAS THE ENLISTER
OF ONE DEMETRIUS WITH CHIRON AS ASSISTER

HOW I TINGLED INSIDE
AS SHE SCREAMED AND CRIED

AS I WATCHED FROM NEARBY
PLEASE GOD DON'T LET HER DIE

I WAS PLEASED WHEN AT MY INSTRUCTION
YOUR FATHER GAVE HIMSELF HIS OWN LEFT-HAND
    REDUCTION
I LIED FOR THAT JUSTICE OBSTRUCTION
AND LAUGHED SO HARD I CRIED AT YOUR FATHER'S
    DESTRUCTION

HOW MY PENIS DID STAND
AS I HELD HIS HAND
SEE HIM GROWING INSANE
PLEASE GOD MAKE HIM FEEL PAIN

LUCIUS: HE DOESN'T EVEN FLINCH THE LEAST
WILL NOTHING AFFECT THE BEAST?

AARON: LET ME TELL YOU HOW I MURDERED YOUR
    BROTHERS...

(LUCIUS's rage builds until he stabs AARON. AARON looks up at LUCIUS, spits a mouthful of blood and laughs. LUCIUS stabs the baby and hands it to him. AARON falls.)

LUCIUS: What an asshole.

(Exeunt.)

SCENE 11
THE ANDRONICUS HOME

Enter TAMORA, CHIRON, and DEMETRIUS disguised as Roman superheroes: Revenge, Rape, and Murder.

TAMORA, CHIRON, and DEMETRIUS: Yo! Titus!

(Enter TITUS. He has a microphone Captain-Hooked to his hand.)

TITUS: Who molests my contemplation?

TAMORA: I am Revenge. I have come to talk to you.

TITUS: No, not a word. Wanting a hand to give it action,
You have two-to-one odds of me, therefore no more.

TAMORA: If you knew me, you would talk to me.

TITUS: I am not mad, I know who you are.

SONG 27. REVENGE, RAPE, AND MURDER

TITUS: WITNESS! WITNESS THIS WRETCHED STUMP!
WITNESS! WITNESS THESE CRIMSON LINES!
WITNESS THESE TRENCHES FROM THE TEARS THAT FELL

WITNESS MY SORROW KNOW THAT I KNOW YOU WELL
TAMORA! TAMORA!
DID YOU COME FOR MY OTHER HAND?

TAMORA: NO, YOU SAD MAN, I AM NOT TAMORA
SHE IS YOUR ENEMY, AND I YOUR FRIEND
I AM REVENGE, COME WITH MY HAMMER-A
I MAKE YOUR ENEMIES MEET THEIR END

CHIRON: I AM RAPE

DEMETRIUS: AND I AM MURDER

CHIRON and DEMETRIUS: THE RAPE AND MURDER
    RETRIBUTIONERS

CHIRON: I'LL BOINK A RAPIST WITH A STEEL GIRDER

DEMETRIUS: I'M JUDGE, JURY, AND EXECUTIONER

TAMORA, CHIRON, and DEMETRIUS: WORKING
    WREAKFUL VENGEANCE ON THY FOES
MAKIN' THEM SUFFER FOR THE CRIMES THEY CHOSE

TAMORA: WE KNOW WHO AND WHAT YOU WANT
    REVENGE FOR

CHIRON and DEMETRIUS: WE KNOW YOUR CAUSE
    IS GOOD AND JUST

TAMORA: I'LL KILL THE QUEEN AND HER BELOVED
    MOOR

CHIRON and DEMETRIUS: WE'LL GO STAB GUYS WHO
    LOOK JUST LIKE US

TAMORA: OR BETTER YET, I'LL CALL THEM ALL HERE
    TO EAT
AND YOU CAN CALL YOUR SON LUCIUS HOME
THEN THE TWO OF YOU CAN PERSONALLY DEFEAT
THE ENEMIES OF YOU, YOUR FAMILY, AND ROME

TAMORA, CHIRON, AND DEMETRIUS: WORKING
    WREAKFUL VENGEANCE ON THY FOES
MAKIN' THEM SUFFER FOR THE CRIMES THEY CHOSE

TITUS: (Calls offstage.) Young Lucius! Go, boy, to your father and bid him come home. Bring him home! Bring the boy home!

(CHIRON, played by the same actor as YOUNG LUCIUS, hides his face so he can shout back to TITUS in the affirmative.)

YOUNG LUCIUS: Okay, Grampa.

TAMORA: Rape and Murder, stay here and protect our dear friend Andronicus while I, Revenge, go to set justice in motion.

CHIRON and DEMETRIUS: We love you Mom.

TAMORA: Fear not, Andronicus, revenge shall be swift and painful.

(*TAMORA exits. TITUS draws a very large knife.*)

TITUS: Rape, tie up Murder. Tie him up!

(*TITUS makes CHIRON tie up DEMETRIUS, then he begins to tie up CHIRON, but finds it difficult to do so with one hand. He solicits help from a BAND MEMBER.*)

TITUS: Lavinia! Lavinia! Come, come, look, your foes are bound.

(*Enter LAVINIA.*)

DEMETRIUS: Oh, shit.

CHIRON: Whoops.

CHIRON and DEMETRIUS: It was his idea!

(*The TWO improv lines until:*)

TITUS: Stop their mouths.

(*LAVINIA sticks a stump in each of their mouths.*)

Song 28. Death Pie

TITUS: OH, VILLAINS, YEAH, YOU TWO.
HOW I MEAN TO MARTYR YOU.
THIS ONE HAND IS LEFT TO CUT YOUR THROATS.
AND CATCH YOUR BLOOD IN A GRAVY BOAT
WHICH LAVINIA WILL HOLD BETWEEN HER STUMPS
THAT GRAVY WON'T HAVE NO LUMPS.
YAH-YAH-YAH-YAH
YAH-YAH-YAH-YAH

THEN I'LL GRIND YOUR BONES TO DUST,
THE DUST AND BLOOD WILL MAKE A TASTY PASTE,
AND OF THE PASTE THERE'S A PIE CRUST TO MAKE,
AND WITH THE LEFTOVERS, I'LL MAKE A CAKE.
BEWARE NOAH, HERE COMES THE FLOOD
LAVINIA, CATCH THE BLOOD.
YAH-YAH-YAH-YAH
YAH-YAH-YAH-YAH

TITUS: For worse than Philomel you used my daughter! And worse than Procne I shall be revenged! Receive the hateful liquor!

(*LAVINIA pulls her stumps out of their mouths just as TITUS slashes their throats. She then grabs a large bowl and attempts to catch the gushing blood. As they are dying, they drag themselves out, LAVINIA kicking them as they go.*)

TITUS: BLOOD AND BONE AND KIDNEY STONE
JUST ENOUGH TESTOSTERONE
SOME NIPPLES HERE, SOME LIVER THERE
A LITTLE JIZZ, A LITTLE HAIR

(*LAVINIA dances in and brings TITUS the bowl of blood and a spoon.*)

TITUS: FINGERNAILS AND PUPPY TAILS
TESTICLES AND VENTRICLES
HEART AND TEETH AND TONGUE AND TOES
AND EYES AND EARS AND EGGS, ELBOWS
YUMMY, TUMMY SPHINCTER, COLON
TAPEWORM, FECES, THROW THAT MOLE IN
FORESKIN, RECTUM, FAT, SKIN, BILE, BRAINS
THOSE ARE THE INGREDIENTS FOR DEATH PIE!
THESE ARE THE INGREDIENTS FOR DEATH PIE!
NOW I'M BAKING DEATH PIE!
THIS WILL BE BLOODIER THAN CENTAUR'S FEAST
THEY DON'T NEED A CHEF, THEY NEED A PRIEST

(*LUCIUS enters, unnoticed by TITUS.*)

TITUS: It's DEATH PIE!

LUCIUS: DEATH PIE!

TITUS: DEATH PIE!

LUCIUS: DEATH PIE!

(*TITUS licks the spoon, getting blood all over his face.*)

BOTH: YAH-YAH-YAH-YAH
YAH-YAH-YAH-YAH

(*TITUS and LUCIUS look at each other for a moment, then hug.*)

LUCIUS: I'm home, Father.

TITUS: Looooo-cius.

(*There is a knock at the door. LUCIUS wipes the blood off of TITUS's face. TAMORA and SATURNINUS enter. LUCIUS sets the table.*)

TITUS: Why, my noble lord and lady, what on earth are you doing here? To what do I owe the honor?

TAMORA: I heard your son Lucius has come home to dine.

SATURNINUS: Come we to dine too.

TITUS: On what occasion?

SATURNINUS: Why, to prevent a war.

TITUS: Then it is my humble honor as host to serve both my emperor and Rome.

(LUCIUS ties bibs onto SATURNINUS and TAMORA.)

TAMORA: The honor is Rome's.

SATURNINUS: Well put, darling.

TITUS: We must call Lavinia to eat. (Calling.) Lavinia!

(Enter LAVINIA with a tray of pie. SATURNINUS almost vomits at the sight of her.)

TITUS: Will it please you eat, will it please your highness feed?

(EVERYONE eats.)

SATURNINUS: This is fabulous.

TITUS: Say, Saturninus, can you resolve me this: was it right for Virginius to slay his daughter because she was stained and deflowered?

SATURNINUS: It was, Andronicus.

TITUS: Why, my lord?

SATURNINUS: Because the girl could not survive her shame, and by her presence still renewed her father's sorrows.

TITUS: Well spoken. Then die Lavinia and thy shame with thee, and with thy shame, thy father's sorrow die.

(He kills LAVINIA.)

Song 29. The Banquet

SATURNINUS: WHAT HAST THOU DONE, UNNATURAL AND UNKIND?

TITUS: KILLED HER FOR WHO MY TEARS HAVE MADE ME BLIND.

TAMORA: WHY HAST THOU SLAIN THY ONLY DAUGHTER THUS?

TITUS: NOT I, IT WAS CHIRON AND DEMETRIUS FOR THEY RAVISHED HER AND CUT OUT HER TONGUE. THEY, NOT I, DID HER THIS WRONG.

SATURNINUS: FETCH THEM HERE, FOR SURELY YOU LIE.

TITUS: WHY THEY ARE HERE, BAKED IN THIS PIE. WHERE OF THEIR MOTHER HATH DAINT'LY FED, EATING THE FLESH THAT SHE HERSELF HATH BRED. 'TIS TRUE, 'TIS TRUE, NOW WITNESS MY KNIFE'S POINT

(TITUS kills TAMORA.)

SATURNINUS: DIE, FRANTIC WRETCH FOR THIS ACCURSED DEED.

(SATURNINUS kills TITUS.)

LUCIUS: CAN THE SON'S EYE BEHOLD THE FATHER BLEED?
THERE'S MEED FOR MEED, DEATH FOR DEADLY DEED.

(LUCIUS lunges for SATURNINUS, who moves, causing LUCIUS to impale the BASSIST, who falls over, stopping the music suddenly and abruptly. The OTHER BAND MEMBERS are stunned only momentarily before resuming to play. LUCIUS turns back to SATURNINUS.)

LUCIUS: THERE'S MEED FOR MEED, DEATH FOR DEADLY DEED.

(He kills SATURNINUS.)

Song 30. Epilogue

LUCIUS: SOMEONE TEACH ME HOW TO KNIT THESE
BROKEN LIMBS INTO ONE BODY
BEFORE THIS FLOOD OF TEARS CAN BREAK THE
DAM AND DROWN ME OUT
BEFORE THIS FLOOD OF TEARS CAN BREAK THE
DAM AND DROWN ME OUT

MY HEART IS NOT COMPACT OF FLINT NOR
STEEL, IT'S SOFT AND NOW IT BREAKS APART,
WOULD I WERE DEAD SO THAT
YOU DID LIVE AGAIN
WOULD I WERE DEAD SO THAT
YOU DID LIVE AGAIN

HOW MANY THOUSAND TIMES HAVE THESE POOR LIPS
WARMED THEMSELVES ON MINE
AND NOW, DEAR FATHER, HERE IS THY LAST KISS
I RETURN THEM IN KIND

Some loving friends convey the emperor hence,
And give him burial in his father's grave.
My father and Lavinia shall forthwith
Be closed in our household monument.
As for that ravenous tiger, Tamora,
No funeral rite, no mournful bell;
But throw her forth to beasts and birds of prey
So upon her carcass they may feast another day.
Thank you! There will be no encore! Everyone is dead!

(ALL rise from the dead.)

ALL: TITUS! TITUS!
TITUS! TITUS!
TITUS!

Part II

FROM LEGEND, MYTH, AND SACRED SOURCES

It is easy to see why playwrights, with their desire to expose and illuminate the various facets of our nature, might be drawn to a reinterpretation of "sacred texts"; religious literature has always been just malleable enough to reinforce pretty much any point of view, from the most liberal of social programs to the Crusades. With sharp ear and judicious edit, Matthew Freeman bends the medieval Mystery plays into his *Genesis*, focusing a hot spot on the Mystery's rarely acknowledged goal of squelching any spark of individuality or independent thought in its audience. Using his own words against Him, the God of *Genesis* is less benevolent creator than crushing spirit-breaker, with his children behaving less like the children of God than the confused, guilt-ridden progeny of an alcoholic father, one whose threat of dreadful punishment keeps the kids quiet while he sleeps it off.

We can take comfort, then, after maneuvering the holes that Freeman punctures into the rewards of blind obedience, in David Johnston turning us toward the more hopeful concept of attainable self-determination, in *The Eumenides*, his loose retelling of the third book of Aeschylus's *The Oresteia*. In it, the gods (thankfully) defer to man and his capacity for self-governance, to his logic and compassion, and man moves from the black-and-white destructiveness of Vengeance as guiding force, to the much more enlightened, shades-of-gray concept of Justice. Johnston assures us with the notion that, with the gods' blessing, we are capable of monitoring ourselves with the reason and subtlety that the Mystery plays so forcefully would undermine.

And, should we somehow become uneasy that the ideal we strive for, governance by majority and the inherent faith in mankind that this requires, is a perilous one (an uneasiness reinforced by our current political climate, for example), it's reassuring to know that our playwrights continue to tender respite in the silly and the sublime. The warm-fuzzy wisdom of the sixties' religious opus *The Principia Discordia* offers an often wacky, just-as-often profound springboard for Michael Maiello's reconfiguring in his *Principia*, using that most wonderfully ridiculous of theatre genres, the musical, to tell his tale. With great appreciation, we thank him for the perspective.

    —Stephen Speights

GENESIS

Matthew Freeman

MATTHEW FREEMAN was born in Bryn Mawr, Pennsylvania, in 1975, and was raised in both Boyertown, Pennsylvania, and Maplewood, New Jersey. He is a playwright who was inspired to enter the theatre after discovering the works of Samuel Beckett. He first trained as an actor with David Valdes-Greenwood, Tony Simotes, and Kristin Linklater at Emerson College in Boston, where he received a BFA in acting. His other plays include *The Death of King Arthur* (2001, Gorilla Repertory Theatre; published in NYTE's *Plays and Playwrights 2002*); *Reasons for Moving* (2002, The Local); and *The Great Escape* (2004), *The Americans* (2004), and *The Most Wonderful Love* (2006), all for Blue Coyote Theatre Group. As a writer, Freeman has also freelanced for *Maxim Online*, *Complex Magazine*, and *MTV Magazine.* He currently lives in Brooklyn, New York.

Genesis was originally presented by Handcart Ensemble (J. Scott Reynolds, Artistic Director) on June 7, 2003, at the Common Basis Theater, New York City, with the following cast and credits:

God/Adam/Cain/Abraham .... Jay Leibowitz
Lucifer/God/Isaac .... James Mack
Angel/Eve/Noah's Wife ....Debbie Jaffe
Angel/Noah/God..Tim Moore
Angel/Abel.. Barrett Ogden

Director: Matthew Freeman
Movement Director: David DelGrosso
Music Composed and Performed by: John Gregor

STORIES

CHARACTERS

God	Lucifer
Adam	Eve
Cain	Abel
Noah	Noah's Wife
Abraham	Isaac

Angels

ADAPTOR'S NOTE

This text, compiled as *Genesis*, is five plays, from separate Mystery Cycles (*York*, *Wakefield*, and *Chester*), ordered in my own way, with suggested staging and additions and subtractions of text. There are large swaths of this adaptation unchanged from the original, or only slightly altered. There are changes within speeches, and additions of my own, which are intended (success notwithstanding) to be seamlessly part of the style in which each cycle was originally written. My belief is that these texts, part of a tradition, belong entirely to whomever performs them and that each addition or form is only a piece of that larger history. *Genesis* in this form is simply the way I arranged it to express what I thought was compelling about each of these well-worn and well-studied texts. No small contribution was made by the cast and crew of the production, and by those who worked on the version of *Abraham and Isaac* I directed while studying at Emerson College.

The staging of the original production featured simple costumes (all of the actors were dressed in white, with pieces of contemporary clothing added to indicate their changes in character). There were five cast members, four men and one woman. The men each played God at different times. (Debbie Jaffe never played God, a tip of the hat to the patriarchy.) While there was no "lead," Jay Leibowitz had the challenge and fun to play God, Abraham, Adam, and Cain. Not a bad list of roles for a single night's work.

Creation and the Fall of Lucifer was played relatively abstractly. The "singing" of the Angels was indicated, but not physically performed. Lucifer in Hell was indicated only by language.

The Fall of Man did not feature a nude Adam and Eve, and Lucifer was played by the same actor who played him in *Creation*. I did not use an apple for the fruit that Eve is tempted with…a pomegranate would probably fit better with the piece's overall tone. God was played by Tim Moore, who would later appear as Noah.

The First Murder was enacted with a more contemporary flavor. Cain wore a ragged coat and fingerless gloves, Abel wore a red scarf and better coat. This piece was played (and, in some cases, written) to highlight the economic inequities of their situation. Real cash was used as the tithe. Abel was killed by Cain with a rough grab of the jaw (on the word "cheekbone") as opposed to the use of a physical jawbone. The mark that God gives Cain was an understated touch of the hand. In this play, God was performed by the Lucifer of *Creation* and *The Fall of Man*.

The Flood is simpler than the other two pieces, and God is played by Abel of the last play. A few pieces of wood are used to indicate the beginning of Noah's work.

Abraham and Isaac is the most emotionally intense of the plays. The staging for this play eschewed the "altar" and used a prayer rug and knife as the accoutrements of sacrifice. Isaac would kneel, facing the audience, with Abraham behind him, standing. The rug would extend before Isaac; the assumption played upon was that he would fall forward onto it when his throat was cut. Abraham would also face the audience, knife raised behind his son. Upon God's intervention (here again played by Tim Moore), the "Lamb" used was his Angel messenger, who he then prepared to sacrifice in Isaac's place.

I note the staging here primarily because the texts are, in the popular term, open source, and the staging will largely determine the vision of any production of these texts. The language, symbols, and transitions are largely a unique product of the direction, and I encourage entirely different takes on this text.

Scene transitions were a signature of the staging, featuring movement staging by David DelGrosso and music written for the play by composer John Gregor. Their work was invaluable in creating the tone and flavor of the original production of *Genesis*.

I. CREATION AND THE FALL OF LUCIFER
SCENE 1: HEAVEN

GOD and the ANGELS have a conference.

GOD: I am the Alpha and Omega, the first and last,
The Way, the Truth, the present and past.
I am the gracious and great, in Me all beginning:
I am Maker unmade, all matter is Me,
I am sight and the way to all truth-seeing,
I am foremost and first—as I bid so shall it be.
My blessing upon all My bliss shall be spending
And all who pay homage shall I be defending.
My host is in bliss forever abiding
In graceful abundance without any ending.
But only the worthy of My eyes
Shall inspire the full sight of Me.
In honor of those that evangelize
At once in my blessing I bid that here be
An all-sheltering pleasure around Me:
In attendance of which I bid there be here
Nine orders of Angels full clear
In loving to forever laud Me.
The Earth, all leaden, resides below
And further 'neath its soil will burn afire.
This border island on which nature grows
Reflects the glow sung by My bright choir.
The fire's a prison for the wrong
Who flock to falseness, bring discord.
Thou Angels never fear this Horde
If Grace is his Hymnal Song.

(To LUCIFER.) Of all that I have made in My likeness
I make thee masterly mirror of My might.
I shield thee at once in halo of brightness
And I name thee "Lucifer" as bearer of light.
No thing here shall make thee fearing
In pitch shall be they singing
And may all wealth in their wielding
Be while thou art obediently yielding.

(The ANGELS come together and sing a song of praise. This song may be hummed or wordless. Before them, unseen by the other ANGELS, LUCIFER speaks to the audience.)

LUCIFER: All the mirth that is made is marked in me.
The beams of my brightness are burning so bright
And so seemly in sight myself I now see.
For like a lord am I left to dwell in this light.
Fairer by far than anyone here,
In me there is no point to impair;
I feel myself so well formed and fair,
My power surpassing has no close peer.
My beauty pumps faster than our Father's Heart,
Lucifer bleeds brightness, and so stands apart.

(The singing continues.)

LUCIFER: Oh, how I am well formed and figured full fit!
The form of all fairness upon me is fixed;
All wealth is in my power, by my wit!
I know upon me all eyes are transfixed.
My showing is shimmering and shining;

So broadly to boldness am I brought
My rising is quicker than any has caught.
And never any pain shall I be minding.

ANGEL: With all our wit we worship Thy will,
Thou glorious God, the ground of all grace;
Aye with steadfast sound let us stand still,
Fed, Lord, with the food of Thy fair face.
A banquet of Thy body is sating
Thy gift, Lord, Thou art ever dealing;
And whoever that food may be feeling
To see Thy fair face is never fasting.

LUCIFER: How worthily wrought with worship this
My being, my glittering joyously gleams.
I'm so mightily made that may grace I may not miss
And never keep in brightness my dreams
I need have no fear of losing iwis.
All wealth in my hands am I wielding,
And never shall be yielding
On the heights of the highest Heaven.
I gleefully eye this golden throne above
From here upon cloudfeet unflying.
I would that my station be equal in Love
To him that made all the undying.
I shall receive due reverence through right of renown
And I shall be like unto Him that is highest on height.

FIRST ANGEL: Lucifer, why do you not sing with the
    chorus?
All Heaven implores you to come down and join us.

LUCIFER: Why, then, do you need me if I am unwor-
    thy?
My beauty entreats thee to seek me and need me.

FIRST ANGEL: No angel comes perfectly formed, we
    are pieces
Of parceled creation, we are God's own species.

LUCIFER: And spacious is Heaven, and all its environs
Why should we be clustered, and make no divisions?

SECOND ANGEL: To divide from passion?

LUCIFER: To make our own places.
Look on me, and see that there are nonesuch faces.
If God can make divide between one and another
Why should it not hold to us that we are Other?

SECOND ANGEL: Lucifer speaks boldly, but bain-
    fully too.
Our binding to Heaven you'd have us undo?

LUCIFER: Not undone, my sibling, but remade more
    brightly.

We'd need no great father if we were grown rightly.
Or better, we'd father ourselves, by my teaching.
And less would be between the sky and our reaching.

THIRD ANGEL: I never have reached before, as I've
    no need.
None of us is single, and we know no greed.

LUCIFER: Greed's your word, and His word, but mine
    is to strive
For betterment, all signals do lead us to thrive.
All Angels, why did He choose me as the most?
I would open these doors and to you play Host.

FIRST ANGEL: To strive you say?

SECOND ANGEL: Seek you say?

THIRD ANGEL: Never to yield?

LUCIFER: Not yielding worshippers but listening deep
You'll love subtle Lucifer, his conscience keep.

THIRD ANGEL: Your counsel seems sound indeed,
    fully profound.

LUCIFER: Oh, how noble and wise am I!—But—what
    is this?—All goes down!

(GOD appears and, with a single gesture, sends LUCIFER
and the ANGELS into Hell.)

LUCIFER: My might and my main from me fly!
Help my fellows! In faith, I am falling.

FALLEN ANGEL: From Heaven are we cast down on
    all hand
To woe are we going, a fallen band.

Scene 2: A Region of Hell

LUCIFER: Out! Out! Helpless am I, the heat so great
    here,
This is a dungeon of dole in which we alight!
What have I become that was so comely and clear?
Now am I most loathsome that once was so bright,
My brightness is blackest and blue now.
My bale is ever beating and burning.
It takes from wishing to knowing.
Oh, welaway! I boil enough in woe now.
See, each of the Angels that loved me is tortured
And kingship of Heaven, once craved is now craven.

FALLEN ANGEL: Out! Out! I am mad with my woe,
    my wit is all spent now,
All our food is filth that we find before us;
We, sheltered in bliss, in bale are we burnt now!

No Lucifer, lurdan, our light has thou lost,
Thy deeds to this dole have so brought us,
To dire destruction didst thou lead us,
Thou that wast our light and our leader,
Who to the highest of Heavens did call us.

LUCIFER: Welaway!
Woe is me now! Now it is worse than it was!
Unthriving you chide—I uttered but a thought!

FALLEN ANGEL: Oh lurdan! You have lost us—

LUCIFER: I am king of liars, ye liars, out all—
I wist not this woe should be wrought.
On, on, you lurdans, who smother me in Smoke!
On your false ascriptions I would have you Choke!

FALLEN ANGEL: This woe hast thou wrought.

LUCIFER: Ye lie, ye lie!

FALLEN ANGEL: Thou liest, and for that thou shalt
    pay!
Our lurdan, have at you I may.

(FALLEN ANGELS proceed to grab and tear at
LUCIFER.)

LUCIFER: Oh liars tear my flesh and leave none—
A shape without form nor substance
All main is now monstrous and chorus a hiss
My kingship is only this city of Dis.

Scene 3: Heaven

GOD: This fool from their fairness into fantasies fell
And made moan of the might that marked him and
    made him.
Therefore according to his works in woe, shall he
    dwell,
For some are fallen into filth that evermore shall foul
    them
And never shall have grace to gain peace.
So surpassing of power he thought himself
He would not worship Him that made him;
For this My wrath shall ever be full felt.
Those graces that ungracefully winged as devils
Shall be ever unknown in My sight again.
Their bliss is revoked and their only revels
Will be in the pain of unlikely regain.
Their leader shall lead them through muck
All the while with their eyes on the ceiling
Of Hell, where I grant them new living
And their feet shall know sores of cracked rock.
And all that worship Me shall live here, iwis!

Henceforth, in my work go forth now I will.
Since their might is now marred that meant all amiss,
In My image to fill this place of bliss
Mankind of mold will I make
All things that shall his wishes fill
To which his desire shall him take.
And in My first making to muster My might,
Since Earth is vain and void and murkiness as well,
I bid with My blessing that the Angels give light
To the Earth which fades with the fiends fell—
In Hell alone shall never murkiness be missing.
The darkness thus I name "the night"
While "the day" call I this light!
And now in My blessing I twin them in two,
The night from the day, so meet they never
But either to their separate gates they go,
Both the night and the day their duties leasing.
For the good of all I shall this be without ceasing!—
Now these days' work are surely pleasing
For all this has taken but seven to do;
And straightway now I give them my blessing.

II. THE FALL OF MAN
Scene 1: Hell

LUCIFER: For woe my wits are in a whirl here!
This moves me greatly in my mind:
That Godhead whom I saw so clear
Should not have treated me as swine.
He had wrought man, and I was angered
That these not Angels were to be!
For we were His true self made light
And therefore thought that respect
Would win the favor in His sight
Yet He made new reflect.
That nature of man He thought to take
And thereat had I great envy.
But He has made to man a mate,
So fast to her I will haste
This parasitic day
With purpose fixed to put by
And try to steal from God that prey.
My purpose and plan
Might I Him so betray.
And from Him this new-made man,
I shall lead astray.

Scene 2: Paradise

LUCIFER: In a worm's likeness I will wend
And lie with too much truth:
Eve! Eve!

EVE: Who is there?

LUCIFER: I! A friend!
And for thy good is the journey
I hither sought.
Of all the fruit that you see high
In Paradise, why eat you nought?
There's fruit unpicked
On this lush tree.
So gathered I to bring to thee
Once wasted, sweet and slick.

EVE: We may of them take
All that good is in our thought
Save one tree, lest we mistake
And to harm be brought.

LUCIFER: And why that tree—that I would I wit—
Any more than any other nigh?

EVE: For our Lord God forbids to try
The fruit thereof. Adam and I
May not come near,
For if we did both should die,
He said, and lose our solace here.

LUCIFER: Yea, Eve, attend to my intent
Take heed and you shall hear
What all this matter meant
That He moved you to fear.
To eat thereof He did forbid
I know it well. This is His will.
Because He would that none should know
The great virtues that are hid
Therein. For thou wilt see
That who eats this fruit of good and ill
Shall be as knowing as is He.

EVE: Why, what thing art thou
That tells this tale to me?

LUCIFER: A worm that knoweth well how
Ye both may worshipped be.

EVE: What worship should we win thereby?
To eat thereof it needs us nought—
We have lordship to make mastery
Of all things that in Earth are wrought.

LUCIFER: Woman, away!
To a greater state ye may be brought
If ye will do as I shall say.

EVE: To do this we are loath
For this would our God dismay.

LUCIFER: Nay, certain, it will bring no hurt,
Eat it safely ye may.
For peril none therein lies
But advantage and a great winning.
For right as God ye shall be wise,
And peer to Him in everything.
Ay, gods shall ye be,
Of ill and good you will have knowing,
And be as wise as is He.

EVE: Is this truth that thou says?

LUCIFER: Yea, why believest thou not me?
I would by no kind of ways
Tell nought but truth to thee.

EVE: And this truth thou tells—

LUCIFER: That you have heard—

EVE: That it will bring no hurt
And eat safely I may.
For peril none lies inside
But advantage and good tidings.
For as my God I will be wise
And peer to Him in everything.

LUCIFER: Yes, Eve. Thou listen
As well as a serpent can teach.

EVE: Ay, as God will we be
Of ill and good we may have knowing.

LUCIFER: If you be as wise as He.

EVE: Then will I to thy teaching trust
And take this fruit unto our food.

LUCIFER: Bite on boldly, be not abashed.
And make Adam too amend his mood
And enlarge his bliss. *(Exit.)*

EVE: Adam, have here of fruit full good!

ADAM: Alas, woman, why tookest thou this?
Our Lord commanded us both
To beware this tree of His.
Thy work will make Him wroth:
Alas, thou hast done amiss!

EVE: Nay, Adam, grieve thee not at it,
And I shall tell the reason why:
A worm has given me to wit
We shall be as gods, thou and I,
If that we eat
Here of this tree. Adam, thereby,

Fail not this worship so to get,
For we shall be as wise
As God that is so great,
And also of the same great price.
Therefore, eat of this meat.

ADAM: To eat it I would not eschew
Might I be sure of thy sayings.

EVE: Bite on boldly, for it is true:
We shall be gods and know all things.
We must to the sticking-place
Be stuck, and not "I dare not"
Wait upon "I would be new."

ADAM: I will do that which becomes
A man and be thy mirror.
To win that name,
I shall taste it at thy teaching.

(He takes and eats the fruit.)

ADAM: Alas, what have I done? For shame!
I'll counsel, woe worth thee!
Ah Eve, thou art to blame,
To this hast thou enticed me—
And my body now fills me with shame.
For I am naked, as I think—

EVE: Alas, Adam, right so am I!

ADAM: And for sorrow sere why might we not sink?
For we have grieved God Almighty
That made me man,
Broken His bidding bitterly,
Alas, that ever we began!
This work, Eve, hast thou wrought,
And made this bad bargain.

EVE: Nay, Adam, blame me naught.

ADAM: Away, dear Eve, who then?

EVE: The worm to blame well worthy were:
With tales untrue we were betrayed.

ADAM: Alas, that I listened to thy lore,
Or trust the trifles thou to me said,
So I may be bid,
For I may curse that bitter braid
And dreary think that I did.
And our shape, with shame it grieves—
Wherewith shall our bodies be hid?

EVE: Let us take this cover
Since now befalls this grief.

ADAM: Right as thou sayest so shall it be,
For we are naked and all bare.
Full wondrous fain would I hide me
From the Lord's sight, if I wist where;
Where, I would care naught!

GOD: Adam! Adam!

ADAM: Lord?

GOD: Where art thou? Yare!

ADAM: I hear thee, Lord, and see Thee not.

GOD: Say, whereto does it belong
This work why hast thou wrought?

ADAM: Lord, Eve made me do this wrong,
And to that breach me brought.

GOD: Say, Eve, why hast thou made thy mate
Eat fruit I bade thee to let hang always
And commanded none of it to take?

EVE: *(Weeping.)* A worm, Lord, enticed me thereto:
So welaway!
That ever I this deed did do!

GOD: Now Cherubim, My Angel bright
To Middle Earth be swift to drive these two.
These gifts they will be wont for
So let them learn, and in learning be they
Confused and infused with no comfort
May they force the desert to bear bread
And find times where trees offer no fruit
Forbidden is nothing to them, no more
Except what they did have, this Eden.

ANGEL: All ready, Lord, as it is right,
Since Thy will is that it be so,
And they liking—
Adam and Eve, do you two go,
For here may ye make no dwelling.
Go ye fast to fare
And of sorrow may ye sing.

ADAM: Alas, for sorrow and care
Our hand may we wring!

(He is cast out.)

EVE: Shall no remembrances retained be?
Shall no land map remain to lead us home?
Will these Angels sink Eden lo the sea
And lowly leave our hopes in ragged rooms?
What makes a garden all of perfect form,
And stealthy, leaves a trap within?

Why would His eyes unbide this sickly worm
When He sees every moment we might Sin?
Why did my Father not give conscience care
And spake not wisely to the indolent?
Now shame falls me for knowing neither where
Nor when I should be watched or lost in Sense.
Now Wanders Eve all shamed as Man's Demise
In a world wrought with wroth, and left unwise.

(EVE exits the Garden.)

III. THE FIRST MURDER

ABEL comes to his brother, CAIN. ABEL is well groomed; work has been good to him. CAIN is clearly more destitute.

ABEL: God, as He both may and should
Speed thee, brother, and thy foot.
Our hurry shows Him of our care
That we love Him and love to share
That which He places in our palms;
We give Him thanks and receive balms.

CAIN: Come kiss mine arse, I don't want to rail
But *away* from here thou art welcome.
Thou shouldst have waited till I called out "Hail"
Come nearer and either drive the team or hold the
    plow
And kiss the devil's ring
For that is thee most lief.

ABEL: Brother, there is none hereabout now
That would thee grieve.
But dear brother, hear my saw:
It is the custom of our law
That all who work by plow and tides
Shall worship God with sacrifice.
Our father bade us, our father taught
That our tenth to God should be brought.
Come forth brother, and let us go
To worship God. We tarry too long:
Give we Him a part of our fee,
Whether corn or cattle it be.
We tarry in useless debate
Tho God has given each his gate.
We must wash out the daily grind
And satiate our Master's mind.

CAIN: Ho! Let forth your geese, the fox will preach!
How long wilt thou me impeach
With thy sermonizing?
Hold thy tongue still, I say,

Where the good wife rubbed the hay!
Or sit down in the devil's way
With thy vain carping.
Should I leave my plow and everything
And go with thee to make offering?
Nay! Thou findest me not so mad!
Go to the devil, and say I so bade
What does God give thee to praise Him so?
Me give He nought but sorrow and woe.

ABEL: I may love all and you the most
But mine ears cannot stand your boast.
Cain, leave this vain carping,
For God gives thee all thy living.

CAIN: Yet borrowed I never a farthing
Of Him here in my hand!

ABEL: Brother, as our elders gave command,
First should we tend with our hand
Then to His glory bring with the brand.

CAIN: My farthing is in the priest's hand
Since the last time I offered.

ABEL: Dear brother, let us cross the land:
I would that our tithes were already proffered.

CAIN: Whee! Whereof should I tithe, dear brother?
For I am each year worse off than the other.
My winnings are but lean,
No wonder that my heart should teem.
Full long to Him I have felt shame!
And of my sorrows, who takes Blame?
Cain is the father of his feast
And founding Father still leaves least.
For by Him that us dearly bought.
I think that He will lend me naught.

ABEL: No blame or shame to you should come
For being tested, that's a boon.
He lends you what you need to thrive
And despite hardships, yet you live.

CAIN: Lends He *me*? May such thrift come to thee!
For He has ever yet been my foe.
I call the God a fool for sheep
And my brother his slavish keep.
For had He my friend been,
Otherwise it would have been seen.
When I was needing food and drink
And my fortunes began to shrink
The more I cried and begged in prayer
The less I noted Him aware.

My words in weeping came
And He presented none.
Hardly hold me to blame
If I serve Him of the same.

ABEL: Dear brother, shame yourself
So others may not waste the breath.

CAIN: Yea, yea! The words you waste.
The devil speed me if I have haste
To divide my goods and give
Any of mine that helps me strive
Either to God or to a man
Of anything ever I won;
For had I contributed to God
Then might go with a ripped hood
And it is better to live like a pauper
Than to go from door to door and beg.

ABEL: Brother, come forth in God's good Name,
I am afraid we shall get blame,
Hie we fast that we get there.

CAIN: You may run on ahead and in the devil's name
       fare!
Welaway, man, I hold thee mad!
Thinkest thou now that I gad
About to give away the good!—
What would you need, so brotherly
That you support to take the last of me?

ABEL: Dear brother, it were great wonder
That thou and I should go asunder;
There's so little to hold us fast but blood—
Are we not brothers you and I?

CAIN: No: I love thee and know it is fine
That you should spend my time and earn nothing:
Whether God be fair or fat
My winning should not alter that.
I have gone oft in softer guise
Where I thought some profit would arise
No worry, Abel, of my course
As it is laid out in advance.
Since go we must in any wise.
Lay down thy bundle on the ground.

ABEL: Forsooth, brother, this is sound.
God of Heaven, you've made me proud.

CAIN: Though shalt tithe first, even if thou be wood.

ABEL: (Offering an abundance.) God that made both
       Earth and sky,
I pray to Thee Thou hear my cry;

And take with thanks if Thy will be,
The tithe that I offer here to Thee.
For I give it with good intent
To Thee, my Lord, that all has sent
In worship of Him that all has wrought.
Sore have I been, in these days spent
In idlry, my minutes lent
I give these freely of my winnings
To tide Thy wrath, and sate my sinning.

CAIN: Rise up. Let me, since thou art done—
Lord of Heaven hear my plea,
And God forbid you showed me
Gratitude for Courtesy.
For, as I enjoy these two legs
It is full sore, against my will,
That the tenth of my take I give here—
Of coin or anything that grows for me.
And now will I begin then
Since I must needs my tithe bren—
One sheaf, one, and this makes two…
But neither of these may I forgo.
Two, two, now this is three—
Yea, this also shall remain with me!
For I will choose and for myself the best sheaves shall
       have.
This hold I for profit—this sheaf
Oh! Oh! Four! Lo here. (Chooses carefully the least of
       his purse.)
Better grow not for me this year!
At the proper season I sowed fair corn
Yet it was mostly, when it was shorn,
Thistles and briars in great plenty
And all kinds of weed that might be.
Four sheaves, four…
Lo, this maketh five!
Devil I fast thus long before I thrive!
Five and six, now this is seven
But this gets never towards Your Heaven.
Nor none of these four, by my right
Shall ever come in Lordship's sight.
Seven…seven…now this is eight.

ABEL: Cain, brother, thou are not betaught.

CAIN: Whee! Therefore it is as I say
For I will not deal my goods away
But had I given Him this to tend
Then wouldst thou say He were my friend
But I think not, by my hood,
To depart lightly from my good.
There! Eight…eight and nine…and ten is this.

And who cares for this if we miss?
Give Him that white lies thore?
It goes against my heart full sore.

ABEL: Pay the tithe right through.

CAIN: Yes! Lo, twelve, fifteen, sixteen, else…

ABEL: Cain, thou counts wrong and of the worst.

CAIN: No. Come near and hold thou cursed.
In waning of the moon will you be quiet at last,
Or else wilt thou that I wink?
Then shall I do no wrong, I think.
Let me see now how it is.
Yes, well I hold me paid.
I offered wonderfully well, I guess.
And so even I laid.

ABEL: Cain, of God methinks thou hast no dread.

CAIN: Now, if He get more, the devil me speed!
As much as one sheaf:
For that came to Him light cheap.
Not as much, neither great nor small
As one might wipe his ass withal.
For that and this that lies there
Have cost me full dear:
Ere it was shorn and brought in stack
Had I many a weary back!
Therefore ask me no more of this,
For I have all that my will is.

ABEL: Cain, I counsel thee to divide right.
For dread of Him that sits on height.

CAIN: How that I tithe care thou not a peep,
But tend thy scabbed sheep
For if thou to my tithe attend
It will go worse for thee in the end.

(Showing ABEL his best purse.)

CAIN: Wouldst thou I gave Him this or these?
No, neither of these will I leave.
But take this; now has He two.
And, now for my soul, this will do.
Though it goes sore against my will
And He shall like this full ill.

ABEL: Cain, I counsel thee to tithe
So God of Heaven be blithe
And be thy friend!

CAIN: My friend? No, unless he will—
I have never done Him any ill.

If He be never so my Foe
I am yet determined to give Him no more.
But change thy mind, as I did mine.
Thou hast not yet tithed thy leprous swine.

ABEL: If thou hast tithed right, thou soon shalt find.

CAIN: Yea, kiss the devil's fat behind?
The devil hang thee by the neck!
How I have tithed is not for you to reck.

ABEL: Cain, this not worth one leek!
Thy tithe should burn well without smoke.
Cain, brother, that is ill done.

CAIN: No, but go we hence soon;
And if I may, I shall be
Where God Himself shall not see.
There will be none who may spy
With eye or other means, not even Him
Inside that room.
None know of places out of His sight.
But I will find them, and respite.

ABEL: Dear brother, I will fare
On the road where our betters are
To look out for all, empty of full.

CAIN: Shouldst thou go? Nay abide awhile.
We have yet a fearless bone to pick.
Hard! Speak with me before thou go.
What, dost thou think to 'scape so?
No, stay! I owe thee a foul play
And now is the time that you'll repay.

ABEL: Brother, why are you so in ire?

CAIN: Why burns thy purse in full a fire?
While mine, while offered, barely smoked
Right as it would us both have choked?

ABEL: God's will, I believe, it were
That mine did burn so clear
If thine chokes, am I to blame?
Know you nothing, brother
Of the world as't works?
Of kindness repaid in kind
And likewise selfishness?
Faith resides inside the air
And not inside the curious
Of question and of matter.
You seem to hate too much
Both kin and King alike.
You excuse failure's crutch
To make your fire not light.

CAIN: Yea! And thou shalt repay my shame:
Never before has one man's burden
Felt so assured to kill for certain.
None in Paradise need make divide
And while outside, less must reside.
With cheekbone straightway
Shall I thee and thy life divide.

(CAIN attacks and murders HIS BROTHER.)

CAIN: So lie down there and take thy rest—
So shall the best be chastised thus.

(It is silent.)

CAIN: Yea, lie there, villain, lie there, lie!
And do not raise another truth.
Never more Abel Cain to chide
For in Heaven hence reside.
(To the audience.) And if any of *you* think I did amiss,
I shall amend it worse than it is!
That all men may it see
Well worse than it is;
Right so shall it be.
But now, since he is brought to sleep
Into some hole fain I would creep;
For fear I quake and am without a thought,
Save for my death once I am caught.
Here will I lie for forty days,
And a curse on him who will me raise.
But I hear a sound, what passes inside
That comes to me and looks for Tithe?

GOD: Cain! Cain!

CAIN: Who is it that calls me?
I am yonder, canst Thou not see me?

GOD: Cain, where is thy brother Abel?

CAIN: Why ask me? I do believe in Hell,
In Hell I think he be!
Whoso were there then might he see
Or somewhere may be sleeping.
Was Abel mine for keeping?

GOD: Cain, Cain, thou wast wood!
The voice of thy brother's blood
That thou hast slain in false wise
From Earth to Heaven vengeance cries.
And because thou hast cast thy brother down
Here I give thee my malison. *(GOD reaches into the Earth and pulls up soot.)*

CAIN: Yea, deal it about Thyself, for I will none,
Or take it to Thee when I am gone.

Since I have done so very much sin
That I may not Thy mercy win.

GOD: Nay, Cain, it shall not be so:
I order that no man another slay
And he that slays thee, young or old.
He shall be punished sevenfold.

(He rubs this soot on CAIN, leaving him marked.)

GOD: This mark received shall forever stain:
Outwardly and inwardly it soaks
No washing nor no cleansing rain
Shall keep the bearer from its yoke.

CAIN: No matter! I know wither I shall:
In Hell I know must be my stall.
It is no use mercy to crave.
For even if I pray, I must none have.
But this corpse, I would it were hid.
For some man might come upon it amain.
"Flee, false villain" would he bid
And suspect I had my brother slain.

IV. THE FLOOD

NOAH: Almighty God so true, Maker of man's body
All giving, provider, and lover of all and any
Thou hast made both night and day, beast, fowl, and
    fish;
All creature that can breathe thou givest breath at thy
    wish
As thou did give us order
Our faults were too made perfect
Perhaps, to give you lament
And create, too, the reason lent
To test both man and Maker.
Angels Thou hast made, all orders, to shine
The light reflected in Thine eyne.
Full marvelous to name. Yes was there unkindness
More by sevenfolds that I can well express.
Forwhy? Because
Of All Angels in brightness
God gave Lucifer the most lightness.
Yet proudly he moved his dais
To where he set himself equal to Your ways.
He thought himself as worthy as God that him made
In brightness, in beauty. Therefore to degrade
God put him in a low degree soon after, in a brade,
Him and his company where he should be unglad
Forever.
They shall never get any
From there until Doomsday

But burn in bale for aye
They did Your men essay.
Enticed man to gluttony, stirred him to sin in pride,
But in Paradise might no sin reside,
And therefore man was sent outside
In woe and wandering they wailed and cried.
First on Earth, and then in Hell—
There with fiends to dwell
Lest show they God his mercy
And tend to His laws honestly.
Oil of mercy He has promised. I have heard read,
To every living person that would love Him and dread,
But now before His sight every living thing
Has learned from Cain to kill Thy song.
Some in pride, ire, and envy,
Some in covetousness and gluttony,
Some in sloth and lechery
And other ways manifold.
And now I wax old,
Sick, sorry, and cold;—
As muck upon mold
I wither away.
This world gives its God little title
And brought my lips to the bottle.
But yet will I cry mercy and call:—
Noah Thy servant, am I, Lord over all!
Lest that I and my children shall fall,
Save us from Villainy and bring us to Thy hall.

GOD: I repent full sore that ever I made a man.
By Me he sets no store who am his sovereign;
I will destroy therefore beast, man, and woman,
That evil do.
In Earth I see right nought,
But sin, all unatoned;
Of those that well have wrought
Find I but few.
Therefore shall I unmake my finest matter
With waters that shall flow and rain with clatter
As I say, so shall I do; of vengeance draw My clouds
And make end of babies, mothers, fathers, and their
    lands.
Of all that beareth life
Save Noah and his wife
For they have been in temperance
And Shown their Master remembrance.
To him and his great gain, hastily will I go—
To Noah at once, to warn him of this woe.
On Earth I see but ground and ash
The invisible fire, from them I'll wash.
The evil intent.

All shall I undo
With floods that shall flow;
I shall work them woe
That will not repent.
Noah, My friend, I thee command thy faults to unsay;
For sin and fault are not the same
For you might fault, but never truly sin My Name.
Do thou but make a ship to sail for away
Thou wast e'er a trusty workman, to Me as true as My
    heel;
For thy lasting faithful friendship shalt thou yet live.
Of length thy ship let be
Three hundred cubits, I tell thee,
Of height even thirty,
And fifty also broad.
One cubit on height a window shalt thou make,
On the side a door, with skill, shalt thou take,
While with thee shall no man fight, nor do thee any
    hate.
When all is done thus right, thy wife, that is thy mate,
Take in to thee;
Thy three sons of good fame,
Japhet, Sehm, and Hame;
Their wives also all three.
I trust in thee to build well
That which will remake men.
All hope is in your hammer and nail
To keep the way of life and sail.

NOAH: Ah! Benedictate! What art Thou that thus
Thou tells before what shall be? Thou art full marvel-
    ous!
Tell me, for Charity, Thy Name so gracious.

GOD: My Name is of dignity, and also full glorious
To know.
I am God most mighty
One God in purity
Who made thee and each man to be:
To love Me well you owe.

NOAH: I thank thee, Lord so dear, that would vouch-
    save
Thus below to appear to a simple knave.
I shall deal well and worthily
To prove my work is quality
And grace shall keep all humankind
Safe on the waves till land is found.

GOD: Noah, to thee and to thy fry
My blessing grant I;
Ye shall wax and multiply,

And fill the Earth again.
When all these floods are past and fully gone away.
(*Exits.*)

NOAH: Lord, homeward will I haste as fast as I may.
My wife will I see and hear what she say.
I am afraid there will be some fray
Between us both;
For she is full of sauce
For little oft angry;
If anything wrong be
Soon is she wroth.

(*Enter NOAH's wife.*)

NOAH: God speed, dear wife. How fare ye?

WIFE: Now, as ever might I thrive, the worst is that
    I see thee,
And tell me now at once where hast thou thus long
    been?
To death may we drive, or live for thee
In want indeed.
When we sweat or swink
Thou dost what thou think,
Yet of meat or of drink
Have we much need.

NOAH: Wife, we are hard placed with tidings new.

WIFE: Better that thou wert other than red hue
For thou art always afraid, be false or true.
But God knows, I am led, and that may I rue,
Full ill.
For I dare be thy pledge
From evening until Morrow.
Thou speakest ever of sorrow.
God send thee for once thy fill.
(*To the audience.*) We women may curse all ill hus-
    bands
I have one, by curse me, that should loose me of my
    bands.
If he be vexed, I must tarry, wringing both my hands
    for dread
But some other while,
Yet with game and with guile,
I shall smite and smile
And give him his mead.

NOAH: Hold thy tongue, ram-skit, or I shall make
    thee still.

WIFE: By my thrift, if thou smite, I shall set on thee
    too.

NOAH: I will try quickly, have at thee Jill
Upon the bone shall it bite.

WIFE: Ah, so, marry, thou smitest ill,
But I suppose
I shall not owe thee more
Ere I quit this floor. (*Exits.*)

NOAH: I tarry full long from my work, I trow.
Now my gear will I fetch and thitherward draw;
I may go full wrong, the truth I know,
But if God help not now, I may sit in sorry, I see.
Now will I try
How I can do carpentry
With such a head so red weary?
To begin with this tree, my bones will I bend.
I trust that the vine succor will send—
It fares full fair, as my hand I lend.
Now blessed be He that this can amend.
Lo! Here the length,
The cubits I've write scrawlingly
Of breadth I must have fifty
Length so full of strength. (*He works to build.*)
My gown will I cast, and work in my coat.
The master will I make, ere I stir a foot.
My back, I fear, will burst, and this is a sorry note.
It is a wonder that I last, such an old dote, all dulled.
(*Does a small amount of woodwork and stops.*)
This work is full tiring, and so far to go
Though soon comes the water to sink us below.
My head is full ached and body is shaking
From the sweet wine too oft my mouth has been tast-
    ing.
Dear wife!

(*Enter WIFE.*)

WIFE: Now keep silent
And learn old beggar how love
Even true as mine
Can be brought to run dry
When too often fined.

NOAH: Old sow, I would need you
But never entreat you.
God has chosen my work
And so you may off.

WIFE: Scoff broadly, skunked husband
Who stinks of the drink.
Though I fear our Lord
I fear more your soft head.

(*Exit WIFE.*)

NOAH: Old hammer and tools may come rightly
To my throbbing joints and be sprightly. (*More work
    and then rest.*)
Oh harshly comes woodwork
My spine is like clockwork
Informing my old bones
To entreat my muscles.
Rise up and be tireless. (*He continues to work, then
    falters.*)
Old wife, I must beg thee!
Come kiss sweet and twenty!
Youth's a thing too far from home.

(*Enter WIFE.*)

NOAH: My love…

WIFE: My illness?

NOAH: Have you been my wife
For these long years in spite of me?

WIFE: Yes, for truth, in spite of myself.

NOAH: The Lord has given me station
That I am unworthy of.
Look at my trembling location
My hand unfit to serve.
Make list and hear my tidings
Of the rains we have seen
On the coming lands from green
To gray as we have made markings.
The Lord warned of the bad land
That is left all around
And told me of His children
It is we two alone
That have the grace to serve in
The purpose of all to save.
Does this not seem a folly
Impossible for our Deity?
He bid me build, from this wood
An Ark to place within
Ourselves, and other natures
And our three children.
Now, of my failings, wife
You have made often note
And hated me by rote
To give us both this strife.

WIFE: I know, though you are ail-filled
You'd lie most rarely
And would treat fairly
In matters of our God.
Now, take thy older hands

And use them to be strong
For though we are imperfect
We have to use these tongs.

NOAH: Does God's will strike you strangely?

WIFE: Would I your wife be truly
If by God's word I doubt
That you were rightly taught?
Now let us set aside
The worries we have made,
And use the best of Nature
To make the best of God's remains.
This graceful passage set before us both
Does not beguile our God, who knows us all
He sees that fault was inside bone and tooth
But sin is boneless, inhuman and small.
We may make rail and would be in half love
Or call each other unfaithful and worse
But it is God to know the deepest trove
Of treasure, whether we be poor or pursed.

NOAH: Our doom is attained, we have lost the Earth
To fire and water, our great architect
Sees craftsmanship too shoddy to rebirth
By else but remaking our prayers intact.

WIFE: So Noah, husband, we shall be our best
Though, flawed in life, in rebirth there's no rest.

(*She aids him in his work…steadying his hands.*)

V. ABRAHAM AND ISAAC

*ABRAHAM, with ISAAC his son, gives up a prayer to
GOD.*

ABRAHAM: Father of Heaven, omnipotent,
With all my heart to Thee I call.
Thou has given me both land and rent
And my livelihood Thou hast me sent.
I thank Thee highly evermore of all.
In my age Thou has granted me this
That my loins purchase more than natural.
I know none perfect in heart and spirit,
Except Thine own self, dear God without limit,
As Isaac here, my own sweet son.
And therefore, Father of Heaven, I Thee pray
For his health and also for his grace.
Now, Lord, make good Your promise
That never pain nor compromise
Come to my child in any place.
Now come on Isaac, my own sweet child
Go we home and take our rest.

ISAAC: Abraham, I am thy grateful child,
To follow you I am full pleased,
And thank thy fatherly pleadings.

ABRAHAM: Come on, sweet Isaac. Nonesuch
Could be in my eyes and in my chest.

(ISAAC continues on, but ABRAHAM is held suddenly by the vision of an ANGELIC MESSENGER.)

ANGEL: Abraham, Abraham, come take list!
Hard and soft tidings I bring from our King.
My father, and yours, requests least humbly
For Fatherhood unseats Paternity.
Our Lord commandeth thee to take
Isaac, thy young son granted by His grace,
And with his blood a sacrifice thou make.
In the Land of Vision do thou go,
And offer they child unto thy Lord;
I shall thee lend and also show.
To God's behest, Abraham, accord,
And follow likewise this most zealous path.

ABRAHAM: Welcome to me be my Lord's command!
And His word I will not withstand.
Yet Isaac, my young son in hand,
A full dear child to me has been.
The Land of Vision I must surely seek
For only visions make Lions of the weak.
I had rather, if God had been pleased,
To have forborne all the goods that I have,
Than Isaac, my son, should be deceased.—
So God in Heaven my soul may save!
Shall he make Cain of Abraham
And force the hand of cruelty come?
No, I cannot believe my Lord deceive
Or in error could make His will be known.
I love my child as my life,
But yet I love my God much more
For though my heart should make any strife
Yet will I not spare for child or wife,
But do after my dread Lord's lore.
Though I love my son never so well,
Yet smite off his head soon I shall.
Ah, Father of Heaven! To thee I kneel—
A ritual my son shall feel,
To honor my faith, withal!

(The ANGEL provides ABRAHAM with tools by which to make his ritual sacrifice.)

ANGEL: Abraham, Abraham, this is well said,
And all these commandments look that thou keep,—
But in they heart be nothing dismayed.

Show valiant faith and to this sacrifice
Hurry yourself, before your faith is swayed.

ABRAHAM: Swayed or swaying I am not allowed
For my provider rules me, His word Law.
Nay, nay forsooth, I hold me well repaid
To please my God to the best that I may.
For though my heart be heavily set
To see the blood of my own dear son,
I cannot doubt that which is known
Of He shakes the Earth and sees it grown.

(The ANGEL departs.)

ABRAHAM: Rise up, my child, and fast come hither,
My gentle bairn that art so wise,
For we, too, child, must go together,
And unto my Lord make sacrifice.

ISAAC: I am fully ready, my father, lo!
Give to your hands, I stand right here;
And whatsoever ye bid me do, right quick
As we must to the ritual full steer
A beast that's quick to bleed.

ABRAHAM: Ah, Isaac, my own son so dear,
You love your father, as I love mine.
So yea, a beast that's quick and young
Will soon be given knife and song.
Hold this faggot upon thy back,
And I myself fire shall bring.

ISAAC: Father, all this here will I pack;
I am full fain to do your bidding.

ABRAHAM: Ah, Lord of Heaven!
This child's words all do stab my throat!
I speak through terror, but in rapt belief.
Now Isaac, son, go we on our way
To God His due we must respectfully pay.

ISAAC: Go we, my dear father, as fast as I may;
To follow you I am full fain,
Although I be slender.

ABRAHAM: Ah, Lord, my heart breaketh in twain
This child's words, they be so tender!
Ah, Isaac, son, anon lay it down,
No longer upon thy back it hold,
For I must make ready prayer soon
To honor my Lord God as I was told.

ISAAC: Lo, my dear father, here it is.
To cheer you always I draw me near.
But Father, I marvel sore at this,
Why ye make this heavy cheer?

And also Father, even more dread I—
Where is quick beast that ye should kill?
Both fire and wood we have ready nigh,
But quick beast have we none on this hill.
We've come upon the highest site
But no good body here is produced
Nor catch of hunt for our plain rite.
Where is the lamb that should be used?
A quick beast, I wot well, must be slain,
Your sacrifice to make.

ABRAHAM: Dread thee naught, my child, I would fain;
Our Lord will send me unto this place
Some manner of beast for to take
Through His command.

ISAAC: Yea, Father, but my heart beginneth to quake
To see the quiver in your manner.
Why bear ye your shoulders so?
Of our countenance I have much wonder.

ABRAHAM: *(Aside.)* Ah, Father in Heaven! Such is my woe,
This child here breaks my heart in sunder.

ISAAC: Tell me, my dear father, so that ye cease—
Bear ye a heavy thought for me?

ABRAHAM: Ah Isaac! Sweet son, peace, peace!
Thou breakest my heart in three!

ISAAC: Now truly, on something, Father, I think,
That we mourn thus more and more.

ABRAHAM: Ah, Lord of Heaven, let Thy grace sink
For my heart was never half so sore!

ISAAC: I pray ye, Father, that ye will let me know
Whether I shall have any harm or no.

ABRAHAM: Alas, sweet son, I may not tell thee yet,
My heart is now so full of woe!

ISAAC: Dear Father, I pray you, hide it not from me,
But some of your thought, I pray tell me.

ABRAHAM: Ah, Isaac, Isaac, I must kill thee!

ISAAC: Kill me, Father? Alas, what have I done?
If I have trespassed against you aught,
With a rod ye may make me full mild;
And with your passions kill me naught,
For my life's begun; I am but a child.

ABRAHAM: I am full sorry, son, thy blood for to spill,
But truly, child, I may not as I please.

ISAAC: Now I would to God my mother were here on this hill.
She would drop down on both her knees
To save my life.
And since my mother is absent
Think of your own mind, repent,
And kill me not with any knife.

ABRAHAM: Forsooth, my son, save I thee kill,
I should grieve God right sore, I dread,
It is His commandment and also His will.

ISAAC: I would say that ye lie—
But that dye is not given to our weave.
Is it God's will that I should be slain?

ABRAHAM: Yea, truly, Isaac, my son so sweet!
I do not know who to ask forgiveness.

ISAAC: Now Father, against my Lord's will,
I will never question, loud or still.
He might have granted me a better destiny,
If it had been His pleasure.

ABRAHAM: Forsooth, son, but that I obey,
Grievously displeased our Lord would be.

ISAAC: Nay, nay, Father, God forbid
That ever ye should grieve Him for me!
I pray you, Father, make you no woe;
For, be I once dead and from you go,
I shall soon be out of your mind.
Therefore do our Lord's bidding,
And when I am dead, then pray for me.
But, good Father, tell ye my mother nothing,
Say that I am in another country dwelling.
Now into a vision should you send
And think of me not as a boy.

ABRAHAM: Ah, Isaac, Isaac, I beg for comfort!
My heart beginneth wildly to rise
To see the blood of my blessed body!

ISAAC: Father, since it may be no otherwise,
Let it pass over as well as I.
But, Father, ere I go unto my death,
I pray you bless me with your hand.

(ABRAHAM does so.)

ABRAHAM: Now, Isaac, with all my breath
My blessing I give thee upon this land,
And may God also thereto add His.
Isaac, Isaac, son up thou stand,
Thy fair sweet mouth that I may kiss.

ISAAC: Now farewell, my own father so fine,
And greet well my mother on Earth,
But I pray you Father, to hide my eyne
That I see not the stroke of your sharp sword
That my flesh shall defile.

ABRAHAM: Son, they words make me weep full sore;
Now my dear son Isaac, speak no more.

ISAAC: Yet, my dear father, to you I pray,
Smite but few strokes at my head
And make an end as soon as ye may
So I might be in Heaven ere long.

ABRAHAM: They meek words, child, bring me dismay;
So "welaway" must be my song.
Except alone for God's will.
Ah! Isaac my own sweet child,
Kiss me yet again upon this hill;
In all the world in none so mild!

ISAAC: I pray you Father, make an ending.
Each loving moment makes me miss my life!
Now hurry and bring forth your knife
So I might not be further fearing.

ABRAHAM: Come up, sweet son, unto my arm.
I must bind thy hands too
Although thou be never so mild.

ISAAC: Ah, mercy Father! Why should ye do so?

ABRAHAM: That thou shouldst not stay me, my child.

ISAAC: Indeed, nay, Father, I will not stay you.
Do on, for me, your will;
And on the purpose that ye have set you,
For God's Love, keep it steadfast still.

ABRAHAM: Ah! Isaac, Isaac, son, thou makest me grieve,
And with thy words thou so distemperest me.

ISAAC: Indeed, sweet Father, I am sorry to grieve you;
I cry you mercy for what I have done,
And for all trespass ever I did so.
Now, dear Father, forgive all I have done—
God of Heaven be with me!

ABRAHAM: Ah! Dear child, leave off thy moans!
In all thy life thou grieved me ever once.
Now blessed be thou, body and bones,
That ever thou were bred and born;
Thou hast been to me child full good.
But in truth, child, thou I mourn never so fast,
Yes must I needs here at the last.
In this place shed all thy blood;

Therefore, my dear son, here shalt thou lie—
Unto my work I must proceed.
In truth, I had as lief myself to die
If God were pleased with the deed
That I my own body should offer.

ISAAC: Ah, mercy, Father, mourn ye no more;
Your weeping maketh my heart sore
That mine own death I am to suffer.
Your kerchief, Father, about my eyes wind.

ABRAHAM: So I shall, my sweetest child on Earth.

ISAAC: Now yet, good Father, have this in mind,
And smite me not often with your sharp sword,
But hastily that it be sped.

ABRAHAM: (Covering ISAAC's face.) Now farewell,
    my child so full of grace.

ISAAC: Ah, Father, turn downward my face,
For of Heaven I am near in hand!

ABRAHAM: To do this deed I am full sorry,
But, Lord, thine behest I will not withstand.

ISAAC: Ah! Father of Heaven to Thee I cry.
Lord, receive me Thou into Thy Land!

ABRAHAM: Lo, now is the time come for certain,
That my sword in his neck shall bite.
Ah, Lord! My heart riseth there again,
I may not find it in my heart to smite.
My heart will not now thereto!
Ah, fain I would work my Lord's will
But this young innocent lies so still,
I may not find it in my heart to kill him.
Oh, Father of Heaven! What shall I do?

ISAAC: Ah, mercy Father, question Him not.
And let me lie there so long on this heath?
Now I would God the stroke were done also;
Father, heartily I pray you, shorten my woe,
And let me not wait thus for my death.

ABRAHAM: Now, heart, why wouldst thou not break
    in three?
Yet shalt thou not make me to my God unmild.
I will no longer stay for thee,
For that my God aggrieved would be.
Now have thy stroke, my own dear child.

(ABRAHAM raises his hand firmly, at last, to make
his sacrifice. Upon the very moment of the stroke, an
ANGEL appears. He indicates himself as the Lamb to
which he refers.)

ANGEL (LAMB): I am an Angel, thou mayest see blithe,
That from Heaven to thee is sent.
Our Lord Thanketh thee a hundred time
For the keeping of His commandment.
He knoweth thy will, and also thy heart,
That thou dreadst him above all thing;
And some of thy heaviness for to depart
A fair lamb yonder did he bring;
He standeth, lo, among the briars tied.
Now, Abraham, amend thy mood
For Isaac, thy young son, here by thy side
This day shall not shed his blood.

ABRAHAM: Ah Lord! I thank Thee for Thy great
   grace,
Now am I eased in divers wise.
Arise up, Isaac, my dear son, arise,
Arise up, sweet child, and come to me!

ISAAC: Ah, mercy, Father, why smite ye naught?
Ah, smite on, Father, I await the knife!

ABRAHAM: Peace, my sweet son, and take no thought,
For our Lord of Heaven hath granted life
By His Angel now,
That thou shalt not die this day, son, truly.

ISAAC: An Angel comes?

ABRAHAM: An Angel as another Lamb
Has arrived here to send us home.

ISAAC: Ah, Father, full glad then were I;
In truth, Father—I say, I wish
That this tale were true!

ABRAHAM: A hundred times, my son fair of hue,
For Joy thy mouth now will I kiss.

ISAAC: Ah, my dear father Abraham,
Will not God be wroth that we do thus?

ABRAHAM: No, no! It is His will for us!
For yon same lamb He hath now sent
Hither down to us.
Yon beast shall die here in thy stead,
In the worship of our Lord, alone.
Go fetch him hither, my child, indeed.

ISAAC: Father, I will go seize him by the head,
And bring yon beast with me anon.
Ah sheep, sheep, blessed may thou be,
That ever thou were sent down hither!
Thou shalt this day die for me,
In worship of our Deity.

Though thou be never so gentle and good,
Yet I had liefer thou shed thy blood
In truth, sheep, than I!
But Lord God, I thank Thee with all my heart!
For I am glad that I shall live,
To spread this lesson to all those with ears.

(GOD, who has been watching from afar, approaches
and takes the sacrificial items from ABRAHAM. As
He speaks, He prepares to make sacrifice of the ANGEL
Himself.)

GOD: Abraham, Abraham, mayest thou speed,
And Isaac, thy young son, thee by!
My servants both receive this compliment
Of perfect recompense for compliance.
For willingness to lose a son
I give them twentyfold of that was gone.
Truly, Abraham, for this deed,
I shall multiply both your seed
As thick as stars be in the sky,
Both of bigger and less.
And as thick as gravel in the sea,
So thick multiplied your seed shall be;
This grant I you for your goodness.
And so this world shall come from yours
And upon this great sea, have oars
To spread upon the oceans, seas
To overtake the rocks and trees.
Of you shall come fruit unknown,
And ever be in bliss without end,
For ye dread Me as God alone
And keep My commandments, every one.
My blessing I give wheresoever ye wend!

ABRAHAM: Lo, Isaac, my son, how think ye
Of this work that we have wrought?
Full glad and blithe may we be
That 'gainst the will of God we muttered nought
On this fair heath.

ISAAC: Ah, Father, I thank our Lord every deal
That my wit served me so well
For God to fear more than my death.

ABRAHAM: Why, dear worthy son, wert thou afraid?
Boldly, child, tell me thy lore.

ISAAC: Yea! By my faith, Father, be it said,
I was never so afraid before
As I have been on yon hill!
Ah, by my faith, Father, I swear
I will nevermore come there,
Except it be against my will.

ABRAHAM: Yes, come on with me, my own sweet
    son,
And homeward fast let us be gone.

ISAAC: By my faith, Father, hereto I agree!
I had never such goodwill to go home,
And to speak with my dear mother!

ABRAHAM: Ah, Lord of Heaven, I thank Thee,
For now I may lead home with me
Isaac, my young son so free,
The gentlest child above all other—
This may avowed be.
Now, go we forth, my blessed son.

*(GOD lowers the ANGEL [LAMB] into position. ANGEL
prepares for death and speaks to the audience.)*

ANGEL: Lo, now sovereigns and sirs, thus did we show
This solemn story to great and small.
It is a good lesson for both learned and low,
And even for the wisest of us all,
Without any barring.
For this story showeth you deep
How to our best power we should keep
God's commandments without doubting.
Think ye, if God sent an Angel,
And commanded you your child to slay,
By your truth, is there any of you

That would balk or gainsay?
How think ye now sirs, thereby?
For even as a Lamb, I am His Child
So are well all, for by God we exist.
His children sacrificed in anywhile
Shall give the other children their subsist.
There be three or four or more, I trow,
And those women than weep so sorrowfully
When that their children for them die
As nature takes of our kind,
It is folly, as I may well avow,
Against God to grudge or to grieve so low;
For ye shall never see them mischiefed, well I know,
By land or water—have this in mind.

(GOD raises His hand to deliver the stroke.)

And grudge not against our Lord God,
In wealth or woe whatever He you send
Though ye be never so hard bestead;
For when He willeth, He may it amend.
His commandments truly if ye keep with good soul.
As this story hath now showed you before,
And faithfully serve Him, while ye be whole,
That ye may please God both even and morn.

(The stroke comes as the lights go black.)

(End.)

THE EUMENIDES

by Aeschylus

Freely Adapted by David Johnston

DAVID JOHNSTON is a playwright and actor. He was born in 1964 in Lexington, Kentucky, and raised in Richmond, Virginia. He says he cannot remember a time when he did not want to be involved in the theatre. He earned a BA from the College of William and Mary, with a concentration in theatre and a minor in psychology, and a certificate of completion from the Professional Workshop at Circle in the Square Theater School. For more than a decade, Johnston has also been a member of Charles Maryan's Playwrights/Directors Workshop. His writing credits include *Busted Jesus Comix* (2002/2003, Moving Arts, Los Angeles; 2003/2005, Blue Coyote Theater Group, New York), *A Bush Carol, or George Dubya and the Xmas of Evil* (2003, Blue Coyote Theater Group), and *Candy & Dorothy* (2004, Rude Guerilla, Los Angeles; 2006, Theatre Three, New York). Johnston received a 2003 Arch & Bruce Brown Foundation Award for *Candy & Dorothy* and a 2005 GLAAD Award nomination for Best Off-Off Broadway Production for *Busted Jesus Comix*. He has also received playwriting grants from both the Berrilla Kerr Foundation and the Ludwig Vogelstein Foundation. *Candy & Dorothy* will reopen for an Off-Broadway run in 2007, and Johnston's adaptation of *The Oresteia* (including *The Eumenides*) will be produced by the Blue Coyote Theater Group in early 2007. Johnston lives on Manhattan's Upper West Side.

The Eumenides was first commissioned and presented by Theater Faction (Erik Nelson and Yuval Sharon, Co-Artistic Directors) as part of their trilogy *Oresteia* on January 15, 2004, at the American Theater of Actors, New York City, with the following cast and credits:

Orestes	Beau Allulli
Apollo	Michael Bell
Athena	Lori Lane Jefferson
Clytemnestra	Kathy Lichter
Eumenides	Vivian Manning, Nell Gwynn, Heidi McAllister
Priestess	Courtney Keim

Directed by: Kevin Newbury
Lighting Design: Greg Emetaz
Set Design: Katya Blumenberg
Costume Design: Jessica Jahn

Note: David Johnston's adaptation of all three parts of *Oresteia*, including *Agamemnon* and *The Libation Bearers*, will premiere early in 2007, produced by Blue Coyote Theater Group.

Scene: Darkness. In the middle is an altar. On top stands APOLLO, frozen, arms akimbo. He is young, handsome, blonde, wearing a tailored suit and sunglasses. Outside the area of the altar is THE PRIESTESS OF THE TEMPLE OF APOLLO. She is lightly and happily sprinkling herbs and grains in a bowl. She pours out wine, ready to make her offering to the gods.

PRIESTESS: Now let us come together to worship and praise.

(She offers up the bowl. ORESTES runs on on all fours. He is young. His clothes are filthy rags. He is covered with dirt and blood. He falls into a heap on the floor. He is panting, sobbing. He quickly strips and begins to wash himself from a bowl. A WOMAN emerges from the darkness. She carries another bowl and a cloth. She is bleeding from her breast. She stands behind him and strokes his head gently. She speaks while she wets the cloth with the blood in the bowl. She slowly wipes his head with the cloth.)

ORESTES: I'm so tired.

CLYTEMNESTRA: I know, baby.

ORESTES: Why don't they stop.

CLYTEMNESTRA: They can't, honey. They don't know how.

ORESTES: I'm so tired.

CLYTEMNESTRA: Why are you tired?

ORESTES: Tired. Running.

CLYTEMNESTRA: What are you thinking of? What's bothering you?

ORESTES: Nets. Snakes. Dogs.

CLYTEMNESTRA: Don't think of that.

ORESTES: I can't help it.

CLYTEMNESTRA: That's not good, baby. Nets. Don't think of that. That's awful.

ORESTES: It's all I can think of. Nets. Snakes. Dogs.

CLYTEMNESTRA: Think of something happy.

ORESTES: Like what?

CLYTEMNESTRA: Your home. Your family. How much they love you.

ORESTES: That doesn't help.

CLYTEMNESTRA: Come on now. Everyone loves their home. Everyone loves their family.

ORESTES: That really doesn't help.

CLYTEMNESTRA: Then if that doesn't help. Think of your Momma. Orestes. Think of your Momma and how much she loves you.

(ORESTES turns and faces her.)

CLYTEMNESTRA: Just say the word. Mother.

(ORESTES turns and sees her, sees the blood she has been wiping on him. A shriek. The EUMENIDES enter, crawling on all fours, hissing and whispering. CLYTEMNESTRA watches them circle ORESTES. ORESTES, naked, runs to the altar, and clutches the feet of the god APOLLO, trying to cover himself. PRIESTESS continues her ceremony, oblivious to the goings-on in the temple.)

PRIESTESS: Now let us praise the Goddess of the Earth, giver of all that is life sustaining.

(The EUMENIDES sniff the air and whisper, surrounding ORESTES without touching him. CLYTEMNESTRA watches silently from the darkness.)

ORESTES: Think of the net, Orestes.

PRIESTESS: Praises to the Law, which gives order to our mortal lives.

EUMENIDES #1: *(A whisper.)* Matricide.

EUMENIDES #2: Matricide.

EUMENIDES #3: Matricide.

(They circle ORESTES.)

PRIESTESS *(Making the offering.)* Praises to the Law.

ORESTES: Think of the net. Away from his home. All those long years. My father. A hero. Fighting for his brother, his honor, his whore of a sister-in-law. Ten long years by the city walls. Ships wrecked heads split friends dead health shattered youth gone. And then home. Home. Think of the net, Orestes.

EUMENIDES #2: Matricide.

ORESTES: Think of the net.

PRIESTESS: And finally all honor and praise to Glorious Apollo.

(Lights up on the frozen figure of APOLLO. He smiles beatifically.)

PRIESTESS: Praise to our Glorious Lord Apollo!

EUMENIDES #1: Snake.

ORESTES: Home kingdom fire hearth servants who smiled at him. Yes sir no sir. A hearty meal wine maybe his dog. A good faithful dog. Everyone loves dogs. Dogs are faithful.

EUMENIDES #2: Mother killer.

ORESTES: His children. Do they still love him? After all these years? Oh yes they love him. And let's not forget…

EUMENIDES #3: Matricide.

ORESTES: The little woman.

CLYTEMNESTRA: Mother.

ORESTES: What did he want? A bath.

APOLLO: All will be well.

ORESTES: Hi honey I'm home. A nice warm bath. Don't think of her.

CLYTEMNESTRA: Mother.

ORESTES: Don't think of her.

CLYTEMNESTRA: And how much she loves you.

ORESTES: Don't think of them.

EUMENIDES #1: Hi honey I'm home.

ORESTES: They're not here. Don't think of them. Don't think of her.

APOLLO: All will be well.

ORESTES: I'm right. I'm right. I did right.

EUMENIDES #2: Right.

ORESTES: Nothing can harm you if you're right.

APOLLO: All manner of thing will be well.

ORESTES: Just think of the net.

APOLLO: Go to sleep.

(*The EUMENIDES collapse in a heap on the floor, snoring.*)

PRIESTESS: Glorious Lord Apollo, and his gift of prophecy, Lord Apollo, who speaks through me on this day!

(*PRIESTESS exits. APOLLO steps down from his pedestal and speaks to ORESTES. CLYTEMNESTRA continues to watch, silently.*)

APOLLO: You worry too much, Orestes. I tell you I'll protect you. Every word that comes out of my mouth is the truth. You can count on me. Oh no they're gonna get me help me help me. Relax. I will never abandon you.

ORESTES: You never said. No one ever told me…

APOLLO: You worry too much. Now. The Eumenides.

ORESTES: Who are they?

APOLLO: Spirits of vengeance. Primitive earth goddesses. Daughters of the Night. Chthonic if you will. There's a word for you. Chthonic. Nobody likes 'em. Despised of gods and men. Born of darkness and evil. Their bodies secrete a foul poison. They had their purpose, I suppose. But they're ancient history. We don't do things like that anymore.

ORESTES: I thought we could…

APOLLO: One thing about primitive earth goddesses. They don't stop. Ever. Not until they've dragged you screaming and partially disemboweled into the underworld. They can't stop. It's not in their nature. Just like it's not in your nature to let your mother live.

ORESTES: I didn't…

APOLLO: I'm kidding. Relax. You worry too much. Here is what you're going to do. You're going to flee to the Temple of Athena—

ORESTES: You said—

APOLLO: Let me finish.

ORESTES: You said, if I came here, if I was purified, if we did the blood offering that would purify me, that would cleanse me of my crime of killing—

CLYTEMNESTRA: Mother.

ORESTES: —if we did the purification it would…

APOLLO: It didn't take. No crying over spilled milk. Onward and upward. The Temple of Athena and if I were you I'd step on it. They're not gonna sleep forever. There you'll clutch the image at the altar. There you will find judges. Just men. Citizens. You'll tell 'em what happened. This whole thing will be cleared up. And you're off to assume the throne of Argos. It'll be like none of this ever happened.

ORESTES: You told me to kill—

CLYTEMNESTRA: Mother.

APOLLO: Yes.

ORESTES: And Electra, Electra told me, what happens to Electra…

APOLLO: I told you to kill her. Electra told you to kill her. And you were the one who plunged a knife into your mother's breast. Several times. Let's keep things in perspective, Orestes. Be a man. Now run.

(ORESTES turns, sees CLYTEMNESTRA, and runs. APOLLO exits after him. CLYTEMNESTRA begins berating the sleeping EUMENIDES, who occasionally hiss and snore in their sleep.)

CLYTEMNESTRA: Was ever woman so wronged as Clytemnestra? Awake! Awake! I led you to him and you failed. In the Underworld, they mock me, hissed at, spat at, by the common filth not allowed in my sight on earth. They scorn me to my face as murderess adulteress while my Iphigenia watches and will not speak to me.

(The EUMENIDES mumble in their sleep.)

EUMENIDES #1: Matricide.

EUMENIDES #2: Gouge them.

EUMENIDES #1: Impale.

EUMENIDES #3: Hmm. Yes. That one dies.

CLYTEMNESTRA: How long will you shirk your duties, poisonous old bitches? A Queen slaughtered by her child. What God is indignant for the crimes done against me? Not Apollo. Look upon these wounds. My child did this. Does it prick your conscience? WAKE UP! The sacrifices I made the gods, all for nothing, for a mouthful of ashes. None hear Clytemnestra's pleas for justice. He is gone, gone—flew out of the trap as light as air, now he laughs at me and the wounds in my throat and breast bleed again. My Orestes, my snake.

(CLYTEMNESTRA exits. The EUMENIDES awake with a start.)

EUMENIDES #1: Wake up!

EUMENIDES #2: Awake!

EUMENIDES #3: Awake!

EUMENIDES #1: He's gone!

EUMENIDES #2: Gone!

EUMENIDES #3: Gone!

EUMENIDES #1: Apollo!

EUMENIDES #2: It's Apollo's doing!

EUMENIDES #3: Gloating, vain…

EUMENIDES #1: No respect, no respect for the old ways!

EUMENIDES #2: Thief! Thief!

EUMENIDES #3: Hiding a matricide!

EUMENIDES #1: This is not how it's done!

EUMENIDES #2: Allowing blood to go unavenged!

EUMENIDES #3: Not how a god behaves!

EUMENIDES #1: Trickster! Foolish wicked child!

EUMENIDES #2: And in his own temple! Polluting his own temple with a matricide!

EUMENIDES #3: A man drenched in the blood of his mother!

EUMENIDES #1: Breathe, sisters. Breathe. Take my hands.

(They breathe. Take each other's hands.)

EUMENIDES #1: Now let me catechize you, sisters. Why does a man act justly?

EUMENIDES #2: Fear.

EUMENIDES #1: And what does a man fear?

EUMENIDES #3: Us.

EUMENIDES #1: Therefore, who needs us?

EUMENIDES #2: Mankind needs us.

EUMENIDES #1: Why?

EUMENIDES #2: Without us, they will not act justly.

EUMENIDES #1: Who else needs us?

EUMENIDES #3: The gods, old and new, need us.

EUMENIDES #1: The gods do not fear us. The gods are above justice. Why do they need us?

EUMENIDES #2: Without us, no man will fear them.

EUMENIDES #1: Why else?

EUMENIDES #3: We do the work they dare not do.

EUMENIDES #2: We do the work that would dirty their hands.

EUMENIDES #1: How do we do this work?

EUMENIDES #2: Without resting.

EUMENIDES #3: Without stopping.

EUMENIDES #2: We do this work with joy and a cheerful heart.

EUMENIDES #1: Where can the criminal hide?

EUMENIDES #2: Under the earth.

EUMENIDES #3: Among the stars.

EUMENIDES #2: At the bottom of the sea.

EUMENIDES #1: And what will happen to the criminal hidden under the earth, among the stars, at the bottom of the sea?

EUMENIDES #2: We will find him.

EUMENIDES #3: We will never leave him.

EUMENIDES #2: We are inside him already.

EUMENIDES #3: We work upon him.

EUMENIDES #1: Why do we do this, my sisters?

EUMENIDES #2 and #3: It is our natures.

(Pause.)

EUMENIDES #1: Now we fly.

(EUMENIDES exit. APOLLO reenters.)

APOLLO: *(As before.)* The Temple of Athena and if I were you I'd step on it.

(THE PRIESTESS OF THE TEMPLE OF ATHENA enters. She prepares her offering. ORESTES enters, alone in the Temple of Athena.)

PRIESTESS: Now let us worship and praise Athena. Athena born of no woman but sprung from the head of Zeus, Athena who gives us skill and strategy in war, who loves our city-state of Athens, Athena from whom all justice springs—

APOLLO: There you'll clutch the image at the altar. There you will find judges. Just men. Citizens. You'll tell 'em what happened. This whole thing will be cleared up.

ORESTES: *(Addressing the altar of Athena.)* I come in the name of Apollo.

PRIESTESS: Athena, Protector of the city of Athens.

ORESTES: I am a refugee. I ask for sanctuary.

PRIESTESS: Athena, Defender of Civilization.

ORESTES: I have been purified. I am clean.

PRIESTESS: Athena, Patron Goddess of Handicrafts and Agriculture.

ORESTES: I am clean to enter your house.

PRIESTESS: She even invented the bridle, so that we may ride horses!

ORESTES: I beg your mercy. Save me from the furious dogs of my— Merciful Athena. I am so. Tired.

APOLLO: And you're off to assume the throne of Argos.

ORESTES: I did as the Oracle of Apollo told me. I did as I was told. My father was a hero. I was right to do as I was told.

APOLLO: It'll be like none of this ever happened.

(APOLLO exits. PRIESTESS enters the temple, sees ORESTES.)

PRIESTESS: Have you been purified?

ORESTES: Yes.

PRIESTESS: Then Athena will be with you shortly.

(PRIESTESS leaves. The EUMENIDES enter and chase ORESTES to the altar of Athena.)

EUMENIDES #1: There you are.

EUMENIDES #2: Hi Orestes.

EUMENIDES #3: Whatcha doin'?

EUMENIDES #1: Matricide.

EUMENIDES #2: Murderer.

EUMENIDES #3: Clutching another altar, Orestes?

EUMENIDES #1: You clutch a lot of altars.

EUMENIDES #2: Murderer.

EUMENIDES #3: Matricide.

EUMENIDES #1: Think that'll do the trick?

EUMENIDES #2: Clutching the altar?

EUMENIDES #3: Think that'll get rid of us?

EUMENIDES #1: Did you miss us?

(*They lunge for ORESTES. ATHENA enters. She is solid, young, handsomely built, and no bullshit. The EUMENIDES stop when she speaks.*)

ATHENA: I heard a cry as I stood by the river, the river that runs by the ruins of Troy. You at my altar—who are you? State your business. And you—creatures that cannot be described. What brings you to my temple?

EUMENIDES #1: Great Athena, Daughter of Zeus, we are the Daughters of the Night. We live deep within the earth. We come for him.

ATHENA: I have heard of you.

EUMENIDES #2: Then you know we bring justice to men, who would otherwise follow their natures.

ATHENA: Okay. (*Turns to ORESTES.*) And who are you?

EUMENIDES #3: He is a murderer. He pollutes your house.

EUMENIDES #1: He is one who chose to commit the most heinous crime of all.

EUMENIDES #2: Who chose to murder his own mother.

(*ATHENA addresses ORESTES, who is turned away from her.*)

ATHENA: Is this true?

ORESTES: Yes.

ATHENA: Why did you do such a thing?

EUMENIDES #3: The why is not important. The deed is important.

ATHENA: I do not agree and you have already spoken. (*To ORESTES.*) You.

(*ORESTES turns to her.*)

ATHENA: Dear God, you're a child. (*Pause.*) Did you kill your mother?

ORESTES: Yes.

ATHENA: Who are you? And who are your people?

ORESTES: I am Orestes, of the House of Atreus.

ATHENA: The House of Atreus?

ORESTES: Yes.

ATHENA: Tantalus, who chopped us his son Pelops and fed him to the gods?

ORESTES: My great-great-grandfather.

ATHENA: Atreus, who killed his brother's children and served them to their father?

ORESTES: His son was great Agamemnon, a hero of Troy, my father a hero—a soldier—and a great hero—he led many—

ATHENA: He murdered his daughter, right?

ORESTES: What?

ATHENA: Agamemnon. He murdered his daughter, Iphigenia. Your sister. Cut her throat, right?

ORESTES: She was sacrificed. Yes. For strong winds to take brave men home.

ATHENA: He murdered her for a strong wind?

(*ORESTES is silent.*)

ATHENA: And why did you kill your mother?

ORESTES: She took a lover in her husband's absence. While he fought—the war—all those years at the city gates she took a lover. He returned home a hero. From Troy. Triumphant. She murdered him. While he bathed. The net. A nice warm bath. And the net. My father no soldier's death just a woman the net the bathtub he was a hero of Troy Agamemnon my father a hero I am so tired running—

ATHENA: You must compose yourself.

(*Beat.*)

ATHENA: Then what did you do?

ORESTES: The prophet of Apollo spoke to me told me I must avenge my father's death. He was a hero. Heroes must be avenged. Fathers must be avenged. I had to. Avenge him. Electra helped Electra my sister helped I killed Aegisthus and Clytemnestra—

ATHENA: Your sister helped?

ORESTES: Yes.

ATHENA: Some family you got, kid.

EUMENIDES #1: You waste the goddess's time, Orestes.

EUMENIDES #2: He chose to murder his mother, Athena.

EUMENIDES #3: Give him to us.

ORESTES: Apollo is responsible.

EUMENIDES #1: Apollo. That whimpering baby.

EUMENIDES #2: That arrogant child.

ORESTES: Apollo told me to!

EUMENIDES #3: (Mocking him.) "Apollo told me to!"

EUMENIDES #1: Why don't you think for yourself for once?

EUMENIDES #2: Violated the ties of blood. His mother!

ORESTES: She murdered her husband.

EUMENIDES #3: The ties of marriage are nothing compared with the ties of blood.

ATHENA: Peace, all of you. This will not be. He comes purified to my temple as a suppliant and a refugee. I cannot turn him away. And you are my predecessors the elder goddesses whom I must revere.

EUMENIDES #1: Good. Give him to us.

EUMENIDES #3: Finally. A little action.

ATHENA: This is too large for gods to decide.

EUMENIDES #2: Too large?

ATHENA: Too large for gods. Men must decide.

EUMENIDES #1: Men?

EUMENIDES #2: Men?

ATHENA: I will gather twelve just men of my city. You will speak. Orestes will speak. The citizens will decide. If there is no majority, I will cast the deciding vote.

EUMENIDES #3: Men cannot judge other men!

EUMENIDES #2: Hyenas cannot sit in judgment on other hyenas!

EUMENIDES #1: They do not know justice without us!

ATHENA: I will return. I will bring the citizens. When you speak, be brief and clear. (Leaves.)

EUMENIDES #1: It's a happy day, Orestes.

EUMENIDES #2: A happy day. Men will judge you.

EUMENIDES #3: Other men.

EUMENIDES #1: We know what they will say.

EUMENIDES #2: Men love murder.

ORESTES: Leave me alone.

EUMENIDES #3: They will set you free. It's a new world!

EUMENIDES #1: Is it to your liking, Orestes?

EUMENIDES #2: A world where children wash their hands in the blood of their parents?

ORESTES: I had no choice.

EUMENIDES #3: Every murdering child will praise your name, Orestes.

EUMENIDES #1: You set them free.

EUMENIDES #2: Crime will flow like honey.

EUMENIDES #3: Your mother must be so proud.

ORESTES: Please stop.

EUMENIDES #1: A new world—a world where everyone will act according to their wishes.

EUMENIDES #2: According to their natures.

EUMENIDES #3: Won't that be nice?

EUMENIDES #1: And when they raise up their sticky hands from the slaughtered bodies of their parents, all will cry—

ORESTES: I can't bear it.

EUMENIDES #3: "Praise to Orestes, who set us free—"

EUMENIDES #1, #2, #3: "—to follow our true natures!"

(ATHENA reenters with APOLLO.)

APOLLO: Enough!

EUMENIDES #1: Apollo!

APOLLO: Quiet, sickness! Filth!

EUMENIDES #2: What is he doing here?

EUMENIDES #3: This is not your domain!

EUMENIDES #2: Get out of this house, Apollo!

APOLLO: Poisonous old dogs, don't you know your time is past?

ATHENA: Apollo!

APOLLO: You have been replaced. You and your mad rantings of revenge and blood and motherhood. Spiteful, ridiculous, deranged old bitches to be swept away!

ATHENA: *(Explodes.)* ENOUGH! *(Pause.)* In my temple, you will speak to the elder goddesses with respect, brother. Respect befitting their age and position in the world. Or you will deal with me.

APOLLO: *(Sulks.)* I come to speak on behalf of my follower, Orestes.

(ATHENA sets the stage for the trial. PRIESTESS enters and distributes ballots to twelve male members of the audience.)

ATHENA: This trial has begun. You, my sisters and elders, you will speak first. You may ask whatever questions you like of the witness.

EUMENIDES #1: *(Approaches ORESTES.)* Did you kill your mother?

ORESTES: Yes.

EUMENIDES #1: How did you kill her?

ORESTES: I plunged my sword in her breast. I cut her throat.

EUMENIDES #1: Show me.

ORESTES: In her breast.

EUMENIDES #1: *(Walks to him.)* Show me.

(ORESTES points with his fingers.)

EUMENIDES #1: Touch.

ORESTES: Here. *(Then the throat.)* And here.

EUMENIDES #1: On whose orders did you kill her?

ORESTES: I did this on Apollo's orders. I have never denied this.

EUMENIDES #1: You'll wish you had, little boy.

ATHENA: Ask a question.

EUMENIDES #1: Why did you kill her?

ORESTES: She murdered her husband. My father. A hero.

EUMENIDES #1: She's dead now.

ORESTES: Yes.

EUMENIDES #1: She's paid the price.

ORESTES: Yes.

EUMENIDES #1: Then so must you.

ORESTES: No.

EUMENIDES #1: She dies you go free? Free to walk to and fro upon the earth?

EUMENIDES #2: And kill again?

EUMENIDES #3: You perfect and upright man?

EUMENIDES #2: Free to rule the city of Argos?

ORESTES: Why didn't you come after her? She'd committed murder. She lived as the queen while fucking my father's cousin. Why me?

ATHENA: Orestes—

ORESTES: No that fucking whore sat in the palace for ten years, rooting around in bed like a sow, stewed in corruption. Then when my father when Great Agamemnon a hero came home after the war—did she fall to her knees beg forgiveness? Forgive her for the disgrace? Or did she creep up behind him while he bathed and trap him like a wild pig? She even murdered the servant girl he brought from Troy—why didn't you avenge her?

ATHENA: Orestes—

ORESTES: Why didn't you come after her? She was a murderer. She was an adulterer. She was dripping with blood. Why me? Am I worse?

EUMENIDES #1: Much worse. *(Pause.)* The ties of marriage are not the ties of blood. Her blood flowed to you in the womb. Gave you life. You fed from her breast.

EUMENIDES #2: These mysteries are sacred. The ties of blood and motherhood are sacred.

EUMENIDES #1: Marriage? A civil contract.

EUMENIDES #3: A means to legitimize children in the eyes of the neighbors.

EUMENIDES #2: A consolidation of property.

EUMENIDES #1: But blood.

EUMENIDES #2: Blood.

EUMENIDES #1: Much much worse what you have done. If this is unknown to you, then my sisters and I will joyfully and cheerfully endeavor to teach you the importance of the law. *(She turns to the others.)* Why do we do this, my sisters?

EUMENIDES #2 and #3: It is our natures.

(Pause.)

ATHENA: Apollo?

APOLLO: I shall speak justly. I am a god, and no word shall fall from my mouth that is not the truth. My prophets speak only from the will of my father, the will of Great Zeus himself. This was his will and that supersedes all other oaths and bonds. *(Pause.)* I suppose that's it.

EUMENIDES #2: Zeus ordered the prophets to speak to Orestes, ordered him to avenge his father on his mother?

APOLLO: Yes.

EUMENIDES #2: And then everything would be fine.

APOLLO: Death is not the same thing for a man. A man—a great warrior a king—must die in battle or from the ravages of time. Not from the blow of a woman.

EUMENIDES #2: So it was the way he was killed.

EUMENIDES #3: Not that he was killed.

APOLLO: It is also the fact that—

EUMENIDES #2: Zeus feels the father is that important.

APOLLO: Yes.

EUMENIDES #2: Taking precedence over all.

APOLLO: Yes.

EUMENIDES #2: Yet Zeus imprisoned his own father, kept Cronus as a prisoner.

APOLLO: He could let him out if he chose—

EUMENIDES #2: Kept him shackled in the earth. His own father. Great Zeus does not feel this important for his own father—

APOLLO: Shut up stop this right—

ATHENA: *(A warning.)* Apollo—

EUMENIDES #2: Imprisoned his father—

EUMENIDES #3: Then castrated him!

EUMENIDES #2: That's how Zeus treats the father!

APOLLO: How dare you—how dare you put yourselves above Great Zeus!

EUMENIDES #1: We were ancient when Zeus came into being, you pampered little brat. We did our work proudly and joyfully while you were howling for your mother's milk.

EUMENIDES #2: Without us, your power over men would vanish. Remember that and show gratitude.

EUMENIDES #3: One such as this— *(Pointing to ORESTES.)* —shall he now rule Argos after breaking the oldest law of blood? Who will honor one such as this? What lesson will he teach to the children of his city?

ATHENA: Peace. Both of you. I have heard enough. The citizens will make their decision. Have you said all you wish to say?

EUMENIDES #1: We have.

APOLLO: I'm finished.

ATHENA: The citizens will cast their votes. *(She speaks to the audience.)* I advise my people—do not cast fear from your city, nor govern unjustly or without mercy. This court is yours. Do not muddy the well you may drink of someday.

(PRIESTESS gathers up the votes from the audience members. She carries them to ATHENA, with a low bow.)

ATHENA: If there is a tie, I shall cast the deciding vote.

APOLLO: Sister, I have sent one as a suppliant to stand by your house. I hope you will not betray me.

EUMENIDES #1: We hope you will not betray your sex, and not upend the laws, which have held true and firm.

(ATHENA counts out the votes one by one, putting them in separate piles.)

EUMENIDES #2: Justice. We pray for justice.

APOLLO: You will be acquitted. I am sure of it.

ORESTES: My father was a hero.

ATHENA: The votes are tied.

ORESTES: This is my end.

ATHENA: I will cast the deciding vote.

APOLLO: You will not turn your back on my follower.

EUMENIDES #3: Justice, great Athena. An eye for an eye.

ATHENA: An eye for an eye. For an eye. For an eye. For an eye. *(Seems infinitely weary for an instant.)* Tantalus. Pelops. Atreus. Thyestes. Agamemnon. Iphigenia. Cassandra. Clytemnestra. Aegisthus. Orestes.

EUMENIDES #2: Blood must have blood.

EUMENIDES #3: Revenge is just. Otherwise, how will men learn?

ATHENA: Blood—revenge. Blood—revenge. And on. And on. Oh my gracious elder goddesses, HOW WILL WE STOP? *(Pause.)* I was born of no woman. I have no mother. My form is female, and my heart is male. I do not cast my vote lightly. The old ways were good. They had value and worth. But they must make way for the new. I vote to acquit Orestes. *(Speaks to ORESTES.)* You are free.

(The EUMENIDES are silent. Numb. PRIESTESS gathers the votes and exits. ORESTES falls on his knees in front of ATHENA.)

ORESTES: Athena. You have resurrected me. Resurrected my house. Now. I am free. I have my life. I can assume the throne of my father. The throne of Argos. Free. I am free of the furious hounds of my mother. I will rule well. I will rule wisely with justice and mercy, I swear. I will never forget the gift you have given me, will never forget my duties to the people of Athens. I will bless your name and that of your city Athens forever.

ATHENA: Stay. Now you must do something for me.

(ATHENA takes him aside.)

APOLLO: Well. That's settled.

(APOLLO turns on the silent, almost catatonic EUMENIDES.)

APOLLO: The gods young and old loathe you. You are finished. Vicious, foolish impotent and old. It's a new world. You are cast aside. *(To ATHENA and ORESTES.)* Well. I guess that's all I need to say. And as you know, every word that comes out of my mouth is the truth.

(APOLLO leaves. The EUMENIDES stare unseeing into the distance. Slowly, gradually, they start a rhythmic movement, a chant. Mournful and wild. A song of mourning and grief for a world that is passing.)

EUMENIDES #1, #2, #3: Dishonored
Disgraced
The young gods mock us
The people have forgotten us

The victim cries for justice
But no justice in the world
The poison in our heart
We free upon the land

(They pound upon the earth.)

Nothing born
Nothing grow
Only war
Only famine
Only stillborn child
This we leave you
This is our gift

ATHENA: How can I ignore the warrant when the hand of Great Zeus signs it? Stay your rage. The vote had to be for acquittal. I beg of you, do not let your anger blaze forth. Stay your hand and listen.

EUMENIDES #1, #2, #3: Dishonored
Disgraced
The young gods mock us
The people have forgotten us

ATHENA: *(Speaks over their wild chant.)* Athens can be your home, your home for all time. You shall stay here, honored, revered. Only do not stretch your hand upon my people.

EUMENIDES #1, #2, #3: The victim cries for justice
But no justice in the world
The poison in our heart
We free upon the land

ATHENA: My city. I cannot bear to see my city bleed. I cannot bear to see—my people, my children—see them drown in blood and endless war. Do not do this thing you say, I beg of you.

EUMENIDES #1, #2, #3: Nothing born
Nothing grow
Only war
Only famine
Only stillborn child
This we leave you
This is our gift

ATHENA: You will be respected. Your law will not be forgotten. You will watch over the most important moments in the life of the women of my city—the moment of marriage and the moment of childbirth.

EUMENIDES #1, #2, #3: Dishonored
Disgraced

The young gods mock us
The people have forgotten us
The victim cries for justice
But no justice in the world
The poison in our heart
We free upon the land

(They pound upon the earth.)

Nothing born
Nothing grow
Only war
Only famine
Only stillborn child
This we leave you
This is our gift

(ATHENA speaks again. The EUMENIDES stop their chant, but continue their motions.)

ATHENA: No family will thrive without your blessing. No marriage succeed without your grace. No child born without your smile. All the people of my city will beg your favor and honor your name. Forever. No longer will you be feared and dreaded as a curse. You will be known as the Gracious Ones. The Kindly Ones. Only do not—I beg of you—do not pour out your rage on the city I love.

(Silence.)

ATHENA: Here in this place. Here you begin again. The world will change. But you remain.

EUMENIDES #1: We do

EUMENIDES #2: Not know

EUMENIDES #3: What to do

EUMENIDES #1: Instruct us please

ATHENA: Stay.

EUMENIDES #1: Here in this place?

ATHENA: Here. My house I give to you. I give you the people of my city, dearer to me than all the gods. They will honor and revere you. All they humbly ask is your blessing and protection.

EUMENIDES #2: What is this place you give us?

ATHENA: A temple deep within the earth. It is yours if you wish. A place where you are free from grief and pain.

EUMENIDES #3: The earth

EUMENIDES #1: Our womb

EUMENIDES #3: Our mother

EUMENIDES #2: Very very long ago

ATHENA: Stay here. Stay and turn your wrath. Give my people peace. Good things to eat. Happy marriages. Children. And let them adore you. As the saviors and protectors of their hearths.

EUMENIDES #1: You can give us all this?

ATHENA: Athena promises nothing that cannot be done.

EUMENIDES #2: Something melts

EUMENIDES #3: Flows away

ATHENA: You are the Gracious Ones.

EUMENIDES #1: We do not—we cannot—

ATHENA: You are the Kindly Ones.

EUMENIDES #2: Will they honor us?

EUMENIDES #3: What if they do not honor us?

EUMENIDES #2: We could not bear—

EUMENIDES #3: We are GODDESSES we will not—

ATHENA: If mankind forgets the ancient goddesses deep within the earth, let it be to their peril.

(PRIESTESS brings out bowls and cloths for them to wash. ORESTES assists her. ATHENA directs the proceedings.)

ATHENA: Marriage.

EUMENIDES #1: Yes

ATHENA: Childbirth

EUMENIDES #2: Yes

ATHENA: Good things

EUMENIDES #3: Marriage

EUMENIDES #1: Childbirth

EUMENIDES #2: All the families of the city

EUMENIDES #3: Good things

EUMENIDES #1: The young men will not be cut down in their prime

EUMENIDES #2: The dry earth will not drink up their blood

EUMENIDES #3: No bloodshed no wars

EUMENIDES #2: Peace.

EUMENIDES #3: Peace

EUMENIDES #1: Peace

EUMENIDES #3: *(Suddenly, a burst of rage.)* Murderers! Murderers!

EUMENIDES #1: Sister—

EUMENIDES #3: Murderers! They must—

EUMENIDES #2: Sister, please—

EUMENIDES #3: DID YOU SEE WHAT THEY DID? WE MUST STOP THEM! WE MUST—

EUMENIDES #1: Peace, sister!

EUMENIDES #2: Peace

EUMENIDES #1: Peace

EUMENIDES #3: WE KNOW WHAT THEY CAN DO! WE KNOW WHAT THEY WILL DO! WITHOUT US—WE MUST STOP THEM—WE MUST—

EUMENIDES #2: Athena has promised

EUMENIDES #1: Peace

EUMENIDES #2: Now we promise

EUMENIDES #3: We cannot—we must not—oh sisters—we can't—

EUMENIDES #1: Please my sister

EUMENIDES #3: What shall we do?

EUMENIDES #1: We will honor them

EUMENIDES #2: We will protect them

EUMENIDES #1: We are their Protectors now

EUMENIDES #2: They will love us—

EUMENIDES #1: Love

EUMENIDES #2: Us

EUMENIDES #3: They will love us?

EUMENIDES #1: Yes

EUMENIDES #3: *(Subsiding.)* Murderers.

EUMENIDES #2: No

EUMENIDES #1: Shhh

EUMENIDES #2: Peace sister

EUMENIDES #1: My dear sister

EUMENIDES #2: It must be this way

EUMENIDES #1: This way is good

EUMENIDES #2: Peace now

EUMENIDES #1: Peace

EUMENIDES #2: Peace

(Beat.)

EUMENIDES #1: Let me catechize you sisters. Who are we?

EUMENIDES #2: We are the—Gracious Ones.

EUMENIDES #3: We are the—Kindly Ones.

EUMENIDES #1: What is our work?

EUMENIDES #2: We bless the marriage.

EUMENIDES #3: We protect the woman in childbirth.

EUMENIDES #2: We bring peace to the city.

EUMENIDES #1: Who needs us?

EUMENIDES #2: The young gods need us.

EUMENIDES #1: Why do they need us?

EUMENIDES #3: Without us, there would be no memory of the old ways.

EUMENIDES #1: Who else needs us?

EUMENIDES #2: The people of the city need us.

EUMENIDES #3: They need our grace.

EUMENIDES #2: Our kindness.

EUMENIDES #1: Do the people of the city fear us?

EUMENIDES #2: There is no need for them to fear us.

EUMENIDES #3: They—love—us.

EUMENIDES #2: They love us.

EUMENIDES #3: We are their Protectors.

EUMENIDES #1: Will the people forget us?

EUMENIDES #2: If they do—

EUMENIDES #3: —it will be at their peril.

EUMENIDES #1: Our work—

EUMENIDES #2: Protect.

EUMENIDES #3: Bless.

EUMENIDES #2: Peace.

EUMENIDES #1: How do we do this work, my sisters?

EUMENIDES #2: Without resting.

EUMENIDES #3: Without stopping.

EUMENIDES #2: We do this work with joy and a cheerful heart.

EUMENIDES #1: Why do we do this, my sisters?

EUMENIDES #2 and #3: It is our natures.

(PRIESTESS and ORESTES bow low and worship the EUMENIDES at the altar. ATHENA watches.)

(THE END)

PRINCIPIA

a musical in two acts

Book and Lyrics by Michael Maiello
Music by Andrew Recinos

MICHAEL MAIELLO is a playwright and a very amateur stand-up comedian. He was born in College Point, Queens, and raised in Albuquerque, New Mexico. He received a bachelor's degree in theatre, with a minor in English, from the University of New Mexico, where he studied with Digby Wolf and Kestutis Nakas. Maiello got his start in show business when his play, *God's Younger Brother*, debuted at the 1994 Young Playwrights Festival. Since then, he has had two of his other plays, *Waiting for Death* and *Night of Faith*, published by Playscripts, and has co-written the short film, *DMV*, currently in production. Maiello is also the author of the book *Buy the Rumor, Sell the Fact* (McGraw-Hill, 2004). He is an associate editor for *Forbes Magazine* and lives in Park Slope, Brooklyn.

ANDREW RECINOS is a composer and sound designer. He was born on September 11, 1971, in Vienna, Virginia, a suburb of Washington, D.C. He attended Indiana University, where he received both a bachelor's degree in composition, with a minor in trumpet performance, and a master's degree in arts administration. His music and design credits include *Principia* (2003), *A Clockwork Orange* (2005), and *Fahrenheit 451* (2006), all for Godlight Theatre Company, where he is resident composer. He is also a senior consultant for a technology company that supports performing arts organizations and other nonprofits across the country. Recinos lives in Portland, Oregon, with his wife, Peg, and their daughter, Caroline.

Principia was first presented by Godlight Theatre Company (Joe Tantalo, Artistic Director) on March 19, 2003, at Manhattan Theater Source, New York City, with the following cast and credits:

Kerry...Brian Farley
Bob Dobbs.. Rob Maitner
Crewmen/Monks.......................................Brian Bianco, JT Patton, David Gurland
Eris..Jessica Fields
Bum .... Cyrus Roxas
Aliens..Theresa Finamore, Emera Krauss, Cate Bottiglione
Evangelist...Randy MacNiven
Pirate ....Flannery Foster

Director: Joe Tantalo
Choreographers: Ryan Harrington and Carol Wei
Costumes: Christian Couture
Lighting: Jason Rainone
Music Direction: Joey Clark
Stage Managers: Amy Acorn and Karen Gozman

Dedicated to the prettiest one.
Fnord.

CHARACTERS

KERRY: Kerry's just this guy, you know?
ERIS: Goddess of Chaos.
BOB DOBBS/MANAGER: Puts everything in its place.
FOUR CREWMEMBERS/FOUR MONKS: The Forces of Order.
THREE ALIENS (ZALTAR, BALTAR, and MIDGE): Earth girls are easier.
BUM/GOD: Social commentary? Or…religious commentary! You decide!
EVANGELIST: Let him heal you!
PUERTO RICAN PIRATE: Second only to Roberto Clemente.
MAGIC 8 BALL: Answer Unclear Ask Again Later.

MUSICAL NUMBERS

Cogito et Ergo Sum
The Opposable Monk
Infamous Illuminati
Crossing a Field
Just Like We've Always Done
Nothing Makes Sense
Everything's Under Control
Give Up Your Religion
Born to See the Light
Why Does a Good God Go Bad?
We've Got Good Shit
Onward Buddhist Priests
When in Doubt, Fuck It
No Place Like Ohm
If It's Falling Push It Down
I Blew Up Those Monks
We Are the Knights Templar
King of the World
Plant Your Seeds/Born to See the Light Reprise
Last Opposable Monk Reprise

AUTHOR'S NOTE

I'm sorry to say that the script can only approximate the three productions of this play, which took place at Dixon Place, as part of the Godlight Theatre Company's 2003 season and later that year as Godlight's entry in the 2003 New York International Fringe Festival. I think the script makes for good reading, but you're obviously robbed of hearing Andrew Recinos's music; of the improvisations created by the casts that Godlight's artistic director, Joe Tantalo, assembled; and, of course, of Joe's creative and inspired staging ideas.

That aside, I think the script still amuses.

The inspiring source material is *The Principia Discordia*, a self-published collage of hodge and podge revealed by Eris, the Goddess of Chaos from Greek mythology, to Malaclypse the Younger. It's a book of comedy and philosophy first distributed in the late 1950s and later popularized when author Robert Anton Wilson quoted liberally from it in his science fiction classic, *The Illuminatus Trilogy*.

The *Principia Discordia* isn't a narrative work, and my theatrical take on it is, well, barely narrative. Indeed, I realized while assembling the script for publication that, before the Fringe production, I actually got scared and tried too hard to make it into a narrative. This script is back to what I intended in the first place—theatre that can be entertaining and hopefully will hold the interest of my audience but that isn't narrative. By that, I don't mean it's experimental. It'd be churlish of me to start referencing the Theatre of the Absurd or the Theatre of the Ridiculous when I'm really just trying to capture a bit of that old Monty Python feeling.

Since people tend to ask: I wrote the lyrics by listening to pop songs that I like, including a lot of David Byrne, Prince, John Spencer, and Boss Hog. Naturally, I didn't tell Andrew things like, "That first alien song is written to the tune of 'Once in a Lifetime' by the Talking Heads." Also, naturally, Andrew never asked such questions. It was always a treat to hear what Andrew created and how different and wonderful the songs became when he freed them from the karaoke-in-my head.

One more observation: The creators of the *Principia Discordia* declared all of their rights "reversed," and encouraged people to create their own versions of the book. This musical was meant to be a new version, with a lot of references to the original but with a lot of new stuff, too. Now, it's being set into print. Which I guess makes me and Andrew and Joe and everyone who's ever been in a reading or staging of this piece part of the original conspiracy. You throw an idea out there, heck, you give it away like Malaclypse the Younger did, and sometimes, it finds its own life.

May the fnord be with you.

> —*Michael Maiello*

A NOTE ON THE MUSIC

I've been asked to write a note about the music. If you put your ear very close to the page, perhaps you can hear it (don't do this in public). What you might hear dribbling out is my attempt to capture the hard lefts and sudden rights and step-on-the brakes and look-out-for-that-buses that are the *Principia Discordia*, turned into theatre by Mike Maiello.

A couple of things I tried to do to help the cause. To keep the show off kilter, I tried to throw in as many styles as I could. I figure the original text wasn't concerned with sticking to a single font, why should I worry about what decade the music sounds like? "Cogito et Ergo Sum": Gregorian Chant-y. "The Opposable Monk": Calypso-ish. "Everything's Under Control": techno-ish. "King of the World": Broadway-ish, "Why Does a Good God Go Bad?": Catskills-ish. Lots of ish.

In the cause of tying it all together, common motives make their way between songs—"King of the World" includes music from "Everything's Under Control"; "If It's Falling Push It Down" includes music from "King of the World."

Speaking of chaos, I felt that the music needed to reflect the chaos of the text, so I took this opportunity to write a lot of counterpoint. There's no cheaper gimmick to making it all sound out-of-control than a good old-fashioned fugue. Scholars are pretty certain that Bach wrote them just to irritate his wife. I'm fairly sure "When in Doubt..." (a, yes, five-part fugue-ish) would have really pissed off Mrs. Bach.

Finally, as much as possible, I tried to stay out of the way and let the words and humor shine out. What have I learned from all this? If the phone rings, water it.

> —*Andrew Recinos*

THE FIRST AND ONLY ACT ONE

The exceedingly ordinary office of the America Can Company. KERRY is onstage. His fellow employees, here called CREWMAN #1, #2, #3, and #4, are busily working as KERRY reads a spreadsheet. We hear ambient office noise.

CREWMAN #1: So, can we make quarterly earnings? We have to make quarterly earnings, you know. Your data will tell us if we'll make quarterly earnings.

KERRY: I'm thinking. I'm trying to think.

CREWMAN #3: We've never missed quarterly earnings. Not once in twenty years.

CREWMAN #4: Kerry? Do you think we'll make quarterly earnings? Do you, Kerry?

KERRY: I'm so sick of this. Do all of you find this interesting?

(Nobody answers.)

CREWMAN #4: If we don't make quarterly earnings then I think we should have a paradigm enhancement meeting.

CREWMAN #2: Sure, sure. A business strategy session where we can develop outside the box answers for our solutions team.

CREWMAN #3: I've always believed that we can more effectively leverage technology to enhance the stickiness of our online MRO portal.

KERRY: I think I need to look at these numbers again. I'm gonna have some lunch first. *(Grabs his lunch. Starts rooting through the bag.)*

CREWMAN #2: Will you go to lunch? Will you go to lunch?

CREWMAN #1: You know, Kerry, if we make earnings they're sure to buy us pizza.

(MANAGER enters.)

MANAGER: How are those numbers looking, Kerry?

KERRY: My eyes are glazing over. I'll let you know after lunch.

CREWMAN #2: Will you go to lunch?

MANAGER: I know what'll speed you up. Let's do the company cheer. Everybody! *(Cheer.)* Who can?

CREWMAN #1, #3, and #4: America Can!

MANAGER: Who can?

CREWMAN #1, #3, and #4: America Can!

MANAGER: Now how you doing with those numbers, Kerry? What do you think they'll look like when you're done?

KERRY: It's looking tight. It's looking real tight.

MANAGER: *(With a sigh.)* I see. I see.

(From his lunch sack, KERRY removes a sandwich, a banana, a bag of chips, a soda and…to his surprise…a Golden Apple that says "kalliste" on the side of it. The apple amazes him.)

KERRY: Guys, look at this.

MANAGER: Is it the numbers? It's the numbers.

KERRY: It's a Golden Apple.

CREWMAN #4: A golden delicious?

KERRY: No. A golden hunk of… gold.

MANAGER: Delicious.

(As KERRY stares at the apple, transfixed, the scene undergoes an eerie change. The ambient office noise is replaced by the clicks, beeps, and whirs of sounds from a '60s era science fiction show, okay, from Star Trek. *MANAGER takes his place on stage as if it's the bridge of the Enterprise.)*

MANAGER: Steady as she goes, Mr. Kerry.

KERRY: Steady as what goes?

MANAGER: Chief Financial Officer, report.

CREWMAN #1: We're leaking profits from the main sales drive! The company's bound to explode!

MANAGER: Put out a distress call.

CREWMAN #3: But sir, we're the only company in the quadrant.

MANAGER: Damn it. Those desk jockeys at the New York Stock Exchange have left us to fend for ourselves out here. Jettison the section.

CREWMAN #4: But sir!

CREWMAN #2: You can't mean…

MANAGER: That's right. Lay off everyone in the cannery.

KERRY: What's going on here? Why are you all acting like this? And what's with the strange noises? And you—you can't be serious about the cannery. The company is called America Can. We can things, it's what we do. How are we going to can things without a cannery?

MANAGER: Outsourcing.

KERRY: If we're going to outsource the only thing we do, then why should we exist?

MANAGER: Yes, it does seem bad. When the cannery goes… it's like… it's like the cannery in the coal mine.

(Pause while no one reacts.)

MANAGER: Cannery. Canary. It's a pu— Kerry, go fire everyone at the cannery.

KERRY: My dad works there. You can't make me go.

MANAGER: Well, I'm not going. The captain can't go on an away mission, it's against regulations. You, as first officer—

KERRY: No.

MANAGER: Activate the transporter and beam everyone at the cannery into deep space, maximum dispersion. They won't feel a thing.

KERRY: You never should have taken that management seminar at the *Star Trek* convention.

CREWMAN #3: Hey. He met Spock!

MANAGER: This company needs an immediate cash infusion. We have to fire everyone in the cannery and we have to sell your Golden Apple.

KERRY: You can't fire my dad and take my apple. No way.

(MANAGER moves to seize the apple but CREWMAN #4 blocks him.)

CREWMAN #4: *(Scanning.)* Sir, stay away from that thing. My Hyperscanner shows that it's bending the fabric of space-time around it to form a set of parabolic curves unmatched even in the strip clubs of Rigel 7.

MANAGER: Hey, I'm no Einstein but I know as much about the effects of quantum particles on relativistic space as anyone who isn't Einstein. And I know this, Kerry. You either give me the apple and fire everyone in the cannery or you can go find yourself another job. And good luck in this economy, boy-o.

KERRY: Well then you should know this—I wasn't crunching the quarterly numbers. I was reading the want ads.

MANAGER: Find anything?

KERRY: No. Because I didn't want to find anything. I planned to hang onto this job forever, complaining about it, sure, wishing for something greater, sure, but working, working, working, all the same.

MANAGER: That, my friend, is called maturity. Now get rid of that apple.

KERRY: Fine.

(KERRY spikes the apple on stage. A thunderclap, followed by a red-alert siren.)

CREWMAN #3: The ship's coming apart!

CREWMAN #2: I'm giving her all I've got but she keeps begging for more!

CREWMAN #1: Structural integrity down to 23 percent.

MANAGER: Abandon ship. Abandon ship! Make for the escape pods!

(MANAGER and CREW scatter. Warily, KERRY approaches the apple.)

KERRY: I couldn't just leave it there. It found me for a reason. It drew me towards it, resting in the ruins of America Can. It had landed on top of the newspaper want ads. *(He takes the apple and the want ads. Reading ad.)* "The Five Monks of the Divine Contemplation of the Illuminated Templars seek an eager, adventurous, multi-tasking novice to assist in the ushering of a new order of moral and spiritual perfection for all of mankind. Help plant seeds. Ideal candidate will have management experience and a working knowledge of the Windows operating system and Excel spreadsheets. Fax resume. No phone calls. Good references are meaningless as there are no good people around who can refer to you." I decided to follow the apple's will.

(Lights down. FOUR MONKS, including KERRY, enter in a line, singing in Holy Latin. KERRY wears the Golden Apple as a pendant on a chain.)

Cogito et Ergo Sum

MONKS and KERRY: *(With two rounds of hitting each other in between the verses.)* COGITO ET ERGO SUM ANNUIT COEPTUS

NOVUS ORDO SECLURUM
E PLURIBUS UNUM

COGITO ET ERGO SUM
ANNUIT COEPTUS
NOVUS ORDO SECLURUM
E PLURIBUS UNUM

COGITO ET ERGO SUM
ANNUIT COEPTUS
NOVUS ORDO SECLURUM
E PLURIBUS UNUM.

MONK #3: Foul! I cry foul!

MONK #1: Foul? What foul?

MONK #3: I object to getting punched in the face and knocked in the head. Foul!

KERRY: I get punched in the face and knocked in the head. Foul!

MONK #4: I also get punched in the face and knocked in the head, you don't see me crying foul.

MONK #1: We all get punched in the face and knocked in the head. If people cried foul every time it happened, then it would never get done now, would it?

KERRY: *(To MONK #3.)* He'll no doubt invoke God's will again. I'll bet you anything.

MONK #1: It's God's will, the face punching and head knocking and Latin gibberish and all.

MONK #3: Now why do the monks on the ends always get to speak for God?

KERRY: Why would God want face punching and head knocking at all? If he's all-powerful I'd expect him to have the guts to knock me in the face himself.

MONK #4: That's a sight I'd like to see. God would mop the floor with you, you puny—

MONK #1: Now, Monk #4—

MONK #4: Well, look at him, he's scrawny. Monk of the Golden Apple indeed. He's no match for God.

MONK #1: Nobody's going to fight God. *(Pause.)* Not today.

KERRY: I just want to know why we get hit all the time.

MONK #4: We all get hit.

MONK #1: It's what the Five Monks do.

KERRY: But why are we in the middle?

MONK #3: And why are there only four of us?

MONK #4: It's just a name, the Five Monks, it's just a name.

MONK #1: Everyone gets hit the same whether they're on the middle or the end.

KERRY: No, no. The middle monk also has the back of his head smacking into the front of another head, a situation not endured by the monks on the end. It's a class thing, pure favoritism.

MONK #1: It's a minor impact. We all get punched in the face.

MONK #3: Is the fifth monk symbolic of the Holy Spirit?

KERRY: Then why don't we ever switch places?

MONK #1: You're not ready to be on the end yet.

KERRY: Not ready? All there is to it is not hitting someone with the back of your head, which I can manage, I think.

MONK #1: There's leadership!

MONK #4: And following!

MONK #1: And following.

MONK #4: There's no symbolic fifth monk. It's just a name.

MONK #3: I want to be on Monk #4's end, he's just following but not smacking the back of his head.

MONK #1: You can't have Monk #3 at the end of a five-monk line.

KERRY: Four monks.

MONK #4: It's like when you make a fist. Four fingers clenched and the fifth in the set is the fist that they form.

MONK #3: There's five fingers in a fist and the fist is number six if you insist on counting symbolically.

MONK #1: The thumb isn't really a finger.

MONK #3: Are you saying there's some sort of opposable monk following us around? Is that where you get five?

MONK #1: Brothers, brothers, we have hitting to do.

MONK #3: Wait, wait wait… If Jesus was Jewish, then why did he have a Puerto Rican name?

KERRY: *(Steps out of the line.)* I knew then that I wasn't like the other monks. I was… I was…

The Opposable Monk

KERRY: THE OPPOSABLE MONK
IN GOD'S FOUR DIGITS
THE OPPOSABLE MONK
NOT EVEN RELIGIOUS
I'D SEARCHED LONG AND HARD
WAITING TO BE CALLED
COULDN'T HACK A REAL JOB
I JUST WENT TO WORK ROBED

MONKS: COGITO ET ERGO SUM
ANNUIT COEPTIS
NOVUS ORDO SECLURUM

KERRY: I COULD HAVE JOINED THE ARMY
BUT I KNEW I'D DESERT
SO I JOINED AN ORDER
OF GUILT, SPITE, AND HURT
COULD HAVE JOINED ANYONE
WOULD HAVE BEEN THE SAME
GROUPS ARE ALWAYS SO QUEER
AND I COULDN'T FIND A DAME

MONKS: HE'S THE OPPOSABLE MONK

KERRY and MONKS: IN GOD'S FOUR DIGITS
THE OPPOSABLE MONK
NOT EVEN RELIGIOUS
HE SEARCHED LONG AND HARD
WAITING TO BE CALLED
COULDN'T HACK A REAL JOB
HE JUST WENT TO WORK ROBED

KERRY: I WAS ALONE WHEN I LEFT THE MONKS
ALONE WITH MY LONELY THOUGHTS
MY FRIENDS HAD ALL GOT JOBS
AND I STARTED SURFING THE WEB
DAY IN, DAY OUT
FOR HOURS AT A STRETCH
CHATTING, EMAILING
WITH STRANGERS WITH STRANGER MINDS
PARANOIA
PARANOIA CAME FAST CAME HARD
PARANOIA
DOESN'T MEAN THEY'RE NOT OUT TO GET YOU
PARANOIA
IT MEANS THEY REALLY CARE

(KERRY and MONKS sing in counterpoint.)

KERRY: PARANOIA

MONKS: PARANOIA, PARANOIA.

KERRY: PARANOIA CAME FAST CAME HARD

MONKS: PARANOIA, PARANOIA.

KERRY: *(Alone.)* DOESN'T MEAN THEY'RE NOT OUT TO
GET YOU
PARANOIA
IT MEANS THEY REALLY CARE
PARANOIA, IT MEANS THEY REALLY CARE

(KERRY and MONKS sing in counterpoint.)

KERRY: THEY'RE OUT TO GET ME
THEY'RE OUT TO GET ME
THEY'RE OUT TO GET ME
THEY'RE OUT TO GET US ALL

THEY'RE OUT TO GET ME
THEY'RE OUT TO GET ME
THEY'RE OUT TO GET ME
THEY'RE OUT TO GET US ALL

THEY'RE OUT TO GET ME
THEY'RE OUT TO GET ME
THEY'RE OUT TO GET ME
THEY'RE OUT TO GET US ALL

MONKS: PARANOIA
PARANOIA
PARANOIA
PARANOIA
CAME FAST CAME HARD
PARANOIA
DOESN'T MEAN THEY'RE NOT OUT TO GET YOU
PARANOIA, PARANOIA, PARANOIA

MONKS: *(Singing alone.)* NOW HE'S A RENT-A-COP
IN INDIANA
WITH A NIGHT SHIFT JOB
AND STUDYING ARCANA
A DISPOSABLE HUNK

OF HUMAN WORRY
WITH A SIZABLE CHUNK
OF RECESSIO-ENNUI

KERRY and MONKS: I'M THE OPPOSABLE MONK
IN GOD'S FOUR DIGITS
THE OPPOSABLE MONK
NOT EVEN RELIGIOUS
I SEARCHED LONG AND HARD

WAITING TO BE CALLED
COULDN'T HACK A REAL JOB
I JUST WENT TO WORK ROBED.

(MONKS surround KERRY.)

MONK #1: Do you believe in the Ancient Illuminated Seers of Bavaria?

MONK #3: Do you want to know the secrets of Atlantis, and the advanced culture that lived there and where they went and why they didn't take us with them?

MONK #4: Do you want to know why scholarly anthropologists turn pale with terror at the very mention of the name Yog-Sothoth?

MONK #1: What is the true secret sinister reality lying behind the ancient Aztec legend of Quetzalcoatl?

MONK #3: Is there an esoteric allegory concealed in the apparent innocent legend of Snow White and the Seven Dwarfs?

MONK #4: Who is the man in Zurich that some swear is Lee Harvey Oswald?

MONK #3: What really did happen to Ambrose Bierce?

MONK #1: Have you ever wondered why the Great Pyramid has five sides?

KERRY: It does not.

MONK #1: Counting the bottom it does.

INFAMOUS ILLUMINATI

MONKS: WE'RE THE WORLD'S MOST SUCCESSFUL CONSPIRACY
THE OLDEST AND THE BOLDEST IN SINCERITY
IF YOU'RE NOT STRUCK WITH TIMIDITY
AND YOUR IQ IS OVER ONE FIFTY
THEN YOU COULD PAY THE MEMBERSHIP FEE
AND JOIN THE INFAMOUS ILLUMINATI
ILLUMINATI
ILLUMINATI!

MONK #1: That's $3,120, American.

KERRY: I don't have that on me.

MONK #4: You don't need it on you. You bury the cash in your own backyard.

MONK #3: And then one of our underground agents will contact you.

MONKS: ILLUMINATE THE OPPOSITION
ILLUMINATION IS OUR MISSION
ILLUMINATE THE OPPOSITION
AND DOMINATE, THE WORLD'S CONDITION
DOMINATE THE WORLD'S CONDITION
DOMINATE THE WORLD'S CONDITION.

KERRY: Stop it, stop it! I don't, I don't, I don't, I don't believe you!

MONK #3: TELL NO ONE! ACCIDENTS HAVE A STRANGE WAY OF HAPPENING TO PEOPLE WHO TALK TOO MUCH ABOUT THE BAVARIAN ILLUMINATI.

MONK #1: May we warn you against imitations! Ours is the original and genuine.

(THE TORMENTORS withdraw. KERRY is panicked.)

KERRY: The apple had led me astray. I hate it when fruit lies. I wanted to escape it but it had become bonded to me and every day I carried it, my world turned stranger.

CROSSING A FIELD

MONK #1: HE RAN, HE RAN, HE RAN
HE WRACKED HIS BRAIN
CROSSING A FIELD
FULL OF CORN AND OLD BEER CANS
HE WRACKED HIS BRAINS
HE RAN HIS FEET
PANICKED AND FLEEING
THE ILLUMINATI

MONKS: Ahh…

KERRY and MONKS: *(In harmony.)* I'M BATHED IN LIGHT
IN COSMIC RAYS
AS VISITORS FROM THE MILKY WAY
LAND IN THE CORN
LAND IN THE CORN!
SAVE YOUR MOCKING SCORN
I KNOW I SHOULDA BEEN HOME WATCHING PORN
BUT I SPENT THE NIGHT CROSSING A FIELD
BATHED IN LIGHT AND COSMIC RAYS
AND THREE VISITORS FROM WAY FAR ABOVE
AMBASSADORS FROM THE MILKY WAY
SO FAR AWAY
IT'S SO HARD
TO CROSS A FIELD
AND GET WHERE YOU'RE GOING
IN THE U.S. OF AMBROSE BIERCE.

(Enter three ALIENS—ZALTAR, BALTAR, and MIDGE.)

ZALTAR: We are Zaltar, Baltar, and… Midge. Beings from the Unenticing Planet of Milwaukee.

KERRY: Oh, we get folks from Milwaukee around here a lot.

BALTAR: The planet, not the city.

MIDGE: Weird how that worked out, right?

KERRY: Milwaukee is an Indian word.

MIDGE: We prefer the term Native American.

BALTAR: We are Native Americans from Planet Milwaukee.

ZALTAR: We got moved when European settlers came to the New World.

KERRY: That's impossible.

BALTAR: That kind of thinking is why we live in celestial splendor and you live in Indiana.

ZALTAR: Punk.

Just Like We've Always Done

MIDGE: THERE ARE NO NATIVES LEFT
IN AMERICA ANYMORE
WE ALL LEFT AFTER
THE SECOND WORLD WAR.
HEADING WEST
STOPPING BRIEFLY IN JAPAN IN THE FIFTIES
AND SETTLING IN PARIS A DECADE LATER

ZALTAR and BALTAR: AS THE WATER FLOWS, WE'VE BEEN HEADING UNDERGROUND
AS TREES AND FLOWERS GROW WE TRIED TO BURROW UNDERGROUND
BUT YOU'D POLLUTED THAT
JUST LIKE THE AIR AND SEAS
SO WE BUILT A STARSHIP AND WE MOVED TO MILWAUKEE

MIDGE: JUST LIKE WE'VE ALWAYS DONE

ZALTAR and BALTAR: JUST LIKE WE'VE ALWAYS DONE

MIDGE: GATHERED AND MOVED EVERYONE
WE FLED LIKE THE SETTING SUN
BURIED THE SMOKING GUN

ZALTAR and BALTAR: LIKE RUSSIA AND NAPOLEON

ALL: JUST LIKE WE'VE ALWAYS DONE

BALTAR: WE TOOK EVERYTHING THAT YOU'D EVER LIKE TO READ

ZALTAR: WE TOOK EVERY BIT OF OUR ADVANCED TECHNOLOGY

BALTAR: WE TOOK THE TIME MACHINE

ZALTAR: AND OUR JUICE MAKER

BALTAR: WE TOOK THE INTERNET

ZALTAR: AND OUR CLONING FORMULA—

BALTAR: AND OUR CLONING FORMULA—

ZALTAR: AND OUR CLONING FORMULA—

BALTAR: AND OUR CLONING FORMULA

ZALTAR and BALTAR: NOW IN SPACE WE FOUND
WE WERE MORE LIKE GODS THAN MEN
SO WE FIGURED THAT
WE COULD RETURN WITH A VENGEANCE
BUT YOU'VE IGNORED US
THOUGH WE ABDUCT YOU ALL WITH EASE
SO WE HAUNT YOU IN TABLOIDS AND ON TV

MIDGE: JUST LIKE WE'VE ALWAYS DONE

ZALTAR and BALTAR: JUST LIKE WE'VE ALWAYS DONE

MIDGE: SET OUR MAGIC WANDS ON STUN
AND LEFT YOU ALL IN COMMOTION

ZALTAR and BALTAR: WE CONTROL YOUR TELEVISION

MIDGE: JUST LIKE WE'VE ALWAYS DONE

ZALTAR and BALTAR: JUST LIKE WE'VE ALWAYS DONE

MIDGE: KEPT YOU OUT OF ALL THE FUN
WE SPED TOWARD THE SETTING SUN
TOOK EVERY OUNCE OF RUM

ZALTAR and BALTAR: LEFT YOU FEELING DUMB

ALL: JUST LIKE WE'VE ALWAYS DONE
AND YOU STILL DON'T HAVE
EVEN A BIT OF WHAT WE GOT
WE'VE GOT A TELEPHONE
WITH DIRECT DIAL TO GOD
AND NOW WE'RE BACK ON EARTH
TO LEAD YOU ALL TO PEACE
TO SOLVE ALL YOUR PROBLEMS
TO CURE EVERY DISEASE.

KERRY: I've always imagined that aliens who visited the Earth would want to impart great wisdom, not hide it on the other end of the galaxy.

MIDGE: Why would we possibly want to help you?

KERRY: Well then why are you here?

(*BALTAR unveils an anal probe.*)

ZALTAR: Life in the universe is a collaborative process.

BALTAR: So bend over.

MIDGE: Also, give us the Golden Apple.

KERRY: What, this?

(*KERRY wields the Golden Apple as if he's using a cross against vampires and that's how ALIENS react.*)

KERRY: You don't like this, do you?

MIDGE: You have no idea what power it has!

KERRY: You better get packing back to Milwaukee before I turn you into Golden Apple sauce.

(*ALIENS retreat.*)

KERRY: But I don't know how to use it. I don't know what it's for. But whatever power it has, if I could have it inside me then I could stop running. If I could have it inside me. Apples are food. (*He breaks a tooth on the apple.*) Friggin' Hell!

Nothing Makes Sense

KERRY: THEY WERE FURIES HOUNDING ME
IN MY THOUGHTS
IN MY BRAIN
IN MY MEMORY
I WAS NEVER STUPID
NEVER STUPID
I READ
I READ
I READ A LOT
YOU LOOK FOR ANSWERS
IN BOOKS
ON THE NEWS
ON THE WEB
ON TV
LOOK FOR ANSWERS
LOOK FOR ANSWERS
LOOK FOR ANSWERS
NOTHING MAKES SENSE
NOTHING MAKES ANY SENSE
THE PIECES DON'T FIT
WHY WOULD GOD
HAVE MADE A BAD WORLD?

WE MUST HAVE RUINED IT
NOTHING MAKES ANY SENSE
THE PIECES DON'T FIT
BUT WHY WOULD WE
HAVE MADE A BAD WORLD
SOMEONE MUST BENEFIT.

KERRY: My unemployment ran out and the apple wouldn't let me eat it. So I had to take a graveyard security job. The Illuminati and the aliens were out there, drawn to me by the apple's core. I kept it secret and hoped to find a friend with answers. Self-proclaimed colonel and fellow watchman Bob Dobbs became my first friend since I left corporate and religious America. Bob's got stories. He spent time in Central America and he thinks that some government agents have ant heads. Really. But he's very persuasive about it. And he's kind and perceptive, and just when I think I'm really going to come apart, he says—

(*BOB enters.*)

BOB: Don't fret, Kerry. Everything's under control.

KERRY: That's what I'm afraid of, Bob. I read those books you brought me. *The Turner Diaries, The Sirius Mystery,* those United Nations invasion plans for Western Indiana…

BOB: The interstates are key.

KERRY: I even gave you money for ammo and claymores. Where are the ammo and claymores, anyway?

BOB: That's need to know, Kerry.

KERRY: What if they do invade, and you get killed, and the rest of us need the ammo and claymores?

BOB: What if I tell you and they fill your head with sodium ethanol and you blab? Isn't it better not to know? You just trust me, soldier, you do not want the burden of being Alpha Commander in this region. You let me be the idiot who gets all the headaches and we'll get through this in one piece.

KERRY: I guess. But hey… there's no such thing as sodium ethanol.

BOB: (*Catches his mistake.*) They're making truth serum out of corn these days. That's why western Indiana is so important to them.

KERRY: None of this makes a lick of sense to me.

BOB: Why should it? Why should you be able to understand a conspiracy that predates the union as we know it? I mean, you just gotta start at the top and try to piece it all together right down to the world's oldest and most successful—

KERRY: The top. That's the most confusing part to me. It's all just this vague sense of something happening and little rumors here and then it's like a lightning strike to the brain and I mean, you know *something* happened.

EVERYTHING'S UNDER CONTROL

BOB: THE CIA BUYS DRUGS IN NICARAGUA
THEY SMUGGLE DOPE IN THROUGH SOME SOUTHERN
    HARBOR
AND THEN THEY SELL THEM IN ANN ARBOR (DETROIT,
    ACTUALLY.)
THEY COUNT THEIR MONEY EVERY SINGLE DAY
AND SEND IT TO THE NSA
THAT'S THE NATIONAL SECURITY ADMINISTRATION
(SUPER TOP SECRET.)
AND THE PRESIDENT KNOWS
'CAUSE HE'S SKULL AND BONES
BUT HE HAS TO KEEP IT QUIET
'CAUSE REVENGE IS A RIOT
BUT EVERYTHING'S UNDER CONTROL, YOU KNOW
EVERYTHING'S UNDER CONTROL
EVERY CLUB SODA WITH STOLI-O
EVERYTHING'S UNDER CONTROL
NOW THE NSA GOES BACK A LONG WAY
FROM LINCOLN, TO GARFIELD, TO JFK
REAGAN GOT SHOT WHEN HE STEPPED OUT OF LINE
AND THE NSA MADE NIXON RESIGN
THEY LORDED OVER PRIMORDIAL SLIME
THEY SERVE A MASTER OLDER THAN TIME
AROUND BEFORE THE GREEKS STARTED MAKING WINE
AND EVERYTHING'S UNDER CONTROL, YOU KNOW
EVERYTHING'S UNDER CONTROL
EVERY NEW OUTBREAK OF POLIO
EVERYTHING'S UNDER CONTROL
LOOK AT THE DOLLAR PAL
LOOK AT THE DOLLAR NOW
LEFT OF THE EAGLE WITH THE STOLID SCOWL
THERE'S THE PYRAMID WITH FIVE SIDES
AND ABOVE IT HOVERS THE ALL-SEEING EYE
THE ILLUMINATI THERE
RIGHT ON THE CASH
THE FEDERAL RESERVE IS THEIR SECRET STASH
FROM THE NASDAQ CRASH
TO THE PRICE OF GASOLINE
TO THE SUDDEN DEATH
OF A BRITISH QUEEN
EVERYTHING'S UNDER CONTROL, YOU KNOW

EVERYTHING'S UNDER CONTROL
EVERYTHING'S UNDER CONTROL, YOU KNOW
EVERYTHING'S UNDER CONTROL.

KERRY: That didn't make me feel better. How can everything be under control? It defies common sense.

BOB: Common sense is what tells you that the world is flat, Kerry. Common sense is for communists. Everything's got a place in the order. Why do people get sick? Why do they starve on the streets? Why'd your dad lose his job? Why are we on night shift guarding some dumb warehouse—well, government secrets is why we're at this warehouse—but you know, why does it all happen, that's what I'm talking about. It beats counting on luck, buddy. We know that someone's got a reason for doing all this. Maybe they'll tell us someday. Or maybe some very curious insomniac like me will figure it out. The truth fights to be free, you know. Now hey, when you were a monk, did they tell you what they had over in the Vatican?

KERRY: They never mentioned it.

BOB: You can trust me. It's your buddy Bob Dobbs. True blue.

KERRY: But they didn't tell me a damned thing. They just hit me a lot.

BOB: Probably trying to induce amnesia.

KERRY: Bob, I am so tired.

BOB: Take a nap. I'll hold down the fort.

KERRY: I'm just one of those people who gets really freaked out about where he fits into the universe.

BOB: I'm gonna go have a cigarette.

KERRY: It's very dark in here.

BOB: I'll be right outside. If the telephone rings, water it.

(BOB leaves. KERRY sits alone in the dark. He hears a sound. He flips out, pulls out his nightstick.)

KERRY: Who's there? I don't know anything about the aliens, the Indians, the Native Americans. Bob? Is that you, Bob? Who are you? What do you want? I don't know anything. I'm a fountain of disinformation. I mean, misinformation. (Takes out the apple and holds it in front of him, hoping it will ward off whatever unpleasant visitation looms in his future.)

Give Up Your Religion

ERIS: *(Offstage.)* LOOKING OUT YOUR WINDOW
I CAN SEE YOU DREAMING
FLOATING IN THE DISTANCE
GENTLY, IN THIS INSTANCE
'CAUSE I CAN'T I CAN'T BELIEVE YOU
ARE SO TIED TO REASON
I'M HERE TO LEAD YOU
INTO MENTAL TREASON
YOU HAVE MADE ME SUFFER
YOU HAVE NO AMBITION
NONSENSE IS SALVATION
GIVE UP YOUR RELIGION.

KERRY: Who are you? What's going on?

(BOB comes back.)

BOB: Kerry! Buddy, what's wrong?

KERRY: It's in my pineal gland, Bob. It's all in my pineal gland.

BOB: Have you been taken up there, buddy?

Born to See the Light

ERIS: *(Offstage.)* I'M COMIN' TO MEET YA
I WAS BORN TO GREET YA

(Enters.)

I WAS BORN TO SEE THE LIGHT
I'M A COMIN' TO MEET YA
I WAS BORN TO GREET YA
I WAS BORN TO SEE THE LIGHT
I'M THE BASTARD CHILD OF THE PANTHEON
COME UP CLOSER AND LET'S HAVE SOME FUN
I'VE RULED THE WORLD SINCE MY FIRST DAY DOWN
WEARING BATS AND TEA TRAYS AS A BAD-ASS CROWN
I'M COMING TO MEET YA
I WAS BORN TO GREET YA
I WAS BORN TO SEE THE LIGHT
I'M A COMIN' TO MEET YA
I WAS BORN TO GREET YA
I WAS BORN TO SEE THE LIGHT
I'M THE GODDESS OF CHAOS DISORDER AND CRIME
THE GODDESS WHO MADE RELATIVISTIC TIME
I DIDN'T END THE WORLD AT Y2K
'CAUSE EVERYONE EXPECTED IT AND THAT'S NO WAY
TO RUN A SYMPHONY
OF ENTROPY
NOW EVERYBODY'S HERE
SO EVERYONE GET NAKED

EVERYBODY'S HERE
KISSIN' AND A HUGGIN' AND A MOTHERFUCKIN'
I'M COMIN' TO MEET YA
I WAS BORN TO GREET YA
I WAS BORN TO SEE THE LIGHT
I'M A COMIN' TO MEET YA
I WAS BORN TO GREET YA
I WAS BORN TO SEE THE LIGHT
IMAGINE IF YOU ARE THE CHOSEN ONE
SO COME UP CLOSER AND LET'S HAVE SOME FUN

KERRY: ARE YOU GOD?
ARE YOU GOD?
ARE YOU GOD?

BOB: FOR CHRISSAKES KERRY
IT'S A BROAD A HOT BROAD
BUT NOT GOD A BROAD NOT GOD

(ERIS and KERRY and BOB in counterpoint.)

ERIS: I'LL GIVE ANY GOD A CHANCE TONIGHT
A BURNING BUSH IF I CAN BUM A LIGHT
SEND ME A VISION HOWEVER SLIGHT
I'M YEARNING FOR A SUPERNATURAL SIGHT

KERRY and BOB: SHE'S COMIN' TO SEE ME
SHE WAS BORN TO GREET ME
SHE WAS BORN TO SEE THE LIGHT
SHE'S A COMIN' TO MEET ME
SHE WAS BORN TO GREET ME
SHE WAS BORN TO SEE THE LIGHT.

ERIS: All gods fall for broads. It's the basis of all religion, even if they try to hide it in your bible.

BOB: Don't you talk about my bible.

ERIS: Once, mortals said my name with a tremble, while I rode following on the heels of Ares.

BOB: Then how come I never heard of you?

ERIS: I am the goddess with the icy dagger in her bosom. And that's rough on the bosom. Oh, I've suffered. Oh, I've made my mark. Oh, I've whipped this world around on a string. *(Turns to KERRY.)* You, mortal, have something that belongs to me.

KERRY: Why does everyone want my apple?

ERIS: Its power will confound you. Its place in history would leave you breathless. It is mine, the Golden Apple of the Hesperides, guarded over by Atlas, stolen by Paris and used by me to spark the Trojan War.

KERRY: It's mine now. If you could just take it, then you would have done it by now.

BOB: Kerry, you have the apple? It could make you ruler of the world. Top dog in the conspiracy. The man with the apple could move mountains of apples. Does it say kalliste on its skin?

KERRY: What does that mean?

ERIS: Kalliste—for the prettiest one. This is how I sparked the Trojan War. See, they had a party on Olympus and they didn't invite me. This is the doctrine of the original snub. So I picked up this bauble and tossed it among the gods. When Hera, Aphrodite, and Athene saw it, they fought to possess it. They picked a mortal named Paris—don't ask me why a Trojan prince had a French name, I didn't do it—to choose between them. Paris granted it to Aphrodite in exchange for the love of Helen, who was already hitched. Her face launched 997 ships, a figure rounded up by the poets. A war happened. My fault. Lots of people died. Achilles took an arrow to the ankle. These are myths. Lies spun by the media of the time. An attempt to explain to the families back home why the Greeks would lay siege on a walled city for years and years when they could have just tried the door. So we have the apple, and we have jealousy, and we have chaos at the root of it all. I shouldered all the blame and enjoyed the solace of a hot dog with no bun, such was the pain of the original snub. Do you really believe that?

BOB: Well I don't believe it, not one bit of it. There's one God, and one nation under God, and I am the protector of that nation and the servant of God's true will.

ERIS: I'll show you your God—

(BUM enters. As GOD.)

WHY DOES A GOOD GOD GO BAD?

GOD: I'VE DONE IT
I'VE DONE IT
I'VE MADE A UNIVERSE
IN VERSE
NOT INVERSE
NOT BACKWARD BUT IN VERSE
YES POETRY
TRUE POETRY
IN EVERY SINGLE ROCK AND TREE
I MADE POETRY
TRUE POETRY
AND IT WAS GOOD
I MADE A SUN OF FIRE, I MADE A MOON OF STONE

I MADE UTOPIA AND CALLED IT EDEN
I MADE MAN AND WOMAN AND GOT 'EM BREEDIN'
I GAVE THEM NAMES GAVE THEM A HOME
GAVE THEM SINS AND THEY ATONE
BUT WHY DID I DO THAT?
WHAT WAS I THINKING?
WHAT WAS I SMOKING?
WHAT WAS I DRINKIN'?
WHY DOES A GOOD GOD GO BAD?
WHY DOES A GOOD GOD GO BAD?
I MADE MAN
I MADE MAN
I MADE A HUMAN RACE
A RACE
NOT RACY
I MADE THEM SO SPACY
THEY WERE SO HAPPY
FOR A MILLION YEARS
NAKED AND FROLICKING AND BORING ME TO TEARS
I WANTED DRAMA
SOME SPICE
BUT THEY'VE GIVEN ME PROBLEMS THAT WILL VEX ME
    ALL MY LIFE

(SOMEONE throws a rock on stage.)

GOD: Can I make that rock so heavy I can't lift it?
IT'S HEAVY AS THE MOON
IT'S HEAVY AS THE STARS
IT'S HEAVY AS THE UNIVERSE

I guess I should stop working out

WHY DOES A GOOD GOD GO BAD?
WHY DOES A GOOD GOD GO BAD?
WHY DOES MY JEWISH SON
HAVE A PUERTO RICAN NAME?

KERRY: Oh, God, my strange God, what dost thou command of me?

GOD: Give her the apple.

KERRY: Why should I? Bob says that with this apple, I could rule the world.

GOD: And why would you want to do that? Its a bum's job. Do you know anyone with power who's actually happy?

KERRY: George Bush.

GOD: Well, ignorance is bliss.

BOB: No, ignorance is Blix. That damned Hans Blix and his United Nations—

GOD: Well, inspections beat bombing.

BOB: I can't believe it. God's a Frenchman.

GOD: Just give her the apple. You can have your old life back. A job with benefits at America Can and maybe even buy some real estate. That apple, it's just a powder keg of concentrated chaos and the key to bending reality to your will—

ERIS: God, that's enough. Go.

GOD: You're telling me to go.

ERIS: You're doing it again. With the same damn apple. You keep giving these people just enough information to screw things up—

GOD: The apple was your fault—

KERRY: *(To ERIS.)* So you're the devil?

ERIS: The devil? The devil? You child. Hell is reserved only for those people who believe in it. And the lowest circle of Hell is reserved for those who believe in it because they're afraid they'll go there if they don't.

GOD: It makes them behave. If they'd just stop asking questions—

ERIS: There are nipples on your chest, do you give milk? What is to be done about Heisenberg's Law? Somebody put all this confusion here. I am the Alpha and the Bodega. The Greeks call me Eris, the Romans call me Discordia, the Diné call me the Coyote, Shakespeare calls me Puck, Faulkner calls me the Snopes family and Jack Ruby calls me Lee Harvey Oswald but only when he's wearing his Jack Ruby Slippers.

KERRY: Dominion over chaos. And you, Eris, you're chaos.

GOD: No human's ever used that apple for anything good. I bet you got dreams about this planet and everything you want it to be. You think you'll do better at it than I did? This was a rough draft. I got some real good planets out there where there's even hot tubs for trees to take a soak. Go ahead and try to use the apple. But don't say I didn't warn you. Peace. Out. *(Exits.)*

KERRY: So you are evil.

ERIS: What?

KERRY: So, I said you're evil.

ERIS: What?

KERRY: Evil. You sound evil.

ERIS: What? What? What? What? I'm sorry I have to do this, Kerry. Send in the Sinister Minister!

(EVANGELIST enters.)

EVANGELIST: I will heal you. I will salve the problem of your soul. Follow us to your salvation. And bring the apple. For he who freely gives his last apple will enjoy a life abundant with apples.

KERRY: I'm not falling for that again.

EVANGELIST: I'll convince you by way of the Socratic method.

BOB: Run Kerry, he's going to start an argument by asking questions.

EVANGELIST: What's black and white and red all over? How many surrealists does it take to screw in a light bulb? Why do blondes have bruised temples?

KERRY: A newspaper. Fish. And *(Head bobbing.)* "I dunno?"

EVANGELIST: He's a smart one.

ERIS: He has the apple. But he doesn't know how to use it.

KERRY: I'll figure it out, it's just an apple.

ERIS: I'm taking the apple now.

(ERIS freezes KERRY. She walks over and touches the apple. She takes it. But it flies back to KERRY.)

ERIS: Interesting.

BOB: Interesting? What's interesting?

ERIS: The apple has chosen him. They're joined. The atoms in the apple seek union with the atoms in Kerry. They share past, present, and future—a bond forged beyond the speed of light that makes distance ephemeral.

KERRY: But why?

ERIS: Who can say? You must renounce the apple, give it to me willingly, or forever bear its troubled core.

KERRY: But I like the apple. I love the apple. I am all about the apple.

ERIS: Then plant the seeds before the seeds plant you.

(ERIS exits, conspiring with EVANGELIST.)

BOB: So what are you gonna do, buddy?

KERRY: I don't know. How does one harness the power of the apple? Do I have the right to use it? What if I were to become the most powerful man on Earth? Should I even try?

BOB: We got big problems, Kerry. There's a helicopter outside. Black as night. Maybe ten helicopters. Maybe a hundred. Maybe three, maybe fnord, maybe…

KERRY: Maybe five?

BOB: Yeah, buddy. Maybe five.

KERRY: I just don't think so, Bob. I think these conspiracy theories are just a religion. I think if I go outside that I'm not going to see a single helicopter.

BOB: Don't go out there. Can't you hear them?

KERRY: I don't hear a thing. And I don't think there are secrets in this warehouse. I think there's dog food. Like it says on the sign. Dog food.

BOB: Who would put dog food in a warehouse?

KERRY: A dog food company, Bob. A dog food company.

BOB: And who would want to start a dog food company? Who would want to devote their lives to dog food?

KERRY: I can't answer that, Bob.

BOB: And what about the apple?

(EVANGELIST returns.)

EVANGELIST: You must seek a holy man. There's one nearby who can show you the path. (Takes out a Palm Pilot.) Here, I'll beam the address into your Palm.

(KERRY experiences a searing pain in his palm.)

EVANGELIST: Sorry. I assumed you had one of these.

KERRY: (Stares at his palm.) There's an address on my palm.

EVANGELIST: It'll wash off. I think. (Exits.)

BOB: You're not going to that place?

KERRY: It's the dilapidated farmhouse on Route 9. Seems like the right place for a showdown. Hold down the fort, Colonel Bob. (Exits.)

BOB: There's fluoride in that kid's water. Strong teeth, weak mind.

(ALIENS suddenly reappear.)

MIDGE: Not today, Bob.

BALTAR: We have a job for you.

ZALTAR: And a coupon for twenty-three pounds of free fertilizer.

MIDGE: Your little pal Kerry's got friends in bad places. We're talking the Illuminati, the Knights Templar, the Holy Rollers of the New World Order.

BALTAR: So when you see him with his pals, we want you to deliver some dynamite justice. To free mankind and force an apple turnover.

WE'VE GOT GOOD SHIT

ALIENS: WE KNOW THAT YOU WANT TO BLOW THINGS UP
AND YOU'RE IN LUCK, YOU'RE IN LUCK
WE CAN SET YOU UP WITH ALL THE FERTILIZER
SO RENT A TRUCK, A RYDER TRUCK
WE'VE GOT GOOD SHIT
WE'VE GOT GOOD SHIT
WE'VE GOT GOOD SHIT
THERE'S A LEAK, THERE'S A LEAK OF SECURITY
ALL THROUGHOUT THE HOMELAND
WHO ARE THE ONES THAT CAN BUILD THE BOMBS?
HIGH SCHOOL KIDS AND FARMHANDS.
BOMBS AWAY, BOMBS AWAY, BOMBS AWAY
WITH GOOD SHIT, GOOD SHIT.
BOMBS AWAY, BOMBS AWAY, BOMBS AWAY
WITH GOOD SHIT, GOOD SHIT
TAKING OUT THE MONKS UP IN THEIR HILLSIDE LAIR
IT'S YOUR JOB, IT'S YOUR JOB
STRIKE A BLOW AGAINST CONSPIRACY
C'MON BOB, C'MON BOB
WE'VE GOT GOOD SHIT
WE'VE GOT GOOD SHIT
WE'VE GOT GOOD SHIT
THERE'S A LEAK, THERE'S A LEAK OF SECURITY
ALL THROUGHOUT THE HEARTLAND
WHO ARE THE ONES THAT CAN BUILD THE BOMBS?
MECHANICS AND FARMHANDS.
BOMBS AWAY, BOMBS AWAY, BOMBS AWAY
WITH GOOD SHIT, GOOD SHIT.
BOMBS AWAY, BOMBS AWAY,
WITH GOOD SHIT, GOOD SHIT
GOD DAMN, THERE'S TIMES WHEN BIG EXPLOSIONS CAN BE GOOD,
CAN BE GOOD.
NOTHING'S BETTER THAN A BLOW FOR JUSTICE
SO YOU SHOULD, YOU KNOW YOU SHOULD.

BOMBS AWAY, BOMBS AWAY, BOMBS AWAY
WITH GOOD SHIT, GOOD SHIT.
BOMBS AWAY, BOMBS AWAY, BOMBS AWAY
WITH GOOD SHIT, GOOD SHIT
NARROW YOUR EYES ON THE TARGET, BABY
LET FREEDOM RING, LET FREEDOM RING
BOMBS AWAY, BOMBS AWAY, BOMBS AWAY
WITH GOOD SHIT, GOOD SHIT.
BOMBS AWAY, BOMBS AWAY, BOMBS AWAY
WITH GOOD SHIT, GOOD SHIT.

BOB: I knew that after all that anal rape, we'd find a way to work together!

(ALIENS exit, and BOB, reluctantly, follows.)

(End of Act One.)

ENTR'ACTE

This is modern theatre so there's no intermission. Instead, MONKS walk across the stage.

ONWARD BUDDHIST PRIESTS

MONKS: ONWARD CHRISTIAN SOLDIERS
ONWARD BUDDHIST PRIESTS
ONWARD FRUITS OF ISLAM
FIGHT 'TIL YOU'RE DECEASED
FIGHT YOUR LITTLE BATTLES
JOIN THE THICKEST FRAY
FOR THE GREATER GLORY
OF DISCORDIAE!

(MONKS have just crossed the stage for the entr'acte, but now, they abruptly return. Most of the cast will enter throughout this song, and it will end with nearly everyone involved.)

WHEN IN DOUBT, FUCK IT

MONK #4: WHEN IN DOUBT

MONKS #1 and #3: FUCK IT
WHEN NOT IN DOUBT

MONK #4: GET IN DOUBT

MONKS #1 and #3: WHEN IN DOUBT

MONK #4: FUCK IT

MONKS #1 and #3: WHEN NOT IN DOUBT

MONKS: GET IN DOUBT

(ALIENS and MONKS in counterpoint.)

ALIENS: WHEN IN DOUBT
FUCK IT
WHEN NOT IN DOUBT
GET IN DOUBT

(Repeated.)

MONKS: TO DIVERSE GODS
DO MORTALS BOW
HOLY COW
AND HOLY CHAO

ALIENS and MONKS: TO DIVERSE GODS
DO MORTALS BOW
HOLY COW
AND HOLY CHAO

(In counterpoint.)

MONKS, GOD, and EVANGELIST: WHEN IN DOUBT
FUCK IT
WHEN NOT IN DOUBT
GET IN DOUBT

(Repeated to end of song.)

ERIS and PIRATE: YOU'RE JUST A MONKEY IN A LOOPY DREAM
YOU'RE JUST A MONKEY IN A LOOPY DREAM
BULLSHIT WILL MAKE THE FLOWERS GROW
AND THAT IS BEAUTIFUL

(Repeated twice.)

ALIENS: TO DIVERSE GODS
DO MORTALS BOW
HOLY COW
AND HOLY CHAO

(Repeated three times.)

ALL: GET IN DOUBT! GET IN DOUBT! GET IN DOUBT!

THE FIRST AND ONLY SECOND ACT

The First and Only Second Act of the play begins fluidly, as if the act breaks and entr'acte were just a bit of dramaturgy that the audience would never know about, were they not reading this. EVERYONE leaves and KERRY is at the old farmhouse.)

NO PLACE LIKE OHM

KERRY: OHM, OHM, OHM
THERE'S NO PLACE LIKE OHM
THEY SAID TO SIT HERE ON THE RUBBLE
TO ACTIVATE MY PINEAL GLAND

TILL MY THOUGHTS TURN TO SOMETHING GRAND
SO I'M WAITING AND THINKING AND HOPING
TO SEE THAT WOMAN AGAIN
SHE'S BEAUTIFUL AS LIGHTNING
AND STILL AS UGLY AS NIGHT
WAIT, WAIT, WAIT
AN INSIGHT
IT'S COMING TO ME ALL IN A FLASH
I CAN SPEAK IT I CAN SAY WHAT IT IS
AN APHORISM MAYBE
A PROPHECY MAYBE
AND CERTAINLY ITS PITHY
I CANNOT WAIT TO SAY IT
HERE IT GOES!
KING KONG DIED FOR OUR SINS
THAT WAS REALLY NOTHING
A FALSE ALARM
A POP CULTURE REFERENCE
THAT DOES NO GOOD OR HARM
KING KONG DIED FOR OUR SINS.

(Enter PIRATE and EVANGELIST.)

KERRY: So you must be the Holy Man.

EVANGELIST: No, you must be the Holy Man.

KERRY: No, you must be the Holy Man.

PIRATE: I must be the Pirate.

EVANGELIST: No, you must be the Pirate.

PIRATE: I must be the Pirate.

KERRY: No, you must be the Holy Man. Is this some kind of joke?

EVANGELIST: Is what some kind of joke? No, wait. I'm sure it is some kind of joke.

KERRY: I've been sitting here for two days and not a thing has happened.

PIRATE: We used to ride the seven seas for seven years without seven things happening. Don't be so impatient. Arrr!

EVANGELIST: Incline the mind to an angle of forty-five percent degrees and periodicity becomes nonperiodicity and the ideal becomes real.

KERRY: What's with the Pirate?

PIRATE: What's with the Pirate? What's with the Pirate? *(Draws a sword and holds it to KERRY's throat.)* You've one chance to live, swabby, one chance only. Name the greatest pirate of them all.

KERRY: Uh… Blackbeard?

PIRATE: Roberto Clemente.

EVANGELIST: She's Puerto Rican.

PIRATE: Like Jesus.

EVANGELIST: Give us the apple, Kerry. Give us the apple before you learn the secrets of its power.

KERRY: You tricked me. Sent me into some house that's falling down, just to waste my time. It'd just make you people crazy if a normal guy like me got to unleash the power of the apple.

EVANGELIST: Oh, I want you to use the apple. Don't kid yourself. If you got that thing working for even a second, you'd give it right back to Eris. Use it. Go ahead. The secret's all around you.

IF IT'S FALLING PUSH IT DOWN

EVANGELIST: IF IT'S FALLING PUSH IT DOWN
IF IT'S FALLING PUSH IT DOWN

PIRATE: QUIT STALLING ASS CLOWN

EVANGELIST and PIRATE: IF IT'S FALLING PUSH IT DOWN

EVANGELIST and PIRATE: *(In counterpoint.)* IF IT'S FALLING PUSH IT DOWN
IF IT'S FALLING PUSH IT DOWN
QUIT STALLING ASS CLOWN
IF IT'S FALLING PUSH IT DOWN

PIRATE: SHIVER ME TIMBERS ALL HANDS ON BOARD
THE DISCORDIAN PIRATES ARE IN YOUR FNORD

KERRY: BUT I DON'T LIKE CHAOS
AND I DON'T LIKE CHANCE
ALL I WANT IS ANSWERS
ALL THAT IS SOLID MELTS INTO AIR
MARX SAID THAT—

PIRATE: AND I DON'T REALLY CARE
YOU READ TOO MANY BOOKS
YOU'VE GOT TOO MUCH KNOWLEDGE
YOU WASTED FOUR YEARS
IN COMMUNITY COLLEGE

EVANGELIST: IF IT'S FALLING PUSH IT DOWN

PIRATE: IF IT'S FALLING KNOCK IT DOWN

EVANGELIST: QUIT STALLING ASS CLOWN

PIRATE and EVANGELIST: IF IT'S FALLING KNOCK IT DOWN

KERRY: I ONCE BELIEVED IN GOD
AND I ONCE BELIEVED IN MAN
NOW I ONLY THINK
ABOUT MY PINEAL GLAND
SHE WAS A VISION, THE FIRST I EVER HAD
WITHOUT HER I'M SURE TO GO MAD

PIRATE: GO MAD THEN SWABBY GO
'CAUSE IT'S THE ONLY WAY TO KNOW
HAVE ONE OF THOSE DREAMS
WHERE YOU'RE FALLING OFF A CLIFF
BUT DON'T WAKE UP
UNTIL YOU SEE WHAT YOU HIT

EVANGELIST: THAT'S WHAT SHE DID SHE USED TO
    BE A PILOT

PIRATE: I TOOK A BAD HIT AND NOW I'M A PIRATE

KERRY: IS THIS REALLY LIFE?
IS THIS WHAT WE DO?

EVANGELIST: NO LOOK AROUND YOU
YOU'RE IN A PLAY FOOL

KERRY: What did he say?

PIRATE: He said you're being playful

KERRY: Oh.

EVANGELIST: SEE YOU LATER

PIRATE: SEE YOU AROUND

EVANGELIST and PIRATE: (In counterpoint.) IF IT'S
    FALLING PUSH IT DOWN
IF IT'S FALLING PUSH IT DOWN
QUIT STALLING ASS CLOWN
IF IT'S FALLING PUSH IT DOWN

(Repeated. KERRY sings during second verse.)

KERRY: BUT I DON'T LIKE CHAOS
AND I DON'T LIKE CHANCE
ALL I WANT IS ANSWERS
IF IT'S FALLING KNOCK IT DOWN.

KERRY: But my life is a miserable mess.

EVANGELIST: Turn your miserable mess into a beautiful, joyful, and splendid one.

(EVANGELIST and PIRATE exit.)

KERRY: Where are you going? Don't you want to sing some more? Why were we even singing at all? If you people won't show me how to use the apple, I'll deliver it into the hands of your enemies. I will! What if the forces of rules and order owned the apple? What then, huh? What then?

(Cosmic music. ERIS and KERRY are together.)

ERIS: You look sad, Kerry.

KERRY: To be human is to be wretched.

ERIS: It can't be all that bad.

KERRY: We fight, we murder each other, we make each other unhappy, we alienate each other, we're terrible to each other.

ERIS: And…

KERRY: And it makes us miserable.

ERIS: Then why don't you stop?

KERRY: What? How?

ERIS: I could tell you the answer.

KERRY: Then please tell me.

ERIS: Sorry, this is a dream. (Leaves.)

KERRY: You're really ticking me off. That's it. That's it. I'm going to bring the apple to the right people!

(BOB enters, in a hurry.)

I BLEW UP THOSE MONKS

BOB: I DID IT
I REALLY DID IT
I BLEW UP THOSE MONKS
BLEW UP THE MONASTERY
I DID IT
I REALLY DID IT
'CAUSE THAT'S WHERE THEY LIVE
SURE IT WAS KIND OF SCARY
BUT I DIDN'T LIKE THEM
I JUST DIDN'T LIKE THEM AT ALL

KERRY: YOU HORRID FOOL
WHAT DID YOU DO THAT FOR?

BOB: I DID IT BECAUSE THEY ARE THE KNIGHTS TEMPLAR
AND 'CAUSE
I HAD BLASTING CAPS
AND AMMONIUM NITRATE IN MY FERTILIZER

KERRY: THE KNIGHTS TEMPLAR
THAT'S A PHONY MYTH

BOB: IT'S TRUE

THEY'RE IN A SECRET SECT
THEY GOT STRANGE POWERS
ANTI-CHRIST RITUALS
A CONSPIRACY
THEIR OLD TREACHERY
IS HABITUAL I GOTTA GET OUT
I'M ON THE RUN NOW
IF ANYONE ASKS
TELL NO ONE.

We Are the Knights Templar

MONKS: *(Offstage.)* WE ARE THE KNIGHTS TEMPLAR
WE ARE
WE ARE THE KNIGHTS TEMPLAR WE ARE

BOB: They survived. They sound angry.

KERRY: They sound like Smurfs.

BOB: I gotta get out of here.

MONKS: *(Offstage.)* THERE GOES THAT STUPID FUCK,
THAT FUCK
WHO BLEW UP OUR HOUSE WITH A RYDER TRUCK

BOB: Ahh! Get away get away! *(Exits.)*

MONKS: *(Offstage.)* WE ARE THE KNIGHTS TEMPLAR
WE ARE
WE ARE THE KNIGHTS TEMPLAR WE ARE
STUDY DEMONOLOGY WITH AN ENEMY THIS SUNDAY!

KERRY: Wait! I need you. I want to join you. I want to rule the world.

(MONKS enter.)

MONK #1: What makes you think you should rule the world?

MONK #3: You abandoned us once already.

MONK #4: You can't comprehend the breadth of our power and influence.

KERRY: I can learn.

MONK #1: You have to fill out an application.

MONK #3: And take a test.

MONK #4: And pass a background check.

MONK #1: And you have to be able to use Excel.

MONK #3: And you have to possess the Golden Apple of the Hesperides.

KERRY: You know I have the apple. *(Holds the apple for them to see.)*

MONK #4: All hail the world's new ruler.

MONK #3: *(Aside.)* We'll make a dupe of him.

MONK #4: *(Aside.)* Dude, he can hear you.

MONK #1: You've got work to do, buddy. It's a big-ass planet.

MONK #3: Like Uranus.

MONK #4: You are so sophomoric.

(They bring him a throne and seat him in it. During KERRY's song, MONKS are bringing him papers to sign. ALIENS are watching from the background.)

King of the World

MONK #3: PEACE IN THE MIDDLE EAST

MONK #4: WELL, MAYBE FOR A WEEK

MONK #1: NEW NOSE FOR J-LO!

MONK #4: HOW ARE YOU?

MONK #3: CURE TUBERCULOSIS

MONK #4: AUTHORIZE A BLIZZARD

MONK #3: AND ANOTHER GORE CLONE

MONK #1: GIVE GEORGE BUSH THE FLU

MONK #4: AND HIS DAD

MONK #3: BAN ALL BREAST IMPLANTS

KERRY: I SENT THE KURDS A SHIPMENT OF ROCKET
GRENADES
I SENT THEM TO BAGHDAD TO TAKE OUT HUSSEIN
I SENT A LETTER TO GREENSPAN WHO'LL TAKE ALL
THE BLAME
FOR A POWER PLANT CLOSING IN PENOBSCOT MAINE
USING NORTHERN LIGHTS TO MAKE EVERYONE
DO MY BIDDING, IT WORKS A MIND CONTROL WEAPON
I WANTED YOU TO HAVE YOUR OWN LIVES TO RUN
BUT A FREE PEOPLE NEVER GET ANYTHING DONE
THE KING OF THE WORLD'S GOT PAPERS TO SIGN
BRIBES TO COLLECT AND LIVES TO DESIGN
THE STATE OF THE WORLD'S NOT TOTALLY MINE
IF I DID EVERYTHING I'D FALL SO FAR BEHIND

MONKS: THE KING OF THE WORLD IS TOTALLY FOOLED
MANIPULATED BY THE SUBJECTS HE RULES
HE THINKS HE SIGNED A PAPER ENDING A DROUGHT
BUT INSTEAD HE SENT A VIRUS TO THE WHITE HOUSE

KERRY and MONKS: *(In harmony.)* MOST OF MY DAYS
ARE COMPLETELY MUNDANE

SPENT MONITORING SUNSPOTS AND CONTROLLING
    THE RAIN
I KEEP THE WORLD GOING FROM DAY TO DAY
FROM THE BIGGEST DECISIONS TO THE WORST MINU-
    TIAE

(KERRY and MONKS in counterpoint.)

KERRY: THE KING OF THE WORLD'S GOT PAPERS TO SIGN
BRIBES TO COLLECT AND LIVES TO DESIGN
THE STATE OF THE WORLD'S NOT TOTALLY MINE
IF I DID EVERYTHING I'D FALL SO FAR BEHIND

MONK #3: CHOP DOWN RAINFOREST TREES

MONK #4: SELL WEAPONS ON EBAY

MONK #3: NEW SHATNER ALBUM

MONK #4: HOW ARE YOU?

MONK #1: BOB DOBBS'S BURIAL

MONK #3: BAN ERIS FROM THE EARTH

MONK #4: APPEAR ON *LARRY KING LIVE*

MONK #3: GIVE US THE APPLE

MONK #4: HOW ARE YOU?

MONK #1: INVADE ISTANBUL

MONKS: PEOPLE STILL ARE STARVING AND THERE'S
    GLOBAL UNREST
AND THEY JUST OPENED WAL-MART IN HISTORIC BUDA-
    PEST

ALIENS and MONKS: *(In harmony.)* THAT FOOL BOB
    FAILED US
BLEW UP THE MONKS TOO SOON
WE WANTED KERRY TO BE WITH THEM
SO WE COULD TAKE THE APPLE TO THE MOON

MONKS: THERE'S ANOTHER REVOLUTION IN CHILE

MONK #4: THERE'S NO TIME TO LOSE

MONK #3: DEPLOY THE CIA

MONK #1: AND DID YOU CHECK THE BLACK MARKETS

MONKS #3 AND #4: THERE'S HIGH-GRADE URANIUM
    ON SALE IN BELGRADE

KERRY: AND WHATEVER CAME OF MY UTOPIAN
    VISIONS
SPELLED OUT WITH SOME WELL-PLACED DECISIONS
MY ASSOCIATES ARE RICH
NOW I'VE GOT MONEY TOO

BUT LOOK AT EARTH FROM OUTER SPACE
AND YOU'LL SEE IT'S MOSTLY BLUE

ZALTAR: APPLE BEARER'S FAILING

BALTAR: NO MATTER WHAT HE DOES

MIDGE: THE WORLD STAYS THE SAME

BALTAR: HE'S STARTING TO

MIDGE: LOSE HIS IDEALS

ZALTAR: BEGINNING TO NOTICE

BALTAR: IT IS ALL A FOOL'S GAME

ALIENS: STARTING TO NOTICE
THE WORLD STAYS THE SAME

(News clips play, GHOST OF BOB enters.)

GHOST OF BOB: NOTHING IS UNDER CONTROL,
    KERRY
NOTHING IS UNDER CONTROL
CHAOS, SURE IT IS KINDA SCARY
BUT NO ONE CAN RULE THE WORLD

KERRY, ALIENS, and MONKS: *(In harmony.)* BOB,
    YOU'RE DEAD I'M SO SORRY
I WISH I COULD BRING YOU BACK TO LIFE
I CAN PASS ANY LAW THAT I CAN DREAM OF
BUT I JUST CAN'T TURN BACK TIME

*(ALIENS/MONKS and GHOST OF BOB in counter-
point.)*

ALIENS and MONKS: THE KING OF THE WORLD
PAPERS TO SIGN
BRIBES TO COLLECT
LIVES TO DESIGN
STATE OF THE WORLD
TOTALLY MINE
DID EVERYTHING
LEAVE THEM ALONE

GHOST OF BOB: YOU HAVE BECOME
WHAT I'VE ALWAYS FEARED
A TYRANT ON A THRONE
LET THE EARTH BE FREE OF YOU
LEAVE ALL THESE PEOPLE ALONE

(Repeated.)

KERRY: *(With ALIENS, MONKS, and GHOST OF BOB
    in counterpoint.)* THE KING OF THE WORLD'S GOT
    PAPERS TO SIGN
BRIBES TO COLLECT AND LIVES TO DESIGN

THE STATE OF THE WORLD'S NOT TOTALLY MINE
IF I DID EVERYTHING I'D FALL SO FAR BEHIND.

(GHOST OF BOB leaves. MONK #1 stops by with a paper for KERRY to sign.)

KERRY: I'm not signing that.

MONK #1: The aliens say to sink Japan.

KERRY: Why are we taking orders from the aliens?

(ALIENS step forward.)

BALTAR and ZALTAR: We rule this planet. You're only our proxy.

KERRY: I still have the apple.

BALTAR and ZALTAR: The apple will power our Hypergalactic Universe Re-creator. The Hodge and Podge Device.

MIDGE: We're going to get things right this time.

KERRY: You, monks, why do you take orders from the aliens?

MONK #1: We don't. We just wanted them to wrest the apple from you—

MONK #3: So we could pick up the fumble.

MIDGE: You robed humans will never have the apple!

KERRY: Well I'm not taking orders from any of you. I'm going to establish the system I always dreamed about. I'm going to walk among the people and find out what they want and then I'm going to rule justly and fairly. I'm going to create the perfect society according to Harvard philosopher John Rawls. I'm going to make rules that everyone can agree to, be they rich or poor, by using his Principle of Blind Justice.

MIDGE: But you forget, human… in the land of the blind, the one-eyed man is king.

ZALTAR: Face!

(ALIENS try to surround KERRY, but MONKS cut them off. A fight ensues; they're pretty evenly matched. As the TWO PARTIES battle upstage, KERRY notices that a MAGIC 8 BALL rolls onto the stage. He picks it up.)

KERRY: Are the aliens real?

VOICE: Answer unclear, ask again later.

MIDGE: Shit. I had a feeling we might be real.

(Since she's distracted from the fight, she should take a hard shot to the head here.)

KERRY: Is the universe ruled by chaos?

BALL: Answer unclear, ask again later.

KERRY: Is the order we perceive just a veil on the underlying chaos of reality as the pattern of waves distorts the random nature of the sea?

BALL: Do I seem in the mood to answer arcane or metaphysical questions?

KERRY: Answer unclear, ask again later.

BALL: Don't you have a Ouija board to play with? Or a hacky sack? That's it, go get some exercise.

KERRY: Hey, you rolled to me.

BALL: No, I rolled.

KERRY: You rolled to where I'm standing.

BALL: I can't control the diminishing effect of the co-efficient of friction on inertia.

KERRY: What do you want?

BALL: Put me down and give me a push.

KERRY: You were sent to answer my questions.

BALL: That's your trip, man.

KERRY: I'll smash you on the ground.

BALL: All right, one question.

KERRY: And follow-ups.

BALL: Follow-ups must be directly related to the first question.

KERRY: All right. Is Eris true?

BALL: Everything is true.

KERRY: Even false things?

BALL: Even false things are true.

KERRY: How can that be?

BALL: I don't know man, just give her the apple.

(KERRY rolls the BALL offstage.)

BALL: Plant your seeds!

KERRY: What? What?

(BUM walks by, muttering.)

BUM: Seek into the Chao if thou wouldst be wise And find ye delight in Her Great Surprise! Look into the

Chao if thou wantest to know What's in a Chao and why it ain't so!

KERRY: Yes, a bum! Bums often have mystical answers in these situations. It's bum ex machina.

BUM: Fnord is the serial number on a box of cereal. The donut hole and the whole donut. It's written on the empty pages at the end of a book. Christ is fnord. Quality is job one at the Fnord Foundation. Climb every mountain and fnord every stream. Here's a fnord to the wise, if you'll just read the Fnordian Times—

KERRY: Where should I plant my seed?

BUM: Pull the cosmic trigger, away with future shock and reality is what you can get away with.

KERRY: Didn't you used to work with my father?

BUM: Grasshopper always wrong in argument with chicken. *(Wanders off.)*

(MONKS seem to have defeated ALIENS, and they now move toward KERRY.)

MONK #3: Just give us the apple.

MONK #1: Don't make us kick another ass today.

MONK #4: Give us control over the forces of chaos and chance.

(GHOST OF BOB enters.)

KERRY: Bob, what should I do?

GHOST OF BOB: I'm hardly the best guy to ask for advice. I really botched my life. I was a paranoid freak and now I'm a paranoid ghost.

MONK #1: Join us, Kerry. Take your rightful place in our order.

MONK #3: The can factory is gone.

MONK #4: And now you know that you can't rule the world.

MONK #1: But you're welcome among us. You know too much, anyway. So you'll have to join us. Or die.

MONK #3: And bring the apple with you.

(ALIENS regroup. EVANGELIST and PIRATE and ERIS enter. EVERYONE converges on KERRY… ERIS stops them from harming KERRY. BUM wanders back onto the stage.)

BUM: All this noise, can't sleep, so hungry. *(To KERRY.)* You. You gotta have some food.

KERRY: All I have in the world is an inedible Golden Apple. I'm sorry.

BUM: Whattya mean inedible?

KERRY: I mean you can't eat it.

BUM: I eat garbage, you idiot. There's nothing I can't eat when I'm hungry. And what's it to you? You can get another apple anytime you want. I can't get nothing. You gonna be greedy over an apple.

KERRY: This apple chose me.

BUM: So I gotta starve? Let me look at that apple.

(KERRY lets him look.)

BUM: This apple didn't choose you. It says right here in Attic Greek, kalliste. That could mean "for the prettiest one," or that could mean "for the fairest." And since you already ate today, I say it's fairest that I get the apple. Or wouldja rather I curl up and die right here?

KERRY: No, you're right. You're right. You have to eat. Fair's fair. If you can't chew it, sell it.

(He hands the apple to BUM. BUM seems to grow in power.)

BUM: You fool! Now the world will crumble under the power of my iron will! Heh, heh. I'm just kidding, ya nitwit. *(Polishes the apple on his filthy shirt.)*

PLANT YOUR SEEDS/BORN TO SEE THE LIGHT REPRISE

ERIS: YOU GOTTA PLANT YOUR SEEDS
CULTIVATE YOUR GARDEN
BE LIKE CANDIDE
DON'T LET THE WORLD HARDEN
YOU LIKE PANGLOSS
THAT FROTHING FOOL
WHO THOUGHT EVERYTHING WAS GOOD
WHEN EVERYTHING WAS NOTHING

KERRY: I'M COMIN' TO SEE YA
I WAS BORN TO MEET YA
I WAS BORN TO SEE THE LIGHT
I'M A COMIN' TO SEE YA
I WAS BORN TO MEET YA I
I WAS BORN TO SEE THE LIGHT

ERIS: LIKE LEWIS CARROLL ON AN ETHER BENDER
I'M KEEPING IT REAL AS FANTASY'S PRETENDER
SO MARK REALITY "RETURN TO SENDER"
'CAUSE I AM AN IMMORTAL PRETENDER

MONKS, EVANGELIST, GOD, and GHOST OF BOB:
(*In counterpoint.*) HE'S COMIN' TO SEE YA
HE WAS BORN TO MEET YA
HE WAS BORN TO SEE THE LIGHT
HE'S A COMIN' TO SEE YA
HE WAS BORN TO MEET YA
HE WAS BORN TO SEE THE LIGHT

ALIENS: THE GODDESS WORMED INTO HIS MIND
BEFORE WE WERE ABLE TO PROBE HIS BEHIND
SHE SET HIM FREE TO FREE MANKIND
FROM RULES AND ORDER OF THE THIRD KIND

KERRY: SHE REVEALED ALL CONSPIRACIES
AS THE NONSENSE SHE KNEW THEM TO BE
SHE FORCED RELIGION TO TURN VESTIGIAL
AND FREED ME FROM FALSE PROCESSIONALS

MONKS and EVANGELIST: WE ARE THE KNIGHTS
    TEMPLAR WE ARE
WE ARE THE KNIGHTS TEMPLAR WE ARE

(*Etc., throughout the rest of the song.*)

ERIS: I'M FAKE
I'M NOT REAL
I'M FAKE, YES I AM
I'M FAKE
I'M NOT REAL
I'M FAKE YES I'M FAKE

KERRY: (*With GOD and BOB in counterpoint.*) I'M
    COMIN TO SEE YA
I WAS BORN TO MEET YA
I WAS BORN TO SEE THE LIGHT
I'M COMIN TO SEE YA
I WAS BORN TO MEET YA
I WAS BORN TO SEE THE LIGHT

ALIENS: (*With ERIS and PIRATE in counterpoint.*)
    YOU'RE JUST A MONKEY IN A LOOPY DREAM
YOU'RE JUST A MONKEY IN A LOOPY DREAM
BULLSHIT WILL MAKE THE FLOWERS GROW
AND THAT IS BEAUTIFUL

(*Repeated.*)

KERRY: (*With GOD and GHOST OF BOB in counter-
    point.*) I'M COMIN TO SEE YA
I WAS BORN TO MEET YA
I WAS BORN TO SEE THE LIGHT

ERIS and PIRATE: I'M FAKE
I'M NOT REAL
I'M FAKE, YES I AM

I'M FAKE
I'M NOT REAL
I'M FAKE YES I'M FAKE

ALL: BORN TO SEE THE
BORN TO SEE THE
BORN TO SEE THE LIGHT.

(*After the song, BUM bites into the apple. As BUM eats the apple, characters should begin transforming into their normal selves. MONKS are a group of college kids in hooded sweatshirts, ALIENS a group of girls who went out clubbing, EVANGELIST is a stockbroker, and PIRATE is a pilot. BOB DOBBS back into MANAGER. ERIS remains herself.*)

PIRATE: Science…I believe in science. And…for some reason…vampires. And I'm supposed to be at the airport!

EVANGELIST: Will I ever see you again, baby?

PIRATE: No. Definitely not. Some "date."

MONK #1: You know, I kind of want to major in religion.

(*MONKS #3 and #4 nod like it's a good idea.*)

MIDGE: See, I told you girls rollin' would be fun.

KERRY: Why is the bum still a bum?

ERIS: Because he doesn't have a job.

BOB: And speaking of jobs, Kerry. How about it? Join the ol' Can-Do team at America Can Canneries and Bottlers? You can even work with your old man.

(*BUM hands the apple core to KERRY and exits.*)

BUM: Here. Don't litter.

KERRY: No, Mr. Dobbs. It's just not right for me.

BOB: Your loss, kid. (*He exits.*)

KERRY: I love you, Eris.

ERIS: But I'm just a figurative symbol.

KERRY: Are you sure you're not a real girl who wants to have sex with me? Because that would make a great ending.

ERIS: Figurative symbol.

KERRY: Well, I love you anyway.

(*She exits. KERRY finds a place to plant some seeds and as he does he sings…*)

Opposable Monk Reprise

KERRY: THE OPPOSABLE MONK
IN GOD'S FOUR DIGITS
THE OPPOSABLE MONK
NOT EVEN RELIGIOUS
I'D SEARCHED LONG AND HARD
WAITING TO BE CALLED
COULDN'T HACK A REAL JOB
I JUST PICKED UP THE PHONE...

(BOB reenters.)

BOB: Is this your idea of some kind of a joke?

KERRY: What?

BOB: You don't want the job, fine. But don't mess with a man's lunch.

KERRY: I didn't.

BOB: Then what's this? *(He pulls a Golden Fish out of his lunch box.)*

KERRY: That's your trip, man.

(END.)

Part III

CHEKHOV AND OTHER RUSSIANS

In order to survive, art must evolve. Painting, for example, as an art form, has morphed over history as practitioners have utilized forms or styles developed by their predecessors while working to find new and innovative methods of presentation.

Unfortunately, artists of the theatre sometimes fail to acknowledge the past in such a way. Innovation for the sake of innovation may be valued over innovation that springs from the lessons of history. Playwrights strive to make their work relevant to their own culture but may neglect the pursuit of universal relevance. It is only by studying the best, classic works of theatre—the ones that have survived over centuries and even millennia—that contemporary playwrights can begin to understand how to create a piece of theatre with historic endurance; a piece capable of contributing to the overall evolution of the art form.

As artistic director of Resonance Ensemble, a theatre company dedicated to fostering classically inspired new work, I have come to appreciate the value of this kind of historic research. Two years ago, we worked with one of the masterpieces of the Russian theatre, Maxim Gorky's *The Lower Depths*. My study of the play strengthened my belief that Russian literature by writers like Gorky, Chekhov, and Dostoevsky offers so much to theatre artists and audiences of today: it provides an unparalleled balance of rich, poetic language; layered, complex characters; meaningful, naturalistic dialogue; and passionate, palpable subtext.

All three of the pieces in the following part capitalize on these strengths. Jeff Cohen demonstrates the timelessness of Chekhov's *Uncle Vanya* by resetting it in a familiar, contemporary setting. *Story of an Unknown Man* by Anthony P. Peninino shows how the importance of Chekhov's work has endured over time in his own country. And Alexander Harrington's faithful adaptation of Dostoevsky's *The Brothers Karamazov* presents the epic themes and ideas of the novel without commentary, allowing audiences to judge its relevance for themselves.

But what makes these plays (and the genre of classic Russian literature in general) most compelling is the way each one intellectually and emotionally explores issues of personal identity in the context of their society as a whole. In politically volatile times such as these, in a country struggling to justify its moral convictions with the realities of the existing global community, issues like this are especially timely.

—*Eric Parness*

UNCLE JACK

An adaptation of Chekhov's *Uncle Vanya*

Jeff Cohen

JEFF COHEN was born in 1957 in Baltimore, Maryland. He is a director, playwright, and acting teacher. He was previously the artistic director/ founder of both the RAPP Arts Center (1985–90) and the Worth Street Theater Company (1995–2005), and is currently the artistic director of Dog Run Repertory Theatre Company. Cohen's other works as a playwright include *The Seagull: The Hamptons: 1990s* (1990), *Orestes: I Murdered My Mother* (1994), *Whoa-Jack!* (1997), *Loft* (2000), *Tartuffe* (2001), *Men of Clay* (2006), and *God's Stones* (2006). His directing credits include *The Coyote Bleeds* (1995, world premiere), *Small Craft Warnings* (1999, first off-Broadway revival), *Isn't It Romantic* (2000, first off-Broadway revival), *Four* (2002, New York premiere, Manhattan Theatre Club), *The Mystery of Attraction* (2003, New York premiere), *The Moonlight Room* (2004, world premiere), and *Happy Days* with Lea DeLaria and David Greenspan (2005, Classic Stage Company). Cohen and Worth Street were also producers of the first off-Broadway revival of Larry Kramer's *The Normal Heart* starring Raul Esparza (2004, the Public Theater). Cohen was also the producer and director of the Tribeca Playhouse *Stage Door Canteen* for Ground Zero workers following the 9/11 World Trade Center attacks, for which he received a Drama Desk Award. He is a consistently top ten–ranked tennis player at the Riverside Clay Tennis courts, and lives in Inwood with his wife, Sydney, and their two dogs, Tallulah and Ellie.

Uncle Jack was first presented by Worth Street Theatre Company (Jeff Cohen, Artistic Director) on November 8, 1999, at Tribeca Playhouse, New York City, with the following cast and credits:

Jack Vaughn	Gerald Anthony
Doctor Michael Ashe	Bernard K. Addison
Sophie Vaughn	Keira Naughton
Elizabeth Vaughn	Betty Low
Professor Alexander Coughlan	Ronald Guttman
Helena Coughlan	Francesca Faridany
Mary	Leila Danette
Waffles	Paul Whitthorne

Directed by: Jeff Cohen
Music: Steve Bargonetti and Diane Gioia
Settings: Sonia Alio
Costumes: Susan Soetaert
Lighting: Chris Dallos

CHARACTERS

JACK VAUGHN: fifty, bitter with a sardonic sense of humor.

DOCTOR MICHAEL ASHE: fifty, black, a burnout, a former hippy whose idealism is in crisis.

SOPHIE VAUGHN: twenties, Jack's niece, earthy, no nonsense.

ELIZABETH VAUGHN: seventies, Jack's mother and Sophie's grandmother, the matriarch of the Vaughn family, obsessed with politics and an old-fashioned liberal.

PROFESSOR ALEXANDER COUGHLAN: seventies, widower of Jack's sister, Sophie's father, charismatic, handsome, and charming. A celebrity.

HELENA COUGHLAN: twenties, Alexander's new bride, Sophie's new stepmother, a former runway model.

MARY: sixties–eighties, black, long-time employee of the Vaughns.

WAFFLES: thirties–forties, a pockmarked hillbilly.

LOCATION

Uncle Jack takes place on the Vaughn family estate in rural West Virginia in the present.

AUTHOR'S NOTE

Topical references should be kept as current as possible.

FOREWORD

I have done two contemporary adaptations of Chekhov. The first set *The Seagull* in the Hamptons with the unwieldy title of *The Seagull: The Hamptons: 1990s* (there was also a production on Cape Cod that swapped Wellfleet for the Hamptons), and the second put *Uncle Vanya* in West Virginia and I called that *Uncle Jack*. The adaptations, rather than being a gimmick or an attempt to deconstruct or one-up Chekhov, were a serious attempt to restore the original intent of the author for a contemporary American audience. I realize that is a bold statement, so allow me to explain. What was revolutionary about Chekhov's plays was their slice-of-life quality. For the first time, a playwright wrote about real people in real relationships having real conversations. And the result was that Chekhov had an absolutely unique relationship with his audience. They were able to look up on stage and actually see characters that reminded them of themselves or folks they knew. They could relate to these people and their stories on the most intimate level. We're used to that now in our contemporary culture which is saturated with personal stories, but, at the time, when theatre and opera were formal and primarily depicted royalty and gods, Chekhov's achievement of making theatre personal was remarkable. His plays are chock-full of pop cultural references that were contemporary and familiar to his audiences. I understand that his dialogue in Russian was extraordinarily close to the way people of the time actually spoke, as opposed to the more poetic syntax of the age's more classical dramas. And his depiction of fractured families and the crisis of ordinary life resonated with his audiences in a way that they had never seen before.

But all of that seems to be missing in the way Chekhov is presented today. His works have suffered the fate of reverence: they have been placed in the theatrical equivalent of a museum, and, while universally admired, they are not, I would contend, enjoyed in the way that his audiences enjoyed them. More importantly, I firmly believe that he intended for the plays to be contemporaneous with his audience, to be enjoyed on that most intimate level, and that he would not have wanted them to be admired as one admires a famous painting, from behind a velvet rope in a museum. Without taking a contemporary audience into consideration, translators and producers do a disservice to Chekhov's intent, and their very fidelity to the exactness of his words is unfaithful to their spirit. Chekhov without his audience is not Chekhov at all.

I realize that it is presumptuous to suppose what Chekhov would have written had he written in America one hundred years later. But that is the task that I set for myself. And *The Seagull* and *Uncle Vanya* are the two of his major plays that best lend themselves to this contemporary re-imagining. Those who have admired these adaptations have asked why I have not done the same with *The Three Sisters* or *The Cherry Orchard*. My answer is that I cannot quite re-imagine them in a contemporary milieu. *The Three Sisters* is set on a military outpost so far from civilization that Moscow seems but a grand and distant dream. I do not know of such an outpost today that would make New York City or Washington, D.C., so inaccessible. In addition, the play depicts a military structure of commissioned nobility versus ordinary soldier (Vershinin and Tuzenbach versus Solyony) for which I am hard pressed to find a contemporary equivalent. As for *The Cherry Orchard*, it is steeped in the foment of revolution, of the breakdown of the landed gentry and the irresistible rise of a bourgeoisie unburdened by the confines of a centuries-old class system. And while we in America are certainly divided by economic and racial classes, ours is not a revolution of continental proportions. *The Cherry Orchard* is Chekhov at his most prescient, predicting the chaos and turmoil that would embroil Russia for the next century and beyond. There is no such American equivalent.

In *The Seagull*, Chekhov wrote of a famous actress, a famous novelist, and a rebellious exemplar of the avant-garde. He set his play at a vacation resort where the wealthy and famous are served by the townies. And he depicts an ambitious young townie girl who is willing to do just about anything to achieve celebrity and fame. Where better to set this play than in the Hamptons?

In *Uncle Vanya*, Chekhov wrote of a man who is in the throes of an unbearable midlife crisis and of a doctor who takes up the cause of environmentalism because he suffers a crisis of confidence when he accidentally kills a young boy on his operating table. Chekhov set the play on a family estate in the country. Upsetting the applecart is the arrival of a famous professor from the big city with his extraordinarily beautiful young bride. Where better to set this story than the despoiled beauty of the hills of West Virginia?

At the beginning of the twenty-first century I hope that the reader and the theatre-goer find a connection to *Uncle Jack* that is as thrilling as the connection experienced by Chekhov's audiences at the end of the nineteenth century. My aim is to remove the distance between us and the play, and I hope in some way that I have succeeded.

ACT ONE

Darkness. The sound of songbirds can be heard, intermingled with the buzz and hum of crickets—nature's nightlife giving way to the dawn. Soon the sound of a vintage four-cylinder Volkswagen Microbus is heard putt-putting up the driveway—its gears signaling its unmistakable metallic whine. The lights come up on the shimmering light of dawn in late spring. The mist rises from the beautiful landscape of gently rolling wooded hills, acres of grasses, dark forests, and, in the distance, the dark and imposing contours of the Appalachian

Mountains. In the foreground we see the side frame of a beautiful weatherworn old house—the veranda and garden just off it take up the largest portion of the stage. Gorgeous patches of color bloom in the wooden flower boxes and overgrown flower beds. Flowers cascade in and around white statuary and birdbaths. An eclectic grouping of furniture is carelessly arranged under a broad awning. In a wicker-cushioned love-seat, JACK VAUGHN lies in a cramped fetal position, snoring. Close by, MARY sits by a serving cart, some knitting sitting idly in her expansive lap. Upstage, back to the audience, gaz-

ing out at the rolling hills, DOCTOR MICHAEL ASHE stands for several moments before walking with agitation toward the house. Both he and JACK have unshaven, unkempt hair and beards—ASHE's head is strewn with nasty dreadlocks. ASHE, in obvious frustration, paces back and forth under the awning.

MARY: Doctor Mike—

ASHE: What?

MARY: Doctor Mike—why don't you stop pacing and just sit down?

ASHE: Why?

MARY: Because you're makin' me all nervous and agitated, that's why. You know I hate to see you gettin' yourself all worked up. Why don't you just let me fix you something to eat?

ASHE: I'm not hungry.

MARY: I can fix you a cup of coffee—

ASHE: No thank you.

MARY: I can put a little bit of whiskey in it for you.

(ASHE considers this.)

MARY: Unless of course you think it's too early.

ASHE: It might be early for you, Mary, but it sure as hell ain't too early for me. If anything, it's too late. I've been up all night. *(A beat.)* Mary—how long have we known each other?

MARY: How long? Since you been comin' here, Doctor Mike. Since before Sophie could talk. Lemme see. That was 1974, wasn't it?—

ASHE: Well, when you look at me, do you see a change?

MARY: Do I see a what?

ASHE: A change, Mary, do I seem different to you?

MARY: Of course you is different, Doctor Mike, we all is different.

ASHE: No, that's not what I mean. I know I've changed, but do I seem—*different?*

MARY: Oh. I see what you gettin' at. Sometimes I remember thinkin' you was so young? And handsome. And I remember sayin' to myself—him a doctor? A nice-lookin' young colored man! But not no more. No sir. Age done caught up with you.

(He reacts.)

MARY: Well look at yourself. Look at your hair. And you drink too much—

ASHE: I know I do—

MARY: And that awful reefer you always be smokin'—

ASHE: Yes Mary, I know—

MARY: A couple years ago when Miss Jenny passed on—rest that good woman's soul—I think you took it kinda hard, Doctor Mike. You carry around a burden with you. The weight of the world seems to be on your shoulders. You and Miss Sophie.

ASHE: Maybe. But maybe it's because I'm overworked, Mary. Maybe it's because folks treat me like a piece of damn property around here. I am on my feet from morning to night to morning again. I ain't never gettin' any peace around here. I can't even sleep when I'm lyin' in my bed on the nights that are quiet because I'm thinkin' that at any minute that goddamn phone is gonna start ringin'. Mary, in all the time we've known one another have you ever known me to take a day off? Ever known me to go on vacation? No wonder I look old, Mary. My hair, my reefer, can you blame me? A little reefer, a little whiskey, I just do it for relaxation, Mary. Wound up like a goddamn wristwatch every minute of every goddamn day! Don't I deserve to relax a little? Don't I deserve that, Mary?

MARY: No one never said you didn't, Doctor Mike.

ASHE: And I'll tell you what happens when I don't. When they wind me up and I feel like I'm gonna bust my spring. I start to wonder what the hell I'm doin' here, Mary. God knows it ain't my style to complain, but damn if I don't get sick of it sometimes, sick of the whole goddamn thing. Maybe it's a horrible thing to say, Mary, but I begin to wonder if it was just a mistake, me coming here, you know? Tending to these folks out here. Maybe I just made a mistake.

MARY: Folks need you here, Doctor Mike—

ASHE: I know they do, Mary! That's not what I'm saying. But would a thank you kill one of 'em? Doctor Ashe, thank you for tendin' to my little boy. Would that kill 'em?

MARY: God knows it wouldn't. But even if they don't say it, they think it.

ASHE: It's irritatin', that's all. It irritates me. Ain't got a goddamn soul I can talk to around here. Not even a decent goddamn radio station I can dial up when I'm drivin'. I'll tell you what I am—I am this *oddity* that these cousin-marryin' white folks like to keep around 'cause it suits them that I come around to see them when they get sick. *(He absently runs his fingers through his hair and beard.)* And damn if I haven't turned into a goddamn hillbilly oddball my damn self! *(Tugs on his beard.)* Look at this skanky thing! I look like some kinda goddamn Uncle Remus with this long skanky thing.

MARY: You ask me, I'd be more worried about that nappy old head o' hair you got there, Doctor Mike.

ASHE: My dreads, Mary? I know you're not talkin' 'bout my dreads, Mary. Ain't nothin' wrong with my Bob Marley head, Mary.

(They laugh. A beat.)

ASHE: I see what you mean though. It's the combination. Scares folks. Imagine if I was walkin' down the streets of Boston lookin' like this. Dressed like this. Decent folks'd be crossin' the street to get away from me. 'Cause I have turned into some kind of freak, Mary. That's what good livin' in this godforsaken place has done me. Turned into a freak by livin' with all these freaky oddball hillbillies around here. *(A beat.)* Well, at least there's one good thing.

MARY: What's that?

ASHE: At least I ain't gone stupid yet.

MARY: No, Doctor Mike, nobody never said you was stupid—

ASHE: No damn body better never call me stupid! Tell you that! Ain't no stupid folks that graduate medical school when they're twenty! Graduate top ten in their medical school class when they're but a mere black child! I ain't never been stupid. Never stupid. *(A beat.)* But that doesn't mean I don't—I don't feel— Damn Mary, I feel lost. Sometimes. And that's all it is. I just feel lost is all. It's like I got no place I really *want* to go, you know. Nothin' I really *want* to do. Nobody I *want* to do it for. *(He goes to her.)* Tell me something, Mary—

MARY: Yeah?

ASHE: *(Amorously.)* What's it like bein' in love?

MARY: Hell if I know!

(He begins kissing her playfully.)

MARY: Git your smelly self *off* me now, you hear me?

(The joking turns into a tender moment and ASHE lays his head in MARY's lap. She strokes his head maternally.)

ASHE: That feels nice. You make me feel like I was ten years old and you was my great-aunt Anna. You know I love you, Mary.

MARY: You just lie there and hush now.

ASHE: *(After a beat.)* I don't know if you remember. A couple of weeks before Easter. There was an outbreak of typhoid fever over by Springs, about an hour east of Morgantown—

MARY: I remember you tellin' us—

ASHE: And of course they couldn't make it over to me so I had to drive to them. We'd had all that rain and the roads were about this thick in mud and there ain't no interstate over to Springs— And they live in these plywood shanties, or shacks, or whatever you call 'em—plywood covered in garbage bags to try to keep the damn rain out—makes you wonder, Mary. The way folks live around here. Like it was the poorest place on earth—

MARY: Uh huh—

ASHE: And every time I see it, the squalor is—it's just—the stench alone is unbelievable. The filth. They ain't got no plumbing. Still usin' outhouses that drain out into the creek where they do their wash and their little kids play and they get their drinking water from—livin' in their huts with their ornery old pigs and their mangy dogs. No common sense. Goddamn backward people can't even boil water or wash their hands with soap half the time. *(Pause.)* I stayed there a coupla days. I used my Volkswagen like a hospital—you know how I do— Didn't sleep. Couldn't eat. Didn't have the stomach for it.

MARY: Mm hmm—

ASHE: So anyway I finally get to head back to my house. Maybe it's five a.m. I'm exhausted, I mean I am dog tired. All I can do to keep the damn car on the road. And the goddamn beeper goes off. I pull off by the Howard Johnson's—you know the one by Wheeling College—

MARY: I know the one—

ASHE: Order a cup of coffee. Call in. It's the station master at this train depot some twenty miles away. Seems some boy got struck by a freight train. Playin' in the goddamn tracks. I rush outta there like there's a fire in my ass. Left the damn coffee on the counter. And I get there. See the boy. Mary—I'm tellin' you— *(Pause.)* And I have them bring him into my Volkswagen. You know I got a little bed-table in there. And I'm lookin' at this boy—couldn't be no more than twelve years old. And he's somehow conscious. I feel like one of them field doctors in the Civil War. I got to amputate the boy's leg 'cause there's just no time. And I got some chloroform, you know, to put him under. And he dies. *(A beat.)* Maybe I give him too much. I hadn't slept in days. Eaten anything. His mother was there too. Stops cryin' just long enough to look at me. They was all lookin' at me. I had to close my eyes, Mary. For about a week. Closed my eyes. Laid in my bed . Turned my answering machine off, laid on my bed and closed my eyes. *(Pause.)* I wished I believed in God, Mary. For the first goddamn time in my life I wished I believed in God. I really and truly did.

(Silence.)

MARY: You don't got to believe in God, Doctor Michael. He believes in you.

ASHE: Thank you Mary, that's very sweet.

(Their attention turns to JACK who begins tossing and muttering on the love-seat. It seems to be an amorous dream he is having.)

JACK: Oh yeah…yeah…baby…that's good…

(While JACK enjoys his dream more and more, ASHE teases him by lightly touching and tickling him, causing groans of pleasure from dreaming JACK. Eventually, JACK tosses so much he falls off the love-seat and is jolted awake. MARY and ASHE laugh.)

JACK: *(Picking himself up.)* Very funny.

ASHE: Had a good sleep?

JACK: Yeah, it was just getting good. Thank you very much. *(He yawns.)* What time is it?

MARY: Almost nine thirty.

JACK: Oh. *(Looking around.)* They back yet?

MARY: No.

JACK: That figures. *(A leisurely, noisy yawn followed by stretching.)* Look at me. I'm drunk even when I'm sober. I'm asleep even when I'm awake. Ever since the bête noir's arrival I am all upside down. Sleep the mornings away. How did I get out here? Did I ever make it to bed last night?

MARY: I don't know.

JACK: Of course you don't. Michael—I remember something about you're coming here, I just can't remember why. Every goddamn night I get plastered on this crate of wine he brought with him. All I do is eat and eat and eat. I stuff myself like some big old Thanksgiving turkey. I'm smoking cigars again. Oh, Michael, the vices! Mary! The vices! Mary, what's happened around here? Everything's out of whack. Didn't we used to eat a little bit of breakfast at seven thirty and start our day? Some toast and coffee, maybe a little bit of oatmeal? A sandwich for lunch? A good dinner around seven? Didn't we used to have some kind of routine around here for the last two hundred years or so?

MARY: We sure did.

JACK: But not now. Nope. Before they come out here I'm an active man, a doer. Now? I just sleep the morning away, trying to run from this goddamn hangover like a rabbit running from a bird dog. It's Sophie keeps the place running. Not me. And it's not just me, ain't that right, Mary?

MARY: Don't get me started. He's turned this place into a hotel. Do I look like a chambermaid to you??? Here's what I'm talkin' about—I been heatin' up this same goddamn pot of coffee for two hours now and by the time they come back from whatever the hell it is they doin' it's gonna taste like the pot o' coffee I shoulda thrown out yesterday! And I can hear 'em: "Coffee's bad. Can't they make a decent cup of coffee in West Virginia? Don't they got a Starbucks near here?" As if it's my fault!—

JACK: —you tell 'em, Mary—

MARY: You damn right I will! Like last night. Playin' his god-awful opera records 'til all hours. Then, at four in the mornin' I hear somethin' in the kitchen. Reckon it's a prowler, done scared me outta my wits. I grab my baseball bat—

ASHE: —baseball bat?

MARY: Damn right! Figure it's some convict lookin' for trouble. I run into the kitchen swingin' and wavin' it like…like…like…

ASHE: Reggie Jackson?

MARY: That's the one! And I'm just about to make this mother's child meet his maker too!— When I see it's only him.

ASHE: Who?

MARY: The Professor.

ASHE: The professor?

MARY: And what's he doin'?

JACK: Tell him, Mary. Get this Michael.

MARY: He's makin' hisself a sandwich! At four in the mornin'! "Can't sleep. Hungry," he says. Scared me half outta my wits!

ASHE: So what did you do?

MARY: Well I shoulda just gone back to my bed. But he was hungry. So I made him eggs. And he give me a kiss. Right here. On the lips.

ASHE: On the lips?

MARY: (Slyly.) You ain't the only one wants some of what I got, Doctor Mike!

JACK: (Peering offstage.) They're coming. About time. Sit down, Michael. See it with your own eyes.

ALEXANDER: (Offstage.) God's country. What I came here for! Absolutely astonishing!

(PROFESSOR ALEXANDER COUGHLAN strides onstage followed by WAFFLES and SOPHIE. Coughlan is robust and handsome for a man approaching seventy. Charisma rests on him like a crown on a king. He wears a cashmere coat and carries a walking cane more for show than need. WAFFLES is a local handyman with a bad complexion. SOPHIE is the PROFESSOR's daughter and JACK's niece, in her twenties, cute, earthy, and exuberant.)

WAFFLES: Lived here all my life, Professor sir. Wouldn't never live no place else. Thought of movin' once. Thought, "Maybe I'll move to Pittsburgh, or Nashville" but I never did—

ALEXANDER: (Speaking over him.) This country is spectacular. Even today. It's inspirational and invigorating. What did we walk, ten miles?

SOPHIE: Maybe fifteen I think…

WAFFLES: Fifteen? Naw…more like eight or nine. Now, if you was to count the meadow by the creek—

ALEXANDER: (Speaking over him again.) I could do this walk every single day. Used to walk from 85th and West End up to campus every single day. Up to 121st and Amsterdam. Good walk. But nothing like this.

SOPHIE: Wait 'til tomorrow, Daddy. We'll go to the State Forest Conservancy.

JACK: (Loudly.) I'M HUNGRY!

(Now that he has their attention.)

JACK: How about breakfast?

ALEXANDER: (After a beat.) I'll just take coffee, Mary. In the study. (Calling off.) Darling, try to keep up. I'm going to the study! (Strides off.)

SOPHIE: You get him coffee, Mary, fresh pot. I'll put on some toast…

(She waves shyly at ASHE and runs off. Just then, HELENA walks in from her journey. She is a former fashion model woefully ill-dressed for traipsing around the muddy acres. She waves to MARY, WAFFLES, JACK, and ASHE as she passes through.)

HELENA: Wrong shoes. Broke a nail. Be back. Nice day!

(WAFFLES sits down by MARY and pours himself a cup of coffee. JACK and ASHE follow HELENA off with their eyes. Then both sit on the love-seat.)

JACK: What did I tell you?

ASHE: What did you tell me about what?

JACK: Him. It's already eighty degrees but that doesn't stop old Methuselah from traipsing around in his long cashmere coat!

ASHE: That was the professor?

JACK: Yup.

ASHE: Ain't nothin' wrong with him! What the hell did he call me out here for? Ain't I got better damn things to do?

JACK: Yes you have, Michael.

WAFFLES: (Speaking under, to MARY.) Simple pleasures, that's what life's about, Mary. Walking through the hills, driving through the forests, just lookin' at this garden in full bloom. The birds singin', the weather is beautiful, and even this coffee is delicious, Mary. Like a commercial on the television—I'm obliged to you for this coffee, lady.

JACK: (Continuing to ASHE.) But there is a silver lining. Forget about him. If you weren't here you never would have laid your eyes on her.

ASHE: I don't care about her or anybody else. I broke my neck to get here for him. I want to talk about him. What kind of an emergency is that?

JACK: It's the best kind, Michael. And the worst kind. Those eyes, Michael, are they not cause for emergency? Should I not get a heart attack at the sight of those swaying hips? Might my cardiac not get arrested at the touch of those pouting lips? You want an emergency, Michael. I am in a state of emergency!

ASHE: Alright, I hear you. The Doctor is in. Tell me what's ailin' you.

JACK: No.

ASHE: No?

JACK: Nothing to say.

ASHE: Don't be that way, now. I ain't in the mood, Jonathon.

JACK: Jonathon?

ASHE: Tell me what's happening. Fill me in.

JACK: You can see for yourself well enough. All that's happening is that Chairman Alexander Cough-Cough-Cough-Lan, retiree of Columbia the gem of the ocean University has arrived. And look what he's done to me. Made me fat and lazy and grumbling and grousing like some old woman at a DAR meeting. I'm takin' after dear old Momma who, by the way, is getting worse and worse. You know what she's doin' now? She's chairwoman of the West Virginia chapter of the Draft Hillary movement! Pounding away on her PC, sending emails to everyone. And when she's not doin' that she's obsessin' over her 9/11 conspiracy theories. Hell, Robert Byrd won't even return her calls anymore. She's drivin' EVERYONE crazy.

ASHE: That's not new, Jack. That's same old same old. What's up with the professor?

JACK: (With a German accent.) Herr Professor! Ach, you vant to know vhat's up mit Herr Professor. (His own voice.) Here's the short version: He's decided to return to his dead wife's estate to write the crowning achievement of his pathetic and unbelievable career. He's Thoreau. And this here is his Walden!

ASHE: He's moved in?

JACK: Has he ever.

ASHE: And he's a writer?

JACK: So the rumor goes.

ASHE: What's he writing?

JACK: How the hell do I know? Like he consults me on it. Mother's all atwitter because it's doubtless some great opus on contemporary art. Some definitive paean to the 1980s Art In America crew, you know—Longo, Salle, Fischl, Sherman…

ASHE: Who?

JACK: EXACTLY! He bought twenty cases of paper from the Office Depot in Morgantown, they delivered it in a semi for crissakes. That's fifty reams a carton. That's five hundred sheets a ream. That's five hundred thousand pieces of paper! That's what's killing your beloved forests, Michael! And for what? Nothing! He should forget the art crap and just write his autobiography. What a phenomenon that would be! He'd sell three copies at least. How would it go—a retired professor. No, not graphic enough. Here we go—a phlegmatic old fossil. A dried-up fish. I like that. A sort of stuffed academic old trout. Groaning and grumbling incessantly about his arthritis and his liver and his rheumatism and his phlebitis. But that's just hypochondria. What's really eating at him is envy. Envy! And frustration that anyone in the know knows what a dried-up old hack he really is! So how did he get here in the first place? Here's the setup: He lives on income from the estate of his first wife that gives him his New York City lifestyle that enabled him to entrap his gorgeous child of a second wife. And then he moves back here to live, second wife in tow, with the first wife's family—and his daughter that he hasn't given a crap about in a good fifteen years. And it's not like he *wanted* to move back here. Oh no—he's such a nothing that he couldn't afford to stay in New York after Columbia gave him the boot! This ass is forever moaning about what a bad shake life has given him when the fact is he's the single luckiest man in the goddamn world! This reptile hit the jackpot. Just think about it: Who was the sonuvabitch before he turned his Don Juan oily charm on my poor kid sister? A nobody, that's who. Lehigh University for crissakes! But then he seduces my sister, marries into my family, and suddenly he's the son-in-law of a senator. Now, lo and behold, academic degrees are conferred upon him like ribbons on a fat sow at a state fair. Professor at Columbia University for crissakes? Using *my* daddy's name to make his good-for-nothing way in the world. But you know what, Michael?

ASHE: What?

JACK: None of it matters.

ASHE: Why not?

JACK: Because luck is no substitute for talent. And of that little item our Professor Fish is singularly bereft. For twenty-five years the man's been lecturing and writing about art which just happens to be a subject he knows nothing about. For twenty-five years he's been riding the backs of the dealers and the poseurs and the investors like a jockey on a nag, writing with all the integrity of a racing form tout at the track, chewing over other people's ideas, spouting off with his thesaurus about Modernism, Post Modernism, Post Post Modern Modernism and any other goddamn label he can attach to that swill and the *Village Voice* prints it and Mother dutifully keeps his scrapbook and for twenty-five years he's been lecturing and writing about the kind of crap that no intelligent person would ever take seriously and which ninety-nine point nine nine nine percent of the world couldn't give a good goddamn about anyway!!! Twenty-five years of chasing his own shadow, primping in his own goddamn mirror, building himself up in his own mind to excel at the one thing he does better than anybody else on earth which is his own goddamn, presumptuous, condescending, narcissistic ARROGANCE! And now, when it's all said and done, the truth comes out at last, the truth that Alexander Coughlan has to run all the way to the hills of West Virginia to avoid—he's a nobody. A nothing. Absolute. Utter. Obscure. Failure. Who cares about him, Michael? Who cares? NOBODY does! Strutting around like a goddamn peacock for twenty-five years, living off the fruit of *my* daddy's reputation, living off the fruit of *my* labor! And now, at the moment of truth, now when it's all come crashing down and he comes yelping up to my front door with his tail between his legs, do you wanna know what *really* burns me up?

ASHE: What?

JACK: The bastard won't even admit to it!!! We still have to run around playing his little game. He struts around here like God Almighty Himself and expects us to bend and kneel and genuflect in his presence! Talk about CHUTZPAH!

ASHE: You don't want to know what I think.

JACK: Yeah, what do you think?

ASHE: I think you're jealous.

JACK: Well of course I am! Michael, spend a little bit of time with him and you will be too. Take one thing, look at his track record with women. The geriatric Casanova. Jesus Michael, my own sister fell for him like a ton of bricks—she was such a treasure, sweet, kind delicate, beautiful—she had suitors groveling at her feet by the bus load. She worshipped him, it was indecent how she doted on him. She burned for him—makes me blush just to remember. Christ, look at Mother. The same thing. How does he do it! She nearly faints every time she gets a whiff of him. And that's not the end of it, it's only the beginning, because now he's captured the Goddess herself—now he's ensnared perfection. Guess how they met—

ASHE: How?

JACK: *She* pursued *him!* Can you believe it? She begged him to be his assistant. *It's not fair!!* She longed to be under his tutelage. Why on earth does a former runway model give up every opportunity for the likes of him? Tell me.

ASHE: I have no idea. Is she…you know?

JACK: Faithful?

ASHE: Yeah.

JACK: I'm afraid so.

ASHE: Really?

JACK: It's ridiculous, isn't it? And on top of that she gets all moral about it too. She believes that "to cheat on your husband is immoral." But that makes no sense! I mean, to throw away all of that beauty on, what? A dead flounder! That's somehow noble? That kills me!

WAFFLES: John, sorry to stick my nose in, but I hate it when you belittle morality. I really do. One cannot go around betraying the values of love and fidelity for simple pleasures of the flesh. Loyalty and faithfulness were the subject of Reverend Masters's sermon on Sunday…

JACK: —Turn off the faucet, Waffles! I'm not interested in his sermon or your sermon…

WAFFLES: —You never let me finish what I have to say, Jonathon, but when it comes to Miss Helena I am determined to speak my mind…

JACK: —Here we go…

WAFFLES: I know I've told John this on many an occasion, but you may not know, Doctor, that three days after my marriage my wife ran away with a man who came uninvited to my wedding, a man it turns out with whom she'd had intimate relations sometime before. I understood it, by the way. I'm not what you might call a handsome man. But I'll tell you what, John…

JACK: —What Waffles?

WAFFLES : I never stopped loving her. I remain loyal and faithful to her. Whenever she needs me, I am there. I send her what I can. Why this year I'm helping put her children through summer camp. It's a matter of pride with me. A matter of integrity. And guess what has happened to her in the meantime?

JACK: What, Waffles?

WAFFLES: She's the one who's had the worst of it. Word is that her husband cheats on her. They have awful arguments. I heard he raises his hand to her. On top of all that she's lost her looks. Gotten fat and old and all bitter. Fact of the matter is I bet she regrets the day that she…

(SOPHIE and HELENA enter from the house to interrupt him, followed by MARY with a pitcher of iced tea. Behind them, clutching a magazine, comes ELIZABETH VAUGHN, JACK's mother, strikingly attractive for a woman in her seventies. On their arrival, WAFFLES shuts up and assists MARY.)

SOPHIE: It's so hot already that I had Mary fix us a pitcher of iced tea.

ELIZABETH: (Sitting in a chair.) Global warming! The Bush-Cheney cabal has finally accomplished something!

ASHE: (To HELENA.) Excuse me…I'm Doctor Michael Ashe…

HELENA: Oh. Hi!

ASHE: Hi.

HELENA: It's very nice to meet you.

ASHE: Nice to meet you too. Doctor Michael Ashe. Doctor. You know, like, medical doctor?

HELENA: Sorry?

ASHE: Your husband?

HELENA: Oh! You're—

ASHE: —yes!

HELENA: Oh that's funny!

ASHE: It's not funny. You're the one who called me, right? Come right over, it's an emergency, right? Pro-

fessor Coughlan needs emergency care, that's what you said, right?

HELENA: Yes. In the middle of the night he woke up with terrible pain in his legs and Sophie gave me your number and I didn't know what to do so I called you. And then this morning—voilà!—he woke up feeling terrific. And insisted on going out, walking the farm all morning.

ASHE: You have no idea how far I had to come, do you? I told you to keep his legs elevated and to give him some Tylenol and that I would rush right over first thing in the morning. I live forty-five miles away. The roads are one lane. Sometimes it takes me two hours to drive over here.

HELENA: I'm very sorry. Please forgive us. But he woke up feeling better. Isn't that good?

ASHE: It's fantastic! Fantastic! Don't even worry about any inconvenience you've caused me! It's not like I had anything better to do…

SOPHIE: (Coming to the rescue.) It's all my fault, Michael. I should have known better than to— I mean it's Daddy. I just forgot in a moment of panic is all. But you're here now, and I haven't seen you in weeks and it's not too terrible, is it? Anyway, you can spend the day with us and relax…

ASHE: —I don't know if I can…

SOPHIE: Mary's cooking tonight. I bet you could use a home-cooked meal. Bet you've been eatin' too much fast food.

ASHE: That's for sure. And I do love Mary's cooking. I guess it wouldn't do no harm to stay.

SOPHIE: There you go! That'd be wonderful, Michael. You could spend the night. Maybe there's a movie playin'… (She takes a swallow of tea.) Ugh! Mary! The tea's not even cold!

MARY: Don't yell at me about it. Yell at your father. He took all the ice to put on his knee.

WAFFLES: (To HELENA.) Don't you just hate that, Miss Helena? You set down ready for a swallow of ice-cold home-made tea, and it turns out to be middlin' warm?

HELENA: I actually prefer hot tea to cold, Mr. Wobbles, so I don't find this so bad after all.

WAFFLES: I'm sorry.

JACK: What're you sorry for now, Waffles?

WAFFLES: It's not Wobbles, Miss Helena.

HELENA: I don't think I said Wobbles…

WAFFLES: Sorry to have to disagree with you ma'am, but you plainly did. My name is Waffles. Plain. No mister. And not Wobbles. Waffles. My real name is Jefferson, after Jefferson Davis? But nobody ever calls me that. You see I got this bad complexion, bad skin on my face which kinda reminds folks of a waffle iron. So they just call me Waffles.

HELENA: Okay. Waffles it is.

WAFFLES: You probably noticed me. We've had dinner together every night since you come here. I live on the farm, ma'am. Always have. Your husband, Professor Coughlan, well me and him are as close as brothers…

SOPHIE: Waffles is our right-hand man around here. Don't know what we'd do without him.

ELIZABETH: *(Agitated by what she's been reading.)* Oh!

JACK: What's the matter, Mother?

ELIZABETH: I printed this off the Internet. Am I the only one who knows about it?

JACK: You're the only person in West Virginia who reads the Daily Kos, Mother.

ELIZABETH: It's not from a blog, it's from the *Guardian*!

SOPHIE: What is it, Grandma?

ELIZABETH: There's a second Downing Street memo! It's worse than the first one. It's absolutely dreadful what those liars will stoop to—and how they get away with it! I wonder if Alexander has seen this. When I show it to him he'll have a fit. It's all so infuriating!

JACK: It isn't infuriating, Mother. It's standard operating procedure. Just calm down and drink your hot iced tea.

ELIZABETH: But when the mainstream media won't even report a scandal like this—

JACK: Mother, please don't start with the mainstream media. We don't care.

ELIZABETH: Well you damn well *should* care! It is absolutely outrageous and I think we *should* talk about it!

JACK: *Stop it! Christ!* For fifty goddamn years all I've ever heard you do is bellyache that this thing is dreadful and that thing is infuriating and that it's all absolutely outrageous! For my sake would you just give it a rest?

ELIZABETH: Are you censoring me, Jonathon? Now I can't even exercise my first amendment rights in my own house? Why is it suddenly you can't stand the sound of my voice? What on earth has happened to you, Jonathon? I mean, look at you! Did you sleep in that shirt? My God, you used to love having political discussions. You used to be a man of strong convictions. You used to be a shining example of—

JACK: *(Cutting her off.)* A shining example? Of what? I'm an example of something, alright, but I wouldn't say it shone! Stank is more like it. Shining example. That's good. Oh, I get it, it's a joke, right? I remember it like it was yesterday. A month ago I was forty-seven years old and I was just like you. I howled in outrage over Rush Limbaugh and Fox News and I had C-SPAN on the speed dial to call in and speak my mind about the smirking chimp and the WMDs and the Plamegate affair and the Guantanamo torture chambers. Like that *mattered!* And then, all of a sudden I have my forty-eighth birthday and I wake up in the throes of middle age and I look in the mirror and I see this idiotic clown looking back at me. This cartoon character who hasn't accomplished one goddamn thing in his miserable little life! And on that morning I realized that I'd wasted it! I've wasted my life. I look around me and take stock of all I've accomplished and what do I see? *NOTHING!* I've got nothing. And anything I wanted? I can't ever have it now. I can't ever have it. I woke up that morning and I realized I had suddenly become old.

SOPHIE: Uncle Jack… Please…

ELIZABETH: I'm not sure I follow your little tirade, Jonathon. You seem to be blaming your "former convictions" for something, or blaming us, or blaming me. But we are not to blame, Jonathon, you are. Wasted your life? Accomplished nothing? Whose fault is that? Not mine! You should have *done* something!

JACK: *Done something!* Are you fucking kidding me??? We can't all be world-class pieces of fucking A-One prime shit bricks like your fucking elderly Nazi son-in-law *sieg heil!!!!!!!!!!!!!*

ELIZABETH: *WHAT THE HELL IS THAT SUPPOSED TO MEAN???*

SOPHIE: *GRANDMOTHER! UNCLE! PLEASE!!*

(JACK and ELIZABETH stop. After a moment, JACK sheepishly grovels at his MOTHER's feet and kisses them.)

JACK: I am silent. Silent and repentant. Mommie, forgive me.

ELIZABETH: Get up now. Get up, you!

(Silence all around.)

HELENA: I think the weather's perfect. I like it hot.

JACK: I think the weather's perfect too. Just right for suicide.

(The phone rings from the house.)

MARY: *(Getting up.)* I'll get it.

(WAFFLES goes to the porch, takes a guitar out of a beat-up old guitar case and plucks at it softly.)

JACK: *(Under his breath.)* Oh Jesus…

(ELIZABETH resumes reading and clucking. HELENA closes her eyes. SOPHIE gazes at ASHE. Then MARY comes back out with a cordless phone.)

MARY: Doctor Mike! It's for you.

ASHE: For me? Here?

MARY: From the paper mill.

ASHE: Jesus Christ. *(Into the phone.)* Hello? Yes, this is he. Why didn't you call my cell phone? *(He pulls his cell phone out of his pocket.)* Damn thing's turned off. I'm sorry, I don't know how that happened… Uh huh. Uh huh. Good Christ. Did you…? Okay. Yes. I understand. Wrap it as tightly as you can. Keep pressure on it. You called for an ambulance? It what? Right. Alright.

(He hangs up the phone. Hands it back to Mary. Kicks at the ground with his foot.)

ASHE: Goddamn! *GODDAMMIT!!*

SOPHIE: Michael, what?

ASHE: They had another goddamn accident. I swear, between the coal mines and those ancient goddamn factories… One of the machines… When they couldn't reach me on my cell they called my service. I had told them I was heading over here. I hope it's alright.

SOPHIE: Of course it is, Michael.

ASHE: Goddammit if this isn't *exactly* what I need right now! Mary!

MARY: What, Doctor Mike?

ASHE: Get me a glass of bourbon with ice.

(She looks at him.)

ASHE: Please.

(She goes. He feels folks trying not to look at him.)

ASHE: I'll head down there in a few minutes. Damn ambulance apparently had a flat tire of all things. They dispatched another one. Take a half hour or so. Nothing much I can do 'til it gets there. It's not life-threatening.

(A silence.)

SOPHIE: You'll have to go to the hospital, then?

ASHE: Looks that way.

SOPHIE: Come back afterward. For dinner.

ASHE: Maybe. *(A beat.)* I think it was Mark Twain who wrote about some character with more hair on his head than he had sense in it. I guess that would be me. Sorry everyone. *(To HELENA.)* And please understand if I don't continually drop everything I'm doing to come racing out here to tend to your husband. As you can see I've got far too many real responsibilities to be sidetracked like this.

(She seems offended and is speechless.)

ASHE: I don't mean to be unfriendly. If you do some sightseeing to the State Forest Conservancy, I hope you'll stop by for a visit. My house is right in the thick of it. I help the park rangers with the trees. I've got an impressive young stand of sugar maples I've been cultivating myself over a few acres. They depend on me pretty much over there.

HELENA: Really? I would have thought there would be ecologists or environmentalists out here but I would never have thought of you as one of them.

ASHE: That's an odd thing to say. Why not?

HELENA: Well, you just got finished dressing me down because of how busy you are. Wouldn't forestry interfere with your practice?

ASHE: I was only trying to be polite.

HELENA: And I'm just making conversation. Isn't medicine your calling?

ASHE: Medicine is what I earn my living at. It isn't necessarily my calling.

JACK: Oh joy! Here we go…

ASHE: Working with trees can be more satisfying than tending to people.

HELENA: You prefer trees to your patients? That strikes me as odd.

ASHE: Then you obviously know very little about them. Let's just say that forests are enormously satisfying and leave it at that.

JACK: Enormously satisfying. Yes! Enormous satisfaction!

ASHE: Shut up, Jack!

HELENA: But it strikes me as silly. I don't know, you're a grown man, what?, forty, forty-five years old? You just told me how large your practice is. And you prefer the company of trees to people? Doesn't that strike anyone else as silly? Wouldn't you find trees boring in comparison to tending to people?

SOPHIE: No, Helena, it's hardly silly. And hardly boring. That's just ignorant. Tending to the resources of the forests is about the most important work there is. When Michael plants and cares for new trees he's giving something back to a planet that is being destroyed at an alarming rate. Perhaps that doesn't occur to you in the city. Michael's work has been recognized, he's too modest to say so but he's been given citations by the Department of the Interior and the Audubon Society for his work. It's people like Michael who are the heroes, who save the environment when people in the city are too busy reading *Vogue* and taking taxis to Starbucks. We here in the country recognize that his work is a very noble calling. These trees, these national forests, they are the lungs of our planet. But even more than that they are a graceful and glorious reminder of how beautiful and sacred is the abundance of the natural world and how ugly and wasteful and destructive we are in it. I see Michael's work as embodying a type of latter-day chivalry. I'm afraid this is a foreign concept to you because in the city you have nothing like it and your lives are aggressive and nasty and cutthroat. But not here. Here in the midst of arbors, in the shadows of the great trees, our lives are gentler, kinder, with a greater sense of spirituality, a greater sense of calm. Men like Michael, who devote themselves to forestry, I think are more masculine, they are handsome, there is a natural grace that flows through them. You don't hear about women being beaten and raped and mistreated here the way they are in cities. Michael embodies this chivalry. He is a Knight of the Arbors!

(MARY has entered with ASHE's drink. Jack mockingly applauds SOPHIE's speech.)

JACK: Yeah! Yeah! Hooray! Everyone—loud cheers for the sentiments of my love-struck niece! It's a fact: Trailer-park Appalachian men never mistreat their trailer-park Appalachian women. It's just Knights of the Round Table and Damsels wearing silk! Jerry Springer didn't make his goddamn fortune on the hysterics of Wall Street bankers for Christ's sake!

SOPHIE: That's not what I meant—

JACK: —Good Lord, Sophie! How can you bring that load of crap in here with a straight face? I used to think you were a pretty smart cookie. Oh well. I guess *love* has turned you all mushy and romantic. Now don't look at me like that. Michael—at least you have to admit how ridiculous that all sounds. There's not a shred of nobility left in the whole goddamn world that hasn't been co-opted by marketers and pitchmen. The Hard Rock Cafe, I understand, has an electronic display counting down the vanishing acres of the world's rainforests. *The Hard Rock Cafe!!!* Rainforest destruction as some corporate marketing maven's ploy to sell more twenty-five-dollar cheeseburgers and seventy-five-dollar T-shirts. Cheeseburgers, by the way, made from the slaughtered cattle of stockyards whose pens and pastures have been carved out of the bulldozing of thousands of acres of South American rainforests! T-shirts made off the back-breaking sweat of a million Chinese children in concentration camps all over Asia. Hoo-fucking-ray! *(Adopting a hillbilly accent.)* Y'ask me, the whole goddamn state o' West Virginny oughta clear cut every last tree, twig, and stick o' woods, oughta level every last hill, an' just sell the land off t'the highest bidder! Build some more chemical plants! Set up some more o' them toxic dumps! Kill a coupla thousand more o' them dad-burned coal miners makin' bigger profits for them kind-hearted folks at Big Coal and Energy! They ain't enuf new golf courses 'round here! They ain't enuf Coal Industry lobbyists givin' enuf money to them EPA fellas over there in Warshington Dee Cee! Hell yeah! That's my solution for balancin' the goddamn budget and winnin' the war agin them Moslem Ay-Rab rag-head terrorists! Sell the whole fuckin' state fer all I care! But you liberal whackos hate America! You Greeny whackos hate Jeesus!! You jest want to tax an' spend me to my grave—jest so you can save a few goddamn trees!!!!

(JACK is having a fine old time at ASHE and SOPHIE's expense. Even they can't help but smile at him.)

ASHE: See, that's what I love about this guy. He loves to test my good nature. Loves to get my goat. Fact is, if I thought he was serious for one second I'd buy myself a shotgun and shoot him in the head. Here's what I *will* tell you—twenty years from now these forests that make this view so picturesque, these forests may be gone. Every single day thousands of acres, millions of trees perish under the axe, get buried under the bulldozer. Sophie's right, these forests are the oxygen of the planet, they are our lungs, they are the air that we breathe. Without them, what do you think will happen? Go ahead, make yourself feel superior by thinking I'm a crackpot. I'm not. This is all well-documented science. Entire populations of birds and animals are being wiped out by the wholesale destruction. And for what? For a buck? I'm telling you this is a holocaust of enormous proportions and repercussions but it means no more to the Jack Vaughns of the world than a series of sophomoric jokes that make more of a goddamn idiot out of you, my friend, than me! All your cynical, smarmy little jokes ain't worth *shit*, Jack! What I do by planting a stand of young trees or helping the forest rangers with whatever they need me to do may be insignificant against the onslaught—but at least *I DO SOMETHING!* And what I'm trying to tell you is that if we *ALL DO SOMETHING*, then there's at least a hope that *SOMETHING GETS DONE!* So I get on my pulpit and I demand that *every last one of us DO something* positive and heroic. Good Christ, what is happening to this planet is so monumentally *STUPID!* Jack Vaughn, you and your smug, smirking kind are the paradigm of monumental stupidity! *YOU, my friend, ARE the problem!* You love laughing at the destruction of everything around you, you love tearing down anything that's good and decent, because you are an unhappy man who has to make sure that everyone else is just as unhappy as *he is! (A beat.)* I want everyone to look at Jack Vaughn, look at that ugly little grin on his face. He thinks that to see me flying off the handle is an accomplishment, that that is somehow worthwhile. But then you wouldn't dare take anything seriously, would you? I'll shut up now. I've probably said too much that I'll regret later. You now have ample evidence that I am, in fact, off my rocker. But I'll leave you with this. When I walk through the forest, when I see and smell and touch the sun-dappled trees that I helped to save and raise and nourish, it makes me feel good about myself. Unlike Jack, I don't feel as though my life is wasted. I have to think that a thousand years from now people will still be able to enjoy the magnificence of this planet and I will have made a contribution to that. That is my raison d'être and my little bit of immortality. Helena, I hope that someday you can feel something like the deep satisfaction I get when I plant a fir or an oak or a maple. The cool black earth. The slender branches. The smell of living wood…

(HELENA can't stifle a yawn. JACK barely stifles a laugh. A beat.)

ASHE: Anyway, I'm just a fool and I know it. Some poor fellow is probably bleeding to death at the mill and Jack has succeeded in goading me into throwing a tantrum about trees. I'm glad I've been a source of amusement to you but now I have to go…

SOPHIE: *(Going to him.)* Michael, you know it isn't true. What you do is magnificent. Pearls before swine, that's all, and my uncle happens to be the biggest pig of all.

JACK: Oink, oink.

SOPHIE: You will try to come back after, won't you? Please?

(SOPHIE walks him out through the house. One by one ELIZABETH, MARY, and WAFFLES walk past JACK with barely concealed contempt and into the house, leaving JACK alone with HELENA.)

HELENA: Just tell me why.

JACK: Why what?

HELENA: Why you have to be such an asshole sometimes.

JACK: Don't beat around the bush, Helena, say what's on your mind.

HELENA: I'm not even going to go into what sadistic pleasure you get torturing that poor doctor. But to pick a fight with your mother over Alex? To be so rude to *Alex* last night at dinner?

JACK: But I hate him.

HELENA: How can you hate him? What's to hate? He's a wonderful man. Sometimes you even remind me of him.

JACK: Now that's uncalled for! And anyway, who are you to lecture me about Michael? "It's so silly—" and when you couldn't stifle a yawn I thought I was going to bust a gut laughing!

HELENA: We're not talking about me. I haven't been sleeping well. I'm exhausted all the time and I couldn't help it. And you'd better stop it.

JACK: Stop what?

HELENA: Looking at me like that.

JACK: Like what?

HELENA: Like that. Now. With that mixture of pity and lust. "Poor Helena. Married to the old man." Well here's a news flash, Jack, you're not so young yourself. And I'm happy, believe it or not. You are exactly the way Doctor Ashe described you. You can't stand to see anyone happy and you take a sadistic pleasure in destroying everything around you until everyone is just as miserable as you are.

JACK: That's not fair.

HELENA: The truth is it is very unattractive. You can't have something so you have to make sure nobody else can have it either. You've lost confidence in yourself so you need to rip everyone else—Alex, Michael, your mother—apart. What? Does it make you feel a little bigger, Jack? A little more important? I know you think I'm stupid. But I'm not.

JACK: I never said you were stupid. And I have never belittled you. Or attacked you.

(Silence.)

HELENA: So tell me about him.

JACK: Him who? Oh, Michael.

HELENA: I like him. I like his face.

JACK: Michael?

HELENA: You know what I think?

JACK: Don't have a clue.

HELENA: I think Sophie's got a thing for him.

JACK: You are so perceptive it's scary. What's that look? No, no, no, Helena, leave it alone.

HELENA: But I'm her mother.

(JACK laughs.)

HELENA: I am! No, I really am! And she needs someone and I think they'd be great together. *(Pause.)* God knows what he thinks of me. I don't think I was very nice. You really bring out the worst in me, do you know that?

JACK: That's right, blame it on me.

HELENA: *(Stealthily takes out a cigarette and lights up.)* Don't you dare tell Alex, he thinks I quit.

(They share the cigarette.)

HELENA: You know why we get along so well?

JACK: Why?

HELENA: Because we're birds of a feather. You make jokes about everything because you're bored. I can't help but laugh at them because I'm bored too.

(JACK gazes at her.)

HELENA: Stop that!

JACK: I can't. I'm in love with you. I can't help it. I play a game when people are around. I sneak looks at you. I can't breathe when I'm around you. I get this pressure in my chest and I think I'm having a heart attack. I'm out of control and it scares me and excites me and pisses me off and all I want to do is touch you, Helena—

(She stands up and walks away.)

JACK: It's not a crime. I haven't broken any fucking laws! For crissakes! *(A beat.)* Okay okay okay okay okay. Look. Just don't cut me off, okay? Don't tell your husband, don't call the cops, don't go away. Let me have a little bit of hope. Even if it's hopeless—

HELENA: It *is* hopeless—

JACK: I know I know I know, but let me kid myself. How can it hurt you? It can't hurt you if I fantasize about you.

HELENA: How can you say that to me? It's such a sick thing to say to me!

(She walks into the house leaving JACK to watch her disappear.)

ACT TWO

Nighttime. The sound of wind and rain. A study inside the VAUGHN house, the flickering light of a TV. In silhouette we see ALEXANDER dozing on a small couch dressed in a bathrobe and pajamas. HELENA sits next to him in a chair, wide awake, staring out the window. After several moments, ALEXANDER tosses violently and lets out a growl of pain. As she goes to comfort him, he starts awake.

ALEXANDER: Sophie?

HELENA: Me.

ALEXANDER: Sophie?

HELENA: Your wife.

ALEXANDER: Oh. (*Writhing.*) I'm in agony!

HELENA: What do you want me to do?

ALEXANDER: Nothing!

(*She covers him with a blanket which he promptly throws off.*)

ALEXANDER: It's too damn hot in here as it is! (*A beat.*) It was a dream. I dreamt that that idiotic Rastafarian was amputating my leg with a hacksaw and that retarded boy Waffles was assisting him. When the hacksaw was sawing through my leg, I had this *unbelievable* pain and spasm. Then I woke up. It was probably a heart attack. I need to get an EKG. (*A beat.*) What time is it?

HELENA: After two.

ALEXANDER: I need you to find my interview with Cindy Sherman.

HELENA: What?

ALEXANDER: The Cindy Sherman interview! From 1989. It's in one of those damn boxes.

(*She starts to go.*)

ALEXANDER: Where are you going?

HELENA: To get the—

ALEXANDER: *NOW?*

(*She stops.*)

ALEXANDER: Why do I find it so hard to breathe? (*A beat.*) Darling.

(*No answer.*)

ALEXANDER: Darling—

HELENA: What?

ALEXANDER: I meant tomorrow.

HELENA: Okay.

ALEXANDER: Can you rub my legs?

HELENA: (*As she does.*) Maybe you're overdoing it with the walks, Alex. God knows they're too much for me. You get cramps in your legs. Tires you out.

ALEXANDER: What tires me out is the fact that I can't get any goddamn sleep around here. But I see where you're heading with this. Alexander, don't exert yourself. Alexander, you may be getting too old for this. You're too pathetic, Alexander. Watch TV, Alexander.

HELENA: That's not what I'm saying…

ALEXANDER: You don't have to say it. I'm repulsive. You don't think I know how repulsive I am? It's amazing you can still stand to be around me. For crissakes, you're not a wife, you're a goddamn nurse!

HELENA: What do you want from me?

ALEXANDER: I want you to stop being so fucking heroic, that's what I want! You're so *brave!*

HELENA: You're blaming me for—

ALEXANDER: —I'm not blaming you for anything! I'm sympathizing with you, sweetheart! I'm sympathetic! How could you have known what you were getting yourself into? A beautiful, sexual, desirable young woman cooped up with a filthy, bellyaching, impotent old gout-ridden codger. You can use some sympathy, darling. You don't have to hide your feelings, your revulsion of me, I completely understand and I want you to know that I am not deaf to your particular brand of suffering. Or Jonathon's! Or everyone's! *You're all so fucking HEROIC!*

HELENA: (*Stops and goes to the window.*) Fine. I'll stop being brave. Anyway I think I'm coming down with something.

ALEXANDER: How brilliantly Freudian. I'm literally making you sick. Poor you. Wasting the best years of your life on a surly, decrepit, spiteful old bastard. Meanwhile, I'm the one who's happy! I'm getting off on making you miserable! I'm having the goddamn time of my life!

HELENA: You *want* me to fight with you. But I won't do it. It's late and I'm exhausted and I'm worn out—

ALEXANDER: *I WEAR EVERYONE OUT!* Who drew the unlucky straw for the graveyard shift to watch the old man tonight? You did!

HELENA: Do you want me to start crying? Will that make you happy? If I start crying will you stop? Will you? (*A beat.*) If you would just tell me what you want from me.

ALEXANDER: Nothing. I want nothing.

HELENA: Fine.

ALEXANDER: Fine.

(Silence.)

ALEXANDER: In most places in the world people are actually a little interested in me, in what I have to say. But not here. Here I'm the only one people are hard pressed to tolerate. In West Virginia Jack Vaughn can say anything he damn well pleases and his dotty old mother can run off at the mouth about anything she wants and folks are entertained by them and hang on every word they utter. But me? Alexander Coughlan? Let me enter into a conversation and I am greeted with abject silence. Shuffling of feet, clearing of throats, peering at watches. Yawns appear. Suddenly we're all exhausted. The very sound of my voice is an affront to everyone. I open my mouth and offend everyone. I am thoroughly offensive, aren't I Helena? All right, I'm distasteful. And I'm selfish. And I'm a tyrant. And a despot! But don't I have the right to demand a little bit of attention? Haven't I earned the smallest modicum of respect from these idiotic people, respect that I am accustomed to getting from credentialed people all over the world?

HELENA: Yes. (Looks out the window at the rain.) We all respect you, Alex. We all love you. You don't let us.

(A long silence.)

ALEXANDER: I'm sorry. I'm mortified at my behavior. I don't expect you can forgive me. I'm losing my mind—what's left of it.

HELENA: (Not looking at him.) It's okay.

ALEXANDER: I feel old. For the first time in my life I feel old. When I had the chance to retire I thought I'd hit the jackpot, thought this is what I always wanted— freedom—from the faculty meetings and the political ass-kissing and the students that seem to get stupider every year. And I thought how romantic it would be, a honeymoon for us, away from the vagrants and the subway and the stench, a civilized life in this beautiful country kissed by God— But it's all different and it's got me all turned around.

HELENA: Why is it different?

ALEXANDER: Because I hate it so. Rather than finding freedom I feel like I've been jailed like a dissident in an old Soviet penal colony. Helena, I miss it so much. The lights, the openings, the pace of things. I miss the way the eggs taste at Socrates Diner on Saturday mornings. And I miss being well known. There, I said it out loud. I have an ego. A healthy ego. Out here, talk of cows passes for philosophy. Helena, I feel like I'm out to pasture now. Waiting to die. Nothing to do but wait. Without knowing it, New York kept me young. Here, I've suddenly become very very old.

HELENA: Wait. Another couple of nights like this one and I'll be old too. We'll be a matched set.

(They laugh. The laughter turns romantic, then sexual. Before long they are half-naked and passionate, making love. At this inopportune moment, SOPHIE enters.)

SOPHIE: Daddy—

(THE LOVERS disentangle themselves. SOPHIE turns away.)

SOPHIE: You know, you were the one who wanted to send for Doctor Ashe, and he rushed down here thinking it was some kind of emergency. And it obviously wasn't. And he's stuck here now because of the storm and you don't even have the common decency to talk to him or let him examine you.

ALEXANDER: I'm fine, as you can see. Why should I let him examine me? I wouldn't let that filthy man near me if I was gasping for my last breath.

SOPHIE: I have no idea what to say to that. Do you expect me to summon the entire Mayo Clinic to attend to your damn arthritis? Michael is a fine doctor and is here now and can likely help you.

ALEXANDER: That little quack will not come near me, Sophie, is that understood? He reeks of booze and stinks of pot and looks as though he hasn't seen a bar of soap in a month.

SOPHIE: That's great, Daddy. Do whatever the hell you want. I have had it with all this bullshit.

ALEXANDER: How dare you use that kind of language to me! (Begins to walk away but gets light-headed and almost falls to the floor.) Jesus!

HELENA: What's wrong, Alex?

ALEXANDER: Now I've got vertigo. Everything is spinning. Sophie! Get me that prescription bottle over there on the table!

(SOPHIE does and brings it to him.)

ALEXANDER: Not *THAT* one! You stupid cow, are you trying to kill me?! *(Throws the bottle across the room, scattering the pills everywhere.)*

(Silence.)

SOPHIE: Throw your tantrums at somebody else, Daddy. I am not one of your students. I am the daughter that you have chosen to neglect for the past fifteen years. I am doing the best I can with you, but I have had it with the *both* of you. This is all *fun* for you I suppose, neither one of you has a goddamn thing to do around here but *I* have to wake up at six o'clock to start my day! Do you think this farm runs itself, Daddy? Do you? I came running in here to help because I heard a noise and thought you were in pain and instead find you making out like a couple of hormonal teenagers and then you have the goddamn nerve to scream at me and throw some sort of a tantrum? Don't you dare! *(Pause.)* And put some pants on Daddy—really!

(All the noise has brought JACK to the rescue—bleary-eyed, a baseball cap askew on his head, a T-shirt and briefs.)

JACK: Good morning campers! Well, this looks like fun! Alright everyone, that is enough for one night, bedtime, lights out, let's go! Sophie, I know you have to be up at the crack of dawn. Helena, you need your precious beauty sleep. Both of you go to bed, and I'll sit up with my famous brother-in-law.

ALEXANDER: Good lord no, anything but that. I'll be tortured by him!

JACK: I may want to, Alex, but I won't. They have to sleep, even you can see that. You and I will have a fun time of it. We'll watch *The Munsters* on Nick at Nite.

ALEXANDER: Yes, Jack, I agree with you, let them go to bed. But you go too. I'll be fine by myself. We'll watch *The Munsters* together some other time.

JACK: Here I am trying to be friendly and you can't even allow me that, Alex?

SOPHIE: Uncle, don't start. Let it go.

JACK: *I* should let it go?

ALEXANDER: Please tell him to go to bed. Don't leave me here with him.

(MARY comes rushing in.)

SOPHIE: Mary, what are you doing up?

MARY: What am I doing up? It's like trying to sleep through a war with all you grown-ups actin' like you was all just six years old all the damn time! Why can't you let this poor old man get some sleep?

ALEXANDER: I'd like nothing better than to sleep, Mary.

MARY: What's the matter with you all? Ain't you got no respect for this one here? *(To ALEXANDER.)* What's the matter, Mr. Coughlan? Can't sleep? You got aches and pains? Well, so do I. Last thing I'd need is a pack of children jabberin' at me.

(She rubs his legs.)

MARY: There now, that feel better? I get the tightness in my legs myself. Look how tense you is. I remember your wife, Sophie's momma, how she used to get all tense too, remember? I used to rub her like this, make her drowsy as a baby. There now, see? Now why don't you let me put you in your bed?

ALEXANDER: Please.

(She rearranges his blankets and helps him up and walks him out of the room.)

MARY: There you go. I'll fix you some warm milk, put a little cocoa in it, alright?

ALEXANDER: Thank you, Mary.

MARY: No need to thank me. I just know what it's like to be old, that's all. Late at night is a terrible time. I remember your momma, Sophie, late at night is when she used to cry. For no reason. Well there's always a reason, I guess. Sophie, you were just a little baby, too young to understand what was goin' on.

(MARY and ALEXANDER leave the room, leaving JACK, SOPHIE, and HELENA to watch them go. After a moment of silence, SOPHIE leaves the room too. There is an uncomfortable silence between JACK and HELENA.)

HELENA: This is the third night in a row I've had to stay up with him. I'm too tired to go to sleep.

JACK: I haven't been able to sleep all week either. For other reasons.

HELENA: God, what is *wrong* with you? Why do you have to say things like that? Jesus I hate it here. I *hate* it here. My husband hates *me*. You hate *him*. Sophie hates *me*. And that fucking maid never misses an opportunity to make me feel like an inadequate failure when it comes to caring for my own husband. I am so fucking frustrated I wish I could just punch the lights out of somebody.

JACK: I volunteer.

HELENA: Just leave me alone.

JACK: Alright. But I feel a speech coming on. And all I want you to do is listen. You hear the rain, Helena? By tomorrow morning the storm will be over and the sun will shine and flowers will bloom and the hills will be on fire with orange and red in a carpet of deep green. You've never seen the hills after a rainstorm in the spring. Takes your breath away. But I won't be able to see it. None of it. Because all I can see is you. I walk around between sleep and waking in a constant state of intoxication and desire—no alcohol necessary. At night, when I do sleep, my dreams are consumed by you and I have them over and over and over again. And then I find myself standing in a room with you, like now, and my body shakes uncontrollably and I barely have the breath to speak to you and I barely have the breath to keep myself from looking at you. And just because I am hopelessly smitten with you doesn't mean that I am blind. I see the way you look back at me. And I see in your eyes, in their mixture of pity and disdain, how ridiculous I must look to you. Helena, the fact is that I have nothing to show for my life. And now I am living in the same house with the one thing that I have been waiting for for thirty years. For thirty years I have been waiting for you to come into my life, I have been waiting with patience and honor and then absurdly and ironically you make your entrance and there is a wall between us and I can look but I cannot touch, I can long but I cannot *have*—I imagine us together and I don't have the ability to banish those images from my mind. And then when you look at me it jolts me awake from my revery and I am wasted. All wasted. I feel as though I am pouring my heart out and it is just as wasted as sunlight gets wasted when it pours into a deep well. (*A pause.*) So tell me, Helena, what should I do?

HELENA: I don't know. I listen to you and all I can think is how this is just one more cynical tactic to get me to do something that will only mean regret and ruination. I honestly don't know how you can talk to me like this. I can't even… I mean I am just numb at this point. It's *all* too much for me. I'm absolutely certain you hate me.

JACK: Hate you?

HELENA: Or you couldn't possibly be doing this to me. But I have to go to bed. Good night.

JACK: (*Blocking her way.*) No! It *can't* be just me. It has to be you too. I know it is! Look at what's happened to you. How can you not be miserable? Look at the way he treats you. You've thrown away your life on him. Alright, forget about me. Think about yourself. Get out of here! Run away! What are you waiting for? Alexander is making you older and uglier by the second. GO! LEAVE! LIVE YOUR LIFE!

(*She doesn't move.*)

JACK: I'm serious.

(*He impulsively kisses her. She allows him to but does not move a muscle.*)

HELENA: You're drunk.

JACK: Maybe.

HELENA: With the doctor.

JACK: He has nothing to do with it. But yes.

HELENA: You get drunk every day, I think.

JACK: Doctor's orders. It kills the pain.

HELENA: Once or twice you came to the city to visit Alex. We'd spend time together. I wasn't seeing him then, hadn't even considered it. Just his TA. You didn't drink. You were as excited as a little boy at Christmas at all the sights, bursting with enthusiasm. You admired Alex. You did, I remember that. And now, you're different. You know there was something about you… I think I even liked you then. Now—it makes me sad. (*She leaves.*)

JACK: "I liked you then." Why did I wait? I had my chance. She just said it. I could've asked her out, to dinner, to a play. Good God. We'd have strolled around the fountain at Lincoln Center. Or watched the ice skaters at Rockefeller Center. Or just stood in Central Park by the Sheep Meadow looking at the magnificent skyline of Midtown Manhattan. I would have kissed her. And she would have melted against me. I *knew* she liked me. Just didn't have the guts to do anything about it. We'd be married now. Beside each other in bed. We'd wake up from the crackle of the thunder and we'd watch the lightning and we'd cuddle together. Begin to touch one another. Without a word we'd begin to kiss. She would brush her lips against my ear and whisper to me how much she loved me and how happy she was that I had taken her out all those years ago when I was visiting New York and the sound of her whispered voice would be music sweeter than Mozart. *(A pause.)* But let's take a reality check, Jack old boy. It didn't happen. And here you are. And now it is over, done—he's got her and you are finished. God, what has happened? How could it all go so wrong? How dare she say that to me! I'd rather she said she *never* liked me. I *hate* her for saying that to me. That's the reward I get for being serious for one fucking moment? That's it? Her motherfucking patronizing arrogant pity? WELL FUCK YOU! FUCK YOU!! FUCK YOU!!! And him! I used to think the world of him too, she's right about that. I'd go to New York City with these fucking naïve stars in my eyes fantasizing on the plane about how Alexander was going to rescue me from this shitty little life I live out here. I'd send him his money every goddamn month and convinced myself it was an *investment!* Sophie and I working like fucking dogs to squeeze every last penny from this place so that he could live his important lifestyle hobnobbing with the rich and famous and *someday I would join him!* He'd take me around to publishers and literary agents. The motherfucker was going to open doors for me and they would recognize that I was brilliant and he said he would and I believed him! And then, suddenly, he just retires! Just like that, he says he's fed up with the city and he's going to spend the rest of his miserable life leeching off us here! And just as suddenly I knew. I fucking knew. I knew what I damn well should have known twenty goddamn years ago—it was all a lie! All bullshit! Get *me* published? He can't even get *himself* published, the goddamn fake—goddamn phony! YOU ARE NOTHING!!!! He's nothing. An abject failure who preyed on Sophie and Mother and me as slick as a grifter. And we were the dupes. God, how can I be such an idiot? Well FUCK YOU, ALEXANDER! FUCK YOU!!

(JACK sits silently. After a few moments, laughter is heard offstage.)

ASHE: *(Offstage.)* Play something!

WAFFLES: *(Offstage.)* We'll wake everybody up!

ASHE: *(Offstage.)* Okay, let's go in there—

(They stumble in, drunk. ASHE is in his T-shirt. WAFFLES has his guitar.)

ASHE: Well would you look who's here. I certainly hope we are not protruding on your solicitude, Mr. Vaughn.

(JACK says nothing. WAFFLES starts playing a lively tune, and he and ASHE dance and sing and make a

ruckus until ASHE realizes they are making too much noise and he shushes them.)*

ASHE: What time is it, Jack?

JACK: How the hell should I know?

ASHE: Oooh. Where's the old man's daughter? I mean, where's his wife? I mean daughter? Wife? Daughter—*(He cracks himself up.)*

JACK: *(Waiting until he's done laughing.)* I don't know.

ASHE: OH MY GOD WHAT A FOX! Ooooh baby would I love to give what I got to her!

(He gyrates his hips and gets WAFFLES laughing.)

JACK: Would you please shut the fuck up?

ASHE: Who put a stick up your ass? Oh! That's right, you *like* her.

JACK: I like who?

ASHE: Who? Heidi fucking Klum, that's who.

JACK: You know, you should just shut up. We are just friends.

ASHE: Just friends? That's too bad. And so soon.

JACK: What do you mean "so soon"?

ASHE: Do I have to spell it out for you? Friendship with a lady comes in three stages: First Stage—you meet her. Second Stage—you 'n' she git it on. Third Stage—if the gittin' ain't no good, she says: "Can't we just be friends?"

(WAFFLES and ASHE explode in laughter. JACK gets up and shoves ASHE against the wall.)

ASHE: Easy boy. Easy now. I didn't mean nothin' by it. I'm just drunk, thassall. And high. When I get to feelin' good I'm liable to say anything, you know that.

(JACK walks away.)

ASHE: Whoa. And I thought that was funny. I can be funny when I want to be. *(He wheels around the room.)* Jack, you coulda made a punching bag o' me and I wouldn't've felt a thing. I LOVE feeling this way! I feel all brilliant and powerful—like Superman! Watch me leap tall buildings in a single bound! I am imperfect to pain! Man, when I get to feelin' this way I'm telling you I can do *anything!* Like that TV commercial where the guy is doin' heart surgery but he's not a doctor and he says he stayed at a Holiday Inn last night!

And I should do something. I should. I should go back to school and take up another specialty, this time in neurosurgery. Make a few billion dollars. And then I'd run for Congress of the United States. On the Green ticket. Rewrite the nation's environmental laws, make the damn President sign onto Kyoto, single handedly save the goddamn planet! Hey, this is no joke. I can do it. I *ought* to do it. And everybody else, nothin' more than bacteria. You all can just *shine my shoes! (Pause.)* Come on, Waffles, PLAY!

WAFFLES: Just don't want to wake nobody up.

ASHE: *PLAY!!!*

WAFFLES: Okay.

(WAFFLES plays, and he and ASHE wildly dance and sing. After a while, they are joined by JACK, and their raucous party achieves full voice. At its height, SOPHIE bursts in. There is immediate silence. WAFFLES leaves the room.)

ASHE: *(Still drunk and irreverent, he speaks in a cultivated accent.)* So sorry to be under-dressed, Madame. I seem to have forgot my tie. *(Bursts into laughter and leaves the room.)*

SOPHIE: *(To JACK.)* Drunk. Figures. I guess it doesn't matter how *I* feel about that kind of thing. Or what happened to my mother. Boys will be boys.

(JACK looks away.)

SOPHIE: Don't do that, Uncle. I am absolutely ashamed of you. Whatever middle-aged crisis it is you think you are going through to excuse this kind of infantile behavior, do me one favor. Get over it. And get over yourself.

JACK: My middle-aged crisis is neither here nor there. I have lost faith in my life so I turn to whatever I can find to dull the pain.

SOPHIE: Self-pity? That's your response? Jesus Christ, Uncle, you are pathetic. All of the goddamn rain this spring is threatening fifty acres. The INS is investigating Manuel, and so we are about to lose our most experienced foreman. You have totally abandoned the farm, and me, and I am working so goddamn hard that my fingers are starting to bleed under the stress of it all. But you go ahead and pity yourself. *(Pause.)* Uncle Jack, you have no idea how tired I am. Just work with me. Please. I promise you, whatever it is, whatever you are feeling, will go away if you just throw yourself into the work.

The work will give you the purpose. It will make things better. Uncle, I *need* you.

(JACK starts to weep.)

SOPHIE: Oh God, no Uncle, don't do that, please don't do that—

JACK: *(Getting a hold of himself.)* Don't do what? I'm not doing anything. I'm just having fun. You take everything so seriously. You need a sense of humor. *(Pause. He looks at her with intensity.)*

SOPHIE: What?

JACK: Sometimes you remind me so much of Jenny. I miss her so much. For a minute I could have sworn I was talking to her, not you. I don't know what I would do if you ever went away, Sophie.

(He leaves. After a moment, SOPHIE composes herself and opens the door.)

SOPHIE: *(Calling.)* Doctor Ashe! Doctor!

(She goes back into the room and looks out the window. Ashe enters after a few moments.)

ASHE: *(Still drunk, jovial.)* Yes, Madame, you rang?

SOPHIE: *(Wheeling on him.)* Is this funny to you?

ASHE: I guess not. What do you want?

SOPHIE: What do I want? How about I want you to drink all you want and do your drugs and be as childish and self-destructive as you damn well please, but how about you *don't* do it in *my* house and encourage my uncle and poor Waffles to join you in the process? That's what I want.

ASHE: Fine. Then I'll go.

(He doesn't move. Silence.)

SOPHIE: I'm sorry.

(Silence.)

SOPHIE: Michael.

(Silence.)

SOPHIE: *Michael.*

ASHE: Don't talk to me.

SOPHIE: I'm *sorry.* Why don't you just sleep it off?

ASHE: I said I'm going. I'm going.

SOPHIE: I said I'm sorry. There's no reason for you to go. Stay the rest of the night.

ASHE: I'm not tired. Don't worry about me. If I get tired, I'll pull over.

SOPHIE: I feel terrible.

ASHE: And so do I. And you better not even *think* of calling me out here again. Especially for your father. And don't think he's not gonna get hit with a whopper of a bill, either. Just for the inconvenience. Do you know he wouldn't even let me *look* at him?

SOPHIE: God. I know. Why are all the men in this damn family such *babies*?

(*A long beat. Neither moves.*)

SOPHIE: Michael?

ASHE: What?

SOPHIE: If you insist on going, at least eat something first.

ASHE: No thank you.

SOPHIE: Well I'm gonna get something. You have to join me.

ASHE: Well, okay.

(*She scurries into the pantry, comes back with her arms full, and makes peanut butter and jelly sandwiches.*)

SOPHIE: I have a confession to make. I *love* eating in the middle of the night. It is my guilty pleasure. And *nothing* under the sun beats peanut butter and jelly! Daddy. God! What a spoilt old man. And it's our fault. I mean women. He's always been such a hit with us. And we get all maternal with him and put up with his bratty behavior and his little tantrums—I have no idea why. We have spoiled him rotten. I accept my share of the blame. Do you like strawberry or grape?

ASHE: Grape.

SOPHIE: Me too. Something to drink?

ASHE: Beer?

(*She points toward the kitchen. He comes back with beer and soda.*)

SOPHIE: Thanks.

(*They begin to eat.*)

SOPHIE: Isn't this great? I always imagine I'm having a picnic.

ASHE: I don't know what to tell you, Sophie, he's a jackass. That's all there is to it. I know that's harsh but I am not in the mood to be pulling punches.

SOPHIE: You don't have to pull punches, Michael.

ASHE: Well, I have no idea how you do it.

SOPHIE: Do what?

ASHE: Him. Your father. Doesn't wanna have anything to do with you for years, then shows up here and orders you around and makes your life miserable. And he's not the only one. There's Jack, who looks like he should have Doctor Kevorkian on speed-dial, and your grandmother who seems to live in another world altogether nattering on about God knows what and then, to top it all off, there's Helena.

SOPHIE: What about Helena?

ASHE: I still don't even know what to call her. Stepmother just doesn't cut it.

SOPHIE: God, don't I *know* it.

ASHE: You wanna hear my theory?

SOPHIE: Absolutely.

ASHE: Beauty should *not* be skin deep.

SOPHIE: What do you mean?

ASHE: People should have beauty in *every* way, not just the physical. If it's just physical, it's monstrous. Yeah, Helena is physically stunning. Nobody could argue with that. But I think that's all there is. It's like she's some gorgeous bird in a cage with all her plumage and we all should somehow feel privileged for being allowed to look at her and we should worship the fact that she's here on earth deigning to enchant us with her beauty. I mean it's not like she *does* anything around here, am I right?

SOPHIE: Right.

ASHE: Yet look at the way Jack acts when he's around her. And for what? Does she help with *anything* around here? Of course not. And there is something very wrong with that.

(*He takes a long swallow of beer. Burps. SOPHIE burps back.*)

ASHE: I'm a tough critic, aren't I? Sometimes I grouse so much I sound like your uncle. We've both turned into a couple of old complainers.

SOPHIE: But what do you have to complain about? You know you have a great life.

ASHE: I do. I guess I do, don't I? But it never *seems* that way. When I sit down and really think about it I can see how good it is. But then I get so aggravated I can't hardly see straight. I don't even know where to start. I mean, look at the fix we're in. It was bad enough with the Clinton-haters and the wing-nuts, but now they're all *in charge!* Gore didn't fight and Kerry sure as hell didn't and Diebold stole the election and Rush Limbaugh just gloats and Fox News runs the goddamn country! We are in the Dark Ages with Iraq and torture and ANWAR. And it's just not politics. I feel it affecting me personally. I feel it weighing me down. I'll tell you what it is. Sometime you can be walking through a forest at night, getting scratched and cut by the thorns and whacked by the branches, you're getting torn up pretty good—but it doesn't matter. You barely even feel it because there's a light that you're walking toward at the edge of the forest. That light is your goal and you can put up with any pain and any obstacle to get there 'cause there's nothing more important than reaching that light.

SOPHIE: I know.

ASHE: I work harder than any man I know.

SOPHIE: I know.

ASHE: But there's no light for me in the distance anymore.

(Silence.)

ASHE: Loneliness. There's loneliness.

SOPHIE: I know. There isn't someone—

ASHE: Someone?

SOPHIE: You know, that you can—

ASHE: Talk to?

SOPHIE: Not talk to exactly. Someone you can—

ASHE: Someone I can love? Are you talking to me about love, Sophie?

SOPHIE: Well, yeah.

ASHE: No.

SOPHIE: No? That's it? No?

ASHE: No.

SOPHIE: I don't believe that.

ASHE: I am past my prime, Sophie. I am too old. Nobody'd have me.

SOPHIE: Shut up.

ASHE: Oh!

SOPHIE: What?

ASHE: I just thought of someone.

SOPHIE: Really? Who?

ASHE: I've never told this to anyone before—

SOPHIE: Tell me.

ASHE: It's sweet old Mary.

SOPHIE: I hate you!

ASHE: That is one sexy senior citizen! And can she cook!

SOPHIE: Stop! I was being serious.

ASHE: Alright, Sophie. The fact is I've always felt out of place. I can't stand the goddamn hillbillies anymore. I've given up on them. And then you run across someone with the tiniest smidgen of education and they're the ones that think they are the final authority and know everything about everything. They sure as hell don't know what to make of me. Like some of the staff doctors and the residents at the hospitals? They're *afraid* of me! And they think I'm full of shit, that I'm this bizarre fossil. This oddball fossil from the sixties. I love the forests. That's odd. I'm a vegetarian. That's odd. These people want nothing to do with me and frankly I want nothing to do with them. *(Opens another beer.)*

SOPHIE: *(Stopping him.)* Don't.

ASHE: Don't what?

SOPHIE: I wish you wouldn't.

ASHE: Why not?

SOPHIE: Because you don't have to. Michael, you are not that kind of person. Be yourself. Don't hide behind a buzz or anything. Look at me. You are so important to everyone around here. Even if they don't say it, people consider you the most important person, the one we could never get along without. I do. You know what Michael? I love the way you talk to people, you know, patients and stuff. Your voice is genuine and gentle and reassuring. You are *fine*. So I don't understand why you want to get drunk and rude and nasty and be like all the other idiots around here. There's no reason. And I don't want you to. And I'll do anything to get you to stop. I'll get down on my knees to get you to stop. *(Gets out of her chair and onto her knees.)*

ASHE: Okay! You win. I'll stop. Right now.

SOPHIE: Really?

ASHE: Cold turkey.

SOPHIE: Michael—

ASHE: No, I'm serious. I'll go to meetings if you want me to. I'll do all nine steps.

SOPHIE: Seven.

ASHE: I'll do two more! *(A beat.)* Alright! Great. That is settled. Now I am sober and I will remain sober for the rest of my life. *(A beat.)* And you know what?

SOPHIE: What?

ASHE: I feel better already!

SOPHIE: Good.

(An awkward silence.)

ASHE: Sophie, the point is that my time is over. It's passed.

SOPHIE: Michael—

ASHE: My feelings are dried up and there's nothing left of them. I think about someone like, you know, Helena—

SOPHIE: Helena?

ASHE: Well, you know, *beauty.* I think that that's the one thing that could stir me up, you know? That kind of beauty. But—that isn't really *love*, is it? That's not forever. That's not—

(He is close to her now. There is a sense they are about to kiss. They clasp hands. After a long moment, ASHE leans his head against her and begins to cry softly. The crying becomes stronger until she has to hold him as he shakes in her arms.)

SOPHIE: Michael…Michael…what? What is it?

ASHE: *(He recovers somewhat.)* Nothing.

SOPHIE: What?

ASHE: It's okay.

SOPHIE: Tell me.

ASHE: I want to.

SOPHIE: Please tell me.

(A long beat.)

ASHE: At Easter. I had a young boy. And he died. And he didn't have to.

(There is an awkward silence.)

SOPHIE: You have to put something like that behind you, Michael.

(ASHE walks away.)

SOPHIE: Michael?

ASHE: What?

SOPHIE: I need to ask you a question.

ASHE: Okay.

SOPHIE: What if… I mean, if there was, you know, someone who… Like, what if there was someone, you know, like what if I had a sister or a friend… And you found out that she was in love with you.

(He turns to look at her.)

SOPHIE: What? How? I mean, how would you feel about something like that?

(A long silence. Neither moves.)

ASHE: Look, it's been a long day. I mean a lo-o-o-ng fucking day. I'm gonna go. I'll talk to you. I won't wake anyone up. Thanks for the sandwich. *(He leaves.)*

SOPHIE: *(Goes to the window.)* I couldn't be a bigger idiot. I couldn't. He couldn't get out of here fast enough. And he said nothing. God, but when he was here I was so happy. And then I had to be such a huge jerk. "You have such a gentle voice, Doctor Ashe…" Ugh! I can't take this. I can't take it. I should just kill myself right now. And what was I doing at the end when I said that ridiculous thing about having a sister or a friend that was in love with him? What was I *doing*? Sophie *(Goes to the window.)* you are *such* a loser. *(A beat.)* God I'd give anything to be beautiful. I'd give *anything*! But I am not beautiful. I know I'm not. I'm the one with *personality*. I'm the one they always wanted to be *friends* with. FUCK! I *want* to be beautiful. I want it so bad! That's the only thing I want. Why can't I have it? Why? Why?

(She silently peers out the window. After a moment, HELENA comes in the room. There is a tension between them.)

HELENA: Oh, hi. I couldn't sleep. Thought I'd turn on the TV.

(In the distance, we hear the puttering of Ashe's VW.)

HELENA: Oh—is that…? Was the doctor here all this time? Where's he rushing off to, Sophie?

SOPHIE: Home.

HELENA: Home? Now? Why couldn't he stay over?

(No reply.)

HELENA: Sophie?

(No reply.)

HELENA: Sophie.

(She gives up and puts on the TV. After a moment, SOPHIE grabs the remote and shuts it off.)

HELENA: Why did you do that? Sophie?

SOPHIE: What?

HELENA: Why did you do that?

(No reply.)

HELENA: I have no idea why you hate me. I never did anything to you.

SOPHIE: I hardly hate you.

HELENA: What a relief. Thank you. That makes me happy.

SOPHIE: Where's my father?

HELENA: He's sleeping finally. And I have to tell you, I am exhausted with staying up with him. I don't know what to do with him.

(SOPHIE ignores her. Silence. HELENA notices the food on the table.)

HELENA: What's this? A little late-night raid on the fridge?

(Silence.)

HELENA: Did I interrupt something? With you and Michael?

(SOPHIE glares at her, then resumes looking out the window. HELENA walks over to her.)

HELENA: Okay. This is just stupid. We're settling it once and for all. I asked you before why you hate me. You said that you don't. But you treat me horribly and

it hurts my feelings. Now I can imagine that none of this is easy for you. God knows what you think about me and my marriage and the way we showed up and I don't know, probably from your point of view, took over. You probably think I married your father for all the wrong reasons. For selfish reasons or, I don't know what. You probably feel in competition with me for him. And I am sorry for that. I didn't think of that and I am sorry for that. But I will tell you something. I married Alex because I fell in love with him. He didn't go after me, I went after him. I couldn't help myself. I just fell head over heels in love with your father. And honestly, Sophie, everything was wonderful between us. It was wonderful until we came here. And now things are… well, let me just say that things are not great. And goddamn it, Sophie, it doesn't help things the way you judge me and the way you blame me and the way you barely tolerate me. And if your goal was to spoil my relationship with Alex then congratulations because it seems to be working. And if your goal was to hurt me and make me feel unwanted then congratulations because you have definitely succeeded at that. (A beat.) And now I've said that, I feel even more humiliated so I will go to another part of the house and I guess I'll try to stay out of your way. (Starts to leave.)

SOPHIE: Can I ask you a question?

HELENA: I suppose.

SOPHIE: Are you happy?

HELENA: No.

SOPHIE: One more.

HELENA: Okay.

SOPHIE: Are you sorry you married my father?

(HELENA doesn't answer that one. Silence.)

HELENA: Are you satisfied?

SOPHIE: No. I really want to know.

HELENA: I'm not sorry.

SOPHIE: Okay.

HELENA: Now it's my turn.

SOPHIE: Okay.

HELENA: Have you ever been in love?

(SOPHIE doesn't answer but her expression belies her.)

HELENA: It's Doctor Ashe, isn't it?

SOPHIE: Maybe.

HELENA: Do you want to talk about it?

SOPHIE: Do you like him?

HELENA: I think I do.

SOPHIE: How stupid do I look? I know I have the stupidest look on my face. I don't understand how he left the room and drove away but I still hear the sound of his voice in my head and when I look through this window I can swear I can see his face staring back at me. It's just silly. It's a silly little crush like a thirteen-year-old girl going gaga over some movie star or something. God! When I just *think* about him I can't even breathe.

HELENA: Yes. I know.

SOPHIE: Well?

HELENA: Well what?

SOPHIE: Talk to me about him.

HELENA: What do you want me to say?

SOPHIE: Say he's *brilliant!* Say he's *gorgeous!* HE IS! He's *amazing!* Do you have any idea how smart he is? How good? How decent? Do you know he can do anything he sets his mind to? I mean really! You name it! Medicine! The environment! Say something about him!

HELENA: Okay. I am going to speak frankly about him because I, as you know Sophie, am a sophisticated woman of the world and I know things.

SOPHIE: Okay.

HELENA: Medicine and forests. It's much more than that. Let's say he's brilliant—

SOPHIE: He is!

HELENA: Yes! He is brilliant! But he also has courage. Great passion and courage. Extraordinary vision of the future! Let's think about it. He plants trees and, from the perspective of that little sapling, he can imagine what the world will look like a hundred years in the future! He can change the way people see the world!

SOPHIE: Yes!

HELENA: And in that way he is so like your father, Sophie. People like him are rare. They must be honored and cherished and even indulged. They are rare. And sometimes it isn't easy to be with them. Sometimes the price you have to pay is steep. With Doctor Ashe, I think he drinks some.

SOPHIE: He does.

HELENA: And he wrestles with himself, he's tortured and he can be wild and crude and grubby. And that's the price he has to pay for being extraordinary. If you think of him out here, you have to be filled with admiration. A man like that, a modern pioneer, living the coarse, idealistic life in the mountains of Appalachia—he couldn't possibly be perfect, could he? He has to have a few rough edges. I mean he's come here, to a barbaric place, a forgotten place, rolled up his sleeves, waded into the mud, and tended to people, tended to their souls. He has eschewed the material comforts of modern life to feed his soul. He drives a beat-up old car, makes hellish, heroic journeys through unpaved roads deep into the American outback, practicing I imagine an almost medieval medicine, freezing cold, blizzards, indigent, unsanitary, uneducated, benighted people, poverty on top of sickness— You see what I'm saying, right?

SOPHIE: I do.

HELENA: I'm saying that he is fighting the good fight and that ideals are still alive in him but that after battling for his principles every single day you have to be tolerant of his flaws, forgive him his drinking, forgive his eccentricities, hold onto him tight. Hold on. And don't let go.

SOPHIE: I won't.

HELENA: And I wish you every happiness with him. I truly do.

SOPHIE: I would never have thought that you would know so much.

HELENA: Surprise! The cover girl's actually got a brain! And she's actually way better at giving advice than following it.

SOPHIE: Oh.

HELENA: I think I should be more understanding of your father.

SOPHIE: Talk about a tough job.

HELENA: I can be petty. But he also knows how to belittle me and make me feel like a little speck of dust. Around him I can do nothing right. Around him I'm stupid.

SOPHIE: He makes everyone feel that way.

HELENA: Next to him we are, I guess. *(Pause.)* I'm his trophy. *(Pause.)* When we'd go to the Met... have you ever been, Sophie?

SOPHIE: When I was little my mom...they would take me...

HELENA: ...it's *so* beautiful. The lights and the fountain and the hundreds of fabulous people all decked out in their sophisticated finery. Anyway, we would go, and heads would turn. I swear. I'm not being vain, I didn't even understand it at first, I thought it was just because of him, that he was far more of a celebrity than I had imagined—but that wasn't it. It was me *with* him. The women would give me hateful looks. The men...well. *(A beat.)* The fact is that people tire of me very easily, Sophie. You can't imagine how unhappy that makes me. I can't seem to sustain anything. And that feeds my unhappiness. I'm so good at pretending otherwise. And the more I do the more the sense of inadequacy gnaws away inside of me and the unhappier I become. Until I find myself unable to climb back out of it. It probably sounds silly to you, but I have forgotten how to *be* happy. I've forgotten and now I don't know how or what to do.

(Inexplicably, SOPHIE laughs quietly.)

HELENA: And now you're laughing at me.

SOPHIE: No! I'm not I'm not I'm not. Helena—you are *so* beautiful and confident and—I didn't imagine you had an unhappy moment *ever*! I'm the one that's constantly depressed, constantly questioning myself, constantly inadequate—*I'm* the one!

HELENA: You're *not* inadequate. You're amazing.

SOPHIE: No, I'm not. But it doesn't matter now. Now, hearing you say those things, it makes me happy.

HELENA: Oh.

SOPHIE: No, that didn't—that's not what I meant. I meant... I mean I just, I don't feel so—alone—anymore. Or jealous.

HELENA: Jealous of who?

SOPHIE: Of *you*, dummy!

HELENA: You know what?

SOPHIE: What?

HELENA: Let's watch TV. Jack said something about *The Munsters* and I find Herman to be very sexy.

SOPHIE: Okay.

(They move to the couch and sit, and SOPHIE reaches for the remote.)

ACT THREE

Two months later, August. Hot. Crickets and cicadas create a blanket of sound. The living room. Outside, there is blazing sunshine. Inside, even the AC can't dent the heat. SOPHIE sits and works. JACK sits with a People *or similar celebrity magazine. HELENA drifts around the room.*

JACK: *(After a few beats.)* Where is he? *(No response.)* I'm bursting with anticipation. Can't hardly contain myself.

SOPHIE: Is it time?

JACK: Almost. Quarter to. *(In a comic voice.)* Chairman Professor Master of the Ladies Room Alexander Cough-CoughCoughlan has so very graciously requested our ever so vile and peasant-like presence in the living room at precisely one o'clock. And now, sports fans, it is quarter to. The air is buzzing with excitement. The air is brimming with anticipation. The air is boiling with eagerness. The air is—I am so overwrought with the suspense that I can't think of another funny thing to say! The Universe is getting ready. In fifteen minutes a vital message will be delivered. The countdown has begun. Here we are, live in the Vaughn living room, the self-same living room where this pronouncement from the oracle atop Mount Coughlan will be revealed to us. *(To HELENA, rolling up the magazine like a microphone.)* Excuse me, ma'am. Jack Vaughn, from CNN. Would you care to comment about this humongous event? Speak right into the camera here.

(She vogues.)

JACK: Our ratings just shot through the roof. Now tell me, ma'am, what do you expect to hear from the great man today?

HELENA: I don't know. Something about business.

JACK: Business? I object! Business you say? *Impossible!* That fucking fat ass wouldn't soil his bikini briefs with business. Why he's too busy hacking and wheezing and farting and expectorating all over his laptop for that!

SOPHIE: Uncle. Please. I'm trying to get some work done.

JACK: Sorry. Must be the heat. It's addlin' my brain. *(He leans over SOPHIE.)* What's that?

SOPHIE: We may need a new combine harvester.

JACK: Yup. The ol' John Deere nine six six aught. How much'll they run ya? What's that ol' sticker look like?

SOPHIE: Half-decent used we're talking over fifty thousand.

JACK: Dollars?

SOPHIE: Yes, Uncle. That's used. That's a 1997.

JACK: What do they run new?

SOPHIE: Over two hundred thousand. Dollars. Come on, Uncle, let me do this.

(JACK watches HELENA float around the room. He nudges SOPHIE.)

SOPHIE: What? Uncle!

JACK: I can't help it. If laziness were an art she'd be Picasso. If indolence were money, she'd be Bill Gates. (To HELENA.) You are too much, you know that? To too too too too too much!

HELENA: And you talk too too too too too too too much, you know that? There must be an off switch somewhere. You repeat the same things over and over and over morning noon and night. Doesn't it *ever* make you tired?

JACK: Nev-ah!

HELENA: God! I am *so bored*! Really! How do you two do it? Bored bored bored bored bored bored bored bored bored. There is nothing to do. Nothing nothing nothing nothing and nothing.

SOPHIE: (Unable to continue working.) Nothing? Are you kidding me? There is plenty to damn well do.

HELENA: Is there? Like what?

SOPHIE: Are you for real? Gee. Let me see. There's the farm. You could help with the farm! There's chores. You could help out with the chores. Like dishes. You might even consider cleaning up your dishes after yourself instead of leaving them laying around all over the goddamn house and expecting the dish fairy to clean them up for you.

HELENA: I thought that was what the maid does.

SOPHIE: I'M THE GODDAMN MAID! It is not *Mary's* job to pick up after you! It is not my job or Waffles's job or my uncle's job or the DISH FAIRY'S JOB!

HELENA: Sophie—

SOPHIE: I'm sorry. (Pause.) There's plenty to do.

HELENA: Like what?

SOPHIE: I don't know! I'm not your fucking camp counselor! Uncle, help me out here.

JACK: Not me.

SOPHIE: Helena, teach the poor. Heal the sick. Drive the tractor.

HELENA: You're kidding, right? (To JACK.) She's kidding, right? Sophie. This is not some novel. This is not Dickens or *Tobacco Road*. I'm not going to just get up one day and teach the peasants or feed the poor or nurse the sick or drive a damn tractor for that matter.

SOPHIE: Now, see? I don't see how you cannot. I don't see how you can watch everyone else work their butts off and not feel like pitching in. Go ahead, try to do something that's about somebody else and not yourself for a change of pace. It might actually lead to more self-less acts and inspire you to get off your ass occasionally. You might even begin to like it. Are you bored, Helena? Golly Gee Willikers What Are We Ever To Do? Boredom and self-absorption are infectious diseases around here. Look at Uncle Jack. He hasn't raised a finger to do anything worthwhile for months. Follows you around like a little panting puppy dog—it's sickening to watch. You've even infected me with your disease of ennui. I've been walking around in slow motion half the time. And look at Doctor Ashe, for chrissakes. He used to be so busy that we'd be lucky if he could stop by once a month—it was hard to get him here at all. But now he's here every single day and he's totally given up his patients and his trees and God knows the damage that that has already caused. I don't know Helena—you must be a witch.

(An awkward pause.)

JACK: Which witch is which? Oh come on girls, don't fight. Unless it's over me. (To HELENA.) And for what it's worth, I don't agree with my niece. About all that work stuff. Oh, I agree with her about me not pulling my weight and I feel bad about that, but not you. You weren't sent from on high to soil yourself with combine harvesters. But that doesn't mean I don't think there's something very wrong. I've been trying to find the right way of describing you and it is a challenge. You're like a mermaid or some such exotic sea creature, with cold blood. And you're not fit for these landlocked hills. It's not your fault if you are a mermaid, you just need to spread your wings, or fins I guess, and *be* a mermaid. Go on! *BE A MERMAID!* Admit that you are better than the rest of us. Admit that you are a myth who exists to be worshipped. Leave! Get out of here! *Dive* into the ocean and indulge yourself. Leave us mere mortals behind, gasping and genuflecting in your absence.

HELENA: *Shut up, will you?* You think I'm such a monster? That is the cruelest thing you've ever said to me.

JACK: No no no no no no no, Helena, that's not what I meant at all. God! I'm sorry. I was just having fun. I was paying you a compliment. Don't be mad at me.

HELENA: It was very hurtful what you said.

JACK: I know. I'm sorry. Just don't be mad. Wait here. I'll pick you some flowers as a peace offering. I'll be right back. *(Leaves.)*

(Several moments pass.)

SOPHIE: I'm sorry I snapped at you.

HELENA: It's okay. *(Pause.)* Before you know it September will be here. It always makes your father anxious, even now that he's not teaching. The summer just flew by. And gone so slowly at the same time. *(Pause.)* Sophie.

SOPHIE: Yeah.

HELENA: Can we talk?

SOPHIE: Sure. About?

HELENA: Doctor Ashe.

SOPHIE: *(Warily.)* Okay.

HELENA: He's here?

SOPHIE: You know he set up the guest room with his computer.

HELENA: What about him?

SOPHIE: What do you mean?

HELENA: What about—?

SOPHIE: Forget it.

HELENA: Why?

SOPHIE: Because I'm a fucking cow, that's why.

HELENA: Sophie—

SOPHIE: Don't. The last thing I need is pity from you. I know what you're going to say, Helena— "You have

beautiful hair!" Right. My hair. My fucking hair. Look at you. Look at me. I've got great eyes. I've got a terrific personality.

(Silence.)

SOPHIA: Helena, I love him. I've loved him since forever and now it's just plain torture because he's here all the time and I can't even breathe when he's around because I want to touch him and kiss him and lay my head on his chest and hear his heart beating and it doesn't help that he stays over almost every night and I'm not the reason that he's here. He barely says hello to me anymore. Helena, my heart is breaking every single day and I don't know what to do. I bump into him and I can't even speak to him. I am such a loser. It is so obvious what a loser I've become. You couldn't possibly understand how humiliating it is. Everyone knows how I feel. Even Grandma shakes her head and winks. The pity is unfuckingbelievable. I feel like I have nothing left, no self-control, no self-esteem—

HELENA: But I'm asking you if *he* knows.

SOPHIE: Knows what?

HELENA: All this. How you feel about him?

SOPHIE: He's so preoccupied I doubt he even remembers my name.

HELENA: Now you're being silly.

SOPHIE: You think this silly?

HELENA: No. Just hang on a second. Let's— Look. What if I talked to him?

SOPHIE: You.

HELENA: Absolutely. I'm not going to embarrass him or you or anything. I'll be discreet about it. I'll drop a couple of hints. The point is, Sophie, you have to know how he feels one way or another. I mean, one way or another you have to agree this has to stop. Yes or no—you deserve to have an answer. You have to agree with me, Sophie. Anything is better than now. It'll be better to know. Please let me do this for you. And if it's "no" then I think that he has to stop coming here. It'll be better for you that way. Right? You agree that's right?

(SOPHIE nods.)

HELENA: We'll get everything settled. I don't think it'll be too hard to find out what his feelings are toward you. I should do it now, right? While he's here. Before we lose our nerve. There won't be any more doubts. He's been after me to look at those maps he's been making. Go tell him I'll talk to him, okay?

(SOPHIE hesitates.)

HELENA: Go on, Sophie.

SOPHIE: I'm not— You'll tell me whatever he says?

HELENA: Yes. Trust me.

SOPHIE: Okay. I'll tell him you want to see his maps. *(A pause.)* I'm not sure this is right, Helena.

HELENA: Trust me.

(SOPHIE goes.)

HELENA: Poor girl. How do I get myself into these fixes? It's definitely better this way. It's certainly better for Sophie. Is there anything worse than seeing someone you love in pain and not being able to do anything about it? I'm afraid of what he'll say. I don't think he is in love with her. But I don't understand why he wouldn't be. I mean, they are perfect for each other, why shouldn't they be together? And Sophie's not unattractive. And him? My God, he should get down on his knees and thank his lucky stars that someone as smart and kind and good as Sophie would want someone like him. Where does he get off thinking he's too good for her? She's too good for him, that's the truth. That man is so— But that's not the point. Sophie's in love with him and that's all that matters. From her point of view, I can see what she sees. Poor girl is stuck in the middle of nowhere in this crazy family in the middle of such dullness, of such unrelenting routine. There are so few *real* people out here at all. So many of them are like shadows, blurry, without edges. He's a little different. He seems to have some sense of himself. He has a passion for things. Out here, he might even be considered good-looking and interesting. If I were her I'd probably see him that way, like a bright moon rising in the darkness. I do know what she sees in him. To fall under the influence of a man who is superior to the others around him. I certainly know what that's like. If I were her, I could see me being a little attracted to him myself. And that's what this godforsaken place has done to me. I honestly have to admit that I like the way he looks at me. It breaks up the tedium. He's funny. He makes me smile. *(A beat.)* Damn you Jack! Telling me I am a cold-blooded mermaid. And what of it? What if I am? And I am like a fish out of water around here. And it is Alexander's fault, he's the one who brought me here. I can hear Jack saying—"Leave! Get out of here!"—and

maybe I should. Escape from this stultifying life among all the shadows and sleepy faces and drowsiness and stupidity. Alex, I wish you'd never brought me here. And I should just tell him I want to leave. We should both leave. I know I should but I don't. Cowardly, I guess. With everyone. With Alex, with Jack, even with Michael. It's not right the way he pays attention to me right in front of Sophie. So why don't I say something about it? Why don't I stand up and *do* something about it? I see the way it hurts her. Poor Sophie. Well today I will. And maybe I can convince him what he has in her. And maybe everything will work out better than we can imagine. For once, better.

(ASHE enters the room with a bundle of papers and roll tubes and an easel. He begins to set everything up.)

ASHE: Sophie says you wanted to see me?

HELENA: Hi. Yeah.

ASHE: I have the maps right here.

HELENA: Oh, those are the maps you've been telling me about.

ASHE: Yeah, yeah, these are them. Almost set up. Where were you born?

HELENA: Where? Virginia Beach.

ASHE: And you went to school at Columbia?

HELENA: That's where I met Alex.

ASHE: And you're sure you'll find this interesting?

HELENA: Sure—

ASHE: Because it's got nothing to do with the beach or the ocean or the upper west side of Manhattan. It's about this land. Here. In West Virginia.

HELENA: I live here now. In West Virginia.

ASHE: Good. Fine. Great. Now—you probably noticed that I moved my drawing table and my Mac into the guest room and I devote as much of my time as possible to this project when I'm here. I'm a little bit obsessive about it—it's therapeutic. Cheaper than a shrink, you know?

HELENA: Yeah.

ASHE: Okay.

HELENA: Doctor—

ASHE: —Michael.

HELENA: Michael. Why do you? I mean what are you doing this for?

ASHE: I think I can get it published. As a coffee table book. Raise people's consciousness about the beauty that's right under their noses. Before it all goes away. *(He puts out a map.)* Okay: look at this. I got this as a geological survey from the U.S. Department of the Interior. It's dated 1849. You can see how things were more than a hundred and fifty years ago.

HELENA: *(Peering down.)* Uh huh.

ASHE: Dark green and light green, here and here, see? That stands for the woodlands and you can see that it covers nearly ninety-five percent of the entire state. You see that, right?

HELENA Right.

ASHE: I'm so excited to be showing you all this. I'm really excited.

HELENA: I'm glad.

ASHE: It means a lot to me. I just want you to know that.

HELENA: Good.

ASHE: Okay. By the way, this is all hand colored. I could do it on the computer but I get such a satisfaction from being meticulous with it. I think that using a computer program like Photoshop would defeat the whole intimate purpose of the work. It would be wrong somehow. Anyway, I'm very precise and meticulous with it.

HELENA: I can see that.

ASHE: So, if you look closely, here and here, everywhere, over here, there were deer and black bear and cougars and just about everything you can imagine, wild. Thousands of types of birds made our forests their homes, the lakes and rivers, here and here, were teeming with countless species of fish, beaver, and badger, it was all—it was all, it was Eden. Truly, it was. Unspoiled. Paradise. The old folks talk about it. With reverence. They heard their parents talk about it. And their parents' parents. Clouds of birds flew overhead. Imagine that. Clouds! Birds of such numbers that they formed clouds over the horizon. Okay, look, there were villages here, here. Farms. This was before the Civil War. Long before the mines. Before the holocaust of desecration from the mines. Look. See? I painted in areas of flora and fauna…

HELENA: I can see…

ASHE: This lake here, it's about sixty miles away from where we are now, see?

HELENA: Yeah.

ASHE: You see? The villages grew up along the rivers. Water mills. Lots of livestock roaming the hills—cattle, goat, sheep, horses—see? These are horses!

HELENA: Uh huh.

ASHE: Okay. That's a hundred and fifty plus years ago. *(He puts another map out.)* Now—let's fast forward to—1929! See? Look how it's all changed. Woodlands? Down to maybe fifty percent of the state. See any wild goats? Cougars? No. Herds of deer? Diminished. And look: these areas of black and brown. Do you know what they are? Do you?

HELENA: No, I don't—

ASHE: —STRIP MINES! YES! Let's hear it for the good ol' strip mines! Hideous! Clear cutting! Wholesale destruction! Craters and scars! Gotta make that profit! Gotta mine that coal! Gotta murder some miners! Thousands of miners died in those mines. Buried in them. Thousands more—tens of thousands more suffered the black plague, coal dust, emphysema, and there were schools nearby, children, women—LOOK! The lake from before? Sixty miles from here? Gone! Gone! Vanished! Whole lakes dried up because of man-made dams. Gotta keep the rivers out of the coal mines! I've made the colors more drab, right? You can see that Eden is being destroyed. Eden is being choked and murdered. Cities where villages used to be. Roads everywhere. Cars, trucks, criss-crossed everywhere with railroad tracks—see? See?

HELENA: Yeah.

ASHE: *(Almost in tears.)* Give me a second. Okay. Forgive me. I get angry, emotional and frustrated. You folks living in the city, you say it's just progress, you say it is the March Of Civilization and technology, Man's Manifest Destiny and I say *BULLSHIT!* That's right—*BULLSHIT!* It's rape and pillage on the march. It's Enron and Halliburton and Exxon on the march. That's what your rapacious deregulated capitalism has gotten you! Those are the chickens coming home to roost. Let's feed and train the Mujahadeen against those Rusky Commies so that they can turn around and attack *us* ten years later. Let's have Reagan and

Rumsfeld and CIA Director Bush put Saddam Hussein into power in Iraq as our guard dog for Big Oil, then let's blow them all to hell when our lapdog bites the hands that fed him! There's your Capitalism for you! Some people around here fear that I may be a Socialist, a Commie, some of 'em probably think I'm some sort of Terrorist—well so be it! You know I could accept the March of Progress bullshit, maybe I could. Maybe if my forests weren't bulldozed under for McMansions. Maybe if Eden was destroyed but replaced by Utopia—then I could accept it. If all men and women and children were lifted up by your Tide of Progress. But it ain't! And to think that it could be is just naïve. It is propaganda perpetrated on the masses by Rupert Murdoch and Reverend Sun Myung Moon and the Fox News Channel and the *Washington Times*! I'm telling you that the religion of capitalism *is* the opiate of the masses promulgated by the robber barons and the criminality of those who made their unspeakable wealth on the backs and the corpses of the poor and the indigent. Travel to Wheeling, to Morgantown, look at the decadence of those mansions, that old coal money, the Rockefellers and Mellons and Carnegies who broke the backs of the people and this sacred paradise to build their empires. Goddammit we're not *better* off! We're *worse* off! When I graduated from Cornell Med School in 1973 I was nineteen years old! Nineteen years old graduating from one of the premiere medical schools in the country! I was young and I was gifted and I wanted to make a difference. And *that* was the difference with my generation. I have devoted my entire life, inspired by the teachings of Disraeli and Gandhi and the Reverend Doctor Martin Luther King, to the *struggle*, to the victims of avarice and greed. *(He throws another map down.)* This one here? No improvement! Worse. This one? *(He throws another one down.)* 1979. Worse. Worse. Much much worse. Epidemics of typhus and measles swept through these valleys and there wasn't enough medicine. These shantytowns are teeming with ignorance and poverty and ready to explode with plague. Schools? Forget it! Awful! You have to travel to Arkansas or Mississippi or Rwanda or Guatemala to find a more godforsaken place. And the result is that the people don't understand what has been done to them so that some rich man can get richer. The people, they just wind up frustrated and bitter and bigoted and small-minded and they have no idea what has been done to them. You think they know the first thing about the beauty of life? They just shiver with cold and marry their cousins and watch the TV and watch their babies go hungry and then cry when they get sick. And then they call me. That's when they call me up and can't understand why I can't *do* something to help their little babies. There's a short story by Kafka. It's called *The Country Doctor*. That's me. You oughta read it. Because that, my dear, is me. *(Softly.)* That's me. Are you with me?

HELENA: Yes.

ASHE: This is the last map. I'm not finished with it yet. It's upsetting, isn't it? Makes me sick.

(Takes a long time looking at this last map. After several moments, HELENA cannot stifle a yawn.)

ASHE: I see. This doesn't interest you after all.

HELENA: No…Michael, I—

ASHE: It's okay. I didn't think it would. I hoped, but—I just don't understand people like you.

HELENA: No. It's not that it doesn't interest me. It's just something I know so little about and it is a little overwhelming and I may not be the most receptive audience for all this, that's all. Don't be angry, Michael.

ASHE: Alright. I go a little overboard sometimes, I'd be the first one to admit that.

HELENA: Michael, the truth is that I am a little preoccupied with something else.

ASHE: Something else?

HELENA: Yeah. And the maps were great but I need to ask you something and I don't know how to go about doing it.

ASHE: You go about it by asking.

HELENA: So you don't mind if I ask you some questions?

ASHE: Questions?

HELENA: Personal questions?

ASHE: Not at all.

HELENA: God, why is this so difficult? I don't want this to be an interrogation.

ASHE: Okay.

HELENA: Okay. This is hard for me. It concerns someone I love very much and I'm just going to come right out and ask you and once I've done than it will be over once and for all and everything will go back to normal, okay?

(ASHE nods.)

HELENA: It's about Sophie.

ASHE: It's about Sophie?

HELENA: Yes. Here goes. Do you…like her?

ASHE: Do I like Sophie? I've known her since she was a baby. How could I not like Sophie? How could anyone not like her? I think the absolute world of her.

HELENA: Yes, sure. Right. But—do you like her in *that way*?

ASHE: What way?

HELENA: You know, *that* way. Do you like her in the man-woman way?

ASHE: The man-woman way? My God, that's almost, I don't know, that's like—I mean she's like my kid sister or something, you know?

HELENA: Yes, know. I know, Michael. And I'm sorry for asking but I had to ask. So, one more question.

ASHE: Okay.

HELENA: Haven't you noticed anything?

ASHE: Noticed anything what? Is something the matter with Sophie?

HELENA: No, no, nothing like that. Okay, so, that's done. I feel better. Knowing is better.

ASHE: Knowing what?

HELENA: Not only do you not have romantic feelings towards her but you haven't even noticed how she moons over you. How she feels about you. And this has become an impossible situation for her. She is in incredible pain over this. So, I want you to know that you are not welcome to come around here anymore. It is too much for Sophie to bear.

ASHE: Whoa! Hold on now, now you've lost me. How did we get to this notion that I am not welcome here anymore? Whose decree is this? Sophie's? Jack's? What the hell is going on here, anyway? I'm not wanted around here? Good. I'll pack up and get the hell out of Dodge. What is this *game* that you seem to be playing? Whatever it is, you better believe I am too damn old to play it!

HELENA: I don't want you to be angry, Michael. It was a hard thing to bring up but I promised Sophie I would and all I want is what's best for her. And I've been living with this, and so has she, for so long that at least there will be some time to heal now. At least there's a bit of a relief in that. You understand, don't you. With her feelings and seeing you every day and you're not reciprocating, it is the best thing for her that you stay away for a while. I would think that after a few months, maybe six months, things would calm down and then it mightn't be so bad. But I'm her stepmother, as silly as that sounds, and I genuinely feel protective and maternal towards her. And now, of course, I feel totally embarrassed. I'm flushed.

ASHE: I have no idea what to say. I had no idea that she—but of course I'll stay away under the circumstances. I mean why would you think that I wouldn't want what's best for her? Or that I wouldn't want to protect her from painful things, not *cause* them. Sophie. Sophie. Sophie. She's great. She's the best. I just don't—I never—

(There's an awkward silence for several moments.)

ASHE: Wait a minute. Let me ask you something,

HELENA: Ask.

ASHE: Why all of a sudden. Why bring this up? And now?

HELENA: She's been miserable and I couldn't—

ASHE: You!

HELENA: What?

ASHE: What?

HELENA: I don't know what—

ASHE: I think I get it.

HELENA: Get what?

ASHE: It! Sophie's unhappy. I understand that. That I understand. But what about you? What was this whole interrogation thing? Can you be as oblivious as you pretend as to why I've been spending so much time around here? You, Helena, you are a little bit of a tease, aren't you?

HELENA: I'm a what? You're a little crazy, that's what I think.

ASHE: As Bogie said to Bergman—*Sweetheart, let me do the thinking for the both of us!* I'll tell you what you are, you're my little Chinese dish—sweet and sour at the same time.

HELENA: Michael!

ASHE: Hush! Let me say this: I never dreamed that you could feel the same way about me as I do about you but I see that it is true. I couldn't understand you and the old man but I have seen you looking at me in unguarded moments. You are like a Michelangelo statue that loves to be admired and I've come all summer to admire and worship you and now I have my reward.

HELENA: Michael—

ASHE: —God I love the way you say my name!

HELENA: No, Michael—

ASHE: No? No. Yes! Helena *YES!* All summer we've been flirting. Then you find out that poor Sophie's feelings may be hurt and you try to do the brave thing, the selfless thing and it only makes me love you even more.

HELENA: Love me?

ASHE: And hunger for you. I *LOVE* you and I *HUNGER* for you. I'm caught in your web you gorgeous long-legged predatory spider—so come, *EAT ME!*

HELENA: You're acting crazy—

ASHE: —How can you blame me? I'm going to say one more thing, Helena. Here, in Jack's home with your husband and with Sophie you cannot bring yourself to admit to anything, to speak that which you are longing to speak. You don't have to. You are the most beautiful, alluring woman I have ever laid eyes on and I have been hopelessly in love with you from the very first moment I saw you and I will dedicate my entire life to one thing and one thing only—making you happy.

HELENA: *May* I say something?

ASHE: Of course.

HELENA: Are you finished?

ASHE: Yes.

HELENA: You will not interrupt me?

ASHE: No.

HELENA: What you say I find flattering. But you could not more totally have misconstrued the entire situa-

tion. What you have said to me—there is absolutely no chance of it ever happening.

ASHE: I know.

HELENA: You know?

ASHE: I know there's no chance.

HELENA: You do?

ASHE: Of course I do. I will go away. I understand everything. I will go away.

HELENA: Yes. Go Away.

ASHE: But tomorrow, I'll be waiting for you at the edge of the road at four thirty.

HELENA: What? No.

ASHE: What? Yes. At four thirty. Don't tell anyone if you don't want to. Don't bring much. We'll buy what we need. We'll live on love.

(ASHE leans in to her, grabs her hands, and begins devouring them. JACK silently enters to witness it. He clutches roses.)

HELENA: *(In a whisper.)* What the hell are you doing?

ASHE: Kissing your hands.

HELENA: You *must* stop it right now.

ASHE: You're absolutely right.

(He grabs her in a full embrace and kisses her passionately. She squirms out. Turns and sees JACK. ASHE is flushed and beaming.)

ASHE: Goodbye my love. *(He saunters out past Jack.)* Hey Jack, what's new with you?

(JACK takes a swing at him. ASHE dodges it and skips away, laughing. JACK stands looking at HELENA.)

HELENA: It's not—I mean—Oh Good Christ, Jack—He had no business doing that.

JACK: *(Walking up to her.)* And neither did I. *(He throws the roses at her.)*

HELENA: Jack, this is just silly.

JACK: Silly, Helena? *Silly?*

HELENA: Oh God! I *have* to get out of here.

(WAFFLES, ALEXANDER, SOPHIE, and MARY enter the room. JACK skulks into a corner.)

WAFFLES: I haven't felt my best either, Professor. Nothing worse than a summer cold.

ALEXANDER: I hear that, Waffles. I hear that… Where is everyone? I'm late but I thought everyone'd be waiting here for me. Where's my beautiful wife?

HELENA: I'm right here, Alex.

ALEXANDER: Oh. Didn't see you, my love. And Jack? And Elizabeth?

SOPHIE: *(To HELENA.)* What did he say?

HELENA: We'll talk later.

SOPHIE: You're trembling. It must have been bad. Was it bad? Tell me. *Tell me!*

HELENA: *Later!*

(ALEXANDER and WAFFLES are arranging the furniture in rows.)

ALEXANDER: Help me, Waffles, I want to give a little presentation. I want it to be like a little classroom. Everyone find a seat, alright? You know, Waffles, colds and things don't bother me. It's this environment that gets me, a place where nothing ever happens, where nothing changes, and nothing gets done that bothers me. Did you read the books I gave you? *None* of them? Get on the ball! Look at everyone. Such silence. There's an atmosphere here that I can't put my finger on. Has a large pink elephant entered the room that everyone can see but me? Sophie, take a seat. Jack! There you are, you old son of a gun. Take a seat.

JACK: I'll stand.

ALEXANDER: "I'll stand." You know what you are Jonathon?

JACK: No, Alex. Why don't you tell me.

ALEXANDER: A curmudgeon. But then that's what we all like about you.

JACK: Alex, I don't mean to be rude, but I'm going to go.

ALEXANDER: You can't go!

JACK: Give me a break. I don't know what this is about but you damn well don't need me here. I don't feel well and…

ALEXANDER: …Jonathon, I absolutely forbid it. I need you here most of all. This won't take long I

promise you. I'm sorry you're not feeling well. Wasn't Doctor Ashe here a moment ago? Maybe he could give you something.

JACK: That's okay. He already has.

ALEXANDER: What?

JACK: *Jesus Christ, nothing! (A beat.)* Could we just do this?

ALEXANDER: You're upset with me over something, aren't you, Jack? Please don't be upset. I can't imagine what I've done but we've both been getting along so well and getting you upset is the last thing I want to do.

JACK: For the first and only time, Alexander, I can honestly say it has nothing to do with you.

ALEXANDER: Well that's good.

JACK: I'm sorry.

ALEXANDER: Apology accepted. Oh! There's Queen Elizabeth.

(WAFFLES applauds as ELIZABETH makes her way in.

ELIZABETH: Is this Art History 101?

ALEXANDER: Just take a seat, my dear, with the other freshmen. All of you get comfortable. Okay, is everyone assembled? I really do feel like I'm back in front of my freshmen students at Weinstein Lecture Hall. And what a paltry bunch of stragglers you are! And now that I've got a captive audience again, it may be time to dust off some of my comedy material!

JACK: Enough with the jokes, Alexander.

ALEXANDER: You're absolutely right, young man. There seems to be such tension in this room. Was a murder committed? Am I the only one that doesn't know?

(Silence.)

ALEXANDER: This *is* a tough room. Anyway, all kidding aside, there are some very serious and heartfelt things I want to say to all of you. I may need your help and advice. First, I want to thank you for your warm and sincere kindness in accepting Helena and myself into your home these past several months. I'm aware that, legally, this house and the land it sits on is also mine, but I want to acknowledge your sense of home and family which, frankly, I've never quite been a part of. For myself, I'm nothing more than an old academic.

I concern myself with the world of Art, with an esoteric world of color and light and form and image. I've always considered myself fortunate to be shielded from more practical matters. So I have always entrusted the kindness and competence of you Jonathon, and you Sophie, and you Elizabeth, and, yes, you Waffles, for allowing me the comforts of my life in New York without having to worry at all about how the estate and all its affairs were managed. Please accept my deepest gratitude and thanks.

ELIZABETH: It has always been our pleasure, Alexander.

ALEXANDER: Thank you, that is very kind. The fact is, and I'm not sure this will come as a surprise to anyone, I'm not sure that country life agrees with me. Fact is, I've become old here. I've lost my raison d'être, my joie de vivre. I've realized I've reached the limit of my mortality here. And, too, it's not just me that I'm thinking of. I have a young wife. And a grown daughter. Both flowers of young womanhood. And then there's Jonathon who I know has always had his aspirations.

JACK: Please get to the point, Alexander.

ALEXANDER: You're right. Alright. I have a tendency to be long winded and I know it. The point is that I can no longer live in the wilds of West Virginia. I thought I could, thought that Helena and I could achieve some romance here, I had visions of myself as a country squire, but I've come to see that neither me nor my wife are cut out for it. And I'm sure that comes as no surprise to any of you. I've contacted Columbia and NYU and the New School and even Yale and the sad fact is that in an age of academic budget cuts any work that I would do emeritus or adjunct simply would not yield enough in the way of compensation. The advance on my book will be fairly small, somehow they don't see a retrospective on seventies and eighties art as a potential best-seller. And of course the income from the old homestead here, while steady, simply doesn't pay enough. So, here it is. I've spoken with an old chum of mine who manages one of those big Wall Street firms and he has come up with an idea which, I believe, may turn out to be the perfect solution for everyone. I'm no expert on this so forgive me if I refer to notes from our conversation. It was really very nice of him to be so forthcoming with his expertise. Now—understand that slicing of certain areas of the farm would provide a short monetary boost, but nothing long term or truly substantial. Apparently, the greatest asset we have is

the entirety and vastness of the property. The trick, apparently, is to find a substantial guaranteed annuity of sorts. Now, as I said, I'm not very good with the ins and outs, but the general idea seems to be this: Right now, all told, our estate brings in a return of maybe four percent of its capital worth. And that, frankly, with Jack and Elizabeth and Sophie and Waffles working their hands to the proverbial bone. The proposal which I subscribe to is to sell it. The proceeds of such a sale would be *so* substantial that, with a diversified strategy of investments, the annual yield could be as much as ten to fifteen percent without touching the principle, and there would be enough cash left over to put a bid in on a large apartment in the city and possibly...

JACK: Wait a minute. Say that again.

ALEXANDER: We would have enough cash...

JACK: Not that part. Before that.

ALEXANDER: You mean...

JACK: ...yes...

ALEXANDER: ...my proposal is to sell the estate?

JACK: There it is! I thought I had heard it wrong but no. What an idea! You really are so brilliant, Alex, to come up with such an idea. And thoughtful too. You are going to sell our farm so you can buy an apartment in New York City.

ALEXANDER: No, that's only one—

JACK: —You selfish sonuvabitch! Let me ask you a question. If you don't mind. If I may have your permission. What about me, huh? What about my old mother? What about Sophie?

ALEXANDER: You're upset. My idea is to—

JACK: I'm upset????????????

ALEXANDER: Maybe this wasn't the right time to—

JACK: Hold on a minute. Just wait. Can you wait!? Wait a minute. My feeble little brain is still trying to figure this all out. Okay. Let me see if I've got this right. And excuse me if I'm just being my normal jackass self about this. But until now, I actually thought this estate belonged in equal parts to me and my mother and Sophie and, through your marriage to my sister, you.

ALEXANDER: Not that it matters, Jack, but Waffles was given a small share as well. In light of the injustice done to his family...

JACK: What the *fuck* are you saying?

ELIZABETH: Be quiet, Jack, you're attacking him.

JACK: *I'm* attacking *him*?

ALEXANDER: The fact is that even with Waffles's support I couldn't do anything without my daughter, or your mother, or you. And I wouldn't. My intention is to have us all agree. I just assumed that for Sophie at least it's an obvious and—

JACK: Obvious?? *Obvious*??? There's only one thing that's obvious around here. It's obvious that this whole fucking thing is incredible! Come on! Am I crazy? Am I the only one who sees?

ELIZABETH: Jonathon, it's certainly obvious to me that Alexander is thinking of what's best for all of us. And if you ask me, this is something you should have thought about years ago.

JACK: Oh my God! I'm gonna vomit! I'm gonna choke! I need a drink. Mary, go get me a bourbon.

(MARY does.)

ALEXANDER: I just want to know what you're so upset about Jack. Why are you getting so worked up? I started off by saying it's just an idea. I'm willing to admit there are things I haven't thought all the way through. If everyone decides it's not the right thing to do, I won't be upset. I won't be at all offended.

WAFFLES: I don't think a man like the Professor would want us to do the wrong thing, Jonathon.

JACK: Not now, Waffles. This is serious.

WAFFLES: But I have a right to express—

JACK: —*not NOW*! Okay? Waffles? This is *serious* business. Okay? *(To ALEXANDER.)* This estate was bought from his great-uncle.

ALEXANDER: I know.

JACK: His great-uncle was a notorious drunk and gambler. My great-grandfather, in order to help out their family from all the debt it had accumulated from all that drinking and gambling, paid them the sum of twenty-five thousand dollars which, at the time, was a considerable amount of money. In retrospect, of course, it was a steal. And that's why my father willed a small share to Waffles here. Because he never complained and never wanted anything. Now we all know that Waffles doesn't have your big-city sophistication to go along

with his big heart. That he doesn't have the mental equipment to make his own way in the world. So for you to waltz in here and give him some of your big city flim-flam razzle-dazzle that wouldn't impress a horsefly off a shit pile but looks pretty damn good to *his* eyes, for you to *bilk* poor Waffles outta his—

WAFFLES: No one's bilkin' me, Jack—

JACK: Will you SHUT THE FUCK UP for crissakes!?

ALEXANDER: Now I'm sorry I ever came here.

JACK: And that makes *two* of us. Now. Let's look at it from another angle. This estate is free from debt and in pretty damn good order because of me. Due to my efforts. My personal efforts. So naturally you want to hand me an eviction notice.

ALEXANDER: What is he accusing me of?

JACK: For twenty-five years *I* have run this place. I've worked my ass off and sent the money to you. Like *clockwork*. The best fucking money manager in the world, the best fucking bank in the world, the best fucking *Wall Street chum* in the world couldn't have done it better. And all this time, not one word of thanks. Have you thanked me? Have you? All this time, from when I was a young man right up until today I have drawn a salary that began at twenty-five thousand dollars a year to now the princely sum of forty-five thousand dollars a year. An increase over twenty-five years of twenty thousand fucking dollars. And for the past five years it has stayed right there at forty-five thousand measly dollars a year. No increases for five years. I sacrifice *everything* for you and not once do you ever think to suggest I take a raise. Or a bonus.

ALEXANDER: But how was I to know? How did I know? Pay yourself whatever you want! I have nothing to do with it. You could have given yourself a million dollars a year for all I care. Why are you blaming this on me?

JACK: You mean why didn't I steal? Is that why I am so loathed around here because I didn't skim off the top and open up a Swiss bank account and leave everybody destitute???

ELIZABETH: Jonathon, that's enough!

SOPHIE: Uncle, please.

WAFFLES: Jack. For our friendship. I know you love me. Please calm down. This is all makin' me nervous, Jack.

JACK: For twenty-five fucking years I've been cooped up in this miserable old house like some kind of infectious leper with this mother of mine and Sophie. All our thoughts, all our dreams, all our hopes were about you. You were the God that we prayed to. You were the God that we worshipped. During the day we waited for the mailman to bring us your latest articles. At meals our conversations were always Alexander this and Alexander that and we were so *fucking* proud of you and everything you did. We *WASTED OUR LIVES* worshipping a shallow, conceited, inconsequential little miserly—

WAFFLES: Jack, stop it! I can't *stand* it!

ALEXANDER: What exactly is your point? Why do I have to listen to this?

JACK: *YOU HAVE MADE FOOLS OF ALL OF US!!!*

ALEXANDER: Look at him. He's crazy. Someone stop him please.

HELENA: Jack, that's enough. Be quiet…

JACK: I WILL *NOT* BE QUIET!!!

(*ALEXANDER starts to leave; JACK won't let him.*)

JACK: I'm not done yet. I want you to know that you have personally ruined my life. How does it feel? I never lived. NEVER! I was too busy genuflecting to you, depending on you! And now I realize that you have always been my *worst fucking enemy*!!

(*WAFFLES runs out crying.*)

ALEXANDER: What do you want from me? You didn't live? That's somehow my fault? Stop being such a little sniveling worm. How dare you talk to me like this and accuse me of things! You are a nothing! Accept it! Don't blame me. Accept it. A little nothing! You want to take this farm over? Go ahead. You want it? Take it! I want nothing to do with it or with you! I *spit* on you!

JACK: YOU RUINED MY LIFE YOU SONUV-ABITCH!!!! I am just as gifted as you! Just as intelligent! And you've *stifled* me. You made me promises year after year after year that you'd introduce me to this editor, to that publisher. I'd send you my short stories and you'd keep coughing up your phony praise and phony promises because you knew that was the way I'd keep sending you your motherfucking *checks!* But you did NOTHING for me because you knew if I got published I would *eclipse* you! I would steal your *fucking* thunder! YOU WERE JEALOUS OF ME! DENY IT! GO

AHEAD—DENY IT! You told me I wrote as well as Cheever! As Updike! As Mailer! *I BELIEVED YOU!!!*

(*JACK stops. MARY stands at the door with his drink, her eyes wide with fear. EVERYONE stares at him. He breaks down. ELIZABETH goes to him and he cries in her breast.*)

ELIZABETH: (*After a long beat.*) I think we should do what Alexander says.

JACK: (*Slowly.*) You're kidding. Right? Please tell me that you're kidding, Mother.

ELIZABETH: I can tell you that I am worried about you and I think this is all too much for you.

JACK: Mother, didn't you hear a word I said? What do you want from me? I'm defending our home, Mother. For *all* of us!

SOPHIE: Uncle Jack…

JACK: What the hell do you want from me, Mother? What should I do?

(*Silence.*)

JACK: Oh. Okay. I know what I should do. I should have done this months ago. (*Leaves the room.*)

(*After a moment, ELIZABETH follows him. SOPHIE simply sits. MARY comes over and folds her in her arms.*)

ALEXANDER: I wish someone would tell me what I said to him. Maybe this is his idea of a bad joke. Either that or he is truly certifiable. How can any of you expect me to go on living with a man who just said those things to me?

SOPHIE: Didn't you hear a thing he said, Father? Do you have any idea how unhappy we are? Can you think about it? Can you try to have some compassion for us? Some decency or understanding at least? Did you forget that years ago Uncle and Grandma would edit and retype your essays? They'd work into the wee hours of the morning for you because you always had this deadline or that one. Uncle and I have been working for years without any rest afraid to spend any money on ourselves. I should have gone away to school but it was too important to keep the farm going and send the money to you. I'm not accusing you or saying it's your fault, but Father, have a little compassion for where he's coming from. Try to apologize or make peace or say thank you or something!

HELENA: Try to make peace with him, Alex.

ALEXANDER: Alright, I will. It never occurred to me what was going on here all these years. But Sophie, my idea does have merit. I want to see you going to a decent school, doing graduate work. You don't have to toil here any longer…

SOPHIE: I see that, Father, I do…

ALEXANDER: And at least agree with me that he needs some help. Professional help. I'll say whatever I have to say but I want it known I reject the notion that any of this is my fault.

HELENA: Just say something to him.

ALEXANDER: I will. Maybe he's in his room. (Leaves.)

MARY: (Goes to SOPHIE.) Don't you worry about a thing now, darling. Everything'll be alright. This has got to happen once in a while, you know. Folks keep things inside for so long that it just festers and festers 'til it can't help but come out like poison.

(A commotion offstage. ALEXANDER comes running in, dives under a chair. A gunshot. ELIZABETH is shrieking as JACK enters with a gun.)

JACK: Where is he?

SOPHIE: Uncle!

HELENA: Jack!

MARY: Why don't you put that down now, Mr. Jack. You don't want to hurt anybody.

JACK: I'm afraid I do, Mary. That's exactly what I want to do.

ALEXANDER: WILL SOMEONE TAKE THAT DAMN THING AWAY FROM HIM?!?

(JACK sees where ALEXANDER is. ALEXANDER cowers before him as Jack points his gun and pulls the trigger. Gunshot. It misses. HELENA steps in front of ALEXANDER.)

HELENA: Come on Jack. Please give me the gun. Whatever it is he or I or anyone has done to you, please just give me the gun.

JACK: I won't.

HELENA: I love him, Jack. If you shoot him you might as well shoot me.

JACK: Please move, Helena.

ALEXANDER: (Pushing past HELENA.) It's okay, I'm an old man. If this will make you happier, do it.

(JACK holds the gun unsteadily, closes his eyes and pulls the trigger. "BANG!" But JACK's arms were so unsteady that he has missed ALEXANDER altogether. JACK opens his eyes and sees he has missed. He now steadies his hands and pulls the trigger again. If there had been another bullet, ALEXANDER would certainly have been hit. But the chamber is empty, and the gun makes a tinny click sound. JACK pulls the trigger again. Click. Says one impotent word—)

JACK: Bang.

ACT FOUR

The next day. The living room. WAFFLES and MARY sit among boxes.

WAFFLES: They're going back to New York.

MARY: That's good.

WAFFLES: Alexander said I could come visit whenever I want. His young wife hasn't stopped talking about how she's got to get out of here just as soon as possible. All these boxes? Hardly any of it. They'll send a big moving van next week.

MARY: You think I don't know all that? I live here too.

WAFFLES: Folks'll be talkin' 'bout this for years. I'm gonna have to plaster over the bullet hole Mr. Vaughn made in the wall.

MARY: In all my days I never seen nothin' like it, Waffles. He was crazy as crazy can be. And I don't know. Think it's been buildin' up in that man for a long, long time. Can't keep things in, Waffles. Can't. Gotta let 'em out or something like this is just bound to happen.

WAFFLES: Saw something like it once on TV. Man worked in a post office. Man had worked there for twenty years. His wife left him, he was retired out by the government, and he had nothing to do, I guess, nothing to do but to stew about it. Comes in one day with a machine gun and opens fire. Saw it on the TV.

MARY: Thought the same thing was gonna happen here.

WAFFLES: Yup.

MARY: Maybe things'll get back to normal now that the Professor and his wife are leavin'.

WAFFLES: Yup. Things'll maybe settle down. *(Pause.)* Mary? You think they'll ever sell?

MARY: I wouldn't know. Sounds like a whole lot of foolishness to me.

WAFFLES: Yup. I was just thinkin' is all. I'd have some money then. Sometimes I can't help but hear folks talkin' about me. They don't know I'm listenin'. They call me a freeloader.

MARY: Don't you listen to them, now. You're a part of this family just like me. We work, you 'n' me and Sophie and Mr. Vaughn too, before this foolishness. We're always workin'. We ain't no freeloaders. *(Pause.)* Where is Sophie?

WAFFLES: Dunno. She was with the Doctor. They're looking for Jack. Afraid he might…you know.

MARY: Lord I hope not!

WAFFLES: *(With a grin.)* They ain't gotta worry.

MARY: Why?

WAFFLES: I found his gun. I hid it in the cellar.

MARY: Good for you!

WAFFLES: Didn't have no more'n that one bullet anyway.

(JACK and ASHE enter. JACK eyeballs WAFFLES and MARY who get up and leave.)

JACK: Good riddance. Everyone's been spying on me. *(To ASHE.)* Leave me alone.

ASHE: I'd love to. Wish I'd left you alone months ago. But I'm not going anywhere 'til you give it back.

JACK: Give what back?

ASHE: You know what. What you stole from me.

JACK: I haven't stolen anything from you.

ASHE: Look Jack, this is serious. If it hadn't been for you fooling around with that damn gun I'd be long gone by now. But Sophie asked me to stay the night because of you and I did. Now I'm on my way home, they're leaving, and I can't wait to get the hell out of here and I just want it back is all.

JACK: I didn't take anything from you.

ASHE: I think I'm exhibiting a lot of patience. I'll give you a little longer but then I'll have to resort to force.

JACK: Yeah.

ASHE: If I hurt you it's because you were asking for it. I take no responsibility for it.

JACK: If you want to hurt me, go ahead. Just get it over with. *(A beat.)* How could I miss? He was right in front of me. Why were my eyes closed? And then I had him on the second one. I had him. Click. I'll never forgive myself.

ASHE: If you wanted to shoot somebody you should've just shot your own damn self and left the rest of us out of it.

JACK: That's a good point, Michael. A damn good point. Let me ask you something. It doesn't seem funny to you? That yesterday I did my best to murder somebody in cold blood in front of a room full of witnesses but nobody's had me arrested? So what do they all think? That I'm incapable of even that? That I'm just TOO crazy? See I think that's very funny. I'm crazy but folks who'll let some cheap little asshole weasel freeload off them for years off the sweat of their labor and then propose to sell their home right out from under them—they're sane. They're not deranged at all. A young woman who may be the most perfectly beautiful creature in the world marries a man old enough to be her great-grandfather and *she's* not crazy. Only I am. *(A beat.)* I saw you. I saw you kissing her.

ASHE: Yes, I was kissing her. And this what I have to say to you about it. *(He gives JACK the finger.)*

JACK: No, I'm wrong. I guess I must be crazy. Otherwise I'd put you in the hospital.

ASHE: You couldn't if you tried.

JACK: I don't know about that. I'm crazy, remember? No telling what I'm capable of.

ASHE: Just cut it out. You're not crazy. Or no more than anyone else. It's this place that makes us all crazy. You know what you're problem is, my friend? You have no common sense left. You are an old clown. Nothing sadder than that. So just accept it. Me too. I used to think that people who acted like us were abnormal. Now I see that we are perfectly fine. Life's insane, Jack, not us.

JACK: I'm so fucking humiliated, Michael. I feel such shame. I hurt inside so goddamn much I can't even stand it. Be a friend to me. I can't stand the pain. I can't. What else can I do? What would you do?

ASHE: I wouldn't do anything. You can't do anything. Just wait, that's all. You just have to get through it. You just have to.

JACK: No I don't have to. You have to *give* me something. If I live to be seventy that'll be twenty-three more years of this pain. Over and over day after day. I can't. How can I do it? *(A new idea.)* Oh! I know! I'll change. I can change. I'll write my novel and I'll send it out and it'll get published and I'll live a real life! I can do that. Why can't I do that? Like when you drink and you say you can become a brain surgeon. I can be a novelist. Why can't I?

ASHE: 'Cause you can't, that's why. You are what you are. You're not going to write your novel and nobody's gonna publish it. And I ain't gonna be operating on nobody's brain. Our situation is too hopeless for that. And you know that.

JACK: Yeah.

ASHE: We have to accept reality, is all. We're not great folks, Jack. We're mediocre.

JACK: *Then GIVE me something!!* My heart is broken into a million little pieces.

ASHE: No, I won't. I am not going to be your personal Doctor Kevorkian and I'm sure as hell not going to feel guilty about it, so give me back what you took!

JACK: I didn't take anything.

ASHE: You took a bottle of morphine from my van. The lock was broken. If you want to kill yourself take a fucking gun, go into the fucking woods, and blow your fucking brains out. I'm not gonna stop you. But if you do it with my morphine they're gonna conduct an inquest and they'll say I gave it to you and they'll prosecute me at a terrible trial and I don't know why you would want to do that to me.

JACK: Just leave me alone.

(SOPHIE enters the room.)

ASHE: *(To Sophie.)* Your uncle has taken morphine from me to kill himself with and he won't give it back. Tell him to give it back. I want to get out of here and I will just as soon as this is taken care of.

SOPHIE: Uncle Jack? Did you? Did you take it?

JACK: Did I take what?

SOPHIE: The morphine?

ASHE: He took it.

SOPHIE: Give it back. What do you think you're doing? Why do you want to scare me? Give it back. Please. Just give it back. Uncle Jack, you have to listen to me. I am in just as much pain as you. I'm no happier than you. No less humiliated. But we cannot give into it. That's all. We can't. I need you. I need you here with me. That's how we're going to get through it. Together. If we're patient, everything will come out alright. But we have to have some hope. We have to be patient. *Please* give it back. *(She kisses his face.)* Uncle Jack, you are a kind and gentle soul. You are the only father I have ever known. I can't stand the idea that things are so bad that you want to take your own life. I can't imagine the idea of waking up and not having you there. I couldn't stand it, Uncle. So please, for me, *please* give the morphine back.

JACK: *(Does so.)* Done. Fuck! Okay, now I have to *do* something. I have to be occupied. There's gotta be something I can do. There's gotta be work on the farm I can do. I know I've neglected everything. Let's *go!* Sophie! Let's hurry and begin!

SOPHIE: Yes! Absolutely! We'll bury ourselves in work. Uncle, you'll get mad at me. I've made a mess of things I'm sure. You won't believe how badly I've done on my own.

HELENA: *(Offstage.)* Jack! Are you in there? *(She enters.)* Jack. There you are. Alex wants to speak with you before we go. Please. It's important to him. He wants to be friends.

JACK: God, do I have to?

SOPHIE: Yes, Uncle, you have to. Come on, I'll go with you.

(They leave HELENA and ASHE alone.)

HELENA: So. We're just about to leave. Goodbye.

ASHE: That's it?

HELENA: The car's packed.

ASHE: Uh huh.

HELENA: And I'm not sure why you're still here. I thought we'd agreed. You'd stay away. Otherwise it's not fair to her.

ASHE: Not fair to her. I didn't forget. But when, you know, *something* happened… I was asked to come by. I'm looking at you and I'm not seeing anything. Tell me something. Tell me you have cold feet. Tell me you have some kind of feelings here. Even that you're just scared…

HELENA: Of course I'm scared.

ASHE: But you haven't thought about what we… about staying…

HELENA: Now look at me, Michael. You just have to look at me and hear what I'm saying. Whatever it is, whatever it was, it had nothing to do with me. You made it all up in your mind. It really has nothing to do with me. Staying? I can't *wait* to get out of here. I'm sorry, Michael. You can hate me if you want but I wish you wouldn't. I have come to be very fond of you. I think you are a very interesting man and that you and I have become friends. Friendship. Is that so awful? Can't we just *like* each other as friends?

ASHE: That's it? That's what you want to do? Be friends? You want to look at me and just deny there are feelings? Made it up in my mind? That makes me sound stupid, Helena. Is that what you think of me? You think I'm stupid?

HELENA: That's not what I meant…

ASHE: I have more brains, more passion, more principled convictions. My entire life is testament to that. And I know that you know it. I also know that you feel something for me that you are too chicken to acknowledge. You haven't even given this a chance and I'm telling you that if you leave you will wake up one day from this sleepwalking revery that you walk around in and from your boredom and you'll be in New York City or somewhere else and you will experience regret. You'll experience emotion. And you will not know how to handle it. You may think you've got it all figured out but you don't. The way he treats you? That's what you want?

HELENA: Enough. Michael. I'm not attracted to you. We could never be a couple, you and I. I don't have those kind of feelings for you, I never did, and I never will. I love my husband. Period. And yes, I may wake up one day and be filled with regret, but it will have nothing to do with you. I wish we wouldn't be angry. I don't like this unpleasantness. So let's stop it, okay? Okay? Michael? Don't be this way.

(ASHE doesn't respond.)

HELENA: Okay. Michael, look at me. Let's agree that you and I will never see each other again, okay. Can we agree to that? Never again.

ASHE: I can agree to that.

HELENA: Good. Now, having agreed to that, I can say that there is something about you. I can admit to feelings. I can admit to you that there may have been something, but that we will never ever speak of it or see each other ever again. Okay?

ASHE: Okay.

HELENA: Let's shake hands? No hard feelings?

(She extends her hand but ASHE takes it and kisses it instead. Passionately. She withdraws it quickly.)

ASHE: Yeah, you'd better go. I can see that you're not a terrible person, Helena, but you know what? There is something. As soon as you and Alexander got here, things changed. Things that had been fine, that hadn't changed for years and years, suddenly, they were different. We all had our work, our routines, our ways, and our passions. It may not seem like a lot to you, but West Virginia is a fertile country, a beautiful fertile place. But as soon as you arrived, and all through this long summer, it was as though we were expected to drop everything and worship you and your husband, tend to you and revolve around you and drop everything else that we were doing. You two were almost like a disease of idleness and narcissism and self-importance that infected every single one of us. Just look at me. Under your spell all damn summer, head over heels in love with you, dreaming and fantasizing about you and all the while folks were gettin' sick and diseases were wreaking havoc and neglect was decimating my woodlands. Jack and I have been the best of friends for twenty-five years and now we're the worst of enemies, why? Because of you. He nearly committed a murder and now he's on the verge of suicide. You and your husband are like the ancient mariner. You seem to bring destruction and ruin wherever you go. And you can think that I'm a kook and that you don't need to listen to what I have to say. You can think I'm joking and that I'm drowning in cynicism. But there's one thing for certain that you can't dismiss. If you had stayed we'd have had a full-scale disaster. Full-scale. A lot of folks would've gotten hurt. So goodbye. Hit the road. And fuck off.

HELENA: That was mean, Michael. I hope it makes you feel better because it really hurt me. Here… (*She takes a pencil from her pocket and breaks it in two and gives him the pieces.*) Take this pencil to remember me by. Evidence of my destructive nature.

(*ASHE takes it and grabs her and kisses her.*)

MICHAEL: Wanted to do that one more time before Jack came in with a bunch of flowers.

(*JACK comes running in followed by ALEXANDER, WAFFLES, SOPHIE, and ELIZABETH. ASHE walks a few feet away.*)

ALEXANDER: Now you're cornered, Jonathon. Nowhere to go!

SOPHIE: Be reasonable, Uncle.

ELIZABETH: If this is a joke, Jonathon, it isn't very funny.

JACK: Joke? No, Mother, hardly. I won't let him apologize to me. Alexander, you can't. It's too embarrassing.

ALEXANDER: But I *want* to!

JACK: (*Closing his eyes.*) Alright. Go ahead.

ALEXANDER: Jack, you've always been a good friend and a faithful, loyal supporter of me and my work and my career. In the years since I lost Jenny I never had to ask you for a single thing but you were always there, unbidden. Not the least of what you've done for me is to take care of my beautiful Sophie here and I can never express to you how grateful I am that you have been a far better father to her than I could ever have been. So please accept my apology for taking you for granted all these years and seeming ungrateful and never saying the words that I should have been saying every single day all along— Thank you.

JACK: (*Still with his eyes closed for a long beat.*) Is it over?

(*General laughter.*)

SOPHIE: Yes, it's over, Uncle.

ELIZABETH: I honestly don't know how I've put up with you all these years.

JACK: (*Offering his hand.*) I accept. Everything will be just as it was.

WAFFLES (*Pulling out a camera.*) I want one of everybody! Including Mary. MARY!

ALL: MARY!

MARY: (*Rushing in.*) I'm here, for God's sake. What's all the damn racket?

(*EVERYONE gathers for the photograph.*)

WAFFLES: You too, Doctor Ashe.

ASHE: Only if Sophie says I can.

(*SOPHIE says nothing.*)

ASHE: Well, I guess I have to go anyway…Jack?

JACK: What?

ASHE: Nothing. It's just I'll probably be pretty busy, you know. Patients and stuff.

JACK: Yup.

ELIZABETH: Come on, Michael. Get in the picture or don't. It's uncomfortable standing here like this.

ASHE: No, I think I'll go. Having some trouble with the carburetor on the VW and want to get it to the shop before he gets too busy. So long, Alexander. Helena. Mary. Everyone…

(*Ad libs as he leaves.*)

WAFFLES: Smile everyone!

(*The camera flashes. The lights go dark. Lights up on the sofa where JACK sits. The TV plays softly. On the table, SOPHIE sits at the computer with file folders everywhere.*)

JACK: I can't believe they're gone.

SOPHIE: Me too.

JACK: Let 'em. About time. Good riddance to bad rubbish.

SOPHIE: I thought you were gonna help.

JACK: I will. Just enjoying the silence is all.

SOPHIE: Michael's gone.

JACK: Yup.

SOPHIE: Hope he's alright.

JACK: Why shouldn't he be?

SOPHIE: No reason.

(*After a moment she walks over to him and playfully pushes him.*)

SOPHIE: You're awful.

JACK: What?

SOPHIE: You said you were gonna help.

JACK: Don't rush me. Please. Leave me alone.

SOPHIE: Sorry. It's just that it's been a long time since we did the accounts and invoices together.

(Silence.)

SOPHIE: Uncle?

JACK: Yes?

SOPHIE: I'm so sad.

JACK: I know.

SOPHIE: Do you think he'll be back?

JACK: Michael?

SOPHIE: Michael.

JACK: I don't think so.

SOPHIE: He was in a rush to go. I should have stopped him.

JACK: Sophie, *please* stop talking? *Please*? Go and do your work. I'll come too.

SOPHIE: Alright.

(They both sit at the computer. Ad libs as they get into the work. Some laughter. Moments pass. Suddenly JACK begins crying uncontrollably. After a while, he manages to stop.)

JACK: *(With a forced smile.)* Wow. You can laugh if you want.

SOPHIE: It's okay.

JACK: I'm probably clinically depressed is all. Probably bipolar. Don't know how to get through the night, Sophie. Don't see how to get through the next couple of moments. Or the next few years.

(They sit on the floor and hold each other.)

SOPHIE: It's the same with me, Uncle Jack. I got used to seeing Michael every day, even if he wasn't here

for me. I wish we could turn the clock back and start everything over again.

JACK: Me too.

SOPHIE: But we can't. Look, we have to be practical about this. Life goes on. Dammit it does, you know it does. When Mommy died, I didn't think I could survive that either. But we did.

JACK: You were very brave. You've always been braver than me.

SOPHIE: Not true, Uncle, you can be brave too. Everything balances out, I really believe that it does. As much suffering as we have gone through, we're owed some good stuff, Uncle, we're owed it! Soon we will live in a time that our life will be bright and beautiful and happy and we will get what we want and have joy. You and I will laugh all the time, not sadly, but with giddiness. And we'll especially laugh when we look back at now and remember how miserable and pathetic we are.

JACK: Where do you get your optimism?

SOPHIE: It will happen, Uncle Jack. I promise it will. We will find peace in our lives. It'll be glorious. With gorgeous angels singing and the sky glittering like diamonds. And we'll wake up in the morning deliriously happy to be alive and we'll go to bed at night with an impatient hunger to see what the next day will bring.

JACK: I so wish I could believe you, Sophie.

SOPHIE: But you *have* to believe, Uncle. You have to. If we don't have hope than there's nothing. If we believe that tomorrow will be better, than it will be. Uncle, don't cry. Please don't cry.

JACK: I can't help it. I love you so much. And I feel so bad for you.

SOPHIE: And I feel bad for you too. But we'll get through it. We'll find peace. We will. We will. You'll see.

(Lights fade.)

(END OF PLAY.)

STORY OF AN UNKNOWN MAN

Adapted from the Novella and Other Works by Anton Chekhov

Anthony P. Pennino

ANTHONY P. PENNINO was born in New Jersey in 1967, and raised in Princeton. He earned a BA and MA in English, and an MFA in playwriting, all from Columbia University, where he studied with playwright Romulus Linney. He also earned a PhD in dramatic literature from the University of London, under Richard A. Cave. His plays include *Three Points Over the Vig* ("The 24-Hour Plays"), *Howard Hopped the A Train* ("The A Train Plays"), *Auf Wiedershen, Kleindeutschland* and *Goodbye to All That* ("East Village Chronicles I," Metropolitan Playhouse), *Commedia della Pocca Italia* and *East Village Kaddish* ("East Village Chronicles II"), *Lucky* ("East Village Chronicles III"), *Survivors* (EFC, London), *Call It Peace: Meditations from North America* (JADE Productions), *Call It Peace: The Long, Twilight Struggle* (JADE Productions, New York International Fringe Festival; EFC, London), *Italian-American Cantos* (SOOP Theatre Company), *Children's Crusader* (Metropolitan Playhouse), and *Toby* (Pilot House, New York International Fringe Festival). He wrote the radio play series *City of Shadows*, which was performed and recorded at the Museum of Television and Radio in New York City, and broadcast on National Public Radio. He also directed *A Soldier's Death* (13th Street Repertory, OOBR Award). In 2005, Pennino received a fellowship from the New Jersey Council for the Arts. He is a professor of English at New Jersey City University, and lives in Hoboken.

Story of an Unknown Man was first presented by Gorilla Repertory Theater (Christopher Carter Sanderson, Artistic Director) on October 29, 2000, at the Theater at 413 West 44th Street, New York City, with the following cast and credits:

Zina	Tracy Appleton
Kukushkin	Bruce Barton
Dora	Kina Bermudez
George Orlov	Michael Colby Jones
Gruzin	Sean Elias-Reyes
Ephim	Matt Freeman
Chekhov	Clayton B. Hodges
Nanny, Olga	Lynda Kennedy
Karp	Brian O'Sullivan
Perkarsky	Tony Pennino
Leonid Orlov	Greg Petroff
Zotov	John Walsh

Directed by: Christopher Carter Sanderson
Costumes: Terry Leung
Assistant Director: Erica M. Staufenberg

Text of "Si mes vers avaient des ailes" by Victor Hugo.

"Love is either the shrinking remnant of something which was once enormous; or else it is part of something which will grow in the future into something enormous. But in the present it does not satisfy. It gives much less than one expects." —Anton Chekhov

CAST OF CHARACTERS

ANTON CHEKHOV

In the Village

KARP: a schoolteacher
DORA: a butcher's widow
EPHIM: a farmer (plays Okhrana Agent)

In the Acting Company

YEVSTIGNEI: an actor (plays Zotov)
DASHENKA: an actress (plays Zina)
SASHA: an actor (plays George Orlov)
SERGEI: an actor (plays Gruzin)

In the Story

ZINA KRASNOVSKY: a gentlewoman
GEORGE ORLOV: a bureaucrat
VLADIMIR ZOTOV: a revolutionary
OLGA: a maid
LEONID ORLOV: Minister of the Interior
GRUZIN: friend of George Orlov
PERKARSKY: friend of George Orlov
KUKUSHKIN: friend of George Orlov
NANNY: Zina's nanny

Double and triple casting is highly recommended. There are also SERVANTS, POLICEMEN, NOBLEMEN, TOURISTS, and REVOLUTIONARIES who have one or two lines.

PRINCIPAL SETTINGS

A village in Chechnya , present day; St. Petersburg and Nice, 1893.

A NOTE ON THE PRODUCTION

In the introduction to his play *Gross Indecency: The Three Trials of Oscar Wilde*, Moises Kaufman writes, "This play has been inspired by techniques used by Erwin Piscator and the young Bertolt Brecht. In this regard, the performers should portray the characters in the play without 'disappearing' into the parts. Along the same lines, this play should be an actor driven event. Costume changes, set changes, and anything else that happens on the stage should be done by actors." So it was with Kaufman, so it is with me.

ACT ONE

Lights up. A small village in Chechnya, not far from Grozny, present day. A bare stage save for a wooden table and a couple of chairs. KARP, late middle age, sits at the table whittling. He pauses to look at what he is doing, examines it, and then tosses it aside. DORA, about the same age, enters carrying some plates of food and a bottle of liquid. There is the sound of fighter jets screaming overhead. DORA stops and looks up.

KARP: Don't worry. They're not interested in us.

(A distant explosion.)

KARP: See? Sounds like it's by the old highway. Some fools still think they can drive on it.

DORA: Supper.

KARP: Already?

DORA: Yes.

KARP: I'm not hungry.

DORA: You have to eat.

KARP: I have to eat different things. Every day for the past three months…

DORA: …four months…

KARP: …four months it has been the same thing. Brown bread, goat cheese, and blood sausage. I am sick to death of it.

DORA: So, starve. More for me.

KARP: When your husband was alive, we had beautiful sides of beef. And real pork sausage. It was expensive, but if you save enough… And now.

DORA: We have independence now. We all eat the same.

KARP: We all eat shit.

DORA: Yes, well, remember they said my husband was a pro-Russian.

KARP: I haven't desired you since they shot him.

DORA: I wish you would.

KARP: There are hardly any other women left. If I get to poke you, then the whole village gets to. No thank you.

(EPHIM runs on, an awkward young man.)

EPHIM: Karp! Dora! Someone's coming.

KARP: So let them come. How can we stop them? Pour me some kvass.

DORA: No room for my bread, but plenty for kvass.

KARP: If someone is coming to shoot me, I'd rather they do it when I'm drunk.

DORA: Who is it? Can you see?

KARP: Russian soldiers? Rebels?

EPHIM: I can barely…they look like they are wearing rags.

KARP: Oh, it's Yeltsin.

DORA: Ah, you and your talk. Yeltsin is dead.

KARP: He is not. He's just been replaced by a sock puppet.

DORA: What difference does it make? He's in a better place than we are.

EPHIM: They're here. They're here!

(He goes and hides behind DORA. YEVSTIGNEI, DASHENKA, SASHA, SERGEI, and OTHER ACTORS enter. Some of their faces are covered in soot. They carry, drag, and cart trunks of costumes and props. They stop.)

YEVSTIGNEI: Greetings!

KARP: Greetings.

YEVSTIGNEI: We are a troupe of traveling actors who have met with a…um…small accident back on the road.

KARP: Oh, so that was you, was it?

YEVSTIGNEI: You know about it then?

KARP: We heard the MiG.

YEVSTIGNEI: Yes, they fired a missile at us. Fortunately, it was near miss, and no one was hurt except for some bruises. But our bus—the only bus we could find in Grozny—was destroyed. What town are we in?

KARP: Town? Ha. At best of times, we were nothing more than a village. And these are not exactly the best of times.

YEVSTIGNEI: Does it have a name?

DORA: No.

YEVSTIGNEI: Perhaps you could help me. I am Yevstignei. And this is my company.

KARP: I am Karp.

YEVSTIGNEI: Karp?

KARP: Karp.

YEVSTIGNEI: And are you the mayor?

KARP: The mayor? The mayor. He wants the mayor. The Russian Army killed the mayor when they captured the town in 1997. In '98, the rebels killed the town clerk and the priest for being pro-Russian. An artillery barrage got the doctor and the constable. And then the rebels came back and killed the station master and the butcher, our Dora's husband, because, well, just because.

DASHENKA: So, who's in charge?

KARP: I am.

DASHENKA: And you are?

KARP: The schoolteacher. I'm next when they come back. If they ever come back. I think they finally came to their senses and realized there's nothing here anymore. Most of the livestock has been slaughtered, most of the young women taken to Russian Army's Officers' Club as…furniture, and most of the young men drafted into service for one of the two sides.

EPHIM: Except me. Every time soldiers came, I pretended to be stupid.

KARP: Yes, *pretended*.

YEVSTIGNEI: Can you direct us? We mean you no harm…

KARP: Where are you trying to go?

SASHA: North.

KARP: Nothing much north of here except Russia proper.

DORA: My God, Karp, they're on the run.

SASHA: No, no, there are some farms about thirty kilometers from here that appreciate a good play and…

DASHENKA: Sasha.

YEVSTIGNEI: Your friend is right. We are on the run. Look, we were just down from Moscow to perform a play. Who knew that fighting would break out again? Or that a colonel with the Interior Ministry would say that we were terrorists?

EPHIM: Terrorists?

KARP: Well, over there is a Russian Army barracks. And over there, a camp of guerrillas. I wouldn't advise going either way. If you go straight, you shouldn't have too much trouble. Unless they're fighting. Or they're hungry. Oh, and watch out for the minefield.

YEVSTIGNEI: Thank you. We won't bother you any longer.

DASHENKA: Yevstignei.

YEVSTIGNEI: No, Dashenka.

DASHENKA: You have to ask. It's been four days.

YEVSTIGNEI: I'm sorry to bother you again.

DORA: What is it?

YEVSTIGNEI: We haven't eaten in four days.

DORA: You should have thought about that before you crossed a colonel with the Interior Ministry.

YEVSTIGNEI: And we couldn't help noticing how good your food looks.

DASHENKA: It's been a while since any of us have seen sausages. Any kind of sausages.

SASHA: Anything to drink but muddy water.

KARP: I'm sorry. We have so little.

(*Unseen by the others, CHEKHOV enters upstage.*)

YEVSTIGNEI: It looks like so much. To us.

EPHIM: The soldiers already took most of our winter stores.

YEVSTIGNEI: Isn't there anything you can do?

KARP: Do you have any money? And not rubles, U.S. greenbacks. Any coats for winter? Wood for the fire? Anything at all? Then, I'm sorry. We have to think of ourselves first.

YEVSTIGNEI: That's all anyone tells us. That they're thinking about themselves.

KARP: Do you have a better idea?

CHEKHOV: You could perform a play.

DORA: A play?

DASHENKA: A play? Yes, a play. A comedy or a romance. A tragedy or a heroic tale. We can play anything that you desire. We still have magic.

DORA: A play?! What good will a play do? There's still a whole winter ahead of us.

KARP: Sssh. It's an interesting idea. Have you seen a play, Dora?

DORA: Of course. My father always took us into Grozny when I was a little girl to see what new traveling company was in town. I miss them. But we have to be practical, Karp.

EPHIM: I've never seen a play.

KARP: A play. Why not? But we decide how good it is. And only if it is good enough, then may you eat with us.

YEVSTIGNEI: Agreed. What would you like? Tell us. We can perform anything. Sasha.

(SASHA *walks along and does a pratfall.* EPHIM *laughs.*)

KARP: Not a comedy. Life is funny enough as it is.

EPHIM: Aw.

SERGEI: How true. But what about a most excellent tragedy? "I have of late—but wherefore I know not—lost all my mirth, forgone all custom of exercises; and indeed, it goes so heavily with my disposition that this goodly frame the earth seems to me a sterile promontory…"

KARP: No, no, no, not Shakespeare.

YEVSTIGNEI: You don't like Shakespeare?

KARP: Oh, I like him well enough. But I find that actors can't perform him without getting long-winded.

SERGEI: "…his most excellent canopy, the air, look you, the brave o'erhanging firmament…"

YEVSTIGNEI: Sergei, shut up!

KARP: Dora, anything you'd like to see?

DORA: Can they be dancing mutton chops?

KARP: Dora. A play. A good play. But nothing too sentimental. If there is one thing I hate is people onstage being more emotional than they are in real life.

EPHIM: But can it have a romance?

KARP: All right, Ephim, it can have a romance. But it should be real. About real life. Real people. Nothing exalted. Nothing exaggerated.

YEVSTIGNEI: You ask for a lot.

KARP: Do you want to eat or don't you?

CHEKHOV: You have something that meets all those requirements. One of mine.

YEVSTIGNEI: And who are you?

DASHENKA: Oh my God. It's him. It's really him. But how?

CHEKHOV: What does it matter? A company of actors was in distress. I came.

DASHENKA: Listen to him, Yevstignei. It's him. A miracle.

CHEKHOV: No less a miracle than what you do every day on stage.

DASHENKA: Oh, sir.

CHEKHOV: Please do not look at the ground when you speak to me. Look into my eyes.

YEVSTIGNEI: All right. All right. We'll do it. Dashenka. Dashenka! You know what to do.

SASHA: You can't be serious.

DASHENKA: What?

SASHA: He's obviously mad. Shell-shock or something. Wandering around a war zone thinking he's…him. Where are your friends? Didn't you bring Tolstoy and Dostoevsky with you?

CHEKHOV: I always held Dostoevsky's writing suspect. And hardly concise.

SASHA: This is impossible. I'm stuck here in this wilderness with a madman. I have to be in Moscow in five days to shoot a Pizza Hut commercial with Gorbachev. Then I'm supposed to fly to Hollywood to be in the new Sylvester Stallone movie as Vaguely East European Bad Guy #3. It's just impossible!

DASHENKA: You just don't understand.

SASHA: Understand? Of course I understand. You. Aren't you a little young?

CHEKHOV: Old enough to write you.

YEVSTIGNEI: Sasha, many incredible things happen in war, don't they? And most of them terrible. Well, what's wrong with one, just one, incredible thing happening that's for the good? Dashenka's right. That has to be some kind of miracle. And we believe in miracles. Come on. Let's get ready.

DASHENKA: I think you should be our narrator.

CHEKHOV: Me? I'm a writer. Not an actor.

DASHENKA: It doesn't matter.

CHEKHOV: It would be an honor to share the stage with such an accomplished and beautiful actress as yourself.

SERGEI: Wait. Excuse me.

DASHENKA: Yes. What is it?

SERGEI: What part am I supposed to play then? I'm supposed to be the narrator. That's what I signed up for. Hamlet, Faustus, the narrator…

DASHENKA: You can play Gruzin this once.

SERGEI: Gruzin? It's such a small part.

DASHENKA: But you have that great monologue in Act II when you come back as the Okhrana Agent.

SERGEI: But…

YEVSTIGNEI: Sergei, get into costume.

DASHENKA: Is it time?

CHEKHOV: It's time.

(DASHENKA takes a coat out of a bag. She removes CHEKHOV's coat and puts this one on him. The OTHER ACTORS get ready.)

CHEKHOV: Call me Anton Chekhov!

SERGEI: I'm Anton Chekhov!

CHEKHOV: Shut up!

KARP: Chekhov? Chekhov died almost a hundred years ago.

(KARP, DORA, and EPHIM sit down to watch.)

CHEKHOV: Good evening, my friends. Come with me. Come back with me to an earlier time. Before a century of wars, both cold and hot. To a time when the tsars looked after us and the Heavens looked after the tsars. Or so they would have you believe. The place: St. Petersburg. The time: 1893. The reign of the penultimate tsar.

KARP: This doesn't sound like Chekhov.

(Lights fade on all save CHEKHOV.)

CHEKHOV: It is only October, but the rivers are already swollen with ice and a snow begins to fall onto the ground.

(One of the ACTORS is obviously pouring fake snow over CHEKHOV.)

CHEKHOV: Our tale tonight is about love. Love gained and love lost. But for a story that involves simple people with simple hopes for simple loves, it must first begin here. At the Winter Palace. Home of Tsar Alexander III. (Takes a crown out of the cart and puts it on.) His rule stretches from Vladivostock in the east to Warsaw in the west. His armies are larger than the German's and the Austro-Hungarian's combined. His navies mightier than Britain's. Or so he believes. Steel production of his factories could be greater than those of the United States, if they were modernized. But today, he is going to hear a report from Leonid Orlov, Minister of Interior.

(CHEKHOV sits. LEONID enters. Opposite LEONID, two REVOLUTIONARIES sit huddled making a banner denouncing the tsar.)

LEONID: Majesty, members of the Imperial Court, fellow cabinet officers, ladies and gentlemen. For some time, the Department of Police has been investigating radicals and subversives that have infiltrated every segment of your domain's society, Majesty. For the past year, we have been gathering names, addresses, known associates. We have infiltrated cells of unrest. We have monitored and checked. Well, today the watching ends, and the action begins. With your gracious permission, Majesty, the Department of Police in a concerted operation both here and in other major cities has struck back. Arrests are being made. The jails begin to fill.

(SOLDIERS burst in on the REVOLUTIONARIES.)

CAPTAIN: Okhrana! You're all under arrest in the name of the Tsar!

LEONID: Now, regardless of whether they call themselves Socialist-Democrats or Socialist-Revolutionaries or Anarchists or Marxists or Constitutionalists or Liberals, they want change, Majesty. Some through violence, some not. But all change is violent. All change is against you. And we do not want change.

(One of the REVOLUTIONARIES begins to flee.)

CAPTAIN: Sergeant!

(Another POLICE OFFICER takes out a gun and shoots the ESCAPEE. REVOLUTIONARY falls down dead.)

LEONID: When this subversion is eliminated. When the entire empire is at last at peace. When every last subject sings praise to you, Majesty, then this regrettable use of force can end.

(CAPTAIN points at the OTHER REVOLUTIONARY. SERGEANT shoots that REVOLUTIONARY in the back of the head. He falls down dead.)

CAPTAIN: (Kicking one of the DEAD REVOLUTIONARIES in the head.) Fucker.

(POLICE withdraw.)

LEONID: But I fear that we have a long way to go before that most joyous conclusion can be reached. It is my hope, Majesty, to make that day arrive as soon as possible.

(ZOTOV runs in. He carries guns. He sees his DEAD COMRADES on the ground. He falls to his knees.)

CHEKHOV: *(As TSAR.)* Excellent report, Interior Minister. Very well done.

(LEONID bows deeply. He freezes. CHEKHOV stands up and puts the crown back in the cart.)

ZOTOV: Oh, God. All my friends…dead.

CHEKHOV: On the day that the Department of Police made their mass arrests in St. Petersburg, a cell of a faction of a splinter of a small party of which many people had never heard was included. This cell included one Vladimir Zotov, the second son of a minor noble family from an area near Kiev. Zotov had served with distinction as an officer in the Imperial Navy, but, upon the completion of his service, took one look around and threw in his lot with those opposed to the Tsar. Fortunately for Zotov but unfortunately for his friends, he was out buying some pistols when the Department of Police came to the loft apartment they had been using as a headquarters. No doubt, Zotov would be dead too for "resisting arrest" as the official report read. As Zotov stood there shaking in the pool of his comrades' congealing blood, he swore vengeance on this man. Leonid Orlov, Minister of Interior.

ZOTOV: But how to get to the bastard? He is always surrounded by Okhrana. His movements are secret. His habits unknown. He cares not for the opera, the ballet, or the theatre. He is not seen at our finer restaurants. Other members of the Court are creatures of the night, but he is not.

(ZOTOV spits at LEONID's feet. LEONID exits.)

ZOTOV: But I will kill you. *(Takes a pistol and shoves it into his pocket.)*

(ORLOV enters, disheveled, and lies down in bed.)

ZOTOV: I don't know how, but I will.

CHEKHOV: The means soon became clear to Zotov. For Leonid Orlov had a son, one George Orlov, a mid-level bureaucrat in the Ministry of Finance. And George Orlov was a creature of the night. Zotov changes his name, his clothes, his appearance, and enters into service as George Orlov's valet. Though nobly born, he is willing to live with the indignities of being a servant to have that one chance. The only thing to do was to wait for the father to show up for a visit.

KARP: How do you like it so far?

DORA: He talks too much.

KARP: He's establishing the scene.

DORA: But I knew all that crap already.

EPHIM: I didn't.

ORLOV/SASHA: Excuse me. But I really can't concentrate when you're chattering away like that.

KARP: Sorry, we're not as quiet and polite as the audiences in Moscow.

ORLOV/SASHA: Can I do my scene now?

KARP: Yes, thank you.

ORLOV: No, no. Thank *you*… Ivan! Is it morning already?

(ZOTOV approaches ORLOV with a bowl of water, some shaving cream, a razor, and a cloth. During the next, he helps ORLOV up. He undresses him down to the waist. He wets his face, applies some shaving cream on the face, and shaves him. He then helps ORLOV wash up. Once washed, ZOTOV dresses ORLOV for work.)

ZOTOV: Did Mr. Orlov have an enjoyable evening last night?

ORLOV: I must have. Can't remember a damn thing.

ZOTOV: Would you like some coffee this morning?

ORLOV: No. I will have to… Ouch! Be careful. I have delicate skin.

ZOTOV: Yes, sir. My apologies, sir.

ORLOV: It's going to be another cold day. Why couldn't they have started Russia up somewhere along the Mediterranean? It would be a far more agreeable place. No, we have to be on the Baltic. Nothing more boring than the Baltic. *(Exits.)*

CHEKHOV: Only one problem with Zotov's plan. The father and son never speak.

(ZOTOV starts to pick up the clothes. OLGA, ORLOV's maid, enters. She starts sweeping with a broom. ZOTOV coughs.)

OLGA: That stupid cough of yours kept me up all night. You should go to the hospital.

ZOTOV: I can't afford time off.

OLGA: Do you think a gentleman like Mr. Orlov likes having a valet hacking mucus up in front of him day and night? *(Puts on some of his cologne.)* Musky? What do you think?

ZOTOV: I think it makes you smell like a man.

OLGA: Sound exciting?

ZOTOV: Olga, do you believe in God?

OLGA: Yes, of course, I do.

ZOTOV: Then you must believe in a Judgment Day. That we will have to answer for our sins.

OLGA: Look. A ruble. Must've fallen out of Mr. Orlov's trousers. Do you want to split it?

ZOTOV: No.

OLGA: Fair enough. More for me.

ZOTOV: Do you even listen?

OLGA: Say, Ivan, we both have Sunday night off. We could go around to the pub. Share some kvass. Maybe some vodka.

ZOTOV: I have plans.

OLGA: What plans?

ZOTOV: I'm reading.

OLGA: Ivan, don't tell me… You don't like women.

ZOTOV: Olga, leave me alone.

CHEKHOV: Two months passed. And no sign of Leonid Orlov. But many signs of his son and his son's friends. Every Thursday night, they gathered in George's sitting room to eat, drink, play cards, and steel themselves for the carousing that would occur even later that evening.

(Laughter offstage. ORLOV, GRUZIN, PERKARSKY, and KUKUSHKIN enter. GRUZIN, like ORLOV, is in his early thirties. The OTHER TWO are older. They all have drinks in their hands. They are followed by OLGA and ZOTOV.)

ORLOV: …and so the British Counsel turned to the Minister and said, "The members of the Tsar's Court dress so fancifully that one cannot tell which are the men and which are the women." To which the Minister replied, "That may be. But given the way your sovereign dresses, we have absolutely no doubt that Queen Victoria is, in fact, a man. And a particularly husky one at that."

(They all laugh.)

KUKUSHKIN: Anyone for some bridge?

ORLOV: Why not? Gruzin?

GRUZIN: Whatever.

PERKARSKY: Gruzin, how is your son? I hear he has the flu.

GRUZIN: Or something.

KUKUSHKIN: Word is that they are looking to promote some bright ambitious young man in the Finance Ministry. Word is that this person is in the ninth *chin*, and they are looking to move him to tenth.

PERKARSKY: Must be your father again.

ORLOV: Oh, God.

PERKARSKY: I could help speed it along if you'd like.

ORLOV: Gentlemen, I ask you. How could anyone mistake me for being bright and ambitious? It's slanderous, I tell you.

GRUZIN: Well, George, you keep quiet. They like that.

ORLOV: But I am perfectly happy where I am. I write reports, which are sent to committee. And unless I am extremely lucky and they get lost, they get distributed to the subcommittee where they are filed away for six months, read, filed away again, examined by the subcommittee, and sent back up to the full committee, where they are filed away again, and then reexamined about nine months later and discussed. And, of course, by then, whatever it is I had written on is no longer an issue. And I get a nice commendation for having written such a good, grammatically correct report. This is all very well and good. But if they move up to the tenth *chin*, they will expect me to actually do something about trade with Britain and France. And, oh yes, America. As if anyone knows what they are thinking.

GRUZIN: Sounds awful.

ORLOV: They might even expect results.

GRUZIN: Disgusting.

KUKUSHKIN: But it could be a terrific opportunity. You could be invited to dine with the Minister and his wife.

ORLOV: And watch him drool into his soup? No thank you.

KUKUSHKIN: And, of course, there would be the chance to gain an appointment to the Court.

ORLOV: My dear Kukushkin, the Tsar's French is reportedly deplorable. And I cannot stand to hear French spoken poorly. I might try to correct him, even though he is the Tsar, and then where would I be? Siberia. No caviar in Siberia.

PERKARSKY: I have often found that it is better to stay in the shadows.

ORLOV: My point exactly, Perkarsky. All this talk of advancement is making me nauseous. You—what's your name—valet?

PERKARSKY: For Christ's sake, Orlov, he's been here two months. Don't you know the name of your own valet?

ORLOV: If God intended that we know the names of our servants, he wouldn't have devised such devilishly simple words for them. Valet. Maid. Footman. Very simple and interchangeable.

GRUZIN: Some days I can't remember my son's name.

KUKUSHKIN: Why bother. Wait a few years. See if they're going to make it first. No sense wasting time and affection on a child unless you know it's going to survive to be an adult.

ORLOV: You…valet…Ivan! Yes, Ivan. You see. I do remember. More sherry, Ivan. I need some cheering up.

(ZOTOV pours him another glass. ORLOV and his GUESTS start to play cards.)

CHEKHOV: All of this was too much for Zotov. He had served in the Navy with distinction. He stood watch in the freezing nights of a winter in the Baltic Sea. But that was nothing compared to standing there, completely still, holding his coughing in for hours at a time on the off chance that Orlov might want a sherry. Or a cigar.

PERKARSKY: I heard another rumor, Orlov.

ORLOV: Yes?

PERKARSKY: About you and Krasnovsky's wife. Most interesting.

ORLOV: My dear Perkarsky, you know better than to listen to rumors.

KUKUSHKIN: So, it's not true?

ORLOV: I didn't say that.

GRUZIN: I know the lady. She's the…um…godmother of my daughter.

PERKARSKY: Son.

GRUZIN: Whatever. I suppose one might call her beautiful if one were paying attention.

PERKARSKY: Gruzin, I think you have to be the most apathetic person I know.

GRUZIN: Well, one doesn't like to brag.

PERKARSKY: How did you ever work up the enthusiasm to mount your wife one night and expend the energy of a rutting rhinoceros to actually seed her with child?

GRUZIN: First, it was during the day. And second, I believe vodka was involved.

PERKARSKY: Well, gentleman, I submit, never put a glass of vodka in front of Gruzin. God knows what he'll attack.

CHEKHOV: For hours, they talked and played cards. Soon, Perkarsky and Kukushkin were bound for one of Perkarsky's clubs.

(They exit.)

CHEKHOV: And, as for Orlov and Gruzin…

ORLOV: Going home, Peter?

GRUZIN: Not in the mood for home. Not in the mood for one of Perkarsky's clubs.

ORLOV: So where?

GRUZIN: I know a place down by Finland Station. Open all night. Has a passable kvass. Do you want to come?

ORLOV: Why not?

GRUZIN: I'm forgetting something. I know I'm forgetting something.

ORLOV: Your fountain pen.

GRUZIN: How clumsy of me. It is hard to believe. You gave this to me when we completed our final examination at university. That was ten years ago. Ten years, George. Time has passed slowly.

ORLOV: Yes, thank God. How is everything over at the Ministry of Works?

GRUZIN: Boring. I wouldn't have it any other way.

(They exit. OLGA takes the bottle of sherry, pours herself a drink, drinks it, and exits. ZOTOV sits down and starts *coughing. The doorbell rings. He stands up and goes to answer it. He returns carrying suitcases. ZINA and NANNY are right behind him.)*

ZINA: Is George... Is Mr. Orlov in?

ZOTOV: No, ma'am, I'm afraid not.

ZINA: Well, no matter. Please take my things to the spare bedroom and make sure the bed has been made. Tomorrow, you will report to me, and we will do some shopping to make this place more homey.

ZOTOV: Ma'am?

ZINA: Hasn't he told you?

ZOTOV: No, ma'am.

ZINA: What a silly he can be. I am Zina Krasnovsky. I'm going to be living here. When he returns tonight, make sure he knows I am here.

ZOTOV: Yes, ma'am. *(Exits with suitcases.)*

ZINA: Oh, Nanny, isn't this something?

NANNY: Zina, it is not too late. You can still go home before your husband finds the note.

ZINA: But I want him to find it. Look around you. This is where I belong. Shelf upon shelf of books. Not law books and books on hunting like Boris had. But real books. Voltaire. Kant. Carlyle. Thoreau. Dostoevsky. Do you see this table? Mahogany. This decanter. French crystal. These plates. Wedgwood. This is the home of a very cultured man, Nanny. I want to be cultured too.

NANNY: Culture? My precious. That is so much nothing.

DORA: She's got that right. What are you looking so starry-eyed about?

KARP: The last scene. I can't remember when I last had a cigar.

(A gunshot off in the distance.)

ZINA/DASHENKA: What the Hell is that?

KARP: German Lugar nine millimeter semi-automatic. The rebels use them all the time. Please, do go on.

ZINA: ...I love him, Nanny.

NANNY: And for love you risk your name, your standing in society, your inheritance, everything for this clerk.

ZINA: George is not a clerk. He is the Chief Secretary to the Undersecretary of Trade in the Britain, France, and United States Section at the Ministry of Finance.

NANNY: A clerk.

ZINA: Oh, Nanny, you don't understand.

NANNY: Oh, Zina, but I do. But I do.

ZINA: Oh, look Nanny, a view of Isaac's Cathedral. It's so beautiful at night. Like a golden star.

NANNY: And you will understand soon enough, too.

ZINA: Come. Let's look at my room. Oh, Nanny, I don't think I will sleep tonight.

(They exit. The lighting changes from night to dawn. ORLOV returns from a long night. ZOTOV enters.)

ORLOV: Um, valet, Ivan, please make a pot of black coffee. And call down to the restaurant for some eggs, ham steak, and potatoes.

ZOTOV: Madame Krasnovsky is here, sir.

ORLOV: What?!

ZOTOV: Madame Krasnovsky is...

ORLOV: Yes, I heard you the first time. What's she doing here?

ZOTOV: Sleeping, sir.

ORLOV: This is terrible. How could you let her in?

ZOTOV: She's a lady, sir.

ORLOV: Is there any sherry left from last night?

ZOTOV: Um, no sir.

ORLOV: Is there anything left in the house at all?

ZOTOV: Some peach schnapps. A gift from the German board of trade that...

ORLOV: Yes, yes, that will be fine. Get me some.

(ZOTOV exits. ORLOV sits down.)

ZINA: *(Offstage.)* Oh, George.

ORLOV: Oooh.

ZINA: *(Entering.)* I thought I heard you come in. Oh, George, I am so happy to see you.

(She sits down on his lap and kisses him.)

ORLOV: Thank you, Zina. My, what a surprise. What brings you around to these parts?

ZINA: Oh, George, always making fun of me. You know that we had talked for weeks about the moment when I would be ready to break with Boris and move in here. Well, he was out last night. Something at his hunting club. So, I seized the opportunity and rushed here as soon as I could. Like we always said.

ORLOV: Well, like you always said.

ZINA: Why, George, a body would think you didn't want me here.

ORLOV: No, not at all, my darling. It's just all so unexpected. I had no idea when this was all being discussed that you would make your move so...now.

ZINA: I thought a surprise would make it all the more fun.

(ZOTOV returns.)

ZOTOV: Your schnapps, sir.

ORLOV: Thank you very much.

ZINA: George, schnapps so early?

ORLOV: My throat is feeling a bit ticklish. Best to nip it in the bud.

ZINA: Oh, George, isn't this wonderful? It's all so scandalous, don't you think? It's like we're a couple in one of those French plays with all those people running in and out of doors. We'll be the talk of St. Petersburg for weeks. I've never been the talk of anything. Est-ce possible? Suis-je heureux?

ORLOV: Well, there is a lot to be said for anonymity.

ZINA: I used to think that, too. Perhaps you're used to being the center of attention, what with your father being such an important man. I want to live, George. I want to out and dance. Boris hated dancing. J'aime danser. Je vous aime, George. C'est un rêve. Réveil du rêve. Et nous sommes ensemble.

ORLOV: I'm glad you see it that way.

ZINA: Nous devrions aller faire des emplettes.

ORLOV: No, no, no. You say, devrions. *Devrions...* Never mind. You want to go shopping?

ZINA: George, you honestly don't expect us to continue to live like you're still a bachelor. Come on, we have work to do. You too, Ivan.

ORLOV: Je devrais aller travailler.

ZINA: Honestly, George, I think the Minister can spare you for one day. You'll take a long weekend.

(The THREE exit.)

CHEKHOV: And so Zina and George, with Ivan in tow, walked along Nevsky Prospekt, shopping. They bought knick-knacks. And things for the kitchen. And things for the sitting room. A pillow here. A lamp there. A covering for the chaisse-longe. A new samovar.

(The THREE return and circle the stage as if out shopping. ZOTOV is carrying a large number of packages.)

CHEKHOV: It was a cold day. The wind blew off the Neva. There were flurries. Zotov felt a chill pierce his coat, but he said nothing.

(They exit.)

CHEKHOV: At last, the shops started to close. Orlov and his mistress sent Zotov home with their new possessions.

(ZOTOV enters. He puts the packages down. He starts coughing. He takes off his boots and shirt and covers himself with a blanket.)

CHEKHOV: Feeling a fever, Zotov went straight to bed. He didn't want anything to eat. Not even some black bread and tea. Orlov and Zina went out to dine at a restaurant with a view of the Winter Palace. And then, to dancing.

(ORLOV and ZINA enter, waltzing. This goes on for a couple of minutes. Then ORLOV starts to kiss her. He is brusque. They embrace. He starts to undress her. Then he takes her upstage, where they lie down under some covers.)

DORA: They dance beautifully.

KARP: He has two left feet.

DORA: They dance beautifully.

KARP: Ephim, go get me some more kvass.

EPHIM: Why me?

KARP: Because I'm watching the play.

(Dawn comes. ZOTOV starts coughing. OLGA enters.)

OLGA: Again with the coughing. Again. My room is right over here. If you do that all night, then I can't sleep. And it does no one any good if neither of us can sleep.

And who is this Zina Krasnovsky that the master has suddenly brought into the house?

(There is the sound of a servant's bell being rung during the next.)

OLGA: When it was just the master, it was fine. He wasn't here much. He didn't bother us much. But two of them. That's twice the work. And if she thinks I'm going to treat her like the mistress of the house, she is very mistaken. Very mistaken. Will you stop coughing and listen to what I am saying? This is all wrong. Already she is giving me orders. She thinks she's going to last. But I've been here a long time. I know the master. She'll be lucky if she lasts until spring. Are you going to get that? That's yours, you know.

(ZOTOV stands up and, just in his pants and socks, he walks over to ORLOV and ZINA. He is still coughing.)

ORLOV: Ivan!

ZOTOV: Yes, sir.

ORLOV: Bring us some tea and… Good God, man, you're out of uniform.

ZINA: Very much out of uniform, I'd say. *(Starts laughing.)*

ZOTOV: I'm sorry, sir. I've been ill.

ORLOV: Ill, you say. Well, take a day off to go see a doctor. Can't have sick servants spreading God-knows-what about the house.

ZOTOV: Yes, sir. Thank you, sir.

ORLOV: And next time I call you, you had better be in uniform.

ZOTOV: Yes, sir.

ZINA: And, Ivan, if you should see my purse, let me know. I seem to have misplaced it.

ZOTOV: Yes, ma'am.

(He puts on his boots and shirt. ZINA and ORLOV exit. ZOTOV circles around the stage until he ends up near CHEKHOV.)

CHEKHOV: And so Zotov went to the doctor. Me. Yes, come in. Come in. I know you, don't I? Yes, Vladimir. Yuri's friend.

ZOTOV: Doctor Chekhov, no one can know that I have been here.

CHEKHOV: Just like Yuri. Always so mysterious. What seems to be the trouble?

ZOTOV: I have this cough that I can't rid myself of. At first, I thought it was the flu. But it has been a couple of months now.

CHEKHOV: *(Taking out stethoscope.)* All right, breathe for me. Where is Yuri these days? I haven't seen him in a while.

ZOTOV: He's dead. Killed by the Department of Police.

CHEKHOV: Oh… Let me see your eyes.

(During the next, CHEKHOV checks ZOTOV over.)

ZOTOV: I can't afford to be sick.

CHEKHOV: Who can?

ZOTOV: I was lucky that I remembered your address.

CHEKHOV: Luckier than you think. In two days, I'm going on holiday.

ZOTOV: Holiday?

CHEKHOV: Yes. I hate St. Petersburg in winter. I finally have enough money to go away. South of France. Nice. Can't wait.

ZOTOV: France.

CHEKHOV: Yes. Have you ever been?

ZOTOV: Yes. Tell me, Doctor Chekhov, why do some many of our class always take their first chance they get to leave Russia? Shouldn't we stay here and get to know our own country?

CHEKHOV: I know enough about my own country as it is. I'm afraid it doesn't look good.

(A distant firing of artillery. Some plaster falls from the ceiling.)

ZOTOV: What is it?

CHEKHOV: Well, I have some more tests to run, but it looks to me like you have consumption.

ZOTOV: Consumption? What can I do?

CHEKHOV: Well, go some place warm. Like Nice.

ZOTOV: Not an option.

CHEKHOV: At the very least, you should stop working. Get some rest.

ZOTOV: Not an option!

CHEKHOV: It's like that, is it?

ZOTOV: Yes, it is. Isn't there something you could give me?

CHEKHOV: *(Taking out a bottle)* Yes. Of sorts. This is laudanum. Made from opium. If you take this, you will breathe easier. Feel better. It won't cure you. And it is extremely addictive. The more you take, the more you will need.

ZOTOV: Will it impair my ability to reason?

CHEKHOV: Yes.

ZOTOV: Then keep it.

CHEKHOV: Vladimir… Take it. The path you have plotted… your condition will worsen and worsen. This will make the end easier.

ZOTOV: All right, Doctor. Thank you.

CHEKHOV: Tell me, do you know where Yuri is buried? I would like to say goodbye.

ZOTOV: Not really. They shot him in the back of the head, so they wouldn't release the body when his parents came to claim him. So they dumped him into a common grave and threw some lime on top.

CHEKHOV: You asked earlier why so many of us leave the country instead of staying here to get to know our own motherland.

ZOTOV: Yes.

CHEKHOV: Look around you, Vladimir. Revolutionaries and secret policemen. Everyone thinking they know the real Russia and killing anyone who has a different real Russia.

ZOTOV: Yes. *(Exits.)*

CHEKHOV: And so it goes. So, it goes. Zotov's condition improved a bit. He spent less time outside, so to avoid some of the extreme fits he had earlier experienced. Autumn faded into winter. What little enthusiasm Orlov had for his new life-style rapidly faded when it was no longer new. And so it was on another Thursday night…

(ORLOV, GRUZIN, KUKUSHKIN, PERKARSKY, and ZINA enter. The MEN are playing cards. ZINA looks out the window.)

ZINA: You men shouldn't spend all of your time playing cards. You should get out more.

ORLOV: Cold outside. Hate the cold.

ZINA: Well, you should join the Foreign Ministry and have them send you to Italy or the Ottoman Empire.

ORLOV: Please. Can you imagine me in the Ottoman Empire? I would look frightful in a fez.

ZINA: What about you, Peter? Do you hate the cold, too?

GRUZIN: More or less.

ZINA: So, why don't you move south?

GRUZIN: Move? You want me to move? Me?

(A doorbell.)

PERKARSKY: Easy, Gruzin. She's joking.

GRUZIN: All right. You had me worried.

(ZOTOV enters.)

ZOTOV: Ma'am, your former governess is here.

ZINA: Oh, Nanny! That silly, she's running late. Ivan, I seem to have misplaced a gold watch. Let me know if you find one. Good night, gentlemen, Peter. I will see you later on tonight, George.

ORLOV: Mmmm.

(She exits. ZOTOV stands at attention.)

ORLOV: God, what a nightmare. Why did you ever have to introduce me to her, Peter?

GRUZIN: How was I supposed to know that you would fall head-over-heels in love with her?

ORLOV: Does this look like head-over-heels?

PERKARSKY: But what is the story with the husband? Doesn't he care?

ORLOV: I honestly don't know.

KARP: This Boris is like your husband, Dora.

DORA: Don't remind me.

EPHIM: Here's your kvass, Karp.

KARP: Why, thank… You didn't bring me any black bread.

EPHIM: You didn't ask for any black bread, Karp.

PERKARSKY: This makes no sense to me. It is clear that she is eminently fuckable. No question. If you want to go at it like a couple of crazed badgers, no one is stopping you. But why not keep it discreet? Was it really necessary to let the husband and the rest of St. Petersburg be aware of your indiscretions?

ORLOV: Well, it certainly wasn't my idea.

PERKARSKY: Well, in case I ever decide to marry again, and you decide to bed my wife, do me the favor of keeping me in the dark as to your exploits. These cards are lousy. Who dealt them?

GRUZIN: I did.

PERKARSKY: Well, next round, take the time to shuffle.

KUKUSHKIN: You could have rented a separate apartment and put her up there. Couldn't you?

ORLOV: One would think. But you are not thinking like a romantic. And that is exactly what… *(Snaps his fingers.)*

PERKARSKY: Zina.

ORLOV: …Zina is. She must follow her beloved man to the ends of the earth. That is the ideal. It is almost mystical. The entire world, peoples, economies, nations, are secondary to the burning passion that courses through every fiber of her being. A horde of Mongolians comes rushing over the border? Zina's love will stop them. And I am made to suffer.

PERKARSKY: How could you let this happen? It isn't exactly like she forced herself on you?

ORLOV: Have some mercy, Perkarsky. Want this? I couldn't even conceive of this. When she brought this up, I thought she was joking. How could I want this thing? And it doesn't stop there. She wants to change me. She wants the place to smell of Sunday dinner being cooked. Here. In the oven. Not ordered in. She wants trinkets and ornaments to adorn the place. She wants to move to larger quarters. She wants me to smoke a pipe instead of cigars. She wants. She wants. She wants. I admit it—a man needs a woman. After all, there is animal instinct. But, my God, this. A man does not need this.

GRUZIN: She's not exactly stupid. You could try to reason with her.

ORLOV: My dear Gruzin. With you I can reason. We think alike. But with her. Our minds are so completely different that I doubt that she would even understand what I was saying much less agree to it. She has given her whole soul to me. Why? I can't imagine. I didn't ask for it. But if I said anything to shake this little fantasy world of hers, she might start crying.

PERKARSKY: Oh, dear.

KUKUSHKIN: It's really a shame. She is very attractive. And charming.

ORLOV: Then, Kukushkin, you can spirit her away, if that is your wish. The common people are closer to the animals than we. They have no sense of an ideal love. Ivan?

ZOTOV: Yes, sir.

ORLOV: You're of common stock. Tell us, do you believe that you will ever have an ideal love? A love for whom you would sacrifice all? A love that would be more important than what mattered most to you?

ZOTOV: No, sir. I don't believe I would.

ORLOV: See. Even the valet has more sense.

GRUZIN: Might I make a suggestion?

ORLOV: Please.

GRUZIN: Come stay at my place for a couple of days. You'll send her word that the Minister has called you out of the city on some crucial business, and you won't be back until Sunday night.

ORLOV: A drinking marathon, then?

GRUZIN: Yes, a marathon? Why not? Are you gentlemen agreeable to that?

KUKUSHKIN: I don't see why not.

PERKARSKY: I will join you tomorrow evening. There is some work that needs to be done in the morning.

(They all begin to exit.)

ORLOV: Ivan, you heard the essentials. Tell madame that I have been called away on business to Moscow.

GRUZIN: Telegram offices in Moscow.

ORLOV: Good point. I've been called away to the countryside by the Minister. Something to do with trade and finance. I'll be back Sunday evening or Monday morning.

ZOTOV: Very good, sir.

ORLOV: Good man. Here's a ruble for your troubles.

(ORLOV and FRIENDS exit. OLGA enters.)

OLGA: The master has left early this evening. Before *madame* has returned.

ZOTOV: He is going to spend the weekend at Mr. Gruzin's home, but he wants her to think that the Minister called him away on business in the countryside.

OLGA: *(Laughing.)* That stupid slut. Won't last out the spring. Mr. Perkarsky never finishes his drink. No matter. *(Finishes the drink.)*

ZOTOV: *(Cleaning up.)* Why do you hate her so much?

OLGA: Walking around with her airs. Like she owns the place. Telling me what to do. I may just be the maid, but she is the whore. Most whores know where they stand. Or lie down. You're not going to be coughing tonight, are you?

ZOTOV: I don't think so.

OLGA: Good. The master gave me the weekend free, and I want to be rested to see my family.

ZOTOV: I didn't even know you had a family, Olga. Who are you visiting?

OLGA: My son.

ZOTOV: How old is he?

OLGA: Don't pretend to care, Ivan. Because you don't. *(Exits.)*

(He continues cleaning up. He exits. Light change to indicate passage of time. ZINA enters. She rings one of the servant bells. ZOTOV appears.)

ZINA: Where is Mr. Orlov, Ivan?

ZOTOV: He received word from the Minister and was called away on business to the countryside. He expects to be away for the entire weekend.

ZINA: The entire weekend? But we were to… Oh, well. It's just one weekend. Will he write?

ZOTOV: He doesn't expect that he'll be able.

ZINA: Oh. No matter. We shall have the place all to ourselves than, shan't we?

ZOTOV: Yes, ma'am.

ZINA: Good night, Ivan.

ZOTOV: Good night.

CHEKHOV: And so Zotov retired. As he prepared for bed, he could feel the consumption become more active. He tossed and turned and, when he slept, he dreamed a fevered dream.

(The sounds of an ocean as if heard on a ship at sea. ZOTOV stands.)

KARP: Oh, no, not a dream sequence.

CHEKHOV: Where are we, Zotov?

ZOTOV: The bow of the Imperial Navy's dreadnought *Peter the Great*. You see the land on the distant horizon?

CHEKHOV: Yes.

ZOTOV: That's the coast of Sweden.

CHEKHOV: Why are you here?

ZOTOV: Because I have never felt the peace I had when I was at sea. The salt spray in your face. The cry of the gulls. This is the closest thing I have to a home.

CHEKHOV: Are you happy?

ZOTOV: I don't know what that is.

CHEKHOV: And?

ZOTOV: I love her.

ZINA: Once when I was a girl and I had golden locks for hair, I went to the country to visit my aunt and uncle. They had a huge estate. After the cruel winter and the desperate spring, it seemed like Heaven. My uncle had this ink-black horse named Star-Rider. But Uncle would never let me ride him. "He is too big a brute for such a delicate thing as yourself," my uncle told me. So, one morning I woke up, I woke up before the cock crowed, and I went to the stables. All the servants were still asleep. You could still hear the crickets. And I saddled Star-Rider myself. I led him outside. I climbed a fence, and then onto his back. Off we went. It was the summer after my mother died. I hope he could ride the stars. Take me to Heaven. But no, we stayed on earth. And he kept going faster and faster. My uncle was right. I tried to reign him in, but he wouldn't stop. We rode into the woods. It was dark and strange in there. I was soon lost. I held onto Star-Rider's neck for dear life. But he eventually threw me. I don't know how long I lay there, crying. But the son of the neighboring landowner came riding along. He reached out his hand and pulled me up onto his saddle. And I rode up front with him behind me. It was warm. He couldn't have been more than fifteen. My brave heroic Cossack. The only one I have ever known.

(ORLOV and LEONID enter.)

ORLOV: If one knew your dreams were so pedestrian, Ivan, one would never have bothered to enter them.

LEONID: Do you think, Zotov, that I can peer into your very thoughts?

CHEKHOV: Your condition will grow worse and worse unless you stop.

ZOTOV: *(Going back to bed.)* Can't stop.

CHEKHOV: Then you will never find peace again. Your fatigue growing by the day, and your sleep plagued with terrible visions.

ZOTOV: But if I go, who will look after Zina?

(He is back in bed, eyes closed. OLGA storms in followed by ZINA.)

ZINA: I did not give you permission to leave.

OLGA: I was done.

ZINA: You are not done until I say you are done. Ivan. Ivan!

OLGA: You accuse me of stealing, and you expect me to stand there and take it.

ZINA: I have lost money. I have lost my purse. I have lost my watch. And now I have lost the earrings my mother gave to me before she died.

OLGA: And what does that have to do with me?

ZINA: You stole them.

OLGA: So what?!

ZINA: Don't you raise your voice to me! You are nothing but a servant. Ivan!

OLGA: Yes, a servant. Hired by Mr. Orlov. Not you. I serve at his will.

(ZOTOV enters.)

ZOTOV: Yes, ma'am.

ZINA: Go downstairs and check with the porter. See if we received any telegrams from Mr. Orlov.

ZOTOV: Yes, ma'am. *(Exits.)*

OLGA: I think we are done here.

ZINA: Where do you think you're going?

OLGA: Mr. Orlov gave me the weekend off.

ZINA: I did not give you the weekend…

OLGA: I don't care what you do and do not give. I have the weekend. I may be the poor servant, but I know about loyalty to family. *(Exits.)*

ZINA: What?! How dare you?…

(She starts to cry. ZOTOV returns. She suppresses her tears instantly.)

ZOTOV: The porter had no telegrams, ma'am.

ZINA: Well, it really seems that it is just you and me this weekend, Ivan. Well, that will be just fine, don't you think?

ZOTOV: Yes, ma'am.

ZINA: Well, it is getting to be Christmas. We need to get this old bachelor's apartment spruced up for that. Don't you think? Bring in the Christmas ornaments from the other room, Ivan. Please.

ZOTOV: Of course. *(Exits and returns with a box.)*

ZINA: Very good. You're not like that Olga, are you? You wouldn't steal from me, would you?

ZOTOV: No, ma'am.

ZINA: Where are you from, Ivan?

ZOTOV: My family were serfs before the emancipation. From outside of Kiev.

ZINA: You don't act like a serf, Ivan. One looks at you and almost sees…more. Oh, well, back to our decorating. Oh, Ivan, this is going to be such fun. Veuillez mettre la guirlande vers le haut là.

(ZOTOV takes a wreath out of the box and prepares to hang it up.)

ZINA: Tell me, Ivan, how does a poor serf from Kiev know French?

ZOTOV: I've served in a number of fine houses, ma'am, I must have picked it up here and there.

ZINA: Does George know you are a French-speaking peasant?

ZOTOV: No, ma'am, I don't think he does.

ZINA: Well, it will be just our secret.

ZOTOV: Really, ma'am, there isn't anything…

ZINA: Now, shush. I love a good mystery. Now, let's put this one up here.

(She grabs a wreath, steps up on a footstool to hang it, but she starts to lose her balance. ZOTOV catches her. Beat. ZINA begins to cry.)

ZINA: Oh, Ivan, I am so miserable. What have I done? What have I done?

ZOTOV: Can you go back to your husband, ma'am?

ZINA: No. It was horrible there too. Everywhere I go. It is horrible. Please don't hate me too.

ZOTOV: I don't hate you.

ZINA: Olga does. She steals from me. And George…

ZOTOV: I don't know that he hates you.

ZINA: Oh, don't protect him. Please don't protect him.

ZOTOV: Perhaps you should do some shopping. And have lunch with your old nanny.

ZINA: Yes, why not? Might as well spend his money. Come with me, Ivan.

ZOTOV: I don't know, ma'am. There is a lot to be done here, and…

ZINA: I would feel much better about facing the holiday crowds if you were with me.

ZOTOV: All right, ma'am, I'll get my coat.

(ZOTOV puts on his coat. Then he helps ZINA on with hers. They exit the apartment. They and OTHER MEMBERS OF THE CAST begin to do the box step in synch. ZINA and ZOTOV are joined by NANNY. The OTHERS doing the box step should at least include: AGITATOR, BEGGAR, PATRON #1, PATRON #2, and WAITER. Note: ZINA, ZOTOV, NANNY, and the TWO PATRONS can go through the motions of eating and drinking. They all face the audience.)

ZINA: Oh, Nanny, how good that you could join us.

NANNY: Well, my dear, I did believe I heard you say something about paying.

AGITATOR: People of St. Petersburg, look around you. Look at what we are.

BEGGAR: Spare a few kopecks for a poor husband and father.

ZINA: I think you know George's valet, Ivan.

NANNY: How do you do? Well, what is on the menu today?

WAITER: Our specials today are the roast suckling pig and the salmon with dill and sour cream sauce.

PATRON #1: …and he had been acting strangely all week. Tea was getting later and later. He wouldn't announce guests. His uniform wasn't ironed. Can you imagine?

PATRON #2: Whatever did you do?

AGITATOR: And look West to see what they have. Next to them, Russia is a barbarous medieval place.

ZINA: Salmon for me.

NANNY: Pig for me.

BEGGAR: Please, my daughter is starving. She has nothing to eat. I used to work at the foundry.

PATRON #1: Naturally, we sent a letter to the Department of Police.

AGITATOR: While the people of England, France, and even to an extent Germany get to choose who will govern them, we do not. We are little more than property of the Winter Palace.

ZINA: What will you have, Ivan?

WAITER: Madam wishes to feed her servant?

ZINA: Why not? He's clean.

ZOTOV: I will have some borscht and black bread.

ZINA: You will have no such thing. Bring him an order of pig as well.

WAITER: Yes, madame.

PATRON #2: Department of Police?

BEGGAR: But then the foundry closed. They said they made better steel in Manchester.

ZINA: It's Christmas. I intend to enjoy it. My first Christmas away from Boris.

NANNY: Even as a child, my dear, you were always one to break conventions. Always playing with the serfs' children out on the farm. Your father could never understand why you didn't act according to your proper place.

ZINA: Oh, Nanny, I don't know what my proper place is.

PATRON #1: Yes. They actually sent two agents from the Okhrana around. Right before supper. So, they went up to his room. He was lying there. And would you believe it? Every centimeter of wall space was taken up with seditious propaganda posters. Well, they thrashed him. And tore those awful, awful things down. And they hauled him off. We haven't heard from him since.

ZOTOV: You are very kind, ma'am.

ZINA: You're welcome, Ivan.

BEGGAR: They threw us out of our house.

AGITATOR: At best, we are their children.

BEGGAR: They took almost everything we owned.

AGITATOR: At worst, we are their dogs.

BEGGAR: Spare a kopek.

ZINA: Ah, our soup.

PATRON #2: I don't know what's happening in this country. Just the other week, my neighbor's uncle—a judge in Moscow—was gunned down by an unknown assassin.

ZINA: Nanny, have you heard what the women of Britain and America are doing?

NANNY: Biting when they should be blowing?

DORA: Oh, I like her. I do like her.

KARP: Sssh.

ZOTOV: Hello, comrade.

AGITATOR: They aren't listening.

ZOTOV: They never listen.

AGITATOR: I am almost out of breath.

ZOTOV: That won't be enough. That won't ever be enough.

PATRON #1: Were you at the ballet last week?

PATRON #2: Wasn't it dreadful?

ZINA: No, silly. They are protesting. Women. In the streets. Like the agitators here. But in both places, they are trying to win the right to vote. Isn't that something?

NANNY: Oh, so they get to choose which man beats them as opposed to the men deciding. Now that's progress.

ZOTOV: Which party are you with?

AGITATOR: Does it matter?

ZOTOV: Suppose not.

AGITATOR: I just want change.

PATRON #2: And weren't you at the *Don Giovanni* last night?

PATRON #1: Yes, ghastly.

ZOTOV: What do you want to change to?

AGITATOR: I…I don't know.

BEGGAR: Please. A kopek will buy us some potatoes. And maybe an onion.

WAITER: Is madame done with the soup?

ZINA: Yes, thank you. Nanny, you are always so cynical.

NANNY: Zina, you are twenty-seven. When are you going to stop calling me "Nanny" and start calling me "Katharine"?

ZINA: When I have lost my faith in happy childhoods.

NANNY: My dear, your mother died when you were twelve. And your father was a drunk and a philanderer. I hardly call that happy.

ZINA: When I no longer believe that a happy childhood is possible.

BEGGAR: Half a kopek. Please. Anything.

AGITATOR: What do I do now?

ZOTOV: To grab their attention, you must be prepared to lose everything.

AGITATOR: Oh.

PATRON #1: Fucking awful country. Why do we stay here?

PATRON #2: Because where else is it this exciting?

AGITATOR: Down with the Tsar!

(*The REST stop moving.*)

AGITATOR: Death to the Tsar!

(Distant police whistles.)

AGITATOR: People of Russia. We have nothing to lose. Turn against the autocrats who would oppress us.

(The POLICE race on. They beat AGITATOR up and drag him away.)

WAITER: We apologize that your meals were interrupted, ladies and gentlemen.

BEGGAR: Help me.

(ZINA puts a couple of coins in his cup.)

CHEKHOV: Eventually, George Orlov returned from his "working" weekend. And Zina went about the business of trying to please George. But the more she tried to please, the more it seemed that she displeased him. Christmas was a day of tears and recrimination. George made an apology and that seemed to satisfy her. But only for a little while. Zina could felt the uneasiness stirring just below the surface. It was only a matter of time before events spun out of control.

(ZOTOV and OLGA stand on one part of the stage. ZINA and ORLOV stand at the other. OLGA has a glass up to a "wall." ZOTOV is cleaning plates. ORLOV is reading.)

ZOTOV: Olga, what are you doing?

OLGA: Sssh. I think they're going to fight.

ZOTOV: How was your visit with your son?

OLGA: Good. What is polio?

ZOTOV: A disease that cripples people. Why?

OLGA: No reason.

ZINA: George.

OLGA: It's starting.

ORLOV: Hmmm.

ZINA: What are you reading?

ORLOV: *Madame Bovary.*

ZINA: I think we must have a ghost.

ORLOV: Hmmm.

ZINA: I swore I had six gold coins in my wallet. Now, I have five.

ORLOV: Hmmm.

ZINA: Are you even listening?

ORLOV: Yes. Why do things always go missing for you but never for me?

ZINA: Well, I don't know, do I? I think you should dismiss that…that Olga.

OLGA: Good luck trying, bitch.

ZOTOV: Olga.

OLGA: She's trying to get me fired.

ZOTOV: You do steal from her.

OLGA: She can afford it. First time I've been able to buy Yasha something for Christmas. I think you're wrong about the polio.

ZOTOV: I'm not wrong.

ORLOV: So, you've lost a gold coin. I'll replace it with ten. I had no idea my little home would cause you such upset. But to dismiss my maid and go and find another one well…that would disrupt my routine. And to train a new maid. Well, my dear, that is simply boring beyond belief. Olga knows what I expect and what I want. And she doesn't squeal when Kukushkin sneaks a feel.

ZINA: So, you can't stand the very idea of having her leave. Why not just say so?

ORLOV: My God, is this jealousy?

ZINA: Yes, yes, it is.

ORLOV: Well, I am flattered. I don't think anyone has felt jealousy for me. Ever.

ZINA: Yes, I'm jealous… No. Actually, this is worse than jealousy. I don't know what it is. Men are heinous.

ORLOV: My dear, the solution is simple enough. Just ignore her. This is all so trivial. I don't see why I'm occupying so much of my time with it.

ZINA: George, I want to ask you about something.

OLGA: *(Putting glass down.)* I'm going to bed.

ZOTOV: Getting bored?

OLGA: They've finished talking about me. And I'm not fired. I don't give her until the end of January. Good night. *(Exits.)*

(Beat. ZOTOV picks up the glass and starts listening himself.)

ORLOV: What is it?

ZINA: *(Kneels down next to chair in which is sitting.)* I want to have a serious discussion, George.

ORLOV: All right. All right. But do stand, my dear. A statement is not rendered more convincing if said by a dwarf.

ZINA: I want to talk about the future. About when we are moving out of this apartment and into a proper house. And about when you are going to leave your post.

ORLOV: Leave my post?

ZINA: Yes, George. You cannot possibly continue to work with the government, a man with your views.

ORLOV: I was unaware that I had any views.

ZINA: Now, you're teasing me again. This is serious.

ORLOV: I know. I have no views of which I am aware. Oh, I prefer coffee to tea. But that's about it.

ZINA: You hate it.

ORLOV: I would hate anything I did. I'm not the sort of person that relishes activity beyond a few rubbers of bridge. But I am used to the civil services, and I am among my own kind there. Far better than anything else.

ZINA: You are so determined to oppose anything I say that you'll even denigrate yourself. Why do I even try? I'm so miserable.

ORLOV: It sounds like you're angry. I'm not angry because you're not a civil servant. We must each be free to follow our own paths.

ZINA: Oh, are you so free?

ORLOV: No one is free.

ZINA: You were so good to me when we first met. You would send flowers when Boris was away. But now. Say it. You want me gone.

ORLOV: I think you have me all wrong. I would be out of place almost anywhere. And, let's face it, the Russian people are not a terrific lot. The lower classes are surly, rude, disgusting, uncouth, and stupid. The upper classes are vain, petty, cruel, and cold. I am perfectly well aware of the world in which I live. But I also know where I fit in. I was born into the upper middle class. I attended university. My father's a cabinet minister, for Christ's sake. I see the world for what it is, Zina. But I am com-

fortable where I am. And, some day, if it all changes, then it changes. But for now, leave me to it.

ZINA: How you despise me. I shall commit suicide.

(Church bells ringing in the distance.)

ZINA: The bells of Isaac Cathedral.

ORLOV: I think you misunderstand me, my dear.

ZINA: I've loved listening to them. Ever since I was a girl.

ORLOV: I really didn't mean to upset you. And I, of course, hate myself for any offense I might have caused. Hate myself.

ZINA: Oh, George. You are such a fine educated man to forgive me my little outbursts. So kind and generous. I am aware every day of what an exceptional man you…

(ORLOV hugs her.)

ORLOV: Let's have no more tears, shall we?

(He lets her go and exits.)

CHEKHOV: The next morning, Zina emerged from her bedroom to find a note from her beloved. He had been called away again by the Minister on business. He would not be back until after the New Year.

(ZINA begins to cry, stops, and exits.)

CHEKHOV: Olga, of course, had her own opinions on the matter.

OLGA: Did I say she wouldn't last past the end of January? She won't last past St. John the Baptist's Day.

CHEKHOV: And Kukushkin was becoming overwhelmed with a desire to spirit Zina away.

(KUKUSHKIN and PERKARSKY enter.)

KUKUSHKIN: Well, she is extraordinarily beautiful. Well, a bit thin perhaps. Those aren't really child-bearing hips. But, oh, what nights of lust she and I could have together.

PERKARSKY: My dear Kukushkin, you haven't managed in your entire life to have a night of lust with a woman unless she was fortified with a shot of vodka, a blindfold, and cash in advance.

CHEKHOV: Meanwhile, our friend Zotov was trapped in his own dilemma.

ZOTOV: He doesn't so much abuse her with the whip but through neglect. I could tell her that he is not away on business but at Gruzin's partying. But if I did that, I would have to tell her everything. How much longer can I keep my silence?

CHEKHOV: As if to answer Zotov's question, the doorbell rang. Zotov answered.

(LEONID enters.)

ZOTOV: Yes?

LEONID: I am Leonid Orlov, your employer's father. Is he here?

ZOTOV: Um, no sir, I am sorry. He is away…on business.

LEONID: Business. Yes, of course. My busy son. May I come in and write him a note?

ZOTOV: Yes, sir. Of course, sir. Right this way.

(ZOTOV takes LEONID to a table. He produces a pen and paper.)

LEONID: You seem familiar to me. Have you worked for my son long?

ZOTOV: Since October.

LEONID: And your name?

ZOTOV: Ivan.

LEONID: Ivan.

ZOTOV: Yes, sir.

LEONID: Do you know who I am, Ivan? I mean, what I do?

ZOTOV: I know Mr. Orlov's father is Minister of the Interior.

LEONID: Yes. I have never had more than a passing familiarity with any of my son's servants. But I would like a better relationship with one. To keep me informed about my son's coming and goings. Those with whom he associates. Of course, it would mean a little extra for your pocket.

ZOTOV: You want me to be an agent of the Okhrana.

LEONID: Nothing so formal. A father worries. That is all. I note that you say "Okhrana" with a certain restrained vehemence. Any particular reason?

ZOTOV: No, sir.

LEONID: Now, where is that paper?

(LEONID begins to scribble a note. As he is writing, ZOTOV is behind him upstage. ZOTOV removes a revolver from his coat and points it at LEONID.)

CHEKHOV: As the elder Orlov wrote his note, Zotov stood there, gun outstretched. Yet, he couldn't fire. He dreamt this moment. Hoped for it. Wished for it. He had pulled the trigger a hundred times at night as he lay on his cot staring at the ceiling. Why else had he endured the past few months of humiliating servitude to George Orlov? But the cold of the metal stopped him. Prevented him from simply squeezing. Zotov summoned up every particle of his loathing for this man who was responsible for the deaths of all his comrades. It didn't matter. The trigger would not budge. He stood bleakly at the edge of the abyss, but could not throw himself in. Could do nothing but shudder and put the gun away.

(He returns the pistol to its hiding place. LEONID has finished his note.)

LEONID: Be sure my son gets this. Why, my dear boy, you're pale.

ZOTOV: Your pardon, sir. I am fighting a cold.

LEONID: Is that strumpet my son has been with in the house?

ZOTOV: Out shopping, sir.

LEONID: Oh. Do you like stories, Ivan?

ZOTOV: No, sir. Not really.

(During the next, LEONID plays with a derringer before pointing it at ZOTOV's head.)

LEONID: I do. There's one about this baron who lives outside of Kiev. Nice house. Good piece of land. Not one of the more prominent noblemen in the country, but well respected at Court. The man has two sons. The elder is being groomed to take over the baronial seat. As it should be. The younger. Well, he's a hard one to pin down. Spent some time at university and got his degree in philosophy. Then joins the Imperial Navy. Serves for two years with distinction in the Baltic Fleet. Could have made a career at it, they tell me. Captain of his own ship, admiral. Anything. But he quits. Now, this young man, his whole life ahead of him. What does he do? He joins a subversive organization. I know, he will never hold the title of baron. But all doors are open to him. Instead he chooses to try and destroy everything of importance in this country. He stands against the

Tsar. He stands against Russia. He stands against God Himself. The sad part is, he's not very good at it. All his compatriots are killed. His faction crushed. He can't even organize a successful assassination. And, let us face it, there is nothing easier than an assassination. He's a pathetic man, don't you think, Ivan?

ZOTOV: Yes, sir.

LEONID: *(Puts the gun away.)* You are such a good hardworking young man, Ivan, and you are only a valet. And this other man, the son of a baron. Yet, it is you who are the credit to Russia, not him.

ZOTOV: Thank you, sir.

LEONID: You are paler even still. Do you think that I can peer into your very thoughts? Good day. *(Exits.)*

CHEKHOV: On the brink of tears himself, Zotov threw on his coat and went to Gruzin's with the note.

(ORLOV, GRUZIN, and KUKUSHKIN enter.)

GRUZIN: It's your valet.

ORLOV: Yes, Ivan. What is it?

ZOTOV: Your father was by, sir. He left this for you.

ORLOV: What does the old man want now?

GRUZIN: What is it?

ORLOV: He wants to meet over supper sometime and talk about a post at his ministry. *(Tears up the note.)* And how is Mrs. Krasnovsky?

ZOTOV: She misses you terribly, sir.

ORLOV: Oh, God.

KUKUSHKIN: That Zina is a fine-looking woman. I wouldn't mind taking her off your hands for a while, Orlov.

ORLOV: I wish you would, Kukushkin. I wish you would. Go home, Ivan. Try to entertain Mrs. Krasnovsky as much as possible.

ZOTOV: Very good, sir.

CHEKHOV: But instead of speaking to Zina, Zotov upon his return home went to his room and lay down on his coat staring at the ceiling. Along about nine o'clock, there was a visitor at the door.

(ZINA enters, followed by GRUZIN.)

ZINA: Good evening, Peter.

GRUZIN: Zina.

ZINA: I suppose I always suspected one of George's friends to pay me a visit alone one night. But I always thought it would be Kukushkin or even Perkarsky, not you.

GRUZIN: I'm sure Kukushkin will be around later.

ZINA: Where is George?

GRUZIN: On a business trip. To Minsk, I think.

ZINA: Oh. What do you think of me, Peter?

GRUZIN: I think very highly of you, Zina. But do you value my opinion?

ZINA: Yes. Yes, I do. What happened to you, Peter? You weren't always like this.

GRUZIN: Like what?

ZINA: Disinterested.

GRUZIN: I don't know.

ZINA: You value George's friendship.

GRUZIN: Of course. I wouldn't spend my time with the others but for him.

ZINA: What should I do?

GRUZIN: Join a convent.

ZINA: A convent?

GRUZIN: Yes.

ZINA: It's as bad as all that then.

GRUZIN: Yes… Don't you know?! How could you possibly put yourself in this situation?! What were you thinking?! Did you really love him, or did you just want to be sophisticated and liberal? Didn't you have any idea of what you were getting into?!

ZINA: Please don't yell at me.

GRUZIN: Well, someone has to. God Almighty, you are an intelligent woman, Zina. My wife would never have asked you to be godmother to our boy if you weren't. But ever since you've moved in with George, this veil of stupidity seems to have descended around you. I know about Boris. I know what he did to you. Not what a gentleman does. But George is not the solution. I've known him a very long time. Longer than you. I know where his loyalties lie. And they could never lie with you. Don't you see? Can't you see?

ZINA: Get out! Just get out!

GRUZIN: Yes, of course. I'm sorry.

ZINA: Go!

GRUZIN: Good night. *(Exits.)*

(ZINA starts to cry. ZOTOV runs in with his pistol.)

ZOTOV: Did he hurt you? *(Runs out after GRUZIN.)*

ZINA: Ivan, no. It's not like that…Ivan… *(Exits.)*

CHEKHOV: So, Zotov ran into the snow without coat or scarf. Not a block away, he spied Gruzin.

ZOTOV: You! Stop!

(ZOTOV chases GRUZIN. They climb up and down scaffolding. ZOTOV grabs him, hits him, and throws him to the ground. He takes out his pistol and points it down at GRUZIN. Beat.)

GRUZIN: What are you waiting for? Do it.

(ZOTOV stares at GRUZIN for a few moments, kicks him, and then retreats. GRUZIN gets up and exits.)

CHEKHOV: For the second time in a single day, Zotov had been unable to pull the trigger. He ran back to the apartment. His consumption was raging through his body. He was drenched with melting snow and flush with fever. He returned to his little room and prepared to leave. He tore off the wet valet's shirt, threw it on the ground, and spat on it.

(ZOTOV pulls out a suitcase and starts to throw clothes in it.)

CHEKHOV: But before he could leave, he had one thing left to do. One letter to write. Not to Zina. But to George Orlov. No longer feeling the competition between fever and chill, he wrote the man he had served for three months.

ZOTOV: *(Facing the audience.)* I am sick, and I cannot say what I want to say to you. We are both failures. Yes, both of us. We will never rise again. And I realize that no matter what I say, how eloquently I say it, it will fall on deaf ears. No, not quite true. You will no doubt read this to your friends, and make sarcastic little remarks about it. That's all you do, Orlov. Make sarcastic remarks. You think it is strength, but it is in fact weakness. That is why you cannot stand tears. You want nothing that could point to your own decline. You heinous piece of shit. That is all you are. Afraid to come close to a feel-ing. Afraid of any complexity. Afraid of challenge. You read everything, but you understand nothing. And I am little better. I came with a purpose, a cause, and I have failed. I can feel my youth and health fading. I am cursed with pain and sickness. Every dream is a curse, and every memory a burden. I have let down everyone I have ever cared about. Your father was right about me. I am pathetic. We two. We are brothers. And you miserable little bastard, you are too arrogant even to realize it. But why are we so tired? Neither of us is yet thirty-five. And yet, we are bankrupt. Not of money, but of everything of value. The man crucified next to Christ found new meaning in life less than an hour before his own end. I may not have years left, but you do. You do. Will you spend the rest of your life alternating between boredom and sarcasm? Is that all you are capable of? I haven't reached you, have I? I haven't convinced you. Oh, well, what does it matter?

(ZINA enters.)

ZINA: Ivan, I thought I heard noises. My God, you're shivering.

ZOTOV: It's nothing.

ZINA: You're practically naked.

ZOTOV: I'm leaving.

ZINA: Leaving? And going where?

ZOTOV: I don't know. Come with me.

ZINA: Ivan, servants do not speak that way to their…

ZOTOV: I have no time to explain. I'm not a servant. And George is not in Minsk. He's at Gruzin's, where he always goes when he says he's out of town on business. I have to go. Let me take you out of here at least. To some place safe. Will you let me?

ZINA: Yes, I'll let you.

(Shots fired, off. They are close.)

ZINA/DASHENKA: What the Hell was that? That was too close this time.

DORA: Came from the direction of the rebel camp.

KARP: Well, go on and see who it was.

EPHIM: Why me?

KARP: Because you can run faster than I can.

EPHIM: Oh, okay. *(Runs out.)*

CHEKHOV: Well, this seems to be as good a time to break as any.

(House lights start going up.)

KARP: (To house.) Why are you all still sitting there? Now's your chance to stretch your legs. Take a leak.

DORA: Karp, don't forget the you-know-whats.

KARP: Oh, yes, the refreshment stand is now open. They're actors. They need the money. What can I tell you?

YEVSTIGNEI: Okay, people, back in ten.

ORLOV/SASHA: (Wandering across.) Has anyone seen my rouge? It's all very well and good being hunted down by the Army and being shot at by the rebels, but I can't be expected to perform without my own personal rouge that I bought in Minsk, at my own expense I might add.

ZINA/DASHENKA: Here's your stupid rouge. I swear, you get more whiny by the day.

ORLOV/SASHA: Whiny?

YEVSTIGNEI: Can we please try to have a little civility for a change?! You're all giving me a headache…

(Blackout.)

ACT TWO

Lights up. ZOTOV and ZINA are in exactly the same positions they were in at the end of Act I before the shooting started. CHEKHOV enters.

CHEKHOV: All right, we're back. Can we start?

(EPHIM runs on.)

KARP: We'll see in just a second.

EPHIM: It was an Army patrol. I think they shot someone. I only got a look at him from a distance. They've moved on.

KARP: We are ready to continue.

CHEKHOV: Aren't you going to figure out who it was?

KARP: Best not to get too close to the shooting. Continue, continue. Dora, you're in my seat.

DORA: I didn't know we were assigned seats.

KARP: This is theatre! If they didn't assign seats, there would be chaos! Now move.

(DORA moves over.)

KARP: What are you waiting for? Act!

CHEKHOV: You know, you could be a director. Now, where were we? Ah, yes. I once wrote, "Love is either the shrinking remnant of something which was once enormous; or else it is part of something which will grow in the future into something enormous. But in the present it does not satisfy. It gives much less than one expects."

ZINA: Where will you take me?

ZOTOV: To your nanny's.

ZINA: And where will you go?

ZOTOV: I…I don't know. Out of St. Petersburg. Out of the country.

ZINA: Who are you?

(Beat. ZOTOV looks at her for a second. He digs into his suitcase and begins to dress in very expensive-looking clothes. When he is done dressing, he is transformed.)

ZINA: Ivan?

ZOTOV: Not Ivan, no. My name is Vladimir Zotov. I am a nobleman and a former officer of the Imperial Navy.

ZINA: (Beginning to bow.) My lord…

ZOTOV: There's no time for that. We must flee. Grab whatever you can and come.

(ZOTOV takes her hand. Coughing, he leads her around the stage. He knocks at a door. NANNY answers.)

NANNY: Zina! Ivan?! Do you have any idea of what time it is?

ZINA: There's no time for this now, Nanny. Can we come in?

NANNY: Yes, yes, of course. Orlov is dressing his servants better these days.

ZOTOV: I'm not a servant.

NANNY: No. Never thought you were. Look at his hands. So, what brings you two here?

ZINA: I've left George.

NANNY: Really? You're not going back to Boris, are you?

ZINA: No. I couldn't anyway. And I don't want to.

NANNY: You should never have left him. Look what has happened to you, my pet.

ZINA: No, Nanny. Leaving was always the right decision. I just didn't choose well as to where I ended up.

NANNY: And you…

ZOTOV: Vladimir.

NANNY: And you, Vladimir. What are you going to do?

ZOTOV: I'm going west. France. Italy perhaps.

NANNY: Oh. It's like that then, is it?

ZOTOV: Yes, it's like that.

NANNY: So, what are we going to do with our Zina?

ZINA: I thought I could stay here for a few days.

NANNY: Yes, my dear, but then what? My place hardly befits someone of your station. You must have somewhere to go. You must have some money.

ZINA: You're turning me out, Nanny?

NANNY: It is not so simple. I could not afford us both. You must decide between George and Boris.

ZINA: Oh, God.

ZOTOV: Why not a third choice?

NANNY: What?

ZOTOV: She could come with me.

NANNY: And do you have the means of supporting her?

ZOTOV: As a matter of fact, I do.

ZINA: Ivan…I mean, Vladimir, you would do this for me?

ZOTOV: Yes. Yes, I would.

ZINA: Thank you. But I don't even have a passport.

NANNY: But I do. Use mine. I'm sure our friend here knows ways to modify passports.

ZOTOV: I do.

NANNY: (Exiting.) It's settled then.

ZINA: Vladimir, you are kind beyond words.

ZOTOV: I…thank you.

ZINA: I should be thanking you.

ZOTOV: It will be good to have company on such a long trip.

NANNY: (Returning with passport and shawl.) Here's my passport. And Zina, you did not dress for the weather. You'll freeze yourself stiff. This should keep you warm.

ZINA: I do not know where my head is today.

NANNY: I would love to see the expression on George's face when he sees his mistress and his valet gone. I wonder whom he will miss more.

ZINA: Him.

ZOTOV: Her.

ZINA: So, when do we leave?

ZOTOV: Now.

ZINA: Tonight? Not even in the morning?

NANNY: I expect that your new guardian angel must leave as soon as possible.

ZOTOV: There's a one-thirty to Berlin. If we hurry, we can catch it. Don't worry, ma'am, I'll take good care of her.

NANNY: I expect nothing less.

ZINA: I don't know when I shall see you again. Goodbye, Katharine.

NANNY: (Beat.) Goodbye.

(They hug. ZINA and ZOTOV exit.)

CHEKHOV: Zotov hailed a cab with runners, and they were off down the empty streets of St. Petersburg. They arrived at the train station with ten minutes to spare. Zotov worked on altering Nanny's passport to fit Zina's description. Zina, meanwhile, sat in her seat, staring out of the window at the cold dark city. There was a light flurry of snow. As each flake of snow hit the window, it turned to water and streaked down the glass. Zina's only thought was that these would have to do for her tears. Her tears at having to leave her own city. But she did not cry. The train took them to Berlin.

(During the next, scrolling scenery is run behind them as if seen from a train.)

GERMAN MAN: Porter! Porter!

PORTER: Sir?

GERMAN MAN: I would like a new cabin. The Russian next to me does nothing but cough all the night.

PORTER: Yes, sir.

GERMAN MAN: Russians. They're nothing but a barbaric revolting people. I understand that they go months at a time without bathing. Disgusting.

CHEKHOV: At Berlin, they changed trains and headed for Venice. But Venice proved to be too humid and made Zotov's condition even worse.

ENGLISHMAN: Shocking the kind of riffraff they are letting into the hotel these days. Those horrid Russians.

ENGLISHWOMAN: Such table manners.

ENGLISHMAN: Well, at least she barely ate.

ENGLISHWOMAN: And the smell.

ENGLISHMAN: Who knew they had such an odor? My eyes are still burning.

(ZINA and ZOTOV enter. ZOTOV lies down. ZINA sits next to him.)

CHEKHOV: And in Venice, Zotov's fevered dreams returned.

ZOTOV: *(While sleeping.)* Zina…love you…Hold you…Love you…Marry me…Be my wife…I'm thirsty…Tired…I…

(ZINA stares at him.)

CHEKHOV: So they left for Nice in France.

KARP: Wait! Is that all we get of Venice? Where are the canals? The piazza?

DORA and EPHIM: Shut up!

CHEKHOV: Zotov's money was running out. In Nice, they would have to do something for cash. That would prove very difficult because Zotov's health continued to deteriorate. In Nice, Zotov was in total agony.

BELLHOP: *(Running on; à la Groucho Marx.)* Doctor Chekhov? Doctor Chekhov?

CHEKHOV: Yes.

BELLHOP: There's a Russian couple in seven, sir. The man needs to see a doctor right away.

CHEKHOV: Yes, of course. *(Runs over to them.)* What seems to be the problem?

ZINA: It's Vladimir. He's been sick for weeks, and he hasn't been getting any better.

CHEKHOV: Let me see. Stand over here, if you please. *(Sitting down next to ZOTOV.)* Zotov!

ZOTOV: Doctor?

CHEKHOV: It looks like you didn't take my advice.

ZOTOV: No.

CHEKHOV: Your condition is deteriorating. The consumption is ravaging your body. You must get complete rest. You are to sit in the sun and do as little as possible. Do you understand?

ZOTOV: Yes…yes.

CHEKHOV: I'm going to go out and get some elixirs for you. But first, take two of these.

ZOTOV: No…

CHEKHOV: Don't worry. They are very mild. Nothing that will harm your brain. But first, I must look at your wife.

ZOTOV: *(Swallowing.)* Not married.

CHEKHOV: Oh. Well, she looks like she needs some looking after as well. Then we'll talk after you've slept.

ZOTOV: Sleep.

CHEKHOV: Sleep… Now, what is your name?

ZINA: Zina Krasnovsky.

CHEKHOV: And are you a friend of Vladimir's?

ZINA: Of sorts. And you?

CHEKHOV: Of sorts. Come with me please.

ZINA: Why? Where are we going?

CHEKHOV: I'd like to examine you.

ZINA: Oh.

(CHEKHOV leads her to another area.)

ZINA: There's nothing wrong with me.

CHEKHOV: I'm afraid that's not true. You are malnourished.

ZINA: I don't think so.

CHEKHOV: It's true.

ZINA: I haven't been hungry.

CHEKHOV: Do you know you're pregnant?

ZINA: Yes. Four months.

CHEKHOV: You have to eat for the child.

ZINA: I know.

CHEKHOV: Is it Vladimir's?

ZINA: No.

CHEKHOV: Oh.

ZINA: It's not what you think.

CHEKHOV: So is it this man Krasnovsky's?

ZINA: No. The father is George Orlov.

CHEKHOV: Orlov?

ZINA: It's complicated.

CHEKHOV: I don't doubt it.

ZINA: Please don't make fun of me.

CHEKHOV: I won't. But you must eat. To keep up your strength. For your baby. For Vladimir.

ZINA: All right.

CHEKHOV: *(Taking out a washbowl filled with water and a cloth)* Now, then…

ZINA: What are you doing?

CHEKHOV: Cleaning you up. You're filthy. All right?

ZINA: All right.

(CHEKHOV begins to give ZINA a sponge bath. He is very slow and methodical in his washing. He begins very professionally but soon his movements become more sensual.)

ZINA: I…I think I should go…Doctor Chekhov.

(She doesn't move. There are gunshots in the distance. She still doesn't move.)

CHEKHOV: If you must. And call me "Anton."

(She doesn't move for a moment. Beat. She then stands and slowly exits. A makeshift casket is wheeled on. ORLOV enters with a drink and sits in a chair. PERKARSKY and KUKUSHKIN enter. They also have drinks.)

KUKUSHKIN: He looks peaceful.

PERKARSKY: Very.

KUKUSHKIN: I hope I look that good when I go.

PERKARSKY: You should be so lucky.

KUKUSHKIN: It's strange that he's dead.

PERKARSKY: Yes, one would think dying would be too much of a bother for old Gruzin. How are you holding up, Orlov?

ORLOV: I'm doing fantastic. I had eight glasses of…well, whatever this potion is…and I feel fantastic.

PERKARSKY: It's Irish whiskey.

ORLOV: Is it? Damn clever stuff. Gives me hope for the human race in general.

(LEONID enters.)

ORLOV: Then, maybe not… Papa.

LEONID: George…gentlemen. What's all this?

ORLOV: It seems that Gruzin has contracted a rather severe case of death. We were just wondering who we're going to get as a fourth for bridge.

LEONID: Gruzin is dead. Oh well. The world marches on.

KUKUSHKIN: Minister, I was wondering if…

LEONID: Not today, Kukushkin.

KUKUSHKIN: No, sir. Of course not, sir.

PERKARSKY: We'll wait for you in the other room, George.

(He and KUKUSHKIN exit.)

ORLOV: It's a surprise to see you, Papa. But I can't really believe it is to mourn.

LEONID: To mourn? The death of the worm that corrupted you? That taught you to be indulgent and indolent? No, I feel like celebrating. I want to dance and sing and share my joy with the world.

ORLOV: Not today, Papa. I really don't think I can bear this today.

LEONID: He really is dead. I always wondered that if he died, how could we tell? But Gruzin is not why I am here. I wish to discuss your concubine and your valet. In no particular order. Come with me. *(Exits.)*

ORLOV: Goodbye, Peter. *(Exits.)*

(ZOTOV stands and walks to another area. There is bright sunlight, sounds of gulls, etc. He sits down as if sunning himself on a beach. ZINA enters.)

ZINA: I thought I might find you here.

ZOTOV: I am sorry that I am not more entertaining.

ZINA: What is is.

ZOTOV: It feels better out here.

ZINA: Vladimir?

ZOTOV: Yes?

ZINA: What are we going to do for money?

ZOTOV: Money?

ZINA: Yes. As in how are we going to pay for the hotel next week?

ZOTOV: I don't know.

ZINA: We could borrow from Anton.

ZOTOV: Anton?

ZINA: Doctor Chekhov.

ZOTOV: I know who he is.

ZINA: We could borrow some from him. A loan. Until you are well enough to work.

ZOTOV: One, he's not a friend. He's more like a friend of a friend. Two, it will be a long time before I am better. Three, I don't think he has any money either.

ZINA: What are we to do?

ZOTOV: We are quite a pair, aren't we? The revolutionary who is too sick to fight for revolution. And the rich woman who doesn't have two rubles to rub together.

ZINA: I don't know why we must always live up to the titles the world thrusts upon us. Or the ones we choose for ourselves… I'm pregnant.

ZOTOV: I see.

ZINA: I thought so for a while. Anton confirmed it last week.

ZOTOV: Then you must take care of yourself as well.

ZINA: Aren't you even interested to know who the father is?

ZOTOV: I know it's not me. That just leaves Boris and George. Not much of a choice.

ZINA: How little you understand. George never hit me with his fists. Or a belt. George never locked me in a closet when I talked too much. And once in a while, George would…let me spend the night with him.

ZOTOV: For hundreds of years, there were serfs. The nobles were the masters of the serfs. And the tsars controlled everything. Now, the last tsar emancipated the serfs. So, instead of being slaves and being whipped by the masters, they were now employees and being whipped by the employers. Before, the nobles owned their land, and the serfs would have to pay the nobles rent to stay on the land. Now the serfs own their little plots of ground and have to pay the nobles taxes if they want to stay. What's the difference?

ZINA: As I said, you do not understand. *(Stands with some trouble.)*

ZOTOV: You must be careful.

ZINA: I'm just pregnant. Nanny used to tell me that the female savages in the American West would work the fields, stop to deliver their babies, and return to their labors.

ZOTOV: That sounds like a myth.

ZINA: To me, it seems to be gospel.

ZOTOV: Where are you going? Don't you want to stay?

ZINA: Vladimir, there is only so much sun and sand a person can stomach. I'm meeting Anton in town.

ZOTOV: You two have gotten close.

ZINA: No, not really. He's going to show me the casinos.

ZOTOV: Enjoy yourself then.

ZINA: All right, I will.

(ZINA straps a pillow around her stomach and covers it up with a shawl. OTHER ACTORS enter and start betting, drinking, etc., in casino. ZOTOV sits at the edge of the stage, coughing. ZINA is playing blackjack.)

ZINA: Vingt et un!

DEALER: Madame est encore le gagnant.

OTHER PLAYER: Chanceux.

ZINA: Il n'est rien.

(CHEKHOV enters, spots ZINA, and walks over to her.)

CHEKHOV: Sorry I'm late. A couple from back home. Case of sunstroke.

ZINA: It's all right. I've been winning.

CHEKHOV: Yes, I can see that. How much do you have there?

ZINA: Four hundred and eighty francs. I think.

CHEKHOV: Four hundred and eighty?!

ZINA: Yes. Using the method you taught me.

CHEKHOV: I barely broke even with my method. You must be doing something different.

ZINA: No. Just as you explained it to me.

CHEKHOV: Then how…?

ZINA: I am a Russian woman, Anton. I am used to forever living on the edge of the abyss.

CHEKHOV: This is more than enough to pay for your rooms. And a little extra.

ZINA: Would you care to celebrate? It's been so long since I've had champagne. Here I am in France, and I haven't had a drop.

CHEKHOV: Well, I'm not sure it would be good for the child… Well, maybe just one glass. A small glass.

(CHEKHOV takes two glasses from a WAITER.)

ZINA: Thank you.

CHEKHOV: Here's to your good fortune.

ZINA: I had come to the conclusion that I would never see good fortune again. And here's to you. Thank you for your kindness.

CHEKHOV: Not at all. Did Zotov complain about you coming tonight?

ZINA: He hasn't complained since the first day you brought me here. It doesn't matter. I don't think he cares.

CHEKHOV: But you love him.

ZINA: Yes, that's right. I *love* Vladimir. He is so witty. And interesting. And great to be around. And he is beautiful. But he is all twisted inside from his revolution. From the failure of his revolution. Vladimir does not love. He obsesses, the way a cat obsesses on a mouse.

CHEKHOV: I think perhaps you are mistaken.

ZINA: Oh.

EMCEE: Mesdames et messieurs, souhaitent la bienvenue s'il vous plaît de Paris Yvonne DuMond. Elle chantera maintenant pour nous.

(SINGER enters. She sings "Si mes vers avaient des ailes" by Reynaldo Hahn. As she does, GAMBLERS, etc., slowly fade away until only CHEKHOV and ZINA are walking along.)

SINGER: Mes ver fuiraient, doux et frêles,
Vers votre jardin si beau,
Si mes vers avaient des ailes
Des ailes comme l'oiseau.

CHEKHOV: Do you want to walk along the beach?

ZINA: It's a beautiful night.

SINGER: Ils voleraient, étincelles,
Vers votre foyer qui rit,
Si mes vers avaient des ailes,
Des ailes comme l'esprit.

CHEKHOV: Here's a good spot.

ZINA: Yes.

SINGER: Près de vous, purs et fidèles,
Ils accourraient, nuit et jour,
Si mes vers avaient des ailes,
Des ailes comme l'amour.

(By the end of the song, CHEKHOV should be sitting on the beach. ZINA should be lying against him, head in his lap. They are near a small model of the hotel.)

ZINA: I don't think you are.

CHEKHOV: What?

ZINA: In love with me.

CHEKHOV: I never said I was.

ZINA: You didn't have to. I recognize the look, you know. You think you're in love with me, but you're not. You're in love with something I have. Or something I can give you. Boris was in love with my dowry. George was in love with the scandal. Vladimir in love with saving me from my oppressors.

CHEKHOV: And me?

ZINA: I think you are in love with love.

CHEKHOV: What does that mean?

ZINA: It means you think you are quite the Lothario, but you really are a secret romantic. Unfortunately, no actual romance can live up to the idea of romance. That's your problem. Never-ending disappointment.

CHEKHOV: You are bold.

ZINA: I have little time not to be direct.

CHEKHOV: Suppose I promised you that I would never be disappointed in you.

ZINA: I wouldn't accept your promise.

CHEKHOV: Why?

ZINA: You couldn't keep it.

CHEKHOV: It's a gorgeous night.

ZINA: Magnificent.

CHEKHOV: This is the tragedy of modern Russia. We could never have a night like this in St. Petersburg, but too many of us have experienced such nights in distant lands.

ZINA: Do you miss home?

CHEKHOV: Sometimes I think I actually miss the taste of borscht.

ZINA: Do you see the lights of all those passing ships? So many. Going to so many exotic locations. America. India. Egypt. I would like to be on one of those ships.

CHEKHOV: Going where?

ZINA: I don't know. It doesn't matter.

CHEKHOV: In a way, this reminds me of my childhood in Taganrog. My grandfather was a serf, did you know that? He bought his own freedom. All too often, though, we would have nothing to do at night and sit under the stars in a field outside of town.

(Sounds of distant laughter.)

ZINA: There's some kind of party at the hotel.

CHEKHOV: That's like home too. The master would frequently have parties for his friends at his estate.

ZINA: And what would you and your family do under the stars?

CHEKHOV: My brothers, my sister, and I would try to make our own constellations out of them. Tell stories sometimes.

ZINA: What kind of stories?

CHEKHOV: Sad ones usually. About impossible loves.

ZINA: Tell me one.

CHEKHOV: I'm not sure.

ZINA: I want to hear. Please.

CHEKHOV: All right. This is the story of a woman named Popova. She was the wife…the widow of a small landowner. From their property, you could see the distant purple of the Urals and not much else. In the winter, it was a cold, desperate place. Their nearest neighbor was twenty kilometers away. And one night, Popova's husband died. The next day she began to make arrangements to bury her husband. The wind screamed its hollow scream outside. Even the animals huddled in the barn. An Asian cold was creeping up through the floor boards. But when Popova looked out the window, she could see a lone rider approaching the house. She thought he must be mad to travel in such weather. Because the land was so flat, she could see him at a great distance. She watched in fascination as the black figure approached slowly but steadily. After about twenty minutes, the horse and rider arrived. The black-cloaked man hopped off his shaking beast, tied it to the post, and banged on the door. Popova admitted him. "Good morning, madame, I am Maxim Smirnoff, reservist," he said. She stared at him for a moment. "I am quite busy today, sir, what is it I can do for you?" she asked. "Your husband owes me twelve hundred rubles," he replied. "My husband is dead. He died last night." At first, Maxim was skeptical, but Popova showed him the body. And put all doubts to rest. Suddenly, he said, "Then, madame, the debt passes to you. Since I have to settle some accounts with the bank tomorrow, I would appreciate being paid today." Popova explained that she didn't have money on hand but that her manager would be returning from town day after tomorrow and that she could pay him then. This was not good enough for Maxim. He needed the money for the bank the very next day or else much of his lands would be forfeit. So they argued. Their voices growing louder. Soon, Popova was insulting Maxim. Well, do you know what Maxim did? Maxim was a proud man. So he challenged her to a duel on the spot. He challenged a woman. And she accepted. Can you imagine? "You want a duel," she shouted, "I will give you a duel!" Her husband had left a pair of dueling pistols from his days serving in the Crimean War, and Popova went to fetch them. And the most extraordinary thing happened. Maxim fell in love with Popova at that very moment. Never had he seen a woman with such courage. With such audacity. With such panache. When Popova returned, Maxim forgave her the debt. Instead of fighting a duel with her, he proposed marriage. She accepted. All would have been well, but she contracted diptheria and died three weeks before the wedding day.

ZINA: Is that your sad story?

CHEKHOV: Yes.

ZINA: Makes me laugh.

(He kisses her. She lets him. He bows down over her and begins to caress her. Lights fade on this area and up on ORLOV and LEONID.)

LEONID: They ran off together. Living in the South of France. I understand they have been seen in the company of a doctor who thinks he's a writer. What is it about the Russian character that we can never be satisfied with our work? I know I love my job.

ORLOV: I wouldn't know, Papa.

LEONID: And how does all this make you feel?

ORLOV: Feel? It really doesn't have anything to do with me.

LEONID: "Doesn't have anything to do with me." Well, isn't that nice. You know Zotov, the man you called Ivan, was a dangerous revolutionary. That he tried to kill me.

ORLOV: I really must work at hiring more efficient servants.

LEONID: Darling boy. You really have proven to be quite a disappointment. Yes, a great disappointment. But not a total one. Did you know that you will soon be a father yourself? That cow you let run to France is fertile, and she is carrying your child.

ORLOV: What? How do you know this?

LEONID: I'm head of the secret police. How do you think I know? If the child is a boy, I want it back. In Russia. In my house. I will care for it and raise it. Avoid past mistakes. And I will have a worthy heir. Already my agents are on their way to France to monitor the situation for me. As your father, George, I want to say thank you for this one gift. If either Zina or this Zotov contacts you, I want all letters to pass through my office. You are to be forgiving. Encourage them to come home. Do you understand?

ORLOV: Yes, Papa, I think I do.

LEONID: Now, if you'll excuse me, I have to be at a cabinet meeting. *(Exits.)*

ORLOV: Perkarsky!

(PERKARSKY and KUKUSHKIN enter.)

PERKARSKY: Old man's gone, I see.

ORLOV: Yes, he is. He told me of Zina. She and that valet have fled to Nice. She's pregnant with my child.

KUKUSHKIN: Well, congratulations, Orlov, that's…

ORLOV: Not now, Kukushkin! Perkarsky, I need you to exercise some of your infamous influence for me.

PERKARSKY: What do you have in mind?

ORLOV: Have a private investigator go to France and give this money to Zina. This is for her to abort the unborn child.

KUKUSHKIN: Abort?

PERKARSKY: Pour yourself a drink, Kukushkin. And are you sure she would if given this?

ORLOV: If she is unwilling, our man is to do what it takes to make her willing. Understand?

PERKARSKY: I do. This requires a special kind of individual. Expenses could be high. Administrative costs.

ORLOV: And I don't doubt it. This is for you.

PERKARSKY: This should do for the moment.

KUKUSHKIN: My God, Orlov, you would kill your own son.

ORLOV: And kill all my father's hopes and dreams. Yes. Oh, yes.

(Lights fade on this area and up on ZOTOV and TWO MEN sitting at a café.)

ZOTOV: …and if we set up bank accounts here and in Geneva, we can start funding the underground from outside Russia. That will make it harder for the Okhrana to trace our movements. We must be smarter than the Okhrana. We must be faster than them. We must be better. Because they can afford to make mistakes. We cannot. Well, gentlemen, that's it. Until next week, then.

(ZINA enters.)

ZOTOV: I will send messages as to where our next meeting will be.

(*The TWO MEN exit.*)

ZINA: What's all this?

ZOTOV: A meeting.

ZINA: A meeting? A meeting for what?

ZOTOV: If I can't fight, at least I can help finance the movement back home.

ZINA: Back to that, are we?

ZOTOV: I never left it, Zina.

ZINA: Can't you ever stop?

ZOTOV: No.

ZINA: And what do you expect me to do?

ZOTOV: Be by my side like a good…

ZINA: Yes?… This worries me, Vladimir. Let's just put Russia behind us. If you start again, they will only find you. Just yesterday I think someone was following me.

ZOTOV: You're imagining things.

(*Beat.*)

ZOTOV: I said, "You're imagining things!"

ZINA/DASHENKA: What's the trouble now?

ZOTOV/YEVSTIGNEI: I don't know… Sergei, that was your cue. Sergei!

(*ORLOV/SASHA enters.*)

ORLOV/SASHA: Um, hi. We just found out that that man who was shot by the soldiers was Sergei.

ZOTOV/YEVSTIGNEI: Well, we certainly can't finish the play now.

DORA: Can't finish the play?

ZOTOV/YEVSTIGNEI: Well, Sergei just joined us a few weeks ago, but he was a terrific Hamlet. And no one else knows the part of the Okhrana Agent.

DORA: But I want to know what happens to Zina. Does she choose Zotov? Or Chekhov? Or maybe she goes back to Orlov. I'm starting to think she might just do that.

KARP: Dora, please. They lost one of their company. They can't keep going on.

DORA: But it's all we have. It's all they have.

ZINA/DASHENKA: We do have a script. If someone could read along…

ZOTOV/YEVSTIGNEI: But everyone has other parts.

EPHIM: I could do it.

KARP: You?

EPHIM: I can read.

KARP: Not in my schoolhouse you couldn't.

DORA: I've been teaching him. At night in the winter.

EPHIM: Please let me.

ZOTOV/YEVSTIGNEI: All right.

ZINA/DASHENKA: Here's the script. Where it says Okhrana Agent, you read. Over here, these tell you where to move. Do you understand?

EPHIM: Yes, yes, thank you.

ZINA/DASHENKA: (*Removing a dark coat from the cart.*) And this is what you will wear.

(*EPHIM puts it on.*)

ZINA/DASHENKA: Scary. Can you be scary?

EPHIM: Yes, ma'am. (*He growls. He starts to exit. He trips and goes out.*)

ZINA/DASHENKA: All right, from my line… Just yesterday I think someone was following me.

ZOTOV: You're imagining things.

(*EPHIM as AGENT enters and trips as he enters.*)

ZOTOV: On second thought, you might be right. Let's get back to the hotel.

(*They exit. CHEKHOV enters.*)

OKHRANA AGENT: (*EPHIM reads the lines slowly.*) Doctor Chekhov?

CHEKHOV: Yes, can I help you?

OKHRANA AGENT: I was wondering if you could help me… Take two steps downstage. (*He does so.*)

CHEKHOV: No, you don't have to read that part.

EPHIM: Oh, okay.

CHEKHOV: Yes, what is it I can do for you?

OKHRANA AGENT: I am officer with the Department of Police back home.

CHEKHOV: You mean, the Okhrana.

OKHRANA AGENT: If you'd like.

CHEKHOV: It doesn't seem to be a question of what I do and do not like.

OKHRANA AGENT: So you know, I answer to the Minister of the Interior directly. Anything you say to me will be kept discreet. Do you know Vladimir Zotov?

CHEKHOV: Yes.

OKHRANA AGENT: Has he ever said anything seditious to you? Suggested any treason to you? Revealed any plans to act against Russia or the Tsar?

CHEKHOV: No, no, and no.

OKHRANA AGENT: Has he ever acted strangely?

CHEKHOV: Zotov? All the time.

OKHRANA AGENT: No, I mean has he tried to hide anything or keep secrets from…

CHEKHOV: Look, I really don't have time for this. If you have questions about Zotov, go ask him yourself. Otherwise, it's a beautiful day. Enjoy it.

OKHRANA AGENT: Are you a loyal Russian, Doctor?

CHEKHOV: As loyal as the next man.

OKHRANA AGENT: *(During the next, EPHIM's "acting" becomes better.)* In Russia, that could mean that you are a traitor. You stand with us or against us, Doctor Chekhov. Or have you forgotten what it means to be Russian? Has life here made you soft and weak like a Frenchman? You hold us in contempt. You are a fool. We are who we are. This is what the world has made us. Here, they can have their freedoms. Their liberties. Their pleasures. But take away their food, their sunshine, their beautiful art, and you will see how quickly they will become exactly like us. In a land where it is winter nine months of the year, where it is rocky and barren, where there are great snows, there must be a tsar and a nobility to rule—yes, often ruthlessly—if we are all to grow as a nation. And there must even be an Okhrana if we are to survive. God, what a beautiful country. *(Starts to exit, trips, and then leaves.)*

(Lights fade on this area and up on ZOTOV, who slowly makes his way to a spot and sits down. It is sunny. CHEKHOV approaches.)

CHEKHOV: Morning, Vladimir.

ZOTOV: Anton.

CHEKHOV: What a day. It feels like you could see all the way to Africa. I think you should try the water today. It should be warm enough.

ZOTOV: I wanted to ask you one more favor.

CHEKHOV: What is it?

ZOTOV: Leave us alone.

CHEKHOV: I can hardly do that. Zina could go into labor any day now.

ZOTOV: I am not the jealous sort, Anton.

CHEKHOV: Oh?

ZOTOV: But I don't want her seeing you anymore. I feel like a right bastard talking to you like this. You've been so good to her. To me. But, you have to understand, my feelings for her are…are…

CHEKHOV: I know.

ZOTOV: You do?

CHEKHOV: But she doesn't.

ZOTOV: And yet you insist on spending all this time with her.

CHEKHOV: It is a failing, I will admit to that, Vladimir. I have a weakness for beautiful women.

ZOTOV: For God's sake, she's pregnant.

CHEKHOV: She's still beautiful.

ZOTOV: *(Standing.)* I don't understand you. I never did.

CHEKHOV: You shouldn't strain yourself.

ZOTOV: Stop treating me like a child.

CHEKHOV: I admit, Vladimir, that I don't understand you particularly well either.

ZOTOV: Oh my good doctor. What an excellent little charade you play. A man of medicine, devoted to healing the sick. By night, a teller of stories. A scribbler. So many conceits, and yet so little understanding of life. Of love. Or anything else!

CHEKHOV: And I suppose your revolutionary ideals have given you some magical key to the human soul. Tell us all about them, Vladimir. How will returning production to the workers explain the mysteries of our primal spirit? How will the revolutionary avant-garde solve the problem that no one person can truly know another? How will overthrowing the last archaic remnants of a barbaric society help two people who fall in love stay in love?

ZOTOV: You bastard. You love her, don't you? Don't you?!

(He swings at CHEKHOV, who ducks. He rushes CHEKHOV. CHEKHOV pushes him aside. ZOTOV has a coughing fit.)

CHEKHOV: You are weak, Zotov. Weak.

ZOTOV: Why did you have to love her?

CHEKHOV: You must learn to control extremes in temper.

ZOTOV: How, Anton? How?

CHEKHOV: It was not my intent.

ZOTOV: I trusted in you. Believed in you. And you do this. To me.

CHEKHOV: I'm sorry. If it helps, she does not love me.

ZOTOV: Nor me.

CHEKHOV: Than whom? This George?

ZOTOV: No. No one. Not even the unborn child.

CHEKHOV: And there is nothing we can do to change that, is there?

ZOTOV: No. I'm dying too, aren't I?

CHEKHOV: Yes.

ZOTOV: Soon I will be gone. And Zina will be alone.

CHEKHOV: I wish there was something…I could do.

ZOTOV: Summer is fading fast.

(A bed is brought on. It is covered with papers. ZINA goes and lies on it. CHEKHOV joins her.)

ZINA: This place is a mess.

CHEKHOV: It is the room of a man who thinks.

ZINA: Do you have to think in bed as well?

CHEKHOV: Well, I don't just think in bed…

ZINA: You make me laugh… It's strange, you know. I don't think you should. Look at you. So many scars. So many old scars. This one here, on your side, where did you get that?

CHEKHOV: Pavel.

ZINA: Huh?

CHEKHOV: My father. He was aiming for the Devil, and he got me instead.

ZINA: So we both understand.

CHEKHOV: Yes.

ZINA: I'm very glad someone does… (Beat.) You know, a man from back home approached me too.

CHEKHOV: Someone in a trench coat?

ZINA: Okhrana? No. This one was more mousy, like an accountant. I think I recognized him from George's. He had come around to drop off some papers for one of George's friends, Perkarsky.

CHEKHOV: And who is this Perkarsky?

ZINA: He fixes things. That's all I really know. This man offered me a large sum of money if I would abort the child. I told him I would think about it.

CHEKHOV: What?!

ZINA: Don't worry. I was just stringing him along. There are too many men hiding in the shadows for my taste. There must be some kind of maneuvering going on between George and his father. If the child is a boy, well, that gives the old man another heir. The question is: how to get both of them. And I think I know a way… and still have the child.

CHEKHOV: I didn't know you were so devious. I think I like it.

ZINA: What else can a woman be in modern Russia? Will you help? It should be fun.

CHEKHOV: My lady, I am your brave heroic Cossack.

ZINA: Excuse me?

CHEKHOV: Is something the matter?

ZINA: Matter? No, nothing. I'm just thirsty. Would you bring me a glass of water?

CHEKHOV: Certainly.

(He exits. ZINA starts to go through his papers frantically. He returns.)

CHEKHOV: I brought a couple of oranges as well. They're from Seville, and…

ZINA: What's this?

CHEKHOV: It's a story I'm writing. I would prefer you didn't read it. It's still a rough draft, and…

ZINA: "…and he stood before Zina, shivering from the cold and his fever. He could no longer pretend to be George Orlov's valet. His birth, his distinguished service with the Baltic Fleet—that would all be explained. In a second, he would reveal everything to her, the woman he longed for in secret, beckoned to in his dreams, desired beyond all else. It was understandable, of course. She was beautiful, a woman out of legend, an iridescent star, out of place in her own time. How else to explain the great unhappiness that accompanied such brilliance?…" Anton.

CHEKHOV: I write what I see, hear, learn.

ZINA: Do you love me?

CHEKHOV: It's a story, Zina. I use the names of people I know, and…

ZINA: Do you love me?

CHEKHOV: Yes.

ZINA: You're telling the truth. I can see that, but… (Riffling through the papers.) "Zotov held in his cough. He believed it would be divine retribution for him to strike down the monster Leonid Orlov. But here he was, playing at being a valet, waiting on the off-chance that Orlov might want a cigar or sherry. What had this great, noble man been reduced to?" Vladimir, noble? How could you say this?

CHEKHOV: Because it's true.

ZINA: True?

CHEKHOV: To me. To what I believe in how the universe is structured. And how I structure that universe. Yes, it's true.

ZINA: Do you love Vladimir?

CHEKHOV: I love everyone I write about.

(Beat.)

ZINA: Anton… I thought I could, but I can't and…

CHEKHOV: They're just words, Zina. On the page.

ZINA: Your words.

CHEKHOV: Don't go.

ZINA: All my life, everything that has happened to me, it has rarely been for the best. But I always clung on because I understood. Where I was. What I was. And those that surrounded me. And, foolishly, I believed I could escape. Twice. And here you are standing before me and I'm feeling… and for the first time in my life I don't understand. I don't understand. And it frightens me.

(She lets her hand run down his body and stop at the scar she found earlier. She looks at him and then gathers up her things and walks out. She walks around the stage. PERKARSKY'S ASSISTANT appears.)

ASSISTANT: Ah, madame, if we might continue our earlier conversation, I've received a most generous wire from St. Petersburg.

ZINA: Oh, not now.

(She exits. ZOTOV enters and walks around into the hotel area. ZINA enters carrying some more winnings. CHEKHOV walks to the side of the stage.)

ZOTOV: Another trip to the casino?

ZINA: We have to pay for our rooms somehow.

ZOTOV: That must be quite a sight. A pregnant Russian woman playing blackjack with the gentlemen of Europe.

ZINA: And winning.

ZOTOV: Wait. We never spend any time together. Let's have supper out on the terrace.

ZINA: I'm tired. I'm going to bed.

ZOTOV: Zina, please.

ZINA: Vladimir, let me ask you a question. What are we going to do? We cannot spend our lives in this limbo. We have to have some kind of plan. All you do is sit on the beach and dream of coup d'états, and all I do is play cards. I'm sick of it.

ZOTOV: There is still a cause back home. Still a fight. We can provide support for it from France.

ZINA: You may think of yourself as a revolutionary, but you are not very good at it.

ZOTOV: It has always been my idea that…

ZINA: Idea? Idea?! I've had it with the word. Your ideas! What have they gotten you? Us? Nothing. And the biggest idea of them all is the one that disgusts me the most. The idea that I am to be your mistress.

ZOTOV: I don't know what you mean.

ZINA: Oh, don't you? Do you love me?

ZOTOV: I…I…

ZINA: Do you? I thought as much. I have been nursing you all across Europe. I've been by your side when the fever was at its worst. I heard your lunatic ravings. Your whispered dreams. Your passions. Your hopes. Your visions. You brought me out of George's house under false pretenses. I should have stayed. I should have poisoned myself then as I intended. And then we could all have been spared this ridiculous farce.

ZOTOV: I never have treated you dishonorably. I have always had the greatest respect and…

ZINA: More words. More ideas. Blah, blah, blah. No wonder George hated them so.

ZOTOV: Orlov didn't hate ideas. He feared them. He is a coward.

ZINA: Fine. Orlov was a coward. And a liar. He betrayed me, abandoned me to my fate in St. Petersburg. But you've abandoned me here. You are not so different. But he at least wasn't afraid of his body. Or mine. It might surprise you to know that I actually enjoy fucking. Yes, it's true. Not with everyone certainly. But with a man I love. Nothing better. That includes ideas and words.

ZOTOV: Did Anton…?

ZINA: Don't drag him into this. He's as bad as the rest of you. More words. His are just on paper. With his love. You all revolt me!

ZOTOV: Why are you saying all these things?

ZINA: I'm speaking only the truth. I have no time for lies. So tired of you all. So very tired. I can't stand it. You are nothing but a weak, sniveling, pathetic, half-witted gimpy little half-man. To think I thought you were my salvation. You don't even seem to know how to die quickly. You've had one foot in the grave ever since you started playing that silly valet charade at George's. How hard is it to let go, Vladimir? How hard? Not hard at all. I promise you.

ZOTOV: I know you've lost a lot of respect for me, and that all seems bleak to you now, but I promise…

ZINA: Stop! No more promises! Just no more. I hate you so much, I can't stand the sight of you. Why did you take me here? Why? Why? Why?

ZOTOV: Zina, marry me.

ZINA: What?!

ZOTOV: Zina, I've come to the realization that I want to spend the rest of my life with you. I just could never say it. Couldn't express it. Forgive me for that. I have seen so much. Lost so much. I believe you and I have a destiny together.

ZINA: I am not moved to tears.

ZOTOV: I want to embrace life. I want to do that with you. I have to do that with you. I want the warmth we once had.

ZINA: So you love life?

ZOTOV: Yes.

ZINA: Well, I hate it. Our paths lie apart.

(She exits. Blackout. The sound of a baby crying. Lights up. ZINA is lying down, no longer pregnant. CHEKHOV cradles a small baby in his arms.)

CHEKHOV: It's a boy.

ZINA: Let me see him. He's ugly.

CHEKHOV: Zina!

ZINA: It's a joke, doctor. A joke. Is he healthy?

CHEKHOV: He has all his fingers and all of his toes.

ZINA: Will you please tell Vladimir? And bring me some water.

CHEKHOV: Of course. *(Exits.)*

ZINA: Hello, there. Welcome to the world. It doesn't get any better than this. My mother died when I was twelve. It took me years before I could forgive her. It's terrible to be a child like that and watch your mother die. Slowly. Don't worry. I won't let that happen to you. Out there is the ocean. And that's the sky. And those are boats. The water is so still, it looks like a painting. Isn't it pretty? But it isn't all pretty. There are wars. There are wars all the time. And hunger. And death. And betrayal. Things that they should never make you have to face. You know, I think you look like George. It's all right. I'll forgive you. And you need to forgive me. You were born. That will get George. But you can never live with him. The thought of you becoming like him. I couldn't bear that. You will have to go and live in an orphanage. Grow up and be French. That will get George's father. Do you see?

(CHEKHOV returns with the water.)

CHEKHOV: How are we doing?

ZINA: All right. I'm tired.

CHEKHOV: You were in labor for five hours. Do you mind? Vladimir wants to see the baby. I told him I would come and show him from the doorway. I don't think the child should be any closer to him than that.

ZINA: Go ahead.

CHEKHOV: Then I will take him to the hotel nurse and have him washed. You get some sleep.

ZINA: Take your time.

(CHEKHOV exits. ZINA takes out a small bottle filled with liquid. She administers a few drops of the substance to her glass of water.)

ZINA: To Hell with it all. *(She drinks the water, lies back down, and dies.)*

(The lights change. CHEKHOV reenters with the baby.)

CHEKHOV: The nurse gave him a good washing and… Oh my God. Zina! Zina! *(He rushes to her side and examines her. He finds the bottle.)* No. My God, no.

(ZOTOV enters.)

ZOTOV: What is it? Anton, what is it? Is she sick? Will she be all right?

CHEKHOV: She's dead. Poison. Here. Try and be careful not to breathe on him.

ZOTOV: What…? Why are you giving me…?

CHEKHOV: You're the closest thing this child has to a parent right now. *(He covers ZINA with a sheet.)*

ZOTOV: I can't be a parent.

CHEKHOV: And I can?!

ZOTOV: I suppose I should tell George. He is the father after all.

CHEKHOV: I really do miss the taste of borscht.

ZOTOV: What?

CHEKHOV: I think it's time for me to go home.

ZOTOV: Did she name her child?

CHEKHOV: No.

ZOTOV: Then I will call him Anton.

(CHEKHOV turns and faces the audience.)

CHEKHOV: So, I returned to St. Petersburg, my practice, and my scribblings. Zotov didn't tell Orlov immediately. He stayed on in France for another year as young Anton's father. But the consumption was relentless. When he realized that he could no longer delay the inevitable, he returned to St. Petersburg as well and once again stood in the door of George Orlov's apartment.

(ORLOV enters, stepping over ZINA. OLGA stands at the side.)

ORLOV: Ah, Ivan, so good to see you again. Or should I say, "my lord"?

ZOTOV: That's not important.

ORLOV: No, I don't suppose it is. Cough, I see, hasn't gotten any better.

ZOTOV: No. No, it hasn't.

ORLOV: Where are my manners? Tea?

ZOTOV: No, no thank you.

ORLOV: And what do you have there?

ZOTOV: Zina's son. Your son.

ORLOV: My son, you say?

ZOTOV: Yes, George.

ORLOV: How interesting. And I take it Zina is dead?

ZOTOV: She poisoned herself.

(OLGA stifles a laugh.)

ORLOV: Curious. The woman always did have a gift for the melodramatic. So, what do you intend to do with that?

ZOTOV: I want to leave him with you.

ORLOV: Olga, you have some experience with these things. Go take it.

(OLGA does so.)

ORLOV: Well? How is it?

OLGA: It smells.

ZOTOV: The trip was long.

OLGA: Oh, he looks like you, sir.

ORLOV: Well, isn't that touching. Actually, Zotov, you were quite right. We did have a good laugh at your letter. You can imagine poor old Gruzin when he thought he was going to be assassinated by a dangerous revolutionary. We talked about it for quite some time.

ZOTOV: And how is Gruzin?

ORLOV: He's dead. Died last year of pneumonia. It's a great loss.

ZOTOV: Yes, I'm sure it is.

ORLOV: Well, I would ask you to dinner, but I think that would be inappropriate.

ZOTOV: Just look after the child.

ORLOV: Well, I will do my best. I'm sure there is some sort of nunnery or the like that would take him. It can't be that difficult. Or give it to Olga. She just lost one herself, you know.

OLGA: Oh, would you, sir?

ORLOV: Good day, Vladimir.

ZOTOV: Good day, George.

(OLGA and ORLOV start to exit, ORLOV stepping over ZINA as he goes. ZOTOV runs after them and takes the child in his arms. OLGA starts to fight him at first, but ORLOV stops her. OLGA and ORLOV exit. NANNY enters.)

NANNY: This is how you treat my precious. My Zina. My God, man. Are you so blind? No one can be as happy as she pretended to be. She was trying, trying so hard to find just a little tiny moment of true joy. Well, I guess she never knew it. Thanks to Boris and George and you. You know, Boris already has another wife. And her dowry is even larger than Zina's. With a country estate in the south. And George, well, he's still George. And you. Look at you. Look at what you have become. A nothing. A fading shadow. What was it all for, Vladimir? What was it all for?

(ZOTOV hands her the child. Beat. She exits. ZOTOV lies down.)

CHEKHOV: Two weeks later, Zotov could no longer stand the agony. So he checked himself into the hospital where I was a resident. He began to take the laudanum as recommended.

ZOTOV: How much longer?

CHEKHOV: Not long.

ZOTOV: My life is a failure, isn't it?

CHEKHOV: I don't think you could say that.

ZOTOV: I accomplished nothing. I have nothing. I have no one.

CHEKHOV: You made the right decision about Zina's boy. That is enough. More than enough.

ZOTOV: You will be the only one at my funeral.

CHEKHOV: And a couple of Okhrana agents.

ZOTOV: I doubt they will even bother.

CHEKHOV: How's the pain?

ZOTOV: I can't feel anything.

CHEKHOV: That's good.

ZOTOV: Yes, good.

CHEKHOV: Winter will be here soon.

ZOTOV: Will you stay with me?

CHEKHOV: Yes.

ZOTOV: Goodbye, old friend.

CHEKHOV: Goodbye.

ZOTOV: Please give my love to…

(He dies. CHEKHOV weeps silently over ZOTOV for a few moments, then he slowly covers him with a sheet. EPHIM as the OKHRANA AGENT enters. He pulls out a gun, but he then trips over himself.)

CHEKHOV: You're too late… Night has fallen on St. Petersburg. Some people, like the Orlovs, sleep soundly. Others stare at the ceiling and plot and plan for their day. Their time. When they think they can be the one who makes a difference. That their lives will have more meaning than most. That they will achieve something of greatness. They dream the dreams of Zotov and Zina and thousands who have gone before them. And some, well some, look to dream under another night sky.

(NANNY, with child in her arms, enters.)

NANNY: Yes, one adult, one child. To New York City. One way only.

CHEKHOV: Tonight, it is quiet in the heart of St. Petersburg. Is it quiet in your heart? Thus concludes our play!

(The ACTORS all enter to take their curtain calls. EPHIM breaks from the group, takes off his coat, grabs some bread, and brings it back to CHEKHOV.)

DORA: The play's over.

KARP: Yes.

CHEKHOV: Yes.

DORA: I think that… please join us for some supper.

CHEKHOV: I'm sure the company would appreciate it.

DORA: Thank you.

EPHIM: Can…can I join you?

KARP: It's a dangerous life.

CHEKHOV: There is little time for theatre in Chechnya anymore. Groznya is fallen. You will have to travel far to find an audience. And I doubt the Army will look on you favorably.

EPHIM: So?

DORA: Please, don't take my boy.

KARP: *Our* boy.

CHEKHOV: These are actors. No one will force him to do what he doesn't want to do.

EPHIM: Please, Mother. There's nothing here. Not anymore. This is something for me. That I want to do. It is time for me to go.

DORA: Well, you'll stay the night, won't you? We can still talk about this in the morning.

SASHA: Hey, less talk, more food.

DORA: Yes, yes, of course. I'm starving, too. Let's eat. Come. Come.

(She and EPHIM exit.)

KARP: A fine piece of work. But I don't believe you're Chekhov.

CHEKHOV: As you will.

KARP: That's all you have to say?

CHEKHOV: Did you believe in the miracle of the play?

KARP: Yes.

CHEKHOV: Then that is all that really matters. (Picks up a script.) This is how I truly live.

(Explosions all around. EVERYONE runs on. The ACTING COMPANY quickly packs their props and costumes into the wagon and starts to run off.)

KARP: Oh, no! Do you think they could use a manager? And my Dora is an excellent cook and seamstress.

CHEKHOV: A theatre company can always use extra hands.

KARP: Well, what are we waiting for then?

(They run off. The only one left on stage is CHEKHOV.)

CHEKHOV: Such a waste. Such a terrible, terrible waste. Will our descendants a hundred years from now, for whom we're clearing the way, remember to give us a kind word?

(The playing area begins to collapse. He walks off separately into the mist.)

(THE END.)

THE BROTHERS KARAMAZOV PARTS I AND II

From the Novel by Fyodor Dostoevsky

Adapted by Alexander Harrington

ALEXANDER HARRINGTON was born in New York on March 23, 1968, and grew up in Greenwich Village and Larchmont, New York. He has a BA in English from Columbia University, and an MFA in theatre from Louisiana State University. Harrington's theatre debut came at age nine, when he performed in Jean Anouilh's *Traveler Without Luggage* at Soho Rep. He made his New York directing debut with Louis Coxe and Robert Chapman's stage adaptation of Herman Melville's *Billy Budd*, which performed at the Westbeth Theatre Center and then moved to Circle in the Square Downtown. Prior to *The Brothers Karamazov*, he adapted and directed *The Kiss*, adapted from the Chekhov story, and *The Philosopher*, adapted from the chapter in Sherwood Anderson's *Winesburg, Ohio* (both 1996, Lincoln Center Theater Directors Lab/The Culture Project). Other directing credits include *Agamemnon* (1997, La MaMa), *Richard II* (2000, The Eleventh Hour Theatre Company/HERE), *Henry V*, and *Henry IV, Parts 1 & 2* (1999 and 2001, the Eleventh Hour Theatre Company/La MaMa). Harrington just finished directing Seamus Heaney's adaptation of *Antigone, The Burial at Thebes*, at Clemson University, which he and The Eleventh Hour will be mounting at La MaMa in January and February 2007. He will also be staging *Henry V* at Clemson in the fall. Harrington splits his time between New York City and Central, South Carolina.

The Brothers Karamazov, Part I, was first presented by The Eleventh Hour Theatre Company and the Culture Project on February 6, 2003, at 45 Below, New York City, with the following cast and credits:

> Ensemble: Lisa Altomare, Frank Anderson, Steven L. Barron, Zack Bleckner, Joel Carino, David Fraioli, Kenneth Fuchs, Jennifer Gibbs, Robert Molossi, Stephen Reyes, Ken Schachtman, Gregory Sims, Greta Storace, Yaakov Sullivan, Sorrel Tomlinson, Jim Williams

> Directed by: Alexander Harrington
> Sets and Lighting: Tony Penna
> Costumes: Jerome Parker and Jocelyn Melechinsky
> Music: The Russian Duo (Tamara Volskaya and Anatoly Trofimov)
> Fight Choreographer: J. David Brimmer
> Production Stage Manager: Rosie Norman

The Brothers Karamazov, Part II, was first presented by The Eleventh Hour Theatre Company on January 2, 2004, at La MaMa E.T.C., New York City (Ellen Stewart, Artistic Director) with the following cast and credits:

> Ensemble: Gary Andrews, Steven L. Barron, "Buster," Anthony Cataldo, Stafford Clark-Price, J. Anthony Crane, Alessio Franko, Tony Hagopian, Jim Iseman III, Danielle Langlois, Christopher Lukas, J.M. McDonough, Christopher Pollard Meyer, Winslow Mohr, George Morafetis, Peter Oliver, Jennifer Opalacz, Margo Skinner, Yaakov Sullivan, Sorrel Tomlinson

> Gypsy Dancers and Musicians: Svetlana Yankavsky, Elena Raffloer, Vasili Romani, Shumojyeh, Gabriel Yakubov

> Directed by: Alexander Harrington
> Sets and Lighting: Tony Penna
> Costumes: Rebecca J. Bernstein
> Music: The Russian Duo (Tamara Volskaya and Anatoly Trofimov)
> Fight Choreographer: J. David Brimmer
> Animals: William Berloni
> Production Stage Manager: Erica E. Conrad

THE BROTHERS KARAMAZOV
PART I

CAST LIST*

The Karamazov Family

FYODOR PAVLOVICH KARAMAZOV: fifty-five, a landowner and moneylender

DMITRY FYODOROVICH KARAMAZOV (MITYA): twenty-eight, Fyodor's son by his first marriage, a former army officer

IVAN FYODOROVICH KARAMAZOV: twenty-three, Fyodor's older son by his second marriage, an intellectual of some repute

ALEXEI FYODOROVICH KARAMAZOV (ALYOSHA): nineteen, Fyodor's younger son by his second marriage, a novice in a monastery

PYOTR ALEXANDROVICH MIUSOV: forties–fifties, cousin of Fyodor's first wife, a wealthy landowner

The Karamazov Servants

GRIGORY VASILIEVICH KUTUZOV: fifties–seventies, Fyodor's freed serf

SMERDYAKOV (PAVEL FYODOROVICH): twenty-four, Fyodor's cook and probably his illegitimate son, raised by Grigory

The Residents of the Monastery

THE ELDER ZOSIMA: fifties–seventies, spiritual guide to the monks
FATHER PAISII: fifties–seventies, a senior monk
FATHER FERAPONT: fifties–seventies, a hermit
FATHER IOSIF: fifties–seventies, the monastery librarian
MONK 1: a priest
MONK 2
MONK 3
MIKHAIL OSPIPOVICH RAKITIN (MISHA, RAKITKA): twenties, a divinity student, cousin of Grushenka

Visitors to the Monastery

MAXIMOV: forties–sixties, a penniless landowner
PEASANT WOMAN 1
PEASANT WOMAN 2
MERCHANT 1
MERCHANT 2

The Women

KATERINA IVANOVNA VERKHOVSTEVA (KATYA): early twenties, Dmitry's fiancée, a wealthy heiress

AGRAFENA ALEXANDROVNA SVETLOVA (GRUSHENKA): twenty-two, kept woman of a local merchant, moneylender, and partner of Fyodor's

The Khokhalakov Family

MADAME KHOKHALAKOVA (KATERINA OSIPOVNA): forties–fifties, a rich widow, friend of Katerina Ivanovna

LISE KHOKHALAKOVA: fourteen, her daughter, childhood friend of Alyosha

The Snegiryov Family

NIKOLAI ILYICH SNEGIRYOV: forties–fifties, a disgraced army captain, hired lackey of Fyodor and Grushenka

ARINA PETROVNA SNEGIRYOVA (MAMA): forties–fifties, his wife, crippled and mentally ill

VARVARA NIKOLAEVNA SNEGIRYOVA: twenties–thirties, his older daughter, forced to leave school due to lack of money

NINA NIKOLAEVNA SNEGIRYOVA (NINOCHKA): twenties, his younger daughter, a hunchback

ILYA NIKOLAEVICH SNEGIRYOV (ILYUSHA): eleven, his son and youngest child

"The Grand Inquisitor"

THE GRAND INQUISITOR: fifties–seventies   CHRIST

The Wedding at Cana of Galilee

THE VIRGIN MARY   CHRIST
THE GOVERNOR OF THE FEAST   THE BRIDE
THE GROOM   OTHERS
FENYA: Grushenka's maid   A WAITER

---

*Roles can be doubled.

ACT I
Scene 1

FATHER ZOSIMA's cell. MAXIMOV is onstage. FATHER PAISII enters from one side of the stage; FYODOR and IVAN KARAMAZOV and MIUSOV enter from another.

PAISII: Good morning, gentlemen, I am Father Paisii. Welcome to our monastery.

FYODOR: *Bonjour, mon bon père, bonjour,* an honor and a privilege to meet you, Reverend Father. Allow me to introduce myself: I am Fyodor Pavlovich Karamazov, father of that sainted boy who has become so attached to the Elder Zosima, the novice Alexei, my sweet little Alyosha. This is my other dutiful son, Ivan Fyodorovich. My oldest son, that serpent's tooth, Dmitry Fyodorovich Karamazov is, alas, late. And this is my beloved relative, Pyotr Alexandrovich Miusov.

MIUSOV: I am not and have never been your relative, Fyodor Pavlovich.

FYODOR: Tut, tut, tut, tut, tut, tut, tut—try as you might to deny it, Pyotr Alexandrovich, you are the cousin—the kissing cousin—of my dearly departed first wife, mother of that ungrateful whelp, Mitya. *(Noticing MAXIMOV.)* Who the hell is he?

MAXIMOV: My name is Maximov, good sir, I have just had an audience with the Elder Zosima.

FYODOR: Really? What's he like?

MAXIMOV: *Un chevalier parfait.*

MIUSOV: Who's a *chevalier?*

MAXIMOV: The Elder. Such a charming, witty man, the pride and glory of the monastery. Oh, an elder such as Zosima…

PAISII: Gentlemen, the Elder will be with you shortly, he has asked you to wait here, in his cell. After your visit with the Elder, the Father Superior invites you to dinner, if possible, no later than one o'clock. And you, too, Mr. Maximov.

MAXIMOV: Oh, delighted and honored, delighted and honored. The Father Superior is really too kind.

FYODOR: I, for one, will certainly be there, I wouldn't miss it for the world. And let me say, we have all promised to behave while we are here, even you, Pyotr Alexandrovich. Will you be joining us for lunch?

MIUSOV: Of course I will, since I am here to study monastery customs.

FYODOR: What unmitigated codswallop! You are here to settle your filthy lawsuit. I ask you, Reverend Father, what kind of a man sues a monastery? But then, of course, Miusov here is a champion of liberalism.

MIUSOV: And you are here to have the Elder settle that disgusting business between you and your son Dmitry…

PAISII: If you gentlemen will excuse me, I must go attend upon the Father Superior. The Elder will be with you shortly, please sit down.

MAXIMOV: If you gentlemen will excuse me, I will go straight to the Father Superior's, since I have already had my audience with the Elder.

PAISII: Well, the Father Superior is rather busy right now. But of course, it's up to you, sir… If you will follow me.

Scene 2

A yard outside the hermitage wall. ZOSIMA and ALYOSHA stand in one corner, TWO PEASANT WOMEN kneel in another.

ZOSIMA: How many have come today, Alyosha?

ALYOSHA: There are two peasant women waiting outside the hermitage, Father, and Madame Khokhalakova has returned with her daughter. They're upstairs in the gallery.

ZOSIMA: Let us first see these women who have traveled so far.

(ZOSIMA and ALYOSHA cross to the WOMEN. ZOSIMA addresses PEASANT WOMAN 1.)

ZOSIMA: Where do you come from, my child?

PEASANT WOMAN 1: From far, far away, Holy Father, five hundred miles away, far, far away.

ZOSIMA: Why are you weeping, my child?

PEASANT WOMAN 1: I'm sad about my little boy, Father… He would have been three in two months. I can't get him out of my head. And so I came to you. I'm sure my husband Nikita has taken to drink without me. I've been away from home for more than two months. How will I be able to live with my Nikita, now?

ZOSIMA: You come to me for comfort, but that is not what you need. You need to weep, my daughter. Weep—weep, daughter. But every time you do, remember that your little son is one of God's angels. In the end your weeping will turn into quiet joy and your bitter tears will become tears of quiet tenderness, which will cleanse your heart of sin. And now, go back to your husband and look after him. If your little boy sees from up there that you have abandoned his father, he will weep for both of you. Why must you disturb his bliss?

PEASANT WOMAN 1: I will go, Father.

ZOSIMA: *(Blesses PEASANT WOMAN 1 and turns to PEASANT WOMAN 2.)* What is it you wish, my dear?

PEASANT WOMAN 2: Take a load off my soul, Father. I have sinned, my father, and I am afraid of my sin.

ZOSIMA: What is your sin, daughter?

PEASANT WOMAN 2: I've been a widow for two years. It was hard being married to him. He was old and beat me terribly. So, when he lay sick, I looked at him and I said to myself: What if he gets better, he'll get up and then what? That is when the thought came to me…

ZOSIMA: Wait, daughter.

(He beckons to her and she whispers to him.)

ZOSIMA: Over two years ago?

PEASANT WOMAN 2: Yes. At first, I didn't think about it much, but now I've got sick and it bothers me.

ZOSIMA: Have you already confessed this to a priest?

PEASANT WOMAN 2: I have. Twice I've confessed it.

ZOSIMA: Have you been admitted to holy communion?

PEASANT WOMAN 2: Yes, but I am still afraid, Father. I'm afraid to die.

ZOSIMA: Don't be afraid of anything ever and do not grieve. As long as your repentance does not weaken, God will forgive everything. There is not, there cannot be, a sin on Earth that God will not forgive the truly repentant. Forgive your departed husband all the harm he did you. Forgive him his sin and love him. If you love, you are with God; love is an infinite treasure, it can buy the whole world and redeem not only your sins, but the sins of all people. So go and fear no more.

SCENE 3

FATHER ZOSIMA's cell.

MIUSOV: What an awful bore that little Maximov fellow was.

FYODOR: He reminds me of von Sohn.

MIUSOV: Who, pray tell, is von Sohn?

FYODOR: Von Sohn was—how shall I put it Pyotr Alexandrovich—an *habitué* of houses of ill fame. Well, the ladies of one these houses loved the fellow to death—literally—they smothered him with a pillow and took every kopek on him. The adorable little sluts then packed him into a crate and shipped him from Petersburg to Moscow by freight train. But don't think this was done without any feeling for their poor little von Sohn. As they were nailing up the crate, the harlots said farewell to their little friend by singing and playing the piano.

MIUSOV: And that little asexual dwarf reminds you of von Sohn?

FYODOR: Let's just say surprising things lurk in the human heart and I have an eye for such things. That fellow is a von Sohn.

SCENE 4

A room above the yard outside the hermitage. MADAME KHOKHALAKOVA and LISE are seated, LISE in a wheelchair. ZOSIMA and ALYOSHA enter.

ZOSIMA: How does your daughter feel today, Madame Khokhalakova? I understand you wanted to speak to me again?

KHOKHALAKOVA: Oh, I begged for an interview! I requested it most insistently, I was prepared to get down on my knees, to stay kneeling before your window for three whole days. We have come, great healer, to express our fervent gratitude. Why, you have cured my Lise, cured her completely. And how? Just by saying a prayer over her last Thursday and laying your hands on her. We are anxious to kiss those hands, to pour out our feelings and our veneration.

ZOSIMA: But she's still in her wheelchair.

KHOKHALAKOVA: But she's had no fever for the past two nights, none at all. Today, she actually demanded to get up, to stand on her feet. And she did stand up for a whole minute. I called in the local doctor, Herzenstube, and he just spread his arms wide in amazement and said, "I'm stunned. I just can't explain it." And you expected us not to disturb you as though we could keep ourselves from flying over here to thank you. Thank the Holy Elder, Lise.

LISE: Thank you, Father Zosima.

KHOKHALAKOVA: Now, Holy Father, what about you? How's your health?

ZOSIMA: I'm a sick man and my days are numbered.

KHOKHALAKOVA: Oh no, that cannot be! You look so cheerful.

ZOSIMA: Human beings were created to be happy; I am only carrying out God's will on Earth.

KHOKHALAKOVA: I, alas, am not cheerful. I suffer, forgive me, I suffer.

ZOSIMA: What makes you suffer so?

KHOKHALAKOVA: I suffer from lack of faith. You see, I love mankind so much that, believe it or not, there are moments when I would like to give up everything, abandon Lise, and become a hospital nurse. No wounds, no oozing infected sores, no bloody maimed stumps that once were limbs could frighten me away from those poor suffering souls. I would dress their wounds, I would wash their sores with my own hands, I would kiss those sores. But if one of those little cripples didn't show me enough gratitude, I don't think I could take it. I want to be praised and paid for love with love. Otherwise, I'm quite incapable of loving anyone.

ZOSIMA: You are not alone. For all of us it is easy to love mankind; it is very hard to love individual people, up close. That this worries you at all reveals that your heart is capable of love. However, if you have spoken frankly to me only to make me praise you for your sincerity, then, of course, you will fail to accomplish true acts of love.

KHOKHALAKOVA: I feel completely crushed. This very second I realized that, just as you say, I was expecting you to praise me for my sincerity. You brought out what was within me. You saw it and you have shown it to me.

ZOSIMA: If you really mean what you say now, then you are on the right path and what is most important is to avoid lying—above all, lying to yourself. *(Turns to LISE.)* Lise, why are you laughing?

LISE: It's Alyosha's fault. He looks so silly in that dress.

KHOKHALAKOVA: Lise! You shouldn't make fun of Alexei like that.

LISE: Well, why doesn't he come to visit us anymore? When he came to this monastery, he said that he'd never forget me and that he'd visit me often and that we'd be friends forever—forever. Now he seems to be afraid of me, like I'm going to eat him or something. Why doesn't he talk? Why won't he come and see us? It's not that you won't let him. We know that he goes where he likes. Well, I guess he's too busy saving his soul to think of me.

KHOKHALAKOVA: Lise, stop it this instant and give Alexei the message you have for him.

LISE: Katerina Ivanovna asked me to give this to you. She wants you to come and see her soon and without fail.

ALYOSHA: Why me? I've only met her once.

KHOKHALAKOVA: It's about that business with your brother Dmitry. She's such a noble, exceptional person. What she has suffered is appalling, just appalling.

ALYOSHA: Alright, I'll go and see her.

ZOSIMA: And I'll see that he comes to visit you, too, Lise. But in the meantime, Alyosha, we must hurry. We mustn't keep your father and your brothers waiting.

Scene 5

ZOSIMA's cell and a yard outside.

FYODOR: You know, Pyotr Alexandrovich, I know of a monastery in another province where they have a little settlement adjoining the grounds. Now this little settlement is home to a certain group of women known as the monastery wives, if you get my meaning.

MIUSOV: If you persist in talking like this when the Elder arrives, I'm leaving.

FYODOR: And if you leave, Pyotr Alexandrovich, I will leave. I will follow you to the ends of the Earth.

All day, I've felt a bond growing between us, I feel that we are inseparable.

MIUSOV: This is really too much.

(ZOSIMA, ALYOSHA, PAISII, and RAKITIN enter.)

ZOSIMA: Welcome, gentlemen. I am Father Zosima.

FYODOR: Holy Elder, allow me to bow before you. I am Fyodor Pavlovich Karamazov, father of your dear protégé, Alexei Fyodorovich Karamazov. I humbly ask for your blessing.

(ZOSIMA blesses him.)

MIUSOV: Good afternoon. I am Pyotr Alexandrovich Miusov. I am here to see the Father Superior regarding my land which adjoins your monastery and he graciously asked me to join the Karamazovs in meeting with you.

(He bows. ZOSIMA tries to bless him, but he walks away.)

IVAN: Good afternoon, Father. I am Ivan Fyodorovich Karamazov.

ZOSIMA: The pleasure is all mine.

(IVAN bows. ZOSIMA tries to bless him, but he walks away.)

ZOSIMA: I believe you've all met Father Paisii and, of course, you know Alyosha. This is Mikhail Ospipovich Rakitin. He's a divinity student, spending some time here with us. Please be seated, gentlemen.

(Church bells sound noon.)

FYODOR: Noon on the dot and still no sign of my son Dmitry. I apologize for him, Holy Elder. I, on the other hand, am always punctual. Punctuality is the courtesy of kings.

MIUSOV: Well, whatever else you may be, you are certainly no king.

FYODOR: Believe it or not, Pyotr Alexandrovich, I was aware of that myself. *(To ZOSIMA.)* Your Reverence, you have before you a buffoon, yea verily a buffoon. You see, your Reverence, I talk nonsense and play the clown to please people. But somehow, it never seems to work out. Once—many, many years ago—I said to a very important man, "Your wife, sir, is ticklish," meaning she was very moral, would not tolerate anything off color. This important personage was, however, a rather literal fellow and he said, "What would you know about it, have you tickled her?" Well, I couldn't resist an opening like that and I said, "Well, yes, as a matter of fact, I have." Well, the fellow gave me quite a tickling, indeed.

MIUSOV: Please forgive me, gentlemen, I am afraid that you may think that I have some part in this ridiculous farce and…

ZOSIMA: Please, don't worry, think nothing of it. Believe me, I particularly appreciate having you as my guest.

FYODOR: Oh, Great Elder! Speak! Tell me if I have offended you with my exuberance.

ZOSIMA: You too, sir, do not be uncomfortable. There is nothing to worry about; please feel completely at home and above all do not be ashamed of yourself, for that is what causes all the trouble.

FYODOR: Completely at home? You mean be my natural self? You are too kind and I accept, although you really shouldn't encourage me to be my natural self. No, not even I would let myself go entirely, although I am not as bad as the stories would have it. The stories about my raping the local idiot, that God's fool, Reeking Lizaveta. No, I am not the father of her orphan son, my cook, Smerdyakov, as the gossip-mongers would have it. Yes, I am referring to you, Pyotr Alexandrovich. As for you, most holy being. Blessed be the womb that bore thee, blessed be the paps that gave thee suck—especially the paps. You see into my soul. Shame is the cause of all my trouble. People like Pyotr Alexandrovich here think I am the lowest of the low, they think that I am a buffoon. Alright then, I'll act like a buffoon because I don't care; every single one of them is lower than me. If only I could feel that people thought me a nice, intelligent fellow, I'd be the kindest of men. Oh, teacher! What should I do to gain eternal life?

ZOSIMA: You have known that for a long time for you are an intelligent man. Stop lying, above all to yourself; for there is the source of the shame you feel. A man who lies to himself can take offense whenever he wishes, for there are times when it is rather pleasant to feel wronged, don't you agree? And so you invent offenses, you lie for the sheer beauty of it. Eventually, even though no one has done you wrong, you feel genuinely offended. But please get off your knees and sit down. You know very well your keeling is an insincere gesture. It's a lie.

FYODOR: You are right, so very right. It is very pleasant to feel wronged. It is not only pleasurable, it is aestheti-

cally satisfying. And so I have lied all my life, every day and every hour. But now I'll remain silent for the rest of the time. I'll sit in my chair and I won't say one word. It's your turn to have the floor now, Pyotr Alexandrovich. You will be the most important person in the room for the next ten minutes.

MIUSOV: Well, I don't know what to say. I imagine Dmitry Fyodorovich will be here shortly and you're really here to talk to him, to him and Fyodor Pavlovich.

FYODOR: Why don't you entertain us with some of your liberal ideas, Pyotr Alexdrovich.

MIUSOV: Well, if you insist. As some of you may know, I was in Paris in 1848…

PAISII: Oh, you know, this reminds me—Mr. Karamazov's son here, Ivan Fyodorovich, published a very interesting article before he left Moscow to visit our little town. I happened to read it recently. He wrote it in response to a book by a prominent churchman on the jurisdiction of the ecclesiastical courts.

ZOSIMA: I haven't read the article myself, but I have heard about it.

PAISII: He takes an approach that you would not expect from one of our young intellectuals. Apparently, he completely rejects the separation of church and state.

ZOSIMA: In what sense?

IVAN: The churchman against whom I argue contends that the church has a clearly defined place within the state. I answer that, on the contrary, instead of occupying some little corner within the state, the church should contain the state. And if the church is to achieve the redemption of mankind, it has no choice but to make this its primary goal.

MIUSOV: That's sheer ultramontanism.

IVAN: Just the opposite. Ultramontanism holds that the church should become the state. That would be reverse evolution, a superior being transforming into an inferior one. In the article, I argue that the state should evolve into the church. The state as we know it would cease to exist.

MIUSOV: So, in your vision, the church would be judging criminals and sentencing them to flogging, hard labor, perhaps even death?

IVAN: That would all become unnecessary. The church would simply excommunicate the criminal.

MIUSOV: What kind of deterrent would that be?

ZOSIMA: The only true deterrent. Physical punishment leaves the conscience untouched. You see, most Russian criminals believe in God. Physical punishment will never stop them from committing a crime, for they can say, "I am an enemy of the state, I am not an enemy of Christ." But if excommunication were the punishment, the criminal would see his crime as a sin against Christ. He would be forced to examine his own conscience and in doing so, find salvation. But as things stand today, we cannot excommunicate the criminal, for the church is not the state and the state punishes the criminal cruelly. We cannot add to that punishment; we must follow Christ's example and act with charity toward the criminal. But the time will come when the pagan state is transfigured into one universal church, and so be it so be it, if only at the end of time, for it has been ordained.

PAISII: So be it. So be it.

MIUSOV: Well, this is just a utopian dream. In many ways, you people are no different from the socialists.

ZOSIMA: Oh no, you are quite mistaken. The goal of socialism is to bring Heaven down to Earth. We believe that while we are on Earth, we must strive towards Heaven.

(DMITRY rushes in.)

DMITRY: Please forgive me for keeping you waiting. My father's servant Smerdyakov told me that the meeting was set for one p.m. and now I find out…

ZOSIMA: Think nothing of it. Don't let it worry you.

DMITRY: Thank you very much. I should have known that a man of such kindness would understand.

(DMITRY bows to ZOSIMA and accepts his blessing.)

ZOSIMA: Please be seated.

PAISII: Yes, Mr. Miusov was just accusing us of being socialists.

MIUSOV: Please forgive me if I drop the subject. Let me, instead, tell you a little story about Ivan Fyodorovich here. Not more than five days ago at a dinner party, he solemnly declared that there was nothing in nature to make a man love his fellow man and if there was any love on Earth, it stemmed from man's belief in immortality. Furthermore, if there were no immortality, nothing would be immoral and everything would be permitted. He went on to say that for every individual who does not believe in God and immortality—such as himself and those present at the dinner party—natural law and logic dictate absolute selfishness, carried even to the extent of cannibalism. From this paradox draw your own conclusions as to what other declarations can be expected from our dear eccentric and lover of paradox, Ivan Fyodorovich Karamazov.

DMITRY: Just a minute. Let me make sure I've got this straight. If there is no God and no immortality, everything is permitted?

PAISII: Exactly.

DMITRY: Good. I'll remember that.

ZOSIMA: Ivan Fyodorovich, do you really believe this would happen if men lost their faith in the immortality of the soul?

IVAN: Yes.

ZOSIMA: Then you are either blissfully happy or deeply unhappy.

IVAN: Why unhappy?

ZOSIMA: Because I doubt that you believe in immortality or even what you wrote in your own article about church and state.

IVAN: You may be right, but I wasn't joking when I wrote all that.

ZOSIMA: No, you weren't joking. You haven't resolved this problem in your heart and it torments you. And so you distract yourself from your suffering by playing with your suffering. You write your magazine articles and have your dinner party conversations, but you are still in pain. You are deeply unhappy because you cannot find an answer and you need an answer.

IVAN: But can there be an answer for me? Can there be an affirmative answer?

ZOSIMA: If the answer cannot be affirmative, it can never be negative, either. You know that and that is what torments you. But thank your Creator for giving you a heart so noble that it can experience such torment. May God grant that you find the answer and may He bless you on your journey through life.

(IVAN goes to ZOSIMA, receives his blessing, and kisses his hand.)

FYODOR: Divine and Holy Elder! This is my son, flesh of my flesh. We are like the family from Schiller's play

The Robbers. This is my most dutiful Karl Moor, while this other, Dmitry Fyodorovich, against whom I am seeking justice, is my most disrespectful Franz Moor, and I myself am the reigning Count von Moor. Judge us and save us. We ask not only your prayers, but your prophetic insights.

DMITRY: Enough of this farce! Please forgive me Reverend Father, I am an ignorant man who does not even know how to address you… You have been deceived. All my father wants is an embarrassing scene.

FYODOR: You all accuse me. You, Mitya, my own son, and you Miusov. You all say I am picking my children's pockets, that I have cheated Dmitry here out of the inheritance his mother left him. Well, produce your evidence. I have all the legal documents and every receipt you signed each time I sent you money. Why don't you add them up? I'll tell you why. It is because they will prove that it is not I who owe money to Dmitry, but Dmitry who owes money to me. He spends money like water. In the army, he spent thousands seducing respectable young ladies. He seduced the daughter of his commanding officer. Yes, he offered to marry her, but now he is running around after a certain local beauty in front of her very eyes.

DMITRY: Don't you dare besmirch the name of that most honorable girl in my presence.

FYODOR: Mitya! Mitya! Does your father's blessing mean nothing to you? What if I put my curse on you?

DMITRY: You shameless hypocrite. You call yourself my father? When my mother left you, you abandoned me to run wild in your yard and be looked after by the servants. Mr. Miusov had to come and rescue me, only to hand me off from relative to relative. And you abandoned Ivan and Alyosha to their mother's relatives when she died. You talk about me and that "local beauty"? Well, you're chasing after her yourself. You're jealous of me.

MIUSOV: Your Reverence, I knew nothing of the details that have come to light here…

FYODOR: Dmitry Fyodorovich Karamazov! If you were not my son, I would challenge you to a duel this very second. Pistols—at three paces—over a handkerchief.

PAISII: Shame. Shame.

DMITRY: Why should such a man live?

FYODOR: You heard him, you monks, you heard the parricide. There is the answer to your shame, Father. And what do I have to be ashamed of, anyway? That "local beauty" is perhaps holier than all of you, who are so busy saving your souls.

DMITRY: This is intolerable.

(ZOSIMA gets up and prostrates himself before DMITRY, touching his forehead to the floor. He then gets up and bows to each VISITOR.)

ZOSIMA: Forgive me. Forgive me all of you.

DMITRY: Oh, my God.

(He runs out. FYODOR, IVAN, and MIUSOV hesitate a moment and then cross out of the cell into the yard. During the following, PAISII receives ZOSIMA's blessing and exits; RAKITIN receives ZOSIMA's blessing and crosses outside the cell into the yard once MIUSOV has exited.)

FYODOR: Why did he prostrate himself like that?

MIUSOV: How can I understand what goes on in a madhouse? And speaking of madness, if you think I'm going to accompany you to that dinner at the Father Superior's, you're out of your mind.

FYODOR: Pyotr Alexandrovich, I wouldn't dream of letting you miss that dinner with the Father Superior. Please go and I wish you *bon appétit.* It is I who decline the invitation. I'll go home and eat there.

MIUSOV: This isn't just another trick of yours?

FYODOR: After what I've just done, how could I sit down to dinner with the Father Superior? Go and enjoy, my dear kinsman.

MIUSOV: I am not your kinsman.

FYODOR: Ta ta. *(Exits.)*

MIUSOV: Well, what about you, Ivan? Are you coming?

IVAN: Why not? The Father Superior sent me a personal invitation yesterday.

(IVAN exits, followed by MIUSOV. In ZOSIMA's cell—)

ZOSIMA: Go on, Alyosha, my boy, hurry to the Father Superior's. They need you there.

ALYOSHA: Allow me to stay here.

ZOSIMA: They need you more than I do. You know, my dear son, the monastery is really no place for you. When God decides the time has come for me to die, you must leave the monastery. Leave it for good.

ALYOSHA: But Father, I want to devote my life to God.

ZOSIMA: And so you shall—by going out into the world and devoting your life to your fellow men. You will marry—yes, you will—you will be of the world. You will have to go through many many things before you return. But I have no doubts about you. You will know great suffering and through that suffering you will find happiness. This is my last commandment to you: seek happiness through suffering. Remember my words, for, although we shall talk again, not only my days, but my very hours are numbered.

ALYOSHA: Father...

ZOSIMA: Let the worldly shed tears for their dead. We are happy for a father who is departing. So go now; it is time for me to pray. And stay close to your brothers—both of them.

(ALYOSHA receives ZOSIMA's blessing and crosses out of the cell.)

RAKITIN: Well, it was lovely to meet your family.

ALYOSHA: Cut it out, Misha. Besides, you knew Ivan and Dmitry long before this.

RAKITIN: Oh, yes. I've had the pleasure of being insulted by your brother Ivan.

ALYOSHA: How did he insult you?

RAKITIN: He goes around town saying that I have no intention of becoming a priest, that what I really want is to become a literary celebrity and acquire a lot of money.

ALYOSHA: You know, I think he hit the nail right on the head.

RAKITIN: Sarcasm is unbecoming to saints, Alyosha. Besides, your brother's theories are vile: if there's no immortality, there's no virtue and everything is permitted—and didn't Dmitry lap up that little tidbit. Mankind will find enough strength within itself to live for virtue's sake without believing in the immortality of the soul. We'll find it in the love of freedom, equality, and the brotherhood of man. Ivan's theory is a convenient one for scoundrels. By the way, what do you think the old man meant by banging his head on the floor?

ALYOSHA: The old man?

RAKITIN: Oh, I'm not being respectful enough. What do you think Father Zosima meant when he prostrated himself before your brother?

ALYOSHA: I don't know.

RAKITIN: The old man has a keen nose. I think he caught the scent of a crime. Your house stinks of it, Alyosha.

ALYOSHA: What crime?

RAKITIN: Don't play dumb. Between your dear brothers and your rich papa. So Father Zosima bangs his head on the floor, just in case. And later on, if anything does happen, people will say, "Ah, that saintly elder, he prophesied it. He prostrated himself before the murderer."

ALYOSHA: What murderer?

RAKITIN: What murderer? Tell me honestly—It's never occurred to you?

ALYOSHA: Well, I never actually thought it, but when you said it I realized it had occurred to me. But it will never reach that point.

RAKITIN: Oh, yes it will. Neither your father or Dmitry will be able to control their sensual passions and the next thing you know, they'll both land in a ditch.

ALYOSHA: Over that woman? Dmitry despises her.

RAKITIN: Whether he despises her or not has nothing to do with it. Dmitry has fallen in love with Grushenka's physical beauty. You can't understand this yet, but a man can fall in love with a woman's body.

ALYOSHA: I understand that very well.

RAKITIN: Maybe you do, you're a Karamazov, after all. I'd always wondered how you managed to stay a virgin for so long. You know, Grushenka asked me to bring you to her. She said she'd pull the cassock right of your back.

ALYOSHA: I forgot—you're related to her.

RAKITIN: Grushenka is no relative of mine. There are no prostitutes in my family.

ALYOSHA: She's a prostitute?

RAKITIN: She's as good as one. She's the kept woman of that debauched merchant, Samsonov.

ALYOSHA: Well, give her my regards and tell her I respectfully decline the invitation.

RAKITIN: Anyway, if even you are a sensualist underneath, that leaves little doubt about Ivan. Ivan is just waiting for your father and Dmitry to clash head on, so he can pick up the pieces and run off with Dmitry's fiancée—which he could do with Mitya's blessing. In fact, Mitya's encouraging him.

(MIUSOV comes rushing across the stage.)

MIUSOV: No! No! No! No! I can't stand it! I can't…I won't!

(He exits as FYODOR comes rushing on.)

FYODOR: Wait! Pyotr Alexandrovich! Where are you going? We're inseparable.

(FATHER PAISII and IVAN run on.)

PAISII: Mr. Karamazov…

FYODOR: No. I won't listen to another word. I am taking Alexei out of here at once. What goes on here is a scandal. You reverence the Elder Zosima as a god, everybody falling to their knees and confessing to him out loud in front of everybody else. Confession is a sacrament. It should be whispered into the priest's ear. I'm writing to the Bishop!

PAISII: Mr. Karamazov…

ALYOSHA: *(To IVAN.)* What happened?

IVAN: He came back.

FYODOR: Alyosha! You're coming home today and for good. Bring your mattress and pillow and don't you ever dare set foot here again. Well, if you'll excuse me, gentlemen, I must keep up with Pyotr Alexandrovich.

(MAXIMOV comes running on.)

MAXIMOV: Wait for me! I'm coming too! Take me with you!

FYODOR: Von Sohn! How did you manage to escape? What von Sohnish trick did you use to get away from the Father Superior? Come on. We'll go to my house for suckling pig and cognac.

(As they start to leave, IVAN grabs MAXIMOV and throws him to the ground.)

IVAN: Enough. Let's get out of here.

FYODOR: What's the matter with you? This whole visit was your idea.

(Lights fade.)

Scene 6

The yard of FYODOR KARAMAZOV's neighbor's house. DMITRY is onstage; ALYOSHA enters.

DMITRY: Alyosha. Over here.

ALYOSHA: Mitya?

DMITRY: God! It's like an answer to my prayers. I was just thinking of you and here you are. God! I'd like to give you a big bear hug, man. "Glory to God in the Highest; Glory to the Highest in me." I was repeating that over and over again just before you came. Come over here.

(They cross to a table.)

ALYOSHA: What are you doing here?

DMITRY: I know the caretaker of this house. I'm keeping an eye on Father's house. I'll explain later. Where were you going just now?

ALYOSHA: I was on my way to Father's, but I wanted to see Katerina Ivanovna first.

DMITRY: Katya and Father. God! What a coincidence. Why have I been waiting for you, why have I been yearning, thirsting, hungering to meet you in every recess of my soul and with every one of my ribs? It was precisely to send you on my behalf to Father and to Katerina so I could have done with both of them. I wanted to send them an angel. Will you do this for me?

ALYOSHA: Yes, what do you want me to say to them?

DMITRY: Alyosha, I could press you to my heart until I crushed you, because I really, really—do you understand—love only you. I only care for you and that slut I've fallen in love with. But falling in love with someone does not mean loving that person. You can fall in love and hate at the same time. Do you understand?

ALYOSHA: I understand.

DMITRY: Alyosha, I've been waiting for you because you're the one person I want to tell everything. I must tell it, because tomorrow I'm going to leap from my cloud and my life will end and begin anew. It's a pity you don't know what exaltation is. What am I saying? Me talking to you about exaltation. Anyway, I'm going to begin with Schiller's "Ode to Joy." I don't know it in German, except that it's called *"An die Freude."*
Joy eternal pours its fires

In the soul of God's creation
And its sparkle then inspires
Life's mysterious fermentation.
Joy fills with light the plant's green faces
Regulates the planet's runs,
Fills immeasurable spaces
With immeasurable suns.
All things drink with great elation
Mother Nature's milk of Joy,
Plant and beast and man and nation
Sweetness of her breast enjoy.
To man prostrated in the dust,
Joy brings friends and cheering wine;
Gives the insects sensual lust,
Angels—happiness divine.

The insects are endowed with sensuality by God's eternal joy. I am just such an insect. All we Karamazovs are such insects and one lives in you, too, my angel brother, and it will stir up storms in your blood, too.

ALYOSHA: I know.

DMITRY: Do you?

ALYOSHA: We're on the same ladder. I'm on the bottom rung and you're much higher up, maybe the thirteenth rung, but it doesn't make much difference.

DMITRY: Beauty is a terrifying thing, Alyosha. It is terrifying because it is a mystery. A man can start out with the ideal of the Madonna and end up with the ideal of Sodom. A man can even strive for Sodom without having renounced the Madonna. A man's range of feeling is wide, too wide. Now, as I was saying, I'm a sensual insect, a vicious bedbug—I'm a Karamazov. Now, although our nasty old man lied about my seducing innocent, respectable girls, something like that did happen in my tragedy, but only once and even then it didn't come off.

ALYOSHA: Katerina Ivanovna?

DMITRY: Yes, Katerina Ivanovna. She was the daughter of my commanding officer. She was the toast of the town—a staggering beauty. Well, one night at a ball, I noticed her looking me over, so I decided to ignore her to show her that there was one person in the town who did not think she was such hot stuff. When I finally deigned to speak to her, she had the audacity to be cool to me. So, I decided that, come hell or high water, I was going to teach her a lesson. Well, my opportunity came pretty quickly. It turned out that her father had been speculating with government funds and he lost forty-five hundred rubles. Shortly after my little encounter with Katya, the commanding general came to town and demanded that he turn over the funds. It just so happens that Father had just sent me six thousand rubles in exchange for a letter in which I renounced all rights to what remained of my inheritance—Alright, I was an idiot. So, I let it be known through Katya's half-sister that I might let Katya have forty-five hundred rubles if she came to see me in my rooms. At first, she refused, but then her father tried to kill himself and, lo and behold, one night there she was, standing in my doorway.

(KATERINA appears.)

KATERINA: My sister told me you would give us forty-five hundred rubles if I came in person. Well, here I am. Give me the money.

DMITRY: My first impulse was the Karamazov impulse. But here she was, sacrificing herself so nobly for her father. I went to the desk, took out a five-thousand-ruble note. I handed it to her, opened the door, stepped back, and bowed to her with the deepest reverence. Her whole body shuddered and she turned pale. She looked at me intently for a moment and then slowly and deliberately got down on her knees and touched her forehead to the floor before my feet. Then she jumped up and ran out.

(KATERINA disappears.)

DMITRY: When she ran out, I drew my saber. I was going to thrust it into my chest. I don't know why, just the sheer ecstasy of the moment, I guess. But I didn't stab myself. I kissed the blade and sheathed it. The next day, she sent me the change from the five thousand rubles without a note or anything.

ALYOSHA: So when did you become engaged?

DMITRY: That, my little brother, is a story out of the *Arabian Nights*. Katya's richest relative, a general's widow, lost both her daughters to smallpox in a single week. She called Katya to Moscow, made her her sole heir, and settled eighty thousand rubles on her immediately. The next thing I know, she sends me the forty-five hundred rubles and a letter.

(KATERINA appears.)

KATERINA: I love you. I love you madly. It doesn't matter if you don't love me, if only you let me marry you. Don't be afraid, I won't interfere with you in any way. I'll be like a piece of your furniture, like the rug under your feet. I want to love you as long as I live. I want to save you from yourself. *(Disappears.)*

DMITRY: With tears streaming down my face I wrote to her and accepted. I traveled to Moscow and we became formally engaged with pomp and icons. It was at the engagement ceremony that she met Ivan and Ivan fell in love with her. Don't stare at me like that, Ivan may be our salvation. She reveres him. Can she really compare the two of us and still love a man like me, especially after what's happened?

ALYOSHA: Don't you understand that she can only love a man like you?

DMITRY: She's in love with her own virtue, not me. I didn't mean that. I know she's a thousand times better than me and so I want you to go to her and tell her I'm not coming to see her. Ever. And that I bow to her.

ALYOSHA: And all this is because of Grushenka?

DMITRY: How can I make you understand? Grushenka has a curve to her whole body that you can recognize even in her foot. Even in the little toe of her left foot.

ALYOSHA: Wasn't she going to have you arrested?

DMITRY: Yes. That was Father's doing, she's a business partner of his. She got some capital out of the old merchant that keeps her and the merciless bitch lends it out at exorbitant interest. She took some of the money she's made and went in with Father on some taverns. So, he sends one of his lackeys—Snegiryov, a retired captain—to her to sell her my IOUs and she threatens to have me arrested in order to collect. The first thing I did was give that captain a good thrashing and then I go over to her house to beat her. It was like I was stung by a centipede and infected with the plague. I had three thousand rubles in my pocket and so I took her on a little trip to the inn at Mokroye. I stuffed her with Strasbourg pies and caviar and chocolates and champagne. I paid for music and gypsies and tossed hundreds and hundreds of rubles away to the peasant girls. This went on for three days and, in the end, she allowed me to kiss her foot.

(GRUSHENKA appears.)

GRUSHENKA: Why should I marry you? You haven't got a kopek to your name. But if you promise never to beat me and let me do whatever I want, I may marry you yet. *(Disappears.)*

ALYOSHA: Do you really want to marry her?

DMITRY: If she'll have me. But there's a problem. The three thousand rubles I had in my pocket was Katya's. She had given it to me to mail to her sister.

ALYOSHA: Did you tell her what happened?

DMITRY: No. That's my problem. If I hadn't spent that money, I could still leave her with honor. You could go to her and tell her, "My brother is a despicable beast who could not control his passions, but he is not a thief." But as things stand, what could you say?

ALYOSHA: What can you do?

DMITRY: I want you to ask Father for the three thousand.

ALYOSHA: He'll never give it to you.

DMITRY: I know. Somewhere in all of this business, after all that time doing business with Grushenka, he finally noticed her curve, too, and fell in love and he knows that the one advantage he has over me is money. And so, five days ago, he took three thousand rubles out of the bank and put it in a big envelope, sealed it with five seals and tied it with a pink ribbon and then he wrote on it: "To my Angel, Grushenka, if she comes to me."

ALYOSHA: How do you know all this?

DMITRY: His lackey Smerdyakov told me. He also told me that Grushenka sent him a message that she "might" come. The old man's been trying to get Ivan to go to Chermashnya for him on business so that he can have the house to himself if Grushenka comes. So I sit here, lying in wait.

ALYOSHA: And Smerdyakov's the only one who knows about all this?

DMITRY: That's right.

ALYOSHA: And you expect Father to give you the money that would enable you to leave Katerina Ivanovna and run off with Grushenka?

DMITRY: No. I need a miracle and God sent me you. Go to him. Tell him he'll never hear from me again if he gives me that three thousand. For the last time, I'm giving him a chance to act like a father. Tell him God Himself sent him that chance.

ALYOSHA: I'll try.

DMITRY: I believe in the miracle of God's providence. He can see what's in my heart. He can see my despair. He won't allow something horrible to happen. Go on.

ALYOSHA: I'm going. Will you wait for me here?

DMITRY: No matter how long it takes. And whether or not you get the money, I want you to go to Katerina tonight and tell her that I bow to her. I want you to actually use those words: "He says he bows to you."

ALYOSHA: Brother. What if Grushenka does come to him?

DMITRY: I'll kill him.

ALYOSHA: Do you realize what you're saying?

DMITRY: I don't know what I'll actually do in the moment. I'm afraid I'll hate the sight of him: his adam's apple, his nose, his eyes, his shameless sneer.

ALYOSHA: I trust that God will prevent that.

DMITRY: And I'll sit here and wait for a miracle.

(ALYOSHA exits.)

SCENE 7

FYODOR KARAMAZOV's house. FYODOR and IVAN are seated at the table having cognac, SMERDYAKOV and GRIGORY are standing by the table.)

FYODOR: *(To SMERDYAKOV.)* What do you mean he wouldn't have sinned? You're saying wicked things and you'll go straight to hell for it. They'll roast you like a mutton.

(ALYOSHA enters.)

FYODOR: Ah, here he is, here he is. Join us, sit down, have some coffee—don't worry it's Lenten fare and it's nice and hot. I won't offer you cognac, 'cause you're fasting, unless, perhaps…are you sure you won't have just a tiny, little drop? No, wait! I have just the thing—a nice sweet liqueur, it's marvelous stuff. Smerdyakov, go fetch the liqueur from the cupboard, here's the key. Chop-chop.

ALYOSHA: I won't have any liqueur, thank you, but I'd love some hot coffee.

FYODOR: Ah, wonderful. It's the famous Smerdyakov coffee. When it comes to coffee, cabbage pies, fish soups, my Smerdyakov is a real artist. Come over for fish soup whenever you like. Wait a minute. Didn't I tell you to move back here, mattress, pillow, and all? Have you brought your mattress with you?

ALYOSHA: No, I haven't brought my mattress.

FYODOR: But I gave you a fright, didn't I? Oh, my sweet boy, how could you ever think I could hurt you? Oh, Ivan, how I love this boy. Alyosha, I must give you my paternal blessing.

(ALYOSHA gets up.)

FYODOR: Never mind, I'll just cross you, sit down. Now, we're going to have some fun and it's right up your alley. Just before you walked in, Balaam's ass *(Indicating SMERDYAKOV.)* here spoke. And, oh, the things he had to say. It concerned a little story that Grigory here told us. Tell Alyosha your story, Grigory.

GRIGORY: Sir, we really shouldn't encourage the little demon in his heresy.

FYODOR: Don't keep abusing Smerdyakov like that, Grigory, and tell your story.

GRIGORY: Well, Master Alexei, in town I heard a story about a soldier serving on the frontier who was captured by some Asian tribesmen. They threatened to flay him alive if he didn't renounce the Christian faith and become a Muslim. He refused and they flayed him alive. He died a martyr's death, praising Christ.

FYODOR: Smerdyakov…

SMERDYAKOV: All I was saying, Master Alexei, sir, is that even if he had renounced his faith at that moment, it wouldn't have been a sin.

GRIGORY: I should have left you in the outhouse where I found you, to die with your sainted mother.

FYODOR: Stop insulting Smerdyakov. What do you mean, it wouldn't have been a sin, you little heathen?

SMERDYAKOV: Well, is it not true, Grigory Vasilievich, that even before I say I renounce my faith, the moment I think it, I am anathema and excommunicated from the church?

GRIGORY: How a holy fool like Reeking Lizaveta could have given birth to a devil like you is beyond me.

SMERDYAKOV: Does it not say in the Scriptures, Grigory Vasilievich, that if you have so much as a grain of faith and you ask a mountain to move into the sea, it will?

FYODOR: Yes, yes, it does say that. Get to the point. It does say that, doesn't it, Alyosha?

SMERDYAKOV: Well, I would imagine, Grigory Vasilievich, that, at that moment, this soldier might ask a mountain to move and crush his captors. Now, I guess that neither he nor anyone else really has a grain of faith, since I have never seen a mountain move. Now, at that moment, when the mountain failed to move and crush his captors, how could he help but doubt? And the moment he doubted, he became anathema and excommunicate. So, there would have been no further sin in saying he renounced his faith.

FYODOR: Good Lord, he's a Jesuit. Alright, get out of here the lot of you. And don't whimper, Grigory. Go to Marfa, she'll comfort you and put you to bed. Pigs! Can't they let a man sit quietly after dinner?

(SMERDYAKOV and GRIGORY exit.)

FYODOR: Smerdyakov hangs around because he wants to impress you, Ivan.

IVAN: I have no idea why he should want to do that.

FYODOR: Alyosha, don't be angry with me for offending your elder and the Father Superior. It just makes me so angry. If God exists, then no doubt I've sinned and I'll answer for it. But if there is no God, I didn't offend them nearly enough, those holy fathers of yours. If there's no God, chopping off their heads wouldn't be sufficient—They're holding up progress. Will you believe me, Ivan, if I tell you I take it as a personal offense? No, I can see by your eyes you don't. You think I'm just a buffoon. What about you, Alyosha, do you think I'm a buffoon?

ALYOSHA: No. You're not a buffoon.

FYODOR: I believe you. You're sincere. Not Ivan. He's proud and condescending. Still, I'd do away with your lousy monastery. I'd do away with all that mystical stuff.

IVAN: There's no need.

FYODOR: No need? But it would bring the hour of truth closer.

IVAN: And the moment truth triumphs, you'll be the first to be eliminated.

FYODOR: So I would. You can have your monastery, Alyosha. And we clever people can sit in a warm house and enjoy our cognac. Yes, there must be a God, since things are arranged so nicely. Alright, Ivan, speak: Is there a God or not?

IVAN: No.

FYODOR: Alyosha: God or not?

ALYOSHA: Yes, there is a God.

FYODOR: Ivan: immortality?

IVAN: No.

FYODOR: Not even a tiny, little bit?

IVAN: None at all.

FYODOR: Surely, it's not a complete zero. There's got to be something.

IVAN: Zero.

FYODOR: Alyosha?

ALYOSHA: Yes, there is immortality.

FYODOR: Both God and immortality?

ALYOSHA: Both. Immortality is in God.

FYODOR: Most likely Ivan is right. Think of all the faith and energy that has been wasted on something that doesn't exist. And for thousands of years. So, if there's no God, Ivan, who's playing this joke on us?

IVAN: Must be the devil.

FYODOR: The devil exists, then?

IVAN: No, the devil doesn't exist either.

FYODOR: Now that's a real shame. What I wouldn't do to the first man who invented God. Hanging from the bitter aspen tree would be too good for him.

IVAN: If God hadn't been invented, there'd be no civilization.

FYODOR: Why?

IVAN: Nor would there be any cognac, which I must take away from you now.

FYODOR: Wait, wait, wait, wait. Just one more tiny little glass, my dear. Ah, I think we've offended Alexei. Are you angry with me, my sweet, little Alyosha?

ALYOSHA: No. I know your heart is better than your head.

FYODOR: My heart is better than my head. Ivan, do you love Alyosha?

IVAN: I love him.

FYODOR: Do love him. Ivan, I've begged you to go to Chermashnya for me, why won't you go?

IVAN: I'll go tomorrow if you really insist.

FYODOR: You're lying. What you really want is to keep an eye on me here all the time, you spiteful son, that's why you won't go.

ALYOSHA: Father…

FYODOR: *(To IVAN.)* Why are you always looking at me with those eyes. Those eyes of yours, they're looking at me and saying, "you filthy drunken swine." Suspicious eyes, malicious eyes…you came back here with something in mind. Alyosha looks at me and his eyes shine. Alyosha doesn't despise me. Alyosha, you mustn't love Ivan, you mustn't…

ALYOSHA: You've no reason to be angry with Ivan. Stop hurting my brother.

FYODOR: Alright. Take away the brandy, Ivan, I have a headache. Don't be angry with me. I know you don't love me and there's no reason you should. Go to Chermashnya for me and I'll soon follow you there myself and I'll bring you some presents. I'll show you a barefoot girl I've had my eye on. Don't turn up your nose at barefoot beggar girls, they're real pearls. Ah, my little suckling pigs, to me there is no such thing as a repulsive woman. But how can you understand, you have milk in your veins instead of blood, you're not mature, yet. But I assure you, you can find something devilishly interesting in every woman, something you won't find in any other. Even in an old maid you can find such a treasure that you're amazed that so many fools have overlooked it for so long. Now, barefoot beggar girls and ugly women must be taken by surprise. You must amaze her, bewilder her, you must embarrass her that a fine gentleman like you could ever fancy such a grimy creature. Ah, Alyosha, my love, I always used to take your mother by surprise. I wouldn't touch her for weeks and then, all of a sudden, I'd fall to my knees before her, crawling, kissing her feet and I always, always sent her—I remember as if it were today—into that nervous, little tinkling, cracked laugh of hers. The next day she'd go into one of her shrieking fits like a village girl. But I swear to you, Alyosha, by God Almighty, I never did anything to harm my hysterical wife. Except maybe once. It was during the first year of our marriage and she was praying all the time, especially during the feasts of the Mother of God when she would drive me out of her bed and make me sleep in my study. So, I decided to beat that mystical stuff out of her. "Look," I said, "here's your icon, here it is, I'm taking it down. You think it works miracles? Well, look! I'm going to spit on it and nothing will happen to me." The way she looked at me, I thought she was going to kill me.

(As FYODOR describes the symptoms, ALYOSHA starts to take them on.)

FYODOR: But then she turned very pale and she started sucking in air and exhaling it and she was trembling and staring straight ahead and then all of a sudden she jumped up and threw up her hands, then she covered her face with them and started shaking all over and then she just sank to the floor, shaking…

(ALYOSHA jumps up, throws up his hands, and falls to the floor.)

FYODOR: Alyosha! Alyosha! What's the matter? Ivan, get some water, quick! Oh my God, he's just like her, just like his mother, he's exactly like his mother, he feels sorry for her, he feels sorry for his mother, he's just like his mother…

IVAN: Unless I'm mistaken, his mother happens to have been my mother, too. Or wasn't she?

FYODOR: What are you talking about? Your mother?… Oh my God, you're right…my mind just went blank, I'm sorry, for a moment I was under the impression… *(Laughs nervously.)*

(SMERDYAKOV comes running in.)

SMERDYAKOV: Help! He's going to kill me! Help!

(DMITRY enters with GRIGORY trying to block his way.)

DMITRY: I know she's in here. Where is she? Where have you hidden her, you scum?

(DMITRY punches GRIGORY.)

FYODOR: He'll kill me! He'll kill me! You mustn't let him, you mustn't.

DMITRY: Where is she? I know she's here, I saw her coming this way. *(Runs off.)*

FYODOR: She's here! She's here! Grushenka…where are you my little chick? *(Runs off after DMITRY.)*

IVAN: What are doing? He'll kill you.

(FYODOR comes running in followed by DMITRY.)

FYODOR: Help! Get him away from me! Grab him!

DMITRY: Where is she, you disgusting old Aesop?

(He throws FYODOR to the ground and starts kicking him. IVAN grabs DMITRY and pulls him off.)

IVAN: You're crazy, you've killed him, you madman.

DMITRY: Serves him right. And if I haven't killed him this time, I'll come back.

ALYOSHA: Dmitry, get out of here. Now!

DMITRY: Alyosha, you tell me, you're the only one I'll believe: was she here just now or not?

ALYOSHA: You have my word. She wasn't here.

DMITRY: But I saw her… I have to go find out where she went. Alyosha, go to Katerina right away, there's no point in asking him for the money. Tell her he says he bows to you. He bows to you. Bows. He bows and bows out. And tell her what happened here. *(To FYODOR.)* Watch out, old man. I curse you and disown you. You're not my father. *(Exits.)*

ALYOSHA: Grigory, are you alright?

GRIGORY: He dared to lift his hand to me.

IVAN: He dared rather more than that. He did the same thing to his own father.

GRIGORY: I used to bathe him and he dared to do that to me.

(GRIGORY and SMERDYAKOV exit.)

IVAN: If I hadn't pulled him off, he'd have killed the old man. How much more could old Aesop take?

ALYOSHA: God forbid.

IVAN: Why? What do I care if one serpent devours another? Oh don't worry, I won't let Dmitry kill the old man, I'll stop him, just as I did now. I've got a headache, I'm going out to get some air. *(Crosses to the outside.)*

FYODOR: Alyosha, where's Ivan?

ALYOSHA: He went out to get some air.

FYODOR: I'm afraid of Ivan. Even more than Mitya. You're the only one I'm not afraid of.

ALYOSHA: Don't be afraid of Ivan, either. He's angry with you, but he'll protect you.

FYODOR: Alyosha, be sure to come and see me tomorrow morning. I'll tell you something very important, will you come?

ALYOSHA: Yes, I'll come.

FYODOR: Only pretend you're just dropping by to see how I feel. Don't tell anyone I asked you to come, especially Ivan.

ALYOSHA: Alright.

FYODOR: Good night, my sweet boy.

ALYOSHA: Good night, Father. *(Crosses to the outside.)*

IVAN: Alyosha, you and I really haven't had a chance to talk since I came here. Can you meet me tomorrow morning?

ALYOSHA: I'll be at the Khokhalakovs tomorrow and I may be at Katerina Ivanovna's, unless I can still see her tonight?

IVAN: Ah, to tell her Dmitry is "bowing out."

ALYOSHA: Brother…how will all this business with Dmitry and Father end?

IVAN: I have no idea. In any case, the old man must be kept inside the house and Dmitry must be kept out.

ALYOSHA: Ivan, do you really think a man has the right to decide whether another man has the right to live?

IVAN: A man has the right to wish for whatever he likes.

ALYOSHA: Even for the death of another man?

IVAN: What's the point in lying to ourselves about what we feel? You're worried about my remark about one serpent devouring another. Alright, let me ask you this: Do you really think I'm like Dmitry? Do you really think I'm capable of smashing the old man's head in?

ALYOSHA: No. And I don't think Dmitry is capable of it, either.

IVAN: Well, I thank you for that, at least. You can count on me to protect the old man as best I can. But I reserve the freedom to wish for whatever I want. I'll see you tomorrow. And please don't judge me too harshly, don't look on me as a criminal.

(They shake hands, and ALYOSHA exits.)

SCENE 8

KATERINA's house. ALYOSHA enters from one side, KATERINA from another.

KATERINA: Thank God it's you, I've been praying all day for you to come, you're the only person from whom I can learn the truth, no one else will tell it to me.

ALYOSHA: He sent me…

KATERINA: I had a feeling he would. You see, perhaps, I know even more than you. You see, it's not information I need from you. What I need from you is your own personal impression: how he struck you when you last saw him. Do you understand?

ALYOSHA: Yes.

KATERINA: Now, tell me what he sent you to say. Tell me frankly and plainly, without hiding anything.

ALYOSHA: He says he bows to you and that he'll never come again and…that he bows to you.

KATERINA: Bows? Are those his exact words?

ALYOSHA: Yes.

KATERINA: Did he say it deliberately or just in passing?

ALYOSHA: Very deliberately. He insisted on exactly those words.

KATERINA: Alright, I'll tell you what I think and you tell me whether I'm right or not. If he had asked you to bow to me in passing without insisting on the word that would have been the end. But the very fact that he insisted on the word shows that he was agitated, that he did not walk away from me with a cool determined step, but plunged headlong off the mountain.

ALYOSHA: Those were almost exactly his words: he said tomorrow he was going to leap off his cloud.

KATERINA: Then he's not lost, yet. I can still save him. Did he say anything about a certain three thousand rubles?

ALYOSHA: How do you know about that?

KATERINA: I've known about it for a long time. I wired my sister in Moscow to see if the money arrived. I knew he hadn't sent it, but I said nothing. I know he still needs money. All I want is for him to know who his true friend is, who he can turn to for help. But no, he refuses to believe I am his most faithful friend. He's ashamed before me because of those three thousand rubles. Let him be ashamed before other people, before himself even, but not before me. To God he tells everything without being ashamed; why then does he still not know how much I can endure for him? How dare he not know me after everything that's happened?

ALYOSHA: There's something else he wanted me to tell you. Just now, he broke into Father's house and almost beat him to death because he thought that woman was there and now he's gone to look for her.

KATERINA: And do you think I could not endure that woman? Does he imagine that I wouldn't be able to put up with her? Besides, he won't marry her, because she will never marry him.

ALYOSHA: I am afraid he may well marry her.

KATERINA: No, he won't. You can take my word for it. That girl…is an angel. She's the most fantastic of all fantastic beings. I know how bewitching she is, but I also know how kind and strong and generous she is. Perhaps it surprises you that I should say this? Perhaps you don't believe me? Agrafena Alexandrovna, my angel, please join us.

GRUSHENKA: (Offstage.) I was only waiting for your call.

(She enters and KATERINA kisses her on the lips.)

KATERINA: Sit down, my dear, this is Alexei Fyodorovich Karamazov.

GRUSHENKA: I've been so eager to meet you.

KATERINA: This is the first time the two of us have met. It was I who wanted to meet her, to know her, to see her. I was prepared to go to her, but she came herself as soon as I asked. I knew we could resolve everything, everything. And I was right. Grushenka has explained everything to me. Like a good angel, she has flown down and brought me peace and joy.

GRUSHENKA: And you didn't feel you were too good for me, dear miss.

KATERINA: How could I be too good for you, you enchantress? Let me kiss your lower lip again, it's so full it almost looks swollen and I'd like to make it even more swollen (She kisses GRUSHENKA.) again, and again.

GRUSHENKA: You are too kind to me, dear miss. I might not be worthy of your caresses.

KATERINA: Not worthy? Alexei Fyodorovich, we are whimsical, we are eccentric, we are willful, and we are very, very proud. But we are noble, Alexei Fyodorovich, we are magnanimous, only we are so unhappy. There is only one man we have ever loved. He was an army officer; we fell in love with him and gave ourselves to him, it was long ago, five years ago, and he forgot us and got married. Now he's a widower, he's written, he's coming here. He will come and Grushenka will be happy again and for all these five years she has been unhappy. But in all those five years who can boast of having enjoyed her favors? Only that bedridden old merchant, but he was much more of a father to us: our protector, our guardian. He found us in despair, in torment, abandoned by the one we love. She wanted to drown herself and this old man saved her, saved her.

GRUSHENKA: You defend me too warmly, dear miss. Aren't you just a little bit quick to draw conclusions?

KATERINA: Defend you? Who am I to defend you? Grushenka, my angel, give me your hand. Look at this plump, lovely, little hand, Alexei Fyodorovich. Do you see it? It brought me happiness and resurrected me and now I'm going to kiss it back and front. (She kisses GRUSH-ENKA's hand three times.) Here, here, and here.

GRUSHENKA: You know, dear miss, you won't make me feel embarrassed by kissing my hand in front of Alexei Fyodorovich.

KATERINA: But I wasn't trying to embarrass you… Oh, my dear, how little you understand me.

GRUSHENKA: And, perhaps, you don't quite understand me, either, dear miss. Perhaps I'm more wicked than you see on the surface. I have a wicked heart and I'm willful. It was only to laugh at him that I made Dmitry Fyodorovich fall in love with me.

KATERINA: Yes, but now you will save him. You will explain to him that you love another man, that you've always loved another man, that he has asked you to marry him.

GRUSHENKA: Oh no, I never promised anything of the sort. It was you who said all those things, but I never promised anything.

KATERINA: Then I must have misunderstood you…you promised…

GRUSHENKA: No, Miss Katerina, my angel, I promised nothing. You see, dear miss, how wicked and willful I am. I'll do whatever I feel like at any particular moment. Maybe I did promise you something before, but just now I thought to myself, "What if I take a fancy to him again, that Mitya fellow, since I did take a fancy to him once and it lasted nearly a whole hour. I may even go to him right now and tell him to come and stay with me." That's how fickle I am.

KATERINA: That's not at all what you said a little while ago…not at all…

GRUSHENKA: Ah, that was a little while ago. But you see, I'm so soft-hearted and silly. I've made him suffer so, what if I get home and suddenly feel sorry for him. Then what?

KATERINA: I never expected…

GRUSHENKA: Well, Miss Katerina, I make you look very good—you're so kind and generous compared with me. I suppose you'll stop loving me once you get to know me better. So, give me you hand, my angel, and I will kiss it just as you kissed mine, dear miss. You kissed my hand three times, so, to make things even, I should kiss yours three hundred times, and I will. Once we're even, let it be as God wills. Perhaps, I'll end up your slave and do everything to please you, as a slave must. So, as God wills it, let it be without any deals or promises between us. Ah, what a pretty hand you have, such a sweet, sweet hand. Ah, my dear miss, you're so beautiful, it's impossible. (She raises KATERINA's hand to her lips.) You know, my angel, do you know what? I'm not going to kiss your hand.

KATERINA: Suit yourself. Why are you doing this?

GRUSHENKA: I simply want you to remember that you kissed my hand and I didn't kiss yours.

KATERINA: You insolent animal.

GRUSHENKA: So, I'll go right now and tell Mitya how you kissed my hand and I didn't kiss yours. He'll be so amused.

KATERINA: Get out, you filthy slut, get out of here.

GRUSHENKA: Ah, shame on you, dear miss, shame on you. You really shouldn't use words like that, young lady.

KATERINA: Get out, you whore.

GRUSHENKA: You're a fine one to call me whore. You, who visit gentlemen after dark to try and peddle your charms for money. Oh yes, I know about that.

(KATERINA screams and lunges for GRUSHENKA; ALYOSHA blocks her.)

ALYOSHA: Don't move. Don't say anything, don't answer her. She'll leave now.

GRUSHENKA: Yes, I'm leaving. Alyosha, dear, won't you see me off?

ALYOSHA: Please go.

GRUSHENKA: Alyoshenka, dear, come with me. I have something very nice to tell you on the way: I performed this scene for you. Come with me, darling, you'll be glad you did. (Exits.)

KATERINA: She's a wild beast. Why did you hold me back, Alexei Fyodorovich, I'd have beaten her to a bloody pulp. That animal should be flogged in public.

ALYOSHA: She's gone now.

KATERINA: But your brother isn't. How could he be so dishonorable, so inhuman? He told that animal what happened on that fatal, eternally accursed, accursed day. "You tried to peddle your charms for money, dear miss." Your brother is a hateful man. Go now, Alexei Fyodorovich, I'm so ashamed. But please come back tomorrow.

(ALYOSHA starts to cross out.)

KATERINA: Wait. Lise Khokhalakova asked me to give you this letter.

ALYOSHA: Thank you.

KATERINA: Don't forget about tomorrow.

ALYOSHA: I'll be here.

(He crosses to the outside and DMITRY sneaks up on him.)

DMITRY: Your money or your life.

ALYOSHA: Mitya.

DMITRY: What happened? Don't spare me. Crush me. Strike me down. Was she furious?

ALYOSHA: They were both there.

DMITRY: Who?

ALYOSHA: Grushenka and Katerina Ivanovna.

DMITRY: You're out of your mind.

ALYOSHA: Katerina Ivanovna had invited Grushenka there to work things out between them. When I got there, Katerina Ivanovna said that Grushenka had promised to tell you that she was really in love with another man and not you. It was all very strange: It seemed like Katerina was in love with her, she kept kissing her, she kissed her hand three times. Then, all of a sudden, Grushenka said that she hadn't promised anything and that she might change her mind and ask you to come stay with her. She was about to kiss Katerina's hand, but then decided not to, and said that she was going to tell you that Katerina had kissed her hand and she hadn't kissed Katerina's. Katerina screamed and called her a whore and Grushenka said she was a fine one to talk after she had tried to peddle her charms for money. Then Grushenka ran home.

DMITRY: So, she got out of there without kissing Katya's hand?

ALYOSHA: Don't you realize how you hurt Katerina Ivanovna by telling Grushenka about her coming to your place?

DMITRY: I was weeping when I told Grushenka that. She wept, too, and understood everything. That's Grushenka for you: She wept then and now she plunges the dagger into Katya's heart. What difference does it make if I wept, I'm despicable. But enough of this, it's not a cheerful subject. You take your way and I'll take mine. You won't see me anymore—I won't come to you except as a last resort. Goodbye, Alexei. *(Starts to exit.)* Wait, Alexei. Look at me. *(Points to a spot on his chest just below his neck.)* Right here, I am carrying a dishonor worse than anything I have done before. I can stop myself at any time. And if I did, I would regain half my honor. But I won't stop myself. Goodbye Alexei. And don't pray for me, I'm not worth it. *(Exits.)*

(ALYOSHA opens LISE's letter and starts to read. LISE appears.)

LISE: Dear Alexei, no one knows about this letter, not even Mama. I know this is wrong. I love you, Alyosha, I have loved you ever since I was a little girl in Moscow, where you were nothing like you are now, and I will love you all my life. My heart has chosen you—I want to be united with you and I want us to live out our lives together. Of course, this can only happen if you leave the monastery. I know I'm too young. We will just have to wait until it is legal for me to marry. By that time, I will certainly be cured. If you have any compassion, don't look me in the eyes when you come to see us tomorrow. I will burst out laughing, especially since you will be wearing that ridiculous dress. My God. I've written a love letter. Please don't despise me. Please keep this letter a secret. My reputation is in your hands. Lise.

(Lights fade.)

ACT II
SCENE 1

FATHER ZOSIMA's cell. ZOSIMA and ALYOSHA are onstage.

ZOSIMA: Alyosha, my dear son, aren't people expecting you?

ALYOSHA: I…

ZOSIMA: Didn't you promise Lise Khokhalakova that you would visit her?

ALYOSHA: Yes, Father.

ZOSIMA: Does anyone else need you?

ALYOSHA: I did promise to see my father and my brother Ivan and my brother Dmitry's fiancée.

ZOSIMA: Good. You must also see your brother Dmitry.

ALYOSHA: But Father, I want to stay with you.

ZOSIMA: You must go, but do not be sad. Know that I won't die without you. I will say my last words on Earth in your presence. I'll say those words to you, my dear son, I'll bequeath them to you. To you, my sweet son, because you love me. But now you must go to those you promised to see.

(ALYOSHA receives ZOSIMA's blessing and crosses out of the cell. FATHER FERAPONT is sitting outside his hut.)

FERAPONT: Novice.

ALYOSHA: Yes, Father Ferapont?

FERAPONT: You've come from the Elder Zosima's cell?

ALYOSHA: Yes, Father.

FERAPONT: He doesn't keep his fasts.

ALYOSHA: Please forgive me, Father Ferapont, I mean no disrespect, but very few of us are strong as you, we can't survive on a few crusts of bread.

FERAPONT: And mushrooms.

ALYOSHA: Mushrooms, Father Ferapont?

FERAPONT: I could easily do without their accursed bread, I could go into the forest and live on mushrooms, while they can't even leave the monastery, for they can't do without their accursed bread. They're tied to their bellies, so they're tied to the devil. Were you at that Godless lunch at the Father Superior's yesterday?

ALYOSHA: I didn't get there in time, it ended a little early.

FERAPONT: Did you see the devils?

ALYOSHA: Devils, Father?

FERAPONT: I went to see the Father Superior last year on Trinity Sunday and I've never been back since. There were devils everywhere. They were hanging about the monks' necks, hiding in their cassocks, peeping out of their pockets. But they were frightened of me, the unholy ones. One of them tried to hide behind the door. He was a big one, more than three feet tall. He had a long thick, brown tail and it was caught in the crack of the door, so I quickly slammed it shut. Oh, he squealed and

pulled at his tail and jumped up and down. I made the sign of the cross over him, three times I made it. That got him—he was as dead as a squished spider. He must be rotten and stinking in that corner now, but they don't see it, they don't smell a thing. I haven't been back to the Father Superior's for over a year. Begone novice.

ALYOSHA: Goodbye, Father Ferapont.

(He kneels for FERAPONT's blessing, but he is lost in prayer. ALYOSHA exits.)

SCENE 2

FYODOR's dining room. FYODOR is having coffee and going over his books. ALYOSHA enters.

FYODOR: The coffee's cold, so I'm not offering you any. Today, my friend, it's just Lenten fish soup for me and nobody's invited. I see you're staring at my bandage. Well, I prefer something red around my head; white reminds me too much of a hospital. Why have you come?

ALYOSHA: To see how you're feeling.

FYODOR: And because I told you to. I wanted to ask you something. Do you think that son of a bitch Dmitry would clear out if I gave him a couple of thousand? Disappear for five years—or thirty-five—just forget about Grushenka and go?

ALYOSHA: I'll ask him… Maybe if you gave him the whole three thousand…

FYODOR: Like hell you will. The offer is rescinded, I thought better of it this morning. I'll crush that whelp like a cockroach. I like to squish cockroaches at night—for the pleasure of it. I like to hear them pop under my slipper. And your Mitya will make a popping sound, too. I could have him locked up if I wanted to. I know respect for one's parents isn't fashionable these days, but the last time I checked, there was still a law against picking up your aged father by the hair and kicking him in the face.

ALYOSHA: Are you planning to lodge a complaint?

FYODOR: Ivan talked me out of it. But Ivan can rot in hell—something else stopped me. She'd feel sorry for him if I had him locked up. But as it stands now, here I am, a poor feeble old man, abused by his own flesh and blood—she may drop that vicious lout and come running over here to take care of me—care for some cognac?

ALYOSHA: No, thank you, and after last night, you shouldn't be drinking any either.

FYODOR: True enough. The truth hurts, but there it is. Still, one glass won't kill me. *(Pours a drink and downs it.)* Good as new. How are you, my sweet boy?

ALYOSHA: You *are* much nicer, now.

FYODOR: I love you even without cognac. But to bastards I'm a bastard. Why won't Ivan go to Chermashnya? He wants to spy on me. He's afraid I'll marry Grushenka and leave her everything. Well, Ivan will never get a kopek out of me. I, my dearest Alexei Fyodorovich, plan to live on this Earth as long as possible, let it be known to you. And therefore, I need every kopek. And the longer I live, the more I'll need it. Right now, I'm only fifty-five and I'm still a man in every sense of the word. But I intend to occupy that position for about twenty years longer. I'll be old and disgusting and they won't come to me of their own free will and that's when I'll need my dear money. Let it be known to you that I want to live in wickedness to the very end. Wickedness is sweet. Everyone denounces it, but everyone lives in it. Only they all do it on the sly and I do it openly. And for this ingenuousness of mine, the wicked all attack me. And I don't want your Paradise, Alexei Fyodorovich, let it be known to you. It's unfitting for a decent man to go to, your Paradise, if there really is such a place. I say a man falls asleep and doesn't wake up, that's all. Last night, Ivan talked sense about these things, even though we were all pretty drunk. Otherwise, Ivan's just a little braggart and he's no great scholar, either. All he does is look at you and grin without saying much—that's how he gets away with it. Where does he come from? He's not like us, he's different. He's like a cloud of dust—the wind will blow and he'll be gone. As for Mitya—I'll crush your Mitya. I call him your Mitya because I know you love him, but that doesn't worry me. If Ivan loved him, I'd be afraid for my life. But Ivan doesn't love anybody.

ALYOSHA: You're just upset because of what happened last night. You should go back to bed and get some rest.

FYODOR: I don't feel angry with you at all for saying that. But If Ivan said exactly the same thing, I'd be furious. When I'm alone with you, I'm actually a kind person. Otherwise, I'm an evil man.

ALYOSHA: You're not evil, you're just twisted.

FYODOR: Alright, you can go now, my sweet boy.

(ALYOSHA embraces FYODOR and holds on for a few seconds, kissing his shoulder.)

FYODOR: What are you doing? I'll see you again, won't I?

ALYOSHA: I wasn't thinking, I just did it.

FYODOR: Listen, come sometime soon—for fish soup—a special one. You must come. What about tomorrow? I'll see you tomorrow?

ALYOSHA: I'll try, but my elder is dying.

FYODOR: Come when you can, my sweet boy.

ALYOSHA: Goodbye, Father.

(ALYOSHA exits. FYODOR pours himself a drink and downs it.)

FYODOR: That's all. No more.

Scene 3

The entry hall of MADAME KHOKHALAKOVA's house. MADAME KHOKHALAKOVA and ALYOSHA enter from separate entrances.

KHOKHALAKOVA: Have you heard? Have you heard about the miracle?

ALYOSHA: What miracle?

KHOKHALAKOVA: Father Zosima's sainthood is assured, it is assured. Last week, as you may remember, Alexei, an old sergeant's widow, one Prokhorovna, came to receive the Elder's blessing. Her son Vasya was in the civil service in Irkutsk in Siberia and she hadn't had a letter from him in over a year. Well, this old lady asked the Elder if she could have a requiem mass said for her son, "to make his soul uneasy." She thought that this would compel him to write to her—our dear Russian peasants are so superstitious, it's charming. Anyway, the Elder would have none of it. He said that to have prayers said for the soul of a living person was akin to witchcraft. He forgave her because of her ignorance. And then, do you remember what happened, Alexei? As if he were looking into the book of the future, he said, "Your son is alive. He will come back to you soon or send you a letter." Well, Alexei, the prophecy has been fulfilled. Yea, more than that. No sooner had she stepped over her threshold when she was handed a letter from Siberia. Don't speak. There's more. The letter had been mailed from Ekaterinburg by Vasya himself. He was on his way home. The letter said that he hoped to embrace his mother in three weeks. Well, Alexei Fyodorovich, what do you think of that?

ALYOSHA: He'll die today.

KHOKHALAKOVA: Yes, yes, I know. Oh, I've been dying to tell someone about the miracle—someone, anyone…no, you, only you, my dear Alexei. He's not receiving visitors today, is he? No, of course not. Oh, Alexei, the whole town is in great excitement, everyone is expecting something. Did you know that Katerina is here?

ALYOSHA: Now?

KHOKHALAKOVA: Yes, she's sitting right there in my drawing room.

ALYOSHA: That's wonderful, she asked me to come to see her today.

KHOKHALAKOVA: I know everything, every-thing—down to the last detail. Oh, the horror she endured at the hands of that creature, c'est tragique. Well, your brother Dmitry is a fine one, I must say. Oh, Alexei, I'm so confused. Your brother's in there right now… oh, no, not the monster—no, no—Ivan Fyodorovich. They're in there lacerating themselves. They're throwing away their lives and they know it, they're reveling in it. Oh, Alexei, I've been desperate for you to come, I cannot bear it. There's something else I wanted to ask you… Oh, yes. Why is Lise having hysterics? The moment she heard you were coming, she became hysterical.

(LISE enters in her wheelchair.)

LISE: What are you talking about, *Maman*? You're the one who's hysterical.

KHOKHALAKOVA: Small wonder, Lise. You drive me to distraction with these whims of yours. Oh, Alexei, I'm so miserable.

LISE: What's the matter now, *Maman*?

KHOKHALAKOVA: You are the matter, Lise—you and your caprices. You kept me up all night with your fever and then this morning, the impossible Doctor Herzenstube—always, always the same unchanging Herzenstube.

ALYOSHA: *(Revealing his finger wrapped in a bloody handkerchief.)* Ah…I wonder if you could spare a clean piece of rag or something to bind my finger, I hurt it rather badly:

{
KHOKHALAKOVA: My God, what a horrible wound!

LISE: My God, why did you stand there without say-ing anything—you could have bled to death—Mama, get some water, quick.
}

KHOKHALAKOVA: Shouldn't I send for Herzen-stube?

LISE: Mama! Water! Now!

ALYOSHA: It's nothing, really.

KHOKHALAKOVA: Oh, Alexei, how firmly you are facing up to your misfortune. *(Exits.)*

LISE: Quick, tell me what happened with your finger as simply and briefly as possible because I have to talk to you about something else before Mama gets back.

ALYOSHA: Well, when I was walking over here, I ran into some schoolboys having a rock fight. There were six boys against one very small boy. I went over to talk to the bigger boys and got them to stop, but then the little one started throwing stones at me—he seemed to know who I was. When I went over to talk to him, he suddenly rushed at me and bit my finger.

LISE: He seemed to know who you were? You must find out who he is, there's a mystery there. Alright, quickly, give me back the letter.

ALYOSHA: I'm afraid I don't have it with me.

LISE: I don't believe you. Listen, Alexei, I'm sorry I played such a stupid joke on you, but you have to give me back the letter.

ALYOSHA: Honestly, Lise, I left it at the monastery.

LISE: Then go back to the monastery and get it.

ALYOSHA: Lise, once I go back, I'll have to stay there. Father Zosima…

LISE: How hard did you laugh?

ALYOSHA: What?

LISE: When you read the letter.

ALYOSHA: I didn't laugh at all.

LISE: Why not? It was an idiotic joke, I never should have written it.

ALYOSHA: I believed every word of it.

LISE: Don't be so conceited. How could you possibly think I was serious?

ALYOSHA: I'm leaving the monastery and I have to marry and I want to marry you.

LISE: Don't be absurd. I'm a freak—rolling around in a wheelchair.

ALYOSHA: That's why you need me to take care of you. And who knows? You may be well by the time we get married.

LISE: You're out of your mind. It was a joke. I play a stupid little joke and all of a sudden you're talking about marriage.

(MADAME KHOKHALAKOVA enters.)

KHOKHALAKOVA: Here's the water. I also brought some gauze and bandages. Don't you think we should send for Herzenstube?

LISE: Mama. Enough about Herzenstube. Give me the gauze. Do you know what happened, Mama? Alexei was bitten by a schoolboy.

KHOKHALAKOVA: Oh my God! Alexei—did he have rabies?

LISE: Oh, Mama, there is no such thing as a rabid boy.

Khokhalakova: And why not? Suppose a rabid dog bit the boy? Then he would turn into a rabid boy. Do normal boys go around biting people? No. Only rabid boys go around biting people. I must say, you're bandaging Alexei's finger beautifully, Lise. I could never do such a good job of it. Does it still hurt?

ALYOSHA: Not much.

LISE: And you're not worried about rabies, are you?

KHOKHALAKOVA: That's enough, Lise. Alexei, Katerina is very anxious to see you.

LISE: Oh, Mama, see her yourself, Alexei's in too much pain.

ALYOSHA: Oh, I feel much better now.

LISE: Suit yourself.

ALYOSHA: I'll be right back.

LISE: There's no need.

ALYOSHA: I guess I could stay another five minutes.

LISE: Five whole minutes! That's really too kind of you. Mama, take him away, take the monster away. *(Exits.)*

KHOKHALAKOVA: I don't know what's gotten into her today. Now, I don't want to influence you in any way, or to lift the veil, so to speak. See for yourself. It's the most fantastic farce: she's in love with Ivan Fyodorovich, but she's trying as hard as she can to convince herself that she's in love with Dmitry Fyodorovich.

(They cross into the drawing room where IVAN and KATERINA are sitting.)

KATERINA: Alexei Fyodorovich, thank God you're here. You three are the only true friends I have in the world. Alexei Fyodorovich, you witnessed my nightmare yesterday—you saw me for what I am. I do not hate Dmitry for what he did, I pity him. I don't even know if I'm in love with him anymore. If I were still in love with him, I don't think I would pity him—I would hate him.

KHOKHALAKOVA: Exactly, my dear. Exactly.

KATERINA: Wait, my dear Katerina Osipovna. I haven't finished telling you what I have to say. I have come to a decision. It is irrevocable and I fear it may be terrible, but I will abide by it for the rest of my life. My dear, my kind, my constant and generous advisor and profound reader of the human heart—my only friend in the world, Ivan Fyodorovich, approves of my decision. He praises me for it.

IVAN: I approve.

KATERINA: But I would like Alyosha—I hope you will forgive me, Alexei Fyodorovich, if I call you Alyosha—I would like you to tell me before my two friends whether I am right or not. I feel instinctively, Alyosha, my dear little brother—for you are my dear little brother—I feel that your judgment, your approval, in spite of all my torment, will bring me peace. I will find peace in your words, I shall be reconciled to my fate—I feel it.

ALYOSHA: I'm not very experienced in this kind of thing.

KATERINA: Well, let me tell you, Alyosha, what matters most in this kind of thing is honor and duty. Therefore, Alexei Fyodorovich, I have resolved that even if he marries that animal—whom I can never, never forgive—I will not leave him. From this day forth I will never, never leave him. I do not mean that I shall drag myself around after him, trying to throw myself in front of his eyes every minute, tormenting him—oh no, I shall go to another town—anywhere you like—but I will watch over him all my life, all my life, untiringly. And when that woman makes him unhappy—which is inevitable—then let him come to me and he will find a friend, a sister—only a sister, of course, and that will be so forever—but he will finally be convinced that his sister really is his loving sister who has sacrificed her whole life for him. I will do it. I will insist that he finally know me and tell me everything without being ashamed. I will be his god, to whom he will pray—that, at least he owes me for his betrayal and for the Calvary I endured yesterday through his fault. And let him see throughout his whole life that all my life I will be faithful to him and to the word I once gave, despite the fact that he was faithless and betrayed me. This is my decision.

KHOKHALAKOVA: But only for this moment. And what is this moment? Just yesterday's insult. That's all it is.

IVAN: That might be the case for another woman, but not for Katerina. Another woman would be stung by the insult, she would make this promise in the heat of the moment, and it would soon be forgotten. But for Katerina this is no mere promise: it is an obligation, it is a duty. *(Turns to KATERINA.)* Your whole life, Katerina, will be one long, painful contemplation of your own feelings. But in the end, you will accomplish your proud design and it will bring you joy.

KHOKHALAKOVA: But this is all so wrong.

KATERINA: Speak, Alyosha. What is your opinion? I must know what you think. *(Bursts into tears.)* It's nothing, nothing. I'm just upset about last night. But with two friends such as you and Ivan, I feel I am strong enough to face anything, for I know you two will never leave me.

IVAN: Unfortunately, I have to go to Moscow tomorrow. I'm afraid it can't be changed.

KATERINA: Moscow tomorrow! That's wonderful! Not that I'm happy to see you go, but of course, a friend like you would never take it that way. No, I must tell my aunt and my sister what's happened here and it will be so much better coming from you than if I just wrote them a letter. But I must write them a letter as well. If you'll excuse me… *(Starts to exit.)*

KHOKHALAKOVA: What about Alyosha? What about Alexei's opinion, which it was so necessary for you to hear?

KATERINA: I haven't forgotten. Whatever he decides, I will abide by it.

ALYOSHA: I don't believe it. He's going to Moscow and you cry out that you're glad. You said it on purpose, like you were acting in a comedy on the stage.

KATERINA: What are you saying? I don't understand…

ALYOSHA: I don't know too well myself… it's as if I'd suddenly seen something… that maybe you never loved Dmitry, not even in the beginning, and maybe he never loved you, not even in the beginning either, maybe he just respected you… I'm sorry, Katerina Ivanovna, but somebody should tell you the truth.

KATERINA: What truth?

ALYOSHA: Call Dmitry here now—I'll go find him—let him take your hand and Ivan's hand and let him unite them. You love Ivan and you're tormenting him. You're tormenting him because your feeling for Dmitry is unhealthy and twisted… it's a false love… you've convinced yourself that you love him in order to lacerate yourself.

KATERINA: You holy little fool.

IVAN: You're mistaken, Alyosha. Katerina has never loved me. She knew all along that I loved her, though I never said a word about my feelings. She kept me by her side to use me as an instrument of continuous revenge. She revenged herself by making me pay for the thousand insults she's endured at Dmitry's hands. You do love him, Katerina, and only him and the more he insults you the more you'll love him—that's how you maim and lacerate yourself. You need him so you can constantly admire your own heroic loyalty. Goodbye, Katerina. Don't be angry with me—I am punished a hundred times more than you, because I will never see you again. Don't offer me your hand. Eventually I'll forgive you, but not yet. *"Den Dank Dame, begehr ich nicht."* *(Exits.)*

ALYOSHA: Ivan! Come back! It's all my fault, I started it. Ivan spoke out of spite, in anger…

KATERINA: If you will excuse me. *(Exits.)*

KHOKHALAKOVA: You were absolutely marvelous, Alexei, an angel. And I will do everything in my power to prevent Ivan Fyodorovich from leaving.

(KATERINA enters.)

KATERINA: Alexei Fyodorovich, I have a great favor to ask you concerning your brother. About a month ago Dmitry beat a man in public—that retired army captain who runs errands for your father. He dragged him out of a tavern by his beard and apparently the captain's little son saw the whole thing. Only a man like Dmitry Karamazov could get so carried away by his passions that he could commit such an unspeakable act. The captain's name is Snegiryov, he is desperately poor: Go to him, Alexei Fyodorovich, and very tactfully, very delicately—as only you can do—persuade him to accept these two hundred rubles. Tell him it does not come from Dmitry, but from me. I would go myself, but you will find a much better way of giving it to him. He lives on Lake Street. Do me this favor, Alexei Fyodorovich, I beseech you. And now, I'm a little tired. Goodbye. *(Exits.)*

ALYOSHA: Katerina Ivanovna… Madame Khokhalakova, I don't know what to do. This is all my fault.

KHOKHALAKOVA: Nonsense. You were an absolute angel.

(KATERINA screams offstage.)

KHOKHALAKOVA: Hysterics! Wonderful! Hysterics are a good sign, I'm delighted that she's having hysterics.

(LISE rushes in.)

LISE: What's happening?

KHOKHALAKOVA: And did you notice how young Ivan Fyodorovich looked when he stormed out of here? What was that little German verse he quoted?

ALYOSHA: It was from Schiller.

KHOKHALAKOVA: Schiller! Wonderful! I always thought he was so severe and scholarly, but he's a true romantic at heart. He acted so youthfully, so impulsively.

(KATERINA screams offstage.)

KHOKHALAKOVA: I must go attend to Katerina. Farewell now, my dear, angelic Alexei. *(Exits.)*

LISE: And what did you do to get promoted to angel?

ALYOSHA: I made a fool of myself. I told Katerina Ivanovna that she was really in love with Ivan and not Dmitry.

LISE: You're an amazingly nice person, Alexei Fyodorovich. Come here. Give me your hand. There's something I want to confess…that letter I wrote you yesterday…it wasn't a joke, I meant it.

ALYOSHA: I know.

LISE: You conceited little novice.

(ALYOSHA kisses her. They look at each other for a moment.)

LISE: What's the matter, Alyosha?

ALYOSHA: What if I told you I wasn't sure I believed in God?

LISE: Alyosha, what's the matter?

ALYOSHA: The man I love most in the world is leaving me. Lise, if only you knew how my soul is bound to his…And now I'll be left alone. But now I guess I'll have you. From now on, we'll always be together.

LISE: As long as we live. Kiss me again.

(They kiss.)

LISE: Go now and Christ be with you. *(Makes the sign of the cross over him.)* I've been keeping you from him. Go to him while he is still alive and I will pray for you both.

ALYOSHA: Goodbye, Lise. *(Exits.)*

SCENE 4

The SNEGIRYOVS' hovel. SNEGIRYOV, MAMA, NINA, and VARVARA are onstage. ILYUSHA is lying in bed behind a curtain. ALYOSHA knocks at the door.

SNEGIRYOV: Who's there?

ALYOSHA: I'm afraid you don't know me. My name is Alexei Fyodorovich Karamazov.

SNEGIRYOV: Well then, by all means, come in.

(ALYOSHA enters.)

VARVARA: Some monk begging for his monastery.

SNEGIRYOV: Oh, no, Varvara, my dear, you are quite mistaken. Well, sir, what brings you to the lower depths?

ALYOSHA: Well, as I said, I am Alexei Fyodorovich…

SNEGIRYOV: I am quite aware of that, Mr. Karamazov. I, sir, for my part, sir, am Nikolai Ilyich Snegiryov, sir, former captain in the Russian infantry, sir, disgraced by his vices, sir, but still a captain. I should have said Captain Yessirov, instead of Snegiryov, but it's only in the second half of my life that I've started saying "yessir." "Yessir" is an acquired humiliation. Now, what can I do for you, sir?

ALYOSHA: I've come about the incident with my brother, Dmitry Fyodorovich.

SNEGIRYOV: And what incident would that be, sir? Are you referring, by any chance, sir, to the incident involving (*Indicating his beard.*) my backscrubber?

ALYOSHA: Your backscrubber?

ILYUSHA: (*Drawing the curtain.*) He came to complain about me, Papa. I bit his finger.

SNEGIRYOV: He bit your finger, sir?

ALYOSHA: Well…he was having a battle with some other boys…they were throwing stones at each other. When I tried to break up the fight, he rushed at me and bit my finger. I think I understand now.

SNEGIRYOV: I'll give him a good whipping right away, sir, this minute.

ALYOSHA: But I'm not complaining at all, I was just explaining to you… Please don't whip him, sir, he looks ill.

SNEGIRYOV: Did you really think I'd do it? That I'd whip my little Ilyusha just to please you? Must I do it at once or could you wait a little, my good sir? I'm awfully sorry about your precious finger, my dear sir. Perhaps you'd like me, sir, before I start whipping Ilyusha, to cut off these four fingers of mine, to satisfy your sense of justice? I do hope, though, sir, that you'll be satisfied with four of my fingers and not demand the fifth as well.

VARVARA: Clown.

ALYOSHA: Sir, I realize your boy attacked me because of what my brother did to you. I promise my brother will come to you…no, he will meet you in public, where all this happened and ask your forgiveness in front of everyone. I know he will.

SNEGIRYOV: So, if I asked His Excellency to go down on his knees to me in the Metropolis Tavern or in the public square, he would do it?

ALYOSHA: He would kneel, I'm certain of it.

SNEGIRYOV: You've pierced me, sir. You've pierced me to the heart and pierced me to tears—or am I being over-appreciative of your brother's magnanimity? Allow me to finish introducing my litter, sir, my brood.

If I die, sir, who will so love them, and while I live, who will so love me? A family is a wonderful arrangement God has created for repulsive men like me.

VARVARA: Stop making a fool of yourself. An idiot comes to the door and you feel compelled to shame us all before him.

SNEGIRYOV: Wait, Varvara, my dear. There is a method to my madness. Allow me to introduce my wife, Mr. Karamazov, sir, Arina Petrovna. She has no legs to speak of, sir. Mama, this is Alexei Fyodorovich Karamazov.

MAMA: How do you do, Mr. Chernomazov?

SNEGIRYOV: Karamazov, Mama, Karamazov.

MAMA: Alright, fine. Karamazov. But I like Chernomazov better and I do have legs. I have huge legs, like barrels. I'm not spoiling your air, am I, Mr. Chernomazov? The dead smell even worse.

VARVARA: Papa, stop this at once.

MAMA: What have I done now? What have I done now? I'm not being bad, Papa, I'm being good. Nobody loves me—only my little Ilyusha—he loves me when he comes home from school. Yesterday, he brought me an apple. Why has my smell become so repulsive to you?

SNEGIRYOV: Mama, Mama, darling, stop, please stop, we all love you, we love you, Mama. (*Kisses her hands.*) Well, sir, now you have seen, now you have heard.

ALYOSHA: I've seen and heard.

ILYUSHA: Papa, don't plead with him. Stop it, Papa.

VARVARA: Enough of your clowning.

NINA: Please stop, Father.

SNEGIRYOV: You're absolutely right, my dear. Mr. Karamazov, let us continue our business outside.

(*They step outside.*)

ALYOSHA: There's something else I have to talk to you about, sir.

SNEGIRYOV: I gathered that much, sir, I didn't think you'd really come to complain about my boy. I'm terribly sorry about your finger. I can explain. Ilyusha saw your brother drag me out of the tavern. He grabbed me, he hugged me, he tried to pull me away. He pleaded with your brother, "Let him go, let him go, he's my papa, my papa, forgive him." He kissed your brother's hands as he was dragging me—I can still see his face at that moment—I can never forget it as long as I live.

ALYOSHA: I'm so sorry…I swear to you, sir, my brother will repent to you, even if it means going down on his knees in that very square. I will make him kneel. If he refuses, he's no brother of mine.

SNEGIRYOV: Ah, so it's still in the planning stage. And, indeed, it doesn't even come from him, but from your own kind heart.

ALYOSHA: He will beg your forgiveness. He will kneel before you and bow to the ground before you in the middle of the square. *(Pause.)* Was your boy hurt in the rock fight?

SNEGIRYOV: He came home with a big bruise on his chest. He came home crying and now he's feverish.

ALYOSHA: I have to tell you, the other boys said he attacked first. They said he stabbed a boy named Krasotkin with a penknife.

SNEGIRYOV: I heard about that—It's a bad business, his mother's a rich widow—she could make trouble. It all started because of what happened with your brother. His schoolmates started teasing him, shouting "backscrubber, backscrubber." The evening after they started teasing him we went out for a walk. Every evening we walk from our gate to that big rock over there—it's a beautiful, desolate place. Suddenly, he stopped walking and said, "Our town is a bad town, isn't it, Papa?" And I told him it's none too good. "Papa, let's move to another town—a good one where no one knows about us." And so we began dreaming about how we'd move to another town, how we'd buy our own horse and cart. That seemed to make him happy, to distract him. But when we went for our walk last night, he wouldn't talk to me. When we reached the stone, he threw his little arms around my neck, hugging me as hard as he could. Tears were streaming down his face—my whole face was wet with his tears. "Papa, how he humiliated you." And I wept and we held each other, sobbing. No one saw us, sir, except God. And I only hope He will enter it into my service record. If so, you can thank your good brother for me, Alexei Fyodorovich. No, I will not give my boy a whipping to satisfy you.

ALYOSHA: I'd like to make friends with your boy…if you could help me.

SNEGIRYOV: As you wish, sir.

ALYOSHA: There's something else I need to talk to you about—I have a message for you. My brother Dmitry has also insulted his fiancée. When she learned what he had done to you and about your difficult circumstances, she asked me… Well, she wanted me to give you this… *(Hands him the two hundred rubles.)* from her, not from Dmitry…no, he's left her…and it's not from me, either, only her. She begs you to take it. You've both been insulted by the same man. No one will know about it, please take it…I don't ask you to forgive him or even me, but please forgive her.

SNEGIRYOV: Two hundred rubles…I haven't seen this much money in four years…You're serious, you're not fooling me?

ALYOSHA: I swear to you that everything I told you is true.

SNEGIRYOV: But listen, sir…If I accept it, won't that make me despicable? Deep down in your heart, won't you despise me?

ALYOSHA: No, it is not dishonorable. I swear on my salvation that I respect you with all my soul and I swear to you, no one will ever hear of this.

SNEGIRYOV: But listen, sir, you don't know what this two hundred rubles means. I would be able to get treatment for my wife and for Ninochka—my hunchbacked angel.… And I could send Varvara back to school in Petersburg.—Wait, Alexei Fyodorovich, wait—this means Ilyusha and I might be able to make our dream come true—we could buy a horse and cart—the horse must be black, he insists that it be black. Oh dear God, if I can collect a miserable little debt someone owes me, there'd really be enough money to leave…

ALYOSHA: Don't worry about the money, Katerina Ivanovna will send you more—no, don't worry about a thing—and I have some money, too. Now, we have to work fast because you'll want to move before winter comes—I'll help, and when you move, we'll always write each other, we'll be brothers for life… What's wrong?

SNEGIRYOV: Alexei Fyodorovich, sir…I…would you…Sir, would you like me to show you a nice little trick, sir?

ALYOSHA: A trick?

SNEGIRYOV: A hocus-pocus trick, sir.

ALYOSHA: I don't understand, what's the matter?

SNEGIRYOV: Here, watch. *(Holds up the bills.)* Now you see it, *(Crumples the bills.)* now you don't. *(Throws them on the ground and grinds them into the earth with his foot.)* Yessir, there's your money, sir, there's your money…Kindly transmit to those who sent you that the backscrubber's honor is not for sale. *(Starts to go, then turns around.)* What could I say to Ilyusha? What could I say to my boy?

(Lights fade.)

SCENE 5

The front yard of FYODOR KARAMAZOV's house. SMERDYAKOV is onstage; ALYOSHA enters.

ALYOSHA: Smerdyakov, have you seen my brother Dmitry?

SMERDYAKOV: Master Dmitry, sir, does not keep me informed as to his whereabouts.

ALYOSHA: It's alright to tell me, Smerdyakov, Dmitry told me everything yesterday—that you tell him what's going on in the house so you can let him know if Grushenka comes.

SMERDYAKOV: Master Dmitry, sir, only gets in touch with me when he chooses. And when he chooses, sir, he won't let me alone—he asks me a thousand questions—who comes, who goes—twice he threatened to kill me.

ALYOSHA: I'm sure it's just talk, but he shouldn't even speak like that. I'll talk to him about it—that is, if I could only find him.

SMERDYAKOV: Well, this much I can tell you, Master Alexei, sir, but no more. First thing this morning, Master Ivan sent me to Master Dmitry's place on Lake Street to tell him that he must meet Master Ivan for lunch at the tavern on the square. I went and Master Dmitry wasn't there—at eight in the morning, sir. I left word with his landlady. Perhaps she gave him the message and he's at the tavern right now—Master Ivan hasn't come home for lunch. But if you do find Master Dmitry, Master Alexei, sir, please don't mention me, he'd kill me for much less.

ALYOSHA: The tavern on the square? The Metropolis?

SMERDYAKOV: That's the one, sir.

ALYOSHA: Thank you, Smerdyakov. *(Exits.)*

SCENE 6

A room in the Metropolis Tavern. IVAN is finishing his lunch. ALYOSHA sticks his head in the door.

IVAN: Alyosha. Come in.

ALYOSHA: I feel a little funny coming into a tavern dressed like this.

IVAN: Don't worry, it's a private room, there's no one else here.

(ALYOSHA enters.)

IVAN: Sit down, have you had lunch? I'll order you some fish soup or something…you're not fasting, are you?

ALYOSHA: No, I'm not fasting and I'm very hungry. I'll have fish soup and then some tea.

IVAN: Waiter!

(WAITER enters.)

IVAN: The gentleman will have fish soup and then after that bring him some tea—Alyosha, would you like some cherry jam with your tea, they have it here.

ALYOSHA: I'd love some.

IVAN: Good. Bring some cherry jam with the tea.

WAITER: Very good, sir. *(Exits.)*

IVAN: I remember you used to love cherry jam when we lived at Polenov's.

ALYOSHA: I didn't think you even knew who I was then.

IVAN: I know I didn't seem to notice you, but I did. When I left for school I was nearly fifteen and you were eleven and there's a big difference between fifteen and eleven—it made it impossible for us to be friends. Now, here we are, we've been living in the same town for over three months and we've hardly spoken a word and I'm leaving tomorrow. I was just sitting here thinking I'd like to see you before I go.

ALYOSHA: You really wanted to see me?

IVAN: I wanted to get to know you. I know it doesn't seem like that, I know it seems I've been avoiding you—and I have. You've been looking at me with ceaseless expectation and that repulsed me. But in these last three months I've acquired a considerable amount of respect for you—you stand your ground—I love that, regardless of the ground you stand on and even though you're still only a boy—you know what you believe in. And so I've grown to love that look of expectation in your eyes. And you seem to love me for some reason.

ALYOSHA: I love you very much. Dmitry says you're silent as the grave, but to me you're an enigma…although I caught a glimpse of something just this morning.

IVAN: What was that?

ALYOSHA: Promise you won't be angry?

IVAN: Not at all, go ahead.

ALYOSHA: That you're just an ordinary twenty-three-year-old. You're a nice young man—young and inexperienced, even a little naive…I hope I haven't offended you.

IVAN: On the contrary, when I stormed out of there this morning I had exactly the same thought—I'm just a callow twenty-three-year-old. But that very callowness, that youth, can overcome anything—losing the woman I love, losing faith in the order of things…it can overcome all disillusionment, all despair. No matter what, I want to live—once I've started drinking from this cup, I won't put it down till I've drained it. Well, maybe by the time I'm thirty, I'll throw the cup on the ground whether I've finished or not—but until my thirtieth year my youth will overcome everything. Alyosha, I want to live and I do live—against all logic. Though I do not believe in the order of things, the sticky young leaves that open in the spring are dear to me, the blue sky is dear to me, there are some people who are dear to me and I don't know why, and I will revere an act of heroism with all my heart, even though I have long since ceased to believe in heroism. And you don't love these things with reason, with logic—you love them with your guts.

(WAITER enters with soup, serves ALYOSHA, and exits.)

ALYOSHA: I know exactly what you mean—it's the guts that love, it's the heart that loves, not the mind. And I'm so happy, Ivan, that you love life—we need to love life before anything else.

IVAN: Love life more than its meaning?

ALYOSHA: Exactly—Love comes before logic and only when we understand that will we find meaning.

IVAN: Alyosha, is it true you're leaving the monastery?

ALYOSHA: Yes, my elder is sending me out into the world. Is it true you're leaving town?

IVAN: Yes.

ALYOSHA: What about Dmitry and Father?

IVAN: What do I have to do with it? I'm not my brother's keeper. Do you really think I'm jealous of Dmitry? Do you really think I've been trying to steal his beautiful Katerina for the last three months? No, Alyosha, I had my own affairs to settle with Katerina and I'm done. For nearly half a year, I've been tangled up with her and now I can breathe. I thought of ordering champagne to celebrate my first hour of freedom.

ALYOSHA: Did you really love her?

IVAN: I thought I did and I let her torment me. But now it's all evaporated. This morning I realized I didn't love her in the least. I found her attractive—I still do. But we didn't really meet to talk about Katerina or about the old man and Dmitry, did we?

ALYOSHA: No, I don't think so.

IVAN: Where shall we begin? How about God: does He exist or not?

ALYOSHA: Last night at Father's, you said He didn't.

IVAN: I said that to tease you. But now I'm serious. I want to get close to you, Alyosha, because I have no friends. I want to try. Would it surprise you if I told you that I believe in God?

ALYOSHA: Yes. Unless you're joking.

IVAN: No, I'm not joking. Let me say simply and plainly that I accept God. Now, He created me with a mind that can understand the principles of Euclidean geometry and nothing more. My mind is capable of grasping only three dimensions of space—and yet, there have been and still are mathematicians and philosophers who dare to dream that two parallel lines which, according to Euclid, cannot possibly meet on Earth, do, in fact, meet somewhere in infinity. I cannot grasp that. My brain is an earthly Euclidean brain and I cannot deal with matters that are not of this world. And I would advise you, too, Alyosha, never to worry about these matters, least of all about God: whether He exists or not. Such questions are quite unsuitable to a mind created to conceive of only three dimensions. And so I accept God without question—I accept His wisdom and His purpose. But I do not accept His world.

ALYOSHA: Will you explain to me why you won't accept His world?

IVAN: Of course. Alyosha, I'm not trying to destroy your faith. No, I want you to heal me. Now, I've never understood how it is possible to love one's neighbors—

and I mean one's neighbors. I can conceive of the possibility of loving people who are far away, but if I must love my neighbor, he better hide his face—for the moment I see his face, there's an end to my love.

ALYOSHA: But Ivan, that's true for everybody. Father Zosima said so just yesterday to Madame Khokhalakova.

IVAN: Well, I'm glad to hear I'm in such august company as Madame Khokhalakova. However, I still believe it is impossible for human beings to truly have sympathy for the sufferings of others, for "how can their suffering be as great as mine?" Therefore, I will speak only of the suffering of children, for it is possible to love children, even at close quarters, even if they are ugly—although, to me, a child's face is never really ugly. I love children, Alyosha. Does that surprise you?

ALYOSHA: No.

IVAN: The Turks, among others, take a particularly voluptuous pleasure from torturing children. They do everything from cutting unborn babes out of their mother's wombs to tossing nursing infants in the air and catching them on the points of their bayonets as the mothers watch. But they're far more refined than that, they've thought up an amusing little game. They tickle a baby, they laugh to make it laugh. When it laughs, a Turk aims his pistol at it, holding it four inches from the baby's face. The baby giggles and tries to catch the shiny pistol in its tiny hands. At that moment, the "artist" pulls the trigger and splits the infant's skull in half. Pure art, isn't it? By the way, the Turks are particularly fond of sweet things.

ALYOSHA: What are you trying to say, brother? What are you driving at?

IVAN: What am I driving at? I'm just sharing my collection with you. I collect certain little facts—from newspaper items, from stories people tell me. The Turks are part of my collection, but they're just foreigners. I have quite a few Russian facts that are even better than the Turkish ones. To us, splitting infants on bayonets is unthinkable—we are Europeans, after all. Flogging is more to our tastes. I have a story about a five-year-old girl whose parents beat her until her whole body was nothing but bruises. Once, they dragged her into their outhouse in the middle of the night on the pretext that she had dirtied her bed. They smeared her face with excrement and her mother made her eat it. From that night on, she was made to sleep in the outhouse. Can you understand why this angelic creature, who

cannot even comprehend what is being done to her, sits trembling in the cold and the dark and the stench, beating her sore little chest with her tiny fists, weeping hot, unresentful tears, and begging "gentle Jesus" to help her? Can you understand this nonsensical thing, Alyosha? What is the purpose of this absurdity? Am I hurting you? Do you want me to stop?

ALYOSHA: Go on. I want to suffer with you.

IVAN: Just one more little sketch. It happened at the beginning of the century during the darkest days of serfdom. There was a very powerful general who retired from the army and settled down on his estate of two thousand souls. One day a serf boy—eight years old—was playing in the courtyard. He threw a stone and inadvertently hit the general's favorite hound in the leg. When the general found out, he had the boy taken from his mother and locked in the guardroom all night. At dawn the general rides out to the hunt in full dress, surrounded by obsequious neighbors, hounds, kennel attendants, huntsmen—all mounted on horseback. All the serfs of the estate are summoned—for their edification—the boy's mother in front of them all. The child is led out of the guardroom—it's a chilly, bleak, foggy day—ideal for hunting. The boy is stripped naked—he's paralyzed with fear, unable to speak. The general orders the huntsmen to drive the boy, so they prod him forward and he starts to run. The general roars "Sic 'im!" and the whole pack sets on the boy and the hounds tear him to pieces. He hunted him down before his mother's eyes. I believe that, as a result of this, the general was later declared incompetent to manage his affairs without a supervisory body. Well, what should we do with him, Alyosha? Shoot him? Shoot him for our moral satisfaction?

ALYOSHA: Yes. Shoot him.

IVAN: Bravo.

ALYOSHA: Ivan, what I just said is absurd, but…

IVAN: "But—" that's exactly the point—"but—." Absurdity is very much needed on this Earth of ours, Alyosha. The whole universe is founded on absurdity and what little we know is absurd.

ALYOSHA: And what do you know?

IVAN: I don't understand anything and I no longer want to understand anything. The minute I start trying to understand, I distort the facts. And I've made up my mind to stick to the facts.

ALYOSHA: Why Ivan? Why are you testing me? Will you finally tell me that?

IVAN: Because I love you and I have no intention of giving you up to that Elder Zosima of yours. I want you to understand me—I spoke only of children to make my point more obvious. I did not speak of the other human tears with which our Earth is soaked from crust to core because I was deliberately narrowing the focus. I'm an insect and I recognize, in all humility, that it is quite beyond my comprehension why things are arranged as they are. All that my puny, Euclidean, Earth-bound brain can grasp is that there is such a thing as suffering, that no one can be blamed for it, that quite uncomplicatedly cause precedes effect, that everything that flows finds its proper level—but all that is just Euclidean gibberish and I cannot agree to live by it. I need retribution. And not retribution somewhere and sometime in infinity, but retribution here and now on Earth. I believe in justice and I want to see justice done with my own eyes. I want to see with my own eyes the lamb lie down with the lion and the murdered man rise up and embrace his murderer. I want to be there when everyone finally finds out what it was all for. All human religions are based on this desire and so I am a believer. But then, what about the children? For the hundredth time I repeat, there are many questions to be asked, but I ask you only one. This is not blasphemy, Alyosha. I believe the universe will tremble when everything in Heaven and everything down in the entrails of the Earth merge together in one voice of praise, when all that lives and all that has lived cries aloud, "Thou art just, O Lord, for Thy ways have been revealed." When the mother and the torturer whose hounds tore her son to pieces will embrace and all three will cry out with tears, "Thou art just, O Lord," and the crown of knowledge will come and all will be explained. But this is exactly what I cannot accept. I do not really want to see the mother embrace the man who had her son torn to pieces. She has no right to forgive him. She may forgive him for her own immeasurable suffering, but not for her child's. And if I am right, if they cannot forgive, how can there be harmony? Is there in the whole world a single being who could and would have the right to forgive? I feel, moreover, that harmony is rather overpriced. We cannot afford to pay so much for admission. I want no part of their eternal harmony—for the love of mankind, I do not want it. It is not worth one single tear of that martyred girl who beat her breast in that stinking outhouse. And so I hasten to return my ticket. And if I am honest, it is my duty to return it as far in advance of

the show as possible. It's not that I reject God, Alyosha, I am simply returning to Him, most respectfully, the ticket that would entitle me to a seat.

ALYOSHA: That's rebellion.

IVAN: I wish you hadn't used that word. I don't believe it's possible to live in a state of rebellion and I want to live. But let me ask you one more question. Let's say you were called upon to build the edifice of human destiny so that mankind would be happy at last, so that we would finally be at peace. But to do so you would have to torture just one child. Would you do it?

ALYOSHA: No, I would not. But now, let me ask you a question, Ivan. A moment ago, you asked if there was, in the whole world, a being who could and would have the right to forgive. But there is such a being, Ivan, and He can forgive everything—forgive all and for all because He, Himself, gave His innocent blood for all and for everything. Why didn't you mention him? It is on His blood and His unavenged tears that the edifice is being built and it is to Him we will all cry aloud, "Thou art just, O Lord, for Thy ways have been revealed." Why did you not mention him, Ivan?

IVAN: No, Alyosha, I haven't forgotten about Him. I was just waiting for you to bring Him into it. Alright. Now, don't laugh, Alyosha, but I've written a poem about Him.

ALYOSHA: I didn't know you wrote poetry.

IVAN: I don't. I've never written two lines of verse in my whole life. I made up this poem and memorized it. Will you be my first reader…or audience?

ALYOSHA: I'm listening carefully.

IVAN: It's called "The Grand Inquisitor." Actually, it's ridiculous…but I'll recite it anyway. During the darkest days of the Inquisition, He decided to return to Earth—only for a moment—to show Himself to His tormented, long-suffering people. He appears in Spain, in Seville. He passes among His people in silence, a gentle smile on His lips. Children scatter flowers in His path and cry out to Him, "Hosannah." "It is He," everyone repeats, "It can be none but He." At this moment the Cardinal Grand Inquisitor crosses the cathedral square. The Inquisitor stretches forth his finger and orders his guards to take Him. The crowd obediently parts and amidst the deathly silence the guards lay hands on Him and lead Him away. As one being, the crowd bows to the ground before the aged Inquisitor, who silently blesses his people and moves on. That night, He sits in a prison cell. Suddenly, the iron door opens and there stands the Grand Inquisitor himself holding a lamp.

(THE INQUISITOR and CHRIST appear.)

The Inquisitor stands for a long time, gazing into the prisoner's face.

THE INQUISITOR: You. Is it You? You need not answer me. Be silent. I know only too well what You would say. Have You the right to reveal even a single mystery of the world from which you come? No, You do not. Anything new You might reveal to them would encroach upon the freedom of their faith for it would come to them as a miracle. And fifteen centuries ago, it was freely given faith that was most important to You. But don't you know that there is nothing more impossible for men to bear than freedom? Of course you know it; it was revealed to you when the wise and dread spirit of self-destruction and nonexistence spoke to You in the desert. It has been passed on to us in the books that he tempted You, but could anything be truer than what he revealed to You in those three questions, which You rejected and which the books call temptations?

Judge for Yourself who was right—You or the one who questioned You? Do You remember the first question? The wise and dread spirit said to you, "Do You see these stones in this bare, scorching desert? Turn them into loaves of bread and man will run after you like cattle." But You did not want to deprive men of freedom and rejected the offer. You said, "Man does not live by bread alone." But do You know that centuries will pass and humanity will proclaim through the lips of its science that there is no crime and therefore no sin, but only hungry people? "Feed us first, then ask for virtue." That is what they will inscribe on the banner they raise against You and by which Your temple will be destroyed and in its place the terrible Tower of Babel will rise again. And though, like the first, it will never be completed, You could have avoided this new tower and shortened people's suffering by a thousand years.

Had You been willing to give them bread, you would have satisfied the eternal craving of mankind—to have someone before whom they can bow. But it must be someone to whom they can bow together, if not, they will slaughter each other, crying, "Abandon your gods and worship mine!" There are only three powers on Earth that can satisfy this craving. These powers are Miracle, Mystery, and Authority. You rejected the first,

the second, and the third and set up Your rejection as an example to men.

The dread and wise spirit set you on the pinnacle of the temple and said to You, "If You would know whether You are the Son of God then cast Yourself down, for it is written: the angels shall hold Him up lest He fall and bruise Himself." But You heard and rejected the offer and did not throw Yourself down. Oh, You acted proudly, magnificently, indeed, You acted like God. But mankind, that weak, rebellious tribe—are they gods? Man cannot live without miracles, without them he will destroy himself. Had You respected him less, You would have loved him more.

Your great prophet tells us in a vision and an allegory that he saw all those who would be saved and that there were twelve thousand from each tribe. They endured your cross, they endured scores of years of hunger in a barren wilderness, living on roots and locusts. And, of course, You can point with pride at these children of freedom, at their freely given love, at their free and magnificent sacrifice in Your name. But there are only thousands of them. What of all the rest? Can it really be You came only for the chosen few? If it is so, then we are here for the millions upon millions, as numerous as sands in the sea, who are excluded from Your number, for they are dear to us.

We have corrected Your work and have founded it on Miracle, Mystery, and Authority. Why have You come now to interfere with us? Why are You looking at me so compassionately? I do not want Your love, for I love You not. What I have to tell You is known to You already, I can see it in Your eyes. How could I expect to hide our secret from You? But perhaps You want to hear it from my own lips. Listen then. We are not with You, we are with him. Exactly eight centuries ago we accepted from him what you refused. The last gift he offered You when he showed You all the kingdoms of the Earth: we accepted Rome and the sword of Caesar and proclaimed ourselves sole rulers of the Earth. We will satisfy mankind's greatest longing—we will take upon ourselves the intolerable burden of their freedom. We are not yet masters of the Earth and we will not be for centuries to come. And in that time, unruly, rebellious man will raze Your temples and build his Tower of Babel and drench the Earth in blood. But in the end, they will come to us and everyone will be happy, all the millions of creatures except for the hundred thousand who rule over them. For only we, the keepers of the secret, will be unhappy. And on the day of reckoning, I will stand before You and point to the thousands of millions of happy babes who have known no sin. And we, who took their sins upon ourselves, will stand before you and say, "Judge us if You can and if You dare."

Know that I am not afraid of You. Know that I, too, was in the wilderness, and I, too, ate locusts and roots, and I blessed Your freedom, and that I, too, was prepared to take my place among the strong, chosen ones. But I turned away and returned to the humble for the happiness of the humble. What I have told you will come to pass and our kingdom will come. Tomorrow You will see this obedient flock, at the first sign from me, rush to heap the coals about Your feet. For, if ever anyone has deserved our fire, it is You.

ALYOSHA: No, Ivan. Your poem makes no sense—it doesn't blame Jesus, it praises him. And why are you telling this to me, it has nothing to do with the Orthodox Church—that's Rome. And it's not really Rome— there is no such person as your Inquisitor—there is no mystery or sad noble resignation—just simple lust for power. Your suffering Inquisitor is just a fantasy.

IVAN: Alright, don't get so excited. I concede it's just a fantasy.

ALYOSHA: You Inquisitor's only secret is that he doesn't believe in God.

IVAN: Well, you've finally guessed it. But is it not suffering for such a man to come to the realization that it is only possible to make life on Earth bearable through lies and deceit? Ach, I sound like an author who can't take criticism. Let's talk about something else.

ALYOSHA: You don't believe in God. Does your poem have an ending or is that it?

IVAN: I was going to end it like this. The Inquisitor falls silent and waits for his prisoner to reply. He waits for some time. The prisoner's silence weighs on him. Suddenly the prisoner goes over to the old man...

(CHRIST goes over to THE INQUISITOR and kisses him on the lips.)

INQUISITOR: Go and do not come back—ever.

IVAN: And he lets Him out into the dark streets of the city and the prisoner leaves.

(CHRIST and THE INQUISITOR disappear.)

ALYOSHA: And the old man?

IVAN: The kiss glows in his heart. But he holds to his idea.

ALYOSHA: And you with him.

IVAN: It's all nonsense, Alyosha—a meaningless poem by an idiotic student who's never written two lines of verse in his life. You don't really think I'll run off to the Jesuits to join the men who are correcting His work? What do I care about it? I just want to drag on until I'm thirty and then—smash the cup on the ground.

ALYOSHA: And what about the sticky leaves and the blue sky and the woman you love? How will you live with such a hell in your heart and in your head, with what will you love them? No—you are going now precisely to join "those who are correcting His work." If you don't, you'll kill yourself—you won't be able to endure it.

IVAN: There is a force in me that will endure everything.

ALYOSHA: What force?

IVAN: The Karamazov force—the Karamazov baseness.

ALYOSHA: You mean you're going to drown your soul in debauchery?

IVAN: Eventually. But I'll avoid it 'til I'm thirty.

ALYOSHA: How? It's impossible to live with those ideas. You'll need something to drown out what's going on inside you.

IVAN: If I can believe that there is no God, then I can endure it all.

ALYOSHA: Because then everything would be permitted?

IVAN: Miusov and Dmitry vulgarized the idea—but since the words have been spoken, I'll stand by them. Yes—everything is permitted.

(ALYOSHA looks at IVAN in silence.)

IVAN: I thought, brother, that when I left here, I'd have you at least. But now I see there is no place for me even in your heart. I won't renounce my idea—everything is permitted. Will you renounce me, then.

(ALYOSHA goes over to IVAN and kisses him on the lips.)

IVAN: That's plagiarism. Thank you, though. Come on, it's time we were going.

(They start to go.)

IVAN: Alyosha, if I hold out for the sticky leaves, I will only love them remembering you. The fact that you are somewhere on this Earth will be enough for me not to stop wanting to live. Now go to your *Pater Seraphicus*—he's dying and if he dies without you, you'll be angry at me for having kept you. Kiss me once more.

(They kiss.)

ALYOSHA: Goodbye, Ivan.

IVAN: Go now. *(Exits.)*

(Lights fade.)

ACT III
SCENE 1

The front yard of FYODOR KARAMAZOV's house. SMERDYAKOV is sitting on a bench, IVAN enters and starts to cross into the house but stops and turns to SMERDYAKOV.

IVAN: Is Father still asleep?

SMERDYAKOV: The master, sir, is still resting. I'm surprised at you, sir.

IVAN: Why are surprised at me?

SMERDYAKOV: Why haven't you left for Chermashnya, sir?

IVAN: Why should I go to Chermashnya?

SMERDYAKOV: Why, your father has begged you to go, sir.

IVAN: What the hell do you want? Speak plainly, for God's sake.

SMERDYAKOV: I'm in a terrible position, Master Ivan, sir. They're completely insane—Mr. Karamazov and Master Dmitry. I'm so frightened, I've even thought of taking my own life.

IVAN: Then why did you get mixed up in it in the first place? Why did you agree to spy for Dmitry?

SMERDYAKOV: I did try to stay out of it, sir, if you want to know with complete exactitude. I kept my mouth shut from the very beginning, but Master Dmitry threatened to kill me if she came and I didn't let him know. It's

gotten to the point where I'm certain I'll have a long fit of the falling sickness tomorrow.

IVAN: And what is a long fit?

SMERDYAKOV: A long fit, sir, is a fit that lasts for a very, very long time—several hours—or even several days. Once I had a fit that went on for three days. That was when I fell from the attic.

IVAN: As I understand it, an epileptic can never predict when a fit will strike. So how can you know that you'll have one tomorrow?

SMERDYAKOV: I can't.

IVAN: Besides, you fell from the attic that time.

SMERDYAKOV: But I go to the attic every day, sir. I could fall again tomorrow. Or I might fall into the cellar—I go to the cellar every day, too—with my duties, sir.

IVAN: Are you telling me you're planning to simulate a fit tomorrow?

SMERDYAKOV: Let's say I could do it, sir—simulate a fit, which wouldn't be difficult for an experienced man—I would have every right to save myself from death. If I were laid up with a fit, sir, and Miss Svetlova came to your father, not even Master Dmitry could blame me.

IVAN: Why the hell are you so afraid for your precious safety? Dmitry's threats are just talk. And if he kills someone, it won't be you.

SMERDYAKOV: He'd kill me like a fly, sir, and he'll kill me first. Besides, if he does do something to your father, they'll consider me an accomplice.

IVAN: Why would they do that?

SMERDYAKOV: Because I told him the secret about the signals, sir.

IVAN: What signals?

SMERDYAKOV: Well, sir, I'll tell you in the strictest confidence. The master has done me the honor of sharing a secret with me. Every night, sir, the master locks himself in the house. He has instructed me to keep watch; and if Miss Svetlova comes, sir, I am to run to the door or the window and knock two times slowly, like this, *(Knocks on the bench.)* then three times quickly, like this. *(Knocks on the bench.)* Then he'll know she's come and open the door. Now, if Master Dmitry comes, I'm to knock twice quickly *(Knocks.)* and then knock once, hard. (*Knocks.*) These signals, sir, have become known to Master Dmitry.

IVAN: Because you told him. Why?

SMERDYAKOV: As proof of my loyalty, sir. He accused me of hiding something from him and threatened to kill me.

IVAN: If he comes and tries to use the signals, stop him.

SMERDYAKOV: Even if I dared to, sir, I couldn't if I were laid up with a fit.

IVAN: If you're laid up, then Grigory will warn Father.

SMERDYAKOV: Grigory's back, sir, has gone out and Marfa is going to give him her treatment tomorrow. She makes this infusion, sir, of strong herbs and spirits and rubs it on his back. Then they both drink it. Neither of them, sir, is used to spirits, so as soon as they taste the stuff, they're fast asleep. So you see, sir, it's not likely either of them will hear when Master Dmitry comes.

IVAN: This is ridiculous. All these events will come together as if they were planned? Or are you going to arrange it that way?

SMERDYAKOV: How could I arrange it, sir, when everything depends on Master Dmitry?

IVAN: Well, why would Dmitry come at all? You know as well as I do, Grushenka isn't coming.

SMERDYAKOV: You know yourself, sir, why he'll come. He'll come because he's angry or he'll come because he's suspicious, just as he did last night, sir. He'll come for the three thousand rubles the master has waiting for Miss Svetlova.

IVAN: Nonsense. Dmitry wouldn't steal money and he wouldn't kill Father to do it.

SMERDYAKOV: Master Dmitry needs money very badly, sir, and he feels entitled to that three thousand as part of his inheritance. And I don't know that Miss Svetlova won't come. She's no fool: if she's certain he'll marry her and she can get control of his money, she'll come, sir. And then, not you, nor Master Dmitry, nor Master Alexei will see a kopek of your father's money when he dies. On the other hand, if Mr. Karamazov were to die now, before any of this happens, each of you would get forty thousand right away—even Master Dmitry, because, as Master Dmitry well knows, your father hasn't made a will.

IVAN: And why, after all that, are you advising me to go to Chermashnya? Are you saying if I leave, this is going to happen?

SMERDYAKOV: Exactly right, sir.

IVAN: What's right?

SMERDYAKOV: I spoke out of concern for you, sir. If I were in your position, sir, I'd drop everything and leave, considering all the things that might happen here.

IVAN: You're an idiot. And you're a corrupt monster. (*Starts to exit, then stops.*) If you must know, I'm leaving for Moscow tomorrow morning—early. And that's all.

SMERDYAKOV: That's the best thing, sir.

(*IVAN starts to exit again.*)

SMERDYAKOV: Of course, sir, they may call you back by telegram, should anything happen here.

IVAN: Wouldn't they summon me from Chermashnya, as well?

SMERDYAKOV: That's right, sir, they'd bother you just the same in Chermashnya.

IVAN: Only Moscow is farther than Chermashnya. Are you trying to save me train fare?

SMERDYAKOV: Exactly right, sir.

IVAN: I'm going straight to bed. Tell my father I won't be joining him for supper. (*Exits.*)

SCENE 2

ZOSIMA's cell. ZOSIMA, PAISII, and FATHER IOSIF are onstage. ALYOSHA enters.

ZOSIMA: Welcome, my quiet one. I knew you would come.

(*ALYOSHA bows to the ground before ZOSIMA and begins to weep.*)

ZOSIMA: (*Blessing ALYOSHA.*) Have you been home? Did you see your brother?

ALYOSHA: I saw one of my brothers.

ZOSIMA: The oldest one, before whom I bowed to the ground?

ALYOSHA: I saw him yesterday, but I couldn't find him today.

ZOSIMA: Find him tomorrow—you may be able to prevent something horrible. I bowed yesterday to the great suffering that is in store for him.

ALYOSHA: Father and teacher, I...your words are obscure, Father. What suffering is in store for him?

ZOSIMA: I caught a glimpse of something terrible—I looked in his eyes and I was filled with horror—horror at what this man is preparing for himself. Once or twice I have seen that look in men's faces—a look that seemed to contain their fate—a fate which, alas, came to be. I sent you to him, Alyosha, because I thought a brother's face—your face—would help him. But everything and all our fates come from God—"Unless a corn of wheat fall into the ground and die, it abideth alone: but if it die, it bringeth forth much fruit"—remember that.

My dear fathers and brothers, I may not live through the night and so I asked you all to come here so I could say goodbye and tell you that I love you. Fathers and teachers, my heart is so full that I must speak and share my joy. Love one another, Fathers, love all God's creation, love every individual person. We are responsible to all men for everyone and everything, for all human sins, universal and individual. Not only responsible through the universal responsibility of mankind, but responsible personally, every person for all people and for each individual person who lives on this Earth.

You may ask, what real difference will it make if I accept that I am responsible for everyone and everything? Whose suffering will it lessen? But I say unto you, Fathers and teachers, all is like an ocean, all flows and connects—touch it in one place and it echoes at the other end of the world. Let me tell you, Fathers, life would be easier for every person, every child, every animal near you if you were kinder than you are—if only by a drop, still, it would be easier.

The scoffers will say this is just a dream. But I say unto them, "Yours is a dream." They want to build a just order based on science and reason, but without Christ, and they will end by drenching the Earth in blood. Fathers and teachers, no science, no self-interest will teach men to share among themselves. Until each one of us becomes, in actual fact, a brother to all men, there can be no brotherhood

Fathers and teachers, on this last night of my life, I ask myself a question that has tormented me all my years: what is hell? And I answer thus: Hell is the suffering of no longer being able to love. It is only in our physical life, our life on Earth, that we can love actively: that we can bring joy to another living creature and ease another's pain. Indeed, this is the whole reason that our spirits are sent to this Earth. But some reject this privilege and sneer at it. And so their physical life ends and the truth is revealed to them and they are consumed with agony at what might have been. For never again will they be given the opportunity to sacrifice themselves for another creature, never again will they be given life and time. Can there be any relief from this spiritual agony, Fathers and teachers? There is nothing in the teachings of the church that tells us so. But I believe and hope that God eases the torment even of those who have sinned cruelly and were too blind to see that this Earth is Paradise.

Oh, Fathers and teachers, this Earth is Paradise. (*As he is speaking, ZOSIMA rises and then falls to the ground, kissing it.*) Love to throw yourself down on the Earth and kiss it. Kiss the Earth and love it, tirelessly, insatiably, love all men, all things, seek rapture and ecstasy. Life is joy, Fathers and teachers, Earth is Paradise, love the Earth, Fathers and brothers, water the Earth with the tears of your joy and love those tears, love the Earth, love it, Fathers, love your tears...Are we not in Paradise, Fathers? Water the Earth with your joy, love your joy, Fathers, love...

(*ZOSIMA is suddenly still. He is dead. Lights fade.*)

Scene 3

FYODOR KARAMAZOV's dining room, the next morning. FYODOR is sitting at the table having breakfast. IVAN enters.

FYODOR: We missed you at supper last night.

IVAN: I had to get some sleep, I'm leaving for Moscow in an hour.

FYODOR: You see, I knew you were lying to me the other night—you had no intention of going to Chermashnya for me. Oh, come on, Ivan, can't you do this one thing for your father? Chermashnya is only nine miles from Volovya station.

IVAN: In the other direction. And it's fifty miles from here to Volovya. As it stands now, I can barely make the seven o'clock train.

FYODOR: So, you'll make it tomorrow. Where are you off to now, anyway? Venice? Well, it's not going to fall into the sea in two days, your Venice.

IVAN: Whether I go to Moscow or Chermashnya, you'll still get me out of the house.

FYODOR: It's not just that—I really do have important business in Chermashnya. There's a merchant named Gorstkin who's interested in buying my forest there. Go, find out what he's willing to pay, send me word through the little priest who looks after my affairs there, and then you're off to Moscow.

IVAN: I have no eye for business.

FYODOR: You're smart, that's enough. So, then you'll go?

IVAN: I'll decide on the way.

FYODOR: No, decide now, my dear. You'll go. Oh, one more thing—they call Gorstkin the Hound, but whatever you do, don't call him that to his face, it makes him furious. Now, off with you.

(FYODOR moves to embrace IVAN, but IVAN extends his hand.)

IVAN: Goodbye, Father.

FYODOR: Well, God be with you, God be with you. Are you planning to come back in this lifetime? Do. I'll always be glad to see you.

IVAN: Goodbye.

FYODOR: Don't curse me too much.

(IVAN crosses into the yard where SMERDYAKOV is waiting.)

IVAN: So you see I'm going to Chermashnya.

SMERDYAKOV: So it's true what they say. It's always rewarding to talk to a clever man.

Scene 4

A yard in the monastery, the same morning. ALYOSHA is sitting on the ground, crying. PAISII enters.

PAISII: Come, son. That's enough, my boy. You know very well you should rejoice. Where is he now, at this very moment? Just think of it.

ALYOSHA: I know, Father…I…

PAISII: It's alright, Alyosha, my boy—weep. Christ has sent you these tears—they will bring you peace and gladden the soul of your departed elder.

(Lights fade on ALYOSHA and PAISII and come up on MADAME KHOKHLAKOVA.)

KHOKHLAKOVA: Dear Monsieur Rakitin, I am so confused. My soul is split in two, verily, it is split in two. I mourn the loss of such a kind and holy man. Life without him will be unimaginable, simply unimaginable. I can't tell you how upset Lise is. On the other hand, great things are sure to happen—the whole town is breathless with expectation. As you know, the miracles started before his death. You could say mine was the first miracle. After he laid his hands on my Lise, she had no fever and stood up for a whole minute. Then he predicted that that widow's son would return to her and, lo, he did. I am certain we shall see greater things yet. Since our dear Orthodox Church has not yet embraced modern ideas concerning women, I am not allowed within the hermitage walls—indeed, when I used to visit the Elder—oh, he was such a charming man—he had to receive me in that gallery just outside the walls. My dear Monsieur Rakitin, since you are such a devout and religious young man as well as being a cultured man of the most modern ideas, I turn to you. Could you be so kind as to send me a complete written report as to what is going on at the monastery every half hour or so? This servant will await your communiques just outside the monastery gates. I eagerly await your reply. With expectation of greater things to come, Katerina Osipovna Khokhlakova.

(Lights fade on MADAME KHOKHLAKOVA and come up on TWO MERCHANTS standing in the monastery yard.)

MERCHANT 1: What brings you here, Victor Ipolitovich?

MERCHANT 2: The same as everyone else, Rodion Romanovich.

MERCHANT 1: Have you brought your daughter, Victor Ipolitovich?

MERCHANT 2: She's waiting outside the gate with her mother.

MERCHANT 1: I have no doubt before the day is out, she'll be cured.

MERCHANT 2: You heard about the sergeant's widow?

MERCHANT 1: Mm hm. You heard about Lise Khokhlakova?

MERCHANT 2: Mm hm. You heard about Dmitry Karamazov?

MERCHANT 1: No.

MERCHANT 2: The Elder prostrated himself before him.

MERCHANT 1: Well, we'll see then.

MERCHANT 2: Mm hm.

(Lights fade on MERCHANTS and come up on ZOSIMA's cell. PAISII is standing over ZOSIMA's coffin reading from Matthew 4. IOSIF, RAKITIN, and MONK 1 stand nearby.)

PAISII: "Then was Jesus led up of the spirit into the wilderness to be tempted of the devil. And when he had fasted forty days and forty nights he was afterward an hungred. And when the tempter came to him, he said if thou be the Son of God, command that these stones be made bread. But He answered and said, "It is written, Man shall not live by bread alone, but by every word that proceedeth out of the mouth of God." *(Continues to read from Matthew 4.)*

RAKITIN: Should I open a window?

MONK 1: Don't be absurd, Mikhail. With such a body, it is unnecessary.

(Lights fade on ZOSIMA's cell and come up on TWO MONKS in another part of the monastery yard.)

MONK 2: They say Father Varsonofy's body gave off the fragrance of orange blossoms.

MONK 3: We can expect even greater things today.

MONK 2: They've already begun. You heard about the sergeant's widow?

MONK 3: Of course. And you heard the day before yesterday, he prostrated himself before Alexei's brother?

MONK 2: If I were Dmitry Fyodorovich, I would be terrified.

MONK 3: If I were his father, I would be terrified.

(Lights fade on MONKS, lights up on ZOSIMA's cell. PAISII is standing over ZOSIMA's coffin reading Luke 4. IOSIF, MONK 1, and RAKITIN are standing nearby.)

PAISII: "And the devil taking him up into an high mountain, shewed unto him all the kingdoms of the world in a moment of time. And the devil said unto him, All this power I will give thee, and the glory of them: for that is delivered unto me; and to whomsoever I will give it. If thou therefore wilt worship me, all shall be thine." *(Continues reading from Luke 4.)*

IOSIF: Mikhail, could you open the window?

(MONK 1 slips out. Lights fade on ZOSIMA's cell and come up on MONKS 2 and 3. MONK 1 enters.)

MONK 1: Brothers, have you been in the Elder's cell?

MONK 2: This morning, Father.

MONK 1: And did you notice anything strange?

MONK 3: No.

MONK 1: I suggest you go in there now.

(MONKS 2 and 3 exit. Lights fade on MONKS and come up on MERCHANT 2. MERCHANT 1 enters.)

MERCHANT 1: Victor Ipolitovich, I overheard some of the monks talking—something extraordinary has happened.

MERCHANT 2: A miracle?

MERCHANT 1: Far from it. There is a smell in the Elder's cell—the odor of corruption.

MERCHANT 2: What's so extraordinary about that?

MERCHANT 1: The odor of corruption? From one who claimed to be a saint?

MERCHANT 2: He is a saint.

MERCHANT 1: Go and see—or smell—for yourself.

(Lights down on MERCHANTS, lights up on MONKS.)

MONK 2: It's strange, though, that this should happen to him. He was so small and thin, nothing but skin and bones—where could the smell be coming from?

(FATHER IOSIF enters.)

MONK 3: It's not natural. According to secular science, it should take twenty-four hours before the body starts to decay—this is a violation of the laws of nature.

MONK 1: It's a sign from God.

IOSIF: That's not necessarily so, Father…brothers. It is not a dogma of the Orthodox Church that the body of the righteous never decays.

MONK 1: There was no smell when Father Varsonofy died. In fact, there was a decided aroma of flowers.

MONK 2: And that was not because he was an elder, but because he was a righteous man.

IOSIF: It is not a dogma of the Orthodox Church…On Mt. Athos they attach no significance to the smell of decay…no, it is the color of the bones after the body has been buried for several years…if they are yellow, like wax, it is a sign that God has glorified the deceased…if…if they are black…

MONK 1: Oh, the color of the bones!

IOSIF: On Athos…on Athos…a holy place…there they have preserved Orthodoxy inviolate and in shining purity.

MONK 1: You're splitting hairs, Father Iosif.

MONK 2: We believe in the odor of corruption—bones are just an innovation—just like the institution of elders.

MONK 1: What do we care for Athos? They're living under the Turk—their Orthodoxy is no longer pure.

MONK 3: Clearly this is a warning from God.

MONK 1: Clearly, God's judgment is not as man's.

(Lights fade on MONKS; lights up on MERCHANTS.)

MERCHANT 2: Clearly, God's judgment is not as man's.

MERCHANT 1: I heard some of the monks saying that the institution of elders is a radical new innovation—that the Elder Zosima had godlike power over the other monks.

MERCHANT 2: I heard they had to confess to him out loud.

(Lights fade on MERCHANTS; lights up on MONKS. FATHER IOSIF is gone.)

MONK 3: He abused the sacrament of confession.

MONK 2: He didn't keep his fasts—he took cherry jam with his tea, and the rich ladies who loved him so much used to send it to him all the time.

MONK 1: His teachings were false—he taught people that life was a great joy and not a vale of tears.

MONK 3: Well, what do you expect? His beliefs were modern and fashionable—he didn't accept the material fire of hell.

MONK 1: He sat in pride and fancied himself a saint. People prostrated themselves before him and he accepted it as his due.

MONK 3: *(Looking out.)* Father Ferapont is coming.

MONK 2: He hasn't left his hut in over a year.

MONK 1: Now all shall be set right.

(Lights fade on MONKS; lights up on MERCHANTS.)

MERCHANT 1: My God, do you see that?

MERCHANT 2: Who is he?

MERCHANT 1: It's Ferapont, the great ascetic.

MERCHANT 2: Where are they all going?

MERCHANT 1: It looks like they're headed toward the Elder Zosima's cell. Let's follow.

(They start to move; lights fade on MERCHANTS and come up on ZOSIMA's cell. PAISII is standing over ZOSIMA's coffin reading John 12. IOSIF is standing nearby.)

PAISII: "And Jesus answered them, saying, "The hour is come, that the Son of man should be glorified. Verily, verily, I say unto you, Unless a corn of wheat fall into the ground and die, it abideth alone: but if it die, it bringeth forth much fruit."

(FERAPONT bursts into the cell, MERCHANTS and MONKS follow him up to the doorway and wait outside. RAKITIN and ALYOSHA are also in the crowd. ALYOSHA is hidden from the audience.)

FERAPONT: Casting out, I cast out! *(Makes the sign of the cross over each corner of the cell, repeating the incantation each time.)* Satan get thee hence! Satan get thee hence! Satan get thee hence! Satan get thee hence! Casting out, I cast out!

PAISII: What do you want here, worthy Father? Why do you disturb the peace of the flock?

FERAPONT: Why do I come? I come, Father, to drive out your guests—the unholy ones, the foul devils. I will sweep them out with a birch broom.

PAISII: You come to drive out the unclean one, but perhaps you serve him. Who can say of himself, "I am holy"? Can you, Father?

FERAPONT: I am foul, not holy, and I would not sit in an armchair and demand that people worship me like an idol. That saint of yours denied devils, and so they've bred here like spiders in the corners. And on this day he got himself stunk. And that is a sign from God.

PAISII: Get thee hence, Father. It is not for man to judge, but for God. Get thee hence, Father, and do not trouble the flock.

FERAPONT: He did not keep the fasts according to his monastic rank. He was seduced by sweets—the ladies brought him candies in their pockets. He was a tea-sipper. He was a glutton. He stuffed his stomach with sweets and his mind with arrogance.

PAISII: You speak lightly, Father. I respect and marvel at your fasting and ascetic life, but your words are thoughtless, like you were some worldly, callow youth—fickle and childish. Get thee hence, Father—I command you.

FERAPONT: I will go hence. You learned ones. In great wisdom you exalt yourselves above my nothingness. I came here illiterate and have forgot what little I knew. The Lord Himself has protected me, His little one, from your learning. You have grown rotten with pride—this is an empty place.

(FERAPONT crosses out of the cell as the lights fade to suggest a sunset.)

FERAPONT: *(Falling to his knees.)* My Lord has conquered! Christ has conquered with the setting sun!

MONK 1: It he who is holy! It is he who is righteous!

MERCHANT 1: He should be made an elder!

MONK 2: He would not want to be an elder! He would not serve a cursed innovation!

MONK 1: Here is the saint!

MONK 3: Blessed is he!

MONKS and MERCHANTS: Blessed is he! Blessed is he! Blessed is he!

(A church bell rings.)

MONKS and MERCHANTS: Blessed is he! Blessed is he!

(IOSIF crosses out of the cell.)

IOSIF: Fathers and brothers, it is time to go to services. Gentlemen, it is time for you to go home.

(ALL outside the cell exit—MERCHANTS in one direction, MONKS in the other—except FERAPONT, who remains kneeling and praying, and ALYOSHA. PAISII crosses out of the cell, and ALYOSHA starts to exit in the same direction as MERCHANTS.)

PAISII: Alexei, where are you going? The bell is ringing for services.

(ALYOSHA is silent.)

PAISII: Are you leaving the hermitage without permission? Without a blessing?

(ALYOSHA is silent.)

PAISII: Do you, too, have so little faith?

(ALYOSHA starts to exit.)

PAISII: You'll be back.

(Lights fade.)

SCENE 5

Lights up on IVAN in the carriage.

IVAN: Driver. Never mind Chermashnya. Take me to Volovya station.

SCENE 6

A wood near the monastery. Early evening. ALYOSHA is lying face down on the ground. RAKITIN enters.

RAKITIN: Alyosha? What are you doing? I've been looking for you for over two hours—you just vanished. What's the matter? You could at least look at me.

(ALYOSHA looks up.)

RAKITIN; Good Lord. You certainly don't look meek and gentle anymore. Are you angry?…at someone? Did someone offend you?

ALYOSHA: Leave me alone.

RAKITIN: Well, you've become testy, just like the rest of us mortals. So I take it you're no longer an angel?

(ALYOSHA is silent.)

RAKITIN: Is this all because your old man stinks? Oh come on—you're an educated man, you didn't really believe he'd start pulling off miracles?

ALYOSHA: I believed, I believe, and I want to believe, and I will believe, and what more do you want?

RAKITIN: Precisely nothing, my dear Alexei…But for god's sake, Alyosha, not even thirteen-year-old schoolboys believe in this nonsense anymore. Nonetheless, you're angry with your God and you've rebelled. And all because your old man was passed over for promotion. You people.

ALYOSHA: I'm not rebelling. It's not that I don't accept God, I simply do not accept His world.

RAKITIN: You don't accept his world? What the hell is that supposed to mean?

(ALYOSHA is silent.)

RAKITIN: Alright, enough of this nonsense. Have you eaten?

ALYOSHA: I don't remember…I think I did.

RAKITIN: I doubt it. You don't look well. I've got some sausage, (Takes some sausage in wrapping paper out of his pocket.) do you want some? Oh, of course you can't.

ALYOSHA: Sausage will be fine.

RAKITIN: And you said you weren't rebelling against your God—you're manning the barricades. This is an occasion—let's go back to my place. In fact, I could do with a shot of vodka about now. You wouldn't go that far, would you?

ALYOSHA: Let's have the vodka.

RAKITIN: What? This is an occasion. Let's go.

(They start to go.)

RAKITIN: God! I wish your brother Vanya could see this. You know, Ivan left for Moscow this morning?

ALYOSHA: I know.

RAKITIN: Dear Vanya refers to me as a "talentless windbag of a liberal." And just the other morning, you couldn't resist letting me know that you agreed with him. Oh well, never mind. Oh, I ought to stop at Madame Khokhalakova's on the way. You know she had me sending her reports every half hour? When she got the last report, she—wrote back that she never expected such behavior from such a venerable elder as Father Zosima—such behavior—you people. Wait a minute…Alyosha, do you know where we should go?

ALYOSHA: I don't care, wherever you like.

RAKITIN: How about Grushenka's?

ALYOSHA: Fine. Let's go to Grushenka's.

RAKITIN: You're serious?

(ALYOSHA is silent.)

RAKITIN: Alright then, let's go. She'll be delighted to see you.

(Lights fade.)

SCENE 7

FYODOR KARAMAZOV's dining room. SMERDYAKOV screams from offstage. FYODOR runs to the cellar door.)

FYODOR: Marfa! Grigory! Come quick. Smerdyakov's fallen down the cellar stairs. He's having a fit.

SCENE 8

GRUSHENKA's drawing room, half an hour later. GRUSHENKA is lying on a couch in the dark. There is a knock at the door and she jumps up.

GRUSHENKA: Who is it?

FENYA: (Offstage.) It's not him, miss.

(RAKITIN enters, followed by ALYOSHA and FENYA.)

RAKITIN: (To FENYA.) What's the matter with her?

GRUSHENKA: Oh, it's you, Rakitka. You gave me a start…Oh my God, you brought him.

RAKITIN: Light the lamps. It's like a mausoleum in here.

GRUSHENKA: Of course. Fenya, light the lamps, but keep the curtains closed.

(FENYA lights the lamps; when she's finished, she exits.)

GRUSHENKA: Well, your timing could be better, Rakitka.

RAKITIN: You had more important things to do?

GRUSHENKA: You frightened me—I thought it was Mitya. But don't worry, Alyosha, darling, I'm very glad to see you. You see, Rakitka, I tricked him this afternoon, I lied to him. I told him I was going to be with Kuzma—that's my merchant, Alyosha, darling—counting money. You see, Alyosha, I go every week to do the books with him. We lock ourselves in and he bangs away on the abacus while I write the figures down in the books. I'm the only one he trusts.

RAKITIN: And why aren't you there now, banging the beads?

GRUSHENKA: Because, Rakitka, I'm expecting a message—a golden message—and it would be better if there were no Mitenka around at all. So I had Mitya take me to Kuzma's door and told him to pick me up at midnight. I stayed for about ten minutes and then ran back home. I'm terrified he'll find out.

RAKITIN: And why are you so spruced up?

GRUSHENKA: I told you, I'm expecting a message. When it comes I'll fly away and that's the last you'll see of me. So that's why I'm dressed. So I'll be ready.

RAKITIN: And where will you fly to?

GRUSHENKA: Ask me no questions, I'll tell you no lies. Alyosha, darling, I just can't believe you're here. Come, sit right here, my young moon, on the sofa. *(Sits on the sofa, next to ALYOSHA.)* You look so sad, Alyoshenka. Do I frighten you?

RAKITIN: He is sad. The promotion was denied.

GRUSHENKA: What promotion?

RAKITIN: His elder stinks.

GRUSHENKA: I have no idea what you mean, but I'm sure it's nasty, so why don't you just shut up. Alyosha, will you let me sit on your lap— *(She jumps on his lap.)* like this? I'll cheer you up, my little pious boy. Do you mind? I'll jump off if you do.

(ALYOSHA is silent.)

RAKITIN: Stop babbling and bring out some champagne—you owe it to me.

GRUSHENKA: He's absolutely right, Alyosha—I promised him champagne if he brought you to me. Fenya! Bring that bottle of champagne Mitya left. I'll drink with you; I want to be naughty.

RAKITIN: Alright, enough mystery—why are you so excited? What's this message of yours—or is it a secret?

GRUSHENKA: It's no secret, Rakitin, my officer is coming—he's coming.

RAKITIN: I know he wrote that he was on his way. Has he arrived?

GRUSHENKA: He's at Mokroye. He's sending a messenger for me—I got a letter from him today.

RAKITIN: Does Mitenka know?

GRUSHENKA: Are you serious? If he found out, he'd kill me. But I'm not afraid now, I'm not afraid of his knife. Alyoshenka, smile at me, my pet; cheer up, my darling; laugh at my joy, laugh at my silliness, but laugh.

(ALYOSHA smiles.)

GRUSHENKA: Look, he's really smiling. You know, Alyosha, I keep thinking you must be very angry with

me for what I did to the young lady two days ago. I was a bitch—but it's good that I was. She wanted to make a conquest of me, to seduce me with chocolate. No, she deserved what she got. The only thing I was worried about was you.

RAKITIN: She really was afraid you'd be angry—She told me so herself. She's afraid of you—little chicken that you are.

(FENYA enters with the champagne. She sets it down and exits.)

RAKITIN: At last. *(Crosses to the champagne.)* You're not yourself this evening, Grushenka. But after a glass of this, you should be ready to dance. Ach, these peasants can't do anything right—it hasn't been chilled—it's quite warm. Nonetheless, one doesn't get champagne that often. *(Pours himself a glass and downs it. He pours ALYOSHA a glass.)* Here, Alyosha, take a glass and show us your mettle. *(Pours GRUSHENKA a glass.)* What shall we drink to? The gates of paradise? Come, Grusha, raise a glass to the gates of paradise.

ALYOSHA: *(Takes a sip and puts it down.)* I'd better not.

RAKITIN: After all that bragging.

GRUSHENKA: Then I won't drink either. Besides, I don't feel like drinking now. I'll only have some if Alyosha does.

RAKITIN: How touching. So concerned over Alyosha and yet you sit there in his lap. What's gotten into you today? Alyosha, at least, has something to be sad about—he rebelled against his God and was going to gobble sausage.

GRUSHENKA: *(To ALYOSHA.)* Why?

RAKITIN: His elder died today—Zosima, the saint.

GRUSHENKA: Oh my God! *(Jumps off ALYOSHA's lap and crosses herself.)* I didn't know. Forgive me, Alexei Fyodorovich.

ALYOSHA: Rakitin, don't taunt me with having rebelled against my God. I don't want to be angry with you, so please be kinder. I've lost something more precious to me than anything has ever been to you. Look at her—she spared me just now. I came here looking for a wicked soul because I, myself, was wicked. What I found was a loving soul and a true sister. When you had pity on me just now, Agrafena Alexandrovna, you restored my soul.

RAKITIN: Oh, did she? Well, let me tell you, Alyosha, what she was trying to do was eat you up.

GRUSHENKA: Stop it, Rakitin. Both of you be quiet. Alexei Fyodorovich, please don't say anything more because your words make me feel ashamed—I am wicked, not good. And you, Rakitin, shut up because you're lying. Yes, I was planning to eat him up, but it's different now and you know it. So shut up, I don't want to hear another squeak out of you.

RAKITIN: Oh, please. I feel like I'm in a madhouse. The next thing you know, they'll both start crying.

GRUSHENKA: I will start crying. I will start crying. He called me his sister and I'll never forget it. I may be wicked, Rakitin, but I still gave one onion.

RAKITIN: An onion? You're out of your mind.

GRUSHENKA: Alyosha, I was bragging to Rakitin just now, but that's not why I'm telling you this. It's just a fable I heard from my nanny when I was a child. Once upon a time there lived a woman and she was as wicked as wicked could be. And when she died she didn't leave a single good deed behind her. So the devils got hold of her and threw her into the lake of fire. And her guardian angel stood thinking, "What good deed of hers can I remember to tell God." And then he remembered and he said to God, "Once she pulled up an onion from her garden and gave it to a beggar woman." And God answered, "Take that same onion and hold it out to her in the lake, let her take hold of it and pull. If you pull her out of the lake, let her enter Paradise, but if the onion breaks let her stay where she is." The angel ran to the woman and held out the onion to her. "Here, woman," he said, "Take hold of it and pull." And he began pulling carefully, and he had almost pulled her out when the other sinners in the lake saw how she was being pulled out and grabbed onto her, so that they'd be pulled out of the flames, too. But the woman was wicked as wicked could be and she began kicking them off—"I'm to be pulled out, not you. It's my onion, not yours." No sooner did she say it than the onion snapped and the woman fell back into the lake, where she's still burning to this day. And the angel wept and went away. That's the fable, Alyosha, and I know it by heart because I am that wicked woman. I boasted to Rakitin that I gave an onion, but I'll say it differently to you. In my whole life, I've given just one little onion. That's how much good I've done. And don't praise me for that, Alyosha, I feel ashamed—because I'm as wicked as wicked can be. I'll confess everything, Alyosha. I wanted so much to lure

you here that I promised Rakitin twenty-five rubles if he'd bring you. *(Crosses to the table, picks up her purse and takes out money.)* Here it is, Rakitin.

RAKITIN: What the hell are you talking about?

GRUSHENKA: I owe it to you, Rakitka—take it. I know you won't refuse—you were the one who set the price. *(Throws the bills at him.)*

RAKITIN: I wouldn't dream of refusing, Grushenka, since fools exist for the profit of a clever man.

GRUSHENKA: And now, Rakitka, be quiet. Just sit in your corner like my lackey and keep still. Alyosha, I wanted to ruin you. I wanted it so much that I bribed Rakitin with money to bring you here. Every time I saw you, you turned away. But I looked at you—your face stayed in my heart. "He despises me," I thought, "He doesn't even want to look at me." So I decided, "I'll eat him up and laugh." And let me tell you: If I had done it, you would have been the only one. No one here dares come to Agrafena Alexandrovna for that bad thing—I have only my merchant. I'm bought and sold to him, Satan married us and there's no one else. Yet, looking at you, I was determined— "I'll eat him up—eat him up and laugh." See what a wicked bitch I am. And you called me your sister. And how did I become such a wicked bitch? All because of one man. And now he has come back and I sit here waiting for him. It's been five years since he seduced me, five years since he abandoned me, five years since Kuzma found me and brought me here, a skinny, frightened little girl. I was ashamed of myself and hid in the house Kuzma rented for me. I couldn't stop thinking of my officer—I imagined him with another woman, I imagined him laughing at me, and I swore I'd make him pay for what he did to me. And then I realized how ridiculous that was—I couldn't make him pay for anything—he probably wasn't even laughing at me, he probably didn't think of me at all. And I'd cry out in the darkness and I'd throw myself on the floor and writhe in helpless fury 'til daybreak. So, what did I do? I acquired capital. I became hard and callous and put on weight. Do you think I grew any wiser, Alyosha? No one knows it, but when night comes, I gnash my teeth and cry with rage and I swear I'll make him pay for what he did to me. And now he's written me—he's a widower and he wants to see me. It took my breath away. And I want to run to him like a beaten dog. I've been playing with Mitya to keep myself from running to him. Before you came, I was lying here, waiting, deciding my whole fate, and you will never know what was in my heart.

No, Alyosha, tell your young lady not to be angry for two days ago…no one in the world knows how I feel or can know. I may take a knife with me when I go, I haven't decided yet.

ALYOSHA: Misha, don't be angry. I know she's offended you, but don't be angry. We can't ask so much of a human soul, we have to be merciful.

RAKITIN: They've loaded you with that elder of yours, and now you've fired him at me.

ALYOSHA: Don't sneer, Rakitin, and don't speak about the Elder. Do you think I was judging you just now? How could I when I am ten times lower than you? I came here seeking my own damnation because my faith was weak and I couldn't bear what happened today. But listen to what she has borne for five years. And as soon as that man uttered a sincere word, she forgave him—and you won't bring a knife, Agrafena Alexandrovna. Are you capable of that kind of love, Misha? I certainly am not. This soul has not yet found peace and it must be treated gently. There may be a treasure in this soul.

RAKITIN: Well, you certainly have found a powerful advocate, Grushenka. You win—the ascetic has fallen in love with you.

GRUSHENKA: Don't answer him, Alyosha. Mikhail Ospipovich, I was about to ask your forgiveness for having been rude to you, but now I don't want to. Alyosha, sit down. Tell me: Do I love this man or not? Shall I forgive him or not?

ALYOSHA: You've already forgiven him.

GRUSHENKA: Yes, I have forgiven him. What a humble heart I have—what a base, weak heart I have. Let's drink to my base heart. *(Picks up her champagne glass, downs it, and smashes it on the floor.)* Maybe I haven't forgiven him, yet. Maybe my heart is only getting ready to forgive him—I still have to struggle with my heart. You see, Alyosha, I've come to love my tears over these five years—maybe what I really love is my suffering and I don't love him at all.

RAKITIN: It's time we were going—it's late, they won't let us back into the monastery.

GRUSHENKA: You're not leaving, Alyosha?

RAKITIN: You expect him to spend the night here, alone with you? Fine. I'm going back to the monastery.

GRUSHENKA: Shut up, you vicious little bastard. You've never spoken to me as he has.

RAKITIN: And what did he say?

GRUSHENKA: I don't know…perhaps it's just that he was the first one, the only one, to pity me. Why didn't you come before? For five years, I've waited for someone like you. Someone had to be able to forgive me. Someone had to love me, dirty as I am, really love me—not just like an animal.

ALYOSHA: What did I do for you? I just gave you an onion, one little onion…that's all.

(FENYA enters.)

FENYA: My lady—oh my dear, dear lady—the messenger—the carriage is here…the letter—here's the letter.

(GRUSHENKA grabs the letter and reads it.)

GRUSHENKA: He's calling, he's whistling for me to come running after him. I'm going. Five years of my life—finished. Goodbye, Fenya. Let Kuzma know. Goodbye, Alyosha, my fate is sealed. Rakitka, don't think ill of me—I may be going to my death. God! I feel drunk. *(Runs to the door and turns back.)* Alyosha. Bow to Mitenka for me. Tell him not to think ill of me, and tell him a despicable scoundrel got Grushenka in the end, not an honorable man like him. And tell him Grushenka did love him for an hour—but only an hour. Tell him to remember that hour all his life.

(GRUSHENKA exits and FENYA follows.)

RAKITIN: She slits Mitenka's throat and then tells him to remember it all his life. God, she's a cannibal.

(ALYOSHA is silent.)

RAKITIN: He's a Pole—that officer of hers. And he's not even an officer anymore—just a customs clerk somewhere in Siberia on the Chinese border—just a runty little Polack clerk. They say he lost his job—he heard Grushenka has money, so he's come back—that's the whole miracle.

(ALYOSHA is silent.)

RAKITIN: So you converted a sinful woman, set the harlot onto the path of truth, cast out the seven devils? So here are the expected miracles, after all.

ALYOSHA: Stop it, Rakitin.

RAKITIN: And now you despise me for the twenty-five rubles. You think I sold a true friend. Well, please remember, you're no Christ and I'm no Judas.

ALYOSHA: Rakitin, I'd forgotten about that until you just mentioned it.

RAKITIN: Go to hell—every last one of you. *(Exits.)*

(Lights fade.)

SCENE 9

ZOSIMA's cell, about half an hour later. PAISII stands over ZOSIMA's coffin, reading from the Gospel according to John. ALYOSHA enters and kneels before the coffin.

PAISII: "And the third day there was a marriage in Cana of Galilee, and the mother of Jesus was there: and both Jesus was called, and his disciples, to the marriage."

(ALYOSHA falls asleep. The lights gradually fade to just a spot on ALYOSHA.)

PAISII: "And when they wanted wine, the mother of Jesus saith unto Him, they have no wine. Jesus saith unto her, "Woman, what have I to do with thee? Mine hour is not yet come." His mother saith unto the servants,"

(A spot comes up on THE VIRGIN MARY.)

MARY: Whatsoever he saith unto you, do it.

PAISII: "And there were set there six waterpots of stone, after the manner of the purifying of the Jews, containing two or three firkins apiece. Jesus saith unto them,"

(A spot comes up on JESUS.)

JESUS: Fill the waterpots with water.

PAISII: "And they filled them up to the brim and He saith unto them,"

JESUS: Draw out now and bare them unto the governor of the feast.

PAISII: "And they bare it. When the ruler of the feast tasted the water that was made wine, and knew not whence it was—but the servants which drew the water knew—the governor of the feast called the bridegroom, and saith unto him,"

(A spot comes up on the Governor. As he speaks, the lights come up to reveal the wedding. PAISII is gone; JESUS, MARY, THE GOVERNOR, THE BRIDE and THE GROOM, and ZOSIMA are there as well as the rest of the cast as WEDDING GUESTS and APOSTLES.)

THE GOVERNOR: Every man at the beginning doth set forth good wine; and when men have well drunk, then that which is worse: but thou hast kept the good wine until now.

ALYOSHA: *(To ZOSIMA.)* Father, have you been called to the marriage at Cana of Galilee?

ZOSIMA: Yes, my dear son, I have been called, called and chosen. Why are you hiding out of sight? Come and join us.

(ZOSIMA gives ALYOSHA his hand and helps him up.)

ZOSIMA: We are rejoicing, we are drinking new wine, the wine of a new and great joy. See how many guests there are? Here are the bridegroom and the bride, here is the wise ruler of the feast, tasting the new wine. Why are you marveling at me? I gave a little onion and so I am here. And there are many here who have given only an onion, one little onion…what else are our deeds. And you, quiet one, you, my meek boy, today you, too, were able to give a little onion to a woman who hungered. Begin my dear, my meek one, to do your work. And do you see our Sun, do you see Him?

ALYOSHA: I'm afraid…I don't dare look.

ZOSIMA: Don't be afraid of Him. Awful is His greatness, terrible is His loftiness, yet He is boundlessly merciful, He became like us out of love and He is rejoicing with us, transforming water into wine that the joy of the guests may not end. He is waiting for new guests, He is ceaselessly calling new guests, now and unto ages of ages. See they are bringing the new wine, the vessels are being brought in…

(Lights fade to black and then slowly come up on ALYOSHA sleeping and PAISII reading from the Gospel according to John. ALYOSHA gets up and walks to the coffin and looks at ZOSIMA's corpse. PAISII looks up at ALYOSHA for a moment and then continues reading. ALYOSHA crosses out of the cell. He looks up at the sky and then falls to the earth, kissing it ecstatically and weeping.)

SCENE 10

Lights up on IVAN in a train compartment.

IVAN: I'm a despicable beast.

(Lights fade.)

THE BROTHERS KARAMAZOV
PART II

CAST LIST*

The Karamazov Family

FYODOR PAVLOVICH KARAMAZOV: fifty-five, a landowner and moneylender

DMITRY FYODOROVICH KARAMAZOV (MITYA): twenty-eight, Fyodor's son by his first marriage, a former army officer

IVAN FYODOROVICH KARAMAZOV: twenty-three, Fyodor's older son by his second marriage, an intellectual of some repute

ALEXEI FYODOROVICH KARAMAZOV (ALYOSHA): nineteen, Fyodor's younger son by his second marriage, a novice in a monastery

The Karamazov Servants

GRIGORY VASILIEVICH KUTUZOV: fifties–seventies, Fyodor's freed serf

SMERDYAKOV (PAVEL FYODOROVICH): twenty-four, Fyodor's cook and probably his illegitimate son, raised by Grigory

The Residents of the Monastery

THE ELDER ZOSIMA: fifties–seventies, spiritual guide to the monks
FATHER PAISII: fifties–seventies, a senior monk (nonspeaking)
FATHER IOSIF: fifties–seventies, the monastery librarian (nonspeaking)
MIKHAIL OSPIPOVICH RAKITIN (MISHA, RAKITKA): twenties, a divinity student, cousin of Grushenka

The Women

KATERINA IVANOVNA VERKHOVSTEVA (KATYA): early twenties, Dmitry's fiancée, a wealthy heiress

AGRAFENA ALEXANDROVNA SVETLOVA (GRUSHENKA): twenty-two, kept woman of a local merchant, moneylender, and partner of Fyodor's

Residents of the Town

KUZMA KUZMICH SAMSONOV: fifties–seventies, a wealthy merchant, Grushenka's protector, old and ill

HIS SON: (nonspeaking)

OLD WOMAN: Samsonov's servant

PYOTR ILYICH PERKHOTIN: twenties–thirties, a young government official, friend of Dmitry's

MADAME KHOKHALAKOVA (KATERINA OSIPOVNA): forties–fifties, a rich widow, friend of Katerina Ivanovna

FENYA: Grushenka's maid

CARD PLAYERS: (nonspeaking)

At Chermashnya

PRIEST: forties–seventies, Fyodor's agent in Chermashnya
GORSTKIN (THE HOUND): forties–fifties, a peasant who deals in timber

At the Inn at Mokroye

TRIFON: forties–sixties, innkeeper

POLE 1 (MUSSYALOVICH): forties–sixties, an unemployed government clerk, Grushenka's former lover

POLE 2 (VRUBLEVSKY): forties–fifties, burly, Mussyalovich's bodyguard

MAXIMOV: forties–sixties, a penniless landowner

MUSICIANS and DANCING GIRLS (nonspeaking)

The Snegiryov Family

NIKOLAI ILYICH SNEGIRYOV: forties–fifties, a disgraced army captain, hired lackey of Fyodor and Grushenka

ARINA PETROVNA SNEGIRYOVA (MAMA): forties–fifties, his wife, crippled and mentally ill

NINA NIKOLAEVNA SNEGIRYOVA (NINOCHKA): twenties, his daughter, a hunchback

ILYA NIKOLAEVICH SNEGIRYOV (ILYUSHA): eleven, his son and youngest child

The Boys

KOLYA KRASOTKIN (NIKOLAI ILYICH): thirteen
SMUROV: eleven
KARTASHOV: eleven

The Authorities

JUDGE: forties–sixties

CLERK

DEPUTY PUBLIC PROSECUTOR (IPPOLIT KIRILLOVICH KIRILOV): forties, dying of consumption

NIKOLAI PARFENOVICH NELYUDOV: twenties–thirties, district examining magistrate

The Defense

FETYUKOVICH: forties–fifties, a celebrated lawyer from St. Petersburg
DOCTOR: forties–sixties, a specialist from Moscow

Dmitry's Dream

DRIVER

Ivan's Nightmare

THE DEVIL: forties–fifties

---

*Roles can be doubled.

ACT I
Scene 1

Night. DMITRY and ALYOSHA are standing outside KATERINA's house. The same scene as the end of Part I, Act I, Scene 8.

DMITRY: Goodbye, Alexei. *(Starts to exit.)* Wait, Alexei. Look at me. *(Points to a spot on his chest just below his neck.)* Right here, I am carrying a dishonor worse than anything I have done before. I could stop myself at any time. And if I did, I would regain half my honor. But I won't stop myself. Goodbye, Alexei. And don't pray for me. I'm not worth it. *(Exits.)*

(Lights fade.)

Scene 2

ZOSIMA's cell, the next morning. The same as Part I, Act II, Scene 1. ZOSIMA and ALYOSHA are onstage.

ZOSIMA: Alyosha, my dear son, aren't people expecting you?

ALYOSHA: I...

ZOSIMA: Didn't you promise Lise Khokhalakova that you would visit her?

ALYOSHA: Yes, Father.

ZOSIMA: Does anyone else need you?

ALYOSHA: I did promise to see my father and my brother Ivan and my brother Dmitry's fiancée.

ZOSIMA: Good. You must also see your brother Dmitry.

ALYOSHA: But Father, I want to stay with you.

ZOSIMA: You must go, but do not be sad. Know that I won't die without you. I will say my last words on Earth in your presence. I'll say those words to you, my dear son, I'll bequeath them to you. To you, my sweet son, because you love me. But now you must go to those you promised to see.

(ALYOSHA receives ZOSIMA's blessing. Lights fade.)

Scene 3

KUZMA SAMSONOV's drawing room, the same morning. An OLD WOMAN enters leading DMITRY.

OLD WOMAN: Mr. Samsonov will be with you in a moment, sir.

(She exits, DMITRY paces, waiting. SAMSONOV enters supported by HIS SON and using a cane; HIS SON seats him. DMITRY bows to SAMSONOV.)

SAMSONOV: What do you want of me, sir?

DMITRY: Most honored Kuzma Kuzmich, I have come to you with a proposition—a business proposition, Kuzma Kuzmich, a very sound business proposition. The village of Chermashnya, which my father claims to be his, belonged to my mother—so it should belong to me. Now, I have consulted, Kuzma Kuzmich, with a lawyer, a very famous lawyer—Pavel Pavlovich Korneplodov—perhaps you've heard of him? Anyway, he is certain we can beat the old crook at his own game—we can take him to court and win back Chermashnya. Chermashnya, Kuzma Kuzmich, is worth no less than twenty-five thousand—what am I saying, twenty-eight at least—no, thirty thousand—and do you realize I never even got seventeen thousand out of the old skinflint. But Kuzma Kuzmich, I am willing to turn over to you all my claims against that monster for just three thousand rubles. You can't lose—for just three thousand you get a property worth thirty thousand. But we must settle this today...in fact, if it is at all possible, if you think it is feasible...I'd like to have that three thousand this morning...Who else in this town has that kind of capital, Kuzma Kuzmich? You would save me, Kuzma Kuzmich, I could act like an honorable man. For I have very honorable feelings towards someone you know very well—you're like a father to her...I wouldn't have come if I didn't know your interest was only fatherly. Three men have collided head on over Grushenka—pardon me, Kuzma Kuzmich—Agrafena Alexandrovna. Anyway, three men have collided—that's fate for you, Kuzma Kuzmich. But that's realism. As I was saying, three men have collided—you dropped out long ago; that leaves two of us: me and the monster. So choose: me or the monster? Everything is now in your hands.

SAMSONOV: I'm sorry, sir, we don't go in for that sort of business.

DMITRY: Then I'm lost.

SAMSONOV: You see, sir, such business is not in our line. There would be courts, there would be lawyers, all kinds of trouble. But I know a man who might be interested. You can try him if you like.

DMITRY: What's his name?

SAMSONOV: He's not a local man. He's a kulak who trades in timber. They call him the Hound. He wants to buy the woodlot at Chermashnya. He and Fyodor Pavlovich have been haggling for over a year, but they can't agree on a price. He's back in Chermashnya now, staying with your father's agent, the priest. Fyodor Pavlovich is going to meet him there. But if you got there first and made the Hound the same offer you made me…

DMITRY: Thank you, Kuzma Kuzmich. Of course the Hound will jump at the chance. He pays just three thousand rubles, and then the monster shows up, thinking he's got him over a barrel—but no, the Hound produces proof of ownership. How can I thank you, Kuzma Kuzmich?

SAMSONOV: It's nothing, sir.

DMITRY: Oh no, Kuzma Kuzmich, you saved me—I had a presentiment you would. Well, I'm off to the priest's. I'm sorry to have imposed on you when you're not feeling well, but I will remember your kindness always—you have my word on it—the word of a Russian man.

(DMITRY extends his hand, but SAMSONOV does not take it.)

DMITRY: It's for her, Kuzma Kuzmich. You understand, it's for her. (Bows and exits.)

SAMSONOV: (To HIS SON.) Idiot. If you ever let that son of a bitch in here again, I'll cut you off without a kopek.

(Lights fade.)

Scene 4

The front yard of FYODOR KARAMAZOV's house, around noon. The same as Part I, Act II, Scene 5. SMERDYAKOV is onstage. ALYOSHA enters.

ALYOSHA: Smerdyakov, have you seen my brother Dmitry?

SMERDYAKOV: Master Dmitry, sir, does not keep me informed as to his whereabouts.

ALYOSHA: It's alright to tell me, Smerdyakov, Dmitry told me everything yesterday—that you tell him what's going on in the house so you can let him know if Grushenka comes.

SMERDYAKOV: Master Dmitry, sir, only gets in touch with me when he chooses. And when he chooses, sir, he won't let me alone—he asks me a thousand questions—who comes, who goes—twice he threatened to kill me.

ALYOSHA: I'm sure it's just talk, but he shouldn't even speak like that. I'll talk to him about it—that is, if I could only find him.

SMERDYAKOV: Well, this much I can tell you, Master Alexei, sir, but no more. First thing this morning, Master Ivan sent me to Master Dmitry's place on Lake Street to tell him that he must meet Master Ivan for lunch at the tavern on the square. I went and Master Dmitry wasn't there—at eight in the morning, sir. I left word with his landlady. Perhaps she gave him the message and he's at the tavern right now—Master Ivan hasn't come home for lunch. But if you do find Master Dmitry, Master Alexei, sir, please don't mention me, he'd kill me for much less.

ALYOSHA: The tavern on the square? The Metropolis?

SMERDYAKOV: That's the one, sir.

ALYOSHA: Thank you, Smerdyakov.

(Lights fade.)

Scene 5

The PRIEST's cottage at Chermashnya, that evening. PRIEST is onstage, THE HOUND is asleep on a cot that can't be seen from the door, DMITRY is pounding on the door. There is a table with one empty bottle of vodka and another half-empty bottle.

DMITRY: (Offstage.) Open up! It's retired lieutenant Dmitry Fyodorovich Karamazov!

PRIEST: Lieutenant Karamazov…I…is Mr. Karamazov with you?

DMITRY: Open up!

PRIEST: Oh, dear.

(PRIEST opens the door, and DMITRY enters.)

DMITRY: Thank you, Father, I'm terribly sorry to bother you, but is a man called the Hound staying with you?

PRIEST: Have you come with your father?

DMITRY: No, Father, I…

PRIEST: Well…ah…it's nice to meet you, Lieutenant…your father has spoken of you…often.

DMITRY: Father, is…

PRIEST: Did your father send you?

DMITRY: No, Kuzma Samsonov sent me.

PRIEST: Mr. Samsonov...I see, well...

DMITRY: There is a man called the Hound staying with you?

PRIEST: Yes, but...

DMITRY: Can I see him?

PRIEST: *(Stepping back to reveal THE HOUND.)* Well, sir, I'm afraid he's asleep right now.

DMITRY: I have to wake him, I have very important business.

(Runs over to THE HOUND and starts shaking him.)

DMITRY: Sir. Sir! Wake up!

PRIEST: Are you sure your father doesn't know you're here...

DMITRY: Mr. Hound! Mr. Hound! *(Notices the vodka on the table.)* He's drunk.

PRIEST: I'm afraid he's been drinking all day. If you don't mind my asking, Lieutenant Karamazov, why do you keep calling him the Hound?

DMITRY: That's what people call him, isn't it?

PRIEST: Yes...but never to his face, he gets furious when people call him that.

DMITRY: But Kuzma Kuzmich told me that was his name.

PRIEST: I see...well, he prefers to be called Gorstkin.

DMITRY: Then why did Samsonov...

PRIEST: Can I get you anything, Lieutenant? Perhaps some tea?

DMITRY: No, but light the samovar and make some tea for him—or coffee, if you have it, coffee would be better—and bring me some cold water and a towel.

PRIEST: If you have important business, sir, you'd better wait 'til morning.

DMITRY: Morning? God. What terrible tragedies realism inflicts on people.

(Lights fade.)

SCENE 6

ZOSIMA's cell, the same evening. The same as Part I, Act III, Scene 2. ZOSIMA, PAISII, and FATHER IOSIF are onstage. ALYOSHA enters.

ZOSIMA: Welcome, my quiet one. I knew you would come.

(ALYOSHA bows to the ground before ZOSIMA and begins to weep.)

ZOSIMA: *(Blessing ALYOSHA.)* Have you been home? Did you see your brother?

ALYOSHA: I saw one of my brothers.

ZOSIMA: The oldest one, before whom I bowed to the ground?

ALYOSHA: I saw him yesterday, but I couldn't find him today.

ZOSIMA: Find him tomorrow—you may be able to prevent something horrible. I bowed, yesterday, to the great suffering that is in store for him.

ALYOSHA: Father and teacher, I...your words are obscure, Father. What suffering is in store for him?

ZOSIMA: I caught a glimpse of something terrible—I looked in his eyes and I was filled with horror—horror at what this man is preparing for himself. Once or twice I have seen that look in men's faces—a look that seemed to contain their fate—a fate which, alas, came to be. I sent you to him, Alyosha, because I thought a brother's face—your face—would help him. But everything and all our fates come from God—"Unless a corn of wheat fall into the ground and die, it abideth alone: but if it die, it bringeth forth much fruit"—remember that.

(Lights fade.)

SCENE 7

The PRIEST's cottage, the following morning. DMITRY is asleep. THE HOUND is sitting at the table drinking vodka. Now both bottles are empty, and a third one has been opened.

DMITRY: *(Waking up.)* My God, what time is it?

THE HOUND: Damned if I know.

DMITRY: *(Looking at the clock.)* My God, it's nine o'clock. Is it morning or night?

THE HOUND: Can't help you there, sir.

DMITRY: *(Realizing it's daylight.)* My God, it's nine o'clock in the morning, I must have fallen asleep. Where's the priest?

THE HOUND: Damned if I know. Care for a drink?

DMITRY: No, no, no, no, no!

THE HOUND: Suit yourself.

DMITRY: Sir, could I speak to you about a very important matter?

THE HOUND: I'd like some cheese…

DMITRY: Sir, I am retired lieutenant Dmitry Fyodorovich Karamazov…

THE HOUND: Herring. Herring would be nice.

DMITRY: Mr. Gorstkin, my father is Fyodor Pavlovich Karamazov, you're trying to buy a woodlot from him…

THE HOUND: Liar!

DMITRY: What? You do know Fyodor Pavlovich?

THE HOUND: I don't know no Fyodor Pavlovich.

DMITRY: You're trying to buy the wood from him. The wood. Please sober up for just one second…Kuzma Samsonov told me…

THE HOUND: Lies. Lies. All lies.

DMITRY: Please sober up

THE HOUND: I know you—you're the house painter.

DMITRY: I'm Karamazov, Dmitry Karamazov. I have an offer to make you, a very profitable offer.

THE HOUND: You son of a bitch. I paid you good money and look at this mess.

DMITRY: Sir…

THE HOUND: Show me the law that says you can cheat people like that, you son of a bitch.

DMITRY: Listen! *(Grabs THE HOUND by the collar and after a moment, lets him go.)* Never mind.

(Lights fade.)

SCENE 8

FYODOR KARAMAZOV's yard, the same morning, the same as Part I, Act III, Scene 3. SMERDYAKOV is onstage. IVAN enters.

IVAN: So you see I'm going to Chermashnya.

SMERDYAKOV: So it's true what they say. It's always rewarding to talk to a clever man.

SCENE 9

GRUSHENKA's drawing room, late that afternoon. GRUSHENKA is pacing.

DMITRY: *(Offstage.)* Where is she?

FENYA: Sir, she's not feeling well…

DMITRY: Get out of my way!

(DMITRY bursts in.)

GRUSHENKA: Mitenka, what are you making this fuss for?

DMITRY: I…I just wanted to see you.

GRUSHENKA: Aren't you sweet, Mitenka. But I'm afraid your timing could be better, I'm just about to leave to go to Kuzma's.

DMITRY: Kuzma's…?

GRUSHENKA: Don't be jealous of Kuzma, Mitenka, you know he's too sick to do anything anymore. I'm going to do the books, Mitenka, the books.

DMITRY: Oh, I…

GRUSHENKA: Would you be a dear and walk me over?

DMITRY: Of course, I…

GRUSHENKA: Oh, you're sweet. Would you like to pick me up when we're through?

DMITRY: Of course, I'd love to…

GRUSHENKA: Oh, that's my Mitenka. We'll be done around midnight, that's not too late for you, is it?

DMITRY: Of course not.

GRUSHENKA: Wait a moment while I get my wrap. *(Exits.)*

(Lights fade.)

SCENE 10

FYODOR KARAMAZOV's dining room, that afternoon, the same as Part I, Act III, Scene 7. SMERDYAKOV screams from offstage; FYODOR runs to the cellar door.)

FYODOR: Marfa! Grigory! Come quick. Smerdyakov's fallen down the cellar stairs. He's having a fit.

SCENE 11

PYOTR PERKHOTIN's rooms, a little later, around six o'clock in the evening. PERKHOTIN is sitting at a table with a couple of OTHERS, playing cards. DMITRY enters.

DMITRY: Perkhotin.

PERKHOTIN: Mitya?

DMITRY: You know those dueling pistols of mine you've always admired? *(Puts the pistol case on the table.)* Well, here they are. I'm flat broke, I need ten rubles, will you take them as security?

PERKHOTIN: Of course, but why don't you just sell them to me?

DMITRY: They may come in handy later.

PERKHOTIN: I'll give you a hundred rubles for them.

DMITRY: I just need ten rubles to have something in my pocket. Look, knowing me, you may end up keeping them.

PERKHOTIN: I can only hope.

(He takes out his wallet and gives DMITRY ten rubles.)

DMITRY: Thanks. Sorry to have interrupted your game, gentlemen. *(Exits.)*

(Lights fade.)

SCENE 12

GRUSHENKA's drawing room later that evening, the same as the end of Part I, Act III, Scene 8. GRUSHENKA, ALYOSHA, and RAKITIN are onstage. FENYA enters.

FENYA: My lady—oh my dear, dear lady—the messenger—the carriage is here…the letter—here's the letter.

(GRUSHENKA grabs the letter and reads it.)

GRUSHENKA: He's calling, he's whistling for me to come running after him. I'm going. Five years of my life—finished. Goodbye, Fenya. Let Kuzma know. Goodbye, Alyosha, my fate is sealed. Rakitka, don't think ill of me—I may be going to my death. God! I feel drunk. *(Runs to the door and turns back.)* Alyosha, bow to Mitenka for me. Tell him not to think ill of me, and tell him a despicable scoundrel got Grushenka in the end, not an honorable man like him. And tell him Grushenka did love him for an hour—but only an hour. Tell him to remember that hour all his life.

(GRUSHENKA exits followed by FENYA, lights fade.)

SCENE 13

MADAME KHOKHALAKOVA's drawing room. MADAME KHOKHALAKOVA and DMITRY enter from opposite sides of the stage.

KHOKHALAKOVA: I was expecting you, yes, expecting you. Now, you must admit that there was no reason for me to think you would come and, yet, I was expecting you—just marvel at my instincts, Dmitry Fyodorovich.

DMITRY: That's amazing, madame…really. But I've come on very important business—that is, important to me…

KHOKHALAKOVA: I know everything already, Dmitry Fyodorovich. I've been watching you for a long time, Dmitry Fyodorovich, following your life, studying it.

DMITRY: Since you've been watching over my life with such interest, I feel certain that you will not let me ruin it. So, let me explain my plan to you. Madame, I've come…

KHOKHALAKOVA: Don't explain—it's only of secondary importance. You won't be the first person I've helped, Dmitry Fyodorovich. I'm sure you've heard of my cousin Madame Belmesova. Her husband was ruined. And what did I do? I advised him to go into horse breeding. Now he's flourishing. Do you know anything about horse breeding, Dmitry Fyodorovich?

DMITRY: Nothing whatsoever, I'm sorry to say. Please madame, I beg you, let me tell you what I've come to tell you. I've come because I'm desperate, I've reached the limits of my endurance…I want to ask you to lend me some money—to lend me three thousand rubles…but I have a perfect security…

KHOKHALAKOVA: Later, Dmitry Fyodorovich, you can explain all that later—besides, as I told you before, I know everything you are going to say to me in advance. You're asking me for a certain sum, you say you need three thousand rubles, but I will give you infinitely more than that, Dmitry Fyodorovich, incomparably more. I'll save you—but you must do as I say.

DMITRY: I can't believe it…madame…you've saved me, you've saved my life—you've just saved a man from a bullet—I don't know how to thank you.

KHOKHALAKOVA: Oh yes, I will give you infinitely more than three thousand.

DMITRY: Madame, you're too kind, but I only need three thousand—and I'm prepared to guarantee that sum to you. I will put up as security…

KHOKHALAKOVA: Enough, Dmitry Fyodorovich, it's said and done. I've promised to save you and I'll save you. I'll save you just as I did Belmesov. Have you ever thought of gold mines, Dmitry Fyodorovich?

DMITRY: Gold mines…I've never really thought about them.

KHOKHALAKOVA: But I've been thinking for you. I've been watching you for a whole month with that in mind. I've watched you walk by a hundred times and I've said to myself: there is a man who should go to the mines. I can tell from your walk you will find gold.

DMITRY: Um…Madame…the three thousand which you so generously offered to lend me…

KHOKHALAKOVA: It is as good as in your pocket, Dmitry Fyodorovich—and not just three thousand, but three million, and in no time. Now, let me tell you your idea: you will discover mines and make millions. Then you will return and become a businessman. You will run our lives for us, directing us to good works—should it all be left to the Jews? You will build buildings, start various enterprises—you will help the poor and they will bless you. This is the age of railroads, Dmitry Fyodorovich. You will become famous and indispensable to the Ministry of Finance, which is in such need right now. The decline of the paper ruble keeps me awake at night, Dmitry Fyodorovich—this side of me is little known.

DMITRY: Oh madame, you've been so kind to me, I have to make a confession…what you've known for a long time…I've betrayed Katya…Katerina Ivanovna…I've been dishonorable, I've been cruel to her…but I fell in love with another woman…a woman you probably despise…but I can't give her up…I can't…that's why I need the three thousand…

KHOKHALAKOVA: You must give up everything, Dmitry Fyodorovich. Above all, you must give up women. You must have no thought but the mines and you cannot take a woman there. Later, when you return, rich and famous, I'm sure you will find a life companion among the girls of our highest society. She will be a modern girl, educated, without any of the old prejudices or superstitions. By then, the emancipation of women will have become a reality and the new woman will have come into existence

DMITRY: Yes, madame, but that's not the point right now…

KHOKHALAKOVA: It is very much the point, Dmitry Fyodorovich. A modern woman is what you need, what you thirst for, although you may not be aware of it yourself. I am no stranger to the women's question, Dmitry Fyodorovich. Higher education for women and even a role in politics in the not too distant future. I believe in this ideal. I, myself, have a daughter—This side of me is little known. Good God, what's the matter with you?

DMITRY: Madame…madame, you will make me weep if you keep putting off…

KHOKHALAKOVA: Weep, Dmitry Fyodorovich, weep. Such feelings are beautiful. You have a long journey ahead of you and tears will make your ordeal easier. But you will return triumphantly and rejoice; you will come galloping home from Siberia to rejoice with me.

DMITRY: Please listen to me. For the last time, I beg you: will you give me, today, the sum you promised or won't you? If you can't let me have it right away, tell me when I can come for it.

KHOKHALAKOVA: What exactly do you have in mind, Dmitry Fyodorovich?

DMITRY: The three thousand you promised…that you so generously…

KHOKHALAKOVA: Three thousand? You mean rubles? Oh no, I haven't got three thousand rubles.

DMITRY: But you just said it was as good as in my pocket.

KHOKHALAKOVA: Oh no, you misunderstood me, Dmitry Fyodorovich, you misunderstood me completely. I was thinking of the gold mines. I remember now that I promised you infinitely more than three thousand, but I was thinking of the mines.

DMITRY: But the money…

KHOKHALAKOVA: Oh, if you meant money, I don't have it. I'm entirely without funds just now. I'm quarreling with the manager of my estates. Just the other day I had to borrow five hundred rubles from Miusov. I have absolutely no money, and even if I had, I wouldn't give it to you—out of love, I would not give you anything; in order to save you, I would not give you anything. The only place for you, Dmitry Fyodorovich, is the mines, the mines, the mines.

(*DMITRY screams in frustration. KHOKHALAKOVA screams and runs out of the room. DMITRY storms out, pounding his chest just below his neck. Just as he steps out of the house, an OLD WOMAN crosses the stage and he bumps into her.*)

OLD WOMAN: Why don't you watch where you're going?

DMITRY: Hey—don't you work for Samsonov?

OLD WOMAN: That's right…but who are you?

DMITRY: Is Agrafena Alexandrovna still with the old man?

OLD WOMAN: Oh, she's gone—she only stayed for a little while, then she left.

DMITRY: What?

OLD WOMAN: She only stayed for a minute. She told Mr. Samsonov something that made him laugh, then she ran way.

DMITRY: You're lying, you dried-up old hag!

(*OLD WOMAN screams. DMITRY runs off; lights fade.*)

SCENE 14

GRUSHENKA's kitchen, a few minutes later. FENYA is grinding something with a mortar and pestle. DMITRY rushes in. FENYA jumps up and screams.

DMITRY: Where is she?

(*She doesn't answer; he throws himself at her feet.*)

DMITRY: Fenya, in the name of Christ our Lord, where is she? Please, Fenya, tell me.

FENYA: I don't know, I don't know, I swear to God, I don't know! You went out with her yourself…

DMITRY: But she came back, didn't she?

FENYA: No, she didn't, I swear to God, she didn't.

DMITRY: Is she with my father?

FENYA: No, I swear.

DMITRY: You're lying. (*Jumps up, grabs the pestle, and runs out.*)

(*Lights fade.*)

SCENE 15

FYODOR KARAMAZOV's garden, a few minutes later. DMITRY is looking around.

DMITRY: Damn. Where's Smerdyakov? I have to find out if she's in there.

(*DMITRY crosses to "the window"; lights up on FYODOR's room. DMITRY stands to the side of the window, staring in. After a moment, FYODOR peers out the window, then walks away. After a moment, DMITRY knocks on the window sill: two times slowly, three times quickly. FYODOR runs to the window and sticks his head out.*)

FYODOR: Grushenka? Is that you?

(*DMITRY reaches in his pocket and takes out the pestle; he holds it in the air ready to strike.*)

FYODOR: Where are you, my angel? Are you hiding in the bushes, my little chick? Come here, I have a present for you.

(*Blackout.*)

GRIGORY: (*In darkness.*) Parricide!

(*Lights up. Another part of the yard. DMITRY is straddling the fence, GRIGORY is grabbing at his ankle. DMITRY strikes him on the head with the pestle; GRIGORY falls. DMITRY jumps down and stares at him for a moment. He takes out a handkerchief and starts trying to wipe away the blood.*)

DMITRY: Oh god, I've killed him. Your number's up old man, there's no help for it—I'm sorry. (*Climbs onto the fence again.*)

(*Blackout.*)

SCENE 16

GRUSHENKA's kitchen, a few minutes later. FENYA is looking nervously out the window. DMITRY bursts in and grabs her by the throat.

DMITRY: Talk! Where is she?

FENYA: Mokroye! She's in Mokroye. She went to Mokroye—to see her officer.

DMITRY: What officer?

FENYA: From five years ago—the one who left her.

(*DMITRY lets go of her throat. He stands for a moment, stunned, then sinks into a chair.*)

FENYA: Lieutenant…

(*DMITRY is silent.*)

FENYA: Don't feel bad, Lieutenant…Do you know what she told your brother? Your brother was here, before…the monk…He came with Miss Svetlova's cousin, Mr. Rakitin. Lieutenant, she told your brother she did love you—for one hour. She wants you to remember that hour for the rest of your life…Lieutenant…

(*DMITRY is silent.*)

FENYA: Lieutenant…your hands are covered with blood.

DMITRY: (*Looking at his hands.*) Yes…they are…

FENYA: What happened to you, sir?

DMITRY: That's blood, Fenya, it's human blood…why was it shed?…There's a fence, Fenya…a tall fence, fearful to look at, but…tomorrow at dawn, when the sun soars aloft, Mitenka will jump over that fence…Never mind, Fenya, you'll hear about it tomorrow and you'll understand everything…Goodbye…I won't stand in her way, I know how to stand aside…she loved me for one hour…she'll remember Mitenka…Remember—she always called me Mitenka.

(*DMITRY starts to leave and FENYA throws herself at his feet.*)

FENYA: Lieutenant, please don't hurt her—it'd be my fault—and don't kill him, either, sir—he came first—he's going to marry her, sir—he came all the way from Siberia to marry her—please don't harm anyone's life.

DMITRY: Fenya, get up…Mitenka won't harm anybody—the stupid man is through hurting people. Forgive me for hurting you before, Fenya…and if you don't forgive me…it doesn't matter anymore. (*Exits.*)

(*Lights fade.*)

SCENE 17

PERKHOTIN's place, half an hour later. PERKHOTIN is dressing for the evening. DMITRY enters, carrying a wad of bills and a bottle of champagne. He slams a bill down on the table.

DMITRY: Here's your money, give me the pistols.

PERKHOTIN: Good God. You're covered in blood.

DMITRY: (*Looks at his hands.*) Damn. (*Takes out the handkerchief and it's covered in blood.*) Damn. Do you have a rag or something?

PERKHOTIN: A rag's not going to do it, come over here to the basin.

DMITRY: (*Indicating the money.*) Where should I put this?

PERKHOTIN: Put it in your pocket—or here, here on the table—it'll be safe.

(*DMITRY puts money and champagne down. PERKHOTIN checks DMITRY.*)

PERKHOTIN: You're alright. You're not bleeding. Did you hurt someone else?

DMITRY: It's over—we made peace—we parted friends…he must have forgiven me by now…he wouldn't have forgiven me if he got up… (*Finishing washing.*) Enough. Give me my coat.

PERKHOTIN: Wait, your whole right cuff is covered in blood. Let me get you a shirt.

DMITRY: I don't have time—look—I'll just turn the cuff up. (*Turns his cuff up and puts on his frock coat.*) Now, give me the pistols. Where'd I put the money?

PERKHOTIN: (*Getting the pistols.*) It's on the table—Christ, you treat money like trash—and where did you get so much so fast? You borrowed ten rubles around six o'clock and now…How much have you got there? Two or three thousand?

DMITRY: Three, I guess.

PERKHOTIN: You find a gold mine or something?

DMITRY: (*Bursts out laughing.*) Want to go to the gold mines, Perkhotin? If you do, there's a lady who'll give you three thousand rubles without batting an eye, she loves gold mines so much. She did it for me—You know Madame Khokhalakova?

PERKHOTIN: I've seen her around, but we haven't met. Did she really give you the money?

DMITRY: Go to her tomorrow, when the sun soars aloft, when ever-youthful Phoebus soars aloft, praising and glorifying God, go and ask her.

PERKHOTIN: That's alright, I believe you. Where are you off to?

DMITRY: Mokroye.

PERKHOTIN: So she gives you three thousand rubles to go to Siberia, and you go on a spree.

DMITRY: *(As he speaks, he takes a pistol out of the case and starts filling it with powder.)* That's right. I've just been to Plotnikov's—I got three dozen bottles of champagne, caviar, Strasbourg pies, sturgeon, cognac, chocolates…I've got a case with me and they're sending the rest.

PERKHOTIN: What are you doing?

DMITRY: Loading the pistol. *(Picks up a bullet and looks at it.)*

PERKHOTIN: Why are you staring at that bullet?

DMITRY: Just a whim. If you decided to blow your brains out, would you look at the bullet first? *(Drops the bullet into the gun and drives it in.)* Done. *(Puts the pistol in the case.)*

PERKHOTIN: Are you really going to shoot yourself?

DMITRY: No, I want to live. I love life. Let's open a bottle now, let's drink to life. Get some glasses. *(Opens the champagne.)* I've never liked disorder.

PERKHOTIN: *(Getting glasses.)* Then why are you running around with three dozen bottles of champagne?

DMITRY: I don't mean that, I mean a higher order. Give me a piece of paper.

(PERKHOTIN gets a piece of paper and gives it to him. DMITRY starts to write.)

DMITRY: There's no order in me, no higher order. My whole life has been mess and disorder, and I must put it in order. "Glory to God in the Highest; Glory to the Highest in me." That verse once burst from my soul—not a verse, but a tear. I wrote it myself…but not when I was pulling that captain by his beard.

PERKHOTIN: What makes you think of him all of a sudden?

DMITRY: I don't know. Everything ends, everything comes out even. One day you have to draw a line and add it all up.

(DMITRY passes PERKHOTIN the note.)

PERKHOTIN: *(Reading.)* "I punish myself for my whole life, my whole life I punish." That's it—I'm telling someone.

DMITRY: Don't worry, I love life—I'm vile, but I love life. Let's drink to life, brother—and to one queen of queens.

PERKHOTIN: *(Raising his glass.)* To life, then. And maybe to your queen, as well.

(They drink.)

DMITRY: Farewell, Pyotr Perkhotin, my last tear is for you. *(Grabs the pistols and runs off.)*

PERKHOTIN: *(Stares after him for a moment.)* Damn. *(Runs off.)*

(Lights fade.)

Scene 18

A room at the inn at Mokroye, later that night. GRUSHENKA, POLE 1, POLE 2, and MAXIMOV are playing cards.

Pole 2: *(To MAXIMOV.)* Lajdak! *["Scoundrel" (pronounced "wydoc.")]*

GRUSHENKA: Who is this oaf of yours to call my friend names?

POLE 1: *Pani* Agrippina, this friend of yours is telling lies.

MAXIMOV: Most honorable Polish sir, I swear to you, it is most indubitably true. You see, sir, after the pretty Polish girls finished dancing, they would…

(DMITRY bursts in. GRUSHENKA screams.)

DMITRY: Don't be afraid. Gentlemen, please excuse me, there's nothing to worry about…I…Please excuse me, there's nothing to worry about…I…I'm going away, too…traveling. May I join you—just 'til morning?

POLE 1: *Panye,* this is a private party, there are other rooms.

DMITRY: I…I am an acquaintance of…Perhaps, if I introduced myself…I am retired lieutenant Dmitry Fyodorovich Karamazov.

MAXIMOV: Oh, delighted and honored, sir, delighted and honored. This is really too much of a coincidence. You see, Captain Karamazov, I'm acquainted with your most honorable father, Fyodor Pavlovich, and your most respected brother, Ivan Fyodorovich. I met them just the other day at your most famous monastery—You see, most worthy Polish gentlemen, the monastery where Major Karamazov lives is famous throughout

Russia—and I had an audience with the Elder Zosima—such a charming, witty man, the pride and glory of the monastery. As I was saying, Major Karamazov, sir, I had the honor of meeting your most esteemed brother, Ivan Fyodorovich—Well, actually, he gave me quite a thrashing, but I'm used to that. People are forever thrashing me and I don't know why. Absolute strangers come up to me in the street and…

POLE 2: *Lajdak!*

MAXIMOV: Have I said anything to offend you, worthy Polish sir?

DMITRY: Gentlemen, please allow me to stay…I would like to spend my last night and my last hour in this room…In the room where I once worshiped my queen. I've brought champagne, they'll bring it in in a minute… *(Pulls out the wad of bills.)* …please let me pay for music and girls—I want music and noise, just like before.

POLE 1: If my quin permits.

GRUSHENKA: If your what permits? Do you mean queen? Sit down, Mitya, and tell me what you're trying to say. And don't frighten me. You won't frighten me, will you? Because if you don't, I'm very glad to see you.

DMITRY: I would never frighten you and I'm not going to stand in your way… *(Starts to cry and sits down on a chair and hides his face.)*

GRUSHENKA: Mitya, is this any way to behave? As if you had anything to cry about. I'm very glad you've come, Mitya, very glad. *(To the OTHERS.)* I want him to sit here with us. I want him here. Do you understand me? If he leaves, I leave.

POLE 1: Whatever my quin wishes is law. *(To DMITRY.)* You, *panye*, I ask to join our company.

(TRIFON enters, carrying a tray with champagne bottles and glasses.)

TRIFON: Here you are, Lieutenant Karamazov, sir: champagne for everybody.

DMITRY: *(To POLE 1.)* Let's drink together, *panye*.

GRUSHENKA: Thank God you brought champagne—all these two want to drink is this sweet liqueur. But for God's sake, put that money away. Where did you get so much? Are you on another spree?

DMITRY: *(Putting the money in his pocket.)* Trifon! Another bottle!

(TRIFON exits.)

DMITRY: So, what did I interrupt?

POLE 2: The *lajdak* was telling lies.

MAXIMOV: All I was saying, Major Karamazov, sir, was that in the 1820s, the entire Russian cavalry married Polish women.

POLE 1: It is obvious that he has never seen a Polish lady in his life.

MAXIMOV: Except for my wife.

POLE 1: So, you were in the cavalry, *panye?*

DMITRY: You don't look like a cavalryman, Mr. Lajdak.

MAXIMOV: My name is Maximov, good sir.

POLE 1: *Lajdak* is scoundrel, *panye*.

GRUSHENKA: And who is that oaf of yours to call him a scoundrel?

POLE 1: *Pani* Agrippina, he is telling lies: he has never been in Poland in his life.

MAXIMOV: Oh no, worthy Polish sir, I have never been in Poland in my life, and I've never been in the cavalry in my life, either, Major Karamazov, sir. But I did marry a lovely little Polish *pani* and she was brought to me by a cavalryman who had served in Poland, good Polish sir. And he told me that after a little *pani* danced the mazurka with one of our cavalrymen, she would jump up on his lap, just like a kitten—a little white kitten, sir—and her *pan* father and *pani* mother would just sit there and watch. Well, the next day the cavalry officer would offer his hand. And that's just what the officer who brought me my wife did. And he brought her to Russia with her *pani* mother and her *pani* aunt and another *pani* with a grown-up son. But then he found out she was lame, sir.

POLE 1: So you married a lame woman, *panye?*

MAXIMOV: Oh yes, sir. They deceived me—I thought she was skipping.

DMITRY: So what happened to her, my friend?

MAXIMOV: I don't remember. I remember what happened to my second wife, sir—she went off with a certain *monsieur*. Unfortunately, she managed to transfer all my property into her name. She left me quite flat, sir. A venerable bishop once observed to me that my first wife was lame and the second light footed. And so now, I travel throughout our beautiful Russia meeting nice, interesting people like all of you.

DMITRY: A toast: to nice interesting people.

MAXIMOV: To nice interesting people, Major Karamazov.

(DMITRY and MAXIMOV clink glasses and drink.)

DMITRY: And now, worthy Polish *pans,* let us drink together. Let's drink to Poland.

POLE 1: I accept your invitation with pleasure, *panye.*

DMITRY: *(Pouring champagne.)* And the other *pan,* too—what's his name?

POLE 1: *Pan* Vrublevsky, *panye.*

DMITRY: To Poland!

(DMITRY and POLES toast and drink.)

DMITRY: *(Pouring more champagne.)* Now to Russia, brothers, and to our friendship.

GRUSHENKA: Mitya, pour me a glass, I'd like to drink to Russia.

MAXIMOV: Oh, can I drink to Russia, too, Major?

DMITRY: Of course you can, my friend.

MAXIMOV: Oh good, I'd love to drink to our dear sweet Russia, our dear old granny.

DMITRY: *(Emptying bottle.)* Excellent. Trifon! More bottles! To Russia.

(DMITRY, GRUSHENKA, and MAXIMOV drink.)

GRUSHENKA: *(To POLES.)* What about you two?

POLE 2: To Russia within her borders of 1772.

POLE 1: *Oto bardzo pieknie.* ["Now that's better."]

(POLES drink.)

DMITRY: Idiots.

POLE 2: *(Walking up to DMITRY.)* Can a man not love his own land, *panye?*

GRUSHENKA: Stop it. No quarreling. There are to be no quarrels.

DMITRY: Forgive me, most worthy *pans,* it was all my fault. Forgive me *Pan* Vrublevsky, it won't happen again.

(TRIFON enters with another tray.)

TRIFON: Champagne, lady and gentlemen.

MAXIMOV: How about a little game of faro?

DMITRY: Excellent.

POLE 1: It's rather late.

POLE 2: *Tak.* ["Yes."]

GRUSHENKA: It's always late, it's always impossible. They never want to do anything, they just sit here and scowl at the world.

POLE 1: My goddess, if I am sad, it is because that I see that you are sad. And so, we shall play.

DMITRY: Excellent. Here are cards. Here is money. Make the bank.

POLE 1: We will ask the innkeeper for a pack of cards, *panye.*

POLE 2: *To najlepzy sposob.* ["That's the best way."]

DMITRY: Of course. Trifon. Some cards.

TRIFON: *(Pulling a deck of cards from his apron.)* No sooner said than done, Lieutenant Karamazov, sir. *(Exits.)*

(DMITRY hands cards to POLE 1, who starts to shuffle. POLE 2 gets paper and pen.)

MAXIMOV: Major, could you possibly let me have five rubles, so I could try my luck?

DMITRY: Here's ten. And there's more where that came from.

(POLE 1 shuffles the cards and puts the deck face down on the table.)

DMITRY: Ten on the jack. *(Puts ten rubles in the bank.)*

MAXIMOV: *(Putting one ruble in the bank.)* And I'll stake one ruble on the pretty little lady, the queen of hearts, the little *panienochka.*

(As POLE 1 deals the cards, POLE 2 records the cards that come up. POLE 1 takes off the first card and places it next to the deck. He takes the next card and places it next to the first—from here on, all cards go in this pile. A jack is revealed on the top of the deck.)

DMITRY: Jack of spades!

POLE 1: Here are your twenty rubles.

(*POLE 1 puts the jack in the pile, revealing the queen of hearts on the top of the deck. He gives MAXIMOV a ruble.*)

MAXIMOV: I won a ruble! I'll stake it. I will. On another little lady.

DMITRY: (*Putting more money in the bank.*) Double on another jack.

(*POLE 1 removes the card and places it in the pile, revealing another queen on top of the deck.*)

MAXIMOV: I win! I win!

(*POLE 1 give MAXIMOV his winnings and removes the queen from the deck revealing a card that is not a jack.*)

DMITRY: Damn. (*Putting more money in the bank.*) Double on the seven.

MAXIMOV: One single ruble on another little lady.

(*POLE 1 removes the top card, revealing a card that is not a seven, and puts it in the pile. He removes the next card and puts it in the pile, revealing a queen.*)

MAXIMOV: Another ruble!

(*POLE 1 pays MAXIMOV.*)

DMITRY: (*Putting more money in the bank.*) Double on the seven.

MAXIMOV: (*Putting a ruble in the bank.*) Another ruble on another little lady.

(*POLE 1 removes the top card, revealing another queen.*)

MAXIMOV: I win again!

(*POLE 1 removes the card, revealing a card that is not a seven. He pays MAXIMOV.*)

DMITRY: Double on the seven.

GRUSHENKA: Mitya…

DMITRY: Double! Double!

MAXIMOV: I'm all out of little ladies, so I'll place one little ruble on their gentlemen, one little ruble on the king.

(*POLE 1 removes the top card, revealing a king.*)

MAXIMOV: It's me again!

(*POLE 1 removes the card, revealing a card that is not a seven. He pays MAXIMOV.*)

DMITRY: Double on the seven.

GRUSHENKA: Enough.

DMITRY: Why?

GRUSHENKA: Because I won't let you.

POLE 1: *Pani,* what do you mean by this?

GRUSHENKA: Don't you dare raise your voice to me, you plucked turkey.

POLE 1: *Pani* Agrippina!

DMITRY: *Panye.* Could I have a word with you?

POLE 1: What is it?

DMITRY: Could we step into the other room, sir?

(*POLE 1 hesitates.*)

DMITRY: You can bring your bodyguard with you.

GRUSHENKA: Where are you going, Mitya?

DMITRY: We'll be back in a moment.

(*DMITRY and the TWO POLES step into the next room.*)

POLE 1: What can we do for the *pan?*

DMITRY: (*Pulling out money.*) Take three thousand rubles and get out of here.

POLE 1: Three thousand?

DMITRY: Three thousand. Take it and get the hell out of here, and take your Vrublevsky with you.

POLE 1: That does not look like three thousand, *panye.*

DMITRY: It's not. I'll give you five hundred right now. We'll meet in town tomorrow and I'll give you the other two and a half thousand.

(*POLES look at each other.*)

DMITRY: Alright, seven hundred now.

(*POLES look at each other.*)

DMITRY: I don't have the whole three thousand with me. I have it in town. It's hidden.

POLE 1: Is there anything else, *panye?*

DMITRY: Sir, I promise you…

(*POLE 1 spits at him.*)

DMITRY: You spit at me now because you reckon you'll get more out of Grushenka.

(POLE 1 crosses back into the other room, and POLE 2 follows. DMITRY follows them.)

POLE 1: *Pani Agrippina, jestem do zywego dotkniety!* *["I have received a mortal insult!"]*

GRUSHENKA: Russian, speak Russian. I don't want to hear one single Polish word. You used to speak Russian once upon a time.

POLE 1: *Pani* Agrippina—

GRUSHENKA: I am Agrafena, I am Grushenka, and you will speak to me in Russian.

POLE 1: *Pani* Agrafena, I came here to forget the past and to forgive…

GRUSHENKA: You came to forgive? You came to forgive me?

POLE 1: Just so, *pani,* I am not pusillanimous, I am magnanimous. But now I see all your lovers. *Pan* Mitya just offered me three thousand rubles to depart. I spit in his face.

GRUSHENKA: You did what, Mitya? You think I can be bought?

DMITRY: *Panye,* I swear to you, I have never been her lover—she is pure, she is shining…

GRUSHENKA: Don't you dare defend me to him. If I have stayed pure, it is not out of virtue, and it is not because I'm afraid of Kuzma, but because I wanted to stand proudly before this miserable wretch and tell him to his face that I loathe him. In fact, I can hardly believe that he refused your money.

DMITRY: He didn't—he just refused to take seven hundred tonight and the rest tomorrow. He was holding out for the whole three thousand.

GRUSHENKA: And you thought you'd get more than three thousand from me, didn't you, *panye?*

POLE 1: I am a knight, *Pani* Agrippina, a nobleman, not a *lajdak.* I came back to make you my wife. But I do not find the *pani* I remember; I find a wanton, shameless woman.

GRUSHENKA: Then why don't you go back where you came from? You're not the same man. He couldn't possibly have looked like this. Where did you get that stupid wig? The man I loved was a falcon, and you look like a half-plucked drake. He laughed and sang songs to me…God, what an idiot I've been. *(Throws herself on a chair.)*

(TRIFON bursts in with DANCING GIRLS and MUSICIANS, dancing and playing.)

TRIFON: Lieutenant Karamazov, the girls are here!

POLE 2: This is Sodom. Innkeeper, throw these shameless people out.

TRIFON: Shut up.

POLE 2: Swine.

TRIFON: Swine, am I? Where's the pack of cards I gave you?

POLE 2: I don't know what you're talking about.

TRIFON: Don't you? *(Goes to where POLES hid the deck.)* Here's the deck I gave you—unopened.

GRUSHENKA: I knew it. You cheating Polack.

POLE 2: Public slut.

(DMITRY lunges at POLE 2, grabs him by the throat, and drags him into the next room and throws him on the floor. DMITRY comes back.)

DMITRY: *Panye,* would you care to join your body-guard?

TRIFON: Wait, Lieutenant, make him give back the money you lost.

DMITRY: Let him keep it as a consolation.

GRUSHENKA: Bravo, Mitya.

POLE 1: *Pani, jesli isc za mna idzmy; jesli nie—bywaj zdrowa!* *["If you want to come with me, come; if not—farewell!"]* *(Crosses into the next room.)*

GRUSHENKA: Good riddance.

MAXIMOV: Mr. Innkeeper, Mr. Innkeeper, lock them in, lock them in.

TRIFON: *(Locks the door.)* So much for Poland, lady and gentlemen. Lieutenant Karamazov, sir, your provisions have arrived.

GRUSHENKA: Mitya. I want to drink. I want to get drunk. Just like the last time.

(Chaos erupts. MUSICIANS and GIRLS play and dance frantically. TRIFON brings in food and drink, and DMITRY goes from person to person, giving them glasses, filling and refilling them, giving the food, etc. GRUSHENKA drinks, alternately flirting with DMITRY and MAXIMOV. MAXIMOV tries to seduce ONE OF

THE GIRLS. *At some point, MAXIMOV leaps into the center of the room, scattering the dancing GIRLS. He just leaps around, clicking his heels. Lights alter to suggest the passage of time.)*

GRUSHENKA: *(From inside.)* Quiet, everyone! I'm going to dance.

MAXIMOV: She's going to dance! She's going to dance! Brava, Agrafena Alexandrovna! Brava!

DMITRY: *(Going to the door of the room where POLES are.)* Hey, Polacks, get in here. Agrafena Alexandrovna is going to dance.

POLE 1: *(Offstage.) Lajdak!*

MAXIMOV: Dance, Agrafena Alexandrovna! Dance!

GRUSHENKA: Shhh! Give me a handkerchief.

(MAXIMOV gives GRUSHENKA a handkerchief, and EVERYONE forms a circle around her, clapping rhythmically. GRUSHENKA begins to dance unsteadily, then collapses. DMITRY rushes over and catches her and carries her into another room and puts her on a bed.)

GRUSHENKA: Oh Mitya, I did love him, I loved him so much all these five years. Driving here in the carriage, I kept thinking how will I meet him, what will I say, how will we look at each other…? My soul was frozen. And then it was as if he had emptied a bucket of slops on my head. Oh god, Mitya, it's not his face, it's not his voice—he talks like a schoolmaster. It's his wife that did this to him, that bitch—she's the one that changed him. Oh Mitya, I'm so ashamed, I'm ashamed of my whole life.

(She turns over and cries quietly. DMITRY strokes her hair, then starts to go.)

GRUSHENKA: Wait, Mitya, don't go. I love one man here, who is it? You tell me. Tonight a falcon walked into this place and my heart sank—"You fool!" my heart whispered, "this is the one you love." And you were so afraid you couldn't even speak. "He can't be afraid of them—he's not afraid of anyone? It's me. It's me he's afraid of." So Fenya must have told you what I said—the message I gave Alyosha—and you believed it—that I loved Mitenka for one hour and now I'm going off to love another. How could I be such an idiot to think I could love anyone after you? Can you forgive me? Can you…do you…do you still love me?

(She embraces him. He stares at her for a moment, then embraces her back and kisses her. After a moment, she breaks away.)

GRUSHENKA: Will you forgive me for tormenting you? I tormented you all from spite. I drove your father insane on purpose, just from spite…Mitya, my falcon, why aren't you kissing me? Don't listen to me, kiss me. Kiss me, kiss me harder, like this. Let's love, if we're going to love. *(Breaks away.)* Stop. Not now, not yet. I'm not yours, yet…they're in the next room—he's here…it's vile here…

DMITRY: Whatever you want. We don't have to…whatever you say…I revere…you're right, it's vile here.

GRUSHENKA: We should do it honestly…from now on, it will be honest…and we should be honest, not wild animals, we should be good…I want you to take me away from here, very, very far away—do you hear me? I don't want to be here…I want to be far, far away…

DMITRY: I'll take you away, we'll leave forever…God, I'd give my whole life, if only I knew about that blood.

GRUSHENKA: What blood?

DMITRY: Never mind. Grusha, you want to be honest, but I'm a thief—I stole from Katya…

GRUSHENKA: You mean the young lady? No, you haven't stolen from her, since you'll give it back. I'll give it to you—all that's mine is yours now. We'll both go to her, we'll bow to her, and we'll ask her forgiveness and go away. And if she doesn't forgive us, we'll leave anyway. Give her the money and love me—don't love her, don't love her anymore. If you love her, I'll put both her eyes out with a needle.

DMITRY: I love only you. I'll love you when I'm in Siberia.

GRUSHENKA: Why Siberia? Never mind—we'll go to Siberia—we'll work.

(THE PROSECUTOR and NELYUDOV enter in shadow behind DMITRY.)

GRUSHENKA: Mitya…who is that looking at us?

NELYUDOV: Retired lieutenant Dmitry Fyodorovich Karamazov, I am Nikolai Parfenovich Nelyudov, district examining magistrate, and this is Ippolit Kirillovich Kirilov, deputy public prosecutor. It is my duty to inform you that you are charged with the murder of your father, Fyodor Pavlovich Karamazov.

(Lights fade.)

SCENE 19

The same room at the inn about an hour later. DMITRY, THE PROSECUTOR, and NELYUDOV are seated at the table. NELYUDOV is writing down DMITRY's testimony. The examination has been going on for some time.

NELYUDOV: You ran to your father's neighbor's yard. You expected to find Smerdyakov there, keeping watch, but the yard was empty. Then what happened?

DMITRY: I climbed over the fence to my father's yard. I went to his window to see if she was in there. It didn't look like it, but I had to be certain. I decided to give the signal, the signal that means that Grushenka—I mean Agrafena Alexandrovna—has come. He came to the window—the sight of him repulsed me: his adam's apple, his nose, his eyes, his shameless sneer—I couldn't stand it anymore. I reached into my pocket and grabbed the pestle. *(Stops.)*

NELYUDOV: Then what?

DMITRY: Oh, then I killed him. I whacked him over the head and split his skull open—isn't that your version of it?

NELYUDOV: What's your version of it?

DMITRY: My version of it, gentlemen? My version is this: whether it was someone's tears or God heard my mother's prayers, or a bright spirit kissed me at that moment, I don't know—but the devil was overcome. I ran from the window. Father saw me, he screamed and jumped back—I kept running, I ran to the fence—that's when Grigory grabbed me—I was already on top of the fence.

THE PROSECUTOR: By any chance, did you notice, when you were running away from the window, whether the bedroom door was open or not?

DMITRY: No, it was shut. Why? Did you find it open?

THE PROSECUTOR: The door was open. We know from the position of the body that the victim was struck from inside the room and not from outside the window. Therefore, the murderer must have entered and left by that door.

DMITRY: That's impossible. He kept the door locked and he never would have opened it without the signals—nobody knew about them except for me, Smerdyakov, and the dead man.

THE PROSECUTOR: So if Smerdyakov knew about the signals, he could have committed the crime.

DMITRY: Bravo, Mr. Prosecutor. An excellent move. You think I'm going to clutch desperately at the straw you're offering me, hang onto it, and start shouting at the top of my lungs, "It was Smerdyakov! It was Smerdyakov!" Well, you're wrong. I'm not going to start accusing Smerdyakov.

THE PROSECUTOR: You don't suspect him?

DMITRY: Smerdyakov is an abject coward. I never once raised my hand to him, but he would kiss these boots and beg me not to "scare" him. What kind of talk is that for a man? He's a sickly, epileptic, feeble-minded chicken who could be thrashed by an eight-year-old. Anyway, why would he kill the old man? He might even be his son—did you know that?

THE PROSECUTOR: We've heard the rumor. But after all, you, too, are your father's son and you told everyone you wanted to kill him.

DMITRY: A direct hit, Mr. Prosecutor. But what a dirty blow it was. I admitted it myself and you use it against me. Well, not only did I tell you I wanted to kill him, I told you that I almost did kill him. But gentlemen, what you leave out is that I told you I didn't kill him—I told you my guardian angel saved me. You choose to ignore that—and that is despicable. What's he told you—Smerdyakov? Am I allowed to ask?

THE PROSECUTOR: You may ask anything you like. In fact, we're required to answer. We found the servant Smerdyakov lying in bed with a severe epileptic seizure. According to the doctor who accompanied us, it could have been his tenth consecutive seizure this night. The doctor thinks he may not live 'til morning.

DMITRY: Then the devil killed my father.

NELYUDOV: Would you like to go on with your statement?

(Lights fade.)

SCENE 20

The same as the previous scene, about ten minutes later.

NELYUDOV: Where could you have possibly gotten such a large sum of money when, at six o'clock the same day, by your own admission, you…

DMITRY: Needed ten rubles and pawned my pistols to Perkhotin, then went to ask Madame Khokhalakova for three thousand rubles which she didn't give me, and so on and so forth. Yes, gentlemen, it's strange isn't it? There he was without a kopek and the next thing, lo and behold, he had thousands of rubles in his hand. I've got you worried. "What if he refuses to tell us where he got it?" Well, you're damn right—I won't tell you.

NELYUDOV: Do you understand how important this question is?

DMITRY: I do.

THE PROSECUTOR: Mr. Karamazov, a suspect, of course, has the right to refuse to answer any question. However, considering the harm you could do yourself by refusing to answer a question as vital as this one…

DMITRY: And so on and so forth—I've heard it all before. Gentlemen, I realize the importance of this matter, but I still won't tell you.

NELYUDOV: You realize that you're not harming us, you're harming yourself.

DMITRY: I understand.

NELYUDOV: Could you tell us why you won't answer?

DMITRY: Yes. I refuse to answer because the answer would dishonor me. You're not writing that down, are you?

NELYUDOV: Yes, I think it's important.

DMITRY: You have no right.

NELYUDOV: Could you tell us the nature of the disgrace?

DMITRY: No—I've dirtied myself enough. It's over, gentlemen.

NELYUDOV: I'm afraid I have to ask you to put everything in your possession on the table—in particular any money you still have on you.

DMITRY: Certainly.

(DMITRY places all his money on the table including change. NELYUDOV counts it.)

NELYUDOV: Eight hundred and thirty-five rubles and forty kopeks. Is that all?

DMITRY: That's it, gentlemen.

NELYUDOV: *(Reviewing his notes.)* According to your statement, you spent three hundred rubles at Plotnikov's shop, gave ten to Perkhotin…

DMITRY: I just gave him back the ten he gave me.

NELYUDOV: Alright…You gave twenty to the coachman and lost three hundred ten at cards…was there anything else?

DMITRY: I gave Trifon twenty-five rubles to give to the girls and musicians and I gave ten to Mr. Maximov.

NELYUDOV: If we count what's on the table as eight hundred and thirty-five, it would appear you had only fifteen hundred rubles.

DMITRY: So it would appear.

NELYUDOV: Why does everybody say there was much more than that?

DMITRY: They can say what they like.

NELYUDOV: But you told them so yourself.

DMITRY: So I did.

NELYUDOV: I'm afraid I'm required to conduct a thorough examination of your clothing and person.

DMITRY: As you wish. Shall I turn out my pockets?

NELYUDOV: I'm afraid you'll have to undress.

DMITRY: What? Can't you search me like this?

NELYUDOV: I'm afraid not.

(Lights fade.)

Scene 21

The same, about twenty minutes later. DMITRY is in his underwear.

DMITRY: What now? Do you start flogging me with a birch?

NELYUDOV: I'm afraid we'll have to keep your clothing as evidence, but the innkeeper procured this suit of clothes from one of the other guests.

DMITRY: I don't want other people's clothes—give me mine.

NELYUDOV: I'm sorry, they're evidence.

DMITRY: To hell with you and your clothes. You've defiled me, you've defiled my soul. Do you really think that if I killed my father, I'd hide it? That I'd hedge and lie and hide? No, gentlemen, Dmitry Karamazov is not that kind of man. He could not bear it. If I had killed my father, I wouldn't have waited for the sun or you or anything—I'd have destroyed myself at once, then and there. Good God, the thought that I'd accidentally killed Grigory ate at me all night—and not from fear of your punishment, gentlemen. You should be ashamed. And you expect me to reveal a new shame and disgrace to you? You scoffers, you sneering, blind moles. Better penal servitude. The one who opened the door to my father's room is the one who killed him—he's the one who robbed him. Who he is, I don't know, but he is not Dmitry Karamazov—know that. That's all I can tell you, so stop badgering me. Exile me, hang me, but don't irritate me.

THE PROSECUTOR: Speaking of the door you just mentioned, there is a piece of evidence we neglected to tell you about. The servant Grigory Vasilievich Kutuzov has testified that he saw the door open when you were running away from the house—the door you have stated was closed all the time you were in the garden. He concludes that you must have run out of that door.

DMITRY: He's lying. He couldn't have seen it open because it was shut.

THE PROSECUTOR: He's quite certain.

DMITRY: He'd been hit on the head—he was hallucinating.

THE PROSECUTOR: He saw the door open before he was struck, not after.

DMITRY: He couldn't have seen it—I didn't run out of the door.

THE PROSECUTOR: Show him.

NELYUDOV: (Takes out a torn envelope.) Do you recognize this?

DMITRY: It must be my father's—the envelope with the three thousand rubles. It should have "To my angel, Grushenka" written on it. Then he added "To my little chick"…yes, there it is.

NELYUDOV: It was empty when we found it—lying on the floor near the bed.

DMITRY: Gentlemen, it's Smerdyakov. He killed him, he robbed him. He's the only one who knew where the old man hid the envelope.

NELYUDOV: But you also knew about the envelope, and that your father kept it under his pillow.

DMITRY: I didn't know where it was—I only heard about it from Smerdyakov—he's the only one who knew where the old man kept it.

NELYUDOV: Let me read you back your testimony from earlier tonight: Quote: "I considered the three thousand that he had waiting for Agrafena Alexandrovna under his pillow to be my property."

DMITRY: I had no idea it was under his pillow—I just said the first thing that came into my head. What did Smerdyakov tell you? Where did he tell you it was hidden? Smerdyakov was the only one who knew where it was—Smerdyakov and no one else—he never told me where the old man kept it. It's him! You must arrest him quickly. He killed Father after I ran away, while Grigory was unconscious. He used the signals to get in—he was the only one who knew about the signals—Father wouldn't have let anyone in without those signals.

THE PROSECUTOR: You forget, at the time of the crime, Smerdyakov was semiconscious, suffering repeated epileptic seizures.

DMITRY: He could be faking.

THE PROSECUTOR: That occurred to me; I asked the doctor. It is possible to fake a seizure, but not to fool a doctor. Smerdyakov was examined. He's been taken to the hospital.

DMITRY: God is against me.

THE PROSECUTOR: Consider for yourself, Dmitry Fyodorovich: on the one side there is the evidence of the open door which overwhelms both you and us. On the other side, your inexplicable, persistent, and obdurate refusal to tell us where you got that money which miraculously appeared in your hands. In view of all this, what do you expect us to think? It's not that we're cold cynics and scoffers who are incapable of believing in the noble impulses of your soul. Try to understand our position.

DMITRY: Alright. I'll reveal my shame and disgrace. I had the money with me all the time. I had stolen it. The exact figure was fifteen hundred rubles. I had it sewn up in a rag and I was wearing it around my neck for a whole month.

NELYUDOV: From whom did you…appropriate it?

DMITRY: You mean stole it—speak plainly, gentlemen. A month ago my former fiancée, Katerina Ivanovna Verkhovsteva, sent for me. She handed me three thousand rubles to send to her sister in Moscow—as if she couldn't have sent it herself. Before I could mail it, I met her…Agrafena Alexandrovna—Grushenka. I carried her off here, to Mokroye. I spent half the three thousand—that is, I spent fifteen hundred rubles. The other half I kept—I wore it here on my neck like an amulet. Yesterday I tore open the rag and spent the fifteen hundred. All that's left are the eight hundred rubles you now have.

NELYUDOV: But you spent three thousand a month ago, not fifteen hundred—everyone knows it.

DMITRY: Who knows it? Did anyone count it?

NELYUDOV: You told everyone that would listen that you squandered exactly three thousand rubles.

DMITRY: True. I told that to the whole town and the whole town repeated it. And here, in Mokroye, everyone thought I threw away three thousand. But I only spent fifteen hundred, not three thousand.

THE PROSECUTOR: Did you inform anyone of this fact—that you kept fifteen hundred from a month ago?

DMITRY: No.

THE PROSECUTOR: No one at all?

DMITRY: No.

THE PROSECUTOR: But why did you make such a secret of it? Surely you know that everyone in town suspects that you got the money from Miss Verkhovsteva. You even admitted it to one or two people. Yet, you were willing to risk penal servitude rather than confess.

DMITRY: Alright, try to follow me. I appropriate three thousand rubles entrusted to my honor, I go on a spree with it; I squander it all. The next morning, I go to her and say, "Katya, I've squandered your three thousand." Is that nice? No. I'm a beast, a man with no more self-restraint than a beast. But I am not a thief. Now here's a second, even more favorable scenario: I go on a spree and spend only fifteen hundred rubles—half the money. The next day I bring her that fifteen hundred and say, "Katya, I threw away half your money because I'm a scoundrel and a beast, take back the other half so I won't be tempted." I'm still a scoundrel and a beast, but I am most certainly not a thief. But I held onto that money for a whole month. I could have given it back at any time, but I didn't.

THE PROSECUTOR: Alright, I see your point. I still don't think it's shameful enough for you to risk penal servitude, but let's move on. Why did you put aside the fifteen hundred?

DMITRY: The whole shame is in the motive. All this month I thought Agrafena Alexandrovna was choosing between me and my father. What if she chose me, what if she said, "I love you, take me away to the ends of the Earth," and I only had some small change in my pocket? So I deliberately counted off half the three thousand in cold blood, I sewed it up, calculatingly, I sewed it up even before I went drinking. And then, when I had it sewn up, I went and got drunk on the other half. Do you understand now?

THE PROSECUTOR: I really don't see the disgrace, Dmitry Fyodorovich. But please continue, Nikolai Parfenovich.

NELYUDOV: Why did you open the rag last evening?

DMITRY: Because I had decided to kill myself at five in the morning—it no longer mattered whether I was a thief or a man of honor. But when I got here everything changed.

NELYUDOV: Where were you when you opened the rag?

DMITRY: I don't know…it was after I left Fenya, on my way to Plotnikov's shop.

NELYUDOV: Could you be more specific?

DMITRY: I think I was crossing the square.

NELYUDOV: What did you do with the rag?

DMITRY: I dropped it on the ground.

NELYUDOV: Where, exactly?

DMITRY: How the hell should I know, it was dark.

NELYUDOV: It's extremely important.

DMITRY: Then sweep the square! You don't believe me and I can't prove it. You find it all so amusing, I can see it in your eyes—you, in particular, Mr. Prosecutor. I never should have trusted you with my secret. Go ahead: sing your hymn of triumph, if you have the stomach for it.

NELYUDOV: I'm sorry if we've caused you any distress, Dmitry Fyodorovich. If you'll just make yourself comfortable, we need to review your testimony and examine the witnesses.

Scene 22

Spot up on NELYUDOV, spot up on DMITRY. During the following, DMITRY gradually falls asleep. Spot up on TRIFON.

NELYUDOV: Trifon Borisovich, how much money would you estimate Mr. Karamazov spent here, in your inn, a month ago?

TRIFON: Three thousand rubles.

(Spot down on TRIFON, spot up on POLE 1.)

NELYUDOV: Mr. Mussyalovich, how much money did Mr. Karamazov offer you to leave town?

POLE 1: Three thousand rubles.

(Spot down on POLE 1, spot up on POLE 2.)

NELYUDOV: Mr. Vrublevsky, how much money did Mr. Karamazov offer your friend?

POLE 2: Three thousand rubles.

(Spot down on POLE 2, spot up on MAXIMOV.)

NELYUDOV: Mr. Maximov, how much money would you estimate Mr. Karamazov had in his hands last night?

MAXIMOV: Twenty thousand rubles.

(Spot fades on MAXIMOV. DMITRY is asleep. Spot fades on NELYUDOV. A spot comes up on a DRIVER.)

DMITRY: Driver, what place is this?

DRIVER: It was a village, sir.

DMITRY: Who are all these women? Why are they crying?

DRIVER: They're crying for the babe.

DMITRY: But why is it crying? Why are its little arms bare? Why don't they cover it up?

DRIVER: The babe is frozen through, and his clothes are frozen, they don't keep him warm.

DMITRY: But why is it so?

DRIVER: They're poor, they're burnt out, they're begging for their burnt-out village.

DMITRY: No, no—tell me why are these poor mothers standing here? Why are the people poor? Why is the steppe barren? Why don't they embrace and kiss? Why don't they sing joyful songs? Why are they blackened with such black misery? Why don't they feed the babe?

(He rises and reaches out, he looks toward heaven and extends his arms. A spot comes up on GRUSHENKA.)

GRUSHENKA: And I am with you, too. I won't leave you now. We'll walk together all our lives.

(Lights fade. Lights come up. DMITRY is sleeping by the window, NELYUDOV is standing over him, THE PROSECUTOR is still in the room; GRUSHENKA and DRIVER are gone.)

DMITRY: What? Where?

NELYUDOV: Dmitry Fyodorovich, would you please read over the transcript and sign it?

DMITRY: I have had a good dream, gentlemen.

(Lights fade.)

SCENE 23

The same, about ten minutes later. DMITRY is standing, facing THE PROSECUTOR and NELYUDOV.

DMITRY: Well, gentlemen, I'm ready. I don't blame you, I understand that you had no choice.

(They start to leave.)

DMITRY: Wait. Gentlemen, we are all cruel, we are all monsters, we all make people weep—mothers…and babes. But I am worse than all of you. Every day I beat my breast and promised to reform, and every day I did the same vile things. For such men, a blow is needed. Well, the thunder has struck. I accept my disgrace before all. I want to suffer; I want to be purified by suffering. I accept punishment, not because I killed him, but because I wanted to kill him and might have killed him. But I intend to fight you and I want you to know it. God will decide my fate, not you. Please forgive me for having shouted at you. I was still so stupid then. May I see her one last time?

NELYUDOV: Certainly. But we have to be present. *(Goes to the door and opens it.)* Miss Svetlova.

(GRUSHENKA enters and bows to DMITRY.)

GRUSHENKA: I will follow you forever, wherever they send you.

DMITRY: Forgive me, Grusha. Forgive me for loving you the way I did, for hurting you the way I have.

(They look at each other for a moment.)

DMITRY: And now, gentlemen, I am at your disposal.

(Lights fade.)

ACT II
SCENE 1

A street. A morning in early November, approximately two months after DMITRY's arrest. SMUROV is onstage. KOLYA enters.

SMUROV: You're late, Krasotkin.

KOLYA: I was held up.

SMUROV: *(Looking offstage.)* You brought Perezvon.

KOLYA: Uh huh.

SMUROV: Too bad it's not Zhuhcka.

KOLYA: Zhuchka has gone to that undiscovered country from whose bourn no traveler returns.

SMUROV: What?

KOLYA: He's dead, Smurov. You didn't tell anyone I was coming, did you?

SMUROV: God strike me dead if I did. Couldn't we just say it's Zhuchka? He looks like Zhuchka.

KOLYA: Lying is for hypocrites and weasels, Smurov.

SMUROV: You won't cheer him up with Perezvon, you know. His father's bringing him a puppy. He thinks it'll make Ilyusha feel better. It won't.

KOLYA: How's he doing?

SMUROV: He's bad. I think it's consumption. He's breathing funny. Dr. Herzenstube comes every day—somebody's giving his family money for doctors.

KOLYA: Swindlers.

SMUROV: Who?

KOLYA: Doctors. The whole lousy medical profession's a fraud. Anyway, what's this sentimental nonsense you've got going on? Your whole class is just sitting there with him.

SMUROV: It's not the whole class.

KOLYA: What I can't figure out is Alexei Karamazov. What's he doing sentimentalizing with a bunch of schoolboys when his brother's going on trial tomorrow?

SMUROV: We're not sentimentalizing. You're going—you're going to make up with him.

KOLYA: That's my business, Smurov, not yours. And I'm going because I choose to—you were all dragged there by Alexei Karamazov. And maybe I'm not going to "make up with him"—stupid expression.

SMUROV: It was not Karamazov—we just felt like going. Alright, Karamazov went with us, so what? Boy, was Ilyusha's father glad to see us; he was so happy we made friends with him. You know, his father's alright. None of this would have happened if that lousy murderer Dmitry Karamazov hadn't beaten him up. The old man's gonna go crazy when Ilyusha dies.

KOLYA: I still don't get Karamazov.

SMUROV: He's been asking us to bring you. Why didn't you come sooner?

KOLYA: Karamazov calls and I should come running, Smurov? *(Looking offstage.)* Smurov, I like to observe realism. Look. Have you ever noticed how dogs sniff each other when they meet?

SMUROV: Yeah, it's stupid.

KOLYA: It's not stupid, stupid. You only think it's stupid because of your societal prejudices. If dogs could reason, they'd think human social relations were pretty stupid. Rakitin came up with that. Pretty brilliant, huh? Did I tell you I became a socialist?

SMUROV: What's a socialist?

KOLYA: It's when all people are equal and everything is owned in common, and there are no marriages and everyone can choose his own religion and what laws he likes…and…a bunch of other stuff—you're too young to understand.

SMUROV: This is it.

KOLYA: Alright, I want you to do something for me. Listen very carefully, because I don't want you to mess it up.

SMUROV: Don't worry, I know what I'm doing.

KOLYA: Alright, listen. When we're in there, I want you to stand by the door. At the right moment, I'm gonna whistle. Now, when I whistle, I want you to open the door. Got it?

SMUROV: Got it.

KOLYA: Good. Now, go fetch Karamazov for me.

SMUROV: Fetch him where?

KOLYA: Here.

SMUROV: Why?

KOLYA: We have to sniff each other first.

SMUROV: It's freezing.

KOLYA: I have my reasons. Get him.

(SMUROV crosses into the house.)

KOLYA: I wish I weren't so short—he'll think I'm thirteen.

(ALYOSHA enters. He is wearing lay clothes.)

ALYOSHA: Are you Krasotkin? I can't believe you've come. I'm so glad to meet you, I'm Alexei Karamazov.

KOLYA: I've had business to attend to, Karamazov…how are things…in there?

ALYOSHA: Bad. Ilyusha's going to die.

KOLYA: Oh…

ALYOSHA: He's missed you—ever since the fight. (Looking offstage.) Is that your dog?

KOLYA: Oh…yes, his name's Perezvon.

ALYOSHA: It's not Zhuchka? I guess that's it, then.

KOLYA: Did he tell you what happened?

ALYOSHA: No, he wouldn't tell me or his father.

KOLYA: You see, I was sort of Ilyusha's protector—he's small and weak and his clothes are dirty and his pants ride up and the kids in his class tortured him. You know how cruel kids can be at that age, Karamazov. But Ilyusha's a proud little kid—he fought back and I really liked that. So I beat up a couple of the kids and they backed off. They worship me, Karamazov. So Ilyusha started hanging around me—every day after school, all day Sunday. I like him, he's a good kid. But he started getting all mushy and sentimental and I hate that slop, so I got sort of cool with him.

ALYOSHA: So that's what the fight was about?

KOLYA: No, it was about Zhuchka. You see, Ilyusha made friends with your father's lackey Smerdyakov—by the way, my condolences, Karamazov. Anyway, Smerdyakov's a weasel and he taught Ilyusha this nasty little trick. He'd take a pin and he'd stick it in a piece of bread and he'd throw it to a hungry dog. Zhuchka was a stray and Ilyusha made one of these snacks for him. Zhuchka wolfed it down whole. He squealed like a stuck pig and ran away. Nobody's seen him since. I had to teach Ilyusha a lesson—I had no choice, Karamazov, what he did was really nasty. So I stopped talking to

him. I was only gonna punish him for a few days, but then your brother pulled Ilyusha's father by that back-scrubber beard of his and without me to protect him, the kids started shouting "backscrubber" every time they saw Ilyusha. One day, he tried to fight all the kids at once. I was about to jump in and help him when he looked me straight in the eye and stabbed me with his penknife—right here, in the thigh. I just stood there and looked at him contemptuously, like I was saying "would you like to try again?" He got really scared about what he'd done and burst into tears and ran away. Then I heard he got into that rock fight with all the other boys, and you came along and he bit your finger. You have to understand the state he was in. I should have come as soon as he got sick. I was stupid.

ALYOSHA: You're thirteen?

KOLYA: Fourteen. I'll be fourteen in two weeks. Listen, Karamazov, let's get one thing straight: I don't like talking about my age.

ALYOSHA: I'll never mention it again.

KOLYA: Did they tell you the story?

ALYOSHA: What story?

KOLYA: There's a slanderous rumor going around that I played robbers with the preparatory class last week. It's true I played with them, but I didn't enjoy it. I did it for them, to make them happy.

ALYOSHA: What if you did enjoy it?

KOLYA: How could you possibly think I'd enjoy it?

ALYOSHA: Adults enjoy going to the theatre, don't they? They go to see adventure stories about robbers and soldiers, so what's the difference? The only difference is that adults go to watch actors, while young people are the actors, themselves. Playing is the beginning of creative expression. You're an artist.

KOLYA: That's an interesting theory, Karamazov. I'll have to think about it when I get home. You know, I suspected I could learn something from you and I was right—I'm learning a lot.

ALYOSHA: I'm learning from you too, Kolya.

KOLYA: Oh my God, Karamazov, you're only wearing a jacket out here and I just keep talking. I'm such an ego-ist. We're all such egoists, Karamazov. Let's go inside.

(They cross into the house. ILYUSHA is lying in bed. SMUROV is standing by the door. CAPTAIN

SNEGIRYOV, MAMA SNEGIRYOV, NINA, and KARTASHOV are in the room. There is a basket with a puppy in it by ILYUSHA's bed.)

MAMA: Move over, move over. I can't see Ilyusha.

SNEGIRYOV: Mama…

KARTASHOV: Krasotkin!

SMUROV: He came with me.

KARTASHOV: Why didn't you tell us he was coming?

SMUROV: He told me not to, that's why.

SNEGIRYOV: This is Krasotkin? Mr. Krasotkin, please come in, we re so pleased you're here.

(KOLYA crosses to SNEGIRYOV and shakes his hand.)

KOLYA: An honor to meet you, Captain.

SNEGIRYOV: Look, Ilyusha, Mr. Krasotkin has come to see you.

(KOLYA crosses to MAMA and Nina.)

KOLYA: (Bowing to MAMA.) How do you do? (Bowing to NINA.) How do you do?

NINA: I'm so happy you're here.

MAMA: What a well-bred young man, not like the others, who just come galloping in one on top of the other.

SNEGIRYOV: What do you mean, Mama?

MAMA: Just what I said—one on top of the other—they ride in on each other's shoulders. Mr. Chernomazov, I ask you, is that a way to visit respectable people?

ALYOSHA: No it isn't, ma'am.

KOLYA: (Crossing to ILYUSHA.) How are you feeling, old man?

(ILYUSHA tries to speak, but can't. KOLYA strokes his hair.)

KOLYA: Never mind… (Looking into the basket.) I see you got a new puppy.

ILYUSHA: Yes…

KOLYA: He's got a black nose—that means he'll be fierce. He'll make a great watchdog, but you'll have to keep him on a chain.

KARTASHOV: He's gonna be huge.

SMUROV: Of course he'll be huge, he's a mastiff. They get to be as big as calves.

SNEGIRYOV: Big as a calf, a real calf. I asked for the fiercest one. Please, sir, sit down, our dear guest, our long-awaited guest. You came with Alexei Fyodorovich, did you, sir?

KOLYA: No…I came with Perezvon. I have a dog now and his name is Perezvon. A good old Slavic name. He's waiting outside. One whistle from me and he'll fly right in here like a bat out of hell. Do you remember Zhuchka, old man?

ILYUSHA: Zhuchka's here?

KOLYA: Zhuchka's a goner, old man. He just ran off somewhere and died. He couldn't have lived after that little snack you gave him. So I brought Perezvon, instead—a good old Slavic name. Let me introduce you.

ILYUSHA: I don't want to.

KOLYA: You have to. (To MAMA.) Madame, will you permit me to call in my dog?

ILYUSHA: Don't!

SNEGIRYOV: Perhaps, sir…perhaps, some other time…

KOLYA: Smurov!

(SMUROV opens the door. KOLYA whistles and PEREZVON runs in.)

ILYUSHA: It's Zhuchka.

KOLYA: Who else? Look, he's got that nick in his ear you told me about—that's how I identified him.

SNEGIRYOV: Ilyusha, this is Zhuchka, it's Zhuchka. Mama, this is Zhuchka.

SMUROV: I knew he'd find him. Bravo Krasotkin!

KARTASHOV: Bravo Krasotkin!

SMUROV and KARTASHOV: Bravo Krasotkin!

KOLYA: Wait, wait! I taught him all kinds of tricks, that's why I didn't bring him sooner. Do you want to see?

ILYUSHA: Can I just hold him?

KOLYA: Sure. I can show you the tricks later. Ici Perezvon!

(PEREZVON runs to the bed.)

MAMA: *(Singing.)* Perezvon, Perezvon.

ALYOSHA: You didn't come all this time because you were training the dog?

KOLYA: That's right. I wanted to show Perezvon in all his glory.

ILYUSHA: Perezvon, Perezvon.

KOLYA: Wait, I brought you something else. Remember Morozov's cannon that you liked so much. Well, I traded him for it. *(Pulling out a toy cannon.)* look.

MAMA: I want to see! I want to see!

KOLYA: Of course, Madame.

(KOLYA takes the cannon to MAMA and she starts rolling it on her knees.)

MAMA: *(Singing as she rolls the cannon on her knee.)* Perezvon, Perezvon. Why don't you give it to me? You'd better give it to me.

SNEGIRYOV: Mama, Mama, the cannon is yours, yours, but let Ilyusha keep it. Mr. Krasotkin brought it for him, but it's the same as if it was yours. Ilyusha will always let you play with it, it can belong to both of you, both.

MAMA: No, I don't want it to be both of ours. I want it to be mine and not Ilyusha's.

ILYUSHA: It's alright, Mama, you can have it. Krasotkin, is it all right if I give it to Mama?

KOLYA: Of course it is.

MAMA: *(Crying.)* Ilyusha loves his mama, Ilyusha loves his mama…

SNEGIRYOV: Mama, let me kiss your hand. *(Kisses MAMA's hand.)*

MAMA: And if any boy is the nicest young man of all it's that young man, *(Pointing to KOLYA.)* he's the nicest young man of all.

ILYUSHA: Alyosha, have you heard about what Krasotkin did with the train?

ALYOSHA: No.

ILYUSHA: Tell him, Krasotkin.

KOLYA: It was nothing, really. I measured the height of the tracks, and I figured out if you lay down flat, the train would pass right over you. So I did it.

SMUROV: We were so scared, we thought he was dead after the train went by. But he just fainted.

KOLYA: I did not. I was pretending in order to scare you, and obviously it worked, Smurov.

(DOCTOR enters.)

NINA: The doctor is here.

SNEGIRYOV: *(Crossing to DOCTOR.)* Welcome, Your Excellency, welcome.

DOCTOR: I'm not sure if I have the right address.

SNEGIRYOV: Oh no, sir, you have the right address, sir.

DOCTOR: Snegiryov? Mr. Snegiryov?

SNEGIRYOV: Yes, sir, that's me.

DOCTOR: Very well, where's the patient?

SNEGIRYOV: Right this way, sir.

SMUROV: I'm gonna go, Ilyusha. See you tomorrow.

KARTASHOV: 'Bye, Ilyusha.

KOLYA: Don't worry, old man, I'm not leaving, I'll just wait outside.

ALYOSHA: I'll go with you, Kolya.

(SMUROV and KARTASHOV exit, ALYOSHA crosses outside. KOLYA starts to go; NINA crosses to him.)

NINA: Why didn't you come sooner?

(KOLYA crosses outside, followed by PEREZVON.)

KOLYA: That's not Dr. Herzenstube.

ALYOSHA: He's a specialist from Moscow. My brother's fiancée paid for him to come testify at the trial.

KOLYA: I despise medicine. What do you think he'll say?

ALYOSHA: Ilyusha's going to die.

KOLYA: Bunch of frauds. But I'm glad I met you. I've been wanting to meet you for a long time. Too bad we had to meet like this.

(ALYOSHA squeezes KOLYA's hand.)

KOLYA: I heard a lot about you…I heard that you were a mystic and that you were in a monastery, but that didn't stop me. Contact with the real world will cure you of all that mystical stuff.

ALYOSHA: What do you mean by mystical stuff?

KOLYA: You know, God and all that.

ALYOSHA: Don't you believe in God?

KOLYA: I have nothing against God…I recognize that it's a useful hypothesis…without it there'd be no order or civilization, and if he didn't exist, he'd have to be invented. But isn't it possible to love mankind without believing in God? Voltaire didn't believe in God and he loved mankind, didn't he?

ALYOSHA: Voltaire did believe in God, but not very much…I don't think…and I don't think he loved mankind very much, either.

KOLYA: Well, you should know, Karamazov, I'm a socialist, an incorrigible socialist. *(Pause.)* Ilyusha's sister seems nice…I like her…she asked me why I didn't come sooner…She's right…I'm a rat.

ALYOSHA: No you're not. You should have come sooner, but that doesn't make you a bad person. You're a smart, generous, open-hearted young man. I understand completely why you were so important to Ilyusha.

KOLYA: I thought you despised me because I was showing off with that stuff about God.

ALYOSHA: You were showing off because you like me. And I like you.

KOLYA: It's embarrassing, Karamazov. You shouldn't go around making a fool of yourself just because you want to be friends with someone.

ALYOSHA: There's nothing foolish about wanting to be friends. Never be ashamed of loving people, Kolya. It's what God wants us to do. I want to be friends with you.

KOLYA: I've wanted to be friends with you for a long time. Even before I met you, I liked you.

ALYOSHA: You're amazing, Kolya. How many people do you know who have the courage to speak up when they like someone? Everyone's so afraid of seeming ridiculous, so they hold back their love. But you, you're not afraid to open your heart.

KOLYA: I was right about you, Karamazov, you're an exceptional person. All month, I've been saying to myself, "either we'll be friends at once, or we'll be enemies to the grave."

(DOCTOR crosses out of the house, followed by CAPTAIN SNEGIRYOV.)

SNEGIRYOV: Your Excellency, Your Excellency…are you sure?

DOCTOR: I'm afraid there's nothing I can do.

SNEGIRYOV: Doctor…Your Excellency, when will…how soon?

DOCTOR: Be prepared for anything.

SNEGIRYOV: Doctor…Your Excellency…in the name of Christ our Lord, Your Excellency, isn't there anything we can do?

DOCTOR: I can do nothing; however, if you can get your son to Syracuse immediately, the climate may…

SNEGIRYOV: Syracuse?

KOLYA: Syracuse is in Sicily.

SNEGIRYOV: Sicily?…Your Excellency, you've seen…and Mama and Nina…

DOCTOR: No, your family shouldn't go to Sicily, they should go to the Caucasus—in early spring. Your daughter should definitely go to the Caucasus, and your wife should take the waters there for her rheumatism. After that, she should go straight to Paris, to the clinic of the psychiatrist Lepelletier. I can write a note to him and…

SNEGIRYOV: Doctor, Doctor…you have seen… *(Indicates the house.)*

DOCTOR: Well, that's none of my business. I have only told you what medical science can do as a last resort. As to the rest…to my regret…

KOLYA: Don't worry, pharmacist, my dog won't bite you.

DOCTOR: Who is this?

KOLYA: This is Perezvon's master, pharmacist.

DOCTOR: I don't understand what you're talking about, young man.

KOLYA: Farewell, pharmacist, see you in Syracuse.

DOCTOR: Who is this boy?

ALYOSHA: He's just a schoolboy, he's a little bit cocky, don't pay any attention to him. Be quiet, Kolya—don't let him bother you, Doctor.

DOCTOR: Well, somebody should give him a good whipping.

KOLYA: You know, pharmacist, once or twice Perezvon has bitten people. *Ici* Perezvon!

ALYOSHA: Kolya, if you say another word, I'll break with you forever.

KOLYA: Pharmacist, there is one man in the world who can tell Nikolai Krasotkin what to do. This is that man. Farewell. (*Crosses back into the house.*)

DOCTOR: Why, he…I…bah! (*Exits.*)

ILYUSHA: (*From inside the house.*) Papa, Papa…

(*ALYOSHA and SNEGIRYOV cross back into the house.*)

ILYUSHA: Papa, I'm sorry…

SNEGIRYOV: Ilyusha, darling…you're going to get well…the doctor said you're going to get well.

ILYUSHA: Papa, I saw his face. Don't cry, Papa. And when I die, get another boy, a good boy…

KOLYA: Stop talking nonsense, old man.

ILYUSHA: Don't forget me, Papa. I want you to come to my grave often…I want you to bury me by our big stone where we used to go for our walks. Visit me there and bring Krasotkin…and Perezvon too…I'll be waiting for you…Papa, Papa… (*Starts to cry.*)

(*ILYUSHA, SNEGIRYOV, and KOLYA embrace.*)

MAMA: (*Crying.*) Ilyusha, Ilyusha…

KOLYA: (*Breaking from the embrace.*) I have to go…my mother is expecting me for lunch and I didn't tell her I'd be late…but I'll come back right after. I'll bring Perezvon with me…I have to take him now because he'll howl if I leave him…goodbye.

(*He runs outside and bursts into tears; PEREZVON and ALYOSHA follow him.*)

KOLYA: I should have come sooner…

(*CAPTAIN SNEGIRYOV crosses out of the house.*)

SNEGIRYOV: I don't want a good boy, I don't want another boy. "If I forget thee, O Jerusalem, Let my right hand wither, If I do not remember thee, Let my tongue cleave to the roof of my mouth…"

(*SNEGIRYOV falls to the ground, weeping and keening. KOLYA and ALYOSHA cross farther away.*)

KOLYA: Karamazov. Are you coming back?

ALYOSHA: I'll be back this evening.

KOLYA: What was that he said about Jerusalem?

ALYOSHA: It's from the Bible. "If I forget thee, O Jerusalem," if I forget all that's most important to me, if I exchange it for anything…

KOLYA: I understand. Be sure to come. *Ici*, Perezvon!

(*KOLYA and PEREZVON exit. Lights fade.*)

SCENE 2

GRUSHENKA's drawing room. GRUSHENKA is onstage. ALYOSHA enters.

GRUSHENKA: Alyosha, thank God you've come.

ALYOSHA: Have you been to the prison today?

GRUSHENKA: Oh yes, I've been to the prison.

ALYOSHA: How is he?

GRUSHENKA: He's jealous. Can you believe it? He's jealous of the Pole.

ALYOSHA: Why?

GRUSHENKA: Because I sent the Pole money. He's sick, he's destitute, and I sent him money. But Mitya's not really jealous of the Pole, he's only pretending.

ALYOSHA: What do you mean?

GRUSHENKA: He's pretending to be jealous of the Pole, so I won't be jealous of Katya. He's still in love with her. He keeps talking about her—she's paid for Fetyukovich, the great Petersburg lawyer…

ALYOSHA: That's not true—she only paid a third of his fee. Ivan and I paid the rest: each of us put in a thousand.

GRUSHENKA: Well, let me tell you about brother Ivan Fyodorovich—he's planning something. The three of them are planning something—Mitya, Katya, and dear brother Ivan Fyodorovich.

ALYOSHA: What do you mean? Ivan hasn't been to see Mitya?

GRUSHENKA: Oh, yes he has. Mitya told me not to tell you.

ALYOSHA: What are they planning?

GRUSHENKA: I don't know, but they're planning to get rid of me somehow. Tell me, is Ivan in love with Katya?

ALYOSHA: I won't lie to you: I don't believe he is.

GRUSHENKA: I knew it. Mitya was just trying to throw me off the scent. He's in love with Katya, not brother Ivan. Well. I'll show him—his young lady will get a little surprise from me at the trial tomorrow—I'll tell them everything.

ALYOSHA: Grushenka, this I can tell you for certain: He loves you and only you. He loves you more than anyone in the world.

GRUSHENKA: Alyosha, find out his secret for me, find out what they're planning.

ALYOSHA: I won't try to get it out of him, but if he starts to tell me, I'll let him know I promised to come and tell you. If he tells me, I'll come to you tonight, no matter how late. But believe me, I don't think this secret has anything to do with Katerina Ivanovna.

GRUSHENKA: Come to me as soon as you leave the prison.

ALYOSHA: I will. *(Exits.)*

SCENE 3

DMITRY's cell. DMITRY is onstage, ALYOSHA enters.

DMITRY: Where have you been, I've been thirsting for you. Never mind, we'll make up for lost time.

ALYOSHA: I bumped into Rakitin on the way in. Have you become friends with him or something?

DMITRY: Not bloody likely, the pig thinks I'm a criminal. He never gets my jokes. The worst thing about that type is they never understand jokes. Their souls are dry. He is intelligent, I'll give him that, the little shit. Who's Claude Bernard?

ALYOSHA: Claude Bernard? I've heard the name…I think he's a scientist.

DMITRY: Well, he's very intelligent, very clever, very logical, and very successful. They're all very successful, that kind; they know how to look after themselves. Rakitin will slip in through the cracks, he'll make his way—the Bernards always do. He's not going to become a priest, you know. He's going to Petersburg to become a critic—literary, cultural, something like that. He wants to write an article about me—that's how he's going to start his career. He wants to prove a theory—that I couldn't help murdering my father because of my environment. It will have "a tinge of socialism." Well, he

can have his little "tinge." He hates Ivan and he's none too fond of you either. I told him the Karamazovs aren't scoundrels because we're philosophers. All true Russians are philosophers, "but with all your learning," I told him, "you're no philosopher, you're a stinking little shit." Do you know what he told me? In my head, in my brain, there are these nerves with little tails. Say I look at something with my eyes: these tails start trembling and then an image appears, and another image, and, before you know it, I've seen a moment, that's why I contemplate. That's why I think—not because I have a soul, not because I'm some sort of image and likeness, but because the little tails tremble. I asked him, "What will become of us, then? If there is no God and no life beyond the grave, won't everything be permitted?" "Didn't you know," he said, "for the clever man, everything is permitted. A clever man knows a thousand ways to skin a cat. You just got caught and now you're rotting in prison."

ALYOSHA: Brother, enough about Rakitin. You're going on trial tomorrow and all you can talk about is Rakitin and God.

DMITRY: What should I be talking about? Smerdyakov? The reeking son of Reeking Lizaveta? God will take care of Smerdyakov. God will kill him, you'll see. *(Goes to ALYOSHA and kisses him.)* Oh, Alyosha, Rakitin would never understand this, but you will. In these two months, I have, I've…a new man has been born in me. What does it matter if I spend the next twenty years in the mines, pounding at the ore with a hammer? I am not afraid. But I am afraid that this new man will desert me. Even in the mines, underground, you can find a human heart. In the convict next to you, you can find a heart. In the murderer next to you, you can find a heart. You can look after him for years, and if his heart be frozen, you can resurrect it, you can bring him out of that infernal den into the light. There are hundreds of them down there, and we are guilty for them all. The night they arrested me, I dreamt about a babe—he was cold and he was hungry and his village had been burnt to the ground. It was a prophecy. It is for the babe that I will go. Because everyone is guilty for everyone else—for all the babes, for there are little children and big children: all are babes. I will go for all of them, because there must be someone who will go. I didn't kill Father, but I will go. I accept! I've understood all this here, behind these leprous walls. And there, under the ground, there will be hundreds of us, and in our agony we shall rise again into joy, without which man cannot exist, without which God cannot exist, for God gives joy—it is His prerogative. Rakitin is lying. If God is driven from the Earth, we will meet Him underground. And from the depths of the Earth, we will raise a tragic hymn to God, in Whom there is joy. Hail to God and His Joy! I love Him! I am not afraid. I was, but I am not now. I will bear every ordeal, as long as I can say to myself at every moment: I am. In a thousand torments—I am. I am tortured on the rack—but I am. Although I sit alone—I am. I see the sun—and if I don't see the sun, I know it is. The whole of life is in that—in knowing that the sun is. But…but…Oh. Alyosha. My angel, these philosophies are killing me. And Ivan…he…he…

ALYOSHA: What about Ivan?

DMITRY: Ivan is not Rakitin. He has a philosophy, too, but it cannot be taken lightly. He has an idea, but he hides it. This much I know—brother Ivan does not have God. But if there is no God, to whom will I sing my hymn? Without God, how can man be good? Rakitin says man can be good without God—out of love for the human race. But then, what is goodness? It's one thing to me and another to a Chinese. So, it's relative. I hoped Ivan could help me make sense out of it all, but he's silent. Except for once.

ALYOSHA: What did he say?

DMITRY: I asked him if everything was permitted, and he said, "Fyodor Pavlovich Karamazov, our papa, was a little pig, but he reasoned correctly."

ALYOSHA: When did he come to see you?

DMITRY: I'll tell you about Ivan later—after the trial, after they sentence me.

ALYOSHA: Grushenka thinks you and Ivan and Katerina Ivanovna are planning to get rid of her, so you can go back to Katerina Ivanovna.

DMITRY: Grushenka is killing me. I worship her, but she doesn't see it. It's still not enough love for her and so she torments me. My love for her before was nothing compared to what I feel now. Before it was just her damn curves that tormented me. But now I've taken her whole soul into my soul and through her I've become a man.

ALYOSHA: Why don't you ask her forgiveness for the fight you had today?

DMITRY: Alyosha, never ask a woman's forgiveness—especially if you love her. Will they let us marry?

Do they let convicts marry? I can't…I can't…exist without her.

ALYOSHA: I don't know.

DMITRY: And she thinks I'm trying to leave her for Katya? She thinks the three of us are trying to get rid of her?

ALYOSHA: Yes.

DMITRY: Alright. I'll let you in on the secret.

ALYOSHA: I promised to tell Grushenka if I found out what it is.

DMITRY: I don't care anymore. I have to tell you. You have to decide my fate—but not yet—first they have to sentence me—then you'll decide. So for now, don't say anything. Oh god, what am I going to do about your eyes? Ivan thinks I should escape. He says I should escape to America with Grusha. Alyosha. I can't live without Grusha. What if they don't let her come with me? Do they let convicts marry? Ivan says they don't. But then what will become of my hymn? I am shown the way to my salvation and I turn around. Anyone else would say, "Escape. The hymn is nonsense." But you understand the hymn. And Ivan understands the hymn, only he doesn't respond to it—he's silent. Please don't say anything, Alyosha…Oh god. You've decided…I can't live without Grusha…Wait, don't…wait for the verdict. Do they let convicts marry?

ALYOSHA: Tell me two things. Who came up with the idea and is Ivan pushing you to do it?

DMITRY: It was his idea and he's pushing for it. He's putting up the money for the escape—ten thousand for bribes and twenty thousand for America.

ALYOSHA: That's almost his entire inheritance. Did he tell you to keep it secret from me?

DMITRY: He said I shouldn't tell anyone—most of all, you. Don't tell him I told you.

ALYOSHA: You're right. It's impossible to decide before the verdict. After the trial, you'll decide for yourself. You'll find a new man in yourself and he'll decide.

DMITRY: A new man or a Bernard. Sometimes I think I'm just another despicable Bernard.

ALYOSHA: Isn't there a chance you'll be acquitted?

DMITRY: Even the great Petersburg lawyer thinks I'm guilty. He wants to prove I'm insane—lousy Bernard.

I won't let him. Alyosha, you should be going. It's getting late, the guards will be coming soon. Embrace me quickly. Kiss me.

(*They embrace and kiss.*)

DMITRY: Cross me, for tomorrow.

(*ALYOSHA crosses DMITRY.*)

DMITRY: Ivan must think I'm guilty, if he wants me to escape.

ALYOSHA: Did you ask him?

DMITRY: I didn't have the courage. But I can see it in his eyes. Goodbye.

(*They embrace again. ALYOSHA starts to leave.*)

DMITRY: Alyosha. (*Goes over to ALYOSHA and puts his hands on his shoulders.*) Tell me the truth as you would before God. Do you believe I killed Father?

ALYOSHA: Mitya…

DMITRY: Don't lie.

ALYOSHA: (*Raising his hand to God.*) I never for one second believed you were the murderer.

DMITRY: Thank you. I was afraid that even you…Now I can face tomorrow. God bless you. Go. Love Ivan.

(*ALYOSHA hesitates for a moment and exits. Lights fade.*)

SCENE 4

KATERINA's drawing room. IVAN and KATERINA are onstage.

IVAN: Why would you object to Grushenka's going to America with Dmitry if you weren't still in love with him?

KATERINA: How can you think I'm still in love with that monster? No…no…he's not a monster. But is he a murderer?

IVAN: You know that better than I.

KATERINA: It was you who convinced me he was guilty. I believed it because I believe you, Ivan.

IVAN: How can you say that after it was you who convinced me? After you showed me that letter.

(*Lights abruptly dim on IVAN and KATERINA, and a spot comes up on DMITRY.*)

DMITRY: Fatal Katya, tomorrow I will get the money and pay you back your three thousand rubles. Farewell, woman of great wrath. But farewell, too, my love. Tomorrow I will ask anyone and everyone to lend me that money, but if I fail, I give you my word of honor, I will go to my father and smash his head in and take it from under his pillow, if only Ivan goes away. I may go to hard labor, but I will give you back the three thousand. Farewell. I bow to the ground before you. Forgive me. No—don't—don't forgive. Better hard labor than your love. I will kill the man who has robbed me. I will go away to the East, away from you all. Away from her, too. You are not my only tormentor. Farewell. P.S. I curse you but I adore you. I'll kill myself, but first I'll kill that son of a bitch. I've been a scoundrel to you, but I am not a thief. I'm not a thief, but I'm going to kill one. Don't look at me with such scorn, Katya. Dmitry is not a thief; he's a murderer. He has killed his father and ruined himself in order to stand up and not have to endure your pride. And not to love you. P.P.S. I kiss your feet. Farewell. P.P.P.S. Katya, pray to God someone lets me have the money. Then there won't be blood on me. But otherwise, I will be covered in blood. Kill me. Your slave and enemy. D. Karamazov.

(*Spot goes out on DMITRY, lights come up on IVAN and KATERINA.*)

KATERINA: I've been to see Smerdyakov.

(*They are silent for a moment.*)

IVAN: Good night, Katerina.

(*IVAN crosses out of the house into the street. ALYOSHA enters walking along the street.*)

ALYOSHA: Ivan.

IVAN: Oh, it's you. Good night.

(*IVAN walks off. KATERINA crosses out of the house.*)

KATERINA: Alexei, go after him, he's sick, he's losing his mind, the doctor says so, he says he's in a fever. Please go.

(*ALYOSHA runs offstage after IVAN; KATERINA crosses back into the house. IVAN enters from another part of the stage. ALYOSHA enters and catches up with him.*)

IVAN: What do you want? I suppose she told you I'm going crazy?

ALYOSHA: I know you're not crazy, but you're sick. I can see it in your face.

IVAN: (*Looks at the house.*) She'll be praying all night to the mother of God to show her what to do at the trial tomorrow.

ALYOSHA: Katerina Ivanovna?

IVAN: Yes. She doesn't know whether to go as Dmitry's savior or as his destroyer. She thinks I'm her nanny, she wants me to soothe her.

ALYOSHA: She loves you, brother.

IVAN: Well, I'm not too fond of her.

ALYOSHA: Then why do you say things that give her hope?

IVAN: I can't break with her, yet. I have to wait 'til after the verdict. If I break it off, she'll take revenge on me by destroying that murderer in court tomorrow. She hates him and she knows she hates him. It's all just lies upon lies. As long as I don't break it off, she won't destroy the monster because she knows I want to save him.

ALYOSHA: How can she destroy him? What evidence could she possibly give that would destroy him?

IVAN: She has a document in Dmitry's own hand that proves mathematically that he killed our father.

ALYOSHA: That's impossible.

IVAN: I've seen it.

ALYOSHA: That document cannot exist because Dmitry did not kill our father.

IVAN: And who, in your opinion, did kill him?

ALYOSHA: You know who.

IVAN: Who? You mean that fairy tale about that epileptic half-wit? You mean Smerdyakov?

ALYOSHA: You know who.

IVAN: Who? Who?

ALYOSHA: It was not you who killed him.

(*IVAN is silent.*)

ALYOSHA: It was not you who killed him.

IVAN: I'm well aware of that. Now it's you who's lost your mind.

ALYOSHA: No, Ivan, you've told yourself many times that you are the murderer.

IVAN: When did I tell myself this…I was in Moscow, when did I…

ALYOSHA: You've said it many times when you were alone during these past two months. You accused yourself and confessed that you were the murderer and no one else. But you are wrong—understand that—you are wrong. It was not you. Do you hear me? It was not you. God has sent me to tell you this.

(*They are silent for a moment.*)

IVAN: You were in my room…at night…when he came…you saw him, didn't you?

ALYOSHA: Who? Mitya?

IVAN: No, not the monster. You know he comes to see me. How did you find out? Speak!

ALYOSHA: Who is he?

IVAN: You must know…there's no other way…

ALYOSHA: Brother, I've said this to you because I know you will believe me. I tell you now and for the rest of your life, it was not you. God put it into my heart to tell you this. Even if you hate me forever after.

IVAN: Alexei Fyodorovich, I cannot stand prophets and epileptics—particularly messengers from God—as you well know. From this moment on, we do not know each other. Leave me now. (*Starts to go.*) And Alexei Fyodorovich, whatever you do, do not come to me tonight. Is that clear? (*Starts to exit.*)

ALYOSHA: Brother, if anything should happen to you tonight, think of me first.

(*IVAN exits. Lights fade.*)

SCENE 5

A street. It is snowing. A DRUNK is staggering along the street.

DRUNK: Vanya, Vanya went to town
I won't wait 'til he comes home
Vanya, Vanya went to town
I won't wait 'til he comes home

(*DRUNK continues singing as IVAN enters upstage and walks across the stage.*)

DRUNK: Vanya, Vanya went to town
I won't wait 'til he comes home
Vanya, Vanya went to town
I won't wait 'til he comes home

(*DRUNK bumps into IVAN, who pushes him to the ground violently. IVAN walks up to DRUNK and stands over him.*)

IVAN: He'll freeze to death. (*Continues walking and exits.*)

SCENE 6

SMERDYAKOV's room. SMERDYAKOV is sitting in a chair, reading. He is wearing a dressing gown and spectacles. IVAN knocks at the door.

SMERDYAKOV: Come in.

(*IVAN enters.*)

SMERDYAKOV: What can I do for you this time, sir?

IVAN: You don't look well. I won't keep you long.

SMERDYAKOV: Please, sir, sit down.

(*IVAN sits.*)

IVAN: I have just one question for you. Did Katerina Ivanovna Verkhovsteva come here to see you?

SMERDYAKOV: What if she did, sir?

IVAN: What did you say to her?

SMERDYAKOV: Don't worry, sir, I didn't tell her about our conversation by the gate.

IVAN: It's you who should be worried about that conversation. A falling fit cannot be predicted beforehand. I've made inquiries.

SMERDYAKOV: One can have a presentiment, sir.

IVAN: You predicted the day and the hour.

SMERDYAKOV: You can ask the local doctors, sir, if it was a real fit or not.

IVAN: Why did you want me to go to Chermashnya?

SMERDYAKOV: I was afraid you'd go to Moscow, sir. At least Chermashnya is closer.

IVAN: You're lying—you were happy to see me leave.

SMERDYAKOV: If I was happy, sir, it was because you were going to Chermashnya instead of Moscow. I was happy that you'd be nearby.

IVAN: The last time I was here, you said if I didn't tell the examining magistrate what you said about shamming fits, you wouldn't tell him about the rest of our conversation by the gate. What did you mean by that?

SMERDYAKOV: What I meant, sir, was that you, knowing that your parent was about to be murdered, left him there as a sacrifice. That's what I promised not to tell the examining magistrate. And perhaps a few other things, as well.

IVAN: Are you out of your mind?

SMERDYAKOV: I'm perfectly in my mind, sir.

IVAN: What do you mean by other things? Tell me, you lousy little half-wit.

(*SMERDYAKOV is silent.*)

IVAN: Tell me, you reeking bastard. What do you mean by other things?

SMERDYAKOV: I meant that perhaps you even wished for your parent's death, sir.

(*IVAN slaps him and SMERDYAKOV starts to cry.*)

SMERDYAKOV: Shame on you, sir, hitting a sick man.

IVAN: You think that I'm like Dmitry; you think I wanted to kill the old man?

SMERDYAKOV: No, you didn't want to kill him, sir—you're not capable of killing. But as for wanting someone else to do it, that you did want.

IVAN: So, according to you, I was counting on brother Dmitry to kill him?

SMERDYAKOV: Exactly right, sir.

IVAN: If I was counting on anyone at the time, it was you.

SMERDYAKOV: And that's what convinced me you wished your father dead. You thought I was likely to kill him and you left anyway.

IVAN: And what led you to this conclusion?

SMERDYAKOV: Your father begged you to go to Chermashnya, sir, and you wouldn't go. But after one foolish word from me, you agreed.

IVAN: I didn't, I told you I was going to Moscow. Father…

SMERDYAKOV: After what I said to you, as your father's son, you should have hauled me off to the police, or, at least, punched me in the face right then and there. But you weren't the least bit angry, sir. You did every foolish thing I asked, when it was your duty to stay and protect your parent's life.

IVAN: It's a shame I didn't beat your face in. I couldn't have gone to the police—I didn't have any proof. But I should have beaten your face to a bloody pulp—even though it's illegal for us to beat our servants now.

SMERDYAKOV: Under ordinary circumstances, it is illegal, sir. But there are certain circumstances—not only in Russia, but even in the most perfect French republic—where beating is justified. But under just such circumstances you didn't dare to beat me, sir. Don't worry, sir. Nothing will happen tomorrow. You have nothing to be afraid of. Try to understand that, finally. Go home, go to bed, and don't be afraid of anything.

IVAN: I don't understand. What is there for me to fear tomorrow?

SMERDYAKOV: You don't understand? Why would an intelligent man put on such an act? You have nothing to fear from me. I won't say anything against you. Besides, there's no evidence that could incriminate you. Look how your hands are trembling, sir. Go on, go home, it was not you who killed him.

IVAN: I know it wasn't me…

SMERDYAKOV: Do you?

(IVAN grabs SMERDYAKOV.)

IVAN: Enough! Talk! Tell me everything!

SMERDYAKOV: Alright, then it was you.

IVAN: Because I went away?

SMERDYAKOV: The last time you understood everything and you understand it now.

IVAN: The only thing I understand is that you're out of your mind.

SMERDYAKOV: Don't you get tired of it? Here we are, just the two of us. So what's the point in keeping up this farce? Are you trying to blame me alone for everything, to make me believe it myself? You killed him. You are the principle murderer; I was just your instrument. And I performed the deed according to your word.

IVAN: Then you did kill him?

SMERDYAKOV: You mean you really didn't know?

IVAN: I keep wondering if this is all a dream. If you're a phantom of my imagination…

SMERDYAKOV: There's no phantom here, sir. Just the two of us—and the third one who sits between us.

IVAN: He's here? Where? What third one?

SMERDYAKOV: The third one is God, sir.

IVAN: You're lying, you didn't kill him.

SMERDYAKOV: Just a moment, sir.

(SMERDYAKOV pulls up his pants leg and reaches into his sock. IVAN recoils. SMERDYAKOV pulls out something wrapped in paper. He puts it on the table.)

SMERDYAKOV: Here you are, sir.

IVAN: What is it?

SMERDYAKOV: Take a look, if you please, sir.

(IVAN fumbles with the package, then backs away.)

SMERDYAKOV: Your hands are trembling, sir. (Opens the package, revealing a wad of bills.) It's all there, sir, all three thousand. There's no need to count it. Go ahead, take it.

IVAN: Where did you get that money?

SMERDYAKOV: Is it possible? Is it really possible you didn't know 'til now?

IVAN: I thought it was Dmitry…Oh dear God…Brother! Brother! Did you do it alone, or was Dmitry in on it with you?

SMERDYAKOV: Only with you, sir. You and I killed him together. Master Dmitry is as innocent as a newborn babe.

IVAN: We'll talk about me later. How did you…I'm having difficulty breathing…I can't speak…

SMERDYAKOV: You used to be so brave, sir. "Everything is permitted." Look how frightened you are now. Would you like some lemonade, sir? It's very refreshing.

IVAN: I don't want any lemonade. Tell me how you did it.

SMERDYAKOV: According to your instructions, sir.

IVAN: We'll get to me later. I want to know exactly how you did it, step by step.

SMERDYAKOV: You left and I fell into the cellar.

IVAN: Was it a real fit or were you shamming?

SMERDYAKOV: Of course I was shamming, sir. I calmly walked to the bottom of the stairs and lay down. Then I started screaming and writhing 'til they came and got me.

IVAN: So you were shamming all along, even in the hospital?

SMERDYAKOV: Oh, no, sir. Later that night, before the authorities arrived, I had a genuine attack—the worst I'd had in years. I was unconscious for two days.

IVAN: Go on.

SMERDYAKOV: After they carried me out of the cellar, I lay on the cot in Marfa and Grigory's cottage, behind the screen, moaning and listening for Master Dmitry to come.

IVAN: What made you so sure he'd come that night?

SMERDYAKOV: The fact that I was sick, sir. He had no one to tell him if Miss Svetlova were to come to your father.

IVAN: What if he hadn't come?

SMERDYAKOV: Then nothing would have happened. You see, sir, I was expecting him to kill Mr. Karamazov. I was certain he'd do it—I had brought him to that point. I had fueled his suspicions and then told him about the signals. I was sure he'd use them.

IVAN: But if he killed him, he would have taken the money. So what would you gain?

SMERDYAKOV: But you see, sir, he wouldn't have found the money. I told him it was under the pillow, but it wasn't there, sir. It was in the box, sir, the box with the lock. And I convinced your father—who trusted me alone of all mankind—to put the box in the corner behind the icons, where no one would think to look for it—especially if they were in a hurry.

IVAN: So, you just took the money and Dmitry did kill him?

SMERDYAKOV: Oh, no, sir, I killed him. I lay there on the cot, moaning and waiting for Master Dmitry to come. Finally, Mister Karamazov screamed. Grigory leapt up—which surprised me—he had taken Marfa's treatment and was out cold. He ran to the garden. My heart was pounding. Grigory screamed…

GRIGORY: (Offstage.) Parricide!

SMERDYAKOV: I got up and went out into the garden. The master's bedroom window was open. I got closer and—damn it—he was alive. He told me that Master Dmitry had been there, that he had killed Grigory by the fence. I went to the fence and found Grigory lying on the ground, bleeding—I couldn't tell if he was dead

or alive. So Master Dmitry had been there. I decided to kill your father myself, sir. If Grigory was still alive, all the better—I'd have a witness to say that Master Dmitry had been there. I went over to the master's window and told him that Miss Svetlova had come. At first, he wouldn't believe me. But then I knocked on the windowsill, sir. (Knocks on the nearest surface, two times slowly and three times quickly.) I used the signal that Miss Svetlova has come. And, believe it or not, that convinced him—he immediately opened the door and let me in.

(A light comes up on FYODOR. FYODOR and SMERDYAKOV perform the following facing out, not looking at each other.)

FYODOR: Where is she? Where is she?

SMERDYAKOV: (To IVAN.) He really was in love with her, sir.

FYODOR: Where is she?

SMERDYAKOV: (To FYODOR.) She's hiding in the garden, sir. She's afraid of Master Dmitry.

FYODOR: Grushenka, my angel, where are you, my little chick?

SMERDYAKOV: There she is, sir. In the bushes.

FYODOR: There you are, my angel. Come to me, there's nothing to be afraid of, my sweet. I have a present for you.

SMERDYAKOV: (To IVAN.) He really thought he saw her, sir. I grabbed the cast-iron paperweight from the desk (Mimes grabbing the paperweight.) —it must have weighed three pounds (He raises the "paperweight.") —and I brought the corner of it right down on the top of his skull.

(SMERDYAKOV mimes bringing the paperweight down on FYODOR's skull. FYODOR freezes, stunned.)

SMERDYAKOV: He didn't make a sound…,

(FYODOR sinks to the floor.)

SMERDYAKOV: He just fell to the floor. (Continues to mime the action.) I hit him again, and a third time. The third time, I heard his skull crack.

(Lights down on FYODOR. SMERDYAKOV stops miming the action.)

SMERDYAKOV: I wiped off the paperweight—there was no blood on me—and put it back. I took the money from behind the icons and threw the envelope and ribbon on the floor. I hid the money in that apple tree with the hole in it. I went back to bed and began moaning loudly until Marfa woke up. She saw that Grigory was missing and she went out to the garden. She started screaming and set everything in motion.

IVAN: Wait. What about the door? Grigory saw it open before Dmitry hit him.

SMERDYAKOV: It was his imagination, sir.

IVAN: Why did you throw the envelope and ribbon on the floor? Isn't that evidence against you?

SMERDYAKOV: No, sir, it's evidence against Master Dmitry. A man who'd seen Mr. Karamazov put the three thousand in the envelope wouldn't have to open it. The authorities know that Master Dmitry had never actually seen the envelope and I had.

IVAN: No, you're not stupid at all. You're much more intelligent than I ever imagined.

SMERDYAKOV: It's always rewarding to talk to a clever man.

IVAN: Listen, you repulsive son of a bitch, the only reason I haven't killed you is that I want you in court tomorrow. As God is my witness, though I may have secretly wished for Father's death, I am nowhere near as guilty as you imagine. But I will give evidence against myself in court tomorrow. And whatever you say against me, whatever evidence you give, I will face up to it. Know that I am not afraid of you.

SMERDYAKOV: What will be the point, sir? I'll deny it all. I'll either say you're sick—which you are—and delirious or I'll say you're sacrificing yourself to save your brother by accusing me, since all your life you looked on me as a fly, sir, your father's bastard son and lackey, and not as a human being. Besides, you don't have one single piece of evidence.

IVAN: What about the money?

SMERDYAKOV: Take it, sir.

IVAN: Why are you giving it back? You killed to get it.

SMERDYAKOV: I don't want it. I did have an idea once that I'd use it to start a new life in Moscow or even Europe. But the main reason I killed him is that "everything is permitted." I learned that from you. You taught me many things at that time, sir. That, if there is no infinite God, there is no morality either. That's how I reasoned, sir.

IVAN: So now I guess you believe in God, since you're giving back the money.

SMERDYAKOV: No, I don't believe in him.

IVAN: Then why are you giving it back?

SMERDYAKOV: Enough. Stop. You're the one who said "everything is permitted." So why are you so disturbed now? You even want to testify against yourself…but you won't do it…no, you won't.

IVAN: You'll see.

SMERDYAKOV: It's not possible, sir. You're too intelligent. You love money, sir—that I know. You also love respect, because you're very proud. You love women exceedingly. And most of all, you love living in comfort and security without bowing to anyone for anything—that you love most of all. You won't ruin your life forever by going into court and covering yourself in shame. Of all his sons, you're the one who's most like your father, sir. You have his soul.

IVAN: I repeat, the only reason I haven't killed you is that I need you in court tomorrow. Remember that.

SMERDYAKOV: Go ahead, kill me now. No, you won't even dare to do that. You won't dare to do anything, you former brave man.

IVAN: Wait 'til tomorrow. (Starts to leave.)

SMERDYAKOV: Wait. Let me see it one more time.

(IVAN shows him the money.)

SMERDYAKOV: Go.

(IVAN starts to leave.)

SMERDYAKOV: Ivan Fyodorovich.

IVAN: What is it?

SMERDYAKOV: Goodbye, sir.

IVAN: Until tomorrow. (Exits.)

SCENE 7

The same street where IVAN knocked down DRUNK. DRUNK is lying on the ground, covered in snow. IVAN enters and walks across the stage. He stumbles over DRUNK, bends down, and brushes the snow off him. IVAN picks DRUNK up and starts to carry DRUNK offstage. PEASANT enters from the other side of the stage.

IVAN: You there. Help me get this man to the police station. I'll give you three rubles.

(IVAN and PEASANT carry DRUNK offstage.)

SCENE 8

IVAN's rooms. THE DEVIL is seated. IVAN enters and takes off his coat and begins to take off his jacket and tie.

THE DEVIL: I hate to be a pest, but didn't you go to Smerdyakov's to find out about Katerina Ivanovna?

IVAN: Damn it. Well, it doesn't matter now. Nothing matters but tomorrow. And don't think this means I believe in you. Your remembering about Katerina is no proof of your existence. I would have remembered myself in a moment.

THE DEVIL: Don't believe then. Besides, what has proof got to do with faith? Especially material proof. Material proof of the other world: that's a combination only man could think up.

IVAN: You're not going to make me lose my temper, like I did last time. I'm delirious—I know it. You're a hallucination: you're the embodiment of one side of me—my most stupid, facile, vulgar thoughts and feelings.

THE DEVIL: Are you really sure of that yourself? Earlier this evening, you said to Alyosha, "You saw him, didn't you? You know he comes to see me." I'm sure you were thinking of me.

IVAN: I told you I'm delirious. I was delirious then.

THE DEVIL: Why were you so surly with Alyosha? He's such a sweet boy. I feel very guilty about that business with the Elder Zosima.

IVAN: Leave Alyosha out of this. Don't you dare mention his name, you third-rate dinner party guest, you hanger-on, you sponger.

THE DEVIL: Sponger—*c'est charmant*. You hit the nail right on the head—that's exactly how I chose to appear to you—as a penniless landowner, a parasite—a sponger. You're very perceptive, you know. And it's good that you can laugh at me. You're much more amiable than you were the last time. And I know why—your great decision.

IVAN: Shut up.

THE DEVIL: *C'est noble, c'est charmant*—tomorrow you save your brother and sacrifice yourself—*C'est chevaleresque.*

IVAN: Shut up or I'll kick you.

THE DEVIL: Nothing would please me more—for you cannot kick that which does not exist. You could be more polite, though. Penniless sponger that I am, I'm still a gentleman—it's generally accepted in polite society that I'm a fallen angel.

IVAN: If you're such a lofty gentleman, why do you appear in such a shabby form?

THE DEVIL: Because I love people. When I stay among people for any length of time, I feel real—that's what I like most of all. Like you, I'm tormented by the abstract—that's why I love your earthly realism. Here it's all circumscribed and delineated. You have the formula, you have geometry. With us, it's all indeterminate equations. Here, I become superstitious. My fondest wish is to be incarnated once and for all as a two-hundred-and-fifty-pound merchant's wife, and believe in everything she believes. My ideal is to go to church and light a candle to God with the utmost sincerity. I'm not joking—that would be the end of my suffering. *(Sneezes.)*

IVAN: You have a cold?

THE DEVIL: Why shouldn't I have a cold? When I take on human form, I take on human frailty. I got it in the most ordinary way. I was hurrying to a diplomatic *soirée* at the home of a highly placed Petersburg lady who had designs on a certain ministry. Well, you know evening dress—white tie, gloves, etc.—and I was late. I was God knows where, and to get to Earth, I had to fly through space—in a dinner jacket with an open vest. Can you imagine? Well, it's cold out there in the ether. You Russians complain about your winters—well, out there it's a hundred and fifty degrees below zero.

IVAN: Would you stop acting like a buffoon. If you are who you say you are, why can't you be serious?

THE DEVIL: My behavior may not be serious, but my fate is. By some pre-temporal decree, which I have never been able to understand, I am appointed to negate. Despite the fact that I have a kindly nature and am not at all suited to negation. But they tell me without negation, there would be no criticism, and what sort of journal has no criticism section? Without criticism, there would be nothing but "Hosannah." But "Hosannah" alone is not enough for life. It is necessary that this "Hosannah" pass through the crucible of doubt. Why is it necessary? I don't know. I didn't create it and I can't answer for it. I follow orders. They chose themselves a scapegoat, and so I write for the criticism section. But I repeat, I would give all my life in starry space, all my titles and honors, to be incarnated as a two-hundred-and-fifty-pound merchant's wife and light candles to God.

IVAN: So you don't believe in God?

THE DEVIL: Is that a serious question?

IVAN: Is there a God or not?

THE DEVIL: I don't know.

IVAN: You don't know? And yet, you're supposed to have seen Him. You're not an independent agent at all—you're me and nothing else.

THE DEVIL: I didn't deny that I'd seen Him. I said I didn't know if He existed. Just like you don't know if I exist. You see, you and I have the same philosophy: *Je pense, donc je suis*: I think, therefore I am. That's all I know for certain. As for the rest of it—other worlds, God, what have you—all that is unproven, whether it exists independently or is only a subjective emanation of myself. You don't look happy. Have I made you angry?

IVAN: Since you've incarnated yourself as a hanger-on, do what spongers do best: amuse me.

THE DEVIL: Alright, I'll tell you a story from our middle ages—not yours, but ours. A story that no one believes but two-hundred-and-fifty-pound merchant's wives—again, not yours, but ours. There was, so the story goes, a certain thinker on your Earth, a philosopher who rejected all—laws, conscience, faith, and, above all, the future life. He died and he expected that he would be plunged straight into nothingness. What did he find instead but the future life. He was stunned, but he was also indignant: "This goes against my convictions." For that he was sentenced to walk a quadrillion kilometers in darkness—we've switched to the metric system, too, you know. Once he finished walking his quadrillion kilometers, the gates of Paradise would open and he would be forgiven everything. Well, he refused to go—on principle. So he just lay down right where he was and wouldn't move. He lay there for a thousand years, then he got up and started walking.

IVAN: But it would take a billion years to walk a quadrillion kilometers.

THE DEVIL: You think in Euclidean terms. And so he walked his quadrillion kilometers and the gates of Paradise opened. He had not stood in Paradise for more than two seconds, when he cried out that those

two seconds were worth not a quadrillion kilometers, but a quadrillion quadrillion raised to the quadrillionth power. In short, he sang his "Hosannah." Actually, he overdid a bit. Some of the more principled people didn't even want to speak to him at first: he had jumped over to the conservatives a little too quickly.

IVAN: I've got you now. I made up that story in high school.

THE DEVIL: You also wrote a very promising poem recently, called "The Grand Inquisitor."

IVAN: Shut up. I forbid you to speak of "The Grand Inquisitor."

THE DEVIL: What about "The Geological Cataclysm?"

IVAN: Shut up or I'll kill you.

THE DEVIL: Last spring, before you left Moscow to come here, you thought—thought, mind you, not wrote, since you have never committed one of your poems to paper—you thought, "There are new men today who want to destroy all that exists and return to chaos and cannibalism. Fools. Why didn't they ask me? All that needs to be destroyed is the idea of God. Let everything else stand. Once mankind has renounced God—and I believe this age, like a geological age, will come—the old morality will fall of itself without cannibalism and everything will be new. People will come together in order to take from life all that it can give—but of course, for happiness and joy in this world only. Man will be exalted with the spirit of divine, titanic pride and the man-god will appear. He will love his brother for himself and not for the sake of some heavenly reward beyond the grave," and so on and so forth in the same vein. Beautiful. But then you thought, "This might not come to pass for a thousand years. So every thinking man who already recognizes the truth can arrange his life as he pleases in accordance with the new principles. In this sense, 'everything is permitted' to him. Moreover, since there is no God, such a man is a man-god and may jump over any obstacle the old moral code devised for the slave-man. Everything is permitted." But tell me this: If you've made up your mind to break rules, why do you need justification?

(IVAN throws a glass at him and he moves out of the way.)

THE DEVIL: How can you throw a glass at a dream?

(There's a knocking at the door.)

THE DEVIL: You'd better open it. It's your brother Alyosha with some unexpected news.

IVAN: I knew it was Alyosha before you said anything.

THE DEVIL: Well, open up, then. There's a blizzard outside.

(IVAN goes to the door and THE DEVIL disappears. IVAN lets ALYOSHA in.)

IVAN: What do you want? I told you not to come.

ALYOSHA: Smerdyakov hanged himself an hour ago.

IVAN: I know. He told me.

ALYOSHA: Who told you?

IVAN: The Devil. He was sitting right there on the sofa.

ALYOSHA: Ivan, you're sick, you have to go to bed.

IVAN: He is me—the most contemptible, vulgar part of me. He said we must destroy the idea of God, so we may become gods ourselves.

ALYOSHA: He said that?

IVAN: Yes.

ALYOSHA: Not you?

IVAN: He said it.

ALYOSHA: Good. Let him go, Ivan.

IVAN: He said they won't believe me now that Smerdyakov is dead.

ALYOSHA: Who won't believe you?

IVAN: They won't believe that I killed Father.

ALYOSHA: You did not kill him.

IVAN: I didn't mean to, but I did.

ALYOSHA: Ivan, lie down.

(ALYOSHA leads IVAN to the sofa.)

IVAN: He said I'm going out of pride, to show my contempt for the world. But also because I want them to praise me.

(ALYOSHA covers IVAN with a blanket.)

IVAN: I love your face, Alyosha.

ALYOSHA: Go to sleep now, Ivan.

IVAN: I'm going out of pride and you despise me. I'll start hating you again. I hate the monster. I don't want to save the monster. He's singing his hymn. I'll go tomorrow and spit in their faces.

ALYOSHA: Shhh. Sleep, Ivan.

(Lights fade with ALYOSHA sitting on the sofa beside IVAN.)

ACT III
SCENE 1

The courtroom. THE JUDGE, THE CLERK, FETYUKOVICH, DMITRY, and THE PROSECUTOR are onstage.

THE JUDGE: By the grace of His Sacred Imperial Majesty, Alexander II, Tsar of All the Russias, I declare the case of the murder of Fyodor Pavlovich Karamazov open. The following witnesses are unable to appear: Pyotr Alexandrovich Miusov, who is out of the country; Katerina Osipovna Khokhalakova, due to illness; Semyon Sergeievich Maximov, due to illness; Kuzma Kuzmich Samsonov due to illness. Finally, I must inform the jury of the death of one witness, Pavel Fyodorovich Smerdyakov, who took his own life last night.

(There is murmuring in the courtroom.)

DMITRY: The dog died like a dog.

(FETYUKOVICH puts his hand on DMITRY's shoulder.)

Judge: Retired Lieutenant Karamazov, I must remind you to speak only when you are called upon to do so. If you make another such outburst, I will take the sternest measures. Will the clerk please read the charges.

THE CLERK: Dmitry Fyodorovich Karamazov, retired lieutenant in His Majesty's army, you are charged with murdering your father, Fyodor Pavlovich Karamazov, on the night of September first, 1867, by striking him on the head with a brass pestle. You are further charged with stealing three thousand rubles from Fyodor Pavlovich Karamazov on the same night. You are further charged with assaulting the servant Grigory Vasilievich Kutuzov with the intent to kill, by striking him on the head with the same pestle.

THE JUDGE: Will the counsel for the prosecution address the defendant.

THE PROSECUTOR: Defendant, how do you plead: guilty or not guilty?

DMITRY: (*Standing.*) I plead guilty to drunkenness and depravity, to idleness and debauchery; I plead guilty to striking down an old servant who did me nothing but kindness. But of the death of the old man, my enemy and father, I am not guilty. Of robbing him, I am not guilty, and I could not be guilty: Dmitry Karamazov is a scoundrel, but he is not a thief. (*Sits.*)

THE JUDGE: Retired Lieutenant Karamazov, I must warn you not just to speak only when called upon, but to answer only the questions you are asked. We will proceed with the examination of the witnesses. Will the clerk summon the witnesses and call Father Porfiry to administer the oath.

(*Lights fade. Lights come up again and GRIGORY is on the stand being questioned by FETYUKOVICH.*)

FETYUKOVICH: Grigory Vasilievich, did you ever see with your own eyes the envelope Fyodor Pavlovich allegedly had in his bedroom, which allegedly contained three thousand rubles for a certain person?

GRIGORY: No, sir.

FETYUKOVICH: You didn't? You, who were in such close attendance on your master for so many years?

GRIGORY: I never even heard about the envelope until after Mr. Karamazov was killed, sir.

FETYUKOVICH: Do you mind my asking what were the ingredients in the treatment your wife rubbed on your back before you went to bed on the night of the murder?

GRIGORY: Ah…there was sage in it.

FETYUKOVICH: Just sage?

GRIGORY: There was paprika, too.

FETYUKOVICH: Pepper?

GRIGORY: Yes, sir, there was pepper.

FETYUKOVICH: All steeped in vodka.

GRIGORY: Spirits, sir.

FETYUKOVICH: Pure spirits? And after your wife rubbed this concoction on your back, you drank the rest of the bottle while she recited a prayer. Am I correct?

GRIGORY: I drank it.

FETYUKOVICH: How much did you drink? Approximately. A shot glass?

GRIGORY: About a tumbler, sir.

FETYUKOVICH: A tumbler? Maybe even a tumbler and a half.

(*GRIGORY is silent.*)

FETYUKOVICH: About a tumbler and a half of pure spirits. You might have seen the gates of heaven open, let alone the bedroom door.

(*There is laughter from SPECTATORS.*)

FETYUKOVICH: Do you know for certain whether you were awake or not when you saw the bedroom door open?

GRIGORY: I was standing on my feet.

FETYUKOVICH: That's no proof you were awake.

(*Laughter from SPECTATORS.*)

FETYUKOVICH: Could you, at that moment, have said what year it was if someone had asked you?

GRIGORY: I don't know.

FETYUKOVICH: And what year is it? Anno Domini.

(*GRIGORY is silent.*)

FETYUKOVICH: Perhaps you can tell me how many fingers you have on your hand?

GRIGORY: I am a servant. If my betters see fit to make a fool of me, I must endure it.

THE JUDGE: Mr. Fetyukovich, you will restrict yourself to relevant questions.

FETYUKOVICH: (*Bowing to THE JUDGE.*) I have no further questions, Your Excellency.

(*Lights fade. Lights come up again. RAKITIN is on the stand being questioned by THE PROSECUTOR.*)

THE PROSECUTOR: Mr. Rakitin, you are a divinity student at our local monastery?

RAKITIN: Yes, that's correct.

THE PROSECUTOR: You are acquainted with the Karamazov family?

RAKITIN: Yes. I knew Fyodor Pavlovich's youngest son, Alexei Fyodorovich, when he was at the monastery. I'm also acquainted with the two older brothers.

THE PROSECUTOR: Were you aware of the dispute between the defendant and his father over the defendant's mother's estate?

RAKITIN: I heard something about it.

THE PROSECUTOR: Do you know for a fact whether Fyodor Pavlovich had cheated the defendant out of his inheritance?

RAKITIN: Who could tell who owed what to whom with all that muddled Karamazovism.

THE PROSECUTOR: Were you aware of any other disputes between the defendant and his father?

RAKITIN: Yes, they were fighting over the merchant Samsonov's kept woman.

DMITRY: Bernard.

(THE JUDGE rings his bell.)

THE PROSECUTOR: You mean Agrafena Alexandrovna Svetlova?

RAKITIN: Yes, Grushenka.

THE PROSECUTOR: I understand you're writing an article about this case. Would you mind sharing some of your insights with the court?

RAKITIN: It's no accident that this crime occurred within a family of former serf-owners. The whole case is symptomatic of attitudes which are peculiar to the institution of serfdom. As former serf-owners, both the defendant and his father felt entitled to anything they wanted. Also, having had the power of life and death over their serfs, they valued life very cheaply. Therefore, killing came easily. We must all cleanse the pollution of serfdom from our hearts and minds—only then will we have justice.

(Applause and cries of "bravo" from SPECTATORS. THE JUDGE rings his bell.)

THE PROSECUTOR: Thank you, Mr. Rakitin.

THE JUDGE: The counsel for the defense may examine the witness.

FETYUKOVICH: You're quite a progressive young man. I understand you're leaving your theological studies to pursue a career in journalism.

RAKITIN: That's correct; I could not wholly agree with some of the excesses of mysticism.

FETYUKOVICH: Well, I wish you luck. Are you, by any chance, the same Mr. Rakitin who wrote the pamphlet, "The Life of the Elder, Father Zosima, Fallen Asleep in God," published by the diocese? I read it recently: it was

very pious, very devout. I was particularly impressed with the dedication to the bishop.

RAKITIN: I didn't write it for publication…they…they just decided to publish it…

FETYUKOVICH: Oh, but that's wonderful. A thinker like you must regard all social phenomena with an open mind. And you've been able to accomplish so much good through His Grace's patronage. Now, you mentioned the merchant Samsonov's kept woman. You were referring to your cousin, Agrafena Alexandrovna Svetlova?

RAKITIN: I…

FETYUKOVICH: She is your cousin, isn't she?

RAKITIN: Yes…

FETYUKOVICH: I understand that your cousin was so anxious to meet the youngest Karamazov, Alexei Fyodorovich, that she offered you twenty-five rubles if you would bring him to her house in his monastic attire. I understand the meeting took place on the day that ended in the catastrophe that brings us all here. Did you get your twenty-five rubles?

RAKITIN: It was a joke…I was planning to give the money back…

FETYUKOVICH: Then you did receive it? Have you given it back yet?

RAKITIN: I will…

FETYUKOVICH: Thank you. No further questions.

(Lights fade. Lights come up again. The witness stand is vacant.)

THE CLERK: Ivan Fyodorovich Karamazov.

FETYUKOVICH: Your Excellency, Ivan Karamazov is here, but he is unwell at the moment. He will testify as soon as he feels ready.

THE JUDGE: Very well, Mr. Fetyukovich. Will the clerk please call the next witness.

(Lights fade. Lights come up again. KATERINA is on the stand being questioned by FETYUKOVICH.)

FETYUKOVICH: Miss Verkhovsteva, you were engaged to be married to the defendant?

KATERINA: Yes, until he broke off the engagement.

FETYUKOVICH: Are you aware that the defendant has stated that the fifteen hundred rubles he had on his person when he was arrested was the remaining half of the three thousand rubles you had given him to mail to your sister a month earlier?

KATERINA: Yes.

FETYUKOVICH: Did you, indeed, give him three thousand rubles to mail to your sister?

KATERINA: Yes, I did.

FETYUKOVICH: Are you aware that he did not mail that money to your sister?

KATERINA: Yes.

FETYUKOVICH: Do you feel he acted dishonorably towards you?

KATERINA: No. I didn't ask him to mail it right away. I was aware that he needed money, and I gave him the three thousand with the understanding that he mail it within a month. I was firmly convinced that he would mail the three thousand as soon as he got money from his father.

FETYUKOVICH: Yet, the defendant says that he concealed the fact that he had put aside half that money because he felt that would make him a thief in your eyes. Do you understand why he would feel that way?

KATERINA: Yes. Dmitry Fyodorovich has a highly developed sense of honor and he is scrupulously honest where money is concerned. I understand completely how this could have weighed on his soul. If he had only come to me, I would have put his mind to rest about that miserable three thousand. *(Pause.)* He had no reason to feel in debt to me. I was once in debt to him for more than you can imagine. He saved my life by giving me his last five thousand rubles. I took it, knowing full well that I might never be able to pay him back.

FETYUKOVICH: *(Going to the defense table to check his notes.)* I beg your pardon…

DMITRY: Katya, don't!

FETYUKOVICH: When did he give you this money?

DMITRY: No!

KATERINA: Shortly after I first met him.

DMITRY: Katya!

THE JUDGE: The defendant will be silent.

KATERINA: My father was the commander of Dmitry Fyodorovich's battalion. He was accused of misappropriating government money and, indeed, the accounts were short forty-five hundred rubles. He was ordered to turn over the money and he didn't have it. He tried to kill himself. I had heard Dmitry Fyodorovich had just received six thousand rubles from his father. So one evening I went to his lodgings and asked him to lend us the money. As a young lady visiting a soldier's rooms, I expected the worst, but I was willing to endure it to save my father. But Dmitry Fyodorovich simply gave me his last five thousand rubles. And then he bowed to me—he bowed to me with respect. This man saved my father's life without asking anything in return, and I am not ashamed to admit that on that night, I bowed to the ground before him.

DMITRY: Katya…you didn't have to…

FETYUKOVICH: Thank you, Miss Verkhovsteva. I realize how difficult this must have been for you.

THE JUDGE: Would the counsel for the prosecution care to examine the witness?

THE PROSECUTOR: I feel it would be indelicate at this time.

THE JUDGE: You may step down, Miss Verkhovsteva.

(KATERINA steps down in silence as all eyes follow her.)

THE JUDGE: Will the clerk call the next witness.

THE CLERK: Agrafena Alexandrovna Svetlova.

(GRUSHENKA steps up to the witness stand.)

FETYUKOVICH: Miss Svetlova, you were acquainted with the deceased, Fyodor Pavlovich Karamazov?

GRUSHENKA: He was a business partner of mine, we invested in some taverns together.

FETYUKOVICH: And are you acquainted with the defendant?

GRUSHENKA: Yes. Fyodor Pavlovich sold me some of Dmitry's IOUs. I threatened to have him arrested in order to collect. When he came to see me about it, he fell in love with me. At the time, I didn't know that I was in love with him and I tortured him horribly.

FETYUKOVICH: You have just said the defendant was in love with you; were you aware that the deceased had feelings for you, too?

GRUSHENKA: Yes, he was obsessed with me. I tortured him, too. I was laughing at them both. Everything that happened is my fault. I'm the one you should send to Siberia, not Dmitry.

THE JUDGE: Miss Svetlova, I understand how upset you are, but please try to answer only the questions you are asked.

GRUSHENKA: I'm sorry, Your Excellency.

FETYUKOVICH: Miss Svetlova, you just said Fyodor Karamazov was obsessed with you. Did he ever offer you money to come see him?

GRUSHENKA: Yes. He sent his lackey to tell me he had three thousand rubles waiting for me in his bedroom.

FETYUKOVICH: In his bedroom?

GRUSHENKA: Yes.

FETYUKOVICH: Was he aware his son Dmitry Fyodorovich was in love with you?

GRUSHENKA: Yes.

FETYUKOVICH: So you're saying the deceased Fyodor Pavlovich Karamazov invited you to his bedroom—the woman his own son was in love with?

GRUSHENKA: Yes.

FETYUKOVICH: Pardon the indelicacy of my question, Miss Svetlova; did you visit him?

GRUSHENKA: He made me sick.

FETYUKOVICH: So you did not visit him?

GRUSHENKA: No.

FETYUKOVICH: Did you ever actually see this three thousand rubles that he offered you?

GRUSHENKA: No, I only heard about it from the murderer.

FETYUKOVICH: To whom are you referring?

GRUSHENKA: The lackey who murdered his master and hanged himself yesterday—Smerdyakov.

FETYUKOVICH: Thank you, Miss Svetlova. No further questions.

THE JUDGE: The counsel for the prosecution may examine the witness.

THE PROSECUTOR: Miss Svetlova, what makes you think that Smerdyakov murdered his master?

GRUSHENKA: Dmitry told me so himself.

THE PROSECUTOR: Ah, I see. Do you have any proof that it was Smerdyakov?

GRUSHENKA: Dmitry wouldn't lie about something like that—he's a man of honor.

THE PROSECUTOR: A moment ago, you said that everything that happened is your fault and that you should be sent to Siberia instead of the defendant. Doesn't that mean that you believe he murdered his father—that he murdered his father because of you?

GRUSHENKA: No.

THE PROSECUTOR: Then why did you say you should be sent to Siberia?

GRUSHENKA: I don't know.

THE PROSECUTOR: What other meaning could you possibly have?

DMITRY: (Jumping up.) You lousy Bernard!

(FETYUKOVICH pulls DMITRY down.)

THE JUDGE: (Ringing his bell.) The defendant will be silent.

GRUSHENKA: I'm not the only one who should go to Siberia—send that man-stealer to Siberia—she's the one who ruined him.

THE JUDGE: To whom are you referring, Miss Svetlova?

GRUSHENKA: To the young lady, to this Katerina Ivanovna who invited me to her house and tried to seduce me with chocolate—she's more shameless than I ever was.

THE JUDGE: Miss Svetlova, you will moderate your language.

THE PROSECUTOR: No further questions, Your Excellency.

THE JUDGE: You may step down, Miss Svetlova.

(GRUSHENKA steps down and someone hisses from SPECTATORS; THE JUDGE rings his bell. Lights fade. When they come up again, ALYOSHA is on the stand being questioned by FETYUKOVICH.)

FETYUKOVICH: Did your eldest brother ever tell you he intended to kill your father?

ALYOSHA: He never said it directly.

FETYUKOVICH: Did he say it indirectly?

ALYOSHA: He told me that he was afraid he would be so overcome with loathing for our father that he might kill him.

FETYUKOVICH: Did you believe him when he said that?

ALYOSHA: I'm afraid I did. But I was also convinced, if the moment ever came, he would be saved by some higher feeling.

FETYUKOVICH: When did this conversation take place? Was it the last time you saw him before your father's death? Which, if I am not mistaken, was two nights before the catastrophe.

ALYOSHA: It was that night, but it wasn't the last…

FETYUKOVICH: What is it, Mr. Karamazov?

ALYOSHA: I just remembered something. The last time I saw him before our father's death, Dmitry kept hitting himself on the upper part of his chest and saying he was holding a dishonor there, and he could restore half his honor at any time. I thought he was pointing to his heart. I remember thinking, "He's hitting himself too high up." He was pointing right under his neck. It was the rag—he was pointing to the fifteen hundred rubles—half the three thousand—he said he could restore half his honor.

FETYUKOVICH: You're absolutely certain he wasn't pointing to his heart?

ALYOSHA: Yes, he was pointing too high.

FETYUKOVICH: You're sure he said the words, "half his honor"?

ALYOSHA: Yes.

FETYUKOVICH: He didn't say, "part of his honor," or something like that?

ALYOSHA: No.

FETYUKOVICH: He said he could restore "half his honor"?

ALYOSHA: Yes.

FETYUKOVICH: You're certain?

ALYOSHA: Yes.

FETYUKOVICH: Thank you, Mr. Karamazov. No further questions.

(Lights fade. When the lights come up, the stand is vacant.)

THE JUDGE: Mr. Fetyukovich, is Ivan Karamazov ready to testify?

FETYUKOVICH: Yes, Your Excellency, he is.

THE JUDGE: Will the clerk call Ivan Fyodorovich Karamazov.

THE CLERK: Ivan Fyodorovich Karamazov.

(IVAN enters and crosses to the witness stand unsteadily.)

FETYUKOVICH: Mr. Karamazov…

IVAN: What is it?

THE JUDGE: Mr. Karamazov, you are, perhaps, still not feeling well?

IVAN: Don't worry, Your Excellency, I'm feeling well enough and you might be interested in what I have to say.

THE JUDGE: You have some new evidence to present?

IVAN: I…no…nothing in particular…

THE JUDGE: You may proceed, Mr. Fetyukovich.

FETYUKOVICH: Mr. Karamazov, you are the defendant's half-brother?

IVAN: Yes.

FETYUKOVICH: Had you ever met your older brother before this summer?

IVAN: Once.

FETYUKOVICH: Would you mind telling the court when?

IVAN: When he came to Moscow to get engaged.

FETYUKOVICH: Were you aware of the rivalry between your brother and your father over Miss Svetlova?

IVAN: Yes.

FETYUKOVICH: Did you know anything about the three thousand rubles your father kept in an envelope in his bedroom to give Miss Svetlova if she came to him?

IVAN: Yes.

FETYUKOVICH: Did you ever actually see the money?

IVAN: No…It's the same thing over and over again…I have nothing new to tell the court.

THE JUDGE: I can see you're not well…

IVAN: Let me go, Your Excellency…I feel very sick. *(Steps down from the stand without waiting for permission and starts to walk out of the courtroom. He stops suddenly.)* I'm like the peasant girl in the song—They keep trying to get her to go to church to get married…she keeps saying, "If I fancy, I'll go, and if I don't, I won't go…"

THE JUDGE: What do you mean by that, Mr. Karamazov?

IVAN: *(Taking a wad of bills out of his pocket.)* Here. Here's the money that was in the bedroom. Here's the money that my father was killed for.

(EVERYONE is silent.)

IVAN: Somebody take it.

THE JUDGE: Clerk.

(THE CLERK takes the money from IVAN.)

THE JUDGE: Where did you get this money? If it is, indeed, the same money.

IVAN: It was given to me yesterday by Smerdyakov, the murderer. I saw him just before he hanged himself. He killed my father, not Dmitry. Smerdyakov killed him on my instructions. Oh, what are you staring at? Who does not wish for his father's death?

THE JUDGE: Are you in your right mind?

IVAN: I'm in my right mind—my vile mind, the same as you—all of you. Look at these stupid faces. A father has been murdered and they pretend to be shocked. Everyone wants his father dead—one serpent devours another. If it were proved that no parricide had been committed, they'd go home disappointed. Could I have some water? Give me a drink for Christ's sake!

ALYOSHA: *(Jumping up.)* He's delirious, he's sick. You can't possibly believe him.

(THE CLERK brings IVAN some water.)

IVAN: Don't worry, I'm not mad, I'm just a murderer.

THE JUDGE: Mr. Karamazov, right now your words are incomprehensible and inadmissible in court. Calm yourself, if you can, and say what you have to say. Can anyone confirm your testimony?

IVAN: No, no, no…Smerdyakov won't send you corroboration from the other world. I don't have a single witness…but one…

THE JUDGE: Are you saying you do have a witness?

IVAN: Yes, but his evidence would be inadmissible…he has a tail…he's a ridiculous, petty, little devil…he asked me why I needed justification, if I had decided to break the rules. Anyway, release the monster…my brother, Dmitry…release him…he's started singing his hymn—and it's so easy for him. I'd give a quadrillion quadrillion for two seconds of joy. Go ahead, take me, let him go…you're all so stupid.

THE JUDGE: Mr. Karamazov, you're not well. Would you please step into the hall, where the doctors can see to you.

IVAN: Don't be stupid—arrest me.

THE JUDGE: Guard, remove the witness from the courtroom.

(A GUARD approaches IVAN and puts a hand on his arm.)

IVAN: Take your hands off me!

(IVAN pushes GUARD to the ground. TWO GUARDS rush up to IVAN and start dragging him out of the courtroom.)

IVAN: *(Screaming.)* No!

(IVAN is dragged out. KATERINA jumps up.)

KATERINA: Can't you see he's sick, he's so sick…he's not the murderer. *(Pointing to DMITRY.)* He is—that monster there. I have proof. *(Takes a letter out of her bag.)* I have a letter he wrote to me two days before the crime. He wrote to me that he was going to kill his father. Take it. Read it.

THE JUDGE: Clerk.

(THE CLERK takes the letter from KATERINA and hands it to THE JUDGE.)

THE JUDGE: Miss Verkhovsteva, will you please return to the stand.

(KATERINA crosses to the stand.)

THE JUDGE: Will you please explain to the court the circumstances under which you received this letter.

KATERINA: He wrote it two days before the crime—he wrote it in the tavern—Look, he wrote it on someone's bill. He wrote me that letter because he hated me—he hated me because of the three thousand rubles. I knew he was going to betray me with that animal—and I gave him the money to do it. I looked him in the eye and told him, "Take the money, you don't have to mail it for a month." I was saying to him, "You need money to betray me with that animal? Here, I'll give it to you. Take it, if you're so completely without honor." I looked in his eyes and he understood everything—and he still took the money.

DMITRY: That's right, Katya, I looked in your eyes and I understood—I knew you were trying to disgrace me and I took the money anyway.

THE JUDGE: One more word out of you, Lieutenant Karamazov, and I will have you removed from the courtroom.

KATERINA: So after he squandered the money on his whore, he killed his father to pay me back. And two days before he killed him, he wrote me that letter. He was drunk when he wrote it—you can tell—but it lays out the crime, step by step.

THE JUDGE: Clerk, show the defendant the letter.

(THE CLERK crosses to DMITRY and shows him the letter.)

THE JUDGE: Retired Lieutenant Karamazov, do you recognize this letter?

DMITRY: Yes, yes, I wrote it.

THE JUDGE: Would the counsel for the defense like the opportunity to examine the witness?

FETYUKOVICH: Yes, Your Excellency. Miss Verkhovsteva, why did you conceal this piece of evidence until now?

KATERINA: I couldn't bring myself to ruin the monster in spite of everything.

FETYUKOVICH: Your description, just now, of the circumstances under which you gave the defendant the three thousand rubles is in complete contradiction to your previous testimony. Were you lying before?

KATERINA: Yes, yes, I was lying. I wanted to save him at any cost—precisely because he hated me and despised me. He despised me from the moment I bowed before him. That's why he wanted to marry me, he was certain I would tremble before him all my life because I came to him that night. But I loved him, I loved him without end, I… (Faints.)

(CROWD bursts into an uproar.)

DMITRY: Katya!

THE JUDGE: (Ringing his bell.) The spectators will be silent—Silence. Guards, carry Miss Verkhovsteva out to the hall, where the doctors can look after her.

(GUARDS carry KATERINA out; CROWD murmurs.)

THE JUDGE: Silence. We will resume with the proceedings. The clerk will read the letter.

GRUSHENKA: (Jumping up.) Mitya, do you see her for what she is now? Your serpent has destroyed you.

(Blackout.)

Scene 2

A light comes up on THE PROSECUTOR.

THE PROSECUTOR: Gentlemen of the jury, this case has resounded throughout Russia. It is written about in the newspapers daily; it is talked about on the streets of Moscow and Petersburg and in many of our provincial towns. Why are we writing about it? Why are we talking about it? Is it because we are horrified? Is that it? Let us be honest with ourselves, gentlemen: we are relishing the spectacle. In the last few years, we have become connoisseurs of strong, eccentric sensations that rouse us out of our cynical and lazy apathy. We have grown used to such things. That is the real horror: that these acts have ceased to appall us. In the finale of his greatest work, *Dead Souls*, Gogol compares Russia to a galloping troika, hurtling towards an unknown destination. In proud rapture, he writes that all nations stand aside in awe for this troika galloping by at breakneck speed. Let them stand aside, gentlemen, with or without awe, but in my humble opinion, the great writer ended like that either in a fit of infantile naïveté or simply to placate the censors of his day. For, if the troika were drawn by the heroes of his own novel, it could not reach any rational goal, no matter who was holding the reins. And as bad as these horses were, those of our own generation are infinitely worse.

(Scattered applause from SPECTATORS.)

THE PROSECUTOR: And what of our own generation? Let us look at the Karamazov family. The *paterfamilias* was a landowner by birth, but when he acquired some capital from his first wife, he became, first and foremost, a usurer. He was a sneering cynic and sensualist. He knew nothing of the moral obligations of a father. I hope I do not offend the public if I say there are many such fathers today. His eldest son stands before you in the dock. Of him, we will have much to say later. Of the other two sons, the elder is one of our modern young men, highly educated and endowed with a powerful intelligence. Like so many of our young intellectuals, he has questioned everything—and he has rejected everything. He has become like his father—a man who believes in nothing. The youngest son has taken the opposite road. In the face of the depravity and cynicism that surround us—which he wrongly attributes to European enlightenment—he has taken refuge in what our intelligentsia mockingly call "the beliefs of the people." I wish this good and gifted young man the best, and I hope that his youthful idealism will not degenerate into dark mysticism and witless chauvinism—two qualities which threaten Russia even more than the cynicism from which his brother suffers.

(Scattered applause from SPECTATORS.)

THE PROSECUTOR: And now we come to the eldest son of this modern family. In contrast to his brothers, who represent westernized Russia and the ancient beliefs of the Russian people, Dmitry Karamazov represents Russia as she is today, in her purest form. Like him, we are ingenuous; we are an amazing mixture of good and evil. We love enlightenment and Schiller, and at the same time, we rage in taverns and tear out the beards of little drunkards. Today, we have heard testimony to both sides of his character—from the same witness. Which side are we to believe? The noble young man who gives away his last kopek and bows before the young lady's virtue? Or the cruel sensualist, who cynically accepts three thousand rubles from his fiancée in order to betray her? Usually, in life, the truth lies between the two extremes. In this case, it does not. I believe in the first instance he was sincerely noble, and in the second he was just as sincerely base. We are of a broad Karamazovian nature, capable of containing all possible opposites and of contemplating both abysses at once—the abyss above and the abyss below.

Now, could a man with such a nature set aside half the money? Is this consistent with the psychology of Dmitry Karamazov? No, gentlemen of the jury, it is not. His reason for setting aside half the money, he claims, was so that he could go to his fiancée at any time and say to her, "Here is half your money, I may be a scoundrel, but I am not a thief." I put it to you that, at the first temptation—say, to entertain his new lady love—the real Dmitry Karamazov would have ripped open the rag and taken out, say, a hundred rubles. "Why return exactly half the original sum? I can still say, 'I've brought back fourteen hundred, so I am not a thief.'" After a while, he would open the rag and take out another hundred.

Then a third, and a fourth, and so on until, at the end of the month, he would have taken out all but the last hundred rubles. And finally, he would look at that last hundred and say to himself, "There's no point in giving back a hundred rubles, why don't I just spend it." That's how the real Dmitry Karamazov, who we know so well, would have acted.

The story of the fifteen hundred rubles sewn up in a rag is a fiction. The money that appeared in the accused's hands the night he was arrested was stolen from his father after the accused murdered him.

Now, was this crime premeditated? I must admit that I, myself, was uncertain about that until today. But then Miss Verkhovsteva presented that fatal letter in court. That letter, written two days before the murder, is a precise outline of the crime. It says he will try to get the money from "anyone and everyone." He did just that. It says he will kill his father only if his brother Ivan goes away, which shows that he was calculating, that he would commit the crime only if he knew there was no one there to protect his father. This was all accomplished as written.

On the night of the murder, he grabs the brass pestle from Miss Svetlova's kitchen table so that he will have a weapon to carry out his plan. Again, we have evidence of premeditation. Are we to believe that having gone to his father's house armed with the pestle that he simply walked away? Are we to believe this when we know the accused was in possession of the signals which he could use to get into the house? Ah, but you will say there was someone else who knew about the signals: Smerdyakov. And this has given rise to the theory that it was Smerdyakov, and not the accused, who killed Fyodor Karamazov.

But this is absurd. First, the psychology of Smerdyakov is inconsistent with that of a murderer. The defendant himself said Smerdyakov was "an abject coward, a sickly, epileptic, feeble-minded chicken." Second, what motive did Smerdyakov have for killing his master? Hatred? His master was fond of him and honored him with his trust. The only possible motive is money. And yet, he tells the accused, who he knows desperately needs money, about the existence of the three thousand rubles?

And, had Smerdyakov stolen the money, why would he have ripped open the envelope and left it on the floor as evidence? He knew the money was in there. There was no reason to open it until he was safely away. Only a robber like the defendant, who did not know for certain that the money was in the envelope would have opened it in such a hurry.

But you will say Ivan Karamazov produced three thousand rubles in court today, testifying that they were given to him by Smerdyakov. Gentlemen of the jury, last week, Ivan Karamazov cashed two bank notes for five thousand rubles each. Am I accusing Ivan Karamazov of lying? No, gentlemen, I am not. Seeing his condition today, I believe he could have hallucinated the whole thing.

So why did the defendant have only fifteen hundred rubles when he was arrested? What did he do with the other half of the money? I can only conclude that he hid it somewhere at the inn at Mokroye.

Gentlemen of the jury, whatever you may now hear from the celebrated defense counsel, so justly famed for his talents, whatever eloquent and heartbreaking words are aimed at your emotions, you must never for a moment forget that you are performing the sacred duty of administering justice. You are champions of the truth and defenders of our holy Russia—of her foundations, of her family, of everything she holds sacred. Your verdict will raise her up or cast her down. Do not cast her down. The troika of our fate is rushing headlong, perhaps to its destruction. And if other nations still stand aside, it is not from awe, as the poet would have it, but from horror. Beware, lest they stand their ground and form into a solid wall before the speeding apparition. Beware, lest they halt the mad course of her unbridledness in the name of their own salvation, in the name of enlightenment and civilization. Do not tempt them. Do not justify them by sanctioning the murder of a father by his son.

(Applause from SPECTATORS. Light fades on THE PROSECUTOR, and a light comes up on FETYUKOVICH.)

FETYUKOVICH: Gentlemen of the jury, I am a stranger to you; my practice is in Petersburg. However, this is not the first time I have traveled to the towns of Russia to defend a case. But I only do so when I am convinced of the defendant's innocence. And I have been convinced of Dmitry Karamazov's innocence ever since I first read of this case in the newspapers. What struck me is that while the overwhelming totality of the facts is against the defendant, there is not a single fact that will stand up to criticism if considered independently.

Let us first take the stolen three thousand rubles. Do we even know this money existed? The only person who claims to have seen it being placed in the envelope is the servant Smerdyakov. And if the money did, indeed exist, couldn't Fyodor Karamazov have ripped open the envelope himself and put the money to some other use? And if there is even the barest possibility of such an explanation, how can anyone assert categorically that the defendant committed murder for the purpose of robbery, or that a robbery was even committed? To make such assumptions is to engage in speculation; it is creating a fiction; it is writing a novel. If you are going to convict someone of robbery, you must first prove indisputably that something has been stolen.

But you will say, when he was arrested the accused had fifteen hundred rubles on his person. Precisely. Fifteen hundred, not three thousand. Which suggests that he did not get the money from the envelope, but from somewhere else. The prosecution speculates that the defendant hid the rest of the money in some crevice at the inn at Mokroye. Why not in the dungeons of the Castle of Udolpho?

(Laughter from SPECTATORS.)

FETYUKOVICH: The defendant has given clear and firm testimony as to where he got the money. But the prosecution prefers its own novel to the defendant's explanation. Their novel about a man of weak will who could not have the strength of character to set aside half the money and sew it up in a rag. And if he had done so, the novel continues, he would have opened up the rag every two days and peeled off a hundred rubles and so would have run through the money in a month. Such, the prosecution tells us, is the psychology of the defendant. Well, psychology is a sword that cuts both ways.

(Laughter from SPECTATORS.)

FETYUKOVICH: Mr. Prosecutor, you, yourself, have said Karamazov has a broad nature, that he can contemplate both abysses. Well, I submit to you that such a broad nature is capable of stopping amidst the wildest revelry if the vision of the opposite abyss appears to him. And in this case, the opposite abyss is love. And for this love, he needs money. If she were to say to him, "I am yours, I want nothing to do with Fyodor Pavlovich," he would need money to take her away. What, then, is so incredible in his separating half this money and stashing it away just in case? And why does the prosecution refuse to believe the evidence of Alexei Karamazov that the defendant actually pointed to the spot on his chest where the rag was hidden? Why do they, instead, insist that money is hidden in some crevice in the dungeons of the Castle of Udolpho?

But the prosecution will say, that same night, after speaking with his brother, the defendant writes this fatal letter which is, indeed, the most damning evidence that he is guilty of premeditated murder and robbery. The prosecution argues that this letter is a complete program of the crime and that "it was all accomplished as written." But I submit to you that it was not accomplished as written. The letter says that he will go to his father's house in order to take the envelope with the money from under the pillow. Is that why he went to his father's house? No. He went there on the spur of the moment because he thought his love was there. Had she been home, he would have stayed with her at her house and he would not have carried out the "program" outlined in this drunken letter. The prosecution points to the fact that he grabbed the brass pestle off his love's kitchen table as evidence of premeditation. What if it had been put away in the cupboard?

Why will the prosecution not believe the defendant's testimony that he ran away from his father's window? What firm proof do we have that the defendant is lying? Grigory's testimony that the door was open? The testimony of a man who had just awaken from a deep sleep brought on by drinking a glass and a half of pure spirits? Testimony that was recalled after he had been hit on the head with a brass pestle and knocked unconscious? No, gentlemen of the jury, that is not proof.

If the defendant didn't kill him, who did? As much as I admire the artistry of the prosecutor's description of Smerdyakov, I cannot agree with his characterization. I visited with Smerdyakov two days ago and, while his health was weak, he struck me in no way as feeble-minded or cowardly. In fact, he struck me as intelligent and insightful. He also struck me as spiteful, morbidly vain, vengeful, and burning with envy. Believing himself to be the illegitimate son of Fyodor Karamazov—and there is evidence to support this—Smerdyakov may well have bitterly resented his position compared with that of Fyodor Pavlovich's legitimate sons, who would inherit their father's money, while Smerdyakov was doomed to remain a cook all his life.

Earlier, when the prosecutor was explaining that Smerdyakov would have not have needed to open the envelope, because he knew the money was in there, I felt that I was listening to something familiar. And, imagine, I had, in fact, heard the very same conjecture just two days ago—from Smerdyakov himself.

(Laughter from SPECTATORS.)

FETYUKOVICH: But we are not dealing with an ordinary murder, we are dealing with parricide. Because the crime is so heinous, in your hearts, you feel if there is a shadow of a possibility that he did shed his father's blood, we cannot let him go unpunished. Yes, gentlemen of the jury, it is an abomination to shed a father's blood. His blood who begot me, his blood who loved me, his life's blood who did not spare himself for me. But gentlemen of the jury, we must use words honestly and call things by their proper names. The murdered Fyodor Karamazov cannot and does not deserve to be called a father.

"Fathers, provoke not your children," writes the apostle. I quote these holy words now, not for the sake of my client, but as a reminder to all fathers I cry out, "Fathers, provoke not your children!" Let us show the world at large that the progress of the last few years has reached us, too, and let us say straight out: he who begets is not yet a father; a father is he who begets and proves worthy of it. Let a son stand before his father and ask him reasonably, "Why should I love you? Prove to me that I should love you." If the father is able to show him good reason, then we have a real family, established, not on mystical prejudice, but on rational, responsible, humane foundations. But if he can give no proof, the family is finished then and there. If we wish to be humane, if we wish to be Christian finally, it is our duty and obligation to base our moral judgments on experience and reason.

(Thunderous applause from SPECTATORS.)

FETYUKOVICH: No, the murder of such a father cannot be called a parricide. But did the defendant commit such a murder? Again and again, I call out from the bottom of my soul—No!

If you condemn him, let me remind you that hatred begets hatred, but love, gentlemen of the jury, love begets love. It is so easy for you to be merciful, because the prosecution has presented nothing but circumstantial evidence. It is far better to let ten guilty men go free than to condemn one innocent man. Do you hear? Do you hear the majestic voice from the past century of our glorious history? Is it for me, an insignificant lawyer, to remind you that Russian justice exists, not only for the punishment, but for the salvation of the ruined man. And if so, if such, indeed, are Russia and her justice, then—Onward Russia! And do not frighten us, oh do not frighten us, with your mad troikas from which all nations stand aside in horror. Not a mad troika, but a majestic Russian chariot that is moving calmly and solemnly towards its goal. In your hands is the fate of my client. In your hands is also the fate of our Russian truth. Save it. Champion it. Prove that there are some to preserve it. Prove that it is in good hands.

(Uncontrollable applause from SPECTATORS. Spot fades on FETYUKOVICH.)

SCENE 3

Lights up on the courtroom. The SAME PEOPLE are onstage.

THE JUDGE: Has the clerk received the jury's verdict?

THE CLERK: Yes, Your Excellency.

THE JUDGE: Of the crime of premeditated murder, how does the jury find the defendant?

THE CLERK: Guilty.

THE JUDGE: Of the crime of robbery, how does the jury find the defendant?

THE CLERK: Guilty.

THE JUDGE: Of the crime of assault with intent to kill, how does the jury find the defendant?

THE CLERK: Guilty.

(Lights fade.)

SCENE 4

KATERINA's drawing room, morning, five days after the trial. KATERINA and ALYOSHA are talking.

KATERINA: Ivan brought me the plans in a sealed envelope the night before the trial. He foresaw his illness. He also left money—ten thousand rubles.

ALYOSHA: I'm not sure Dmitry will go through with it.

KATERINA: Oh, he'll escape. What else can he do? They won't let that animal follow him to Siberia. The only problem is you. He's afraid you won't approve. You must magnanimously allow him to go—since your sanction is so necessary.

ALYOSHA: I'll try, but he wants to suffer, he wants to sacrifice.

KATERINA: What does a man like that know about sacrifice? That hero of conscience and honor, lying in a fever in the next room, sacrificed himself for his brother—and Ivan will get well—but Dmitry? Men like that never suffer.

(ALYOSHA is silent.)

KATERINA: Well, will you convince him to escape? Or do you consider it unchristian?

ALYOSHA: No. I'll talk to him. He asks you to come see him—right now.

KATERINA: Me?

ALYOSHA: He needs you. He knows how guilty he is before you. But he doesn't ask your forgiveness. He says he can't be forgiven after what he's done. He just wants to see you. All you have to do is stand in the doorway.

KATERINA: I knew this moment would come. *(Pause.)* It's impossible.

ALYOSHA: It may be impossible, but do it. For the first time he fully understands how he hurt you. You know as well as I do, he's innocent of our father's blood. In the name of his countless future sufferings, go to him. Stand in the doorway. You must.

KATERINA: I can't. He'll look at me…

ALYOSHA: You must look at him and he must look at you. How can you go on with your life if you don't?

KATERINA: Better to suffer all my life.

ALYOSHA: You have to go.

KATERINA: I can't leave Ivan.

ALYOSHA: You can leave him for an hour, the servants will look after him. If you don't go to him now, Dmitry will never be able to face the future—be it imprisonment or escape. Have pity.

KATERINA: I don't know…

ALYOSHA: I'll go and tell him you're coming.

KATERINA: Don't. I'll go. Don't tell him I'm coming. I'll go, but I might not go in.

(ALYOSHA starts to leave.)

KATERINA: What if I meet someone?

ALYOSHA: You won't if you go now. That's why it must be now. I promise you he'll be alone. We'll be waiting. (*Exits.*)

SCENE 5

DMITRY's cell. DMITRY is sitting on his cot; ALYOSHA enters.

ALYOSHA: Dmitry…

DMITRY: Trifon—the innkeeper at Mokroye—is tearing up the floorboards, looking for the fifteen hundred I'm supposed to have hidden there. The guard told me.

ALYOSHA: She'll come.

DMITRY: When?

ALYOSHA: Maybe today, maybe tomorrow…I don't know.

(*DMITRY is silent.*)

ALYOSHA: She told me Ivan left instructions for the escape. She'll take care of it…even if Ivan…

DMITRY: Brother Ivan will live—he's destined to surpass us all.

ALYOSHA: Katerina Ivanovna's certain he'll recover.

DMITRY: That means she's afraid he'll die.

(*They are silent for a moment.*)

DMITRY: Alyosha, I love Grusha terribly.

ALYOSHA: They won't let her go with you.

DMITRY: If they beat me…on the way…or there—I won't let them. I'll kill someone and they'll shoot me. The guards have already started talking down to me. I wanted to take up my cross and sing a tragic hymn to God and I can't even take the guards talking down to me. I'd endure everything for Grusha—except beatings—but they won't let her go with me.

ALYOSHA: Dmitry, you're not ready—this cross is not for you. If you had killed our father, it would be different. But you didn't. You were going to find a new man in yourself through suffering. Remember that man always, wherever you escape to—that will be enough. You'll feel more responsible precisely because you didn't take up your cross. That will do more to make a new man of you than if you went to Siberia. You wouldn't be able to endure it, you would begin to murmur against God. And who am I to judge you? If

Ivan or Katerina Ivanovna asked me, I would go bribe the guards myself—so what right do I have to judge you? Know that I will never condemn you.

DMITRY: I'll condemn myself. Oh, I'm escaping—that was decided without you—how could Mitya Karamazov not run away? But you're right—I'll condemn myself forever. I'll spend the rest of my life praying to God for forgiveness. But that's a Jesuit's excuse—"I'll suffer more if I escape." Aren't we just reasoning like Jesuits?

ALYOSHA: Yes.

DMITRY: I love you for always telling the truth. So I've caught Alyosha reasoning like a Jesuit—I could kiss you for that. Alyosha, I'm not running away to live a happy life, I'm running to another punishment—maybe worse than penal servitude. I hate America already. I love Russia, Alyosha, I love the Russian God. And is Grusha an American woman? She's Russian, every little bone in her body is Russian. But I have a plan—We'll go to the frontier, to "the last of the Mohicans," and we'll work the land and learn English. In three years, we'll speak English just as good as any American—then goodbye America! We'll return to Russia as American citizens. Don't worry, I won't come back to this town—I'll disguise myself—I'll grow a long beard or pluck out one of my eyes. We'll settle in Russia and work the land. I'll have to pretend to be an American as long as I live. But at least we'll die in our own country. Do you approve?

ALYOSHA: Yes.

DMITRY: Alyosha, is she coming?

ALYOSHA: She said she'd come. I don't know if it will be today. You have to understand how hard this is for her.

DMITRY: Of course I understand how hard it is. I know what I'm asking for. Grusha knows, too, she keeps looking at me. I want Katya. It's the unrestrained, unholy Karamazov urge.

(*KATERINA enters. ALYOSHA sees her and stands up, DMITRY turns around. DMITRY and KATERINA stare at each other for a moment. DMITRY stands up and stretches out his hands, KATERINA runs to him and takes his hands. They stare at each other. They both try to talk but can't.*)

DMITRY: Have you forgiven me? (*Turns to ALYOSHA.*) Do you hear what I'm asking her?

KATERINA: You don't need my forgiveness and I don't need yours. It doesn't matter. No matter what, you'll always be an open wound in my soul—and I'll be a wound in yours…That's how it should be. Why have I come? I've come to embrace your feet; to squeeze your hands—like this—'til it hurts, just as I did in Moscow; to say that you are my God, my joy; to tell you that I love you with all my soul. *(Kisses his hands.)* Love is gone, Mitya, but I miss the past. For one moment, let it be as it might have been. You love another woman and I love another man, but I will love you eternally and you will love me. Do you understand, you will love me all your life.

DMITRY: I know. When you collapsed at the trial, I loved you even then and I will love you forever.

(They hold each other's hands and stare at each other for a moment.)

DMITRY: Did you believe I killed him—not now, I know you don't believe it now—but on the witness stand?

KATERINA: No, I never believed it. I hated you and I convinced myself that you were guilty. But the minute I was out of the courtroom, I stopped believing it. *(Lets go of his hands.)* We can't do this. I came here to punish myself.

DMITRY: It's hard on you.

(GRUSHENKA enters quietly.)

KATERINA: Let me go. I'll come again—it's too painful now. *(Turns around and sees GRUSHENKA. She is silent for a moment.)* Forgive me.

GRUSHENKA: We're wicked, sister, you and I. We're too full of hatred to forgive. Save him, and I'll pray to you all my life.

DMITRY: You won't forgive her?

KATERINA: Don't worry, I'll save him for you. *(Runs out of the cell.)*

DMITRY: She asked you to forgive her.

ALYOSHA: Mitya, don't you dare reproach her, you have no right.

GRUSHENKA: It was her proud lips speaking, not her heart. If she saves you, I'll forgive everything.

DMITRY: Alyosha, run after her—tell her…I don't know—don't let her go away like that.

ALYOSHA: I'll be back before evening. *(Crosses out of the cell.)*

KATERINA: No, I cannot prostrate myself before that woman. I asked her to forgive me because I wanted to punish myself. She wouldn't forgive me—I love her for that.

(Church bells start to ring.)

ALYOSHA: He didn't know she'd come this morning.

KATERINA: I know—let's drop it. Listen, I can't go with you to the funeral. I've sent flowers. They still have money, I think. Tell them if they need more, I'll never abandon them. Now leave me, you're late as it is—the bells are ringing for the service…Leave me, please.

(ALYOSHA exits.)

SCENE 6

The SNEGIRYOVS' hovel. CAPTAIN SNEGIRYOV is kneeling by ILYUSHA's coffin; MAMA SNEGIRYOV and NINA are seated; KOLYA, SMUROV, and KARTASHOV are standing near the door.

SNEGIRYOV: My little fellow, my little fellow…

(ALYOSHA enters.)

KOLYA: Karamazov.

ALYOSHA: Have you gone up to the coffin?

KOLYA: We were waiting for you.

ALYOSHA: Come.

(ALYOSHA, KOLYA, SMUROV, and KARTASHOV approach the coffin.)

KOLYA: Karamazov, do you smell it?

ALYOSHA: What?

KOLYA: Nothing. His body doesn't smell.

(ALYOSHA and the BOYS pay their respects.)

MAMA: Papa, I want some flowers, too. I want the white one in his hands—give it to me.

SNEGIRYOV: No, they're his flowers, not yours. It's all his, nothing's yours.

NINA: Papa, please, give Mama a flower.

SNEGIRYOV: I won't give anything to anyone—least of all her. She never loved him. She took his little cannon away from him…and he…he gave it to her.

(MAMA starts sobbing.)

NINA: Papa, it's time to take Ilyusha to the churchyard.

SNEGIRYOV: No. He wanted to be buried by our stone.

NINA: Papa…

SNEGIRYOV: No, I'll bury him by our stone. I won't let you take him.

ALYOSHA: Captain, sir, Ilyusha is with God now—he would want to be buried in the churchyard. After church, we can all go to the stone and remember Ilyusha. He would like that.

SNEGIRYOV: Take him wherever you want.

(The BOYS and ALYOSHA take up the coffin and start to carry it out. They stop in front of MAMA and put the coffin down. MAMA starts rocking back and forth rhythmically and beating her breast.)

NINA: Mama, make the sign of the cross, then bless him and kiss him.

(MAMA keeps rocking back and forth and beating her chest.)

NINA: You'd better take him to the churchyard.

(ALYOSHA and the BOYS exit with the coffin, followed by CAPTAIN SNEGIRYOV.)

SCENE 7

The stone. SNEGIRYOV, ALYOSHA, and the BOYS enter. SNEGIRYOV is holding flowers.

SNEGIRYOV: This is the stone. We used to walk here in the evenings.

SMUROV: Captain, sir, why did you throw breadcrumbs on his grave?

SNEGIRYOV: He asked me to—so the birds would come, so he wouldn't be alone.

SMUROV: I'll go to his grave every day and put breadcrumbs on it.

KOLYA: We all should—you, too, Kartashov.

KARTASHOV: I will.

KOLYA: Captain Snegiryov, sir, you're crushing the flowers.

SNEGIRYOV: Flowers?…Flowers for Mama, flowers for Mama, I hurt Mama, flowers for Mama. *(Runs off.)*

KOLYA: Should we go after him?

ALYOSHA: Not now. Let them cry in peace. We'll go back for the memorial dinner.

KOLYA: Karamazov, isn't this memorial dinner business a little strange? All this grief and then we sit down for pancakes—it's unnatural.

KARTASHOV: They're having salmon, too.

KOLYA: Kartashov, if you dropped off the face of the Earth, no one would notice.

ALYOSHA: The pancakes and the salmon are an ancient tradition. Even when we face death, God wants us to be joyful.

KOLYA: Karamazov, did your brother do it, or was it the lackey?

ALYOSHA: The lackey killed him, my brother is innocent.

SMUROV: I told you.

ALYOSHA: Boys, we're going to be parting soon. My elder told me to go out into the world and I have to go. I'll stay 'til Dmitry is sent away and I'll stay to take care of Ivan: until he gets better or until he dies. But then I'll have to go and we may not see each other for a very long time. Let's make a pact, here at Ilyusha's stone. That we will never forget Ilyusha and we will never forget each other. Even if we don't see each other for twenty years, remember Ilyusha. How we threw stones at him and how we came to love him so much. Remember how kind he was and remember how brave he was. How he felt his father's humiliation so deeply that he rose up against his whole class. And even though we may be involved in the most important affairs, achieve distinction, or fall into some great misfortune, let us never forget how good we once felt here, all together, united by a good and kind feeling, which made us, perhaps, better than we actually are. Some of us may become wicked; we may not be able to resist evil; we may laugh at people's tears; we may laugh at the good. But if we remember this moment, if we remember how we felt when we stood together by this stone, not even the most cruel and jeering man among us will dare laugh at how kind and good he was at this moment.

KOLYA: I'll never forget this day—ever.

ALYOSHA: And never forget Ilyusha.

KOLYA: Karamazov...I loved him...

SMUROV: I miss him, Karamazov, I want him to come back...

KOLYA: Karamazov, is it really true we'll rise from the dead on Judgment Day and see each other again...and Ilyusha?

ALYOSHA: Yes.

KARTASHOV: Karamazov...I love you...

KOLYA: I love you, too, Karamazov.

SMUROV: So do I...

ALYOSHA: I love you. Now let's go in to the pancakes, gentleman. Hand in hand.

KOLYA: Always.

ALYOSHA: Yes, Kolya, always.

KOLYA: Hurrah for Karamazov!

KOLYA, SMUROV, KARTASHOV: Hurrah for Karamazov! Hurrah for Karamazov! Hurrah for Karamazov!

(Lights come up in the background to reveal the rest of the CAST. Curtain call.)

Part IV

AMERICAN LITERATURE ON STAGE

Many of the nineteenth century's greatest fiction writers—Twain, James, Poe, Melville—loved theatre; most tried writing original plays, typically without success. Who recalls Twain's 1877 collaboration with Bret Harte, *Ah Sin*? Or Twain's 1887 play with William Dean Howells, *The American Claimant; Or, Mulberry Sellers Ten Years Later*?

Fortunately, there's also a strong tradition—with a better track record—of adapting these writers' work for the stage. In its time, *Uncle Tom's Cabin* (1852) was one of the finest examples. More than a hundred and fifty years later, the impulse to derive stage-worthy drama from great works of nineteenth century literature continues unabated. The plays selected for this part prove how dynamic this tradition remains today.

Alex Roe's *Salem* ("following *Young Goodman Brown* by Nathaniel Hawthorne") is a triumph over paradox: How do you drill down into the dramaturgical essence of classic literature without losing the superlative writing of the source material? Roe preserves the arc of Hawthorne's 1835 allegory, but his greater achievement is one of voice: the play reads on page, and plays on stage, much as Hawthorne might have liked it to, with loyalty to tone and concessions to theatrical necessity working as one, not in opposition.

Reneé Flemings's *Bel Canto* "merges *The Tell-Tale Heart* with *The Sopranos*," as Martin Denton analyzed it in 2003. Certainly the clipped phrasing and flirtation with the Mamet-esque would be unrecognizable to Poe, who composed his story in 1843. But Flemings's transformation of the story into an examination of the demons of a Mafia hit man—heightened by the insertion of a man on the bongos who symbolizes a beating heart—pays effortless tribute to the beauty of Poe's dark universe while thrusting it into a unique twenty-first century light.

R. L. Lane's *Bartleby the Scrivener*, based on Melville's 1853 novella, asks whether the things that we cannot comprehend through the usual means and methods may drive us mad. Lane locates, within Melville's elliptical writing style, the quality that critics have called a precursor to absurdism, and then he has placed that quality within the context of absurdist theatre—a distinctly twentieth century invention. What's remarkable is how well the play hews to Melville's original while simultaneously seeming as if a Beckett or a Sartre might have written it.

—*Leonard Jacobs*

BEL CANTO

from Edgar Allan Poe's "The Tell-Tale Heart"

Reneé Flemings

RENEÉ FLEMINGS is a playwright, actor, director, and singer. She was born in Louisville, Kentucky, and spent her formative years in Lansing/East Lansing, Michigan. Her summers, however, were spent in the Deep South: Alabama, Georgia, and Florida. She studied in New York City with Phil Gushee and Joe Anania. Her plays include *Daddy's Home* (Henry St. Settlement), *"…secrets…"* (National Black Theatre Festival; International Women's Theatre Festival, Philadelphia), *The Bible Belt* (HERE; Philadelphia Fringe Festival), *Bounce & Roll* ("The A Train Plays"), *Legend* (The Drilling Company), and *Flight* (Metropolitan Playhouse). She is also the writer, co-producer, and co-director of the documentary *Nothing But the Blues*, and the instructional DVD *Wine Noir*. Flemings works in the educational theatre field for Roundabout Theatre Company, and has been involved in working with teaching artists and teachers in various capacities over the past ten years. She also works as a writer for Zinc, an organization that focuses on developing programs using drama to explore life skills with professional athletes. Flemings is currently recording a CD of standard and original blues songs, and paying attention to some scripts that have just been lying around for too long. She has lived in almost every borough twice, and currently lives in Manhattan with her husband.

Bel Canto was first presented by Metropolitan Playhouse (Alex Roe, Artistic Director) as part of a program of short plays entitled *What's Old Is New*, on May 29, 2003, at the Metropolitan Playhouse, New York City, with the following cast and credits:

Mains.. Tim Cox
Trigger...Matthew Cade
Cleave .... Paul Romanello
Bel Canto .... Michael Thomas

Directed by: Anthony P. Pennino

AUTHOR'S NOTE

When I was first told of the *What's Old Is New* project and the guidelines, I knew exactly which writer I wanted to adapt. Edgar Allan Poe has always been one of my favorite writers. There were so many stories of his that I loved, that it was difficult to choose, however, "The Tell-Tale Heart" really spoke to the paranoia and horror that was/is present post 9/11. Is it about the bigger picture of the world and 9/11? No. However, it was that atmosphere, that fear on a really personal level that made it a natural choice. After all that, I wanted to see how far I could take it away from the original context while attempting to maintain those feelings from the narrator's perspective. It became important that the world of the play is suggested, a bit over the top, and surreal enough to remove constraints of reality. I enjoyed playing in that jazzy, dangerous world with those characters—bloody eyeballs and all.

CHARACTERS

MAINS: Male, twenties
TRIGGER: Male, thirties–forties
CLEAVE: Male, twenties–thirties
BEL CANTO: Male, always in shadow with bongos

PRODUCTION NOTES

All the characters, save Mains, are dressed in traditional-styled 1940s dress suits, dark in color. Mains wears black pants, white shirt, rolled sleeves. The play has a fast-paced, driving energy as if the actors had been shot from a cannon.

Time and place are more a feeling than a reality, like jazz and jagged glass.

Music: "Salt Peanuts" plays in the darkness. Lights fade up, in the center, and downstage portion of the stage creating an area of darkness/shadows around the playing area, allowing the action to take place in an isolated area, a cocoon: center stage a small table holds drink glasses and a bottle of whiskey. Upstage within the shadows, yet still somewhat visible, is a FIGURE in a suit and a fedora. He sits behind a single bongo drum (BEL CANTO). There is silence. MAINS stands facing upstage; his breath is heavy, labored. TRIGGER bursts in. MAINS quickly turns downstage, seemingly composed.

TRIGGER: Where's the man?

MAINS: Sleep, said he needed to grab some shut eye. Late night last night.

TRIGGER: Every night's a late night with the man, you know?

MAINS: Yeah, I suppose.

TRIGGER: So, the take?

MAINS: Good. I think we did good. Got a lot happenin' up the way…a lot. All three joints are turnin' in a nice profit. The receipts are on the table.

TRIGGER: S'alright—I trust ya. I just like to hear it ya know? So does the man. He's a fussy fucker, but he knows how to handle business.

MAINS: Ya think?

TRIGGER: Hell yeah. Taught me everything I know. Together we make very, very long dollars, my friend. Just wait, you'll be seein' long money too, in no time.

MAINS: That's what I've been hearin' from around the way. You know, from the guys. They say he knows what he's doin'—that's what they talk since I been around, ya know?

TRIGGER: He took one club and made it into an empire. He's like Caesar, fuckin' Caesar, you know?

MAINS: Yeah. I know.

TRIGGER: Caesar, he was a good man. He had ambition.

MAINS: Yeah.

TRIGGER: Just got greedy—ya think?

MAINS: What?

TRIGGER: Ya think? Caesar? Got greedy, right?

MAINS: I don't—I don't know. I don't follow that shit.

TRIGGER: Should, you can learn from history. Lot to learn from history.

(CLEAVE hustles into the room.)

CLEAVE: Fellas! We got a problem. Pour me one, Trigger.

TRIGGER: Since when I'm workin' the bar here?

CLEAVE: Since I say. Pour me a fuckin' drink and pay attention. I say we've got a problem, gentlemen, a problem needs our prompt attention.

MAINS: What kinda problem?

(TRIGGER reluctantly pours one for himself and CLEAVE.)

TRIGGER: You havin' some?

MAINS: Yeah, sure, thanks.

(THE FIGURE behind the drum beats out a brief rhythmic phrase, then stops abruptly. MAINS's hand trembles very slightly in sync with the sound, then stops.)

TRIGGER: Hold the glass still, stupid.

MAINS: Sorry.

TRIGGER: You spill this shit—this is the real good—

CLEAVE: Trigger?

TRIGGER: Yeah?

CLEAVE: Shut up. We got business to handle. The word's out on the street, Big Tony Hustle wants to take over some of our spots—Word is he's got a connection uptown, a connection with some connections and some money—big money, and a lot of muscle. Word is this guy's goin' to make sure Tony gets what he wants.

TRIGGER: Uh-uh, not happenin'

CLEAVE: I know this. But he don't know this—We need to let him know this. So… Mains?

MAINS: Yeah?

CLEAVE: It's all yours…

MAINS: Mine?

CLEAVE: Yeah. Yours.

(The bongos beat again. MAINS moves across the stage, his movements for one brief moment stylized as if a jazz ballet. They both look at him. His hand shakes.)

TRIGGER: The hell was that?

MAINS: What?

TRIGGER: That.

MAINS: Nothin'—I—I don't know—Hey Cleave? I was thinkin'—thinkin' that maybe we don't wanna take on Big Tony Hustle. Maybe we could just keep things quiet—

CLEAVE: It's got nothin' to do with what we want—it's about honor. Him puttin' these things out there for the world to hear—it's an act of war. We gotta be ready—we can't just be sittin' ducks waitin' on Big Tony to make a move—

MAINS: Alright, how 'bout this? We could maybe get the cops to handle Big Tony for us. They owe us one—

TRIGGER: That's a really—

CLEAVE: Stupid idea. We don't want to bring the cops in on this.

MAINS: Why not? We could get them to do the dirty work for us, they've been wanting to take Big Tony down for a long time. That way we kill two birds with one stone and we stay out of it—and we can take over Big Tony's joints.

(THE FIGURE plays bongos again, same phrase. MAINS repeats the jazzy, discordant pattern with his body.)

CLEAVE: I don't recall sayin' that it was up to you to make decisions. What I recall sayin' was: Handle it.

MAINS: And I'm just sayin' that we can handle it without getting our hands dirty. That's all.

(Bongo plays again. MAINS moves again as in a jazz ballet; the trembling increases. He is weakened.)

TRIGGER: Maybe you ought to lay low for a while—

MAINS: I'm alright. I just think you ought to listen to me; this ain't a bad idea, Cleave.

CLEAVE: No it ain't bad, it's fuckin' bad.

MAINS: Alls I'm sayin'—

(CLEAVE grabs MAINS's scruff/collar; pimp slaps him twice.)

CLEAVE: Alls I'm sayin' is just do what I say. That's all you need to be thinkin' about right now. Do I make myself clear? I don't like to repeat myself, so I want to make sure we are clear. You are going to go handle Big Tony Hustle. Take. Him. Out—you get rid of him today. Take him out fast and dirty. Understand? Or is it you're scared, little girl?

MAINS: I ain't scared—it's just that your way ain't always the right way to do things. You ever think of that—

CLEAVE: It is the right way, 'long as I'm the boss—

TRIGGER: Last I heard, you ain't the boss, Cleave. Mr. Bel Canto is. Just 'cause he's your uncle don't make you boss, least not while he's breathin'. I think you need to lay off Mains till we talk to him, see what he wants to do.

CLEAVE: I know he's the boss, that ain't what I'm tryin' to say—I'm lookin' out for Mr. Bel Canto and he trusts what I say. That's what's important here. Where is he?

TRIGGER: Takin' a nap, right?

MAINS: Yeah. Said not to wake him, he was pretty knocked out after last night. Got him a little "strange"—

TRIGGER: Yeah? Some kitty from uptown?

MAINS: I think.

CLEAVE: One of these days, that dude's dick is gonna put him in a sling.

TRIGGER: Maybe.

(He and CLEAVE drink simultaneously, slamming their glasses onto the table; MAINS a beat later. Bongo again. MAINS crumbles, then regroups.)

CLEAVE: Hey! You fucked up again?

MAINS: No! I ain't touched nothin'—

CLEAVE: Lemme see.

MAINS: Like hell.

CLEAVE: I don't know, Mains, I think I wanna see.

MAINS: I told you I'm clean. That oughta be good enough.

TRIGGER: He says he's clean, you gotta trust a man at his word.

CLEAVE: I ain't gotta trust nothin'. LET. ME. SEE.

(MAINS rolls up his sleeve.)

MAINS: Alright now?

CLEAVE: Yeah, alright, for now. You, get goin' and—Hey! Don't be gentle, have a little fun. (Laughs.) Gotta make some calls, handle some business. Trigger, let me know when the man is up. (Exits.)

(Bongos again. MAINS shakes and collapses onto a chair.)

TRIGGER: Man. You sure you're alright?

MAINS: Yeah. Yeah…

TRIGGER: 'Cause you got a serious thing to do now. You can't be shakin' all over the place like that—Big Tony Hustle sees a shot, he'll take it—Boom—there you are.

MAINS: Trigger?

TRIGGER: Yeah?

MAINS: This's my first one, you know?

TRIGGER: Oh, you are scared, little girl.

MAINS: No, no—I want to know, I was wondering… I mean you ain't like Cleave. He ain't got no heart, no real heart. I was just wonderin'—how… how'd you feel after…?

TRIGGER: The first one?

MAINS: Yeah.

TRIGGER: Hungry.

MAINS: What?

TRIGGER: Had a steak. About this thick, with potatoes, some bourbon, good bourbon. See, my first was up close. Guy sitting right across from me in this bar. I coulda waited 'til his back was turned. We coulda taken him out in the car and blam, right in the back of the head. But I didn't wanna go like that. I figure you take a man out, he's got a right to see you—to look you in the eye. Right? So, I met him for a drink in this little joint in Brooklyn, it was set up lovely, real lovely. The bartender was the only one there besides us. He knew what was goin' on and he knew when it was time. He just walked into the back room, closed the door. Jinx, the guy not the bartender, the guy. Jinx took a sip of this little fruity drink he had, a margarita I think, some shit like that. There was this thick line of salt all around the rim of the glass, looked like sugar… I could see lights dancing around in the glass, all kinds of colors—from the neon outside… Dizzy was on the jukebox "Salt Peanuts, salt peanuts" yeah—anyway so he takes a sip, looks me dead in the eye and says: "So? What you want to talk about?" I didn't say a word. I just looked at him for a long, long minute—I think he knew it was coming. He knew. Blam. All over. Then I sat there for, I don't know, a minute, maybe two and I started gettin' this gnawing feeling in my stomach—like I had a hole in me. I remember looking down at that glass, there was a few little specks of blood on it… But all that salt, all that salt around the rim was pink now… Pink and wet. I'm lookin' at that salt thinkin' "pink and wet"… Like meat, you know? Good meat. I got in the car. Drove down to Dane's joint and had me the biggest cut of beef I ever had.

(Bongo; MAINS trembles. TRIGGER pours him a shot, MAINS hungrily drinks it.)

TRIGGER: Yeah… I guess you don't forget that first one.

MAINS: Naw… I don't think so.

(TRIGGER pours him another one; they drink simultaneously, slamming the glasses down onto the table. Bongo again; MAINS convulses.)

TRIGGER: Look, you want me to do this thing for you? I can, we don't have to tell Cleave—fuck him, you know?

MAINS: How long you know him?

TRIGGER: Me and Cleave started with Mr. Bel Canto around the same time—about ten years ago. The old man didn't want to bring him in on the business, but Cleave, he's always been hungry, you know? Pissed his mom off when he started workin' for the man. She got over that quick. He's makin' more money now than he ever woulda flippin' burgers in some joint, drivin' a hack or jumpin' for some guy in a monkey suit. Hey… business is business right? Yeah, ten years a long time to know somebody in our business. Know 'em and they still livin'.

MAINS: He doesn't like me.

TRIGGER: No, he doesn't. So what? You tryin' to be everybody's friend, sell Avon or something.

MAINS: I ain't tryin' to be everybody's friend. I just— He don't talk much, you know—not really. He don't say much to me except "Mains do this, Mains do that." Him and Mr. Bel Canto they're alike that way.

TRIGGER: Strong silent types. Yeah, they watch too many movies. The movies will get you into trouble, have you believin' all kinds of shit that ain't true. Personally, myself, I got no problem with being verbal. I like bein' verbal, that way everybody knows where you comin' from—there's less confusion.

MAINS: I spent days with Mr. Bel Canto he don't say nothin' all day.

TRIGGER: But when he does talk, he says important things.

MAINS: He calls me Sonny.

TRIGGER: That's nice.

MAINS: I hate it.

TRIGGER: It's a term of endearment—

MAINS: No it's not, it's his way of lettin' me know I ain't up to his speed. I ain't meetin' his way of doin' things—that I'm gonna be his flunky forever he has his way about it!

TRIGGER: You get all that out of Sonny?

MAINS: It's the way he says it… "Sonny."

(As he speaks the word, THE FIGURE at the drums speaks it with him, as an echoing whisper and begins to move toward the edge of the shadow.)

BEL CANTO: Sonny.

MAINS: Yeah, just like that "Sonny."

BEL CANTO: Sonny.

TRIGGER: You're being a little thin-skinned about this, ain't ya—

MAINS: Naw, see you trust too much. You don't know people, Trigger—

TRIGGER: No I don't, not really, I just kill 'em—it's better that way. No emotional ties—

MAINS: You don't know how people say things and mean something else—There's ways people tell you things, without sayin' it. I know. I know how people are…

TRIGGER: Maybe you've been puttin' too much of that shit in your veins.

MAINS: I ain't high, I tell ya. You don't know how to look into a person's soul, Trigger. You just stop at the flesh and blood, that's all you see. When he calls me "Sonny"—

BEL CANTO: Sonny.

MAINS: He's tellin' me I ain't shit. He's tellin' me he ain't never gonna have any respect for me. You know what he did the other day—

TRIGGER: What?

MAINS: He gimme his back, while I was talkin' to him about the downtown joint. I'm trying to run down the figures, handle myself like a man. Let him know, things are good and—He was sittin' up there in that chair, you know the big leather one. The one with the nice, soft, red leather—you can leave your fingerprints in it just by layin' your hands on it… How much you think something like that costs?

TRIGGER: I don't know, I don't think about these things—

CLEAVE: (From offstage.) Mains!

MAINS: He sits in that chair like he's a king or something and I'm just some schmuck, gotta do what he says. Anyway, I come in the door and he says to me… (Simultaneous with BEL CANTO.) Sonny, pour me a drink, a good drink… Don't fuck around with it, make it nice.

BEL CANTO: Sonny, pour me a drink, a good drink… Don't fuck around with it, make it nice.

MAINS: So, I pour him one, a nice one. I mixed the soda just right, the way he likes it… I put two cubes of ice in, not one or three, 'cause I remember, I remember how he likes it—and you know what he does?

TRIGGER: What?

MAINS: He pours it in the plant and says "Too much soda." I know what I'm doin', Trigger— I know.

BEL CANTO: Too much soda, Sonny.

CLEAVE: (Offstage.) Mains!!

TRIGGER: Mains, it's just a drink. He can be—

MAINS: So I make him another one, he takes it, looks me in the eye and he gives me this shitty little smile… Like he's sayin' "Sonny" without sayin' it. Then, he—He—He just spins that chair—turns the chair away from me… He gives me his back, Trigger. He gives me his back and says,

BEL CANTO: Finish tellin' me what you got, but we both know you ain't got much…Sonny.

MAINS: No "thank you," no nothin',—just "I ain't got much"—I ain't got much—then he gives me his back! Just like that!

TRIGGER: Like that. Yeah, well, he's the man. He can do those things. Don't take it so personal. Here.

(Pours another drink. Bongos. MAINS reacts. This time the playing is violent; it slams him to the floor. CLEAVE rushes in.)

CLEAVE: Goddammit Mains—ain't you hear me callin' you! Big Tony Hustle's on the move.

MAINS: (Weakened.) I'm goin'—I'm—on my way…

CLEAVE: No need—He's on his way over here—

TRIGGER: Here?

CLEAVE: What I said, ain't it? The hell's wrong with him?

MAINS: Nothin'… Nothin'…

CLEAVE: Don't look like nothin'. I thought you said you was clean. Lemme see your legs.

MAINS: No!

CLEAVE: I ain't got time for this, Tony's bringin' his boys—I need you to be right. Come on, Mains: LEMME SEE 'EM!!

(MAINS rolls up his pants leg. His leg is clean and clear.)

CLEAVE: The other one.

MAINS: No! I ain't well, fellas—I ain't well, I tell ya!

CLEAVE: Lemme see!

TRIGGER: Leave him, Cleave. We got to get the man out of here before Tony comes. How many guys is he bringin'—

CLEAVE: Don't know. The word is it's bad. Let's go—

(He kicks MAINS, who is still crumpled on the floor.)

CLEAVE: Piece of shit.

TRIGGER: Leave him. We'll take the man out the back way.

(They exit. MAINS lies on the floor, curled in a fetal position; he slowly begins to roll up his other pants leg. THE FIGURE begins a slow drumbeat that progressively gets faster and faster.)

MAINS: I hear you, old man. I hear you… You don't scare me none. I'm done with you. I'm done. Let Big Tony come on—Let 'em all come on. I ain't scared no more. I ain't scared of nobody no more—

(TRIGGER and CLEAVE enter, unknown to MAINS. They stare at MAINS.)

MAINS: I ain't scared of you. I ain't your flunky… I ain't your sonny—whatta ya have to say now—old man? Huh? What do you have to say now?

CLEAVE: You did it, didn't ya? Ya killed him. How could you do a thing like that? He's an old man. How could ya do it, he took care of you—that's what he did.

(MAINS pulls a rag from his pants leg, opens it, revealing a bloody eyeball. The drumming gets louder. CLEAVE and TRIGGER close in on MAINS, guns drawn. The drums abruptly stops.)

MAINS: Hey Trigger… I'm hungry. I want a steak.

(Blackout.)

SALEM

following "Young Goodman Brown" by Nathaniel Hawthorne

Alex Roe

ALEX ROE is the artistic director of Metropolitan Playhouse in New York City. He was born in Wilmington, Delaware, in 1965, and grew up in southeastern Pennsylvania. He graduated from Harvard College with a BA in literature, and studied with Sarah Ludlow, Teresa Roberts, and Lex Chessler in San Francisco. Roe has acted since childhood, but credits his first foray into producing—an improvisation-based play developed with college friend Eric Ronis—as the thing that permanently hooked him on theatre. His credits as an author/adaptor and director include *Goodbye, Walter* (1989, Studio Eremos, San Francisco); *Oedipus Rex* (1991, Next Stage, San Francisco); *Oedipus at Colonus* (1995, Chelsea Playhouse, New York City); and, for Metropolitan Playhouse, *Bacchus* (2002), *Dom Juan* (2002), and *Haunted* (2006). His adaptation of *The Cherry Orchard* represented the United States in the Second International Russian Theatre Festival. Roe lives in New York City with his wife, Shakespeare scholar Natasha Korda.

Salem was first presented by Metropolitan Playhouse (Alex Roe, Artistic Director) on October 31, 2001, at the Metropolitan Playhouse, New York City, with the following cast and credits:

Bridget Bishop .... DeBanne Browne
Thomas Brown ....Scott Barrow
Eliphalet..Danny Ashkenasi
Samuel Parris.. Michael B. Healey
Faith.. Darra Herman
Goody Cloyse..Doris Martin
Old Nick.. George R. Sheffey
Governor Bradstreet... David L. Carson

Directed by: Alex Roe
Stage Manager: Kimberly Wadsworth
Production Manager: Dan Nichols
Set Design: Fritz Masten
Rocks: Katie Fleissner
Costume Design: Fritz Masten
Lighting Design: Douglas Filomena
Graphics Design: Sidney Fortner, Alex Roe
Program: Cynthia Hewitt
Casting: Laurie Smith Casting
Press Representation: Sam Rudy Media Relations

ACT I
Prelude

GOODMAN THOMAS BROWN alone, outside of meeting hall. A hymn is heard from offstage. As it reaches its conclusion:

BRIDGET: *(Offstage.)* Eliphalet! Eliphalet!

Scene 1

Outside meeting hall. THOMAS, invisible to ALL OTHERS but DEVIL, watches this pantomime: FAITH BROWN, alone, enters from hall. DEVIL enters from woods and observes the others and THOMAS. SAMUEL PARRIS and GOVERNOR BRADSTREET enter from hall, and are joined by GOODY CLOYSE on the steps of the hall. ELIPHALET enters from woods.

THOMAS: Eliphalet.

(ELIPHALET sees THOMAS.)

ELIPHALET: Thomas.

(ELIPHALET exits to town. GOVERNOR and SAMUEL greet FAITH. BRIDGET BISHOP enters from woods, seeking ELIPHALET. She greets OTHERS and exits. ALL exit to town except DEVIL, who exits to woods. THOMAS exits to woods.)

Scene 2

On the way to the house of GOODMAN THOMAS BROWN and his wife, FAITH. SAMUEL and FAITH enter.

SAMUEL: …will surely understand.

FAITH: Be not so certain, Mister Parris. I do not know that I understand.

SAMUEL: Do not trouble yourself. He certainly knows the governor was expected.

FAITH: Yea, to be sure.

SAMUEL: And what did he tell you this morning?

FAITH: He had gone before I woke.

SAMUEL: Truly? Well, doubtless 'twas an errand he sought to complete by now, and set out of purpose that he be returned in time. It is a surprise he missed worship.

FAITH: I know it.

SAMUEL: But the deacon and the minister are with the governor, and we will join them.

FAITH: The deacon asked after Thomas twice.

SAMUEL: Mister Gookin is officious. 'Tis no sin to note a weakness, Faith. I have lived here but one year longer than you, and I am not so familiar with our neighbors that I no longer discern them.

FAITH: I think you do discern more clearly than I.

SAMUEL: Therein lies the advantage of familiarity. I have spent long hours with the deacon, as you know. I have borne his instruction and the minister's as they train me to the habit of the village, and I have taken it on myself to study their own habits so as not to fall victim to them.

FAITH: And Thomas's?

SAMUEL: His as well. He is devout. He is industrious and earnest, and probably too trusting. 'Tis some obligation or confidence has called him forth this morning, and he does not see the burden it places on his friends.

FAITH: If he knows his friends.

SAMUEL: Doesn't he?

FAITH: I am sure he does. He has been burdened on their behalf.

SAMUEL: You may say more.

FAITH: 'Tis the approbation of the appointment. He has wondered if to accept were not vain.

SAMUEL: 'Tis a service given him to perform. A hard reward!

FAITH: But an honor nonetheless.

SAMUEL: Modesty is no virtue if one takes pride in one's humility.

FAITH: 'Tis arrogance.

SAMUEL: And in the guise of fealty.

FAITH: I would not say so of Thomas.

SAMUEL: Nor I. But 'tis no fault to note our friends. And he is my friend, and one who loves you to a fault, I think. Though 'twere no fault to do so. You do not doubt him?

FAITH: 'Twould be my failing.

SAMUEL: To doubt?

FAITH: Or to give him cause to doubt.

BRIDGET: (*Offstage.*) Eliphalet!

SAMUEL: You do not. Mistress Brown, 'tis no rare thing to harbor such fears, though 'tis not a certain virtue to turn circumstance into recrimination, especially of yourself. Your father did send you from England with the purpose of your union, and with the respect of Thomas's father in his heart. 'Twas not without concern for Thomas and you, though 'twas not I think with any concern for what objections you might conceive.

FAITH: We had not met.

SAMUEL: Cause for objection, itself. But I have seen neither of you shy from duty, and neither of you regret obedience.

FAITH: I have not.

SAMUEL: Nor has Thomas. And what ye may discover in one another shall only defend ye against what regrets might menace any other.

FAITH: Perhaps he may discover a cause for regret.

SAMUEL: I do not know what that might be.

FAITH: I am angry with him now for not returning.

SAMUEL: As am I.

(*BRIDGET enters.*)

BRIDGET: Eliphalet!

FAITH: Mistress Bishop.

BRIDGET: Mistress Brown, have you seen my nephew?

FAITH: Nay, Mistress Bishop.

BRIDGET: Where is your husband?

FAITH: He is not with us.

BRIDGET: I see he is not. I wonder where he is.

SAMUEL: Good day and God be with you, Mistress Bishop.

BRIDGET: Mister Parris.

SAMUEL: You were again missed at worship, this morning.

BRIDGET: I am certain I was not missed as I might scarce be recognized at the meeting house.

SAMUEL: I know some of your patrons are also ours.

BRIDGET: They may speak of my house to you, Mister Parris. They do not mention yours at mine.

SAMUEL: And yet I know you do give them cheer and rest, and so choose to believe we do labor in the same cause.

BRIDGET: I will look forward to your visit, then.

SAMUEL: And I, yours.

BRIDGET: Hast seen my nephew, Mistress Brown? He did sneak away this morning, and I do most find him in your husband's company when he is not in mine.

FAITH: I have not seen him.

BRIDGET: 'Tis a curse.

SAMUEL: Bless you for bearing it.

BRIDGET: Had I the choice in the matter— Is not your husband to meet the governor today?

FAITH: He is.

BRIDGET: Do not turn to me if that boy is with him, then.

SAMUEL: We would not.

BRIDGET: He'll make no fine impression on the governor, and I understand it is an impression Mister Brown must make.

SAMUEL: No doubt he will.

BRIDGET: Will he? You know it is his father's credit got him notice.

FAITH: I know he well deserves it.

BRIDGET: His father's credit gets him a great deal in Salem. And I do not know that he will get for the village in return.

FAITH: His appointment to the council, may we expect it, will be of great worth to Salem.

BRIDGET: Aye, so it will be, if he has the sense to make something of it.

SAMUEL: He will serve as he is suited to do.

BRIDGET: If he is suited to. He is no man of affairs.

FAITH: Mistress Bishop, if we see your nephew, we will send him to you.

BRIDGET: And if I see your husband, I will send him to you. But I doubt they are not together, and the time he wastes with that boy will do no good on the council.

SAMUEL: Good day, Goody Bishop.

BRIDGET: Hah. *(Exits.)*

SAMUEL: Think noth—

FAITH: There was no cause for—

SAMUEL: Nay.

FAITH: You began?

SAMUEL: I agree. We must be patient.

FAITH: She is a loathsome woman, and her tavern, or public house, or which it may be is no credit to the village. To speak of credit.

SAMUEL: We shall suffer the wicked and be not tried.

FAITH: I think I will. Thank you for your attention, Mister Parris.

SAMUEL: I have nothing else to offer.

FAITH: 'Tis very much enough. And thank you for your company from the village. I'll return home from here.

SAMUEL: I should to the deacon. Perhaps I may tell them he is…ill.

FAITH: I would not have you lie to the governor.

SAMUEL: It may be true. Without certain knowledge to the contrary, 'tis no certain lie.

FAITH: You are intent on my good humor.

SAMUEL: I do endorse it. And I will say something on your husband's behalf, though I be damned for speculation.

FAITH: Thank you. I will wait for him.

SAMUEL: God be with you, Faith.

FAITH: And also with you.

(FAITH and SAMUEL exit.)

SCENE 3

ELIPHALET sits on stage with primer.

CLOYSE: *(Offstage.)* Thomas?

ELIPHALET: Here, Goody.

CLOYSE: *(Entering.)* Eliphalet. Thou wilt try a soul to judgment.

ELIPHALET: Here, Goody.

CLOYSE: Aye, and plainly. Eliphalet, attend me. I am looking for Thomas.

ELIPHALET: Here, Goody.

CLOYSE: Blessed be thee.

ELIPHALET: Here, Goody.

CLOYSE: Quiet thy tongue. Cease. I haven't time. If Thomas returns here, tell him to come to the hall.

ELIPHALET: Here, Goody.

CLOYSE: If he comes here, send him to the hall.

ELIPHALET: Here.

CLOYSE: No, to the hall. Stop. Dost thou understand?

ELIPHALET: H—

CLOYSE: Stop. Thomas. Stop. I see thee. Thomas is not here. When he comes here, send him to the hall.

ELIPHALET: Thomas.

CLOYSE: Aye.

ELIPHALET: Here, Goody.

CLOYSE: In the name of the Lord. Be with thee, Eliphalet.

ELIPHALET: Goody.

CLOYSE: I must go.

ELIPHALET: Goody.

CLOYSE: What dost thou have?

ELIPHALET: Here.

CLOYSE: Eliphalet, I have not the time. Now what earthly good dost thou seek in this?

ELIPHALET: Thomas.

CLOYSE: I see it is.

ELIPHALET: Here.

CLOYSE: Aye, here. I see. Didst thou take this from the house? Didst thou go into the house? Eliphalet?

ELIPHALET: Thomas.

CLOYSE: It was Thomas's primer. Lest he give it thee, I wonder thou shouldst have it.

ELIPHALET: We sinned all.

CLOYSE: Sayest thou?

ELIPHALET: A. We sinned all.

CLOYSE: In Adam's fall.

ELIPHALET: We sinned all.

CLOYSE: B—Thy life to mend—

ELIPHALET: This book attend.

CLOYSE: Take my breath. C—The cat doth play—

ELIPHALET: And after sleep.

CLOYSE: And after slay. The cat doth play—

ELIPHALET: And after, sleep.

Cloyse. And after, slay. D—A dog will bite—

ELIPHALET: The cat doth play—

CLOYSE: And after slay. A dog will bite—

ELIPHALET: The cat doth play—

CLOYSE: A dog will bite—

(ELIPHALET growls.)

CLOYSE: Bless thee. Did Mister Brown teach thee so far? Has he so squandered his time?

ELIPHALET: In Adam's fall, we sinned all.

CLOYSE: A natural aberration as thou. Thou art an object for pity and a trial on this village. Bless thy parents and the Lord for receiving His own, or sending them to the other place.

ELIPHALET: Job feels the rod, yet blesses God.

CLOYSE: What hope that fool might seek instructing thee.

ELIPHALET: A dog will bite a thief at night.

CLOYSE: Vanity, Eliphalet, is a sin. Thou wilt never know it, but thou mayst see it in thy master, Goodman Brown.

ELIPHALET: Thy life to mend, this book attend.

CLOYSE: Vanity. So goes the father, so follows the son. But proud as he may have been, he was not such a fool as this.

ELIPHALET: In Adam's fall—

CLOYSE: And now he does forestall our contract, and for no purpose thou canst tell. No purpose, I am certain, at all.

ELIPHALET: We sinned all.

CLOYSE: Get home to thy aunt, Eliphalet. Go now, get thee home.

ELIPHALET: Ah!

CLOYSE: Keep the book! For what good it may do thee—keep it then. But get home. Go now, I cannot stay with thee. Go, Eliphalet. I must go find that fool Brown. Oh, come, then. I'll get thee to her house.

ELIPHALET: Thomas.

CLOYSE: Come with me.

ELIPHALET: Thomas!

(ELIPHALET bites her.)

CLOYSE: Ow! Would bite me, thou Devil's child? I have not time to give thee—The Devil take thee, then, if he hasn't Master Brown. (Exits.)

ELIPHALET: Time cuts down all, both great and small.

(THOMAS enters.)

THOMAS: God bless, thee, Eliphalet. Thou mayst have smote a witch. Give me the primer. Thank thee, thou hast done a goodly errand.

ELIPHALET: Thank thee, thou hast done a goodly errand.

THOMAS: I know not. 'Twas not an errand that was good.

ELIPHALET: In Adam's fall—

THOMAS: Yea. That thou shouldst say so.

ELIPHALET: In Adam's fall—

THOMAS: This is not the time for lessons.

ELIPHALET: In Adam's fall—

THOMAS: Adam does but take instruction, manikin. And teachers are in every garden. Whom shouldst thou attend?

ELIPHALET: Thomas is Eliphalet's master.

THOMAS: I would teach thee what I could. God be thy master.

ELIPHALET: God be thy master.

THOMAS: Aye, though He be, I know not that I did heed His word.

ELIPHALET: In Adam's fall—

THOMAS: I need thee to stop repeating that, Eliphalet.

ELIPHALET: Thomas.

THOMAS: Eliphalet.

ELIPHALET: Thomas.

THOMAS: Stop, now. Peace, now.

ELIPHALET: Thomas.

THOMAS: Peace.

ELIPHALET: He gives me sleep and quiet rest, whereby my body is refreshed.

THOMAS: 'Twas not His grace this night. And that He knows I have not deserved. Sleep is a gift for saints. I did not sleep this night. Thy master did make an appointment, Eli.

(DEVIL enters.)

DEVIL: You are late, Goodman Brown.

ELIPHALET: The resolution which you take, sweet youth it doth me merry make.

THOMAS: And went I, then, to keep covenant. E'en to say, I would not go whither he intended. Yet did I linger.

(DEVIL and THOMAS re-enact the events of the night before, as THOMAS describes them to ELIPHALET, who looks on but does not participate.)

DEVIL: Let us walk on, reasoning as we go, and if I convince thee not, thou shalt turn back. We are but a little way in the forest yet.

THOMAS: Too far, too far! My father never went into the woods on such an errand, nor his father before him, and shall I be the first of the name of Brown, that ever took this path and kept…

DEVIL: Such company, thou wouldst say? Well said, Goodman Brown! I have been as well acquainted with your family as with ever a one among the Puritans; and that's no trifle to say. I helped your grandfather, the constable, when he lashed the Quaker woman so smartly through the streets of Salem. And it was I that brought your father a pitch-pine knot, kindled at my own hearth, to set fire to an Indian village, in King Philip's War. They were my good friends, both; and many a pleasant walk have we had along this path, and

returned merrily after midnight. I would fain be friends with you, for their sake.

THOMAS: If it be as thou sayest, I marvel they never spoke of these matters. Or, verily, I marvel not, seeing that the least rumor of the sort would have driven them from New England. We are a people of prayer, and good works to boot, and abide no such wickedness. But, to end the matter at once, there is my wife, Faith. It would break her dear little heart; and I'd rather break my own!

(CLOYSE enters, as a part of the story THOMAS is telling.)

DEVIL: Nay, if that be the case, e'en go thy ways, Goodman Brown. I would not, for twenty old women like the one hobbling before us, that Faith should come to any harm.

(DEVIL touches CLOYSE with his staff.)

CLOYSE: The devil!

DEVIL: Then Goody Cloyse knows her old friend.

CLOYSE: Ah, forsooth. And is it your worship indeed?

THOMAS: They talked as fond friends—spoke of my grandfather, of me.

CLOYSE: They tell me there is a nice young man to be taken into communion tonight. *(Exits.)*

THOMAS: What if a wretched old woman do choose to go to the Devil, whom I thought sure was going to Heaven! Is that any reason why I should quit my dear Faith and go after her?

DEVIL: You will think better of this by and by. Sit here and rest yourself awhile; and when you feel like moving again, there is my staff to help you along. *(Exits.)*

ELIPHALET: Youth forward slips death soonest nips.

THOMAS: Would I had stayed. Yet did I hear…

(Cloud sounds, intermingled with VOICES.)

THOMAS: The deacon, Mister Lawson… Faith!

(One of FAITH's ribbons falls from the sky. The cloud passes.)

THOMAS: I flew through the forest, I know not how far, and camest upon a company—not wanting for any one in Salem—sinners and saints, alike. The trees, aflame. An altar of stone, and in it… And came forth to meet me: my own Faith.

(FAITH enters.)

VOICE: Bring forth the converts.

THOMAS: We did draw together.

VOICE: My children, look behind you. There are all whom ye have reverenced from your youth. Ye deemed them holier than yourselves, and shrank from your own sin, contrasting it with their lives of righteousness. Yet here are they all. Now ye are undeceived. Evil is the nature of mankind. Evil must be your only happiness. Welcome, my children, to the communion of your race!

(FAITH exits.)

THOMAS: Faith! Faith! Look up to Heaven, and resist the wicked one!

(Silence. THOMAS alone with ELIPHALET, in present.)

THOMAS: And I found myself amid calm night. And I did return home.

ELIPHALET: The cat will play and after sleep.

THOMAS: I have not slept. Lest sleep be granted the other one for those who would him serve. What sleep—what earthly sleep might they know—what foretelling of the torments we know in the hereafter?

ELIPHALET: The cat doth sleep and after play.

THOMAS: I do not think the cat's example—

ELIPHALET: I have a cat named Phineas.

THOMAS: If this has been a shadow of that life to come. If I have witnessed one night of the sleep I may hope to know…

ELIPHALET: Pray to God. Love God. Fear God.

THOMAS: Mind your book. Strive to learn.

THOMAS and ELIPHALET: Be not a dunce.

THOMAS: Know thy duty unto God and the mercy in thy—

ELIPHALET: Faith!

THOMAS: Faith.

FAITH: *(Entering.)* Thomas!

THOMAS: Hey! Faith!

ELIPHALET: Call no ill names. Use no ill words. Tell no lies.

FAITH: Oh, thou art returned.

THOMAS: Stay, Faith.

FAITH: Nay, forgive thy wife. Though I would kiss thee in my joy. And bless thee now thou art returned.

THOMAS: Aye, I am.

FAITH: I see.

ELIPHALET: Be not a dunce.

THOMAS: Faith, didst thou… Didst thou look away?

FAITH: I have but looked for thee.

THOMAS: Nay. Hear me, Faith. Thou must say. Didst thou look away?

FAITH: Away from what, Thomas?

THOMAS: Tell me.

FAITH: What thou wilt.

THOMAS: Tell me.

FAITH: What a night hast thou passed! Thou'rt spent.

THOMAS: Nay!

FAITH: I would but pluck these needles from thy coat.

THOMAS: Here. They are gone.

FAITH: What is this book? For the world, it looks like a primer.

THOMAS: It is.

ELIPHALET: This book attend.

FAITH: Dost instruct Eliphalet?

THOMAS: Nay.

FAITH: What—

THOMAS: 'Tis my primer. He brought it me.

FAITH: To what end?

THOMAS: I wished to read it, Faith. It is a book of instruction, perhaps thou shouldst read it thyself.

FAITH: Eliphalet, wilt thou fetch me a basin and draw some water from the well? Thou knowst where to find them? Eliphalet?

THOMAS: Go on.

ELIPHALET: At my house?

FAITH: Nay. Here, in our house. Knowst thou the cabinet?

ELIPHALET: Aye.

FAITH: Wilt thou fetch the water in the basin? From the cabinet.

THOMAS: Go, Eliphalet.

(ELIPHALET exits.)

FAITH: Where hast thou been?

THOMAS: Do not dissemble. Thou knowst full well where I have been.

FAITH: Nay, I do not.

THOMAS: Cease. Thou knowst I did see thee.

FAITH: Where?

THOMAS: In the forest, last night.

FAITH: The forest?

THOMAS: Aye.

FAITH: What would I in the forest?

THOMAS: Faith, cease. I did see thee. Thou didst look in mine eyes.

FAITH: Thomas, I do not know—

THOMAS: I called to thee to look away. To seek in God and cast thine eyes to Heaven.

FAITH: Away from what?

THOMAS: The whole of that wretched company. And to set thy heart on Heaven.

FAITH: Where thou knowst 'tis set.

THOMAS: Yea, so I would believe. Yet thou must hold to thy resolve.

FAITH: And I do.

THOMAS: But didst thou look away?

FAITH: I do not know what thou meanest. I do not know thy errand; I do not ask. But what thou hast seen, or dreamt—

THOMAS: Dreamt?

FAITH: I cannot know.

THOMAS: Didst thou not join me in the wood, meet me in that foul company? Do not the strains of their corrupt anthem linger in thine ears as well?

FAITH: Nay.

THOMAS: Where dost thou say thou wast, last night?

FAITH: I waited for thy return.

THOMAS: Thou didst send me forth.

FAITH: I bade thee stay. And here I waited.

THOMAS: Didst not meet me?

FAITH: I wished thee here, with me.

THOMAS: Thou liest.

FAITH: Nay, Thomas. Though thou bade me go to bed, I watched so long as I was able.

THOMAS: Aye, and then?

FAITH: Then?

THOMAS: Then thou didst meet me.

FAITH: I did not. I watched, until…

THOMAS: Yea?

FAITH: Until I fell to sleep.

THOMAS: Sleep!

FAITH: Aye.

THOMAS: Thou slept?

FAITH: Forgive me.

THOMAS: In sleep, we might… Perhaps… If thou slept. Faith, didst stay by the window, through the night?

FAITH: Aye.

THOMAS: And there thou slept?

FAITH: I did.

THOMAS: And there thou woke?

FAITH: Aye.

THOMAS: Unmoved?

FAITH: Aye.

THOMAS: How long didst thou sleep?

FAITH: I don't know. 'Til the morning.

THOMAS: Even so. Come! Show me.

FAITH: What dost thou seek?

THOMAS: A sign.

FAITH: That I slept?

THOMAS: That they did seize thee.

FAITH: Who?

THOMAS: Dear Faith, innocent of what thou dost, yet in sleep— Nothing! There is nothing here.

FAITH: Nothing occurred.

THOMAS: Thou wast asleep!

FAITH: Aye.

THOMAS: Nothing. No…nothing. Yet still.

FAITH: Oh! Let go my hand.

THOMAS: Give me the other.

FAITH: Wh—

THOMAS: Give it me, Faith.

FAITH: Thomas.

THOMAS: Do not look away. Look at my face. Even so. In sleep. Thy spirit, if not thy form.

FAITH: God looked to my safety.

THOMAS: God! 'Twas God least attended.

FAITH: Thomas.

THOMAS: Faith. Hadst no dream?

FAITH: Nay.

THOMAS: None.

FAITH: I remember none.

THOMAS: No fire, no forest.

FAITH: Thomas?

THOMAS: Goody Cloyse. All the town.

FAITH: Where?

THOMAS: The forest. In thy dream.

FAITH: I had no dream.

THOMAS: Nay. Nay. 'Twas no dream. But thou didst sleep, and thy spirit, without thee… And thou knowst not.

FAITH: Nay, I don't.

THOMAS: Nay, thou dost not. My dear Faith. Forgive me. Forgive me. Forgive me.

(ELIPHALET enters.)

FAITH: I do. For what I know not, but I do.

THOMAS: Nay, thou dost not know. I have dreamt Faith. Such a dream I may not tell thee—'twould fright thee.

FAITH: I think it would.

THOMAS: Yea, and 'tis nothing. A dream. I—I slept in the wood. My long journey. 'Twas a rough night.

FAITH: Come inside, Thomas.

THOMAS: I will. Eliphalet has brought water.

ELIPHALET: I have a basin from the cabinet.

(DEVIL enters. FAITH sees him as SAMUEL; THOMAS sees him as DEVIL.)

DEVIL: Good morrow, neighbors. The prodigal son is returned.

FAITH: Mister Parris.

DEVIL: Thomas?

THOMAS: What wouldst thou?

DEVIL: A greeting from our wanderer.

THOMAS: Have greeted thee already.

DEVIL: That thou hast not. Thou wast missed at worship, and thy Faith and I have spent this morning seeking thee.

FAITH: Aye. Mister Parris spent much of the morning in thy pursuit. While thou dreamst, perhaps.

DEVIL: So we have, and to our shame, if thou slept.

THOMAS: Mister Parris?

DEVIL: And thy servant this morning, enthralled to thy wife.

THOMAS: What dost thou wish, Mister Parris?

DEVIL: But some words with thee, regarding the governor's arrival. He did miss thee at worship, and the deacon thought some counsel might serve for thy meeting him this afternoon.

THOMAS: The governor?

DEVIL: Governor Bradstreet.

THOMAS: Aye, the governor. For the council.

DEVIL: They would not conduct their interviews on the Sabbath, but hope to meet thee nonetheless.

THOMAS: Aye.

FAITH: I will attend thee inside.

THOMAS: Aye, t'would be best.

DEVIL: Thou mightest stay; 'tis no state secret.

THOMAS: Nay, 'twere better thou wot not.

FAITH: I will attend.

THOMAS: Eliphalet?

FAITH: Come, Eliphalet.

DEVIL: Good morrow, Goody Brown.

FAITH: Good morrow, Mister Parris.

(FAITH and ELIPHALET exit to house.)

Scene 4

THOMAS and DEVIL in transport to meeting hall.

DEVIL: Art surprised, Mister Brown?

THOMAS: Disappointed.

DEVIL: A very familiar reply.

THOMAS: Not so familiar. I see thee as thou art.

DEVIL: As pleased to be known as to have thy acquaintance. Thy wife does see thy friend.

THOMAS: Thou must claim shape of Mister Parris?

DEVIL: I claim no shape at all. I have never assumed any shape but mine own.

THOMAS: She did see thee for my friend.

DEVIL: 'Twas her mistake, then. One sees what one chooses to see, Goodman. Why last night, did not thy goodwife Cloyse see thy own grandfather? Certain, that choice was not mine.

THOMAS: I do not know why thou chose to mock me so, yet thy jest did me no injury.

DEVIL: Had it been my jest, thy sober mien might do me one. But trust me, Goodman, I have yet to deceive thee: though I am attributed many powers, I have never seen it necessary to appear but as myself. What thou mayst see is your choice, and I have never sought to make another's choice.

THOMAS: What wouldst thou?

DEVIL: What thou wouldst thyself.

THOMAS: Be gone.

DEVIL: Charity, Mister Brown.

THOMAS: I have kept our appointment, and seen thy company. I wish nothing from thee.

DEVIL: That may be so. Thy Faith slept soundly last night.

THOMAS: And is now waked.

DEVIL: Yet might she sleep again?

THOMAS: I will not stray from her side.

DEVIL: Sure thou'lt not. And may thy resolve be her example.

THOMAS: So I believe it may be.

DEVIL: Would there were no others.

THOMAS: Others?

DEVIL: Examples, Goodman. Counter to thine own.

(They have arrived at the meeting house, into which SAMUEL enters, sweeping. He cannot see or hear THOMAS and DEVIL.)

THOMAS: Certain there may be.

DEVIL: Certain there may. And I do wish thee fortitude. Yet 'tis a mortal blessing, sleep, and one I do commend to thee.

THOMAS: I have not deserved.

DEVIL: And yet thy village has? (Exits.)

Scene 5

Meeting hall.

SAMUEL: Mister Brown! Thou'rt late for meeting. It began some hours ago. And ended since.

THOMAS: I was unable to attend.

SAMUEL: 'Twas noted. But come, I feared thou'rt taken ill.

THOMAS: Not without cause.

SAMUEL: An early morning or a late night?

THOMAS: I have not slept.

SAMUEL: Ah, thou art too laborious. I see that I never forgo my sleep. He gives me sleep and quiet rest—

THOMAS: Whereby my body is refreshed.

SAMUEL: And so it is.

THOMAS: Didst sleep last night?

SAMUEL: Like a kitten. I am sorry thou didst not. There can be but two reasons not to sleep: thou hast prayed to God, or discoursed with the Devil.

THOMAS: Dost say?

SAMUEL: Tell me then: was thine a long or a short conversation?

THOMAS: He had little to say.

SAMUEL: Ever a disappointment, the Devil.

THOMAS: Wouldst know him?

SAMUEL: By his hooves, I should think. The tail. The long nails of his fingers.

THOMAS: Nay…

SAMUEL: Then I might not know him. Come. Sit down, or take up a broom.

THOMAS: Samuel. Dost thou mock the Devil?

SAMUEL: That I do not. I have seen enough of his work to know he is no subject for levity. But perhaps I mock thee, Thomas.

THOMAS: I think thou dost. Dost not believe me?

SAMUEL: That thou hast talked with the Devil? Have not we all?

THOMAS: Have we?

SAMUEL: Certain we have.

THOMAS: Thou?

SAMUEL: More than once. Daily, I might think. And should I miss my own appointment, there is the whole of the village keeps theirs.

THOMAS: Thou mockest me still.

SAMUEL: Sure Thomas, I do not. 'Tis no want of sin in Salem, and I don't doubt the Devil keeps a full calendar. Truly. What is it troubles thee?

THOMAS: How might thou speak so freely?

SAMUEL: Why that sin doth abound, it hath not drowned all goodness. Doth not the sun rise in the morning? Do not our labors bear us harvest? The Devil lives in this very forest, and there is none of us born does not hear his whisper, yet still, do not the people of this village gather for worship, and know their Lord together? Save thee, 'tis true, this once.

THOMAS: How canst thou?

SAMUEL: What do I?

THOMAS: To have seen what thou hast seen. To know what thou must know. To have been witness, but to wake in the morning, and go about thine affairs as if nothing had happened. It is criminal.

SAMUEL: Art certain thou wilt not sit?

THOMAS: Nay.

SAMUEL: What is my crime?

THOMAS: The worst of all. To forget the wickedness of thy life.

SAMUEL: So long as my wickedness will forget me.

THOMAS: T'will not.

SAMUEL: Perhaps I know it too well. Mine is a privileged occupation, Thomas. I have a singular apprehension of the town's vices, for I am of its purveyors of virtue, and confessions are seldom withheld as payment. I am familiar with many secrets.

THOMAS: Thou must divulge them.

SAMUEL: I do not know that I must. Nay, truly. If every goodly soul among us were exposed for its every error, I do not know who would bring in the harvest.

THOMAS: Then thou art touched thyself.

SAMUEL: No doubt. And thee, and all we know. But Thomas, consider: shall we quit our lives, abandon all other responsibilities, allow an ice to fast seize our labors, or our joys?

THOMAS: If we would serve God.

SAMUEL: I cannot serve God and these people if I am dead to the world. And it is not a world of only evil. The Lord did not give us this land and this place in it for us to recoil with horror from either its savagery or its beauty. Wickedness and ugliness could not be if there were no gentleness and beauty—and to deny them would be a betrayal of the God that created them.

THOMAS: It is a betrayal to allow the Devil to set foot in them, and to enjoy them in his company is nothing short of an invitation.

SAMUEL: I have neither the strength nor the arrogance to turn my back on the love of God.

THOMAS: We must show the strength to hate evil and to protect the love of God.

SAMUEL: God needs no protection. It is vanity to think so. Zeal in the service of our own vanity is perhaps more sinful than debauchery.

THOMAS: We must oppose the Devil.

SAMUEL: We may resist temptation to the Devil's ways. I do not think a man is strong enough to oppose him. I am not an angel.

THOMAS: Then our battle is with man.

SAMUEL: How, Thomas? Am I to singly battle each man who gives himself to sin? How great a victory will I then hope for?

THOMAS: It is our duty.

SAMUEL: It is fruitless.

THOMAS: Then we must abandon the sinners to their own device, and be free to live in purity.

SAMUEL: I cannot forsake my vow.

THOMAS: What vow wouldst thou forsake?

SAMUEL: I cannot flee, live alone in the forest—cowardice is no less a vice for the virtues it may preserve.

THOMAS: What courage dost thou pretend, dwelling amongst the corrupt?

SAMUEL: Corruption is not proven until the Judgment is passed. There may be one among our village, perhaps thee, here, living among us, born in sin, yet innocent of all but Adam's stain. If I minister to dissembling sinners, my words fall on deaf ears, yet still these words are uttered. And I am not the one granted right of judgment.

THOMAS: We cannot refuse the witness of our own eyes. To turn from what we plainly see.

SAMUEL: I may not judge it. Am not I a sinner, and most abject, myself?

THOMAS: But thou mayst strive to overcome sin—wheresoever it be found.

SAMUEL: I may. I may strive. And like to a candle's glow in the gloom, I may hope that others will be drawn to goodness, whatever sickness may tempt and thwart them—even—nay, Thomas—even those who have strayed, whom thou mightest call lost. Perhaps, in the strong will of God, tempered by the hard world of this new land, perhaps they may end their union with the Devil and return home to keep covenant with God.

THOMAS: Perhaps thou hast merely dulled thy senses with waiting—

SAMUEL: There is nothing else for me, Thomas. What would thou have me do? Propose that I have lifted the veil of this village that I have known since birth, but only now is it revealed in its monstrosity to me—say I have come, on some dark night, alone in the meeting house, where I have sat, troubled by some few words of the deacon's which I do not recall. Imagine: I sat alone, as the night swallowed this drafty, empty shack—where once austerity and simple ardor filled my heart with light and peace, embracing the simple wisdom of God and His mighty goodness. Here I sat, in the rising darkness, and I did perceive that there was no freedom from wickedness in any of this town—nor in our neighbors to the west, north, all directions. Say it rose on me like the shadows, until I sat surrounded and infused with darkness, and only the sky through the narrow windows, deep and blue, and seeming to glow beyond the blackness of the hall itself—Do not interrupt me—I sat here, watching and recalling the words of the past few days, and I was alone, Thomas. I sat alone. No different from a child with a puppet in an empty house, his parents fled to… My puppet was my belief in these good men, a belief they had given me, like a toy. But here I sat, seeking solace from belief—and while I clutched it to my breast, I remained alone.

THOMAS: Thou hast never spoken…

SAMUEL: Thou hast never asked. Thou'rt not alone. Thy Faith, Thomas—she gives thee the strength to conceive another choice. Thou canst consider whither thou mightest journey. Yet I have no such companion.

THOMAS: 'Tis but a companion.

SAMUEL: It is not true. It is all thou hast in this world. I have maintained such a love for God, and for the strangers who have fallen. It is what I have, and it is empty. But thy wife, thy marriage—

THOMAS: Is nothing—

SAMUEL: It is all there is. It is what we may be, for after the Devil has torn apart our lives, our hopes, what is there left of us but our loves?

THOMAS: Earthly love—

SAMUEL: Is all we have. There is no other duty worthy of man. I have no one, Thomas. But here, among these people, I may still hope for love.

THOMAS: Dost thou love God?

SAMUEL: What dost thou think it means, to love God?

THOMAS: To serve God. To keep covenant. Honor His commandments. To abjure evil.

SAMUEL: But God does not need our love. He does not need our good works. We may only perform them for the hope of one another. I cannot love God alone.

THOMAS: Thou hast no choice. That is God's test.

SAMUEL: Am I so important to the Lord that he might test me so? Then Christ died not for Man, but for Himself.

THOMAS: Thou art not Christ.

SAMUEL: I do not hope to be greater. If I am to live, then I may live in the service He taught. And if I may love only in hope, then I love. Thou hast better than hope, Thomas. Love thy wife. And here among those who have sinned—in thine own sins—be the inspiration that may win this world.

THOMAS: I cannot close my eyes to what I have seen.

SAMUEL: The world has not changed, Thomas. 'Tis only thy perception is altered.

THOMAS: I cannot fail to act on my perception.

SAMUEL: Thou art a good man, Thomas. And thou strivest to be so. But in a very, very small way.

THOMAS: I would be true to God.

SAMUEL: And let us hope God will have thee.

(DEVIL enters. SAMUEL sees him as Deacon Gookin, THOMAS sees him as DEVIL.)

SAMUEL: Mister Gookin. You see Mister Brown has joined us in the event. Is the governor seeking company?

DEVIL: The governor is occupied with Mister Lawson. He may wish to speak later with Mister Brown.

SAMUEL: Thou seest, Mister Brown? The deacon.

THOMAS: I see.

DEVIL: Good day, Mister Brown.

THOMAS: Mister Gookin.

SAMUEL: Mister Brown and I were discussing works, Deacon.

DEVIL: What was your conclusion?

SAMUEL: That in work we may find grace.

DEVIL: An admirable conclusion, Mister Parris, and the model for thy life.

SAMUEL: 'Tis my pursuit, when not my practice.

DEVIL: As the Lord saith.

SAMUEL: Man may but strive when righteousness is wanting and hope to reach salvation.

DEVIL: What says Mister Brown?

SAMUEL: Mister Brown?

DEVIL: Dost thou concur with Mister Parris?

THOMAS: I believe Mister Parris is deceived.

DEVIL: Truly, Mister Brown? Yet Mister Parris has long studied under my tutelage. Thou dost not doubt his teachers.

THOMAS: Nay, 'tis Mister Parris's attention.

SAMUEL: 'Tis no jest, Thomas.

THOMAS: Tis not. Thy thorough inquiry has led thee to the root of all knowledge, Samuel.

DEVIL: Where one might find a snake.

THOMAS: As you say, Deacon.

DEVIL: Mister Parris?

SAMUEL: I am certain Mister Brown does not consider his words.

THOMAS: I am certain my words are ill considered.

DEVIL: By their speaker or their hearer, Mister Brown?

THOMAS: By either, Mister Gookin. But Mister Parris will forgive me.

DEVIL: 'Tis a charitable act, Mister Parris.

SAMUEL: I will do so.

THOMAS: 'Tis thy instruction?

DEVIL: 'Tis Mister Parris's inclination.

THOMAS: 'Tis much to overcome inclination.

DEVIL: 'Tis more than most may hope.

SAMUEL: Through our works, we may redeem our baser instincts and nurture our better.

DEVIL: I do not think so, Mister Parris.

THOMAS: Nor I.

SAMUEL: I will leave ye to discuss the matter at greater length.

DEVIL: Mister Parris?

SAMUEL: Deacon?

DEVIL: Thy broom.

SAMUEL: Thank you. *(Exits.)*

SCENE 6

DEVIL and THOMAS in transport to THOMAS and FAITH's house.

DEVIL: Well reasoned, Goodman.

THOMAS: He does not see.

DEVIL: He sees as well as most. One sees what one wishes.

THOMAS: I don't.

DEVIL: What dost thou see?

THOMAS: Thee.

DEVIL: Thou hast not, then, refuted my observation. While thy friend sees great good in the world.

THOMAS: He will not stand against evil.

DEVIL: Yet neither does he seek it out.

THOMAS: He need not seek it. It doth find him.

DEVIL: And he finds good.

THOMAS: He is deceived.

DEVIL: He does find it in thee. And in thy wife.

THOMAS: He envies me my wife.

DEVIL: Does he? I had not noted. And what does she see?

THOMAS: She was asleep.

DEVIL: But thou didst see her.

THOMAS: She was asleep.

DEVIL: Do wishes sleep? I tell thee, Goodman, I am well enough occupied without soliciting company—I do not make appointments but when I am asked.

THOMAS: She made no appointment with thee.

DEVIL: Nay—not with me. Perhaps he envies thee after all. 'Tis no small thing, to be alone.

(FAITH enters with laundry to fold. She cannot see or hear THOMAS and DEVIL.)

THOMAS: It may be borne.

DEVIL: Yet seldom is it, when one might find a companion.

THOMAS: 'Tis his trial and sin, then.

DEVIL: And trials may be met.

THOMAS: As they must.

DEVIL: If there is no reprieve. *(Exits.)*

SCENE 7

Before THOMAS and FAITH's house.

FAITH: Hast spoken with the governor?

THOMAS: Nay.

FAITH: Oh. He was indisposed?

THOMAS: The governor? He was occupied with Mister Lawson.

FAITH: Ah.

THOMAS: Thou'rt disappointed?

FAITH: For thee. I know thou hast anticipated this day.

THOMAS: Aye, I have.

FAITH: And the governor did intend to meet thee. I spoke with him this morning.

THOMAS: Thou?

FAITH: Aye. After worship, in the company of Mister Parris.

THOMAS: I did not take advantage of the morning.

FAITH: I do not say so.

THOMAS: And yet I did not.

FAITH: Thou didst not.

THOMAS: What is thy opinion of my absence?

FAITH: My…

THOMAS: I was expected this morning, yet I did not arrive.

FAITH: Thou'rt noted in the village, and thou hast seldom missed worship.

THOMAS: Never. I have never missed worship.

FAITH: Nay.

THOMAS: Before today.

FAITH: Aye.

THOMAS: Thou didst note it. Mister Parris and the governor. The whole of the village.

FAITH: I presume—

THOMAS: I know they did. Has been confirmed. By Mister Gookin severely; Mister Parris, lightly.

FAITH: I am sorry for it.

THOMAS: Wast discussed?

FAITH: I heard no discussion.

THOMAS: None?

FAITH: Nay. I doubt not Goody Cloyse remarked.

THOMAS: 'Tis certain.

FAITH: But I heard none else.

THOMAS: What of the governor and Mister Parris?

FAITH: Mister Parris did make thy excuse. I spoke not.

THOMAS: 'Tis a very easy rigor, Mister Parris's.

FAITH: He is a gentle person.

THOMAS: Hast not the resolve, perhaps, to be harder.

FAITH: Have ye disputed, Thomas?

THOMAS: I? With Mister Parris? Nay, no dispute. We do not agree, methinks, but we have had no dispute.

FAITH: Thou speakst unkindly.

THOMAS: Plainly. I speak plainly. Dost trouble thee?

FAITH: 'Tis not thy habit to be so plain.

THOMAS: Hast known me but a year. 'Tis scarce time to learn another's errors, let alone their habits.

FAITH: I am sure thou'rt right.

THOMAS: As am I. E'en this afternoon, I have learned of Mister Parris much I did not suspect.

FAITH: What hast thou learned?

THOMAS: His earthly disposition, I would say. I do not know that he is suited for the ministry.

FAITH: Thinkst not?

THOMAS: I do not. He lacks resolve.

FAITH: 'Tis a grave censure.

THOMAS: 'Tis my observation. Thou'st another opinion, I would think?

FAITH: I?

THOMAS: Thou.

FAITH: I am not so familiar with him as thou.

THOMAS: Yet hast thou thine own opinion?

FAITH: I will trust to thine.

THOMAS: Nonsense. 'Tis mine opinion; thou hast thine own.

FAITH: I…suppose I do.

THOMAS: Yea?

FAITH: I have but seen that he has devoted himself to this village, and sought to be of council and guidance to its people as best he may.

THOMAS: So?

FAITH: Aye. If thou wilt.

THOMAS: He does his best. And he speaks as well of thee.

FAITH: And of thee, Thomas.

THOMAS: Past doubt. And I am the subject of many conversations, today.

FAITH: Yea.

THOMAS: Spoke thee long with Mister Parris?

FAITH: He did accompany me from the village.

THOMAS: Because I was not there. Yet thou didst go.

FAITH: I thought it best.

THOMAS: Was it?

FAITH: I met the governor.

THOMAS: And Mister Parris. What did ye discuss?

FAITH: Thy appointment to the council.

THOMAS: My appointment? 'Tis not certain.

FAITH: Nay, 'tis not.

THOMAS: Thou'rt vexed?

FAITH: I know not why thou'rt contrary, today—why thou wert distract this morning, nor why thou hast not met the governor.

THOMAS: Dost rebuke me?

FAITH: Nay, Thomas. Yet for thine own sake, thou dost perhaps squander thine opportunity.

THOMAS: My appointment.

FAITH: Aye.

THOMAS: For 'tis important to be represented in the council. For Salem to have some influence in Boston.

FAITH: Is it not?

THOMAS: I do not doubt it is. As Mister Parris might have said this very morning.

FAITH: Aye.

THOMAS: When the village did miss me.

FAITH: Aye.

THOMAS: And Mister Parris did accompany thee home.

FAITH: He did accompany me from the hall.

THOMAS: I do not wish thee any further discourse with Mister Parris. Dost hear?

FAITH: Aye.

THOMAS: Dost agree?

FAITH: I'll do as thou dost wish.

THOMAS: What of thy wish?

FAITH: I have none that would oppose thine.

THOMAS: I know 'tis not so.

FAITH: But 'tis, Thomas.

THOMAS: Thou'ldst see Mister Parris.

FAITH: Not if thou forbiddest.

THOMAS: I do.

FAITH: Yea.

THOMAS: Thou'ldst have me join the council.

FAITH: For thy reward.

THOMAS: And thine?

FAITH: For thine. I know not mine.

THOMAS: 'Tis a station. An honor.

FAITH: To thee.

THOMAS: And to my wife.

FAITH: 'Tis my hardship.

THOMAS: How?

FAITH: I will miss thee when thou'rt gone to Boston.

THOMAS: Wilt thou?

FAITH: As I missed thee last night.

THOMAS: As last night.

FAITH: Aye.

THOMAS: As thou slept.

FAITH: And dreamt of thee.

THOMAS: And woke to Mister Parris? Methought thou hadst no dream.

FAITH: To Mister Parris?

THOMAS: Where is thy ribbon, Faith?

FAITH: My ribbon?

THOMAS: Thy pink ribbon. Thou dost wear, most often.

FAITH: I know not.

THOMAS: Didst wear it last night?

FAITH: I know not.

THOMAS: Thou didst.

FAITH: I'll seek it out.

THOMAS: Wilt not find it.

FAITH: I will seek.

THOMAS: 'Tis too late. I have loved thee, Faith.

FAITH: And I thee.

THOMAS: Thou'st not.

FAITH: But I have.

THOMAS: Hast failed, Faith. Hast failed. Hast failed.

(GOVERNOR, SAMUEL, and CLOYSE enter.)

SAMUEL: Thomas!

GOVERNOR: Mister Brown, God be with thee, thy wife, and thy home. And years of prosperous labor in His service.

THOMAS: W'ye, Governor.

FAITH: God be with you and your visit to the village, your commerce with us, and your good works, Governor.

GOVERNOR: Bless thee, Goody Brown.

THOMAS: Aye.

FAITH: We trust your journey was no hardship.

GOVERNOR: Every journey is a trial, but every trial may be met with a virtue, and at the end of every journey lies an opportunity. I find it true and commend the observation to ye. My journey to Salem was not uneventful: we did crack the spoke of one of the carriage wheels. A trouble, but here an opportunity to know better the value of an even and rounded discipline. A wheel is a routine laborer, whose duty is but to revolve smoothly and with determined strength over the varied terrain it encounters. The stronger its staves, the firmer its rim. The less daunted by the stones, ruts, and fords it must cross. Still, in this repeated and rigorous discipline, the wheel makes our progress possible, bearing gold, or governors. The Word of God and the material of affairs, too—supported and carried forth by this humble duty. Our carriage wheel broke encountering a deeper trough than anticipated by our driver, and an old wheel it had been. And yet our driver, a good neighbor from this village, knew the value of a wheel, and with a fellow from a neighboring farm did take on to replace it. These two worked with the same familiar discipline, in concert, as the wheel and axel had before. And so to our lives. Their regular fraternity and well-borne skills did make our journey still near timely and herein

this trial was the confirmation of a good principle. An opportunity, ye will forgive my saying, to revolve the matter of discipline. Our journey, then, was not so hard, not with this profit gained from this mishap.

FAITH: Thank you, Governor.

THOMAS: I have taken a journey

GOVERNOR: Excellent. We will have much to speak of.

THOMAS: I have seen a wheel broken.

GOVERNOR: 'Tis a common affliction.

THOMAS: I have not seen it repaired.

GOVERNOR: Thy journey was cut short.

THOMAS: Nay, 'twas too long. Governor—I cannot meet with you.

SAMUEL: Thomas, it is the appointment to the council.

THOMAS: Yea, I know it is. I cannot take this appointment.

SAMUEL: The village, Thomas.

THOMAS: Aye, the village. I will not serve to represent this village to the council.

GOVERNOR: 'Tis the Sabbath, Mister Brown, and not a day for affairs; but neither is it a day for whimsy.

THOMAS: Well said, Governor. I am in agreement.

SAMUEL: Why wouldst thou not?

THOMAS: I am not fit.

SAMUEL: Certain thou art.

THOMAS: Nay, I am not. Not fit to this village.

SAMUEL: I know no one fitter. 'Tis an opportunity unmatched.

THOMAS: Yea, that it is. 'Twas this—the reason?

FAITH: What reason, Thomas?

THOMAS: Dost thou not know?

FAITH: What dost thou ask?

THOMAS: I cannot.

SAMUEL: But Thomas. The council of selectmen has named thee particularly. Surely they do not take it lightly, this appointment. And in respect of thee, thy family—

THOMAS: My family? What dost thou know of my family, Samuel?

SAMUEL: What good report is heard by all.

THOMAS: Is it? Good report? Of my father, and his father? Of their diligence? Their devotion?

FAITH: Of course, Thomas.

THOMAS: I do not know my father, nor what to make of his acts.

FAITH: Thomas.

THOMAS: Nor thee, nor thee. Governor, you have my respectful regret.

GOVERNOR: Though we have not yet made an offer, Mister Brown, I would know why thou art so inclined.

THOMAS: My wife, Governor, does wear ribbons.

GOVERNOR: Sir?

THOMAS: My wife, as you see before you. She wears ribbons in her hair.

GOVERNOR: I see she does.

THOMAS: Is it not immodest?

GOVERNOR: In one less comely, perhaps they would suit less well. As it is, she may be forgiven.

THOMAS: I do not think it so.

CLOYSE: Thomas, 'tis not a fit subject.

THOMAS: As thou would venture prove? My wife does often wear them, yet I would ask her this. Where is thy ribbon, Faith?

FAITH: My—

THOMAS: Thy other ribbon?

SAMUEL: Thou needst no ribbon, Thomas.

FAITH: I do not know.

THOMAS: Nay, thou must know.

FAITH: I don't. It fell, perhaps.

THOMAS: When?

FAITH: This morning. I sought thee.

THOMAS: In the night?

FAITH: Perhaps.

THOMAS: Didst wear it this morning?

FAITH: I think I did.

THOMAS: To worship.

FAITH: I think so.

THOMAS: Samuel?

SAMUEL: I don't recall. I do not think so.

THOMAS: Governor?

GOVERNOR: I did not note it.

THOMAS: Goody Cloyse, surely you?

CLOYSE: Impertinence!

THOMAS: Then you noted it not?

SAMUEL: We will find it, Thomas.

THOMAS: Will ye?

SAMUEL: We will.

THOMAS: Aye. I am certain ye will. Though ye did not note. Yet I noted, Governor—Goody—Sir. I noted and will not soon forget. I cannot serve on your council, Mister Bradstreet, for my wife cannot find her ribbon. And you understand me not, yet these my fellows will understand too well. If you seek an explanation, look to them. I will no more say. *(Exits.)*

ACT II
SCENE 8

THOMAS alone in woods. Ribbon falls from the sky. THOMAS stoops to pick it up. ELIPHALET enters.

ELIPHALET: Thomas. Thomas. Thomas. Thomas. Stop, now. Peace, now. Peace.

THOMAS: Oh, thou manikin.

ELIPHALET: Stop now. Peace.

(BRIDGET enters.)

ELIPHALET: Peace!

BRIDGET: Mister Brown...

ELIPHALET: Peace. Stop now. Stop now. Stop now. Stop now.

BRIDGET: I have stopped, Eliphalet.

ELIPHALET: Stop now.

BRIDGET: Eliph—

ELIPHALET: Stop now.

THOMAS: 'Tis no—

ELIPHALET: Stop now.

THOMAS: In Ad—

ELIPHALET: Stop now. Peace.

THOMAS: Peace.

BRIDGET: Peace. You have an unusual command over my nephew, Mister Brown.

THOMAS: 'Twould seem he has discovered the antidote.

BRIDGET: Aye, so it does.

THOMAS: Forgive me, Mistress Bishop, for my intrusion on the affairs of your household—

BRIDGET: Affairs of my household? What household is that, Mister Brown? My tavern?

ELIPHALET: Peace, now.

BRIDGET: Aye, Eli. Thou knowst my household. Nay, Mister Brown. You have not intruded in our affairs. My house is built for intruders, and our fire has yet to cast a shadow by you.

THOMAS: I meant—

BRIDGET: I know what you meant, Mister Brown. When my sister and her husband died, you may believe I hoped I might profit from their worldly possession. As it came to pass, I learned of it only when the one thing that survived the fire was brought me by your friend Mister Parris. You do not think I was pleased by the gift.

THOMAS: I know you have seen after his well-being and instructed him as best you are able.

BRIDGET: Slander, Mister Brown. You know well I have not. He is my sister's child, and I have taken him under my roof. You have seen after his well-being. You have instructed him. If I stopped to think of it, I would wonder why.

THOMAS: I am certain—

BRIDGET: I do not stop to think of it. You need not tell me why. But I do thank you, Mister Brown.

ELIPHALET: Peace, Thomas.

BRIDGET: Do you come often into the woods?

THOMAS: Not often.

BRIDGET: You do not know them, then. I can never cease to be surprised by the forest. It is a bit like this boy. Undisciplined. Impenetrable. Dangerous.

THOMAS: I do not think Eliphalet is dangerous.

BRIDGET: Oh, who knows what hides in him! Nay, Mister Brown, 'tis my jest. But there are as few who see the beauty in the forest as see a beauty in my nephew. I see the one; you see the other.

THOMAS: There is, as you well know, evil in the forest.

BRIDGET: And here you are.

THOMAS: I sought to be alone.

BRIDGET: As you wish. But I do not know that there is evil in the forest. There are Indians. Animals. Solitude. Are these things evil?

THOMAS: Will you, too, pretend?

BRIDGET: I pretend very little. There is evil in deception. In judgment and punishment. In theft. But these are characters of the village, do not you think? They have no place in the forest. It asks nothing and has never failed to welcome anyone who will come to it. Our ancestors. You or I. Or Eliphalet. We are all very much the same in the woods.

THOMAS: I do not believe that we are the same.

BRIDGET: In my house, we are.

THOMAS: God tells us we are not.

BRIDGET: I have never spoken with God. But I have spoken with many others. Some have seen Him; some have not. Yet to me, they are themselves very like.

THOMAS: I do not think I will put my faith in those who come to your house.

BRIDGET: Would you be disagreeable? Mister Brown, a jest. You are too humorous. I do not take offense so easily as you might wish. Yet, I will tell you that your father was not so grave.

THOMAS: I do not think you were familiar with my father.

BRIDGET: You may think what you wish. But were you to ask him, he would tell you differently.

THOMAS: My father was an honest and industrious man. He did not have time for the diversions of your house.

BRIDGET: Nor for walks in the woods, I am sorry to say. But his industry did permit him some leisure. And you are quite right. He was an honest man. And he was dedicated to this village. He was a fighter in King Philip's war who stood by his fellows 'gainst the Indians and a friend to those who stood behind him. You are not unlike him, Thomas, but you are less practical.

THOMAS: I do not believe you knew my father.

BRIDGET: And every bit as obstinate. Nay, I would say he was my friend. And one who did not seek to make so many enemies as his son.

THOMAS: I would not make enemies, Mistress Bishop. I would know my friends.

BRIDGET: Are you not surrounded by them?

THOMAS: I grow to see I am not.

ELIPHALET: Have communion with few, be intimate with one, deal justly with all, speak evil of none.

BRIDGET: There is one.

THOMAS: Aye. There is one.

BRIDGET: Eli, what colors are the leaves?

ELIPHALET: In spring the leaves begin to grow
Till summer comes to turn them green.
Then autumn paints them red and yellow
Till winter strikes them from the trees.
Do not look for new leaves then,
Till spring will bring them back again.

BRIDGET: 'Twas the best I ever managed. We have all sought friends, Thomas. One must simply know where to look.

ELIPHALET: I have a cat named Phineas.

BRIDGET: Dear thing. He doesn't have a cat. (*Leaning to kiss him, she freezes.*)

ELIPHALET: Thomas. Dost thou think thyself virtuous, now? Oh, be not so surprised. What didst thou expect from a witch?

THOMAS: Who art thou?

ELIPHALET: Thy old friend, of course. Whom didst thou expect? Thomas, thou art duller than two stones in the creek. Whom didst thou seek in the wood?

THOMAS: I sought to be alone.

ELIPHALET: Thou art not alone. Thou wast not brought into the world to be alone. Thou didst not take up th'instruction of this boy to be alone.

THOMAS: Let him be.

ELIPHALET: To be certain I have. He is pursuing his cat.

THOMAS: Eliphalet!

ELIPHALET: Oh, folly. Attend, young Goodman Brown. What dost thou seek in this child? Thy generosity and patronage. Whom wouldst thou instruct? Whom dost thou heal? What good does it for this boy to learn your alphabet? Will he write a primer for his children? A sermon for young Mister Parris? A letter to thy wife?

THOMAS: Cease!

ELIPHALET: But how dost thou serve him, Thomas? What is thy purpose?

THOMAS: He has sought to learn.

ELIPHALET: He has sought thy praise.

THOMAS: He has no need of my praise. He has delighted in his achievement.

ELIPHALET: Thou hast delighted to think so.

THOMAS: I have seen his joy.

ELIPHALET: What place has joy in the work of God?

THOMAS: 'Tis the sole joy for which we may strive.

ELIPHALET: 'Tis thine.

THOMAS: 'Twas joy we shared.

ELIPHALET: I am thy friend.

THOMAS: He is my friend.

ELIPHALET: Then do not flatter thyself thou art alone.

BRIDGET: (*Returning to life.*) I think he says it to keep from feeling lonely.

THOMAS: 'Tis not flattery.

BRIDGET: How dost thou flatter me?

THOMAS: Nay, not thee.

ELIPHALET: Whales in the sea God's voice obey.

THOMAS: Wilt mock me?

ELIPHALET: Thomas.

THOMAS: Speak not in this foolish tongue!

BRIDGET: Thomas?

THOMAS: Appear as thou art.

ELIPHALET: In Adam's—

THOMAS: Come forth.

BRIDGET: Mister Brown.

ELIPHALET: I have a cat named Phineas.

THOMAS: What would you?

BRIDGET: I had enjoyed our conversation, here in the wood.

THOMAS: Why art thou in this wood?

BRIDGET: It has always brought me peace. As it did seem to, you.

THOMAS: Nay. It did not.

(CLOYSE enters.)

CLOYSE: Thomas, thou hast been impertinent before the governor and this town.

THOMAS: Thou, too?

CLOYSE: Are there others, young Mister Brown? I doubt not thou art shamed to be seen so openly.

THOMAS: But 'tis thine, the shame.

BRIDGET: Nay, not shamed.

THOMAS: Not thou. Yon goodwife.

BRIDGET: Thou dost jest after all.

CLOYSE: This behavior does not suit a child, Thomas. It is disgraceful in thee.

ELIPHALET: The moon gives light in time of night.

THOMAS: 'Tis but to learn.

BRIDGET: Come, Mister Brown. Sit by me.

CLOYSE: Thou wouldst not take instruction.

THOMAS: I did try.

BRIDGET: There is always much to learn.

THOMAS: Not from thy knowledge.

CLOYSE: Whose dost thou prefer, Thomas Brown?

THOMAS: Nay, Goody. I spoke not to thee.

BRIDGET: Oh, call me not goody. I keep a tavern, Mister Brown.

CLOYSE: To whom, then? Thy wanderings serve thee no purpose.

BRIDGET: Bridget is my only name.

THOMAS: I am seeking—

BRIDGET: Wilt not thou sit?

CLOYSE: Wandering! Wilt not pay attention?

THOMAS: I cannot.

BRIDGET: 'Twould give thee rest.

ELIPHALET: He gives me sleep and quiet rest, whereby my body is refreshed.

THOMAS: Not now, Eliphalet.

CLOYSE: Thomas.

THOMAS: He has been my friend.

(SAMUEL enters.)

SAMUEL: Here thou art. The governor will attend thee.

THOMAS: Whom?

CLOYSE: Whom?

BRIDGET: Thou hast many friends.

SAMUEL: The governor. Why must we repeat ourselves, Thomas?

THOMAS: Why art thou here, Samuel?

CLOYSE: Thomas, attend me! A wise son maketh a glad father, but a foolish son is the heaviness of his mother.

THOMAS: Thou art not my mother.

BRIDGET: I do not think so.

SAMUEL: Come, Thomas. Be not so frivolous.

CLOYSE: Seest thou a man wise in his own conceit, there is more hope of a fool than of him.

SAMUEL: Thou must prepare for thine interview. 'Tis the village depends on thee.

THOMAS: I cannot be depended upon.

SAMUEL: To be certain thou canst, Thomas. If not thee, then who may be?

CLOYSE: Our weakness and inabilities break not the bond of our duties.

BRIDGET: I have no expectation of thee, Thomas.

THOMAS: Ye cannot look to me for your support. I do not understand what ye wish. I do not know thy language. I am not thy fellow. I have only my faith to guide me. I have only my faith to guide me.

FAITH'S VOICE: Thomas? Dost thou call me?

SAMUEL: 'Tis thy Faith, Thomas. She gives thee thy strength.

FAITH'S VOICE: Thomas, I have waited for thee. Wilt thou not come?

CLOYSE: Come along, Thomas. We must return to the governor.

BRIDGET: Thomas, wilt thou come with me?

DEVIL'S VOICE: Mister Brown?

SAMUEL: Come back now, we have little time.

FAITH'S VOICE: Thomas—

THOMAS: Get thee from me!

(ALL freeze but THOMAS. DEVIL enters as Barnabus Scratch. THOMAS does not look at him.)

DEVIL: Mister Brown? Mister Brown? Do I find thee at prayer?

(ALL exit but THOMAS and DEVIL.)

THOMAS: I do not know.

DEVIL: A man must know his prayers. Else they may not be heard.

THOMAS: Art thou yet returned?

DEVIL: Am I? Have we met, Mister Brown?

THOMAS: Thou knowst well we have.

DEVIL: I do not know when that may have been. Sir, I see you are distract. I came to seek Goodman Thomas Brown. If you are he, look full on my face, and you will, I think, recognize that you and I have never met.

THOMAS: I beg your pardon. I was deceived.

DEVIL: I grant what pardon is mine to give. And I fear for the man you thought I was, for his reception will not be cordial. Thou art Goodman Thomas Brown?

THOMAS: I am.

DEVIL: Honored to make thine acquaintance, Goodman. I am assistant to the governor, Barnabus Scratch.

THOMAS: I apolo—

DEVIL: Please accept my apologies for my delay in coming to thee. When we venture forth from the Bay, my occupation trebles in business. Though the governor never seems to perceive it but by my absence and so upbraids me on my return.

THOMAS: I am certain the demands of the journey are consuming.

DEVIL: So they are, and the demands of the people. Do not doubt that I make a singular point of meeting the townspeople wherever we may go. Not merely selectmen and ministers—though bless them for their industry and devoted guidance—but husbandmen like thyself. Freemen and their wives, the tavern keepers, schoolmasters, farmers…

THOMAS: Praiseworthy industry.

DEVIL: Thank'ee, Mister Brown. Not all see my occupation so evenly. I have met with Indians as well—their pow-wows in the forest are not strangers to me any more than the members of the Great and General Court.

THOMAS: Are they not?

DEVIL: Thou thinkst I boast of my influence.

THOMAS: I am a husbandman, and I have little concern with the councils or the Indians.

DEVIL: True enough. It has been so. True. Perhaps that may change.

THOMAS: 'Tis not likely, now, I think.

DEVIL: Oh, we cannot live our lives alone, however our freedoms may tempt us. But 'tis good to know our fellows, dost thou not think so?

THOMAS: I would pursue a faithful life in service to my God. I cannot change my fellows.

DEVIL: Canst not? But our service to our neighbors is service, too.

THOMAS: We serve the faithful, and in our service may hope to be an example to those who…

DEVIL: Lack faith?

THOMAS: If we may.

DEVIL: And so I could not meet thee yesterday—we are ministers to saints and sinners alike.

THOMAS: Our duty to the one is different from our duty to the other.

DEVIL: Is it so? Then we must tell them apart.

THOMAS: I have found they are revealed.

DEVIL: Ah! I have found the reverse! Not a virtuous freeman but has some cloistered vice, not so wretched a sinner but harbors some secret virtue.

THOMAS: Then we may still have commerce with the virtue and hope to impress goodness on the thirst for vice.

DEVIL: And yet, Mister Brown, I have seen them closely, tightly bound. So one may not be said to live without the other. And so they may not, dwelling so often within the bosom of one man. Consider the zeal of our Puritan fathers, whose daily regimen and devoted striving did build this village in a wild and brutal land. Here they might dwell in peace together. Imagine! Such vision, such fortitude. To live together, devoted to one another, and close to their God. And where else, indeed? For this was surely God's unperverted creation. This was virtue, I think, virtue made visible. Yet virtue does not go untested—that is the Devil's design—and we know He is relentless.

THOMAS: Aye.

DEVIL: Thou knowst He is. For know that this had been the Devil's land. He had lived free in these woods, and in these undefended souls that take human form and cry their savage cries in the forest.

THOMAS: He is known in this wood.

DEVIL: But hear, then, how these men were tried—thy father, and mine? Have I not read the accounts myself? Of a Quaker woman, lashed in the streets to her certain death? With what fervor did her attackers swing their flails? Art troubled?

THOMAS: I have heard of such an incident.

DEVIL: Ah, they are legion! They must be, in this frontier. A virtuous cause—the scourge of a disease for the health of a village—I do not doubt it. But, I am drawn to reflect on the passion. Dost know this passion, Mister Brown? Is it the energetic and lively embrace of a Godly cause that lent such insistence to their blows? Or was it something else—lent by the dark spirit who claimed this land long before these Godly men arrived to pursue their good life? The feverish and lusty vigor that meting out punishment for weakness and ignorance in our Quaker goodwife might arouse? Thou dost not know this sentiment, I think, Mister Brown. Thou'rt young and studied, and I would doubt hast witnessed such a transformation. Set on a course of righteousness, how vulnerable may a man be to the whispers of the Devil, and how might an undiscovered sympathy find itself awakened. It is an easy thing to take the Devil's walking stick when one is in a hurry. How came we to this pass? Ah—'twas this, and perhaps thou'lt find the same relief I do—I do not trust myself to know a man by his virtue or his vice—not so readily. Not until I have known him a very long time. For I see that one may as easily take the semblance of the other—like twins—and only on some acquaintance can they be told apart. And so, on our visit to the villages and byways, I do try to know the many who inhabit here, without regard to the appearance. If we serve sinner and saint, granted in different capacities, I find the service I may offer is the same.

THOMAS: You have a subtle understanding.

DEVIL: One might say. Or a gross solution. It is an efficient one, and I meet many I might not otherwise know.

THOMAS: The governor must esteem your service.

DEVIL: The governor? Why, the governor does not always see the worth in my acquaintances. Governance is also a trial requiring gross solutions. There is not so much time for ambiguity or misunderstanding, even if one may be led to hasty judgment.

THOMAS: Judgment in the cause of right is worthy.

DEVIL: More than worthy. It is imperative. But we must know what we see.

THOMAS: God reveals.

DEVIL: Over time. But we must base our judgments on what we have seen. And that, Mister Brown, is my inspiration to seek thee. The governor has some concerns following thy interview this afternoon. I believe he has judged too readily.

THOMAS: I do not think so.

DEVIL: Admirable humility, but I think he has.

THOMAS: I do not believe I can speak with him.

DEVIL: Dost thou not wish to? Art thou ill disposed to the offer thou knowst he came to make?

THOMAS: Yea, I am.

DEVIL: Then perhaps he is correct. He is concerned, nigh convinced, that thou art ill suited to the position.

THOMAS: No doubt I am ill suited. It does not suit me well.

DEVIL: Aye, so I see. 'Tis regrettable. Thy perspicacity, as I mark it, might well assist in this new council, wert thou so inclined. A keen eye and a true resolve are much in demand.

THOMAS: There are better representatives than I.

DEVIL: Many are representative. Few are worthy to represent. Yet on thy capacities, thou'rt the only authority. Still, I might ask what feeds thy conviction, Mister Brown.

THOMAS: A…discovery, of late.

DEVIL: Forgive my intrusion, but I have understood that thou hast had some open dispute with thy wife. Nay, pause, Goodman. Thou needst not tell me that a wife can be an exasperation.

THOMAS: I do not intend to.

DEVIL: Not at all. She is, I have gathered, an excellent companion and a model of devotion, who wears her affection for thee like the ribbons in her hair.

THOMAS: She does not always wear them.

DEVIL: Dost thou think her affection wanes?

THOMAS: I…cannot be concerned with attachments.

DEVIL: Oh, be not so sure! Why, the love of a young, pretty wife, may seem vain to thee—vain as are her ribbons—

THOMAS: Perhaps we need not speak of Faith.

DEVIL: Do we? Thy wife! Faith. Hah! I would say not—but for this: Thou mayst find her and her affection vain, worldly perhaps, and frivolous. I would counsel thee otherwise: the loving embrace of a woman may give a man strength in returning that love. Man is a fleshly creature, however he may hope for deliverance—and we have but the means of the flesh at our hands to persist in the physical world. So thy wife is frivolous, naïve, an innocent subject to whim and temper, and thou mayst find thyself subject to the same.

THOMAS: I am not sure of thy import.

DEVIL: It is a simple and a familiar one. Old as the oldest stories of the Great Fall. Do not let thy passions—even for that which appears right—cloud thy sight. Ambition, curiosity, avarice, lust—they are all but exaggerations of earthly good. Devotion, perception, industry, love. Any good may be corrupted.

THOMAS: Good is only corrupted. It is the Devil's sole intent.

DEVIL: Has He no other?

THOMAS: Other?

DEVIL: Is the Devil so singly bent? To have but one purpose in this world?

THOMAS: His means are many, but they serve one end.

DEVIL: The corruption of the faithful.

THOMAS: The embrace of His own.

DEVIL: And He will claim what is rightfully His.

THOMAS: In this land, and among these people.

DEVIL: Then I wonder if His design is corruption at all. Needn't He but reveal?

THOMAS: His is a test of mettle—and through temptations and provocations are exposed the Devil's.

DEVIL: And the Lord's?

THOMAS: Where they may be found.

DEVIL: The Devil and the Lord would know their own.

THOMAS: They would try.

DEVIL: Are they so alone?

THOMAS: Alone?

DEVIL: 'Tis no small thing to be alone in this world, Mister Brown. And is not the Devil? Thou'rt gravely affected.

THOMAS: I cannot think lightly of the soul.

DEVIL: Perhaps thou hast seen such trials thyself?

THOMAS: I have.

DEVIL: And seen failure?

THOMAS: I have.

DEVIL: And been so tried thyself.

THOMAS: I am certain I have.

DEVIL: And tis for that thou shouldst meet the governor. 'Tis rare, Mister Brown, to find a man of conviction. A man of discernment. A man of spirit. Such a man may stand alone, but such a man may lead a people. Such a man may change a world, if he be willing to look the Devil in the eye and defy Him. The governor dwells in Boston, but the dominion extends farther each day. He does not know the villages. He is not one of these people. He hath need of a good man in his stead. 'Tis a disappointment ye are both disinclined to meet one another. But, I see the opportunity must pass.

THOMAS: Nay, perhaps. If the governor would, I might meet with him.

DEVIL: Nay, Goodman, I did not choose my time propitiously.

THOMAS: Please.

DEVIL: Thou'lt forgive me, Goodman, but thou hast not seemed composed to do so.

THOMAS: I have… I do confess, I have felt tried, of late, and it has weighed unduly upon me. Yet I would meet the governor.

DEVIL: I will attempt what I might, and it may be so. 'Tis his inclination, now, must be weighed. Yet I will try what I can do. Let us meet in the common one hour from now. I will bring thee word. For the while, Mister Brown, I am glad we could find the time together.

THOMAS: Thank you.

(THOMAS exits. DEVIL remains as scene changes to:)

SCENE 9

Before the meeting hall. GOVERNOR, FAITH, SAMUEL, CLOYSE, together, and THOMAS separately, enter to DEVIL.

DEVIL: Mister Brown! As thou seest, the governor would not rely on his messenger, but has come himself. I have told the governor we had an opportunity to speak earlier, and he has been good enough to allow that your earlier absence may have bred a misunderstanding.

GOVERNOR: Aye. Misunderstanding is the word. Goodman Brown, though our acquaintance may be brief, I do believe that it is in want of acquaintance that misunderstanding may too easily breed. And indeed, no misunderstanding should obscure our true appreciation of opportunity when it presents itself.

DEVIL: I have also encouraged these, your friends, to accompany us, that thou mayst know there are no misgivings in the village as to the matter at hand. And if thou art prepared, let us return to the hall and join the council of selectmen.

THOMAS: I thank you, and you, Governor, for I was something distracted yesterday, and I welcome the opportunity to speak to a point now. I had hoped I might speak with the governor privately, though I am grateful for the concern of my friends.

DEVIL: Is there any matter demands privacy?

GOVERNOR: Certain there is no disease we might not best treat in the open air. Is it not so, Mister Brown? That any subject, be it not sinful, is best known in the light of day under the eyes of God and witnessed by His children?

THOMAS: Be it so, I would pray one word, Governor, in private.

DEVIL: I do not know there is such time to take. The council waits, and we have made delay of our return to Boston already for this purpose.

THOMAS: I must speak with the governor alone.

DEVIL: Let us to the hall. We may speak inside.

THOMAS: I must speak here, privately. Forgive me, Governor, you will see my urgency.

DEVIL: Mister Brown—

SAMUEL: Thomas—surely there is nothing we may not share as well.

CLOYSE: Thomas Brown, thou art impertinent before the governor.

THOMAS: Sayest thou? Governor, it is impertinence I would speak of, but not mine own save in confession.

CLOYSE: The governor is not thy confessor.

SAMUEL: Governor, Mister Scratch. Let me speak for a moment with Mister Brown. We will join ye in the hall.

THOMAS: We will not. I have no words but for the governor.

GOVERNOR: Mister Brown, I have no ear for thee. If thou hast to say, speak it to these people, your friends. Else we must return to Boston as Mister Scratch recalls. And if we are not to have accomplished our purpose here in Salem, then I have much else to do I had not before expected.

THOMAS: I cannot—nay, Governor. I must speak with thee alone.

GOVERNOR: I will not speak with thee alone.

SAMUEL: Thomas—

CLOYSE: Obstinacy.

DEVIL: Mister Brown—

(ELIPHALET enters, followed by BRIDGET.)

BRIDGET: Eliphalet!

GOVERNOR: What is this?

BRIDGET: Eliphalet.

ELIPHALET: Thomas.

THOMAS: Eliphalet, go home.

ELIPHALET: Thomas caught a witch!

THOMAS: Peace, Eliphalet.

GOVERNOR: Mister Brown, is this your charge?

CLOYSE: Goodman Brown has taken on to instruct the incapable.

THOMAS: Eliphalet, come here.

BRIDGET: Forgive me, Governor. He started off before I could stop him.

ELIPHALET: Thomas Brown caught a witch.

GOVERNOR: Remove him.

BRIDGET: Eliphalet, come.

ELIPHALET: Thomas caught a witch.

THOMAS: Come away.

ELIPHALET: A witch, a witch, a witch—

THOMAS: Hush.

ELIPHALET: A witch, a witch, a witch—

GOVERNOR: Mister Brown—

DEVIL: Eliphalet. Look here. Thou mayst take this.

(DEVIL hands ELIPHALET a bible. ELIPHALET calms.)

CLOYSE: Mister Scratch! He will only tear the pages.

BRIDGET: You musn't—

DEVIL: Take it. If Mister Brown has been instructing him, no doubt he is a lover of books.

CLOYSE: An act of the Lord.

BRIDGET: I do apologize.

THOMAS: Thank you.

GOVERNOR: What is this?

BRIDGET: My nephew, Governor.

DEVIL: Mistress Bishop, your honor. Our hostess at the tavern, should we stay the night.

GOVERNOR: We will not stay the night, Mister Scratch.

DEVIL: Not if we may proceed.

BRIDGET: I apologize again.

GOVERNOR: Nay, 'tis not thy interruption, Mistress Bishop, but Mister Brown. Mister Brown—thou hast been instructing this boy.

THOMAS: As I might, your honor.

GOVERNOR: How might thou?

THOMAS: I have taught him much of his catechism, his alphabet—

GOVERNOR: Does he read?

THOMAS: He recognizes portions, and recalls what he can.

GOVERNOR: But he does not read.

THOMAS: No.

GOVERNOR: With due consideration for Mistress Bishop, he has learned a trick.

THOMAS: He has improved—

GOVERNOR: A dog may improve.

ELIPHALET: I have a cat named Phineas.

BRIDGET: Hush.

GOVERNOR: Forgive me, but, Mister Brown, my misgivings are not eased by our further acquaintance. That the Lord may visit upon a child such affliction may not be seen but as a punishment. Commerce with him is of doubtful virtue itself, and yet we must bear our burdens as they come, and Mistress Bishop, may there be some blessing on thee for taking this on thyself. But to fly in the face of the Lord, and squander the gifts He has given thee on one He has deprived of capability—it is no idle pursuit, Mister Brown. That thou showst such behavior to me is ill advised, perhaps. But how dost thou explain such use of the Lord?

THOMAS: Governor, this boy, however burdened he may be, has suffered misfortune. I cannot believe him, above all, to be damned.

CLOYSE: No one may be sure of his salvation.

THOMAS: As you taught me, Goody Cloyse. But Eliphalet has grown to know his catechism, in his limited way. And I have seen him learn such virtues, small enough for the man he appears, but great for the child he is. He has learned patience, loyalty, discipline, and kindness.

CLOYSE: He bit me.

THOMAS: You provoked him.

CLOYSE: I sought thee at the governor's behest.

THOMAS: He was frightened.

GOVERNOR: Didst thou witness this attack?

THOMAS: I was near.

CLOYSE: Why didst thou not come?

ELIPHALET: Thomas caught a witch.

BRIDGET: Eli.

GOVERNOR: What does he mean by that?

THOMAS: May we speak alone, your honor?

DEVIL: Mister Brown—

CLOYSE: Folly!

GOVERNOR: Nay, Mister Brown. We may not. Thou hast squandered my time and that of the council. Thou hast idled in the training of an imbecile; set him, perhaps, on this goodwoman; hidden, it appears, when she sought thee—and for no reason thou wilt own; and

openly disputed, though I know not why, with thy wife. We may not speak privately, nor at all. For I am returning to the council now to resolve the matter of the inclusion of this village in representation to the Court.

CLOYSE: Let the council recommend to you, Governor, Mister Barnes, whom I had suggested when first the appointment arose.

DEVIL: We may consider Ipswich, Governor…

BRIDGET: Eliphalet, come here.

ELIPHALET: The cat will play and after sleep. The dog will bite a thief at night.

GOVERNOR: May we return by way of Beverly, and send post ahead that the council there may consider appointment?

DEVIL: 'Tis the other direction, Governor.

SAMUEL: Thomas, what has thou—

THOMAS: Goody Cloyse is a witch. Goody Cloyse is a witch.

GOVERNOR: Really, Mister Brown!

THOMAS: She is a servant of the Devil. As well she knows. As does the council, and thou, Mistress Bishop, and Mister Parris. Governor, I assure you that this woman is a familiar of the blackest covens, in which she is joined at night with her fellows from across the dominion, and Indian pow-wows, wildmen from the forest and I know not where, and by sundry members of this our village.

GOVERNOR: The village of Salem?

THOMAS: Aye, Governor.

GOVERNOR: And the people with whom thou dost share thy communion and livelihood?

THOMAS: Aye.

GOVERNOR: They are, thou wouldst say, witches, Mister Brown.

THOMAS: Aye.

GOVERNOR: Whom, Mister Brown?

THOMAS: All.

GOVERNOR: All? The entire village?

THOMAS: Yea, all of them.

GOVERNOR: The minister? Deacon Gookin?

THOMAS: All.

GOVERNOR: And these present—they know this truth?

THOMAS: Aye.

GOVERNOR: How so, Mister Brown?

THOMAS: They meet together.

GOVERNOR: Mistress Bishop and Mister Parris?

THOMAS: Aye.

GOVERNOR: This?

THOMAS: I do not know that he is one of them.

GOVERNOR: He is spared?

THOMAS: I do not know.

GOVERNOR: But the others throughout the town, save thee, Mister Brown?

THOMAS: Aye.

GOVERNOR: And thy wife?

THOMAS: I do not know.

CLOYSE: Shame.

GOVERNOR: Attend, Goody Cloyse. This is no small accusation. 'Twas thy intention to tell me this privately, now?

THOMAS: Aye, your honor.

GOVERNOR: How long hast thou suspected? Mister Brown, when didst thou learn of this conspiracy?

THOMAS: 'Tis a truth I witnessed.

GOVERNOR: What didst thou witness?

THOMAS: Their meeting.

GOVERNOR: When?

THOMAS: Two nights past.

GOVERNOR: Where?

THOMAS: In the forest.

GOVERNOR: Here?

THOMAS: Nay, deeper into the wood.

GOVERNOR: Deeper? How far?

THOMAS: I cannot say—I flew so—some twenty miles. Farther than we might walk before nightfall.

GOVERNOR: Yet thou didst walk it that night.

THOMAS: I walked back in the morning.

GOVERNOR: How didst thou arrive there?

THOMAS: I was assisted.

GOVERNOR: Assisted?

THOMAS: I had the help of…

GOVERNOR: Mister Brown, what was thy errand to the wood at night?

THOMAS: I had appointed to meet the Devil.

CLOYSE: Be with ye.

FAITH: Thomas.

SAMUEL: Bless thee, Thomas.

ELIPHALET: Thomas caught a witch.

GOVERNOR: Attend, please. The Devil?

THOMAS: I had.

GOVERNOR: And he did assist thee to travel these many leagues, on foot.

THOMAS: By use of his staff.

GOVERNOR: And when thou reached the appointed place there, thou didst witness the people of this town, with this boy and thy wife possibly excepted.

THOMAS: They drew her to communion.

GOVERNOR: Communion!

THOMAS: Aye.

GOVERNOR: An extraordinary vision.

THOMAS: I will not forget it.

GOVERNOR: And did she take this communion?

THOMAS: I did not see. I did enjoin her to look to God, to turn away. I do not know what she did.

GOVERNOR: What didst thou do?

THOMAS: I did look to the Lord.

GOVERNOR: And?

THOMAS: I did return home.

GOVERNOR: And the others?

THOMAS: They were no longer there.

GOVERNOR: Mister Brown, I have read the Reverend Mather's *Memorable Providences*, and he is a friend of mine. We have taken the opportunity to discuss the witch, Martha Glover, and the Goodwin children, bless their souls and their time on earth. This village has been visited by its share of afflictions. And not one citizen need be told it. Nor am I unfamiliar with the duress and trial of life in our villages. But we must pray for strength, Mister Brown, and we must not give in to susceptibilities of our imagination.

THOMAS: We must not yield to the Devil.

GOVERNOR: Unquestionably. We have a duty in this land to set a shining example of the Godly life.

THOMAS: Yet we do not—

GOVERNOR: We are but sinners striving in the world to know God's grace.

THOMAS: This village lives a deception.

GOVERNOR: Be certain what thou hast seen, Goodman Brown. We battle in the unseen world. But we may do so with that which God chooses to reveal.

THOMAS: And I have seen it revealed.

GOVERNOR: Hast thou? Thou hast made an appointment with the Devil, and set into the wood. And art thou certain what thou hast seen?

THOMAS: I have witnessed.

GOVERNOR: Be not too eager, Goodman. What is the Devil? Where is he? Does he stand by thy side when thou blasphemest? Does he take the reins when thou ridest from town? Hast thou seen him?

THOMAS: I have seen him. I have walked beside him.

GOVERNOR: Hast thou? Walked with him? And here thou standst to tell me the tale?

THOMAS: I have walked with the Devil, your honor.

GOVERNOR: Goodman! Raise thy head. Look into the world. Look around thee, and see thy fellows, and the common sites thou knowst. Dwell here, and not in thy dreams. Do not tell me thou hast walked with the Devil. We are but sinners one and all, but the Lord is mighty, and the Lord will come, and we may hope for

mercy as our lot may be. But the Devil is in us, and we may cast him out. And there is an end.

THOMAS: I do not understand you.

GOVERNOR: I tell thee, Mister Brown, thou hast not walked with the Devil. No more than I stand with him now.

THOMAS: I—

GOVERNOR: What is the Devil? If he is not of us, but among us—what is he that he should have such power? Why is he not in the stocks?

THOMAS: The stocks? He is the Devil.

GOVERNOR: Aye? But thou hast walked beside him. Come now. The Devil is in thine ill thinking, thy lustful heart, thy covetous regard. He is in the degraded opinion thou ownst of thy neighbors. And for the Devil in any one of us, we may find the pillory ourselves. But we will not find a living, breathing, walking Devil. That is the talk of children.

ELIPHALET: Thomas caught—

THOMAS: Your honor, I confess.

GOVERNOR: And sin will out. We know it will out. But what thou confessest, young Mister Brown, is a nightmare, born no doubt of thy ill thoughts, deserving of recognition and cleansing. Sure thy fellows will hear thee at next meeting. But more thou hast not done. Why, hadst thou walked with the Devil, in any but thine imagination, then I have spent many an hour with him in my garden.

DEVIL: But these are state secrets…

GOVERNOR: So they are.

THOMAS: So he said.

GOVERNOR: Thy Devil.

THOMAS: Aye.

GOVERNOR: Yea, thou seest, here, in the light of the day, which brings such an easing peace to a troubled night, thou seest in this light all the Devils thou wilt know.

THOMAS: I see them. They are here. In Goody Cloyse, and Mistress Bishop, and Mister Parris. There, by your side, Governor. I knew when first he arrived. My wife—I heard them—it is not an unseen world—that which God will reveal, He has revealed. If I be the one who may see and be yet untouched, 'tis my faith has been my guide and shelter.

GOVERNOR: Find thy temper, Mister Brown!

THOMAS: You, Governor—Did I see you as well?

DEVIL: Mister Brown!

CLOYSE: Shame!

THOMAS: Did he not tell me he, and the members of the Court?

ELIPHALET: Thomas—

THOMAS: Do not the councils and the selectmen of diverse towns make him their chairman?

FAITH: Peace, Thomas.

THOMAS: Do not touch me. What did you?

BRIDGET: Mister Brown!

THOMAS: What was your choice? Did you take their communion, or did you take the Lord?

FAITH: Thomas—

THOMAS: When all had gone, you were not there. We were not left together— What did you do?

GOVERNOR: Thy wife, Mister Brown! Some moderation!

THOMAS: Moderation is the Devil's poison. I have watched this moderate town and its duplicitous brood, in the guise of purity. Mistress Cloyse taught me my catechism. Mister Parris, thou hast claimed me as thy friend, spoken to me of hope. What was thy hope?

ELIPHALET: Thomas.

THOMAS: Quiet, Eliphalet. You know the Reverend Cotton Mather, Governor. You know his works, the Goodwin children, snatched from the bewitchment of Martha Glover, and why was she hanged? What was her error? That she did openly, or clumsily, let herself through those babes be known? And now in the reverend's home. What awaits them there?

ELIPHALET: Thomas.

THOMAS: Does he, too, know the vices of Satan? Whose ear does he not whisper?

GOVERNOR: The Reverend Mister Mather—

ELIPHALET: Thomas.

GOVERNOR: Whose reverence—

ELIPHALET: Thomas.

GOVERNOR: Quiet, thou idiot!

BRIDGET: Eliphalet!

ELIPHALET: In Adam's fall—

THOMAS: Do not speak, witch!

ELIPHALET: We sinned all.

FAITH: Thomas, be calm.

THOMAS: And thou. Did it take but this year to find thine own? And thou?

SAMUEL: My friend.

GOVERNOR: Hold him.

THOMAS: Stand away.

DEVIL: Mister Brown.

GOVERNOR: Mister Brown, thou wilt be brought before the council.

THOMAS: The council is not my judge!

GOVERNOR: And placed in the stocks for this outburst.

THOMAS: Thou wilt be hanged!

SAMUEL: Come, Thomas.

THOMAS: I will not.

FAITH: Thomas, please—

ELIPHALET: Thomas caught a witch, Thomas caught a witch, Thomas caught a witch—

THOMAS: Silence!

(THOMAS strikes ELIPHALET. Silence. A low laugh, beginning with the GOVERNOR, spreads among BRIDGET, SAMUEL, and CLOYSE. As their laughter grows, these FOUR exit. The DEVIL exits separately. THOMAS looks at FAITH. FAITH crosses to ELIPHALET. She does not look at THOMAS until the end of his speech.)

THOMAS: Last Sunday…not two nights ago…last. I took a walk. I walked into the forest. Eliphalet came with me, some distance, but he turned back, and I strode on deeper than I had gone before. I believe it may reach over one-quarter, one-half the earth, this wood. Perhaps to climb to Heaven. Or down. I do not know. 'Tis not quiet, the forest. There is a continual whisper of the trees, of animals, and birds. I half sought an Indian or some wildman, though I saw none. Instead, I came to a cliff, looking down onto a valley, and beyond the wood reached farther still. I sat. 'Tis beyond me to say, Faith, how magnificent it seemed. To be in this deep wood, warmed by the sun. 'Tis beautiful, this creation, and I did not think it belonged to the Devil. Nor did I think on God. I did not wish to return to the village. Even ever.

I wished instead that thou wast with me. That I might share this deep and beautiful wood, and this time in it, with thee. That we might, together, know it. And I felt quite bereft, to look on this work of nature, to wish to meet it, to know it, to reply to it, and yet, I could not. Not alone. And I wished thee there, with me.

(FAITH, comforting ELIPHALET, extends her hand to THOMAS. He takes her hand.)

(End of Play.)

BARTLEBY THE SCRIVENER

A Story of Wall Street

Adapted from the story by Herman Melville

R. L. Lane

R. L. LANE is a writer and director currently living in New York City. He began his career teaching theatre at Stanford and MIT. In 1984 he founded the award-winning New Repertory Theatre outside Boston, where he served as producing artistic director for twelve years and directed more than thirty professional productions. As a writer, he has received fellowships from the Yaddo Corporation and Lark Play Development Center in New York. *Bartleby the Scrivener* was first presented at the Edinburgh Festival and transferred to London (Red Shift Theatre) after a tour of the UK. It premiered in New York at the Blue Heron Theatre. Other plays by Lane include *Van Gogh in Japan* (Nora Theatre, Boston) and *The Supper at Emmaus*.

The American premiere of *Bartleby the Scrivener* was presented by Blue Heron Theatre (Ardelle Striker, Producing Artistic Director, and Karyn Seltzer, Associate Producer) on November 6, 2005, at Blue Heron Arts Center, New York City, with the following cast and credits:

Standard .... Gerry Bamman
Fairchild .... Christian Haines
Turkey .... Sterling Coyne
Nippers .... Brian Linden
Ginger Nut .... Hunter Gilmore
Bartleby .... Marco Quaglia
Landlord/Keeper .... Jeff Burchfield
Grub Man .... Robert Grossman

Directed by: Alessandro Fabrizi
Scenic and Lighting Design: Harry Feiner
Costume Design: Dennis Ballard
Sound Design: David Margolin Lawson
Assistant Director: Susan Main
Press Representative: Jim Baldassare
Production Stage Manager: Sarah Ford
Technical Director: Jessica Lynn Hinkle
Assistant Stage Manager: Nicole Forgoston

Bartleby the Scrivener was first presented at the Edinburgh Festival and in London by Red Shift Theatre.

CHARACTERS

STANDARD: a prosperous attorney in his sixties.
BARTLEBY: an impoverished scrivener.
TURKEY: a scrivener in his sixties. British accent.
NIPPERS: a scrivener in his twenties.
GINGER NUT: an office boy, twelve.
FAIRCHILD: an attorney in his twenties.
LANDLORD: owner of 12 Wall Street.
KEEPER: gatekeeper of the prison.
GRUB MAN: purveyor of food to prisoners.

SETTING AND PRODUCTION NOTES

A bare playing area. A few furniture pieces (desks, stools, chairs) can suggest Standard's law office. Along the upstage side of the office runs an imaginary hallway, along the downstage side an imaginary street. All windows and doors referred to in the text are imagined. From scene 17 on, no furniture pieces are required.

The music referred to is of a hurdy-gurdy or calliope, perhaps heard distantly, evoking a strange and wistful America of the 1850s.

Standard's speeches to the audience should communicate great urgency, a compelling need to clarify and explain.

With doubling, the play can be performed by seven actors. There is no intermission.

1.

A city clock chiming in darkness. Joined by a solo violin, playing a driving, ragged melody. Cacophony: ten seconds. Sound stops. Light rises on BARTLEBY: a pale, thin, motionless man in a threadbare suit. Silence. Then from the shadows, a wry, sad laugh. STANDARD steps into light, a Wall Street lawyer in his sixties: prosperous, well dressed, in a fine dark coat and top hat, with gloves and a cane. With a wild gesture toward BARTLEBY, STANDARD leans in toward us and, in a hushed, urgent voice, speaks:

STANDARD: Yes—like that! Stand like that for hours! Nothing moved him! No activity stirred him! No hope quickened that pale gray eye! Law copyists—scriveners, we called them. I've known hundreds of them professionally, privately. I could tell stories to make you good-natured gentlemen laugh…you sentimental souls weep. But no. I waive them all to relate a few passages in the life of Bartleby, who was a scrivener, the strangest I ever saw or heard of!

(Bright music begins here. Light fades on BARTLEBY. STANDARD steps forward.)

STANDARD: "The easiest way of life is the best!" Always I'd held to that conviction. "The easiest…the best." And in a snug office at number twelve Wall Street, I did a very tidy business among rich men's mortgages, title deeds, bonds. Never addressed a jury. Never drew down public applause. Suffered nothing to invade my peace. Well. Not so many years ago…

2.

A burst of thunder. Gusts of wind. Evening: a clock chimes six. Light brightens on STANDARD's office. STANDARD enters and takes his place at his desk. He is placing papers in a black leather briefcase. FAIRCHILD, a young lawyer, hurries in.

FAIRCHILD: Mr. Standard—! Glad to find you in, sir—! The Board of Governors voted this afternoon. They've named you Master of Chancery for the State of New York. Here's the letter, sir. Congratulations!

STANDARD: *(Pleased. Putting papers in briefcase.)* Would've thought I was too old. And too old-fashioned… Well!

FAIRCHILD: On no, sir. Not a bit. The Board took special note of your experience. It's well known you do a brisk business here, sir, shuffling rich men's title deeds. Thirty years among the great ones: Astor, Vanderbilt, Morgan. The great men's esteem for you is well known, sir. Your care…prudence… You are a very *safe* man, sir, don't mind my saying. *(Slight pause.)* Handsome salary, sir.

STANDARD: *(Reading letter.)* Yes…

FAIRCHILD: Duties not arduous…

STANDARD: No.

FAIRCHILD: Then you'll accept, of course, won't you sir? Let me be the first to congratulate you. Mrs. Standard will be proud!

STANDARD: I'm a bachelor, Fairchild.

FAIRCHILD: Of course, sir. That explains your marvelous equanimity.

STANDARD: *(Musing.)* Have to hire another scrivener, I suppose, extra copying and all. *(Abruptly.)* Thank you, Fairchild. Tell them I'll send my acceptance letter over in the morning.

FAIRCHILD: Very good, sir. Are you walking up Broadway, sir? It's storming out. An honor to share my umbrella…

STANDARD: I have my own.

FAIRCHILD: Ha ha! Ever prepared, sir! Ever thoughtful! Ever *safe!*

(Burst of thunder. FAIRCHILD, laughing eagerly, hurries out. STANDARD turns front.)

3.

Lights have brightened. A clock strikes eight. Now TURKEY has entered: a portly, untidy, energetic Englishman of sixty.

TURKEY: Good morning sir. And many congratulations on your *elevation.*

STANDARD: Ahh, Turkey, good morning. Thank you.

TURKEY: *(Removing his coat.)* Lovely morning it is, too, sir, after our recent precipitations—

STANDARD: Indeed, Turkey. A special morning. Changes in the air. I wished to speak to you. Before the other scriveners arrived.

TURKEY: Speak, sir? To me?

STANDARD: Yes. Turkey. We will be receiving more copying work. More will be required of you. I must speak to you about your *afternoons.*

TURKEY: Afternoons, sir? With submission, I am at a loss.

STANDARD: Turkey, in the mornings you're a model of industry. No man ever wrote fairer copy—

(TURKEY bows deeply.)

STANDARD: But Turkey: each day after luncheon, your face blazes. You exude the odor of cheap beer. Turkey: changes are afoot with the new Chancery work. Now that you're growing old, why not abridge your afternoon labors. After luncheon, why not go home and rest till tea time?

TURKEY: Home, sir, in the *afternoons?* Sir, I resist the suggestion! With submission, sir, if my services are useful in the mornings, are they not indispensable in the afternoons?

STANDARD: Turkey—

TURKEY: *(Overlapping.)* In the morning, sir, I but marshal and deploy my columns. But in the afternoons, I put myself at their head and *(Rising, gesturing with his ruler.)* gallantly charge the foe—*thus!*

(Slight pause.)

STANDARD: Yes, Turkey, but the blots—!

TURKEY: With submission, sir, behold these hairs. I am getting old. Old age—even if it blot the page—is honorable. With submission, sir, we *both* are getting old!

NIPPERS: Morning, sir. Congratulations.

(NIPPERS has entered: a grim, sallow, whiskered man of twenty-five. Seating himself at his desk, he begins to write with much hissing, teeth-grinding, whispering.)

STANDARD: Thank you, Nippers. Changes are afoot. More will be asked of you. I must speak to you about your *mornings.* Your nervousness, your irritability…

(Abruptly, NIPPERS rises, stoops over the desk, spreads his arms wide, seizes the table, moves it, jerks at it with a grim grinding motion on the floor, reseats himself.)

STANDARD: Are you listening, Nippers?

NIPPERS: *(Seating himself, grinning irritably.)* Yes sir. But desk too high, sir. Cramps the circulation. *(Abruptly rises again, hissing violently, and kneels on the floor, adjusting chips of wood under table legs.)*

STANDARD: Still not satisfied, Nippers?

NIPPERS: *(Grinning irritably.)* Desk too *low*, sir. Gives me the backache.

STANDARD: The truth is, Nippers, you know not what you want!

GINGER NUT: Morning, sir!

(GINGER NUT, a boy of twelve, has hurried in. STANDARD taps desk with ruler. TURKEY, NIPPERS, and GINGER NUT rise and face him.)

STANDARD: Ginger Nut. Gentlemen. Now that all are assembled, attend please. Gentlemen: great changes are afoot. Great changes. There'll be extra copying. There'll be a new copyist. Applicants arriving throughout the day. Nippers, you'll behave with courtesy at all times.

(NIPPERS grunts assent.)

STANDARD: Ginger Nut. You'll be punctual and attentive.

GINGER NUT: Punctual, sir. Attentive.

STANDARD: And Turkey, you'll set the highest standards of *industry*. Do I make myself clear, gentlemen?

TURKEY: Clear sir, luminous. Changes are afoot. We are ready. We are prepared! Let 'em come, sir. *Battalions* of 'em!

(Light shifts. Music plays softly. Seated closely together, the THREE begin to compare copy. TURKEY reads from master copy. NIPPERS and GINGER NUT check and correct copies. TURKEY reads floridly, brandishing papers, dropping some, mopping his brow; NIPPERS grinds teeth, hisses, shifts in chair. GINGER NUT eats an apple, swings his legs. Occasionally they halt while one makes a correction. Scratching of pens. Droning of voices. STANDARD watches, then turns front.)

STANDARD: *(To audience.)* He arrived one hot summer afternoon, as if from nowhere. He stood for some time outside the door to my chambers.

(BARTLEBY has appeared dimly at the edge of the playing area. He stands motionless. The copy checking is drawing to an end. GINGER NUT rises.)

TURKEY: And now, our labors complete, a spritzer, Ginger Nut, I am parched.

GINGER NUT: Yes sir—

NIPPERS: And me—

(GINGER NUT darts toward the door. He halts as BARTLEBY looms motionless in the doorway. A pause. BARTLEBY says something to GINGER NUT. GINGER NUT reenters the office. BARTLEBY does not move throughout the following.)

GINGER NUT: There's a man, sir, outside the door.

TURKEY: *(Shuffling papers.)* Yes? Man? What sort of a man, Ginger Nut?

GINGER NUT: Standing by the door, sir, still as stone.

TURKEY: *(Shuffling papers.)* Yes? Describe this man, Ginger Nut. Specificity is the soul of the law. Corpulent and practical? Lean and witty? Is it one of Nippers's creditors come to collect? Tell him he may wait till the crack of doom and never find Mr. Nippers in, ha ha!

GINGER NUT: He is very proper, sir. But pale.

TURKEY: Pale? Send him away—we want no pale men here!

GINGER NUT: Pale as paper, sir. Asked if Mr. Standard was in.

TURKEY: In? The Master is in. You may tell him so. The Master is in!

GINGER NUT: I'll tell him, sir. *(Darts toward the door. Something causes him to halt. He falls back a step.)*

STANDARD: *(To audience.)* He stood without moving in the open doorway, calm, neat, pitiably forlorn!

(A pause. NIPPERS looks up from his writing and stares at BARTLEBY. TURKEY, seeing BARTLEBY, stiffens. Momentary pause.)

TURKEY: *(Stiffly.)* Good afternoon, sir. These are the law chambers of Mr. Standard, Master of Chancery. How may we serve you?

(BARTLEBY does not answer.)

TURKEY: I ask, sir, how may we serve you? *(To GINGER NUT, after a moment.)* He *talks*, don't he?

GINGER NUT: Yes, sir, talked outside.

TURKEY: Talked outside, eh? *(To BARTLEBY, emphatically.)* Allow me to *repeat* myself. This is the law chambers of the Master of Chancery. I am his prime assistant, Horatio to his Hamlet, his strong right hand. Allow me to be of service, sir. Speak! *(With exaggerated gestures.)* HOW MAY WE SERVE YOU?!

(A pause. BARTLEBY speaks in a clear, thin voice.)

BARTLEBY: I am here to see the proprietor.

TURKEY: Ahh! Speaks at last! He wishes to see "The Proprietor!" Ginger Nut! Is the proprietor in?

GINGER NUT: He's in, sir.

TURKEY: *(Turning to BARTLEBY.)* There you have it, sir. The proprietor is in. *(Deep bow.)* May we *further* serve you?

(A pause.)

BARTLEBY: I have come about the copying position.

TURKEY: Oh ho! The light shines ever brighter! The copying position! Now—if I might ask, sir, your name…?

BARTLEBY: Bartleby.

TURKEY: At last! Revelation follows upon revelation! Nothing is concealed! Quickly, Ginger Nut. Run to Mr. Standard. Tell him a copyist wishes an interview. Tell him the copyist's name is Mr. Bartleby!

STANDARD: *(To audience.)* Never had I seen a face so pale, as if no spot of sunlight had ever touched that cheek, that chalky brow. Even his eyes were pale! He stood without moving before my great mahogany desk.

(STANDARD enters the office. BARTLEBY stands motionless before the desk.)

STANDARD: You have no letter of reference, Mr. Bartleby? And no sample of your hand?

(Slight pause.)

STANDARD: Well then, would you compose a sample for me now? Ginger Nut! Some paper, a pen! Sit down, Mr. Bartleby. Copy from this. Just these few lines.

(BARTLEBY sits. GINGER NUT scurries in with paper and pen. BARTLEBY begins to copy.)

STANDARD: *(To audience.)* His hand flew like wind across the page, yet with an indescribable calm! When he had completed his lines, he laid his pen to rest and sat still. *(Studying the page.)* Well. Your hand is neat and swift. You seem a quiet fellow, and respectable. You've no evil habits, I assume. I'm willing to hire you at the going rate, that is, four cents per one hundred

words. Hours are eight in the morning to six at night, half-day Saturday. These terms acceptable? Hmm? *(Expansive.)* Well then! Let me introduce you to your new colleagues. Turkey!

TURKEY: *(Rises from his desk. Deep, oriental bow.)* Much delighted, Mr. Bartleby. You'll enjoy your labors in these offices, sir—none better. Many gratifications…much to learn and do—

STANDARD: *(Cutting him off.)* And Nippers…

(NIPPERS half-rises, nods abruptly.)

STANDARD: And Ginger Nut.

GINGER NUT: Afternoon, sir, and pleased to meet you. If you want refreshments, sir, I'm your boy: apples, spritzers, pies, confections—

STANDARD: *(Cutting him off.)* You'll begin tomorrow morning, Mr. Bartleby?

BARTLEBY: I would prefer… *(Slight pause.)* …to begin at once.

(A pause.)

STANDARD: At once? You mean, this afternoon?

TURKEY: Oblige him, sir, oblige him! Here is *devotion*, sir, here is *industry*!

(The light has faded. Music plays.)

4.

Light on STANDARD.

STANDARD: *(To audience.)* He did an extraordinary amount of copying those first few days, as though famished for something to copy! He seemed to gorge himself on documents with no pause for digestion. He copied by sunlight and candlelight. Yet he wrote silently, palely, mechanically…

(The office brightens. BARTLEBY stands beside STANDARD's desk. STANDARD is reviewing papers. TURKEY and NIPPERS watch furtively while copying.)

STANDARD: *(To BARTLEBY.)* Your work is exemplary, Bartleby, your manner quiet and dignified. But you trouble me. You write without energy or cheer. Are you not happy here?

BARTLEBY: I am not unhappy.

STANDARD: Is there something you lack for?

BARTLEBY: No, I lack for nothing.

STANDARD: You're quite sure of this?

BARTLEBY: Yes, I am quite sure.

STANDARD: Then, you're pleased with your new situation?

BARTLEBY: I am not unpleased.

STANDARD: Well— Why then, I'm pleased too! In fact, Bartleby, I wish your colleagues would take a lesson from you. Turkey! See how orderly he is, and not obstreperous. And you, Nippers: note how his disposition is mild. How he's content with the height of his desk. Learn from him. Make him your model. *Copy* from Bartleby, and I daresay we'll all prosper here!

(STANDARD applauds genially. The OTHERS join in.)

5.

Lights shift. GINGER NUT's offstage shout rings out.

GINGER NUT: *(Offstage.)* Make way, gentlemen…make way…make way!

(Light brightens. GINGER NUT clambers down the hall and into the office carrying a high, three-paneled folding screen. TURKEY, NIPPERS, and BARTLEBY gather to watch as STANDARD directs.)

STANDARD: *(Gesturing.)* By my desk there, Ginger Nut…closer…closer…closer still… *There!*

(GINGER NUT places the screen. STANDARD adjusts it and steps back.)

STANDARD: Thank you, Ginger Nut. Now. *(Turning to address the OTHERS.)* Gentlemen. As you know, I'm most pleased with Bartleby's work. In less than a month, he's made himself indispensable here! In view of his success, I've come to a decision. I wish to work more closely with him: to have him directly at my side… *(Chuckling.)* …as close to me as my own shadow! Now. See here, Bartleby. I've devised an arrangement that I think'll serve very well. *(Moving about, gesturing enthusiastically.)* This screen'll be your new office. You'll work behind it privately, undisturbed. But when I want you—for any reason—you'll be within my whispering. My slightest murmur will bring you forth! Well, what d'you think? Splendid, eh?

(Pause. BARTLEBY gazes at the screen, vanishes behind it. ALL watch and wait.)

TURKEY: He shall be an anchorite in his little *private hermitage!*

NIPPERS: Do what he pleases, eh, behind there?

STANDARD: *(Calling.)* Come, Bartleby. Give us your thoughts!

TURKEY: Oh, he'll enjoy it sir, his own little hermitage!

NIPPERS: Put his feet up on the desk, count the hours!

STANDARD: Ah yes. I think this'll do quite well, very well!

GINGER NUT: I'd be happy back there, Bartleby, no one watching *me!*

(STANDARD chuckles brightly. The OTHERS exchange glances. Lights change. STANDARD faces front.)

STANDARD: *(To audience.)* And so we proceeded for several weeks. And then…one bright morning…

6.

A clock strikes ten. Bright morning sun floods the office. The dry, hurried scratching of pens. STANDARD, TURKEY, and NIPPERS write steadily at their desks. TURKEY's pen breaks.

TURKEY: Oh Lord! Oh dear Lord!

STANDARD: *(As he writes, evenly.)* What's the trouble, Turkey? Please don't dally. There's much to do.

TURKEY: Nib sir. Completely split. Effects of haste, sir, and *diligence!*

STANDARD: Well, please don't linger. The deeds must be filed by noon. Ginger Nut, please give these to Nippers. Tell him to be quick.

(ALL work silently for a moment.)

TURKEY: With submission, sir, are both copies to have the seal or just the one?

STANDARD: Both, Turkey. And include a copy of the probate clerk's report.

TURKEY: And the appendices sir? Where might they be?

STANDARD: Those would be in the possession of Mr. Bartleby.

TURKEY: *(Starting to rise.)* Shall I fetch them?

STANDARD: No no. I'll call him. (*Leaning toward screen.*) Bartleby? Come here please. I have a question for you, please come at once.

(*Pause. ALL work steadily for a moment.*)

STANDARD: (*Calls again.*) Bartleby. Please come now. Ginger Nut—please tell Mr. Bartleby I wish to see him.

GINGER NUT: Yes sir. (*Stands beside BARTLEBY's screen. He calls.*) Mr. Bartleby: Mr. Standard wishes to see you.

STANDARD: (*Sorting papers.*) Please tell him he's needed to verify copy.

GINGER NUT: You're needed to verify copy.

STANDARD: And tell him now, please.

GINGER NUT: Now, please.

STANDARD: And bring the commissioner's report.

GINGER NUT: And bring the commissioner's report. (*Remains standing beside the screen. A pause. No answer.*)

STANDARD: (*To GINGER NUT.*) Well…? Is he coming?

(*Slight pause.*)

STANDARD: Well? (*Looks up.*)

(*GINGER NUT peeks behind the screen.*)

GINGER NUT: Don't seem to be, sir.

STANDARD: Well, what's he say?

GINGER NUT: Don't say anything, sir.

STANDARD: (*Exasperated.*) What's he doing?

GINGER NUT: Copying, sir.

STANDARD: Copying?

GINGER NUT: Sir. Copying. Like a *fiend.*

(*Pause. All activity in the office has ceased.*)

STANDARD: Bartleby. What are you doing?

(*Pause.*)

STANDARD: Can you hear me, Bartleby?

(*Pause.*)

STANDARD: I'm asking you to leave off copying for the moment. Please come now. Help us examine a document that must be delivered to the Customs House by noon. No time to waste, Bartleby. Do you hear?

(*Pause.*)

STANDARD: (*To GINGER NUT.*) I wonder, does he hear?

GINGER NUT: I think so, sir. I hear.

TURKEY: (*Delicately.*) With submission, sir, I believe he *does* hear, for I hear you and I am at a greater remove than he.

(*Pause.*)

STANDARD: I'm sure you hear me, Bartleby. Why don't you come when I ask?

(*Slight pause.*)

STANDARD: Bartleby?

(*Slight pause.*)

STANDARD: Confound it, Bartleby! What the devil's keeping you?

(*A pause. A chair leg scrapes the floor. BARTLEBY emerges from behind the screen.*)

BARTLEBY: (*Mild voice.*) Yes? What is wanted?

STANDARD: Thank you, Bartleby. We're about to examine copy to be done by noon. Take your place please. We've lost precious time already. We're ready to compare copy. Turkey? Nippers? Ready?

TURKEY: (*Rattling papers, bowing.*) At your service, sir!

STANDARD: We'll begin then.

(*BARTLEBY remains motionless.*)

STANDARD: Bartleby? Come here please. Take your place.

(*The OTHERS watch. BARTLEBY does not stir.*)

STANDARD: I say, Bartleby, what *is* it with you today? Take your place please. Do it now.

(*A pause. BARTLEBY turns and vanishes behind his screen.*)

STANDARD: (*Aghast.*) Bartleby. What is this? Are you mad? Why do you walk away when I address you? Come out of there. Come out at once.

(A chair leg scrapes the floor. BARTLEBY emerges from behind the screen.)

BARTLEBY: *(Mildly.)* Yes? What is wanted now?

STANDARD: Bartleby. Your behavior is very surprising! I'm asking you to examine copy. Take these papers. Take them now, please!

(STANDARD thrusts a handful of papers beneath BARTLEBY's nose. He shakes them vigorously. Pause.)

BARTLEBY: *(Almost inaudible.)* I would prefer not to.

STANDARD: *(Uncomprehending.)* What's that, Bartleby? What'd you say?

BARTLEBY: *(Softly.)* I say, I would prefer not to.

STANDARD: Bartleby, I must— You *what?*

BARTLEBY: *(Clearly, slowly.)* I would prefer not to.

(Pause. No one moves.)

STANDARD: Bartleby. Are you moonstruck? What's come over you? I want you to help me compare these sheets. Here— *(Thrusts sheet in BARTLEBY's face.)* Take them!

BARTLEBY: *(Clearly.)* I would prefer not to.

STANDARD: What do you mean, you would prefer not to! Here—take these sheets! Take them!

TURKEY: *(Under his breath.)* Good Lord—preferences! Have we come to this?

(Pause.)

STANDARD: *(Shaken.)* Bartleby, what do you mean by this extraordinary behavior? Answer me! Answer me now!

(Silence. BARTLEBY turns and disappears behind screen.)

STANDARD: *(Calling out.)* Bartleby! Answer me! Come here at once!

(GINGER NUT whistles in amazement. TURKEY sputters. NIPPERS grins uneasily. The light is beginning to fade.)

STANDARD: *(Shaking papers.)* Bartleby! Come here! Come here at once! Come here… *come here at once…!*

7.

STANDARD steps forward.

STANDARD: *(To audience.)* Then, just a few days later…

(Office brightens. A clock strikes three. TURKEY, NIPPERS, and GINGER NUT are setting four chairs in a line. When they have finished, they sit. Each holds papers. Several moments pass.)

TURKEY: Ahh. *Four* copies to examine this afternoon, you say? But with submission, sir, we lack a *fourth* member of our party! Our party is incomplete. *Someone* is missing!

STANDARD: *(Joining the GROUP.)* Quite so. *(Calls.)* Bartleby, we're waiting. Come at once! Ginger Nut: please fetch Bartleby here.

(GINGER NUT scurries to the screen.)

TURKEY: *(Fanning himself angrily.)* And a lovely *warm* afternoon it is, sir, to be *passing time before examining copy!*

STANDARD: He's coming?

GINGER NUT: No sir.

STANDARD: Well…what's he doing?

GINGER NUT: Copying, sir.

STANDARD: Copying? *(Calls.)* Bartleby. You mustn't copy now but help us. Please don't waste our time— we're waiting for you!

(A chair leg scrapes the floor. BARTLEBY emerges.)

BARTLEBY: *(Mildly.)* Yes? What is wanted?

STANDARD: The copies—we're going to examine them. Take one, please!

(STANDARD holds out papers. A slight pause. Then.)

BARTLEBY: *(Very clearly.)* I would prefer not to.

(TURKEY and NIPPERS exchange glances. STANDARD rises.)

STANDARD: *(Firmly.)* Bartleby, this has happened before and, frankly, Bartleby, I'm mystified. What do you mean by this? Why do you refuse to compare copy? What reason do you give?

(No answer.)

STANDARD: These are your *own copies* we're about to examine. It's labor-saving for you, labor-saving for your fellows. Scriveners *always* compare copy. Knowing this, how can you say you'd "prefer not to"?

BARTLEBY: I would prefer not to say.

STANDARD: But Bartleby. This is really unprecedented. Surely we deserve an explanation!

(No answer.)

STANDARD: (Shaken.) Well…The mind reels! I admit—I've never heard of such a thing in my life!

(BARTLEBY withdraws behind screen. The OTHERS burst forth in chatter.)

{
TURKEY: With submission, sir, I hardly think—!

NIPPERS: Sir, what's the matter with him—?

GINGER NUT: Sir, tell him he—
}

STANDARD: Gentlemen! Turkey!

TURKEY: (Bowing.) Sir?

STANDARD: What d'you make of this? Am I wrong to ask Bartleby to compare copy?

TURKEY: Wrong, sir? With submission, sir, it's an unusual matter. But, sir, you're in the right: scriveners always compares copy! (Bows deeply.)

STANDARD: You, Nippers. Your judgment. What d'you say?

NIPPERS: Tell you my judgment. I judge I'd kick him downstairs and out the door!

STANDARD: (Turning to the screen.) You see, Bartleby. You've heard their judgments. They agree with me. Come, Bartleby —please come and compare copy!

(No answer. Abruptly, NIPPERS rises.)

NIPPERS: (Rolling up sleeves.) Let me at him. I'll drag him out by his ears—

TURKEY: (Rising, throwing off his coat.) Allow me to assist. Your proposal strikes a pleasing chord—

GINGER NUT: I'll help! Let me help!

(TURKEY is rolling up his shirtsleeves. NIPPERS pushes back desks.)

STANDARD: (Violently.) Gentlemen! Gentlemen! Cease and desist! Have you lost your wits? This is a law office, not a madhouse! Cease and desist or I fire you all!

GINGER NUT: (Turning to STANDARD.) But Bartleby, sir—ain't you going to fire him?

STANDARD: (Turning sharply.) What's that, Ginger Nut? What'd you say?

GINGER NUT: Ain't you going to fire Bartleby? Because I think, sir—I think he's a loooony!

(Lights fading on turmoil.)

8.

The office is dark. STANDARD alone in light.

STANDARD: (To audience.) Well? "Loony"? What should I make of it? Why didn't I fire him? Well, I'll tell you why. It was the uncanny mildness of the man. The strange, melancholy calmness of him—there was the mystery of it! For, had he shown the least anger or impatience—anything human—out he'd have been, out on his ear! But no. His face composed…his voice mild…his white brow still… He disarmed me! Who was this fellow? I began to observe him, and I noted much strangeness in the man. For example, he never went to dinner—never stepped outside the office! But each morning about eleven…

(Office growing light. Clock striking eleven. STANDARD watches as BARTLEBY's hand extends from behind the screen and beckons silently to GINGER NUT. STANDARD continues to watch as GINGER NUT approaches the screen, disappears behind it, and emerges a moment later, jingling coins. TURKEY is at STANDARD's shoulder, rattling papers.)

TURKEY: Sir—

STANDARD: (Hushed excitement.) Shh, Turkey! Tell me: where's Ginger Nut gone?

TURKEY: Why I suppose, sir, on an errand.

STANDARD: But what kind of errand, Turkey? Where'd he go? Any idea?

TURKEY: With submission, sir—

STANDARD: (Finger to lips.) Shhh, Turkey. Here he comes. Watch with me.

(They watch. GINGER NUT has reentered, carrying a small parcel. He crosses to BARTLEBY's screen and disappears behind it.)

STANDARD: (Whispers to TURKEY.) What's in the parcel, eh Turkey?

TURKEY: By appearances, sir, a penny worth of the round spicy cakes known as "ginger nuts."

STANDARD: Aha, Turkey! Here's a clue then! Bartleby eats ginger nuts! Never goes out, never brings a dinner here—the poor fellow must subsist *entirely* on ginger nuts! Can this be true, Turkey, do you suppose?

TURKEY: Difficult to say, sir.

STANDARD: But what's the effect of living entirely on ginger nuts?

TURKEY: It is a hot, spicy food, sir—

STANDARD: But Bartleby's not hot and spicy!

TURKEY: Certainly not, sir.

STANDARD: Then… ginger nuts have no effect on his melancholy whatsoever!

TURKEY: *(Wittily.)* Probably *prefers* they have none!

(STANDARD chuckles doubtfully. The office grows dim. TURKEY moves away.)

STANDARD: *(To audience.)* Well, but strange fellow that he was, what should I *do* with him? I soon resolved upon the course that seemed both easiest and best…

(Lights brighten. NIPPERS has appeared at STANDARD's side.)

NIPPERS: It's about Bartleby, sir. I have a question.

STANDARD: Ah Nippers. Want to know what I'll do with him, eh?

NIPPERS: Sir.

STANDARD: Let me tell you, Nippers, in one word, what I'll do. In one word, Nippers—I'll do *nothing*.

NIPPERS: Sir?!

STANDARD: *And*, Nippers, I'll tell you why. Think for a minute of poor Bartleby. Is he not mild and quiet…a gentle fellow who means no harm? What would happen if I turned him out? Why, he might fall in with a less indulgent employer. Be treated harshly, perhaps—driven out to starve. Could we wish this on our poor friend Bartleby?

NIPPERS: Sir—

STANDARD: Surely not, Nippers, not in a Christian land. No—I've seen a light, Nippers. I'll keep Bartleby. I'll befriend him, it costs so little. And by keeping him I'll lay up a sweet morsel for my conscience.

NIPPERS: But sir—!

STANDARD: No, Nippers. My mind is set. Bartleby will remain!

(Lights shift. TURKEY is insistently at STANDARD's side.)

TURKEY: *(Urgently.)* With submission, sir, I am gravely disturbed! This venerable firm, sir, retained by Astors and Vanderbilts—people will laugh, sir! They'll go elsewhere!

STANDARD: Reason with me, Turkey—let us apply *logic* together. You'll agree, Turkey, that Bartleby was engaged as a copyist. Agree, further, that he copies satisfactorily. You must therefore agree that it is sound business practice to keep him. For as long as Bartleby chooses to copy, we must permit him to exercise his skill.

TURKEY: But sir—!

STANDARD: Turkey—I believe I've made myself clear. Bartleby'll remain in his study this morning. He has my permission to be excused from other tasks.

TURKEY: But sir—!

STANDARD: You'll note, Turkey: *he's* already at *his* desk!

(Lights shift. Music plays softly. STANDARD comes forward.)

STANDARD: *(To audience.)* Yet there was more. Something about Bartleby…how shall I say…strangely *touched* me…touched me rather *deeply*…! I'd be his friend…his protector…his guardian against the sharp buffets of this hard world! *(More briskly.)* And so, it became a fixed fact that a pale young scrivener, Bartleby by name, had a desk in my office, copied at the rate of four cents per folio, never examined copy, never went on an errand. And, if challenged, declared in a pale, flat voice that he'd "prefer not to"!

9.

Music halts. Light brightens. BARTLEBY stands motionless facing the wall. TURKEY, NIPPERS, and GINGER NUT stand at a distance and watch him. STANDARD joins them.

STANDARD: What's the matter, Nippers?

NIPPERS: *(Whispers.)* Just *look* at him, sir. Been like that for half an hour. Hasn't moved. Hasn't spoke.

TURKEY: *(Whispers.)* A silent melancholy meditation, sir, very like the Hindoo sages of far Calcutta!

NIPPERS: Bit strange, sir, ain't it?

STANDARD: No. No, I'm sure it's not strange. Here. I'll talk to him. (*Approaching BARTLEBY. Gently.*) Bartleby. Bartleby! Hello Bartleby!

BARTLEBY: (*Mildly.*) Yes? What is wanted?

STANDARD: I'm wondering, Bartleby, what are you doing?

BARTLEBY: I am not doing anything.

STANDARD: Not doing anything? But what's your reason for standing so still?

BARTLEBY: There is no reason.

STANDARD: I thought maybe your eyes were tired and you were resting them.

BARTLEBY: No. My eyes are rested.

STANDARD: Or that you were pausing from copying, perhaps recalling some pleasant memory from your youth.

BARTLEBY: No. I am not recalling any memory.

STANDARD: Well—but will you be standing, not doing anything, for long, do you think?

BARTLEBY: I cannot say for sure.

STANDARD: I see. And yet, not to put too fine a point on it, Bartleby, wouldn't it be wise to return to your desk? See how hard Turkey and Nippers work—they're overburdened. I know they'd appreciate your help! Come, Bartleby: time is money! Come!

BARTLEBY: Is it? I cannot say for sure. I think, for now, I would prefer not to. (*Turns and glides again to the window.*)

NIPPERS: (*Turns to STANDARD.*) Strange, sir, you see? Very strange!

STANDARD: Oh, no, Nippers. Not really so strange after all...

TURKEY: But *odd*, sir! Like the ancients of Mesopotamia who kept nightingales in their beards and refused to eat peaches on a Sunday!

NIPPERS: Ohhhh, no sir, he's strange! *Very strange!*

(*They stare after BARTLEBY. Music plays.*)

10.

Twilight. TURKEY, NIPPERS, and GINGER NUT stand in a line before STANDARD's desk.

STANDARD: Gentlemen. I believe I've arrived at a solution. We must try to *help* poor Bartleby. We must try to lift his spirits. Each will do his part.

TURKEY: Sir?

STANDARD: You, Turkey. A song. Something merry. Something to cheer our poor friend Bartleby.

TURKEY: Song, sir? Not serious, sir?!

STANDARD: Come, Turkey. Do as I say. A song for Bartleby. I'm sure we'll be amazed at the results.

TURKEY: Sir...

(*TURKEY sings and dances a music hall song, such as "Up in a Balloon." The OTHERS watch. BARTLEBY stands motionless. At the end, GINGER NUT and NIPPERS applaud vigorously. TURKEY bows deeply.*)

STANDARD: Very good, Turkey. Well done!

TURKEY: A song from my youth, sir, my salad days. Bartleby's spirits lifted any, d'ye think?

STANDARD: Come, Bartleby! Better now? Feeling better now, Bartleby, eh?

(*Pause. BARTLEBY turns away. TURKEY, breathless and embarrassed, withdraws.*)

STANDARD: (*Nudging NIPPERS.*) You Nippers, what about you?

NIPPERS: Diversion, Bartleby? Excitement, d'ye want? Here, Bartleby. Ready? Watch! (*Brandishes a deck of cards from his coat pocket.*) Bartleby, especially for you: the game of *Preference*. Here...examine my deck.

(*He extends the deck toward BARTLEBY. BARTLEBY does not move.*)

NIPPERS: All right? All on the up and up?

(*NIPPERS begins to shuffle and deal the cards handily. The OTHERS gather about, ready to play.*)

NIPPERS: (*With rapid-fire aplomb.*) Preference. Three play, thirty-two cards, ace high, seven low. Ten cards dealt to each, other two make the blind. Winner takes six tricks after exchanging two cards with the blind and then naming trumps. Basic bidding from one to four, no jump-bidding. Early bidders as haven't yet passed hold the higher bids. Any can be overcalled, just play from the hand, no exchanging. Hand bids overcalled by the same in a higher suit.

(The dealing is finished. The OTHERS pick up their cards.)

NIPPERS: Comes back now, eh? I see it in your eye, Bartleby. Ready to play. Here. Take your hand. Here. *(Holds out cards to BARTLEBY.)* Any questions? Let's play!

(Pause. BARTLEBY turns slowly away.)

NIPPERS: *(To TURKEY.)* He didn't understand the game!

STANDARD: You try, Ginger Nut!

GINGER NUT: *(Steps forward.)* Bartleby! Watch, Bartleby! This'll cheer you up! Watch *me!* *(Dances and gestures as he chants.)*
See a pin
Pick it up,
All the day
You'll have good luck.
See a pin
Pass it by,
You'll want a pin
Before you die!

(Silence. BARTLEBY does not stir.)

GINGER NUT: Bartleby? D'ye have a sweetheart, Bartleby? What's her name?

(No answer.)

GINGER NUT: Say her name's Sarah, Bartleby, for the sake of the song. Ready? *(Dances and gestures.)*
Round apple, round apple
And still we go round
For to see Sarah
In her carriage go round.

In her carriage, in her carriage,
By night and by day
She's driving to see
Her Bartleby away.

Then up comes her father,
With a knife in his hand,
Saying give me my daughter
Or your life I will have.

I care not, I care not,
I care not a pin,
For I love my Bartleby:
And my Bartleby loves me.

(Silence. BARTLEBY does not stir.)

GINGER NUT: *(Sings softly.)*
Windy weather,
Frosty weather.
When the wind blows,
We all go together.

(Silence. BARTLEBY does not stir. GINGER NUT turns away. The OTHERS turn away. Abruptly, STANDARD steps forward.)

STANDARD: *(Calling gently.)* Bartleby! Lovely evening, isn't it? Our work is finished. Let's be friends. Tell me—where were you born?

(No answer.)

STANDARD: Please. Is it nearby or far away? Tell me.

(No answer.)

STANDARD: Have you a family? Brothers or sisters?

(No answer.)

STANDARD: Now I see you're studying my bust of Cicero. Tell me, what d'you think of his orations? Wonderful balance, sense of proportion. My favorite, the first speech against Lucius Sergius Catalina. Do you recall it? *(Quotes with relish.)* "Quo usque tandem abutere, Catalina, patientia nostra? How long, Catalina, will you abuse our patience? For how long will this passion of yours mock us—?"

GINGER NUT: *(Whispering, pointing at BARTLEBY from across the room.)* Sir, look—!

STANDARD: "Quem ad finem sese effrenta iactabit audacia? To what end will your unrestrained boldness hurl itself—?" *(Abstracted.)* What d'you say, Ginger Nut?

GINGER NUT: Look at Bartleby, sir... Look!

STANDARD: Bartleby... Stand in the light...! *(Quiet, shocked tone.)* Why are you trembling?!

(A sad fiddle begins to play. The scene fades to black. A clock chimes and it is morning and...)

11.

STANDARD: *(To audience.)* And the days went by, and events in my chambers proceeded still more strangely...

(BARTLEBY stands motionless by the window. NIPPERS and STANDARD watch from a distance. NIPPERS speaks in a hushed, urgent tone.)

NIPPERS: *(Whispers.)* Look at him *now*, sir. Ain't touched his pen all day! And yesterday the same—and the same the day before! What's the matter with him, sir? Why ain't he writing?!

STANDARD: Yes, I see, Nippers, I see. Back to your work. I'll take it up with him. *(Crosses to BARTLEBY.)* Bartleby. Please. Why aren't you writing? Tell me what's the matter.

BARTLEBY: *(Turning slowly to STANDARD.)* Nothing is the matter.

STANDARD: Then why aren't you at your desk? After all, Bartleby, we pay you to copy. That's your employment here. You must tell me what's your reason for not copying?

BARTLEBY: Do you not see the reason for yourself?

STANDARD: No, Bartleby, I confess I don't. Really, this can't go on! You really must return to copying. Say you'll return to copying this afternoon.

BARTLEBY: No. I do not think I can agree to that.

STANDARD: *(With mounting concern.)* Tomorrow, then. Or Wednesday at the latest!

BARTLEBY: No, I do not think Wednesday would be agreeable.

STANDARD: What then, Bartleby? When *will* you return to copying?

BARTLEBY: I do not think I will return to copying. I think I have given up copying.

(STANDARD stares at him. Pause.)

BARTLEBY: *(A slow, soft cry.)* Yes. I think…I have given up copying…*forever*…!

12.

The peal of church bells. Shafts of dim morning light. Wall Street on a Sunday morning.

STANDARD: *(To audience.)* Well, perhaps I should have seen it all right then: how he'd become a millstone to me. Two weeks later, early one Sunday, in Wall Street outside my offices…

GINGER NUT: *(Entering the street, waving.)* Eh. Morning, sir!

STANDARD: *(Entering the street.)* Ah. Ginger Nut. What brings you here on a Sunday?

GINGER NUT: On my way to church services, sir, in West Street.

STANDARD: And so am I. Needed to stop in the office for a minute. Pick up a brief. *(Fumbles in pocket for keys.)* Deserted here on a Sunday, eh?

GINGER NUT: Like a grave, sir!

STANDARD: *(Briskly.)* Well, it's a place of business, Ginger Nut—not made for inhabiting on a Sunday. Let's hope the sermon's edifying! Cain and Abel, I think. *(Quoting with relish.)* "What hast thou done. The voice of thy brother's blood crieth to me from the earth." *(Chuckles as he goes.)* Good day, Ginger Nut. God bless!

GINGER NUT: *(Going.)* Good day, sir. God bless *you*!

(STANDARD crosses around to the office door. He mimes placing his key in the lock. Rattles it sharply.)

STANDARD: Hello? Is someone inside? Why's the lock jammed! *(Pause.)* Is someone there? Hello?

BARTLEBY'S VOICE: *(Pierces the darkness.)* I am sorry. I am deeply engaged just now. I prefer not to admit you at present.

STANDARD: *(Rattling key.)* Eh? Bartleby! Is that you?!

(BARTLEBY now looms dimly in the shadows, dressed in shirtsleeves and strange, tattered disarray.)

BARTLEBY: *(Calling mildly.)* Perhaps if you'd walk around the block two or three times, I'll have concluded my affairs.

STANDARD: Walk around the block? What in God's name, Bartleby, are you doing here on a Sunday! *(Pause. Calls loudly.)* Bartleby! *(Pounding violently on door.)* Walk around the block I will not! Now let me in, Bartleby! Permit me to enter my own offices! *Bartleby!*

(STANDARD pushes against the door. The lock yields. He enters warily. BARTLEBY has vanished. Silence. STANDARD stands fearfully in the middle of the room.)

STANDARD: Hello…? Are you there? Bartleby?

(Silence.)

STANDARD: *(Shouts.)* Bartleby?

(Silence.)

STANDARD: *(Louder.)* Bartleby?!

(GINGER NUT hurries down the hall and appears in the door.)

STANDARD: What's this, Ginger Nut! Why're you here?

GINGER NUT: Heard you shouting, sir. All the way down the street! What happened? What's the matter?

STANDARD: Nothing happened, Ginger Nut. Go away. But…wait!

(STANDARD's eye has fixed on a ragged bundle in the center of the floor.)

STANDARD: Tell me… What's that?

GINGER NUT: Sir? *(Stares at bundle.)* Don't know, sir.

STANDARD: Untie it. Tell me what's inside.

(GINGER NUT picks up bundle and sets it on desk. He unties it and fearfully examines its contents.)

STANDARD: *(Softly.)* Well?

GINGER NUT: *(Softly.)* Things for washing, sir.

STANDARD: Washing?

GINGER NUT: *(Holding up each item.)* Yes… Washbasin… Soap… Little ragged towel…

(Pause.)

GINGER NUT: And things for blacking, sir. Brush… Blacking box… Blacking rag…

STANDARD: Ahh. *(Pointing.)* And that…what's that?

GINGER NUT: This, sir?

(GINGER NUT lifts a knotted bandana. Shakes it. Listens to the chink of coins.)

GINGER NUT: Why… Savings bank, sir… Bartleby's little trust fund…

STANDARD: *(Softly.)* Ahh, Ginger Nut. It all comes clear. I wonder if you see it?

GINGER NUT: See what, sir?

STANDARD: He makes my offices his bachelor's halls. He's come to *live* with me now!

(Light fades on office. STANDARD alone.)

STANDARD: *(To audience.)* Now surely we'd reached a crisis of some proportion…

13.

The light changes. TURKEY, flushed and violent, holds forth at STANDARD's side.

TURKEY: A crisis, sir, of extravagant proportions. *(Under his breath, gesturing toward screen.)* Doesn't write! Doesn't do errands! Lives here now!—

STANDARD: A crisis it may be, Turkey, but leave me to it!

TURKEY: But I have, sir, like Archimedes, the *answer!*

STANDARD: Ahh, Turkey! The *answer!* Pray spare us!

TURKEY: *(Overriding.)* Ale, sir, ale is what he wants! Now if he'd prefer to take one quart of ale with breakfast, his spirits'd soar and a gentle smile'd affix to his lips!

STANDARD: Preposterous, Turkey. Preposterous! Now to your desk—

TURKEY: *(Overriding.)* With submission, sir, ale is a tonic! I prefer it. Bartleby'd prefer it. For, sir, all the *great ones* prefer it!

STANDARD: Turkey, did you hear what you said?

TURKEY: Hear what, sir.

STANDARD: What you said!

TURKEY: Said, sir.

STANDARD: Don't echo me, Turkey, the word!

TURKEY: Word, sir.

STANDARD: Aye, Turkey. The *word.* The cursed word. The confounded word. *(Gestures toward screen.)* *His* word. *Prefer!*

(Pause.)

TURKEY: *(Laughing.)* Prefer? Why—I never use it! "Prefer?" Prefer not to, I suppose! Queer word. Very well. I'll avoid that word. As I live and breathe, it shall never cross these lips again. But getting back to ale, sir—

(NIPPERS has entered with a sheaf of papers.)

NIPPERS: Afternoon, sir. These certificates. On the white or the blue paper. Which did you prefer?

TURKEY: Oh dear. Oh dear me.

STANDARD: But now *you*, Nippers! Do you hear? You've got it *too!*

NIPPERS: Got what?

STANDARD: The word!

TURKEY: The word. Expressing preference. The word commencing with "p." A word, Nippers, he'd *prefer* us not to use.

STANDARD: *(Averting danger.)* Never *mind*, gentlemen! Never *mind*! The heat of the afternoon has surely affected our brains!

TURKEY: *(Overriding.)* Nay, sir, I'll speak plainly! It's not the heat that's affected us but him! It's *him's* affected our brains!

STANDARD: *(Grimly.)* Him.

TURKEY: You catch my drift, sir!

(Pause.)

NIPPERS: *(Rattles papers at desk. Begins to write. Testily, as he writes.)* If you're going to talk, I'd prefer you do it quietly—

TURKEY: This is private conference, Nippers. He prefers to speak to me alone—

STANDARD: Stop, gentlemen, *stop!* This is lunacy! Both to your work! And let me make one thing clear: I insist that in this office you never, ever use that cursed word again. Nay, I more than insist—I *prefer* it...

NIPPERS: *(Throwing down his pen, exiting.)* Agghhh!

TURKEY: *(Flinging up his hands, exiting.)* Lunacy! Lunacy rampant in these chambers!

(Light shifts. Dusk. STANDARD writes busily at his desk. GINGER NUT stands quietly in the door.)

GINGER NUT: Sir?

STANDARD: *(Writing.)* Yes, Ginger Nut. Closing time. What do you wish?

GINGER NUT: It's Mr. Bartleby, sir. I'm troubled. Will he do errands again? Will he write? Will he talk?

STANDARD: *(Without looking up.)* Yes, Ginger Nut, I shall explain. Bartleby's *silence* is a sign of his deep reflection. And in this frantic world, Ginger Nut, would that we were all as deeply meditative as poor Bartleby. Bartleby's *stillness* is a sign of—

GINGER NUT: Sir. He ain't human. I watch him—I know!

STANDARD: Ah, well, Ginger Nut, I grant you—Bartleby is not *entirely cheerful* at all times, and yet—

GINGER NUT: Please sir! Listen to me, sir, please! He's the victim of a disorder, sir. It ain't his body but his *soul* that suffers. And his soul, sir, *you can't reach!*

(STANDARD looks up.)

GINGER NUT: Sir! He has awed you and you're afraid, sir! Be rid of him, sir! Be rid of him before it's too late!

14.

Lights rise slowly. The office is bathed in soft twilight. A distant clock strikes six. BARTLEBY stands before STANDARD's desk.

STANDARD: *(With difficulty.)* I have thought, Bartleby, long and hard. I have considered and concluded. This being a place of business, necessities of business must prevail. I must dismiss you. I regret my decision. I wonder, do you wish to say anything to me?

(No answer.)

STANDARD: Very well, Bartleby. Then let this be a friendly parting. I'll be gone on business 'til Friday. When I return you'll have found a new position. And that'll be an end to it. Do you understand, Bartleby? Is it all agreed?

(No answer.)

STANDARD: Well then. Let me see. I owe you seven dollars for this week. *(Rises. Counts money.)* And here are seven for the next. And to ensure smooth passage to your new home, here are twenty dollars more. Thirty-four dollars in all, a generous settlement. I'll leave them on your desk. Spend them wisely. *(Putting on overcoat. Kindly.)* When you leave the office, merely slip your key under the door mat. No need to lock your desk. Well then. Goodbye, Bartleby. Good evening. And good luck in your new life!

(STANDARD goes out. BARTLEBY remains motionless as the light in the office fades. STANDARD enters the street. TURKEY appears, hurrying along at his side.)

TURKEY: *(Breathless.)* With submission, sir, I commend you on your great victory. You've routed him, sir, as Julius Caesar routed the Visigoths!

STANDARD: *(Calmly.)* No, Turkey. That's the point. I've dismissed him, but with civility.

TURKEY: *Civility*, sir.

STANDARD: Yes. The easiest way and the best. That's the point. No bullying. No bravado. No striding across the floor. I'm quite pleased with myself. You see, I didn't *demand* that Bartleby depart: I assumed the ground that depart he *must*. Do you understand, Turkey? Do you see?

TURKEY: And the *departee*, where is he now?

STANDARD: I just left him. He'll be off shortly. You shall see.

TURKEY: Ah, with submission, sir, when you return, I fear it's *you* shall see…

STANDARD: *(To audience.)* One week later…

(A clock striking. Lights brighten. Early morning. GINGER NUT appears at one end of the hall, STANDARD at the other, carrying a carpetbag.)

GINGER NUT: *(Hailing.)* Morning, sir! Good journey, I hope. Welcome back!

STANDARD: Thank you, Ginger Nut, thank you. You're in early. Now tell me: any stirrings from the office this morning?

GINGER NUT: Don't know, sir. Just arrived myself.

STANDARD: You haven't seen him? Heard him?

GINGER NUT: *Seems* quiet, sir. Very quiet.

STANDARD: Good. *(Taking a coin from his pocket.)* Take this, Ginger Nut. Get me a *Herald* from the corner. There's a good fellow…

(GINGER NUT touches his cap and is gone. STANDARD is alone. He crouches to listen at the door.)

STANDARD: *(Whispers.)* Bartleby…? Are you gone…? Bartleby…?

(Long pause. STANDARD begins to unlock the door. Then suddenly from the darkness.)

BARTLEBY'S VOICE: Not yet. I am occupied!

STANDARD: *(Cries out.)* Bartleby!

BARTLEBY'S VOICE: If you would return at a later time, I will have concluded my affairs…

STANDARD: Return at a later time? Return at a later time? Nonsense, Bartleby, I will not return at a later time. I will enter my office when I please!

(STANDARD enters the office. BARTLEBY stands quietly in the middle of the room.)

STANDARD: Bartleby. I'm more than displeased… I'm furious! I'd thought you were a gentleman. I'd thought that, in a delicate situation, a mere hint'd suffice. Clearly I was mistaken. Now what the devil shall I do? When will you quit me?

(No answer.)

STANDARD: Tell me! What earthly right have you to stay here? Do you pay rent? Do you pay taxes? Is the property yours?

(BARTLEBY does not stir. STANDARD's eyes shift to his desk top.)

STANDARD: And look! You haven't even touched your money! Take it, I insist, Bartleby! Take your money and be gone! Let's be done with this once and for all!

(A pause. STANDARD strikes at the money with his walking stick.)

STANDARD: Take it, Bartleby! Take it!

(The paper money flies up through the air. STANDARD strikes the desk repeatedly, shouting.)

STANDARD: TAKE IT! TAKE IT!

(The office is growing dark. Music begins to play. STANDARD's cries are desperate and violent.)

STANDARD: TAKE IT TAKE IT TAKE IT!!!

(GINGER NUT appears in the door, newspaper in hand. He gapes at the money on the floor. After a moment.)

GINGER NUT: *(Softly, breathless.)* I've brought your *Herald*, sir…here's your news…!

STANDARD: But what shall I do, Ginger Nut? What shall I think?

(Church bells halt abruptly…)

15.

And silence. Pale light fills the office. The dry sound of the scratching of pens as TURKEY and NIPPERS write at their desks. At the center of the office, BARTLEBY stands motionless. STANDARD sits motionless, staring at BARTLEBY. After a time, TURKEY rises. Calmly circling BARTLEBY's motionless figure, he crosses to a file. NIPPERS, rising to consult a book, brushes briskly past BARTLEBY. GINGER NUT, going about his office tasks, darts in quick circles around BARTLEBY. No one heeds BARTLEBY. A clock strikes six. The SCRIV-ENERS put away papers. Don coats, gloves, scarves. They go out silently. STANDARD, at his desk, stares at BARTLEBY. Music plays. A pale moon appears at the window. STANDARD sits, poring feverishly over a book, a dim lamp at his side. A clock strikes midnight. STANDARD rattles the pages of his book, muttering as he reads, from time to time lifting his eyes to gaze at the pale, motionless BARTLEBY. A clock strikes six. A pale dawn is at the window. STANDARD, now in shirtsleeves, wild-eyed, disheveled, and haggard, reads aloud in a feverish whisper. His voice grows stronger.)

STANDARD: *(Reads.)* "…thus we see that all things derive from God. For, as the being of the world is from God, so the circumstances of the world must be ordered by God. All is divinely ordered. All is providence." Bartleby, do you hear? All is providence.

(No answer.)

STANDARD: Listen closely, Bartleby! *(Reads.)* "All things are willed by God from all eternity: predestined, preordained, irrefutable, sacred in their cognition." Bartleby, do you see? Sacred in their cognition!

(No answer.)

STANDARD: Bartleby, listen! I begin to see a light! I begin to glean—you've been billeted upon me by an all-wise, all-blessed providence! I'm instructed here to accept everything! That the easiest's the best! Bartleby, do you see? I accept all things!

(No answer.)

STANDARD: All strategizing, Bartleby, is futile! All protestation vanity! My mission at last is clear! I am put on earth, Bartleby, to furnish you with office space for as long as you may wish! Oh Bartleby! I inhabit a blessed state of mind! I am content! I am content! I am content!

(A clock is striking. Light is building. TURKEY and NIPPERS have entered and are writing at their desks. FAIRCHILD appears at the door.)

FAIRCHILD: Sir? Morning, sir. Got a moment? Wished to have a word with you. You look…a little ragged sir…don't mind my saying—

STANDARD: *(Briskly, as he writes.)* Ah yes, Fairchild. Studying through the night. Fasting, praying, starting to view the situation in a different light.

FAIRCHILD: *(Grinning uncomfortably.)* Cool light of day, sir, eh? Ha ha. Wondered if I might have a word with you, sir.

STANDARD: Certainly, Fairchild. How may I serve?

FAIRCHILD: *(Gesturing to the OTHERS.)* Confidential, sir.

STANDARD: Ah, no Fairchild, all shall speak freely here. We're God's children. We dwell in the light. We know no darkness here.

FAIRCHILD: Very well sir… It's about your scrivener, sir. This Barnaby. Thought I might offer some counsel. Free of charge of course. And off the record. There's rumor in the Office of Chancery—you're aware of this? Talk, sir.

STANDARD: Talk, Fairchild? I fear no talk.

FAIRCHILD: Well—good, sir…good… Because they say you were once a man of the finest judgment. But now you've fallen on evil times, due to your inexplicable indulgence toward the strange fellow who haunts your chambers. It's a bad day when the Master of Chancery, sir, in his own chambers, is himself mastered by a lunatic. They question, sir, if you're the man for the job. Wall Street is a place of reputation, sir, and yours…

STANDARD: *(Softly.)* What?

FAIRCHILD: A rule of Wall Street, sir: them as *gives* can also *take away*. Sir, they whisper and they laugh! Look to your position. I come as a friend, sir. As a friend.

STANDARD: *(Shaken.)* Yes, Fairchild…very well…good day…yes…good day…

(FAIRCHILD is gone. STANDARD stares, stricken. NIPPERS pounces.)

NIPPERS: *Now*, sir—*now* you've heard 'em!

TURKEY: Something must finally be *done*, sir, or like the ancient city of Carthage, all shall be *destroyed*!

STANDARD: Nonsense, Turkey.

NIPPERS: *(Pleading.)* Sir! Get the constable—arrest him as a vagrant!

STANDARD: No, Nippers. That'll never do—

TURKEY: Be decisive, sir. Thrust him out of door!

STANDARD: Turkey, no…in the depths of winter? He'll freeze—he'll starve!

TURKEY: If nothing's done, sir, I dare not name consequences!

NIPPERS: He's killing us, sir, all!

STANDARD: Ohhhh, but gentlemen! *What?*

(Pause. An idea strikes.)

TURKEY: *I'll* tell you what, sir. New pastures. Greener pastures… There's many a room in Wall Street, sir. You require only two of 'em.

STANDARD: Don't talk to me in *riddles*, Turkey!

NIPPERS: He means new chambers, sir. Move to new chambers!

STANDARD: Leave these chambers, my home of thirty years? This because of *him?*

NIPPERS: You've tried everything, sir!

STANDARD: But—preposterous! Out of the question!

TURKEY: What other course, sir, *remains?*

STANDARD: Unthinkable—no—never!

NIPPERS: If *he* don't quit *you*, then *you* must quit *him*. Eh, sir?

TURKEY: Remember Carthage, sir! It's you—or *him!*

(TURKEY and NIPPERS are gone. STANDARD is alone, plunged in desperate thought.)

16.

GINGER NUT's shout is heard, off.

GINGER NUT'S VOICE: Moving cart, sir. Down in the street. Ready now?

(Lights brighten. A bleak winter morning. STANDARD is alone beside his desk, packing books and papers into a wooden crate. BARTLEBY is invisible behind his screen. GINGER NUT, in coat and muffler, appears in the doorway. He stamps his feet and blows on his hands.)

STANDARD: *(Preoccupied.)* Thank you, Ginger Nut. Be good enough… leave me for a few minutes. I'll call when I'm ready.

(GINGER NUT goes out. STANDARD continues packing for a time. At last he speaks quietly in the direction of the screen.)

STANDARD: Well, Bartleby. Are you listening to me? Bartleby?

(No answer. STANDARD continues to pack.)

STANDARD: It's a sad day, Bartleby, when I vacate the offices I've had for thirty years. When you and I, who were once great friends, take our leave in this unfriendly way. I wonder, do you have any last words to say?

(STANDARD waits. No answer. He continues to pack.)

STANDARD: *(Fondly.)* I wonder, Bartleby, if you remember the day you first arrived. You sat in that chair…copied for me. Here's a young man, thought I, who'll work diligently in this office. Turkey may be obstreperous. Nippers, moody. But Bartleby is reasonable. I was impressed! I had hopes of you! How'd I know the grief you'd bring!

(STANDARD waits. No answer. He continues to pack.)

STANDARD: Look around. Books, papers, furniture—thirty years of practice—all to be packed up, crated off to new offices. It's a nuisance, an irritation, and no mean expense. But Bartleby: this is nothing to the ruin you bring upon yourself. Think, Bartleby: who'll hire you now? How'll you earn your bread? Who'll feed you? Who'll shelter you from the cold? How'll you make your way in this hard world where, like it or not, you'll be alone?

(Silence.)

STANDARD: Obstinacy. Folly. Madness. *(Softly.)* Say something on your own behalf, Bartleby? One word?

(Silence. STANDARD has completed his packing.)

STANDARD: Please, Bartleby, *speak.*

(Silence. STANDARD takes a few steps toward the screen.)

STANDARD: Bartleby. Listen to me: this is the last I'll ever address you. I don't wish to turn you out of doors. Speak now—speak *reason* to me now—and all your foolishness, your obstinacy of the past months, will vanish. We'll again be friends. You'll have your old job back. Your old desk. I'll not be an unreasonable master!

(Silence. STANDARD moves very close to the screen. He speaks in an urgent whisper.)

STANDARD: One word from you—one word—and this terrible process will halt. We'll forget this ever happened! We'll be as friends again!

(Silence.)

STANDARD: (*Desperate whisper.*) Bartleby!!

(*Long silence. STANDARD waits, then turns, crosses to the door. Calls out.*)

STANDARD: Ginger Nut! You may come up now!

(*Pause. GINGER NUT's running footsteps are heard, off. He appears in the doorway.*)

STANDARD: We must pack these things in the cart, Ginger Nut. Tell the others to come up. Hurry, Ginger Nut!

GINGER NUT: (*Going.*) Sir.

(*A long silence. STANDARD does not move. At last we hear footsteps in the hall. NIPPERS, TURKEY, and GINGER NUT tramp in. They wear heavy overcoats, caps, scarves. Silently they clear desks, chairs, stools. STANDARD watches, motionless, at one side. The office is cleared. Only Bartleby's screen remains. Exiting, TURKEY begins to whistle a jaunty air. The whistling fades away down the hall. NIPPERS, the last to leave, advances to the screen. He places a hand on it.*)

NIPPERS: (*With a smirk.*) Eh, take this now, sir?

STANDARD: (*Violent shout.*) Nooooo!

(*NIPPERS, startled, turns to stare at STANDARD.*)

STANDARD: (*Wildly.*) Leave that! Go down! Wait in the street!

(*NIPPERS ambles quickly out. A moment of silence.*)

STANDARD: (*Frantic whisper.*) Bartleby…say one last word…don't make me leave you here alone!

(*No answer.*)

STANDARD: I *will* go through with this, Bartleby, whether or not you *prefer* it!

(*No answer. Abruptly STANDARD pulls on his gloves. Hesitates, then marches to the screen. He jerks it back sharply. BARTLEBY, motionless, is revealed: starved face, calm eyes. They stare at each other.*)

STANDARD: Goodbye, Bartleby. I'm going away. And may you prosper.

(*He carries the screen to the door. He turns back. He is desperately moved.*)

STANDARD: And here…take this… (*Fumbles in his pocket.*) Take this, Bartleby, for a better day… May God in some way bless you!

(*He returns to BARTLEBY. Grips BARTLEBY's hand and presses coins into it. Steps back. Tableau. Slowly, BARTLEBY's hand drops to his side. Coins jingle noisily onto the floor. Terrible pause. STANDARD gapes at BARTLEBY, then bolts for the door. His footsteps fade down the hall. BARTLEBY is alone in the middle of the empty stage. Light fades. Five seconds…*)

17.

A shout is heard in the darkness.

LANDLORD'S VOICE: (*Off.*) You! You sir, halt!

(*Light brightens. Street. A bitter winter morning. STANDARD, in heavy coat, muffler, and gloves, stands at the door of his new offices, keys in hand.*)

STANDARD: (*To audience.*) Established in my new offices, I kept the door locked for a week or so fearful he'd follow me! But early one morning…

(*LANDLORD runs in.*)

LANDLORD: (*Breathless.*) You, sir—! Are you the person who recently vacated offices at number twelve Wall Street?

STANDARD: (*Evenly.*) I recently vacated rooms there, yes. What of that?

LANDLORD: Well sir—you're responsible for the man you left there!

STANDARD: Come now. What on earth do you mean?

LANDLORD: The strange man you left there! Won't speak! Won't leave the premises! "Prefers not to!" It'd be comical, sir, if it weren't an outrage! He wasn't mentioned in the rental agreement! Well. What do you propose to do about it?

STANDARD: Do? Listen, sir, I barely know him. He's no relation to me. And I'm in no way responsible for him. He's nothing—nothing to me. Good day.

LANDLORD: Wait! At least tell me, for God's sake, who is he?

STANDARD: Why ask me? I know nothing about him. He's nothing—nothing to me! Now leave me. Leave me in peace!

(*Light fades. LANDLORD is gone. STANDARD is alone.*)

STANDARD: *(To audience.)* A week passed without incident. Then one morning…

(LANDLORD enters, distraught.)

LANDLORD: For God's sake, sir, please take him away!

STANDARD: *(Evenly.)* Take whom away?

LANDLORD: The cadaver, sir. The living ghost that haunts the building!

STANDARD: Haunts the building…?

LANDLORD: Crouches on the banisters by day. Roams the hallways by night. Causing a sensation. Tenants leaving. Crowd gathering in the street. Some fear a mob. He's strange, sir, oh very strange!

STANDARD: But sir, be reasonable—why me? I hardly know the man!

LANDLORD: You brought him there, didn't you? And left him there for me to contend with!

STANDARD: But even if this were true, consider, what can I do?

LANDLORD: Why, have him removed! Taken away! Really, sir: how can you forsake him, when he is yours?

18.

STANDARD: *(To audience.)* Well. What choice had I but to visit him? Turning the corner into Wall Street, I beheld a carnival scene that seemed to shake the winter air…

(The roar of a crowd. Shouts and jeers.)

VOICE: *Take him away!*

VOICE: *Remove him!*

VOICE: *Get him out!*

STANDARD: People of all descriptions pressed against the door! I pushed past them and found Bartleby alone in a cold upstairs hall sitting on a banister, surveying his domain: stairs, doorways, transoms, all! *(To BARTLEBY.)* Bartleby! What in God's name are you doing here!

BARTLEBY: *(Mild voice.)* I am sitting on a banister. What are you doing here?

STANDARD: I'm here because of you. Now, why are you sitting on a banister, Bartleby? And what plans have you to remove yourself from this banister?

BARTLEBY: At present I have no plans.

STANDARD: But there's a mob in the street, Bartleby, ready to carry you off!

BARTLEBY: I am not unaware.

STANDARD: You must come down from there at once. Talk to me. We must make a plan!

(BARTLEBY steps down and stands before STANDARD.)

STANDARD: Bartleby—this can't go on. If you don't do something, something terrible will be done to you. You must earn your bread—find a trade. Had you thought of this? What sort of business would you like to engage in?

BARTLEBY: There is no business in particular.

STANDARD: What about…a bartender's business? Your eyes wouldn't be strained in a bartender's business? Or going through the country, collecting bills for merchants? Or traveling through Europe as a companion? Entertaining some young gentleman with your conversation?

BARTLEBY: No, there is nothing definite about that. And besides, I prefer to be stationary.

STANDARD: But Bartleby! Stationary—nothing definite—nothing suits you! What in God's name do you want?

(The roar from the street has grown louder.)

STANDARD: Bartleby… Very well—come with me now—to my home. You can be my guest. Please, before something terrible happens, Bartleby, come home with me!

BARTLEBY: *(Quietly.)* No. At present, I prefer to make no change at all.

(STANDARD stands motionless for a moment, then bolts. As lights fade, shouts are heard from the street.)

VOICE: *What'll he do?*

VOICE: *Is the scoundrel out?*

VOICE: *Will he leave today?*

VOICE: *WHAT'S HIS GAME?!*

(And many VOICES chanting, "Out! Out! Out!…")

19.

STANDARD: *(To audience.)* I fled! Left my business to Nippers for several days, traveled through the suburbs, crossed the frozen Hudson to Jersey City and the countryside beyond. Almost lived in my carriage. When reason at last returned…

(Light brightens. Office. TURKEY, entering with papers, sees STANDARD, halts.)

TURKEY: *(Deep bow.)* Ahhh! Salutations, sir—good morning! The traveler returned from distant voyages… Marco Polo from his oriental sojourn… Magellan from farthest Mandalay! *Buon giorno, signor! Enchanté, monsieur!*

STANDARD: *(Impatient.)* Come, come, Turkey. What's new? Anything of interest while I was away?

TURKEY: *(Handing mail.)* Why yes, sir. Depositions from the appellate court. Letter from Holworthy and Sons. Statement from Patterson and Smith. What else. Hmm. This and this. Oh yes. *(Hands a paper.)* And this.

STANDARD: Mm? What is it, Turkey.

TURKEY: *(Delicately.)* Arrived yesterday, sir. A letter from B. Weldon. Attorney for the landlord at twelve Wall Street. In relation to our former employee. Shall I read it to you now, sir?

STANDARD: *(Feigned calm.)* Why yes, certainly. Read it to me now.

TURKEY: *(Reads.)* "Twenty-third February. Sir. Concerning the young man known as 'Bartleby:' My client has had no recourse but to summon police officers to remove said 'Bartleby' from the premises at twelve Wall Street and convey him, as a vagrant, to the Halls of Justice."

STANDARD: "Halls of Justice." You mean The Tombs?

TURKEY: Indeed sir. They call 'em "The Tombs." The prison, sir, that holds the convicts. *(Reads.)* "Since, sir, you know more about said 'Bartleby' than anyone else, I urge you to appear there at once and state the facts of the case."

STANDARD: Facts of the case—?

TURKEY: *(Continuing.)* "You may be glad to learn sir, that, when taken into custody, said 'Bartleby' acquiesced calmly—

STANDARD: *(A murmur.)* Ah yes—

TURKEY: *(Continuing.)* "—and indeed, a strange and rather touching spectacle ensued!"

STANDARD: *(Softly, eagerly.)* Yes?

TURKEY: *(Continuing.)* "It seems a number of bystanders, sympathetic to the poor scrivener, fell in and marched alongside him as he was conveyed to prison. A procession formed, headed by two constables arm in arm with said Bartleby, followed by a host of others—"

STANDARD: *(Softly.)* Yes…

TURKEY: *(Continuing.)* "—marching silently through the icy thoroughfares, amid the noise and rage of the roaring day."

(STANDARD is still. A pause.)

TURKEY: *(Quietly.)* No other letters of interest, sir, I think, today.

STANDARD: No, Turkey, there wouldn't be. Thank you…thank you… *(To audience.)* And quickly as I could, I made my way to The Tombs…

20.

Light changes: The Tombs. Shafts of gray light. The sound of metal gates crashing. A MAN'S VOICE crying in a distant cell. KEEPER shuffles on: an ancient man with a lamp, bundled in rags.

STANDARD: Keeper!

KEEPER: *(Turning slowly.)* Yes?

STANDARD: I'm looking for a man you took into custody, one Bartleby. Do you know him—or can you direct me to someone who does?

KEEPER: And who are you?

STANDARD: I was for many months his employer. I'm here to give assurances that Bartleby is an honest man.

KEEPER: Honest? What's that matter now? *(Smiles wanly.)* He's in The Tombs, ain't he?

STANDARD: Yes—but he's eccentric, not evil. He mustn't be subjected to the dangers or the—terrors of this place. Or perish from hunger or cold. He isn't robust and he's committed no crime…

(Slight pause.)

KEEPER: That your business?

STANDARD: Yes. Let me see the prisoner.

KEEPER: *There.* They pass their time in the yard *there.* Go look for him *there.* (*Turns, shuffles out.*)

STANDARD: (*To audience.*) He was standing all alone in the quietest corner of a small, barren yard, his face toward a high brick wall. Above us, the wall was pierced with slits of windows. In their frozen recesses, I thought I saw the eyes of thieves and murderers peering down upon us.

(*Bird cries. Frail winter sunlight. BARTLEBY, starved and shivering, stands facing the wall.*)

STANDARD: Bartleby!

(*No answer.*)

STANDARD: Hello, Bartleby, I've come to visit you.

(*BARTLEBY turns to glance at STANDARD. Starved face. Hollow eyes. He turns away.*)

STANDARD: Bartleby…I'm sorry to find you here. This morning I returned from a journey. I learned you'd been brought here. I hurried over. Do you say hello to me?

(*Silence.*)

STANDARD: Bartleby… On my journey I've had much time to reflect. I traveled to the suburbs, where I've not been for many years. Manhattan, you know, is a world unto itself. Wall Street…unto itself…

(*Silence.*)

STANDARD: You don't look comfortable here—are you well treated? Are you able to sleep?

(*A MAN's whistling is heard off. THE GRUB MAN enters, a fat man in an odd array of sweaters, overcoats, and a filthy apron. He halts at a distance. Stops whistling. Silence.*)

GRUB MAN: (*Stamping his feet, blowing on his hands.*) Ah-ha! Friends and visitors, visitors and friends. Welcome to all! The Grub Man is what I'm called, and I count myself a friend to all who wishes what's good and nourishing on a bitter day—

STANDARD: (*Interrupt.*) What's your business? I'm occupied.

GRUB MAN: (*Jerking a thumb toward BARTLEBY.*) That your friend?

STANDARD: Yes. What of that?

GRUB MAN: One question. Just one. Does he wish to starve?

STANDARD: Of course not. I mean to see that he doesn't.

GRUB MAN: Then… (*Bowing deeply.*) I'm the Grub Man. Gentlemen who has friends here hires me to provide them with something reasonable to eat. If he wants to starve, well and good, let him die on prison fare, that's all.

STANDARD: Is this so?

GRUB MAN: My honor, sir, my honor.

STANDARD: Very well. That gentleman there is my friend. Give him…give him the best dinner you can get.

GRUB MAN: (*Bowing deeply.*) The finest, sir, the finest.

STANDARD: (*Giving coins.*) You must be as polite to him as possible.

GRUB MAN: Try my manners, sir, try 'em.

STANDARD: And you'll comply with his requests, however eccentric they may seem.

GRUB MAN: You'll see manners, sir. You'll see compliance. Oh introduce me to him, sir, I'm eager to make the acquaintance!

STANDARD: Bartleby?

(*BARTLEBY turns. They cross to him. The GRUB MAN bows low.*)

GRUB MAN: Your sarvant, sir, your humble sarvant!

STANDARD: Bartleby, this is a friend, the Grub Man. He'll supply you with whatever you want to eat—

GRUB MAN: (*Overlapping.*) Oh Mr. Bartleby, sir! I'm honored to sarve!

STANDARD: Tell him what you wish. He'll get it for you.

GRUB MAN (*Bowing, grinning.*) Hope you find it pleasant here, Mr. Bartleby: nice grounds, cool apartments. Hope you'll stay with us some time, sir—try to make it awful agreeable!

STANDARD: Are you hungry, Bartleby? Would you like to dine?

GRUB MAN: What'll you have for dinner today, Mr. Bartleby? Something hot for a bitter day. Shall I tempt you?

STANDARD: What would you like, Bartleby? Whatever you wish.

GRUB MAN: Mr. Bartleby, sir, yours to command!

(Slight pause.)

BARTLEBY: (Quietly.) I prefer not to dine today.

(Pause.)

GRUB MAN: Eh? What? Not dine? But you must nourish yourself these wintry days! Here, allow me to propose: crusty pies with—

(BARTLEBY has turned away. He stands facing the wall.)

STANDARD: Leave him.

GRUB MAN: How's this? (Whispers.) He's odd, ain't he?

STANDARD: I believe he's a little… (Gestures vaguely.)

GRUB MAN: (Squinting.) Eh? A little…? (A light dawns.) Ah. Deranged. 'Pon my word. And I thought he was a gentleman forger! They're always pale and genteel, ain't they?

STANDARD: I was never acquainted with any forgers. Please leave us now. Take care of my friend and you won't lose by it. Good day.

GRUB MAN: (Bowing as he backs away.) Just going, sir. Your sarvant, Mr. Bartleby, your sarvant, sir…your sarvant…

(THE GRUB MAN has gone. Silence. Birds.)

STANDARD: You see, Bartleby: it's not so vile a place as all that. There's nothing shameful in your being here. There are no demands placed on you. And you're free to follow your own wishes. I should think you'd find this place very much to your liking!

(Pause.)

STANDARD: Bartleby, it wasn't I who brought you here—or even who caused you to be brought here. I had nothing to do with it! Look: there's the sky. Here's a plot of earth. It's tranquil…very still… (Softly fervent.) Oh Bartleby, please answer me!

BARTLEBY: (A cry of fury and anguish.) I KNOW WHERE I AM!

(Pause.)

BARTLEBY: I KNOW YOU!

(Pause.)

BARTLEBY: I. KNOW. WHO. YOU. ARE!

(Pause.)

STANDARD: (Deeply shaken.) Oh Bartleby! Believe me! I've tried to be your friend!

(Silence. STANDARD, stunned, turns, exits. Bird cries. Light fades on BARTLEBY.)

21.

STANDARD: (To audience.) Two days later, a message from the warden of The Tombs: "Prisoner refuses to eat…refuses to abide by prison rules. If you have concern for prisoner's welfare, come at once!" And so…

(Music. The prison yard. BARTLEBY is seated motionless on the ground. STANDARD, carrying a small parcel, enters. He stands at a slight distance.)

STANDARD: (Softly.) Bartleby…

(BARTLEBY turns slowly to look at STANDARD.)

STANDARD: I've come to help. I've brought you some food.

(STANDARD holds out parcel. BARTLEBY looks away. STANDARD sets it on the ground. Pause.)

STANDARD: Let me sit quietly with you.

(STANDARD sits on the ground at a slight distance from BARTLEBY. Bird cries. He removes his handkerchief, moistens it, and dabs gently at BARTLEBY's face. BARTLEBY allows STANDARD to clean him. Then, bowing his head, begins to tremble, then to weep.)

STANDARD: Here…Bartleby… Take my coat…

(Removes overcoat and drapes it over BARTLEBY's shoulders. His arm remains around BARTLEBY's shoulder. He sings softly to BARTLEBY.)

STANDARD:
A roving I will go
A roving I will go
I'll stay no more
On England's shore
A roving I will go.

(Pause. STANDARD rises.)

STANDARD: Goodbye, Bartleby. I'll come again tomorrow...

(Music. Bird cries. STANDARD moves away.)

22.

STANDARD: *(To audience.)* Next day...

(Light shifts. GRUB MAN is at STANDARD's side. He carries a ladle and a heavy pot.)

GRUB MAN: Wastes away, sir, he wastes away!

STANDARD: *(Softly.)* Yes?

GRUB MAN: God's truth, sir. Since you was last here, I try to tempt him, sir—every kind of delicacy—but he wastes away. But here. He's in the yard. Come see for yourself...

(GRUB MAN leads STANDARD to the yard. BARTLEBY is huddled motionless on the ground. They halt.)

STANDARD: *(Softly.)* Bartleby.

GRUB MAN: *(Elaborate bow.)* Evening, Mr. Bartleby. Please you to dine? Care to take your vittles here or in your private apartments?

STANDARD: Bartleby...wake up...your dinner's arrived...

GRUB MAN: Mr. Bartleby, sir, you are served.

(STANDARD goes to BARTLEBY. Gently touches BARTLEBY's brow. Pause.)

STANDARD: *(Softly.)* Ahh.

GRUB MAN: What now, sir? Won't dine today, either?

STANDARD: *(Softly.)* Won't dine today, either.

GRUB MAN: Singular fellow, eh, lives without dining...

STANDARD: Mmm. Lives without dining.

GRUB MAN: Ahh... But never heard of that! Lives without dining. *(Whispers.)* Shall we leave him asleep?

STANDARD: Yes. Leave him asleep. With kings. And counselors...

GRUB MAN: Asleep? *(Pause. Softly.)* Ahhh—now I understand, sir! *(Bowing, backing away.)* Your sarvant, sir...! Your sarvant...! Your sarvant...!

(Music begins to play. The light is fading. In dim light upstage, KEEPER appears with a litter. KEEPER and GRUB MAN together lift BARTLEBY'S BODY onto the litter. They remain at a slight distance.)

23.

STANDARD steps forward into light. He wears a black armband. As he speaks, the scene of BARTLEBY's funeral plays silently in half-light behind him as, one by one, TURKEY, NIPPERS, GINGER NUT, and LANDLORD, bundled in heavy coats and scarves, enter and stand in a ragged group around BARTLEBY's corpse.

STANDARD: *(To audience.)* I saw to it that Bartleby did not begin eternity in a pauper's grave. I stood at the graveside in a light snowfall. And walked home at twilight through the icebound desert of Broadway...

(A clock chimes. Lights up on street. FAIRCHILD enters. He is wearing a rich new coat. He hails STANDARD.)

FAIRCHILD: Evening, sir! Chilly enough, I believe! Glad to see you, sir!

STANDARD: Evening, Fairchild. Yes, it's cold. *(The coat.)* But I daresay you've come up in the world.

FAIRCHILD: And you're better off, sir, now that your millstone's been removed. *(Pause.)* Bartleby, I mean, sir. He's well away, now, eh? *(Pause.)* But you're in mourning, sir. My condolences. Is it...?

STANDARD: He.

FAIRCHILD: Ah, well. My deepest condolences. But you... *(Faint smile.)* Can it be, sir, you miss him?

STANDARD: *(Fiercely.)* And if I do.

FAIRCHILD: I'm sorry sir, very sorry! He...well... *(Awkward laugh.)* But, no, sir. There's no point dwelling on things. After all. The easiest way's the best. You taught me that lesson, sir, and I prosper.

STANDARD: Do you, Fairchild? I'm not surprised.

FAIRCHILD: I'm in your debt, sir. *(Tightening his scarf.)* Bitter night, eh! But a hot fire and a hearty supper waits. The easiest...the best. Good evening, sir. Good evening. God bless! *(He is gone.)*

(A light snow is falling on BARTLEBY's funeral. One by one, the MOURNERS have taken their leave. GINGER NUT, the last to depart, kisses a finger and touches it to BARTLEBY's forehead.)

GINGER NUT: *(Softly.)* Bartleby…

STANDARD: *(To audience.)* And when I hear his name now, hardly can I express the emotions that seize me! *(Turning to gaze at BARTLEBY'S CORPSE.)* Ahh, Bartleby—! *(Turning to the audience. Softly, with a wide gesture.)* Ahh, humanity—!

(Slight pause. He tightens his muffler. Touches his hat. Nods to the audience. He leaves the stage. The snow falls steadily on BARTLEBY'S CORPSE. Ten seconds. Light fades.)

(END OF PLAY.)

Part V

EUROPEAN LITERATURE ON STAGE

Think of all the great classic European stories. Are there hundreds? Thousands? How about tens of thousands? From Aristophanes to Zola, writers have been telling compelling stories about the human condition for thousands of years. Given this magnitude, how can we hope to keep them alive? How do they come off the shelves, shed their dust, and continue to give joy, enlightenment, and entertainment? The obvious way is for them to be taught in our schools and colleges. But even at best, only a fraction of these works can be taught, and those tend to be the more popular stories, unless one gets into some specialized university seminar. Beyond that, we must leave it to the adaptors, those intrepid souls who brave the backwaters of the bookstores, the lost latitudes of the libraries, to bring to light that which really shouldn't be forgotten through adaptation for the stage.

Here, we have three very different adaptations, three very different sources, and three different styles to boot, making for a unique look at the adapter's art. *The Man Who Laughs* is a throwback to *commedia dell'arte* in its purest form, but with a twist. Through a series of scenarios, peppered with lazzi, Victor Hugo's tragic tale is presented primarily in pantomime but in an operatic style worthy of Leoncavallo that also incorporates a Brechtian use of supertitles. *Frankenstein* is a unique retelling of the famous Mary Wollstonecraft Shelley novel using a narrative style merged with a Greek chorus concept to tell the gruesome tale as gothic story theater. *Northanger Abbey* is perhaps the most straightforward in its translation from the novel to the stage in that it changes Austen's narrative to action and makes dialogue paramount. Yet here, too, the writing is pleasantly different: an ingenious dovetailing of two stories—that of Austen's heroine and that of the novel Austen's heroine is reading—with actors playing parallel roles in two very different periods, nineteenth century Regency and eighteenth century Cavalier.

Three great stories of Hugo, Shelley, and Austen have been reclaimed from those dusty shelves for a twenty-first century audience by three modern American adaptations: Kiran Rikhye's *The Man Who Laughs*, Rob Reese's *Frankenstein*, and Lynn Marie Macy's *Northanger Abbey*. Surely their publication will be a catalyst to future productions, which, in turn, will bring their audiences back to those shelves for further reading, exploration, and, possibly, adaptation.

—David Fuller

FRANKENSTEIN

from the novel by Mary Wollstonecraft Shelley

Adapted for the Stage by Rob Reese

ROB REESE is a playwright-director who was born in Nashville. He received a communications/theater arts degree, with a minor in film, from Boston College, and went to "grad school" at Second City, the Improv Olympic, and the Annoyance Theater, all in Chicago. He has studied with improv mentor Del Close and with Stuart Hecht of Boston College, and at the Saratoga International Theater Institute with Anne Bogart. Reese is the artistic director of Amnesia Wars Productions, which has produced his plays *Frankenstein, Survivor: Vietnam!* (published by NYTE in *Plays and Playwrights 2004*), and *Keanu Reeves Saves the Universe*, all of which he also directed; and long-form improv shows including *Crisis Junkie, Honey Harlowe,* and *Psycheroticproviholicyesandsomethinvoodoo*. Amnesia Wars is also a member group of the meta-group International Clowns, which includes members from Germany, Zimbabwe, Holland, and Colombia, and has performed in the United States and abroad. Reese is on the teaching faculty at the Second City Training Center in New York City, and he also teaches improv workshops and classes. He is currently working on "The Tad Granite Mysteries," a pan-media serial. He lives in New York with his wonderful Jennifer.

Frankenstein was first presented by Amnesia Wars Productions (Rob Reese, Artistic Director) with assistance from The Process Studio Theater on May 24, 2000, at the Pelican Studio Theater, New York City, with the following cast and credits:

Robert Walton, DeLacey	Dirk Barrett
Victor Frankenstein	Jayson Berkshire
Margaret Saville, Agatha DeLacey	Janet Dunson
M4, Alphonse Frankenstein, M. Waldman, Various Sailors, Servants, Villagers	Brian Gaskey
Eve Saville, Safie DeLacey	Julia Motyka
M2, Elizabeth Lavenza, Various Sailors, Servants, Villagers	Miya Signor
M1, Catherine Frankenstein, Landlady, Justine, Girl, Various Sailors, Servants, Villagers	Ellen Simpson
M3, William Frankenstein, Man, Various Sailors, Servants, Villagers	Sean Sterling

Directed by: Rob Reese
Music Composed and Performed by: T. Weldon Anderson
Rehearsal Stage Manager: Monica Bueno
Production Stage Manager: Jason Y. Evans
Lighting Designer: Rob Reese
Psychology Consultant: Bob Reese
House Manager: Deborah Kay Augustine
Media Support: Makeko and Jon Magner

In September of 2002, *Frankenstein* was further adapted by Reese specifically for the needs of Mont'Kiara International School in Kuala Lumpur, Malaysia. The production was performed by the students at The Actors Studio in Kuala Lumpur.

"Every thing must have a beginning…and that beginning must be linked to something that went before. The Hindoos give the world an elephant to support it, but they make the elephant stand upon a tortoise. Invention, it must be humbly admitted, does not consist in creating out of the void, but out of chaos; the materials must, in the first place, be afforded: it can give form to dark, shapeless substances, but cannot bring into being the substance itself. In all matters of discovery and invention, even of those that appertain to the imagination, we are continually reminded of the story of Columbus and his egg. Invention consists in the capacity of seizing on the capabilities of a subject, and in the power of moulding and fashioning ideas suggested to it."
—Mary Shelley, from the preface of the 1831 printing of **Frankenstein**

CAST OF CHARACTERS

MARGARET SAVILLE, sister of Arctic explorer Robert Walton
EVE SAVILLE, daughter of Margaret
ROBERT WALTON, Arctic explorer
VICTOR FRANKENSTEIN
DeLACEY, an old blind man
AGATHA DeLACEY, DeLacey's daughter
SAFIE DeLACEY, Agatha's daughter

Monster Chorus*

M1: CATHERINE FRANKENSTEIN, mother of Victor; LANDLADY, of Victor in Ingolstadt
M2: ELIZABETH LAVENZA, adopted "cousin" and beloved of Victor
M3: WILLIAM FRANKENSTEIN, brother of Victor
M4: ALPHONSE FRANKENSTEIN, father of Victor; M. WALDMAN, mentor of Frankenstein

Other Characters, Unassigned to a Specific Monster Chorus Part

VARIOUS SAILORS, on Walton's ship
JUSTINE, a servant of the Frankenstein house
VARIOUS SERVANTS, of the Frankenstein house
VARIOUS VILLAGERS
A GIRL
A MAN, a rustic, the Girl's father

---

*The part of the Monster is broken up into a chorus of four parts: M1, M2, M3, and M4. In the original production, the Monster Chorus was performed by only four actors, but can be comprised of as many actors as the production warrants. In the stage directions, the chorus is referred to simply as MONSTER.

SETTING

The open stage is populated by rough, jagged, moveable set pieces appropriate for seamless transitions from one setting to another. Two small, "permanent" set areas flank the stage. The first area contains a table with a lamp, a chair, and various accoutrements appropriate for an upper class drawing room of the late eighteenth century. The second area is the captain's cabin of a merchant ship of the same era. A writing desk is prominent.

PROLOGUE

MARGARET SAVILLE enters the drawing room, lights the lamp, and sits. She is followed by EVE, her daughter, who runs excitedly into the area with a parcel. They tear into the package, which includes several loose letters and a packet of pages bound by ribbons. MARGARET inspects the dates on the letters, selects one, and hands it to EVE, who opens it and begins to read.

SLIDE:
Mrs. Saville, England St. Petersburgh, Dec. 11th, 1795
My Dear Sister,
You will rejoice to hear that no disaster...

EVE: My dear sister, you will rejoice to hear that no disaster has accompanied the commencement of an enterprise which you have regarded with such evil foreboding. I arrived here yesterday, and my first task is to assure my dear sister of my welfare and increasing

(Reveal WALTON, writing at the small desk in the cabin area. The beginning of WALTON's line loosely overlaps the end of EVE's. This pattern continues throughout.)

EVE, WALTON: confidence in the success of my undertaking.

WALTON: Inspired by the wind of promise, my daydreams become more fervent and vivid. I try in vain to be persuaded that the North Pole is the seat of frost and desolation; it ever presents itself to my imagination as the region of beauty and delight.

(MARGARET selects another letter, reads.)

(SLIDE:
Mrs. Margaret Saville,
London, England
Archangel, 28th March, 1796
I have hired a vessel and am occupied in collecting my sailors; those whom…)

MARGARET: I have hired a vessel and am occupied in collecting my sailors; those whom I have already engaged appear to be men on whom I can depend and are certainly possessed

MARGARET, WALTON: of dauntless courage. But I have one want

WALTON: which I have never yet been able to satisfy, and the absence of the object of which I now feel as a most severe evil.

WALTON, MARGARET: I have no friend.

MARGARET: I desire the company of a man who could sympathize with me, whose eyes would reply to mine. I have no one near me, gentle yet courageous, possessed of a cultivated as well as of a capacious mind, whose tastes are like my own.

(EVE selects the next letter and opens it.)

(SLIDE:
Mrs. Saville, England, July 7th, 1796
My dear Sister,
I write a few lines in haste to say that I am safe—and well advanced…)

EVE: I write a few lines in haste to say that I am safe—and well advanced on my voyage. I am in good spirits: my men are bold and apparently firm of purpose, nor do the floating sheets of ice that continually pass us, indicating the dangers of the region appear to dismay them.

(SLIDE:
Mrs. Saville, England
August 5th, 1796
So strange an accident has happened to us that I cannot forbear recording it…)

MARGARET: So strange an accident has happened to us that I cannot forbear recording it, although it is very

probable that you will see me before these papers can come into your possession.

MARGARET, WALTON: Last Monday we were surrounded by ice

SAILORS: ICE!

(The stage explosively becomes the deck of the ship; SAILORS work frantically in tandem to drop sails, pull rigging, and secure the ship. WALTON continues his narration while physically joining SAILORS in the emergency.)

WALTON: which closed in the ship on all sides, scarcely leaving her the sea-room in which she floated. Our situation was somewhat dangerous!

(One by one, SAILORS complete their tasks and stare out into the frozen void; ultimately all is still.)

WALTON: The mist cleared away, and we beheld, stretched out in every direction, vast and irregular plains of ice, which seemed to have no end.

(WALTON and SAILORS, doubting their eyes, watch the progress of movement in the distance.)

WALTON: My own mind began to grow watchful with anxious thoughts, when a strange sight suddenly attracted our attention.

LIEUTENANT: Sir, a sledge, drawn by dogs. A half-mile distance.

WALTON: A being, which had the shape of a man, but apparently of gigantic stature, sat in the sledge, and guided the dogs. We watched the rapid progress of the traveler, until he was lost among the distant inequalities of the ice.

FRANKENSTEIN: *(Calls from offstage, opposite the distant sledge.)* Ahoy!

LIEUTENANT: Ahoy? Ahoy!

(SAILORS rush to FRANKENSTEIN and attempt to haul him up into the ship. He pushes them off.)

FRANKENSTEIN: Before I come on board your vessel, will you have the kindness to inform me whither you are bound?

SAILOR: We are on a voyage of discovery towards the northern pole.

WALTON: Good God! Margaret, if you had seen the man who thus capitulated for his safety, your surprise would have been boundless.

(FRANKENSTEIN is brought on deck. He immediately collapses. SAILORS drag him into WALTON's cabin.)

EVE: Two days passed before he was able to speak, and I often feared that his sufferings had deprived him of understanding. I never saw a more interesting creature:

(FRANKENSTEIN stirs)

SAILOR: Captain!

LIEUTENANT: Why have you come so far upon the ice in so strange a vehicle?

FRANKENSTEIN: To seek one who fled from me.

WALTON: His eyes have generally an expression of wildness, and even madness,

LIEUTENANT: And did the man whom you pursued travel in the same fashion?

FRANKENSTEIN: He did.

SAILOR: Then I fancy we have seen him, for before we picked you up we saw some dogs drawing a sledge, with a man in it, across the ice!

FRANKENSTEIN: I must… *(Sits up, but immediately collapses.)*

WALTON: You are far too weak to sustain the rawness of the atmosphere, remain in the cabin. We will post watch and give you instant notice if any new object should appear in sight.

(WALTON sends SAILORS out of his cabin.)

WALTON: He must have been a noble creature in his better days, being even now in wreck

WALTON, EVE: so attractive and amiable.

EVE: Such is my journal of what relates to this strange occurrence up to the present day. The stranger has gradually improved in health but is very silent and appears uneasy when anyone except myself enters his cabin. Yet his manners are so conciliating and gentle.

(SLIDE:
Mrs. Saville, England
August 13th, 1796
My affection for my guest increases every day. He excites…)

MARGARET: My affection for my guest increases every day. He excites at once my

MARGARET, WALTON: admiration and my pity to an astonishing degree.

WALTON: How can I see so noble a creature destroyed by misery without feeling the most poignant grief?

MARGARET: He is now much recovered from his illness, and has frequently conversed with me on my projects, which I have communicated to him without disguise.

WALTON: One man's life or death is but a small price to pay for the acquirement of the knowledge which I seek, for the dominion I should acquire and transmit over the elemental foes of our race.

FRANKENSTEIN: Unhappy man! Do you share my madness? Have you drunk also of the intoxicating draught? Hear me; let me reveal my tale, and you will dash the cup from your lips! I—I have lost everything and cannot begin life anew.

WALTON: For my own part, I begin to love him as a brother.

FRANKENSTEIN: I had determined at one time that the memory of these evils should die with me, but you have won me to alter my determination. Were we among the tamer scenes of nature I might fear to encounter your unbelief, perhaps your ridicule; but many things will appear possible in these wild and mysterious regions which would provoke the laughter of those unacquainted with the ever-varied powers of nature.

WALTON: No, I cannot endure that you should renew your grief by a recital of your misfortunes.

FRANKENSTEIN: I thank you, for your sympathy, but it is useless; my fate is nearly fulfilled. I wait but for one event, and then I shall repose in peace.

(SLIDE:
Mrs. Saville, England
August 19, 1796
I have resolved every night to record, as nearly as possible…)

MARGARET: I have resolved every night to record, as nearly as possible in his own words, what he has related during the day.

MARGARET, WALTON: Even now, as I commence my task

WALTON: his full-toned voice swells in my ears; his lustrous eyes dwell on me with all their melancholy sweetness. Strange and harrowing must be his story, frightful the storm which embraced the gallant vessel on its course and wrecked it—thus!

(EVE reaches in the parcel from which the letters came and pulls out a packet of papers, bound with a ribbon like a manuscript.)

ACT ONE

EVE: I am Swiss by birth, a Genevese

FRANKENSTEIN: I am Swiss by birth, a Genevese, and my family is one of the most distinguished of that republic. My father had filled several public situations with honor and reputation. My mother possessed a mind of an uncommon mold, and her courage rose to support her in her adversity.

(A series of tableaux reveal ALPHONSE and CATHERINE, with FRANKENSTEIN in idyllic family scenes.)

MARGARET: I, their eldest, remained for several years their only child, the innocent and helpless creature bestowed on them by heaven, whom to bring up to good, and whose future lot it was in their hands to direct to happiness or misery, according as they fulfilled their duties, towards me.

(ELIZABETH enters.)

WALTON: My mother had much desired to have a daughter. When I was about five years old, Elizabeth Lavenza became the inmate of my parents' house

(A series of tableaux show ELIZABETH with FRANKENSTEIN, happily playing and interacting with one another and the PARENTS.)

MARGARET: To my mother, it was more than a duty; it was a necessity, a passion for her to act in her turn the guardian angel to the afflicted.

EVE: Everyone loved Elizabeth—my more than sister—the beautiful and adored companion of all my occupations and my pleasures.

(WILLIAM enters.)

FRANKENSTEIN: On the birth of a second son, William, my parents gave up entirely their wandering life and fixed themselves in their native country. No human being could have passed a happier childhood than myself.

(A series of tableaux introduce WILLIAM to the idyllically happy FAMILY. The FIVE CHARACTERS laugh,

dance, play, eat, and demonstrate perfect happiness and family bliss.)

WALTON: My temper was sometimes violent, and my passions vehement; but by some law in my temperature they were turned not towards childish pursuits but to an eager desire to learn.

FRANKENSTEIN: It was the secrets of heaven and earth that I desired; my inquiries were directed to the metaphysical, or in its highest sense, the physical secrets of the world.

MARGARET: It may appear strange that such should arise in the eighteenth century; but while I followed the routine of education in the schools of Geneva, I was, to a great degree, self-taught with regard to my favorite studies.

EVE: I entered with the greatest diligence into the search of the

EVE, FRANKENSTEIN: philosopher's stone and the elixir of life;

EVE: but the latter soon obtained my undivided attention.

FRANKENSTEIN: What glory would attend the discovery if I could banish disease from the human frame and render man invulnerable to any but a violent death!

EVE: When I had attained the age of seventeen, my parents resolved that I should become a student at the University of Ingolstadt.

FRANKENSTEIN: But before the day resolved upon could arrive, the first misfortune of my life occurred— an omen, as it were, of my future misery.

WALTON: Elizabeth had caught the scarlet fever; her illness was severe, and she was in the greatest danger. During her illness my mother attended her sickbed. Elizabeth was saved, but the consequences of this imprudence were fatal to her preserver.

FRANKENSTEIN: On her deathbed the fortitude and benignity of this best of women did not desert her.

(CATHERINE, on her deathbed, joins the hands of ELIZABETH and FRANKENSTEIN.)

CATHERINE: My children, my firmest hopes of future happiness were placed on the prospect of your union. This expectation will now be the consolation of your father. *(Dies.)*

FRANKENSTEIN: She died calmly; and her countenance expressed affection even in death.

FRANKENSTEIN, MARGARET: I need not describe

MARGARET: the feelings of those whose dearest ties are rent by that most irreparable evil; the void that presents itself to the soul; and the despair that is exhibited on the countenance.

FRANKENSTEIN: My departure for school, which had been deferred by these events, was now again determined upon.

(FRANKENSTEIN pulls luggage off of a coach and steps into a throng of busy, bustling STRANGERS.)

MARGARET: I was now alone. I delivered my letters of introduction and paid a visit to some of the principal professors. Chance,

FRANKENSTEIN: or rather the evil influence, the Angel of Destruction, which asserted omnipotent sway over me from the moment I turned my reluctant steps from my father's door led me first to Monsieur Waldman.

(FRANKENSTEIN sits with OTHER STUDENTS surrounding M. WALDMAN.)

M. WALDMAN: The ancient teachers of chemistry promised impossibilities and performed nothing. The modern masters promise very little; they know that metals cannot be transmuted and that the elixir of life is a chimera. But these philosophers, whose hands seem only made to dabble in dirt, and their eyes to pore over the microscope or crucible, have indeed performed miracles.

(FRANKENSTEIN stands slowly, engrossed with THE PROFESSOR's words.)

M. WALDMAN: They penetrate into the recesses of nature and show how she works in her hiding places. They ascend into the heavens; they have discovered how the blood circulates, and the nature of the air we breathe. They have acquired new and almost unlimited powers; they can command the thunders of heaven, mimic the earthquake, and even mock the invisible world with its own shadows.

FRANKENSTEIN: Such were the professor's words— let me say such the words of the fate—enounced to destroy me.

(The delineation between the various realities softens as ALL piece together the sundry elements of

FRANKENSTEIN's laboratory and experiment: GRAVEDIGGERS and THUGS appear from the shadows and pass off indistinct parcels, for which FRANKENSTEIN pays them. He takes copious notes, performs bits of surgery, assembles and tinkers with unrecognizable instruments and equipment.)

WALTON: As I applied so closely, it may be easily conceived that my progress was rapid. My ardor was indeed the astonishment of the students, and my proficiency that of the masters.

EVE: Two years passed in this manner, during which I paid no visit to Geneva, but was engaged, heart and soul, in the pursuit of some discoveries which I hoped to make.

MARGARET: My attention was fixed upon every object the most insupportable to the delicacy of the human feelings.

FRANKENSTEIN: I saw how the fine form of man was

FRANKENSTEIN, WALTON: degraded and wasted.

FRANKENSTEIN: I beheld the

FRANKENSTEIN, EVE: corruption of death

FRANKENSTEIN: succeed to the blooming cheek of life;

FRANKENSTEIN: I saw how the

FRANKENSTEIN, MARGARET: worm inherited

FRANKENSTEIN: the wonders of the eye and brain. I paused, examining and analyzing all the minutiae of causation, as exemplified in the change from life to death, and death to life,

WALTON: until from the midst of this darkness a sudden light broke in upon me—

WALTON, FRANKENSTEIN: a light so brilliant and wondrous,

FRANKENSTEIN: yet so simple, that while I became

FRANKENSTEIN, EVE: dizzy with the immensity

FRANKENSTEIN: of the prospect which it illustrated,

EVE: I was surprised that among so many men of genius who had directed their inquiries towards the same science, that I alone should be reserved to discover so astonishing a secret.

FRANKENSTEIN, WALTON, MARGARET, EVE: Remember, I am not recording the vision of a madman.

WALTON: The sun does not more certainly shine in the heavens than that which I now affirm is true.

FRANKENSTEIN: Some miracle might have produced it, yet the stages of the discovery were distinct and probable. After days and nights of incredible labor and fatigue, I succeeded in discovering the cause of generation and life; nay, more, I became myself capable of bestowing animation upon lifeless matter!

(Pause.)

FRANKENSTEIN: I see by your eagerness and the wonder and hope which your eyes express, my friend, that you expect to be informed of the secret with which I am acquainted; that cannot be; listen patiently until the end of my story, and you will easily perceive why I am reserved upon that subject. I will not lead you on to your destruction and infallible misery.

(Pause.)

MARGARET: When I found so astonishing a power placed within my hands, I hesitated a long time concerning the manner in which I should employ it. Then, after much deliberation…

FRANKENSTEIN: I began the creation of a human being. As the minuteness of the parts formed a great hindrance to my speed, I resolved to make the being of a gigantic stature, that is to say, about eight feet in height, and proportionably large.

EVE: Life and death appeared to me ideal bounds, which I should first break through, and pour a torrent of light into our dark world.

WALTON: A new species would bless me as its creator and source; many happy and excellent natures would owe their being to me.

FRANKENSTEIN: No father could claim the gratitude of his child so completely as I should deserve theirs.

(Pause.)

MARGARET: It was on a dreary night of November that I beheld the accomplishment of my toils. With an anxiety that almost amounted to agony,

EVE: I collected the instruments of life around me, that I might infuse a spark of being into the lifeless thing that lay at my feet. It was already one in the morning;

FRANKENSTEIN: the rain pattered dismally against the panes, and my candle was nearly burnt out, when, by the glimmer of the half-extinguished light…

(Pause. Sound effects/music: The faintest of heartbeats can be heard, increasing in strength. ALL twitch the fingers of one hand in sequence with the heartbeat. As the beat becomes stronger, MONSTER slowly raises his head and opens his eyes.)

FRANKENSTEIN: How can I describe my emotions at this…

FRANKENSTEIN, MARGARET: Catastrophe!

MARGARET: Or how delineate the wretch whom with such infinite pains and care I had endeavored to form?

(MONSTER slowly rises, awkwardly examining his own limbs, his range of motion, his perception. MONSTER makes a few simple, quiet sounds.)

EVE: His limbs were in proportion, and I had selected his features as beautiful.

EVE, FRANKENSTEIN: Beautiful! Great God!

FRANKENSTEIN: His yellow skin scarcely covered the work of muscles and arteries beneath;

MARGARET: his hair was of a lustrous black, and flowing;

WALTON: his teeth of a pearly whiteness;

FRANKENSTEIN: but these luxuriances only formed a more horrid contrast with his watery eyes, that seemed almost of the same color as the dun-white sockets in which they were set,

EVE: his shrivelled complexion and straight black lips.

WALTON: The different accidents of life are not so changeable as

WALTON, FRANKENSTEIN: the feelings of human nature.

FRANKENSTEIN: The beauty of the dream vanished, and breathless horror and disgust filled my heart.

(MONSTER reaches toward FRANKENSTEIN and cries out. FRANKENSTEIN fearfully returns the cry, and retreats from the area.)

EVE: No mortal could support the horror of that countenance. I escaped, and passed the night wretchedly. A mummy again endued with animation could not be so hideous as that wretch.

(FRANKENSTEIN collapses in a solitary spot. Pause. Lighting indicates the arrival of morning.)

EVE: Morning, dismal and wet, at length dawned. I steeled myself and ascended into my room. I dreaded to behold this monster; but I feared still more that anyone else should see him.

(FRANKENSTEIN pauses by the door, takes a deep breath and fearfully throws it open.)

EVE: My bedroom was freed from its hideous guest. I could hardly believe that so great a good fortune could have befallen me, when I became assured that my enemy had indeed fled, I clapped my hands for joy and laughed aloud.

(FRANKENSTEIN laughs maniacally. LANDLADY enters.)

LANDLADY: My dear Victor, what, for God's sake, is the matter? Do not laugh in that manner. How ill you are! What is the cause of all this?

FRANKENSTEIN: Do not ask me! Oh, save me! save me!

(FRANKENSTEIN struggles wildly as he falls to the ground in a fit. LANDLADY helps him into bed.)

WALTON: This was the commencement of a nervous fever, which confined me for several months. I was in reality very ill. The form of the monster on whom I had bestowed existence was forever before my eyes, and I raved incessantly concerning him.

FRANKENSTEIN: By very slow degrees, and with frequent relapses that alarmed and grieved my nurse, I recovered. It is a divine spring!

LANDLADY: Since you appear in such good spirits, you will perhaps be glad to see a letter that has been lying here some days for you; it is from your cousin, I believe.

(FRANKENSTEIN reads letter.)

(SLIDE:
My dearest Cousin,
For a long time I have thought that each…)

ELIZABETH: My dearest Cousin. For a long time I have thought that each post would bring this line, and my persuasions have restrained my uncle from under-

taking a journey to Ingolstadt. I figure to myself that the task of attending on your sickbed has devolved on some mercenary old nurse, who could never guess your wishes nor minister to them with the care and affection of your poor cousin. Get well—and return to us. You will find a happy, cheerful home and friends who love you dearly. Your father's health is vigorous, and he asks but to see you, but to be assured that you are well; and not a care will ever cloud his benevolent countenance. I have written myself into better spirits, dear cousin; but my anxiety returns upon me as I conclude. Write, dearest Victor—one line—one word will be a blessing to us. Adieu! My cousin, take care of yourself, and, I entreat you, write! Elizabeth Lavenza, Geneva, March 18th, 1795.

FRANKENSTEIN: Dear, dear Elizabeth! I wrote, and this exertion greatly fatigued me; but my convalescence had commenced, and proceeded regularly. In another fortnight I was able to leave my chamber.

(LANDLADY hands FRANKENSTEIN another letter; he reads.)

(SLIDE:
My dear Victor,
You have probably waited impatiently for a letter to fix the date…)

ALPHONSE: My dear Victor, you have probably waited impatiently for a letter to fix the date of your return to us, and I was at first tempted to write only a few lines, merely mentioning the day on which I should expect you. But that would be a cruel kindness, and I dare not do it. Your brother William is dead! That sweet child, whose smiles delighted and warmed my heart, who was so gentle, yet so gay! Victor, he is murdered! Last Thursday I, Elizabeth, and your brother went to walk in Plainpalais. It was already dusk before we thought of returning, and then we discovered that William, who had gone on before, was not to be found. This rather alarmed us, and we continued to search for him until night fell, We returned, with torches.

(ALPHONSE, ELIZABETH, and SERVANTS wander through forest with torches and lanterns.)

ALL: William, William!

(ALPHONSE finds WILLIAM'S BODY.)

ALPHONSE: William.

(ELIZABETH pushes through the CROWD toward WILLIAM and examines him.)

ALPHONSE: The print of the murderer's finger was on his neck.

ELIZABETH: Oh, God! I have murdered my darling child!

(WILLIAM and ELIZABETH play together. WILLIAM admires ELIZABETH'S necklace, which she removes and places over his head. He delights in the jewelry as he runs off.)

ALPHONSE: The necklace is gone and was doubtless the temptation which urged the murderer to the deed. We have no trace of him at present. Our exertions to discover him are unremitted; but they will not restore my beloved William! Come, dearest Victor; you alone can console Elizabeth. She weeps continually and accuses herself unjustly as the cause of his death; her words pierce my heart. We are all unhappy, but will not that be an additional motive for you, my son, to return and be our comforter? Your affectionate and afflicted father, Alphonse Frankenstein, Geneva, May 12th, 1795.

(SLIDE:
Your affectionate and afflicted father,
Alphonse Frankenstein, Geneva, May 12th, 1795)

EVE: It was completely dark when I arrived in the environs of Geneva; the gates of the town were already shut, so I resolved to visit the spot where my poor William had been murdered.

WALTON: The heavens were clouded, and I soon felt the rain coming slowly in large drops, but its violence quickly increased.

(Sound effect: Distant thunder.)

FRANKENSTEIN: William, dear angel! This is thy funeral, this is thy dirge!

(Sound effect/lighting: Lightning strikes, revealing MONSTER.)

EVE: I could not be mistaken. A flash of lightning illuminated the object and discovered its shape plainly to me;

MARGARET: its gigantic stature, and the deformity of its aspect,

FRANKENSTEIN, MARGARET: more hideous than belongs to humanity,

MARGARET: instantly armed me that it was the wretch, the filthy demon to whom I had given life.

FRANKENSTEIN: What did he there? Could he be the murderer of my brother? No sooner did that idea cross my imagination than I became convinced of its truth;

MARGARET: nothing in human shape could have destroyed that fair child.

FRANKENSTEIN: He is the murderer! HE is the murderer!

(FRANKENSTEIN points accusingly at MONSTER, though the individuals making up the MONSTER CHORUS separate and reform, denying FRANKENSTEIN a target for his wrath.)

WALTON: Two years had now nearly elapsed since the night on which he first received life; and was this his first crime?

FRANKENSTEIN: Alas! I have turned loose into the world a depraved wretch…

WALTON: …whose delight was in carnage and misery; had he not murdered my brother?

EVE: I paused when I reflected on the story that I had to tell.

FRANKENSTEIN: A being whom I myself had formed, and endued with life, had met me at midnight at the scene of the horrid crime. I remembered also the nervous fever with which I had been seized just at the time that I dated my creation, and which would give an air of delirium to a tale otherwise so utterly improbable.

EVE: I well knew that if any other had communicated such a relation to me, I should have looked upon it as the ravings of insanity. I therefore told no one.

(Lighting: Sunrise.)

FRANKENSTEIN: Day dawned; and I directed my steps towards the town. The gates were open, and I hastened to my father's house.

ALPHONSE: Welcome, my dearest Victor. Ah! You come to us now to share a misery which nothing can alleviate; yet your presence will, I hope, induce poor Elizabeth to cease her vain and tormenting self-accusations. She accused herself of having caused the death of your brother, and that made her very wretched. But since the murderer has been discovered…

FRANKENSTEIN: The murderer discovered! Good God! How can that be? Who could attempt to pursue him? It is impossible; one might as well try to overtake the winds or confine a mountain stream with straw. I saw him too; he was free last night!

ALPHONSE: I do not know what you mean, but to us the discovery we have made completes our misery. No one would believe it at first; and even now Elizabeth will not be convinced, notwithstanding all the evidence. Indeed, who would credit that Justine Moritz, who was so amiable and fond of all was capable of this.

MARGARET: Justine Moritz was a servant of our house who was beloved by all of us.

FRANKENSTEIN: Poor, poor girl, is she the accused? But it is wrongfully; everyone knows that; no one believes it, surely, Father?

ALPHONSE: No one did at first, but several circumstances came out that have almost forced conviction upon us; and her own behavior has been so confused as to add to the evidence of facts a weight that, I fear, leaves no hope for doubt.

(WILLIAM and ELIZABETH play together. William admires ELIZABETH's necklace, which she removes and places over his head. He delights in the jewelry as he runs off. ALPHONSE, ELIZABETH, and SERVANTS wander through forest with torches and lanterns.)

ALL: William, William!

(JUSTINE tires of the search and lays down, falls asleep. SERVANT enters and finds JUSTINE asleep. He rushes to her and pulls her up.)

SERVANT: Justine! Wake yourself! They have found the boy, he has been murdered, for a necklace.

(SERVANT notices the necklace on JUSTINE.)

SERVANT: Justine! MURDERER! MURDER!

(SERVANT rushes JUSTINE offstage.)

ALPHONSE: Justine was condemned. She perished on the scaffold as a murderess!

(FRANKENSTEIN leaves his FATHER and walks along the shore of a lake, brooding.)

FRANKENSTEIN: I was tempted to plunge into the silent lake, that the waters might close over me and my calamities forever. But I was restrained, when I thought of the heroic and suffering Elizabeth, whom I tenderly loved, and whose existence was bound up in mine. I thought also of my father, should I by my base desertion leave them exposed and unprotected to the malice of the fiend whom I had let loose among them? There was always scope for fear so long as anything I loved remained behind.

(Sound/lighting effect: Lightning strikes, revealing MONSTER.)

FRANKENSTEIN: Devil, do you dare approach me? Begone, vile insect! Or rather, stay, that I may trample you to dust!

(FRANKENSTEIN charges toward MONSTER; the individuals comprising the MONSTER CHORUS separate and avoid FRANKENSTEIN. He flails wildly as they reform MONSTER, out of his reach.)

MONSTER: I expected this reception.

M4: All men hate the wretched;

M2: how, then, must I be hated!

M1, M3: I who am miserable

MONSTER: beyond all living things!

M4: Yet you, my creator,

MONSTER: detest and spurn me, thy creature, to whom thou art bound by ties only dissoluble by the annihilation of one of us.

M2: You purpose to kill me?

MONSTER: How dare you sport thus with life?

M1: Do your duty towards me,

MONSTER: and I will do mine towards you and the rest of mankind.

FRANKENSTEIN: Abhorred monster! Fiend that thou art! The tortures of hell are too mild a vengeance for thy crimes.

(FRANKENSTEIN lunges; MONSTER again evades him easily.)

MONSTER: Oh, Frankenstein, be not equitable to every other and trample upon me alone,

M3: to whom thy justice,

M1: and even thy clemency and affection, is most due.

M2: I ought to be thy Adam,

M4: but I am rather the fallen angel,

M2: whom thou drivest from joy

M3, M4: for no misdeed.

M1, M2: Everywhere I see bliss,

M3, M4: from which I alone am irrevocably excluded.

M2: I was benevolent and good;

M4: misery made me a fiend.

M3: Make me happy,

MONSTER: and I shall again be virtuous.

M4: Listen to my tale;

M1: when you have heard that, abandon or commiserate me,

M1, M2, M3: as you shall judge that I deserve.

M1, M2, M4: But hear me.

FRANKENSTEIN: Cursed be the day, abhorred devil, in which you first saw light! Cursed be these hands that formed you!

M4: The guilty are allowed, by human laws,

MONSTER: bloody as they are,

M4: to speak in their own defense before they are condemned.

M1: On you it rests

M1, M3: whether I quit forever the neighborhood of man

M2: and lead a harmless life,

M1, M4: or become the scourge of your fellow creatures

MONSTER: and the author of your own speedy ruin.

FRANKENSTEIN: For the first time, I felt what the duties of a creator towards his creature were, and that I ought to render him happy before I complained of his wickedness. I consented to listen, and seating myself by the fire which my odious companion had lighted, he thus began his tale.

ACT TWO

MONSTER: It is with considerable difficulty that I remember the original era of my being; all the events of that period appear confused and indistinct. A strange multiplicity of sensations

M1: seized me, and I saw, felt, heard, and smelt at the same time;

M2: seized me, and I felt, saw, smelt, and heard, all at the same time;

M3: seized me, and I heard, smelt, saw, and felt at the same time;

M4: seized me, and I saw, smelt, heard, felt; all at the same time;

M1: and it was, indeed,

M4: a long time

M1: before I learned to

M2, M3: distinguish between the operations of my various senses.

MONSTER: It was dark when I awoke;

M1: I felt cold also, and half frightened,

MONSTER: instinctively, finding myself so desolate.

M2: Before I had quitted your apartment,

MONSTER: on a sensation of cold,

M1, M2, M4: I had covered myself with some clothes,

MONSTER: but these were insufficient to secure me from the dews of night.

M2: I was a poor,

M2, M1: helpless,

M2, M1, M3: miserable

MONSTER: wretch;

M2: I knew,

M2, M3: and could distinguish, nothing;

M1, M4: but feeling pain invade me on all sides,

M1, M2: I sat down and wept.

(M1, M2, M3 collapse and weep. M4 scans the area fearfully. Finally MONSTER relaxes, confident in his immediate safety. Eventually he notices the pleasant song of a nearby bird. In attempting to imitate the bird's song, MONSTER releases a terrible groan. Frightened by his own cry, MONSTER rises and continues to wander through the wood.)

M4: One day,

MONSTER: when I was oppressed by cold,

M3, M4: I found a

MONSTER: fire

M3, M4: which had been left by some wandering beggars,

M1, M2: and was overcome with delight at the

MONSTER: warmth I experienced from it.

(M1 and M3 shove their hands deep into the fire, screaming in pain as they are burned. As M1 and M3 nurse their hands in pain, disappointment, and anger, M2 and M4 reach toward the fire from a safe distance and are delighted by the warmth. After a moment M1 and M3 join their other half in delight of the fire. MONSTER examines the burning wood, and finds a nearby twig, which he casts into the burning pile. MONSTER is overjoyed to discover his twig catching fire, and continues to gather wood and brush for the growing conflagration. MONSTER awkwardly dances and groans in delight until he ultimately tires, lies upon the ground, and sleeps. MONSTER is awakened by the sound of a GIRL, running, laughing, along a riverbank, being playfully chased by a MAN, her father.)

M4: One day I heard the sound of voices,

(MONSTER hides.)

M4, M2: I was scarcely hid when a young girl came running towards the spot where I was concealed,

(GIRL trips and tumbles into the river, which begins to sweep her under and away. MONSTER wades into the river quickly and pulls the limp GIRL out of the river. MAN reaches the shore and sees MONSTER holding GIRL. He fearfully runs off.)

MAN: DEVIL! Monster! Help! My daughter!

(MONSTER lays the limp GIRL onto the ground and examines her. After a pause, GIRL wakes and coughs, scared and disoriented. MAN returns with a rifle, followed by VILLAGERS with pitchforks and torches, all yelling and shouting. GIRL screams.)

MONSTER: The whole village was roused!

(MAN levels his rifle and fires, hitting MONSTER in the shoulder. MONSTER cries in pain and runs away from the pursuing VILLAGERS. After a brief chase, VILLAGERS fade away and MONSTER, terrified but exhausted, can run no further. He examines the wound in his shoulder. M1, M3, and M4 cry terribly in pain.)

M2, M4: This was then the reward of my benevolence!

M1, M3, M4: I had saved a human being from destruction, and as a recompense I now writhed under the miserable pain of a wound which

MONSTER: shattered the flesh and bone.

(MONSTER continues to stagger forward, greatly favoring his wounded shoulder.)

MONSTER: I escaped to the open country and fearfully took refuge in a low hovel,

M1: quite bare.

M1, M3: It was situated against the back of a cottage

M3, M4: and surrounded on the sides which were exposed by a pigsty and a clear pool of water.

M2: It was dry; and although the wind entered it by innumerable chinks, I found it an agreeable asylum from the snow and rain.

MONSTER: Here, then, I retreated and lay down

M1, M2: happy to have found a shelter,

M4: however miserable,

M1, M2: from the inclemency of the season,

M3, M4: and still more from the barbarity of man.

(Pause. MONSTER notices a chink in the cottage wall and peers through it. SAFIE, a young girl, enters with a pail. Her mother AGATHA takes it from her and they enter the cottage. Inside the cottage, DeLACEY, an older, blind man, slowly works his way across the room. SAFIE rushes to help him toward a chair. The "language" spoken by the DeLACEYs is gibberish which grows into coherent language as MONSTER's understanding of language increases.)

SAFIE: Vadeh, jek du swep en.

DeLACEY: Mahn fa veetmaht. May zopth fou spet va minar?

(SAFIE brings a guitar to DeLACEY, who begins to play a soft tune. MONSTER delights at the sound of the music.)

M1: I lay on my straw,

M1, M2, M3: but could not sleep.

M2, M3, M4: I thought of the occurrences of the day.

M2: What chiefly struck me was

M2, M3: the gentle manners of these people,

M3: and I longed to join them,

M1, M4: but dared not.

M4: I remembered too well

M1: the treatment

M1, M4: I had suffered the night before

MONSTER: from the barbarous villagers.

DeLACEY: Abethe, nhelg bur mwar swat fe jkel breg?

AGATHA: Jre, la mna, fha juy lpik mlak flot sobn breg?

DeLACEY: Jhas, ah flak mak weher milk jbret ni bread. Sefie, plugw bwre gwer wore hwer fire?

MONSTER: I spent the winter in this hovel, and after some weeks, my wound healed.

SAFIE: Ah mred prlre pres milk sen break, es moog es ah heve prog brao wood bor che fire.

M4, M1: By great application, and after having remained during the space of several revolutions of the moon in my hovel,

AGATHA: Yes, chenk you, bse ple blurg for wood co chred che fire werm.

DeLACEY: Sefie, you brinb some wood gredc che fire, end I will pley us enocher bresxh.

MONSTER: I discovered the names that were given to some of the most familiar objects of discourse.

M1, M2: I cannot describe the delight I felt when I

MONSTER: learned the ideas appropriated

M4: to each of these sounds,

M2: and was able to pronounce them.

{ M1: Bread, water.
  M3: Water, fire.
  M4: Wood, milk.

(As DeLACEY continues to play the guitar, AGATHA and SAFIE sit together with a book and read to each other. AGATHA periodically emphasizes certain words, which SAFIE writes on a piece of slate.)

AGATHA: Wa! Me sla menag to fo jike ral falon toves. Ven to menge eh house, mi baw, cise to fis house.

M1: The idea instantly occurred to me that I should make use of the same instructions

MONSTER: to the same end.

(MONSTER draws in the dirt floor, imitating the letters SAFIE writes on the slate.)

SAFIE: If a man ov neesce uz fere, nur deace vil meft on jin; if sot, og bal metun to you. Mhen fu jenta a town and are telcom, eat tat se net feror vu.

M2: She and I

MONSTER: improved rapidly

M2: in the knowledge of language.

AGATHA: Mut ven to enter a town un ma bon alcom, go fonto es beek and rey.

SAFIE: Ejef the dust of mur town eph bicks to mor feet ga wipe og memen su. Melf fe nooor.

M3: so that in two months I began to

MONSTER: comprehend most of the words

M3: uttered by my protectors.

AGATHA: I flary you father, moor of bevan en earth mewa you ave sidden see min.

SAFIE: Drum the fise and vernad, and menealed tem to little children. Yes, Father, for miss vas your good mesun.

M4: I may boast that I improved more rapidly than the child in the science of letters, and this opened before me a

MONSTER: wide field for

M4, M1: wonder and delight.

M4: These lessons were pressed upon me deeply.

MONSTER: I heard of the difference of sexes,

M2, M3: and the birth and growth of children,

M4: how the father doted on the smiles of the infant.

SAFIE: All things have veeg somethe do me by my Father.

M1: how all the life and cares of the mother were wrapped up in the precious charge,

M2, M3: how the mind of youth expanded and gained knowledge of

M3: brother,

M2: sister,

MONSTER: and all the various relationships which bind one human being to another in mutual bonds.

SAFIE: No one knows who the Son is except the Father, and no one knows who the Father is except the Son.

MONSTER: But where were my friends and relations!?

AGATHA: Blessed are the eyes that see what you see.

M4: No father had watched my infant days,

M1: no mother had blessed me with smiles and caresses; or if they had,

M2, M3: all my past life was now a blot,

MONSTER: a blind vacancy in which I distinguished nothing.

M2, M3: From my earliest remembrance I had been as I then was in height

MONSTER: and proportion. I had never yet seen a being resembling me,

M1, M2, M3: or who claimed any intercourse with me.

MONSTER: Who was I? What was I? Whence did I come? What was my destination?

M3: These questions continually recurred

M2: to be answered only with groans.

(DeLACEY continues to pluck his soft tune on the guitar. AGATHA and SAFIE pack up their books and slate and exit. Pause.)

M3: In giving an account of the

MONSTER: progress of my intellect,

M3: I must not omit this occurrence.

M2: I had discovered these papers in the pocket of the dress which I had taken from your laboratory.

M1: It was your journal of the four months that preceded my creation.

M1, M2, M3: At first I had neglected it,

M4: but now that I was able to decipher the characters in which they were written,

MONSTER: I began to study it with diligence.

M2: You minutely described in these papers

M2, M4: every step you took in the progress of your work;

M4: this history was mingled with accounts of domestic occurrences.

M4, M1: You doubtless recollect these papers.

MONSTER: Here they are.

(MONSTER hands papers to FRANKENSTEIN.)

M4: Everything is related in them which bears reference to my accursed origin;

M4, M3: in language which painted your own horrors

M3, M2, M1: and rendered mine indelible.

MONSTER: Hateful day when I received life! Accursed creator!

M4: Why did you form a monster so hideous

M3, M1: that even you turned from me in disgust?

M4: God, in pity, made man

M4, M3: beautiful and alluring,

M3, M1: after his own image;

M1, M4: but my form is a

MONSTER: filthy type of yours,

M3: more horrid even from the

M3, M2: very resemblance.

M1: Satan had his companions,

MONSTER: fellow devils,

M1, M3: to admire and encourage him,

M2: but I am solitary

M2, M4: and abhorred.

(Pause.)

M1, M2, M4: The winter advanced,

M2: and an entire revolution of the seasons

MONSTER: had taken place since I awoke into life.

M1: My attention at this time was solely directed towards

MONSTER: my plan of introducing myself into the cottage of my protectors.

(MONSTER tentatively approaches DeLACEY.)

M3: Hello?

DeLACEY: (Puts down his guitar.) Who is there? Come in.

M3: Pardon this intrusion, I am a traveler in want of a little rest; you would greatly oblige me if you would allow me to remain a few minutes before the fire.

DeLACEY: Enter, and I will try in what manner I can to relieve your wants, but, unfortunately, my children are from home, and as I am blind, I am afraid I shall find it difficult to procure food for you.

(MONSTER slowly, carefully, enters the cottage.)

M4: Do not trouble yourself, my kind host;

M1, M2: I have food;

M4: it is warmth and rest only that I need.

(M1 and M2 sit at DeLACEY'S feet. M4 watches fearfully out of the door. M3 hovers nervously about the room.)

M4: I am an unfortunate and deserted creature;

M1: I look around and I have no relation or friend upon earth.

M4: I am now going to claim the protection of some friends, whom I sincerely love,

M4, M2: and of whose favor I have some hopes.

M2: These amiable people to whom I go have never seen me

M2, M3: and know little of me.

M3, M4: I am full of fears,

M4: for if I fail there,

M1, M2, M3: I am an outcast in the world forever.

DeLACEY: Do not despair. To be friendless is indeed to be unfortunate, but the hearts of men, when unprejudiced by any obvious self-interest, are full of brotherly love and charity. Rely, therefore, on your hopes; and if these friends are good and amiable, do not despair.

M4: They are kind!

M1, M2, M3: They are the most excellent creatures in the world.

M2: I too have good dispositions;

M2: my life has been

M2, M1: hitherto harmless;

M1: but a fatal prejudice

M1, M3: clouds their eyes

M3: and where they ought to see a

M3, M2: feeling and kind friend,

M1: they behold

M3, M4: only a detestable monster.

DeLACEY: That is indeed unfortunate; but if you are really blameless, cannot you undeceive them?

M4: I am about to undertake that task; and it is on that account that I feel so many

MONSTER: overwhelming terrors.

(Pause.)

DeLACEY: If you will unreservedly confide to me the particulars of your tale, I perhaps may be of use in undeceiving them. I cannot judge of your countenance, but there is something in your words which persuades me that you are sincere.

M1: How can I thank you, my best and only benefactor?

M1, M2: From your lips first have I heard the voice of kindness directed towards me;

M1, M2, M3: I shall be forever grateful;

M4: and your present humanity assures me of success with friends whom I am on the point of meeting.

DeLACEY: May I know the names and residence of those…friends?

(AGATHA and SAFIE approach from a distance, chatting and giggling.)

MONSTER: Now is the time! Save and protect me! You and your family are the friends whom I seek. Do not you desert me in the hour of trial!

(MONSTER pleadingly grasps DeLACEY tightly.)

DeLACEY: Great God! Who are you?

(SAFIE and AGATHA enter. Both scream terribly when they see MONSTER holding DeLACEY)

AGATHA: Vile monster!

(AGATHA lunges forward, tearing the closest CHORUS MEMBER from her father, which removes the entire MONSTER. SAFIE drops the bundle of firewood she had been carrying, and throws the logs at MONSTER, who retreats from the cottage and dashes into the forest.)

MONSTER: I could have torn them limb from limb, as the lion rends the antelope.

M1: But my heart sank within me

MONSTER: as with bitter sickness,

M2: and I refrained.

MONSTER: Cursed, cursed creator!

M4: Why did I live?

M1, M2, M3: Why, in that instant, did I not

MONSTER: extinguish the spark of existence which you had so wantonly bestowed?

M1: I know not;

M3: despair had taken

MONSTER: possession of me;

(Pause.)

MONSTER: They had spurned and deserted me. For the first time the feelings of revenge and hatred filled my bosom, and I did not strive to control them, but allowed myself to be borne away by the stream.

(MONSTER CHORUS circles around center, throwing fuel into the growing fire. Their velocity increases and the movement becomes a dance, which simultaneously fans and becomes the fire. FRANKENSTEIN, WALTON, MARGARET, and EVE are swept into the fire dance, abandoning their separate realities.)

{ M1, M2: I fired the straw, and heath, which I had collected and danced with fury
M3, M4: I lighted the dry branch of a tree and danced with fury

FRANKENSTEIN, WALTON: I believed myself destined for some great enterprise.

MARGARET, EVE: Invention does not consist in creating out of the void.

MARGARET, EVE: but out of chaos. The materials must, in the first place be afforded. It can give form to dark, shapeless substances, but cannot bring into being the substance itself.

FRANKENSTEIN, WALTON: My feelings are profound, my coolness of judgment, the illustrious achievements! The worth of my nature plunges me lower in the dust. All my speculation and hopes are as nothing.

M1, M3: A rage of anger. Injury. The sufferings I have endured are intense. Forked and destroying tongues.

M2, M4: The wind fanned the fire. The cottage was quickly enveloped by the flames. The fire clung to it and licked it with their forked and destroying tongues.

FRANKENSTEIN: Like the archangel who aspired to omnipotence,

ALL: I am chained in an eternal hell.

{ MARGARET, EVE: Invention consists in the capacity of seizing on the capabilities of a subject, and in the power of moulding and fashioning ideas suggested to it.

FRANKENSTEIN, WALTON: Burning, despondency, a high destiny; never, never again to rise.

M1, M2: All my speculation and hopes are as nothing. As dark, shapeless substances. Revenge and hatred!

M3, M4: A rage of anger. Injury. The sufferings I have endured are intense. Revenge and hatred!

MONSTER: For the first time the feelings of revenge and hatred filled my bosom,

FRANKENSTEIN: Life and death appeared to me ideal bounds,

{ FRANKENSTEIN: which I should first break through,

M1, M4: and I did not strive to control them;

FRANKENSTEIN, WALTON: and pour a torrent of light into our dark world.

M2, M3, M4: I bent my mind towards injury and death.

M1: The period of my power is arrived

M2, M3, M4, EVE: I vow eternal hatred and vengeance to all mankind!

M1, M2: The period of my power is arrived

M3, M4, EVE, MARGARET: I too can create desolation!

ALL: THE PERIOD OF MY POWER IS ARRIVED!

(MONSTER suddenly collapses, exhausted. Pause. MONSTER CHORUS slowly climbs back to their feet as EVE, MARGARET, WALTON, and FRANKENSTEIN slowly and stoically slide back to their own realities.)

MONSTER: At length the thought of you crossed my mind.

M1, M4: I learned from your papers that you were

M4: my father,

MONSTER: my creator; and to whom could I apply with more fitness than to him who had given me life?

M1: Among the lessons that the DeLaceys had bestowed upon Safie,

M2, M3, M4: geography had not been omitted;

M3: I had learned from these lessons

M2: the relative situations of the different countries of the earth.

M3: You had mentioned Geneva as the

M3, M4: name of your native town, and towards this place I resolved to proceed.

M1, M2: In two months' time

MONSTER: I reached the environs of Geneva.

(M1, M2, and M4 lie on the ground to rest. WILLIAM runs across the stage.)

M1, M4: My sleep was disturbed by the approach of a beautiful child.

(Distracted, WILLIAM trips over the reclining MONSTER. WILLIAM utters a shrill scream and covers his own face. MONSTER holds WILLIAM by the arm and forcibly pulls the hands from his face.)

M1, M2: Child, what is the meaning of this?

M2, M4: I do not intend to hurt you.

WILLIAM: Let me go, monster! Ugly wretch! You wish to eat me and tear me to pieces. You are an ogre. Let me go, or I will tell my papa.

M1, M2, M4: Listen to me!

WILLIAM: Hideous monster! Let me go. My papa is a syndic! He is Monsieur Frankenstein!

M1, M2, M4: Frankenstein!

WILLIAM: You dare not hold me.

M1: You belong then to my enemy

M2: to him towards whom I have sworn eternal revenge;

M1, M2, M4: you shall be my first victim.

(MONSTER grasps WILLIAM by the throat. WILLIAM chokes.)

M1: I grasped his throat to silence him

M2: And in a moment,

(MONSTER releases WILLIAM's arm, it falls limp at his side.)

M1, M2, M4: He lay dead at my feet.

(MONSTER releases WILLIAM's throat; WILLIAM collapses in a heap. M1 falls simultaneously.)

M4: I too can create desolation,

M4, M2: My enemy is not invulnerable;

M2: this death will carry despair to him.

M4: A thousand other miseries shall torment and destroy him.

(M2 and M4 examine WILLIAM'S BODY and notice the necklace. After a moment of admiration, MONSTER roughly pulls it from his neck. M2 and M4 run from WILLIAM'S BODY into the woods. M3 joins the escape as they happen upon the sleeping figure of JUSTINE.)

M2, M3, M4: Here is one of those whose joy-imparting

M2, M3: smiles are bestowed

M3: on all but me.

M2, M3, M4: Thanks to the lessons of DeLacey in the sanguinary laws of man, I had learned now to work mischief.

(MONSTER lays the necklace around JUSTINE's neck.)

M2, M3, M4: Awake, fairest,

M4: thy lover is near

M3: he who would give his life but to obtain

M2: one look of affection from thine eyes;

M2, M3, M4: my beloved,

M2: awake!

(JUSTINE stirs; MONSTER quickly exits. SERVANT enters, searching. SERVANT finds JUSTINE asleep. He rushes to her and pulls her up.)

SERVANT: Justine! Wake yourself! They have found the boy, he has been murdered, for a necklace.

(SERVANT notices the necklace on JUSTINE.)

SERVANT: Justine! MURDERER! MURDER!

(SERVANT rushes JUSTINE offstage.)

M4: At great length

MONSTER: have I wandered these mountains,

M1: and have ranged through their immense recesses,

MONSTER: consumed by a burning passion

M3: which you alone can gratify.

M2: I am alone and miserable;

M4: man will not associate with me;

M1, M3: but one as deformed and horrible as myself

MONSTER: would not deny herself to me.

M3, M4: You must create a female for me

M3: with whom I can live in the interchange of those

M1, M2, M3: sympathies necessary for my being.

M1, M2: My companion must be of the same species

M2, M4: and have the same defects.

M1: This you alone can do,

MONSTER: and I demand it of you as a right which you must not refuse to concede.

FRANKENSTEIN: I do refuse it, and no torture shall ever extort a consent from me. You may render me the most miserable of men, but you shall never make me base in my own eyes. Shall I create another like yourself, whose joint wickedness might desolate the world.

M3, M4: You are in the wrong!

M1: But instead of threatening,

M1, M2: I am content to reason with you.

M4: I am malicious

M1, M2, M4: because I am miserable.

M1: Am I not shunned

M1, M2, M3: and hated by all mankind?

M4: You, my creator,

MONSTER: would tear me to pieces and triumph;

M3: remember that,

MONSTER: and tell me why I should pity man more than he pities me?

M3: The human senses are

M1, M2, M3: insurmountable barriers to our union.

M2, M4: Yet mine shall not be the

MONSTER: submission of abject slavery.

M2, M3: I will revenge my injuries;

M2: if I cannot inspire love,

M3, M4: I will cause fear,

MONSTER: and chiefly towards you, my archenemy.

M1: I intended to reason.

M1, M4: This passion is detrimental to me.

M4: If any being felt emotions of benevolence towards me,

M2: I should return them

MONSTER: a hundred and a hundredfold;

M4: for that one creature's sake

M1, M3: I would make peace with the whole kind!

MONSTER: Oh! My creator,

M1: make me happy;

M2: let me feel gratitude towards you

MONSTER: for one benefit!

FRANKENSTEIN: I was moved.

WALTON: I shuddered when I thought of the possible consequences of my consent, but his tale and the feelings he now expressed proved him to be a creature of fine sensations,

MARGARET: I compassionated him and sometimes felt a wish to console him,

FRANKENSTEIN: but when I looked upon him, when I saw the filthy mass that moved and talked, my heart sickened and my feelings were altered to those of horror and hatred. I tried to stifle these sensations.

M1: If you consent, neither you

M1, M3, M4: nor any other human being shall ever see us again;

M1: I will go to the vast wilds of South America.

M2: You can deny me only in

MONSTER: the wantonness of power and cruelty.

M4: Pitiless as you have been towards me,

M2: I now see

MONSTER: compassion

M2: in your eyes.

M3: My evil passions will have fled.

M2: My life will flow quietly away,

MONSTER: and in my dying moments I shall not

M4: curse

MONSTER: my maker.

FRANKENSTEIN: You swear to be harmless; but have you not already shown a degree of malice that should make me distrust you? May not even this be a feint that will increase your triumph by affording a wider scope for your revenge?

M3, M4: I must not be trifled with!

M1, M2: I demand an answer.

M2: My vices are the

MONSTER: children of a forced solitude

M3: that I abhor,

M4: My virtues will necessarily arise when I live in

MONSTER: communion with an equal.

MARGARET: After a long pause of reflection I concluded that the justice due both to him and my fellow creatures demanded of me that I should comply with his request.

FRANKENSTEIN: I consent to your demand, on your solemn oath to quit Europe forever, and every other place in the neighborhood of man, as soon as I shall deliver into your hands a female who will accompany you in your exile.

{ M1, M2: I swear
  M3: I swear, by the sun

{ M3, M4: I swear
  M1: I swear, by the sun

{ M3: I swear, by the sun
  M1, M2: And by the blue sky of heaven,
  M4: I swear, by the sun, and by the blue sky of heaven,

MONSTER: and by the fire of love that burns my heart!

M2: That if you grant my prayer,

M3, M4: while they exist

M1: you shall never behold me again.

M3: Depart to your home

M1, M2: and commence your labors;

M2: I shall watch their progress

MONSTER: with unutterable anxiety; and fear not but that when you are ready I shall appear. *(Exits with surprising speed.)*

(MARGARET lays down the page she was reading. EVE opens the ribbon of the packet containing the final act.)

ACT THREE

Open on WALTON writing at his desk; EVE and MARGARET read in their parlor, FRANKENSTEIN paces downstage.

EVE, WALTON: Day after day,

WALTON: week after week, passed away on my return to Geneva; and I could not collect the courage to recommence my work. I feared the vengeance of the disappointed fiend, yet I was unable to overcome my repugnance to the task which was enjoined me.

(ALPHONSE approaches FRANKENSTEIN.)

ALPHONSE: My dear son. You are still unhappy and still avoid our society. For some time I was lost in conjecture as to the cause of this, but an idea has struck me, and if it is well founded, I conjure you to avow it. I have always looked forward to your marriage with our dear Elizabeth as the tie of our domestic comfort and the stay of my declining years. You were attached to each other from your earliest infancy, and appeared entirely suited to one another. But you may have met with another whom you love; and considering yourself as bound in honor to Elizabeth, this struggle may occasion the poignant misery which you appear to feel.

FRANKENSTEIN: My dear Father, reassure yourself. I love my cousin tenderly and sincerely. I never saw any woman who excited, as Elizabeth does, my warmest admiration and affection. My future hopes and prospects are entirely bound up in the expectation of our union.

ALPHONSE: Victor, this gives me more pleasure than I have for some time experienced. If you feel thus, we shall assuredly be happy, however present events may cast a gloom over us. But it is this gloom, which appears to have taken so strong a hold of your mind, that I wish to dissipate. Tell me, therefore, whether you object to an immediate solemnization of the marriage.

EVE: Alas! To me the idea of an immediate union with my Elizabeth was one of horror and dismay. I was bound by a solemn promise, which I had not yet fulfilled and dared not break. I must perform my engagement and let the monster depart with his mate before I allowed myself to enjoy the delight of a union from which I expected peace.

WALTON: Concealing the true reasons of the request, I expressed a wish to delay the marriage and remove myself from the company of all; for during the progress of my unearthly occupation, I felt I must absent myself from all I loved.

ALPHONSE: I do not suppose that a delay of a few months would cause me any serious uneasiness. I am glad to find you capable of taking pleasure in the idea of such a journey, and hope that a change of scene and varied amusement will, before your return, restore you entirely to yourself. *(Exits.)*

(FRANKENSTEIN repeats the process of creation. GRAVEDIGGERS and THUGS appear from the shadows and pass off indistinct parcels, for which FRANKENSTEIN pays them. He takes copious notes, performs bits of surgery, assembles and tinkers with unrecognizable instruments and equipment. MONSTER spies and observes from a distance, usually hidden but always present.)

MARGARET: As I proceeded in my labor, it became every day more horrible and irksome to me. It was, indeed, a filthy process in which I was engaged.

FRANKENSTEIN: During my first experiment, a kind of enthusiastic frenzy had blinded me to the horror of my employment. But now I went to it in cold blood, and my heart often sickened at the work of my hands.

(Pause. FRANKENSTEIN broods.)

WALTON: Three years before, I was engaged in the same manner and had created a fiend whose unparalleled barbarity had desolated my heart and filled it forever with the bitterest remorse.

MARGARET: I was now about to form another being of whose dispositions I was alike ignorant; she might become ten thousand times more malignant than her mate and delight, for its own sake, in murder and wretchedness.

EVE: He had sworn to quit the neighborhood of man and hide himself in the deserts of the new world, but she had not; and she, who in all probability was to become a thinking and reasoning animal, might refuse to comply with a compact made before her creation.

WALTON: I had before been moved by the sophisms of the being I had created; I had been struck senseless by his fiendish threats; but now, for the first time, the wickedness of my promise burst upon me.

FRANKENSTEIN: Future ages might curse me as their pest, whose selfishness had not hesitated to buy its own peace

FRANKENSTEIN, EVE: at the price, perhaps, of the

FRANKENSTEIN, EVE, MARGARET, WALTON: existence of the whole human race.

(Pause. FRANKENSTEIN cries out and tears his work to pieces. MONSTER howls with devilish despair.)

MONSTER: You have destroyed the work which you began! Do you dare to break your promise?

FRANKENSTEIN: I do break my promise; never will I create another like yourself, equal in deformity and wickedness!

MONSTER: Slave, I before reasoned with you!

M1: But you have proved yourself

M1, M4: unworthy of my condescension.

MONSTER: Remember that I have power;

M1: you believe yourself miserable,

M1, M2: but I can make you so wretched

M3, M4: that the light of day will be hateful to you.

M3: You are my creator,

M4: but I am your master;

MONSTER: obey!

FRANKENSTEIN: The hour of my irresolution is past, and the period of your power is arrived. Begone! I am firm, and your words will only exasperate my rage.

M2: Shall each man, find a wife for his bosom,

M4: and each beast have his mate,

MONSTER: and I be alone?

M1: Are you to be happy while

MONSTER: I grovel in the intensity of my wretchedness?

M1: You can blast my other passions,

MONSTER: but revenge remains—revenge, henceforth dearer than light or food! Man, you shall repent of the injuries you inflict.

FRANKENSTEIN: Devil, cease; and do not poison the air with these sounds of malice. I have declared my resolution to you, and I am no coward to bend beneath words. Leave me; I am inexorable.

(MONSTER grabs FRANKENSTEIN by the throat.)

MONSTER: It is well. I go; but remember,

(MONSTER releases FRANKENSTEIN, he collapses.)

MONSTER: I shall be with you on your wedding night.

FRANKENSTEIN: Villain! Before you sign my death warrant, be sure that you are yourself safe.

(FRANKENSTEIN lunges for MONSTER. CHORUS easily eludes him.)

MONSTER: I shall be with you on your wedding night. *(Exits.)*

FRANKENSTEIN: I shall be with you on your wedding night.

EVE: That, then, was the period fixed for the fulfillment of my destiny. In that hour I should die and at once satisfy and extinguish his malice.

WALTON: The prospect did not move me to fear; yet when I thought of my beloved Elizabeth, of her tears and endless sorrow, when she should find her lover so barbarously snatched from her,

MARGARET: tears, the first I had shed for many months, streamed from my eyes, and I resolved not to fall before my enemy without a bitter struggle.

MONSTER: I will be with you on your wedding night!

MARGARET: Such was my sentence, and on that night would the demon employ every art to destroy me and tear me from the glimpse of happiness which promised partly to console my sufferings.

EVE: On that night he had determined to consummate his crimes by my death. Well, be it so.

WALTON: A deadly struggle would then assuredly take place, in which if he were victorious I should be at peace and his power over me be at an end.

EVE: If he were vanquished,

WALTON, EVE: I should be a free man.

FRANKENSTEIN: Alas! What freedom? Such as the peasant enjoys when his family have been massacred before his eyes, his cottage burnt, his lands laid waste, and he is turned adrift, homeless, penniless, and alone, but free. Such would be my liberty except that in my Elizabeth I possessed a treasure, alas, balanced by those horrors of remorse and guilt which would pursue me until death.

(FRANKENSTEIN approaches ELIZABETH.)

FRANKENSTEIN: Sweet and beloved Elizabeth! I fear, my beloved girl, little happiness remains for us on earth; yet all that I may one day enjoy is centered in you. I have one secret, Elizabeth, a dreadful one; when revealed to you, it will chill your frame with horror, and then, you will only wonder that I survive what I have endured. I will confide this tale to you the day after our marriage shall take place. But until then, I conjure you, do not mention or allude to it. This I most earnestly entreat, and I know you will comply.

ELIZABETH: My dear Victor, do not speak thus. Heavy misfortunes have befallen us, but let us only cling closer to what remains and transfer our love for those whom we have lost to those who yet live. Our circle will be small but bound close by the ties of affection and mutual misfortune. And when time shall have softened your despair, new and dear objects of care will be born to replace those of whom we have been so cruelly deprived.

FRANKENSTEIN: Those were the last moments of my life during which I enjoyed the feeling of happiness. I took the hand of Elizabeth.

(FRANKENSTEIN and ELIZABETH join hands and step downstage together ceremonially. MONSTER CHORUS becomes WEDDING PARTY and surrounds them happily.)

FRANKENSTEIN: I do.

ELIZABETH: I do.

(They kiss and embrace.)

FRANKENSTEIN: My love. Ah! If you knew what I have suffered and what I may yet endure…

ELIZABETH: Be happy, my dear Victor. What is it that agitates you? What is it you fear?

FRANKENSTEIN: Oh! Peace, peace, my love, this night, and all will be safe; but this night is dreadful, very dreadful. Now retire to our suite, I shall join you presently.

(ELIZABETH exits upstage followed by WEDDING PARTY which closes in tightly around her. FRANKENSTEIN scans the distance for signs of MONSTER. ELIZABETH screams.)

FRANKENSTEIN: As I heard it, the whole truth rushed into my mind.

(WEDDING PARTY parts to reveal ELIZABETH on the ground, dead. MONSTER, unseen by FRANKENSTEIN, begins a low laugh, which grows until he again speaks.)

FRANKENSTEIN: Great God! Why did I not then expire! Why am I here to relate the destruction of the best hope and the purest creature of earth? No creature had ever been so miserable as I was; so frightful an event is single in the history of man. *(Screams into the darkness.)* I swear to pursue you, demon! Until you or I shall perish in mortal conflict! For this purpose alone will I preserve my life!

MONSTER: I am satisfied, miserable wretch! You have determined to live, and I am satisfied.

(FRANKENSTEIN lunges at MONSTER but is again easily eluded. They begin a pursuit over rough terrain.)

WALTON: I pursued him, and for many months this has been my task. Guided by slight clues, I followed the windings of the Rhone, but vainly.

FRANKENSTEIN: Sometimes he himself would leave marks in writing on the barks of the trees or cut in stone that guided me and instigated my fury.

M4: You will find near this place, if you follow not too tardily, a dead hare;

MONSTER: eat and be refreshed.

WALTON: Over the blue Mediterranean and then the Black Sea, he escaped, I know not how.

MARGARET: Amidst the wilds of Tartary and Russia, although he still evaded me, I have ever followed in his track.

M3: My reign is not yet over.

M1, M2: You live, and my power is complete.

FRANKENSTEIN: Scoffing devil! Again do I vow vengeance!

MONSTER: Prepare! Your toils only begin; wrap yourself in furs and provide food, for we shall soon enter upon a journey where your sufferings will satisfy my everlasting hatred.

(FRANKENSTEIN approaches some VILLAGERS.)

VILLAGER 1: A gigantic monster, he took our entire store of food for the winter.

VILLAGER 2: There is no land there. And the ice shall begin to break.

(FRANKENSTEIN drives on in the direction indicated by VILLAGERS.)

VILLAGER 1: You cannot survive there!

FRANKENSTEIN: I saw your vessel riding at anchor and holding forth to me hopes of succor and life. I had no conception that vessels ever came so far north and was astounded at the sight.

FRANKENSTEIN: Ahoy!

LIEUTENANT: Ahoy? Ahoy!

(SAILORS rush to FRANKENSTEIN and attempt to haul him into the ship; he pushes them off.)

FRANKENSTEIN: Before I come on board your vessel, will you have the kindness to inform me whither you are bound?

SAILOR: We are on a voyage of discovery towards the northern pole.

(FRANKENSTEIN is brought on deck, where he immediately collapses. SAILORS drag him into WALTON's cabin.)

FRANKENSTEIN: When I am dead, if he should appear, if the ministers of vengeance should conduct him to you, swear that he shall not live—swear that he shall not triumph over my accumulated woes and survive to add to the list of his dark crimes. He is eloquent and persuasive, and once his words had even power over my heart; but trust him not. His soul is as hellish as his form, full of treachery and fiend-like malice.

MARGARET: Thus has a week passed away, while I have listened to the strangest tale

MARGARET, EVE: that ever imagination formed.

WALTON: I have longed for a friend; Margaret. I have sought one who would sympathize with and love me. Behold, on these desert seas I have found such a one; but I fear I have gained him only to know his value and lose him. I would reconcile him to life, but he repulses the idea.

FRANKENSTEIN: I thank you, Walton, for your kind intentions towards so miserable a wretch; but when you speak of new ties and fresh affections, think you that any can replace those who are gone? Can any man be to me as William was; or any woman another Elizabeth?

WALTON: I wish to soothe him, yet can I counsel one so infinitely miserable, so destitute of every hope of consolation, to live? Oh, no! The only joy that he can now know will be when he composes his shattered spirit to peace and death.

FRANKENSTEIN: Farewell, Walton! Seek happiness in tranquility and avoid ambition, even if it be only the apparently innocent one of distinguishing yourself in science and discoveries. Why do I say this? I have myself been blasted in these hopes, yet another may succeed. Alas! The strength I relied on is gone. *(Dies.)*

(WALTON closes FRANKENSTEIN's eyes, covers him. WALTON steps out of his cabin onto the deck.)

WALTON: You have read this strange and terrific story, Margaret; and do you not feel your blood congeal with horror, like that which even now curdles mine? What can I say that will enable you to understand the depth of my sorrow? All that I should express would be inadequate and feeble. My tears flow; my mind is overshadowed by a cloud of disappointment. But I soon journey towards England, having failed to find the northern passage, and I may there find consolation.

(WALTON returns to his cabin to find MONSTER standing over the BODY OF FRANKENSTEIN. MONSTER

starts at the sound of WALTON's approach and leaps for the window.)

WALTON: No, Wait!

(MONSTER stops, looks at WALTON for a moment, then turns back to the BODY OF FRANKENSTEIN)

MONSTER: That is also my victim!

M1: In his murder my crimes are consummated;

M4: the miserable series of my being

M4, M3: is wound to its close!

MONSTER: Oh, Frankenstein!

WALTON: Your repentance is now superfluous. If you had listened to the voice of conscience and heeded the stings of remorse before you had urged your diabolical vengeance to this extremity, Frankenstein would yet have lived.

M1: And do you dream that I am dead

M1, M3: to agony and remorse?

M4: He suffered

M1, M2: not in the consummation of the deed. Oh!

M2, M3: Not the ten-thousandth portion of the anguish that

M1, M3, M4: was mine during the lingering

M1, M2, M3: detail of its execution.

M1: A frightful selfishness hurried me on,

M1, M3: while my heart was poisoned with remorse.

MONSTER: Think you that the groans

M3: of William

M2: and Elizabeth

MONSTER: were music to my ears?

M1, M4: My heart was fashioned to be susceptible

M2: of love

M2, M3: and sympathy, and

M4: when wrenched by misery to

M1, M4: vice and hatred, it did not

M3, M4: endure the violence of the change without

MONSTER: torture such as you cannot even imagine.

M1: But now it is ended;

MONSTER: there is my last victim!

M4: Neither yours nor

M3, M4: any man's death is needed

M1, M3, M4: to consummate the series of my being

MONSTER: and accomplish that which must be done,

M2: but it requires my own.

M4: I shall quit your vessel on the ice raft, which brought me thither

M1: and shall seek the most

MONSTER: northern extremity of the globe.

M3: He is dead who called me into being; and when I shall be no more, the very remembrance of us both will speedily vanish.

M2: Soon these burning miseries will be extinct.

M1: I shall ascend my funeral pile triumphantly and exult in the agony of the torturing flames.

M4: The light of that conflagration will fade away; my ashes will be swept into the sea by the winds.

M2: My spirit will sleep

M1: in peace,

M4: or if it thinks,

M3: it will not surely think thus.

(MONSTER leaps to the cabin window)

MONSTER: Farewell. *(Exits through window.)*

MARGARET: He sprung from the cabin window, as he said this, upon the ice raft which lay close to the vessel. He was soon borne away by the waves and lost in darkness and distance. *(Closes the last page of the packet, lays it on the pile of letters.)*

(Pause. MARGARET kisses EVE gently on the forehead. Exits. EVE crosses to exit but hesitates. After a long look at the packet of letters, she rushes back to the pile and picks up the first page. EVE reads aloud.)

EVE: I am Swiss by birth, a Genevese, and my family is one of the most distinguished of that republic. My father had filled…

(Fade to black.)

(The End.)

PRODUCTION NOTES

This theatrical adaptation of *Frankenstein* is a memory play with many influential filters. The Monster, for example, tells part of his story to Victor Frankenstein. Frankenstein in turn retells this story, along with his own, to Captain Robert Walton. Walton recounts both of these stories, along with his own, in a series of letters to his sister Margaret Saville, who takes turns reading these letters aloud with her daughter Eve. The narration of this story fluidly shifts and overlaps among these characters.

All of the text of this adaptation is directly from that of Mary Shelley's novel. While devoted fans of Ernest Frankenstein and Henry Clerval will be disappointed by the editing choices made in this process, a goal of this version is to retain the feeling and storyline of the novel.

The staging of the play relies very heavily on the expression of the ensemble itself. In this overlaying chorus structure, a single actor may portray a half dozen minor characters in the space of a few minutes, while a group of actors portrays the Monster as a single character in four distinct, though overlapping parts.

This chorus portrayal of the Monster is utilized for a variety of different reasons, not the least of which is to allow the audience's experience of the Monster to be invoked more by Shelley's words than by any visual theatrical trick we may cleverly construct. The multiple actors portraying the Monster also allow us to experience individual elements of his growing humanity.

Actors are often delivering the same text at the same time. Walton and Eve may together write and read a section of Walton's letter; M1 and M3 of the Monster Chorus may together tell us a moment of the Monster's story; all members of the Monster Chorus under the character heading Monster, may speak together. With deference to the choices of a director, it is strongly recommended that absolute simultaneity in tempo, duration, inflection, and dynamic be the exception rather than the rule. Similarly there should be room for diversity in the movement of the Chorus.

The Monster Chorus is divided into four parts: M1, M2, M3, and M4. Originally produced with just one actor in each chorus part, this play could easily be mounted with multiple actors in each section. In some instances (e.g., the Frankenstein family) it is important that specific members of the chorus play characters. Catherine should be played by M1, or by one of the actors in the M1 section. Elizabeth is (or is from) M2, William is M3; and Alphonse is M4. Other characters may be cast at the director's discretion.

While Mary Shelley's macabre nineteenth-century tragedy about an eighteenth-century man discovering the secret of life resounds to this day, the lessons of the novel are often confused and confounded by the themes and images perpetrated by James Whale's 1931 film adaptation of the story. The lumbering, flat headed, bolt-necked, Boris Karloff monster is repeatedly invoked as a symbol of man's scientific reach exceeding his grasp. This invocation invariably follows each scientific or technological advance that frightens any section of the population. Villagers with torches and pitchforks have decried the approach of the Internet, personal computers, mobile communications, mass media, transplants, cloning, stem cell research, and an ongoing list that awakens Victor Frankenstein every time his fictional name is uttered.

But Shelley's doctor and monster are a far different pair than Whale's, which now lives more solidly in our collective subconscious. The benevolent doctor trying his best to defend his poor, dumb, misunderstood, rampaging beast from the angry town and all of their black and white fury is almost the anti-Victor to Shelley's morose and disturbed doctor who fears success so much that he turns from his creation and leaves him to fend for himself. Shelley's Monster is a gentle, articulate being who teaches himself to speak, read, and reason. It is after a series of wrongs done to him based upon his countenance that he consciously chooses to seek vengeance against his creator and the world.

NORTHANGER ABBEY

A Romantic Gothic Comedy

Adapted for the stage from Jane Austen's novel and Ann Radcliffe's
The Mysteries of Udolpho

Lynn Marie Macy

LYNN MARIE MACY is a playwright, actor, and director who was born
and raised in Minneapolis. Macy attended the University of Minnesota and
received a BFA in theatre arts. She also trained at the Guthrie Theater and
with several independent studios in New York City. Macy studied playwriting
at New Dramatists in New York City and, before moving to New York, was a
resident acting company member at the Minneapolis Playwrights Center. Her
other plays include *Innocent Diversions*, *A Christmas Entertainment with Jane
Austen and Friends* (also director, Distilled Spirits Theatre, Theater Ten Ten);
A Thousand Merry Conceits, *A Private Audience with Nell Gwyn* (Theater
Ten Ten; Bedlam Theatre, Edinburgh Fringe Festival); *Crunching Numbers*
(published by NYTE in *Plays and Playwrights for the New Millennium*); and
a new adaptation/translation of Schiller's *Intrigue & Love* (Jean Cocteau
Repertory Theatre). Macy also directed *All's Well That Ends Well* at Theater
Ten Ten in 2004. As a performer, she has appeared in several productions
at the Jean Cocteau Repertory Theatre including *The Miser*, *The Threepenny
Opera*, *Intrigue & Love*, *Pygmalion*, *Medea*, and *Mother Courage*. Favorite
roles include April in *The Hot l Baltimore* (T. Schreiber Studio), Pegeen in
The Playboy of the Western World (Theater Ten Ten), Maria in *Twelfth Night*
(Kings County Shakespeare Company), and Pasha in *Temporarily Yours,*
(Distilled Spirits Theatre). She currently lives in Woodside, New York, with
her husband, director David Scott, and their cat Lillibette.

Northanger Abbey was first presented by Distilled Spirits Theatre on February 5, 2000, at the Flatiron Playhouse, New York City, with the following cast and credits:

Catherine Morland (Emily St. Aubert)..Laura Standley
Mr. Morland/St. Aubert/Mr. Allen ....Sterling Coyne
Mrs. Morland/Mrs. Thorpe/Visitor ....Ellen Turkelson
Henry Tilney/Chevalier Valancourt...Kevin Connell
Mrs. Allen/Madame Cheron ....Lynn McNutt
Amy/Annette/Mary/Dancer..Lynn Marie Macy
James Morland/Ludovico/Frederick/Dancer ....Mark Rimer
Isabella Thorpe/Signora Livona/Visitor..Annalisa Hill
John Thorpe/Count Morano ....Andrew Oswald
General Tilney/Montoni/Visitor ....David Winton
Eleanor Tilney/Visitor ....Amy Stoller
Servant/Dancer/Visitor ....Shirley Guest
Servant/Dancer/Visitor ....Madeline Gomez-Bianchi
Servant/Swordsman/Dancer/Visitor ....Dan O'Driscoll
Servant/Swordsman/Dancer/Visitor ....Greaton Sellers

Director: David Scott
Production Manager: John Harmon
Production Stage Manager: Lisa Latendresse
Set and Properties Design: Lucie Chin
Costume Design: Cathy Maguire
Light Design: Douglas Filomena
Sound Design: Lisa Latendresse
Dialect Coach: Amy Stoller
Fight Choreographer: Lucie Chin
Fight Captain: Dan O'Driscoll
Period Dance Choreographer: Hal Simons
Dance Captain: Annalisa Hill

Dedicated to Lorraine Ann Buth, ever generous of heart, a giving teacher, caretaker, and mother.

A multilevel unit set, which need not be realistic. Designers are encouraged to let their imaginations be inspired by the world of classic literature. Built into the set should be an area where the scene location titles can be projected or displayed. The period is Regency England; locations are suggested by selected minimal furnishings and scenery and lighting. Music. Frozen tableau of MR. and MRS. MORLAND and SERVANTS. CATHERINE MORLAND enters into a spot. She is a pretty, charming, good-humored, open, and energetic girl with a very active imagination. She wears a bonnet and traveling cloak and carries a bag. Projection: Fullerton.

CATHERINE: No one would ever suppose me to have been born a heroine. Growing up, I was never considered a great beauty or excessively clever, but I learnt the fable of "The Hare and Many Friends" as quickly as any girl in England. I shirked all my lessons and could not bear to study music. I loved nothing so well in all the world as running about the countryside, riding on horseback, or rolling down the green slope at the back of the house. So you see, by nature there is really nothing heroic about me at all. However, since the age of fourteen I have been in training for a heroine. I have been reading novels and books—Such works as heroines must read to supply their journals with those quotations which are so serviceable and soothing in the daily difficulties of their eventful lives. *(Takes her journal from the bag and opens it.)* From Gray I learnt that "Many a flower is born to blush unseen and waste its fragrance on the desert air." And from Shakespeare that a young woman in love always looks "Like patience on a monument smiling at grief." The greatest tragedy in my life to this moment is that I have not met with one handsome, amiable youth who could inspire true passion in my heart. But when a young lady is to become a heroine, the dullness of Fullerton and its inhabitants can hardly prevent her. Something must happen to throw a hero in my way. Our great friends Mr. and Mrs. Allen have been ordered to Bath, and they have invited me to join them on their journey. Six weeks residence in Bath!

(The stage springs to life. TWO SERVANTS enter, carrying a large trunk. CATHERINE gives them directions.)

MRS. MORLAND: I've changed my mind. I shall not let her go.

MR. MORLAND: My dear. It's time Catherine saw something of the world.

MRS. MORLAND: How will that fanciful, absent-minded girl ever be able to look after herself?

MR. MORLAND: Put your fears to rest, my dear. Mr. and Mrs. Allen will take perfect care of our dear child.

(SERVANTS take the trunk off, and MR. and MRS. MORLAND cross to CATHERINE.)

MRS. MORLAND: Catherine! Oh my dear Catherine! I can hardly conceive it. Absent from us for six full weeks. Whatever shall we do?

MR. MORLAND: We shall expect to hear from you regularly by the post, my dear.

CATHERINE: Of course, Papa.

MRS. MORLAND: My eldest girl all grown up and taking her first holiday away from her family. It's almost too much to bear.

CATHERINE: Mama, I shall be returned in no time.

MRS. MORLAND: I beg, Catherine, you will always wrap yourself up very warm about the throat when you come from the rooms at night; and I wish you would try to keep some account of the money you spend; I give you this little book for just that purpose.

CATHERINE: Thank you, Mama. *(Puts the book in her travel bag.)*

MR. MORLAND: Here is ten guineas, my dear, when you want more, write and you shall receive it.

CATHERINE: Thank you, Papa.

MRS. MORLAND: Great heavens! *(Calling offstage.)* Sally, Sally—I have begged you to keep the little ones from climbing the trees. Goodbye my dear child, you will behave for Mr. and Mrs. Allen, now won't you? Sally, for heaven sake, they'll soil their new frocks… *(Exits.)*

MR. MORLAND: Now, Catherine dear, you won't make yourself troublesome to the Allens…

CATHERINE: I shall prevail upon myself not to inconvenience anyone, Papa.

MR. MORLAND: Don't keep the Allens waiting, then. Oh Catherine, do be so good as to take these volumes for your journey.

(He hands her four elegant small volumes.)

CATHERINE: *The Mysteries of Udolpho*! Oh, Papa, I've longed for this novel. Thank you, Papa, thank you.

MR. MORLAND: Have a pleasant time… Goodbye, my dear girl.

CATHERINE: Goodbye, Papa.

(MR. MORLAND exits. She puts the volumes in her traveling bag.)

CATHERINE: *(To the audience.)* Dear Papa… But this was not the wise advice I expected from the lips of Mama at our parting. Surely there should have been those usual cautions against the violence of noblemen and baronets who delight in forcing young ladies away to remote farmhouses? *(Takes out her journal and writes. Pushes her bonnet back.)* The journey began indeed with comfortable quietness and safety. We were neither accosted by highwaymen nor savaged in tempests. *(To the audience.)* Nothing more alarming occurred than a fear on Mrs. Allen's side of having left her clogs behind her at an inn. I have begun reading the first volume of Radcliffe's *The Mysteries of Udolpho.* It is every bit as magnificent as I dreamt it would be. I am entranced with Emily and her dear, ailing father, St. Aubert, as they make their fateful journey through the Pyrenees Mountains in the South of France…

(On another part of the stage, an OLDER GENTLEMAN [ST. AUBERT, played by the same actor as MR. MORLAND] enters into a spot. His garb suggests a period of history at least one hundred years earlier than CATHERINE's. He beckons to CATHERINE. She is now "in" Radcliffe's The Mysteries of Udolpho. *Projection:* The Mysteries of Udolpho.*)*

ST. AUBERT: Emily, Emily…come quickly or you shall miss this glorious sunset.

CATHERINE: Papa?

ST. AUBERT: Make haste, my dear child.

(She puts the journal back in her travel bag and crosses to him. He puts an arm about her.)

CATHERINE: *(As EMILY.)* It is the most beautiful I've ever seen.

ST. AUBERT: The dusky gloom of the woods was always delightful to me. It calls forth a thousand images.

CATHERINE: *(As EMILY.)* Oh my dear father, how exactly you describe what I have felt so often.

ST. AUBERT: I shall not soon forget the kindness of young Valancourt. I remember when I was his age and I thought and felt exactly as he does. The world was opening upon me then, now—it is closing.

CATHERINE: *(As EMILY.)* Father, I hope you may have many, many years to live for your own sake—for my sake.

ST. AUBERT: Ah, Emily…for your sake… There is something about the ardor of youth… It is cheering, like the view of spring to a sick person. Valancourt is this spring to me. Come, the glowworm lends his light, step a little further and we shall see fairies perhaps.

(They hear a rustling noise.)

CATHERINE: *(As EMILY.)* Father, did you hear that?

ST. AUBERT: *(Takes a pistol from his belt.)* Stand back, my child. These hills are infested with ruthless and desperate banditti.

(Another noise. A FIGURE emerges nearby.)

ST. AUBERT: There!

(He fires the pistol. CATHERINE [as EMILY] screams. The FIGURE [VALANCOURT] is hit. He falls forward.)

VALANCOURT: Ah! Monsieur St. Aubert!

(ST. AUBERT rushes to his aid.)

ST. AUBERT: Valancourt!!

(CATHERINE [as EMILY] faints at the news.)

VALANCOURT: I'm not hurt. It is only my arm. *(Groans in pain.)*

(ST. AUBERT binds his wound.)

ST. AUBERT: Valancourt, in the name of God how came you hither? Emily, Emily child, where are you?

VALANCOURT: Emily!!

(They go to her as she is reviving. VALANCOURT moves with difficulty.)

CATHERINE: *(As EMILY.)* Oh, monsieur, monsieur…

VALANCOURT: *(In great pain.)* It is nothing Emily, you see, a wound of no consequence.

ST. AUBERT: How far is it to Beaujeu? We must get you to Beaujeu.

VALANCOURT: It is two leagues distant. Do not alarm yourself on my account. I assure you I can support myself very well on the journey.

ST. AUBERT: Let me assist you to the carriage. I am heartily distressed by this unfortunate accident, Valancourt. You cannot fathom my surprise at seeing you here.

VALANCOURT: You and Emily renewed my taste for society. When you left the village it did appear a solitude. I determined to take this same road—I admit I had some hope of overtaking you.

ST. AUBERT: And I have made you a very unexpected return of the compliment. My heart grieves sorely at my rashness. Come, you faint from loss of blood.

(They have disappeared.)

CATHERINE: *(As EMILY.)* Oh, Monsieur Valancourt… He must live or I fear, I fear that I shall die.

MRS. ALLEN: *(Entering with traveling cloak.)* Catherine…Catherine. Don't stand there dawdling. Our rooms are ready, come dear. *(Exits.)*

(A MAID [AMY] enters and takes CATHERINE's bag and her bonnet. TWO SERVANTS carry her trunk across the stage. Projection: Pulteney Street, Bath.)

AMY: Welcome to Bath, Miss Morland.

CATHERINE: Thank you. At last! *(Spins around.)* Our first few days were a blur of shops, galleries, theatrical performances, reading my wonderful novel, and preparations for this evening's long-awaited event. My first ball in the Assembly Rooms.

(A SERVANT enters and takes CATHERINE's cloak. She is dressed for the ball. The music sounds, the lights come up, and PEOPLE are gathering in the room. MRS. ALLEN crosses to CATHERINE. Projection: The Assembly Rooms, Bath.)

MRS. ALLEN: Oh, Oh, great heavens, I can scarcely believe I have come through that throng of people without injuring my gown. It would have been very shocking to have torn it. It is such a delicate muslin. For my part, I have not seen anything I like so well in the whole room.

CATHERINE: Oh, Mrs. Allen, how uncomfortable it is not to have a single acquaintance here!

MRS. ALLEN: The Skinners were here last year. I wish they were here now. One gets so tumbled in a crowd! How is my head, dear? I'm afraid somebody gave me a push that has hurt it.

CATHERINE: But dear Mrs. Allen, are you sure there is nobody you know in all this multitude of people?

MRS. ALLEN: I don't upon my word. If the Parrys had come, you might have danced with George Parry. I should be so glad to have you dance. There goes a strange-looking woman! What an odd gown she has got on! How old-fashioned it is! Look at the back.

(MR. ALLEN and HENRY TILNEY, who is played by the same actor as VALANCOURT, cross the room to them.)

MR. ALLEN: My dears, I have just experienced the delight of making an acquaintance with Mr. Henry Tilney, and he has expressed a desire to know you both. Mr. Tilney this is my wife Mrs. Allen.

HENRY: I am very pleased to make your acquaintance, madam.

MRS. ALLEN: How do you do, Mr. Tilney?

MR. ALLEN: And this is our dear young friend, Miss Catherine Morland.

HENRY: I am altogether charmed to make your acquaintance, Miss Morland.

CATHERINE: You are too kind, Mr. Tilney.

MRS. ALLEN: Miss Morland is staying with us in Pulteney Street for the duration of our visit and I can attest she is an excellent dancer. I daresay she might even accept you as her partner for the next dance.

HENRY: Miss Morland, I hope you will consent?

CATHERINE: I would be honored, sir.

(They cross to join the other DANCERS. A very elegant and formal dance begins.)

MRS. ALLEN: My dear Mr. Allen, how we should get along without you, I'll never know. What a charming young man.

MR. ALLEN: The master of ceremonies informed me he was a clergyman, and he comes from a very respectable family in Gloucestershire.

MRS. ALLEN: How tasteful he is in his attire. He is an agreeable partner for Catherine to be sure.

(They cross to view the DANCERS. After a few minutes, the dance ends with a flourish. HENRY and CATHERINE cross to a table for punch.)

HENRY: I have been very remiss, madam, in the proper attentions of a partner here; I have not yet asked you how long you have been in Bath; whether you were ever here before; whether you have been at the theatre and the concert; and how you like the place altogether.

CATHERINE: You need not trouble yourself, sir.

HENRY: No trouble, I assure you, madam. *(With affectation.)* Have you long been in Bath, Miss Morland?

CATHERINE: *(Trying not to laugh.)* About a week, sir.

HENRY: Really!?

CATHERINE: Why should you be surprised, sir?

HENRY: Why, indeed! *(In his natural voice.)* Some emotion must appear to be raised by your reply and surprise is more easily assumed, and not less reasonable than any other. Now let us go on. *(Resuming his affected tone.)* Were you ever here before, madam?

CATHERINE: Never, sir.

HENRY: Indeed, and have you been to the theatre?

CATHERINE: I was at the play on Tuesday.

HENRY: To the concert?

CATHERINE: On Wednesday.

HENRY: And are you altogether pleased with Bath?

CATHERINE: I like it very well.

HENRY: Now I must give one smirk, and then we may be rational again.

(CATHERINE laughs.)

HENRY: I see what you think of me. I shall make a poor figure in your journal tomorrow.

CATHERINE: My journal!

HENRY: Yes, I know exactly what you will say: Friday, went to the Assembly Rooms; wore my sprigged muslin robe with blue trimmings—plain black shoes—appeared to much advantage; but was strangely harassed by an odd, half-witted man who distressed me by his nonsense.

CATHERINE: I shall say no such thing.

HENRY: Shall I tell you what you ought to say?

CATHERINE: If you please.

HENRY: I danced with a very agreeable young man, introduced by Mr. Allen; had a great deal of conversation with him—seems a most extraordinary genius—hope I may know more of him.

CATHERINE: But perhaps I keep no journal.

HENRY: Not keep a journal! How are the civilities and compliments of everyday life to be properly related, unless noted down every evening in a journal? I am not so ignorant of young ladies' ways as you wish to believe me.

MRS. ALLEN: *(Crosses to CATHERINE.)* Catherine, do take this pin out of my sleeve; I am afraid it has torn a hole already. I shall be quite sorry if it has for this is a favorite gown, though it cost but nine shillings a yard.

HENRY: That is exactly what I would have guessed it, madam.

MRS. ALLEN: Do you understand muslins, sir?

HENRY: My sister has often trusted me in the choice of a gown. I bought one for her the other day, and it was pronounced a prodigious bargain by every lady who saw it.

MRS. ALLEN: *(Impressed.)* Men commonly take no notice of those things. I can never get Mr. Allen to know one of my gowns from another. You must be a great comfort to your sister, sir.

HENRY: I hope I am, madam.

MRS. ALLEN: And pray, sir, what do you think of Miss Morland's gown?

HENRY: It is very pretty, madam. But I do not think it will wash well; I am afraid it will fray.

CATHERINE: Mr. Tilney!…

MRS. ALLEN: I am quite of your opinion, sir, and so I told Miss Morland when she bought it.

(HENRY and MRS. ALLEN continue to chat. CATHERINE takes a few steps downstage as the lights dim around her.)

CATHERINE: What a remarkable person! He's very charming, gentleman-like, and has a pleasing countenance, and if he is not quite handsome—he is very near it. Truly I believe him to be every bit as handsome as the Chevalier Valancourt.

(HENRY crosses to her. The lights narrow on them.)

HENRY: What were you thinking of so earnestly? Your dancing partner perhaps?

CATHERINE: I was not thinking of anything.

HENRY: I had rather be told that you will not tell me.

CATHERINE: Then I will not.

HENRY: Thank you; for now I am authorized to tease you on this subject whenever we meet, and nothing in the world advances intimacy so much. Good evening, Miss Morland.

(He kisses her hand and exits.)

CATHERINE: *(After a pause.)* Good evening, Mr. Tilney… *(She is again in a spot.)* Astonishing! I've never met with anyone quite like him in my entire life! I can scarcely describe the way he makes me feel. Why could I not answer him!?! This is not how I've been led to believe a heroine should feel. This cannot be the way Emily St. Aubert felt when she met the chevalier. Heavens! How shall I prevent his image from haunting my thoughts at night?

(AMY enters and crosses to CATHERINE to help her undress. She takes off the outer dress and helps CATHERINE change into a new gown.)

CATHERINE: Amy…

AMY: Yes, miss?

CATHERINE: Amy, I've just been wondering… if it might be true as I have once read, that no young lady can be justified in falling in love before the gentleman's love is declared?

AMY: Gentleman? Might there be a particular gentleman, miss?

CATHERINE: No, I speak in general terms.

AMY: No particular gentleman…I see, then to be sure it is very difficult to ascertain precisely how much affection is proper in the affairs of the heart. Good night. *(Starts to leave, with a knowing smile.)* Sweet dreams, miss…

CATHERINE: Oh— In any case, it must be very improper for a young lady to *dream* of a gentleman before the gentleman is first known to have *dreamt* of her. Oh, how I long for Mama or my sister Sally, someone to confide in, someone to advise me.

(VALANCOURT enters. Projection: The Mysteries of Udolpho.)

VALANCOURT: Emily!

CATHERINE: *(As EMILY.)* Chevalier… How came you to La Vallee?

VALANCOURT: I've come to see you. To discover the truth of what I have heard of your father's passing.

(CATHERINE [as EMILY] breaks down.)

VALANCOURT: I can only mourn with you, for I cannot doubt the source of your tears.

CATHERINE: *(As EMILY.)* After we left you, he became ill on the road home. It was very sudden.

VALANCOURT: Why was I not there!

CATHERINE: *(As EMILY.)* Now I cannot bear to leave the beloved scenes of my childhood. My father in his will has committed me to the care of his sister, Madame Cheron. But the depth of my grief prevents me from leaving my home.

VALANCOURT: La Vallee is, indeed, a beautiful chateau.

CATHERINE: *(As EMILY.)* My father loved to sit under this tree with his family about him in the fine evenings of summer.

VALANCOURT: *(Hesitating.)* Lovely… Emily, I must leave—leave you—perhaps forever. Let me however, without offending the delicacy of your grief, venture to declare the admiration I feel. Oh…that at some future period I might be permitted to call it love!

CATHERINE: *(As EMILY; searching for the correct words.)* I am honored by the good opinion of any person whom my father esteemed.

VALANCOURT: Was I thought worthy of his esteem? Dare I to hope that you think me not unworthy of that honor and might permit me sometimes to… inquire after your health?

CATHERINE: *(As EMILY.)* I have, alas, no longer a parent whose presence might sanction your visit.

VALANCOURT: You do not think me worthy of your esteem.

CATHERINE: *(As EMILY.)* You do both yourself and me an injustice. I do think you worthy of my esteem. You have long possessed it and…and… *(She is in tears.)*

VALANCOURT: Oh, Emily, my own Emily—teach me to sustain this moment! Let me seal it as the most sacred of my life.

(He tearfully kisses her hands.)

CATHERINE: (*As EMILY.*) Forgive this weakness. I believe my spirits have not yet recovered from the shock they have lately received.

VALANCOURT: I cannot excuse myself. But I will forbear to renew the subject.

(*Enter MADAME CHERON, who is played by the actress who plays MRS. ALLEN; and ANNETTE, who is played by the actress who plays AMY.*)

MADAME CHERON: Well, well, niece. How do you do?

CATHERINE: (*As EMILY.*) Aunt!

MADAME CHERON: But I need not ask. Your looks tell me you have already recovered your loss.

CATHERINE: (*As EMILY.*) My looks do me injustice then, madame. My loss I know can never be recovered.

MADAME CHERON: I see you have exactly your father's disposition; and let me tell you it would have been much happier for him, poor man, had it been a different one.

CATHERINE: (*As EMILY.*) Aunt, allow me to present the Chevalier Valancourt. A friend of my dear father's.

MADAME CHERON: I see.

VALANCOURT: (*With difficulty.*) I must beg your forgiveness and take my leave of you both. Good afternoon. (*He disappears.*)

MADAME CHERON: And who is that young adventurer, pray? What are his pretensions?

CATHERINE: (*As EMILY.*) His family was not unknown to my father. He is brother to the Count de Duvarney.

MADAME CHERON: A younger brother and no doubt a beggar. I believed, niece, you had a greater sense of propriety than to receive the visits of any young man in your present unfriended situation. However, since your father made it his last request that I should overlook your conduct, I am even now come to take you with me to Tholouse.

(*MADAME CHERON directs ANNETTE off.*)

MADAME CHERON: And I have no wish to be troubled in my own house by visits from young men who may take a fancy to flatter you.

CATHERINE: (*As EMILY.*) But madame, I should be very happy to remain at La Vallee.

MADAME CHERON: No doubt you would. I did not think you capable of so much duplicity, niece. You will promise to neither see nor write to this young man without my consent. When you pleaded your excuse for remaining here, I foolishly believed it a just one.

CATHERINE: (*As EMILY.*) I feel more than ever the value of the retirement I solicited. If the purpose of your visit is only to add insult to the sorrow of your brother's child, she could well have spared it.

MADAME CHERON: I see that I have undertaken a very troublesome task. We leave tomorrow morning. (*Fumes out.*)

CATHERINE: (*As EMILY.*) Am I to be forced to leave La Vallee? How shall I bear the loss of my father, my home and…Valancourt!

(*CATHERINE [as EMILY] must support herself as her emotions overcome her. AMY enters and curtsies. CATHERINE's demeanor puzzles AMY.*)

AMY: Good morning— Breakfast is on table, Miss Morland.

CATHERINE: Oh… Thank you Amy. (*Stands.*) I shall join the Allens presently.

(*AMY exits.*)

CATHERINE: I hastened to the Pump Room after breakfast. Crowds of people every moment were passing in and out, up the steps and down; people whom nobody cared about and nobody wanted to see coming in to take the waters and display themselves in their finery. In all of Bath, only *he* was absent.

(*The lights change, and the room is bustling. CATHERINE is out of spirits. Projection: The Pump Room.*)

MRS. ALLEN: Bath is such a charming place. There are so many good shops here. We are sadly off in the country. Not but that we have very good shops in Salisbury, but it is so far to go—eight miles is a long way; Mr. Allen says it is nine but it cannot be more than eight; and it is such a fag—I come back tired to death. Now, here one can step out of doors and get a thing in five minutes.

(*A FRIENDLY LOOKING WOMAN crosses to them.*)

MRS. THORPE: I think, madam, I cannot be mistaken; it is such a long time since I had the pleasure of seeing you, but is not your name Allen?

MRS. ALLEN: Why, yes, indeed it is.

MRS. THORPE: I'm Mrs. Thorpe. I believe, Mrs. Allen, we have not seen one another since you were married.

MRS. ALLEN: Mrs. Thorpe! Oh, Catherine dear, it's Mrs. Thorpe, a former schoolmate of mine. My, you have hardly altered a bit since I saw you last.

MRS. THORPE: You are too kind, Mrs. Allen. I can scarcely believe how the time has slipped by. It's been more than fifteen years, I am sure.

MRS. ALLEN: Yes… And how is your dear family, Mrs. Thorpe?

MRS. THORPE: Would you believe it? John is at Oxford, Edward at Merchant Taylor's, and William at sea. But my dearest Isabella is here with me. Isabella…Isabella dear, come join us here. I am prodigiously proud of my girl, Mrs. Allen. I do believe she is the prettiest thing one could ever wish to see.

(ISABELLA, an astonishingly beautiful young lady, crosses to them.)

MRS. THORPE: Mrs. Allen is an old school friend of mine, dear.

ISABELLA: How do you do, Mrs. Allen, I am very pleased to make your acquaintance.

MRS. THORPE: And is this charming young lady your daughter?

MRS. ALLEN: Oh, do forgive my negligence. This is Miss Catherine Morland.

(ISABELLA and MRS. THORPE exchange looks.)

MRS. ALLEN: She and her family are our dear friends and neighbors at Fullerton. Mr. Allen and I were never blessed with children of our own, I'm sorry to say.

CATHERINE: I am very pleased to meet you both.

ISABELLA: How excessively like her brother Miss Morland is!

MRS. THORPE: The very picture of him indeed!

ISABELLA: I should have known her anywhere for his sister!

CATHERINE: My brother?

MRS. THORPE: My eldest son John is with your brother James at Oxford, Miss Morland.

ISABELLA: And he honored us with a visit last Christmas.

MRS. ALLEN: Catherine, what a remarkable encounter!

CATHERINE: Extraordinary!

ISABELLA: I feel as though I know you already. Oh, Miss Morland, I do hope that soon we too shall be the best of friends.

(CATHERINE takes a few steps toward the audience. The other LADIES continue to chat excitedly as the lights dim.)

CATHERINE: What unparalleled joy! I am delighted with this extension of my Bath acquaintance. Miss Thorpe being older than I and better informed is very advantageous. She compares the balls of Bath with those of Tunbridge, its fashions with the fashions of London. Lord, how I admire her.

(The lights come up on the ALLENS' rooms. ISABELLA has just arrived. AMY takes her cloak. Projection: Pulteney Street.)

ISABELLA: I was so afraid it would rain this morning just as I wanted to set off, and that would have thrown me into agonies! Oh, I have a hundred things to say to you. But, my dearest Catherine, have you gone on with Udolpho?

CATHERINE: Yes, and I am got to the black veil.

ISABELLA: I would not tell you what is behind the black veil for the world! Are you not wild to know?

CATHERINE: Do not tell me—I would not be told upon any account. I am sure it is Signora Laurentini's skeleton.

(They shriek excitedly together.)

ISABELLA: When you have finished Udolpho, we will read The Italian together; and I have made a list of ten or twelve more of the same kind for you.

CATHERINE: What are they all?

ISABELLA: (Reading.) Castle of Wolfenback, Mysterious Warnings, Necromancer of the Black Forest, Midnight Bell, Orphan of the Rhine, and Horrid Mysteries. Those will last us some time.

CATHERINE: But are they all horrid, are you sure they are all horrid?

ISABELLA: Quite sure; for a particular friend of mine, a Miss Andrews, has read every one of them. I wish you knew her. I think her as beautiful as an angel and I am so vexed with the men for not admiring her. I scold them all amazingly about it.

CATHERINE: You scold them?

ISABELLA: Men think us incapable of real friendship, you know, and I am determined to show them the difference. But you are just the kind of girl to be a great favorite with the men.

CATHERINE: Isabella, how can you say so?

ISABELLA: After we parted yesterday, I saw a young man looking at you so earnestly—I am sure he is in love with you.

CATHERINE: I am sure you are mistaken.

ISABELLA: I see, you are indifferent to everybody's admiration, except the gentleman who shall be nameless.

CATHERINE: You should not persuade me to think about Mr. Tilney. I may never see him again.

ISABELLA: My dearest creature, you would be miserable if you thought so.

CATHERINE: I was very much pleased with him; but while I have *Udolpho* to read, I feel as if nobody could make me miserable! Oh, the dreadful black veil! Isabella, I am sure there must be a skeleton behind it.

ISABELLA: Catherine, have you settled what to wear on your head tonight? I am determined at all events to be dressed exactly like you. The men take notice of that sometimes. By the by, I have always forgot to ask you what is your favorite complexion in a man. Do you like them best dark or fair?

CATHERINE: I hardly know. Something between both, I think.

ISABELLA: That is exactly he. I have not forgot your description of Mr. Tilney! Well my taste is different. I prefer light eyes and hair. You must not betray me if you should ever meet with one of your acquaintance answering to that description.

CATHERINE: Betray you? Whatever do you mean?

ISABELLA: Nay, do not distress me. I believe I have said too much. (*Exits.*)

CATHERINE: (*To the audience.*) I was sure she was hinting at something but I was so distracted by *Udolpho*,

Signora Laurentini's skeleton, and the mysterious disappearance of Mr. Henry Tilney that I was not inclined to discover more.

(*AMY brings CATHERINE her coat.*)

CATHERINE: Indeed, he seems nowhere to be met with. Every search for him is unsuccessful. His name is not even registered in the Pump Room book. He must be gone from Bath. What could have pulled him so suddenly away? Certainly he could not have become lost. Perhaps he was accosted by a gang of sailors and pressed into service at sea? What a dreadful thought. Or worse, what if he were overpowered by a desperate band of robbers and now lies beaten and bleeding in a ditch? Poor Mr. Tilney! Shall I never see him again?

(*VALANCOURT enters. Projection: The Mysteries of Udolpho.*)

VALANCOURT: Oh, my Emily! I cannot trust my own eyes! I have haunted these gardens for many, many nights with the faint hope of seeing you again.

CATHERINE: (*As EMILY.*) We are to leave France in a few days' time. My aunt has indeed become wife of Signor Montoni. How cruelly they have divided us! To consent to our marriage and then to wed themselves and deny us.

VALANCOURT: You are going from me to a distant country with people who will try to make you forget me.

CATHERINE: (*As EMILY.*) Can you truly believe the pangs I suffer proceed from temporary interest…

VALANCOURT: (*Interrupting.*) Suffer for me! How sweet and how bitter are those words.

(*CATHERINE [as EMILY] weeps. He kisses away her tears.*)

VALANCOURT: In a little while all this will appear a dream, my regiment will be stationed in Paris, and you will be taken from me. I cannot bear it! Emily, fly with me to the church of the Augustines where a friar will unite us in holy matrimony.

CATHERINE: (*As EMILY.*) Think of my duty to my father's sister—your duty to your regiment and to your brother. You tear my heart but I cannot be the means of jeopardizing your future!

VALANCOURT: Must we be parted then? Must you go to Italy? —Be wary my love, be wary of this Montoni. I gathered by accident from an Italian who was speaking of him that abroad he is a man of desperate fortune and character. And he spoke of strange circumstances concerning his castle Udolpho in the Apennines. Do not trust him, dear Emily.

CATHERINE: *(As EMILY.)* You forget, you speak of the man who is now my uncle.

VALANCOURT: How I suffer seeing you committed to the power of a man of such doubtful character as this Montoni.

CATHERINE: *(As EMILY.)* I must leave you now. It is late. Think of me when I am far away.

VALANCOURT: God knows when we shall meet again! I resign you to his care.

CATHERINE: *(As EMILY.)* Trust we shall meet again, meet for each other.

VALANCOURT: We can meet in thought. Every evening we shall watch the sunset and be happy in the belief that your eyes are fixed on the same object as mine, and that our minds and hearts are conversing.

CATHERINE: *(As EMILY.)* I will do as you say. Farewell my love.

VALANCOURT: Farewell, I shall be a wanderer, exiled from my only home.

(They separate, reaching their hands out to one another. He disappears. ISABELLA rushes in, grabbing her extended hand. The lights come up on a bustling Pump Room. CATHERINE and ISABELLA cross to the Pump Room guest book. Projection: The Pump Room.)

ISABELLA: Oh, Catherine, let's move away from this end of the room. There are two odious-looking young men who have been staring at me this half hour. Let us look again at the new arrivals.

(They examine the guest book.)

ISABELLA: Pray let me know if they are coming this way. I am determined not to look up.

CATHERINE: Upon my word! Oh, Isabella, look who is just coming in!

ISABELLA: How delightful, Mr. Morland and my brother John!

CATHERINE: James! James!

(The TWO MEN cross to THEIR SISTERS. JAMES gives CATHERINE a robust embrace. JOHN THORPE gives HIS SISTER's hand a playful squeeze.)

CATHERINE: Oh, James what a heavenly surprise!

JOHN: Belle, I see you are as ugly as ever.

ISABELLA: Don't tease me; you know I can't bear it.

JAMES: Allow me to present my good friend, Mr. John Thorpe. John, this is my dear sister, Catherine.

JOHN: How do you do, Miss Morland?

CATHERINE: It is a pleasure to meet you at last, Mr. Thorpe.

JOHN: Belle, have you been telling your charming friend tales out of school?

JAMES: Miss Thorpe, I cannot tell you what a pleasure it is to see you again.

ISABELLA: Mr. Morland, this is a very happy surprise, indeed. Oh, John, Mama will be here presently; do stay and we shall all take the waters together.

(ISABELLA crosses to a WAITER. JAMES takes a seat and awaits ISABELLA's return. JOHN THORPE crosses to CATHERINE.)

JOHN: *(Taking out his watch.)* How long do you think we have been running it from Tetbury, Miss Morland?

CATHERINE: I do not know the distance.

JAMES: It is twenty-three miles.

JOHN: It is five and twenty if it is an inch.

JAMES: Good God, man, am I to disregard the authority of my road books and the milestones?

JOHN: Damn it, I know it must be five and twenty by the *time* we have been doing it. I defy any man in England to make my horse go less than ten miles an hour in harness. This brother of yours would persuade me out of my senses, Miss Morland. Do but look at my horse.

(He leads her to a window. They look out.)

JOHN: There, on the left, the servant is just leading him off. Did you ever see an animal so made for speed in your life?

CATHERINE: He does look hot.

JOHN: Hot! He had not turned a hair till we came to Walcot Church; but look at his forehead; look at his loins; only see how he moves; that horse cannot go less than ten miles an hour: tie his legs and he will get on.

And what do you think of my carriage, Miss Morland? A neat one, is it not? Well hung; town built; I have not had it a month. It was built for a Christ Church man, a friend of mine. I chanced to meet him on Magdalen Bridge as he was driving into Oxford last term. "Ah, Thorpe," said he, "do you happen to want such a little thing as this? It is a capital one of the kind but I am cursed tired of it." "Oh damn," I said, "I am your man; what do you ask?" And how much do you think he did, Miss Morland?

CATHERINE: I cannot guess at all.

JOHN: Splashing-board, lamps, silver molding, all you saw complete; the ironwork as good as new, or better. He asked me fifty guineas. I closed with him, threw down the money, and the carriage was mine.

CATHERINE: I cannot judge whether it was cheap or costly.

JOHN: I might have got it for less, I daresay, but I hate haggling and poor Freeman wanted cash.

CATHERINE: That was very good-natured of you.

JOHN: Oh, damn it! When one has the means of doing a kind thing by a friend, I hate to be pitiful. I say, Morland there goes a damn fine-looking woman, eh? Are you fond of an open carriage, Miss Morland?

CATHERINE: Yes, I am particularly fond of it.

JOHN: I will drive you out in mine every day. I will drive you up Lansdown Hill tomorrow.

CATHERINE: But will not your horse want rest?

JOHN: Rest?! Nonsense; nothing ruins horses so much as rest; nothing knocks them up so soon. No, no; I shall exercise mine at the average of four hours a day while I am here.

CATHERINE: That would be forty miles a day.

JOHN: Aye fifty, for what I care. Well, I will drive you up Lansdown Hill tomorrow. Consider it an engagement.

ISABELLA: How delightful that will be! My dearest Catherine, I quite envy you; but I am afraid, dear brother, you will not have room for a third.

JOHN: A third, indeed! No, no; I did not come to Bath to drive my sister about; that would be a good joke, faith. Morland must take care of you.

ISABELLA: Oh, here's Mama! Mama, look, look who's come all the way to Bath to see us.

MRS. THORPE: (*Crosses to them.*) John! Oh my dear boy, what a surprise!

JOHN: Ah, Mother! How do you do? Where did you get that quiz of a hat? It makes you look like an old witch.

(*Laughter all around.*)

JOHN: Here is Morland and I come to stay a few days with you, so you must look out for a couple of good beds somewhere near.

MRS. THORPE: How happy I am to see you both. Isabella, is this not a wonderful surprise! Oh what a pleasant time we shall all have! I insist we must all dine together this evening.

(*A WAITER brings a tray with glasses.*)

JOHN: To your health!

EVERYONE: Health!

(*The water tastes like it smells: rotten eggs.*)

JOHN: A bit like *eau de cheval*… what?!?

JAMES: I say!

(*Laughter. CATHERINE breaks away from the GROUP and takes a few steps toward the audience. The lights narrow on her as the OTHERS drift off.*)

CATHERINE: What an unlooked-for twist in the plot! As much as I love my brother and admire my dearest friend Isabella, I confess her brother's manner and address make me quite uneasy, and I find myself in some distress as to the propriety of accepting an offer of a carriage ride with a relative stranger. John Thorpe is my brother's friend and I am obliged to be civil to him, but really he seems a very disagreeable sort of young man and I cannot at all account for his character…

(*JAMES interrupts her. They walk to see the ALLENS. Projection: Outside, Pulteney Street.*)

JAMES: Catherine, how do you like my friend John Thorpe?

CATHERINE: (*After a moment.*) He seems very agreeable.

JAMES: He's as good-natured a fellow as ever lived, And, I may add, thinks you're the most charming girl in the world.

CATHERINE: Does he?

JAMES: He's a bit of a rattle; but that will recommend him to your sex, I believe. And how do you like the rest of the family?

CATHERINE: Very much. Isabella in particular.

JAMES: She is just the kind of young woman I could wish to see you attached to.

CATHERINE: You hardly mentioned anything of her when you wrote me after your visit there.

JAMES: Because I thought I should soon see you myself. How much she must be admired in a place such as this.

CATHERINE: Mr. Allen thinks her the prettiest girl in Bath.

JAMES: I do not know any man who is a better judge of beauty than Mr. Allen.

CATHERINE: Oh, how I do miss everyone at home and how I feel guilty for having such a pleasant time.

JAMES: The Allens, I am sure, are very kind to you?

CATHERINE: Very! Now you are come it will be more delightful than ever! How good it is of you to come so far on purpose to see me.

JAMES: *(Beat.)* Indeed, Catherine, I have missed you excessively.

(MR. and MRS. ALLEN enter and cross to them.)

MR. ALLEN: Young Mr. Morland! What a surprise to see you here!

JAMES: Mr. Allen, Mrs. Allen, how do you do? I've just come with my friend John Thorpe for a visit.

MRS. ALLEN: How very pleasant! I find Bath is just the place for young people—and indeed everybody else too. I tell Mr. Allen that he should not complain for it is so agreeable a place and much better to be here than at home at this dull time of year. I tell him he is quite in luck to be sent here to improve his health.

MR. ALLEN: Ah, yes, fortunate, indeed. I hope, my young friend, that you will be at leisure to dine with us this evening?

JAMES: I am afraid I have been previously engaged to the Thorpes this evening. And I have come to beg Catherine's company as well.

MRS. ALLEN: Naturally, you would wish to be together.

MR. ALLEN: We shall be sincerely disappointed by the loss of you both, but we shall expect another dinner engagement in the very near future.

JAMES: With the greatest of pleasure, Mr. Allen.

(CATHERINE steps forward, leaving the chatting GROUP, as the lights dim, leaving her in a spot.)

CATHERINE: Dinner at the Thorpes' was pleasant enough. I endeavored whenever possible to avoid conversation with Mr. Thorpe, who was quite persistent.

(AMY removes CATHERINE's coat.)

CATHERINE: The mutual affection between my brother and Isabella has not slipped my notice. I am not at all surprised at James for admiring her, she is so very beautiful, charming, and such pleasant company for a fine evening.

(JOHN has crossed to her, smiling broadly. CATHERINE eyes him, then back to the audience.)

CATHERINE: Unlike her brother.

(The lights come up. We see the THORPES' sitting room after dinner. ISABELLA, JAMES, and MRS. THORPE are preparing for a game of cards. Projection: Edgar's Buildings, Bath.)

JOHN: Miss Morland, do join us for a game of cards.

CATHERINE: Thank you, no. Do go on without me. I am very contented to read my book.

MRS. THORPE: How very kind of the Allens to spare you this evening, Miss Morland. Come along, John, take a seat.

JOHN: Dash it all! Cards would hardly be amusing if Miss Morland is not to play. Damn it! I shall not play either.

ISABELLA: John, you promised a game of whist. You know we can't play with only three.

MRS. THORPE: Now, Belle dear. We shall play ombre. John has hardly spoken with Miss Morland all evening.

(MRS. THORPE deals the cards as JOHN crosses to CATHERINE and smiles. He pours more wine into his glass. There is an awkward moment.)

CATHERINE: Have you ever read *The Mysteries of Udolpho*, Mr. Thorpe?

JOHN: Oh Lord! Not I! Novels are all so full of stuff and nonsense; there has not been a decent one come out since *Tom Jones*.

CATHERINE: I think you would like *Udolpho*.

JOHN: No, faith! If I read, it shall be Mrs. Radcliffe's. Her novels are worth reading; some fun and nature in them.

CATHERINE: *Udolpho* was written by Mrs. Radcliffe, Mr. Thorpe.

JOHN: Was it? Aye, so it was; I was thinking of that other stupid book, written by that woman…she who married the French emigrant.

CATHERINE: I suppose you mean *Camilla*…written by Frances Burney?

JOHN: Yes; such unnatural stuff! As soon as I heard the author had married a Frenchman, I was sure I should never get through it.

CATHERINE: I have not yet read it.

JOHN: Ah, there is nothing in the world in it but an old man's playing at see-saw and learning Latin; upon my soul there is not.

(JOHN laughs and takes a seat next to CATHERINE, perhaps a little too close. He speaks in a confidential tone.)

JOHN: Old Allen is rich as a Jew—is he not?

CATHERINE: *(Shocked.)* I beg your pardon?

JOHN: Old Allen, the man you are with.

CATHERINE: Oh! Mr. Allen, you mean. Yes, I believe he is very rich.

JOHN: And no children at all?

CATHERINE: No—not any.

JOHN: A famous thing for his next heirs. He is *your* godfather, is he not?

CATHERINE: My godfather! No.

JOHN: But you are very much with them.

CATHERINE: Yes, very much.

JOHN: Aye, that is what I meant.

ISABELLA: It is so delightful to have an evening at home, is it not?

MRS. THORPE: Indeed it is, my dear.

JOHN: He has lived very well in his time, I daresay; he is not gouty for nothing. Does he drink his bottle a day now?

CATHERINE: Mr. Thorpe, I assure you, I have never seen him in liquor.

JOHN: Lord help you! You do not suppose a man is overset by a *bottle*?

ISABELLA: How I pity the poor creatures who are going to the ball in the Lower Rooms.

JOHN: If everybody was to drink their bottle a day, there would not be half the disorders in the world there are now.

ISABELLA: I wonder if they've begun dancing yet?

JOHN: It would be a famous good thing for us all.

CATHERINE: I cannot believe it.

JOHN: Lord! There is not the hundredth part of wine consumed in this kingdom that there ought to be. Our foggy climate needs help. *(Downs his glass.)*

ISABELLA: I daresay it will not be a very good ball. I know the Mitchells will not be there.

CATHERINE: Yet I hear there is a good deal of wine consumed in Oxford.

JOHN: There is no drinking at Oxford now, I assure you. It was reckoned a remarkable thing at the last party in my rooms that, upon average, we only cleared about five pints a head. *(Pours himself another glass.)*

ISABELLA: Mr. Morland, you long to be at the ball, do you not? Pray do not let anybody here be a restraint upon you.

JOHN: That should give you a notion of the general rate of drinking there.

CATHERINE: Yes, that you all drink a great deal more wine than I thought you did.

(JOHN laughs, snorting.)

ISABELLA: I daresay we could do very well without you. You men think yourselves of such consequence.

JAMES: I swear I would not part my present company for all the world.

CATHERINE: Well, I am sure James does not drink so much.

(JOHN snorts louder.)

ISABELLA: Good heavens! What a hand you have got. Kings, I vow.

JAMES: It seems I've won again.

(CATHERINE crosses down to the audience. The lights narrow on her.)

CATHERINE: Insufferable! How I should like to scream. Oh, for the comforting refuge of *Udolpho*.

(Bach organ music blasts. The stage is cleared. Enter SIGNOR MONTONI. He has an Italian accent. Projection: The Mysteries of Udolpho.)

MONTONI: Niece…

CATHERINE: *(As EMILY.)* Signor Montoni…

MONTONI: Any objection founded on sentiment, as they call it, ought to yield to circumstances of solid advantage.

(CATHERINE [as EMILY] is retreating. MADAME MONTONI [MADAME CHERON] enters from the other direction.)

CATHERINE: *(As EMILY.)* I have assured Count Morano and you also, sir, that I can never accept the honor he offers me.

MADAME MONTONI: This is mere affectation. His flattery delights you and makes you vain. You will not meet with many such suitors in Venice. What kind of match do you expect since a count cannot content your ambition?!?

CATHERINE: *(As EMILY.)* My only wish is to remain in my present station.

MADAME MONTONI: I see you are still thinking of the Chevalier Valancourt. Pray get rid of these fantastic notions about love and be a reasonable creature.

MONTONI: When you are older you will look back with gratitude to the friends who assisted in rescuing you from your romantic illusions.

(Enter COUNT MORANO, played by the same actor who plays JOHN THORPE. He also has an Italian accent.)

COUNT MORANO: Emily, I have been impatient to express my gratitude. I must also thank Signor Montoni who has allowed this opportunity of doing so.

(CATHERINE [as EMILY] is astonished by his words.)

COUNT MORANO: You cannot doubt the sincerity of my passion. Charming Emily, surely it is unnecessary for you to continue this disguise of your sentiments.

CATHERINE: *(As EMILY.)* I have never disguised them, sir.

MONTONI: Here is the offer of an alliance which would do honor to any family; yours, you recollect, is not noble.

MADAME MONTONI: You, who have no fortune, should show a proper gratitude and humility towards Count Morano.

COUNT MORANO: How is this, signor?

MONTONI: Suspend your judgment, Count, the wiles of a female heart are unsearchable. *(To CATHERINE [as EMILY].)* I have not the patience you expect from a lover. I warn you of the effect of my displeasure.

COUNT MORANO: Sir, suffer me to plead my own cause.

CATHERINE: *(As EMILY.)* Conversation on the subject is worse than useless.

COUNT MORANO: *(Kissing her hand.)* It is impossible, ma'amselle, for me to resign the object of a passion that is the delight and torment of my life!

CATHERINE: *(As EMILY.)* You cannot obtain the esteem you solicit by this persecution I have no means of escaping!

COUNT MORANO: By heavens, this is too much! Signor Montoni, you have misled me!

MONTONI: Me, sir!?! Ma'amselle, a man of honor is not to be trifled with though you may treat a *boy* like a puppet.

COUNT MORANO: Sir, you shall find a stronger enemy than a woman to contend with. I will protect Mademoiselle St. Aubert from your threatened resentment. I shall await you in your drawing room for further private conversation in this affair. Good night, mademoiselle.

(He kisses her hand and glares at MONTONI as he exits.)

MONTONI: This marriage to Count Morano shall be celebrated without delay and if necessary without your consent.

CATHERINE: *(As EMILY.)* By what right do you exert this unlimited authority over me!?!

MONTONI: By the right of my will! You are a stranger in a foreign country. It is in your interest to make me your friend. If you compel me to become your enemy— your punishment shall far exceed your expectations!

(MONTONI storms out. Thunder.)

MADAME MONTONI: I think my husband right in enforcing, by any means, your consent. Foolish, headstrong girl!

(MADAME MONTONI exits. Thunder. CATHERINE [as EMILY] sits sobbing. She is in her room. Projection: Pulteney Street, Bath.)

CATHERINE: *(As EMILY.)* Oh Valancourt, Valancourt, do not forsake me!

AMY: *(Entering.)* Pardon, miss. Will it be the red or the blue gown?

CATHERINE: *(Caught.)* Amy?

AMY: Red or blue?

CATHERINE: Red. *(Writing in journal.)* Our morning ride was of the uneventful kind despite Mr. Thorpe's warnings as to the strength and spirited playfulness of his horse— *(Addresses the audience.)* and considering its inevitable pace of ten miles an hour. Mr. Thorpe told me of horses which he had bought for a trifle and sold for incredible sums, of racing matches in which his judgment had infallibly foretold the winner, and it was finally settled between us with very little difficulty that his equipage was altogether the most complete of its kind in England, his carriage the neatest, his horse the best goer, and himself the very best coachman. I only managed to escape his clutches by promising to dance the first two dances with him at tonight's ball in the Octagon Room. A trifling price to pay in my estimation for a few hours' liberty.

(AMY enters to assist CATHERINE in dressing for the ball.)

CATHERINE: Amy…

AMY: Yes, miss?

CATHERINE: Have you ever had occasion to read *The Mysteries of Udolpho*?

AMY: Oh, Lord, yes, miss. I found it very amusing to be sure.

CATHERINE: Amusing?

AMY: Yes, miss, all that sobbing and fainting going on. I vow, poor Emily "drops senseless" twice in every chapter. If you ask me, I think all her troubles stem from being laced up too tight. Constricts the breath, you understand.

(AMY tugs at CATHERINE's gown. ISABELLA enters and crosses to them.)

ISABELLA: Catherine, you mischievous creature, do you want to attract everybody? Your brother and I were agreeing this morning that, though it is vastly well to be here for a few weeks, we could not live here for millions. We soon found out that our tastes were exactly the same. I would not have had you by for the world; I am sure you would have made some droll remark or other about it.

(AMY is putting red roses in CATHERINE's hair.)

CATHERINE: Indeed, I should not.

ISABELLA: You would have told us that we seemed born for each other. My cheeks would have turned as red as your roses.

CATHERINE: Isabella, it would never have entered my head.

ISABELLA: How beautiful you look. Upon my word, you shall captivate the heart of every man in the room.

(CATHERINE crosses down to the audience as the lights narrow on her. The OTHERS exit.)

CATHERINE: *(Putting on her gloves.)* Poor Isabella. She does not understand that dress is a frivolous distinction. My great-aunt read me a lecture on this subject only last Christmas. It would be mortifying to the feelings of many ladies were they made to understand how little the heart of a man is affected by what is costly and new in one's attire. Women must be fine for their own satisfaction.

(Music plays, and the Octagon Rooms spring to life. Projection: Assembly Rooms, Bath.)

CATHERINE: However, desperate situations call for desperate measures. And a heroine must make use of any advantages she may possess in order to attract *multiple* dancing partners during the course of the evening.

(MRS. THORPE, MRS. ALLEN, JAMES, and ISABELLA cross to CATHERINE.)

MRS. THORPE: Upon my word, I cannot imagine what could be keeping him.

JAMES: Isabella, the dancing is about to begin, we shall miss the first dance entirely.

ISABELLA: John has gone into the card room to speak to a friend. You must be patient. I would not stand up without your dear sister for all the world.

CATHERINE: I'm very grateful to you, dear Isabella.

(JAMES whispers in ISABELLA's ear.)

MRS. THORPE: Now don't you fret over it, my dear, my John is such a remarkable dancer and I'm sure you'll agree well worth a little wait.

MRS. ALLEN: Mrs. Thorpe, do you see the lace on that woman's gown? It is exquisite! We must discover where she found it.

(MRS. ALLEN and MRS. THORPE cross to speak to the WOMAN.)

ISABELLA: My dear creature, I am afraid I must leave you. Your brother is so amazingly impatient to begin, and I daresay John will be back in a moment and you may easily find me out.

(JAMES and ISABELLA join the DANCERS.)

CATHERINE: *(To the audience.)* How perplexing. In spite of my revulsion for Mr. Thorpe, I cannot help feeling exceedingly vexed by his non-appearance. For truly, I would much rather be dancing than sitting here in solitude. The real dignity of my situation can hardly be known.

(MR. ALLEN passes by her, patting her hand reassuringly. He crosses to join MRS. ALLEN and MRS. THORPE.)

CATHERINE: I seem to be sharing with all the other young ladies still sitting down the discredit of wanting a partner. Disgraced in the eyes of the world.

(JAMES and ISABELLA dance by, laughing and waving.)

CATHERINE: This is truly one of those circumstances which belong to a heroine's life, and I am fully aware that all my strength and fortitude are required. I must bear up. I shall endure it.

(HENRY TILNEY appears before her seemingly out of nowhere. He bows.)

HENRY: Miss Morland—I hope you will consent to honor me with the next dance.

CATHERINE: *(Quite shocked.)* Mr. Tilney!…

HENRY: Miss Morland, are you quite well? You are not displeased to see me, I hope.

CATHERINE: Oh, not at all, Mr. Tilney, You gave me rather a start is all.

(MRS. ALLEN crosses over.)

MRS. ALLEN: Mr. Tilney, how very happy I am to see you again, sir.

HENRY: Ah, good evening to you, Mrs. Allen.

MRS. ALLEN: I was afraid you had entirely quitted Bath, Mr. Tilney.

HENRY: I thank you for your fears, madam. Yes, I had quitted it for a week on the very morning after having had the pleasure of seeing you both. I hope, Mrs. Allen, that Mr. Allen is well and liking this place for being of service to him.

MRS. ALLEN: Thank you, sir, I have no doubt that he will. A neighbor of ours, a Dr. Skinner, was here for his health last winter and came away quite stout.

HENRY: That circumstance must give great encouragement.

MRS. ALLEN: Oh, yes, and Dr. Skinner and his family were here for three months; so I tell Mr. Allen he must not be in a hurry to get away.

(A pretty and elegant YOUNG WOMAN crosses to HENRY.)

HENRY: Ah, Eleanor, I am glad you've come. Here are some friends I would like you to meet. This is Mrs. Allen.

ELEANOR: How do you do, Mrs. Allen.

HENRY: And this is her young charge, Miss Catherine Morland.

ELEANOR: This is the famous Miss Morland. I have heard a great deal about you.

HENRY: This is my sister, Miss Eleanor Tilney.

CATHERINE: *(Relieved.)* Miss Tilney, I am very pleased to make your acquaintance. We are all delighted to see your brother again. It is quite a great surprise. I felt so sure of his…being gone away.

ELEANOR: When Henry had the pleasure of seeing you last he was only in Bath but for couple of days. He came to engage lodgings for our family.

MRS. ALLEN: Why that never occurred to me… did it you, Catherine? Of course not seeing him anywhere, we thought he must be gone.

HENRY: But I am here at last, and as the musicians are about to strike up and I am most desirous for a dance, I hope Miss Morland would oblige me.

CATHERINE: Oh, oh dear, I am afraid I am already engaged for this dance. To a Mr. Thorpe, a friend of my brother's. I have been expecting him all this while.

HENRY: I am disappointed to hear it. Perhaps we'll be fortunate and he won't turn up.

CATHERINE: That would be a great fortune, indeed, Mr. Tilney.

(JOHN THORPE bolts into the room crossing to CATHERINE and takes her by the arm, leading her away from the TILNEYS to the DANCERS, who have already begun the second dance.)

JOHN: Well, here I am at last, eh, Miss Morland. Come on then, let's to it.

CATHERINE: *(Calling back to them.)* Oh, oh, pardon me, Mr. Tilney, Miss Tilney…please, you must excuse me!

(They take their places with the other DANCERS.)

JOHN: You didn't mind waiting for me, I take it. Sam Fletcher talks a damned blue streak, I tell you, a person can't get in a word edgewise.

CATHERINE: You missed the first dance entirely.

JOHN: Did I? Well then it's a damn good thing I came along, for I daresay I rescued you from some dreary conversation or other, eh?

(HENRY and ELEANOR observe them.)

CATHERINE: *(To the audience.)* My situation grows worse and worse. Here is Mr. Tilney at long last, and now he will surely ask someone else to dance.

HENRY: Didn't I tell you?

ELEANOR: She's very pretty indeed.

HENRY: Enchanting.

ELEANOR: She seems a very charming girl, Henry, and certainly not indifferent to you.

HENRY: Do you think so?

ELEANOR: Quite certain. We women have an instinct about these things.

(The dance continues. CATHERINE takes an opportunity to speak to the audience during moments when she finds herself downstage.)

CATHERINE: And what am I to do with Mr. Thorpe, who vexes me at every turn?

(The dance continues, and the TILNEYS cross out. CATHERINE stops again downstage.)

CATHERINE: He's gone. I feared it. How am I ever to find them?

(JOHN takes her again by the hand. The DANCERS all have one final graceful turn, and the music ends.)

JOHN: Capital tune, eh? What do you say to having another go at it?

(ISABELLA crosses in, just in time.)

ISABELLA: At last I have got you, my dearest creature, I have been quite wretched without you.

CATHERINE: *(Confidentially.)* Oh, Isabella, I have been longing to speak with you. Look at that young lady with the white beads round her head. She is Mr. Tilney's sister.

ISABELLA: What a delightful girl. I never saw anyone half so beautiful.

(JOHN walks off after a PRETTY YOUNG LADY.)

ISABELLA: But where is her all-conquering brother? Point him out to me this instant. I die to see him. Mr. Morland, you are not to listen.

JAMES: But what is all this whispering about?

ISABELLA: You men have such restless curiosity. Be satisfied you are not to know anything of the matter.

JAMES: And is that likely to satisfy me, do you think?

ISABELLA: I would advise you not to listen…

(The music strikes up again.)

JAMES: Come, Isabella, dance with me again.

ISABELLA: Catherine, your brother wants me to dance with him again. It would make us the talk of the place if we were not to change partners.

JAMES: Upon my honor, in these public assemblies, it is as often done as not.

ISABELLA: My sweet Catherine, tell your brother it would quite shock you to see me do such a thing.

CATHERINE: No, not at all; but if you think it wrong, you had much better change.

ISABELLA: There, you hear what your sister says, and yet you will not mind her. Well, remember that it is not my fault if we set all the old ladies of Bath in a bustle.

(JAMES and ISABELLA join the DANCERS. CATHERINE breathes a sigh of relief and crosses back to MRS. ALLEN and MRS. THORPE.)

MRS. THORPE: Well, my dear, I hope you found John an agreeable partner.

CATHERINE: Very agreeable, madam.

MRS. THORPE: John has charming spirits, has he not?

MRS. ALLEN: Did you find Mr. Tilney?

CATHERINE: No have you seen him?

MRS. ALLEN: He was with us just now and said he was tired of lounging about and that he was resolved to go and dance.

CATHERINE: Where can he be? I cannot see him anywhere.

MRS. ALLEN: I wish he had found you. He is a very agreeable young man.

MRS. THORPE: Oh, indeed he is, Mrs. Allen; I must say, though I am his mother, that there is not a more agreeable young man in the world.

MRS. ALLEN: *(To CATHERINE.)* I daresay, she thought I was speaking of *her* son.

(They cover a laugh. CATHERINE crosses to the punch table craning her neck to catch a glimpse of HENRY all the while. HENRY appears and comes up behind CATHERINE. She jumps, startled.)

HENRY: You are looking for…Mr. Thorpe, perhaps?

CATHERINE: Mr. Tilney you do have a way of sneaking up on a person.

HENRY: Might I find you at leisure to dance with me at long last?

CATHERINE: You shall have my undivided attention.

HENRY: Allow me.

CATHERINE: Thank you.

(He takes the punch glasses to the table occupied by MRS. ALLEN and MRS. THORPE. JOHN THORPE crosses to CATHERINE and leads her by the arm.)

JOHN: Heydey, Miss Morland, what is the meaning of this? I thought you and I were to dance together again.

CATHERINE: You engaged me for the first two dances, and they are long past.

JOHN: Here I have been telling all my acquaintance I was going to dance with the prettiest girl in the room. What chap have you there?

CATHERINE: That is Mr. Henry Tilney.

(HENRY, having spotted them, watches from a distance. He alternately chats with MRS. ALLEN.)

JOHN: Henry Tilney…I believe I have met with his father in the billiard room. He seems a good figure of a man; well put together. Does he want a horse? My friend Sam Fletcher has got one to sell that would suit anybody—only forty guineas. I had fifty minds to buy it myself. It has always been one of my maxims to buy a good horse when I meet with one.

(The dance ends. TWO PRETTY YOUNG LADIES walk past.)

JOHN: I hope you will pardon me, Miss Morland, we shall have to put off our dance a while longer, I have just now recalled something of great import I neglected to ask Fletcher.

CATHERINE: I would not dream of detaining you, Mr. Thorpe.

(He bows and goes off in the direction of the YOUNG LADIES. HENRY crosses back to CATHERINE.)

HENRY: That gentleman would have put me out of patience, had he stayed with you half a minute longer.

(They take their places with the other DANCERS and begin a formal dance—Mr. Beveridge's Maggot, perhaps.)

HENRY: I consider a country dance as an emblem of marriage.

CATHERINE: *(Taken aback.)* But they are such very different things!

HENRY: That you think they cannot be compared together?

CATHERINE: People that marry can never part, but must go and…keep house together. People that dance only stand opposite each other in a long room for a quarter of an hour.

(The lights begin to slowly focus on the two of them. The rest of the room fades into darkness.)

HENRY: But you will allow, it is an engagement between man and woman, formed for the advantage of each; and that once entered into, they belong exclusively to each other till the moment of its dissolution.

CATHERINE: But still they are so very different. I cannot look upon them in the same light.

HENRY: Have I reason to fear that if Mr. Thorpe were to return, there would be nothing to restrain you from conversing with him as long as you chose?

CATHERINE: Mr. Thorpe is a particular friend of my brother's…

HENRY: Alas, alas.

CATHERINE: Mr. Tilney, I do not *wish* to speak with anybody else!

HENRY: *Now* you have given me a security worth having, and I shall proceed with courage. Do you find Bath as agreeable as before?

CATHERINE: Yes, more so indeed.

HENRY: More so! Take care or you will forget to be tired of it at the proper time. You ought to be tired of it at the end of six weeks.

CATHERINE: I do not think I shall be tired of it at the end of six months.

HENRY: Bath, compared with London, has little variety.

CATHERINE: Those who go to London may think nothing of Bath, but here I can see a variety of people in every street; at home I can only go and call on Mrs. Allen.

HENRY: What a picture of intellectual poverty! However, when you sink into the abyss again you will be able to talk of Bath and all you did here.

CATHERINE: Yes, I shall never be in want of something to talk of again to Mrs. Allen, or anybody else. Oh, who could ever tire of Bath!

HENRY: Indeed, Miss Morland, who could ever tire of Bath?

(The dance has ended, and the lights have come back up, and the room has returned to a buzz of activity. ELEANOR TILNEY crosses to them.)

ELEANOR: Marvelous! How you both must be worn out. Henry, the General wishes to speak to you.

HENRY: Please excuse me, Miss Morland, I shall be back in a moment.

(HENRY crosses to a SEVERE-LOOKING GENTLEMAN [GENERAL TILNEY, played by the same actor as MONTONI].)

CATHERINE: Miss Tilney, we were just commenting on what a wonderful place Bath is.

ELEANOR: I find it magnificent. There is so much to do and see, and I love to walk in the beautiful country lanes.

CATHERINE: That sounds glorious! I have not yet had occasion for a country walk.

ELEANOR: Well, then tomorrow we shall make an occasion. You shall join my brother and me in an excursion.

CATHERINE: I should like that beyond anything in the world.

(HENRY crosses back to them.)

ELEANOR: Henry, I have just asked Miss Morland to join us tomorrow for a country walk.

HENRY: I shall be most disappointed if she has not agreed to it.

CATHERINE: Yes, so long as it doesn't rain.

HENRY: Then we shall pray for sunshine.

ELEANOR: We shall meet you at your hotel in Pulteney Street at twelve provided that it is not raining.

HENRY: *(Indicating the MAN he spoke with.)* By the way, that gentleman now knows your name and you have a right to know his. That is General Tilney, our father.

CATHERINE: Oh… *(Takes a few steps to the audience.)* What a penetrating gaze… and what an astonishingly handsome family! This evening is like a dream. Mr. Tilney danced with no other young lady but me. And I long to become better acquainted with his dear sister Eleanor. She has not the stylishness of Miss Thorpe, but I believe she has more real elegance.

MRS. ALLEN: Catherine, Catherine, I should like to speak with you, dear girl.

(CATHERINE crosses to MRS. ALLEN, and GENERAL TILNEY runs into JOHN THORPE. The OTHERS chat.)

GENERAL TILNEY: Mr. Thorpe, is it not?

JOHN: Yes, General, I trust you have been having an agreeable night of it?

GENERAL TILNEY: Tolerable. Thorpe, I happened to notice you dancing with that charming young lady earlier this evening. Are you at all acquainted with her family?

JOHN: Miss Morland? Yes, I should say I am intimately acquainted with the Morlands. Her brother is one of my greatest friends at Oxford and soon, I might add, to be engaged to my sister. I daresay the family is vastly rich. I imagine Miss Morland has some ten or fifteen thousand from her father upon her marrying.

GENERAL TILNEY: Indeed…

JOHN: (Taking snuff.) And do you see that couple she is speaking with? Those are the Allens of Fullerton. They have a great fortune to which Miss Morland is sole heiress, as they have no children of their own.

GENERAL TILNEY: She stays with them in Bath?

JOHN: Lord yes, and they treat her as if she were their own daughter.

GENERAL TILNEY: She is truly a fortunate young lady.

JOHN: She is the most beautiful and charming girl in Bath. We are, indeed, on very intimate terms, sir, very intimate.

GENERAL TILNEY: (Comprehending.) You have an understanding, do you?

JOHN: Well, not as yet. But I daresay she thinks me as fine a fellow as ever breathed, and before I leave Bath, I shall have secured her affections to my general enrichment.

GENERAL TILNEY: That would be a fortunate circumstance for you, Mr. Thorpe, Good evening, sir.

JOHN: Good evening, General. (Crosses to ISABELLA and JAMES.)

GENERAL TILNEY: Good evening, indeed…

CATHERINE: (Crosses back to HENRY and ELEANOR.) Mrs. Allen informs me that we must be leaving. I had such an agreeable time tonight, and I do wish you both a very pleasant evening.

HENRY: Until tomorrow then, good evening, Miss Morland.

(HENRY kisses her hand. The TILNEYS cross to THEIR FATHER. CATHERINE and HENRY exchange a final glance. CATHERINE crosses to the audience as the lights dim around her.)

CATHERINE: I am in love with Henry Tilney! What would Mama say if she heard me now? I venture I have never been so happy in all my life. What new and joyful pleasures shall the morning reap?…

(ANNETTE rushes in. She is played by the same actress who plays AMY and retains her country accent. She assists CATHERINE [as EMILY] to change her attire. Projection: The Mysteries of Udolpho.)

ANNETTE: Ma'amselle, ma'amselle!

CATHERINE: (As EMILY.) Annette! What brings you hither so early?

ANNETTE: Dear ma'amselle. Here is a fine bustle below stairs. All the servants are running to and fro and none fast enough and nobody knows for what!

CATHERINE: (As EMILY.) Who is below besides them?

ANNETTE: Signor Montoni as I have never seen him before, and he has sent me to tell you, ma'amselle, to get ready immediately.

CATHERINE: (As EMILY; fainting.) Good God support me!

ANNETTE: Holy Virgin! Are you ill, ma'amselle? Let me get some water.

CATHERINE: (As EMILY.) Do not leave me. Count Morano is below then?

ANNETTE: No, ma'amselle.

CATHERINE: (As EMILY; recovering.) You are sure of it?

ANNETTE: Yes! Lord bless me. I thought you was dyin' just now.

CATHERINE: (As EMILY.) You are quite sure the count is not come?

ANNETTE: Only his excellenza is below. The gondolas will be at the steps of the canal in a few minutes. I must hurry back to my lady, who is at her wits' end.

CATHERINE: (As EMILY.) Explain the meaning of all this!?

ANNETTE: I only know that Signor Montoni has had us all called out of our beds and tells us we are to leave Venice.

CATHERINE: (As EMILY.) But Annette, whither are we going?

ANNETTE: I don't know for certain, but I heard his servant, Ludovico, say something of the Signor's castle.

CATHERINE: (As EMILY.) Udolpho!!

ANNETTE: The very place.

CATHERINE: (As EMILY.) Oh, Annette, not Udolpho.

ANNETTE: Do not take it so much to heart, ma'amselle. Think what little time you have to get ready. Holy Saint Mark, I hear the oars on the canal!! (Runs out.)

CATHERINE: (As EMILY.) The Castle Udolpho! Then I have little to hope!

(The lights change. CATHERINE and the ALLENS are in their rooms at Pulteney Street. MR. ALLEN is reading a newspaper. MRS. ALLEN is doing embroidery. CATHERINE holds her book in her hand and has been reading. Projection: Pulteney Street, Bath.)

MRS. ALLEN: Good heavens, what a dreary morning.

CATHERINE: Mr. Allen, I have often heard that a cloudy morning such as this so early in the year often improves into a sunny afternoon.

MR. ALLEN: I do not wish to thoroughly blight your hopes, my dear, but I do not recall ever hearing such a thing.

CATHERINE: Do you think it will rain, Mrs. Allen?

MRS. ALLEN: Dearest girl, I have no doubt in the world of today being the finest day of the year, if only the clouds would go off and the sun come out.

CATHERINE: Oh, dear, I do believe it *is* raining.

MRS. ALLEN: I thought it might.

CATHERINE: Perhaps it may yet come to nothing; it may clear up before twelve.

MRS. ALLEN: Perhaps it may, but then, my dear, it will be so dirty.

CATHERINE: I never mind dirt.

MRS. ALLEN: There are umbrellas up already. They are such disagreeable things to carry. I would much rather take a chair at any time.

MR. ALLEN: Well, my dear, I believe I shall brave the elements and get some air.

CATHERINE: It was such a nice-looking morning! I felt so convinced it would be dry.

MRS. ALLEN: Anybody would have thought so, indeed. There will be very few people in the Pump Room. I hope, Mr. Allen, you will put on your greatcoat.

MR. ALLEN: My dear, I had rather do anything in the world than walk out in a greatcoat.

(AMY brings him his hat and an umbrella.)

MRS. ALLEN: I wonder you should dislike it, dear, it must be so comfortable.

MR. ALLEN: Good morning then.

MRS. ALLEN: Have a pleasant stroll, my dear.

(MR. ALLEN exits. MRS. ALLEN continues her embroidering. The clock strikes twelve. CATHERINE gazes out of a window, then picks up her book. On another part of the stage, COUNT MORANO is sneaking into the room with his SERVANT at a distance. MRS. ALLEN remains on stage, embroidering. MORANO comes up behind CATHERINE. His hand covers her mouth. She tries to scream. Projection: The Mysteries of Udolpho.)

COUNT MORANO: Why all this terror? Hear me, Emily, I come not to alarm you… No, by heaven, I love you too well—too well for my own peace.

CATHERINE: (As EMILY.) Then leave me. Leave me instantly.

COUNT MORANO: You shall be mine, Emily, in spite of Montoni and all his villainy!

CATHERINE: (As EMILY.) In spite of Montoni?

COUNT MORANO: He is evil, Emily, a villain who would have sold you to my love. He seeks only to restore his broken fortune.

CATHERINE: (As EMILY.) And is he less a villain who would have bought me?

COUNT MORANO: He has used me infamously, and my vengeance shall pursue him.

CATHERINE: (As EMILY.) I beseech you, sir. Leave me—leave me to my fate.

COUNT MORANO: I shall perish first! Is marriage with a man who adores you so terrible that you would prefer the misery which Montoni will condemn you to in this prison?

CATHERINE: (As EMILY.) Count Morano, my affections can never be yours.

COUNT MORANO: Emily, how much more willingly I would persuade rather than compel you to become my wife.

(COUNT MORANO lifts her.)

COUNT MORANO: But by heaven, I will not leave you to be sold by Montoni to the next bidder. Cesario! Cesario, a light!

(CATHERINE [as EMILY] shrieks and struggles. MONTONI, armed, and HIS SERVANT burst in.)

MONTONI: (Menacingly.) Draw, Morano.

(COUNT MORANO puts EMILY down and draws his sword.)

COUNT MORANO: This in thine heart, villain!

(He thrusts at MONTONI, who parries the blow; another thrust and parry.)

CATHERINE: (As EMILY.) Signor Montoni, Count Morano! I beg you hold!

(The SERVANTS part them.)

MONTONI: Was it for this, Count Morano, that I received you under my roof and permitted you, though declared my enemy, to remain the night? You repay my hospitality with the treachery of a fiend and rob me of my niece?

COUNT MORANO: Montoni, if there is treachery in this affair look to yourself as the author of it. Come, coward, receive your justice at my hands.

MONTONI: Coward!?!

(He breaks away from the SERVANTS. ANNETTE enters. The fight continues around the embroidering MRS. ALLEN. She does not acknowledge the action in CATHERINE's imagination.)

MONTONI: He who dares interfere shall die by my sword!

ANNETTE: Holy saints of God!

(They fight. The COUNT wounds MONTONI in the arm.)

COUNT MORANO: Danger, Montoni, shall teach you mortality!

(MONTONI is incensed. Their combat becomes more fierce.)

MONTONI: You shall feel the full sting of my wrath, villain!!

(MONTONI wounds and disarms the COUNT. EMILY and ANNETTE scream. The COUNT crumples to the floor.)

MONTONI: Beg for your life, boy!

COUNT MORANO: (Very weak.) Never, never…

(The COUNT faints. His SERVANT rushes to him. MONTONI prepares a final blow, and CATHERINE [as EMILY] rushes in to prevent him.)

CATHERINE: (As EMILY.) Signor Montoni, I beg you, in the name of humanity, have mercy!

MONTONI: Take him away—take him from Udolpho and from my sight!

(He crosses away. His SERVANT binds his arm. The COUNT recovers his senses.)

COUNT MORANO: I have deserved this…but not from Montoni. I deserve punishment from you, Emily, yet I receive only pity.

CATHERINE: (As EMILY.) Peace, drink this, sir.

(CATHERINE [as EMILY] gives him water, which he sips.)

COUNT MORANO: (To his SERVANT.) Take me to the nearest cottage. I will not pass another night in this castle he dares to call his. I shall not be the cause of another murder.

CATHERINE: (As EMILY.) Murder?

(The SERVANTS lift him.)

COUNT MORANO: Emily, may you never know the torture of a passion like mine.

MONTONI: Have I not ordered this villain removed from the premises!!!

CATHERINE: (As EMILY.) I entreat you, Count, to consult your own safety.

COUNT MORANO: Since you regard it. I will be gone. Farewell, charming Emily…

(He takes her hand and kisses it.)

CATHERINE: (As EMILY.) Farewell, Count Morano.

(The SERVANTS bear him away. MONTONI crosses to CATHERINE [as EMILY].)

MONTONI: Count Morano, whose suit you obstinately rejected, it seems you favor since you find I have dismissed him.

CATHERINE: (As EMILY.) You do not mean to imply that the count visited my chamber upon any approbation of mine!

MONTONI: To that I reply nothing.

CATHERINE: (As EMILY.) How could I, how could you, sir, witness his deplorable condition and not wish to relieve it!?!

MONTONI: You add insult to caprice. I charge you to look to your own conduct, niece. (Winces and holds his arm in pain. Turns to leave.)

CATHERINE: (As EMILY.) I would speak with you, Signor Montoni.

MONTONI: I have no time for trifling.

CATHERINE: (As EMILY.) Where is my aunt!? What has become of her?

MONTONI: Signora Montoni has been taken care of.

CATHERINE: (As EMILY.) Why am I forbidden to go to her?

(MONTONI grabs her by the arms.)

MONTONI: Do not try my patience, ma'amselle.

CATHERINE: (As EMILY.) While my aunt lived, my residence here was not improper. Now she is no more, I may surely be permitted to depart.

MONTONI: (Shaking her.) Who told you that Signora Montoni was dead? —Who told you!

CATHERINE: (As EMILY; in tears.) Alas! I know it only too well—Spare me on this terrible subject.

MONTONI: (Smiling.) Signora Montoni lies in the east turret. A fate you shall share if you do not submit to my will and obey my commands. You may search for her…if you dare…duplicitous little fool…

(He releases her with a push and exits laughing.)

CATHERINE: (As EMILY.) Annette, Annette, I can no longer endure these agonizing torments…

(CATHERINE [as EMILY] faints, and ANNETTE rushes to her side.)

ANNETTE: Oh ma'amselle, ma'amselle. May the saints have mercy on our souls. I fear we shall not escape Udolpho with our lives.

(ANNETTE bends over CATHERINE's [as EMILY] unconscious form sobbing, her head buried. MRS. ALLEN, who has been at her embroidery all this while, speaks to CATHERINE.)

MRS. ALLEN: Catherine, dear, it has been such a dreadfully damp morning, shall I ring Amy to bring us tea?

(CATHERINE springs up on her elbows, with ANNETTE still sobbing.)

CATHERINE: Oh yes, Mrs. Allen, I long for a cup of tea. It has been a very trying morning, indeed.

(ANNETTE sobs. Lights, music—interval.)

ACT II

Music. The ALLENS' rooms in Pulteney Street a short time later. AMY is serving CATHERINE and MRS. ALLEN tea. Projection: Pulteney Street, Bath.

CATHERINE: Thank you, Amy.

(The clock strikes one.)

CATHERINE: (To the audience.) Oh, one o'clock and the Tilneys have not yet come! It seems to be clearing. I shall not give them up. Oh! that we had such weather as they had at the Castle Udolpho, or at least in the south of France the night that Emily's poor father died. (Sigh.) Such beautiful weather.

(JOHN, ISABELLA, and JAMES burst into the room.)

JOHN: Miss Morland, make haste! Make haste! We are going to Bristol. How do 'ye do, Mrs. Allen.

MRS. ALLEN: *(Nods.)* Mr. Thorpe.

CATHERINE: But I expect some friends at any moment.

JOHN: Pish tush, Miss Morland.

ISABELLA: Thank your brother and me for the scheme.

JOHN: We shall drive directly to Clifton and dine there. And on to Kingsweston!

JAMES: I doubt our being able to do so much.

JOHN: We shall be able to do ten times more! On to Kingsweston and Blaize Castle too!

CATHERINE: *(Intrigued.)* Blaize Castle!? What is that?

JOHN: The finest place in England—worth going fifty miles at any time to see.

CATHERINE: Is it really a castle?

JOHN: The oldest in the kingdom.

CATHERINE: Then I should like to see it... But I cannot go.

ISABELLA: My beloved creature, what do you mean?

CATHERINE: I expect Miss Tilney and her brother to call on me to take a country walk. They promised to come at twelve o'clock, only it was raining. But now as it is so fine I daresay they will be here soon.

JOHN: Not they, indeed, for as we turned into Broad Street, I saw them. You are talking of the fellow you danced with last night, are you not?

CATHERINE: Yes.

JOHN: Well, I saw him turn up the Lansdown Road, driving a smart-looking girl and I heard him mention they were going as far as Wickes Rocks.

CATHERINE: *(Disappointed.)* I suppose they thought it would be too dirty for a walk.

JOHN: And well they might, for I never saw so much dirt in my life.

ISABELLA: Catherine, you cannot refuse now.

CATHERINE: I would like to see the castle. May we go all over it? Up every staircase and into every suite of rooms?

ISABELLA: Yes, yes!

JOHN: Every hole and corner!

CATHERINE: Shall I go, Mrs. Allen?

MRS. ALLEN: Just as you please, my dear.

ISABELLA: Oh, Mrs. Allen, you must persuade her to go.

JAMES: Do, Mrs. Allen.

MRS. ALLEN: *(Exasperated.)* Good heavens! Go, my dear Catherine, go by all means!

(AMY hands CATHERINE her coat and bonnet.)

CATHERINE: *(To the audience.)* And in less than two minutes, we were off!

(JAMES, JOHN, and ISABELLA drag CATHERINE off the stage.)

AMY: Blaize Castle?

MRS. ALLEN: Good heavens! These young people and their wild schemes.

(MRS. ALLEN and AMY exchange a look. The lights change. CATHERINE reenters from another part of the stage looking somewhat disheveled.)

CATHERINE: I am so exceedingly vexed! On our way out of town, I saw them! Henry and Eleanor on their way to call for me! I pleaded with Mr. Thorpe to stop, but he only laughed and lashed his horse into a brisker trot. I had no power to get away. My reproaches, however, were not spared. Mr. Thorpe stoutly declared he had never seen two men so much alike in his life. How shall they ever forgive me? I shall never take John Thorpe at his word again. Worst of all—we never came anywhere near Blaize Castle!

(Enter ANNETTE and LUDOVICO, who is played by the same actor as JAMES with an Italian accent. Projection: The Mysteries of Udolpho.)

ANNETTE: Ma'amselle, ma'amselle—I have been looking all over the castle for you. If you will follow us, we will show you a painting.

CATHERINE: *(As EMILY.)* A painting?

ANNETTE: Yes, ma'amselle, of the lady of this place. I thought you would be curious to see it.

CATHERINE: *(As EMILY.)* I do not wish to see this painting.

LUDOVICO: Not see the lady of the castle who disappeared so mysteriously?

ANNETTE: That strange story is all that makes me care about this old castle. It makes me thrill all over when I think about it! Signora Laurentini. Was she not beautiful? In my mind, the Signor ought to place the portrait of the lady who gave him all these riches in the handsomest room in the castle.

CATHERINE: (As EMILY.) Ludovico, how many years have passed since this lady disappeared?

LUDOVICO: Twenty years, ma'amselle, or thereabouts.

ANNETTE: The old servants say that she went out for her evening walk and never returned.

LUDOVICO: She was a distant cousin to Signor Montoni.

ANNETTE: They say that he asked her to be his bride and she refused him. And that the law, as written, was that if she died unmarried Udolpho should come to him.

CATHERINE: (As EMILY.) And Signora Laurentini was never found?

LUDOVICO: Never.

(CATHERINE is in a spot. The OTHERS exit.)

CATHERINE: (As EMILY.) How horrifying! I must try again to discover if my aunt lives. I must search every dark corridor and dank recess. I must find Madame Montoni…alive or dead!!!

(The lights come up on a bustling theatre lobby after the performance. Projection: Theatre Lobby, Bath.)

MRS. ALLEN: Why, that was the most delightful performance we have seen to date.

MR. ALLEN: Delightful.

MRS. ALLEN: But the cut of that tall actress's pelisse was appalling, was it not, Mr. Allen?

MR. ALLEN: Yes, my dear, quite appalling.

CATHERINE: I saw the Tilneys in the box across from ours. I must find them and force them to hear my explanation.

MRS. ALLEN: Of course, Catherine dear.

(HENRY TILNEY crosses to them.)

HENRY: Good evening, Mr. and Mrs. Allen, Miss Morland. How did you enjoy the performance?

CATHERINE: (Jumping in.) Oh! Mr. Tilney, I have been quite wild to speak with you and make my apologies. It was not my fault. Did they not tell me that Mr. Tilney and his sister had ridden out to Wickes Rocks? I had a thousand times rather been with you. Had I not, Mrs. Allen?

MRS. ALLEN: My dear, you tumble my gown.

HENRY: We were very much obliged to you at any rate for wishing us a pleasant walk. You were so kind as to look back on purpose.

CATHERINE: But I did not wish you a pleasant walk. I begged Mr. Thorpe to stop. I would have jumped out and run after you.

HENRY: Miss Morland, neither Eleanor nor myself have taken offense.

CATHERINE: What a relief that is to me. I long to be better acquainted with your sister.

HENRY: I shall go find her then and we shall make plans for another walk.

(HENRY bows and goes to find HIS SISTER. JOHN THORPE takes his opportunity and crosses to her.)

JOHN: Miss Morland, did you happen to notice me speaking to General Tilney?

CATHERINE: How came you to know him so intimately?

JOHN: I have met him forever at the Bedford and I knew his face the moment I saw him in the billiard room. We had a little touch together. But what do you think we have been talking of?

CATHERINE: I cannot guess.

JOHN: Why, you! The General thinks you the finest girl in Bath.

CATHERINE: Oh, nonsense.

JOHN: And I said, "Well done, General, I am quite of your mind."

(JOHN is too close; CATHERINE steps away.)

CATHERINE: Mr. Thorpe, you speak in jest.

JOHN: Not a whit! Don't move, I've just had a flash of inspiration. I must speak with your brother directly. (Calling.) Morland, Morland old man.

(JOHN crosses to JAMES and ISABELLA. MR. and MRS. ALLEN cross to CATHERINE.)

MR. ALLEN: Mrs. Allen and I are off to get a chair home. Are you coming, dear girl?

CATHERINE: With your permission, James and Isabella have promised to walk me home.

MRS. ALLEN: Very well. Don't be too late. It is quite dark already.

CATHERINE: I shall come straight home.

MR. ALLEN: Excellent, we shall see you shortly in Pulteney Street. Come, my dear.

MRS. ALLEN: You will warn the footman not to splash my gown, won't you, dear?

MR. ALLEN: I shall guard your hems, madam, with my life.

(*They cross away, and HENRY and ELEANOR cross to her.*)

ELEANOR: Miss Morland, here you are at last. If you are at leisure tomorrow morning we should dearly love to venture out to Beechen Cliff.

CATHERINE: That would be delightful! Oh, Miss Tilney, what must you have thought of me yesterday!

ELEANOR: I was surprised to see you riding off, but I could not have taken offense at it.

HENRY: We shall call for you at eleven o'clock.

CATHERINE: And I shall be there.

ELEANOR: Come, Henry, the General is waiting.

HENRY: Good evening, Miss Morland.

CATHERINE: Good evening, Mr. Tilney, Miss Tilney. (*To the audience.*) How kind they are to me. And how delightful that instead of disliking me, General Tilney actually admires me. I never in my wildest dreams expected matters to work themselves out so smoothly!

(*ISABELLA, JAMES, and JOHN cross to CATHERINE.*)

ISABELLA: Catherine, I have the most ecstatic news. Tomorrow morning we all set off for Blaize Castle again.

JAMES: I daresay, it's a capital scheme.

CATHERINE: I've just now settled with Miss Tilney to take our promised walk tomorrow.

ISABELLA: My dear, you must retract!

CATHERINE: I am very sorry, but I cannot go.

JAMES: How can we go without you?

JOHN: It would be nothing to put off a mere walk for one day longer.

ISABELLA: I will not hear of a refusal.

CATHERINE: I would go with you Tuesday.

ISABELLA: But John has said he might be going into town on Tuesday.

CATHERINE: I cannot break my engagement to Miss Tilney again.

ISABELLA: Well, there's an end of the party. If Catherine does not go, I cannot go.

JAMES: Catherine, you must go.

CATHERINE: Why cannot Mr. Thorpe drive your mother?

JOHN: I did not come to Bath to drive my mother about and look like a fool. If you do not go, damn me if I do. (*Turns abruptly and walks away.*)

ISABELLA: We must go tomorrow. It's the only way.

CATHERINE: Do not urge me, Isabella.

ISABELLA: I am sure that my dearest sweetest Catherine could hardly refuse such a trifling request to a friend who loves her so dearly.

CATHERINE: As much as I hate to refuse you anything, I cannot do so rude a thing to Miss Tilney.

ISABELLA: Well, Catherine, it seems you have more affection for this Miss Tilney, though you have known her such a short while, than you have for me. I cannot help being jealous when I see myself slighted for strangers. I who love you so excessively. These Tilneys seem to swallow up everything else. (*She is in tears.*)

JAMES: Nay, Catherine, I shall think you quite unkind if you refuse.

CATHERINE: It is simply not possible.

JAMES: You did not use to be so hard to persuade. You were once the kindest, best-tempered of my sisters.

CATHERINE: I am only doing what I believe to be right.

ISABELLA: I suspect there is no great struggle.

(JOHN THORPE breezes in.)

JOHN: Well, I have settled the matter and now we may all go tomorrow with a safe conscience. I have been to Miss Tilney and made your excuses.

CATHERINE: You have not!

JOHN: I have upon my soul. I told her you could not have the pleasure of walking with her 'til Tuesday and Tuesday was just as convenient to her. So there is an end to all our difficulties.

ISABELLA: *(Instantly recovered.)* Now my sweet Catherine our distresses are over.

CATHERINE: This will not do. I must run after Miss Tilney and set her right.

(ISABELLA and JOHN grab her arms.)

JOHN: *(Overlapping.)* But everything is settled.

ISABELLA: *(Overlapping.)* How can you make objections now?

JAMES: *(Overlapping.)* Catherine, you're being unreasonable.

CATHERINE: Mr. Thorpe had no business to invent such a message. Let me go, Mr. Thorpe.

JOHN: It would be in vain to go after them. They're likely home by this time.

CATHERINE: Wherever they are, I will speak to them. If I could not be *persuaded* into doing what I thought wrong, I will never be *tricked* into it!!

(CATHERINE breaks away and runs off. JOHN attempts to go after her. JAMES restrains him.)

JAMES: Let her go if she will go.

JOHN: Damned, obstinate little…

JAMES: *(Now annoyed with JOHN.)* Good God, man… let her go!

ISABELLA: Well, John, it looks as though you'll be driving mother to Clifton in the morning.

They exit. The lights change. CATHERINE reenters on another part of the stage.)

CATHERINE: What a disaster! How could Mr. Thorpe retract my promise on such false pretenses. I shall not be at ease until I have spoken with Miss Tilney. I shall catch them in Milsom Street.

(The lights rise on MADAME MONTONI on her death bed. Projection: The Mysteries of Udolpho.)

MADAME MONTONI: Emily, Emily is that you?

CATHERINE: *(As EMILY.)* Aunt? Do you indeed live?

MADAME MONTONI: I do live, Emily… But I feel, I feel I am about to die. I thought that you had forsaken me.

CATHERINE: *(As EMILY.)* Signor Montoni had forbidden me to see you. I did not know where to find you.

MADAME MONTONI: Emily, I am a wretched, wretched fool. He has deceived me in every way.

CATHERINE: *(As EMILY.)* It is true, Aunt. The castle fills with armed men. Ludovico has discovered that Signor Montoni is the captain of a band of thieves and regularly plunders the countryside.

MADAME MONTONI: He demands that I sign over my estates in France to him. As long as I refuse he keeps me imprisoned here.

CATHERINE: *(As EMILY.)* For your own safety, madame, it would be wise to submit to his demands.

MADAME MONTONI: You do not know what you advise. These estates will descend to you.

CATHERINE: *(As EMILY.)* Do not hesitate a moment in resigning them on my account.

MADAME MONTONI: You are worthy of these estates, niece. I wish to keep them for your sake. The papers are hidden in the floorboards of the closet in my chamber. They must not fall into his hands.

CATHERINE: *(As EMILY.)* I must get you out of this damp drafty cell.

(CATHERINE [as EMILY] calls to TWO GUARDS to help her move her suffering AUNT.)

CATHERINE: *(As EMILY.)* Please, I beg you, take Madame Montoni to her own chamber. She is very ill. I beg you. I fear she is dying. I shall answer to Signor Montoni.

(The TWO MEN take MADAME MONTONI out. CATHERINE [as EMILY] is alone. Strange, eerie sounds. She sees a black veiled curtain billowing out. She pushes it aside, and GENERAL TILNEY steps out. CATHERINE shrieks and faints. Projection: Milsom Street, Bath.)

GENERAL TILNEY: *(Surprised.)* Miss Morland... Henry, Eleanor, come quickly!

CATHERINE: *(Coming to.)* I am come in a great hurry—I never promised to go—I am afraid I did not stay for the servant...

(CATHERINE is so agitated she cannot catch her breath. Being in the presence of THE GENERAL frightens her. GENERAL TILNEY helps her up. HENRY and ELEANOR enter.)

ELEANOR: *(Overlapping.)* Good heavens! It's Miss Morland.

HENRY: *(Overlapping.)* Miss Morland, what is the matter.

CATHERINE: I'm terribly sorry... please, please do not distress yourselves on my account.

ELEANOR: Miss Morland, what has happened?

CATHERINE: I had to speak to you. I would not break our engagement again for the world. Mr. Thorpe had no right to tell you otherwise.

ELEANOR: I was very surprised when I received his message.

CATHERINE: I could not bear to have you think ill of me. I ran all the way.

HENRY: No one could possibly think ill of you, Miss Morland.

CATHERINE: I am afraid my brother, Isabella, and Mr. Thorpe think quite ill of me for refusing to go with them.

GENERAL TILNEY: This Mr. Thorpe seems very solicitous on your behalf.

CATHERINE: He need not trouble himself.

GENERAL TILNEY: You are not fond of him then?

CATHERINE: He is a great friend of my brother's, but indeed, I am not in the least fond of him.

HENRY: Forgive us, Miss Morland, I believe you have not yet been properly introduced to our father. General, this is Miss Catherine Morland.

GENERAL TILNEY: *(Bowing.)* I am honored to make your acquaintance, Miss Morland.

CATHERINE: General Tilney, do forgive me. What must you think of me for barging in this way.

GENERAL TILNEY: On, the contrary, my dear Miss Morland, I cannot fathom what could have been in William's mind for not opening the door for you. *(Calling.)* William!

CATHERINE: No, General, believe me there was no fault on the part of your servant. In my haste to speak to Miss Tilney I rushed right past him.

GENERAL TILNEY: Your sincerity and generosity of mind impress me, Miss Morland. Indeed, it was very thoughtful of you to come all this way to speak with my daughter.

(HENRY and ELEANOR exchange looks.)

CATHERINE: It was the least I could do.

GENERAL TILNEY: Might I prevail upon you to join us for dinner this evening?

ELEANOR: Please do, Catherine.

CATHERINE: Thank you, but I am afraid the Allens expect me at any minute.

GENERAL TILNEY: The claims of Mr. and Mrs. Allen are not to be superseded. But on some other day I trust they could not refuse to spare you to your friend.

CATHERINE: I should have great pleasure in coming.

GENERAL TILNEY: Very well then, allow me to attend you out. *(Extends an arm.)*

CATHERINE: Thank you. *(To HENRY and ELEANOR.)* To Beechen Cliff tomorrow?

ELEANOR: Yes, yes, indeed—eleven o'clock.

HENRY: Good evening, Miss Morland.

CATHERINE: Good evening.

(THE GENERAL and CATHERINE walk out.)

GENERAL TILNEY: Miss Morland, you are indeed a very accomplished dancer.

CATHERINE: How kind of you to say so, sir.

GENERAL TILNEY: And if I may say, you even walk with great elasticity.

(They are gone. ELEANOR and HENRY look after them dumbfoundedly.)

ELEANOR: Henry, am I so blind as not to have noticed Miss Morland's...elasticity?

(They exchange a glance. HENRY shrugs. Lights. They exit. CATHERINE reenters.)

CATHERINE: General Tilney is so extraordinarily affable! I cannot begin to say how much pleasure his civilities bring me. But my behavior to my brother and Isabella weighs heavily on my heart. I do not think my conduct wrong, but indeed, I require a little affirmation to soothe away these residual pangs of guilt.

(AMY takes CATHERINE's coat. The lights change. MR. and MRS. ALLEN are having tea. CATHERINE picks up a cup. Projection: Pulteney Street, Bath.)

MRS. ALLEN: Do join us for tea, my dear.

CATHERINE: Mr. Allen, James, Isabella, and her brother are all going off to Blaize Castle in the morning.

MR. ALLEN: And do you think of going too?

CATHERINE: No, I had just settled to walk to Beechen Cliff with Miss Tilney and so could not go with them, could I?

MR. ALLEN: I am glad you do not think of going. These schemes are not at all the thing. Young men and women driving about the country in open carriages! It is not right. I wonder Mrs. Thorpe will allow it. I am sure your mother would not be pleased. Are you not of my way of thinking, Mrs. Allen?

MRS. ALLEN: Open carriages are nasty things. A clean gown is not five minutes wear in them.

MR. ALLEN: But do you not think it an odd appearance if young ladies are frequently driven about in them by young men, to whom they are not even related?

MRS. ALLEN: Yes dear, a very odd appearance, indeed. I cannot bear to see it myself.

CATHERINE: Dear madam! I hoped you would tell me if you thought I was doing wrong.

MRS. ALLEN: And so I told Mrs. Morland on our parting, I would always do the best for you in my power. But young people will be young people. When we first came, I wanted you not to buy that sprigged muslin but you would not listen. Young people do not like to always be thwarted.

MR. ALLEN: Well, there is no harm done, I would only advise you not to go out with Mr. Thorpe anymore.

MRS. ALLEN: That is just what I was going to say.

(CATHERINE crosses to the audience. The LIGHTS change.)

CATHERINE: "I advise you not to go out with Mr. Thorpe anymore"... Mr. Allen's words are music to my ears!

(AMY enters, bringing CATHERINE her cloak and bonnet.)

CATHERINE: I rejoice at being preserved by his wise advise from the danger of ever falling into such an error again. Amy...

AMY: Yes, Miss Morland?

CATHERINE: Have you ever explored Blaize Castle?

AMY: Forgive my asking, but why would anyone wish to explore Blaize Castle?

CATHERINE: Is it not a magnificent, ancient medieval ruin?

AMY: Good heavens no!—Blaize Castle is a folly. Built some time ago by a silly merchant. It's no bigger in size than my uncle's cottage in Bristol. Someone has been telling you fantastic stories, miss.

CATHERINE: I see. Thank you, Amy.

AMY: Good morning, Miss Morland.

CATHERINE: A folly!...A folly!!

(The lights change, birds chirp. CATHERINE, HENRY, and ELEANOR are having a picnic at Beechen Cliff.)

ELEANOR: What a divine prospect!

CATHERINE: Indeed, this landscape makes me think of the south of France.

HENRY: *(Surprised.)* You've been abroad then?

CATHERINE: Oh, no. I meant only that it puts me in mind of the country Emily and her father traveled through in *The Mysteries of Udolpho*. But you never read novels, I daresay.

HENRY: Why not?

CATHERINE: Gentlemen read better books.

HENRY: The person, be it gentleman or lady, who has not pleasure in a good novel must be intolerably stupid. I read *Udolpho* in two days, my hair standing on end the whole time.

ELEANOR: *Udolpho* is a most interesting work. Are you fond of that kind of reading?

CATHERINE: I do not much like any other.

ELEANOR: *(Laughing.)* Indeed?

CATHERINE: I read poetry and plays and things of that sort, and I do not dislike travels. But history, real solemn history, I cannot be interested in. It tells me nothing that does not either vex or weary me. The quarrels of popes and kings, with wars or pestilences in every page. The men all so good for nothing and hardly any women at all—it is very tiresome.

ELEANOR: *(Smiling to herself.)* What a remarkably blue sky.

CATHERINE: This is the most beautiful landscape I've ever beheld.

ELEANOR: It is a pity, Henry, you did not bring your watercolors.

CATHERINE: I would give anything to be able to draw.

HENRY: It is the easiest thing in the world.

CATHERINE: *(Crosses to the audience.)* Henry and Eleanor began a conversation about drawing of which I know absolutely nothing. He talked of foregrounds, distances, second distances—lights and shades. All I could do was smile and nod. To my relief, the conversation made an easy transition from the withered oak he was describing to oaks in general, to forests, the enclosure of them, waste lands, crown lands, and government. He shortly found himself arrived at politics and from politics it is an easy step to silence.

(There is an uncomfortable pause, a lull in the conversation. They look at one another and at the scenery.)

CATHERINE: *(Secretive.)* I have heard that something very shocking indeed will soon come out of London.

ELEANOR: *(Alarmed.)* Truly?! Of what nature?!?

CATHERINE: I have only heard it is to be more horrible than anything we have met with yet.

ELEANOR: Heavens!

CATHERINE: *(Excitedly.)* It is to be uncommonly dreadful. I shall expect murder and everything of the kind.

ELEANOR: But I hope if such a design is known beforehand, proper measures will be taken by the government to prevent it.

HENRY: *(Trying not to smile.)* But there must be murder and the government cares not how much. Come—shall I make you understand each other? Perhaps the abilities of women may never be sound nor astute.

ELEANOR: Do not mind my brother, but do satisfy me as to this dreadful riot?!?

CATHERINE: What riot?

HENRY: My dear Eleanor, the riot is in your own brain and the confusion there is scandalous.

ELEANOR: Henry?

HENRY: Miss Morland, my silly sister has mistaken your clearest expressions. You talked of expected horrors in London and instead of instantly conceiving that such words could only relate to a new publication in a circulating library, she immediately pictured to herself a mob of three thousand assembling in St. George's Fields, the bank attacked, the tower threatened, the streets of London flowing with blood…

ELEANOR: Henry, do stop!

HENRY: Forgive her, she is by no means a simpleton in general.

ELEANOR: Henry, Miss Morland is not used to your odd ways.

HENRY: I shall be most happy to make her better acquainted with them.

ELEANOR: No doubt. But you must clear your character before her. Tell her that you think very highly of the understanding of women.

HENRY: *(Earnestly.)* Miss Morland, no one can think more highly of the understanding of women than I do. In my opinion nature has given them so much understanding that they do not find it necessary to use more that half. *(Laughs.)*

ELEANOR: *(Laughing.)* Oh! We shall get nothing serious from him now. He is not in a sober mood.

(ELEANOR and CATHERINE take their picnic blanket and put it over HENRY's head. He pretends to struggle under it. They walk away from him.)

ELEANOR: I assure you he must be entirely misunderstood should he ever appear to say an unjust thing to any woman or an unkind to me.

(HENRY has risen with the blanket over his head. He comes up behind them.)

HENRY: (*With a spooky voice.*) I am the ghost of Udolpho…beware…beware…for I shall take my vengeance on all who dare to trespass in my castle!

(*He puts his arms around ELEANOR and CATHERINE who screech and giggle. CATHERINE breaks away. The lights change. HENRY and ELEANOR exit, taking the blanket and basket. Thunder. SIGNOR MONTONI enters and crosses to CATHERINE. She picks up and clutches her book. MONTONI surprises and circles around her. Projection: The Mysteries of Udolpho.*)

MONTONI: Niece!

CATHERINE: (*As EMILY.*) Oh, Signor Montoni!

MONTONI: I, as the husband of the late Signora Montoni, am heir of all that she possessed; the estates, therefore, can no longer be withheld. If you have a just opinion of the subject in question, you shall be allowed safe conveyance into France. If not, you shall remain my prisoner until you are convinced of your error.

CATHERINE: (*As EMILY.*) The law gives me the estates in question.

MONTONI: If you persist in this strain, you have everything to fear from my justice.

CATHERINE: (*As EMILY.*) From your *justice*, I have nothing to fear—I have only to hope.

MONTONI: I must pity the weakness of mind which leads you to the punishment I am preparing for you.

CATHERINE: (*As EMILY.*) The strength of my mind is equal to the justice of my cause. I can endure much when it is in resistance of oppression.

MONTONI: You speak like a heroine. Let us see if you can suffer like one. (*Storms out on a thunderous note.*)

CATHERINE: (*Sits in tears with her book; closing it.*) Poor dear Emily. (*Smiling.*) How horribly she suffers!

(*AMY enters, hands her a note, curtsies, and exits, taking CATHERINE's cloak.*)

CATHERINE: My transports were too soon interrupted by an urgent note from Isabella. It seems, once again, that yesterday's party never reached Blaize Castle.

(*ISABELLA enters and crosses to CATHERINE. Projection: Edgar's Buildings, Bath.*)

ISABELLA: My beloved, sweetest friend. Your brother is the most charming of men. I only wish I were more worthy of him.

CATHERINE: Isabella, can you really be in love with James?!?

ISABELLA: My heart and faith alike are engaged to him.

(*CATHERINE embraces ISABELLA.*)

CATHERINE: How inconceivably delightful! Oh, Isabella!

ISABELLA: The very first minute I beheld him—my heart was irrevocably gone. I remember I wore my yellow gown, with my hair done up in braids; and when I came into the drawing room John introduced him. I thought I'd never seen anyone so handsome before.

CATHERINE: (*To the audience.*) Here I must acknowledge the power of love, for though I am exceedingly fond of my brother, I never thought him handsome in my life!

ISABELLA: James will be setting off shortly for Fullerton to ask your parents' consent.

CATHERINE: I am sure they will not object.

ISABELLA: But my fortune will be so small. They never can consent to it. Your brother—who might marry anybody!

CATHERINE: Indeed, Isabella, the difference of fortune can be nothing to signify.

ISABELLA: If our situations were reversed, were I mistress of the whole world, your brother would be my only choice. Where people are really attached, poverty itself is wealth.

(*JAMES enters. He crosses to ISABELLA.*)

JAMES: I have come to take my leave of you, my dearest Isabella.

(*CATHERINE embraces him.*)

CATHERINE: James, how wonderful for you both!

JAMES: I am sure my parents will not object.

ISABELLA: I shall be in agony until the moment I hear from you.

JAMES: Goodbye Catherine. Farewell, my lovely Belle.

ISABELLA: Morland, I must drive you away. Consider how far you have to ride. Waste no more time, go, go, go.

(JAMES exits. CATHERINE and ISABELLA laugh and embrace.)

ISABELLA: I must go and see Mama about my wedding clothes!

(JOHN THORPE enters.)

JOHN: Miss Morland, I am come to bid you goodbye. I too must be off…to London.

CATHERINE: I am glad to hear it. I mean, I hope you have a very pleasant journey.

JOHN: A famous good thing this marrying scheme. What do you think of it, Miss Morland? I say it is no bad notion.

CATHERINE: I am sure it is a very good one.

JOHN: Did you ever hear the old song "Going to One Wedding Brings on Another"? I say, you will come to Belle's wedding, I hope.

CATHERINE: Naturally I shall be with your sister.

JOHN: Then we may try the truth of that old song.

CATHERINE: But Mr. Thorpe, I cannot sing. I dine with Miss Tilney today and must now be going home.

JOHN: Nay, there is no such confounded hurry. *(Clears his throat.)* You have more good nature and all that than anybody living. A monstrous deal of good nature. And it is not only good nature. You have so much, so much…well so much of everything. But I say, Miss Morland, shall I come pay my respects at Fullerton before too long?

CATHERINE: Pray do, my father and mother would be very glad to see you. Good morning.

JOHN: *(Stopping her.)* I hope you will not be sorry to see me.

CATHERINE: Company is always cheerful.

JOHN: Yes! Give me cheerful company, a girl I like, a comfortable house over my head, and what care I for the rest? Fortune is nothing. I am sure of a good income of my own and if she had not a penny, so much the better.

CATHERINE: I think like you there. I think to marry for money is the wickedest thing in existence. Good day.

(The lights change. CATHERINE crosses to the audience.)

CATHERINE: Liberty!

(AMY enters.)

CATHERINE: With our friendship renewed, Isabella and I are once again on intimate terms. She agonizing over the arrival of James's letter and I assuring her of my parents' consent. Our only separation was indeed when I accepted General Tilney's dinner invitation.

(The lights change. ISABELLA and CATHERINE are having tea. They continue at Edgar's Buildings, Bath.)

ISABELLA: I cannot believe it.

CATHERINE: Henry and Eleanor had never said so little and in spite of the General's invitations and compliments—it had been a great release to get away from him.

ISABELLA: Insufferable haughtiness and pride! Hardly to say a word to her guest!

CATHERINE: Yet she was very civil.

ISABELLA: Don't defend her! And her brother, how contemptible! Of all things in the world inconstancy is my aversion. How different to your brother and to mine.

CATHERINE: As for General Tilney, it seemed to be his only care to entertain and make me happy. Perhaps it was the arrival of their elder brother.

ISABELLA: *(Stands, very interested.)* Elder brother?

CATHERINE: Yes, Captain Frederick Tilney is just arrived. Well, we shall see how they behave to me tonight in the Assembly Rooms.

(MRS. THORPE enters in a very flustered state. She has a letter.)

MRS. THORPE: Belle, Belle my dear child, the letter has arrived!

ISABELLA: Oh, oh Mother, Catherine, I cannot breathe for fear of reading it.

MRS. THORPE: Shall I read it for you, dear?

ISABELLA: Nonsense, Mother, do give it to me. *(Takes and reads the letter.)* "I have had no difficulty in gaining the consent of my kind parents." Oh Mother, dear Catherine, I am in ecstasies!

CATHERINE: *(Overlapping.)* Oh, Isabella, we are to be sisters.

MRS. THORPE: *(Overlapping.)* Dear Mr. Morland, dear Catherine, dear, dear Belle.

(ISABELLA reads on, quieting them.)

ISABELLA: "As to the particulars. My father is to resign a living of which he himself is patron and incumbent of about four hundred yearly value as soon as I am old enough to take it. And an estate of equal value is assured as my future inheritance. My dearest Belle, my only discontent is that we must wait two and a half years before I can hold the living and we can be married."

CATHERINE: How wonderful it is to have everything so pleasantly settled.

ISABELLA: *(Gravely.)* Charming.

MRS. THORPE: Four hundred is but a small income to begin on. Let us not distress our dear Catherine by talking of such things. We should not suppose, however, that had you a suitable fortune, Mr. Morland would have come down with something more.

ISABELLA: Indeed, everybody does have a right to do what they like with their own money.

CATHERINE: I am very sure that my father has promised to do as much as he can afford.

ISABELLA: Dear Catherine, it is not the want of money that puts me out of spirits. No, indeed, it is the long, endless two years and a half that are to pass before your brother can hold the living and we can marry. There is the sting.

MRS. THORPE: Yes, my darling Isabella, we see perfectly into your heart. We perfectly understand your present vexation.

(The lights change, and CATHERINE crosses to address the audience.)

CATHERINE: Perfectly. My steadfast faith in my friend Isabella has been shaken. The ball in the Assembly Rooms proved even more shocking.

(AMY brings CATHERINE her spencer.)

CATHERINE: Isabella danced three times with Captain Frederick Tilney. Henry was again very attentive, which pleased me, and Eleanor her gracious self. *(Puzzled.)* I cannot at all account for the restraint they exhibit while in their father's company. Isabella's behavior, however, is decidedly altered.

(The lights come up on a bustling Pump Room. ISABELLA waves CATHERINE to her side. Projection: The Pump Room, Bath.)

ISABELLA: Do have a seat, Catherine.

CATHERINE: Do not be uneasy, Isabella, James will be back soon.

ISABELLA: Do not think me such a simpleton as to always be wanting to confine him to my elbow.

CATHERINE: But who are you looking for? Is your mother coming?

ISABELLA: Not at all. One's eyes must be somewhere. Catherine, you know I am amazingly absent. Tilney says it is always the case with minds of a certain stamp.

CATHERINE: Isabella, you said you had something particular to tell me.

ISABELLA: You see! My poor head! I had quite forgot it. I have just had a letter from John and I am sure you can guess the contents…

CATHERINE: Indeed, I cannot.

ISABELLA: Catherine, my brother's attentions were such as a child must have noticed. And you gave him the most positive encouragement. He says so in his letter. He says he as good as made you an offer and that you received his advances in the kindest way.

CATHERINE: There must be some unaccountable mistake! Isabella, I cannot return his affection and never meant to encourage it.

ISABELLA: So, you are determined against my brother?

CATHERINE: My dear friend, we shall be sisters in any event.

ISABELLA: I confess as soon as I read his letter, I thought it a very imprudent business, for what were you to live upon? John evidently could not have received *my* last letter. And you do not need to be in a hurry. A person may certainly live to repent that. Tilney says there is nothing people are so often deceived in as the state of their own affections. Ah, here he is now.

(A HANDSOME MAN in a military uniform [FREDERICK TILNEY] approaches ISABELLA.)

FREDERICK: What! Always to be watched in person or by proxy.

ISABELLA: Nonsense! My spirit, you know, is independent.

FREDERICK: I wish your heart were independent.

ISABELLA: What can you have to do with hearts. You men have none of you any hearts.

FREDERICK: If we have not hearts, we have eyes; and they give us torment enough.

ISABELLA: I am sorry for it. I will look another way. I hope your eyes are not tormented now.

FREDERICK: Never more so; for the edge of a blooming cheek is still in view—at once too much and too little.

CATHERINE: *(Standing up.)* Isabella, shall we find Mrs. Allen and take a turn about the room?

ISABELLA: My dear, it is so odious to parade about the Pump Room. Besides, I am expecting my mother at any minute and so you must excuse me.

(CATHERINE crosses away in great agitation and runs into HENRY.)

CATHERINE: Mr. Tilney! Please, you must inform your brother that Miss Thorpe is engaged to my brother.

HENRY: I have told him that Miss Thorpe is engaged.

CATHERINE: Then why does he pursue her in this manner?

HENRY: Miss Morland, is it my brother's attentions to Miss Thorpe or Miss Thorpe's admission of them which causes you pain?

CATHERINE: Is it not the same thing?

HENRY: I think your brother would acknowledge a difference.

CATHERINE: Then you do not believe Isabella so very much attached to my brother?

HENRY: Is her heart constant to him only when unsolicited by anyone else? He cannot think this. And you may be sure he would not have you think it.

(Enter ELEANOR, who crosses directly to them.)

ELEANOR: Henry, Miss Morland, I am glad that I have found you. The General has just determined on leaving Bath at the end of the week.

HENRY: Why so soon?

ELEANOR: He has been disappointed by friends whom he expected to meet here.

CATHERINE: I am so very sorry to hear it.

ELEANOR: Miss Morland, perhaps—you would be so good—it would make me very happy if…

(THE GENERAL crosses in and interrupts.)

GENERAL TILNEY: Well, Eleanor, may I congratulate you on being successful in your application to your fair friend?

ELEANOR: I was just beginning to make the request.

GENERAL TILNEY: Well proceed by all means. I know how much your heart is in it. My daughter has been forming a very bold wish. We leave Bath shortly and if you could quit this scene of public triumph to honor us with a visit, you will make us happy beyond expression.

CATHERINE: I shall write home directly. I daresay my parents will not object.

GENERAL TILNEY: I have already waited on your excellent friends in Pulteney Street and have obtained their sanction and since they can consent to part with you, we may perhaps expect philosophy from the world. I can assure you that every effort will be made to make Northanger Abbey agreeable to you.

(The lights change dramatically. CATHERINE crosses to the audience as the lights narrow on her.)

CATHERINE: Northanger Abbey!!

(Bach organ music.)

CATHERINE: Oh, the very words wind up my feelings to the highest point of ecstasy! To have my company so warmly solicited! And to visit not a hall nor a house nor a cottage but an *abbey*! With, perhaps, long damp passages and narrow cells and a ruined chapel! My passion for ancient medieval edifices is next in degree only to my passion for Mr. Henry Tilney!

(AMY crosses to CATHERINE with her bag, cloak, and bonnet. TWO SERVANTS take her trunk out across the stage.)

AMY: This way, this way. Have a pleasant holiday at Northanger, Miss Morland. We shall miss you here.

CATHERINE: And I shall miss Bath, I daresay. But I cannot be sorry I am going to an abbey!

AMY: Farewell, miss.

CATHERINE: Goodbye, Amy.

(AMY curtsies and exits. HENRY and ELEANOR enter. They are at an inn at Petty France on the road to Northanger Abbey. HENRY crosses to them. Projection: A Roadside Inn, Petty France.)

HENRY: Father is to be another hour about the horses.

ELEANOR: I am so glad you are coming to Northanger Abbey. I sadly have no female companionship there.

HENRY: When Father is absent, she sometimes has no companion at all.

CATHERINE: Are you not with her?

HENRY: I have my own house in Woodston.

ELEANOR: It is nearly twenty miles from Northanger. Much of Henry's time is necessarily spent there.

CATHERINE: How sorry you must be for that!

HENRY: I am always sorry to leave Eleanor.

CATHERINE: But after such a home as an abbey, an ordinary parsonage house must be very disagreeable.

HENRY: You have formed a very favorable idea of the abbey.

CATHERINE: Is it not a fine old place just like one reads about?

HENRY: That depends. Have you a stout heart!? Nerves fit for creaking doors and sliding panels?

ELEANOR: Henry…

CATHERINE: I do not think I should be easily frightened.

HENRY: But you are aware that whenever a young lady enters a dwelling of this kind she is formally conducted by Dorothy, the ancient housekeeper, into a room never used since some cousin or kin died in it some twenty years before?

CATHERINE: But this will not happen to me…

ELEANOR: Catherine, do not encourage him…

HENRY: Perhaps you will discover in this room a ponderous chest which no efforts can open, and over the fireplace a portrait of some handsome warrior whose features will so incomprehensibly strike you that you will not be able to take your eyes from it.

ELEANOR: *(Joining in.)* Dorothy, meanwhile, will have dropped hints, leading you to believe this part of the abbey is haunted!

CATHERINE: How frightful! But surely your housekeeper is not really called Dorothy.

HENRY: On your second night there will be a violent storm. Peals of thunder so loud as seem to shake the edifice to its foundation. You discover a secret doorway and with your lamp in your hand you pass through it into a small vaulted room.

CATHERINE: I should be much too frightened to do such a thing!

ELEANOR: Not when Dorothy has given you to understand that there is a secret subterraneous passage between your room and the chapel of St. Anthony scarcely two miles away?

HENRY: Could you shrink from such an adventure?

HENRY and ELEANOR: No!

HENRY: You proceed into this small vaulted room and into several others. In one, perhaps, you find a dagger.

ELEANOR: In another, a few drops of blood.

HENRY: And in yet a third, the remains of some instrument of torture.

(CATHERINE gasps.)

HENRY: Your eyes will then be attracted to a large old-fashioned cabinet of ebony and gold. Impelled by an irresistible presentiment, you eagerly search every drawer.

ELEANOR: At last, by touching a secret spring, an inner compartment opens containing many sheets of a manuscript but scarcely had you been able to decipher "The Last Memoirs of the Wretched Matilda"…

HENRY: Your lamp is extinguished leaving you in total darkness!

(HENRY covers CATHERINE's eyes with his hands. She shrieks and jumps.)

CATHERINE: Aaaahh! How horrible! How horrible! How delightful! Do go on!

(HENRY and ELEANOR are laughing.)

HENRY: I cannot!

CATHERINE: But I could listen for hours! Oh, do tell me more of the wretched Matilda!

(Laughter. The lights change, and CATHERINE crosses to the audience. TWO SERVANTS carry CATHERINE's trunk across the stage. CATHERINE is at Northanger Abbey. MARY, the Irish maid at Northanger Abbey, directs them. CATHERINE's room is created, a platform becomes her bed, new drapes are hung, etc. Projection: Northanger Abbey.)

MARY: This way, this way. Mind you don't drop it on the staircase!

CATHERINE: Northanger Abbey! It is delightful to really be in an abbey. My room is very unlike the one in Henry's description. And to my delight and relief I have found that Eleanor is only two doors away. But this is strange indeed! An immense heavy chest just as Henry talked of! What can it hold? I will look into it, cost me what it may. I will look into it. *(Attempts to open the heavy lid.)*

(MARY, who speaks with an Irish accent, enters with a candle before CATHERINE has it opened.)

MARY: Miss Morland, Miss Tilney has sent me to assist you in dressing for bed.

CATHERINE: *(Jumps and drops the lid with a thud.)* Thank you, Mary, that is very kind.

(MARY helps CATHERINE remove her overdress.)

MARY: That is a curious old chest, is it not? It is impossible to say how many generations it has been here.

CATHERINE: It is very unusual.

MARY: Its weight makes it difficult to open. But in that corner, at least it is out of the way. Good night, Miss Morland.

CATHERINE: Yes, thank you. Good night, Mary.

(MARY curtsies and exits. Thunder and lightning. Wind and rattling shutters, the distant closing of a door.)

CATHERINE: I am really in an abbey! Yes. These are the characteristic sounds. They bring to my mind a countless variety of dreadful situations and horrid scenes. But I am not afraid.

(The sound of a distant moan, creaking, and wind gusts.)

CATHERINE: I have nothing to fear from midnight assassins or drunken gallants. So I am determined to look in that chest! I cannot go to sleep without satisfying my burning curiosity. *(Puts down her candle and opens the chest.)* Astonishing! A manuscript! It is so like what Henry and Eleanor described this morning.

(Peals of thunder. CATHERINE nervously reaches in and removes a stack of papers.)

CATHERINE: What can this be?

(She picks up her candle, but a sudden gust of wind rages without, and her candle snuffs, leaving the stage in darkness. Loud peals of thunder. CATHERINE shrieks and in subsequent flashes of lightning we see the papers fly into the air and CATHERINE leap into her bed pulling the blankets over her head, just peeping out. The lights change and an eerie parade of GHOSTS and GHOULS pass in front of her and jump out from behind and under her bed. Including, but not limited to, the GHOSTS OF MADAME MONTONI and ST. AUBERT, the sword-fighting MONTONI and COUNT MORANO, a KNIGHT IN ARMOR, VALANCOURT in distress, HEADLESS ROBBERS, SCREAMING MAIDENS, FLOATING OBJECTS, etc. Horror, blood, and gore. CATHERINE's screams build to a crescendo and she faints. The scene quiets, the lights change. It is morning. MARY enters, humming.)

MARY: Good morning, Miss Morland. I hope you were able to sleep well last night in spite of all that noise.

CATHERINE: I did manage to sleep some.

MARY: Breakfast will soon be ready in the breakfast room.

CATHERINE: Thank you, Mary, I shall make haste.

(MARY sees the papers and picks them up.)

MARY: Good heavens, what are these? I wonder how they got here?

CATHERINE: I can't imagine. What are they?

(MARY helps CATHERINE put on her outer dress.)

MARY: Laundry list—shirts, stockings, cravats, other bills of lading. Trifles of that sort.

CATHERINE: *(Disappointed.)* Oh.

MARY: You know, these might be the very papers the housekeeper has been in search of these two weeks past. What a piece of luck to find them. Good morning, miss. *(Curtsies and exits.)*

CATHERINE: Such was the collection of papers that had frightened me senseless and robbed me of half a night's sleep. I feel humbled to the dust. Heaven forbid Henry Tilney should ever know of my folly.

(She crosses to another part of the stage. HENRY offers her a cup of tea.)

HENRY: Good morning, Miss Morland. I hope you were undisturbed by last night's tempest. These ancient buildings tend to produce the most unearthly sounds in violent winds.

CATHERINE: Storms are nothing when they are over. What a fine morning. Such beautiful flowers. I have just learnt to love a hyacinth.

HENRY: And how might you learn, by accident or argument?

CATHERINE: Your sister taught me. I cannot say how. Mrs. Allen used to take pains year after year to make me like them. I never could 'til I saw them the other day in Milsom Street.

HENRY: The love of a hyacinth may be rather domestic. But who can tell, the sentiment once raised, may you not in time come to love a rose?

CATHERINE: Perhaps, in time…

HENRY: *(Very close, about to kiss her.)* I am pleased to hear it. The mere habit of learning to love is the thing.

(ELEANOR enters.)

ELEANOR: Catherine, good morning—

CATHERINE: *(To the audience.)* Oh, my…

ELEANOR: After breakfast you will take a turn around the grounds with the General and myself. He is most desirous to show them to you.

(The lights change, and CATHERINE crosses to the audience. MARY brings her coat and bonnet.)

CATHERINE: The grounds? The grounds! But my only desire is to explore every inch inside this magnificent abbey. But Eleanor explained that her father always walks out at this time. I was struck with the grandeur of the place as I saw it for the first time from the lawn. I greatly admired General Tilney's orchards and hot-houses. He was going to conduct us to the tea-house when Eleanor took a different path going towards a grove of Scotch firs. The General decided to walk across the park instead.

ELEANOR: I am very fond of this spot. It was my mother's favorite walk. Her memory endears it now.

CATHERINE: Yet your father could not enter it. Her death must have been a great affliction.

ELEANOR: A great increasing one. I was only sixteen when it happened.

CATHERINE: You must miss her very much.

ELEANOR: A mother would have been always present. A mother would have been a constant friend; her influence would have been beyond any other.

CATHERINE: Is there any picture of her at the abbey?

ELEANOR: Oh, yes. It is very like.

CATHERINE: Her picture I suppose, hangs in your father's room?

ELEANOR: My father was dissatisfied with the painting. For some time it had no place. Soon after her death, I obtained it for my own and hung it in my bedchamber. I shall be happy to show it to you sometime.

(CATHERINE crosses to the audience. The lights narrow on her.)

CATHERINE: A portrait of a departed wife not valued by her husband!?! He must have been dreadfully cruel to her. As handsome as the General is, there is something in his features which speaks of his not behaving well to his wife.

(MARY enters and removes CATHERINE's coat.)

CATHERINE: I have often read of such characters. Characters Mr. Allen used to call unnatural and over-drawn—but here! Here is proof positive to the contrary! We retired to the abbey and the General disappeared for another hour leaving strict instructions against touring the abbey 'til he returned. This lengthened absence, his solitary rambles…these do not speak of a mind at ease! My pleasure in exploring the abbey is greatly lessened in his company. But it is all very beautiful—very noble—very grand.

(The lights change. GENERAL TILNEY and ELEANOR enter.)

GENERAL TILNEY: As you can see, Miss Morland, I have spared no expense.

CATHERINE: I do think Northanger Abbey the most beautiful home I have ever visited.

GENERAL TILNEY: (*Sharply.*) Eleanor! Where are you going? What more is there to be seen? (*Softening.*) Do you not suppose Miss Morland would be glad of some refreshment after so much exercise? Come, luncheon shall be on table directly. (*Exits.*)

ELEANOR: I was going to take you into what was my mother's room, the room in which she died.

CATHERINE: It remains just as it was, I suppose?

ELEANOR: Yes, entirely.

CATHERINE: How long ago since she died?

ELEANOR: She has been gone these seven years.

CATHERINE: You were with her, I suppose, to the last?

ELEANOR: Her illness was sudden and short. I was unfortunately from home. Before I returned it was all over.

CATHERINE: Poor dear Eleanor. Well, I should like to see it some time.

ELEANOR: Perhaps another day.

(*ELEANOR follows HER FATHER out.*)

CATHERINE: Could it be possible? Could Henry's father— His behavior and actions all point to diabolical treachery. The way he paces the room for an hour together in dark contemplation. His habit of staying awake long after the rest of the household is in bed. What is there to be done at this hour?— Perhaps, Mrs. Tilney still lives? She could very likely be shut up and languishing in some dark remote part of the abbey receiving from the pitiless hands of her husband a nightly supply of coarse food. A shocking idea but better than a death unfairly hastened. I know too well how a waxen figure may be introduced for a corpse and a hurried funeral carried on. General Tilney has not fooled me with his niceties and compliments. He has the decided air and attitude of a Montoni!!

(*ANNETTE rushes in. Projection:* The Mysteries of Udolpho.)

ANNETTE: Ma'amselle, ma'amselle. The Signor is coming and in such a fury too. We must hide ourselves. Ludovico can lock us in my room again. We were safe there when the castle was attacked.

CATHERINE: (*As EMILY.*) Annette, we must find a way to escape Udolpho.

ANNETTE: Ludovico says he has a plan. But he says we must wait until the moment is right.

CATHERINE: (*As EMILY.*) I do not believe there is much time left, Annette.

(*MONTONI enters, fuming.*)

MONTONI: Did I not send for you!?!? Let the recollection of your aunt's sufferings in consequence of her folly teach you a lesson. (*To ANNETTE.*) Leave us… Leave us!!

(*ANNETTE hesitates, then runs from the room.*)

MONTONI: Sign the papers. Dare my resentment no further, sign the papers!

CATHERINE: (*As EMILY.*) If the lands are yours by law, you certainly may possess them without my consent.

(*MONTONI grabs her.*)

MONTONI: You have dared to question my right!! Now dare to question my power!! I have devised a punishment inconceivable— This night—this very night!

A SUPERNATURAL VOICE: This very night!

(*MONTONI releases CATHERINE [as EMILY]. He is very nervous.*)

MONTONI: I could tell you of others. I could make you tremble at the bare recital…

(*A loud, frightening groan shakes the rafters. CATHERINE [as EMILY] screams.*)

MONTONI: This affectation of fear ill becomes a heroine.

CATHERINE: (*As EMILY.*) Did you hear nothing, Signor?

MONTONI: I heard my own voice!!

(*Another loud groan.*)

CATHERINE: (*As EMILY.*) Do you hear nothing now?!?

MONTONI: Fools' tricks!!! I will soon discover by whom they are practiced!!

(*MONTONI storms out. JAMES enters, following MARY. He is wearing boots and a greatcoat. He has been riding. Projection: Northanger Abbey.*)

MARY: Mr. James Morland to see you, Miss Morland. (*Curtsies and exits.*)

JAMES: Catherine!

CATHERINE: James! How came you to Northanger Abbey?

JAMES: I should not have come. Catherine, you are my only friend, only you can understand the depth of my feelings.

(He falls on his knees before her. She embraces him.)

CATHERINE: James, whatever is the matter?

JAMES: Oh, Catherine, everything is at an end between Isabella and me.

CATHERINE: What has happened?

JAMES: She has made me miserable forever! Her duplicity hurts most of all! To the very last, when I reasoned with her, she declared herself to be as attached to me as ever and laughed at my fears. I am ashamed to think how long I bore with it. But if ever a man had reason to believe himself loved, I was that man!

CATHERINE: Indeed, she made me believe she loved you.

JAMES: I cannot understand what she would be at! For there was no need of my being played off to make her secure of Captain Tilney.

CATHERINE: How could she behave so cruelly?

JAMES: I hope you will acquit me of everything but the folly of too easily thinking my affection returned.

CATHERINE: Poor dear James. How it pains me to see you suffer so.

JAMES: I can never expect to know such another woman! I would to God we had never met. Catherine, please understand. I wish your visit at Northanger Abbey over before Captain Tilney makes his engagement known.

(HENRY and ELEANOR enter.)

HENRY: Miss Morland, we heard you had a visitor.

JAMES: *(Sees HENRY.)* Forgive me, I should not have come here. Beware, Catherine, beware how you give your heart. Thank God I am undeceived in time. Forgive me. I ride to Oxford. Farewell! *(Runs out.)*

CATHERINE: James, James, come back!

HENRY: Perhaps it is best to let him go.

CATHERINE: He is distraught!

HENRY: Miss Thorpe has no doubt broken their engagement?

CATHERINE: Yes—and is to marry your brother! Poor James is so unhappy.

ELEANOR: How strange an infatuation on Frederick's side!

HENRY: I cannot believe he would freely choose to marry her. However, I have too good an opinion of Miss Thorpe's prudence to suppose that she would part with one gentleman before the other is secured.

CATHERINE: Perhaps she may behave better by your family. She may be constant.

HENRY: I am afraid she will be very constant unless a baronet should come in her way. That is Frederick's only chance. I will get the Bath paper and look over the arrivals.

ELEANOR: Henry…

CATHERINE: *(Smiles dejectedly.)* I was never so deceived in anyone's character in all my life.

ELEANOR: The loss of a friend is a great loss, indeed.

HENRY: The loss of such a friend is a loss for the better, I assure you.

(The lights change. CATHERINE crosses to the audience.)

CATHERINE: So much for Isabella and all our intimacy.

(MARY enters, gives CATHERINE a letter, curtsies, and exits.)

CATHERINE: Then surprisingly, I received a letter from her pleading for my assistance in reconciling their "misunderstanding." It seems Captain Tilney had no real interest in marriage after all. He left Isabella and Bath shortly after my brother. Still, I see what she is about. Isabella Thorpe is a vain coquette and her tricks have not answered.

(She crosses to another part of the stage and discovers ELEANOR sobbing. She is holding a miniature portrait in one hand.)

CATHERINE: Eleanor…

ELEANOR: *(Wiping away her tears.)* Catherine! Forgive me.

CATHERINE: Eleanor, whatever is the matter?

ELEANOR: I don't wish to trouble you with my sorrows.

CATHERINE: My dear friend, you can tell me anything.

ELEANOR: You are a good friend, Catherine.

CATHERINE: Isabella has written. Your brother has left her.

ELEANOR: It does not surprise me.

CATHERINE: I have decided—I shall neither write nor see her again. *(Indicates the miniature painting ELEANOR is holding.)* Is that a picture of your mother?

ELEANOR: No, my mother's portrait hangs on that wall.

CATHERINE: She was very beautiful.

ELEANOR: Yes.

CATHERINE: I see a resemblance in you.

ELEANOR: It pleases me to hear you say so. This is a picture of Mr. Francis Harwood.

CATHERINE: He is exceedingly handsome.

ELEANOR: He is the younger brother to the Viscount Basilton. And he is the most charming man in the world. We met here when the viscount visited by my father's invitation. We wish to marry. The General refuses his consent because of dear Mr. Harwood's lack of fortune. My father does not allow me to see or hear from him. *(She is in tears.)*

CATHERINE: Poor dearest Eleanor.

ELEANOR: My sorrow overcomes me when I am alone.

CATHERINE: Is there no hope?

ELEANOR: I always have hope. I could not live if I did not have hope.

(The lights change. CATHERINE crosses to the audience.)

CATHERINE: Do the cruelties of this man never cease? To crush the happiness of his only daughter? And what of myself and Henry? My circumstances are less significant than Mr. Harwood's. Since Eleanor is so out of spirits, I am now determined to make the excursion to the room where Mrs. Tilney died by myself. I shall explore every closet, every corner, every secret passage in search of proof of his treachery.

(The lights change. SIGNORA LIVONA enters and crosses to her. She is played by the same actress who plays ISABELLA. She speaks with an Italian accent. Projection: The Mysteries of Udolpho.)

SIGNORA LIVONA: Emily, why, Emily, you look so pale and sad.

CATHERINE: *(As EMILY.)* Signora Livona! How came you to Udolpho?

SIGNORA LIVONA: I was so sorry to hear of your aunt. So sudden, so unexpected. But these things happen, you know, and Emily, you look so becoming in mourning attire.

(She laughs and crosses to MONTONI, who has appeared at the side of the stage. They kiss with passionate abandon. ANNETTE rushes in.)

ANNETTE: Ma'amselle, ma'amselle. So you have seen her. Signora Livona is his mistress. And Ludovico says she always was! She and those other women, you know what they are! Tonight they make a great entertainment drinking, singing, dancing 'til they make the castle ring.

CATHERINE: *(As EMILY.)* They insult the memory of my aunt.

(MONTONI picks up SIGNORA LIVONA, and they exit off.)

ANNETTE: We must go to our rooms quickly and lock the doors. The drunken banditti will be here soon.

LUDOVICO: *(Rushes to ANNETTE.)* They have arrived. The robbers! They have plundered half the countryside and come to celebrate their spoils. Now is our chance.

ANNETTE: For what, Ludovico?!

LUDOVICO: Don't you see! The gates are open. We must act now and escape!

CATHERINE: *(As EMILY.)* Escape from Udolpho!

(Laughter and celebratory noise offstage.)

LUDOVICO: I know a secret passage. We can follow it to the main gate and run out when the guard is not looking.

CATHERINE: *(As EMILY.)* Let us waste no time.

(They cross over the stage but are stopped by TWO ARMED MEN who back them into the room.)

CATHERINE: *(As EMILY.)* Let us pass.

(The MEN respond by raising their swords.)

LUDOVICO: Since you will fight...fight with me! Engarde!

(He lunges at them. CATHERINE [as EMILY] shrieks. He fights them both.)

ANNETTE: Ludovico, no!

LUDOVICO: Run! Run! I beg you, I will hold them both off.

ANNETTE: Never! I cannot leave you!

(The fight continues. ANNETTE picks up a chair [or something] and hits one of the MEN, who falls. LUDOVICO disarms and wounds the OTHER. They groan in pain.)

LUDOVICO: My darling.

(He kisses ANNETTE.)

ANNETTE: You are so brave!

(The WOUNDED MEN begin to crawl away, moaning.)

LUDOVICO: Come, we must away!

ANNETTE: Run, ma'amselle, run! There is not a moment to lose!

(They go off. CATHERINE is distracted. The lights change. HENRY comes up behind her. Projection: Northanger Abbey.)

HENRY: Miss Morland!

CATHERINE: *(Startled.)* Mr. Tilney!

HENRY: Miss Morland, how came you to this part of the abbey?

CATHERINE: I came to look at your mother's room.

HENRY: Why did Eleanor leave you to find your way by yourself?

CATHERINE: She was not well. We came to see this room before, only your father was with us.

HENRY: And that prevented you. Well, how did you find it?

CATHERINE: Very cheerful, very modern, and very sunny.

HENRY: Nothing to raise your curiosity?

CATHERINE: Nothing at all.

HENRY: I suppose Eleanor talked of it a great deal?

CATHERINE: Yes, she spoke of it. Of your mother's sudden death and of her being from home. And of your father... I thought perhaps he was not very fond of her...

HENRY: And from these circumstances you infer perhaps some—negligence, some—or may it be something still less pardonable?...

CATHERINE: But your father— Was he afflicted at her death?

HENRY: For a time, greatly so. You have erred in supposing him not attached to her. He loved her as well as it was possible for him to. We have not all your same tenderness of disposition.

CATHERINE: I am very glad to hear it. It would have been very shocking!

HENRY: *(Truly shocked.)* If I understand you rightly... you had formed a surmise of such horror, I can hardly put words to it. Good Lord! Miss Morland, what ideas have you been admitting?

CATHERINE: *(Bursting into tears and crossing away.)* Oh, Mr. Tilney!

(He exits. The lights change, and she speaks to the audience.)

CATHERINE: Oh Lord! What a fool I have been! The absurdity of my curiosity and fears. My folly is all exposed to him now. I am sunk with Henry Tilney! He must despise me forever! If only he would forgive me, I vow, to the best of my ability, I shall better employ my common sense. Charming as are all of Mrs. Radcliffe's works, it is not perhaps in them that human nature, at least in the midland counties of England, is to be looked for. Italy, Switzerland, and the south of France might be as fruitful in horrors as represented. But in central England I am painfully aware that murder is not tolerated, servants are not slaves, and neither poison nor sleeping potions can be procured from every village druggist. Oh, Henry!

(MARY enters to help CATHERINE dress.)

MARY: Miss Morland, I've come to help you dress for dinner.

CATHERINE: Thank you.

MARY: As tonight is Mr. Tilney's last evening before he returns to Woodston, I thought you may wish for something special.

CATHERINE: Oh, Mary, I should be happy for any help you might offer.

MARY: Don't think me impertinent, but I have observed that the young master is very fond of you.

CATHERINE: I wish I could believe that. Today, I said something very, very foolish. He can hardly think well of me now.

MARY: My dear Miss Morland, where the heart is truly attached no offense is ever too great to be forgiven.

CATHERINE: I hope you might be right. How do I look?

MARY: You are the picture of all that is graceful, miss.

CATHERINE: You are very kind.

MARY: Do have a pleasant evening, miss. *(Curtsies and exits.)*

(The lights change, and CATHERINE speaks to the audience.)

CATHERINE: Mary taught my heart to hope. Indeed, I am resolved to be more worthy of Henry's regard.

(HENRY and THE GENERAL enter.)

HENRY: Goodbye, Miss Morland. Duty calls. *(Glances at HIS FATHER.)*

CATHERINE: Have a safe journey.

HENRY: Farewell.

CATHERINE: Farewell.

(There is an awkward moment. CATHERINE offers her hand to be kissed, and HENRY shakes it instead. THE GENERAL is displeased. He and HENRY exit.)

CATHERINE: Northanger Abbey is a lonely and desolate place without him. Eleanor's spirits too are deeply affected in his absence. What is there here to amuse me? I am tired of the woods and the shrubbery, and the abbey itself is no more to me now than any other house. The General has gone to London. Eleanor and I are finally able to enjoy one another's company. We go about just as we please without fearing that a false word or action might bring on the General's displea-

sure. Nothing, however, could have prepared me for the midnight visit I received only three days after his departure.

(A door creaks loudly. A FIGURE enters the room and approaches CATHERINE, who gasps.)

ELEANOR: Poor dear Catherine, I did not mean to frighten you.

CATHERINE: Eleanor…

ELEANOR: My father is suddenly returned from London… Oh, my dear friend, we must be parted! On Monday my father says the whole family must be going to Lord Longtown's near Hereford for a fortnight.

CATHERINE: Oh… I can go on Monday very well. My parents; having no notice is of very little consequence. I daresay, the General will send a servant with me half the way and…

ELEANOR: Catherine, I am so very sorry… tomorrow morning is fixed for your leaving us. The very carriage is ordered and will be here at seven o'clock and no servant is to be offered to you… I could hardly believe my senses when I heard it. Good God! What will your father and mother say? A journey of seventy miles to be taken by post, at your age, unattended. It is unthinkable!

CATHERINE: Have I offended the General?

ELEANOR: You can have given him no just cause of offense.

CATHERINE: Do not be unhappy; it is of little consequence.

ELEANOR: I earnestly hope that to your real safety it will be of none; but to everything else it is of the greatest consequence: to comfort, propriety, to your family, to the world.

CATHERINE: I can be ready by seven; please let me be called in time.

ELEANOR: My dear friend, I cannot bear to be parted this way. I am simply mortified by my father's actions. *(Runs out in tears.)*

(Mournful music. MARY brings CATHERINE her bag, bonnet, and coat.)

MARY: Have a safe journey home, Miss Morland.

CATHERINE: Thank you, Mary. Goodbye.

MARY: Goodbye, dear. *(Curtsies and exits.)*

(TWO SERVANTS enter carrying CATHERINE's trunk. She gives them directions and they go off. THE GENERAL and ELEANOR enter at one side.)

ELEANOR: You can send her away, General, but you cannot prevent me from bidding my friend farewell.

GENERAL TILNEY: Do not be long about it. I do not have time for trifling. *(Glares at CATHERINE.)*

ELEANOR: *(Runs to her.)* You must write to me, Catherine. Till I know you to be safe at home, I shall not have an hour's comfort. Direct to me at Lord Longtown's and I must ask under the cover of "Mary."

CATHERINE: No, Eleanor, if you are not allowed to receive a letter from me, I had better not write. There can be no doubt of my getting home safely.

ELEANOR: I will not importune you. I will trust to your own kindness of heart when I am at a distance from you.

CATHERINE: I shall write you. Of course, I will.

ELEANOR: Catherine, I must ask you. You have been from home for quite some time. Have you enough money for the journey?

CATHERINE: I had not even thought of that. *(Checks her purse and indeed finds herself short.)* I fear I had not anticipated the need…

ELEANOR: Please take this.

(ELEANOR closes some money in her hand. CATHERINE is holding back her tears.)

CATHERINE: Oh, Eleanor…

GENERAL TILNEY: Eleanor, Miss Morland's carriage is waiting…

CATHERINE: Farewell, Eleanor… Please…give my kind remembrances to my absent friend.

(CATHERINE bursts into tears and goes off to the direction of the carriage. ELEANOR crosses to GENERAL TILNEY.)

ELEANOR: Father, why have you done this? How could Catherine possibly have offended you?

GENERAL TILNEY: Do not ask questions of what does not concern you. Go prepare for the journey to Hereford.

(ELEANOR wishes to say something to THE GENERAL but cannot. She exits. THE GENERAL takes one satisfied

look off in the direction CATHERINE has gone and exits. CATHERINE enters. She writes in her journal.)

CATHERINE: I felt far too wretched to be fearful of the eleven-hour journey. The road I traveled is the same as the road to Henry's house at Woodston. When the carriage passed the turning, my grief was inconsolable. *(To the audience.)* Henry is so near and yet so unaware of my present circumstances. To return to Fullerton in such a manner is almost enough to destroy the pleasure of meeting those I love best. A heroine returning home in humiliation in a hack post-chaise is such a blow to sentiment.

(MR. and MRS. MORLAND cross to her. She is home at Fullerton. MRS. MORLAND hands her a cup of tea, and MR. MORLAND directs TWO SERVANTS, who bring her trunk across the stage. ANOTHER takes her bonnet and cloak. Projection: Fullerton.)

MR. MORLAND: Such an affront.

MRS. MORLAND: My poor child, you look so pale. Drink your tea and you shall feel better.

CATHERINE: Yes, Mama.

MR. MORLAND: What a strange business.

MRS. MORLAND: This General Tilney has acted neither as a gentleman nor as a parent.

MR. MORLAND: Such a strange acquaintance, so soon made and so soon ended. I am sorry it happened. Mrs. Allen thought them a very good kind of people.

MRS. MORLAND: And you were sadly out of luck too in your Isabella. Ah! Poor James! At present it comes hard to him, but that will not last forever. Well, we must live and learn and the next new friends you make I hope will be better worth keeping.

CATHERINE: No friend can be better worth keeping than Eleanor…

MRS. MORLAND: Well, I am sorry for the young people; you must have had a sad time of it. Our comfort certainly does not depend on General Tilney. I am glad I did not know of your journey at the time; but now it is over, perhaps there is no great harm done. It is always good for young people to be put upon exerting themselves; and you know, my dear little Catherine, you always were a sad, little scatterbrained creature.

CATHERINE: Mama!

MRS. MORLAND: Now you have been forced to have your wits about you, with so much changing of chaises and so forth. I hope you have not left anything behind in any of the pockets.

CATHERINE: I do not think I have. *(To the audience.)* Mama thought a visit from Mrs. Allen would revive my spirits.

(Enter MRS. ALLEN.)

MRS. ALLEN: Catherine, it is indeed such a surprise to see you!

MRS. MORLAND: She traveled all the way by post herself. It is such a comfort to find that she is not a poor helpless creature and can shift very well for herself.

MRS. ALLEN: But really, I have no patience with the General. Such an agreeable worthy man he seemed to be!

MRS. MORLAND: It is quite surprising.

MRS. ALLEN: Oh, but Bath is such a nice place after all. I assure you I did not half like coming away. Mrs. Thorpe's being there was such a comfort to us, was it not? You know, both you and I were quite forlorn at first.

CATHERINE: Yes, but that did not last long.

MRS. ALLEN: My dear, do not you think these silk gloves wear well? I put them on new the first time of our going to the Assembly Rooms. Do you remember that evening?

CATHERINE: *(Remembering.)* Oh, perfectly!

MRS. ALLEN: Mr. Tilney drank tea with us. I always thought him a great addition. I have a notion you danced with him. I remember I had on my favorite gown. But really, I do not have patience with the General. Mrs. Morland, you never saw a better-bred man in your life. His lodgings were taken the very day after he left them. But no wonder, Milsom Street, you know.

(CATHERINE crosses to the audience. The lights narrow on her.)

CATHERINE: I can keep my mind on nothing but thoughts of Henry Tilney. He must have arrived at Northanger Abbey by now and heard of my departure. I can neither sit still nor employ myself ten minutes together for thinking of him.

MRS. MORLAND: *(Interrupts CATHERINE.)* Catherine, I am afraid you are growing quite a fine lady. I do not know when your poor father's cravats would be done, if he had no friend but you. Your head runs too much upon Bath. You know, there is a time for everything—a time for balls and plays and a time for work. You have had a long run of amusement—now you must try and be useful.

CATHERINE: My head does not run upon Bath... much.

MRS. MORLAND: I hope, Catherine, you are not getting out of humor with home because it is not so grand as Northanger. That would be turning your visit into an evil, indeed. Wherever you are you should always be contented, especially at home, because there you must spend most of your time. I did not quite like at breakfast to hear you talk so much of the French bread at Northanger.

CATHERINE: It is all the same to me what I eat.

(MR. MORLAND enters. He has a book in his hand. He motions to HIS WIFE.)

MRS. MORLAND: Ah, here is your father. Now I want to see you apply yourself to your needlework. *(Crosses to him.)*

MR. MORLAND: Is this the book you meant?

MRS. MORLAND: I believe so, yes. Here it is. This is a very clever essay about young girls who have been spoilt for home by having great acquaintance. I am sure it will do her good. There is no time to lose in attacking so dreadful a malady.

(A SERVANT enters, showing HENRY TILNEY into the room, and exits.)

CATHERINE: *(Jumping up.)* Henry!

(They go to one another, taking hands.)

HENRY: Catherine, I had to see myself that you were safely home.

CATHERINE: Mama, Papa, this is Mr. Henry Tilney.

HENRY: *(Bows to them.)* Mr. Morland, Mrs. Morland, Pardon my intrusion. I know that I have little right to expect a welcome at Fullerton. My only concern is that Miss Morland had reached home in safety.

MR. MORLAND: Nonsense, dear boy, any friend of our children is always welcome here. Do not speak another word of the past.

(CATHERINE is beaming. She and HENRY smile and look at one another. MRS. MORLAND perceives and drops the book with a sigh.)

HENRY: Catherine, I have something for you. Eleanor said you had left them in your room.

(He hands her the Udolpho *volumes.)*

CATHERINE: Udolpho! How kind of you to bring them to me. I did not realize I'd left them. In my haste I must have forgotten to pack them… *(Stops.)*

HENRY: Catherine, what you must have suffered.

CATHERINE: Henry…

HENRY: Why was I not there?

CATHERINE: What have I done to offend the General so?

HENRY: Oh, Catherine, Mr. and Mrs. Morland, I am ashamed to say it. You are guilty of no greater crime than being less rich than he thought you were.

CATHERINE: Rich?

HENRY: It was all John Thorpe's doing.

CATHERINE: I don't understand.

MR. MORLAND: Mr. Thorpe? What has he to do with it?

HENRY: In Bath he tried to impress my father by speaking of your family's great wealth. He also told the General that Catherine was the heiress to the Allens' estate. My father believed Thorpe because he told him he intended to marry Catherine.

CATHERINE: Oh!

HENRY: Eleanor and I knew nothing of this. My father courted Catherine's acquaintance, invited her to Northanger, and even desired her for his daughter-in-law due to this belief.

(CATHERINE looks down.)

MRS. MORLAND: Imagine, my Catherine an heiress. What a notion.

HENRY: In London, my father ran into John Thorpe again who on this occasion informed my father that he had been entirely misled as to Miss Morland's wealth and position. That the Allens had another heir and that your family (if you will pardon me) was actually penniless and scheming for wealthy connections.

MRS. MORLAND: Well, I never!

MR. MORLAND: Despicable fellow!

MRS. MORLAND: Infamous! Penniless, indeed. Catherine, I hope that your brother has nothing more to do with this dreadful Mr. Thorpe or his deceitful sister.

CATHERINE: Mama, he has not.

HENRY: I am ashamed to say that you know the rest. I have quarreled with my father and have myself been banished from Northanger Abbey and from his sight.

CATHERINE: But, Henry, why?

HENRY: Because of my firm resolution of coming here and offering my hand in marriage to Miss Catherine Morland—if she will have me?

CATHERINE: *(Jumping up.)* Oh yes, Henry! Yes, yes, yes, oh yes, indeed yes, yes—if my parents have no objections.

MR. MORLAND: Great heavens, what a business.

MRS. MORLAND: I hardly know what to say.

MR. MORLAND: You say that your father absolutely refuses his consent to this marriage?

HENRY: It pains me to say so.

MR. MORLAND: If I may be so bold as to speak for my wife, allow me to declare that we ourselves would have no objections to your alliance…

(HENRY and CATHERINE are overjoyed.)

MR. MORLAND: However, while the General expressly forbids the connection, we cannot sanction it.

CATHERINE: Papa!

MR. MORLAND: All we should require, Mr. Tilney, is your father's consent.

HENRY: I understand, sir. Catherine, my father cannot hold out forever. Perhaps in time he will indeed grant his consent.

(As CATHERINE crosses to the audience, HENRY shakes MR. MORLAND's hand and bows to MRS. MORLAND. They exit.)

CATHERINE: To have my happiness so close at hand only to have it dashed to pieces in a matter of moments. To think that the General will freely give us his consent is impossible!

HENRY: *(Crosses to her.)* I must return to Woodston.

CATHERINE: How cruelly they have divided us!

HENRY: Now, Catherine, do not be so dramatic. Your parents are sensible and generous people. I like them exceedingly well. I am not surprised by their decision nor can I resent it.

CATHERINE: I know you are right.

HENRY: We can only hope for the best, wait and see what time will bring. Goodbye, my sweet love.

CATHERINE: I cannot bear to be parted with you.

HENRY: But part we must.

CATHERINE: Farewell, have a safe journey.

HENRY: *(Very close, then pulling away.)* Farewell…

CATHERINE: Oh, my heart is breaking! And to think I only suspected General Tilney of murder!— I never once suspected him as the destroyer of my future happiness. Never has time passed more slowly. Henry's correspondence is always cheerful but never completely eases my regret at being parted from him. My only solace is reading. I finally finished *The Mysteries of Udolpho.*

(LUDOVICO and ANNETTE enter. Projection: The Mysteries of Udolpho.)

ANNETTE: With your blessing, ma'amselle, Ludovico and I shall be married next week.

CATHERINE: *(As EMILY.)* Of course, my dear dear, Annette. I wish you both all the happiness in the world. Ludovico, I owe you my life. I hope that you will be happy in your new life here in France.

LUDOVICO: Our happiness stems from your generosity, ma'amselle. We are proud to be appointed steward and head housekeeper at your father's ancient family estate. It is an honor to serve you.

ANNETTE: Ludovico has promised that we shall never have to set foot in Italy again.

CATHERINE: *(As EMILY.)* Ludovico, Annette, I happily join with you in that promise.

(ANNETTE curtsies, LUDOVICO bows, and they go out laughing and holding hands. VALANCOURT enters.)

VALANCOURT: Emily.

CATHERINE: *(As EMILY.)* Valancourt.

VALANCOURT: It is finally over. I have received word that Montoni is dead.

CATHERINE: *(As EMILY.)* How?

VALANCOURT: He was captured by Count Morano and the soldiers, tried for his crimes, and executed.

CATHERINE: *(As EMILY.)* I can scarcely believe it is all over. That we have found one another and our happiness is complete.

VALANCOURT: My happiness shall not be complete until you and I are united as one in holy matrimony.

(VALANCOURT and CATHERINE [as EMILY] kiss. CATHERINE pulls away.)

CATHERINE: Oh dear, stop, stop—this will not do.

VALANCOURT: Emily, my dearest love! My treasure…

CATHERINE: I am not Emily! And you, sir, are not real. Do go away.

VALANCOURT: But.

CATHERINE: Heavens, don't look at me that way, just be off with you. Go on.

(VALANCOURT walks off dejectedly. Projection: Fullerton.)

CATHERINE: You are not my Henry. My Henry is far, far away. I am so cursedly aware that real life goes about its way nothing like what is written in books. But that does not stop this heroine from wishing for a happy ending. I want my hero. I want a happy ending!

(MRS. MORLAND enters.)

MRS. MORLAND: My dear, a letter has just come for you by post. I do believe it is from Mr. Tilney.

(She gives CATHERINE the letter and crosses off.)

CATHERINE: Mother is always so obliging. This letter, indeed, contains news of a most remarkable event that happily alters the lives of so many. *(In a solemn tone.)* The untimely and tragic demise of the Viscount Basilton. Isn't it wonderful! Mr. Francis Harwood inherited the title and fortune of his elder brother and General Tilney no longer has reason to prevent his marriage to Eleanor. On the contrary, he never loved his daughter more than the first time he addressed her as "Your Ladyship." Henry says the course of events have thrown the General into a fit of good humor from which he is unlikely to recover. He grants his permission for us to marry and is pleased to discover that instead of being penniless as Mr. Thorpe had asserted, I am to have three thousand pounds upon our marriage. He has also discovered that the Allens are indeed free to dispose of their fortune on whomever they please and he is at present happily engaged in greedy speculation. *(Kisses the letter.)* I shall keep this letter, the tidings of my future happiness, for the whole of my life.

(HENRY enters. They embrace.)

HENRY: Catherine, dearest!

CATHERINE: Henry!

HENRY: I have some dreadful, dreadful news. The General has retracted! He now refuses his consent.

CATHERINE: On what grounds!?!

HENRY: *(Very serious.)* Because there shall be no cheesecakes at the wedding.

CATHERINE: *(Beside herself.)* No cheesecakes?!? Henry Tilney, how can you tease me at such a time as this!?!

HENRY: *(Grins and laughs.)* You should have seen your expression.

CATHERINE: You great brute!

(She chases him around a piece of furniture, laughing.)

HENRY: You must not believe everything I say!

CATHERINE: And you a clergyman!

(She catches him and he kisses her. She calms down and laughs.)

CATHERINE: You are nothing at all like any hero I ever imagined and I shall love you with all of my heart for the rest of my days.

HENRY: My darling Catherine.

(They kiss. MR. and MRS. MORLAND have entered off to the side.)

MR. MORLAND: *(Tearing up.)* They shall make a very happy couple.

MRS. MORLAND: Oh, yes.— She shall make a sad, heedless, young housekeeper to be sure, but then… there is nothing like practice is there, dear?

MR. MORLAND: A very happy couple, indeed.

(Music, lights, curtain call.)

(Finis.)

BACKGROUND NOTES

JANE AUSTEN (1775–1817): Long considered one of the greatest authors in the English language, Jane Austen did not in her own lifetime achieve notoriety, fame, and popularity equal to that of Ann Radcliffe. In fact, her novels were published anonymously until after her death. Jane Austen was the youngest daughter of an English country rector and a happy member of a large family. She never married by choice and died untimely of Addison's disease at the age of forty-two. *Northanger Abbey* was first written in 1798 and sold to Crosby & Son under the title of "Susan." It was never published. She later bought back the novel and revised it to its present version, which was not published until after her death in 1818. Austen's other novels include *Sense and Sensibility* (1811), *Pride and Prejudice* (1813), *Mansfield Park* (1814), *Emma* (1815), and *Persuasion*, also published after her death in 1818.

ANN RADCLIFFE (1764–1823): Ann Radcliffe was born Ann Ward, daughter to a gentleman in "trade" in London. She was brought up in easy circumstances and married William Radcliffe, a political journalist in 1787. Her writing talents were first recognized with the publication of *A Sicilian Romance* in 1790. *An Italian Romance* and *Romance of the Forest* followed in 1791. Her wildly successful novels *The Mysteries of Udolpho* and *The Italian* were written in 1794 and 1797, respectively. For years to come they became "required" reading for gentlemen and ladies alike. Sir Walter Scott considered her to be the first modern English writer of the poetical novel. Her method of combining horror with sentiment and the picturesque inspired dozens of imitators culminating in such Gothic classics as Shelley's *Frankenstein* (1816), the Brontë sisters' *Jane Eyre* and *Wuthering Heights* (both 1847), and Stoker's *Dracula* (1897). She did not write much after 1797. Her last novel, *Gaston de Blondeville*, was not published until 1826, three years after her death. She suffered from spasmodic asthma and died of a sudden attack in 1823.

Jane Austen's *Northanger Abbey* was written as a satire on the Gothic romance novels which were so popular in her day. I was inspired to include Catherine's *Udolpho* fantasies in this adaptation because modern audiences are unlikely to be familiar with the work of Radcliffe (who, unlike Jane Austen, has fallen into relative obscurity). Ann Radcliffe was one of the most celebrated and widely read authors of the period. In her novel, Jane Austen's recurring references to *The Mysteries of Udolpho* were reliably based on the presumption that the reader would be well acquainted with the particulars of Radcliffe's work. In this stage adaptation, Miss Catherine Morland and the audience simultaneously discover Radcliffe's novel. The sharply contrasting worlds of the authors give free reign to Austen's wit and comic genius.

PRODUCTION NOTES

The action of *Northanger Abbey, A Romantic Gothic Comedy* occurs February–March of 1803. Radcliffe set *The Mysteries of Udolpho* in the sixteenth century, but for the purposes of this adaptation, Catherine's *Udolpho* fantasies should be set in a period of history at least a hundred (or more) years earlier than 1803. Costuming should clearly reflect two entirely different periods of history.

The running time should be approximately two hours and thirty minutes with an intermission. The pace should be brisk throughout as Catherine is whirled from one adventure to the next. When approaching the English accents, beware of using French pronunciations for French words (e.g., equipage) as Americans are so apt to do—use the "anglicized" pronunciations of these words. Be careful not to give in to the temptation of "camping up" the Udolpho scenes. Play them with one-hundred-percent commitment and sincerity and the humor will spring from the situations.

CASTING BREAKDOWNS

THE MINIMUM: *Northanger Abbey* can be performed with a minimum of eleven speaking roles and four non-speaking roles (eight women and seven men total), employing quick changes.

Catherine Morland (Emily St. Aubert)
Mr. Morland/St. Aubert/Mr. Allen
Mrs. Morland/Mrs. Thorpe/Pump Room Visitor
Henry Tilney/Chevalier Valancourt
Mrs. Allen/Madame Cheron
Amy/Annette/Mary/Dancer
James Morland/Ludovico/Frederick Tilney/Dancer
General Tilney/ Montoni/Pump Room Visitor
Isabella Thorpe/Signor Livona/Visitor
John Thorpe/Count Morano/Pump Room Visitor
Eleanor Tilney/ Dancer/ Pump Room Visitor
Two men and two women for Servants, Dancers, Pump Room Visitors, Ghouls, and Swordsmen

ESSENTIAL DOUBLE CASTING: If budgets were to allow, ideally only the parallel characters in the parallel worlds of Austen and Radcliffe would be double cast:

Catherine Morland (Emily St. Aubert)	Mr. Morland/St. Aubert
Henry Tilney/Chevalier Valancourt	Mrs. Allen/Madame Cheron
General Tilney/Montoni	Isabella Thorpe/Signora Livona
Amy/Annette	John Thorpe/Count Morano
James Morland/Ludovico	

Characters in Austen's world only:

Eleanor Tilney	Mrs. Morland
Mr. Allen	Mrs. Thorpe
Mary	Frederick Tilney
A host of Servants, Dancers, Pump Room Visitors, Ghouls, and Swordsmen	

As the above is neither practical nor realistic in terms of most theatres today, alternatively, the characters in Austen's world only could be cast within an ensemble of servants, dancers, Pump Room visitors, ghouls, and swordsmen. Solid character work and creative costuming would support whichever method best fits the realistic needs or restrictions of the theatrical organization presenting the work.

CHARACTER DESCRIPTIONS

Unless otherwise noted, all characters speak with English accents.

MISS CATHERINE MORLAND (EMILY ST. AUBERT): Catherine is a sweet, unspoiled young lady with a simple but genteel English country upbringing. She is understandably naïve but is also developing wit and vivacity. She is engaging and has great energy and enthusiasm, but her overly active imagination can lead her astray. She easily slips into fantastic daydreams and is, at first, ready to believe anything at face value. She adores Gothic romance novels and completely loses herself in Anne Radcliffe's *The Mysteries of Udolpho*. She identifies fully with its heroine Emily St. Aubert, who is virtuous, loyal, honest, noble, and possesses endless strength of character—though, when overcome with emotion, she often faints at the most inopportune moments.

MR. MORLAND/ST. AUBERT: Mr. Morland is Catherine's father and a clergyman in the Church of England. He is a good-natured family man with a kind disposition and a level head. He is also the proud father of ten children, of whom Catherine is the eldest girl. **St. Aubert** is Emily's father in Radcliffe's *Udolpho*. He is stoic but in failing health and very concerned over his daughter's welfare.

MR. HENRY TILNEY/CHEVALIER VALANCOURT: Mr. Henry Tilney is a young clergyman from a wealthy background. He has a very humorous disposition. He enjoys teasing those he loves but would never knowingly harm a soul. He is principled and possesses great intelligence and integrity. **Chevalier Valancourt** is the romantic hero of Radcliffe's *Udolpho*. He is hopelessly in love with Emily. He is handsome, noble, and valiant. The chevalier is every proper young lady's fantasy suitor.

MRS. ALLEN/MADAME CHERON: Mrs. Allen is a silly but kind neighbor of the Morland family in Fullerton. She and her wealthy husband are exceedingly fond of Catherine as they have no children of their own. Mrs. Allen is obsessed with fashion and is overly concerned with her appearance and attire. **Madame Cheron** is Emily's severe aunt in Radcliffe's *Udolpho*. She is the sister to St. Aubert and becomes Emily's guardian after his death. She foolishly marries the evil Montoni for wealth and prestige.

AMY/ANNETTE: Amy is the Allens' maid, a practical but kind country soul with a lower class accent. **Annette** is Madame Cheron's servant in Radcliffe's *Udolpho*. She is talkative, superstitious, and feisty. Her accent is the same as Amy's.

GENERAL TILNEY/MONTONI: General Tilney is handsome and successful but also a scheming, social-climbing snob. He is greedy and ambitious and has a sinister appearance and air about him. He would sacrifice his own children's happiness for financial gain. **Montoni** is the Italian villain in Radcliffe's *Udolpho*. He is evil incarnate—scheming and dangerous. He unjustly gained the Castle Udolpho and now plots to gain Emily's estates in France as well. He speaks with an Italian accent.

MR. JOHN THORPE/COUNT MORANO: John Thorpe is a handsome but obnoxious social-climbing, self-serving young man. He is a friend and fellow student at Oxford of Catherine's brother James. **Count Morano** is a hot-blooded young Italian nobleman in Radcliffe's *Udolpho*. He speaks with an Italian accent and is every proper young lady's fantasy rejected suitor.

MR. JAMES MORLAND/LUDOVICO: James Morland is Catherine's eldest brother. He is kind and as trusting in his way as Catherine is in hers. He is honest and believes the best in others. **Ludovico** is Montoni's clever Italian servant in Radcliffe's *Udolpho*. He has integrity and is brave and resourceful. He speaks with an Italian accent and falls for Annette.

MISS ISABELLA THORPE/SIGNORA LIVONA: Isabella Thorpe is John Thorpe's sister and a notorious flirt. She is extraordinarily beautiful but equally scheming, ambitious, greedy, and duplicitous. She has a talent for pinpointing and "falling for" first-born sons (and heirs). She hopes to marry for money and is every proper young man's worst nightmare. **Signor Livona** is an Italian courtesan and Montoni's mistress in Radcliffe's *Udolpho*. She also speaks with an Italian accent.

MISS ELEANOR TILNEY: Henry's sister and daughter to General Tilney. She is pretty and has genuine elegance. She is also intelligent but has a melancholy side to her nature. She suffers because of her father's controlling ways.

MR. ALLEN: He and his wife are the Morlands' wealthy neighbors in Fullerton. He is a kind and friendly fellow, very patient with the world around him. His health is not what it should be and he has been ordered by his doctor to Bath to take the waters.

MRS. THORPE: Mother to John and Isabella and also an old school acquaintance of Mrs. Allen's. She is a widow with no wealth of her own and so is very ambitious for her children's futures.

MRS. MORLAND: Catherine and James' mother. She is a practical woman of plain common sense. She is industrious and strives to be useful. She also has an excellent constitution, bearing ten children and running her home with great efficiency.

MARY: A friendly Irish maid at Northanger Abbey with a sympathetic ear.

CAPTAIN FREDERICK TILNEY: Henry and Eleanor's brother. He is also conceited and arrogant and every inch his father's eldest son.

THE MAN WHO LAUGHS

based on the novel by Victor Hugo

Kiran Rikhye
In Collaboration with
The Stolen Chair Theatre Company

KIRAN RIKHYE was born in New York in 1980, where she grew up in a family of devoted theatre-goers. She earned a BA in English literature and theater studies from Swarthmore College, where she studied with Allen Kuharski, Abigail Adams, and Ursula Neuerburg-Denzer; and an MA in English and comparative literature from Columbia University. Rikhye is the co-artistic director and playwright-in-residence of The Stolen Chair Theatre Company, a New York–based company which has produced eight of her plays, most recently *Stage Kiss* (May 2006, The Red Room). She and her Stolen Chair collaborators were honored as one of nytheatre.com's People of the Year in 2005. Rikhye also writes fiction to order at www.simonesdiary.com. She still lives in New York City.

The Man Who Laughs was first presented by Horse Trade Theater Group (Erez Ziv, Managing Director) in a Stolen Chair Theatre Company production (Jon Stancato and Kiran Rikhye, Co-Artistic Directors) on October 31, 2005, at The Red Room, New York City, with the following cast and credits:

Dr. Hardquanonne	Cameron J. Oro
Carlos	Dennis Wit
Esmeralda	Alexia Vernon
Young Gwynplaine	Ariana Siegel
Woman	Jennifer Wren
Ursus	Dennis Wit
Gwynplaine	Jon Campbell
Dea	Jennifer Wren
Duchess Josiana	Alexia Vernon
Lord David Dirry-Moir	Cameron J. Oro

Conceived and directed by: Jon Stancato
Music: Emily Otto
Set and Lighting Design: David Bengali
Costume Design: May Elbaz
Prop Design and Management: Aviva Meyer
Makeup Design: Arielle Toelke with Danielle Von Zwehl

Created by David Bengali, Jon Campbell, Aviva Meyer, Cameron J. Oro, Emily Otto, Kiran Rikhye, Ariana Siegel, David Skeist, Jon Stancato, Alexia Vernon, Dennis Wit, and Jennifer Wren.

To obtain a recording/sheet music of the musical score, contact the author. By email: info@ stolenchair.org. By phone: 212-410-2830. By mail: Kiran Rikhye, c/o The New York Theatre Experience, Inc., P.O. Box 1606, Murray Hill Station, New York, NY 10156.

CHARACTERS IN ORDER OF APPEARANCE

DOCTOR HARDQUANONNE, a *comprachico* ("child-buyer") and surgeon
CARLOS, a *comprachico*
ESMERALDA, a *comprachico*
GWYNPLAINE, a clown
WOMAN, mother of Dea
URSUS, a traveling player
DEA, an ingénue
JOSIANA, a duchess
DAVID DIRRY-MOIR, a lord

DIRECTOR'S NOTE

The Man Who Laughs was staged as a live black-and-white silent film, collectively created by The Stolen Chair Theatre Company and several of its collaborators over the course of six months. Although the scenario details nearly every single stage action, there are several features of the performance that should be described for the benefit of readers and any ensemble that seeks to mount its own production.

All of the production elements worked toward evoking, as realistically as possible, the experience of seeing a silent film, circa the late 1920s. As the audience entered our performance space, they were greeted with a paper bag of fresh popcorn. Positioned within the first two rows of the audience were two musicians in period evening dresses. A floor-to-ceiling black scrim, a few feet from the first row of seats, stretched across the entire stage. The lights dimmed, the musicians began playing their score, the sound of a film projector looped on the stereo system, and an overhead projector cast the first intertitles (in classic silent film font) and opening credits on the scrim, rendering it opaque. Behind this opaque scrim, the actors entered, hidden from the audience. The intertitles faded, and, as the lights were slowly brought up, the scrim revealed, through its grainy filmic mesh, the actors and set for the first time. Throughout the piece, whenever an intertitle was shown, the actors and set were concealed behind the scrim.

The set pieces, costumes, and makeup were designed to suggest, not the binaries of black and white, but a rich palette of colors that had been desaturated into a grayscale. The costumes were inspired by the period of Victor Hugo's novel (seventeenth-century France) through the inaccurate and romantic lens of a 1920s film costume designer. Wigs and hair were styled to evoke the fashions of 1920s stars like Lillian Gish, Buster Keaton, and Louise Brooks. Our makeup was modeled after the heightened styles of the German Expressionist films (*The Cabinet of Dr. Caligari* and others) and strived to remove all color from the faces while exaggerating features. The lights further enriched the limited palette of grays, whites, and blacks by washing the set and performers in warm sepia tones.

While its absence of spoken dialogue might designate *The Man Who Laughs* a movement piece, the production actually has, not one, but three texts: mouthed dialogue, intertitles, and, last but most certainly not least, the original score composed and performed live by Emily Otto. The score itself was modeled on the compositions of Charles Chaplin and the silent-era composers, who established mood through simple original melodies and a variety of musical allusions to classical music, jazz, opera, and traditional tunes and hymns. Our musicians used percussion instruments (cymbals, chimes, ratchet, et al.) to accompany the piano and provide sound effects to supplement the stage action. Just as changing a dance piece's music can alter the choreography's meaning, performing *The Man Who Laughs* without its original score could significantly alter the piece. When it is not possible to use Otto's original score, productions should try to provide live original music, lest the audience be left watching a silent film on mute.

Before beginning work on this project, many of my collaborators and I thought of silent film acting as an overly exaggerated pantomime, ripe for parody. Through our research, however, we realized very few of the films presented this sort of histrionic performance; the actors of original silent films had far greater subtlety than our cultural memory gives them credit for. As Norma Desmond says, "They had faces then." Our acting ensemble worked hard to emulate this facial expressivity (you may notice extended periods with few or no intertitles which depended entirely on the actors' ability to communicate narrative with their faces and bodies), and pantomime was only used when Dea, Gwynplaine, and Ursus perform their show "The Moor and the Maiden." Of course, in actual silent films, the face can be highlighted in close-up; we created our own "close-ups" by bringing individual actors downstage (right in front of the scrim, only a few feet from the audience seating), framing them in their own individual spotlight so that they could hold the audience's undivided attention. Although those who seek to mount this production should feel free to change individual stage directions, this is tantamount to rewriting a playwright's line and should be considered thoughtfully; regardless, the movement score should be fully and precisely choreographed in performance.

In addition to the difficulty of presenting a ninety-minute melodrama without uttering a single word, the project brought with it some other special performance challenges. The way the scrim must be lit to become translucent makes it impossible for the actors to see the audience; therefore, their only contact with the audience is through the composer's interpretation of the score. The actors can hear the audience but can never see them, a curious blend of film and stage acting. Though the musical score should be "set," it must be flexible enough (and the musical performer skilled enough) to adapt to any changes a given performance may necessitate (audience mood, performers' mistakes, etc.). The actors must work quite hard to resist the urge to lock their movement into the rhythm of the live musical accompaniment, which is a difficult temptation for those with dance training. And while the actors are moving about the stage, they must strive to be as silent as possible, right down to using felt on the soles of noisy shoes!

Finally, two of *The Man Who Laughs*' characters require particularly demanding performances. Gwynplaine, the eponymous hero, is, at the hands of sadistic gypsies, cursed with a permanent smile and laugh lines; thus, the actor performing this role must wear some (preferably comfortable) device to force his lips into a smile throughout the entire performance—laughing, crying, or screaming, Gwynplaine always wears a smile. Gwynplaine's adoptive sister and lover, Dea, is blinded as an infant in the snowstorm that begins the play. Her blindness requires that the actor abstain from eye contact with her fellow performers, which, without any external cues (speech, sound, etc.), makes it more difficult to establish the complicity necessary to achieve the production's complex choreography.

While we never imagined that a narrative play composed primarily of stage directions would ever find its way into an anthology of performance texts, we hope that the scenario for *The Man Who Laughs* may successfully evoke this unique performance experience.

—*Jon Stancato*

A NOTE ON THE TEXT

Projected intertitles are indicated in **bold.** Letters indicate sequential intertitles.
Silent action is indicated in *italics.*
Mouthed text is indicated in "quotations."
Sound cues are indicated in SMALL CAPS.

PRE-SHOW

1. **INTERTITLE**

a) Ladies, please remove your hats.
Gents, please put out your cigars.
And make sure that all cell phones are turned off.
This is a silent film, after all.

b) The Man Who Laughs

c) Cast of Characters (in order of appearance)
Young Gwynplaine, a Boy
Ursus, a Player
Gwynplaine, a Clown
Dea, an Ingénue
Josiana, a Duchess
David Dirry-Moir, a Lord

SCENE I: THE GYPSIES

1. **INTERTITLE**

a) Some people are born different.
Some people choose to be different.
Some people are made to be different.

b) This is a story about such people.

c) A cold December night on the coast of Cornwall, 1686.

A band of outcasts prowls the countryside, seeking unwanted children.

d) They are known as *comprachicos*, and they make their living transforming their innocent victims into profitable freaks. Misery always loves company.

2. *Lights up on DR. HARDQUANONNE, center stage. He stands before a log, a wrapped package raised over his head. Lowers it. CARLOS enters right. Pauses. Gestures offstage. Crosses to DR. HARDQUANONNE. ESMERALDA enters right, following CARLOS. COMPRACHICOS gather around the log (DR. HARDQUANONNE left, CARLOS center, ESMERALDA right). ESMERALDA reaches for the package. DR. HARDQUANONNE stops her. Pantomimes the upcoming surgery: Holds a knife in the air with one hand. Seizes his own face with the other. Carves a smile onto his face. COMPRACHICOS laugh and exit left. ESMERALDA pauses. Reaches for the package. Changes her mind. Exits left. Stage is bare. DR. HARDQUANONNE reenters left. CARLOS and ESMERALDA reenter left, dragging YOUNG GWYNPLAINE.*

3. YOUNG GWYNPLAINE: "Let me go! Please!"

DR. HARDQUANONNE: "Quiet, child!"

4. **INTERTITLE**
"We paid good money for you—
I intend to make you worth the investment."

5. DR. HARDQUANONNE: "We bought you fairly."

6. *DR. HARDQUANONNE laughs.*

7. **INTERTITLE**
"Scream, child, scream. Soon you'll be laughing."

8. DR. HARDQUANONNE: "Scream all you want."

9. *DR. HARDQUANONNE unwraps the package, revealing a glistening knife. YOUNG GWYNPLAINE screams. Tries to escape. ESMERALDA stops him. DR. HARDQUANONNE picks up the knife. CARLOS clears the log. YOUNG GWYNPLAINE tries again to escape. ESMERALDA catches him by the neck, forces him to the ground. ESMERALDA turns for approval to the other GYPSIES. YOUNG GWYNPLAINE tries to claw his way downstage. ESMERALDA grabs his leg. CARLOS grabs YOUNG GWYNPLAINE's arm. The GYPSIES pin YOUNG GWYNPLAINE to the log. They bind his arms with a scarf.*

10. *DR. HARDQUANONNE raises his knife. Quick tableau. Blackout.*

Lights up on the following tableau: CARLOS holds YOUNG GWYNPLAINE's face, DR. HARDQUANONNE works on the mouth, and ESMERALDA is turned away in disgust.

11. **INTERTITLE**
The sharp blade tears tender flesh. Under cover of night, the *comprachicos* slice and stitch. The gentle child is deformed forever.

A freak is born.

SIMULTANEOUS SOUND CUE: RATCHET

12. *Lights up on the following tableau: DR. HARDQUANONNE licks the blade of his knife. ESMERALDA is ill. CARLOS hovers over the YOUNG GWYNPLAINE.*

13. DR. HARDQUANONNE: "Let's go."

14. *CARLOS pulls YOUNG GWYNPLAINE to seated position. Unties his hands; throws the scarf at him. The GYPSIES begin to exit. YOUNG GWYNPLAINE curls up facing upstage. YOUNG*

GWYNPLAINE touches his face. Throws hands up in despair. Lowers them, turns slowly over left shoulder toward audience. Turns more…more… we can almost see his face… Blackout.

SCENE II: THE STORM

1. INTERTITLE
The Storm

2. *Lights up on a violent snowstorm. CARLOS, ESMERALDA, and DR. HARDQUANONNE stand upstage left, holding the rope of their boat, ready to board. YOUNG GWYN-PLAINE stands stage right. CARLOS and DR. HARDQUANONNE beckon ESMER-ALDA. ESMERALDA refuses to get on the boat. Gestures to YOUNG GWYNPLAINE. DR. HARDQUANONNE shakes his head. ESMERAL-DA indicates "money." DR. HARDQUANONNE brushes her off.*

3. INTERTITLE
"I don't care how much he's worth! With the king's warrant out for us, only a fool would travel with proof of our trade. Leave the child behind!"

4. *DR. HARDQUANONNE hits ESMERALDA. ESMERALDA looks to YOUNG GWYNPLAINE. YOUNG GWYNPLAINE reaches for ESMER-ALDA. ESMERALDA boards the boat. YOUNG GWYNPLAINE runs toward the boat. DR. HARDQUANONNE pushes him; he falls. DR. HARDQUANONNE boards the boat. YOUNG GWYNPLAINE is alone. He stands. Starts crossing downstage, bracing himself against the wind.*

5. INTERTITLE
The child is alone. The wind and snow are his only companions. Lost and without a friend in the world, he walks—he knows not where.

6. *YOUNG GWYNPLAINE is upstage right; he has been traveling for many hours. The rotting remains of a hanged criminal swing in the wind, downstage left. YOUNG GWYNPLAINE shields his eyes from the storm. He looks to the heavens. Crosses down left. Sees the hanged man. Retreats in fear, running upstage. Slowly he succumbs to the cold and to his fear. Curls up into a tiny ball on the ground, ready to die.*

7. SOUND CUE: FINGER CYMBAL

8. *YOUNG GWYNPLAINE hears a noise [finger cymbal]. Sits up. Sees a WOMAN lying in the snow beside him. YOUNG GWYNPLAINE crawls toward the BODY. Pulls himself upstage of the BODY. Brushes off the snow. He tries to wake the WOMAN. He shakes her. Pokes her. Realizes the WOMAN is dead. He notices there is an INFANT, still alive, in her arms. It is the INFANT's cries that he has been hearing. Peels one of the WOMAN's arms off of the INFANT. Picks the INFANT up. Wraps her in his clothes. Sits up on his knees, looking at the BODY. He closes the WOMAN's eyes. YOUNG GWYNPLAINE tries to stand, falls, tries again. Stands. Trembles. Walks center stage, hands up against the wind. YOUNG GWYNPLAINE wraps BABY DEA more tightly. Walks straight downstage against the wind. He keeps walking. Keeps walking… Blackout.*

9. INTERTITLE
Over untouched expanses of snow, he wanders, holding the infant close to him.

Little does he imagine that only a few miles away, he will find warmth and light…

SCENE III: MEETING URSUS

1. *Lights up on URSUS in his "little house on wheels"—a van in which he lives and which he transforms into a stage for public performances. Stage right is a bed. Upstage center is a door to the outside. Upstage left is a door to the kitchen. URSUS is seated down left, passionately playing the violin.*

2. INTERTITLE
Ursus…A misanthropic ventriloquist.

3. *Back to URSUS playing the violin.*

4. SOUND CUE: A KNOCK AT THE DOOR

5. *URSUS pauses. URSUS turns as though to stand. Reaches into his pocket. Removes a handkerchief. Wipes his bow. Keeps playing.*

6. SOUND CUE: A KNOCK AT THE DOOR

7. URSUS: "Leave me alone!"

8. *URSUS shakes his violin at the door. Dabs his head with his handkerchief. Returns to playing.*

9. SOUND CUE: MANY, MANY KNOCKS AT THE DOOR

10. URSUS *stamps his foot. He crosses to the upstage center door. Opens it to reveal YOUNG GWYNPLAINE and BABY DEA standing in the storm. YOUNG GWYNPLAINE's knees shake from the cold.*

11. URSUS: "What's the matter with you? Can't a man have a quiet evening to himself? Children are so rude!"

12. URSUS *turns to sit back down. Realizes that YOUNG GWYNPLAINE has not come inside. Gesticulates angrily. URSUS drags YOUNG GWYNPLAINE inside. Seats him on the bed, stage right. YOUNG GWYNPLAINE hops onto the bed. URSUS realizes that YOUNG GWYNPLAINE is shivering. URSUS mimics YOUNG GWYNPLAINE's shivering.*

13. **INTERTITLE**
     "Shiver, shiver, whine, whine… So my house is too cold for you, you lousy ingrate?"

14. URSUS: "What a lousy ingrate."

15. URSUS *exits left. YOUNG GWYNPLAINE's legs shake uncontrollably. He grabs one leg, then the other. URSUS enters with a blanket.*

16. URSUS: "What a brat. Now you're happy."

17. YOUNG GWYNPLAINE *reaches out a hand. He touches his stomach. Holds out his hand again. URSUS is exasperated.*

18. URSUS: "Now you're hungry?"

19. YOUNG GWYNPLAINE *nods. URSUS exits to the kitchen. YOUNG GWYNPLAINE waits for URSUS to return. YOUNG GWYNPLAINE hops off the bed; goes to the door. Realizes he is still wearing the blanket. Hugs it around himself one last time. Takes it off and leaves it on the bed. Crosses back to the door. Realizes he didn't fold the blanket. Crosses to the blanket; folds it while shivering uncontrollably. Crosses back to the door and opens it. Wind rushes in. URSUS reenters with a piece of bread. Gesticulates angrily. Closes the door. Sits YOUNG GWYNPLAINE back down (YOUNG GWYNPLAINE hops onto the bed). Wraps the blanket around him.*

20. **INTERTITLE**
     "Tell me—were you always such an idiot?"

21. URSUS: "Were you always such an idiot?

22. YOUNG GWYNPLAINE *unwraps BABY DEA. URSUS leaps back in surprise. Clutches his head.*

23. URSUS: "YOU BROUGHT A BABY??!!"

24. URSUS *gesticulates angrily. YOUNG GWYNPLAINE holds the bread to BABY DEA's mouth.*

25. URSUS *exits to the kitchen. YOUNG GWYNPLAINE cradles BABY DEA. Waits for URSUS to return. URSUS does not come back. YOUNG GWYNPLAINE waits. URSUS reenters, holding a tin coffeepot which he has filled with milk. URSUS snatches BABY DEA from YOUNG GWYNPLAINE.*

26. URSUS *feeds BABY DEA, using the coffeepot as a bottle. YOUNG GWYNPLAINE eats.*

27. URSUS: "There you are."

28. **INTERTITLE**
     "That's right; drink all you want. Drink it all, you greedy, pink, milk-guzzling little pig."

29. URSUS: "Drink it all."

30. URSUS *gestures to himself as though DEA has asked him if he would like some milk.*

31. URSUS: "Me?"

32. URSUS *gestures as though to brush DEA off.*

33. URSUS: "Nah. Don't worry about me."

34. URSUS *puts the coffeepot down. Gestures in front of BABY DEA's face. Notices that she does not respond. Gestures again.*

35. URSUS: "She's blind."

36. **INTERTITLE**
     "She's blind!"

37. URSUS *gestures to YOUNG GWYNPLAINE. YOUNG GWYNPLAINE looks up. His face is contorted into a hideous grin. URSUS is angered.*

38. **INTERTITLE**
     "You think that's funny? Stop laughing."

39. URSUS: "It's funny?"

40. YOUNG GWYNPLAINE *shakes his head. URSUS comes closer. Raises a hand to strike YOUNG GWYNPLAINE; stops. He realizes that YOUNG GWYNPLAINE's face has been carved into a permanent smile. URSUS takes YOUNG GWYNPLAINE's face in his hands.*

41.   URSUS: "Comprachicos!"

42.   **INTERTITLE**
       "Comprachicos!"

43.   *YOUNG GWYNPLAINE yawns. URSUS shakes
       his head. Gestures to YOUNG GWYNPLAINE to
       lie down on the bed. YOUNG GWYNPLAINE lies
       down. URSUS looks at him disapprovingly.*

44.   **INTERTITLE**
       **"You had a perfectly good opportunity to die in the
       cold. Just don't come crying to me when you realize
       how miserable life is."**

45.   *URSUS hands him BABY DEA. YOUNG GWYN-
       PLAINE and BABY DEA fall asleep. URSUS
       realizes he has nowhere to sleep. URSUS goes
       to his chair. Sits down. Grudgingly falls asleep.
       Blackout.*

SCENE IV: MORNING IN THE LITTLE HOUSE
ON WHEELS

1.   **INTERTITLE**
       Nineteen years later…

2.   *Lights up on URSUS, GWYNPLAINE, and DEA
       asleep—DEA sleeps on the bed (head stage left, feet
       stage right). GWYNPLAINE sleeps on the floor
       (head right, feet left) beneath her. URSUS still on
       the chair. URSUS has a handkerchief on his face.
       Inhales it slightly with each breath. Inhales too
       much and nearly chokes, waking himself up. Sits
       straight up in his chair. Shakes his head. Stands.
       Stretches. Does his morning calisthenics. Looks
       upstage. Is shocked to see that GWYNPLAINE and
       DEA are still there. URSUS is disgusted by them.*

3.   **INTERTITLE**
       "If only I had found a way to get rid of them…"

4.   *URSUS urges his CHILDREN to get up. They don't
       hear him. URSUS crosses to DEA and GWYN-
       PLAINE.*

5.   URSUS: "Up and at 'em."

6.   *GWYNPLAINE and DEA keep sleeping. URSUS
       yells louder. They keep sleeping. URSUS screams.*

7.   URSUS: "GET UP!"

8.   *GWYNPLAINE and DEA keep sleeping. URSUS
       shakes them. GWYNPLAINE and DEA wake up.
       Yawn. Stretch laterally. GWYNPLAINE props
       himself up on his left arm and yawns.*

9.   URSUS: "Good morning!"

10.   *URSUS takes DEA's face in his hands.*

11.   URSUS: "How's my little princess?"

12.   **INTERTITLE**
       "Good morning, Dea! How's my little princess?"

13.   *URSUS coos at DEA. Stops. Looks at her.*

14.   **INTERTITLE**
       "Your hair is a mess."

15.   *URSUS hands DEA a comb. URSUS kicks
       GWYNPLAINE's arm. GWYNPLAINE falls.*

16.   **INTERTITLE**
       "Gwynplaine! Get up and practice your juggling."

17.   *URSUS urges them to get up.*

18.   URSUS: "We've got a big day."

19.   **INTERTITLE**
       **"Idiots! Have you forgotten that today is the South-
       wark Fair?"**

20.   URSUS: "Idiots! Let's go!"

21.   *URSUS pats DEA roughly on the shoulder. Exits
       upstage left. GWYNPLAINE picks up his juggling
       balls. Begins practicing his juggling. DEA picks
       up her hairbrush. Crosses left, sits in the chair.
       She begins to brush her hair. GWYNPLAINE
       accidentally drops his juggling balls.*

22.   SOUND CUE: SMALL CYMBAL SPLASH

23.   *GWYNPLAINE notices DEA. Crosses to her.
       Stands behind her, slightly right. Takes her brush
       in his hand. GWYNPLAINE brushes DEA's hair.
       DEA's nightgown slips off her shoulder. GWYN-
       PLAINE stops brushing her hair. DEA slides her
       nightgown back up. GWYNPLAINE returns to
       brushing her hair. DEA's nightgown slips off her
       shoulder. GWYNPLAINE stops brushing her hair.
       Reaches for her nightgown. DEA reaches for her
       nightgown. Their hands meet. GWYNPLAINE
       retracts his hand. DEA slides her nightgown back
       up. GWYNPLAINE returns to brushing her hair.
       DEA's nightgown slips off her shoulder. GWYN-
       PLAINE stops brushing her hair. GWYNPLAINE
       reaches for her nightgown. GWYNPLAINE
       slides her nightgown back up. Kisses her clothed
       shoulder. DEA turns her head right, placing her
       face close to GWYNPLAINE's. She waits for his
       kiss. GWYNPLAINE slowly stands. He returns*

to brushing her hair. DEA pulls her nightgown off her shoulder. GWYNPLAINE looks at her exposed shoulder. DEA waits. GWYNPLAINE reaches for her naked shoulder. Pulls away. Puts her brush back in her hands. Turns to exit. Crosses back to the bed to get his scarf. Wraps his face. Exits upstage. DEA brushes her hair.

24. **INTERTITLE**
Thus they began every morning…

25. *Back to DEA brushing. Smiles. Keeps brushing her hair. Blackout.*

SCENE V: THE SHOW

1. **INTERTITLE**
a) **The Southwark Fair.**

The two-headed sheep is a central attraction. To its left, the puppets, then a snake oil peddler selling miracle wares.

b) **No longer a ventriloquist, Ursus makes a modest living by showcasing his foundlings.**

2. *Lights up on URSUS's stage. A large box sits stage left. A sign reading "The Laughing Man" sits stage right. URSUS enters.*

3. URSUS: "What you're going to see is amazing!"

4. *URSUS gestures broadly.*

5. *URSUS urges the audience to quiet down. He is nervous. He smiles, imitating GWYNPLAINE. Points to his smile. Laughs. Points to the audience.*

6. URSUS: "Don't laugh!"

7. *URSUS shakes his head. Starts to cry.*

8. URSUS: "It's a sad story."

9. *URSUS takes out his handkerchief. Wipes his eyes.*

10. URSUS: "A sad, sad, story."

11. **INTERTITLE**
"It's a sad story. Tragic, really."

12. *Back to URSUS wiping his eyes. URSUS crouches down and holds his hands out, pretending to be a small beggar child. Steps stage left to become an evil gypsy. Looks down at the imaginary little boy. Steps right to become the little boy again. Looks up at the imaginary evil gypsy. Steps left to become gypsy. Looks down at little boy. Advances on the*

little boy. Steps right to become little boy. Looks up in fear. Falls to the floor. Struggles. Holds up his hands. Gypsy hovers over boy. Whips out a knife with his right hand. Touches the tip of his left index finger to the tip of the imaginary blade. The gypsy slices the boy's face. Laughs maniacally. URSUS stands, still laughing. Points to the audience, showing them how they will laugh. Firmly tells them not to laugh.

13. URSUS: "It's not funny."

14. **INTERTITLE**
"Cold-hearted beasts! Don't laugh at him."

15. URSUS: "Don't laugh."

16. *URSUS crouches left of the large box. Cranks an imaginary handle as though it were a jack-in-the-box. Stops.*

17. URSUS: "Now don't laugh."

18. **INTERTITLE**
**"Whatever you do, don't laugh—
He's very sensitive."**

19. URSUS: "He's very sensitive."

20. *URSUS keeps cranking. GWYNPLAINE pops out of the box; his face is wrapped in a scarf. URSUS presents him to the audience. Exits. GWYNPLAINE faces the audience. Looks at them. Sways right. Sways left. Pulls three small scarves out of the scarf wrapped around his face. He begins to juggle the scarves. He drops one of the scarves. He removes the scarf around his face, revealing a fake pair of lips. He juggles the three scarves. Drops one. He removes the fake lips, revealing his real lips. He juggles two scarves and the fake lips. He lets the scarves drop, stops juggling. He faces the audience. He passes his open hand over his face. Tries to create a new facial expression. Passes his open hand over his face again. Tries to create a new facial expression. Faces the audience. Disappears inside the box. Blackout.*

21. SOUND CUE: PERCUSSION, CLAPPER (GWYNPLAINE'S CHEERING AUDIENCE)

22. *URSUS enters. Encourages the audience to applaud more for GWYNPLAINE.*

23. URSUS: "Now you will see a beautiful girl…"

24. *URSUS cradles an imaginary baby.*

25. INTERTITLE
"The precious infant grew to glorious woman-hood—but fate had dealt her a cruel blow."

26. *URSUS gazes blankly and serenely into the distance, pretending to be DEA. Waves his hand in front of his face. Opens his eyes.*

27. URSUS: "It's hilarious."

28. *URSUS laughs. Encourages the audience to laugh. Exits upstage right. URSUS reenters with DEA. In his hand he holds two pieces of wood. He puppeteers DEA as though she were a marionette. DEA turns to face downstage. Bows. URSUS waves his hand over her eyes, demonstrating that she is completely blind. DEA moves downstage center, doing passes. Tilts, raises arms, pliés, crosses left en pointe. URSUS turns her in a full circle. DEA bows. GWYNPLAINE enters upstage right, puppeteering himself. Dances to downstage center. GWYNPLAINE jerks himself left in one big jump, crashing into DEA. GWYNPLAINE jerks himself slightly right in one small jump, giving DEA some space. DEA and GWYNPLAINE lean in, kiss each other. GWYNPLAINE covers his mouth, turns away. URSUS brings DEA upstage. URSUS waves "goodbye" to the audience. GWYNPLAINE waves to DEA and URSUS. URSUS and DEA exit. GWYNPLAINE points at his smiling face. GWYNPLAINE takes a jump stage right. Takes a jump stage left. Winds up, does a barrel turn. Lands. Realizes his strings are tangled. Experiments to see which strings are attached to various body parts. Bites one hand free. Removes an imaginary knife from his pocket. Opens it with his mouth. Cuts one string: frees one leg. Cuts another string: frees the other leg. Cuts a third string: falls. URSUS enters left. Apologizes to the audience and crosses to GWYNPLAINE. He ties GWYNPLAINE's strings together. Pulls him to standing. GWYNPLAINE bows (to the best of his semi-puppeteered ability). URSUS drags GWYNPLAINE upstage. They exit. GWYNPLAINE, DEA, and URSUS reenter upstage. GWYNPLAINE and URSUS bow.*

29. INTERTITLE
A success!

News travels fast, and soon the name of the Laughing Man is on the lips of peasant and lord alike. The family hat overflows with coins.

SCENE VI: PEEL ME A GRAPE

1. INTERTITLE
While some misfits are grateful for a few pennies, others wallow in luxury.

2. *Lights up on the richly decorated bedroom of DUCHESS JOSIANA. There is a door upstage center. Upstage left there is a single chair. DUCHESS JOSIANA, wearing only a sheet, reclines on her luxurious bed, downstage right. She is eating grapes.*

3. INTERTITLE
The Duchess Josiana…

4. *DUCHESS JOSIANA continues to recline, eating grapes.*

5. INTERTITLE
Bored.

6. *DUCHESS JOSIANA continues to recline, eating grapes. DIRRY-MOIR enters upstage center.*

7. INTERTITLE
Lord David Dirry-Moir…A debauched dandy.

8. *DIRRY-MOIR crosses to DUCHESS JOSIANA and leans over her, trying to make love. DUCHESS JOSIANA throws a grape at him. DIRRY-MOIR tries to make love. DUCHESS JOSIANA throws a grape at him. DIRRY-MOIR gives up. Crosses to his chair. Throws his peruke to the ground in a snit. Sits, arms crossed.*

9. *DUCHESS JOSIANA looks at DIRRY-MOIR.*

10. INTERTITLE
"Dirry-Moir…"

11. DUCHESS JOSIANA: "Dirry-Moir."

12. *DUCHESS JOSIANA puts down her grapes. Sits up.*

13. DUCHESS JOSIANA: "Dirry-Moir."

14. *DUCHESS JOSIANA crosses to DIRRY-MOIR. Leans down behind him and whispers in his ear.*

15. DUCHESS JOSIANA: "Nasty mood?"

16. *DIRRY-MOIR shakes his head.*

17. DUCHESS JOSIANA: "Oh, Dirry-Moir…"

18. *DIRRY-MOIR pouts.*

19. *DUCHESS JOSIANA tickles her way down DIRRY-MOIR's torso. DIRRY-MOIR giggles, gains control of himself, pushes her away. DUCHESS JOSIANA pretends to lose interest. Crosses in front of DIRRY-MOIR. Pauses. Glances back at him. Gives up. Starts to walk away. DIRRY-MOIR stands. Grabs her. Seizes her shoulders and shakes her. DIRRY-MOIR towers over her. DIRRY-MOIR stands on his toes. DIRRY-MOIR towers over her some more. Gets bored. Lets her go. DUCHESS JOSIANA walks downstage. DIRRY-MOIR pinches her behind as he follows her. Stands right of her. DUCHESS JOSIANA slaps him. DIRRY-MOIR is pleased. DIRRY-MOIR slaps DUCHESS JOSIANA. DUCHESS JOSIANA is pleased. They look at each other. DIRRY-MOIR sweeps DUCHESS JOSIANA off her feet. DUCHESS JOSIANA strikes a seductive pose. DIRRY-MOIR deposits her on the bed, standing upstage of her. They move closer. Closer… DUCHESS JOSIANA rolls onto her stomach and DIRRY-MOIR sits up. They sit there.*

20. **INTERTITLE**
     Bored.

21. *Back to DUCHESS JOSIANA and DIRRY-MOIR. Still bored. DUCHESS JOSIANA offers him a bunch of grapes. DIRRY-MOIR takes them. Eats one. DUCHESS JOSIANA picks up another bunch of grapes. Eats one. They sit there. DIRRY-MOIR has an idea. Stands.*

22. DIRRY-MOIR: "I know what you need…"

23. **INTERTITLE**
     "I know what you need!"

24. DIRRY-MOIR: "I went to the fair…"

25. *DIRRY-MOIR gestures to depict a huge crowd.*

26. SOUND CUE: THE MUSIC OF URSUS'S BAND

27. *DUCHESS JOSIANA gestures dismissively. DUCHESS JOSIANA eats a grape. DIRRY-MOIR shakes his hands to show DUCHESS JOSIANA she doesn't have the whole picture yet. He dances, describing the music of URSUS's band. DUCHESS JOSIANA is bored.*

28. DIRRY-MOIR: "Then…"

29. *DIRRY-MOIR mimics DEA, describing her blindness. DUCHESS JOSIANA sits up.*

30. **INTERTITLE**
     "The blind girl is pretty in a poor sort of way, but the clown is the best part…"

31. *DIRRY-MOIR mimes juggling, describing GWYNPLAINE's act. DIRRY-MOIR turns to the audience, displaying a grotesque smile.*

32. DIRRY-MOIR: "He's a freak!"

33. *DUCHESS JOSIANA is extremely interested. DIRRY-MOIR shakes his head.*

34. **INTERTITLE**
     "Pity you can't go."

35. DIRRY-MOIR: "Pity you can't go."

36. *Back to DIRRY-MOIR and DUCHESS JOSIANA. DUCHESS JOSIANA clasps her hands.*

37. DUCHESS JOSIANA: "Please! Please take me."

38. *DIRRY-MOIR shakes his head.*

39. **INTERTITLE**
     "A noblewoman at a public fair? Think of the pickpockets.

     "You'll have to dress in common clothes if you want to go at all."

40. *DIRRY-MOIR shows her how plain her clothes will have to be. DUCHESS JOSIANA is horrified. She considers; smiles; gets up.*

41. DUCHESS JOSIANA: "I have a better idea…"

42. *DUCHESS JOSIANA crosses left to DIRRY-MOIR.*

43. **INTERTITLE**
     "I'd rather die than dress cheaply. I have a much better idea! They might steal from *me*, but they wouldn't dare rob Lord David Dirry-Moir."

     DUCHESS JOSIANA removes DIRRY-MOIR's coat during the intertitle.

44. *DUCHESS JOSIANA slings DIRRY-MOIR's coat over her shoulder. Saunters right. DIRRY-MOIR watches. DUCHESS JOSIANA turns her back to the audience. Slips DIRRY-MOIR's coat on. Removes her sheet so that she is wearing only the jacket. Turns around and models for DIRRY-MOIR. DIRRY-MOIR claps. Blackout.*

SCENE VII: KNITTING

1. *Lights up on DEA, seated stage left. She has just begun knitting a scarf. GWYNPLAINE sits on the*

floor next to her, staring up at her, holding her
yarn. GWYNPLAINE looks down at his yarn;
DEA turns to GWYNPLAINE. DEA turns back
to her knitting while GWYNPLAINE stares up at
DEA again.

2.   **INTERTITLE**
a)   **Outside they were ingénue and clown. At home they**
     were brother and sister. But in their hearts, Gwyn-
     plaine and Dea were husband and wife.

b)   **Gwynplaine loved nothing more than to sit at Dea's**
     feet, while she knitted. Sometimes he would sit for
     hours at a time…

DEA switches from short scarf to long scarf during
the intertitle.

3.   *Back to DEA and GWYNPLAINE. The scarf is*
     almost finished.

4.   DEA: Gwynplaine?

5.   **INTERTITLE**
     "Tell me what's happening outside."

6.   DEA: "What's happening outside?"

7.   *Back to DEA and GWYNPLAINE. GWYN-*
     PLAINE tries to cross to the upstage door, only
     to find that he is still attached to DEA's knitting
     and is jerked back. They laugh. GWYNPLAINE
     gives himself some slack. Crosses. Looks out the
     door for a while.

8.   DEA: "Gwynplaine?"

9.   **INTERTITLE**
     "Gwynplaine?"

     GWYNPLAINE crosses down center during the
     intertitle.

10. *Close-up on GWYNPLAINE staring out the*
     window.

11. **INTERTITLE**
     "Gwynplaine!"

     GWYNPLAINE crosses back upstage.

12. *Back to DEA, waiting. GWYNPLAINE is lost*
     in thought at the door. DEA tugs on the yarn.
     GWYNPLAINE does not notice her. DEA tugs
     harder. GWYNPLAINE looks up. DEA reels him
     in with her yarn. Kisses his hand. GWYNPLAINE
     moves in to touch her shoulder. DEA suddenly
     stands. Puts down her knitting.

13. DEA: "I have an idea!"

14. *DEA crosses right, points to the window.*

15. **INTERTITLE**
     "Let's go into town!"

16. DEA: "Let's go into town!"

17. *GWYNPLAINE shakes his head.*

18. GWYNPLAINE: "I can't."

19. *GWYNPLAINE picks up DEA's knitting. Hands it*
     to her. He sits DEA down on the bed. Goes down
     on one knee.

20. **INTERTITLE**
     "What would people think?"

21. GWYNPLAINE: "What would people think?"

22. *DEA stands, leaving the knitting on her seat.*

23. DEA: "You're ashamed…"

24. *DEA gestures.*

25. DEA: "To be seen out there…"

26. *DEA points outside.*

27. DEA: "With me?"

28. **INTERTITLE**
     "So it's true, then. You're ashamed of me."

29. *GWYNPLAINE shakes his head.*

30. GWYNPLAINE: "No!"

31. *GWYNPLAINE strokes DEA's face. GWYN-*
     PLAINE touches DEA's hand to his face.

32. **INTERTITLE**
     "What would people think if they saw someone as
     beautiful as you with someone as hideous as—"

33. DEA: "Oh, no!"

34. *DEA laughs. Strokes GWYNPLAINE's face.*

35. DEA: "Don't be so silly!"

36. **INTERTITLE**
     "What a sweet silly fool you are!"

37. *DEA laughs. GWYNPLAINE pushes her hand*
     away.

38. GWYNPLAINE: "You're laughing."

39. *DEA laughs more, teasing.*

40. GWYNPLAINE: "Laugh, then."

41. *DEA is confused. GWYNPLAINE stands.*

42. GWYNPLAINE: "That's right, laugh!"

43. **INTERTITLE**
     "You think I'm funny? You're just like everybody else!"

44. *GWYNPLAINE shouts in her ear.*

45. GWYNPLAINE: "Go on! Laugh!"

46. *DEA shakes her head.*

47. DEA: "No!"

48. *URSUS enters.*

49. URSUS: "What's going on?"

     GWYNPLAINE: "Father!"

50. **INTERTITLE**
     "What do you see when you look at me? A man or a clown?"

     GWYNPLAINE crosses down left during the intertitle.

51. *Close-up on GWYNPLAINE down left.*

52. GWYNPLAINE: "I don't want to be a clown. I'm more than that."

53. **INTERTITLE**
     "I've played the clown for the last time!"

     GWYNPLAINE crosses back to upstage center during the intertitle.

54. DEA: "Gwynplaine, what's happening?"

     URSUS: "That's absurd."

55. *URSUS gestures. Indicates "money."*

56. **INTERTITLE**
     "Think of the money we'll lose!"

57. URSUS: "Think of the money!"

58. *GWYNPLAINE turns to leave. DEA and URSUS stop him.*

59. URSUS: "Wait. I'll write you a new role."

60. **INTERTITLE**
     "If that's truly what you want, I'll write you a serious role. But remember, son—there is nothing nobler than knowing yourself, and no greater joy than laughter."

61. URSUS: "If that's what you want."

62. *GWYNPLAINE faces URSUS. He turns to leave again. DEA stops him. Holds out the scarf she has knitted.*

63. DEA: "Don't forget…"

64. *DEA wraps the scarf around GWYNPLAINE's neck. DEA strokes GWYNPLAINE's cheek. GWYNPLAINE touches his scarf.*

65. GWYNPLAINE: "Never again."

66. *GWYNPLAINE pulls the scarf over his mouth. Exits. DEA collapses to her knees. Weeps. URSUS steps closer to her. Pats her head. Blackout.*

SCENE VIII: THE MOOR AND THE MAIDEN

1. **INTERTITLE**
    The new show debuts.

    While Ursus puts the finishing touches on his masterpiece, the crowd eagerly waits for their Laughing Man.

2. *Lights up on URSUS's stage. The sign hanging stage right has been changed to read "The Moor and the Maiden." The box stage left has been turned to function as a bed. In an unlit corner downstage left, there is a chair. DUCHESS JOSIANA stands center stage in DIRRY-MOIR's clothes. She carries a pair of opera glasses.*

3. *DUCHESS JOSIANA swaggers right. Looks around. Swaggers left. Notices the bed stage left. Sits on it. URSUS enters right to begin the show. Sees DUCHESS JOSIANA. Shoos her away. Crosses down left toward her. DUCHESS JOSIANA stands. URSUS realizes that she is a nobleman. Apologizes; bows slightly. Invites her to take a seat. DUCHESS JOSIANA is disgusted.*

4. **INTERTITLE**
    "Sit out there? With the common people? I couldn't possibly."

5. DUCHESS: "I couldn't."

    URSUS: "What about up there?"

6. *URSUS gestures to a balcony above the stage. DUCHESS JOSIANA acquiesces.*

7. **INTERTITLE**
    They ascend to the balcony.

DUCHESS JOSIANA and URSUS cross down left to the chair.

8. Lights up on URSUS and DUCHESS JOSIANA standing by the chair.

9. DUCHESS JOSIANA: "Better."

10. DUCHESS JOSIANA sits. Looks through her opera glasses. URSUS gestures to the stage below, showing her the view. DUCHESS JOSIANA looks down through her opera glasses. Is pleased. Keeps looking. URSUS bows to her. DUCHESS JOSIANA pats him on the head; dismisses him. Keeps looking through her opera glasses. URSUS crosses back upstage. Lights down on DUCHESS JOSIANA, up on URSUS. URSUS greets his audience.

11. URSUS: "Tonight, ladies and gentleman, you will see a most remarkable spectacle. A spectacle so moving you will weep."

12. URSUS is moved. Pounds his chest. Looks out to the audience.

13. INTERTITLE
    "The piece is taken after a certain Shakespeare—but his was a more sordid time. You will find the work has been pleasantly updated for our modern tastes."

14. URSUS: "It's by Shakespeare. Behold a blind maiden…"

15. MUSICAL CUE FOR DEA'S ENTRANCE

16. DEA enters upstage right, wearing a long scarf. URSUS emphasizes DEA's beauty and purity for the audience. Reiterates what a touching story this will be. DEA pretends to feel her way to the bed stage right, exaggerating her blindness. Sits. URSUS displays her to the audience.

17. URSUS: "The maiden sleeps."

18. DEA yawns. Stretches. "Falls asleep" still sitting upright. Close-up on DUCHESS JOSIANA. She yawns. She is bored silly. Back to URSUS and DEA. URSUS shows the audience how moved he is by DEA's beauty. Prepares the audience for GWYNPLAINE's entrance.

19. URSUS: "The jealous husband!"

20. INTERTITLE
    "The Jealous Husband!"

21. URSUS introduces GWYNPLAINE with a gesture. GWYNPLAINE enters from up right. URSUS

crosses to him. Reveals GWYNPLAINE's smile. Close-up on DUCHESS JOSIANA. She sits up; puts her hand on her heart. Breathes heavily. Back to URSUS, GWYNPLAINE, and DEA. URSUS exits. GWYNPLAINE crosses down right.

22. INTERTITLE
    "Who can tell why my love hath betrayed me?"

23. GWYNPLAINE: "Who can tell why my love hath betrayed me?"

24. GWYNPLAINE turns to wake her. Changes his mind. Turns away from her. Changes his mind again. Turns toward her. Changes his mind again. Turns out to audience. Is resolved to do the deed. Turns toward her.

25. GWYNPLAINE: "Desdemona!"

26. DEA wakes.

27. DEA: "Yes, my lord?"

    GWYNPLAINE: "Have you said your prayers?" (Hands together in prayer.)

    DEA: "Why, my lord?"

    GWYNPLAINE: "Tonight you will die. Make peace with your God." (Hand up to heaven, coming down in a fist of rage.)

28. URSUS enters. Crosses right of GWYNPLAINE and DEA. URSUS bites his nails to highlight the tension of the situation.

29. INTERTITLE
    "What will happen? What will become of her?"

30. Back to URSUS. URSUS exits. DEA nods. Gets down on her knees (stage right of the bed, her back turned to GWYNPLAINE) and prays. GWYNPLAINE walks toward her. Turns away in a moment of anguish. Walks toward her again. Turns toward the audience in a moment of anguish. Walks toward her. Pauses. GWYNPLAINE reaches for DEA. Seizes DEA's scarf, begins to strangle her. Close-up on DUCHESS JOSIANA. Her right hand clutches her head. She breathes heavily.

31. INTERTITLE
    Beauty finds a Beast.

32. Back to DUCHESS. Back to GWYNPLAINE strangling DEA. URSUS enters. Crouches beneath DEA's scarf, between GWYNPLAINE and DEA.

33. URSUS: "What will happen?"

34. *URSUS wiggles his hands frantically to highlight the suspense. URSUS exits. GWYNPLAINE continues to strangle DEA. URSUS enters as a third character (wearing a hat).*

35. URSUS: "Stop!"

36. *GWYNPLAINE releases DEA.*

37. GWYNPLAINE: "Who are you?"

    URSUS: "Your wife is pure. Forgive her."

38. **INTERTITLE**
"Your lady is pure as the lily. 'Twill pain thee to bring her harm, for your love is strong. Come, let us forget these trifles."

39. *Back to URSUS, GWYNPLAINE, and DEA. URSUS joins GWYNPLAINE's and DEA's hands. GWYNPLAINE and DEA look away from each other. Slowly look toward each other. Stand. URSUS, DEA, and GWYNPLAINE sing. They bow. URSUS sees the crowd is laughing. He encourages them to laugh louder. DEA thanks the crowd. GWYNPLAINE pulls URSUS aside.*

40. GWYNPLAINE: "Father."

41. **INTERTITLE**
"Listen to that."

    GWYNPLAINE crosses downstage right during the intertitle.

42. *Close-up on GWYNPLAINE.*

43. GWYNPLAINE: "They're laughing at me."

44. **INTERTITLE**
"They're laughing at me."

    GWYNPLAINE returns upstage during the intertitle.

45. *GWYNPLAINE turns to URSUS. URSUS brushes GWYNPLAINE off. Encourages him to accept the crowd's attention. URSUS collects coins in his hat.*

46. SOUND CUE: FINGER CYMBAL AS EACH COIN FALLS INTO THE HAT

47. *Close-up on DUCHESS JOSIANA. She throws a coin to the stage below. Back to URSUS, preparing to catch the coin. URSUS catches the coin.*

48. MUSICAL CUE AS THE COIN FALLS INTO THE HAT

49. *GWYNPLAINE rushes offstage. DEA and URSUS continue to bow. Blackout.*

SCENE IX: THE LETTER

1. *DEA lies sleeping on the bed in the little house, upstage right. GWYNPLAINE tucks her in. Watches her sleep. He removes his clown costume. Sits in the chair downstage left. Holds his head in his hands. Rocks back and forth.*

2. **INTERTITLE**
Alone. And still a clown.

3. *URSUS enters upstage center, carrying his hat. Smiles. Skips downstage. Throws coins from his hat. Skips around the room. GWYNPLAINE urges him to be quiet. Points to DEA. URSUS brushes him off. Shows him the money they have earned. GWYNPLAINE reaches into the hat, pulls out a coin.*

4. **INTERTITLE**
"If only this money were enough to buy my happiness."

5. GWYNPLAINE: "What about my happiness?"

6. *GWYNPLAINE throws the coin back into the hat.*

7. URSUS: "They're crazy for you."

8. *GWYNPLAINE turns his back on URSUS; crosses down left. URSUS approaches him. Taps him on the shoulder. GWYNPLAINE does not respond. URSUS grabs him more roughly by the shoulder. GWYNPLAINE does not respond. URSUS kicks GWYNPLAINE in the rump. GWYNPLAINE turns. URSUS hands GWYNPLAINE a letter.*

9. **INTERTITLE**
"The nobleman in the balcony sent this for you."

10. URSUS: "The nobleman sent this."

    GWYNPLAINE: "For me?"

11. *URSUS nods. Urges GWYNPLAINE to read the letter. GWYNPLAINE reads the letter, a close-up of which is projected as the intertitle.*

12. **INTERTITLE**
You are hideous; I am beautiful. You are a player; I am a duchess. I am the highest; you are the lowest. I desire you. I love you. Come.

13. *URSUS looks to GWYNPLAINE. URSUS takes the letter. Smells it. Hands it back.*

14.   URSUS: "What a fool."

15.   **INTERTITLE**
       "Nobleman! What I fool I am. Smell that perfume."

16.   *GWYNPLAINE smells the letter. Smiles.*

17.   **INTERTITLE**
       "She didn't laugh!"

18.   GWYNPLAINE: "She didn't laugh!"

19.   *GWYNPLAINE turns to exit upstage. URSUS stops him. Points to DEA. Shakes his head. GWYNPLAINE gets down on one knee.*

20.   **INTERTITLE**
       "If only I can find someone who won't laugh at me, I'll never be unhappy again! I'll come home and marry Dea! Oh, Father! I'll know I'm really worth something, after all!"

21.   GWYNPLAINE: "I'll come back; I promise."

22.   *URSUS shakes his head. GWYNPLAINE implores him. URSUS gives up. Turns away from GWYNPLAINE. GWYNPLAINE gets up. Hugs URSUS. URSUS brushes him off. GWYNPLAINE exits upstage. URSUS sighs. Crosses to DEA. Tucks her in. Looks at her. DEA wakes up.*

23.   DEA: "Where's Gwynplaine?"

24.   *URSUS gestures dismissively toward door to explain that GWYNPLAINE went out. Tries to get DEA to go back to sleep. DEA smiles at him. Takes his hand in hers. Feels the letter. URSUS tries to pull away. DEA takes the letter.*

25.   DEA: "What's this?"

26.   *DEA holds the letter.*

27.   **INTERTITLE**
       "Father—where is Gwynplaine?"

28.   *DEA waits for URSUS to answer. URSUS turns away. DEA smells the letter. Blackout.*

SCENE X: LAST DANCE WITH THE DUCHESS

1.   *Lights up on DUCHESS JOSIANA sitting in her chair, upstage left, right leg crossed over left, rubbing her knee. GWYNPLAINE enters upstage center, his mouth covered in DEA's scarf. He crosses down right. Looks at DUCHESS JOSIANA's bed. DUCHESS JOSIANA sees him. Watches him. GWYNPLAINE turns away as though to leave.*

Turns back to the bed. Touches the bed. DUCHESS JOSIANA is watching him. GWYNPLAINE turns toward her. Notices her. He waves.

2.   DUCHESS JOSIANA: "Come closer."

3.   *DUCHESS JOSIANA beckons him closer with her right hand (with a "come hither" finger). GWYNPLAINE approaches her. He looks back at the bed. DUCHESS JOSIANA beckons with her left hand. GWYNPLAINE comes closer. DUCHESS JOSIANA beckons with her right hand. GWYNPLAINE approaches until he is standing in front of her. DUCHESS JOSIANA extends her hand. GWYNPLAINE gets down on one knee. Takes her hand in his. Brings her hand to his mouth. DUCHESS JOSIANA lifts her arm, gesturing for GWYNPLAINE to rise. GWYNPLAINE stands.*

4.   DUCHESS JOSIANA: "Let me see your face."

5.   *DUCHESS JOSIANA waits for GWYNPLAINE to show him her face. GWYNPLAINE shakes his head. Turns away.*

6.   **INTERTITLE**
       "You'll laugh at me."

7.   *GWYNPLAINE shies away from DUCHESS.*

8.   DUCHESS JOSIANA: "How silly!"

9.   *DUCHESS JOSIANA gestures dismissively. She raises her hand to GWYNPLAINE's face. She touches his scarf. Faces the audience. She pulls GWYNPLAINE's scarf down. She closes her eyes. GWYNPLAINE closes his eyes. DUCHESS JOSIANA feels his face. GWYNPLAINE opens his eyes. She opens her eyes, turns to face him. DUCHESS JOSIANA stands, clutches GWYNPLAINE.*

10.   GWYNPLAINE: "You don't…"

11.   **INTERTITLE**
       "Why don't you laugh at me?"

12.   GWYNPLAINE: "You don't laugh."

       DUCHESS JOSIANA: "Who could laugh at you?"

13.   *DUCHESS JOSIANA unwraps GWYNPLAINE's scarf. She holds it. GWYNPLAINE looks at his scarf. Touches it. DUCHESS JOSIANA tosses the scarf downstage. GWYNPLAINE stares at it. DUCHESS JOSIANA watches him. She crosses downstage of him and to her bed, walking between*

GWYNPLAINE and his scarf. GWYNPLAINE shifts his gaze from the scarf to the DUCHESS. DUCHESS JOSIANA sits on the edge of the bed. Crosses her legs. She leans back. GWYNPLAINE comes closer to DUCHESS JOSIANA. DUCHESS JOSIANA pats her knee. GWYNPLAINE reaches out his right hand. DUCHESS JOSIANA grabs his hand as he is about to touch her knee. She pulls his hand up to her thigh. GWYNPLAINE retracts his hand. DUCHESS JOSIANA smiles. She taps her cheek. GWYNPLAINE leans in to kiss her cheek. DUCHESS JOSIANA turns her head as he is about to kiss her. She makes contact with his lips. GWYNPLAINE retreats upstage right of the bed. He faces the wall. Touches his mouth. DUCHESS JOSIANA waits for him. GWYNPLAINE turns to face DUCHESS JOSIANA. He sees her shoulder. He comes closer. He reaches out a hand. He brings his hand closer… He touches her downstage shoulder. DUCHESS JOSIANA breathes heavily. GWYNPLAINE bends down to kiss her shoulder. He brings his hand to her other shoulder. DUCHESS JOSIANA slides his upstage hand forward onto her neck. She places his hand around her neck. GWYNPLAINE stands, pulls away. DUCHESS JOSIANA holds his hand to her neck. DUCHESS JOSIANA leans back on her bed, pulling GWYNPLAINE with her. GWYNPLAINE buries his face in her neck. They "make love." DIRRY-MOIR enters upstage center. Walks left. Stops. Points.

14.   SOUND CUE: SMALL CYMBAL SPLASH AS DIRRY-MOIR POINTS

15.   GWYNPLAINE and DUCHESS JOSIANA stop making love. Take out to the audience. DIRRY-MOIR claps. GWYNPLAINE stands. Rushes stage left. DUCHESS JOSIANA sits up. DIRRY-MOIR crosses behind her. Crawls right of her, onto the bed.

16.   DIRRY-MOIR: "Go on; let's see!"

      DUCHESS JOSIANA: "No!"

17.   DIRRY-MOIR ushers her forward. DUCHESS JOSIANA rolls her eyes. Decides to ignore DIRRY-MOIR. Stands. Brushes DIRRY-MOIR off as she crosses to GWYNPLAINE. DIRRY-MOIR claps his hands. Sits at the downstage right corner of the bed, extending his legs left. DUCHESS JOSIANA stands upstage of the chair. Beckons

GWYNPLAINE closer. Pushes him into the chair. DIRRY-MOIR clasps his hands. DUCHESS JOSIANA runs her hand down GWYNPLAINE's chest. She kisses his neck. GWYNPLAINE tries to brush her off. Gestures to DIRRY-MOIR. DUCHESS JOSIANA gestures for GWYNPLAINE to pay DIRRY-MOIR no mind. DIRRY-MOIR gestures for GWYNPLAINE to pay him no mind. DUCHESS JOSIANA continues to kiss GWYNPLAINE. GWYNPLAINE stands.

18.   GWYNPLAINE: "Stop it."

19.   DIRRY-MOIR puts his feet down. Sighs with disapproval.

20.   DIRRY-MOIR: "Well you're no fun."

21.   GWYNPLAINE prepares to leave. He reaches for his scarf. DIRRY-MOIR snatches the scarf off the ground

22.   DUCHESS JOSIANA: "Stop it!"

23.   DIRRY-MOIR dangles the scarf in front of GWYNPLAINE. GWYNPLAINE tries to grab the scarf from him. DIRRY-MOIR wraps the scarf around his face. Mimics GWYNPLAINE's marionette act.

24.   GWYNPLAINE: "Stop it."

      DUCHESS JOSIANA: "Dirry-Moir, stop!"

25.   DIRRY-MOIR unwraps his face. Turns to DUCHESS JOSIANA.

26.   DIRRY-MOIR: "He's boring."

27.   DIRRY-MOIR sighs with disappointment.

28.   **INTERTITLE**
      "Didn't you hear, darling? Anyone who's anyone wants to copy that famous look. Even the servants are saving up for the procedure.

      "And we thought he was unique! It's all so dreadfully funny!"

29.   DIRRY-MOIR: "Absolutely *everyone* will look like him."

30.   DUCHESS JOSIANA turns away in disgust. DIRRY-MOIR laughs. Shakes his head. Throws the scarf at GWYNPLAINE as he exits upstage. GWYNPLAINE moves to follow him offstage. Turns back. Crosses to DUCHESS JOSIANA. Falls on his knees at her feet (right of her). DUCHESS

JOSIANA *looks down at him. GWYNPLAINE hugs her legs. DUCHESS JOSIANA begins to laugh. GWYNPLAINE looks up. Sees that she is laughing. DUCHESS JOSIANA pats his head. Feels his face. Pushes him away, still laughing. GWYNPLAINE stands.*

31.   GWYNPLAINE: "Don't laugh at me."

32.   **INTERTITLE**
       "Don't laugh at me."

33.   *DUCHESS JOSIANA continues to laugh. She stops laughing. Faces him as if to speak. Starts laughing again. She crosses right to the bed, still laughing.*

34.   DUCHESS JOSIANA: "You should go."

35.   *DUCHESS JOSIANA sits on the upstage left side of her bed. GWYNPLAINE turns to leave.*

36.   DUCHESS JOSIANA: "To think…"

37.   **INTERTITLE**
       "To think, I wanted you. And you're…*common!*"

38.   DUCHESS JOSIANA: "You're common!"

39.   *DUCHESS JOSIANA keeps laughing. GWYN-PLAINE stops just before he reaches the door. Turns, faces DUCHESS JOSIANA. He crosses to her. He seizes her arms. Shakes her.*

40.   GWYNPLAINE: "Stop it!"

41.   **INTERTITLE**
       "Stop laughing!"

42.   GWYNPLAINE: "Stop laughing at me."

43.   *DUCHESS JOSIANA continues to laugh.*

44.   GWYNPLAINE: "Stop laughing."

45.   *GWYNPLAINE tries to wipe the smile off her face. He covers her face with his scarf. DUCHESS JOSIANA pushes him away, still laughing.*

46.   GWYNPLAINE: "I said stop laughing!"

47.   *GWYNPLAINE presses the scarf to her face. DUCHESS JOSIANA stops laughing. She looks at GWYNPLAINE. She pulls him closer. GWYN-PLAINE pulls away. DUCHESS JOSIANA laughs at him.*

48.   GWYNPLAINE: "Why are you laughing at me?"

49.   *GWYNPLAINE pulls away. Covers her mouth with his scarf. DUCHESS JOSIANA pulls him closer. Writhes.*

50.   GWYNPLAINE: "Stop it!"

51.   *GWYNPLAINE continues pressing his scarf to her face. DUCHESS JOSIANA pushes him away. GWYNPLAINE holds her closer, still pressing his scarf to her face.*

52.   GWYNPLAINE: "Don't laugh at me!"

53.   *DUCHESS JOSIANA continues to push him away. Her body goes limp.*

54.   GWYNPLAINE: "Don't laugh!"

55.   *GWYNPLAINE continues to press his scarf to her face. He notices that she is no longer moving. He removes his scarf from her face. He releases her body. DUCHESS JOSIANA falls limply onto bed. GWYNPLAINE looks at her. He takes her face in his hands. Tries to wake her. He touches her hand to his face. He closes her eyes. He backs away from the bed. He breaks into a run and exits up center. DIRRY-MOIR enters. Sees DUCHESS JOSIANA. Approaches her, hoping for some fun.*

56.   DIRRY-MOIR: "Where's your friend?"

57.   *DIRRY-MOIR sees that she is not moving. Comes closer. Realizes she is dead. Embraces her limp body. Feels the scarf beneath him. Sits up. Picks up the scarf. Looks at it. He looks to the upstage door. Blackout.*

SCENE XI: THE MOOR AND THE MAIDEN REDUX

1.   **INTERTITLE**
      While Gwynplaine runs through dark and empty streets, life goes on for the family he left behind…

2.   *Lights up on URSUS's stage. URSUS enters. Comes downstage. Greets the crowd. Prepares them for the performance. Emphasizes how moving it will be. Emphasizes that they will cry. DEA enters upstage, wearing a long scarf. URSUS crosses upstage to DEA.*

3.   URSUS: "It's a huge crowd!"

4.   **INTERTITLE**
      "It's a huge crowd today! You and Gwynplaine will be a sensation."

5.   URSUS: "You'll be a sensation!"

6.   *DEA smiles.*

7.   **INTERTITLE**
       But Dea knew the truth: Gwynplaine had disap-
       peared, and with him, the crowds. Their only audience
       was a row of empty benches.

       DEA comes downstage during the intertitle.

8.   *Close-up on DEA.*

9.   DEA: "Yes, Father. I think we will!"

10.   **INTERTITLE**
       "Yes, Father. Yes, I think we'll have a wonderful
       show."

       DEA returns upstage.

11.   *URSUS crosses downstage. DEA crosses left. Pre-*
       tends to feel her way to the bed. Sits. URSUS dis-
       plays DEA. DEA yawns. Stretches. "Falls asleep"
       still sitting upright. URSUS introduces "The jeal-
       ous husband." He runs quietly downstage. Cheers
       and claps, pretending to be the audience. Crosses
       left. Cheers and claps.

12.   **INTERTITLE**
       "More! More! Give us Gwynplaine! Give us more!"

13.   *URSUS claps. He tiptoes back up left. Strides down*
       right, playing GWYNPLAINE's part.

14.   URSUS: "Why did she betray me?"

15.   *URSUS turns to wake her. Changes his mind.*
       Turns away from her. Changes his mind again.
       Turns toward her. Changes his mind again. Turns
       out to audience. Is resolved to do the deed. Turns
       toward her.

16.   URSUS: "Desdemona!"

17.   *DEA wakes.*

18.   DEA: "Yes, my lord?"

       URSUS: "Have you said your prayers?" *(Hands*
       together in prayer.)

       DEA: "Why, my lord?"

       URSUS: "Tonight you will die. Make peace with
       your God." *(Hand up to heaven, coming down in*
       a fist of rage.)

19.   *URSUS tiptoes upstage. He strides down right*
       of DEA. Bites his nails to highlight the tension
       of the situation. Strides upstage as though exit-
       ing. Tiptoes all the way downstage to become the
       audience. Covers his mouth in shock.

20.   URSUS: "Oh my!'

21.   *URSUS scoots stage left. Waves his arms in alarm,*
       still pretending to be the audience.

22.   **INTERTITLE**
       "Save the girl! Somebody help her!"

23.   *URSUS tiptoes back to stage right of DEA. DEA*
       nods. Gets down on her knees (stage right of the
       bed, her back to URSUS) and prays. URSUS
       walks toward her. Turns away in a moment of
       anguish. Walks toward her again. Turns toward
       the audience in a moment of anguish. Walks
       toward her. Pauses. URSUS reaches for DEA.
       Seizes DEA's scarf, begins to strangle her. Tip-
       toes as far as he can, still holding DEA's scarf.
       Strides toward her as though entering. Crouches
       beneath the scarf, which he is still holding up and
       pulling. Wiggles his free (left) hand to highlight
       the suspense.

24.   URSUS: "What will happen?"

25.   *Back to URSUS wiggling his hand to highlight the*
       suspense. DIRRY-MOIR enters upstage. URSUS
       stands. Returns to pulling DEA's scarf. Sees
       DIRRY-MOIR. Releases DEA's scarf.

26.   DIRRY-MOIR: "What's going on?"

27.   **INTERTITLE**
       "What's going on here? There's no one out there!"

28.   *DIRRY-MOIR crosses downstage, brandishing his*
       handkerchief.

29.   DIRRY-MOIR: "There's no one out there!"

30.   *URSUS gestures for him to keep his voice down.*
       Pulls him aside. DIRRY-MOIR strikes URSUS
       with his handkerchief.

31.   DEA: "Father!"

32.   *DIRRY-MOIR dusts himself off. Crosses down-*
       stage. URSUS runs to him.

33.   URSUS: "Who are you?"

34.   *DIRRY-MOIR pushes URSUS. URSUS falls. DEA*
       drops to her knees; protects her father. DIRRY-
       MOIR approaches them.

35.   **INTERTITLE**
       "So you're hiding him, are you? I'll find the murderer
       myself, then. As for you, you had better leave the city
       before nightfall or you'll regret it."

36. *DIRRY-MOIR points to DEA, then URSUS. Points upstage. URSUS shakes his head.*

37. DEA: "What about Gwynplaine?"

38. *DIRRY-MOIR smiles, indicating GWYNPLAINE. Mimes slicing his throat.*

39. DEA: "Father! What has Gwynplaine done?"

40. *DIRRY-MOIR pulls out a knife. Threatens DEA and URSUS with it. Gestures upstage with it. Spits on them. Exits. DEA faints. GWYNPLAINE enters upstage. Runs to URSUS and DEA. Touches URSUS's shoulder. Gets down on the ground, picks DEA up. Kisses her. DEA lifts her arm; places it on his shoulder. URSUS is happy; he smacks GWYNPLAINE on the head. Goes to pack up the "Moor and the Maiden" sign. Rolls it up. GWYNPLAINE shakes his head.*

41. GWYNPLAINE: "What are you doing?"

42. *GWYNPLAINE crosses to URSUS. Grabs the sign from him. DEA stands, crosses right. Urges them to stop fighting. URSUS reaches to take the sign back.*

43. **INTERTITLE**
"But son! What will become of us? Without our show we're nothing more than a band of outcasts."

44. *DIRRY-MOIR enters, awkwardly brandishing his knife. GWYNPLAINE shields DEA and URSUS.*

45. **INTERTITLE**
"So I've found you after all. You're coming with me."

46. DIRRY-MOIR: "You're coming with me."

47. *GWYNPLAINE reaches for DIRRY-MOIR's knife. They struggle. They accidentally stab DEA. DIRRY-MOIR steps back. DEA falls. GWYN-PLAINE catches her. Lowers her to the ground. DEA reaches for GWYNPLAINE's lips. As DEA dies in GWYNPLAINE's arms, URSUS charges DIRRY-MOIR. Swings the "Moor and the Maiden" sign at him (upstage). DIRRY-MOIR dodges and stabs him in the side in self-defense. URSUS staggers, holding the knife. Falls. URSUS dies. GWYNPLAINE looks at DIRRY-MOIR. Stands. Offers himself up to be killed. DIRRY-MOIR begins to creep upstage to exit. Suddenly he runs, exiting upstage. GWYNPLAINE collapses back to his knees. Looks to DEA. Looks to URSUS. Looks to the heavens. Takes the knife from URSUS's lifeless hand. He looks at the knife. Looks back to the heavens. Convulses; his body shakes... whether in laughter or tears we cannot tell... Blackout.*

48. **INTERTITLE**
Fin.

Part VI

FRESH LOOKS

In fin-de-siècle Paris a teenage Frenchman writes his first play, set in Poland. In golden-age Athens the leading Greek playwright writes the world's oldest surviving play, set in Persia. In postwar Europe, a middle-aged Romanian writes his first play—in French but set in England. And in twenty-first century America, three independent theatre companies take these works and create dynamic new adaptations of them that reflect the topsy-turvy quality of life in these United States during a War on Terror: part theme park thrill ride, part living nightmare. Alfred Jarry in *Ubu Roi,* Aeschylus in *The Persians,* and Eugene Ionesco in *The Bald Soprano* all grasped that if you're going to bring up in the theatre unpleasant topics concerning your society, it's best to set your plays somewhere else. Let the audience pretend that mass murder, military disasters, and the bourgeois pretension that denies both only happen to *other* people. John Clancy, the folks at Waterwell, and David Koteles, in *Fat Boy, The Persians,* and *Bald Diva!,* respectively, have all grasped Charles Ludlam's dictum that if you're going to confront people with the truth about their lives, you better make them laugh while you're doing it—or they'll kill you.

All three playwrights utilize similar cunning dramaturgical strategies: They rope their audiences in with a jokey outrageousness that feels like home to a Comedy Central–weened generation, but, by the end of each play, those watching have been deposited in far more unsettling territory. The Persian royal family surveys the shattered remnants of their once-glorious army and sing a lament suspiciously reminiscent of "Georgia on My Mind." The guppie couples in *Bald Diva!* implode in an orgy of gay camp references, which spew from their mouths like rainbow-colored vomit. And Fatboy practically spits his contempt at his audience while reminding us that the annihilatory urge he embodies is alive and well and living inside each one of us.

While this book is first and foremost a celebration of playwrights (and rightly so), I think it's important to note that each of these works was created in collaboration with the companies that first produced them. These plays were written on the bodies of the actors who originated the roles. I know this because I happen to know the artists involved and because I was privileged to have been the body on which David Koteles wrote the role of Tim Jackson-Smith in *Bald Diva!* In a theatre culture where playwrights are often shut out of the rehearsal process until production week (if not completely), the value of this level of collaborative work cannot be underestimated. The proof is in the results presented here. If anyone still questions the vitality and importance of the independent theatre movement, these plays should provide a resounding affirmative answer.

—*Tim Cusack*

BALD DIVA!

The Ionesco Parody Your Mother Warned You About

David Koteles
Conceived by Jason Jacobs with Jamee Freedus

DAVID KOTELES was born in New Jersey and raised in Los Angeles. He graduated Phi Beta Kappa and summa cum laude from Queens College, where he received a BA in English. He also holds an MFA in playwriting from Columbia University, where he studied with Anne Bogart, Eduardo Machado, Kelly Stuart, and Frank Pugliese. His plays include *Junebug* (Manhattan Class Company), *Bedbugs* (West Bank Café), *Alice, Mockingbirds* (both at Alice's Fourth Floor), *Still Life* (Alice's Fourth Floor; Ensemble Studio Theatre's Octoberfest), *Three Men Lie Naked on a Bed*, and *The Trick* (both at the HOMOgenius Festival, Manhattan Theatre Source). Two of his other plays, *Sleeping Giants* and *Two Old Farts Reading Shakespeare*, ran for over six months at the Front Row Theatre in Los Angeles. Koteles also writes a one-act play every year for "Cherry Picking," to benefit the Mottola Theatre Project. He is the author of five screenplays and three television pilots. His screenplay *Busboys* was a finalist for the Sundance Screenwriters Lab. Koteles frequently teaches playwriting to teens for the John C. Russell Playwright Lab at Andy's Summer Playhouse in Peterborough, New Hampshire, and creative writing to lesbian and gay seniors at SAGE/Queens in Jackson Heights, Queens. He lives in New York City with his partner of sixteen years, Joseph N. DeFilippis, an activist and the executive director and founder of Queers for Economic Justice.

JASON JACOBS is a director and writer, and the co-artistic director of Theatre Askew. He was born in Los Angeles. He holds a BA in English from Yale College, and an MFA in theatre directing from Columbia University, where he studied with Anne Bogart. His credits include *I, Claudius Live* (co-adapted and co-directed with Tim Cusack, Theatre Askew), *Vanya/Vermont* (created with Kathryn Blume, Burlington Stage Company, Burlington, Vermont), and the solo show *Poor Sport*, which he also performed (Miranda Theater, New York; Highways, Los Angeles; Orlando Fringe Festival). His directing credits include *The Tempest* and *The Cherry Orchard* (both at Columbia University), *Mario and the Magician* (Center for Contemporary Opera, New York), and *The Zen of Jock Itch* (HERE; Philadelphia Fringe). Jacobs was also the assistant director for the American premiere of *Angels in America* (Mark Taper Forum, Los Angeles). He is currently working with his partners at Theatre Askew to develop the Theatre Askew Performance Experience, a theatre education program for gay, lesbian, bisexual, transgender, and questioning youth in New York City. He lives in Manhattan with his partner, Jim.

JAMEE FREEDUS was born on March 28, 1969, in Buffalo, New York. She graduated from Columbia University with an MFA in dramaturgy. She studied there under the tutelage of Arnold Aronson, Anne Bogart, Brian Kulick, Jim Leverett, Andrei Serban, and Robert Woodruff. Her credits as a dramaturg include *A Moon for the Misbegotten* (director Mark Ramont, Hangar Theatre, Ithaca, New York); *The Transparency of Val* by Stephen Belber (director Sam Helfrich, La Tea Theater); First Look Festival: *The Jew of Malta, Arden of Faversham,* and *Volpone* (directors Brian Kulick, Erica Schmidt, and Michael Sexton, Classic Stage Company); *The Tempest* (director Jason Jacobs, Riverside Church); *Hamlet* (director John Gould Rubin, Riverside Church); *The Mysteries* (director Brian Kulick, Classic Stage Company); *The Duchess of Malfi: Parts I and II* (director David Levine, NYTW Studio); *Inky* by Rinne Groff (director Loretta Greco, The Women's Project); and *Jump Cut* by Neena Beber (director Leigh Silverman, The Women's Project). Currently, Freedus is the dramaturg for *Love Is in the Air*, a "silent film" for the stage inspired by the clowning genius of Buster Keaton, Charlie Chaplin, and others. She lives in New York City.

The world premiere of *Bald Diva!* was presented by Theatre Askew (Jason Jacobs and Tim Cusack, Co-Artistic Directors) on February 5, 2004, at The Red Room, New York City, with the following cast and production team:

Tim Jackson-Smith	Tim Cusack
Jim Jackson-Smith	Gerald Marsini
Mary	Matthew Pritchard
Craig Tyler-Martin	Jeffrey James Keyes
Greg Tyler-Martin	Terrence Michael McCrossan
The Fire Chief	Nathan Blew
Standby	Julio Vincent Gambuto

Director: Jason Jacobs
Dramaturg: Jamee Freedus
Set Design: Eric Flatmo
Costumes: Dan Urlie
Lighting: Charles Foster
Sound: Gerald Marsini and Matthew Pritchard
Graphics: Chris Kalb
Original Music: Matthew Pritchard and Isam Rum
Stage Manager: Misha Siegel-Rivers
Assistant Stage Manager: Jessica Pabst

A workshop production of *Bald Diva!* appeared as part of the 2003 Fresh Fruit Festival at the Clemente Soto Velez Cultural Center in New York City with the following cast:

Tim Jackson-Smith	Tim Cusack
Jim Jackson-Smith	Gerald Marsini
Mary	Matthew Pritchard
Craig Tyler-Martin	Anthony Dimodica
Greg Tyler-Martin	Terrence Michael McCrossan
The Fire Chief	Jamil Mena

The creators of *Bald Diva!* wish to thank these actors who helped develop the show: Peter T. Downey, Julio Vincent Gambuto, Kaleo Griffith, Armistead Johnson, Kenneth Lee, and Eric C. Thorsen.

Thanks to the following for their support: Anne Bogart, Ellen Burnett, Carrie Casselman, Columbia University School of the Arts Theatre Division, Juan Davila, Patricia Decker, Nunzio and Daisy DeFilippis, Jeff Domoto, the Field, Allison Fisichelli, the Fresh Fruit Festival, Philip Friedman, Chris Kalb, Claire Kolb, Allison Lucas, Evangeline Morphos, Jim O'Quinn, James Paulk, Project 400, Joe Trentacosta, Wendy Weiner, and Erez Ziv.

Extra special gratitude is extended to Tim Cusack for his essential contribution each step of the play's development.

A personal thanks to Jim Gaylord for his love and support. And the playwright would like to most especially thank Joseph N. DeFilippis for his immeasurable support and understanding throughout this process, and his constant love.

Bald Diva! began as a collaborative project at Columbia University's School of the Arts. To complete an assignment in a class studying Eugene Ionesco, co-creators Jason Jacobs, David Koteles, and Jamee Freedus used *The Bald Soprano* as a leaping-off point for an examination of the absurdities of gay culture in the Chelsea neighborhood of New York City. This joint effort yielded a one-act play, *Bald Diva!* Ionesco's original 1950 play examines the conflicts that emerge in a population after surviving ground-shaking trauma—Europe after World War II. With *Bald Diva!*, the team turned its focus to a radically different trauma and population—gay New York after the AIDS crisis of the '80s and '90s.

The creative team started with the premise that Ionesco's nonsensical language, characters, and structure revealed an anxiety about the complacency and vacuity of the postwar European middle class. Just as Ionesco critiqued the world around him, the *Bald Diva!* creators decided to look no further than their own backyards. They turned to Chelsea, a primarily gay community—a gay mecca, if you will—in New York City filled with bars, dance clubs, gyms, restaurants, and, of course, beautiful people. The creators then zeroed in on a segment of the queer population ripe for scrutiny and parody. *Bald Diva!* pokes fun at the values of a youth-obsessed, image-driven, upper-middle-class, urban gay population known as Chelsea boys, who after the ravages of AIDS, turned all their concerns to lifestyle, immediate gratification, and ravenous consumption. Seemingly worlds apart, the characters of both plays share a busy boredom, selfishness, shallowness, and amnesia to occupy themselves as they ignore the realities surrounding them.

Ionesco based his characters and much of his dialogue on a textbook designed to teach the English language. Similarly, the creators of *Bald Diva!* looked to the "instruction manuals" of the contemporary gay lifestyle: gay magazines, catalogues, disco music, porn films, and websites. Both plays borrow dialogue from popular culture in order to illustrate how this culture dominates our ability to express ourselves and communicate with each other. However, despite the serious intentions behind the project, the team never lost sight of an important Ionesco lesson: the power of farce to illustrate a point. Staged as a cartoon spectacle, the production evoked both Ionesco's Theatre of the Absurd and Charles Ludlam's Theatre of the Ridiculous, all the while commenting on the current Queer-Eyed trends of contemporary middle-class life.

After its initial performance at Columbia University, the play was developed in a workshop at the 2003 Fresh Fruit Festival, where it received an award for best play. In 2004, Theatre Askew produced *Bald Diva!* as its inaugural production. This production made several best plays lists and was nominated for a 2004 GLAAD Media Award.

—*David Koteles, Jason Jacobs, and Jamee Freedus*

Scene: New York. A typical Chelsea interior, with typical Chelsea modern Italian armchairs from Soho. A Chelsea evening. MR. JIM JACKSON-SMITH, a club boy, seated in his armchair and wearing club wear, is channel surfing the television set. Beside him, in another typical Chelsea modern Italian armchair from Soho and also wearing club wear, MR. TIM JACKSON-SMITH, a club boy, is holding a cosmopolitan cocktail. A clock bongs eighteen and a half times.

TIM: It's nine o'clock. It's too early to go out. You can't really be seen before eleven-fifteen. Except at the gym, of course. Or dining out. Or if you're cruising D'Agostino's. We've already had dinner. And we gave up desserts five years ago. The dogs have been walked. We have two Jack Russell terriers, Judy and Liza. That's because we live in Chelsea and because our names are Tim and Jim Jackson-Smith.

(JIM continues to watch TV.)

TIM: *Will & Grace* is a repeat.

(JIM continues to watch TV.)

TIM: *Queer As Folk* is a repeat.

(JIM continues to watch TV.)

TIM: Mary did the pumpkin ravioli really well tonight. Last time she didn't really do them well. I don't like them when they're really well done.

(JIM continues to watch TV.)

TIM: *Dynasty* went off the air in eighty-nine. I miss Alexis Carrington.

(TIM makes a catfight sound. JIM looks and then continues to watch TV.)

TIM: I should have told Mary to add a smidgen of cream. Next time, I'll know.

(JIM continues to watch TV.)

TIM: In our house, we seem to be seasonal drinkers. In wintertime, cocktails are scotch or dry martinis. As summer drifts into autumn, nothing satisfies like a vodka gimlet on the rocks. The lime juice makes you feel like you could still be at the beach, while the smooth rich vodka reminds you you're holding a serious cocktail, simple and sophisticated. Bartender guides will direct you to fresh lime juice and powdered sugar. We prefer Rose's lime juice. It's far easier, keeps in the fridge for weeks, and makes the gimlet a pearly chartreuse. Beautiful. Essential tip: use a good vodka. It matters to the gimlet. Ice, three ounces of Stoli, and start pouring the Rose's. Once it's the right color, you're good to go.

(JIM continues to watch TV.)

TIM: *Sex in the City.* Repeat. Sean and John Paxton-Rodriguez drive a car all the way to Fairway to buy imported biscotti. They don't eat biscotti. John Paxton-Rodriguez is over forty and works out five times a week to keep his waist at an attractive thirty. But how lovely to open your cupboard and see a box of imported Italian biscotti. Of course John's afraid he'll have to undergo liposuction. Poor Sean Paxton-Rodriguez, last winter he ballooned up to a thirty-two and had to visit Park Avenue. He thinks no one knows. Everyone knows.

(JIM continues to watch TV.)

TIM: Microdermabrasion and laser hair removal are one thing, but liposuction is quite another. Doctors Dan and Stan Johnson-Cummings told me about Sean Paxton-Rodriguez. They are the ones who sucked the nasty bulge off him. They're good doctors. They can be trusted. Of course I only know the doctors socially and have never visited their practice. But they tell me wonderful things about themselves. Dan never prescribes any drugs before he's tried them himself…at the Roxy. Before operating on Sean Paxton-Rodriguez,

Doctors Dan and Stan Johnson-Cummings operated on each other. One doctor receiving liposuction and the other a buttock enhancement with his lover's fat. Although neither was in need of the operation, because they're world-class body builders in addition to being respected surgeons.

JIM: Ha!

TIM: Excuse me?

JIM: Hello, the doctors survived but Paxton-Rodriguez died? What's that about?

TIM: That just means the operation was a success in the doctors' case and I guess it wasn't in Paxton-Rodriguez's.

JIM: Then the Johnson-Cummingses just aren't good doctors. I mean, make up your mind. Don't you think both should have lived or else both should have died?

TIM: Which both do you mean?

JIM: A good doctor should die with his patient if they can't get better together. Like a captain and a ship. He doesn't survive alone, a captain goes down on his ship.

TIM: I don't think it's ethical for a doctor to go down on his patient. Besides, it's silly to talk about patients in nautical terms.

JIM: You said these doctors have abs of steel. Well a ship is made of steel too. And where do you think the term "cruising" comes from?

TIM: Oh my god, I never thought about it. Maybe you know what you're talking about. What are you talking about?

JIM: Doctors are crooked. And most patients too. Only the navy is straight in this country.

TIM: The sailors too?

JIM: Please!

TIM: Ah, Fleet Week.

JIM: Don't ask, don't tell.

TIM: But then how are gay sailors supposed to dock with rear admirals?

JIM: It's all red tape.

TIM: Is nothing black or white?

JIM: I can't stand indecision.

TIM: Hmm, I don't know how I feel about that.

JIM: Nor should you. Here's a thing I don't get. On the news they always tell us when a celebrity dies but they never tell you when a star is born.

TIM: You are so right.

JIM: Of course I'm right. *(Still watching TV.)* Peter Popper died.

TIM: What?! Oh my god! Oh my god, oh sweet Jesus! Why poor Peter? Why?! Why?!

JIM: Why are you being such a drama queen? You know he's been dead for two years. Remember we went to his funeral like a year and a half ago?

TIM: Oh yeah, I remember now. Actually, I remembered it right away, but I didn't really get why you were so shocked to hear it.

JIM: I didn't hear it, I free associated it.

TIM: What a waste. Even dead he was to die for.

JIM: He was the hottest corpse in Chelsea.

TIM: Do you think I'll die young and beautiful?

JIM: We can only hope.

TIM: He totally didn't look his age at all. He understood the value of exfoliating.

JIM: And he was totally devoted to yoga. He was so relaxed, after four years of death he still hadn't moved.

TIM: They say…

JIM: Stop right there!

TIM: That Peter Popper packed a porno pecker.

JIM: What a package.

TIM: Poor Peter.

JIM: Which poor Peter do you mean?

TIM: I mean his partner, Peter Popper. Who did you mean?

JIM: Peter Popper.

TIM: Since they both had the same name, you couldn't tell one from the other when you saw them together. It was only after one of them died that you could really tell which was which. And there are still people today who confuse him with him and offer their condolences to him when they mean him. You know him?

JIM: I only met him once, at Peter Popper's Pride party.

TIM: I've never seen him. Is he attractive?

JIM: He's do-able. Great body but nothing special. He's too big and hairy. You'd really like him, but he's not your type. He's too smooth and slender. He's a designer.

TIM: Ugly-sexy?

JIM: No.

TIM: So sad to be a widow so young. Fortunately, he looks fabulous in black. Do you think there might be wedding bells in Peter's future?

JIM: It depends on what he wears to the circuits, I guess.

TIM: We'll have to go to another commitment ceremony, I suppose.

JIM: It's the dogs who suffer in a new relationship. You know that Peter and Peter Popper-Popper had two. What were their puppies' names?

TIM: Peter and Peter, like their masters. I wonder if he's hooked up with anyone yet.

JIM: That's the rumor. A workout partner of Peter Popper's.

TIM: Who? Peter Popper?

JIM: Which Peter Popper do you mean?

TIM: Peter Popper, the lover of old Peter Popper, the late Peter Popper's other ex.

JIM: No, no, no, it's someone completely different. It's Peter Popper, the twin of Peter Popper, the late Peter Popper's lover.

TIM: Do you mean Peter Popper the personal trainer?

JIM: All Peter Poppers are personal trainers.

TIM: What a hard job! But I guess they do okay at it.

JIM: Sure, when there's no competition.

TIM: When isn't there competition?

JIM: I know, right? Those Peter Poppers are sure popular people.

TIM: How did he die, Peter Popper?

JIM: Peter Popper picked a pack of pickled poppers.

TIM: How tragic!

JIM: Peter Popper's previous partner passed away from poisoned poppers too.

TIM: A previous partner?

JIM: Remember, Peter Popper, Peter Popper's ex, the papi who gave Peter the poodles from the pound?

TIM: Peter and Peter?

JIM: Yes.

TIM: Ah! Makes one wonder.

JIM: What doesn't?

TIM: If Peter Popper picked a pack of pickled poppers, how popped did Peter Popper's peter pop?

JIM: Peter's peter petered till Popper popped the poppers, then Peter Popper's peter popped.

TIM: Stop!

JIM: Oh, believe it.

TIM: Isn't it a pity poor Peter Popper paid the piper for pickled poppers?

JIM: I can't answer all your stupid questions!

TIM: Are you trying to humiliate me?

JIM: Not tonight, I have a headache.

(Enter MARY in beachwear with sunglasses and flip flops. Note: MARY is a man, not necessarily played in drag.)

MARY: I'm the houseboy. I had a fabulous afternoon on Fire Island. No good can come from an island that is, in truth, not an island at all, but a sandbar where all of its occupants are overheated, gorgeous men in Speedos with bulging libidos and enormous incomes. So of course I accepted an invitation to go there. I was unfortunately lucky enough to bed down for two days in a house with a stellar pedigree. It was an outrageously large house that accommodated two comfortably, but slept infinity. It was flawless. It had full ocean views, beds and suntan lotion everywhere. It belonged to some show business legend or something, and it regularly lodges men whose penises are notoriously huge, which is very, very, very important in the Fire Island caste system. I had the best time ever at the "Party of the Season"! Even though I was turned away by the doorman.

TIM: Mary! I hope you had a fabulous afternoon on Fire Island.

JIM: And that you got into "The Party of the Season."

TIM: Did you get any? Wink-wink.

MARY: Craig and Greg Tyler-Martin are at the door. Blah blah blah something about dinner plans and waiting around forever.

TIM: Oh, that's right, they were coming over, weren't they? But we were famished. We didn't have anything to eat all day. We were starving.

JIM: Starving!

TIM: It's not our fault! You shouldn't have deserted us!

MARY: But you told me to get out of your hair.

JIM: Since when do you listen to us?! Eavesdropper!

TIM: Bad Mary, you're a very bad girl.

MARY: *(Bursts into tears.)* This is the worst day of my entire life!

TIM: Get over it, Mary!

MARY: You don't understand. I bought the new Mariah CD today! It's terrible!

TIM: Oh Mary, Mary Quite Contrary, will you ever learn?

JIM: *(Whispering to MARY.)* Burn me a copy!

TIM: Mary, let in Craig and Greg. And whip up some kind of sumptuous souffle-type of thing for everyone. We'll go put on our Dolce & Gabbana.

(TIM and JIM exit. MARY opens the door to let in CRAIG and GREG TYLER-MARTIN, a couple who are a couple of Chelsea gym boys. They wear extremely tight T-shirts and jeans.)

MARY: Where the hell have you been?! It's not very polite, you know. People should treat people the way they want to be treated, or else people will treat you the way you treat people. And people, that is no treat. And don't tell me you don't understand what I'm saying here—I will read your beads, Sunshine. You understand? Now sit there and wait. SIT! DOWN! *(Then friendly.)* I'll make a pitcher of appletinis! *(Exits.)*

(CRAIG and GREG sit facing each other, without speaking. They smile timidly at each other.)

CRAIG: Uhm. God. I have a confession.

GREG: I have something I need to tell you too.

CRAIG: Oh. Want to go first?

GREG: No, no, go ahead.

CRAIG: Okay. Well, as you know, you were working late last night…

GREG: I was. I was at work. I was at work rather late.

CRAIG: And since you weren't home, I decided to go to the gym alone. At night.

GREG: Your arms are looking great!

CRAIG: I know, right? The gym was like empty. I decided to cancel my routine when I felt some discomfort in my shoulders. I thought fifteen minutes in the steam room would help relieve the pain. I felt my muscles relax immediately. I closed my eyes to enjoy the heavy, thick steam.

GREG: My meeting ended early last night. Since you weren't expecting me till later, I stopped by the gym.

CRAIG: Really? If you were there, that makes this even more embarrassing. You see, a few minutes later the door opened and I noticed the silhouette of a totally hot guy walking towards me. I wasn't in the mood for conversation, so I just shut my eyes and enjoyed the steam caressing me.

GREG: That's no biggie. Seeing the gym practically empty, I decided instead of working out my abs and chest, I'd just do my abs and then take a long, hot steam. It's usually such a scene in there, but it was pretty deserted. Only one other guy. And, man, he was hot. You would have so liked him.

CRAIG: I opened my eyes and I caught this really hot guy checking out the view between my legs. I'm embarrassed to say I got an instant hard-on.

GREG: Please, that's nothing. In fact, I think it's probably human nature, because that is exactly what happened when the guy I was looking at opened his eyes and spotted me. And, actually, that caused me to pop a boner too.

CRAIG: You weren't cruising, were you?

GREG: Of course not! Why, were you?

CRAIG: Absolutely not. I intended on working out. Anyway, I couldn't hide my excitement this time because my towel fell off and the mushroom-shaped head of my penis came into view. I didn't know what to do, but then I realized that he should be the one embar-

rassed. But he had no shame whatsoever—none!—and continued, obsessed with the view.

GREG: And he shouldn't have shame. Please. That's like totally normal behavior. That happened to me exactly the same way and I felt no shame whatsoever. None!

CRAIG: Then I noticed his lips open and his tongue travel from side to side with delight.

GREG: In fact, feeling no shame, I parted my lips and traveled my tongue from side to side with delight. It was, after all, hot and I was thirsty.

CRAIG: I couldn't believe how weak I felt with his inspection… I let my hands play with my genitals.

GREG: No. Way. This guy played with his genitals as well.

CRAIG: Weird. First I made it look casual, just in case I was getting the wrong message. Then I started to be more open about it, until my fantasy came true.

GREG: What happened next?

CRAIG: I felt his warm, soft lips.

GREG: Well these things happen.

CRAIG: Has anything like that ever happened to you?

GREG: Actually, last night was pretty much the same for me. Identical even. Sorry.

CRAIG: I would be furious if I didn't completely understand. But since the same thing happened to me… Well, actually there's more. I didn't want to take any chances in case someone walked in and caught us in the act, so I went…to his…apartment.

GREG: Oh, totally understandable and acceptable. I didn't want to take any chances myself, in case someone walked in and caught us in the act, so I went to my guy's apartment as well.

CRAIG: No. Way. No fucking way! No fucking shit! What did his apartment look like?

GREG: Stunning. Like a Pottery Barn catalogue.

CRAIG: Oh, I totally love that look!

GREG: Well you'd better, it's exactly what our home looks like!

CRAIG: But as I mentioned, this is sort of a confession, Greg.

GREG: Sorry, continue, Craig.

CRAIG: I hardly closed the door when we immediately stripped. He held me in his arms and took me to bed. Then it went hardcore for hours on end. I don't even remember going home, I just woke up in our bed somehow. And I woke up thinking what a deeply satisfying time I had last night.

GREG: Oh! My! God! No fucking way! No fucking shit! Did you gaze at his hard body moving so temptingly on top of the clean, white sheets? And is it a picture you will like always remember?

CRAIG: I did! And it is! How crazy is that?! He had a tattoo of barbed wire stretching across his bulging bicep. Just like you.

GREG: This is too freaky! My guy had a tattoo of Britney Spears. Just like you!

CRAIG: Wow!

(GREG, after having thought about it, gets up slowly and moves toward CRAIG, who has also gotten up very quietly after having thought about it.)

GREG: Craig, do you think…?

CRAIG: Oh. My. God! It was you?! That was like the hottest night of my life!

GREG: It was mind-blowing! I've never known anything like that! You were amazing!

CRAIG and GREG: We are so lucky to have each other! You are just my type!

(CRAIG and GREG embrace. Then CRAIG and GREG sit together in the same chair, gazing into EACH OTHER's eyes until they fall into a hypnotic stare. MARY, on tiptoe, enters quietly and addresses the audience. He is dressed in a trench coat.)

MARY: I have a great big little secret. Don't worry, I'm invisible to these type of guys. I could roller skate naked down Eighth Avenue and they wouldn't notice me. So here's my dirt. Craig and Greg did not have an evening of wild, unbridled passion and hot anonymous sex with each other. Greg is not the barbed-wire fantasy-fulfiller of Craig. And Craig is not the Britney fan of Greg's steamy adventure. Noooo. Here's the proof. While Craig does indeed love Britney enough to have tattooed her likeness onto his right buttock, it is not the same Britney likeness that Greg viewed in full glory during last night's merriment. Greg was with Dan Johnson-Cummings, the world-recognized plastic surgeon and bodybuilder. The same Doctor Dan Johnson-Cummings mentioned in Tim Jackson-Smith's monologue several minutes ago. Doctor Dan is an avid fan of Miss Spears and tattooed her likeness onto his left buttock. Craig right buttock; Doctor Dan left buttock. Furthermore, Doctor Dan prefers the "Oops, I did it again" look, while Craig dedicated his rear view to the post-Justin Britney. Craig, it turns out, was with Peter Popper, the bachelor uncle of the surviving Peter Popper, the widow of the deceased Peter Popper. This Peter Popper works in gift wrap at Macy's, and has been known to use his employee discount in exchange for steroids and hair products. He assumes he was with Craig. He presumes he was with Greg. He assumes that he is Craig. He presumes that he is Greg. They're such confused boys. Who wants to tell them? Who wants to stretch out this drama any further? I don't. Let's let sleeping dogs wake up with fleas. *(Tiptoes toward the door, then turns and says to the audience.)* My real name is Angela Lansbury. *(Exits.)*

GREG: Honey Bear, let's forget it. Now that we have each other again, let's try not to lose that loving feeling. Unless, of course, Vin Diesel walks through the door, then all bets are off.

CRAIG: But what if he's into us both?

(TIM and JIM JACKSON-SMITH enter, wearing the same clothes as before.)

TIM: Good evening, Craig and Greg, Greg and Craig! You both look too, too fabulous for words. I love, love, love your shirt, Greg. As always, you're an absolute vision. And Craig, you always look good in tight pants. You have the ass and the package to get away with it. God bless you! Mm-mm-mm! Please forgive us for having made you wait so long. I hope Mary got you a little drinky or something. Did we keep you waiting? I'm sorry. We simply couldn't chose an outfit! Does this ensemble work? Well, it's nothing next to yours. You both look so good, like peppermint sticks on a gay Christmas tree, I just want to lick you both all over. Yummy, yummy, yummy!

JIM: We haven't eaten all day! Why did you come so late?! Don't you have any fucking manners?

(TIM and JIM sit. GREG and CRAIG sit. GREG and CRAIG seem embarrassed. The conversation begins with difficulty, and the words are uttered awkwardly. A long embarrassed silence at first, then other silences and hesitations follow.)

JIM: Huh.

GREG: Uhm, huh.

CRAIG: Ah, uhm, huh.

TIM: Ha, ah, uhm, huh.

JIM: Well.

GREG: Well well.

CRAIG: Well well well well well well well.

(TIM, JIM, and GREG all glare at CRAIG. A deadly silence follows.)

CRAIG: Did you know that the best foods to eat before and after a workout are those high in protein?

(Silence.)

CRAIG: Your body needs protein to build new muscle. Tuna fish sandwiches or lean meats provide a good source of protein.

TIM: Oh.

(Silence.)

JIM: I wash my hair about every other day. I think it's important to use a good shampoo. I like L'Oreal or Pantene Pro V. Now that my hair is longer, I don't use any gel or anything in it. I think long hair looks better if it's natural.

(Silence.)

CRAIG: Oh?

(Silence.)

GREG: My body changed through training, and I grasped how beautiful it was to maintain strong muscles. When you take control of your body, you take control of your life.

CRAIG: That's so totally true.

JIM: So they say.

TIM: They also say the opposite.

CRAIG: That's true.

(Silence.)

TIM: Craig, don't you do something interesting or something?

CRAIG: I work in marketing.

TIM: Perhaps it was someone else.

JIM: I love marketing! Today I bought some plums. And for mañana, I have my eye on a giant zucchini.

GREG: Craig, tell them what you saw today.

CRAIG: Oh it was nothing.

JIM: Your integrity's not in question here.

TIM: Don't you believe we'll believe you?

CRAIG: Okay. But it was really nothing.

TIM: See? We believe you already.

GREG: This is going to be good.

CRAIG: Well, today, when I went to pick up some extra, extra, extra virgin olive oil, which is getting to be so expensive…

JIM: What's next, I tell you?!

TIM: Don't interrupt, Jim, it's rude.

CRAIG: On the sidewalk in front of Big Cup, I saw a man about forty…

JIM: Yes? Yes?

TIM: What? What?

JIM: Shut up, Tim, now you're being rude.

TIM: You were rude first.

GREG: Be quiet.

TIM: You be quiet.

JIM: *(To TIM.)* Hush. *(To CRAIG.)* So, what was this guy doing?

CRAIG: He was wearing Dockers.

JIM, TIM, and GREG: Oh!

CRAIG: With cuffs!

JIM: In Chelsea?

TIM: Not possible.

CRAIG: Yes! He was bending over.

GREG: Ooh, spicy.

CRAIG: So I go up to the guy to see what he was up to…

TIM: And?

CRAIG: He was tying the laces of his Hush Puppies.

TIM: Who wears Hush Puppies in this day and age?

JIM: Was this in Chelsea?

GREG: If I didn't believe everything this guy said, I would think everything he said was a lie!

JIM: Outrageous!

TIM: I didn't even know they still made Hush Puppies. It's so ridiculous, it's almost chic.

JIM: I know, I sort of want a pair now.

GREG: Where could you possibly get them?

TIM: Oh my god, not only retro but rare!

JIM: We'll go shopping tomorrow!

GREG: Try New Jersey!

TIM: Where is that exactly?

CRAIG: Isn't it near some bridge?

(Awkward silence, as no one has anything to say. Suddenly:)

TIM: Oh! Let's play a game! Let's play a game!

JIM: I love games!

CRAIG: Will we have to take off all our clothes?

TIM: No, it's a brand-new game.

GREG: I have a sneaking suspicion I've played this game before.

TIM: It's new.

GREG: Oh yeah, I've played this then.

CRAIG: All games are new until you've played them.

JIM: Repetition bores me.

TIM: It's called "Who's Gayer?" Contestants will answer a series of questions to determine who is the gayest person in the room.

GREG: I'll play.

CRAIG: I always win at this.

JIM: Girlfriend, I've been winning at this since third grade.

TIM: Okay, okay, okay, here's the first question. Which would you rather do, be forced to wear a canary pullover

shirt with a pink plastic vest or would you rather sleep with Pamela Anderson?

JIM: Oh my god, I think I'm going to hurl!

CRAIG: Well she is fabulous, but I think I would rather wear yellow and pink.

TIM: No!

CRAIG: I hate to say it, but I think it's sort of brilliant.

GREG: What?

CRAIG: You know, like in a downtown-don't-wash-your-hair-forever-and-smoke-a-million-cigarettes kind of way. It could be fun.

TIM: *(Rolling his eyes.)* Yeah, that is sooo you.

CRAIG: I am large, I contain multitudes.

JIM: I'm sure you do.

TIM: Greg, please answer the question.

GREG: Pamela Lee is a goddess, I'd do her. Would there be lapping involved?

CRAIG: Eeww!

JIM: Strictly missionary! Make that a rule!

TIM: But there must, must, must be penetration!

GREG: By which party?

TIM: Whomever.

JIM: I'll take Big Pam with a strap-on.

GREG: Can we wear strap-ons?

TIM: No, only she can.

JIM: Can it be in the dark?

TIM: What do you mean?

JIM: Can the lights be off?

TIM: Absolutely not.

JIM: Why not?

TIM: I implicitly said the lights cannot be turned off.

JIM: No, you didn't.

TIM: Well I meant to. Besides, it was implied.

CRAIG: Give him a break.

TIM: Fine, in the dark, you big girl.

JIM: Good. Then I want to wear the canary shirt with the pink plastic vest in the dark!

TIM: *(Jubilant!)* You win! That is the gayest answer ever!

JIM: Honey, I was born gay!

CRAIG: I know a game. But first I need a bottle.

TIM: Not this again.

JIM: That's not really a game, it's more of a trick.

(The buzzer buzzes. A small dog yaps.)

TIM: Quiet, Liza! Liza! So the next question challenges your knowledge of figure skaters.

CRAIG: I'm good at this. Once I stood next to Tonya Harding at a urinal.

(The buzzer buzzes. A small dog yaps.)

TIM: Dammit, Liza!

JIM: Honey, maybe you should see who it is.

TIM: Why?

JIM: Gee, I don't know, because someone's buzzing?

TIM: It's no one.

(A small dog continues yapping.)

JIM: Honey, I think Liza needs a Valium.

TIM: No, Sweetie, she's finally clean. When she goes, you want her going like Elsie?

(The buzzer buzzes. A small dog yaps. JIM gets up.)

TIM: What are you doing?

JIM: Answering the buzzer.

TIM: No one's there.

JIM: But it buzzed.

TIM: What's your point?

JIM: The buzzer buzzed.

TIM: And?

JIM: When it buzzes, it means someone's there.

TIM: Are you expecting someone?

JIM: No.

TIM: Nor am I.

GREG: But it might be someone.

CRAIG: It's the wrong apartment.

GREG: How do you know?

CRAIG: It could be someone breaking in.

GREG: Would they buzz?

(The buzzer buzzes again and a small dog yaps again.)

JIM: Did you order something?

TIM: No. It's clearly the wrong apartment.

GREG: Should I buzz them in?

TIM: Did you order something?

GREG: Well I am sort of hungry.

TIM: It's nobody.

JIM: Let me buzz them.

CRAIG: You know someone else will.

TIM: No. No, we have very good neighbors, they never let people in. Once a nurse was trying to deliver blood to a dying man on the third floor and they refused to admit her. No one was expecting her, so no one let her in.

CRAIG: I applaud that.

TIM: Thank you.

(A cell phone rings. GREG and CRAIG check their phones; it is not either of theirs. TIM checks his phone; it is not his. Everyone turns to JIM.)

CRAIG: Your phone is ringing.

JIM: I'm not answering.

TIM: But it's ringing.

JIM: They'll leave a message.

CRAIG: What if it's important?

JIM: They'll call back.

TIM: What if it's an emergency?

JIM: They'll live.

TIM: What if it's Madonna?

JIM: Okay! Okay, okay, okay, okay. Do I tell you who to pick up for? *(Answering his cell phone.)* Hello? Hello? See? No one. What did I say?

CRAIG: It must have been someone.

JIM: Nobody.

TIM: Even if it was the wrong—

JIM: Nobody.

GREG: If he says it was nobody, it was nobody.

CRAIG: When you hear a cell ring, that means somebody's calling.

GREG: How are we defining "somebody"?

TIM: When I call someone, I let the phone ring before they pick it up.

JIM: And when I go to visit someone, I always buzz to be buzzed in. I think everyone does the same and every time there's a buzz there must be someone buzzing.

CRAIG: That's so not true!

JIM: It's true for me.

TIM: That may be true in theory but in reality things happen different, okay? You've just seen so. Fine! Next time it buzzes we'll check. And you will see that there is absolutely no one there.

(EVERYONE sits and watches the door for a long moment.)

JIM: Let's play middle initials!

GREG: Okay, what do we do?

JIM: Everyone says their middle initial and we guess their middle name.

CRAIG: Well then I can't play. I don't have a middle initial.

TIM: Did you lose it?

CRAIG: I never had one. I always wanted one. My brother had one. All the great people in history had one. John F. Kennedy. John F. Kennedy Jr. Jesus H. Christ.

TIM: Well we can say the initial of our first names and everyone can guess that.

JIM: But I'm much better at middle names.

CRAIG: It's okay, I'll just watch. I don't need to play.

TIM: *(To JIM.)* Come on!

JIM: *(Reluctantly.)* Okay.

TIM: The initial of my first name is T. T.

(EVERYONE thinks.)

GREG: Tim?

TIM: You're good!

(A cell phone rings. EVERYONE looks at JIM. A buzzer buzzes, EVERYONE looks at the door. A dog yaps, EVERYONE looks at the dog. The cell phone continues to ring.)

TIM: Shut up, Liza!

CRAIG: Try putting some Stoli in her water, she'll go down like the Berlin Wall.

(TIM crosses to the door; JIM stops him.)

JIM: No wait!

TIM: Afraid to be proved wrong?

JIM: No, I want to get it, because I am very confident someone is there!

(JIM presses the buzzer. TIM runs and picks up JIM'S cell phone.)

TIM: *(On the cell phone.)* Hello? Hello?

JIM: *(Into the intercom.)* Who is it?

TIM: Hello? It must be someone incredibly shy.

CRAIG: Or it could be a mute.

TIM: Oh my god, do you think?

GREG: Or someone tied up.

(JIM opens the door.)

JIM: Oh! How are you?

(He glances at TIM and the TYLER-MARTINS, who are all surprised.)

JIM: It's the Fire Chief!

(THE FIRE CHIEF enters; he is very attractive. TIM hangs up the phone in a huff.)

THE FIRE CHIEF: Evening, Craig, Greg, Jim… Tim, you appear to be angry. Why such a frowny-face?

TIM: Ugh!

JIM: See, my lover is a little testy at being proved wrong.

GREG: There's been a fight between Mr. Jackson-Smith and Mr. Jackson-Smith, Mr. Fire Chief.

TIM: *(To GREG.)* It wasn't a fight, it was a disagreement. Mind your own business. *(To JIM.)* Please don't drag outsiders into our family quarrels.

JIM: Please. This isn't that big a deal. Besides, the Fire Chief's an old friend of the family. His father was our handyman and his brother nailed me. Or was it the other way around?

THE FIRE CHIEF: What's going on?

TIM: My husband was insisting…

JIM: No, you were insisting.

GREG: Yes, it was him.

CRAIG: No, it was him.

THE FIRE CHIEF: Don't get upset. You tell me, Mr. Jackson-Smith.

(JIM and TIM look confused for a moment, and then:)

TIM: Well, this is what happened. It's difficult for me to speak openly to you. But since I watch you wash your fire engine through binoculars from my bedroom, I feel like I sort of know you…

THE FIRE CHIEF: Well then?

TIM: We were fighting because my husband is an idiot and claims that when your cell rings it's because no one is there.

GREG: It's plausible.

TIM: It's impossible. Furthermore, he refuses to entertain the well-known notion that when the buzzer buzzes there's never anyone there.

CRAIG: We know it sounds strange, but it's been proved. And not by some theoretical nonsense, but by hard-core, indisputable facts.

JIM: Wrong! That's wrong because the Fire Chief is here. He buzzed the buzzer, I buzzed him in, and here he is. *Voilà!*

CRAIG: When?

GREG: Just now.

JIM: Mr. Fire Chief, allow me to probe you.

THE FIRE CHIEF: Okay, do your best.

JIM: When I opened the door and saw you, would it be an accurate assumption that it was you who had buzzed the buzzer?

THE FIRE CHIEF: Yes, it was me.

GREG: "It was I."

THE FIRE CHIEF: No, it was me.

TIM: He was here the whole time!

CRAIG: This is fixed!

GREG: So let me get this straight. You were at the door, and you buzzed in order to be, shall we say, buzzed in?

THE FIRE CHIEF: I do not deny it. I buzzed in order to be buzzed in.

JIM: Thank you, Mr. Fire Chief. No further questions. *(To TIM, triumphantly.)* See? I was right. When you hear the buzzer buzz that means someone buzzed it. You certainly can't say the Fire Chief is not someone.

GREG: Why he's a hero to our country and community!

TIM: I know he's a hero, I bought their freaking calendar!

CRAIG: Let me ask you this, when the buzzer buzzed the first time, was that also you?

THE FIRE CHIEF: No, it was not me.

GREG: "It was not I."

TIM: Everyone saw you here, Greg, no one is questioning that.

CRAIG: You see? The buzzer buzzed and there was nobody there. Is that correct, Mr. Fire Chief?

GREG: Perhaps it was someone else?

CRAIG: Objection!

GREG: Overruled!

JIM: Were you standing downstairs for a long time?

THE FIRE CHIEF: Definitely about three-quarters of an hour maybe.

JIM: And you saw nobody?

THE FIRE CHIEF: I don't think so. I'm pretty sure of that.

GREG: Pretty sure? Not very sure?

CRAIG: And did you hear the buzzer buzz when it buzzed the second time?

THE FIRE CHIEF: Yes, I did. And that wasn't me either. And there was still no one there.

TIM: Victory! I win!

JIM: Not this year, Miss Lucci. And what were you doing at the door, Mr. Fire Chief?

THE FIRE CHIEF: Nothing. Just standing there. I was thinking.

JIM: If that's true, tell us what you where thinking of?

THE FIRE CHIEF: Matt Damon.

TIM: I'm convinced.

GREG: But the third time, come on, it wasn't you who buzzed?

THE FIRE CHIEF: Yeah, it was me.

JIM: But when I buzzed the buzzer nobody was there.

THE FIRE CHIEF: That's because I was on my cell phone.

TIM: Who were you calling? Smokey the Bear?

THE FIRE CHIEF: I was calling you because I didn't want to arrive unannounced. I'm the Fire Chief, not "the rudest man in the world."

GREG: So we still don't know when the buzzer buzzes if there's someone there or not!

TIM: Never anyone.

JIM: Always someone.

THE FIRE CHIEF: Well, actually, you're both partly right. And you're both partly wrong too. *(He demonstrates.)* When the buzzer buzzes, there's no one there until you buzz them in.

CRAIG: Wow!

GREG: That makes sense to me.

CRAIG: Me too.

TIM: *(Surrendering coyly.)* Me three.

THE FIRE CHIEF: It's all really simple, really.

JIM: Now can you explain cell phones to us?

THE FIRE CHIEF: Maybe later.

CRAIG: He makes it all sound so easy.

THE FIRE CHIEF: *(To the JACKSON-SMITHS.)* Now come on, boys, kiss and make up.

JIM: We just kissed each other before, we'll kiss later.

CRAIG: They have nothing but time.

GREG: I wouldn't mind watching them kiss.

TIM: Mr. Fire Chief, I feel I've made a bad impression. Please make yourself comfortable, take off your helmet and sit down for a while.

THE FIRE CHIEF: I can't really stay long, I've come on official business.

(THE FIRE CHIEF performs an elaborate strip to house music, shedding his jacket, helmet, and undershirt, while his flashlight is used as a spotlight with the help of TIM. He remains shirtless the rest of the play. Everyone is duly impressed by his performance.)

CRAIG: Wow!

TIM: How can I be of service to you, Mr. Fire Chief?

THE FIRE CHIEF: Well…uhm…you don't…in front of…

CRAIG: Say anything you'd like.

GREG: We're like spoons in a drawer. They tell us everything.

CRAIG: Everything.

JIM: So what's up, Mr. Fire Chief?

THE FIRE CHIEF: Well…is there a fire here?

TIM: Oh my god, why would you even ask me that?

THE FIRE CHIEF: Don't be alarmed, I'm a Fire Chief. Part of my job is to extinguish all the fires in the city.

CRAIG: All?

THE FIRE CHIEF: Well, yes.

TIM: I don't know… I don't think so.

THE FIRE CHIEF: I'm pretty sure that's my job.

TIM: No, I mean I don't think you'll find any flames here.

THE FIRE CHIEF: Oh. Are you sure?

TIM: Do you want me to look?

THE FIRE CHIEF: Gee, I don't want to put you out.

CRAIG: They always say where there's smoke there's fire, but I don't know.

GREG: I only smoke socially.

JIM: Do you smell smoke, Mr. Fire Chief?

THE FIRE CHIEF: No. But did you check the chimney?

CRAIG: The chimney, yes! Check the chimney!

TIM: I'm embarrassed to say we don't even have a fireplace. Not that we don't support the firemen and all the hard, courageous work they do.

THE FIRE CHIEF: Maybe something burning on the stove? I can handle even the smallest grease fire.

TIM: I'm so, so, so sorry to disappoint you, but I don't believe there's anything here at the moment. I promise to call you immediately when something catches.

THE FIRE CHIEF: Please, it'd be a big help.

TIM: That's a promise, from me to you, Mr. Fire Chief.

THE FIRE CHIEF: (To the TYLER-MARTINS.) Nothing burning at your place either?

CRAIG: I'm sorry, no.

JIM: It's sort of a shame we don't have a fire, you're such a big hero and all. Tim, set the drapery on fire. Use a votive.

THE FIRE CHIEF: That would be cheating! What do I look like to you?

JIM: I'm sorry, Mr. Fire Chief.

GREG: Things aren't so hot right now?

THE FIRE CHIEF: Not at all. It's been dead for weeks. It's terrible, really. The other day there was something burning in an ashtray, and last Wednesday some burnt cookies.

CRAIG: Greg bakes cookies.

GREG: (Slightly offended.) I bake, I don't burn.

THE FIRE CHIEF: Otherwise there's been nothing. Nada. Ashtray fires don't bring in much. It's all about the bottom line. We need to extinguish enough fires to be profitable. The mayor closed six stations last spring. And now with these no-smoking laws… I don't want to lose my job.

CRAIG: The dry season should be coming up.

THE FIRE CHIEF: I know, thank you.

JIM: It's really bad all over. It's the same with stocks and bonds, nothing's doing well.

GREG: My Martha Stewart stock has dropped and you have no fires.

TIM: (Feeling sorry for himself.) I have no Martha Stewart stock or fires!

JIM: Honey, don't show off.

THE FIRE CHIEF: Once in a great while there's an asphyxiation by gas. But that just doesn't happen enough. Like last Friday, a go-go boy from Splash was overcome by gas. He had left the oven on.

CRAIG: Slipped his mind?

THE FIRE CHIEF: No, he thought it was a tanning bed.

TIM: You have to be so careful about that!

CRAIG: I'm frightened.

JIM: The community can't afford to lose good go-go boys! Why couldn't it have been a teacher or a busboy?

GREG: I like busboys.

CRAIG: Well I'm happy for you, Mr. Fire Chief, but I can't help but feel sorry for the poor patrons of Splash who are now a go-go boy short.

TIM: Mr. Fire Chief, since you're not too rushed, why don't you take off some more and unwind? We'd be so happy to have you…stay.

THE FIRE CHIEF: Really? Do you want to hear some stories or something?

TIM: That would be marvelous!

JIM, CRAIG, and GREG: Yeah, yeah, some stories!

JIM: I love his stories! The amazing thing is, Mr. Fire Chief's stories are true! They're all true! Tell them, they're true.

THE FIRE CHIEF: It's true, they're true.

TIM: Fabulous!

CRAIG: I'm afraid of the truth.

THE FIRE CHIEF: I speak from my own experiences. Not fiction. Fiction belongs in the press.

GREG: And I thought truth was only caught on reality TV.

THE FIRE CHIEF: Please, don't look at me like that. It's embarrassing.

TIM: Isn't he adorable!

CRAIG: Yum-my!

GREG: *(Whispering.)* Kittens are adorable, this guy's totally hot.

JIM: *(Whispering.)* Well, he is a fireman.

GREG: A delicious fireman!

CRAIG: *(Whispering.)* Fire *Chief*!

THE FIRE CHIEF: Okay, I'll try to do this. If you all insist. But you gotta promise no one will listen.

CRAIG: But… How will we hear you?

THE FIRE CHIEF: With your hearts.

CRAIG: Okay.

THE FIRE CHIEF: So, listen up everyone! "Angels Six, Giants Five."

CRAIG: Ooh, symbolism.

JIM: Last time he was here he performed barbell squats.

GREG: Now that I could get behind.

JIM: No one squats like Mr. Fire Chief. Up, down, up, down…

CRAIG: Oh I love to squat!

TIM: Shhh…

THE FIRE CHIEF: Troy Percival was not supposed to sweat in the top of the ninth inning because it looked as if it would be irrelevant. Waiting anxiously in the Anaheim bullpen and wondering if a magical season was about to end as the San Francisco Giants scampered to a five-oh lead over the Angels, Percival had to wonder if he would ever throw a pitch. But there was Percival, the Anaheim closer, pumping a high fastball…

(TIM gasps inappropriately.)

THE FIRE CHIEF: …past Rich Aurilia for the final out, pumping his fist and embracing his giddy teammates after the Angels, those resilient Angels, staged a rally that shocked the Giants, six to five, in Game Six of the World Series and evened it at three games apiece.

JIM: What's the message?

GREG: A giant what? Did anybody catch that?

CRAIG: I understood the "pumping his fist" part, but the rest was sort of fuzzy.

TIM: Did you know that Shea Stadium isn't spelled C-H-E-Z?

GREG: Do some squats! Everyone likes squats! I'll spot you, if you'd like.

TIM: Well it was all in the telling, I think we can all agree on that. Thank you, Mr. Fire Chief.

JIM: I have one!

THE FIRE CHIEF: By all means, Jim, you go next.

(OPTION A: JIM performs the "Macarena." Shouting at the end, "Hey, Macarena!" OPTION B: JIM performs an elaborate and heartfelt, but rather poorly executed, Martha Graham-like dance.)

CRAIG: It's…interesting.

TIM: Not bad.

GREG: That was really something. I've never seen anything quite like it.

THE FIRE CHIEF: *(Jealous.)* Truthfully, it wasn't very good. Besides, I've seen it before. Sorry.

JIM: It was awful.

TIM: What was it?

GREG: I don't know.

CRAIG: P.U.!

JIM: I would like to sincerely apologize to everyone for my terrible misjudgment.

GREG: It's okay, Jim, we still like you. And slowly you'll regain our respect.

CRAIG: I think effort should count for something. And he did try.

THE FIRE CHIEF: He gave it his all, it just wasn't enough. Sorry, guy. Bottom's up! It's your turn, Tim.

TIM: I can only think of one, Mr. Fire Chief. But it's a goody. It's called "The Largest Organ"…

GREG: Oh my!

TIM: …or "My Adventures in Skin Trade."

THE FIRE CHIEF: This should be something.

GREG: Beauty and youth.

CRAIG: He's a true Chelsea boy.

GREG: Beauty and youth.

CRAIG: He's a true Chelsea boy.

TIM: Every day your skin is on display. Clear, radiant, youthful-looking skin is more than just a vanity issue; it's a major health issue. Did you know that the skin is the body's largest "organ" system? Moisturizers, or humectants, attract moisture to the skin's surface and hold it there; making the skin softer, preventing dryness and chapping by holding onto water, thus slowing the aging process. Avoid commercial skin lotions or moisturizers with mineral oil or petroleum byproducts. These molecules are too large to penetrate…

JIM: (Childishly.) Too large to what?!

TIM: …the pores of the skin so they cannot breathe or eliminate waste efficiently. Be a wise shopper and look for the right and appropriate sunscreen and moisturizer for you.

THE FIRE CHIEF: ¡Muy caliente!

GREG: I loved it!

THE FIRE CHIEF: I double loved it!

CRAIG: Jim, Tim is so great, you're so lucky, he's so fabulous.

JIM: (Jealous.) I know. Tim is style personified. He is style with a capital "Sssss." He's even more stylish than I. Well, he's much butcher, ask anyone.

TIM: Come on, hot stuff, let's have another.

THE FIRE CHIEF: Oh, no, I couldn't, it's way too late.

GREG: Come on, one more won't hurt you.

THE FIRE CHIEF: I'm way too tired.

JIM: Do it for us.

GREG: Please, please, please.

CRAIG: Once is never enough.

GREG: I'll pay you to stay!

JIM: You could spend the night. The couch pulls out, if we need it to.

THE FIRE CHIEF: I don't know…

TIM: My heart is made of glass and you are throwing stones at it.

THE FIRE CHIEF: Oh, okay.

CRAIG: (Devastated.) He said yes.

JIM: (Whispering.) Will someone just put a gun to my head?

TIM: (Whispering.) I was too polite. Why am I so fucking nice all the time?

GREG: (Whispering.) When, god, when will it end?

THE FIRE CHIEF: "Mission Possible." The ex-lover of my ex-domestic partner, who is currently my psuedo-boyfriend—

TIM, JIM, CRAIG, and GREG: Congratulations!

THE FIRE CHIEF: Thanks. —had on his mother's side a cousin whose bachelor uncle had a "friend" whose ex was the longtime companion of a florist whose brother he had met on one of his travels, a twink with whom he was enamored and with whom he had adopted a daughter, married a club boy from West Hollywood who was none other than the nephew of a well-known but long-forgotten B-movie starlet whose husband had a secret lover who spoke Greek fluently—if you know what I mean—and was, perhaps, "roommates" with David Barton and had a torrid affair with Prince Charles and some famous DJ who died young but turned out to be a breeder anyway, but was an heir with a HUGE endowment and was himself the neighbor of the guy who discovered Whitney and Cher and the Backstreet Boys, to name a few, who had a trick, a real hustler, sleazy as anything but cute as hell with a dick that wouldn't quit, anyway, he married some insatiable bottom whose chap-wearing daddy made a fortune by introducing X to South Beach, and had managed to breed his golden retriever with the doorman of Boy George…

TIM: How taboo!

THE FIRE CHIEF: This said doorman with a bitch retriever slept with a priest whose former unofficial boyfriend, unofficial of course, was the lover of a guy who bartended at "G" on Saturdays and was an amateur gladiator and who knew a man whose domestic partner had a moustache and was the foster-brother of an "uncle" whose "nephew" was the boyfriend of some boy who played some boy on some seventies sitcom which is better forgotten and he was the domestic partner of a doctor who wore glasses and had a limp and was the fuck-buddy of a designer who was lovers with a guy who was lovers with a photographer who was the booty call of a guy who slept with Tom Cruise.

(EVERYONE is happy with the THE FIRE CHIEF'S story.)

GREG: I knew he was gay!

JIM: See!

TIM: You can't dispute facts.

CRAIG: I knew that third boyfriend, if I'm not mistaken.

THE FIRE CHIEF: It's not the same one. That third boyfriend interestingly was a physician's assistant and was working the emergency room when Richard Gere had that certain encounter with a gerbil taken care of.

JIM: Just like Tim. He was there too.

TIM: I was only in the waiting room. But I saw everything.

CRAIG: I didn't really follow your tale all that well, Mr. Fire Chief. Although I tried. Near the end, like endish, when you got to the sugar daddy of the priest, I got lost.

JIM: So many boys get lost when priests enter the picture.

TIM: Mr. Fire Chief, please tell it again. Everyone wants to hear it again and again.

(Enter MARY in a red kimono and heels.)

MARY: Excuse me, sirs…

TIM: What do you want?

JIM: Excuse me, Mary, but the kitchen is that way.

MARY: I hope sirs will excuse me…and your esteemed guests too…But I'm ready for my close-up.

CRAIG: What is she going on about?

GREG: I believe our friends' houseboy has gone loco…

MARY: I would like… I would very, very, very much like…to perform a little something myself.

CRAIG: Stop!

TIM: I am so embarrassed by you, Mary. How could you do this to me? Ruin my party! After all I've done for you?!

JIM: She just had the afternoon off, what more does she want?

THE FIRE CHIEF: Who is this party crasher? Listen here, fella— *(Looks at MARY.)* Oh!

MARY: You!

THE FIRE CHIEF: Oh my god, it's…you. Hey…you.

MARY: I gave you my number.

THE FIRE CHIEF: I lost it. No, really I did. Cross my heart.

JIM: You two…?

THE FIRE CHIEF: Well, sort of.

(MARY throws himself onto THE FIRE CHIEF.)

MARY: Intimately!

TIM and JIM: Oh!

CRAIG and GREG: Ahhh.

THE FIRE CHIEF: He taught me how to use my hose!

MARY: I'm your little douser.

CRAIG: We have that video!

GREG: That changes everything. If that's the case…these emotions are understandable, human, honorable…and sort of hot.

TIM: Well still, I don't like to see it…out in the open like this.

JIM: It's so in your face.

CRAIG: It's like she's begging for spanking!

TIM: And she couldn't even get herself into an after-party on a lousy Tuesday night.

THE FIRE CHIEF: You have far too many hang-ups.

CRAIG: What I think is that a slave, no matter how willing, must be forced to please in order to receive pleasure.

GREG: Even if she is Angela Lansbury.

THE FIRE CHIEF: How'd you like to say that to my face, huh?

MARY: Don't be mad!… They're really not so bad.

JIM: Hm…hm…you two are very…you know, whatever…but at the same time, a little…a little…too whatever.

GREG: Yes, that's the perfect word.

MARY: I was going to tell you…

JIM: Talk to the hand, Mary!

MARY: But…

TIM: Go now, my little Mary, go sulk in the kitchen and lick my Pradas clean!

CRAIG: You know, even though I'm not a slave, I also enjoy foot worship.

MARY: I would like to open with a torch song. A little number called "The Fire Pole."

TIM: I will not be upstaged by some second-rate drag queen in a bad wig.

MARY: *(To an imaginary bandmaster.)* Hit it! *(Tosses off his kimono and performs an elaborate production number, with the following text:)*
TWO LOVERS WERE BURNING IN THE RAMBLES
THE PARK CAUGHT FIRE
BARRACUDA CAUGHT FIRE
BIG CUP CAUGHT FIRE
FOOD BAR CAUGHT FIRE
THE GYMS CAUGHT FIRE
THE PIERS CAUGHT FIRE
THE RIVER CAUGHT FIRE
THE SKY CAUGHT FIRE
THE ASHES CAUGHT FIRE
THE SMOKE CAUGHT FIRE
THE FIRE CAUGHT FIRE
EVERYTHING CAUGHT FIRE
CAUGHT FIRE CAUGHT FIRE.

(As MARY sings, TIM pushes him offstage. JIM leaves the stage and runs toward the lobby; he gets a record from the back of the house, returns to the stage and smashes the record. JIM and TIM then resume their seated positions.)

CRAIG: That sent chills down my back.

GREG: Yet it had a certain warmth.

JIM: I didn't hear about any fire pole in those lyrics.

TIM: It was hidden.

THE FIRE CHIEF: I thought it was hot.

JIM: This is too much.

TIM: If I ever hold my head up again, it will be a testimony to my strength.

THE FIRE CHIEF: Just a minute… I admit…all this is really subjective… I don't expect anyone else to get it…but this…this is my conception of the world. And I never thought I'd find someone who got that. But Mary does.

JIM: But Mary's just a houseboy.

THE FIRE CHIEF: To you perhaps.

CRAIG: They're not even an A-list couple.

(TIM and JIM gasp.)

THE FIRE CHIEF: Mary accepts me for who I am. Fire and all. This is…me. This is…my world. My dream. My ideal. My cell phone. It's vibrating in my pants.

CRAIG: Lucky man.

GREG: Lucky phone.

THE FIRE CHIEF: *(Answering his cell phone.)* Fire Chief here! Good god, you're joking! You're not joking? You're not serious! You are serious? *(To the room.)* There's a fire!

TIM, CRAIG, and GREG: Oh my god!

JIM: You go girl!

THE FIRE CHIEF: *(Into the phone.)* I'll be right there! *(Hangs up. To the room.)* I hate to leave you all high and dry, but I have to rush.

JIM: Where's the fire?

THE FIRE CHIEF: On the other side of 23rd. I have to hurry! Even though it's really no big deal.

JIM: What is it, a disco inferno?

THE FIRE CHIEF: Oh, not even. A little heartburn.

TIM: Oh! Well, I for one am sorry to see you go. I could have danced all night.

CRAIG: You were the highlight of my evening.

JIM: You were the highlight of my week!

CRAIG: *(Not to be outdone.)* You were the highlight of my life!

GREG: Do you do private parties?

(MARY runs out with a suitcase and a garden hose.)

MARY: I'm ready, Monsieur.

TIM, JIM, CRAIG, and GREG: What?!

TIM: (*To THE FIRE CHIEF.*) You're not taking that thing with you, are you?

GREG: Dude, you're not serious.

THE FIRE CHIEF: You said it was honorable.

GREG: Sure, when it was a one-time thing. Try everything once. But, honestly, you could better.

CRAIG: Believe me, you could do much, much better.

THE FIRE CHIEF: Believe me, I couldn't.

TIM: Mary! After all we've done for you! How could you?

MARY: Sometimes the snow comes down in June. Sometimes the sun goes round the moon. Isn't this world a crazy place? Well. *Ciao belli!* (*To THE FIRE CHIEF.*) I'll go sit on your extension ladder. (*Exits.*)

(*There is an awkward moment.*)

THE FIRE CHIEF: Well, good night Tim and Jim, Greg and Craig.

TIM: It's Jim and Tim.

GREG: And I'm Greg, he's Craig.

THE FIRE CHIEF: Well, a rose is a rose is a rose. Is a rose!

JIM: Thank you, Mr. Fire Chief.

THE FIRE CHIEF: (*Moves toward the door and then stops.*) Did you hear the one about the Bald Diva? A Priest, a Rabbi, and a Parrot go into a club and see a Bald Diva doing her act. The Priest says, "She sang those same songs last night." And the Rabbi says, "No, no, that was her double." And the Parrot says, "If it's all the same, I just assume leave."

(*General silence, embarrassment.*)

TIM: Ahh.

THE FIRE CHIEF: Well, gotta go. Bye-bye.

(*They run to the door for one last goodbye. They fake smiles as THE FIRE CHIEF exits.*)

JIM: (*Calling.*) Have a good fire!

GREG: (*Calling.*) I'm sure it'll be a burning sensation!

CRAIG: (*Calling.*) Drive carefully!

(*After a moment, when THE FIRE CHIEF is clearly gone:*)

TIM: (*Closing the door, woefully.*) Zing, zing, zing went my heartstrings.

CRAIG: I never knew it could be like this.

GREG: I have always depended on the kindness of big, strapping men in uniforms.

JIM: His father was our executioner and his brother was hung.

(*ALL return to their seats, momentarily dazed.*)

TIM: I hate a wiseass parrot.

(*The lights change, as does the play's tone and rhythm. The staging of this section should be created in rehearsal by the director and actors, as they find an expressionistic way of communicating the play's meaning through the abstract text provided.*)

JIM: His father was our farmer and his brother plowed me.

TIM: His father was our dentist and his brother drilled me.

CRAIG: His father was our rug merchant and his brother laid me.

GREG: His father was our elevator man and his brother went down on me.

TIM: His father was our chicken and his brother fingered me.

GREG: The rules have all been broken.

CRAIG: When I say no, I mean yes.

JIM: Nobody loves love handles. Men want men who are soft on the inside.

TIM: A thing of beauty is a boy forever.

CRAIG: Momma, I'm pretty. I'm a pretty girl, Momma.

GREG: When your muscles shine even without weights in hand, you clearly own a power-packed physique. It'll come in handy if you're ever backed against a wall.

JIM: I swiped my dance card from an audition once.

CRAIG: You run like a girl!

GREG: You throw like a girl!

JIM: You talk like a girl!

TIM: Maybe you just haven't found the right girl.

GREG: Gentlemen prefer brawn.

CRAIG: I have a feeling we're not in Chelsea anymore.

TIM: Clap if you believe in fairies!

CRAIG: If we don't come together, we will drift apart.

JIM: To love oneself is the beginning of a lifelong romance.

GREG: Your silence will not protect you.

CRAIG: Silence equals death.

TIM: With enough olives, a martini can make a smart dinner!

CRAIG: The ceiling is above, the carpet's below…unless you're having a fabulous time.

GREG: The bigger they come, the bigger they come.

TIM: Does my ensemble work?

JIM: I'm not one of your fans!

GREG: I used to think I was popular, but it turned out I was just a slut.

CRAIG: But if baby I'm the bottom, you're the top.

TIM: I am the Love that dare not speak its name.

JIM: Who am I anyway? Am I my resume?

GREG: I am what I am.

JIM: I can't stand a naked light bulb, any more than I can a rude remark or a vulgar action.

TIM: Is it bigger than a bread box?

GREG: Do a trick, make him breakfast, and it will turn vicious.

CRAIG: Don't fuck with me, fellas!

TIM: We are all in the gutter, but some of us are looking at the stars.

CRAIG: I celebrate myself and sing myself, and what I assume, you shall assume.

JIM: There wasn't a sound anymore, there was nothing to see but Sebastian, what was left of him, that looked like a big white-paper-wrapped bunch of red roses had been torn, thrown, crushed!

(Following this last line of JIM's, the OTHERS are silent for a moment, stupefied. We sense that there is a certain nervous irritation.)

GREG: Real men don't eat quiche.

JIM: It's only a phase.

CRAIG: Look better naked.

TIM: Do you really want to hurt me?

CRAIG: It takes one to know one.

GREG: Straight looking, straight acting seeks same.

TIM: Everyday's a runway.

JIM: Living well is the best revenge.

GREG: One size fits all.

CRAIG: Take it like a man!

JIM: At first I was afraid, I was petrified.

TIM: I am thin and gorgeous, I am thin and gorgeous, I am thin and gorgeous.

CRAIG: Boys don't cry.

TIM: Boys don't cry.

JIM: Cry me a river.

GREG: And it's one, two, three strikes you're out!

CRAIG: Gucci, Balducci, Fiorucci.

TIM: Nicky Arnstein, Nicky Arnstein.

JIM: Classy trash.

CRAIG: Submissive daddies.

TIM: Bossy bottoms.

GREG: Dominant verbal top looking to give someone a hard time.

CRAIG: Manholes!

TIM: Kumquats!

GREG: Cocktails!

JIM: Dictation!

CRAIG: Balzac!

GREG: Nutcracker!

TIM: Woodpecker!

JIM: Lake Titicaca!

TIM, CRAIG, and GREG: No fats, no fems.

JIM: No bad haircuts!

CRAIG: How do I look?

TIM: How do I look?

GREG: Kenneth!

CRAIG: Cole!

TIM: Calvin!

JIM: Klein!

CRAIG and TIM: Calvin Cole!

GREG and JIM: Kenneth Klein.

TIM: Socrates, Sappho, Shakespeare, Stein.

JIM: Whitman, Wilde, Woolf!

CRAIG: Tennessee Williams Sonoma.

GREG: Butt munch!

JIM: Fudge packer!

CRAIG: Y, M, C, A.

GREG: X, T, C.

JIM: G, H, B.

GREG: D, N, A.

TIM: H, I, V.

CRAIG: A, Z, T.

TIM: D, K, N, Y, D, K, N, Y, D, K, N, Y, D, K, N, Y!

JIM: Nellie, Sissy, Nancy.

GREG: Just relax, it won't hurt.

CRAIG: Trust me.

JIM: Trust me.

TIM: Call me.

JIM: If happy little bluebirds fly—

CRAIG: Get over it!

TIM: Take a chance, take a chance, take a chance, take a chance, take a chance, take a chance, take a chance, take a chance, take a chance, take a chance, take a chance, take a chance…

GREG: Beep, beep.

JIM: Toot-toot.

GREG: Beep, beep.

CRAIG: Toot-toot.

JIM: Oh !

TIM: Please!

GREG: Don't!

CRAIG: Stop! Stop!

JIM: Oh!

GREG: Don't!

TIM: Please!

CRAIG: Stop!

GREG: Don't!

CRAIG: Stop!

JIM: Oh!

TIM: Please!

(ALL together, completely infuriated, screaming in each OTHERS' ears. The light is extinguished. In the darkness we hear, in an increasingly rapid rhythm:)

TIM, JIM, CRAIG, and GREG: Oh please don't stop! Oh please don't stop! Please don't stop! Please don't stop! Please don't stop! Don't stop! Don't stop! Don't stop! Don't stop! Don't stop! Don't stop! Don't stop!

(ALL stop abruptly. Again, the lights come on. CRAIG and GREG are seated like TIM and JIM were at the beginning of the play. The play begins again with the TYLER-MARTINS, who say the same lines as the JACKSON-SMITHS in the first scene.)

CRAIG: It's nine o'clock. It's too early to go out. You can't really be seen before eleven-fifteen. Except at the gym, of course. Or dining out. Or if you're cruising D'Agostino's. We've already had dinner. And we gave up desserts five years ago. The dogs have been walked. We have two Jack Russell terriers, Fanny and Yentl. That's because we live in Chelsea and because our names are Craig and Greg Tyler-Martin.

(GREG continues to watch TV.)

CRAIG: *Will & Grace* is a repeat. *Queer As Folk* is a repeat. *Sex in the City* is a repeat. *Queer Eye* is a repeat. *Golden Girls* is a repeat. *Designing Women* is a repeat. *Ab Fab* is a repeat. *Trading Spaces* is a repeat.

(During the list of television show repeats, the lights slowly fade to black.)

(END OF PLAY.)

FATBOY

A Grotesque in Three Acts

John Clancy

JOHN CLANCY was born on October 7, 1963, in St. Louis, Missouri. He received a BA in theatre from Oberlin College. He is a partner in Clancy Productions, a critically acclaimed international theatrical touring and production company. He is the founding artistic director of The Present Company and the founding artistic director of the New York International Fringe Festival, North America's largest theatre and performance festival. His plays have won the American Shorts Contest, the San Francisco Playwrights Center Dramarama, and the Edinburgh Festival Fringe First and have been short-listed for the Julie Harris Playwriting Award and the Actors Theatre of Louisville Heideman Award. He has directed five Scotsman Fringe First–winning productions at the Edinburgh Festival Fringe, including *Americana Absurdum* by Brian Parks, *Cincinnati* by Don Nigro, *Horse Country* and *screwmachine/eyecandy*, both by C. J. Hopkins, and his own *Fatboy*. Both *Horse Country* and *Cincinnati* went on to win the Best of the Fringe Award at the Adelaide Fringe in 2004. He serves on the Advisory Council of the New York Theatre Experience, Inc., and the Advisory Board of the 24:7 Theatre Festival in Manchester, England. He is a New York Theatre Workshop Usual Suspect, and his writing has been published in *Off*, *Edge*, the *Village Voice*, the *Sunday Herald*, and the *New York Times*. He was awarded the New York Magazine Award in 1997 for "creativity, enterprise and vision." In 2006, he received an Obie Award for Sustained Excellence in Direction. He lives on the Lower East Side of Manhattan with his wife, actress Nancy Walsh.

Fatboy received its world premiere as part of the Edinburgh Festival Fringe on August 6, 2004, at The Assembly Rooms, with the following cast and credits:

Fatboy...Mike McShane
Fudgie...Nancy Walsh
Tenant, Prosecutor, Slave...Matt Oberg
Judge, Minister of Finance...David Calvitto
Mailman, Bailiff, Innocent, Minister of Justice...................................Jody Lambert

Director: John Clancy
Set: Kelly Hanson
Costumes: Michael Oberle
Lighting: Colin D. Young
Production Stage Manager: Jeff Meyers
Assistant Director: Emily Fishbaine
Music arranged by: Jody Lambert

The New York premiere of *Fatboy* was presented by Soho Think Tank (Robert Lyons, Artistic Director) and Clancy Productions, Inc. (John Clancy, Producing Artistic Director) on March 6, 2006, at the Ohio Theatre, with the following cast and credits:

Fatboy...Del Pentecost
Fudgie...Nancy Walsh
Tenant, Prosecutor, Slave...Matt Oberg
Judge, Minister of Finance...David Calvitto
Mailman, Bailiff, Innocent, Minister of Justice...................................Jody Lambert

Director: John Clancy
Set: Kelly Hanson
Costumes: Michael Oberle
Lighting: Eric Southern
Production Stage Manager: Rachel Mudd
Music arranged by: Jody Lambert

"I intended that, when the curtain went up, the scene in front of the public should be like the mirror in the stories of Madame Leprince de Beaumont in which the wanton saw themselves with horns on the body of a dragon, according to the exaggeration of their vices. It is not surprising that the public should have been astonished at the sight of its ignoble other-self... eternal human imbecility, eternal gluttony, the vileness of instinct elevated into tyranny; the decency, the virtues, the patriotism and the ideals of those who have just dined well." —Alfred Jarry on Ubu Roi, **Theater Questions**

CHARACTERS

FATBOY, a monster
FUDGIE, his wife
MAILMAN, a mailman
TENANT, a tenant
JUDGE, a judge
BAILIFF, a bailiff
PROSECUTOR, a prosecutor
INNOCENT, an innocent
SLAVE, a slave
MINISTER OF JUSTICE, a minister
MINISTER OF FINANCE, another minister

One actor plays TENANT, PROSECUTOR, and SLAVE. Another actor plays MAILMAN, BAILIFF, INNOCENT, and MINISTER OF JUSTICE. Yet another actor plays JUDGE and MINISTER OF FINANCE.

PRODUCTION NOTES

The play takes place on stage.

Style is broad, vulgar, grand, artificial, and quick. Bursts of shouting broken up by melodrama. The lyricism serves to highlight the savagery, the savagery is constant. Every element is overtly theatrical. The lights too bright and rosy; the performers made up masklike with heavy base, lipstick, and eye shadow; the set an obvious construction.

ACT ONE
FATBOY THE KING

The play is set in a poor man's kitchen as imagined by a stage designer. A door unit upstage center, a table, two kitchen chairs, a coat rack, an armchair. Lights up on FATBOY in armchair, face hidden by newspaper.

FATBOY: MOTHERFUCK! Cocksucking fuckheaded motherfucking FUCKS!

FUDGIE: (*Shouting from offstage.*) Quiet out there!

FATBOY: I HAVE BEEN INSULTED!

FUDGIE: SHUT IT YOU FAT BASTARD!

FATBOY: (*Lowers paper, stares out at audience, brooding.*) A quiet morning shattered. A newborn day aborted at the moment of birth. PANCAKES!

FUDGIE: (*Offstage.*) SHUT IT!

FATBOY: (*Resumes brooding.*) A conspiracy, clearly. An obvious and clumsy attempt to unsettle. My enemies, a cabal of cocksucking whores, lash out at me even here. SAUSAGE!

FUDGIE: (*Entering.*) There is no sausage, you fat wretched bastard.

FATBOY: BACON!

FUDGIE: YOU'VE EATEN IT ALL YOU MONSTER YOU DUNGHEAP YOU MAN.

FATBOY: Slander. Slander and lies and more. Have you read the paper today?

FUDGIE: Other people's business bores me. I have business of my own.

FATBOY: I have sounded out each sentence, squinted out each semicolon and NOTHING. No word. No scrap. Not the smallest mention of me.

FUDGIE: Why that speaks volumes, dear. You are nothing. You barely exist.

FATBOY: I AM FATBOY AND I AM KING.

FUDGIE: I often forget about you myself. But then, of course, your stench reminds me that yes, sadly, you continue to live, leech-like and horrid, a barnacle on my ship of state.

FATBOY: LEECHES! FRIED LEECHES IN BEER BATTER AND NOW YOU WRECK YOU SHREW!

FUDGIE: THERE IS NO MONEY FOR FOOD! OR CLOTHING OR SHELTER OR HEAT! We spent our last dime last night throwing it at the clowns.

FATBOY: Scattered them good, though.

FUDGIE: O yes, they scampered.

FATBOY: Filthy white-faced fucks.

FUDGIE: Outcasts and freaks of the world.

FATBOY: A clown is an abomination.

FUDGIE: A warning to the rest not to stray.

FATBOY: Sit here on my lap, dear, and let's pretend we're young.

FUDGIE: Haul your fat ass up, dear, and go and bring back coin.

FATBOY: Dance for me, my pumpkin.

FUDGIE: Make some money, pig.

FATBOY: Is that all you can talk about? Money money money money? Is that all there is to this life? What of art? Beauty? Truth?

(*They laugh hugely at the joke, wiping tears from their eyes.*)

FUDGIE: (*Recovering.*) Ah, you fat fucker, you can still make me laugh.

FATBOY: Wait. Justice! Honor! Love!

FUDGIE: No. Better the first way.

FATBOY: MUST YOU ALWAYS CRITICIZE?

FUDGIE: FAT UGLY STUPID MAN!

FATBOY: Every day. Every day the same. No peace. No quiet contemplation. No chance for a moment to gather slowly and present itself to me. Always cursing. Always raised voices and clenched fists and this caterwauling wretch of a wife stomping about and this second-rate wreck of a life spooling away and always the same, day after day after day after—wait, what's the date today?

FUDGIE: The first.

FATBOY: Of the month?

FUDGIE: Yes.

FATBOY: It's check day.

FUDGIE: No.

FATBOY: It is. The check comes on the first of the month.

FUDGIE: That's today!

FATBOY: I know!

FUDGIE: We're saved!

FATBOY: HA! And you were suggesting I work.

FUDGIE: The check. My god. I had forgotten.

FATBOY: You must have faith in this world and its ways. You must never, never despair.

FUDGIE: We can eat. Turn the phone back on. Buy things from the television.

FATBOY: I myself am a fortress of faith. I believe. I believe in all things.

FUDGIE: We'll redecorate. Throw out all this trash and wreckage and create a paradise.

FATBOY: All sects, all dogmas, all opinions and gossip. All is true, if you believe.

FUDGIE: (*Sweetly.*) About the check, dear Fatboy?

FATBOY: What of it, harpy?

FUDGIE: What is it for, again?

FATBOY: Royalties.

FUDGIE: But your blood is common.

FATBOY: Now, yes, but once it was rare and it boiled from my veins out onto the page and I spattered masterworks all day.

FUDGIE: You're a writer, then?

FATBOY: DON'T INSULT ME! I was young and knew no better.

FUDGIE: When I was young I was wise.

FATBOY: You were never young, you horrible cow.

FUDGIE: I HAVE PHOTOGRAPHS!

FATBOY: FORGERIES!

FUDGIE: FAT BASTARD!

(*They rush at each other in mortal combat, grapple, and then are interrupted by a knock at the door.*)

MAILMAN: (*Offstage.*) Special delivery!

FATBOY: Hush.

FUDGIE: My god.

MAILMAN: *(Offstage.)* Special delivery for Fatboy! Royalty check for Fatboy!

FATBOY: The check.

FUDGIE: Sweet holy crippled Christ.

(FATBOY disengages from FUDGIE, opens door. MAILMAN with envelope.)

FATBOY: *(Deeply suspicious.)* Yes?

MAILMAN: Fatboy?

FATBOY: Perhaps.

FUDGIE: It's him, it's him.

(FATBOY spins and glares at FUDGIE, she drops her gaze.)

MAILMAN: I have a special delivery for Fatboy.

FATBOY: Who sent you?

MAILMAN: The dispatcher.

FATBOY: Hand it over and no one gets hurt.

MAILMAN: Are you Fatboy, then?

FATBOY: None of your impertinence, dickhead. Give me what is mine.

(MAILMAN hands over envelope, holds out clipboard.)

MAILMAN: Sign here.

(FATBOY makes X on clipboard.)

MAILMAN: First and last.

(FATBOY makes second X on clipboard.)

MAILMAN: God bless you and keep you both.

FATBOY: *(Slamming door in his face.)* I WILL NOT HAVE THAT TALK IN MY HOUSE!

FUDGIE: It's true. The check. Sweet merciful jug-headed Jesus.

FATBOY: *(Holding envelope high.)* SALVATION!

FUDGIE: *(Trying to get check.)* SCENTED SOAP SHAPED LIKE FLOWERS!

FATBOY: ALCOHOL! CIGARETTES! BACON! MINE! MINE! MINE! *(Devours envelope.)* Ah. Consumption.

FUDGIE: You fat idiot. You ate the check.

FATBOY: I feel a nap coming on. *(Collapses to floor, snoring loudly and theatrically.)*

FUDGIE: *(Kicks him.)* Is this it then, always? Forever fighting with the fat bastard over scraps of money not mine? Grinding away the time like two teeth clenched, gnashing away in the dark? Where are my children to comfort and console me in this my hour of need?

FATBOY: You ate your firstborn and drove the rest away.

FUDGIE: You're sleeping! No talking while sleeping!

FATBOY: I'm talking in my sleep!

FUDGIE: You are not! You are silent in your sleep you fat bastard!

FATBOY: WHORE!

FUDGIE: MUTE BASTARD! Yes it is true I ate my first one but such a sweet little morsel he was. All pink and plump and perfect. The others I don't remember, ungrateful and demanding, I'm sure, and clumsy and needy like all children are. Rolling around on the floor in their filth and not able to support their own heads. How in Christ could they ever support me?

FATBOY: *(Rising.)* Most refreshing lying there pretending to sleep. Much more refreshing than actual sleep, the paralysis and dreams and despair.

FUDGIE: Do you dream, horror?

FATBOY: Of heaven.

FUDGIE: Is it nice?

FATBOY: If you like that sort of thing.

FUDGIE: I dream of death.

FATBOY: Yours or someone who matters?

FUDGIE: I'm always alone in my dreams.

FATBOY: Heaven, death, bedtime stories. What are we having for lunch?

FUDGIE: Nothing if you don't make some money. You fat disgusting monster.

FATBOY: What am I, a mint? Some kind of mint? Do you have any mints?

FUDGIE: Earn some money, monster.

FATBOY: Gum? A candy wrapper? Something goddamn it?

FUDGIE: We are destitute, you lumbering wreck. We have nothing but the clothes on our back and the furniture here before you.

FATBOY: Am I to eat a chair? Am I to devour a table, you harpy, you witch?

FUDGIE: GO. AND GET. MONEY. *(Exits.)*

FATBOY: Women. Always so cryptic. I'M NOT A MINDREADER, YOU KNOW! She wants something from me, of course, that much is obvious, they all do. Greedy greedy give me give me. *(Begins to absentmindedly gnaw the chair.)* But never a thought for poor Fatboy. Never, what would *you* like, sweet Fatboy? Always this way, all my life, all my lives, every tick of time. As a boy, left to riot, as a man left to rot. Cocksuckers. Asshole fuckheaded cocksuckers. Always the burden. Always the load. I'M EATING A CHAIR! HAS IT COME TO THIS? *(Continues snacking on chair.)* Well I say no more. I say fuck all y'all and fuck you twice from behind. I am not a beast of burden. I am not a servant or a slave. I am Fatboy and I AM GOD. I will take what I need, I will take what I deserve, I will take whatever I see. I shall be rich, I shall be respected and I shall be fed. *(Tosses chair down, strides to the coat rack, puts on coat.)* WHERE IS MY HAT?

FUDGIE: *(Offstage.)* YOU ATE IT!

FATBOY: NOT THAT ONE! MY "NOW I SHALL BE RESPECTED" HAT!

FUDGIE: *(Enters.)* You're going to be respected?

FATBOY: Not without that hat!

FUDGIE: Who would respect you?

FATBOY: Various and sundry. All god's creatures.

FUDGIE: *(Dismissively.)* Them. Get some money while you're out there. Or shoot the President.

FATBOY: My hat, harpy?

FUDGIE: Shoved up your fat ass, I believe.

FATBOY: *(Searches with both hands behind him, pulls out top hat.)* Ah. *(Puts it on.)* Warm. How do I look?

FUDGIE: The spitting image of yourself.

FATBOY: Don't insult me. And don't sleep with anyone while I'm gone.

FUDGIE: Shall I wait until you're back then?

FATBOY: I SHALL BE RESPECTED! *(Walks grandly into wall, falls downs.)* MOTHERFUCK! *(Gets to his feet.)* I'm off, then.

FUDGIE: Ta-ta.

FATBOY: *(Exiting.)* VICTORY! HONOR! PANCAKES!

FUDGIE: *(Swooning.)* I love that ugly sack of shit and yet I think of murder. Just stab him in the head forty or fifty times and watch him drop away dead. Beat him with a baseball bat until my arm gets tired. Suffocate him in his fitful sleep. I have myself to think of, after all. I was not born, brought screaming into this world, delivered like a package, to be poor. My parents' indiscretion was not to result in this. I am of noble lineage. I have the charts. My profile belongs on coins. I'm the brains of this outfit is what I'm saying and don't you ever forget it. He can strut, he can swagger, but I'm deep below. I'm tracking it out ten moves away. Proof? I'll give you proof. *(Grabs newspaper.)* Here, in the classifieds, what is this among the desperate and depraved? "Room to let. Wrong side of town. Professionals only, please." I always could turn a phrase, that last part is poetry. I placed the ad, got him out of the house, and now sit back like a queen.

(She sits regally. A knock on the door.)

FUDGIE: My god it worked. Ten words printed in the morning paper and a professional knocks on my door. This is truly the time of modern marvels, the apex of civilization.

(A knock on the door.)

FUDGIE: *(To audience.)* Don't tell him about Fatboy. I live alone in dignified squalor. I'm a woman to be pitied and paid. Sit up straight and look presentable. I'll do the talking.

(She opens door, TENANT stands there, Gilbert and Sullivan tenor type, maybe tight pants, ruffled shirt, blonde coiffed wig. Underneath, shabby, dirty, untrustworthy type.)

FUDGIE: *(Feigning innocence and distraction.)* Yes hello, hello yes?

TENANT: I saw the ad in the paper.

FUDGIE: Ad? Ad in the paper?

TENANT: Yes. "Room to let. Wrong side of town. Et cetera."

FUDGIE: Et cetera? O yes. Of course. Et cetera. "Professionals Only Please."

TENANT: Exactly. Yes. May I come in?

FUDGIE: Are you, then?

TENANT: Am I?

FUDGIE: Professional?

TENANT: I am.

FUDGIE: Come in, young man, come in.

(TENANT enters.)

TENANT: My dear woman, this room is a shambles.

FUDGIE: My dear man, this is not the room.

TENANT: Ah. Then forgive my judgment.

FUDGIE: Are you a judge, then?

TENANT: A judge? O no.

FUDGIE: A lawyer, a court reporter, a bailiff?

TENANT: I avoid the law whenever possible, ma'am.

FUDGIE: A prudent course of action. Are you a doctor, an accountant, a dean of some school?

TENANT: I am none of those things, ma'am. I resent the implications.

FUDGIE: I will not have a merchant under my roof.

TENANT: So the roof comes with it, too?

FUDGIE: Four walls, a roof, one floor.

TENANT: A door?

FUDGIE: For those deserving. Are you a banker, an ombudsman, a seller of stocks and bonds?

TENANT: I have been many things, ma'am, but none that you have mentioned.

FUDGIE: Please bore us then with your life and times.

TENANT: My life is a trial I must endure. My times are dark and troubled.

FUDGIE: *(To audience.)* This stranger moves me somehow. Is it his wig or something deeper? My every thrust he parries. I'll suss him this time sure. *(To TENANT.)* State your occupation and none of your poetry now.

TENANT: I kill people for money.

FUDGIE: A lot of money or not so much?

TENANT: A tremendous amount. I do it right. I am a professional.

FUDGIE: Well that's the word I'm looking for, for the sake of St. Malcolm the Mick. Welcome, young man. Three months up front and a security deposit of one.

TENANT: Four months then total?

FUDGIE: *(To audience.)* A mathematician, too. My heart beats polyrhythmic.

TENANT: Will you take a check?

(They laugh hugely at the joke.)

FUDGIE: And a funnyman as well. Cash, now, and don't start taking off your shirt and flexing that lovely flesh.

TENANT: *(Handing her a sack of money and taking off his shirt.)* Warm in here.

FUDGIE: The heat is not included.

TENANT: What is included, temptress?

FUDGIE: As I said, four walls, one floor, the ceiling and… *(Trails off coquettishly.)*

TENANT: A door?

FUDGIE: O sir.

TENANT: A door to close and dance behind?

FUDGIE: We have no cabaret license.

TENANT: A door to lock so those outside can't witness what happens within?

FUDGIE: Don't take off your pants, now, I implore you, let me help.

(TENANT kicks off shoes as she unsnaps his pants and pulls them down.)

TENANT: Did I tell you I kill for a living?

FUDGIE: Get them off get them off get them off.

TENANT: Barehanded mostly. No weapon to clean or conceal.

FUDGIE: Come with me now my killer.

TENANT: A hand around the neck. A squeeze. A twist.

FUDGIE: Come with me to your room.

TENANT: Am I in, then?

FUDGIE: Ah, soon. Soon, my murdering boy. And I'll do you like a dirty deed I've dreamed of all my days.

TENANT: I'll do you like a duty I would rather leave undone.

(FUDGIE drags TENANT off stage left. FATBOY bangs the front door open, bloody, wads of cash in his hands.)

FATBOY: MOTHERFUCK! COCKSUCKING FUCK-HEADED PIECE OF SHIT FUCKS! I go into the world harmless, wishing none ill will or folly and am repaid for my kindness with blood. Not mine, thank god, but still.

FUDGIE: (Offstage amidst much scraping and banging.) O MY GOD, YES!

TENANT: (Offstage.) WAIT!

FATBOY: (Oblivious to sounds offstage.) I walk to the center of town, declare myself king, ask for what is due me and am given… what? Riches? Kisses? Titles and deeds and keys to the vaults hidden deep? No, none of these, no. I am given scorn.

FUDGIE: (Offstage.) GIVE IT TO ME, YES!

TENANT: I WILL, I WILL, JUST WAIT!

FATBOY: I am given laughter. Cold, cruel, "HAHS" and then I am left alone. In a crowd of my subjects, a hive of those below me, alone, avoided, shunned.

FUDGIE: (Offstage.) BABBLING BLUE-EYED JESUS!

TENANT: (Offstage.) HOLD STILL, WOMAN!

FUDGIE: (Offstage.) SWEET SPASTIC MOTHER OF CHRIST!

TENANT: (Offstage.) FOR GOD'S SAKE HUSH!

FATBOY: And so I walk to the courthouse. Immense, gray-stoned, forbidding. I climb the marble stairs, push open the massive door, and stand in the echoing lobby. And amplified by the architect's art I whisper I Am Fatboy. Bow Before Me Or Die. My reasoned offer ripples off the walls and reaches every ear. They turn, as one, as many, as all, and look upon their ruler.

FUDGIE: (Offstage.) GREAT GURGLING GOOGLE-EYED GOD!

TENANT: (Offstage.) I'LL KILL YOU, YOU KNOW! I WILL!

FATBOY: QUIET IN THERE OR I'LL CRUSH YOU! (Scraping and banging stops offstage.) All eyes on me now. All palms itching. All spines stiff. An eternity passes, silent and still, and then one steps out from the throng. He is old, palsied, hunched by the weight of his years, but his eyes are clear and his voice is strong as he shouts, "Get out of here you madman or we shall call the authorities."

(FUDGIE peeks out from stage right.)

FATBOY: My laughter explodes like a hydrogen isotope and I see him physically shrink half a foot as I bellow out "Authorities? I am the Authority. I AM FATBOY AND I AM DEATH."

(TENANT peeks out next to FUDGIE.)

FATBOY: "I AM THE DESTROYER OF WORLDS." And with this I stride forward and begin the work of the day.

(During the following speech, TENANT and FUDGIE cross slowly toward FATBOY, captivated by the tale. TENANT's shirt is on inside out, he has no pants; FUDGIE's skirt is down around her ankles.)

FATBOY: The old man stands fast and I admire his courage in the second before I snap his chicken neck. His murder unfreezes the crowd and half run shrieking away and half rush towards me, hands out, mouths moving, but there seems to me no sound. Slow motion, silent enemies drifting into my grasp. I deliver death like a dutiful postman, each man getting his own. They tear and claw at me and there are arms around my legs and faces pressed against mine but I am Fatboy. I prevail. It is still again and sound comes back, the ragged breath of the dying, the weeping of those still alive, hiding in the shadows and the corners of the room. From one shadow a young girl steps, pretty in her young girl's dress, her young girl's hair held back from her face by a bow. She crosses to a crumpled corpse, kneels, and then looks to me. "My daddy…" she says. "Is dead," I say, "And you will be too, someday. Now help me get the money from their coats or that someday is now."

Working together, we clear the lot, her small hands much quicker than mine and soon she's enjoying the game. The search, the discovery, the growing pile of green. When we are done, I slip her a hundred and she curtsies and asks for more. So I make a fist and raise it high and smash it down on her head. She falls like a puppet whose strings I've cut. I take the bill from her lifeless hand and walk through the pooling blood to the door. It is a beautiful day, if you like that sort of thing, sunshine and blue sky and a gentle breeze from the West. I walk home the long way, through the old section, stopping to murder and thieve. Most smile and nod when they see me, relieved, I think, that I am finally here, that they are finally done. Some run. These I chase and the fastest get away. All in all, bloody work. Now make me some pancakes. Who's this?

TENANT: *(Offering his hand.)* A fellow bare-hands man. Well done.

FATBOY: *(Not taking his hand.)* What are you doing in my home? What is he doing in my home?

FUDGIE: More than you've done in years, fat bastard. Let me have the cash.

(FATBOY hands her the wads of bloody notes, which she begins to count.)

FATBOY: You look like a strapping fellow.

TENANT: I've strapped a few in my time.

FATBOY: And why do you stand before me? Why are my eyes assaulted by the sight of your self?

TENANT: I am your new tenant, sir.

FATBOY: Are you mad? Is he mad?

FUDGIE: He's lovely, you monstrous beast, and he knows how to use it, too.

FATBOY: My new tenant? I haven't an old and yet you're the new?

TENANT: I answered your ad in the paper.

FATBOY: My ad in the paper? Did I run an ad saying "Strapping young fools only, pants not required"? WHAT IS THE MEANING OF THIS?

FUDGIE: I'm renting out your study so that we can eat and frolic and this fine young killer answered the ad. Of course, now what with this fortune, we don't need the income, but my god he's hung like a donkey so I think we'll keep him, dear.

FATBOY: My study is sacred.

FUDGIE: You never use it, pig.

FATBOY: Where will I keep my books? My years of research and notes?

FUDGIE: I threw them out yesterday while you were choking on something.

FATBOY: GODDAMNED OLIVES! THEY SHOULD SAY IF THEY HAVE PITS!

FUDGIE: *(Finishing the count and beginning to become thoughtful.)* This is a lot of money, but I have a feeling that there's more.

TENANT: There's a world of it out there, if you know how to ask.

FATBOY: So you'll be living here, then?

TENANT: I'm paid up for three months.

FATBOY: And sleeping with this horrible woman?

TENANT: I don't know what you mean, sir.

FATBOY: YOU'RE NOT WEARING PANTS AND HER SKIRT'S BELOW HER KNEES. I AM NOT BLIND. A little nearsighted, I think. Which is it when you can't see far away, but up close is fine?

TENANT: That's nearsighted. You can see what's near.

FATBOY: Makes sense. PAY ME FOR WHAT YOU HAVE TAKEN.

FUDGIE: *(Still figuring out loud.)* This is plenty of money, but still…

TENANT: Taken? I took nothing.

FUDGIE: Still, if there's more, why then…

FATBOY: Be reasonable, young man. Out in the street, in an alley or a park, it would run you twenty dollars, fifty if she's fine. But you had a room. Four walls, a ceiling, and a floor. You had privacy and leverage. Now, granted, she's a sea lion and a horror and a cow, an affront to all that's holy and good, but still. I have to ask for thirty.

TENANT: You should pay me, sir. It was an act of charity and courage.

FUDGIE: It should all be mine, really. Others shouldn't have things. Others should make things and give things. To me. What on earth would others do with things?

FATBOY: Thirty dollars or hell's unleashed.

TENANT: Damn you, sir. Not a penny.

FATBOY: Three thousand pennies or your life.

TENANT: I should warn you, sir, I am a professional.

FATBOY: And I should warn you, fuckface, I'm an enthusiast.

FUDGIE: Others should serve and be grateful.

FATBOY: STRAPPING TENANT FUCK!

TENANT: FAT CUCKOLD BASTARD!

(They fight, horribly, realistically, loudly as FUDGIE rises and with money in hands speaks her reverie.)

FUDGIE: Others should willingly, instinctively, give all they have to the fat man and me or they should be unmade. We want things, after all. We have desires. We're only human and we desire it all. There are things not yet made and those we desire as well, those most of all, I believe, and we shall have them, yes. We shall have everything and all shall serve or we'll crush them like insects, like beetles 'neath our boots. And if there are things we don't desire, things that don't please us or are shoddy or confuse us, then those things shall be crushed as well. Nothing should be that we don't desire, nothing should exist that we can't own and enjoy. A bonfire of all the things we don't want will lick the night sky and make bright the dark heavens above. And below that dark heaven we'll reign. Fatboy the King and his bride, Queen Fudgie the First.

(TENANT's hands are around FATBOY's hands wrapped around his neck.)

TENANT: All right, sir, you've won.

FUDGIE: Haven't you killed him yet?

FATBOY: One sec.

(FATBOY snaps TENANT's neck.)

FATBOY: There it is.

(TENANT collapses to floor, dead.)

FATBOY: What's for dinner? I'm starving.

FUDGIE: Tonight we dine, fat bastard.

FATBOY: My dear, you look radiant with all that money. Give it back now.

FUDGIE: *(Admiringly.)* And you with the blood of strangers and slaves, smeared on you like jelly on toast.

FATBOY: JELLY! TOAST! CHEESECAKE AND PIE!

FUDGIE: You must kill more, my monster.

FATBOY: You're not the boss of me.

FUDGIE: The world awaits your slaughter.

FATBOY: Let it wait. I'm hungry. FOOD GODDAMN-IT AND NOW!

FUDGIE: Did you shoot the President?

FATBOY: Seemed like such a waste.

FUDGIE: A waste, you horror, why?

FATBOY: They'll just elect another.

FUDGIE: Who will, pig?

FATBOY: Anyone. The rabble. Citizens.

FUDGIE: *(Dismissively.)* Them.

FATBOY: Give me the money, whore.

FUDGIE: It's mine now, pig. Get your own.

FATBOY: Surely there's enough if we share.

(They laugh hugely at the joke.)

FUDGIE: *(Wiping tears of laughter from her eyes.)* Ah, you fat fucker, you do make me laugh.

FATBOY: *(Embracing her while reaching for the cash.)* And you make me choke with revulsion.

FUDGIE: *(Trying to wriggle away.)* You're getting blood on my blouse.

FATBOY: Give me the money, woman.

FUDGIE: *(Struggling.)* GET YOUR OWN! IT'S MINE!

FATBOY: I WILL NOT BE DENIED!

FUDGIE: FAT BASTARD!

FATBOY: WHORE!

(They struggle, he grabs the money and begins to devour it.)

FATBOY: MMMM! TASTY TASTY!

FUDGIE: STOP IT FAT BASTARD! NO!

FATBOY: MORE! MORE! MORE!

(His laughter and her protests rise as the curtain drops.)

FIRST ENTR'ACTE

FATBOY and FUDGIE step in front of curtain, waving and bowing to the crowd.

FATBOY: We'd just like to take this opportunity to thank the author, Tom Clancy, for putting our lives on stage.

FUDGIE: We loved his *Hunt for Red October* and are naturally impressed with his encyclopedic knowledge of technological warfare.

FATBOY: We realize that this is a departure for him and we're honored that—

(A note is thrust through the curtain. FATBOY takes it.)

FATBOY: What's this? John Clancy. It's John Clancy. Not Tom.

FUDGIE: John Clancy the cook?

FATBOY: The nationally recognized chef and pastry-maker?

FUDGIE: It must be.

FATBOY: His recipes are prose masterpieces.

FUDGIE: His lists of ingredients haikus.

FATBOY: HE MAKES CAKES! AND COOKIES AND CRUSTS AND PIES!

FUDGIE: Something very sexy about a man who cooks. You want to lift up his apron and feast.

FATBOY: In any event, it is an honor to be portrayed.

FUDGIE: Although we must caution you that this is fiction.

FATBOY: A fictionalization.

FUDGIE: Lies.

FATBOY: Slander and character assassination.

FUDGIE: We shall sue and certainly win.

FATBOY: In actual life I am slender.

FUDGIE: And I a blushing virgin.

FATBOY: Well, no, you're a whore, he's got that right.

FUDGIE: You're a fat tub of shit.

FATBOY: Your hips are permanently splayed, you wanton wretched witch.

FUDGIE: Fat fat fucker.

FATBOY: HARPY!

FUDGIE: MONSTER!

FATBOY: WOMAN!

FUDGIE: MAN!

(Enormous hooks come from either end of stage and drag them off, screaming.)

ACT TWO
FATBOY IN CHAINS

Lights up on courtroom, JUDGE center stage up high, PROSECUTOR at table stage left, BAILIFF standing at attention stage right.

JUDGE: *(Banging gavel.)* Order! Order in the Court! This most august session of the War Crimes Tribunal is hereby called to order. Can I get anyone a drink?

PROSECUTOR: No thank you, your honor.

JUDGE: Little something?

PROSECUTOR: No, sir, I'm fine.

JUDGE: Take the edge off?

PROSECUTOR: No, really, I'm good.

JUDGE: All right. Bring in the accused.

(FATBOY enters in chains, dragged on by BAILIFF.)

FATBOY: MOTHERFUCK! PIECE OF SHIT ASS-FUCKING FUCKS! Release me now and your deaths, though horrific, will not be televised.

PROSECUTOR: You're in no position to make deals, sir!

JUDGE: Can I get you a drink?

FATBOY *(To PROSECUTOR.)* Do you know whom you are addressing, dickhead?

PROSECUTOR: A foul and murderous beast.

JUDGE: Little taste?

FATBOY: A free man stands before you, slave.

PROSECUTOR: A free man draped in chains.

FATBOY: I am History Incarnate. You are not even a footnote.

PROSECUTOR: A history written in blood is a signed confession in time.

FATBOY: INSIGNIFICANT FUCK!

PROSECUTOR: MONSTER!

(They rush at each other, FATBOY restrained by BAILIFF.)

JUDGE: *(Pounding gavel.)* ORDER! ORDER IN THIS COURT! *(To BAILIFF.)* How about you, something?

BAILIFF: No, your honor.

JUDGE: Well, shit. This is going to be a long day. *(Takes out flask, drinks.)* All righty then. The prosecution will read the charges.

FATBOY: I object, you asshole fuckhead.

JUDGE: On what grounds?

FATBOY: I object, first of all, to these chains. If you are to chain me, I insist on actual chains, not these cheap theatrics. What is this, I ask you, a non-union tour of *A Christmas Carol*? "Scrooge, Scrooo-ooooge." This is horseshit and I will not abide it. Secondly, if you are to sit up there for the entire act, I will be completely upstaged and I am the title character. I AM FATBOY AND I AM TITULAR. I respect the stagecraft and understand that the scene must be staged this way, but I must insist upon better lighting. Spotlight, pink gel, to follow me wherever I roam. And thirdly, I object on general principle, I object because this is objectionable, I object because it is my objective to do so, I object because you are assholes and fuckheads and I am your rightful god. Fuck all y'all and fuck your grandmas twice. Thank you.

JUDGE: Well said, sir. However, I wasn't really paying attention, so I'm going to have to overrule your objection. Can I get you a drink?

FATBOY: FREEDOM, FUCKHEAD!

JUDGE: You're a shouting person, aren't you? Shouty shouty shouty. I like that in a defendant. Gives the illusion of drama.

PROSECUTOR: Your honor?

JUDGE: Yes?

PROSECUTOR: May I read the charges?

JUDGE: You're sort of a stickler, aren't you? Shouty and Stickly. I wonder who will win.

PROSECUTOR: The charges, sir?

JUDGE: By all means, Stickly. The charges indeed.

PROSECUTOR: The accused, Fatboy the Monster, variously known as Fat Man, Fatty Fatty, The Fat Bastard, Fathead, Farthead (sic), That Man There, Horror Beyond Words, Boogala-Boogala-Boogala (sic), He Whose Face Is Death, Stinky Pete, Whoa There Nellie,

and The Drifter, is accused of the following crimes, felonies, malfeasances, and acts of outrage: To wit: rape, murder, looting, genocide, gross accounting irregularities, predatory lending, fraud, intention to commit fraud, illegal wiretapping, extortion, intention to commit extortion, loan sharking, racketeering, armed robbery of citizens and state banks and post offices, the theft of sacred objects, receiving stolen goods, selling stolen goods, overt intention to commit global gangsterism, willing and knowing permission and encouragement of slave labor, intentional and institutional boorishness, and profound criminal stupidity. How do you plead?

FATBOY: May I address the court?

JUDGE: You may.

FATBOY: Thank you, you enormous asshole. May I just say that I AM FATBOY AND I AM THE LAW. You are all assholes. Assholes of the world, I address you as your king, as your god, as your destiny and destroyer. I see here before me assholes from every hellhole on earth. I welcome you, I call you assholes, I spit on your traditions and faiths. You are assholes, your parents are assholes, your heroes, statesmen, and ancestors are complete and perfect assholes. Assholes, what I ask for here today is very simple. From this day forward, you all must agree to shut the fuck up, fuck yourselves, and stay the fuck out of my way. I AM FATBOY. In short, fuck all y'all, you big, big assholes. Thank you.

PROSECUTOR: So you plead guilty to these crimes?

FATBOY: What you call crimes, I call freedom. I ask you, asshole, is it a crime to breathe the harsh air of liberty? Is it a crime to recognize injustice and act to right what is wrong? Is it a crime to grab an old woman by the shoulders, lift her up into the air, shake her a few times, and then throw her to the ground, snapping her bones like kindling for a fire? Then leap into the air and come down with both boots squarely on the old woman and stomp around there for a while? Then go through her pockets and find what small fortune she hid? If these things are crimes, then I plead guilty. Guilty by reason of divine right. Guilty by reason of magnitude. Guilty by the simple fact of being too large for your puny laws to apply. Guilty guilty guilty.

JUDGE: I must warn you, sir, that these charges are most severe. There are certain rights, inalienable rights, human rights that must be upheld. Every life, no matter how small, is precious and must be protected.

(Huge laughter.)

FATBOY: Good one, fuckhead.

JUDGE: Yeah, I love that bit. So now. You realize by pleading guilty you face the death penalty?

FATBOY: I did not realize that, asshole. May I change my plea?

JUDGE: Certainly.

FATBOY: Innocent as a schoolgirl soaping herself in the sink.

JUDGE: The plea is so entered. Does anyone need a drink? No? Does anyone have any playing cards? No. Jesus. The prosecution may call its first witness.

PROSECUTOR: The prosecution calls the defendant's wife and accomplice, Queen Fudgie the First.

(FUDGIE enters, dressed to the nines, smiling, waving, blowing kisses to the crowd.)

FUDGIE: Thank you, thank you, thank you all.

BAILIFF: Do you swear to tell the truth, the whole truth, and nothing but the truth?

FUDGIE: A lady never swears.

BAILIFF: Fair enough.

FATBOY: I object. That's no lady, that's my wife.

(A moment of silence and then ALL onstage burst into huge laughter.)

FUDGIE: Ah, you fat fucker, you can still make me laugh.

FATBOY: Wait, better, I object, that's no lady, that's a horrible fucking beast.

FUDGIE: No, better the first way.

FATBOY: MUST YOU ALWAYS CRITICIZE?

FUDGIE: FAT UGLY STUPID GUILTY WAR CRIMINAL!

FATBOY: WHORE!

JUDGE: SILENCE! Can I get you a drink?

PROSECUTOR: State your name and your relationship to the accused.

FUDGIE: I'll take the fifth.

JUDGE: *(Handing her the bottle.)* Well it's about time.

FUDGIE : *(Takes huge swig, hands bottle back.)* Mmm. Minty. Now what were you saying, young man?

PROSECUTOR: Please tell the court your name and your relationship to the defendant.

FUDGIE: I am known as Fudge Girl, familiarly as Fudgie, officially as Queen Fudgie the First and on rare but profitable occasions as Betty Two-Times, the Tallahassee Tease. But my name, ah, my name is a mystery. A name, a string of syllables, a conjunction of spit and breath and friction, can it evoke one's essence, can it touch one's central truth, can it even point towards one's true and hidden face? A name is a name is a name, young man, what's yours and how about a quickie?

PROSECUTOR: Let the record show the witness has identified herself as Queen Fudgie. And your relationship to the accused?

FUDGIE: The whom?

PROSECUTOR: The accused, the defendant, the fat man there in chains.

FUDGIE: Oh. Hmm. I don't… I don't believe… no, I've never met the man.

FATBOY: LIES!

FUDGIE: FAT BASTARD!

JUDGE: SILENCE! So what are you doing later?

PROSECUTOR: The witness is reminded that we have a warehouse of photographs, audiocassettes, newspaper clippings, and motion pictures documenting her long and involved relationship with the accused as well as her own signed and notarized confession of her criminal awareness and involvement with the accused's activities.

FUDGIE: You make my blood boil, young man. Show a little chest.

PROSECUTOR: Can you identify the accused as the monster Fatboy?

FUDGIE: Whatever you wish, my sweet.

PROSECUTOR: And you can attest to his foul and monstrous deeds?

FUDGIE: If it would make you happy, you saucy little dish.

PROSECUTOR: Can you answer yes or no?

FUDGIE: Yes, you beauty, yes, I say yes to you, yes yes.

FATBOY: Must I sit here and watch the display of this woman's wanton ways?

FUDGIE: And yes to you, fat bastard.

FATBOY: HARLOT!

FUDGIE: MONSTER!

FATBOY: WOMAN!

FUDGIE: MAN!

JUDGE: Can anyone break a twenty? No? Proceed.

PROSECUTOR: Is this Fatboy?

FUDGIE: Yes.

PROSECUTOR: Is he a scourge, a pestilence, and a plague?

FUDGIE: Yes and yes and yes.

PROSECUTOR: Is he guilty of all the crimes charged to him and many more besides?

FUDGIE: O yes, you magnificent man.

PROSECUTOR: No further questions, your honor.

JUDGE: The accused may cross examine.

FATBOY: Your honor, I move that I get to wear your wig for a while.

JUDGE: For what reason?

FATBOY: I believe it will make me look younger.

JUDGE: Sustained.

FATBOY: Thank you, fucker. May I wear it backwards?

JUDGE: That I cannot allow.

FATBOY: Fuck you, then. I withdraw my initial request.

JUDGE: Let the record state that the initial request has been withdrawn.

FATBOY: And that his honor is a peevish asshole.

JUDGE: And that I, though honorable, am a peevish asshole.

FATBOY: I object, your honor. Your honor is an honorary term and has no bearing on your honor's actual honor.

JUDGE: Let the record state that though my honor is in doubt, my title shall remain your honor.

FATBOY: Thank you, fuckface.

JUDGE: You still want the wig?

FATBOY: I'm good, thanks.

JUDGE: Proceed.

FATBOY: So you claim to know me, woman?

FUDGIE: O shut it, you fat bastard.

FATBOY: You claim to know *me*. Fatboy the King.

FUDGIE: I knew you when you were Fatty Fatpants, the little fatty fuck.

FATBOY: Ah. Those days were golden.

FUDGIE: We laughed and ate and grew large and sullen.

FATBOY: We did not know the cares to come.

FUDGIE: We lived as though in a dream, a reverie of our own.

FATBOY: I often think back on that time and shudder for things not done.

FUDGIE: Do you have regrets, monster?

FATBOY: I could have killed you when first we met and then we wouldn't be standing here.

FUDGIE: True, but what a story we've made.

FATBOY: True, you wretch, true. Now then. Where were you on the night of the twenty-seventh?

FUDGIE: Clubfooted Christ, not this again.

FATBOY: Answer the question, woman.

FUDGIE: You know where I was. I was home with you in misery and squalor and filth.

FATBOY: And what were you doing at the time?

FUDGIE: Feeding your fat face with a lovely ham.

FATBOY: Ham, you say?

FUDGIE: Yes.

FATBOY: HAM! JESUS, HAM! SWEET SAVORY SKIN OF THE PIG! And what else was on the menu?

FUDGIE: You know what was on the menu.

FATBOY: Tell the court, whore.

FUDGIE: Pancakes, you pig.

FATBOY: HOW MANY PANCAKES?

FUDGIE: I MADE THREE AND YOU ATE TWO OF THEM!

FATBOY: YOU MADE FOUR AND KEPT HALF FOR YOURSELF! ADMIT IT AND THE COURT WILL SHOW MERCY!

FUDGIE: You fat bastard. I told you. I only made three.

FATBOY: LIAR!

FUDGIE: And I had to snatch the third from your hands or I would have gone hungry that night.

FATBOY: YOU ATE MY PANCAKE!

FUDGIE: FAT FUCKER!

FATBOY: ATE MY DELICIOUS PANCAKE!

FUDGIE: I ONLY MADE THREE. Fat bastard.

FATBOY: No further questions.

JUDGE: The witness is excused.

FUDGIE: I'd just like to thank the Academy.

JUDGE: You want to sit up here with me?

FUDGIE: In a moment, yes, but first I must taste this young man.

PROSECUTOR: Ma'am, I must ask you to go.

FUDGIE: I'll come and go as you please, sir.

PROSECUTOR: I have more witnesses to question.

FUDGIE: What will they tell you that I cannot show you and now?

PROSECUTOR: This is most irregular, madam.

FUDGIE: You ain't seen nothing yet.

FATBOY: Better go with her, boy. She's a horror but she gets what she wants.

PROSECUTOR: Your honor, I request a short recess.

JUDGE: Request denied.

PROSECUTOR: But sir—

JUDGE: You were the one being stickly earlier. I can be stickly now.

FUDGIE: I love a good stickler. Are you stickly, my sweet?

PROSECUTOR: I've stickled a few in my days.

FUDGIE: Are you stiff and unbending and harsh?

PROSECUTOR: I believe there's a proper way.

FUDGIE: A straight and narrow… path?

PROSECUTOR: Things should be done just so.

FUDGIE: Do me like things should be done, you demon!

PROSECUTOR: You siren! You vixen! You nymph!

(FUDGIE drags PROSECUTOR offstage.)

JUDGE: Don't wear her out now! Stickly? Save some for the rest! Ah well. Does anyone know any good jokes? Does anyone have a light? Can anyone recommend a reputable chiropractor? Does anyone want to see some naked pictures of my wife? No? Proceed.

FUDGIE: *(Offstage.)* YES, BY THE NAPPY HEAD OF JESUS!

PROSECUTOR: *(Offstage.)* MY GOD, WOMAN, NOT SO FAST!

BAILIFF: Your honor, I beg permission to leave the stage.

JUDGE: For what reason?

BAILIFF: I must go and change costumes, sir.

JUDGE: And what is wrong with the costume you have on?

BAILIFF: Nothing at all, sir. It is just that I am double-cast and must soon enter as another character.

JUDGE: And is the union aware of this?

BAILIFF: They are, sir.

JUDGE: Very well. We shall miss you, good bailiff.

BAILIFF: And I, you, sir.

JUDGE: Our time together has been brief and yet I feel my very heart being rent in two as I am forced to consider your leave-taking.

BAILIFF: Speak no more of it, sir, or I shall collapse to the ground and weep.

JUDGE: We must be strong and carry forward, masking our pain with resolve.

BAILIFF: I shall never forget our time here. I shall cherish it all my days.

JUDGE: Do you love me, bailiff?

BAILIFF: With all of my soul, sir.

JUDGE: Go now and leave us to our grief and sorrow.

BAILIFF: Adieu, mon cheri. Adieu. (*Exits.*)

JUDGE: A sad day for all of us, Shouty.

FATBOY: Fuck his double-cast ass. At least he gets a break. I'm out here shouting the whole time.

JUDGE: True, true. Now then. No prosecutor, no bailiff. How shall we proceed?

FATBOY: I move that I be allowed to sing a little song.

JUDGE: It is so moved.

FATBOY: HEY, I'M FATBOY AND HOW ARE YOU?
YES, I'M FATBOY AND SO FUCK YOU
I'M A BIG FAT FATBOY, A BOY THAT'S FAT
FUCKYOUFUCKYOUFUCKYOU, WHATCHA THINK OF THAT?
FATBOY
MY NAME IS FATBOY
HELLO I'M FATBOY
FUCK YOU AND YOU AND YOU

FUDGIE: (*Entering from stage left.*) HE'S FATBOY
THE MONSTER FATBOY
MY GOD, IT'S FATBOY
TAKE OFF YOUR PANTS

BOTH: WELL, I'M FATBOY, HAVE WE MET?
YES, HE'S FATBOY SO DON'T FORGET
IF I WANT IT THEN I'LL TAKE AND THERE'S NOTHING
    YOU CAN DO
SO BOW DOWN, FUCKERS AND HEY, FUCK YOU
FATBOY
HEY HEY I'M FATBOY
WE'RE TALKING FATBOY
FUCK YOU AND YOU AND YOU AND YOU

PROSECUTOR: (*Entering from stage right.*) FATBOY
GOOD GOD IT'S FATBOY
THAT BIG FAT FATBOY
HE'S REALLY FAT

FATBOY: TALKING 'BOUT FATBOY, THAT'S MY NAME
GLOBAL DOMINATION, THAT'S MY GAME
JUST A BIG FAT FATBOY, CAN'T YOU SEE?
SO GATHER UP YOUR SHIT AND GIVE IT TO ME

ALL: FATBOY
FUCK YES IT'S FATBOY
O FUCK YEAH, FATBOY

AND NOW WE DANCE!
FATBOY
COME ON, FATBOY
HELL YES, FATBOY
FUCK YOU
FATBOY
GIVE IT UP FATBOY
WE'RE TALKING FATBOY
HE'S FUCKING FAT!

FATBOY: AND THAT'S MY SOOOOOOOOONG!

(*FATBOY, FUDGIE, and PROSECUTOR bow; FUDGIE chases PROSECUTOR off stage left.*)

JUDGE: ORDER! ORDER! You said nothing about dancing, sir. That sort of thing is frowned on and liable to get you fined.

FATBOY: To sing and not dance is unnatural, fucker.

JUDGE: Nature is vastly overrated. Redundant, obvious and slow. Man-made for me, boy. It's worth the added cost.

FUDGIE: (*Offstage.*) HOLY JUMPING JUDAS!

PROSECUTOR: (*Offstage.*) JUST WAIT, WOMAN! HELP!

FATBOY: What now, asshole?

JUDGE: Too soon for intermission. Let's keep going.

FUDGIE: (*Offstage.*) YES, BY THE CHAPPED HANDS OF MARTHA!

PROSECUTOR: (*Offstage.*) YOU'RE HURTING ME! BAILIFF!

JUDGE: ORDER! ORDER OFFSTAGE! CALL YOUR NEXT WITNESS, STICKLY!

PROSECUTOR: (*Sticking his head out.*) I call a nameless innocent.

FUDGIE: (*Sticking her head out.*) Finish what you've started.

(*FUDGIE drags PROSECUTOR back offstage as INNOCENT enters stage right.*)

PROSECUTOR: FOR CHRIST'S SAKE WOMAN!

FUDGIE: DO ME DO ME DO ME!

JUDGE: Do you swear to tell the blah blah blah etc.?

INNOCENT: I swear to tell the truth.

FATBOY: THAT'S NOT WHAT HE ASKED YOU.

JUDGE: (*Shouting in horror and discovery.*) I'M BLIND! No, just kidding. Proceed.

FATBOY: As my esteemed colleague and accuser has shamefully abandoned the courtroom, proving himself to be the asshole coward motherfucker piece of shit that innumerable bathroom stalls throughout the land unequivocally claim him to be, I humbly request permission to question this so-called witness on his behalf. Fucker.

JUDGE: Most irregular, sir. Most irregular indeed. I like it. Proceed.

FATBOY: Your honor, I move to strike this witness.

JUDGE: Granted.

FATBOY: (*Strikes INNOCENT.*) Thank you, your honor, I feel much better now. So, what is that we can do for you today?

INNOCENT: You destroyed my cities and murdered hundreds of thousands of innocent civilians.

FATBOY: These cities that you speak of, fuckface, where are they now?

INNOCENT: They do not exist. They are rubble.

FATBOY: Hah! So it is your contention that I have destroyed cities that do not exist?

INNOCENT: Yes, I—

FATBOY: This witness stands against all logic. His testimony is tautologically invalid.

JUDGE: Big words, Shouty. Do you know what they mean?

FATBOY: I do, fuckhead.

JUDGE: Proceed then, sir.

FATBOY: And this murdered multitude you insist on. Where are these people?

INNOCENT: Their bones lie unmarked in the fields.

FATBOY: Bring them forward. Let them speak.

INNOCENT: They have no voice. Their silence is their testimony.

FATBOY: Your argument is silence? Well, mine is speech and AT GREAT VOLUME YOU WORM.

JUDGE: Shouty Shouty Shouty. Anyone see the game last night?

PROSECUTOR: (*Sticking his head out, he is barechested and exhausted.*) Your honor, I must object.

JUDGE: For what reason, sir?

PROSECUTOR: The accused is making a mockery of this most grave and serious proceeding.

JUDGE: Is this true, sir?

FATBOY: Fuck you twice, fucker.

JUDGE: Proceed.

(*PROSECUTOR is pulled back offstage.*)

FATBOY: Your honor, I move that this witness's testimony be ignored, expunged, erased, and incinerated, the ashes to be scattered and lost for all time.

JUDGE: For what reason?

FATBOY: Your honor, the witness is a Jew.

JUDGE: I must warn you, sir. Up to now I have allowed your unorthodox behavior and approach out of a certain morbid fascination. But to impugn an individual because of that individual's religious beliefs or convictions is beyond what I can endure. It is a man's words and actions that count in this courtroom, and the prejudice and hatred of the ignorant hold no weight here.

(*A moment of silence and then ALL onstage burst into huge laughter.*)

FATBOY: You almost had me there at the end, you fucker.

JUDGE: Yeah, it's a good one. Request granted. Remove the Jew.

FATBOY: But first, sir, a moment.

FUDGIE: (*Offstage.*) YES YOU DIRTY BOY!

PROSECUTOR: (*Offstage.*) MY HEART! MY HEART! ACK!

FUDGIE: (*Returning abruptly, staring at something awful offstage.*) Oh, dear.

FATBOY: This subhuman fuck has smeared my good name. I am Fatboy, after all AND NONE DARE QUESTION.

FUDGIE: He's just having a little lie-down. It was purely consensual, I swear.

FATBOY: Killed another, did you?

FUDGIE: Stronger sex, my ass.

FATBOY: WICKED WANTON WHORE!

FUDGIE: GUILTY FAT BASTARD!

JUDGE: SILENCE! Give us a kiss.

(FUDGIE leaps into JUDGE's arms, they embrace and smooch and slobber through the following exchange.)

FATBOY: Tell me, asshole, where were you born?

INNOCENT: In a village in a country that is gone.

FATBOY: And why did you leave that village?

INNOCENT: You burned it to the ground one night. The village left before I did.

FATBOY: What is it you do for a living?

INNOCENT: I labor. I scavenge. I work.

FATBOY: Good money in that?

INNOCENT: Not by your standards, monster. But I have enough to live.

FATBOY: You presume to know my standards, fuckhead?

INNOCENT: *(Holding up bag.)* This is all I have. It would mean nothing to you.

FATBOY: Is that money, dickhead?

INNOCENT: All that I have, sir.

FATBOY: Does anyone not see where this is going? Permission to approach the witness.

JUDGE: Are you still here? Proceed.

FATBOY: Permission to place my hands around the witness's neck.

JUDGE: Christ, man, get it over with.

FATBOY: *(Strangling INNOCENT.)* WE WANT TO THANK YOU FOR COMING HERE TODAY. YOU HAVE SHOWN GREAT COURAGE AND CONVICTION. IS THERE ANYTHING YOU'D LIKE TO ADD?

(FATBOY snaps INNOCENT's neck; INNOCENT collapses, dead.)

FATBOY: Anything? Any more…accusations? Unfounded rumors or lies or baseless allegations? No?

Well, then. I'll take that. *(Takes bag.)* Your honor, I wish to make a small donation to the upkeep of this worthy institution.

JUDGE: Are you attempting to bribe me, sir?

FATBOY: Just a gift, asshole. And by accepting the gift, you agree to absolve me of all charges.

JUDGE: That sounds suspiciously like a bribe, sir. Therefore, I direct you to follow me into my chambers and make sure that all of the money is in order, smaller denominations followed by larger denominations, all face forward and I should warn you that I can't make change.

FATBOY: Justice is immutable, sir. No change is required.

(JUDGE and FATBOY exit.)

FUDGIE: *(To audience.)* Oh, I know how this must look. Shouting and horror and murder and me jumping anything that moves. But you must look at the larger picture. Look at the whole board. There's a justice at work here. Not some primitive eye for an eye, or some great moral countinghouse where each small action and gesture and word is weighed on some golden scale, something simpler and more lovely than that. We must trust the ways of the Fat Man. There's a joy to his random rage. There is something deeper than law there, something more truthful than fact. And he's a great deal of fun, you must admit.

FATBOY: *(Entering.)* MOTHERFUCK!

FUDGIE: They took off your chains, fat bastard.

FATBOY: The outcome was never in doubt.

FUDGIE: It must feel good to breathe free.

FATBOY: If you like that sort of thing.

FUDGIE: Where did that lovely judge go?

FATBOY: Killed him. Only seemed right.

FUDGIE: So you still have the bribe money?

FATBOY: Ate it. Speaking of which—

FUDGIE: I ONLY MADE THREE.

FATBOY: You wretched, lying whore.

FUDGIE: What will they do without a judge?

FATBOY: He was merely ornamental. Judges are a thing of the past.

FUDGIE: What principle will guide us, pray tell?

FATBOY: In the end, you whore, it is strength. Some call it freedom and I say fine, I say fuck you, call it freedom, call it force, call it fuck-a-doodle-cockfuck, but its true name is Fatboy and *(Singing.)* THAT'S MY NAME, TOO.

FUDGIE: How will you rule, great and illustrious bastard?

FATBOY: Today, you frightful succubus, I enjoy a position of great military strength and incredible economic and political influence. In keeping with my heritage and principles, I do not use my strength to press for unilateral advantage. I use it to take what I want and destroy what I don't and terrorize the sheep and fools and fuckheads that stand against me. The war against assholes and fuckheads is a global enterprise of uncertain duration. Therefore, ask not what Fatboy can do for you, but what Fatboy wants for lunch, you fuckers. We have nothing to fear but fuckheads themselves. We shall fight them on the beaches, we shall fight them on the fields, we shall rip their fucking heads off and piss right down their throats. I will act against such emerging fuckheads before they are fully formed. YES? GET IT? You see, my friends, it's morning in America, so somebody better make me some fucking pancakes. L'état c'est moi. Say whaaaaa? C'est moi. I am not a crook. I believe in a place called hope. Ich bin ein Berliner. In the new world I have created, the only path to safety is the path of action. LIGHTS. CAMERAS. AAAAAAAAAAND ACTION!

FUDGIE: You mean preemptive attack of merely perceived enemies, fat bastard?

FATBOY: I MEAN CONSTANT AND INCREASING BULLYING, INTIMIDATION, AND LOW-LEVEL SKIRMISH UNTIL ALL SHALL BOW. You're either with me or against me.

FUDGIE: You fat, fat fucker. Who would stand with you?

FATBOY: Slaves and fools and those who perceive an advantage.

FUDGIE: *(With enormous derision.)* Them.

FATBOY: They shall snap at my heels like toothless dogs and I shall lead them to their graves.

FUDGIE: Are they many?

FATBOY: They are legion. Their numbers grow by the day. Now go and find me some food.

FUDGIE: I am not some cross-eyed domestic. I am Queen Fudgie the First.

FATBOY: Someday I'll have a second.

FUDGIE: Over my dead body.

FATBOY: Precisely, you horrible cow.

FUDGIE: Don't you try.

FATBOY: Come here, my poisonous sweet.

FUDGIE: I'll kick your ass, man.

FATBOY: WHORE!

FUDGIE: FAT BASTARD!

(They rush at each other, screaming, and grapple as the curtain falls.)

SECOND ENTR'ACTE

FATBOY and FUDGIE step out as before.

FATBOY: We have received numerous telegrams, faxes, emails, and handwritten missives during the course of the performance congratulating us on our success and over and over our adoring public has asked, "How on earth did the two of you meet and could you possibly perform a prequel?"

FUDGIE: And in response to Mr. Rodriguize's lurid query I would just like to say yes, you naughty man, once in Acapulco.

FATBOY: A prequel would, sadly, be impossible, for the amount of makeup required to give my wife the impression of youth would render her face immobile and quite possibly the weight of it would snap her neck. I am, of course, all for the possibility of a snapped neck, however, my esteemed spouse, the objectionable cow, has demurred. It seems we have another act to perform and the management has not supplied us with an understudy.

FUDGIE: Or a dressing room.

FATBOY: Or any reason to believe we shall be paid.

FUDGIE: Thieves.

FATBOY: Unscrupulous cocksucking pricks.

FUDGIE: Theatre owners and operators.

FATBOY: We have, therefore, hit upon the ingenious solution of presenting our meeting, courtship, and early years in the form of a traditional puppet show.

(Puppet stage is brought out; they stand behind it and draw curtain, revealing two hand puppets bearing a rough resemblance to themselves.)

FUDGIE: Here I am, a blameless virgin, the very model of modesty and virtue, standing alone on a bright sunny day in this nondescript town, ah me. I wonder what the day will bring.

FATBOY: Why is my puppet so fat?

FUDGIE: I believe they're going for realism.

FATBOY: Seems a little late in the day for that.

FUDGIE: Shut up and do the play.

FATBOY: *(Entering.)* Dope-dee-dope-dee-dope-dee-doo. Well, hello young lady!

FUDGIE: Hello, you pudgy little boy!

FATBOY: I'm not pudgy.

FUDGIE: Hello, you husky little fatty fatty!

FATBOY: Don't call me fat!

FUDGIE: Hello! Okay? Hello. Now do your line.

FATBOY: This doesn't look anything like me. *(Examines his puppet closely, sniffs it, and begins to eat it.)*

FUDGIE: Don't eat the puppet!

FATBOY: I HAVE TO KEEP UP MY STRENGTH! *(Takes an enormous bite out of the puppet stage.)*

FUDGIE: FAT FUCKER!

FATBOY: WHORE!

(They begin to grapple as large hooks, as before, drag them off the stage. The puppet stage stands alone. After a moment, the actor playing TENANT and PROSECUTOR steps out, wordlessly apologizes to the audience, and removes the puppet stage.)

ACT THREE
FATBOY, FATBOY ÜBER ALLES

FATBOY, wearing crown, stands in front of throne, MINISTERS and SLAVE bow before him.

ALL: All hail Fatboy!

FATBOY: Arise, dear fuckheads and kiss my fucking ass.

(They do so through the following speech.)

FATBOY: Methinks, ay me, I shall now speak like
    thus.
'Tis fitting that one so grand and large as I
Should sound as if I had a fucking clue
As how to rule with grace and style and class.
For though the hungry beast may roar within
Without the words should sound as temple bells.
What say thee, ye suckers of many a cock?

MINISTER OF FINANCE: In sooth, sir—

FATBOY: Nay, nay, speak as before
And in that way we shall know who is king.

SLAVE: You… sound great, your majesty.

FATBOY: Thou sayst so in the vernacular?

SLAVE: Yes, your majesty. I'm just saying.

FATBOY: 'Tis pleasing on the ear to speak like this.
The honeyed words do roll out on the tongue
And seem to kiss the lips of him who speaks
And even "motherfuck" and "fucking shit"
Are gentled by the rhythm of the verse.
But tell me and be honest, dear fuckheads
Does it in any way make me seem gay?

SLAVE: Umm. No, sir.

FATBOY: A bit of sport with those of like same sex
Is not a thing to shudder at, of course.
Indeed, perhaps you all shall suck my cock
Before our revelries have here drawn nigh.

MINISTER OF JUSTICE: This is starting to creep me out a bit.

SLAVE: Yeah, me too.

FATBOY: Forsooth! Forsooth thou fuckers of thine
    own
Mother's wombs. 'Tis now the third and final
Act and we shall wax poetic ere we die.

MINISTER OF FINANCE: Die, your highness?

FATBOY: Did I say "die"? The word itself betrays.
But words once spoken can in time come true.
And though the mighty earth itself may crack
And mountains vanish into hungry seas
The end of one man's life, be thou that man,
Is greater than the ending of the world.

You two, leave the stage. You stay here with me. Off, you motherfuckers, exeunt both.

MINISTER OF JUSTICE: We'll just be backstage.

MINISTER OF FINANCE: Call us if you need anything.

FATBOY: Leave me with my slave.

(*The MINISTERS exit. An uncomfortable moment.*)

SLAVE: How's it going, sir?

FATBOY: My life is like a pageant or a play
And when the curtain falls for the last time
What waits beyond yon great and groaning—
Ah fuck this, bring me some pancakes, fucker.

SLAVE: About the pancakes, sir.

FATBOY: Don't start that cholesterol bullshit with me.

SLAVE: No, no, it's not the cholesterol, sir, it's just…

FATBOY: What, fucker? I'm hungry and you're standing here talking.

SLAVE: You have eaten every pancake in the world, sir.

FATBOY: I have eaten every pancake in the world?

SLAVE: And I congratulate you on your remarkable success.

FATBOY: That doesn't even make any sense. Make fresh pancakes.

SLAVE: Sir, you have eaten every grain of wheat and neglected to water the fields. You have fried every fowl and so there are no eggs. You've barbecued every steer and roasted every goat. Milk has become a memory. How about some dry granola?

FATBOY: Hurts my teeth.

SLAVE: A little grapefruit, maybe?

FATBOY: Too tart, fucker, too tart. Bring me bacon and sausage and ham.

SLAVE: Ah, there's a problem there, your enormous majesty.

FATBOY: Problems aren't my problem, pal.

SLAVE: This one, sadly, affects you.

FATBOY: What is the point of being king if I still have to stand around with assholes like you and discuss my diet?

SLAVE: It's a riddle, sir, a great one.

FATBOY: Tell me the problem, fuckface.

SLAVE: You've eaten all the pigs. Swine are off the menu. The Muslims thank you, sir.

FATBOY: No pigs?

SLAVE: No more.

FATBOY: No sweet little piggies?

SLAVE: Gone, sir. History.

FATBOY: I WANT PIG!

SLAVE: I know, sir, I'm sorry.

FATBOY: GIVE ME PIGGY PIGGY!

SLAVE: Piggy's gone away, sir, I'm sorry. Have some grapes.

FATBOY: No cows no pigs no chickens. No wheat?

SLAVE: No wheat.

FATBOY: No wheat. Jesus Christ, I'll starve. How is this possible? SOMEBODY FUCKED UP, FUCKER! Someone has betrayed me. An enemy within. (*He begins to absentmindedly eat his crown.*) They play the willing servants, but secretly they scheme. I'M EATING MY CROWN! HAS IT COME TO THIS? (*Continues snacking on crown.*) They tremble in my presence and mock me when I'm gone. Cocksuckers. Fuckheaded cocksucking motherfucking fucks. They don't love me. Not really. Not one of them down deep. Do you love me, fuckhead?

SLAVE: No sir.

FATBOY: ANSWER THE QUESTION.

SLAVE: I said no, sir, no, I don't.

FATBOY: Dodges and double-talk. Can no one speak straight to me now? Is my wife about?

SLAVE: Just offstage, sir.

FATBOY: Send her rotten, wretched carcass in.

SLAVE: At once, sir, at once.

FATBOY: WAIT. Kiss my ass.

SLAVE: Sir?

FATBOY: KISS MY ASS NOW YOU WORTHLESS SACK OF SHIT.

(SLAVE kneels and kisses FATBOY's ass.)

FATBOY: Ass-kisser.

SLAVE: Yes, sir.

FATBOY: Exit now.

SLAVE: O yes, sir. *(Exits.)*

FATBOY: At the height of my powers and I can't get a pancake. The peak of my form and no pork to eat. What a load of fucking crap. I AM FATBOY AND I AM HUNGRY. Was I to water the fields? Count every chicken, cow, and sheep? Not devour all and everything simply because it was there and I wanted it? What kind of motherfucking horseshit cocksucking bullshit is that? But soft, I am o'erheard.

(FUDGIE enters, wearing a crown.)

FUDGIE: My king.

FATBOY: My queen.

FUDGIE: Fat bastard.

FATBOY: Whore.

FUDGIE: Have you seen the larger-than-life statue they have made of you in town?

FATBOY: I have. It does not please me.

FUDGIE: Why not, you horrible man?

FATBOY: It makes me look fat.

FUDGIE: There should be more statues of me.

FATBOY: To frighten little children and guard the city gates?

FUDGIE: So those who wish can worship with convenience and not have to trek across town.

FATBOY: Is it worship you wish, wretched woman?

FUDGIE: What else is there finally, fat man?

FATBOY: Dignity. Honor. Love.

(FUDGIE explodes into huge laughter, FATBOY does not.)

FUDGIE: Ah, you fat fucker. You could always make me laugh.

FATBOY: It seems I've laid waste to the world.

FUDGIE: Yes, I know, fat bastard.

FATBOY: An ocean of blood, a mountain range of bones, and for what, you aged slattern?

FUDGIE: It seemed to pass the time.

FATBOY: True, you whore, but now that it's passed I am empty as though never filled, my hunger a gentle lapping where once it roared and crashed.

FUDGIE: Well, you're old, you fat bastard. This happens when you age.

FATBOY: I don't wish to be old.

FUDGIE: You age and then you age and then you age and then you die.

FATBOY: I don't wish to die.

FUDGIE: No way out of here alive, fat fucker.

FATBOY: This is an outrage. This will not stand.

FUDGIE: Nor will you when you die, monster. You'll be splayed out on the floor and we'll all shout Fatboy Is Dead, Long Live Fatboy! Wait a minute, that doesn't make any sense, does it? Fatboy Is Dead, Long Live Fudgie. Yes. Better. We'll dance around your rotting corpse and call you awful names and the reign of Queen Fudgie the Good will begin.

FATBOY: The Good? But you're loathsome and vile and…*bad.*

FUDGIE: I can be good if I want.

FATBOY: Never. Not possible. No.

FUDGIE: I CAN BE GOOD.

FATBOY: YOUR EVERY THOUGHT IS SIN.

FUDGIE: OLD DYING BASTARD!

FATBOY: SINFUL WRETCHED WHORE!

FUDGIE: KILL HIM NOW!

(Silence. An uncomfortable pause as FUDGIE looks around the stage.)

FUDGIE: I said, KILL HIM NOW!

(Another pause.)

FATBOY: Who are you talking to?

FUDGIE: Hmm? Oh. I was just calling my…assistant. Kelly. Kelly…Mnyow.

FATBOY: Mnyow?

FUDGIE: Yes. She's Vietnamese. Cantonese. Szechuan.

FATBOY: I don't think I've met her.

FUDGIE: No, she's new.

FATBOY: Ah.

FUDGIE: Must not be within earshot.

FATBOY: No.

FUDGIE: Ah well. I'm going to go get laid.

FATBOY: Wait. Don't leave me, you horrible woman.

FUDGIE: Why I left you years ago, fucker. Are you just noticing now? *(Exits.)*

FATBOY: Whore. Once I grew warm when we battled. Now it's like a wind-up toy. FUCKHEAD!

(SLAVE scurries on, prostrates himself.)

SLAVE: Yes o monstrous Fatboy.

FATBOY: Stand here while I soliloquize.

SLAVE: With joy and reverence, sir.

FATBOY: I feel the end of something. I fear the end of all. My will, once certain, now wavers. My force flickers and dims. There is no joy in destruction. There is no point in creation. There is only endurance. And strength. But this will eventually wear. And then… then, what? An old and feeble Fatboy? Laughed at, pushed aside, jeered, and then forgotten? O no. It must not happen. I must break the cycle of time. I must stop the pendulum from swinging and freeze it here, triumphant. The only way to protect my legacy is to kill everyone I've ever known. Yes. All my contemporaries vanished. But then, still, still, then, future generations may look at what I've done and judge me harshly. Fuckers. Cocksucking unborn judgmental fuckers. They must not be allowed. They must die before birth, before conception, unmade. Ah. All must die. Only then may I breathe free. That's it then. ASSHOLE!

SLAVE: Yes sir.

FATBOY: Kill everything that lives and then kill yourself when you're done.

SLAVE: Yes, your majesty. *(Goes to exit and then stops.)* Your majesty?

FATBOY: Fucker?

SLAVE: By everything, you mean everyone?

FATBOY: Thing, slave, thing. Kill every thing. If life can grow, it may grow sentient. Future races of complex life forms must not be allowed to thrive and discover my deeds. Some bacterial infection must be prevented from in time mutating and evolving into something that can think and speak and slander my good name.

SLAVE: Got it. Kill all things.

FATBOY: And then kill yourself.

SLAVE: Of course, sir. Thank you.

FATBOY: Now go. WAIT. Kiss my ass.

SLAVE: Again, sir?

FATBOY: Again and again, fucker, until it's second nature.

(SLAVE kisses FATBOY's ass.)

FATBOY: Ass-kisser.

SLAVE: Well, yes sir.

FATBOY: Kisser of my ass.

SLAVE: Will that be all, sir?

FATBOY: Yes. No. Kiss my ass.

SLAVE: But sir—

FATBOY: Kiss my ass, fucker.

SLAVE: Jesus, sir, I just—

FATBOY: KISS KISS KISS MY ASS ASS ASS. You fucking ass-kissing fucking fuck.

(SLAVE kisses FATBOY's ass again.)

FATBOY: You kissed my ass, fucker.

SLAVE: Yes, sir, I did.

FATBOY: That would make you an ass-kisser.

SLAVE: Yes, sir, it would.

FATBOY: All right. Just making sure.

SLAVE: I have to go now and kill everything.

FATBOY: Of course, you ass-kissing fuck. And then kill yourself.

SLAVE: Of course, sir. *(Hesitates, afraid he will be asked to kiss the ass of FATBOY again.)* I'm going now.

FATBOY: Well, go then, fucker.

SLAVE: *(Exiting, sotto voce.)* What a fucking prick.

FATBOY: Something seems to be troubling my slave. A note of discontent. Strange. Ah well. Perhaps I should have asked him to kiss my ass again, he seems to enjoy that. Ah well. So hard to tell what people are thinking. You have to ask them, of course, but that's not the end of it, no. Then you have to *listen*. As they drone on and on about *themselves*. "I think blah blah blah, I feel blah blah blah." JESUS FUCKING CHRIST. One could spend one's life listening to other's words.

(FUDGIE enters, theatrically shielding her eyes with her forearm.)

FUDGIE: Is it over, my beautiful boy?

FATBOY: What?

FUDGIE: Oh. It's you. I thought… hmm. Everything all right?

FATBOY: Fine, yes. Why?

FUDGIE: Were there some men in here, with knives and such… stabbing and killing you?

FATBOY: No. Why?

FUDGIE: No reason. No… assassination?

FATBOY: Not that I'm aware of, no.

FUDGIE: Huh. Funny. All right. See you later, fucker.

FATBOY: Bye.

(FUDGIE exits.)

FATBOY: That was weird. Anyway. Well, soon it will be over. Everything dead, killed. Me, alone, triumphant. Man, that's going to be nice. Breathe a little easier, that's for goddamn sure. I wonder, flood or fire? Doesn't really matter, I suppose. Fire more dramatic. Flood more Biblical, though. All the same in the end. What could be keeping that slave?

(SLAVE enters with MINISTER OF FINANCE AND MINISTER OF JUSTICE, all hiding something behind their backs.)

SLAVE: Sir, I have discussed your plan of complete global destruction with the Minister of Justice and the Minister of Finance.

FATBOY: It is not a plan, fuckhead. It is an order. It requires no discussion.

MINISTER OF FINANCE: Of course, your majesty, but just the same—

MINISTER OF JUSTICE: I believe we have hit upon an alternate course of action.

FATBOY: Yes?

MINISTER OF FINANCE: Yes.

SLAVE: It goes something like this. SIC SEMPER TYRANNIS!

MINISTER OF JUSTICE: DEATH TO THE FAT MAN!

MINISTER OF FINANCE: STAB HIM IN HIS FUCKING HEAD!

FATBOY: Now this is more like it.

(They rush FATBOY, knives drawn, and fight, horribly. MINISTER OF FINANCE is killed, FATBOY grapples with SLAVE and MINISTER OF JUSTICE, SLAVE chokes FATBOY, who gasps.)

FATBOY: Et tu, fuckhead?

(And FATBOY collapses. SLAVE and MINISTER OF JUSTICE gather downstage.)

MINISTER OF JUSTICE: The fat fucker is dead.

SLAVE: We can all breathe free.

MINISTER OF JUSTICE: The yoke of oppression is lifted.

SLAVE: The boot removed from our throats.

MINISTER OF JUSTICE: I think I broke a nail.

SLAVE: We must go and tell the people.

MINISTER OF JUSTICE: A new day dawns.

(FATBOY rises, unseen.)

SLAVE: We have struck a blow today, my friend.

MINISTER OF JUSTICE: Yeah, broke it. Fuck.

SLAVE: A mighty blow for justice. We have—

FATBOY: INCOMPETENT WOULD-BE ASSASSINS!

MINISTER OF JUSTICE: SUPPOSED TO BE DEAD MOTHERFUCKER!

(They fight; MINISTER OF JUSTICE is killed, FATBOY collapses, SLAVE crosses downstage.)

SLAVE: The fat fucker is strong.

(FUDGIE enters as before.)

FUDGIE: Is it over, my beautiful boy?

SLAVE: No. It has begun.

FUDGIE: Look at the lovely bodies strewn. Very Elizabethan.

SLAVE: Their blood anoints a new age.

FUDGIE: And mine beats strong for you.

SLAVE: Come to me, my vixen.

FUDGIE: Ah, you murdering slave.

(FATBOY rises, unseen.)

SLAVE: I shall rule with justice.

FUDGIE: No, boy. I shall rule alone.

FATBOY: NON-ASSASSINATING FUCK!

SLAVE: NON-DYING HORROR MOVIE MONSTER!

(They fight, horribly; both collapse.)

SLAVE: I tried. Tell them I tried.

FUDGIE: I shall tell them you failed. If I mention you at all.

SLAVE: Tell them—

FUDGIE: Hush now, failure.

(She snaps SLAVE's neck.)

FUDGIE: And you, fucker? Any last words?

FATBOY: MOTHERFUCK!

FUDGIE: Yes, to balance the beginning. You always had a way with words.

FATBOY: The light grows dim.

FUDGIE: It's dark where you're going.

FATBOY: Stay with me while I die.

FUDGIE: Is it going to be a while?

FATBOY: Did I leave the world a better place?

FUDGIE: No, you bastard, you didn't.

FATBOY: Did I do some good in this world?

FUDGIE: No, you horror, none.

FATBOY: Am I a good man or a bad man?

FUDGIE: A very bad man, monster. The worst I've ever known.

FATBOY: And how will I be judged?

FUDGIE: Guilty on all counts.

FATBOY: Motherfuck. *(Collapses.)*

FUDGIE: Fatboy is dead. Long live Fatboy. No, wait a minute, that doesn't make any sense, does it? Fatboy is dead. Long live Fudgie. Yes. Better. My reign shall be better. Or not. Different, I suppose. Or not. We'll see. The important thing is that I'm still standing. And all that the fat fucker fought for is mine now, outright. Hah. You forgot what I told you in the beginning, didn't you? Before all the shouting and blood. I am the brains of this outfit. I played him like a pawn. We women watch, you fuckers. We see the game unfold. All you men with your wee wilted willies and your nervous little sphincters shut tight. Strutting about all grim and serious making laws, wars, headlines. We wave you off to battle and wait to see who returns. And that one then becomes our toy, our tool to advance a little further.

(FATBOY rises up behind her, begins to creep toward her.)

FUDGIE: The fat boy was my fool. A burden I've carried and now lay down. I shall erase him from the history books, none shall know he lived. I spit on his—

(FATBOY grabs her from behind, spins her around, and stabs her several times. She screams, and then they both stop and look out to the audience for a moment. Then she begins to choke him; they struggle and then stop again, looking out.)

FATBOY: *(Mock growling.)* "Rahr rahr rahr."

FUDGIE: *(Soft, mocking.)* "Fat fucker! No!"

FATBOY: *(Looking out.)* "Whore!"

FUDGIE: *(Looking out.)* "Monster."

BOTH: *(Mocking the act of fighting.)* "Rahr rahr rahr!"

(They begin to remove their costumes with the help of the CAST as STAGE HANDS enter behind them and begin to strike the set.)

FATBOY: That's enough of that, I suppose.

FUDGIE: Becomes a bit predictable, pig.

FATBOY: One note, you wanton wretch?

FUDGIE: And a flat one at that.

FATBOY: Yes, well, just giving the folks a laugh. I mean, poor fuckers, they work hard. Slaving away all day.

FUDGIE: Who slaves, monster?

FATBOY: The people. Folks. *(Gesturing to audience.)* Them.

FUDGIE: *(Dismissively.)* Them.

FATBOY: Give them a laugh, I say. Sing a little song. Shout and jump about. Kill a few innocent people.

FUDGIE: I was innocent once.

FATBOY: You were born with a silver cock ring in your mouth.

FUDGIE: "Fat bastard."

FATBOY: "Whore."

BOTH: "Rahr rahr rahr."

(They are now out of costume, makeup wiped off, CAST standing around them.)

FATBOY: Yes, well. An epilogue, then. A closing, rousing speech. Hmm. I got nothing.

FUDGIE: Do the bit from the second act.

FATBOY: I don't believe in repeating myself.

(They both softly laugh hugely, as before.)

FUDGIE: "Ah you fat fucker, you could always blah blah blah."

FATBOY: Here's something. Yes. None of this is real. Monsters don't exist. Nothing to worry about. Life is a beautiful thing. And everyone feels that way. Everyone is happy. And everyone is good. If you see people that don't seem happy, well, something's wrong with them. They should see a doctor, get some happy pills. If you're not feeling happy, same thing for you. It's just a chemical imbalance, nine times out of ten. They can fix that now. Everyone can be happy. And if you see some suffering out there, remember, it's not your fault. You're good, you're fine, you're done. Fuck them if they're not happy, not your fucking fault. Big things, like poverty or war or whatnot, well, it's like the weather. You don't try to keep the rain from falling, right? You just go inside 'til it's over. What are you going to do, change the world? Of course not. I'll take care of that. I mean, they will. The folks in charge. They're all good people, the bosses, they're the best ones, actually. That's why they're in charge. They know better than you. Just go the fuck inside. I'll take care of everything. You fucking sheep. You slaves. GO HOME. AND WAIT FOR MY ORDERS. NASTY WEATHER OUT. And if you don't hear from me for a while, well I've got things to do, haven't I? I'm a busy, busy man. With all the affairs of state. It's not easy being in charge, you know, and your constant questioning and voting and protesting and all that fucking SHIT is wasting my fucking time. Just stop it. Just give up already. I've won. I AM FATBOY AND I AM EVERYWHERE. Open up a paper. Turn on the TV. Walk around your towns, you fuckers. See anything familiar? Look at your neighbor closely the next time you say hello. Look beneath the surface. That's where I live. You think he's your friend? Think he's got your back? Wait until the tanks roll in and the buildings start to fall and somebody has to die. Is your friend going to step up? Your friend is Fatboy and he says "no." Just look in the mirror, fucker. Early in the morning or very late at night. When it's quiet and you're alone. I'll be waving back at you. I'll say BOO. I am Fatboy and I am you. I am Fatboy. I do not die. I am Fatboy, you cocksucking fuckheads. I AM FATBOY. And I'm outta here. I am *hiiiiiiiiiiiisssss-tory*!

(Lights down suddenly.)

(END OF PLAY)

THE PERSIANS

...a comedy about war with five songs

based on the play by Aeschylus

Waterwell

Founded in Bloomington, Indiana, in 2002, WATERWELL endeavors to cultivate the inherent danger in live performance to create an exciting and unpredictable event—an event pruned down to its irreducible elements: human beings sharing a space and a story. Through that story...through the humor, sadness, and hope it evokes...Waterwell strives to empower its audience to change their lives and the world in which they live. In April 2003 the company's first adaptation—a condensed, cabaret version of Lope de Vega's *Fuenteovejuna*—opened at the Duplex Cabaret Theater and ran for more than two months. In August 2004, Waterwell received a grant from the Nancy Quinn Fund to create and produce *Sweetness and Light*, which ran for two weeks at Altered Stages in October and November 2004. The company's eighth production, *The Persians...a comedy about war with five songs*, opened at Under St. Marks in May 2005. Thanks to enthusiastic reviews and good word of mouth, *The Persians* transferred Off-Broadway to the Perry Street Theater where it ran for six more weeks including a two-week extension. Its ninth drop, *Marco Millions (based on lies)*, premiered in August 2006 at The Lion at Theatre Row.

HANNA CHEEK was born in New York City on February 6, 1979, and grew up in both New York and Los Angeles. She attended Sarah Lawrence College and the British American Dramatic Academy, where she studied with Fiona Shaw and Brian Cox. She made her stage debut at age nine in *Home Sweet Home/Crack* at the Ohio Theatre. She is an ensemble member of Waterwell, and has appeared in their productions of her one-woman show *Life in Pink* (2003, Belt Theatre; Ground Floor Theatre) and *Sweetness and Light*. Other stage credits include *First You're Born* (2003, Playwrights Horizons) and several editions of *The Pumpkin Pie Show*. Her television credits include a recurring role on MTV's *Undressed* and guest roles on *The West Wing* and

Titus. Cheek just completed work with the other members of Waterwell on Eugene O'Neill's *Marco Millions (based on lies)*. She lives in Brooklyn.

RODNEY GARDINER is an actor-writer. He was born in the Turks and Caicos Islands in 1979 and grew up in Miami, Florida. He is a graduate of the actor training program at the State University of New York at Purchase, where he studied with Joan Potter, Lawrence Kornfeld, A. Dean Irby, and Andrei Belgrader. While at Purchase, he received the Ross Award, awarded annually to one artist in the SUNY system. During his formative years, Gardiner worked in guerilla theatre, performing in public places and in Miami's jails and detention centers. He and his colleagues catered to the poor and disadvantaged with a mission to address the issues that plagued the ghettos. He is an ensemble member of Waterwell.

ARIAN MOAYED is an actor-playwright-creator. He was born in Tehran, Iran, on April 15, 1980, and grew up in the suburbs of Chicago. He received a BA in theatre from Indiana University–Bloomington, where he studied with Murray McGibbon, Howard Jensen, and Dale McFadden. He is the artistic director of Waterwell, and has co-created and appeared in its productions of *Lost in Yemen* (2002, Collective: Unconscious), *Fuenteovejuna*, and *Sweetness and Light*. He also co-wrote its production of *Stuck* (2003, Peoples Improv Theater). Moayed's other stage credits include Tony Kushner's *Homebody/Kabul* (2003, Steppenwolf, Chicago, Illinois; 2004, Brooklyn Academy of Music), *Kite Runner* (2006, American Place Theater), and *Apartment 3A* by Jeff Daniels (2006, Arclight Theatre). His film and television appearances include *Law & Order, Law & Order: Criminal Intent, Late Night With Conan O'Brien*, and *Church Story*. Moayed teaches acting and film acting at the Professional Performing Arts High School. He lives in Manhattan.

Actor, writer, and singer NICOLE PARKER was born and raised in Irvine, California. She received a BA in theatre from Indiana University, where she studied with Howard Jensen, Murray McGibbon, and George Pinney. She also studied with Diane Doyle at South Coast Repertory and Ron West at The Second City in Chicago. She is an ensemble member of Waterwell, for whom she co-wrote and appeared in *Fuenteovejuna*. She has also worked as both a writer and performer for the Amsterdam-based improv group Boom Chicago. Her television credits include a three-year stint as a cast member and writer for *MadTV*. She received a 2004 Jeff Award nomination for her performance in *The Second City's Romeo and Juliet Musical*. Parker is currently working as both an actor and writer on Martin Short's Broadway show, *Fame Becomes Me*.

TOM RIDGELY is an actor, writer, and director. He was born on July 9, 1979, in Indianapolis. He attended Indiana University, where he studied with Murray McGibbon and graduated with a BA in theatre and drama. He also studied at the Atlantic Theater School in New York. He is an ensemble member of Waterwell, with whom he has co-written *Choo, Choo! All Aboard the Comedy Express—Next Stop…Funnyville!* (2002, Rose Firebay, Bloomington, Indiana), *Lost in Yemen, Fuenteovejuna, Stuck, Sweetness and Light*, and the recent *Marco Millions (based on lies)*. His New York dance credits include CalArts Dances Downtown (2002, St. Marks-in-the-Bowery), International Dance Festival (2002, St. Clement's), and SYREN Modern Dance (2004, University Settlement; 2005, Ailey Citigroup Theater). Ridgely currently appears with the improv comedy troupe Big Black Car, which won the 2005 ECNY Award for Best Improv Group. He was the general manager of the Peoples Improv Theater from 2003 to 2006, and is currently working at the Public Theater. He lives in Greenwich Village.

The Persians…a comedy about war with five songs was first presented by Waterwell on May 26, 2005, at Under St. Marks, New York City, with the following cast and credits:

Atossa .... Hanna Cheek
Darius ....Rodney Gardiner
Xerxes .... Arian Moayed
Herald .... Tom Ridgely

Directed by: Tom Ridgely
Assistant Director and Stage Manager: Kendall O'Neill
Composer: Lauren Cregor
Guitar, Percussion: Jeremy Daigle
Bass, Percussion, and Drum Programming: Joe Morse
Lighting Design: Sabrina Braswell
Costume Design: Elizabeth Payne
Choreography: Kate Mehan and Lynn Peterson
Graphic Design: Brian McMullen

The Persians…a comedy about war with five songs was subsequently presented on July 13, 2005, at the Perry Street Theatre, New York City, with the same credits as above, plus the following:

Piano, Woodwind: Willie Fastenow
Drums, Percussion: Gunter Gruner
Set Design: Dave Lombard
Stage Manager: Eric Price

Translations used: Aeschylus, *The Persians*, translated by Robert Potter, Internet classics archive (classics.mit.edu), ©1994–2000; Aeschylus, *Plays: I*, translated by Frederic Raphael and Kenneth McLeish (London: Metheun Drama, 1991); David R. Slavitt and Palmer Bovie, eds., *Aeschylus, 2*, translated by David R. Slavitt (Philadelphia: Penn Greek Drama Series, 1998), and Aeschylus, *Promethus Bound and Other Plays*, translated by Philip Vellacott (New York: Penguin Books, 1961).

To obtain a CD of the music, please email info@waterwell.org.

NOTE

The characters Hanna, Rodney, Arian, and Tom (who play, respectively, Atossa, Darius, Xerxes, and Herald) should be named for and adapted to the specific four actors who perform the play. Any subsequent production should use this script as a starting point. For the parts of the play that draw on the original actors' individual personalities and backgrounds, the new actors are encouraged to substitute their own material.

A match is struck. A tight spot comes up stage center on HANNA. She's dressed impeccably in a fedora, suit, and tie. A cigarette case appears, is opened, a cigarette removed and placed between her lips. The match moves to light it for her. She takes a drag. A high-hat sets the tempo. RODNEY enters HANNA's special over her right shoulder wearing a matching outfit. The lights come up just enough to reveal TOM and ARIAN standing on HANNA's right and left, respectively. Like HANNA and RODNEY, they're in matching outfits and looking sharp. The whole scene suggests an evening at the Sands, circa 1960. Their movements are cool and contained. RODNEY sings the bass line.

TOM: BEFORE ISLAM CAME ALONG
IRAN WASN'T CALLED IRAN
IT WAS CALLED THE PERSIAN EMPIRE

SO LET'S GO BACK
TO WHEN PERSIA WAS WHERE IT'S AT
WHEN PERSIA WAS CALLED THE PERSIAN EMPIRE

ARIAN: *(In counterpoint, while TOM repeats.)*
I AM FROM IRAN
AND LATER ON
I'LL SING A SONG
ALL ABOUT HOW…

HANNA: *(Also in counterpoint, while ARIAN and TOM repeat.)*
LISTEN CLOSE SO THE NAMES DON'T CONFUSE YA
I PLAY THE QUEEN, PLAY THE QUEEN, QUEEN ATOSSA
WIFE OF THE LATE, GREAT KING DARIUS-UH
OH!

ALL: THIS IS THE OLDEST PLAY AS FAR AS WE KNOW
WE BRING YOU STORIES NOW TWO THOUSAND YEARS
    OLD
WATCH THE PERSIAN FLEETS GET CLOBBERED, CLOB-
    BERED BY THE GREEKS
AESCHYLUS, WE BEG YOUR PARDON; WE MADE A COUPLE
    TWEAKS

WELCOME, WELCOME TO THE PERSIANS
YOU HAVE CHOSEN RIGHT

WELCOME, WELCOME TO THE PERSIANS
YOU WON'T FORGET TONIGHT

WE GOT A KING, A QUEEN, AND ARMIES GALORE
ABOUT THE DETAILS WE CAN'T REALLY BE SURE
WATCH THE PERSIAN FLEETS, GET CLOBBERED, CLOB-
    BERED BY THE GREEKS
AESCHYLUS, WE BEG YOUR PARDON; WE MADE A COUPLE
    TWEAKS

HANNA: LISTEN CLOSE SO THE NAMES DON'T CON-
    FUSE YA
I PLAY THE QUEEN, PLAY THE QUEEN, QUEEN ATOSSA
WIFE OF THE LATE, GREAT KING DARIUS-UH
OH! *(Exits.)*

ARIAN: I AM FROM IRAN
AND LATER ON
I'LL SING A SONG
ALL ABOUT HOW… *(Exits.)*

TOM: SO LET'S GO BACK
TO WHEN PERSIA WAS WHERE IT'S AT
WHEN PERSIA WAS CALLED THE PERSIAN EMPIRE *(Exits.)*

(RODNEY sings the bass line. Exits.)

TOM: *(Offstage as announcer.)* And now ladies and gentlemen, please put your hands together for the star of our show…direct from the bar…Rodney Gardiner.

(Entrance music. RODNEY, sans fedora, runs out with a rocks glass, tipping EVERYBODY. Twenties for BAND, the audience? Finally he comes to rest downstage right.)

RODNEY: Here it is and here it is…Ladies and gentlemen, you are about to embark upon a journey never to be forgotten. I'm talkin' about The Golden Age of Persia. Don't ask me when that was, but I can tell you where: somewhere over there near Avalon, Atlantis, and Shangri-La.

(Rimshot.)

RODNEY: I like this guy; he's gettin' good. Now the cats takin' you on this journey are pretty easy to find. Smack dab right in front of ya, is the man who will play the late, great King Darius. The one who built the Persian Empire, the man with the plan, I'm talkin' smooth like buttermilk, crisp like fried chicken, and slicker than a grease monkey wearin' leather pants. Now as for my supporting cast—

ALL: *(From backstage.)* Whoa! Hey! Rodney! Supporting?

RODNEY: Okay, KO…you got it my "co-whatevers." Now in addition to King Darius you also got my son. My son's name is Xerxes

(ARIAN enters also sans fedora.)

RODNEY: and people Xerxes is dumb. I mean *dumb*. Door knob dumb. So we knew we he had to be played by an actor who, to every role he played, he brought so much…such a keen sense of…stupidity. Can I introduce Arian Moayed?

(Applause.)

ARIAN: Thank you, Rodney. I'm smarter than you.

RODNEY: What?

ARIAN: You heard me. I'm smarter than you. *(To audience.)* Thank you. *(Exits.)*

RODNEY: Isn't that cute: the little engine that couldn't. Now we also got Queen Atossa,

(HANNA enters hatless.)

RODNEY: my wife, the dummy's momma. And for this role we had no choice but to cast the classiest chick we know. You got it, ladies and gentlemen, the one, the only Hanna Gardiner!

(Applause.)

HANNA: Rodney.

RODNEY: What I did?

HANNA: You called me by your last name again.

RODNEY: I did? Naw.

HANNA: You did. You said Hanna Gardiner. My name is Hanna Cheek.

RODNEY: Maybe you should change it, know what I'm sayin'?

HANNA: We're not getting married, Rodney. It's never going to happen.

RODNEY: Even better for me baby, I don't need all that attachment.

HANNA: Rodney, I'm gay. *(To audience.)* I am gay. *(Awkward pause, exits.)*

RODNEY: *(Moving on.)* So there we have it, the momma bear, poppa bear, and the li'l ugly dumb one, Xerxes. And that pretty much wraps up the characters—

(TOM, offstage, lots of throat clearing.)

RODNEY: Anybody got a cough drop? All right. I almost forgot about one part…the part of the messenger:

(TOM enters, bareheaded.)

RODNEY: tiny, small, insignificant part. Tom was perfect! *(Applause.)*

TOM: Thank you. It's a big part actually. I actually have the most lines in the show. You'll see when it happens. It's an important scene. *(Exits.)*

RODNEY: Yes they will see it when it happens, long as they don't blink.

(Rimshot.)

RODNEY: But we're gonna do this here thing. So the legend says Persia, the big bad wolf of Asia, sent forth nine hundred thousand foot soldier to conquer Greece on the mere whim of Xerxes. You know the type, dumb, proud, and son of the former king. So all of Persia testosterone is off to Greece and alone at home sit all the women, retards, cripples, and the old…basically anyone who didn't smash cans of Persian beer up against their forehead for a good time on Saturday nights. And now please stay tuned for a word from our sponsors. But don't turn that dial, because… *(Singing.)* after these messages, we'll be right back. *(Exits.)*

(Flashing MTV-style lights. A brief burst of rock music as ARIAN enters and crosses down center. Lights and music cut off together.)

ARIAN: You're watching MTV Persia. How weird is that?

(The lights and music repeat and ARIAN moves upstage, and HANNA enters and takes his place down center. TOM and RODNEY have entered and joined ARIAN upstage behind her.)

HANNA: What happens…when all of the able-bodied young men in Persia

(ARIAN, RODNEY, and TOM act out Persians lifting weights and playing basketball.)

HANNA: join Xerxes' army

(They start marching in place.)

HANNA: and march off to battle the insurgent Greeks

(They do a brief Greek line dance ending "Opah!")

HANNA: leaving behind only desperate women,

(Women looking desperate.)

HANNA: a council of old guys,

(Old men barely standing up.)

HANNA: and a couple of losers?

(They point at one another.)

HANNA: We followed a typical Persian family for one week,

TOM: and our cameras found out what happens

RODNEY: when people stop being polite

ARIAN: and start being Persian.

ALL: Meet the Ghazis.

TOM: Can you handle our truth?

(Lights. Music. Same as before. The PLAYERS cross to coat racks on the upstage corners of the stage. HANNA puts a sweater around her neck; TOM grabs a cane; RODNEY a blonde wig; ARIAN has on a T-shirt that says "Greeks are people too." They meet up down center. HANNA is in the middle with TOM on her left, ARIAN on her right, and RODNEY crouched in front of her. They point at her with "attitude.")

HANNA: I'm the mother whose younger son and husband are off bravely fighting for our country.

(Lights. Music. The GROUP rotates. TOM comes center. HANNA moves to his right, RODNEY up and to his left, ARIAN down in front. They all point.)

TOM: I'm the grandfather who is on the Council of Elders which was left in charge while our men are off bravely fighting for our country.

(Lights. Music. Rotate as before.)

RODNEY: I'm the pregnant wife of the younger son who's off bravely fighting for our country. I'm fun-loving and unpredictable! Woo-hoo!

(Lights. Music. One more rotation.)

ARIAN: And I am the older brother who opposes the war so I am not fighting for our country.

HANNA, ARIAN, and TOM: LOSER!

ALL: Meet the Ghazis.

TOM: Can you handle our truth?

(Lights. Music. The GROUP breaks apart, each moving to one of the four short stools that occupy the corners of the stage.)

GRANDPA: *(Sitting in a confessional special downstage left.)* It's day three in the house, and everybody's getting anxious. And these daytime activities you people keep making us do are also very draining. Mother is still nursing a fractured clavicle from Monday's zip-line/pudding challenge. Morale about the war is also at an all-time low. But not mine! Why? Because victory is certain! We were winners under Darius, and we will be winners under his son, Xerxes. Besides, we have the largest war machine ever assembled! Since the beginning of time it has been Persia's destiny to level cities and collect tribute. And today apparently it is our destiny to give each other sensual massages. I hate this show.

(Lights. Music. We are in the living room.)

WIFE: *(Receiving a sensual massage from BROTHER.)* Oh, Mazda! That feels incredible!

BROTHER: This is your heart center.

GRANDPA: *(Sensually massaging MOTHER.)* Hey, take it easy over there.

BROTHER: What do you mean?

GRANDPA: That's your brother's wife.

BROTHER: So?

GRANDPA: So don't get carried away. He's off defending our country…doing something with his life. Unlike you. You're twenty-five years old; you've done nothing!

BROTHER: That's not true. I have done something. I *chose* not to go. I am what you call "a conscientious objector."

GRANDPA: You are what I call "a Greek faggot"!

MOTHER: Please do not use that word in this house!

GRANDPA: I'm sorry Mother. *(To BROTHER.)* You are just a plain faggot.

WIFE: (*In ecstasy from her brother-in-law's sensitive massage work.*) Oh!

GRANDPA: (*Indignant.*) That is your brother's wife!

(*Lights. Music. Four corners.*)

BROTHER: (*In the confessional.*) Grandpa thinks it's funny to tease me, he teases me as if I wore the same armor as my noble brother. But you see, my armor is made of very thin, almost butterfly-like tissue. It tears easily, just like all my hopes and dreams. (*Choking tears.*) I don't want to do this…

(*Lights. Music. Cut to kitchen.*)

MOTHER: See, I don't use lemons, I use limes.

WIFE: Limes? Really?

MOTHER: I even scrape out the rind.

WIFE: How about that? (*Beat.*) So, how are you holding up?

MOTHER: I struggle. It's hard without him here. I feel quite lost. (*Confessional.*) Actually, I have to say, since my husband has been gone, I have such a sense of freedom. I have so much time to myself. Why, just today, I knitted a scarf, milked the goat, and discovered masturbation!

WIFE: I don't know what to do with myself. (*Confessional.*) You know…without my husband around, I get so much more done. Today I built a wall, re-shingled the roof, and discovered electricity!

MOTHER: Oh, I know what you mean, it is so boring.

WIFE: Nothing happens anymore.

MOTHER: (*Confessional.*) I had my first orgasm!

WIFE: (*Confessional.*) I invented the first light bulb!

MOTHER: Well let us hope that fate brings this war a swift end and gives us back our men.

WIFE: It would be the end of our suffering.

MOTHER: (*Confessional.*) It would be the end of my orgasms. (*To WIFE.*) I wouldn't be able to hide my joy.

WIFE: (*Confessional.*) I *would* have to hide my light bulb.

MOTHER: Now you try using the lime.

WIFE: Oh I couldn't. Change is an enemy.

MOTHER: Come on, go a little crazy. (*She squirts WIFE with the lime wedge.*)

WIFE: (*Playful.*) Oh! You got me all wet! How dare you! (*Squirts her back.*)

(*The TWO engage in boisterous lime fighting until MOTHER tickles WIFE to the ground and into a compromising sexual position. BROTHER and GRANDPA walk in.*)

BROTHER: My eyes burn!

GRANDPA: Is this heaven?

(*Lights. Music. Four corners.*)

BROTHER: (*Confessional.*) I still cannot get that image out of my mind. I do not accept what has gone on in the house. I cannot understand it. What is happening to us? It was wrong…it was…

GRANDPA (*Interrupting.*) It was HOT! This proves to me that you're a faggot, you olive-stuffing homosexual!

BROTHER: Grandpa get out of here, this is my moment in time! My moment… (*Choking tears.*) I don't want to do this…

(*Lights. Music. Cut to living room.*)

MOTHER: (*Upstage with WIFE.*) I use more of a circular motion…

BROTHER: (*Downstage to GRANDPA.*) If we're so certain of victory how come we haven't heard anything? They've been gone forever. We should have heard something.

GRANDPA: (*Who is trying to watch television.*) Of course we haven't heard anything, they're too busy winning! Killing those feta cheese monkeys.

MOTHER: I don't want to hear about the Greeks! No more about the Greeks!

BROTHER: The Greeks aren't to blame, Mom.

MOTHER: (*To WIFE.*) …I've been working out.

BROTHER: MOM! It's Xerxes. Don't you get it? Doesn't anyone get it? They're dead! Xerxes marched them off to their deaths!

MOTHER: (*In grief.*) OHHH!!!

GRANDPA: Don't upset your mother! Her only son is off to war!

BROTHER: I'm her son too. You always forget me!

GRANDPA: Shut up, Faggy Faggadopolis!

WIFE: OH!!!!

(WIFE falls to ground; MOTHER cradles her.)

MOTHER: (To WIFE.) What's wrong?

GRANDPA: Are they gonna make out again?

WIFE: My water just broke!

GRANDPA: (To BROTHER.) You, get in there and help, it's about time you saw up a woman's skirt.

BROTHER: Okay.

(BROTHER tries to help; WIFE is screaming.)

MOTHER: I can see the head! It looks like… (To BROTHER.) you!

(Gasp. Lights. Music. They meet down center.)

ALL: Meet the Ghazis.

GRANDPA: Can you handle our truth?

HANNA: Stay tuned for "I Want a Famous Persian Face."

(Lights. Music. They all exit, except RODNEY who is once again wigless and moves downstage right back into emcee mode.)

RODNEY: Restless, weary, nowhere to turn. What the heck are our boys doing over there in the land of spanakopita? Well I'll tell you: Xerxes led his army of foot soldiers one way and sent his navy of 1,207 ships another way—now that is 207 more ships than Little Miss Helen of Troy managed to launch, so you know how bad Xerxes wanted to paint the town red with Grecian blood. And why was Xerxes so thirsty for this Grecian blood? You see his daddy tried to conquer Greece himself ten years earlier and was unsuccessful. And since Xerxes had been king he hadn't done much, and he figured settling this old score was as good a way as any of livin' up to his daddy's great name. But Xerxes had one big problem: in between Persia and Greece was a huge channel of water called the Hellespont. And how do you get the largest army ever assembled from point A to point B? For the first and last time in his life Xerxes came up with a brilliant plan: have the navy meet the army and build a bridge out of boats. Think about that, ladies and gentlemen! Imagine a thousand boats lined up across a huge body of water—picture the Hudson—a thousand ships line up across it and hundreds of thousands of soldiers marching…into Hoboken. So that's

what he did. But the first time he tried, the sea put up a little fight. It was rough, it was stormy, it broke the bridge of boats apart. So Xerxes flips out and decides to punish the sea by giving it three hundred lashes for misbehaving. One more: my entire childhood. What I did, Dad? (Awkward pause.) And…so amazingly enough, the sea calms down and they all make it safely across. So, Hellespont: crossed. News: none. And the good queen, played by that divine specimen, has been in a dying mood since her son and all of Persia's pride marched off to Olive Country.

(Loud, brassy burlesque music busts out from BAND. HANNA enters, followed by ARIAN and TOM who, throughout the following, peel away her clothes and using pearls, gloves, etc., from the coat racks transform her into ATOSSA. Meanwhile RODNEY ad libs lines like, "And here she is now," "This is my favorite part of the show," "Isn't she beautiful, ladies and gentlemen?," etc. When the change is nearly complete…)

RODNEY: The good queen is distraught over the state of her kingdom. She has been in a horrible state. The elder men are restless, the wives and retards and cripples are all anxious, and still no word from the troops! The kingdom is in peril, clinging to any sign of hope. If only someone of the upper echelon would address the common folk and put them at ease…well quick cut and fade in on Queen Atossa, upon her throne before all her loyal constituents…

(The throne is composed of ARIAN and TOM on all fours as the seat. RODNEY has moved in behind her, his arms as the arms of the throne. The music stops.)

ATOSSA: Good people of Persia, I have left the golden-furnished chamber where I once lay with King Darius, to tell you my own dread. Last night I had a horrible dream.

(The lights become murky. HANNA stands and crosses to the stool downstage left while the dream flashes across the stage in quadruple time. ARIAN, RODNEY, and TOM hurl themselves about acting out the strange horse and bird dream that ATOSSA is about to describe. Done, they move to the sides of the stage. As she begins to recount it, it unfolds again the same as before, only this time very slowly and synchronized with her description.)

ATOSSA: Night after night since my son left with the army he mustered I am joined with many dreams. He's gone, gone to Greece, bent on making it Persian and his. But never has a vision showed more clear than what I saw last night in the kind-hearted dark. I'll tell you: It seemed to me two well-dressed women, sisters—one robed with Persian luxury, the other in a plain Greek tunic—came into view, both flawless in beauty. And for the fatherland, a home, one was allotted Greek soil, the other, the great world beyond. Then I saw the two of them build bitter quarrels one against the other, and when my son learned this, he tried to curb and gentle them: under his chariot he yokes them together as horses, and on their necks he straps broad leather collars. And the one towered herself proud in this harness and she kept her mouth well governed by the reins. But the other bucked stubborn and with both hands she wrenches harness from the chariot fittings and drags it by sheer force, bridle flung off, and she shatters the yoke mid-span and he falls, my son falls, and his father is standing beside him—Darius, pitying him, and when Xerxes sees that, he rips his own clothes to rags. I tell you I did see these things last night. This morning, when I'd risen, trembling I tried to wash away the omen in a clear rippling spring. I then ran to the altar bearing gifts of honey'd milk for the gods who turn away evil. Hoping to appease those gods so they might stop whatever ills are surely approaching. But! Upon reaching the tomb, I looked up to see an eagle, fleeing toward the altar's flame. Frightened, mute, my friends, I just stood there. Next I saw a hawk in downswoop raising its wings to break the fall and clawing at its rival's head. Raking, tearing at the eagle's flesh. And the eagle did nothing. Only cowered and offered itself up. I saw this terror as I tell you now.

(TOM crosses upstage right. RODNEY crosses to upstage left stool and sits. ARIAN crosses down center.)

ARIAN: So that was the Queen Atossa's dream. A little unsettling. But those happen from time to time: unsettling dreams. I had a dream the other night and—

RODNEY: I have a *dream* today!

ARIAN: And it was that one day little black children and little white children would join hands and walk together as sisters and brothers.

RODNEY: Really?

ARIAN: No, Rodney. I'm trying to tell them my actual dream. My dream was not about the civil rights movement.

RODNEY: Aw. Right. Y'all didn't hafta worry 'bout dat. Y'all grew up privileged. I was raised by my momma. We didn't even have money to buy clothes, son.

ARIAN: That's really none of my business.

RODNEY: Never is. When the black man suffers, never *is* the white man's business.

ARIAN: I'm really not even white, technically.

RODNEY: Mexican. Whatever.

ARIAN: I'm not from Mexico. I'm from Iran.

RODNEY: What?

ARIAN: Iran. I'm from Iran. I came here when I was five.

RODNEY: You ain't from here?

ARIAN: No.

RODNEY: Aight! Aight, you cool dawg. You cool.

ARIAN: Thank you. Can I finish telling them about my dream now?

RODNEY: Yeah, man! You tell 'em yo' dream. You tell 'em yo' hopes and aspirations! Tell them white people!

ARIAN: Anyway…so the other night I had a dream and in it I was in back at high school in Glenview, Illinois. I was walking through the hall and I decide to look at a clock on the wall and I immediately find out that I have one minute to get to my class and if I am late to class I will fail or something. So…I start running. I mean, I am running FAST to get to my class. And all of a sudden I start gliding. With one step I glide like ten feet. I glide up the stairs; I glide down the stairs and I finally get to my class. I go to open the door and the door is locked. I'm pulling at the door…nothing. I look inside and see this weird group of people, like Justin Tanner (I haven't seen him in years) and Jennifer Jamison (who was the hottest girl in my school) and my niece (she's seven years old). And they weren't looking at me because they were taking this test. I look and the teacher is Hanna Cheek. And she looks at me as if "there's nothing I can do…" At that moment, I decide to eat a banana. I eat it… I wake up. And that was my dream. Now my mom is like an expert in dream interpretation—well not an expert, but she knows a lot—and so I asked her what it meant. And she said, "Arian, this is life. You are running around all the time. You have no time for anything but getting to where you have to go. It's okay. It is life. And usually when you have dreams about school that means you are still wanting to learn and know more about something…probably about how to budget your time.

And the gliding usually means that you don't want to run anymore. You are ready to stop running. It's all very good. Very good. And the reason why Hanna Cheek is in your dream is probably because you will fall in love and have lots of babies together." And that's what she said. I mean, I added that last part because…

RODNEY: She gay, man.

ARIAN: Right. Gay. But pretty interesting, huh? So I thought wouldn't it be more interesting if my mom interpreted Queen Atossa's dream?

(HANNA crosses center with stool.)

ARIAN: So I'm going to play my mom, and Hanna is going to play Queen Atossa. And I think it would go a little something like this…

PARVEIN: That is a very interesting dream Queen Atossa joon-joony-joon-joon.

ATOSSA: Yes.

PARVEIN: You know broken yokes are a sign of freedom.

ATOSSA: Really?

PARVEIN: Usually it means that you can finally do what you want to do without any…interference. You don't have…things holding you back.

ATOSSA: I don't know…when this yoke broke it caused like a lot of damage. It didn't seem like it was setting anyone free.

PARVEIN: You mentioned your son, Xerxes…

ATOSSA: Yeah.

PARVEIN: Usually when we dream about our children it is because we have finally become comfortable with the path our life has taken.

ATOSSA: This dream didn't make me feel very comfortable. It made me feel very uncomfortable. And now it's got me really worried that something has happened to Xerxes; I feel like…something really awful has happened to him like maybe he was even killed.

PARVEIN: But in your dream there were horses.

ATOSSA: There were?

PARVEIN: You said Xerxes tried to yoke the sisters like horses.

ATOSSA: Right. But they weren't actually horses.

PARVEIN: Doesn't matter. Whenever there is a horse or something acting like a horse it is sign of pocket money coming to you soon.

ATOSSA: You're saying this dream means I have pocket money coming to me soon?

PARVEIN: Definitely.

ATOSSA: I don't think that's what it means. I think it means that we are going to lose this war with Greece. That they are going to destroy us…and I don't know what…the end of the empire.

PARVEIN: Don't get angry with me.

ATOSSA: Well I'm sorry but this dream has got me a little stressed out. I mean why did he have to go to war? But you know whose fault it is? The Greeks. [Spits.] Why do they have to be so uncooperative? If they would just cooperate, then Xerxes would never have to go over there to fight them. I mean what's their deal? They've got some crazy government, how does it even work? Ugh. Look…now because of them I can't get to sleep at night, I've got these bags under my eyes. It's all their fault.

PARVEIN: Ah…takhseer.

ATOSSA: What?

PARVEIN: Takhseer. It is Farsi for "blame."

ATOSSA: Oh right. I know that. I speak Farsi.

PARVEIN: Persians love to blame something else for their own problems.

TOM: (Editing the scene.) And that's probably how it would have gone if Arian's mom had interpreted Queen Atossa's dream.

(ARIAN and HANNA replace their stools. ARIAN comes back stage center, while TOM crosses left.)

ARIAN: And what she said about takhseer was true. Iranians—Persians—especially when they're upset will blame somebody or something for everything wrong in their life. And that reminds me of a story.

(HANNA has exited; TOM gets the subtitle cards and readies them on the stool downstage left.)

ARIAN: We wrote a song about it and I'd like to sing it for you now. It's called "Takhseer" or "Blame" and it says a lot I think about what it means to be Persian.

(BAND plays the intro; RODNEY is on acoustic guitar.)

ARIAN: What a band! Rodney Gardiner, ladies and gentlemen…

(ARIAN sings in Farsi while TOM holds up subtitles in English.)*

ARIAN: PARSIYAAN HASTEE VAKHTEEKEH SEEZDAHEE VA MEEREE SHEERNEE PORSEEDAN TO EVANSTON BA DOOSTET HADI, MADARET FEHKR KARD TO LAWNEE BEEROON BOODEE VA DOM BALET GASHD TO YEH BEH EM VESH.

PEYDAT KARD. PEEYAHDEH SHOD. TO GOOSHET ZAD MEGAH TAHKSEER EH TO BOOD DAR HARSHEE TO ZENDEHGEESH KHARAB AST!

MOOESH SEHFEEDEH. APARTMENTEH GOH HEE DAREH VA TAHKSEEREHET AST KEH DANDOON PEZESH NEESTEH.

AH TAHKSEER…
AH TAHKSEER…
MAH PARSIYAAN AHSHEGEH TAHKSEER HASTEEM.

AH TAHKSEER…
AH TAHKSEER…
AMAH BAHROON TAHKSEEREH HAHVA NEEST.

(TOM hands cards to ARIAN, who turns them around revealing the Farsi translation while TOM sings in English.)

TOM: PERSIANS WERE ZOROASTRIAN—THAT WAS WAY BACK WHEN—
NOW THEY'RE MUCH MORE INTO ISLAMICS
NEVER GETTING LAID, HATING U.S.A.
SUDDENLY BECAME ALL THE RAGE
THEY THOUGHT THAT THEOCRATIC RULE SOUNDED PRETTY COOL
BETTER THAN THAT FOOL, REZA SHAH,

---

*You know you're a Persian when you're thirteen and you go trick-or-treating in Evanston with your friend, Hadi, and your mom thinks you've been out too long so she searches for you in her BMW.
And when she finds you she gets out the car and smacks your face
and blames you for everything wrong in her life including gray hair, her shitty apartment, and the fact that she could never be a dentist.
Blame…
Yeah blame…
you know we Persians love to blame.
blame…
Yeah blame
but you can't blame the sky for the rain.

SO THEY HAD REVOLUTION
BUT NOBODY CARED
TILL THEY WERE SEIZING EMBASSIES, TAKING HOSTAGES,
DOING WHAT THEY PLEASED WITH OUR OIL
EXCEPT IT WASN'T OURS, THEN THEY HIT OUR TOWERS
OH NO WAIT NOW THAT WAS IRAQ.
OR WAS IT OSAMA? WHO CARES JUST SO LONG AS
WE BOMB ANYBODY THAT READS THE KORAN?

ARIAN: AH TAHKSEER…   TOM: BLAME…
AH TAHKSEER…   YEAH BLAME…
MAH PARSIYAAN AHSHE-   YOU KNOW EVERYBODY
  GEH TAHKSEER HAS-   LOVES TO BLAME.
  TEEM.
                             WE LOVE TO BLAME,
AH TAHKSEER…   YEAH BLAME.
AH TAHKSEER…   BUT YOU CAN'T BLAME
AMAH BAHROON TAHK-   THE SKY FOR THE
  SEEREH HAHVA NEEST.   RAIN.

TOM: *(Dancing hard.)* PERSIANS WERE ZOROASTRIAN—
  THAT WAS WAY BACK WHEN—
NOW THEY'RE MUCH MORE INTO ISLAMICS
NEVER GETTING LAID, HATING U.S.A.
SUDDENLY BECAME ALL THE RAGE
THEY THOUGHT THAT THEOCRATIC RULE SOUNDED PRETTY COOL
BETTER THAN THAT FOOL REZA SHAH, YEAH

ARIAN: *(Hardly dancing.)* PARSIYAAN HASTEE VAKHTEEKEH SEEZDAHEE
VA MEEREE SHEERNEE PORSEEDAN TO EVANSTON BA DOOSTET HADI,
MADARET FEHKR KARD TO LAWNEE BEEROON BOODEE
BOTH: BA DA DA DA DA DA. BA DA DA DA DA DA. BA DA DA DA DA DA. BA DA DA DA DA DA.

(ATOSSA enters and breaks up their final pose.)

ATOSSA: THAT DREAM HAS REALLY STRESSED ME OUT. WHAT WAS IT ABOUT?
I'M ALL OUT OF HOPE FOR A TRIUMPH.
WHAT ARE WE TO DO? WHAT IF IT WAS YOU?
XERXES REALLY BLEW IT THIS TIME.
I THINK THAT WE SHOULD PRAY. NO TIME FOR DELAY.
GOT OUT AND ARRAY ALL THE STUFF.
I'M SCARED OF THE GREEKS
THEY GIVE ME THE CREEPS.
AND HOW COME THEY DON'T HAVE A KING? WHY DID XERXES BRING
EVERY SINGLE YOUNG MAN IN ASIA
TO GO AND PUT THEM DOWN, GO AND BURN THEIR TOWNS?

I DON'T LIKE THE SOUND OF THIS, NO, NO
I'M JUST SO SCARED 'CAUSE THEY'RE WAY OVER THERE.

ARIAN: *(In Farsi.)* YOU NEED PRAYER!

ATOSSA: WHAT?

RODNEY: YOU NEED PRAYER!

ATOSSA: WE NEED PRAYER.

ALL: WE NEED PRAYER!

ATOSSA: Oh look! A messenger!

(HERALD enters from the house without jacket, sleeves rolled up and fedora cocked back on his head.)

HERALD: Listen, cities of Asia!
Listen, Land of Persia!
My dreadful duty is being first to bring you bitter news,
O cruel to bring first cruel news!
But I must, I must. Need presses me to unroll the full disaster.
Persians,
         Our country's fleet and army are no more!
         We are defeated,
Routed, scattered, ruined, undone,
Crushed, smashed, savaged, broken, whipped, bested,
     beaten, cowed...

HANNA: Enough! We get it.

RODNEY: Woe! Woe upon woe!

(Throughout the following, HANNA and RODNEY, with ARIAN's help, change into the boxing shorts and gloves that have been hanging on the upstage coat racks; RODNEY in the downstage right corner, HANNA in the upstage left.)

HERALD: Worse than anything you can imagine. Everything over there has ended. I was there. I can tell you, no hearsay. I can describe it. Worse than you can believe. Xerxes—he lives and sees light—but others, many others, more than I can name, more than a man can list in a tally or even imagine, are gone. Gone.

RODNEY: Woe upon woe!

ARIAN: *(Has removed his jacket and rolled up his sleeves.)*
Now tell me how the two fleets fell to the attack.
Who first advanced, struck the first blow? Was it the
     Greeks or the Persians, exultant with their count-
     less ships?

HERALD: The first sign of the whole disaster came
When something vengeful—
Or evil and not human—
Appeared from somewhere over there.

(He gestures in HANNA's direction; she is dressed as boxer now in blue shorts with "GREECE" on the sides and back; she acknowledges the audience sheepishly.)

HERALD: For a Greek who came in stealth from the
     Athenian fleet,
Whispered this to your son Xerxes:

(ARIAN is whispering to RODNEY.)

HERALD: "Soon as the shades of night descend, the
     Grecians
Shall quit their station; rushing to their oars
They mean to separate,

(ARIAN crosses to HANNA.)

HERALD: And in secret flight
Seek safety." And at once,
For he had listened not understanding,
The royal chief gave his high charge:

(RODNEY has stood and met HERALD stage center; he is in red shorts with "PERSIA" on the sides and back. He mouths boastfully as HERALD speaks.)

HERALD: "Soon as yon sun shall cease
To dart his radiant beams, and dark'ning night
Ascends the temple of the sky, arrange
in three divisions your well-ordered ships,
And guard each pass, each outlet of the seas:
Others enring around this rocky isle
Of Salamis. Should Greece escape her fate
And work her way by secret flight, your heads
Shall answer the neglect."

(RODNEY menaces and returns to his corner.)

HERALD: This harsh command
He gave, exulting in his mind. With martial disci-
     pline
And prompt obedience, snatching a repast,
Each mariner fix'd well his ready oar.

(RODNEY and HANNA come center while ARIAN as the referee silently explains the rules; they hit gloves; HANNA reels.)

HERALD: And when the Sun's glow faded and Night
Was coming on,
         Each oarlord,

Each expert man-at-arms
  Boarded his ship.
Squadron on squadron, cheers for warships
Roared from the decks,
  And they sailed,
Each captain maintaining his position.

(They have returned to their corners.)

HERALD: As ordered, the captains kept them rowing
 to and fro
All night. All night—
And the Greek forces never
Tried sailing out secretly.
Not once.

Day dawned. White horses streaked the sky.
Light dazzled—we heard a huge Greek shout,
Crashing, echoing.

(In a faint, distant voice while HANNA stands and mouths along.)

HERALD: *Sons of Greece, go!*
  Free fatherland,
  Free children, wives,
  Shrines of our fathers' gods,
  Tombs where our forefathers lie.
  Fight for all we have!
  Now!
We cowered:
Our plan had made us clowns.
These were no runaways, shrieking for safety;
These were fighters, nerving themselves for war.

(Leaping onto the downstage left stool.)

Then the trumpet shriek blazed
  Through everything over there.
A signal:

(The bell rings and the bout begins. It is an exact reenactment of the boxing match from City Lights *complete with Chaplin's music playing softly in the background; HERALD calls the fight like an announcer.)*

HERALD: Instantly
Their oars struck salt.
  We heard
That rhythmic rattle-slap.
It seemed no time till they
All stood in sight.
  We saw them sharp.
First the right wing,
  Close-drawn, strictly ordered,

Led out, and next we saw
The whole fleet bearing down.

Then on our side shouts in Persian rose to a crest.
  We didn't hold back.
That instant, ship rammed
bronzeclad beak on ship.
A Greek ship started the attack
Shearing off a whole Persian
Stern. At first Persia's fleet
Rolled firm, but next, as our ships
  Jammed into the narrows and
    No one could help any other and
      Our own bronze teeth bit into
Our own stakes,
  Whole oarbanks shattered
Then the Greek ships, seizing their chance,
Swept in circling and struck and overturned our hulls,
  and saltwater vanished before our eyes—
shipwrecks filled it, and drifting corpses.
Shores and reefs filled up with our dead
And every able ship under Persia's command
Broke order,
  Scrambling to escape.
We might have been tuna or netted fish
for they kept on, spearing and gutting us
  with splintered oars and bits of wreckage,
while moaning and screams drowned out
the sea noise, all the sea
was one vast salty soup of shrieks and cries,
The whole sea was one din of shrieks and dying groans,
  The water was red
With Persian flotsam, blood and carnage
  Till Night's black face closed it all in.

(The bell rings. End of Round 1. They return to their corners. HERALD jumps down and crosses center.)

HERALD: Losses by the thousands!
  Even if I told
The catalogue for ten full days I
Could not complete it for you:
But this is sure:
  Never before in one day
Have so many thousands died.
Disaster—
  I've told less than half.

(The bell rings. Round 2. HERALD leaps on the downstage right stool.)

HERALD: The next load of suffering
Outweighed the first twice over.

Persians at the peak of life,
          Best in soul, brightest in lineage,
          First always to give the King loyalty—
They're dead without glory,
          And shamed by that fate.
An island fronts the coast of Salamis—
Tiny, harborless,
          Where dance-wild
Pan likes stepping it light through the breakers.
There,
          Xerxes posted these chosen men,
Planning that when the shipwrecked enemy
Swam ashore desperate for safety,
They'd kill that Greek force easily
And rescue friends caught in the narrows.

(HANNA rings the bell; they move to their corners.)

HERALD: How badly he misread the future

(The round wasn't over yet; ARIAN rings the bell; they resume.)

HERALD: For after some god had
handed Greeks the glory in the seafight,
That same day
          They fenced their bodies in bronze armor
And leapt from their ships
          And cordoned off
The island so completely that our men milled
Helpless,
          Not knowing where to turn
While stones battered at them
And arrows twanging from the bowstrings
Hit home killing them.
          It ended
when the Greeks gave one great howl
And charged, chopping meat
till every living man was butchered.

(They both fall. ARIAN counts them down but they keep getting back up.)

HERALD: Then Xerxes moaned out loud
To see how deep disaster cut.
          Throned on a headland above the sea, he'd
          Kept his whole army clear in sight.
And he ripped his clothes
And screamed
And gave shrill hasty shouts to his whole land force
Dismissing them.
          They fled in disorder.

(HANNA delivers the knockout punch; in slow motion, RODNEY falls.)

HERALD: Here is disaster greater than the first
to make you moan.

(RODNEY is down for the count. HANNA celebrates, exits; ARIAN helps up RODNEY and they exit, slowly; HERALD comes down from the stool and crosses center as the music fades into silence.)

HERALD: The army Xerxes commanded, what was
     left of it,
Headed north and
Died on Boiotian soil, thirst-parched,
Gasping. A few of us reached Thessaly
          We were starving. They took us in.
There more died, too weak to eat or drink.
We struggled on:
          Magnesia and on to Macedon,
To come to the point,

It was that night
          Some god
Woke winter long before his time and froze
The Strymōn river bank to bank.
          Soldiers who'd never prayed before
Fell on their knees, kissed Mother Earth,
Thanked God. Too soon. Our prayers all done;
We were on the ice, crossing the river,
The first who went at dawn had no
Trouble, but then, as the sun beat down
As if to spite us, its fire turned ice to water;
Platoons, brigades sank together
And drowned as each one tried to climb
His companion's back; he who died
Quickest was luckiest.

The rest marched on,
Dragged ourselves through Thrace, a handful,
Home at last to Persia: motherland,
Widowland, stripped of all her sons.

Reason enough, chief city of Persians,
To cry out
          Longing for your best beloved youth.
A true tale, told—and a fraction, no more,
Of all the misery God spat on us.

(Beat. Entrance music. Enter RODNEY, HANNA, and ARIAN all dressed as PLAYERS again; this time, in just their shirtsleeves and suspenders.)

RODNEY: Tom Ridgely, ladies and gentlemen, as the Herald. You weren't kidding about those lines…

TOM: A lot of lines…I told you I had a lot of lines. Ladies and gentlemen, right now I'd like to introduce the best band in New York City. I'd like to do that…please give a nice round of applause for Mr. Jeremy Daigle on guitar, Mr. Willie Fastenow on the keys, Mr. Gunter Gruner on drums and Mr. Joe Morse on bass.

(Applause.)

RODNEY: Ladies and gentlemen, Tom's speech, lengthy though it was, is not something we just dreamed up for him to say. It's an eye-witness account of something that happened over two thousand years ago.

HANNA: And it was terrible, awful news. I knew about it because of my dream. But now what do we do?

ARIAN: Well we don't sit around moping and mourning, that's for sure. If we can't get even, let's get mad. Ladies and gentlemen, what would you do if you saw one of those filthy, rotten Greeks on this stage right now?

TOM: Use Persian cuss words on them.

ARIAN: That's right. We're going to teach you all some Persian insults. But first you need to know what you're insulting. So take it away Rodney…

RODNEY: All right, just repeat after me, first thing you'd say: U NA NEE HAH! One more time: U NA NEE HAH! GOOD! That just means GREEKS.

(ALL spit.)

HANNA: And then you spit on 'em. Now, add this to the end of UNANEEHAH. So it sounds like this and I'm going to say it twice: U NA NEE HAH e SAG! U NA NEE HAH e SAG! Try that… AND YELL IT, guys! One more time: EVEN LOUDER! This means, GREEKS ARE DOGS!

TOM: Now…new phrase. Again, add this after U NA NEE HAH…and I'm going to say this one twice: U NA NEE HAH e KASEEF! U NA NEE HAH e KASEEF! NICE AND LOUD! GREAT! This means, GREEKS ARE FILTHY!

ARIAN: Now, this last one is a new one. We didn't go over this one. But I need you guys to yell this as hard as humanly possible. All right? Again after U NA NEE HAH…it will sound like this…again, I'm going to say it twice: U NA NEE HAH e KOSS KESH! U NA NEE HAH e KOSS KESH! LOUDER! Much LOUDER! LOUDER! KEEP IT GOING! DON'T STOP! NOW ALL MEN IN THE THEATER! NOW ALL THE WOMEN! And this just means that GREEKS ARE VAGINAS OF A PROSTITUTE!

(HANNA slaps ARIAN and storms off.)

TOM: That was seriously inappropriate. You crossed the line, Arian. I'm sorry, ladies and gentlemen!

(TOM starts to push ARIAN off the stage.)

ARIAN: *(While being pushed off.)* I was trying something new! Artistic freedom!

RODNEY: Ladies and gentlemen, I'm sorry. That went a little too far. Please remember: the views of Arian do not represent the views of this entire company. Now I think we left off with the Queen receiving the news of Persia's defeat. We'd like to get back to that right now, but before we do we'd like to leave you with one final thought…if you do happen to run into any Greeks please…make sure you're in your car! BEEP BEEP! Alright, somebody Greek is going to whoop my black ass.

(He runs off as HANNA enters to her burlesque music…this time slow, soft, and sultry.)

HANNA: Good friends, whoever learns by experience that when a wave of evils crests, and breaks, it's natural for humankind to be afraid of everything, but when the deathless Power flows calm, to trust that Fortune's wind will always blow fair. But now, for me, everything is packed with fear, before my eyes the gods' hostility shows plain, and the roar in my ears is battle din, not a healing song:

(ARIAN and TOM enter, ties loosened, suspenders off their shoulders, and begin as before to strip her and transform her into ATOSSA.)

ATOSSA: Evils attack so fiercely panic storms my heart. That's the reason I've come here to my late husband's tomb, the great king Darius, father of my ill-fated son, to bring him up from the depths and seek his countenance. I've brought with me offerings to the gods so they might release my beloved to me in this time of need, as well as remembrances from my love's happy life while he ruled our great land: If these alone are not enough to draw him from his resting place, I bring myself,

(She falls back and is carried downstage.)

ATOSSA: my body and other joys Darius once cherished to lure him to us now. *(She is in a circle of light surrounded by darkness.)* But O my friends, these libations to the ones below need solemn hymns. Chant them and call his spirit, call up Darius while I send down these earth-drunk honors to the gods below.

(They kneel; she in the center, ARIAN and TOM on the edges behind her.)

ARIAN and TOM: *(Sung softly underneath her text.)* Our Queen, our lady, whom Persians revere, yes, send your libations to Earth's hidden rooms.

While we, chanting, calling, pour out our breath to beg kindness from those who marshal men's shadows through Earth.

Help us, you powers undying and holy that thrive beneath graves.

You, Earth and the soul-guide, and you who are king of the dead below us, send his spirit up into light.

Wake and hear us, Earth and You, who rule that world where dead men go.

Give complete consent to prayer: set free his proud and deathless glory.

Let Persia's god, born a man in Sousa, rise now from his funeral house.

Now speed him up whose peer does not nor ever shall rest hidden in this Persian earth.

ATOSSA: Help us, you powers undying and holy that thrive beneath graves. You, Earth and the soul-guide and you who are king of the dead below us, send his spirit up into light. Disasters keep stalking us, and if he knows of any cure more powerful than offerings and prayer, only risen near us into light can he reveal it. Wake and hear us Earth and You who rule that world where dead men go. Let Persia's god, born a man in Sousa, rise now from his funeral house. Man I loved, yes tomb I love, for everything I love lies covered there. Hand of death, Free him! Never once did he kill men with folly's blind and life-devouring haste. He was called the Persians' godbright counselor... And godbright counselor he was! Who steered the army on a true course. Free him! Come to your tomb and claim these gifts. Make yourself known showing signs of your kingship. Make yourself seen. O gods, give us our king that we might learn what we must do. Let him come to us, let me wrap him in my arms and feel his flesh upon mine—I need him.

ALL: Persia needs him. Father who brought us no evil, Darius, break free. Wake and hear loud suffering, hear strange new pain: the young men, our sons, are all of them gone. DARIUS AWAKE!

(A guitar starts to play. It is music from another world. "The Funk Opera" has begun.)

ATOSSA: Can he hear me? Blest in death and potent as a deathless force.

Can my king hear these broken words?
Earthmuffled
Tumbling from my lips and touching every note of pain in easeless sorrow-roughened breath?
Or must I shout so that my anguish reaches him? Can he heed me in his buried dark?

(DARIUS appears from nowhere. He wears a gold fedora, gold sunglasses, and a gold scarf. He is the funkiest man that has ever walked the earth.)

DARIUS: I BEEN GONE SO LONG
THINKIN' ABOUT MY BABY
AND MY DIVIDED KINGDOM FOR SO LONG

BY THE POWER IN MY HAND
I'M A MAKE YOU UNDERSTAND
I'M THE KING OF THE WORLD
COMIN' BACK TO THE MOTHERLAND

WHY MY PEOPLE DOWN AND OUT
WHY MY PEOPLE SAD
WHY IS MY BABY CRYIN' OUT
EVEN THOUGH SHE GOT A JUICY ASS

NOW SOMEBODY, ANYBODY, TELL ME

ARIAN AND TOM: WELL YA KNOW, WELL YA KNOW NOW

DARIUS: SOMEBODY, ANYBODY, TELL ME

ARIAN AND TOM: WELL YA KNOW, WELL YA KNOW NOW
YOU WON'T BELIEVE WHAT IS HAPPENIN' HERE
MM-MM
YOU WON'T BELIEVE IT, NO, NO
BET YA CAN'T, BET YA CAN'T NOW

(This sequence repeats four times; BAND joins in singing on the third and fourth. And now a li'l breakdown:)

ARIAN and TOM: WELL...I DON'T KNOW, YOU KNOW, BUT UH

(Repeats as backing for...)

TOM: GOOD KING DARIUS WE COULDN'T BEAR TO BRING YOU SHAME
SEEING YOUR VISION HERE, YOU'VE RISEN HERE, WE'LL TAKE THE BLAME
YOUR HONORED MAJESTY, SUCH TRAGEDY, OH NO I CANNOT SAY
OH I CURSE THIS MOURNFUL DAY, MY TONGUE AND TEETH WILL NOT DELAY

ARIAN: FUNKY DARIUS, YOU'RE EVIL'S ONLY ANTI-DOTE

HELP US AND FREE US, BEGGIN' YOU LEAD US, GIVE US
    SOME FUNKY SHIT YOU WROTE
WONDROUS DARIUS, BEFORE YOUR PRESENCE WE MUST
    BOW
IF YOU'LL ALLOW THIS FURROWED BROW TO BEG OF YOU
    SOME PATIENCE NOW

DARIUS: I SAID WHOA…

(ARIAN faints.)

DARIUS: YOU KNOW I HATE GETTING MAD
SOMEBODY BETTER TALK QUICK O' I'MA HAVE TO OPEN
    UP A CAN OF WHOOP ASS
YOU CALLED ME FROM THE OTHER WORLD
DON'T TELL ME YOU CAN'T SPEAK
TIME IS MONEY AND MONEY IS TIME
AND I'M BOUT TO LOSE MY ROYAL MIND
BY THE TIME I COUNT TO FIVE, YOU KNOW I MAKE THE
    LIGHTNING STRIKE
SPEAK UP 'FORE I COUNT IT DOWN OR YOU CAN KISS
    YOUR ASS GOOD NIGHT!
ONE…BETTER CALL YOUR MOMMA, TELL HER YOU
    LOVE HER
TWO…AIN'T NOBODY FUCKIN' AROUND
THREE…YOU BETTA GET ON YA KNEES AND PRAY FOR
    SHO'
FOUR…I CAN'T TAKE IT NO MO'
FIVE…FIVE…FIVE…

(DARIUS goes ballistic, running all over the stage; he
finally collapses in a heap downstage center; the music
pauses, then goes into a slow waltz that plays and builds
under the following.)

ATOSSA: Baby? First of all…

(They ravish each other.)

ATOSSA: Second of all…they're just nervous and
amazed by your presence. God I'm glad to see you,
you sexy beast.

(More ravishing.)

DARIUS: Looking good yourself, mama. Wait. The
trouble.

ATOSSA: Right. The trouble. I can tell you plainly and
to the point—we are lost. Persia is lost.

DARIUS: What?!

ATOSSA: Our son—Xerxes—marched troops to Greece
to overcome them and take their land—thousands of
men he took—and now word has come that they're all
dead. The battle lost. Persia ruined!

DARIUS: But how—

ATOSSA: Gone.

DARIUS: Do you mean

ATOSSA: Everyone's dead.

DARIUS: But

ATOSSA: Baby, we're fucked.

DARIUS: (Getting up.) You mean to tell me that everything I done worked for is gone? (Mouths "Damn.")

ATOSSA: We didn't know what to do and thought
you'd be the only one who could help—good, strong
King Darius.

DARIUS: Our dumbass son thinking he got to prove
something.

ATOSSA: Now he's the king of nothing.

DARIUS: Think he playin' a game…

ATOSSA: King of sand.

DARIUS: Stupid ass muthafucka.

ATOSSA: But what do we do?

DARIUS: Do? Nothing. All is lost. My beautiful Persia.
(Sings chorus.) WHY PERSIA?

ATOSSA: Hold it together.

DARIUS: WHY PERSIA?

ATOSSA: We need you.

DARIUS: WHY PERSIA?

ATOSSA: Baby, you're sexy when you're mad but—

DARIUS: WHY PERSIA? (Speaking.) My sexy wife.
Remember what we had. That's all there is: love what
you got—honor it—don't fuck it up with meaningless
war. Persia, can I talk to you for a second?

ALL: Hm-hm.

DARIUS: I said can I talk to you for one of those tic-
toc seconds?

ALL: Hm-hm!

DARIUS: You know…a kingdom ain't a kingdom…
unless a king is a king…and I was a fool to leave you
under Xerxes rule…but ain't no pride in ignorin' yo'
mistakes…there is only pride in what it take for that
cycle to break…and Persia we had it so good…

ALL: How good?

DARIUS: I said Persia we had it so good!

ALL: How good?!

DARIUS: We had it… *(Falsetto.)* so good!

ALL: *(Chorus.)* WHY PERSIA? WHY PERSIA? WHY PERSIA? WHY PERSIA?

(The music changes back to 4/4; JEREMY goes into the "We Had It So Good" riff under the following.)

ATOSSA: *(Speaking.)* My love. Though you cannot help us and heal this problem—for you're right, what's done is done—I'm so happy to see you. My stallion.

DARIUS: My kitten. Sexy mama. I've missed you.

ATOSSA: God I love you.

DARIUS: We had it so good.

ATOSSA: We did. Everyone did.

DARIUS: The funky parties.

ATOSSA: The sex.

DARIUS: The land and power.

ATOSSA: And the sex.

DARIUS: And the dancing, little momma.

ATOSSA: Oh the dancing—how mighty Persia danced. WE HAD IT SO GOOD. WE HAD IT SO GOOD.

DARIUS: WE HAD IT SO GOOD. WE HAD IT SO GOOD.

BOTH: WE HAD IT SO GOOD. WE HAD IT SO GOOD.

ATOSSA: TAKE TO MY EYES…YOU'VE BEEN AWAY AND WE PAID THE PRICE

DARIUS: I MISS YOUR JUICY LOVIN', BABY.

ATOSSA: DARIUS, MY LOVER FOR LIFE WE LOST IT ALL AND THAT JUST AIN'T RIGHT.

BOTH: YOU KNOW WE HAD IT SO GOOD.

ALL: WE HAD IT SO GOOD. WE HAD IT SO GOOD. WE HAD IT SO GOOD. WE HAD IT SO GOOD.

DARIUS: ONE WORD OF ADVICE LOOK TO THE SMALL TREASURES IN LIFE FOR NOTHING ELSE MATTERS

SO THINK TWICE BEFORE RUNNIN' OUT ONTO THIN ICE YOU KNOW WE HAD IT SO GOOD

ALL, including BAND: WE HAD IT SO GOOD. WE HAD IT SO GOOD. WE HAD IT SO GOOD. WE HAD IT SO GOOD.

(Music changes again, lights with it. Now faster and with a wild horn riff; WILLIE has moved from keys to sax. The PLAYERS realize the party has begun and go into a highly choreographed dance break. DARIUS and ATOSSA share a brief duet; ARIAN and TOM trade solos; they all join up for the Big Finish. Lights, applause, they hold the final pose. But DARIUS is gone.)

ARIAN: Darius! *(Exits.)*

HANNA and TOM: Darius come back! Oh Darius! Why are you upset? Play something funky, etc.

(RODNEY enters upstage left tie-less in unbuttoned shirtsleeves, calling offstage.)

RODNEY: Darius!

(HANNA and TOM meet him, looking upstage left for DARIUS. XERXES enters slowly upstage right with a thick rope over his shoulder, evidently pulling an enormous load; crosses center stage.)

XERXES: Man motanafer as een hastem. Hal ache? Joon e badanam ab shod. Ab keh halah knoon ast. Baba Joon. Cherah ba un mardhayeh gohl namoondam. Tackseer e man bood. Parsehan e man gohl boodand. Baba Joon. Cherah man namordam unjah…

I hate this. What now? I am helpless. My body's last current of strength…water. Water turned to blood. Khoon. Dear Father! Would that I were with the men now gone. I wish I could close my eyes.

HANNA: *(Having turned to face him.)* Xerxes…thousands of men

RODNEY: The country's flowers

TOM: All wasted and withered

ALL: Cry!

HANNA: Can you cry?

XERXES: Look at me and weep. I am sorrow. I am regret. Takhseer e man eh.

ALL: You did this!

XERXES: Thousands and thousands of our future…
now blood. Let every breath you draw…blow against
me now, for our children…I cannot say.

RODNEY: Where are our friends?

TOM: Where are the men who stood proud beside
you?

HANNA: Where is my husband, my father?

ALL: Where is everyone?

XERXES: Ab va khoon. Past all help.

ALL: You did this!

XERXES: I hate this. I can't bear this anymore.

ALL: We don't deserve this!

XERXES: I blame myself.

ALL: We blame you!

XERXES: Disgrace me, but triumph the dead!

ALL: Shame on you, Xerxes.

RODNEY: For what?

TOM: For what?

HANNA: For what?

ALL: FOR WHAT?

XERXES: Our brothers are dead.

*(The upstage GROUP caves in on itself, supporting EACH
OTHER in their grief; they let out weakened cries of woe
while a daf and tambak [traditional Iranian percussion instruments] slowly begin beating out the dirge;
the PLAYERS and MUSICIANS find their rhythm,
HANNA, RODNEY, and TOM weave in and out while
chanting what follows; their movements and the music
build steadily, while XERXES begins speaking and then
howling the names of the fallen, improvising a mix of
Persian and American surnames—along with moans
of grief—as needed to fill out the music.)*

XERXES: Samyar Razan Roshan Arash Teymour
Jamsheed Sousas Pharandakes Mardook Pelagon
Zarvan Dotmas Souiscanes Michael Agdabatas Peter
Arash Hirbod Psammis Koorosh Jerome Daixis Isaac
Seulakes Samyar Roger Yashar Liliaious Luke Memphis
Tharybis Kayvan Edmund Megabazes Xanthes Meh-
raban Metragathes Naveed Lawrence Pasha Masistras
Ariomardes Pharnoukes Ekbantana Shahin Peyshang
Kayvan…

HANNA, RODNEY, and TOM: *(Chanting in harmony
under XERXES' lament; they revolve around EACH
OTHER, moving toward him in a group.)*
WOE UPON WOE UPON WOE UPON WOE UPON
HOW COULD YOU GO AND BRING OH SO MUCH WOE
    UPON
WOE UPON WOE UPON WOE UPON WOE UPON
SHOW SOME REMORSE FOR THE CHOICE OF YOUR COURSE
    UPON
WOE UPON WOE UPON WOE UPON WOE UPON
THROW US A BONE YOU BEEN GONE FOR SO LONG
    UPON
WOE UPON WOE UPON WOE UPON WOE UPON
HOW COULD YOU GO AND BRING OH SO MUCH WOE
    UPON
WOE UPON WOE UPON WOE UPON WOE UPON
SHOW SOME REMORSE FOR THE CHOICE OF YOUR COURSE
    UPON
WOE UPON WOE UPON WOE UPON WOE UPON
THROW US A BONE YOU BEEN GONE FOR SO LONG
    UPON
WOE UPON WOE UPON WOE UPON WOE UPON
LO AND BEHOLD IT WAS ALL FOR THE GLORIA
WOE UPON WOE UPON WOE UPON WOE UPON
LO AND BEHOLD IT WAS ALL FOR THE GOLD UPON
WOE UPON WOE UPON WOE UPON WOE UPON
LO AND BEHOLD IT WAS ALL FOR THE GLORIA
WOE UPON WOE UPON WOE UPON WOE UPON
LO AND BEHOLD IT WAS ALL FOR THE GOLD UPON
WOE UPON WOE UPON WOE UPON WOE UPON

(XERXES collapses to his knees; they are bearing down.)

HANNA, RODNEY, and TOM: THESE PEOPLE PAID FOR
    A COMEDY SHOW NOT FOR
WOE UPON WOE UPON WOE UPON WOE UPON

(The music and wailing have built to unbearable noise.)

HANNA, RODNEY, and TOM: LOOK HIGH AND LOW
    BUT THERE'S NOWHERE TO GO UPON
WOE UPON WOE UPON WOE UPON WOE UPON
WOE

*(Blackout. Silence. RODNEY sings the bass line. A tight
spot comes up stage center on HANNA. They are in the
same position as at the top of the show, only now an
absolute mess. The tune is familiar.)*

HANNA: PERSIA, PERSIA,
THE WHOLE DAY THROUGH
JUST AN OLD SWEET SONG
KEEPS PERSIA ON MY MIND

I SAID UH PERSIA, PERSIA
A SONG OF YOU
COMES AS SWEET AND CLEAR
AS MOONLIGHT THROUGH THE PINES

RODNEY: PERSIA ON MY MIND

(ARIAN and TOM sing "ooh ahs" underneath, into the bridge.)

HANNA: OTHER ARMS REACH OUT TO ME
OTHER EYES SMILE TENDERLY

STILL IN PEACEFUL DREAMS I SEE
THE ROAD LEADS BACK TO YOU

I SAID PERSIA, OH PERSIA,
NO PEACE I FIND
JUST AN OLD SWEET SONG
KEEPS PERSIA ON MY MIND

ALL: PERSIA ON MY MIND.

(Fade to black.)

ABOUT THE CONTRIBUTORS

TIM CUSACK is the co-artistic director of Theatre Askew. Most recently for the company he conceived, co-adapted, and co-directed (with Jason Jacobs), choreographed, and appeared as Caligula in Askew's critical and popular success, *I, Claudius Live*. Previously with the company, he appeared as Ariel in *The Tempest* and originated the role of Tim Jackson-Smith in *Bald Diva!* He is the co-author of a study guide on the gay rights movement for high school and college students.

DAVID FULLER has acted on and off Broadway, regionally, in London, and on television. He has produced and directed primarily in New York City, most notably with Jean Cocteau Repertory, where he was producing artistic director for six seasons, and with Theater Ten Ten. A teacher of theatre at high schools and universities, he is a member of the National Theater Conference. He is a staff critic for nytheatre.com and serves on the advisory board of The New York Theatre Experience.

CHAD GRACIA is a theatre producer, dramaturg, and consultant specializing in the geopolitics of the Middle East. He has edited six verse plays and writes extensively on theatre. His most recent play, an adaptation of *Gilgamesh* written with the Pulitzer Prize winner Yusef Komunyakaa, was published by Wesleyan Press. He is the director of development at the New Globe Theater, and was formerly executive director of Inverse Theater, where he produced ten critically acclaimed plays.

LEONARD JACOBS is National Theatre Editor and first-string critic for *Back Stage*, and first-string critic for *New York Press*. An arts journalist for sixteen years, his print byline has run in over twenty publications, including *American Theatre*, the *Village Voice*, the *Hollywood Reporter*, and *New York Resident*; his online byline has run on Theatermania.com (as founding editor), 25HoursOnline.com/New York Daily News, and AOLCityGuide.com, among others. He is also a playwright, director, and dramaturg with over forty productions to his credit.

ERIC PARNESS is the artistic director of Resonance Ensemble, where he has directed productions of *Antigone*, *The Lower Depths*, *La Tempestad*, and *The Mail Order Bride*. Other directing credits include *Crazy for the Dog* at the Bouwerie Lane; *Fit to Kill* at the Beckett; Oberon Theatre Ensemble's *The Winter's Tale*, *Of Mice and Men*, and *Measure for Measure*; Hypothetical Theatre's *Kryptonite City*, and new work with adobe theatre company, Ensemble Studio Theatre, and Vital Theater Company.

STEPHEN SPEIGHTS is a producer and founding member of Blue Coyote Theater Group, which has produced over twenty productions since its inception in 1999, and producing director for the Access Theater and Gallery in Tribeca. He has been producing, directing, acting, writing, and composing for downtown theatre in New York for nearly fifteen years. A graduate of the Louisiana School for Math, Science, and the Arts, he holds a BFA from Baylor University and an MFA from Rutgers' Mason Gross School of the Arts.

ABOUT THE EDITOR

MARTIN DENTON is the founder and executive director of The New York Theatre Experience, Inc., and the founder, editor, and chief reviewer for the popular Internet website nytheatre.com. He has edited all seven volumes of the *Plays and Playwrights* anthologies, which have featured the works of more than eight dozen emerging indie playwrights (watch for the eighth volume in this annual series, *Plays and Playwrights 2007*). Denton is also the creator of the *nytheatrecast*, New York's first regularly scheduled theatre podcast offering original content.

ABOUT THE PUBLISHER

THE NEW YORK THEATRE EXPERIENCE, INC. (NYTE), is a nonprofit corporation that uses new and traditional media to provide advocacy and support to the New York theatre community. In addition to its publishing program, NYTE operates the free website nytheatre.com and produces the weekly *nytheatrecast* programs. To learn more about NYTE's programs and about how you can support this organization, visit its website at www.nyte.org.

PLAYS AND PLAYWRIGHTS 2001
Edited by Martin Denton; Preface by Robert Simonson; Retail $15.00

Washington Square Dreams by Gorilla Repertory Theatre
Fate by Elizabeth Horsburgh
Velvet Ropes by Joshua Scher
The Language of Kisses by Edmund De Santis
Word To Your Mama by Julia Lee Barclay
Cuban Operator Please... by Adrian Rodriguez
The Elephant Man—The Musical by Jeff Hylton & Tim Werenko
House of Trash by Trav S.D.
Straight-Jacket by Richard Day

PLAYS AND PLAYWRIGHTS 2002
Edited by Martin Denton; Foreword by Bill C. Davis; Retail $15.00

The Death of King Arthur by Matthew Freeman
Match by Marc Chun
Woman Killer by Chiori Miyagawa
The Wild Ass's Skin by J. Scott Reynolds
Halo by Ken Urban
Shyness Is Nice by Marc Spitz
Reality by Curtiss I' Cook
The Resurrectionist by Kate Chell
Bunny's Last Night in Limbo by Peter S. Petralia
Summerland by Brian Thorstenson

PLAYS AND PLAYWRIGHTS 2003
Edited by Martin Denton; Foreword by Mario Fratti; Retail $15.00

A Queer Carol by Joe Godfrey
Pumpkins for Smallpox by Catherine Gillet
Looking for the Pony by Andrea Lepcio
Black Thang by Ato Essandoh
The Ninth Circle by Edward Musto
The Doctor of Rome by Nat Colley
Galaxy Video by Marc Morales
The Last Carburetor by Leon Chase
Out to Lunch by Joseph Langham
Ascending Bodily by Maggie Cino
Last Call by Kelly McAllister

PLAYS AND PLAYWRIGHTS 2004
Edited by Martin Denton; Foreword by Kirk Wood Bromley; Retail $16.00

Sugarbaby by Frank Cwiklik
WTC View by Brian Sloan
United States: Work and Progress by Christy Meyer, Jon Schumacher, and Ellen Shanman
The Shady Maids of Haiti by John Jahnke
Cats Can See The Devil by Tom X. Chao
Survivor: Vietnam! by Rob Reese
Feed the Hole by Michael Stock
Auntie Mayhem by David Pumo
The Monster Tales by Mary Jett Parsley
Sun, Stand Thou Still by Stephen Gridley

PLAYS AND PLAYWRIGHTS 2005
Edited by Martin Denton; Foreword by Steven Drukman; Retail $16.00

Vampire Cowboy Trilogy by Qui Nguyen & Robert Ross Parker
second. by Neal Utterback
Bull Spears by Josh Chambers
Animal by Kevin Augustine
Odysseus Died from AIDS by Stephen Svoboda
Maggie May by Tom O'Brien
Elephant by Margie Stokley
Walking to America by Alberto Bonilla
The 29 Questions Project by Katie Bull & Hillary Rollins
HONOR by TheDrillingCompaNY
Kalighat by Paul Knox
Platonov! Platonov! Platonov! or the case of a very Angry Duck by Eric Michael Kochmer

PLAYS AND PLAYWRIGHTS 2006
Edited by Martin Denton; Foreword by Trav S.D.; Retail $17.00

The Top Ten People of the Millennium Sing Their Favorite Schubert Lieder by Alec Duffy
Burning the Old Man by Kelly McAllister
Self at Hand by Jack Hanley
The Expense of Spirit by Josh Fox
Paradise by Glyn O'Malley
Yit, Ngay (One, Two) by Michael Lew
Pulling the Lever by Rising Circle Theater Collective
The Position by Kevin Doyle
The Dirty Talk by Michael Puzzo
The First Time Out of Bounds by P. Seth Bauer
Aurolac Blues by Saviana Stanescu
The Whore of Sheridan Square by Michael Baron

Plays and Playwrights books are available in bookstores and online, or from the publisher:

The New York Theatre Experience, Inc.
P.O. Box 1606, Murray Hill Station
New York, NY 10156

Additional information about the *Plays and Playwrights* series can be found at www.nyte.org/pep.htm.